CHINESE HISTORY

A MANUAL

Revised and Enlarged

D1091341

Harvard-Yenching Institute Monograph Series, 52

Also by Endymion Wilkinson

Japan Versus the West
Japan Versus Europe: A History of Misunderstanding
Studies in Chinese Price History
The History of Imperial China: A Research Guide

Translated from the Chinese

Landlord and Labour in Late Imperial China
The People's Comic Book

CHINESE HISTORY

A MANUAL

Revised and Enlarged

Endymion Wilkinson

Published by the Harvard University Asia Center
for the Harvard-Yenching Institute
and distributed by Harvard University Press
Cambridge (Massachusetts) and London
2000

Printed in the United States of America

The Harvard-Yenching Institute, founded in 1928 and headquartered at Harvard University, is a foundation dedicated to the advancement of higher education in the humanities and social sciences in East and Southeast Asia. The Institute supports advanced research at Harvard by faculty members of certain Asian universities and doctoral studies at Harvard and other universities by junior faculty at the same universities. It also supports East Asian studies at Harvard through contributions to the Harvard-Yenching Library and publication of the *Harvard Journal of Asiatic Studies* and books on premodern East Asian history and literature.

Library of Congress Cataloging-in-Publication Data

Wilkinson, Endymion Porter.
Chinese history : a manual / Endymion Wilkinson -- Rev. & enl.
   p. cm. -- (Harvard-Yenching Institute monograph series ; 52)
Includes bibliographical references and index.
ISBN 0-674-00247-4 (alk. paper) -- ISBN 0-674-00249-0 (pbk. : alk. paper)
1. China--History--Handbooks, manuals, etc. I. Title. II. Series

DS735.W695 2000
951--dc21
                            99-056876
                                 CIP

Indexes by the author

☺ Printed on acid-free paper

Last number below indicates this year of printing

10 09 08 07 06 05 04 03 02 01

Printed from camera-ready copy supplied by the author

Note to

Revised and Enlarged

Edition

The revised and enlarged edition (2000) of the manual comes to a total of 418,000 words—95,000 more than in the first edition (1998). The changes and additions represent about 250 additional pages. In order to fit them all in, the point size of the main text has had to be reduced and the entire manual reset.

There is a new chapter on the Republic (51) and research tools for Republican history have been inserted in the chapters dealing with horizontal problems (1–11). References to Taiwan research institutes and publications have been updated throughout. There are also new sections on Self-Deprecatory and Honorific Forms of Address (3.2.5), Non-Verbal Salutations (3.2.6), Weights and Measures (7.3), Money and Prices (7.4–5), Transplantation of Modern Science (37.2), Furniture (37.4.3), and Qing Newspapers (50.8).

Other chapters and sections have been revised and expanded, notably Language (1), Etymology (2.3), People (3), Geography (4), Chronology (5), Archaeology (12), Shang and Zhou (13), War (28), *Leishu* (31), Food (35.2), Women's Studies (39) Non-Han Peoples Outside China (41), and the Qing (50).

There are nine new tables.

A separate index of some 2,000 terms explained in the manual has been added and all the other indexes have been redone.

The manual discusses 4,300 primary and secondary sources, including periodicals and scholarly journals. About 1,500 titles have been added to the new edition and 200 dropped.

Acknowledgments

I am most grateful to those readers who corrected careless grammatical and typographical mistakes in the first (1998) edition, notably Timothy Connor, Charles Aylmer, Roger Greatrex, Liu Xueshun 劉學順, Ken'ichi Takashima 高嶋謙一, and James Z. Lee (Li Zhongqing 李中清). The following very generously shared their knowledge by commenting, correcting, raising questions or sending materials on particular sections or references:

Robert Bagley (archaeology and epigraphy)
James H. Cole (bibliogaphy)
Roger Greatrex (various)
Charles W. Hayford (bibliography)
Gail Hershatter (Women's studies)
David N. Keightley (Shang)
Lin Xiaoan 林小安 (characters)
Liu Shangci 劉尚慈 (Dictionaries)
Joseph P. MacDermott (ritual)
Pornchai Mahaisavariya (layout and indexes)
Alfreda Murck (painting)
Andrew Nathan (Republican period)
Ogawa Hiromitsu 小川裕元 (painting)
Edwin G. Pulleyblank (language)
Robert L. Thorp (archaeology)
Michael Tsin (Republican period)
Sun Ji 孫機 (art and archaeology)
Hans Ulrich Vogel (weights and measures)
Arthur Waldron (Republican period)
Pierre-Etienne Will (Official handbooks)
Alexander Woodside (Vietnamese dates)
Xing Yongfu 邢永福 (Ming-Qing archives)
You Rujie 游汝杰 (language)

In no sense are any of the above in any way responsible for errors of omission or commission in the Manual. Yang Feng 楊楓, Li Lei 李蕾, and Wang Jingyan 王京彥 very kindly helped me construct some rare characters on the computer. Once again, I should like to express my thanks to John R. Ziemer for the speed, accuracy, and consistency of his editorial comments on the entire text.

Acknowledgments to First Edition (1998)

I am most grateful to Timothy Connor, who not only made many fruitful suggestions and supplied the draft of section 11.6 but also corrected an enormous number of mistaken characters and other orthographic faults in a careful reading of the entire draft. Many others generously shared their learning, including William Jenner and Diana Lary, who commented on the first draft; Charles Aylmer, Beatrice S. Bartlett, Peter Bol, Karine Chemla, Hubert Durt, Roger Greatrex, Christian Lamouroux, John D. Langlois, D.C. Lau (Liu Dianjue 劉殿爵), James Z. Lee (Li Zhongqing 李中清), Liu Xueshun 劉學順, Michael Loewe, Alfreda Murck, Edwin G. Pulleyblank, Qi Wenxin 齊文心, Jessica Rawson, Shi Yanting 史延廷, Takashima Ken'ichi 高嶋謙一 and Chün-fang Yü (Yu Junfang 于君方), all of whom generously advised on and corrected one or more chapters; An Zuozhang 安作璋, Chu Shibin 初世賓, Craig Clunas, Hu Pingsheng 胡平生, Roderick MacFarquhar, Pavel Ostrov, Elisabeth Rochat de la Vallée, David Schaberg, Edward Shaughnessy, Frank Joseph Shulman, Song Zhenhao 宋鎮豪, Wang Lixing 王立興, Wang Weixin 王維新, Pierre-Etienne Will, Zhang Xiujun 張秀軍 and Zhao Keqin 趙克勤, who generously gave advice or sent materials.

John R. Ziemer not only edited the text but showed me how to prepare the camera-copy pages ready for printing; Laura Carter patiently corrected my orthography. He Jin 何晋, Zhao Dongmei 趙冬梅, and Li Xinfeng 李新峰 proofread the final draft. Pornchai Mahaisavariya helped me compile the indexes.

At Cambridge (England) in the early 1960s I had the good fortune to sit at the feet of Chang Hsin-chang (Zhang Xinzhang 張新章), Cheng Te-k'un (Zheng Dekun 鄭德坤), Paul Kratochvil, Michael Loewe, Edwin Pulleyblank, and Piet van der Loon. As a Ph.D. student at Princeton, James T. C. Liu and Fritz Mote were my teachers. Yamane Yukio 山根幸夫 accepted me into his seminar on Ming law in Tokyo, despite my incompetence and the student struggles raging at that time (1968–69).

I should never have sustained a lasting interest in Chinese history without the inspiration of these exceptionally learned and generous teachers, and I am therefore delighted to have this opportunity to express my thanks to them.

Contents

Introduction

I   Basics

II *Pre-Qin Sources*

III *Historical Genres*

IV *Other Primary Sources*

V *Primary Sources by Period*

Boxes

Tables

Preface

The manual has five principal aims:

> to suggest solutions to basic problems encountered in doing research on traditional Chinese civilization and history;
>
> to introduce the main primary sources for all periods from the Shang to the foundation of the People's Republic in 1949;
>
> to introduce the main reference works for all periods from the Shang to the foundation of the People's Republic in 1949;
>
> to give readers a sense of the spectacular changes that took place in the course of Chinese history;
>
> to suggest ways to avoid anachronistic interpretations of the past.

None of these aims includes the desire to compile a bibliography of secondary scholarship (10.4.1).[1]

The first three aims are straightforward. The fourth and fifth need some explanation.

When we look back from today, it is easy to forget that the Chinese, their language, and their culture were "ever in the process of becoming." The main reason that it is easy to overlook this is that the modern Western image of China was not formed at different stages of the process but at the end of the imperial era. Moreover, the last phases of the tradition were taken mistakenly as being accurate reflections of all previous stages. Encouragement for this view came from Chinese higher culture itself, which constantly invoked the models of the classical age. Starting with the Zhou and repeated in a systematic way in the Han, the past was rewritten in the light of contemporary cosmological beliefs and political agendas. The practice continued in the Tang, with the establishment of a new historical office with official historians whose principal duty was to enforce the legitimacy of the dynasty by showing that past precedent was respected and continuity maintained. Thereafter, be-

---

[1] A quarter of a century ago, I wrote *The History of Imperial China: A Research Guide*, HUP, 1973. It was intended for students of the economic and social history of imperial China (about 65% of China's recorded history). The present manual is a new and much larger work with different aims, a much more thorough examination of research problems, and a longer time span (about 99% of China's recorded history), and so it has a different title.

cause the literary style of the scholars remained essentially unaltered, and officials deliberately used old terms for new institutions, this, too, gave rise to the erroneous impression that Chinese civilization was not only ancient but also unchanging. It was an impression that influenced the first scholarly interpreters of China to the West, the Jesuits, who stressed literary and philosophical continuity with the classical age. The impression was powerfully reinforced in the nineteenth century, because China, by comparison with the changes in the newly industrializing countries of the West, seemed like a country caught in an unchanging time warp. Seen from a distance, the landscape appeared flat and, it was assumed, unchanging over time. In the twentieth century, Chinese intellectuals and politicians indirectly reinforced these views. They were impatient with their own past and completely rejected the old notion that it was a mirror for the present. Nevertheless, they continued to foreshorten the past and to use it—selectively, anachronistically and teleologically—to legitimize the present, a practice that nationalism reinforces today. It is not unusual, for example, for contemporary historians to write about "national minorities" in China in the Shang dynasty even though neither China nor the concept of national minority existed at that time.

For all these reasons, it is easy to fall into ahistorical interpretations of Chinese history. So, my fourth and final aim in writing the manual is to suggest some ways of avoiding this. For example, check the official written record with unofficial sources and newly discovered epigraphic evidence. Check written records of all kinds with the archaeological record. Avoid the nationalistic belief that ancient China was unique and therefore there is no need to compare it with other civilizations. On the contrary, use information about other societies as a means to understand China better and compare institutions and other phenomena in China with those found elsewhere. Above all, try to understand how Chinese civilization was perceived by those people creating it and living in it. To achieve this perspective, it is essential to grasp that the same words and terms could mean different things in different hands and in different periods and places in China. This is a plea not for philology, nor even for historical linguistics, useful though these may be, but for historical imagination and accuracy. As a first step in this direction, every effort is made to pinpoint the changing meanings of words and terms at different periods in the past.

In writing the manual I had in mind to produce the sort of book that I would have appreciated, but which did not exist, when I started Chinese studies in 1962. It is written, however, at a time of increasing specialization. This makes it difficult for students to have a good grasp of the primary sources and research tools for periods and fields outside their own. I hope therefore that it may prove useful not only for beginners but even for those more advanced.

It is possible to arrange a historical manual either by research problems, by the different types of primary sources, by period or by subject—or by all four, which is the course followed here: research problems are dealt with mainly in Part I; Parts III and IV are on genres and to a certain extent on subjects; Parts II and V are on periods, subdivided mainly by genres. Cross-referencing has been used throughout to avoid repetition.

Part I deals with basic knowledge. Since the historian of Chinese civilization needs a good mastery of all forms of written Chinese, the first chapter is on the language, and the second is on dictionaries. The rest of Part I covers people, places, time, numbers, and bibliography, including advice on how to master the characters, how to convert dates, how to find places, how to trace people, and how to evaluate historical statistics. This is followed by a discussion of where to find primary sources (including rare, lost, recovered, forged and banned books), what is in them, and how to find the meanings of difficult titles. The main index and concordance series are also introduced. Part I concludes with chapters on guides and bibliographies for using and locating secondary sources in Chinese, Japanese and Western languages and on the main libraries of Chinese books in China, Japan, the United States, Europe, and Russia.

Part II introduces the sources for the pre-Qin: archaeological, epigraphic, and textual. There are also chapters on archaeology in general and on the early script and its possible precursors.

Part III describes the different branches of historical writing and compilation in imperial China (primary and secondary sources, annals, the Standard Histories, topically arranged histories, miscellaneous histories, official communications, government institutions, penal and administrative law, army administration, and warfare).

Part IV deals with other primary sources, including myth and religion, anthologies of elite literature, encyclopaedias of various kinds, miscellaneous notes, philosophy, and popular literature; particular subjects such as agriculture, food, the environment, water control, natural disasters, medicine, technology and science, geomancy, architecture, furniture, and gardens, painting, calligraphy, and music, women's studies, non-Han peoples (both inside and outside of the country), and foreign accounts of China.

Part V presents the main primary sources and research tools for each of eight historical periods from the Qin to the end of the Republic.

The five parts of the manual are divided into 51 chapters. These are in turn subdivided into 500 sections and subsections.

Because some research problems addressed in Part I are already well discussed in the literature (for example, biography and historical geography), these chapters are shorter than those on chronology and keeping the time, which are neglected subjects. Likewise, because some sources are important, others less so, and some are plentiful, while others are rare, the chapters in Parts II through V are sometimes long, sometimes short. For example, the chapter on the Standard Histories is much longer than the one dealing with topically arranged histories. In other places more space has deliberately been given to newly discovered sources, such as documents on bamboo and wooden strips or from the archives, on the grounds that these often new sources are the ones with which students will be least familiar. Finally, in elaborating the thesis that China was ever in the process of becoming, I have deliberately gone into more detail on some of the basic elements of Chinese civilization such as the diverse origins of the Chinese people (13.1), changes in the language (Chapter 1), changes in the writing system (1.3 and Chapters 14–16), changes in the diet and cuisine (35.2), changes in nonverbal communications (3.2.3), changes in sitting (from a mat-level to a chair-level culture; 37.3.3), and the origins and changes of Han and non-Han toponyms (4.1) and ethnonyms (40.1, 41.2, and 42.1).

I have brought together the scholarship of many generations of students of Chinese civilization. In doing so, my role has been "to compile and to transmit, not to innovate." I only hope that I have done so accurately and with due acknowledgment. In fairness to me, I trust the reader will bear in mind that a chapter of the manual is not intended as a full account but as a pointer along the way.

Endymion Wilkinson

Beijing

Conventions

Romanization

Today it is hard to imagine that not so long ago one of the first problems facing Western students of the Chinese language was the number of different systems of romanization that had to be mastered. British and American textbooks alone came in a bewildering variety of transcriptions of Chinese. Having mastered Wade-Giles, students had to learn the various modifications to it in Mathews' dictionary, in the *Postal Atlas of China*, and in library catalogs. Shortly thereafter they began to study spoken Chinese using the completely different American Army system as developed at Yale. Next, there were the Chinese systems to master, starting with *Gwoyeu Romatzyh* (*Guoyu Luomazi* 國語羅馬字, National Romanization, 1928, 1986) and the *Zhuyin zimu* 注音字母 (Mandarin Phonetic Letters, 1918; called *Zhuyin fuhao* 注音符號, Mandarin Phonetic Symbols after 1930). When reading about China in the other European languages, students had to learn how to decode yet more systems of romanization.

To add insult to injury, there were always those scholars who invented personal modifications (and there are some still at it). Giles' own comment on the Wade-Giles system holds true today: "It is," he said, "anything but scientifically exact. In some respects it is cumbersome; in others it is inconsistent." The same could be said of *Hanyu pinyin* 漢語拼音 (Chinese Phonetic Alphabet, *pinyin* for short, 1958). But at least it is now the one system that is used by most scholars, both Chinese and foreign alike. Although sinological library collections in Europe and North America have still not completed the expensive process of converting to *pinyin*, they have begun.

So, *pinyin* is used throughout the manual. Not because it is linguistically superior to its numerous predecessors, but because as the normative system, it has become the standard for the romanization of Chinese in English and the other languages written in the Roman alphabet.

Some of the most familiar names in modern Chinese history are best known in English and other languages by their Cantonese pronunciation or by their Wade Giles romanizations, for example, Sun

Yatsen (Cantonese for Sun Yixian 孫逸仙) or KMT (short form of
Wade-Giles transcription of Kuomintang, i.e., Guomindang 國民
黨, referred to as GMD). In general, names throughout the manual,
including these examples, are given in *pinyin* transcriptions of their
Standard Chinese form (with an indication at first occurrence of earlier transcriptions if these had previously been commonly used or
an explanation, if necessary, at the main entry for the person or institution). The only occasions when *pinyin* is not used are for names
that have become part of the English language, for example, Confucius (not Kong fuzi 孔夫子) or Mencius (not Mengzi 孟子), and
Cantonese for *Guangzhouhua* 廣州話.

Note on Romanization of Dynastic Names

The names of dynasties and historic periods, as with other proper
names in Chinese, are capped but not italicized. For example, the
Zhanguo (Warring States) period, not *Zhanguo*.

In modern Chinese two dynasties are often linked together (e.g.,
Qin Han 秦漢, or Ming Qing 明清), but they are not hyphenated in
romanization in the manual, even though they may be translated
into English as Qin-Han or Ming-Qing. Likewise, dynastic names
that are customarily modified by a temporal or directional word are
not hyphenated (e.g., 前漢 is written as Qian Han), but note Nan-
Bei Chao 南北朝.

When dynasties are referred to in numbered clusters, they are
written as one capitalized word, for example, Sanguo 三國 (but Wudai Shiguo 五代十國, not Wudaishiguo). Numerical expressions
such as 兩漢 or 兩宋 are not hyphenated, but written Liang Han
and Liang Song. Pre-Qin (*xian-Qin* 先秦) is hyphenated.

For further comments on romanization, see Box 2, Chapter 2;
and section 4.1, *Romanization of Chinese Place-Names*. Note the large
number of concordances of the different ways of transcribing the
sounds of Chinese into Western languages.[1]

---

[1] The most comprehensive concordance contains 50 different systems: Ireneus Laszlo Legeza, *Guide to Transliterated Chinese in the Modern Peking Dialect*, 2 vols., Brill, 1968–69. Vol. 1 shows equivalents in 21 current systems and
vol. 2 lists equivalents in 29 defunct systems.

If you are uncertain of the orthography of *pinyin*, where, for example, to
use spaces, hyphens, or apostrophes (*zuqiu chang* or *zuqiuchang* 足球場? *Renyi
daode* or *renyi-daode* 仁義道德? *Lao er wugong* or *lao'erwugong* 勞而無功?),
Footnote continued on next page

Characters

Characters are given in their complex form throughout.

Notes

Readers should not be surprised if the points made in the text are not necessarily the same as those made in the references cited in the footnotes.

Abbreviations of Journal Titles

The abbreviations used throughout the manual for journals are listed in 10.2.4, 10.3.3, and 10.4.2.

Book Titles

All Chinese book titles are given first in *pinyin* in *italics*, then in characters followed by an English translation in brackets. For example, *Yijing* 易經 (Classic of changes). Edited or compiled works, for example, most of the Standard Histories, are identified by their titles. For this reason, their titles are listed first, followed by the editor or compiler.

Abbreviations of Book Titles

CHAC *The Cambridge History of Ancient China*, Michael Loewe and Edward L. Shaughnessy, eds., New York: CUP, 1999 (Chapter 12)

CHC *The Cambridge History of China*, John K. Fairbank and Denis Twitchett, general editors, 15 vols., CUP, 1978– (Chapter 43)

CHKSK *Chûgoku hôseishi kihon shiryô no kenkyû* 中國法制史基本資料の研究 (Chinese legal history, studies on basic source materials), Shiga Shûzô 滋賀秀三, ed., Tôkyô daigaku, 1993, 1994 (27, *Introduction*)

CZS *Chûgoku zuihitsu sakuin* 中國隨筆索引 (index to Chinese *suibi*), Saeki Tomi 佐伯富 ed., Nihon gakujutsu shinkôkai, 1954 (Chapter 31)

CZZS *Chûgoku zuihitsu zatcho sakuin* 中國隨筆雜著索引 (Index to Chinese *suibi* and miscellaneous works), Tôyôshi kenkyûkai, 1960 (Chapter 31)

---

consult the authoritative *Hanyu pinyin cihui* 漢語拼音詞匯, 1989; 2nd rev. ed., Yuwen, 1991; 2nd prnt., 1995. In these examples, the second spelling is the recommended one.

DMB	*Dictionary of Ming Biography 1368–1644*, Luther Carrington Goodrich and Chaoying Fang, eds., 2 vols., Col. UP, 1976 (49.5)
DOTIC	Charles O. Hucker, *A Dictionary of Official Titles in Imperial China*, SUP, 1985; SMC rpnt., 1988 (22.3)
ECCP	*Eminent Chinese of the Ch'ing Period*, Arthur W. Hummel, ed., 2 vols., Washington, DC: Government Printing Office, 1943–44; SMC rpnt., 1991 (50.8.3)
ECT	*Early Chinese Texts: A Bibliographical Guide*, Michael Loewe, ed., *Early China* Special Monograph Series, SSEC and IEAS, 1993 (19.1)
H-Y Index	*Harvard-Yenching Institute Sinological Index Series* (9.10)
HCJ	*Historians of China and Japan*, William G. Beasley and Edwin G. Pulleyblank, eds., OUP, 1961
ICS Concordance	*Institute of Chinese Studies Ancient Chinese Texts Concordance Series* (9.10)
ISMH	*An Introduction to the Sources of Ming History*, Wolfgang Franke, ed., Kuala Lumpur and Singapore: University of Malaya Press, 1968 (49.5.1)
ICTCL	*Indiana Companion to Traditional Chinese Literature*, William H. Nienhauser, Jr., ed. and comp.; Charles Hartman, Y. W. Ma, Stephen H. West, associate eds., IUP, vol. 1, 1986; rev. rpnt., SMC; 1988; vol. 2, William H. Nienhauser, ed. and comp., Charles Hartman and Scott W. Galer, associate eds., IUP, 1998 (30.1)
NSECH	*New Sources of Early Chinese History: An Introduction to the Reading of Inscriptions and Manuscripts*, Edward L. Shaughnessy, ed., SSEC and IEAS, 1997 (12.2)
OCCG	Edwin G. Pulleyblank, *Outline of Classical Chinese Grammar*, UBC Press, 1995
SB	*A Sung Bibliography*, initiated by Etienne Balazs; Yves Hervouet, ed., HKCU Press, 1978 (47.4.1)
SCC	*Science and Civilisation in China*, Joseph Needham, ed., CUP, 1954–95; 1996– (Chapter 37)
ZZFDJ	*Zhongguo zhenxi falü dianji jicheng* 中國珍稀法律典籍集成 (Collection of rare works of Chinese law), Liu Hainian 劉海年 and Yang Yifan 楊一凡, series eds., 14 vols., Kexue, 1994 (27, *Introduction*)

Publishers

Publishers are indicated after every book title. In some cases, the name has been shortened by dropping words such as *shuju* or *chubanshe*, so Zhonghua Shuju 中華書局, Hunan Renmin Chubanshe 湖南人民出版社, and Chengdu Chubanshe 成都出版社 appear as Zhonghua, Hunan renmin, and Chengdu.

Full names of all publishers, with principal place of business and Chinese or Japanese characters, where appropriate, are given in the Appendix. The only exceptions are a small number of Western publishers that, if they are only referred to once, are cited in full in the text. No attempt has been made to list pirated editions.

Western university presses are abbreviated as follows:

ANUP	Australian National University Press
Col. UP	Columbia University Press
Corn. UP	Cornell University Press
CUP	Cambridge University Press
DUP	Duke University Press
HKCUP	Hong Kong: Chinese University Press
HKUP	Hong Kong University Press
HUP	Harvard University Press
IUP	Indiana University Press
OUP	Oxford University Press
PUF	Presses Universitaires de France
PUP	Princeton University Press
SUP	Stanford University Press
SUNY	State University of New York Press
UAP	University of Arizona Press
UBCP	University of British Columbia Press
UChP	University of Chicago Press
UCP	University of California Press
UHP	University of Hawaii Press
UMP	University of Michigan Press
UWP	University of Washington Press
YUP	Yale University Press

Abbreviations of Institutions

Abbreviations of institutions in China and Japan are normally given in the manual according to the standard abbreviations used in Chinese and Japanese; not according to the many abbreviations for them sometimes found in Western languages.

Guotu 國圖	Guojia tushuguan 國家圖書館 (National Library); previously Beijing tushuguan 北京圖書館; 11.1
CCS	Center for Chinese Studies (various)
EFEO	Ecole française d'Extrême Orient, Paris

Ershiguan 二史館	Zhongguo di'er lishi dang'anguan 中國第二歷史檔案館 (Second Historical Archives of China), Nanjing; 51.1.2
ICS	Institute of Chinese Studies, Chinese University of Hong Kong, Shatin
IEAS	Institute of East Asian Studies, University of California, Berkeley
Jinbun 人文	Kyôto daigaku Jinbun kagaku kenkyûjo 京都大學人文科學研究所 (Institute for Humanistic Studies, Kyoto University); 11.3 (Kyoto)
Jindaishisuo 近代史所	Zhongguo shehui kexueyuan, Jindaishi yanjiusuo 中國社會科學院近代史研究所 (Institute of Modern Historical Research, Shekeyuan), Beijing (1840–1949)
Jinshisuo 近史所	Zhongyang yanjiuyuan Jindaishi yanjiusuo 中央研究院近代史研究所 (Institute of Modern History, Academia Sinica), Taibei; 11.2
Kaogusuo 考古所	Zhongguo shehui kexueyuan, Kaogu yanjiusuo 中國社會科學院考古研究所 (Institute of Archaeology, Shekeyuan), Beijing; 12.3
MFEA	Museum of Far Eastern Antiquities (Östasiatiska Samlingarna), Stockholm
Lishisuo 歷史所	Zhongguo shehui kexueyuan, Lishi yanjiusuo 中國社會科學院歷史研究所 (Institute of Historical Research, Shekeyuan), Beijing (pre-Qin to Qing)
Shekeyuan 社科院	Zhongguo shehui kexueyuan 中國社會科學院 (Chinese Academy of Social Sciences [CASS]), Beijing
Shiyusuo 史語所	Zhongyang yanjiuyuan, Lishi yuyan yanjiusuo 中央研究院歷史語言研究所 (Institute of History and Philology, Academia Sinica), Taibei (pre-Qin to Qing); 11.2
SOAS	School of Oriental and African Studies, University of London
SSEC	Society for the Study of Early China, USA
Tôbunken 東文研	Tôkyo daigaku, Tôyô bunka kenkyûjo 東京大學東洋文化研究所 (The Institute of Oriental Studies, Tokyo University); 11.3 (Tokyo)
Wenkaosuo 文考所	Wenwu kaogu yanjiusuo 文物考古研究所 (Cultural Relics and Archaeology Institute), various places, China
Yishiguan 一史館	Zhongguo diyi lishi dang'an guan 中國第一歷史檔案館 (First Historical Archives, Beijing); 50.1.2

CHINESE HISTORY

A MANUAL

Revised and Enlarged

Introduction

Recent Historiographical Trends

Sinology and the writing of Chinese history in the West are both heavily dependent upon scholarly output in China, whether this output is understood in the broad sense of the editing and publishing of ancient texts or in the more narrow sense of archaeology, epigraphy, or historical writing. Western students are also able to draw on Japanese secondary scholarship. However, the fine line between making the findings of Chinese or Japanese scholarship available in a Western language (a useful activity) and the writing of original work based on Chinese sources written before the twentieth century is not always made explicit. Throughout the manual it is assumed that there is a community of scholars writing in many different languages about Chinese history. Entry into this community is based on original research or interpretation of Chinese primary sources with due recognition and acknowledgment of the secondary work of others in the field.

From 1949 to 1979, the writing of history in China became even more directly subordinate to politics than it had been in imperial China. However, the past was no longer regarded as a mirror for the present, but as the dark night at the end of which, following liberation in 1949, a new era had dawned. What happened during the course of the long night of Chinese "feudal" history (and even during the "pre-class" millennia before then) was analyzed in Marxist-Maoist terms. All other forms of historical studies were proscribed and the research agenda limited to five themes: peasant rebellions (because it was believed that peasant uprisings were the major driving force of the development of China's feudal society); the formation of the Han nation; the landholding systems of feudal China; capitalist sprouts in the Ming and Qing; periodization. Despite the fact that the research agenda had the backing of the state and was watched over by a handful of politically approved historians, not every question was resolved. For example, no final decision was reached on how to deal with Marx's slippery concept of the Asiatic mode of production. Nor is there to this day a consensus on periodization, a subject discussed below.

During the entire 1949–79 period Chinese historians were cut off from historical studies in the West. Foreign publications, if available at all, were severely restricted.

Much work of tremendous value was done, sometimes at the direct command of Mao Zedong, as when, for example, a group of leading historians were assigned to produce variorum punctuated editions of the *Zizhi tongjian* 資治通鑑 and of the Standard Histories.

Some of the varieties of historical writing that flourished during these years have since been labeled by Chinese historians as teleological history (*mudilun shixue* 目的論史學), according to which everything of value in the past was a preparation for the glorious present; weathervane history (*fengpai shixue* 風派史學), which was as influenced by present political fads as by historical evidence; hot-air history (*yilun shixue* 議論史學), another name for the previous genre; Aesopian history (*yingshe shixue* 影射史學), whose practitioners, following an old Chinese tradition, criticized the present indirectly by using historical precedents.

Many avoided controversy by engaging in compilation of excerpts on the approved themes or by writing pot-boiler history (*huiguorou shixue* 回鍋肉史學), rehashing other people's work (in the name of popularization, as acceptable an activity as independent research was suspicious). At times of heightened tension, such as during the Cultural Revolution, all forms of study and writing stopped.

The end of nation building in a Maoist framework in 1979 began to free Chinese historians from the necessity to work within such narrow margins. During the 1980s and early 1990s, scholarship blossomed. New journals were founded. Manuscripts that had been unpublishable for decades saw the light of day. Pre-1949 works were for the first time given their due. The barriers that had previously divided historical studies abroad from those in China were removed. For the first time in a generation, foreign journals and books started to become available. Travel abroad was allowed. Access for foreign scholars to colleagues in China opened up. Fruitful contacts multiplied. New interpretations began to emerge.

Regional and local history are now booming, as pride in local traditions is fortified and financed by economic growth and by the discovery of a huge variety of archaeological treasures, including whole settlements from villages to cities, attesting to distinct, and in many cases unsuspected, Neolithic and Bronze Age cultures.

Greater attention is being paid to the role of the non-Han peoples, both in the formation of Chinese civilization in its earliest stages and at later periods of Chinese history.

Gender studies are beginning to make their mark.

Historical archives have opened doors that until the 1980s were shut. Joint archaeological digs have been permitted since 1991 after a hiatus of more than 40 years.

Previously Chinese history was seen either as part of world history in a Marxist-Leninist framework or as the glorious story of the formation of the modern Chinese nation-state. There are some signs that new cross-border and cross-cultural comparisons are now being made, even though many still have a predilection to regard history principally as a means to evoke national pride.

In these more open times, the volume and diversity of historical works, compilations, and reprints of historical texts have increased enormously. Although there is more private wealth in society, there are ever diminishing public funds available to support scholarly research and publication. The use of the computer to edit, analyze, index, and disseminate research results may mitigate such difficulties. For example, searching for bibliographic references has become much more efficient with the availability of online library catalogs, in some cases allowing access to major Chinese and Japanese collections all over the world. Hundreds of Chinese journals are distributed on CD-ROM, which allows checking current research trends much more rapidly and at less cost to the scholar or library than would have been thought possible only a few years ago.

Primary sources too (including even epigraphic materials), are becoming more accessible. Even if the originals may still be scattered in collections in many countries, transcriptions have been made and comprehensive editions published, and CD-ROM versions are becoming available. Ironically, greater ease of access comes just at the moment when the ability to handle Classical or Literary Chinese, not to speak of the difficult ancient scripts of the Shang and Zhou inscriptions, is declining.

Historians of imperial China (from Qin to Qing) in China itself, as well as in Japan and Korea, have usually concentrated on the classical age or periods when China was strong (such as the Han, the Tang or more recent dynasties) and they continue to do so. Conversely they usually neglected periods of alien rule or division, except in special cases, for example, the Manchu interest in the Jin dynasty because it was founded by their Jurchen (Nüzhen 女真) ancestors. Today, there are many more specialized fields and disciplines, covering not only the dynasties when China was strong but also the periods of disunity.

That Chinese historical studies in the West should become more specialized is also entirely fitting. In the study of European and American history, it is considered normal for historians to concentrate on one period—the Tudors or the antebellum South, or even on a single event such as the French Revolution—and certainly to specialize in a discipline such as economic history or the history of science. The old idea that a historian of China should cover three or four thousand years of history in all its manifestations was an indication of the immaturity of the field, or simply a reliance on received interpretations.

One result of increased specialization is that works covering all of Chinese history are written by large teams.[1]

Today, although there is increased specialization, the periods covered are still vast. A historian who takes the Han as his special field is after all taking a period longer than that which separates the first Queen Elizabeth of England from the second, or the Pilgrim Fathers from the moon landing. No subsequent dynasty lasted as long as the Han (although its predecessor, the Zhou, was twice as long), but the volume of extant primary sources grows larger as we approach the present, and even the Qing (the shortest of China's major dynasties) lasted for 267 years.

The blossoming of historical studies in the new, more open atmosphere of the 1980s and early 1990s in China was made possible by the contributions of scholars of an older generation, many of

---

[1] For example, more than one hundred scholars contributed to the most comprehensive and detailed account of Chinese history ever attempted in a Western language, the 15-volume *Cambridge History of China*, CUP, 1978– (Chapter 43); several hundred historians contributed to the 22 volumes of *Zhongguo tongshi* 中國通史 (General history of China), Shanghai renmin, 1989–99; 75 historians wrote the chapters in the four-volume *Chûgoku shigaku no kihon mondai* 中國史學の基本問題 (Basic problems in Chinese history), Kyûko, 4 vols., 1996–2000.

The collecting, writing, and copying of large-scale reference books and compilations of all sorts by teams of scholars often working on behalf of, if not inspired by, prestigious editorial committees or powerful patrons has been a feature of Chinese intellectual and official life since the Han dynasty.

whom for the first time in 30 years were left in peace to do their research. However, historical studies reached a watershed in the mid-
1990s due to the near breakdown of the state-supported systems of
academic and university scholarship and publication in a society
where the pursuit of wealth made the slow acquisition of the skills
to study history seem beside the point.

Center and Periphery

We now know that the Shang was probably one of several advanced
bronze cultures in the China area although we know very little
about the other ones there. The Zhou succeeded in imposing a central administration on part of north China. But during the Warring
States this broke down into many individual kingdoms. Much of
pre-Qin history is therefore "regional history." After the Qin unification, China on many occasions again divided into regional and local powers. At such times, by definition, history becomes regional
history. Quite apart from this rather formal definition, even when
China was centralized, there remained great pride in regional and
local traditions. Local identities were expressed in local dialects, local customs, local cuisines, and local products. Pride in local culture
is reflected in the local gazetteers and in genealogies. In this sense,
all of Chinese history, apart from the history of the imperial court
and the central institutions of government through which it ruled,
is in the words of William Skinner "an internested hierarchy of local and regional histories."[2]

Traditional scholars not infrequently produced collections of
documents and excerpts (culled from both national and local
sources) on a particular province, city, or locality. Many such collections are mentioned in the manual. Modern scholars have continued this tradition, often more thoroughly—take, for example,
Taiwan wenxian congkan 臺灣文獻叢刊 (51.2.5). The compilers of
this collection brought together all known references to Taiwan in
both official and unofficial sources from the earliest times to 1949.

---

[2] G. William Skinner, "Presidential Address: The Structure of Chinese History," *JAS* 44.2: 288 (1985), quoted in "Regional Societies," in Evelyn S. Rawski
and Susan Naquin, *Chinese Society in the Eighteenth Century*, YUP, 1987, 139–
216.

The excerpts and texts are punctuated and annotated. Such collections can be a useful starting point for the study of local history.

Recent years have seen the first attempts to write comprehensive histories of regional cultures linking archaeological discoveries with the later histories of local kingdoms based on textual traditions, in some cases even tracing shared boundaries with the commanderies, circuits and provinces of the empire.[3]

Sometimes the sources and often the reference works for local history are more detailed and accurate than what is available on a national level. Thus, for example, studies of place names of a province or region are usually of a higher standard and often more detailed than those compiled nationally and the same applies to biographies. There is a third possible definition of local history. In the nineteenth and twentieth centuries the establishment of separate political regimes or administrations in various parts of China had the indirect consequence of encouraging the writing of local history. This is particularly true of Hong Kong, Macao, Manshûkoku, and Taiwan, because their governments employed professional archaeologists and historians to conduct research and to teach, not only national history, but also the history of these places.

Periodization

History since at least the Han dynasty has been broadly divided using the relative terms *gu* 古 and *jin* 近, ancient and modern, with the definitions changing as each new generation sees itself as modern and an ever larger stretch of the past as ancient. Currently in China political criteria are applied: ancient history (*gudaishi* 古代史) covers antiquity to the early nineteenth century; early modern history (*jindaishi* 近代史) is from 1840 to 1919 (according to some, 1911); modern history (*xiandaishi* 現代史) is from 1919 to 1949 (or from 1912 to post-1949); and contemporary history (*dangdaishi* 當代史) is from 1949 to the present. As 1949 fades into the past and as the "contemporary" looks "modern" at best, these demarcation lines have already begun to shift.[4]

---

[3] For example, *Chuxue wenku* 楚學文庫 (18.1.1); *Changjiang wenhuashi* 長江文化史 (14.5); *Wu wenhua shicong* 吳文化史叢, 2 vols., Jiangsu renmin, 1995.

[4] 1840 is the beginning of the Opium War; 1919 is the May Fourth Movement; 1949 is the founding of the People's Republic.

Yuangu 遠古, remote antiquity, sometimes refers to the legendary time before the use of writing. Thereafter, within the vast time span of "ancient," divisions are usually made in one of three ways. By tradition, the *Sandai* 三代 (the three dynasties of Xia, Shang, and Zhou) are simply lumped together as *xian-Qin* 先秦 (pre-Qin, i.e., before the Qin unification) or *shanggu* 上古 (high antiquity; archaic China, ancient history), a period that covers in all about 1,900 years. Since the Han, this is usually divided into the Western and Eastern Zhou (following the forced removal of the dynasty from its principal to secondary capital; see the table of dynasties on pp. 9–11). The Eastern Zhou is subdivided into the Spring and Autumn and the Warring States periods (also referred to as the Chunqiu and the Zhanguo). Thereafter, the following 2,200 years (often called "imperial China") are divided into six or seven main dynastic periods, alternating between those that ruled over a united empire and those that existed in a period of weakness and disunity. The drawback of this convention is that it still leads to the uncritical acceptance of what might be called "the Zhou interpretation of history," whereby all of the Chinese past is seen as having originated from one (mythological) source leading inexorably to the Zhou and continuing thereafter in an unbroken succession of "legitimate" dynasties, each founded by an upright and capable ruler who gains the mandate of heaven as the result of the corruptness and disorder under the last ruler of the previous dynasty. This teleological approach to the past focused almost exclusively on court politics and the concerns of the imperial government ever conscious of the need to justify its actions in moral terms.[5]

The second way of dividing Chinese history is to use Marxist-Leninist stage theory (still applied in China) of primitive society,[6] slave society, feudal society,[7] semi-colonial, semi-feudal society (*ban-*

---

[5] See section 13.1 for the first challenges to the "Zhou interpretation of history."

[6] Primitive society (*yuanshi shehui* 原始社會) is defined as pre-class society and subdivided into pre-clan, matriarchal clan, and patriarchal clan. What effect the application of these categories has had on Chinese archaeology is discussed at the end of 13.2.

[7] Arif Dirlik, "Feudalism in 20th Century Chinese Historiography," *China Report*, 33.1: 35–66 (1997); Cho-yun Hsu, "Early Chinese History: The State of the Field," *JAS* 38.3: 453–75 (1979).

zhimindi, banfengjian shehui 半殖民地半封建社會), and capitalist
society (*ziben zhuyi shehui* 資本主義社會).[8]

The timing of the transition to slave society (*nuli shehui* 奴隸社
會) varies according to the historian from different periods of the
Longshan culture (third millennium BC), the Xia, or the Shang dynasties. The end of slave and the beginning of feudal society (*feng-
jian shehui* 封建社會) are variously placed in the Western Zhou, the
Spring and Autumn, the Warring States, the Qin unification, the
Later Han, or the Wei-Jin periods. The beginnings of the end of the
feudal are usually placed in the Ming and Qing with the appearance
of capitalist sprouts (*ziben zhuyi mengya* 資本主義萌芽), nipped in
the bud by the arrival of the imperialists.[9]

The third method of periodization (often used by Western and
Japanese historians) is to apply the conventional categories of European history: ancient, medieval, and modern.[10] The Nan-Bei Chao
are usually taken to mark the transition to medieval, and the Song
(or the Ming), the transition to modern.[11] The disadvantage is not so
much that these categories cannot be made to fit the Chinese experience, but that their familiarity in the European context suggests
false connotations.

A simplification found in many Western textbooks is to lump
everything which happened before the Qin unification as the formative age, from the Qin to the Song as the early empire, and from
the Song to the Qing as the later empire, thus creating three massive
and rather indigestible slices of one thousand years each.

[8] Albert Feuerwerker, *History in Communist China*, MIT Press, 1968, covers the formative years up to 1959.

[9] Timothy Brook, "Capitalism, Modern History, and the Chinese Premodern," in *Culture and Economy: The Shaping of Capitalism in East Asia*, Timothy
Brook and Hy Van Luong, eds., UCP, 1997.

[10] Tanigawa Michio, "Problems Concerning the Japanese Periodization of
Chinese History," Joshua A. Fogel, tr., *JAH* 21.2: 150–68 (1987).

[11] In Japan, the Kyoto school regarded the Song as marking the transition
to the modern; the Tokyo school identified the late Ming in this role (see
10.3.1). The Chinese orthodoxy chose the Ming. Recent Western scholarship
has developed the "early modern paradigm" (coinciding with and characterized
by the increasing monetization of society in the late Ming); see Philip C. C.
Huang, "The Paradigmatic Crisis in Chinese Studies: Paradoxes in Social and
Economic History," *Modern China* 17.3: 299–341 (1991).

Controversies have raged as to which method to use and where the demarcation lines should be drawn, but periodization is not a science. Whichever method is chosen (and each has drawbacks and advantages), it should serve to clarify analysis and to assist the memory, not to provide a straitjacket into which to fit the data.

The manual follows the first approach: the pre-Qin is taken as a whole, followed by seven dynastic periods and the short period of the Republic. The advantage is that most of the primary sources fit neatly into this scheme.

The Dynasties

Pre-Qin: The Three Dynasties (Sandai 三代)

	BC
Xia 夏[1]	ca. 21st–16th c.
Shang 商	ca. 1600–1045
Early Shang (Erligang 二里崗 period)	ca. 16th–14th c.
Yin Shang 殷商 (Anyang 安陽 period)	14th c.–1045
Zhou 周[2]	1045–256
Western Zhou 西周	1045–771
Eastern Zhou 東周	770–256
Spring and Autumn (Chunqiu 春秋)[3]	770–476
Warring States (Zhanguo 戰國)[4]	475–221
Six Kingdoms (Liuguo 六國)[5]	

[1] The historicity of the Xia is generally accepted in China, although no contemporary written evidence has been found.

[2] 1045 is one of many estimates for the Zhou conquest of the Shang. In the year 256 Qin killed the last Zhou ruler.

[3] Chunqiu 春秋 comes from the chronicle of that name (21.1), which covered the years 722–481 BC. By modern convention the Chunqiu period has been extended to cover the years 770–476, that is, from the start of the Eastern Zhou (marked by the removal of the Zhou capital to Luoyi 雒邑, modern Luoyang) to the start of the Warring States period.

[4] Zhanguo comes from the *Zhanguoce* 戰國策 (see Table 21, 19.1). Its beginning was traditionally put either in 475 (*Shiji* 史記) or in 403 (*Zizhi tongjian* 資治通鑑; this latter date marks the formal recognition by the Zhou of the rulers of Han 韓, Zhao 趙, and Wei 魏, who had earlier dismembered Jin 晉 into three [San Jin 三晉]). Modern convention normally uses 475.

[5] The Six Kingdoms at the end of the Warring States were Han 韓 (403–230), Zhao 趙 (403–222), Wei 魏 (403–225), Chu 楚 (?–223), Qi 齊 (11th c. BC–221), and Yan 燕 (11th c. BC–222). They were all conquered by Qin 秦.

Dynasties of Imperial China

Qin 秦	221–206 BC
Han 漢	202 BC–AD 220
Former Han 前漢 (also called Western Han)	202 BC–AD 23
Xin 新 (Wang Mang 王莽 reign)	AD 9–23
Later Han 後漢 (also called Eastern Han)	25–220
Wei, Jin, Nan-Bei Chao 魏晉南北朝	220–589
Sanguo 三國 (Three Kingdoms)	220–280
Wei 魏 (commonly known as Cao Wei 曹魏)	220–265
Han 漢 (commonly known as Shu Han 蜀漢)	221–263
Wu 吳 (commonly known as Sun Wu 孫吳)	222–280
Jin 晉	265–420
Western Jin 西晉	265–316
Eastern Jin 東晉	317–420
Six Dynasties 六朝[6]	222–589
Sixteen Kingdoms 十六國[7]	304–439
Nan-Bei Chao 南北朝 (Northern and Southern Dynasties)	420–589
Southern Dynasties 南朝	420–579
Liu Song 劉宋	420–479
Qi 齊	479–502
Liang 梁	502–557
Chen 陳	557–589

[6] The Six Dynasties (Liuchao 六朝) of the years 222–589 were Wu 吳, Dong Jin 東晉, and the four Southern dynasties of Song 宋, Qi 齊, Liang 梁, and Chen 陳. They were grouped together because they had their capitals in the South at Jiankang 建康 (Nanjing). They are sometimes called the southern Six Dynasties to distinguish them from another definition of the term, the northern Six Dynasties (Wei 魏, Xi Jin 西晉, Bei Wei 北魏, Bei Qi 北齊, Bei Zhou 北周, and Sui 隋). Occasionally, too, the whole period of Sanguo, Jin, and Nan-Bei Chao is called the Six Dynasties.

[7] Conventional term for the sixteen states established over most of North China and Sichuan between 304 and 439, of which five were Xianbei 鮮卑; three Han 漢; three Xiongnu 匈奴; two Di 氐; and one each Qiang 羌, Jie 羯, and Ba-Di 巴氐. Collectively the non-Han peoples who ruled in the North at this time were known as the "five barbarians" (*wuhu* 五胡). They were not counted in the legitimate succession of dynasties (*zhengtong* 正統); see 20.4.

Northern Dynasties 北朝[8]	386–581
Northern Wei 北魏[9]	386–534
Eastern Wei 東魏	534–550
Western Wei 西魏	535–556
Northern Qi 北齊	550–577
Northern Zhou 北周	557–581
Sui 隋	581–618
Tang 唐	618–907
Wudai Shiguo 五代十國	902–979
(The Five Dynasties and Ten Kingdoms)	
Five Dynasties 五代 (North China)[10]	907–960
Ten Kingdoms 十國 (South China)[11]	902–979
Song 宋	960–1279
Northern Song 北宋 period	960–1127
Southern Song 南宋 period	1127–1279
Liao 遼 (*Qidan* 契丹, Khitan)	916–1125
Jin 金 (*Nüzhen* 女真, Jurchen)	1115–1234
Xia 夏 [Xixia 西夏] (*Dangxiang* 黨項, Tangut)[12]	1038–1227
Yuan 元 (*Menggu* 蒙古, Mongol)	1279–1368
Ming 明	1368–1644
Qing 清 (*Manzhou* 滿洲, Manchu)[13]	1644–1912

[8] The founders and rulers of the Northern Dynasties were all Xianbei 鮮卑 (a non-Han people) with the exception of the Northern Qi, whose ruling house was founded by a Han from Bohai 渤海. Another convention is to date the Northern Dynasties to the years 439–581 (from the Wei unification of North China to the establishment of the Sui dynasty).

[9] Also called Tuoba Wei 拓拔魏.

[10] The Five Dynasties were Later Liang 後梁 (907–23), Later Tang 後唐 (Shatuo 沙陀, a Turkic people, 923–36), Later Jin 後晉 (Shatuo, 936–46), Later Han 後漢 (Shatuo, 947–50), and Later Zhou 後周 (951–60).

[11] The Ten Kingdoms were Wu 吳 (902–37), Southern Tang 南唐 (937–75), Wu-Yue 吳越 (907–78), Chu 楚 (907–51), Min 閩 (909–45), Southern Han 南漢 (917–71), Former Shu 前蜀 (903–25), Later Shu 後蜀 (933–65), Jingnan 荊南 (924–63), and Northern Han 北漢 (Shatuo 沙陀, 951–79). Most were conquered by the Song.

[12] Not counted in the legitimate succession.

[13] The Qing court announced the abdication of Puyi on February 12 1912.

Note on Cycles of Rule

There are several theories as to what caused the rise and fall of Chinese dynasties.[14] Some have seen the creation of nomadic empires and the consequent ripple effect across the Eurasian continent as a prime cause, not only in China but also in Europe.[15] Others, concentrating on the Chinese end of the Continent, have noted that Chinese and steppe empires influenced each other in an interactive way from the Qin to the Ming, from the Xiongnu to the Manchu and have tried to construct an all-embracing explanation, suggesting that when there were strong dynasties in China, this led to the creation of steppe empires to the North and Northwest. These theories do not fit the later empire when much or all of China was ruled by sinicized peoples originating from the steppe.[16]

Note on Dynastic Names (Guohao 國號)

Nearly all the names of states and fiefs up to and including the Han were taken from place-names. Between the fall of the Han and the establishment of the Jin in the twelfth century, the same names for dynasties were used over and over again. Most were taken from the previous place of enfeoffment of the dynastic founder, which in turn perpetuated the names and titles of Zhou dynasty states or fiefs (*guo* 國). There were also those states that claimed a restoration by using the dynastic title of an immediately previous dynasty (the Later Tang, 923–36, for example). The Liao and the Jin followed the old traditions in that they took their *guohao* from place-names, albeit not those of ancient states, but the names of rivers in the homelands of their dynastic founders. Thereafter, for reasons explained at the beginning of Chapter 48, starting with the Yuan, an entirely

[14] L. S. Yang (楊聯陞), "Toward a Study of Dynastic Configurations in Chinese History," in his *Studies in Chinese Institutional History*, HUP, 1963.

[15] The classic study was Frederick J. Teggart, *Rome and China: A Study in Correlations in Historical Events*, UCP, 1939.

[16] See Gary Ledyard, in Rossabi, 1983 (41.1); also the table in Thomas J. Barfield, *The Perilous Frontier: Nomadic Empires and China, 221 BC to AD 1757*, Blackwell, 1989; rpnt., 1996, 13. For a critique of these theories, see Ruth Dunnell's review of Barfield (1989) in *JAS* 50.1: 126–27 (1991), and also her review of Juha Jankunen, *Manchuria: An Ethnic History*, Helsinki: The Finno-Ugrian Society, 1996, in *JSYS* 28: 264–72 (1998). For the view from the steppe, see David Christian, 1998 (41.3.1).

new course was followed. Khubilai Khan adopted the term "Fundamental force" (*Yuan* 元) for the name of his dynasty. It was taken not from history but from the beginning of the *Yijing* 易經 (Classic of changes). The first emperor of the Ming 明 decided to perpetuate the title of the Red Turban leader Xiao Mingwang 小明王 (Young Prince of Radiance), whose mantle he inherited. The name had strong messianic overtones (see Chapter 49, note 1). Hong Taiji 洪太極 (Abahai), the ruler of Da Jin 大金 (or Hou Jin 後金), in 1635 changed his dynasty's name to Qing 清. The reasons why he did so are not known, but probably included *wuxing* 五行 beliefs (Box 8).

To distinguish between dynasties with the same name later generations qualified them by time (Former and Later Han) or by place (often the relative situation of the capital, as Western and Eastern Han); or by the names of their ruling houses (Cao Wei 曹魏, Zhu Ming 朱明, or Man Qing 滿清.

Dynasties were often grouped together in sets that were revised as time went by. There were, for example, two sets of Six Dynasties (*Liuchao* 六朝, see note 6), not to speak of four definitions of the *Liudai* 六代 (Six Dynasties), the fourth of which is the Liuchao.

Note on the Dates of Dynasties

The dynastic tables can be misleading because they suggest that each period followed the preceding one in an unbroken succession. In reality, this was not the case. New powers and contenders for power often overlapped with established rulers. It was only later that historians constructed a legitimate succession of dynasties, each neatly following its predecessor (20.4). This pattern was then projected into the pre-dynastic past. To take a later example, the Former Han is usually listed as beginning in 206 BC. That was the year in which the last Qin ruler died and Liu Bang, the founder of the Han, was marginalized with a provincial command. He did not become emperor until 202 BC. Yet many historical works list the Han dynasty as beginning in 206 BC.

The date for the ending of a failed dynasty was often prolonged after it had ceased to rule over most of China. To avoid confusion when this happened the old dynasty was usually given a new name (for example, the Southern Ming, Nan-Ming 南明, 1644–61).

I

BASICS

1

Language

Language is one of the most sensitive barometers of change in society. It is also the basic tool for doing historical research. So, the manual begins with a brief overview of the history of Chinese (1.1). This is followed by an examination of two of the main problems in reading Chinese sources: the many meanings of a single word (1.2) and the large number of characters to be learned (1.3).

The discussion of the first problem covers not only multiple meanings (1.2.1) but also the shift from monosyllabic to polysyllabic words (1.2.2) and the ways of creating new words (1.2.3), including with compounds (1.2.4), affixes (1.2.5), and loans (1.2.6). The section ends with the relationship between words, syllables, and characters (1.2.7).

The discussion of the second problem starts with the number of characters to be mastered (1.3.1), then turns to how students learned them in old China (1.3.2) and how to learn them today (1.3.3). The chapter concludes with short sections on punctuation (1.3.4) and textbooks (1.3.5).

Dictionaries, including etymologies and word families (2.3), are the subject of Chapter 2. The specialized subjects of the origins and changing structure of the characters are discussed in Part II (Chapters 14–17).

Note that all works to do with the study of language and the characters (*xiaoxue* 小學) were placed in the Classics branch of the traditional fourfold bibliographical classification (*Sibu* 四部, on which see 9.3).

1.1   *Historical Changes*

The official belief in an uninterrupted legitimate succession from ancient times to the dynasty of the day and the unbroken use of a learned written language reinforced the impression of an unchanging China. It is a false impression. A good demonstration is the history of the changes that took place in the spoken language. Over the course of the past three millennia, the pronunciation changed radically: initial consonant clusters were lost, and consonant finals virtually disappeared from the standard language; there was a general move toward homophony, and tones were introduced. Monosyllabic words account for about two-thirds of the words in Classical Chinese texts. In Modern Chinese, both spoken and written, they have been largely replaced by polysyllabic words. Old Chinese was an isolating language using word order and particles to show grammatical relations, not inflections. It also has traces of an earlier system of sub-syllabic morphological affixes. Modern Chinese has gained greater precision using many varieties of syllabic affixes. It retains the same basic word order and remains largely uninflected.[1]

There is no generally agreed way of describing the different stages of the Chinese language during its recorded history. A widely accepted convention is to divide its development into four stages. The terms are all modern:

Shanggu Hanyu 上古漢語 (Old Chinese)
Zhonggu Hanyu 中古漢語 (Middle Chinese)
Jindai Hanyu 近代漢語 (Mandarin)
Xiandai Hanyu 現代漢語 (Modern Chinese)

The fit between the beginning of Modern Chinese and the modern period of Chinese history is a close one because the inauguration of both is defined in terms of political events or decisions. How the other stages of the development of the language fit the periodization of Chinese history based on cultural or other criteria (see Introduction, *Periodization*) is a fascinating question which deserves more attention than it has so far attracted, either from linguists or from historians.

---

[1] The best historical survey of the Chinese language in English is Jerry Norman, *Chinese*, CUP, 1988; 5th prnt., 1997. For a comprehensive 1,300 page history in Chinese, see Xiang Xi 向熹, *Jianming Hanyushi* 簡明漢語史 (Concise history of Chinese), 2 vols., Gaodeng jiaoyu, 1993, 1998. The main trends of modern research on the Chinese language in all periods are introduced in *Ershi shiji de Zhongguo yuyanxue* 二十世紀的中國語言學 (The study of the Chinese language in the twentieth century), Liu Jian 劉堅, ed. in chief, Beijing daxue, 1998.

"Old," "Middle," and "Mandarin" refer to stages of spoken Chinese as reconstructed largely on the basis of extant written texts. The style found in the texts that have survived from the period of Old Chinese—principally the Confucian classics—is referred to as Classical Chinese.[2]

From the Han onward, Literary Chinese (*wenyan* 文言) modeled on Classical Chinese developed. As time went by it was left behind by developments in the standard vernacular and in the dialects. But it retained its importance because it was used by the court and government for all official written business. Its mastery was a matter of survival and advancement for every scholar and official in the empire. The maintenance of a unified nonphonetic script was also crucial to the survival of the Chinese empire, whose rule extended over peoples who shared no common tongue.[3] Its role (but obviously not its form) is therefore often compared to that of Latin during the European middle ages. *Wenyan* was by no means immobile; indeed it was refined in numerous literary movements. It was also influenced by developments in the spoken language and in the vernacular literature. Its styles differed. Private correspondence, for ex-

---

[2] Chou Fa-kao (Zhou Fagao 周法高, 1915–94), "Stages in the Development of the Chinese Language," in *Papers in Chinese Linguistics and Epigraphy*, HKCUP, 1986, 1–3. Zhou uses the terms "archaic," "medieval," and "modern" instead of Old, Middle and Mandarin.

An enormous number of different and often overlapping terms have been used to describe and analyze the Chinese language. No less than 11,000 from all periods are briefly defined in *Hanyu zhishi cidian* 漢語知識辭典 (Dictionary of erudition on the Chinese language), Dong Shaoke 董紹克 and Yan Junjie 閻俊杰, eds. in chief, Jingguan, 1996.

For definitions of the special terms relating to Classical Chinese, consult: *Gu Hanyu zhishi xiangjie cidian* 古漢語知識詳解辭典 (Dictionary of detailed definitions of Classical Chinese knowledge), Ma Wenxi 馬文熙 and Zhang Guibi 張歸璧, eds. in chief, Zhonghua, 1996. It contains 3,600 entries divided between philology (700), phonology (270), semantics (660), grammar (930), rhetorical and stylistic devices in literature (400), literary genres (168), and bibliography (484), as well as brief biographies of 298 linguists and philologists, both ancient and modern. The entries scrupulously quote the often contradictory theories and views of the leading authorities. There are four-corner and *pinyin* indexes.

[3] Mark Edward Lewis, *Writing and Authority in Early China*, SUNY, 1999, is the best study of writing in early China as an instrument of power and control.

ample, was less formal than an examination essay or a memorial addressed to the emperor. It remained in use well into the twentieth century. Almost without exception, the primary sources that the historian of imperial China will be handling are written in it.

Throughout the manual Classical Chinese is used to refer to the written language of the sixth to second century BC. Literary Chinese (*wenyan* 文言) refers to the elite written language used from the Han to the mid-twentieth century. There is some risk of confusion because the current expression *Gudai Hanyu* 古代漢語 (ancient Chinese) in its broadest sense embraces all forms of Chinese before the twentieth century. Even in the narrow sense of the written language of the elite, it makes no distinction between Classical and Literary Chinese. Another possible source of confusion is that the term *guwen* 古文 is sometimes used as a synonym for *Gudai Hanyu*, yet *guwen* has at least three other distinct meanings (16.1, note 6). The pre-modern written vernacular is called *baihua* 白話 (unadorned speech), as opposed to *wenyan* 文言 (ornate speech), terms that were coined in the early twentieth century.

Baihua 白話 is the written form of the post-Han spoken language of which the first traces appear in the devotional tracts, popular literature, and vernacular stories of the Tang. It reached its most developed form in the great novels of the later empire such as *Hongloumeng* 紅樓夢 (Dream of the red chamber). It was normally based on the relatively educated spoken language of north China (*Hongloumeng* is the best available record of eighteenth-century Beijing dialect) although some *baihua* fiction uses the spoken tongues of the lower Yangzi (34.2).[4] *Baihua* was adopted as the written form of the language in the early part of the twentieth century and at the same time, along with the spoken language, transformed by the import of lexical and grammatical elements from foreign languages, chiefly English and Japanese (1.1.4).

The only European language which is still in use and has a recorded history as long as Chinese is Greek, whose earliest traces,

---

[4] Jiang Jicheng 蔣冀騁 and Wu Fuxiang 吳福祥, *Jindai Hanyu gangyao* 近代漢語綱要 (Essentials of Mandarin Chinese), Hunan jiaoyu, 1997; Jiang Shaoyu 蔣紹愚, *Jindai Hanyu yanjiu gaikuang* 近代漢語研究概況 (Outline of research on Mandarin Chinese), Beijing daxue, 1996, summarizes primary sources and research (1930s to 1990) under the headings of phonology, grammar, and lexicon.

Mycenaean Linear B, are roughly contemporary with the oracle-bone script of Shang China (1200 BC). There are other similarities between the histories of Greek and Chinese; for example, both had learned written languages, which changed much more slowly than the spoken language and its written forms; both based their literary languages on a canonized corpus of classical texts; both created national standard languages in the twentieth century only after lengthy debates on the merits of their respective demotic and literary traditions; and both drew heavily on their respective classics to create modern scientific vocabularies (as also did their neighbors).

1.1.1 Shanggu Hanyu 上古漢語 (Old Chinese)

Historical linguists have tried to identify the pre-Shang constituents of Old Chinese and its relationships with other languages and language groups. The evidence comes from a variety of scattered data derived from archaeology, genetics, comparative linguistics, inscriptions, and early texts. Some have even hypothesized that an early form of Tibeto-Burman was the language of the Yangshao 仰韶 culture, at least in the middle and upper reaches of the Yellow river; the language of the Shang was influenced by the Austroasiatic language of the Dongyi 東夷 peoples in Shandong and to the south, and an early form of Miao-Yao 苗瑤 was spoken in the middle Yangzi. Awaiting further research and more evidence, such hypotheses must remain tentative.[5] It is a controversial field with tantalizing pointers; for example, most of the languages of Inner Asia right across to Japan have since they first appeared been subject-object-verb, agglutinating, and polysyllabic. Chinese, on the other hand, along with most of the other languages of the Sino-Tibetan family (but not Tibetan itself), has been predominantly a subject-verb-object, isolating, mainly monosyllabic, language.[6]

---

[5] Wu Anqi 吳安其, "Han-Zangyu tongyuan wenti yanjiu" 漢藏語同源問題研究 (A study of questions of genetic affinity in Sino-Tibetan languages), *Minzu yuwen* 2: 18–25 (1996); George van Driem, "Neolithic Correlates of Ancient Tibeto-Burman Migrations," in *Archaeology and Language II*, Roger Blench and Mathew Spriggs, eds., CUP, 1998, 67–93. On the Yangshao and other Neolithic cultures, see 13.1.

[6] James A. Matisoff, "Sino-Tibetan Linguistics: Present State and Future Prospects," *Annual Review of Anthropology* 20: 469–504 (1991); George van Driem in "Sino-Bodic," *BSOAS* 60.3: 455–88 (1997), argues that Chinese may

Footnote continued on next page

The language of the Shang and early Western Zhou is recognizably Chinese, but incompletely known because it has been preserved only in the divinatory formulae carved on the Shang and early Zhou oracle bones (the longest no more than 200 characters), on the slightly longer inscriptions on bronze (the longest no more than 500 characters), and in the earliest parts of the *Shangshu* 尚書 (Venerated documents) and of the *Shijing* 詩經 (Classic of poetry). These are the concise records of the shaman, the archivist, or the minstrel, each representing quite different uses of the language. With the possible exception of the oracle-bone inscriptions, they were far removed from the spoken languages of their day. Some scholars include these early traces of Chinese in the definition of Classical Chinese. Others prefer to classify them as *Yuangu* 遠古 or *Taigu* 太古 *Hanyu* 漢語 (Chinese of remote antiquity, pre-classical or archaic Chinese, ca. 1200–600 BC).[7]

The *Shijing* and the main works of Classical Chinese circulated by word of mouth for years, if not for centuries, before being written down. Even after they were recorded, the practice of memorization and chanting of texts was the norm until the advent of printing in the Song, and it persisted until the twentieth century. Classical Chinese is therefore probably a rather special form of the language, whose short words and brief sentences were designed for easy memorization, a style close to ritual poetry. Indeed many of the works of the pre-Qin thinkers are notable for their brevity, and most are rhymed in whole or in part. The longest entry in the *Chunqiu* 春秋 (Spring and Autumn annals) is only 47 characters; the entire *Lunyu* 論語 (Analects) consists of short sections with a com-

---

have developed from an earlier form of Tibetan. Note *Bibliography of the International Conferences on Sino-Tibetan Languages and Linguistics I–XXV*, Randy J. LaPolla and John B. Lowe, eds., 2nd ed., Sino-Tibetan Etymological Dictionary and Thesaurus Project, UC, Berkeley, 1994. Covers the first twenty-five International Conferences on Sino-Tibetan Languages and Linguistics, from the first held at Yale in 1968 to the 25th held at Berkeley in 1992. In addition to a full bibliography of all papers presented, it includes indexes by author, subject, title, and Chinese character. A chronological listing of papers by conference is also provided.

[7] William Boltz offers a good description of the development of the language and the script between 1200 and 200 BC in "Language and Writing," *CHAC*, chapter 2, 74–123. See also Christoph Harbsmeier, *Language and Logic in Traditional China* (*SCC*, vol. 7, part 1), CUP, 1998.

bined total of only 15,883 characters. The *Shisanjing* 十三經 (Thirteen classics) altogether contain only 589,283 characters (Table 26, 19.2). New works written in the Han were beginning to become much longer, more like prose than poetry. The *Shiji* 史記 (Records of the historian), for example, is almost as long as the classics and 33 times longer than the *Lunyu*. One reason that it is so much longer is that it is closer to the spoken language of the day. This resulted in more polysyllabic words than are found in the pre-Qin texts.[8] The difference in styles can be seen clearly in the reworking in the *benji* 本紀 and *shijia* 世家 chapters of the *Shiji* (22.1; 44.1) of earlier texts such as the *Shangshu*, *Zuozhuan* 左傳 (Zuo's tradition) and *Guoyu* 國語 (Sayings of the states).

The idea that the need to memorize many of the early texts influenced their form is a hypothesis. It and other views as to the nature of the language of the pre-Qin texts need to be further tested, a task made easier by the discovery of new epigraphic materials and excavated texts that predate the transmitted texts (usually edited in the Han).

Even if the pre-Qin texts may be far removed from the spoken language of their day, the rhymes they contain have been used by Qing philologists (50.6.4) and modern historical linguists in an effort to reconstruct the pronunciation of Old Chinese by working back from the sounds of Middle Chinese (for which rhyme books are available, notably the *Qieyun* 切韵, AD 601).[9] The task is a con-

---

[8] Zhu Minche 祝敏徹, "Cong *Shiji Hanshu Lunheng* kan Hanyu duoyinci de goucifa" 從史記漢書論衡看漢語多音詞的構詞法 (Polysyllabic word formation in Chinese as seen in the *Shiji*, *Hanshu*, and *Lunheng*), *Hanyuxue luncong*, 8, Shangwu, 1981, 142–56; *Liang Han Hanyu yanjiu* 兩漢漢語研究 (Research on the Chinese language during the Former and Later Han), Cheng Xiangqing 程湘清, ed. in chief, Shandong jiaoyu, 1992, 1994, 262–364.

[9] Bernhard Karlgren (Gao Benhan 高本漢, 1889–1978) summed up his reconstructions of Old Chinese phonology (which he and some others refer to as "Archaic" Chinese) in *Grammata Serica Recensa*, *BMFEA*, 29: 1–332 (1957). For an account of Karlgren's work, see S. Robert Ramsey, *The Languages of China*, PUP, 1987; rpnt., with corrections, 1989, 136–48.

Jerry Norman and South Coblin argue that the *Qieyun* and other rhyme tables cannot be used as the key to unlocking the stages in the history of Chinese phonology, as they were by the Qing phonologists and later by Bernhard Karlgren, Edwin G. Pulleyblank, and others. See "A New Approach to Chinese Historical Linguistics," *JAOS* 115.4: 576–84 (1995). In a convincing rebut-

Footnote continued on next page

troversial one because it has to rely mainly on an analysis of the
rhymes in the *Shijing* and their comparison with the word classes
implied by characters sharing the same phonetic (*xiesheng* 諧聲) or
used as phonetic loans (*jiajie* 假借; see 16.2). Moreover, the odes in
the *Shijing* were created over a 500-year period and then recorded in
the standard cultivated language of the north, which was not necessarily directly related to the southern dialects of the Middle Chinese
rhyme books. Indeed, in the present state of knowledge it is not
possible to give a complete and reliable reconstruction of the sounds
or other features of Old Chinese. All that can be said with any certainty is that it was different from its written form, Classical Chinese (itself no monolith).[10]

The *yayan* 雅言 (cultivated speech or received pronunciation) of
the Spring and Autumn period was based on the dialect of the Eastern Zhou royal domain, whose center was Luoyi 雒邑 (Luoyang).
As the prestige pronunciation of the day, it served as a standard for
interstate diplomacy, as a means of communication across dialect
boundaries, and as the correct pronunciation for reciting the classics
(*Lunyu*, vii.18). The *yayan* in the sense of standard speech was contrasted with the regional languages, *fangyan* 方言 (conventionally
regarded as "dialects"), found in other parts of China. In the sense of
cultivated speech, *yayan* was contrasted with *suyan* 俗言 (everyday
speech). By the end of the Spring and Autumn period, the Austroasiatic Yi 夷 of Shandong and the Huai valley had mostly been sinicized, as had also the other early languages spoken along the Yangzi
River, in Wu 吳 and Yue 越, and by the Man 蠻 of Chu 楚, a process accelerated by the forced migrations of northern speakers to the
south and southwest (7.2.2).

By the Han, only a scattering of montagnards would have spok-
en in the old indigenous languages. The exceptions were the peoples
in the southwest, many of whose languages belonged to the Tibeto-
Burman branch of the Sino-Tibetan family. Their partial sinification was to come much later. In the rest of the south, the six major

---

tal Pulleyblank replies that all available sources should be used; see *JAOS* 118.2:
200–216 (1998).

   [10] Students of Old Chinese are just beginning to distinguish the different
dialects reflected in the classics. See Wang Qiming 汪啓明, *Xian-Qin liang Han
Qiyu yanjiu* 先秦兩漢齊語研究 (Research on the language of Qi in the Han
and pre-Qin), Ba-Shu, 1998.

regional dialects of today gradually began to take on their distinctive forms as the result of the language of the settlers from different parts of the north merging with the various sinicized and semi-sinicized languages of the places in which they settled. By the end of the Song the pattern of today's southern dialects had become established.[11]

In the larger dialect areas, the main cities set the model or standard form of the dialect (as does, for example, Guangzhou for Cantonese). Each dialect also had (and still has) many subdialects and brogues (*tuhua* 土話, *difanghua* 地方話). These often coexist alongside non-Han tongues, such as the eight branches and 28 subbranches of the Kam-Tai languages in southern China.

In the north, Chinese was influenced by the Turkic and Altaic languages of the Xianbei 鮮卑, Khitan, Jurchen, Mongol, and Manchu conquerors, all of whom made their languages the official language (*guoyu* 國語) while at the same time making lesser or greater efforts to master the language of their subjects.[12] In the south the dialects were less influenced by these northern conquerors and in

---

[11] The earliest dialect geography was written by Yang Xiong 揚雄 (53 BC–AD 18), *Fangyan* 方言. In it he listed words in use in various cities which differed from those in *tongyu* 通語 (the commonly used language based on the court and capital). Arrangement is by subject category. See Paul M. Serruys, *The Chinese Dialects of Han Times According to Fang Yan*, UCP, 1959, and South Coblin in *ECT*, 94–99; see also "Yang Xiong *Fangyan* zhong de shaoshu minzu yuci" 揚雄方言中的少數民族語詞 (Analysis of the vocabulary of national minorities in Yang Xiong's *Fangyan*) in Li Jingzhong 李敬忠, *Yuyan yanbian lun* 語言演變論 (Linguistic change), Guangzhou, 1996, 265–276 (first published in *Minzu yuwen* 1987.3).

For the distribution of the dialects in the twentieth century, see *Language Atlas of China*, S. A. Wurm, B. K. Tsou, and D. Bradley, eds., HK: Longmans, Parts 1 and 2, 1987 and 1991, and for description, Ramsey (1989). Zhou Zhenhe 周振鶴 and You Rujie 游汝杰, *Fangyan yu Zhongguo wenhua* 方言與中國文化 (Dialects and Chinese culture), Shanghai renmin, 1986; 4th prnt. with revisions, 1997, is fascinating and accessible.

[12] Mantaro Hashimoto, "The Altaicization of Northern Chinese," in *Contributions to Sino-Tibetan Studies*, Brill, 1986, 76–97; Jerry Norman, "Four Notes on Chinese-Altaic Linguistic Contents," *Tsing Hua Journal of Chinese Studies* 14: 243–47 (1982). The overall effect of migration on the late formation of dialects is examined in James Lee and R. Bin Wong, "Population Movements in Qing China and Their Linguistic Legacy," in *Language and Dialects of China*, William S. Y. Wang, ed., *JCL* Monograph Series 3, Berkeley, 1991, 52–77.

some cases retain to this day traces of Old Chinese brought to the south by settlers between the Han and Song.[13]

As the power of the central state waxed and waned, the influence of the language of the capital (*jingyu* 京語) rose or fell. In the Han, apart from being called *tongyu* 通語, it was also known as *changyu* 常語 or *fanyu* 凡語 and remained centered on Luoyang, a direct descendant of the *yayan* of the Zhou. Again in the Tang, the Song, the Ming, and the Qing, a common vernacular and literary standard grew up based on the dialect of the capital, from which Modern Chinese grew.

1.1.2 Zhonggu Hanyu 中古漢語 *(Middle Chinese)*

Zhonggu Hanyu broadly refers to Chinese as reconstructed using the *Qieyun* 切韵.[14] It covers the mainstream, cultivated, spoken language from the end of the Han to the end of the Tang. It has been further divided by some scholars into Early Middle Chinese (the cultivated spoken language of the Nan-Bei Chao as represented in the *Qieyun*) and Late Middle Chinese (the standard spoken language of the Tang probably based on Chang'an 長安, modern Xi'an, as represented by the *Yunjing* 韵鏡 and other rhyme tables in the same tradition). During these centuries, many lexical items took on grammatical functions as new particles and measure-words (sometimes called noun classifiers) were introduced.

The translation of more than 55 million characters of Buddhist scriptures provided a powerful stimulus for linguistic innovation and change (1.2.6). Buddhist literature broke the monopoly of *wenyan* on written Chinese. This helped prepare the way for the

---

[13] Cantonese and southern Min (Fujian) are the dialects considered closest to Old Chinese because of the retention of the finals 'p,' 't,' 'k,' and 'm,' which had begun to disappear from Mandarin already in the Song. They also retain more tones and still use many Classical words and characters, for example, *zou* 走, *shi* 食, and *wen* 蚊 in Cantonese instead of their equivalents in Standard Chinese, *pao* 跑, *chi* 吃, and *wenzi* 蚊子.

[14] The *Qieyun* also systematized the *fanqie* 反切 method of indicating pronunciation by giving two characters, the first showing the *shengmu* 聲母 (initial), the second, the *yunmu* 韵母 (final). For example, *dan: de an qie* 旦: 得安切. Previously, homophones or near-homophones had been used. *Fanqie* remained the standard method until the twentieth century. On Middle Chinese, see Pulleyblank, 1984 and 1991, and Baxter, 1992 (2.5.1).

growth of a vernacular literature in the Song (34.3). The desire to produce as many texts as possible to gain merit was also a major stimulus leading to the invention of printing (18.4).

Along with many other aspects of Chinese higher culture, the Chinese writing system was adopted by Korea, Japan, and Vietnam during this period. Classical pronunciation of the characters in these languages therefore provides important clues to the sounds of Middle Chinese.[15]

1.1.3　Jindai Hanyu 近代漢語 *(Mandarin)*

Jindai Hanyu 近代漢語 covers the cultivated spoken language from the end of the Tang to the mid-Qing. Some scholars subdivide it into Early (Song to Yuan), Middle (Ming to Qing), and Late (nineteenth to twentieth century) Mandarin. Everyday speech was called *suyu* 俗語 or *liyu* 俚語.

Guanhua 官話 (Mandarin) was the *lingua franca* of officials. It had begun to develop in the Liao, Jin, and Yuan and was based on the spoken Chinese of north China, gradually shifting from the Central Plains to Nanjing in the Ming and to Beijing at the end of the Qing. This *jingyu* 京語 of the later empire formed the basis of Modern Chinese. It was able to do so as the result of the north's having set the standard for so many centuries and also as the result of huge migrations to the south during the Qing.[16] Moreover, from the eighteenth century, examination candidates from Guangdong and Fujian were required to use *guanhua* and efforts were made to teach them in especially established schools called *zhengyin shuyuan* 正音書院.

1.1.4　Xiandai Hanyu 現代漢語 *(Modern Chinese)*

Modern Chinese (*Xiandai Hanyu* 現代漢語) is the general term for the Chinese language since the May Fourth Movement. It is used to

---

[15] The Japanese reading of Chinese characters based on an approximation of the pronunciation of the lower Yangzi region as introduced into Japan in the sixth century and before is called *Go on* 吳音, that based on the seventh, and eighth-century pronunciation of the Tang capital region is called *Kan on* 漢音, and the pronunciation introduced into Japan by Zen Buddhist monks from the Song to the Ming, *Tô on* 唐音.

[16] Lee and Wong, 1991 (1.1.1).

refer to both the spoken language and its written forms. In its broadest sense it embraces all the dialects of Chinese. In its narrow sense it is increasingly used to mean the standard form of Modern Chinese. In the 1920s and 1930s, *Guoyu* 國語 (National Language) was used in this sense. It was the successor of Mandarin (*guanhua* 官話). The term *Guoyu* is still used in Taiwan. In Singapore and elsewhere in Southeast Asia it is called *Huayu* 華語. It is also often called *Beifang hua* 北方話. The officially created *lingua franca* of the People's Republic was named *Putonghua* 普通話 (common speech). It is based on *Guoyu* and is the current, standard spoken form of *Xiandai Hanyu*.

Both the spoken and written languages have undergone greater changes in the twentieth century than at any time in Chinese history. This has meant not only the introduction of huge numbers of foreign loanwords, but also the adoption of grammatical structures. The process began during the New Culture and May Fourth Movements. Deliberate efforts were made to Europeanize or modernize the Chinese language. *Baihua* was introduced as the new written form to replace *wenyan* and *baihua* itself was "Europeanized." Accordingly it is sometimes called new-style *baihua* to distinguish it from old or traditional *baihua*.[17] Despite these changes, Modern Chinese still retains a far greater portion of its ancient roots than any other world language (most clearly seen in its written form, *shumianyu* 書面語), possibly because of the continuous history of the language and thanks to the late survival of *wenyan*.

1.2 Words

1.2.1 Multiple Meanings

As with all other languages, many Chinese lexemes have more than one meaning (polysemy). This is perhaps more common than in other languages because words continued in use for such a long time, accumulating as they did so an unusually large number of

---

[17] Ping Chen, *Modern Chinese: History and Sociolinguistics*, CUP, 1999, is a good introduction to the transformations of the language between the 1890s and the 1990s; see also Edward Gunn, *Rewriting Chinese: Style and Innovation in Twentieth Century Chinese Prose*, SUP, 1991; Cornelius C. Kubler, *A Study of Europeanized Grammar in Modern Written Chinese*, Student Book Co., 1985.

meanings. Many words and terms in *wenyan* not only changed their meanings but were retained in Modern Chinese, sometimes with new definitions (1.2.6) or with some new and some old ones. The fact that the characters stayed basically the same can mask the extent of these changes.[18]

One of the main difficulties in reading both Classical and Literary Chinese is that many characters have multiple meanings; this is the result of the less than perfect match between words and characters or, to put it in another way, the fact that many different lexemes have the same written form. They do so because there were always more words than characters in early China, so a single character was pressed into use for different words. This is most clearly seen in the oracle-bone script, which uses, to take but one example, the original form of the character *shi* 史 (scribe) for *shi* 事 (carry out an official duty), *shi* 史 (record official acts), *li* 吏 (the person who does an official duty), *shi* 使 (send somebody on an official errand), and *shi* 使 (envoy). Over the millennium between the end of the Shang and the Eastern Han, many more characters came into use in an increasingly standardized manner. Nevertheless, one character could still be used for several words, different characters were often used for a single word, and individual characters could have many variant forms (16.4).

A related difficulty is caused by the common occurrence of homographs (the same character, but pronounced in a different way; cf. the difference between English to <u>wind</u> wool and the <u>wind</u> blows). In Old Chinese, such differences in pronunciation or tone are the traces of an earlier system of sub-syllabic derivational affixes, but because of the nature of the characters these traces are barely discernable (1.2.2).

Not infrequently, the distinct meanings of both syllables in a disyllabic phrase in Classical or Literary Chinese (*qiutian* 秋天: autumn skies) are merged into one in Modern Chinese (*qiutian* 秋天: autumn). Indeed, it is not easy to decide when two characters still represent two words or have become a compound. Take the example of *baixing* 百姓. To translate it as "the hundred names" is a mistake. Not only because *bai* 百 is used as a hyperbolic number (7.1.2)

---

[18] For introductions to lexicology, see Zhao Keqin 趙克勤, *Gudai Hanyu cihuixue* 古代漢語詞匯學 (The lexicology of Classical Chinese), Shangwu, 1994.

meaning "many," but also because it had early become a compound whose meaning had changed radically in the classical period and was more than the separate meanings of its two constituent root morphemes. There are no rules: the process leading from two separate words to one compound was not uniform (1.2.5).

The names of institutions and titles are a trap for the unwary because they often continued in use long after the reality that they had originally described had changed. *Baixing* 百姓 in the earliest classical texts meant "the clan leaders." It was then extended to mean the "the senior officials" (*baiguan zuxing* 百官族姓). During the Warring States, it took on the sense of "the ordinary people," as in modern *laobaixing* 老百姓. In post-Han texts it is also sometimes used to mean "many sons." The changes in the meaning of *Zhongguo* 中國 or *Hanzi* 漢子 in later Chinese history are other good examples (Box 2 and 42.1).

Allusions in a foreign language are never easy. Classical and Literary Chinese abound in them (called *dian* 典 or *diangu* 典故 and their use, *yongdian* 用典, *yongshi* 用事). They often require knowledge of the original context from which they are condensed to fully understand the sense. A further complication is that *diangu* themselves were often abbreviated, for example, into set phrases (*chengyu* 成語). These in turn were frequently reduced to two characters or split into two disyllabic words making the original allusion even more elusive. *Diangu* were often used for personal names (3.2.2) and in book titles (9.9). More difficult are formations such as *zangci* 藏詞, in which one part of a phrase takes its meaning from the unstated part, for example, *erli* 而立 meaning thirty years old (from the sentence in the *Lunyu*, "*Sanshi erli*" 三十而立; Table 4, 3.2).

Fortunately, there are many other more straightforward kinds of abbreviation (*lüeyu* 略語 or *shengzi* 省字 are the modern terms), including the Chinese equivalents of clippings, acronyms, and initialisms—of personal names and toponyms (Table 6), of book titles (9.9), of official titles (22.3), of loanwords (1.2.6), of numerological sets and correspondences (2.5). Once recognized as such, they can serve their original purpose as a shortcut in speech and as an aid to memorization. It is, after all, easier to say the clipping Meiguo 美國 than Yameilijia hezhongguo 亞美理駕合衆國, just as it is easier in English to say the initialism USA than the United States of America (41.2.3). No doubt because they are all-pervasive, nobody has ever thought to compile a dictionary of abbreviations in Literary Chinese, although there are individual reference books for particular types of abbreviation (2.4, items 12–15). Large comprehensive dictionaries such as the *Hanyu da cidian* 漢語大辭典 contain definitions of huge numbers of abbreviated words and phrases, including *diangu* and *chengyu*.

The challenge for students of Chinese history is to recognize the changed meanings of words, phrases, and titles in different periods, in different genres, and, in some cases, in different dialects and, having recognized them, to explain them. One should never assume that because a word, character, or compound is familiar from a modern context that its meaning in an earlier period was the same.

1.2.2   Polysyllabic Words in Classical Chinese

The use of polysyllabic words was quite advanced in Classical Chinese, up to 25–30 percent of whose lexicon is composed of them. Most were disyllabic compounds (trisyllables are only occasionally found in nouns and adjectives, never in verbs).

Disyllabic words occur much less frequently in Classical Chinese than monosyllabic words (which as a result score 80–90 percent in word frequency counts of early works such as the *Shijing* or the *Mengzi*).[19] Most scholars argue that Old Chinese was close to the written language of the day, Classical Chinese, and therefore, like it, mainly monosyllabic. In Middle Chinese, the number and frequency of disyllabic words increased greatly. The main explanations of this change pinpoint semantic needs, phonological attrition, historical influences, and prosodic requirements. Probably all four played their part.

As society becomes more complex, the need to specify things more accurately is increasingly felt. Take the example of plant names in the *Shijing*. They are usually monosyllabic. But even in those early days of the written language the need to distinguish dif-

---

[19] The *Mengzi* contains 713 polysyllabic compounds (of which 200 are proper names or titles) out of a total of 2,278 words; so 78 percent of its lexicon is monosyllabic. Many of the monosyllabic words occur more than 500 times, while few of the disyllabic words occur more than 10 times. See "Xian-Qin shuangyinci yanjiu" 先秦雙音詞研究 (Research on disyllabic words in the pre-Qin), in *Xian-Qin Hanyu yanjiu* 先秦漢語研究 (Research on the Chinese language in the pre-Qin period), Cheng Xiangqing 程湘清, ed., Shandong jiaoyu, 1992, 1994, 45–113.

ferent varieties led to the creation of disyllabic words, for example *tangdi* 唐棣 (possibly *prunus triloba*) and *changdi* 常棣 (possibly *prunus tomentosa*). From the Later Han, hundreds and thousands of words were formed in a similar way and for similar reasons.

All languages undergo phonological attrition over time (e.g., Latin *vinum* → French *vin*). In the case of Old Chinese this involved the loss of initial consonant clusters, loss of morphological affixation, and a reduction in the number of consonant finals. By the Later Han the only way to avoid ambiguity caused by the increase in homophones was to increase the number of polysyllabic words (1.2.4–5). The change was perhaps also influenced by the polysyllabilism of China's northern conquerors and by the new vocabulary of Buddhism (1.2.6). A fourth hypothesis downplays functional, semantic, or historical explanations of the shift from monosyllabic to polysyllabic words, arguing instead in terms of prosodic phonology.[20] The transition from Old to Middle Chinese was characterized by the reduction of syllable weight. Since the new syllables were insufficient to form minimal independent prosodic units, thereafter such units needed to be formed by two syllables, not one.

The lexicon of Modern Chinese is overwhelmingly disyllabic. Yet, as with nearly all other languages, including English and even German, most of the most frequently used words remain monosyllabic. In the course of time, many disyllabic words also found their way into *wenyan*.[21]

1.2.3   Ways of Creating New Words

The ways of creating new words in Chinese were the same as in other languages, namely, by extending the meanings of existing words, by combining existing words to form compounds (1.2.4), by affixation (1.2.5), by borrowing from other languages, and by importing dialect words into the language of the capital (1.2.6). Exten-

[20] Shengli Feng (馮勝利), "Prosodic Structure and Compound Words in Classical Chinese," in *New Approaches to Chinese Word Formation*, Jerome L. Packard, ed., de Gruyter, 1998, 197–260.

[21] Of the 3,000 most commonly used words today, 1,337 are monosyllabic. Of the remaining 1,663 polysyllabic words, 724 contain characters from the monosyllabic list. The *Hanyu da cidian* 漢語大辭典 contains a total of 369,000 words from all periods of the language. Of these 94 percent are polysyllabic (and 80 percent of these are disyllabic). Only 6 percent are monosyllabic.

sion was typical of Old Chinese, compounding and affixation grew in importance in Middle Chinese, and borrowing took place on a large scale in Middle Chinese and to an even greater extent from the late Qing onward. One result of these changes is the shift from the monosyllabism of Old Chinese to the polysyllabism of Modern Chinese examined in 1.2.2.

The lexicon of the Shang already contains much of the core vocabulary of Chinese. Judging from the evidence available in oracle-bone script, it was mainly monosyllabic, and words tended to have single meanings (16.3). Given the special nature of the inscriptions the vocabulary is extremely limited. Most words are nouns. There are only slightly over 300 verbs (by the Later Han, there are over 3,000). As China entered the iron age, society became more complex and new words were needed. As literature became more sophisticated, greater precision was required. During the Zhou many new words were created, including ones for new objects and concepts, including for indicating grammatical relations. The different ways in which the characters were adapted to write the new words are examined in section 16.2.

One of the features of Classical Chinese is that the different meanings or parts of speech of a word are sometimes indicated by differences in pronunciation, in tone, or in both. These were recorded by commentators in the Han and subsequent dynasties and in some cases have survived to the present day (*hao* 好 as an adjective meaning "good" is read in its original third tone, *benyin* 本音; in the departing or fourth tone, it becomes the verb "to like"). Linguists refer to this as *sisheng bieyi* 四聲別義 (derivation by tone change). Sometimes a change in meaning (and in part of speech) is indicated by changes in both the sound and the tone (*chang* 長 in the second tone means "long," and *zhang* 長 in the third tone means "to grow"). Sometimes the changes in meaning or usage were later indicated by alterations in the character (*dao* 道 in the fourth tone means "road"; when it was extended to mean "to guide," the new character *dao* 導 was eventually introduced).

Traditional scholars believed that the same original word had been deliberately split up in pronunciation or given different tones in order to distinguish shades of meaning (*pozi* 破字). Modern scholars starting with Karlgren and others have shown that the different pronunciations are probably traces of a system of sub-syllabic affixation used in a pre-classical stage of the language. For example, the suffix *-s appears to have been added to adjectives or verbs to make them nouns (*drjon* 傳 "to transmit" becomes the postulated *drjon-s* 傳 "a record," a distinction still reflected in Modern Chinese 傳 *chuan* and 傳 *zhuan*). As more is discovered about the phonology of Old Chinese, it may be possible to discern the morphological rules governing such changes.[22] Some of the difficulties of reconstructing such derivational processes are that many of the old readings have long since been forgotten, the practice of reading Classical Chinese in modern spoken Chinese (because the characters look the same) masks many of the old distinctions, and different readings for different meanings of a character are often dropped in modern editions and dictionaries.

1.2.4   Compounds

Bound compounds (formed according to rhyme) have been common in Chinese since the earliest Zhou texts. They predate compounds formed according to grammar, which enter the language in large numbers during and after the Han.

The earliest bound compounds were onomatopoeic reduplicates (e.g., *jiangjiang* 將將 for the sound of a carriage) or simple repetitions (usually descriptives, e.g., *pengpeng* 蓬蓬, abundant). Others include alliterative semi-reduplicates, such as *pipa* 琵琶 (lute) or *linglong* 玲瓏 (nimble); rhyming ones, such as *paihuai* 徘佪 (waver); or those that are neither alliterative nor rhyming, such as *furong* 芙蓉 (cottonrose hibiscus). The names of birds, insects, plants, fruits, animals, and fish were sometimes of this type.[23] With the exception

---

[22] Edwin G. Pulleyblank, "Morphology in Old Chinese," *JCL* 28.1 (2000); William H. Baxter and Laurent Sagart, "Word Formation in Old Chinese," in *New Approaches to Chinese Word Formation*, Jerome L. Packard, ed., de Gruyter, 1998, 45–64.

[23] It may be that many such words were imported into Old Chinese along with the things they represented. Or, as You Rujie 游汝杰 suggests, generic noun prefixes may have been one of the shared features of Old Chinese, Tai, and Miao-Yao. Traces may still be found in some of the southern dialects or in those languages which put the general name for birds, insects, and trees, first as in the Dai for fruit (*ma*) followed by the specific as in *maman* (pear), *matau* (peach), *masan* (persimmon); You Rujie, "Zhongguo nanfang yuyan li de niaochong lei mingci citou ji xiangguan wenti" 中國南方語言里的鳥蟲類名詞詞頭及相關問題 (Noun prefixes in southern Chinese languages for birds and in-

Footnote continued on next page

of simple repetitions, all the reduplicates (*dieci* 叠詞) and semi-reduplicates have one thing in common: their meaning cannot be deduced from the individual words. It is for this reason that they are called bound compounds (*lianmianzi* 連[聯]綿字). They were often written with various characters because these were used for their sounds, not their meanings. For special dictionaries of *dieci*, see 2.4, item 12; and of *lianmianzi*, 2.4, item 13). Another category of disyllabic words was composed of proper names or official titles.

The most common type of compound in Literary Chinese was not bound. The two constituent words had equal weight and were usually synonyms or near synonyms, such as *daolu* 道路 (avenue + road = highway). This type was already beginning to make an appearance in Classical Chinese. Not infrequently, the two synonyms were also cognates (e.g., *rouruo* 柔弱 "weak" or *shaoxiao* 少小 "young"). Others were antonyms, e.g., *daxiao* 大小 (big + small = size); another common type was when the first word modified the second, as in *daji* 大計 (big + plan = strategy); *tiaozao* 跳蚤 (jump + flea = flea), or the second modified the first, as in *shuoming* 説明 (speak + clear = explain). Many of the compounds at first had more abstract meanings than their constituent parts (e.g., *pengyou* 朋友, *guojia* 國家). Synonym compounds may have arisen as a means of avoiding ambiguity by identifying which word a speaker was referring to. For example, in order to avoid confusing *chu* 初 with another word having the same pronunciation, the speaker might have said (as did Xu Shen 許慎 in the *Shuowen jiezi* 説文解字), *chu shi ye* 初始也 (start is begin).[24] The two words gradually became linked to form the compound *chushi* 初始. Likewise, a speaker would have avoided confusing *zao* 蚤 (flea) with other words having the same pronunciation (and for which 蚤 had been pressed into service to represent), by saying something along the lines of "*tiaozao*

---

sects and related questions), in *The Ancestry of the Chinese Language*, William S. Y. Wang, ed., *JCL*, Monograph series 8 (1995), 253–68. Benjamin K. Ts'ou, "Some Remarks on Entolomogical Terms in Chinese and the Austroasiatic Link Revisited," in *Studies on Chinese Historical Syntax and Morphology: Linguistic Essays in Honor of Mei Tsu-lin*, Alain Peyraube and Sun Chaofen, eds., École des Hautes Etudes en Sciences Sociales, Centre de Recherches Linguistiques sur l'Asie Orientale, Paris, 1999, 203–21. Note that the *Shijing* contains about 340 names of plants, birds, insects, and animals. However, only 10 percent are disyllabic words of this or any other kind.

[24] The *Shuowen* was completed in AD 100 (2.2.1 and 16.2).

zhi zao ye" 跳蚤之蚤也 (flea as in jumping flea). Eventually it was easier just to use the compound *tiaozao* for flea (this is sometimes called the "clear identification of meaning theory" of the origin of disyllabic words, *mingque biaoyi shuo* 明確表義説). Early dictionaries and glosses on the classics in the Wei, Jin, and Nan-Bei Chao used the same method.[25] Since these works were intensively studied or even committed to memory by the wordsmiths (the literati), the definitions themselves may often have been the source of new disyllabic words or increased their currency.

In Classical Chinese, disyllabic compounds usually had only one meaning, and their constituent syllables were rather loosely connected, for example, *renmin* 人民 (A-B) could also be written *minren* 民人 (B-A), and both *ren* 人 and *min* 民 could represent independent words. In some cases, the reverse order of the syllables served to indicate different parts of speech, as in *yanyu* 言語 (speak, a verb) and *yuyan* 語言 (language, a noun). As time went by, the link between the words in a compound became stronger and their order irreversible. Today there are a still a number of A-B, B-A compounds. Usually the B-A alternative is less used (e.g., *zhishuang* 直爽 and *shuangzhi* 爽直, candid). Occasionally, a reverse order has been retained in a dialect, as in *huanxi* 歡喜 (to like) in the Wu dialect as opposed to the standard *xihuan* 喜歡.

1.2.5 Affixes

In line with the trend towards bisyllabism, syllabic affixation (represented by a separate character) becomes increasingly common from Middle Chinese onward. It was done by adding either prefixes (for example, *a* 阿 or *lao* 老) or suffixes (*tou* 頭, *zi* 子, *shi* 師, *jia* 家, *bian* 邊, *mian* 面) to a word. Many of these affixes were meaningless

---

[25] For example, *xing wei xingxiang* 形爲形象, gloss by Guo Pu 郭璞 (276–324) on *Erya*, II.1. Xu De'an 徐德庵 has a list of 839 examples of such disyllabic glosses by Guo on monosyllabic words in the *Erya* and in the *Fangyan* 方言 in his *Gudai Hanwen lunwenji* 古代漢文論文集, Ba-Shu, 1989, 225–74. Xu Shen also defines many pairs of words in terms of each other: *sheng yin ye* 聲音也 and under the entry *yin* 音: *yin sheng ye* 音聲也, probably indicating that whatever differences there may once have been between the two words had been lost by his day. Other words defined by a synonym or chain of near synonyms often emerge as compounds, if they had not already done so (in this case *sheng-yin* 聲音).

(e.g., the noun suffix *zi* 子 as in *beizi* 杯子, *yizi* 椅子, *wenzi* 蚊子). They created a more balanced rhythm (possibly compensating for some lost feature such as a final consonant). Being unstressed, they enabled an alternation of stressed and unstressed syllables that is easier to speak than a string of stressed ones (1.2.2). They also functioned to differentiate the meanings of homophones. For example, in the late Tang, to distinguish *yi* 椅 (the word for the newly introduced high-standing, high-backed chair) from the previous meanings of *yi* 椅 and from other words pronounced *yi*, you said *yizi* 椅子. There are many such affixes. The *Hanyu da cidian* lists 1,200 compounds ending in *zi* 子 (and *zi* is only the most common). Another large class of disyllabic words was formed using grammatical affixes, such as *liao* 了 (*laile* 來了), *li* 里 (*jiali* 家里) or *qu* 去 (*zouqu* 走去).

1.2.6 Loanwords

The fourth important source of new words was loanwords from other languages (*wailaici* 外來詞 is the modern term). Reflecting their origins, they tended to be polysyllabic. There were, and still are, four main types:

jieci 借詞 (loanwords based on a transcription of the sound, *yinyi* 音譯), what might be termed "aliens"

yici 譯詞 (semantic loans based on a translation of the meaning, *yiyi* 意譯), what might be termed "denizens"

banyin banyi 半音半意 (hybrids, a mixture of the two previous types)

direct borrowings of the form (almost entirely from Japanese, for example, *changhe* from *baai* 場合)

Over time, if an "alien" moved from the dialect of first transcription to general use, it usually moved from the first to the second type (from "alien" to "denizen"), a transition found in most languages as words are gradually assimilated to the standard pronunciation and other features of the language of their adoption. The difference in Chinese is that the transition meant shifting from the demotic to the literary language. The reason is that people found it easier to recognize and to pronounce a new word based on two familiar *wenyan* characters than a jumble of characters not necessarily even representing the foreign sounds because of dialect differences. Thus, for example, in the early twentieth century, *linggan* 靈感 (inspiration) quickly replaced its earlier transcription, *yanshipilichun* 烟士披里

純, and *kexue* 科學 (science) prevailed over the earlier transcription *saiensi* 賽恩斯. In the course of time, most loanwords were gradually sinicized and standardized. But many lingered on in their original form in the dialect of first transcription. Thus dialects often have different sets of loanwords—for example, Hakka is rich in Malay and Malay-Dutch loans, and Cantonese is strong in English loans. Indeed, today, given the prestige of Cantonese, the dialect word sometimes prevails over the translated term and enters the standard language, e.g., *digxi* 的士 (taxi) rather than *chuzu qiche* 出租汽車, even though *dishi*, or *di* for short (*putonghua* for *digxi*) gives little or no indication of the original sound. Note that even with those words that remained transcriptions, some margin was possible in the choice of characters, allowing not only an approximation of the sound but also a particular meaning. This can be seen in the flattering characters chosen for transcribing the names of the Western powers in the nineteenth century (e.g., Meiguo 美國) as compared to the graphic pejoratives selected for aborigines and barbarians (40.1 and 41.2).

At the formative period of Chinese in prehistoric times, a huge amount of the vocabulary no doubt came from non-Huaxia 華夏 tribes.[26] There are glimpses of foreign loans even in some of the basic vocabulary. The earliest forms of *hu* 虎 (tiger) are possibly derived from Austroasiatic, and *xiang* 象 (elephant) from one of the early Tibeto-Burman languages. As pointed out in 1.2.4, some of the early bound reduplicates may also have been loans. It is not easy to discern such pre-Qin loans because of the remoteness of the time and because they were assigned Chinese characters whose pronunciation has changed and whose phonetic origin has long since been forgotten. Under the empire, most loanwords were from languages spoken outside China or from the language of those who conquered and settled in China; few were from the languages of the non-Han peoples in the China area except toponyms (4.1) and ethnonyms

[26] Norman, 1988, 6–22; *The Ancestry of the Chinese Language*, William S. Y. Wang, ed., *JCL* Monograph series 8 (1995), especially Edwin G. Pulleyblank, "The Historical and Prehistorical Relationships of Chinese," and the same author's "Zou and Lu and the Sinification of Shandong," in *Chinese Language, Thought and Culture: Nivison and His Critics*, Philip J. Ivanhoe, ed., Open Court, 1996, 39–57; for the possible connections of Chinese with Indo-European via the Tarim Basin, see 12.1.

(40.1). For general vocabulary items, because of the complexity of the intermingling of peoples and their languages over many centuries, it is often no easy matter to establish which language is the lender and which the borrower.[27]

The first easily identifiable wave of loanwords dates from the Former Han dynasty, during which new goods (along with new words for them) were imported from the Xiongnu and from Western Asia. They are easily known, not only because many were listed, but also because they are clearly transcriptions of foreign sounds, e.g., *tuotuo* 橐駝 (camel; later *luotuo*, eventually orthographically standardized in the Tang by writing it in the dictionaries with the appropriate signific [*ma* 馬] to form *luotuo* 駱駝); *musu* 目宿 (lucerne, alfalfa; later standardized as *musu* 苜蓿); *putao* 蒲桃[陶] (grape; later standardized as 葡萄). Another common way to make a new word for a new product was to form a disyllabic compound consisting of the current word for barbarian (at this time, *hu* 胡) tacked on to an existing Chinese word, e.g., *gua* 瓜 (generic for gourds), to form *hugua* 胡瓜 (cucumber). Centuries later such compounds often lost their alien identifier for a neutral term (the *hugua* 胡瓜 became a *huanggua* 黄瓜).

Sanskrit (*Fanwen* 梵文, from the abbreviated transcription of Brahmâ, *Fanmo* 梵摩) was the next major source of loanwords, not only for things but also for ideas, mainly conveyed during the process of translating the Buddhist scriptures between the Later Han and the Tang.[28] The desire to propagate the faith to the general public

---

[27] Laurent Sagart, "Chinese 'Buy' and 'Sell' and the Direction of Borrowings Between Chinese and Hmong-Mien: Response to Haudricourt and Strecker," *TP* 81.4–5: 328–42 (1995); David Strecker and André G. Haudricourt, "Hmong-Mien (Miao-Yao) Loans in Chinese," *TP* 77.4–5: 335–41 (1991). It has often been argued that *jiang* 江 (river) and *he* 河 (river) are derived from Austroasiatic and Altaic, respectively (e.g., by Norman, 1988). Zhang Hongming 張洪明 shows convincingly that it was the other way round; see "Chinese Etyma for River," *JCL* 26.1: 1–47 (1997).

[28] See Liang Xiaohong 梁曉虹, *Fojiao ciyu de gouzao yu Hanyu cihui de fazhan* 佛教詞語的構造與漢語詞匯的發展 (The structure of Buddhist words and the development of Chinese vocabulary), Beijing yuyan xueyuan, 1994; Zhu Qingzhi 朱慶之, *Fodian yu zhonggu Hanyu cihui yanjiu* 佛典與中古漢語詞匯研究 (Researches on the Buddhist Canon and the vocabulary of Middle Chinese), Wenjin, 1992, 1996; Victor H. Mair, "Buddhism and the Rise of the
Footnote continued on next page

(not just to the educated) led to the choice of the spoken language. The originals were in a rhythmic, polysyllabic form of Sanskrit intended for easy memorization. The translators emulated the originals. A huge new lexicon was created (comparable in size to the 12,000 words having German etymologies in the English language). The new words were mainly polysyllabic, reflecting both the Sanskrit from which they were translated and long-term trends in the Chinese language. Transcriptions circulated for centuries in a profusion of phonetic approximations. *Futu* 浮屠 (the earliest official transcription for Buddha) appeared with other characters depending on the dialect of the scribe. *Fotuo* 佛陀, reflecting the Luoyang dialect of the second and third century, eventually emerged during the early Tang as the standard. Soon thereafter it was abbreviated as *Fo* 佛 and then coupled with existing Chinese monosyllabic words to form dozens of new disyllabic compound hybrid loans for Buddhist concepts such as *Fofa* 佛法 (Buddha dharma), *Fojiao* 佛教 (Buddhism), *Fojing* 佛經 (sutra), *Fosi* 佛寺 (Buddhist temple), and so forth; all of which are still in common use. Such words are readily identifiable as originally part-Sanskrit imports. Other new words from Sanskrit were not transcribed but translated using different combinations of sound and meaning as well as affixes, for example, *huashi* 畫師 (from *citara-kara*, painter). Many thousands of new words were created using existing Chinese words to invent new compounds. They very quickly became part of the general language (often with extended meanings). Take, for example,

fangbian 方便 (*upâya* "opportune, expedient"; modern "convenient")

pingdeng 平等 (*upeksâ* "space and time have the same form"; modern "equal")

shiji 實際 (*koti*; *tathatâ* "the frontier of consciousness"; modern "real")

shijie 世界 (*loka-dhâtu* "time and space," replaced the Classical Chinese word *tianxia* 天下; modern "world")

xianzai 現在, *guoqu* 過去, *weilai* 未來 ("present," "past," and "future," replaced *jin* 今, *xi* 昔, and *lai* 來)

Written Vernacular in East Asia: The Making of National Languages," *JAS* 53.3; 707–51 (1994).

Because words such as these are not transcriptions, their foreign origin is not obvious. As a result, few people today have any idea of their non-Chinese origin.[29]

A thousand years went by before the next major wave of loanwords. It reached an initial high point at the end of the Qing and has been accelerating ever since. It started with the arrival of the Westerners in south China in the Ming. *Fan* 番 was often used to indicate foreign instead of the earlier *hu* 胡 (as in *fangua* 番瓜, pumpkin, and *fanqie* 番茄, tomato). In the nineteenth century, the meaning of *xi* 西 was extended to mean "western" in general (previously it had referred to the Western Regions, i.e., Inner Asia, or to India). *Yang* 洋 served the same purpose. Both *yang* and *xi* 西 were typical of Shanghai coinages. As in previous periods, alien loanwords became denizens, in this case by changing the prefixes for a descriptive with no sense of foreign. But the dialect into which they had been first introduced sometimes retained the original transcriptions (e.g., Cantonese *fanjian* 番梘 for soap instead of *feizao* 肥皂; see 35.2 for more examples). There are even a few examples of reverse imports of words with *fan* into English: fangwei/fankwae (foreigner: *fangui* 蕃鬼) or fantan 蕃攤 (a card game).

The missionaries exerted a considerable influence in creating loanwords. They would translate the text into spoken Chinese, and a Chinese collaborator would then write down his understanding in *wenyan*. The method, known as *kouyi bishou* 口譯筆受, had also been used during the translation of the Buddhist scriptures. Some of the neologisms invented, even at the first arrival of the missionaries in the early seventeenth century, are still in use today—for example, the translations of geometrical terms such as "triangle" (*sanjiaoxing* 三角形) by Matteo Ricci (1552–1610) and Xu Guangqi 徐光啓 (1562–1633) in their Chinese version of the first six chapters of Euclid's *Elements*.[30] It was also Ricci and his Chinese collaborators who invented the translations for names such as Mediterranean (Di-

---

[29] Zhu Qingzhi (1996) lists 248 examples of Chinese words that began as translations from Sanskrit in the *Zhongbenqi jing* 中本起經 (Madhyametyukta-sutra, a life of Sakyamuni), of which only 128 are identified as translations in the *Hanyu da cidian* 漢語大詞典; and of these, 105 are cited as originating in later, non-Buddhist sources. *Zhongbenqi jing* was translated in AD 207.

[30] For a study of the background and course of their translation, see Peter M. Engelfriet, *Euclid in China*, Leiden, 1998. On Ricci, see 29.7.1.

zhonghai 地中海), Atlantic (Da Xiyang 大西洋), or terms such as North and South Poles (Nan Beiji 南北極), and equator (*chidao* 赤道). In the nineteenth century, the missionaries translated many more scientific and medical texts into Chinese using neologisms like *luosiding* 螺螄釘 (lit. snail nail, i.e., screw); *gongsi* 公司 (company), or calques such as *tielu* 鐵路 (railroad, from Fr. *chemin de fer*). Popular works by Chinese authors explaining one or other aspect of the West, such as the *Haiguo tuzhi* 海國圖志, were often based on these early translations, thus giving them a wider circulation both in China and Japan (29.7.1 and 29.7.3). Chinese scientific translators working alone or with the missionary educators or in the College of Interpreters or at the Kiangnan Arsenal also invented many words (37.2). Xu Shou 徐壽 (1818–84) was responsible, for example, for the characters for the chemical elements, and Li Shanlan 李善蘭 (1810–82) coined hundreds of terms, including *daishuxue* 代數學 (algebra) and *weifen* 微分 (differential). These were quickly adopted in Japan. Neologisms were also drawn from a number of early English-Chinese dictionaries, long since forgotten, e.g., Wilhelm Lobschied, *English and Chinese Dictionary*, HK: *China Express*, 1866–69; rpnt., Bikashoin, 1997.

Typically, both in China and in Japan, different versions of a new word circulated for several decades before a winner emerged. In the case of the rival terms for mathematics (*suanxue* 算學 and *shuxue* 數學), the two were in use for a century before a national conference in China in 1938 decided by a narrow margin to settle for *shuxue*. *Kuangwu* 礦物 (minerals) was coined in 1853, but it replaced *jinshi* 金石 (also used at this time for minerals) only in 1902. These examples show that the establishment of a loanword was in two main stages: first, the transcription or coining of the new word; second, its gaining acceptance as the standard term for the new product or concept. Once it had emerged, the variants gradually disappeared, although not infrequently in China some have been retained to this day in one or other of the southern dialects.

In many thousands of cases, those terms that emerged as standard for new scientific, legal, and other concepts in Japan were then imported into China at the beginning of the twentieth century, where there too they became the standard, replacing earlier translations or transcriptions. The reason that the Chinese readily accepted these loans was that they could be regarded as "denizens," not "aliens." No doubt, too, the vogue in China for things Japanese in the 1900s (37.2) increased the value attached to the loans. Some of the loans were well-established Japanese words, for example, *baai* 場合 (*changhe*) for "occasion"; or had just been created using old Chinese words such as *zu* 足 (foot) to form calques like *zuqiu* 足球 (football); or were old phrases with a new meaning, for example *kagaku* 科學 (*kexue*) for science (original meaning in *wenyan*: "study for the official examinations") or *keizai* 經濟 (*jingji*) for economy (original meaning: "to govern and assist the people"). Many were taken from the Japanese versions of English-Chinese dictionaries, where they had first appeared in their modern sense, e.g., *guanxi* 關係 (relation, now used in the sense of "special connections"), *xingwei* 行爲 (action), *liyi* 利益 (profit), *lixi* 利息 (interest), *falü* 法律 (law). Hundreds of others were affix compounds, such as *yan* 炎 (*weiyan* 胃炎, gastri<u>tis</u>); *zhuyi* 主義 (*shehuizhuyi* 社會主義, social<u>ism</u>); *hua* 化 (*xiandaihua* 現代化, moderni<u>zation</u>). Only occasionally did Japanese supply aliens, such as the curious Chinese word *wasi* 瓦斯 for "gas" (from the Japanese pronunciation of *wa* as *ga*). European languages, chiefly English, on the other hand, provided large numbers of such loans (Masini [1993] and Liu [1995] have appendixes with many examples of the different categories of missionary and Japanese loans; see 2.7).

In a passage that captures the haphazard way in which new words were coined, the great educationist and popularizer of the West Fukuzawa Yukichi 福澤諭吉 (1835–1901) explains how he found the new word for steam: "Up to this time [ca. 1860], the English word 'steam' had been translated by *zhengqi* 蒸氣. But, I thought, is it possible to shorten this to one character? So, I got out the *Kangxi zidian* 康熙字典 and glanced over the characters with fire and water significs. There I came across the character *qi* 汽 with the annotation, 'the vapor of water.' I thought this was not bad, so, I began to use it [in *Seiyô jijô* 西洋事情, 1866]." Actually, *qiche* 汽車 had already appeared in China in 1855 and in Japan in 1864. But given the popularity of his works, Fukuzawa may have been right in claiming that he was the one who ensured that it became the standard in Japan (replacing *kasha* 火車 and *karinsha* 火輪車).

Words flew backward and forward between China and Japan, and the process by which, and at what time, one or other transcription or translation became the standard is often not clear. Not surprisingly, in many cases, the Chinese and Japanese eventually chose different neologisms, of which the words for "train" and "automobile" are but two of many examples (*huoche* 火車 and *qiche* 汽車 in Chinese; *kisha* 汽車 and *jidôsha* 自動車 in Japanese).

Throughout Chinese history large numbers of loanwords fell out of use after the influence of the people who had introduced them declined. This was the fate of many Xiongnu, Xianbei, Khitan, Jurchen, Mongolian, Manchu, and Soviet loans. Finally, because translation of the meaning rather than transcription of the sound was the preferred form for loans, with the passage of time their foreign origin was often forgotten (who now remembers that *nucai* 奴才 was probably derived from the Mongolian for dog [*noqai*]?). One way of spotting a loan from earlier times (especially a proper name) is if it has an unusual pronunciation and is composed of two or more characters. For example, the kingdom at modern Kuqa (Kuche 庫車) is pronounced Kuci or Qiuci 龜茲 (618–732), not Guici. It is clearly a loan (4.1). Much easier to spot as transcriptions are loanwords to which the mouth classifier (*kou* 口) has been attached to indicate that the character is used for its sound, not for its sense. The practice began in the Nan-Bei Chao and was common in the Qing, by which time it has been claimed, this use of *kou* 口 had acquired a derogatory sense.[31] This was certainly not always the case, witness the late-Qing practice of writing weights and measures with the mouth classifier to indicate "English" or "foreign" inches, miles, and so forth (7.3), or its use for novelties such as *kafei* 咖啡 (from French café).

1.2.7 Words, Syllables, and Characters

Compared with the million-year development of the neurological basis for language in humans, the appearance of writing took place very suddenly and almost simultaneously within the time span 7000—1500 BC, first in ancient Mesopotamia and Egypt, next in northern India, and then in China (for the antecedents of the characters, see Chapter 14). As with the other ancient writing systems, the Chinese script was used to record words or parts of words, not directly things or ideas: that is to say, even though many of the earliest characters may have been derived from symbols or drawings of things, they were neither pictographs nor ideographs, but logo-

[31] The claim is made by Zhou Zhenhe 周振鶴, *Yiyan shuyu* 逸言殊語 (Anecdotes and unusual phrases), Zhejiang sheying, 1998, 12–14.

graphs. This was pithily expressed in the *Yijing* 易經 (Classic of changes), "Shu bujin yan, yan bujin yi" 書不盡言言不盡意 (Writing cannot express all words, words cannot encompass all ideas), i.12. To this day, there is no agreement on how to define Chinese characters. Some stress their meaning, some their sound, some both. Some emphasize the change from single-morpheme words in Classical Chinese to disyllabic words (*shuangyinci* 雙音詞) in Modern Chinese. All are agreed that characters can be analyzed in terms of three essential elements: form, meaning, and sound.

Almost without exception classical philologists after the Han called "words" characters (*zi* 字), a usage first recorded in the *Shiji*. They did so because they were analyzing the literary language in which most words were single morphemes represented by single characters (*ci* 詞, the modern word for "word" was used for "grammatical particle," *xuci* 虛詞, empty word). Characters are of course not the same as words. In a polysyllabic word they stand for syllables, not for the word; the same character was not infrequently used for two quite different words, and likewise two or more characters were on different occasions written for the same word.

1.3   On Studying Chinese Characters

1.3.1   The Number of Characters

At first sight the main hurdle in studying written Chinese, including Classical Chinese, is the large number of characters to be mastered. It has been on the rise since the second millennium BC, but there were far fewer characters in general use at any one time than the figures in Table 1 suggest.

An unchanging core of no more than a few hundred basic characters has remained the most frequently used since the Shang dynasty to the present day. They account for up to 70 percent of all characters employed at any given time. Another 1,000 to 2,000 characters were in the frequently used category, accounting for 30 percent and more of the total. Finally, a large number of characters only rarely make an appearance. They account for no more than 5 percent of all characters in use in a particular period. The remainder formed a growing pool of graphic variants (*yitizi* 異體字; 16.4.1) and dead characters (*sizi* 死字) long since discarded except in successive dictionaries or rhyme books, each of which not only added new characters but absorbed those found in its predecessors.

Table 1: The Number of Characters

1000 BC	4,500	*jiaguwen* 甲骨文 (15.4)
AD 100	9,353	*Shuowen* 説文 (2.2.1 and 16.2)
1066	31,319	*Leipian* 類篇[32]
1716	47,035	*Kangxi zidian* 康熙字典 (2.2)
1990	54,678	*Hanyu da zidian* 漢語大字典 (2.3)
1994	85,568	*Zhonghua zihai* 中華字海[33]

To get a sense of proportion, the *Lunyu* has only 1,382 different characters in a total of 15,883. Only about 10 percent of the different characters (not counting the 88 particles) appear more than 10 times, but they occur so frequently that they account for 70 percent of the total characters. Sixty-seven percent of the characters appear less than five times, but they account for only 10 percent of the total characters. Of the most common characters in the *Lunyu*, about 100 have remained among the most frequently used to this day, retaining the same forms and basic meanings (but not pronunciation). In addition, even some of the characters that appear infrequently in the *Lunyu* have in the meantime joined the core of most frequently used characters.

A traditional scholar would have had an active knowledge (the ability to write) at least 6,000 or 7,000 characters (in the Han dynasty, a knowledge of 9,000 characters was required as a condition to qualify as a scribe, *shi* 史). His passive knowledge (the ability to read), on the other hand, would have covered many more, because before the advent of Qing philology and modern scholarship, much of his reading ability depended on recognizing borrowed characters, graphic variants, and changed meanings. The 6,000 or 7,000 characters could of course be arranged in different combinations to form tens of thousands of different words and phrases. So, the total num-

[32] The *Leipian* is a dictionary containing many characters newly coined in the Tang and Song. Final editing was done by Sima Guang 司馬光 (1019–86).

[33] (The Chinese sea of characters), Zhonghua, 1994. The large increase in characters in this dictionary is accounted for by the inclusion of variants found in Buddhist and Daoist texts and new epigraphic sources, as well as characters unique to Hong Kong, Taiwan, Singapore, Korea, and Japan.

ber of words that a scholar knew would have far surpassed the total number of characters he had mastered.[34]

1.3.2 Traditional Ways of Learning the Characters

Fu yu dushu bi xian shizi yu shizi bi xian chaxing 夫欲讀書必先識字欲識字必先察形 (If you wish to read books, you must first be able to recognize characters; and to recognize characters, you must first scrutinize their forms), Gu Aiji 顧藹吉 (Kangxi period), in *Preface* to *Libian* 隸辨 (Analysis of chancery script), 1718; Zhonghua, 1985.

Nowadays children in China begin to study the characters by learning to spell their sounds using an alphabetic writing system (*pinyin wenzi* 拼音文字). In the old days there was no such system, and they began by memorizing the characters for everyday words often using the equivalent of "flash cards" (individual characters on separate bits of paper or wood) with a homophonous character, a picture, or both on the back.[35] Long before school they usually began

---

[34] Today, adult literacy is defined as having a knowledge of at least 3,000 characters (of which 45 percent are monosyllabic words and 44 percent are used in the most common 1,663 compounds). Since 1988, there has been an official listing of 3,500 frequently used characters (*changyongzi* 常用字). Primary-school children have to learn 2,535 by the time they graduate at age 12 *sui*, the remaining 1,000 are acquired at junior high school along with a further 2,000 or so to bring the total to 5,000–6,000. A knowledge of 3,500 characters is enough to enable comprehension of 99 percent of everyday printed matter in modern China; knowledge of 3,800 would enable comprehension to be increased to 99.9 percent, and of 5,200 to 99.99 percent. Character counts say nothing directly about the number of words (especially in Modern Chinese) mastered by an individual since some frequently used characters (*xue* 學, for example) often reappear in different words, while others (*de* 的, for example) do not. Frequency counts have therefore to take into account not only how frequently a character is used in isolation, but also its "word formation capability"; Yin Binyong 尹斌庸, *Modern Chinese Characters*, John S. Rohsenow, tr., Sinolingua, 1994, 45–89.

[35] There is a good account in Evelyn Sakakida Rawski, "Elementary Education," and "Popular Education Materials," Chapters 2 and 6 of *Education and Popular Literacy in Ch'ing China*, UMP, 1979, 24–53, 125–54. See also the article "Children's Literature" by Xiong Bingzhen 熊秉真 in *ICTCL*, vol. 2, 31–38 and Pei-yi Wu, "Education of Children in the Sung," in *Neo-Confucian Education*, William Theodore de Bary and John W. Chaffee, eds., UCP, 1989; SMC, 1994, 307–24.

with pictographic characters such as *ri* 日 (sun) or *yue* 月 (moon) and those with the fewest strokes such as *yi* 一 (one) or *er* 二 (two). Later, they also used lists of characters for common words in rhyming doggerel arranged by categories such as heaven and earth, trees and flowers, fruits and nuts, animals and birds, pots and pans, farm tools, toponyms, and official titles, and much else besides. The first reference to such lists of miscellaneous characters (*zazi* 雜字) is in the Song. Normally they either circulated separately or were included in almanacs and encyclopaedias for everyday use (31.3). One of the first to survive dates from the fifteenth century. It is the earliest illustrated primer in the world.[36] Only one is known to have been written by a famous writer (Pu Songling 蒲松齡, 1640–1715, *Riyong suzi* 日用俗字).

Those village children who were lucky enough to have the opportunity to study did so part-time in the winter slack season. No doubt they stopped once they had learned enough basic characters for everyday use. But children from wealthy or educated families, studied full-time at a private school (*sishu* 私塾) run by the family or clan. They began formal studies at the age of eight *sui*. The first step was to memorize one of several of the famous character primers (*zishu* 字書), which not only listed characters but also contained edifying stories and other materials. The primers were referred to as *cunshu* 村書 (village school books) or as *mengshu* 蒙書 (beginners' books). The children chanted the primers aloud, either singly, in turn, or in unison. They also used the primers as copy-books for learning the characters. Dozens are extant. They are an important source for the history of education and the transmission of received ideas.[37] They were often written and rewritten by eminent scholars and statesmen or at least attributed to them. The chancellor of Qin, Li Si 李斯 (280–208 BC), was the author of *Cang Jie* 倉頡, the first

[36] Luther Carrington Goodrich introduces the *Xinbian duixiang siyan* 新編對象四言 (Newly compiled and illustrated four-word primer), 1436, in *15th Century Illustrated Chinese Primer*, HKUP, 1967, 1975. This contains 326 illustrations of 244 single-character words and 82 two-character compounds.

[37] *Zhongguo mengxue jicheng* 中國蒙學集成 (Anthology of Chinese elementary primers), Han Xiduo 韓錫鐸, ed., Liaoning jiaoyu, 1993. This massive tome contains the original texts of 74 primers with detailed notes on their content and language. The editor has also compiled a bibliography of the editions of all known extant primers, 2083–98.

primer of which fragments survive.[38] More than a millennium later, Zhu Xi 朱熹 carried on the tradition with his *Tongmeng xuzhi* 童蒙須知 (What children should know).

From the Han to the Six Dynasties, the most popular character primer was the *Jijiu pian* 急就篇.[39] It introduced everyday characters for basic vocabulary arranged in groups. By the Tang, this had been replaced by the *Qianziwen* 千字文 (Thousand-character text).[40] Another popular primer was the *Baijiaxing* 百家姓 (Myriad family names). It lists 438 of the most common surnames arranged in six-character rhyming couplets. Both the *Qianziwen* and the *Baijiaxing* were deliberately written so that almost no character they contain occurs more than once. They were memorized generation after generation for well over 1,000 years. Starting in the Song, the first eight characters of the *Qianziwen* were also used for archival classification (20.1). From the Yuan to the Qing, the single most popular primer was the *Sanzijing* 三字經 (Three-character classic).[41] In the later empire, these three primers—the *Sanzijing*, the *Baijiaxing*, and the *Qianziwen*—were known as the *San Bai Qian* 三百千. They were also known as the *San Bai Qian Qian* 三百千千 (the *Sanbaiqian* plus

---

[38] It was expanded under the title *Cang Jie pian* 倉頡篇 (on Cang Jie, see 14.1). Fragments were discovered at Fuyang in Anhui (44.4.2), at Juyan (44.4.3), and at Dunhuang (46.3); see Roger Greatrex, "An Early Western Han Synonymicon: The Fuyang Copy of the *Cang Jie Pian*," in *Outstretched Leaves on His Bamboo Staff: Essays in Honour of Göran Malmqvist on His 70th Birthday*, Joakim Enwall, ed., Stockholm: Association of Oriental Studies, 1994, 97–113.

[39] (Quick mastery of the characters), Shi You 史游 (fl. 43–33 BC), comp.; punctuated and collated edition, Zeng Zhongshan 曾仲珊, Yuelu, 1989.

[40] The *Qianziwen* was written in the early sixth century. It consists of 250 four-character lines (only one character appears more than once). See *Ch'ien tzu wen, The Thousand Character Classic, A Chinese Primer*, Francis W. Paar, ed., Frederick Ungar, 1963. This includes the original Chinese in several Chinese scripts plus English, French, German, and Latin translations by various nineteenth-century hands.

[41] *San Tzu Ching*, Herbert A. Giles, tr. and annotated, 1900; 2nd ed., rev., Kelly and Walsh, 1910. The *Sanzijing* contains 356 alternating rhyming lines of three characters each. It has 514 separate characters. See James T. C. Liu, "The Classical Chinese Primer: Its Three-Character Style and Authorship," *JAOS* 105.2: 191–96 (1985), who argues that the *Sanzijing* was probably not written by the Southern Song scholar Wang Yinglin 王應麟 to whom it is usually attributed.

the *Qianjiashi* 千家詩, the myriad poems). Some are still in use (albeit in rewritten versions).

Many other primers came into common use, sometimes on more specialized themes, such as history or poetry. They are usually in rhyming, balanced phrases with very short lines to make them easy to memorize and to do away with the need for punctuation.[42] In the preface to his translation of the *Sanzijing*, the first professor of Chinese at Cambridge, Herbert Giles, stressed that "to foreigners who wish to study the book-language of China, and to be able to follow out Chinese trains of thought, [its importance] can hardly be over-estimated. Serious students would do well to imitate the schoolboy, and commit the whole to memory." The first professor of Chinese at Oxford, James Legge, used the *Sanzijing* to teach his beginning students, who were required to memorize it. If this seems asking too much, then at least memorize the opening lines.[43]

The characters for numbers were learned early and repeated in the arithmetic lessons, which were an important part of the primary school curriculum.[44]

Although girls were not allowed to attend government schools until the reforms of 1906, they too used the same primers if they attended clan schools or were privately educated at home. In addition

[42] *Meng Ch'iu: Famous Episodes from Chinese History and Legend*, Burton L. Watson, tr., Tuttle, 1979. The *Mengqiu* 蒙求 is a primer in the form of a history story book. It was written by Li Han 李翰 (Tang).

[43] 人之初性本善, 性相近習相遠, 苟不教性乃遷, 教之道貴以專 (At birth human nature is basically good; our natures are the same, but our behavior differs. If foolishly there is no teaching, nature will deteriorate. The right way of teaching is to pay attention to the details). The first two lines were based on *Lunyu*, xvii. 2. They have been on the lips of every Chinese schoolchild ever since the Yuan dynasty. After 1949, and especially during the Cultural Revolution, a different message was taught: the class background of one's parents makes people different; the right way of teaching is to be not just expert (*gui yi zhuan* 貴以專) as taught in the *Sanzijing*, but also, and above all, politically correct (*youhong youzhuan* 又紅又專).

[44] Man-Keung Siu, "Mathematics Education in Ancient China," *Historia Scientiarum* 2nd series, 4: 223-32 (1995). Catherine Jamie, "Learning Mathematical Sciences During the Early and Mid-Ch'ing," in *Education and Social Change in Late Imperial China*, Benjamin Elman and Alexander Woodside, eds., UCP, 1994, 223-56. The mathematics textbook for more advanced students was the *Jiuzhang suanshu* 九章算術 (37.1).

there were special primers with characters and sentiments considered appropriate for them (39.2).

As an integral part of learning to read the characters (*shizi* 識字), students also learned to write them (*xiezi* 寫字). They started, as they do today, with the strokes (*bihua* 筆畫) and the stroke order (*bishun* 筆順). They practiced them over and over again (*xizi* 習字), first by imitating the red (*miaohong* 描紅, i.e., filling in in black the red outlines written by the teacher on *miaohongzhi* 描紅紙), then by tracing from the primers, and finally by copying the calligraphic models of accepted masters (a practice known as *lintie* 臨帖). To help get the proportions right, they used *jiugongge* 九宮格 (paper marked out in squares with each square subdivided into nine small ones).

By the time they had memorized the primers (which together contained from 400 to 1,500 different characters), students would have been seven or eight years old and ready to begin to read simple books. It was commonly held that a person's ability to memorize was at its strongest up to the age of 15 *sui*; so there was great pressure to pack in as much as possible by then. The technique used was constant repetition. First on the list was the *Xiaojing* 孝經 (Classic of filial piety), which was used as a character primer, soon followed by the *Sishu* 四書 (Four books), specially selected for their brevity and correct Confucian thinking by Zhu Xi 朱熹 (19.2). Girls also had to memorize the *Xiaojing* as well as one or other of the ethical texts for women (39.2). Reading took several forms: explanations by the teacher (including the difficult characters, punctuation, and key passages); reading aloud or silently by the students (*du* 讀 or *kan* 看); punctuating the texts for themselves, and finally, and above all, recitation and chanting from memory (*langsong* 朗誦, *langdu* 朗讀). After the basic classics and poetry came extracts from well-known works from the Qin and the Han periods (*wen bi Qin Han* 文必秦漢). Students also memorized the classifiers (often referred to in English as radicals; see 16.3). Composition of literary and moral essays and poetry was the final stage of study. Here the emphasis was on the imitation of the styles of the ancient masters with a premium on quotations and allusions from the classics (*yongdian* 用典, *diangu* 典故).

A late Qing poet satirizes a village school:

一陣烏鴉噪晚風，諸徒齊逞好喉嚨。
趙錢孫李周吳鄭，天地元[玄]黃宇宙洪。

千字文完翻鑒略，百家姓畢理神音。
就中有個超群者，一目三行讀大中。

Like a flock of crows cawing in the evening breeze, the students
show the quality of their lungs: 'Zhao, Qian, Sun, Li, Zhou, Wu,
Zheng' [opening of the *Baijiaxing*], 'Heaven and earth, dark and yellow, the universe vast and great' [the beginning of the *Qianziwen*].
When the *Qianziwen* is finished, they go over the *Jianlüe* (Abbreviated mirror), when the *Baijiaxing* is done, they do the *Shentong shi*
(Poems of an infant prodigy). An outstanding student reads at high
speed the *Daxue* (Great learning) and the *Zhongyong* (Doctrine of the
mean).[45]

Throughout the entire process of learning the characters, students were (and still are) taught to dissect them into their graphic
components, for example, *hong shi jiangbian niao* 鴻是江邊鳥 (the
goose [character] is a bird beside the river; more succinctly, *jiang-
niao hong* 江鳥鴻). In the same way they learned to distinguish
common names such as Zhang 張 or Li 李 by referring to them as
gongchang Zhang 弓長張 or *muzi Li* 木子李. They were also taught
character riddles (*zimi* 字謎, *miyu* 謎語), such as *ban'ge pengyou bu
jianle* 半個朋友不見了 (half a friend you can't see; answer, *yue* 月).
Dissecting compound characters *hetizi* 合體字 into their component
parts was used not only by students as a mnemonic but also by
scholars as a literary device (*xizi* 析字)[46] and as an influential approach to etymology (2.3.1), and by all levels of society as a popular
form of fortune-telling (*chaizi* 拆字, *cezi* 測字, *xiangzi* 相字). Such
practices no doubt began when the first *hetizi* were put together.
The earliest references are in the Zhou period. Several are recorded
in the *Zuozhuan*, one under the year 542 BC: *Yuwen min chong wei
gu* 于文皿蟲爲蠱 ("the character for 'ultra-venomous insect' is made

---

[45] *Cunxue shi* 村學詩 (Village school poem) from Guo Chenyao 郭臣堯,
Pengfuji 捧腹集 (Comic collection), ca. 1810, as quoted by Liang Shaoren 梁紹
壬 (1792–1837) in his *Liangban qiuyu an suibi* 兩般秋雨庵隨筆 (Miscellaneous
writings in Autumn Rain Study), Shanghai guji, 1982, 214; see Angela Leung,
"Elementary Education in the Lower Yangtze Region in the Seventeenth and
Eighteenth Centuries," in Elman and Woodside, 1994 (1.3.2), 396.

[46] There is a thorough description of the different forms of *xizi* in Karl S.
Y. Kao, "Rhetoric," in *ICTCL*, vol. 1, 134–35. Anagram poetry developed dur-
ing the Southern Dynasties and remained a popular minor art thereafter; see
John Marney, *Chinese Anagrams and Anagram Verse*, CMC, 1993.

up of insects [above the character for] bronze vessel"). Xu Shen in the *Postface* of the *Shuowen* deplores the faulty analyses of the component parts of characters, which were common in his day. He cites several, for example, *ma tou ren wei chang* 馬頭人爲長 ([The character for] "long" [is incorrectly] written with the [characters for the] top part of the horse and man), see 16.2.

1.3.3 Learning the Characters Today

The old method of committing the characters to memory by writing them over and over again has much to commend it. On the other hand, rote learning of long lists or whole books is unacceptable to foreign students, most of whom will have long since passed their infancy by the time they start studying Chinese. A good teacher will introduce readings that contain the most common characters. In parallel, it pays to develop an analytical way of looking at the characters (Table 2).

Table 2: Component Parts of Characters
Example: zhang 蟑 as in zhanglang 蟑螂, *cockroach*

Bushou 部首 (classifiers or radicals)	虫
Pianpang 偏旁 (side components)[47]	虫 章
Xingfu 形符 [*xingpang* 形旁] (significs)	虫
Shengfu 聲符 [*shengpang* 聲旁] (phonetic indicators)	章
Bujian 部件 (constituent parts)	虫 立 日 十
Zigen 字根 (roots)[48]	虫 立 日 十

Note that the majority of characters consist of pairs of components, which in turn can be subdivided into pairs of constituent parts. Thus *zhang* 蟑 is composed of *chong* 虫 and *zhang* 章; *zhang* 章 is composed of *li* 立 and *zao* 早; and *zao* 早 combines *ri* 日 and *shi* 十.

---

[47] *Pianpang* 偏旁 (side components) refers to both *xingfu* 形符 and *shengfu* 聲符. Although they can occur in any position in a character, they are referred to in this way because they occur on the left and right side of more than 60 percent of *xingsheng* 形聲 compounds.

[48] *Zigen* 字根 are used in computer coding. The concept is very similar to the *bujian* 部件. There is no agreed count of the number of *zigen*. The system used in China, the Big-5, has 125.

Character riddles, graphic puns, anagrams, and other such diversions have the merit of making you think of the characters in terms of their components. But because there are so many characters, it is not possible to rely solely on specific mnemonics, especially such fanciful inventions as "what he <u>wants</u> (*yao* 要) is a Western (*xi* 西) girl (*nü* 女)." Apart from writing the characters, most students find there is a much better way to reinforce the learning of the characters encountered in their reading and study. It is to master the few hundred components, mainly significs and phonetic indicators that can provide the key to the meanings and sounds of tens of thousands of characters. Next, to group them in one of three ways—by signific, by phonetic indicator, or by word family. The most common components of compound characters (*hetizi* 合體字) are usually themselves single-component characters (*dutizi* 獨體字). Almost without exception their original pictographic form indicated the words for everyday objects or ideas, which by definition form the core vocabulary of all languages, for example, *ri* 日, *yue* 月, *shang* 上, and *xia* 下 (sun, moon, up, and down). They account for only 3 percent of all characters in use today, but they are the oldest, and they have been among the most frequently used at every stage of the language. Moreover, the most common ones feature as significs or phonetic indicators in thousands of other characters. They are also used as classifiers in dictionaries; so it makes good sense to begin by mastering the *dutizi*, starting with the most frequently used classifiers (16.3). Having mastered these, the next step is to dissect and analyze compound characters (*hetizi* 合體字).

Most *hetizi* (which make up the vast majority of all Chinese characters) are composed of a signific (*xingfu* 形符) and a phonetic indicator (*shengfu* 聲符). They are therefore called *xingshengzi* 形聲字 (16.1). They can be grouped either by signific or by phonetic indicator. As an example of the first type, take, *chong* 虫:

蟑 *zhang* (cockroach)   蚊 *wen* (mosquito)
蟪 *hui* (cicada)   蚤 *zao* (flea)

As an example of the second type, take *zhang* 章 (seal, stamp):

zhang 蟑 (cockroach)   *zhang* 障 (obstruct)
zhang 樟 (camphor wood)   *zhang* 彰 (bright; outstanding)

Karlgren's *Grammata Serica Recensa* is a listing of 8,398 characters in Old Chinese grouped together by phonetic indicator on the basis of their reconstructed sounds (2.5). *Lishi Zhongwen zidian* 李氏中文字典 is a dictionary of Modern Chinese organized by phonetic indicator, using modern pronunciations (2.8).[49]

A third method of grouping the characters is by identifying those that have not only a semantic relation, but also a shared phonetic origin, for example, those containing *zhang* 長 (stretch), namely *zhang* 張 (stretch a bow), *zhang* 帳 (canopy), *zhang* 漲 (increase of water), *zhang* 脹 (distended stomach). The study of such cognate words or word families is an excellent way of learning them. It is discussed in section 2.3.2.

For computer coding the characters are dissected into smaller units than the *pianpang*. These are usually called *bujian* 部件 or *zigen* 字根.[50] They include graphemes (*zisu* 字素, *ziwei* 字位), defined as the smallest units in the script capable of causing a contrast in meaning. *Bujian* can also be single-component characters (*dutizi*).

There is no agreed number of *bujian*. It depends into how many graphic components the characters are split and for what period of the script the analysis is made. Throughout most of Chinese history there were something fewer than 400. There are, then, only limited numbers of component parts to be learned—the dozen or so basic strokes, the 214 classifiers, the 1,000 or so *pianpang* from which most compound characters are constructed, and the 350 to 600 or so *bujian* into which all characters of whatever type can be dissected.[51] Each method overlaps with the others, so the total number of component parts is less than their sum.

---

[49] Because the script by its nature was ill-suited to keep pace with changes in the spoken language, today the phonetic indicators of only about 18 percent of the characters give an exact indication of their pronunciation; 59 percent give a hint; and 23 percent give no indication at all. The scores would be slightly higher in Cantonese and much higher in Old Chinese.

[50] In one large sample of several million characters, the 10 most frequently used *bujian* were all classifiers, namely, *kou* 口, *ren* 人, *tu* 土, *ri* 日, *huo* 火, *ren* 亻 (usually called *danliren* 單立人), *quan* 犬, *bai* 白, *gou* 勹 and *mu* 木. They accounted for 23 percent of the total sample.

[51] One scholar has counted 348 *bujian* in the oracle bones; modern characters are dissected into 623 *bujian* for electronic communications. See *Yitizi zidian* 異體字字典 (Dictionary of graphic variants), Li Pu 李圃, ed., Xuelin, 1995; rev., 1997, Introduction, 3) and *Hanzi xinxi zidian* 漢字信息字典 (A dictionary of Chinese character information), Kexue, 1988.

1.3.4 *Punctuating a Text*

As with other ancient writing systems, pre-Qin texts had no punctuation, and most later ones had none either. It was left to each reader to mark pauses in a sentence (with a pause mark, *dou* 讀, inserted between characters), and the end of a sentence with a small circle " 。" (*quan* 圈) or dot (*dian* 點) called *ju* 句 that was placed beside the last character. The process was called *judou* 句讀 from the Han onward (also *judu* 句度, *jujüe* 句絕, *juduan* 句斷, or *duanju* 斷句). One of the hallmarks of a good scholar was how easily and accurately he could punctuate a text.

In everyday life, scribes or other writers did provide some punctuation, as can be seen even as early as the oracle bones, where sentences are sometimes divided by straight lines drawn under the last character. In imperial times, characters such as *ju* 句 (stop) or *dou* 逗 (pause) were occasionally used in place of the circles and dots. Sometimes only *quan* were used. Sometimes a blank space was left at the end of a sentence. Ticks were also used as a sort of paragraph indicator or sentence divider. Instead of repeating a phrase, or occasionally a character, an equals sign was used. Many other punctuation marks were inserted, as can be seen on excavated texts written on bamboo, wood, and silk (19.1). If the same character had several tones, this was often indicated by writing a little circle at the corners of the character: the level tone (*ping* 平) in the bottom left-hand corner; the rising tone (*shang* 上), top left; the departing tone (*qu* 去), top right; the entering tone (*ru* 入), bottom right.

Various clues can be used to help mark sentences and pauses. For example, introductory and final particles indicate the beginnings and endings of sentences, and interlinear notes were always placed at the end of a sentence. Rhythm and parallelism are also important indicators.

There were, of course, no capital letters at the beginning of a sentence, and proper nouns were not marked. A reader would emphasize a passage with a row of circles, one to the left of each character. Occasionally in the Song and more frequently in the Qing, editions were printed with punctuation already added.

The lack of punctuation is a real difficulty in reading an old text. Modified Western punctuation (*biaodian* 標點) was gradually introduced in the twentieth century. Fortunately, modern editions of old texts are usually punctuated. But there are many mistakes. They arise from failing to understand institutional terms, personal names and toponyms, book titles, grammar, and special terms.

1.3.5 Textbooks and Readers

It is best to study Classical Chinese having mastered Modern Chinese. A convenient way to start is to go through one of the many excellent annotated texts of the classics that give the original text in complex characters, a translation into Modern Chinese, and notes. Or use a good bilingual text of one of the classics such as *Lunyu* 論語 or the *Mengzi* 孟子 (Table 26, 19.2). While doing so, be guided by a good grammar (such as Pulleyblank's *Outline of Classical Chinese Grammar*, UBCP, 1995; hereafter abbreviated as *OCCG*), and try one of the many beginner's dictionaries such as *Jianming gu Hanyu zidian* 簡明古漢語字典 or *Gu Hanyu changyongzi zidian* 古漢語常用字字典 (2.4). More structured approaches are available in the sampling of textbooks of Classical Chinese listed below.

Modern editions of Han and pre-Han works can help overcome many difficulties, such as indicating alternative characters (16.4.4) or the special readings of a character in a particular context, and they invariably provide punctuation. But not all texts that a historian will be reading will have modern editions or translations.

To study different genres of Chinese, start with a textbook or reader. Each generation to visit China, from the first missionaries through the consuls and customs inspectors to modern scholars, has produced its own. Some are still worth using; for example, there is much to interest the economic historian in a perusal of Friedrich Hirth (1845–1927), *Textbook*. It includes 240 documents, including contracts with translation, notes, and vocabularies:

Textbook of Documentary Chinese, 2 vols., Statistical Department of the Inspectorate General of Customs, 1885; 2nd enlarged edition, 1909; rpnt. in 1 vol., Ch'eng-wen, 1968.

There are plenty of more recent textbooks for non-Chinese students, some of which incorporate the latest analyses of the language, for example, the first item below:

Michael A. Fuller, *An Introduction to Literary Chinese*, HUP, 1999. Excellent for beginning students of Classical Chinese (with annotated excerpts up to the Tang and Song). Also introductory chapters on the history of the language and grammar (further elaborated in appendixes). Aims to bring the student to think in Literary Chinese.

Xu Zongcai 徐宗才, *Gudai Hanyu keben* 古代漢語課本 (Classical Chinese textbook), 3 vols., Beijing yuyan wenhua daxue, 1998. Excerpts ranging from the easy to the difficult, from the short to the long; bilingual annotations in vols. 1–2 and Chinese only in vol. 3.

Raymond Dawson, *A New Introduction to Classical Chinese*, OUP, 1984, 1986.

Note also the annotated readers with excerpts from historical texts of a particular dynasty or style, for example,

A Classical Chinese Reader: The Hanshu Biography of Huo Guang [霍光, d. 68 BC], Donald Wagner, ed., Curzon, 1997.

The History of the Han Dynasty: Selections with a Preface, Kan Lao, ed. (44.6.1).

A Handbook for T'ang History, Denis C. Twitchett and Howard L. Goodman, eds. (46.5.1).

Selected Readings in Yuan History, Lao Yanshan, ed. (48.1).

Ming History: An Introductory Guide to Research, Edward L. Farmer, Romeyn Taylor, and Ann Waltner, eds. (49.5.1).

Introduction to Ch'ing Documents, Philip Kuhn and John King Fairbank (1907–91), eds. (50.10.2).

State and Economy in Republican China: A Handbook for Scholars, William C. Kirby, Man-houng Lin, Jame Chin Shih, and David A. Pietz, eds. (51.14.1).

Try using one of the many textbooks and readers compiled for Chinese students. Some contain excerpts from all branches of literature, including history, while others concentrate more on historical texts (the last two of the examples given below):

Gudai Hanyu 古代漢語 (Classical Chinese), Wang Li 王力, ed. in chief, 4 vols., Zhonghua, 1962; 2nd rev. edition, 1981; 3rd rev. edition, 1999 (for many years the standard for Chinese universities). Its threefold arrangement (selected readings, frequent words, and general surveys of particular topics) is still the most widely used.

Gu Hanyu wenxian daodu 古漢語文獻導讀 (A reader of Classical Chinese texts), Han Zhengrong 韓崢嶸, ed. in chief, Jilin daxue, 1994. Excerpts for reading are given with their original commentaries and without punctuation.

Zhongguo lishi wenxuan 中國歷史文選 (Selected readings in Chinese history), Zhang Yantian 張衍田, ed., Beijing daxue, 1996. The course book for teaching Classical Chinese to students in the history department of Peking University. Contains brief introductions to primary sources arranged under archaeology and the four branches (*Sibu*). There are 80 excerpts.

Zhongguo jingji sixiangshi ziliao xuanji 中國經濟思想史資料選輯 (Selected materials on the history of Chinese economic thought), Wu Baosan 巫寶三, ed. in chief, Shehui kexue, 1982-96: *Xian Qin*, 2 vols., 1985; *Qin Han*, 2 vols., 1982; *Sanguo Liang Jin Nan-Bei Chao Sui Tang*, 2 vols., 1992; *Song Jin Yuan*, 2 vols., 1996; *Ming Qing*, 2 vols., 1992. This series contains extracts from a wide variety of sources; each extract is followed by notes and a translation into Modern Chinese.

2

Dictionaries

New insights into character formation and meanings have been gained from the study of epigraphic sources discovered in the twentieth century. The work of integrating the new evidence with the pre-Qin textual sources will be greatly accelerated by the availability of both in database form. Special dictionaries for oracle-bone inscriptions and other epigraphic sources are given in Chapters 15–17.

There has been a great improvement in dictionaries of Classical Chinese thanks to the collaborative efforts of lexicographers and the use of computer databases (2.4 and 2.5). These modern efforts have been able to build on a tradition of dictionary making that goes back to the Han dynasty and beyond (2.2). Traditional etymology and modern studies of word families are examined in 2.3. There has been no major dictionary of Classical or Literary Chinese into English or any other Western language (2.6) since those of the nineteenth century. Some of these are still useful as repositories of late Qing Mandarin, but are outdated for other purposes (see Box 1 at the end of the chapter). There are, however, excellent new comprehensive Chinese-English and Chinese-French dictionaries (2.9). Recent years have seen the compilation of many special-purpose dictionaries, devoted, for example, to literary styles, to individual literary and historical works, to Buddhist and Daoist terminology, to the secret language of the trades, to economic terminology, or to the language of specific periods. A dozen are presented in 2.7. A further 60 appear in the relevant sections of the manual. For biographical and geographical dictionaries, see Chapters 3 and 4, respectively, and for a full listing of all the many different types of dictionary introduced in this chapter and in the other sections of the manual, see under the entry "dictionaries" in the subject index.

Note that dictionaries, as all works to do with the study of language and the characters (*xiaoxue* 小學), were placed in the Classics branch of the traditional fourfold bibliographical classification (*Sibu* 四部, on which see 9.3).

2.1   The Criteria for a Good Dictionary

The scope of the dictionary should be clearly indicated. For example, is it intended to be synchronic (that is to cover all genres of a particular period of the language), diachronic (all genres from the earliest times to the present), or restricted to a particular genre at or during a specific time? Whichever the case, the corpus of literature upon which it is based should be made clear.

Ideally, comprehensive diachronic dictionaries should be able to build on more specialized synchronic dictionaries. In China, this is not yet always the case, but publishers still produce diachronic dictionaries whose focus as a result is often fuzzy.

Having defined its scope and ambitions, a good dictionary will avoid putting definitions together in a single list, but will divide them into categories, starting with the root meaning or etymon (*benyi* 本義), then moving in a systematic and clearly indicated manner through the alternative (*tongjia* 通假), special (*tezhi* 特指), general (*fanzhi* 泛指), derived (*yinshenyi* 引申義), and metaphorical (*biyu* 比喻) meanings. It will also indicate variant, ancient and modern, and alternative characters (*yitizi* 異體字, *gujinzi* 古今字, *tong-jiazi* 通假字; see Chapter 16) and different pronunciations. Parts of speech should be indicated, as also style (for example, literary or spoken; Buddhist or Daoist). The definitions should be illustrated with citations (*yinzheng* 引證), whose sources should be clearly indicated. The date of first-known appearance of a word or usage should be given.

If it is a comprehensive dictionary, it should give maximum help with words by providing examples of usage of a character whether it stands alone or at the head, middle, or end of a compound or phrase. It should also list homophones and either quote or cross-reference cognates.[1]

---

[1] The usual practice in Chinese dictionaries is to list multi-character compounds under their first character, e.g., *lishi* 歷史 appears under its head character *li*. In recent years, several *nixu* 逆序 or *daoxu* 倒序 (reverse-head character) dictionaries have been published listing compound words under their last character (2.4, 2.7, and 2.8). Thus *lishi* would be found under *shi* along with all the other compounds ending in *shi*. This has the advantage of showing the usage of characters in contexts which are not immediately apparent in normally arranged dictionaries. In traditional China, rhyming phrase books were also arranged in this manner. It is possible to list compounds under their head charac-

Footnote continued on next page

One of the chief criteria for a good dictionary is not that it defines more characters and words than its predecessors. Rather, it is how thoroughly, accurately, and clearly the editors have been able to combine explanations of the forms, sounds, and meanings (*jiexing* 解形, *zhuyin* 注音, and *shiyi* 釋義) of words (characters, compounds, phrases). Such explanations should include, but not be limited to, examples of usage.

The dictionary should be available in both print form and on CD-ROM. The CD-ROM search engine should be powerful and flexible enough to allow searches on characters wherever they appear in a phrase, but also on etymologies and quotations. It should be possible to assemble cognates, synonyms, and antonyms. If it is in print, the characters should be sufficiently large to ensure that those with many strokes are legible.

Last but not least, a good dictionary will have several indexes (*pinyin*, classifier and stroke count).

2.2   Ancient Dictionaries

Chinese dictionaries customarily concentrated on meanings, forms, or phonology and were arranged by semantic category, by classifier, or by rhyme.[2] The earliest lexicographical work, the *Erya* 爾雅 (Examples of refined usage), third century BC, contains brief definitions of some 4,300 words and phrases arranged by semantic category. It was made one of the classics in the Tang in 837. This greatly enhanced the influence of the *Erya* on the interpretation of the classics, and no doubt also on the development of the language itself since generations of scholars memorized it. Many supplements and corrections to the *Erya* were written, but the thesaurus-like ap-

---

ters and to show in index when they appear at the end or middle of words and phrases (see, for example, *Duo gongneng Hanyu da cidian suoyin* 多功能漢語大詞典索引, 2.3). Dictionaries on CD-ROM or other computer media open the possibility for the first time of instantaneously finding characters wherever they appear in words or phrases.

[2] The generic term for dictionary from the sixth to the eighteenth centuries was *zishu* 字書 (a term also applied to character primers). After the publication of the *Kangxi zidian* 康熙字典 (1716), the term *zidian* 字典 gradually replaced *zishu*. *Cidian* 辭典 (or *cidian* 詞典) is the modern expression for dictionary. Such works include definitions of words (both *zi* 字 and *ci* 詞).

proach it uses was not developed. Later dictionaries were organized by rhyme or by classifier.[3]

The earliest comprehensive dictionary of Chinese characters to have survived is the *Shuowen jiezi* 說文解字 by the Han scholar Xu Shen 許慎.[4] His aim was to record and preserve the small seal script forms of the characters because he believed this was their earliest form and therefore the best guarantee of analyzing correctly the meanings of the classics (16.2).[5] Xu was the first to make systematic use of the significs as classifiers (*bushou* 部首).[6] This breakthrough was made possible by the predominant position achieved by the Han of characters with both a signific (*xingfu* 形符) and a phonetic indicator (*shengfu* 聲符), the *xingshengzi* 形聲字. Had Xu himself had access to the earliest known scripts, he would certainly have devised a more simple classification scheme than he did (in principle, he lists as separate classifiers the significs of all *xingsheng* and *xingyi* characters, thus, for example, he makes *zhui* 隹, *chou* 雠 and *za* 雥

---

[3] *Erya gulin* 爾雅詁林 (Collected glosses on the *Erya*), Zhu Zuyan 朱祖延, ed. in chief, 5 vols., Hubei jiaoyu, 1994–98.

[4] *Shuowen jiezi* (Explaining single-component graphs and analyzing compound characters), completed in AD 100, but presented to the emperor only in 121. See Boltz in *ECT* (1993), 429–42. *Shuowen jiezi jizhu* 說文解字集注 (Collected commentaries on the *Shuowen jiezi*), Jiang Renjie 蔣人傑, comp., 3 vols., Shanghai guji, 1996, adds paleographic evidence and commentary since the last major edition, that of Ding Fubao 丁福保 (1874–1952): *Shuowen jiezi gulin* 說文解字詁林 (Collected commentaries on the *Shuowen jiezi*), Shangwu, 1930; 1932; Dingwen, 12 vols., 1967 (the 12th volume is an index). For a convenient index by modern pronunciation to the *Shuowen* and the works of the four main Qing commentators, Duan Yucai 段玉裁 (50.6.4), Zhu Junsheng 朱駿聲 (1788–1858), Gui Fu 桂馥 (1736–1805), and Wang Yun 王筠 (1784–1854), see *Shuowen jindu ji wujia tongjian* 說文近讀暨五家通檢, Li Xingjie 李行杰, ed., Qi-Lu, 1997.

[5] Zhu Junsheng 朱駿聲 estimated that Xu had left out 1,844 characters from written texts available in his day. But Xu's aim was to analyze small seal characters; so he did not include many Han characters invented after small seal had fallen out of use. He was not aware of the oracle-bone and early Zhou bronze inscriptions, which have enabled modern scholars to correct between 20 and 30 percent of the etymologies in the *Shuowen*.

[6] Earlier works had used the classifiers as a basis of organization; for example, the character primers, *Cang Jie* 倉頡 (third century BC) or *Jijiu pian* 急就篇 (first century BC), see 1.3.2. Both were arranged by subject categories (*yilei fenbu* 義類分部), and hence in practice by *xingpang* (classifiers).

into three separate classifiers; moreover, not all his classifiers are
significs). Be that as it may, such was Xu Shen's influence that his
system of 540 classifiers (under each of which, words were grouped
according to their meaning) was followed with minor modifications
in most dictionaries (except rhyming ones) for the next 1,500 years
up to the *Zihui* 字彙 (Lexicon), a Ming dictionary completed in
1615 by Mei Yingzuo 梅膺祚 (fl. 1570–1615). Mei included 33,179
characters and turned the classifiers into an index tool by reducing
their number to 214 and by listing characters under each classifier
by the number of residual strokes, still today the most widely used
system. In recent years, the simplification of the characters has enabled editors to further reduce the number of classifiers (to 201, 200,
189, or even 180), but most modern dictionaries of ancient scripts
are still arranged by the *Shuowen* classifiers (Chapters 15–17).[7]

After the *Shuowen* (containing 10,516 different characters, of
which 1,163 are graphic variants), dozens of dictionaries were compiled over the following centuries, each drawing from its predecessors and also increasing the number of characters defined. The largest of all the character dictionaries, the *Kangxi zidian* 康熙字典
(1716), contains a total of 47,035 characters, out of which as many as
20,000 (40 percent) are graphic variants. There are also many dead
characters or characters that were used rarely or only once. Leaving
aside the graphic variants, the *Kangxi zidian* contains nearly three
times as many characters as the *Shuowen*.[8]

The most comprehensive premodern collection of phrases was
compiled under imperial auspices and presented in 1711: *Peiwen
yunfu* 佩文韵府.[9] To this day no Chinese dictionary has included as
many words. All 700,000 are arranged under the rhyme of their last
character. Each compound is followed by quotations (with references) showing the different uses of the word or phrase, but no def-

[7] Paul L-M. Serruys, "On the System of the *Pu Shou* (部首) in the *Shuo-wen
chieh-tzu* 説文解字," *SYSJK* 55: 651–754 (1984). Serruys translates Xu's definitions of all 540 *bushou*.

[8] *Kangxi zidian* (Kangxi character dictionary), Zhang Yushu 張玉書 (1642–
1711), et al., eds., 1716.

[9] (Rhyming treasury of the honoring literature library [Peiwenzhai was the
name of the Kangxi emperor's library]), Zhang Yushu 張玉書 (1642–1711) et
al., eds., 1711 and (supplement) 1720; 7 vols., Wanyou wenku, 2nd series, 1937
(vol. 7 is an index); 4 vols., Shanghai guji, 1983 (vol. 4 is an index).

initions as such are given. The *Peiwen yunfu* is an enlargement of Yuan and Ming dynasty predecessors, and like them, it was intended as an aid to literary composition. There are modern indexes available. Another (and complementary) eighteenth-century collection of literary phrases is the *Pianzi leibian* 駢字類編.[10]

In the opinion of the *Siku* editors (9.5), there was no phrase or allusion that could not be found in either the *Peiwen yunfu* or in the *Pianzi leibian*. They were referring to *literary* phrases.

2.3 Etymology and Word Families

2.3.1 Etymology

Ever since the Han the origins and meanings of words have been traced by analyzing the forms of the characters, reconstructing their sounds, or comparing their usage in early texts (*xingxun* 形訓, *yin-xun* 音訓, *yixun* 義訓). Scholars stressed now one, now the other, method.

The analysis of single-component characters (whose origin was usually pictographic) has customarily been based on the analysis of their graphic structure (*xingxun* 形訓). The starting point was the *Shuowen jiezi* 説文解字, with examples of usage taken from the classics. The discovery of new epigraphic material from the Shang and early Zhou has given a whole new life to this approach. For an excellent example of just how much can be learned about archaic Chinese society using iconographic analysis of the oracle-bone script and bronze characters (checked against later written sources and insights from anthropology), see James C. H. Hsu (Xu Jinxiong 許進雄), *The Written Word in Ancient China*, 2 vols., published by Tan Hock Seng (Chen Fucheng 陳福成), HK, 1996.

Graphic analysis can be used for single-component characters or those with significs, but it obviously does not work for characters that were borrowed for their sounds and whose forms therefore

---

[10] *Pianzi leibian* (Compound phrases arranged by category), Zhang Tingyu 張廷玉 et al., eds., 1726; 8 vols., Xuesheng, 1963. Zhuang Weisi 莊為斯 (Wallace S. Johnson, Jr.), *Pianzi leibian yinde* 駢字類編引得 (Index to the *Pianzi leibian*), Taibei, 1966. There is also an index to rhyming groups: *Pianzi leibian yinxu suoyin* 駢字類編音序索引, Wuhan daxue, 1995, and to the Zhongguo shudian reprint (1988).

usually bear no relation to their meaning (see 16.1 for the distinction between these different types of characters). Etymologies based on a fanciful or wrong reading of the form of a character (a characteristically Chinese type of folk etymology) were castigated by the Qing philologists as *wangwen shengyi* 望文生義 or *wangwen shengxun* 望文生訓 (an expression which has come to mean in modern Chinese "taking words too literally"). Even when it was not good etymology, the breaking down of the characters into their component parts has always served as a way of committing them to memory (1.3.3).

The second method (*yinxun* 音訓) is based on the analysis of the sounds of a word and is summed up in the phrases *yinjin yitong* 音近義通 (if the sound is close, the meaning is the same) or *yinsheng qiuyi* 因聲求義 (find the meaning through the sound). It was initiated by Liu Xi 劉熙, who compiled the first etymological dictionary, the *Shiming* 釋名 (Explanation of words), ca. 200. Liu used rhyming puns and both the literary and the spoken languages of his day to trace the origins of 1,500 words under 27 subject categories.[11]

During the Qing, the great phonologist Duan Yucai 段玉裁 (1735–1815) recommended using both these approaches as well as tracing usage over time. Linguists today follow his advice, using both the pre-Qin *guwen* 古文 script forms of a character (Table 24, Chapter 16), its reconstructed sounds in Old Chinese, and examples of usage. The final step is to check that the meaning assigned to a character fits with other examples from similar contexts. The same approach is used for reading texts from later stages of the language, which often present their own particular difficulties (the more vernacular the style, the less fixed the characters). Linguists today have the advantage that a great deal more is now known about the ancient scripts. Comparative phonology has also contributed to improving the analysis of the sounds of Old Chinese.

The words whose meaning and usage have been most systematically studied are those traditionally classified as *xuzi* 虛字 ("empty characters," that is to say grammatical function words, also called *ci* 詞). A comprehensive dictionary of Classical Chinese particles covering all styles of *wenyan* would contain about 800 of them; the core

---

[11] *A Concordance to the Shiming and Jijiu pian* 釋名急救篇逐字索引, D. C. Lau and Chen Fong Ching (Chen Fangzheng 陳方正), eds. HK: Shangwu, forthcoming.

particles number between 150 to 200. They changed considerably over time. Pulleyblank examines 330 in *OCCG*. All other words were classified as *shizi* 實字 (content words). Their changing meanings have been less intensively studied, although important dictionaries of Chinese along historical lines, notably the *Hanyu da cidian* 漢語大詞典, have been published (2.3 and 2.4). These are a great step forward because they illustrate with citations how words changed their meanings over time.

Specialized branches of etymology such as onomastics (the origin and history of proper names) are essential tools for the student of Chinese history. Toponyms and ethnonyms, for example, can reveal evidence of migration and settlement and hitherto unsuspected traces of non-Han cultures. Later sections deal with toponyms (4.1), personal names (3.2, 3.3), ethnonyms (3.1, 40.1, 41.2, 42.1), eponymous dates (5.4.1), and the names of foodstuffs (35.2.3).

2.3.2 Word Families

As explained in 1.3.3 (and in Chapter 16), significs (*xingfu* 形符) give a broad indication of the semantic category of a *xingsheng* 形聲 character; phonetic indicators (*shengfu* 聲符) suggest the pronunciation. One obvious way of learning the characters is therefore to remember them in groups sharing the same classifier for example, the willow, pine, and poplar (*liu* 柳, *song* 松, *yang* 楊) and most other trees all share the wood classifier, *mu* 木. A less obvious way to learn *xingsheng* characters is by using the *shengfu* to group together characters that have similar meanings and sounds in Old Chinese (but not necessarily the same form).[12] Such groups are called word families (*tong yuanci* 同源詞), and the characters for them, *tongyuanzi* 同源字.[13] In the examples below, the members of each group

---

[12] There are a number of dictionaries arranged not by classifiers but by phonetic indicators; for Modern Chinese, see *Lishi Zhongwen zidian* 李氏中文字典 (2.8); for Classical Chinese, see *Grammata Serica Recensa* (2.6.1).

[13] Bernhard Karlgren used the term "word families" for groups of words that appear to be related but for which he could not propose any regular processes of affixation to explain the nature of the relationship. Karlgren, "Word Families in Chinese," *BMFEA* 5: 1–120 (1933); "Cognate Words in the Chinese Phonetic Series," *BMFEA* 28: 1–18 (1956); William G. Boltz, *The Origin and Early Development of the Chinese Writing System*, American Oriental Series, vol., 78, New Haven, Conn.: American Oriental Society, 1994, 95–101.

were derived from the root words (placed at the beginning). In many cases, as the meanings of the root words were extended, they had significs added to differentiate the new meanings. Thus, the root came frequently to serve as the *shengfu*, while continuing to carry the original meaning. In other cases, completely different characters were used (see the *rou* 柔 set). In most of the examples below, the *xingfu* is on the left and the *shengfu* on the right:

bing (OC *pieng*) 并 (combine): 餅 *bing* (pancake; water and flour combined), *pian* 駢 (double-horses harnessed together), *pian* 胼 (callus, i.e., double skin on hands and feet), *pin* 姘 (man and woman living together out of wedlock)

fen 分 (divide): *ban* 半 (half), *pian* 片 (one part; half), *pan* 泮 (half), *pan* 胖 (half a piece of meat), *pan* 判 (chop wood in half), *bie* 別 (separate; divide), *bian* 辨 (distinguish; separate), *bian* 辯 (distinguish)

rou 柔 (soft): *ruo* 弱 (weak), *ruan* 軟 (soft), *rou* 揉 (knead; make malleable), *rou* 鞣 (tanning and dressing leather)

zeng 曾 (add): *zeng* 增 (increase), *zeng* 甑 (double cooking vessel), *zeng* 罾 (extra high fishing net), *zeng* 贈 (contribute; add to someone's wealth), *ceng* 層 (second story of a building)

Constructing word families can serve not only as a mnemonic, but also as one of the best ways of finding the origins and the different shades of meanings of words.[14] Not all characters sharing the same phonetic are *tong yuanzi*, nor are all synonyms necessarily derived from the same root. Substituting one member of a word family for another happened more often than using alternative characters (*yitizi* 異體字), for which they are often mistaken. The various classifications of characters and their relationship with *tong yuanzi* are specialized subjects dealt with in 16.4. The main dictionary of *tongyuanzi* was edited by Wang Li 王力 (1900–86):

Wang Li 王力, *Tongyuan zidian* 同源字典 (Dictionary of cognate words), Zhonghua, 1982; 4th prnt., 1997.

Liu Junjie 劉鈞杰, *Tongyuan zidian bu* 同源字典補 (Additions and corrections to the *Tongyuan zidian*), Shangwu, 1999, and idem, *Tongyuan zidian zaibu* 同源字典再補 (More additions and corrections to the *Tongyuan zidian*), Yuwen, 1999.

[14] Tsu-lin Mei, "Notes on the Morphology of Ideas in Ancient China," in *The Power of Culture: Studies in Chinese Cultural History*, Willard J. Peterson et al., eds., HKCUP, 1994, 37–46.

Two interesting works have since extended the scope of Wang's dictionary by examining the phonological basis and the structure of the characters, respectively:

Qi Chongtian 齊冲天, *Shengyun yuyuan zidian* 聲韵語源字典 (Dictionary of etymologies based on initials and rhymes), Chongqing, 1997.

Wang Yunzhi 王蘊智, *Yin-Zhou guwen tongyuan fenhua xianxiang tansuo* 殷周古文同源分化現象探索 (Investigation of the division of cognate characters in Yin-Zhou scripts), Jilin renmin, 1996.

2.4 *Modern Comprehensive Dictionaries*

Modern Chinese dictionaries concentrate on characters, on words, or on both. Some focus on the language of a specific work, style, or period, for example, Classical Chinese in the strict sense, or are more general in scope, trying to cover everything written between the *Shijing* 詩經 and the *Qingshi* 清史 or, even more ambitiously, all varieties of written Chinese from the earliest times to the present day. Many publishers put out small, medium, and large versions of a dictionary in order to cater for different segments of what is a lucrative market. Table 3 gives a quantitative idea of the scope of many of the dictionaries discussed in the following sections.

The most comprehensive dictionary of Chinese available is the *Hanyu da cidian* 漢語大詞典.[15] It is a diachronic dictionary, that is to say, it defines not only the language of today, but also records usage at all periods and in all styles from the Zhou dynasty Confucian classics to the speeches of Mao Zedong. It does so by means of definitions and quotations from a huge range of historical sources. In this sense it is comparable to the *Oxford English Dictionary on Historic Principles*, and it was compiled in much the same way. In one sense the editors of the *OED* had an easy task: they had only to cover the development of written English over the relatively short time span of 850 years. The editors of the *Hanyu da cidian*, on the other hand, had to record changes in written Chinese over nearly 3,000 years. Hundreds of scholars were assigned different words and given the task not only of defining them, but also of tracking their first and subsequent meanings and uses from ancient times to the

---

[15] *Hanyu da cidian* (Great Chinese word dictionary), 13 vols., Hanyu da cidian, 1986–90; 1990–3; 5th prnt., 1995; 3-vol., small-print edition, 1997.

Table 3: Definitions of Dao 道

Note: The reference in the left-hand column indicates in which section of this chapter the dictionary is discussed. The first figure after the title indicates the number of meanings each dictionary defines for *dao* 道 (a large number does not necessarily mean the dictionary contains more information; it sometimes means that related meanings are listed separately). The second figure shows how many words it contains with *dao* as the head (or tail) character.

2.4	漢語大詞典	45	1,291	(345 head + 922 tail positions; 598 in disyllabic words and 324 in polysyllabic words. Available on CD-ROM)
	大漢和辭典	47	410	(+ 100 books, toponyms etc.)
	中文大辭典	47	290	(+ 10 Western phrases)
2.5	王力古漢語字典	12		
	漢語大字典	45	0	
	字通	7	204	(of which 62 have no citations)
	簡明古漢語字典	28	0	
	古漢語常用字字典	9	2	
2.5	辭源	12	68	(of which 15 are book titles)
	實用古漢語大詞典	12	20	
	古代漢語詞典	14	16	
	逆序類聚古漢語辭典	6	86	
	連綿字典	0	15	
	古辭辨	4	0	(articles on the meanings of *dao*)
2.7	近代漢語辭典	7	21	
2.8	新華字典	11	0	
	現代漢語詞典	17	47	(192 if used with the next entry)
	倒序現代漢語詞典	17	145	
	李氏中文字典	8	9	
2.9	漢英詞典	13	46	
	漢英逆引詞典	7	134	
	Ricci (1976)	13	44	
	Le Grand Ricci	35	250	
Box 1				
	Morrison	0	11	
	Williams	0	33	(incl. 19 in which *dao* is a suffix; examples, but no citations)
	Couvreur	15	0	
	Giles	10	261	(no citations)
	Mathews	6	147	(+ 77 words in which *dao* is used as a suffix; no citations)

present day.[16] As a first step, words and examples of their usage were selected from over 10,000 works, both ancient and modern. These were then recorded on eight million filing cards from which a first selection of two million was made. Next, definitions and explanations were written for a total of some 370,000 words. These are arranged under 23,000 head characters, whose definitions are no less copious than in the standard large-scale character dictionary, the *Hanyu da zidian* 漢語大字典 (2.5, item 1), but far fewer characters are included because obsolete ones have deliberately been excluded. Nor is any attempt made to trace the development of the forms of the characters using the ancient scripts (a feature of the *Hanyu da zidian*). Despite the fact that it weighs over 20 kilos and contains a total of 50 million characters spread over 20,000 large double-column pages, the *Hanyu da cidian* is an easy dictionary to use to the full because it is unusually well indexed. There is also an abbreviated CD-ROM version.[17]

Overall arrangement is by 200 classifiers. Volume 13 contains convenient *pinyin* and stroke-count indexes. In addition, the full use of this important dictionary is greatly enhanced by the publication of a multi-purpose index in a separate volume, *Duo gongneng Hanyu da cidian suoyin* 多功能漢語大詞典索引.[18] This lists the appearance of all characters whether they appear at the head, tail, or middle positions of words or phrases. Altogether the index contains 728,000 entries clearly arranged on 1,700 eight-column pages. There is a *pinyin* finding index.

---

[16] Unlike the *OED*, the *Hanyu da cidian* had the support of the government and took 11, not 70, years to complete. The decision to compile it (as well as the *Hanyu da zidian* 漢語大字典, see 2.4) was taken at the highest levels in Beijing in 1975. Four hundred scholars worked on the former; three hundred on the latter. Real work was able to begin only in 1979.

[17] *Hanyu da cidian*, CD-ROM version, Hanyu da cidian and HK: Shangwu, 1998. Contains 29,952 different head characters; 346,000 word entries, and 23,700 *chengyu* and sayings, with a combined total of 516,000 definitions. Head characters are in complex forms; the remainder, not. Variants are shown. Printing is easy. However, nearly all the citations in the printed edition have been dropped.

[18] *Duo gongneng Hanyu da cidian suoyin* (General-purpose index to the *Hanyu da cidian*), Hanyu da cidian chubanshe and Zen bunka kenkyûjo, eds., Hanyu da cidian, 1997.

In the body of the dictionary, head characters are given in *fanti*
繁體 (complex forms), although *jianti* 簡體 (simplified forms) are
also indicated. Pronunciation of head characters is given in *fanqie*
and in *pinyin*. Polysyllabic words are given in their complex forms
and are arranged by order of the second character's stroke count
and classifier. The quickest search method is to use the *Duo gongneng* index. This lists page references for every character and word.
In the dictionary itself the number of strokes in the second character of a polysyllabic word is always given beside the first definition
in the top left-hand column of each page and also beside the phrase
when the number of strokes changes.

Definitions and explanations are in simplified characters. Fortunately, quotations from old Chinese works use the original complex
characters (even if these are graphic variants), while modern works
are quoted in simplified characters. Quotations are arranged chronologically. Sources are clearly indicated, although a full listing of
authors and publications cited is not given. Single- and multi-
character words are included as well as phrases, idioms, *diangu* 典故
(classical allusions), proverbs, colloquial sayings, slang, and important institutions from all periods. All genres of literature are included.

There are 2,503 illustrations of apparel, accoutrements, and architectural details. People and book titles, except for the most famous, are for the most part not included.[19] Modern specialist vocabulary is excluded unless it has become part of the general language.

Apart from the indexes to head characters, volume 13 contains
detailed appendixes on the evolution of Chinese weights and measures (7.3.3), as well as chronological tables giving era and reign-name
years with their cyclical characters and Western year equivalents
from 841 BC to 1909.

In a comprehensive dictionary that aims to cover all genres of
Chinese from the classics to the present, there are bound to be some
areas that are less well covered than others (one weakness noted in
1.2.6 is the failure to incorporate thoroughly the language of Buddhism from the Han to the Tang, a time when its influence on the
development of Chinese was particularly strong). Nor do the edi-

---

[19] To locate a book or check a title, see Chapter 9.

tors always give the first occurrence of words.[20] The quality of the volumes is not the same, reflecting the different standards of the volume editors. Nevertheless the *Hanyu da cidian* is the leading dictionary of the Chinese language. Students of Chinese history and civilization will no doubt wish to start their search for the changing meanings of words in this dictionary before proceeding to other more specialized ones.

The only other dictionary of Chinese on a similar scale (but different in scope) is Morohashi Tetsuji 諸橋轍次, *Dai Kan-Wa jiten* 大漢和辭典.[21] This great work, usually referred to in the West as "Morohashi," includes 49,964 individual characters with many quotations, mainly from Classical Chinese, showing their usage. In addition there is a great deal of encyclopaedic information, especially on book titles, official titles, and toponyms, and 130,000 phrases mainly from Modern Chinese, including names of foreign people and places and Buddhist terms to give a grand total of 500,000 words (the original edition of 1955–60 contained 370,000 words). Despite these additions, Morohashi remains essentially a dictionary of Classical and Literary Chinese. Also, despite an attempt to add root meanings based on oracle-bone and bronze inscriptions, it remains

[20] For example, the *Hanyu da cidian*'s first citation of the phrase *Hanyu* 漢語 is from Yu Xin 庾信 (513–81), but this is at least 100 years after the first-known occurrence of the term (in a story about the early fourth-century monk Srimitra (Gaozuo 高座), of whom it was said that he did not study the language of the Han (*Hanyu* 漢語) in order to avoid being pestered by others (*Shishuo xinyu* 世説新語, II.39; see 45.2).

[21] *Dai Kan-Wa jiten* (The great Chinese-Japanese dictionary), 13 vols., Taishûkan, 1955–60; rpnt. in smaller format and with revisions, 1966–88; rev. and enlarged edition, 1984–86; a 14th volume is a glossary indexing all words and phrases alphabetically according to Japanese syllabary, Taishûkan 1989; 5th prnt., 1997. A Chinese version of the first edition of Morohashi was produced in Taibei: *Zhongwen da cidian* 中文大辭典 (The encyclopaedic dictionary of the Chinese language), 38 vols., 2 vols. index, Zhongguo wenhua yanjiu suo, 1962–68; rev. edition, 10 vols., 1973.

The editing of Morohashi was completed in 1943, in which year the first volume was published to coincide with the editor's 60th birthday. Vol. 2 was in print and the remaining 11 vols. ready for print when, along with all the fonts, they were completely destroyed by firebombs in 1945. Morohashi had kept three sets of the proofs, so he and his fellow workers reedited these. They were soon ready, but it took the best part of 10 years to make another set of fonts and to print the dictionary.

weak in this area. Entries are arranged by classifiers, and there are good indexes. Under each head character, words are arranged in the order of the Japanese pronunciation of the second character.

In his autobiography, Morohashi explained his original motives in wanting to compile a Chinese-Japanese dictionary. As an overseas student in China in 1917–19, he had to spend between a quarter and a third of his study time trying to find the meanings of words and phrases. This tedium he felt could be avoided if there were a dictionary that provided both citations and definitions (the two largest Chinese dictionaries then available had their limitations: the *Kangxi zidian* gives definitions of characters but contains no phrases, while the *Peiwen yunfu* contains phrases but has no definitions). By the time he returned to Japan, he had filled 20 notebooks with vocabulary. It was in 1928 that he signed the contract to edit a Chinese-Japanese dictionary. Within four years students under his direction had culled phrases from the main Han and pre-Han texts and filled 400,000 cards. It became clear to Morohashi and to his publisher (who fortunately by this time had become a personal friend) that this was going to be a very large dictionary. He spent the rest of his long life lecturing on Chinese literature, acting as curator of the Seikadô Library (11.2, item 6), and above all editing, reediting, and revising his dictionary until his death in 1982 at the age of 99.

2.5   *Dictionaries of Classical Chinese*

Each of the 17 dictionaries of Classical and Literary Chinese introduced below is as different as the different varieties of the language it attempts to define. The first (*Wang Li gu Hanyu zidian* 王力古漢語字典) is the most thorough and linguistically sophisticated dictionary of ancient Chinese currently available. It alone comes anywhere near meeting the criteria for a good dictionary set out in section 2.1; the second (*Hanyu da zidian* 漢語大字典) is the standard modern large-scale dictionary of characters; the third (*Jitsû* 字通) innovates in a number of important ways, not least by incorporating insights based on ancient inscriptions. Item 6 (*Gu Hanyu changyongzi ziyuan zidian* 古漢語常用字字源字典) is a similar effort but on a much smaller scale. Most of the remainder concentrate on the explanation of meanings. Numbers 4 (*Jianming gu Hanyu zidian* 簡明古漢語字典) and 5 (*Gu Hanyu changyongzi zidian* 古漢語常用字字典) are among the best medium- and small-sized dictionaries of frequently used characters; number 9 (*Ciyuan* 辭源) was the first modern phrase dictionary but is now superseded by *Hanyu da cidian* 漢語大詞典 (2.4). Number 8 (*Shiyong gu Hanyu da cidian* 實用古漢語大詞典) is a medium-large dictionary with definitions and citations both in Modern Chinese. Number 7 (*Gudai Hanyu cidian* 古代漢語詞典) is similar but more advanced; number 10 (*Nixu leiju gu Hanyu cidian* 逆序類聚古漢語辭典) is a reverse-head character dictionary; number 11 (*Lianmian zidian* 聯綿字典) is the standard work on early bound compounds; number 12 (*Hanyu chongyanci cidian* 漢語重言詞詞典) is the first large-scale dictionary of reduplicates (*dieci* 叠詞); and numbers 13 (*Gucibian* 古辭辨) and 14 (*Gu Hanyu tongshi yiming cidian* 古漢語同實異名辭典) are studies of near-synonyms. Many other dictionaries of the classical language covering a particular type of phrase, literary genre, or period are listed in the relevant sections of the manual. Only three examples are included here (items 15–17 on four-character phrases and allusions). A sampling of special-purpose dictionaries for other branches of the language is given in 2.7.[22]

1. *Wang Li gu Hanyu zidian* 王力古漢語字典 (Wang Li's Dictionary of ancient Chinese characters), Wang Li 王力, ed. in chief, Tang Zuofan 唐作藩, Guo Xiliang 郭錫良, Cao Xianzhuo 曹先擢, He Jiuying 何九盈, Jiang Shaoyu 蔣紹愚, and Zhang Shuangdi 張雙棣, eds., Zhonghua, 2000. The dictionary was started by the influential linguist Wang Li and after his death in 1986 completed by his principal students, themselves by now leaders in the field.

   This innovative work makes most previous dictionaries of Classical Chinese appear as mere compilations based on their predecessors rather than on fresh scholarship. There are nearly 12,000 head characters. Simplified characters are not used. Bound phrases (*lianmianzi* 聯綿字) are included. Particular attention is paid to the following: indication of changing pronunciation, tracing the root meaning (and hence the extended, metaphorical and other meanings of a character), the period in which a meaning was used, listing of *hapax legomenon* (*piyi* 僻義), analysis and cross-referencing of synonyms, and indication of the word family to which characters belong. There is a short introduction to almost all the classifiers. The dictionary contains a total of three million characters and is 2,000 double-column pages in length. It was over ten years in the making.

---

[22] For dictionaries of ancient scripts, *guwenzi* 古文字, see Chapters 16–18.

2. *Hanyu da zidian* 漢語大字典 (Dictionary of Chinese characters), 8
   vols., Sichuan cishu and Hubei cishu, 1986–90; 3 vols., with corrections, 1995; reduced-size, one vol. rpnt., 1992.

   One of the largest *zidian* 字典 (character dictionaries) ever compiled; it contains explanations of the form, the sounds, and the meanings of 54,678 characters. Each head character is given in regular
   script, below which examples are drawn from oracle-bone, bronze,
   seal, jade, bamboo, and chancery scripts. Pronunciation is given for
   Old Chinese (rhyme categories, *yun* 韵); Middle Chinese (*fanqie*);
   and Modern Chinese (*pinyin*). Characters were drawn from the main
   traditional *zidian* (although some modern characters, for example,
   for the chemical elements, are included). Definitions begin by citing
   the *Shuowen* and later classical dictionaries. Arrangement is by 200
   classifiers. The index is by stroke count (vol. 1, 1–112). A handy
   pocket edition (*Hanyu da zidian xiuzhenben* 漢語大字典袖珍本) was
   published by the same publishers in 1999. It contains the same number of head characters but not the examples of different scripts and
   the definitions and citations have been greatly reduced. Nevertheless,
   this is a handy one-volume treasure trove of character forms.

3. *Jitsû* 字通 (Comprehensive character dictionary), Shirakawa Shizuka
   白川靜, ed., Heibonsha, 1996.

   Large, comprehensive dictionary that achieves a number of aims.
   It defines the meanings of some 9,500 characters in depth by tracing
   the development of their forms, starting with oracle-bone and bronze
   scripts, as well as changes in their pronunciation. Next, words in
   which the character occurs in the head position are listed with brief
   definitions but no citations. This is followed by a simple listing of
   two-character words in which the character appears in the tail position (these words are mainly drawn from the *Peiwen yunfu*). Finally,
   the most important disyllabic words in which the character appears
   in the head position are defined. There are 223,000 such entries. Examples of usage are drawn from some 500 works from the Zhou classics to the Qing (an appendix lists and describes each work and its
   author when known). The citations are given in Japanese translation,
   not in the original Chinese. Arrangement is by Japanese syllabary.
   There are indexes by classifier, stroke count, and the four-corner system. The editor has integrated much of the new work on Old Chinese based on the analysis of the expanding epigraphic record, to the
   interpretation of which he himself has made important contributions. This is a beautifully printed and presented work with over
   2,000 pages, each divided into four rows of text.

4. *Jianming gu Hanyu zidian* 簡明古漢語字典 (Simplified dictionary of Classical Chinese), Zhang Yongyan 張永言 et al., eds., Sichuan daxue, 1986; 8th prnt., 1995.

Contains 8,500 frequently used characters (with an additional 2,233 simplified ones) and also a small number of disyllabic words. It uses examples not only from *wenyan*, but also from old *baihua*. Arrangement by *pinyin*. Accurate and handy. The complete text contains 1.7 million rather small characters.

5. *Gu Hanyu changyongzi zidian* 古漢語常用字字典 (A dictionary of commonly used characters in Classical Chinese), Shangwu, 1979; rev. and enlarged edition, 1993; rev. ed. (33rd prnt.), 1998.

Small dictionary of the most frequently used characters. It carries a surprising amount of information and almost succeeds in avoiding the weakness of most such dictionaries, namely, that they seem never to have the infrequently used character (it turns out) that you were looking up. Its success is based on a very long list of frequently used characters in Classical Chinese (a total of just over 4,100) and an appendix of an additional 2,500 "difficult," less frequently used characters. It was written by linguists at Peking University working under Wang Li 王力 in the 1960s and 1970s and grew out of the list of 1,086 frequently used characters analyzed in *Gudai Hanyu* 古代漢語 (1.3. 5). Difficult citations are translated into Modern Chinese. An excellent little dictionary that contains reliable information and manages to pack in 900,000 very small characters. Use with the next item.

6. *Gu Hanyu changyongzi ziyuan zidian* 古漢語常用字字源字典 (Dictionary of the origins of the characters in commonly used characters in Classical Chinese), Da Shiping 達世平 and Shen Guanghai 沈光海, comp., Shanghai shudian, 1989; 3rd prnt., 1997.

Compiled to complement *Gu Hanyu chang yongzi zidian* by giving the earliest forms of each character (oracle bone, bronze, large seal, small seal); the basic meaning; the sound in Middle Chinese and Modern Chinese; and differentiated, vulgar, and alternative characters. It does not quite meet its targets, but nevertheless it packs in an extraordinary amount of information (handwritten) in a tight space.

7. *Gudai Hanyu cidian* 古代漢語詞典 (Dictionary of ancient Chinese words and phrases), Shangwu, 1998.

A medium-sized dictionary of Classical and Literary Chinese (11,000 head characters plus 24,000 compounds). Along with *Xiandai Hanyu cidian* 現代漢語詞典 (2.7), the two form a handy pair covering Classical, Literary and Modern Chinese.

8. *Shiyong gu Hanyu da cidian* 實用古漢語大詞典 (Large practical dictionary of Classical Chinese), Henan renmin, 1995.

Written for high-school teachers and their students with special attention to providing definitions of pre-Qin words and phrases in Modern Chinese. *Pinyin* is used to indicate the pronunciation of the 11,000 head characters (shown in simplified and complex forms) and the 50,000 words defined. Usage of characters and words is shown by means of quotations, all of which, and this is the key distinctive feature, are translated into Modern Chinese. Despite this excellent feature, the dictionary risks falling into the category of "neither-nor": a fraction the size of the *Hanyu da cidian*, it cannot begin to include the riches of that work, nor is it small enough to be as handy as the *Jianming gu Hanyu zidian*, let alone the *Gu Hanyu changyongzi zidian*. But if you want your citations translated into Modern Chinese, this is the work for you. In addition, it has large-size (B-5), triple-column, clearly printed pages and is arranged by *pinyin*.

9. *Ciyuan* 辭源 (The roots of words), 4 vols., Shangwu, 1915; rev. edition, 4 vols., 1979–84; reduced-size, single vol. ed., 1988.

   The editors of the 1979 edition of this, the first modern encyclopaedic phrase dictionary, deliberately cut out the technical and international words that had crept in during 60 years of revisions and updates (it was originally published as a classical phrase dictionary in 1915), so it now covers the Chinese language up to 1840. There are 12,980 head characters under which are defined 84,134 words. Volume 4 has a *pinyin* index attached. The only reason for using this rather old-fashioned, classical dictionary rather than plunge straight into the riches of the *Hanyu da cidian*, *Jitsû*, or Morohashi is that it is cheaper.

10. *Nixu leiju gu Hanyu cidian* 逆序類聚古漢語辭典 (Dictionary of ancient Chinese with characters arranged in reverse order by categories), An Deyi 安德義, ed. in chief, Hubei renmin, 1994.

    Unique in being a reverse-head character dictionary of Classical Chinese. It contains 2,500 head characters and 22,300 words, all of whose readings are given in *pinyin*. After a brief definition arranged by grammatical category, there are citations showing usage drawn from the main texts of the classical corpus. Arrangement is by classifiers. It carries more information than a conventional dictionary because in addition to the main 1,600-page text there is a 200-page index giving compounds by *pinyin* reading of head characters. This enables the reader to find, for example, 15 compounds in which *shi* 史 appears (in nine compounds as the second character under the main entry for *shi*, and in six compounds as the head character accessed through the index). This is a small-sized, fat work with a total of 1.9 million characters.

11. *Lianmian zidian* 聯綿字典 (Dictionary of reduplicate characters), 11 *ce*, Beiping: Jinghua yinshuju, 1943; 2nd ed., 4 vols., Zhonghua, 1954; 3rd rpnt., 1983.

Fu Dingyi 符定一 spent 30 years compiling this unique dictionary. It contains about 15,000 bound disyllabic compounds from the classics up to the Six Dynasties and about another 5,000 regular compounds. *Lianmianzi* (more correctly *lianmianci* 連[聯]綿詞) are total or partial reduplicates and typically alliterative or rhyming. Pronunciations are given according to the *Shuowen* and rhyme books and variant characters listed (for example, 83 ways of writing *weiyi* 委蛇, meandering). The strength of the dictionary lies in the amount of data gathered rather than in the explanations. If ever this rich data were to be put on computer and arranged by sound, it would be much more useful than the present arrangement by Kangxi classifiers. Index: by classifiers with pronunciation shown in *Zhuyin zimu*. For a similar dictionary that *is* arranged by sound, see *Citong* 辭通, Zhu Qifeng 朱起鳳, comp., Kaiming, 1934; Shanghai guji, 1982. The first draft was completed in 1896, the final one, in 1930. Contains about 40,000 entries. Based on the principle that the meaning of a phrase can be found through its sound (*yinsheng qiuyi* 因聲求義). Has been criticized for the inconsistent quality of the editor's annotations. Has a four-corner index.

12. *Hanyu chongyanci cidian* 漢語重言詞詞典 (Dictionary of Chinese reduplicate words), Wang Weimao 汪維懋, ed., Junshi yiwen, 1999.

A labor of love 20 years in the making, this is the first large-scale dictionary of two-character reduplicates (*dieci* 疊詞 or, as the editor of the dictionary prefers, *chongyanci* 重言詞). It contains 7,800 of them drawn largely from Classical and Literary Chinese, although it includes some from Modern Chinese.

13. *Gucibian* 古辭辨 (Analysis of ancient near-synonyms), Wang Feng-yang 王風陽, comp., Jilin wenshi, 1994.

Examines the sets of lexemes (usually characters) belonging to a particular area of meaning or semantic field. This method is especially effective for Classical Chinese, in which characters were often used interchangeably, so that the conventional approach of defining individual words in isolation is less helpful. The success of *Gucibian* also derives from its concentration on a specific lexicon (3,800 of the most frequently used characters based on the word counts in the concordances to 19 of the Han and pre-Qin texts). Near-synonyms are organized into 1,400 groups divided into 50 semantic fields such as movements of the hands (60 entries, each analyzing between two and six near-synonyms), of the eyes (12 entries), of the mouth (19), of the tongue (41), of the body (52), of the heart (46), and of time (21). One of the entries on time, to take an example, is a brief article of 1,500 characters analyzing the changing meanings and interrelations of *sui* 歲, *nian* 年, *si* 祀, and *zai* 載 (see 5.2, note 21 for a summary). The explanations are in clear Modern Chinese with plenty of examples of usage. Characters are in simplified form, but complex forms are given for the head characters. Finding your way around this excellent work is easy. In addition to a detailed table of contents, there are classifier and *pinyin* indexes. This is a large-size, clearly printed book containing a total of over 1.8 million characters.

14. *Gu Hanyu tongshi yiming cidian* 古漢語同實異名辭典 (Dictionary of synonymy in ancient Chinese), Yang Shishou 楊士首 and Yang Beining 楊北寧, eds., Jilin jiaoyu, 1994, 1995.

    Useful both for historians and readers of Chinese literature. It is an attempt to put together in dictionary form a collection of different phrases used to describe the same reality in Classical Chinese. There is a table of contents showing the 600 head phrases by *pinyin* and a stroke-count index of the 10,000 alternative phrases. Many such dictionaries were compiled in imperial China; see, for example, the Qing work, *Shiwu yiming lu* 事物異名錄 (Record of different words for events and things), Li Quan 厲荃, ed., indexed edition, Shanxi guji, 1993.

15. *Hanyu chengyu kaoshi cidian* 漢語成語考釋詞典 (Dictionary of the origins of Chinese *chengyu*), Liu Jiexiu 劉潔修, comp., Shangwu, 1989, 1996.

    Careful examination of the origins and changing meanings of 7,600 four-character or set phrases (*chengyu* 成語) and 10,000 of their variant forms. About 2,500 commonly used bisyllabic abbreviations of *chengyu* are noted at the end of each entry. In addition there is an appendix of 5,000 proverbs and other special phrases of various types.

16. *Zhonghua chengyu cihai* 中華成語辭海 (Dictionary of Chinese four-character phrases), Jilin daxue, 1994, 1995.

    Contains altogether 40,000 entries. One of the largest of the many *chengyu* dictionaries. The huge number of entries is achieved by including proverbs and other types of set phrase that more exact editors (see previous item) do not count as *chengyu*.

17. *Zhonghua diangu quanshu* 中華典故全書 (Dictionary of Chinese classical allusions), Yu Changjiang 俞長江 et al., eds., Zhongguo guoji guangbo, 1994. Contains explanations and citations for 22,000 classical allusions (*diangu* 典故).

2.6   Bilingual Dictionaries of Premodern Chinese

2.6.1   Classical and Wenyan Dictionaries

There has been no major new dictionary of Classical Chinese into English or other European languages since Séraphin Couvreur compiled his *Dictionnaire classique de la langue chinoise* at the end of the nineteenth century (see Box 1). The problem was less one of funding than of the very concept of trying to produce a comprehensive dictionary before detailed synchronic, diachronic, and genre dictionaries were available in China itself. The difficulties are illustrated by the fate of two projects initiated in the 1930s—the Harvard-Yenching Institute Chinese-English dictionary project and the Zhongshan Chinese dictionary. Both sank under their own weight.

Chinese-English Dictionary, Preliminary Print, Fascicle 39.0.1-3, H-Y Institute, 1953. Work on the H-Y dictionary was initiated in 1936 by pasting together the contents of 16 dictionaries from the *Shuowen* to Karlgren, 1940 (see below). Two trial fascicles were published in 1953-54. The first covers the character *zi* 子. After defining 30 different meanings, it gives 68 pages of compounds with *zi* as head character. The project was abandoned in 1955.

Zhongshan da cidian "yi" zi changbian 中山大辭典"一"字長編 (Long draft of the Zhongshan dictionary: character *yi*), Wang Yunwu 王雲五 (1888-1979), ed. in chief, HK: Shangwu, 1938, 3rd prnt., 1939; Taibei, 1967. After giving 58 definitions of *yi* 一, the editors define 5,474 words and phrases beginning with *yi* (pp. 6-472). Arrangement, as to be expected, is by the four-corner system (Wang was the inventor). The project was not continued.

Important specialized bilingual dictionaries of Classical Chinese and reconstructions of its pronunciation at various stages have, however, been published for example:

A Dictionary of Early Zhou Chinese, Axel Schuessler, UHP, 1987. One of the few attempts in the last hundred years to compile a synchronic dictionary of Chinese into a foreign language. Examples of usage from early Zhou texts or inscriptions are translated into English and parts of speech are indicated. The readings are those reconstructed by Li Fanggui 李方桂 (1902-87), "Studies in Archaic Chinese Phonology," Gilbert L. Mattos, tr. of Li (1971), *University of Hawaii Working Papers in Linguistics* 6.1: 171-282 (1974).

Dictionnaire Ricci de caractères singuliers, Paris: Ricci Institute and Desclée de Brouwer, 1999. Defines 16,000 separate characters (taken from *Le Grand Ricci*, 2.8). One of the many excellent features of this work is that homophones are shown at the beginning of each section with their reference number, tone, classifier, frequency count, and stroke count indicated. Simplified, alternative, vulgar, and wrong forms are also given. Arrangement is by Wade transcription. The dictionary is fully indexed. It also traces in detail the semantic evolution of 2,000 of the characters from the Shang to the Han. Changing meanings of these characters are defined, from the oracle-bone and bronze inscriptions and the main classical texts up to the *Shuowen* definition. Inscriptional forms of the characters are indicated with examples.

Grammata Serica Recensa, Bernhard Karlgren, *BMFEA*, 29: 1–332 (1957); rpnt., Elanders, 1972; SMC, 1996. Replaces the author's earlier *Grammata Serica*, *BMFEA*, 12 (1940). Karlgren's reconstruction of the pronunciation of Old Chinese (which he termed "Archaic" Chinese). Also indicates the pronunciation of around AD 601 and Modern Chinese. Arrangement of the 8,398 characters is by 1,260 phonetic indicators. A classifier index is included. A pioneering monument in its day, *GSR* has been superseded by more recent works. For a Chinese translation with a *pinyin* index, see *Hanwendian* 漢文典, Shanghai cishu, 1997; also Avishai Gil, *Character Index to Grammata Serica Recensa*, CUP, 1974; Ulving Tor, *Dictionary of Old and Middle Chinese: Bernhard Karlgren's Grammata Serica Recensa Alphabetically Arranged*, Goteborg, 1997.

A Handbook of Old Chinese Phonology, William H. Baxter, Mouton de Gruyter, 1992.

Lexicon of Reconstructed Pronunciation in Early Middle Chinese, Late Middle Chinese and Early Mandarin, Edwin G. Pulleyblank, UBCP, 1991. Complements the author's earlier *Middle Chinese*, UBCP, 1984, by providing reconstructed pronunciation for approximately 8,000 characters (with meanings in English) at three historical stages: Early Middle Chinese (based on the language of the *Qieyun*); Late Middle Chinese (the standard language of the High Tang, based on the dialect of Changan); Early Mandarin (the language of the Yuan capital Dadu around 1300). Arranged in alphabetical order by modern pronunciation in *pinyin*. Intended not only for students of historical phonology, but also to help interpret Chinese transcriptions of foreign names and to appreciate the rhymes of Chinese poetry during the three periods.

Hanzi gujin yinbiao 漢字古今音標 (Table of ancient and modern pronunciations of Chinese characters), Li Zhenhua 李珍華 and Zhou
Changji 周長楫, comps., Zhonghua, 1993; corrected ed., 1999. Contains about 9,000 characters, including the 2,826 in the *Shijing* and the
5,869 in the *Zhongyuan yinyun* 中原音韵. Gives not only reconstructed pronunciations of Old, Middle, and Mandarin Chinese, but
also the pronunciations of seven dialects and Modern Chinese. Arrangement is by rhyme. There is a stroke-count index.

Han Ying duizhao chengyu cidian 漢英對照成語辭典 (Comparative dictionary of sayings in Chinese and English), Chen Yongzhen 陳永禎
and Chen Shanci 陳善慈, comps., HK: Shangwu, 1983. Gives English
equivalents of 4,000 *chengyu*. Synonyms and antonyms also noted.

Chinese-English Dictionary of Chinese Historical Terminology, David Y.
Hu (Hu Yingyuan 胡應元), 2 vols., Huaxiang yuan, 1992. Translations and definitions of 11,811 historical terms, mainly famous sayings and classical allusions (*diangu* 典故), names, titles, and institutions. Arrangement is by Wade-Giles with an index to terms used in
the definitions.

2.6.2   Bilingual Dictionaries of the Colloquial Language

*A Dictionary of Colloquial Terms and Expressions in Chinese Vernacular
Fictions* (*Zhongguo huaben xiaoshuo suyu cidian* 中國話本小説俗語辭
典), Tian Zongyao 田宗堯, comp., Lianjing, 1983; rev. and enl., 1985.
The first Chinese-English dictionary for old *baihua* ever published. It
examines about 22,000 character combinations (the author claims
32,000) and gives an English translation, sometimes with a short explanation. Arrangement is by *pinyin*. There is a classifier index. References are noted to examples in *baihua* fiction, but there are no citations. This appears to be based on two earlier works by Lu Dan'an
陸澹安, *Xiaoshuo ciyu huishi* 小説詞語會釋 and *Xiqu ciyu huishi* 戲曲
詞語匯釋, but it does not entirely replace them, because Lu quotes
examples of usage for all, or nearly all, the 8,000 entries. See 34.2 for
other dictionaries of the colloquial language.[23]

---

[23] *Xiaoshuo ciyu huishi* (Collected explanations of phrases found in Chinese
ficton), Zhonghua, 1964; HK: Zhonghua, 1973; Shanghai guji, 1981, and *Xiqu
ciyu huishi* (Collected explanations of phrases found in Chinese drama), Shanghai guji, 1981.

2.7 Special-Purpose Dictionaries

There are thousands of special-purpose dictionaries, dictionary-like compilations, and glossaries available. Their contents are not necessarily included even in the largest of the comprehensive dictionaries. A dozen examples follow:

Cooking: *Zhongguo pengren cidian* 中國烹飪辭典 (Dictionary of Chinese cooking), Xiao Fan 蕭帆, ed. in chief, Shangye, 1992. Contains *inter alia* many of the huge number of different regional names for the same foodstuff as well as a listing of some 2,000 recipes by dynasty with sources indicated and over 400 dishes of 31 non-Han peoples.

Dialects: *Hanyu fangyan da cidian* 漢語方言大辭典 (Dictionary of Chinese dialects), compiled by Fudan University 復旦大學, Shanghai and Kyoto Foreign Languages University (Kyoto gaikokugo daigaku 京都外國語大學), Xu Baohua 徐寶華 and Miyata Ichirô 宮田一郎, eds. in chief, 5 vols., Zhonghua, 1999. This huge work of over 7,500 double-column pages draws on 1,200 previous dictionaries and studies of Chinese dialects published from earliest times to 1988 (titles are listed in an appendix). Arrangement is by stroke order. There are *pinyin* and four-corner indexes at the end of volume 5.

Economic history terminology: *Zhongguo jingjishi cidian* 中國經濟史辭典 (Dictionary of Chinese economic history), Zhao Dexin 趙德馨, comp., Hubei cishu, 1990.

Economic and social history terminology: *Chûgoku shakai keizaishi goi* 中國社會經濟史語彙 (22.3).

Enigmatic folk similes (*xiehouyu* 歇後語): John S. Rohsenow: *A Chinese-English Dictionary of Enigmatic Folk Similes (xiehouyu)*, UAP, 1991.

Euphemisms, see below under "Taboo, linguistic."

Loanwords (*wailaici* 外來詞): see *Hanyu wailaici cidian* 漢語外來詞辭典 (Dictionary of loanwords and hybrid words in Chinese), Gao Ming-kai 高名凱 et al., eds., Shanghai cishu, 1984. This contains over 10,000 loanwords ("aliens" and "hybrids," not "denizens"; see 1.2.6 for a definition of these terms). It is not always accurate; see also the following three studies of loanwords from the West and from Japan:

Federico Masini, *The Formation of Modern Chinese Lexicon and Its Evolution Toward a National Language: The Period from 1840 to 1898*, Berkeley, 1993.

Lydia H. Liu, *Translingual Practice*, SUP, 1995, contains a good discussion of loanwords in Chinese as well as appendixes showing neologisms derived from various sources, 265–378.

Mantic and medical arts (*fangshu* 方術): *Zhongguo fangshu da cidian* 中國
方術大辭典 (Dictionary of Chinese mantic arts), Chen Yongzheng
陳永正, ed. in chief, Zhongshan daxue, 1991. Contains 6,393 clear
entries on the special phrases used in 25 mantic arts from *qixiang
zhanbu* 氣象占卜 (aeromancy or divination by the weather) to *meng-
bu* 夢卜 (oneiromancy or divination by dreams), from *zhanxingbu* 占
星卜 (astrology) to *guxiangxue* 骨相學 (phrenology), from *bagua* 八
卦 (Eight Trigrams) to *fengshui* 風水 (geomancy). Arrangement is by
topic. There is a thematic as well as a comprehensive index.

Myth and legend (*shenhua chuanshuo* 神話傳説): *Zhongguo shenhua da cidian* 中國神話大辭典 (29.1).

Numerical phrases; numerological correspondences (*shumuci* 數目詞):
Hanyu shumuci cidian 漢語數目詞辭典 (A dictionary of Chinese numerical phrases), Yin Xiaolin 尹小林, comp., Zhonghua, 1993. From
the Three Dynasties to the Four Modernizations, from the Five
Drums to the Five Classics, from ancient times to the present day,
the Chinese language is peppered with numerological correspondences and affinities at one end of the scale and numerical mnemonics intended for primary students at the other. The trouble is that
there are so many, and not a few were used with different meanings
in different periods. There is a rich tradition of dictionaries of numerical phrases written for children. The present dictionary goes a
long way toward sorting things out with its clear arrangement and
definitions of 2,760 numerical phrases (including 700 different
phrases beginning with "the three ..."). One of the earliest to survive
was compiled by Wang Yinglin 王應麟, *Xiaoxue ganzhu* 小學紺珠
(Purple pearls for elementary studies), Zhonghua facs. edition, 1987.
A 60-page table of contents has been added, showing each of the
2,257 entries divided by the author into 17 main subject categories.
For a study of numerology in Chinese society, see Ye and Tian, 1998
(7.1.2).

Secret languages and tradesmen's jargon (*heihua* 黑話, *qiekou* 切口, *yinyu*
隱語, *hanghua* 行話): *Zhongguo yinyu hanghua da cidian* 中國隱語行
話大辭典 (A comprehensive dictionary of China's enigmatic language
and jargon), Qu Yanbin 曲嚴斌, ed., Liaoning jiaoyu, 1995; or the
smaller *Yuhai: Mimi yu fence* 語海秘密語分冊 (An encyclopaedia of
Chinese folk language: volume 1, Chinese secret languages), Wenyi,
1994. Both have *pinyin* indexes.

Symbols (*xiangzheng* 象徵): *Zhongguo xiangzheng cidian* 中國象徵辭典
(Dictionary of Chinese symbols), Liu Xicheng 劉錫誠 and Wang
Wenbao 王文寶, eds., Tianjin jiaoyu, 1991. The editors were able to
call on more than 60 experts to help them define 2,900 symbols using

not only book knowledge but also recent archaeological findings and in some cases interviews. The results can be appreciated by comparing an entry (e.g., the three pages on "dragon") with the entries on dragon in two earlier dictionaries of Chinese symbols, Eberhard (1986) and Williams (1941). The interpretations in *Zhongguo xiang-zheng cidian* are fuller and more rigorous. There are illustrations and a bibliography of works consulted. Arrangement is alphabetical by *pinyin*, and the entries are also indexed by stroke count.[24]

Taboo, linguistic (*bihui* 避諱): *Lidai bihuizi huidian* 歷代避諱字匯典 (3.3). Best known is the taboo (found in many primitive tribes) against using the names of the ruler in speech, in personal names, toponyms, titles, book titles, even in ordinary words. Many different strategies were used, including substituting alternative characters (3.3) or leaving out a stroke (16.4.1). There were stringent punishments in the codes for infringement of imperial name taboos. There were also taboos on referring to one's seniors (especially family members) by their given names.

Of a different nature were words for sex, excretion, and death. As in most other cultures, they were used for swearing, but otherwise avoided. Each dialect had its own inventory of such taboo words (*ji-hui* 忌諱). For example, *dan* 蛋 (egg) was used for swearing in the Beijing dialect and hence taboo for anything else, so instead of saying *ji-dan* 鷄蛋 (chicken egg) or *pidan* 皮蛋 (thousand-year old egg), the words *jizi'er* 鷄子兒 and *songhua* 松花 were used. In Shanghai, it was *luan* 卵 (ovum, egg) that was used for swearing and hence taboo. *Dan* 蛋 was used normally. *Hu* 虎 (tiger) in many contexts was a taboo word. In the north, it was replaced with *dachong* 大蟲; in many southern dialects with *damao* 大猫 (big cat). Such taboos easily extended to words with similar pronunciations. In Hunan, for example, *hu* is pronounced *fu*, so a word like *furu* 腐乳 (fermented beancurd) became *maoru* 猫乳.[25] Very often a word with the opposite meaning was chosen to the one considered unfortunate as exemplified by the Ming neologism *kuaizi* 快子 for chopsticks (35.2.5). Note that local

[24] Wolfram Eberhard (1986) and Wolfram Eberhard, *A Dictionary of Chinese Symbols*, Routledge, 1988; 4th prnt., 1993; C. A. S. Williams, *Outlines of Chinese Symbolism and Art Motives*, 3rd rev. edition, Kelly and Walsh, 1941, rpnt., under the title *Chinese Symbolism and Art Motives*, Julian Press, 1960; Tuttle, 1974; Dover, 1976.

[25] See Zhou Zhenhe 周振鶴 and You Rujie 游汝杰, *Fangyan yu Zhongguo wenhua* 方言與中國文化 (Dialects and Chinese culture), Shanghai renmin, 4th prnt. with revisions, 1997, 231–35.

gazetteers often record dialect taboo words. The normal way of avoiding everyday taboo words was the same in Classical and Literary Chinese as in other languages, namely, to use euphemisms. For an innovative dictionary of nearly 3,000, see *Hanyu weiwanyu cidian* 漢語委婉語辭典 (Dictionary of Chinese euphemisms), Zhang Gonggui 張拱貴, ed., Zhongguo wenhua yuyan daxue, 1996. It is arranged and indexed by category. For example, it has 117 entries containing euphemisms for urine, excreta, toilets, menstruation, tears, and sweat from the pre-Qin to the present day. Examples of usage with citations are included. There are stroke-count and *pinyin* indexes.

Vernacular literature: In addition to *A Dictionary of Colloquial Terms and Expressions in Chinese Vernacular Fictions* (item 5 of the previous section), note *Jindai Hanyu cidian* 近代漢語辭典, Xu Shaofeng 許少峰, comp., Tuanjie, 1997. It covers the language of vernacular literature from the late Tang to the end of the Qing. All 25,000 entries include examples of usage with references cited. Arrangement is by *pinyin* with every phrase spelled out in full (Chapter 34).

Many other special-purpose dictionaries, devoted to literary styles, to individual literary and historical works, to Buddhist and Daoist terminology, or to specific periods are discussed in the appropriate sections. For biographical and geographical dictionaries, see Chapters 3 and 4, respectively.

2.8   *Dictionaries of Modern Chinese*

The standard medium-sized dictionary of Modern Chinese is the *Xiandai Hanyu cidian* 現代漢語詞典 (*XHC*, for short).[26] It is arranged by *pinyin* and gives authoritative pronunciations for all 61,000 entries (in *pinyin*). The definitions are noted for their accuracy. There is a "reverse-head character" version of the second (1983) edition: *Daoxu XHC* 倒序現代漢語詞典.[27] Arrangement is by rhymes (it is partly intended for those wishing to write poetry). There are also *pinyin* and classifier indexes. The *Daoxu XHC* unlocks many of

[26] *XHC* (Dictionary of modern Chinese), Shangwu, 1978; 2nd rev. edition, 1983; 3rd rev. edition, 1996; 186th prnt., 1996. The draft was completed in 1963. Between 1978 and 1995, 25 million copies were sold. The 1996 revision cut out 4,000 out-of-date phrases and added 9,000 new ones. As a sign of the times, the four-corner index was dropped. Arrangement is by 189 classifiers.

[27] *Daoxu XHC* (Reverse-order *XHC*), Shangwu, 1987; 5th prnt., 1997.

the riches of the original dictionary, for example, *XHC* only lists 47 words in which *dao* 道 features (as the head character). The *Daoxu XHC* lists an additional 145 words (in which *dao* is the end character). These words are in the *XHC*, but before the appearance of the *Daoxu XHC* there was no means of accessing them. The Classical and Literary Chinese companion to *XHC* is *Gudai Hanyu cidian* 古代漢語詞典 (2.5, item 7).

The standard pocket dictionary of characters is the *Xinhua zidian* 新華字典.[28] Despite its small size, this dictionary has been immensely influential. Since the 1950s, more than 300 million copies have been printed. Two generations of Chinese primary and middle school students and their teachers have been brought up on it. *XHZD* is also useful to foreign students of Chinese, and not only beginners (there is a bilingual version of the ninth edition available: *Han Ying shuangjie Xinhua zidian* 漢英雙解新華字典, Shangwu International, 2000). *XHZD* contains authoritative pronunciations of its more than 10,000 head characters, and clear, concise definitions of them (plus another 3,500 compounds and phrases). Arrangement is by *pinyin*. Simple characters are used throughout, but complex characters are also indicated (in brackets after each head character), as well as alternative characters (16.4.1). *XHZD* has gone through six major revisions and continuous minor ones. During the Cultural Revolution years (1966–72), as with all other standard dictionaries in China, it was heavily influenced by changes in the political climate. The last major revisions (1979, 1992, and 1998) have been more influenced by the search for lexicographical perfection than politics. The 1998 edition (of which the first printing was 5 million copies) is on especially manufactured paper with a slightly yellow hue to make it easier on the eyes.[29]

---

[28] *Xinhua zidian* (New Chinese character dictionary), Renmin jiaoyu, 1953; 9th ed., Shangwu, 1998; 119th prnt. (in Beijing), 1998. The first edition was compiled in the early 1950s by veteran editors, some of whom had worked in the early part of the century on the *Zhonghua da zidian* 中華大字典, Zhonghua, 1915; 2 vols., 1995 (with over 48,000 separate characters, this was the first dictionary to contain more characters than the *Kangxi zidian*—and to correct 2,000 errors in it).

[29] The 1965 revised edition was ready and printed but not released. It was only in 1970, on the direct orders of the prime minister, Zhou Enlai, that a revised version was finally published, but not before Zhou had personally read over the draft and agreed on the inclusion of words related to such controver-

Footnote continued on next page

Lishi Zhongwen zidian 李氏中文字典[30] is an unusual dictionary for a number of reasons: the 12,800 characters it defines are organized under about 1,100 phonetic indicators (*shengfu* 聲符) and 60 or so *xingfu* 形符. This is useful for seeing characters that are pronunced in the same or a similar way. In addition, the Cantonese pronunciation is also given for every character and compound. Definitions are short but include examples of usage and common compounds. There are *pinyin*, Cantonese, stroke-count, and *shengfu* indexes that obviate the necessity of mastering the author's unique "fan system" of arranging the phonetic indicators.

The *Cihai* 辭海[31] began life as Zhonghua's answer to its rival, Shangwu's *Ciyuan* (2.5, item 8). Today, it serves a different purpose. From the second revised edition (1979), it deliberately covered mainly modern China and international matters as much as China's past. In other words, it became a general-purpose encyclopaedic dictionary of Modern Chinese and world knowledge and as such is less useful than the *Ciyuan* for the purposes of historical research. The latest edition (1999) has been completely revised. It contains 17,674 head characters and 122,835 entries. Many new entries have been added and many old ones have been rewritten. There are numerous tables and illustrations. Arrangement is by classifiers and there are stroke-count, four-corner, *pinyin*, and foreign-language indexes.

2.9   Bilingual Dictionaries of Modern Chinese

General-purpose dictionaries of Modern Chinese into English and other languages have improved greatly in recent years:

---

sial matters as the *diwang-jiangxiang* 帝王將相 (emperors, kings, generals, and chancellors, i.e., the feudal rulers), e.g., *bixia* 陛下 (Your Majesty). After the fall of Lin Biao 林彪 in 1971, all expressions associated with him (e.g., *sige diyi* 四個第一; *wuhao zhanshi* 五好戰士; *xue Maozhu* 學毛主) were weeded out (*wagai* 挖改), a process that continued between printings according to the changing political climate. In the 1979 revision most of the Cultural Revolution phrases were cut, a process completed in later revisions.

[30] *Lishi Zhongwen zidian* (Li's Chinese dictionary), Li Choh-ming (Li Zhuomin 李卓敏), ed., HKCUP, 1980; Xuelin, 1980; 2nd ed., 1989.

[31] *Cihai* (Sea of words), Zhonghua, 1936; revised ed., 3 vols., Shanghai cishu, 1979; 1989 revised and enlarged ed., 1989; 1999 revised and enlarged edition, 3 vols., 1999 (total 17,080,000 characters).

Grand dictionnaire Ricci de la langue chinoise (Chinese-French), Paris, 2001. The main dictionary of Chinese into a foreign language. It is an encyclopaedic, diachronic dictionary containing 16,000 individual head characters and 300,000 compounds. It has been in the making on and off for 50 years.[32] The single characters and their definitions have been published as a separate dictionary (see 2.5). Some 200,000 of the words defined are from standard colloquial Chinese; the remainder range from ancient to modern Chinese culture. They cover many specialist vocabularies, from aviation to zoology, from Buddhism to television. There are a large number of appendixes with information on diverse subjects such as the 24 seasons of the year or the 64 hexagrams. One advantage of the *Grand Ricci* is that it is available on CD-ROM. Early on, the editors decided to use Wade-Giles as the system of romanization, a decision that they have maintained.

Han Ying da cidian 漢英大詞典 (Large Chinese-English dictionary), Wu Guanghua 吳光華, ed. in chief, 2 vols., Jiaotong daxue, 1993, translates no fewer than 220,000 Chinese words and characters, many of them modern scientific compounds. It is arranged alphabetically by *pinyin*. The *pinyin* readings for all compounds are given. In addition, it has the welcome luxury of three indexes: by *pinyin*, classifiers, and stroke count.

ABC (Alphabetically Based Computerized) Chinese-English Dictionary, John DeFrancis, ed., UHP, 1996. Covers Modern Chinese arranging the words in *pinyin* in strict alphabetic sequence. The advantage is that if you know the pronunciation of the word you are looking for (but perhaps you cannot remember the characters), this is the fastest way to find it. On the other hand, if you do not know the pronunciation of a word, you are lost (there is no stroke-count or classifier index). If you know only the first character of a two-character phrase, you are partially lost. The *ABC* manages to pack its more than 71,300 entries into a relatively small-sized book, partly by using exceptionally clear, small typefaces, and partly by giving one-word, or very brief definitions, and almost no parts of speech or examples of usage. There are also 50 pages of appendixes containing orthography rules for *pinyin*, etc. The *ABC* is exceptionally handy to use and a much larger version

---

[32] See the earlier *Dictionnaire français de la langue chinoise*, Ricci Institute, ed., Paris: Institut Ricci-Kuangchi Press [Guangqi chubanshe 光啓出版社], 1976. This is a good, medium-size Chinese-French dictionary. It contains 6,500 head characters under which are listed 50,000 polysyllabic words. Arrangement is by Wade (with *pinyin* and other transcriptions indicated).

is forthcoming. It is not yet quite up to the standard of the best Japanese bilingual dictionaries of Modern Chinese (see, for example, the *Chû-Nichi jiten* below).

Han Ying cidian 漢英詞典 (Chinese-English dictionary), 1978; rev. and enlarged edition, Waiyu jiaoxue yu yanjiu, 1995. A good single-volume dictionary of Modern Chinese that contains about 80,000 entries. Eight hundred new head characters and 18,000 phrases have been added, and much of the political jargon included previously has been excised. Definitions are under head characters arranged by *pinyin*. Also includes *pinyin* readings for all compounds and examples of usage. There is a classifier index.

Han Ying niyin cidian 漢英逆引詞典 (Reverse Chinese-English dictionary), Shangwu, 1986, 1993. Arrangement is by *pinyin* with *pinyin* readings for all 67,000 entries. It was based on the first (1978) edition of the *Xiandai Hanyu cidian*.

Bol'shoj Kitajsko-Russkij slovar', I. M. Oshanin, ed., 4 vols., Moscow, 1983–84. On and off this Chinese-Russian dictionary was more than 50 years in the making.

Chû-Nichi jiten 中日辭典, Shogakukan and Shangwu, eds., 1992; 17th prnt., 1998. This is probably the best available medium-sized bilingual dictionary of Modern Chinese. It contains 80,000 entries and over 60,000 examples of usage (giving both the Chinese original and a Japanese translation). There are also many useful insets and line drawings illustrating special vocabulary and various aspects of the modern language. A CD-ROM version available. Shogakukan's *Chû-nichi jiten* is more up-to-date than Aichi University's *Chû-Nichi dai-jiten* 中日大辭典, 1968; rev. and enl., 1994.

Box 1: Early Bilingual Dictionaries

The classics contain references to interpreters facilitating the exchanges between northern tribes and the Huaxia 華夏 (early term for Chinese, see 3.1). There is no mention of any lists of equivalent words, and none has survived. The earliest extant such reference works are the bilingual glossaries compiled to help deal with the alien dynasties in the north. They date from the twelfth century and are from Chinese to Tangut. More are extant from the Yuan, Ming, and Qing (40.1). Some of the primers of Chinese and glossaries compiled by Vietnamese, Koreans, Japanese, and Ryûkyûans have survived. Chinese scholars engaged in the detailed study of their own language including its lexicon, but they appear not to have been too interested in the languages of non-Han peoples.

The Jesuits were the first Westerners to compile bilingual dictionaries (from Chinese into Latin, Portuguese, Spanish, French and Manchu). They also made the first systematic attempts to devise systems of romanization and glossaries, such as Nicolas Trigault (1577–1628) and Wang Zheng 王徵, *Xiru ermuzi* 西儒耳目資 (Helps for the eyes and ears of Western literati), Hangzhou, 1626. Thereafter, sinologists gradually improved the quality of dictionaries of Chinese into Western languages.

The first Chinese-English, English-Chinese dictionary was compiled by the pioneer Protestant missionary to China, a young Scot who started learning Chinese on arrival in Canton in 1807 at age 25: Robert Morrison (1782–1834), *A Dictionary of the Chinese Language in Three Parts*, 6 vols., Macao: East India Company Press, 1815–23; rpnt., London Missionary Press, 1865. This contains more than 40,000 head characters and sold at the princely sum of 20 guineas. Arrangement is both by Kangxi classifiers (part 1, vols. 1–3) and by pronunciation (part 2, vols. 4–5). Aspirations are not shown. The sixth volume (part 3) is from English into Chinese.

Morrison was superseded by the work of a younger contemporary and one-time colleague, the American missionary and diplomat-scholar Samuel Wells Williams (1812–84), whose *Syllabic Dictionary of the Chinese Language*, Kelly and Walsh, 1874, was less bulky (and cheaper). The organizing principle was to list characters under 858 phonetic indicators. Williams retired to become the first professor of Chinese at Yale, having earlier published an influential work, *The Middle Kingdom*, 1848; rev. edition, 2 vols., Allen, 1883.

Box 1—Continued

A number of early English-Chinese dictionaries were translated into Japanese and played an important role as a source of neologisms for scientific and other words, see 1.2.6.

In an 1874 review of Williams' dictionary, an irascible 29-year old British consular official described its author as "the lexicographer, not for the future, but of the past." It took Herbert A. Giles (1845–1935) another 20 years to show that he could do better with his *Chinese-English Dictionary*, Kelly and Walsh, 1892; rev. and enl., 3 vols., 1912; rpnt., Ch'engwen, 1968. Giles (1912) is still interesting as a repository of late Qing documentary Chinese, although there is little or no indication of the citations (mainly from the *Kangxi zidian*). Shortly after retiring from the consular service, Giles became the second professor of Chinese at Cambridge in succession to Thomas Wade, the inventor of what became the Wade-Giles system of romanization (based on the Beijing pronunciation of Mandarin as recorded in the 1912 edition of the Giles dictionary). Most libraries that still use Wade-Giles omit the breve and circumflex diacriticals.

For French speakers there was Séraphin Couvreur SJ (1835–1919), *Dictionnaire classique de la langue chinoise*, 1890; 3rd rev. edition, Ho Kien Fou: Imprimerie de la Mission Catholique, 1911. The author based his work on the Confucian classics and on Tang and Song *guwen* using works such as the *Peiwen yunfu*. Sources for the citations in the 21,400 entries are indicated. Arrangement is either alphabetic (3rd ed.) or by Kangxi classifier (2nd ed., 1904). The French romanization system reflects the Nanjing pronunciation of Mandarin as based on Joseph Prémare (1666–1736), *Notitia linguae sinicae*, completed, 1730; published, Malacca, 1831.

Giles (1912) was replaced by Robert H. Mathews (1877–1970), *A Chinese-English Dictionary Compiled for the China Inland Mission*, Shanghai, 1931. Based on Giles. Arrangement is by syllabic order of modified Wade-Giles under which 7,785 different characters and 104,000 character combinations are defined. Over 15,000 phrases were added for the revised US edition published under the title *Mathews' Chinese-English Dictionary*, HUP, 1943; 18th prnt., 1996; a *Revised English Index* was published as a separate volume by HUP in 1947. *Mathews'* continues in use, especially by students of *wenyan*. For other purposes it has been outdated by the many excellent dictionaries cited in 2.9.

3

People

The chapter begins by examining the ethnonyms (collective names) used by the Chinese people (Chinese names for China are summarized in Box 2, 4.1; Chinese names for non-Han peoples and foreigners and foreign countries are dealt with in 40.1 and 41.2; foreign names for the Chinese and China are covered in 42.1).

Next come the family and given names of men, women, and children from both the elite and the non-elite (3.2), as well as the names, forms of address, and titles of the ruler (3.3), and a selection of modern biographical dictionaries (3.4). Salutations are briefly introduced in 3.2.5. The *koutou* 叩頭 and other non-verbal salutations are dealt with in 3.2.6.

An enormous quantity of biographical writing is extant, especially from the last 500 years of imperial history. Published indexes alone refer to biographical materials on more than 250,000 people who lived from the Qin to the Qing (3.4). The greater part of these materials served a ritual or social function, to commemorate, praise, or commend deceased family members or friends. The main categories of biographical writing were genealogies, family instructions, and wills (3.5); diaries, autobiographies, and letters (3.6); commemorative writings (3.7); and various types of biography, including historical and other biographies; chronological biographies; biographies in local gazetteers and biographical collections (3.8). The chapter ends with a brief section on portraits (3.9). Many of those whose biographies survive served as officials; therefore official titles and lists of examination graduates are essential to the biographer (25.3.1).

Biographical works (*zhuanji* 傳記) were placed in the History branch of the traditional fourfold bibliographical classification (*Sibu* 四部, on which see 9.3).

3.1   The Chinese

The Xia 夏, Shang 商, and Zhou 周 dynasties (and later their peoples) were named after Xia, Shang and Zhou, the places that they
counted as their homelands.[1] The Shang and the Zhou also referred
to each other by these names. By the end of the Western Zhou, the
practice had grown of calling the Shang dynasty and people *Yin* 殷
(perhaps after the last Shang cult center), or sometimes *Yi* 衣 (a dialect reading of Yin), and their own people, Xia (after the first dynasty). The people of the Zhou fiefs were called collectively *Xia* 夏
or *Zhuxia* 諸夏. They were also known as the *Hua* 華, which was
probably originally the name of an earlier tribe or possibly an alternative for Xia 夏, but was later glossed as meaning "cultivated" as in
Huaxia 華夏.[2] *Hua* and *Yi* 夷 were common adjectives in the Spring
and Autumn period for Chinese and barbarian, respectively. The
words were linked from the early Tang in the phrase *Huayi* 華夷
(Chinese and barbarians). See 40, *Introduction* for some of the background to these and similar expressions.

During the Warring States, people referred to themselves and to
each other by the names of their kingdoms: *Songren* 宋人, *Weiren*
魏人, and so forth. After the Qin unification, for most of the rest of
Chinese history, the Chinese continued to refer to themselves collectively as the Xia 夏 (or Hua 華, Huaxia 華夏, or Zhongxia 中夏).
They also used the name of a dynasty to refer to the people of that
dynasty. After the Tang, Han 漢 or *Hanren* 漢人 was used in this
sense and also as an alternative for Huaxia (42.1).

People of the Ming and Qing sometimes referred to themselves
as *Mingren* 明人 or *Qingren* 清人. *Qiren* 旗人 (bannermen) referred

---

[1] Kwang-chih Chang (Zhang Guangzhi 張光直, 1931–), "On the Meaning
of *Shang* in the Shang Dynasty," *EC* 20: 69–77 (1995). Traditionally, the Xia
were said to have come from western Henan, and the Shang and Zhou from
Shaanxi. Archaeological evidence is not conclusive but seems to point to either
western Henan or southern Shanxi as being the original home of the Xia; the
area encompassing the borders of Shanxi, Henan, and Hebei, for the Shang
(who may earlier have been a branch of the Dongyi and migrated from eastern
Shandong to western Shandong and southern Henan); and the western part of
Shaanxi for the Zhou, who in any event had before that been semi-nomads outside the China area. On the controversy over the Zhou origins, see Edward L.
Shaughnessy, *CHAC*, 299–307, and Jessica Rawson, *CHAC*, 375–85.

[2] Another equally spurious gloss is on the character *man* 蠻 (40.1).

to members of the Manchu elite (although as the dynasty wore on, its meaning more readily included the Mongol and Han bannermen). The Manchus continued to call the Huaxia *Han'er* 漢兒 (see 42.1 on the changing nuances of this term). Zhongguoren 中國人 and Hanzu 漢族 are modern expressions.

3.2   Family Names and Given Names

3.2.1   Family Names

Some 12,000 family names (surnames) have been recorded in the course of Chinese history.[3] This statistic, like that for the total number of Chinese characters, is true but misleading (on the total number of characters and of the much smaller number actually in use, see 1.3.1). At any given time, there were probably no more than a total of a couple of thousand surnames in use, even including the most obscure ones. And of these, the vast majority of the population used no more than a few hundred. This is a good example of a random drift trend by which many thousands of choices become narrowed down to a few, in this case, more and more people using fewer and fewer names. Today the total of Han surnames is about 3,000, of which the three most common (Li 李, Wang 王, and Zhang 張) account for something on the order of one-quarter of the twenty most commonly used ones and hence 16 percent of the total. One reason for this is that for most of the twenty names, there is no other with an identical pronunciation. Conversely, the surnames that have many other names with an identical pronunciation are rarely used (e.g., *Ji* in the fourth tone: 計, 記, 季, 薊, 冀, 暨). Whatever the reasons, there are today, as there were in the past, an extraordinarily small number of names in use by a very large number of people. Some of the consequences of this imbalance are examined in the following pages.[4]

---

[3] This is the number traced in *Zhonghua gujin xingshi da cidian* 中華古今 姓氏大詞典 (Dictionary of Chinese surnames, past and present), Dou Xuetian 竇學田, ed. in chief, Jingguan, 1997.

[4] The twenty most commonly used surnames in the 1990s were Li 李, Wang 王, Zhang 張, Liu 劉, Yang 楊, Chen 陳, Zhao 趙, Huang 黃, Zhou 周, Wu 吳, Xu 徐, Sun 孫, Hu 胡, Zhu 朱, Gao 高, Lin 林, He 何, Guo 郭, Ma 馬, and Luo 羅.

Most surnames were by origin the names of ancient states, topographical features, official titles, or occupations. Given the large number of surnames that have accumulated over the centuries, it is not unusual to come across words once used as surnames, but now more familiar for their meaning, for example, Fu 父, Mu 母, Xiong 兄, and Di 弟. Such unexpected names are sometimes called *qixing* 奇姓 or *xixing* 希姓.[5] Fortunately modern punctuated texts of old Chinese books include conventions for indicating proper nouns.

During the Zhou, nobles had tribal (*xing* 姓) or clan (*shi* 氏) names; ordinary people only had given names (*ming* 名).[6] Gradually, as the use of *xing* were extended, including to women, even of humble origin, the nobles began to use titles or places of enfeoffment as branch clan names (*shi*) marking their status. The *shi* were also taken from honorific titles (*jue* 爵), official titles, or posthumous names (*shi* 謚). As time passed, the *shi* became used by all members of the kin. Eventually, by the Qin and Han the old distinctions between *xing* and *shi* were lost. Thereafter, the use of surnames (*xing* 姓), at least for administrative records, seems to have spread quickly.

Since the Qin, the typical Chinese family name (*xing* 姓) has been a single character. Several thousand double-character *xing* are known to have existed, although they were not nearly as frequently used as single-character ones. Triple-character and above *xing* account for less than 1 percent and nearly always represent transcriptions of the names of non-Han peoples and foreign names. The long-term trend was for more and more people to have three character names, so people with a double-character *xing* tend to have a single-character given name (*ming* 名). The most common *xing* have often been those having a royal or imperial connection. Li 李, the most common of all, came to popularity during the early Tang, whose founding emperor was a Li (there are more than 100 million Li's in China today). In the Northern Song, Zhao 趙 became the

---

[5] Others include Dong* 東, Nan 南, Xi 西, Bei 北; Qian 前, Hou 後, Zuo* 左, You 右; Jin* 金, Mu* 木, Shui* 水, Huo 火, Tu 土 (those still in use as names are marked with an asterisk).

[6] Li Xueqin 李學勤, "Xian-Qin renming de jige wenti" 先秦人名的幾個問題 (Various questions concerning pre-Qin personal names), in *Gu wenxian conglun* 古文獻叢論 (Collected essays on ancient documents), Shanghai yuandong, 1996, 128–36 (originally in *Lishi yanjiu*, 1991.5).

most popular name for the same reason. Until modern times, surname changes were not infrequent (for example, to avoid taboos or adapt from a non-Han multi-character transliteration to a single-character surname), and so people reinforced the trend by choosing the most common or simple ones to write.

3.2.2   Given Names

The main given names that became the norm from the Han onward can be summarized as follows:

1. *Xiaoming* 小名 (for infants)
2. *Ming* 名 (for children)
3. *Zi* 字 (given on coming of age)
4. *Hao* 號 (nicknames for adults)
5. *Shihao* 謚號 (honorific; given after death)

The different names were used at different stages of a person's life. The *xiaoming* in infancy, the *daming* in youth, the *zi* and *hao* in adulthood and the *shihao* after a person's death. In modern times, the *xiaoming* has been retained; the *ming* and the *zi* have been combined to form the *mingzi* 名字. The *hao* and *shihao* have fallen out of use. Shortly after birth, children, from emperor to peasant without exception, were given a milk name (*ruming* 乳名, *xiaoming* 小名, or *xiaozi* 小字) by their parents or wet nurse. The *ruming* were the familiar terms for infants still used today such as Xiaobao 小寶 in Mandarin or Abao 阿寶 in Cantonese (little treasure); Xiao-sanzi 小三子 or Asan 阿三 (little no. 3). A common type of *ruming* are those made up of a prefix such as *a* 阿 or *xiao* 小 plus the last character of the *ming*, as in A-lin 阿林 for Wang Hailin 王海林.

Three months after birth, it was the normal practice for the father to choose the given name (*ming*, sometimes called *xueming* 學名 or *daming* 大名 to distinguish it from the *xiaoming*). Within a family, the seniority among brothers or sisters was often indicated by using ranking characters in the *ming* or *zi* (a practice known as *paihang* 排行). For example, starting from the Zhou period, *bo* 伯 (*meng* 孟),[7] *zhong* 仲, *shu* 叔, and *ji* 季 were used for eldest, second, third and youngest (7.1.1, *Ordinal Numbers*). Thus Confucius's *zi*,

---

[7] *Meng* 孟 was used for the eldest child of the secondary wife. It was also used for the first month of each season (3.2).

Zhongni 仲尼, indicates that he was the second son. Later, *bo*, *zhong*, *shu*, and *ji* were used in the different terms for relatives, for example to distinguish between *bofu* 伯父 (elder brother of one's father) and *shufu* 叔父 (younger brother of one's father). In the Tang, numbers came into fashion among the literati who used them instead of given names in their poems to refer to junior friends of the same generation (who were therefore called *hangdi* 行第). For a special list, see *Tangren hangdi lu* 唐人行第錄 (46.5.2). The practice had died out by the Southern Song.

Numbers in earlier Chinese history were used by ordinary people in place of given names (a practice that declined as they began using *ming* and *zi* in the later empire). Numbers 1–10 were all used in the earlier centuries for surnames; Liu 六, Qi 七, Bai 百, Qian 千 and Wan 萬 were among the most common. They were also not infrequently used in given names by all types of people. The highest digit (*jiu* 九, nine) was the favorite. Parents often referred to their own children (as they still do) by order of birth, for example, *lao'er* 老二 or *laosan* 老三 (second or third born). The eldest today is called *laoda* 老大 (a modern expression; in Literary Chinese it meant "old").

Table 4: The Ages of Man

Years Old	
>1	*ying'er* 嬰兒
10	*youxue* 幼學, *you* 幼
(15)	*tong* 童; *tongzi* 童子; *ertong* 兒童
20	*ruoguan* 弱冠; *shaonian* 少年 (young men)
30	*zhuangshi* 狀室; *erli* 而立 (*Lunyu* 論語, "Weizheng" 爲政)
40	*qiangshi* 强仕; *buhuo* 不惑 (*Lunyu* 論語, "Weizheng" 爲政)
50	*aifu* 艾服; *zhiming* 知命 (*Lunyu* 論語, "Weizheng" 爲政)
60	*huajia* 花甲
70	*laozhuan* 老傳; *guxi* 古稀 (杜甫, "Qujiang ershou" 曲江二手)
80	*mao* 耄
90	*mao* 耄; *taibei* 鮐背; *dongli* 凍李
100	*qi'yi* 期頤

Note: The first word or phrase on the left (with the exception of that for 15) can be traced to the *Liji* 禮記 (Records of ritual), "Quji" 曲記.

A shared character in a two-character *ming* or *zi* was often used for all the brothers and fraternal cousins to indicate that they belonged to the same generation. If they had a single-character *ming*, then a character with the same classifier would often be used (as with the brothers Su Shi 蘇軾 and Su Che 蘇轍). In the Han it was not uncommon to identify all males of the same generation with the same character in their *ming*. From the Tang, and increasingly from the Song, it became the common practice. After the Song, genealogies contained the rules (and the names) for use by later generations in a particular lineage.

Throughout Chinese history not only the ranking, but also the choice of characters for given names was heavily influenced by *bagua* 八卦 (Eight Trigrams) and *wuxing* 五行 (Five Phases) beliefs and practices.[8] Not infrequently given names were derived from the place name where a person was born. In literary families it was common to use classical allusions, for example, the given name of the Tang historian Liu Zhiji 劉知幾 (20.3) was taken from a phrase in the *Yijing* and the name of the Yuan scholar Hu Sanxing 胡三省 was from the *Lunyu*.

The *ming* could be one character or two. Fashions changed. During the reign of Wang Mang 王莽 (AD 9–23) it was forbidden to use disyllabic given names. This prohibition lasted more or less until the third century. From then until the Ming both disyllabic and one-syllable given names were in use. In the Qing, disyllabic ones became more popular. Since the 1950s, one-syllable given names have staged a comeback, especially since the 1970s.

Translating the meanings of given names (a common practice in treaty port writing) almost invariably gives a false or cute impression. Do not translate them, although studio and other alternative names need explanations.

At coming of age young men and women got married. Those of social standing were given a courtesy name (*zi* 字) at this juncture for use outside the family (hence also called *biaozi* 表字). The *zi* was disyllabic and usually chosen to extend the meaning of the *ming*.[9]

---

[8] On the *bagua*, see 14.1 and on Five-Phases theory, see Box 7, 22.3.3. On its and *bagua* influence on the choice of names, see Wolfgang Bauer (1930–97), *Der chinesiche Personenname: Die Bildungsgesetze und hauptächlichsten Bedeutungsinhalte von Ming, Tzu und Hsiao-ming*, Harrassowitz, 1959.

[9] Girls came of age at 15 *sui* (named after the ancient ceremony *jiji* 及笄, binding up and securing the hair with a clasp), and boys at 20 *sui* (*jiguan* 及冠, binding up the hair and wearing a cap).

For the use of the *ming* and *zi* in addressing others, see 3.2.5, *Self-deprecatory Expressions and Salutations*.

Given the minutely small stock of commonly used Chinese surnames and the habit of choosing again and again the same optimistic and fortunate given names, there are enormous numbers of people in Chinese history bearing the same names. Many lists of these were made over the ages. *Gujin tong xingming da cidian* 古今同姓名大辭典[10] contains 56,700 people with the same names from antiquity to 1936. Arrangement is by stroke count. Sources are given.

3.2.3 Women's Names

It is a sign of the lower status of women that in general they had fewer names than men.[11] Within their own family, they were usually referred to by their *xiaoming* until they married. The Dunhuang manuscripts show that reduplicates such as Maomao 毛毛, Xinxin 心心, Dandan 丹丹, and so forth were popular for girls' *xiaoming*, as they have remained to this day. Outsiders called them by their father's name, as in Zhang *nüzi* 張女子 (daughter of Zhang) or Zhang *ermei* 張二妹 (the third Zhang girl). Women high in the social scale received a *ming* and a *zi*, but this was often not recorded for reasons explained in a much quoted passage from the *Yili* (Etiquette and rites): "Women have no business outside the home, therefore their names are not known by outsiders." After marriage, they were ranked according to their husband's ranking among the brothers in his own family and called *dasao* 大嫂, *ersao* 二嫂, *sansao* 三嫂 ... and, when they became older, *daniang* 大娘, *erniang* 二娘, *sanniang* 三娘 ... . Outside their household, they were referred to in formal documents by their original family name followed by a gender indicative, as in Zhang *nü* 張女, Zhang *mu* 張母, Zhang *qi* 張妻, or, most commonly, Zhang *shi* 張氏, or in everyday speech, Zhang

---

[10] *Gujin tong xingming da cidian* (Large dictionary of ancient and modern same names), Peng Zuozhen 彭作楨, ed., Beijing haowang shudian, 1936; rpnt., Shanghai shudian, 1983.

[11] For a discussion of women's given names, see Viviane Alleton, *Les Chinois et la passion des noms*, Aubier, 1993, 205–22. This fascinating study concentrates mainly on given names in Chinese society. See also Rubie S. Watson, "The Named and the Nameless: Gender and Person in Chinese Society," in *Gender in Cross-Cultural Perspective*, Caroline B. Brettel and Carolyn F. Sargent, eds., Prentice Hall, 1993, 120–33.

sao 張嫂 (in a similar way *fu* 父 or *fu* 甫 after a name indicates the male sex). To indicate seniority between women of the same generation, ranking characters were also sometimes used before the *xing*—for example, *shao* Zhang 少張 (the younger Zhang) or after it, as in Zhang *sisao* 四嫂 (Zhang four). Often the family name of the husband was also indicated (first), as in Liu Zhang *shi* 劉張氏, Miss Zhang, wife of Liu (or Mrs. Liu, née Zhang).

3.2.4   Alternative Names

It may well be that because so many people had the same name, the literati usually chose to adopt several additional alternative names, often embodying recondite allusions or rare characters. Such literary names (*hao* 號, *biehao* 別號) could be a single character or more usually three or four. From the Tang, *shiming* 室名 (house names), or *zhaiming* 齋名 (studio names), became popular, and by the Qing studio names had overtaken *biehao*. The choice was personal and often whimsical. It had no special connection with a writer's or painter's *ming* or *zi*. *Shiming* or *zhaiming* were often used by a writer in the title of his collected works.

   Nicknames or sobriquets (*chuohao* 綽號, *hunhao* 渾號, *hunming* 渾名, *waiming* 外名, or *waihao* 外號) were common. Unlike the *biehao*, they were not chosen by the individual, but given by others, and they were usually in direct, not refined, language. For example, the Han soldier Li Guang 李廣, famed for his rapid maneuvers, was given the nickname the flying general (*fei jiangjun* 飛將軍); Zhuge Liang 諸葛亮, before his talents were given full rein, was known as the sleeping dragon (*wolong* 臥龍), and the Tang expert in the small seal script Li Yangbing 李陽冰 was known as the brush tiger (*bihu* 筆虎). *Chuohao yicheng cidian* 綽號異稱辭典[12] is an interestingly arranged collection of 9,000 nicknames of personalities from the Zhou to the early Republic grouped by category (e.g., appearance; gifted talkers; leaders of peasant uprisings; doctors; great travelers).

   In addition to the above types of name, officials took official names (*guanming* 官名), Buddhist monks and nuns and Daoist

---

[12] *Chuohao yicheng cidian* (Dictionary of nicknames), Xie Canglin 謝蒼霖, ed., Jiangxi gaoxiao, 1999. There is a stroke-count index.

priests took religious names (*faming* 法名 or *fahao* 法號),[13] and kin groups frequently used ancestral hall names (*tangming* 堂名). Another important type of name was the posthumous name or title (*shi* 謚, *shihao* 謚號). For ranking officials this was bestowed by the court; for others by the family or clan. The practice may go back as far as the Shang.

Many of the biographical dictionaries contain lists of alternative names, but it usually saves time to turn directly to one of the comprehensive separate indexes of alternative names:

Gudai mingren zihao cidian 古代名人字號辭典 (Dictionary of styles and alternative names of ancient personalities), Zhongguo shudian, 1996. Over 40,000 alternative names are listed by *pinyin* and identified with their owners. There is also a *pinyin* index of regular names.

Gujin renwu bieming suoyin 古今人物別名索引 (An index to alternative personal names, ancient and modern), Chan Takwan (Chen Deyun 陳德蕓), comp., Lingnan, 1937; Xinwenfeng, 1965, 1978; Shanghai shudian, 1984, 1987. Lists 70,000 alternative names of some 40,000 people who lived from the Zhou to 1936. Arrangement is by stroke count with index.

Shiming biehao suoyin (zengdingben) 室名別號索引 (增訂本), Chen Naiqian 陳乃乾, Ding Ning 丁寧 et al., comps., Zhonghua, 1982 (this revised and enlarged a 1957 work that had combined two of Chen's previous books into one: *Shiming suoyin* 室名索引, 1933, and *Bieming suoyin* 別名索引, 1936). Some 34,000 studio and alternative names are listed by stroke count, but only those containing three or more characters are included.

None of these works contains biographical information, and so if you are looking up somebody reasonably famous, try

Lidai mingren shiming biehao cidian 歷代名人室名別號辭典 (Studio and alternative names of historical personages), Chi Xiuyun 池秀雲, ed., Shanxi guji, 1996; rev. edition, 1998. It contains over 13,500 entries indexing alternative names as well as dates, domicile, and writings of about the same number of people from the Zhou to 1840.

---

[13] The surname of Buddhist monks was *Shi* 釋 (derived from Shishi 釋氏, the abbreviated Chinese transcription of Sakyamuni 釋迦牟尼) plus a two-character personal name bestowed at ordination. Daoist masters and recluses sometimes took nicknames, *Daohao* 道號.

Table 5: Self-Deprecatory Expressions and Honorific Salutations

Self-Deprecatory Expressions (Beicheng 卑稱)

guaren 寡人 (the bereft one, We); see 3.3 for other expressions used by rulers

chen 臣 (your subject); used by a minister to his ruler (cf. *bichen* 鄙臣)

bi 鄙 (rustic, your humble servant), as in *biren* 鄙人, *bilao* 鄙老, *bifu* 鄙婦

bei 卑 (lowly, I); as in *beiren* 卑人, *beiguan* 卑官, *beizhi* 卑職, *beifu* 卑府

pu 僕 (your humble servant); cf. Japanese *boku* 僕

yu 愚 (foolish, your unworthy, I), as in *yulao* 愚老, *yuxiong* 愚兄, *yudi* 愚弟

bucai 不才 (lacking ability, I); cf. *buxiao* 不肖 (untalented, I)

xiao 小...; as in *xiaoren* 小人, *xiaosi* 小廝 (your page), *xiaosheng* 小生 (your
    junior), *xiaomin* 小民, *xiaoke* 小可, *xiaozi* 小子

menxia 門下 (your retainer), *mensheng* 門生 (regularly forbidden, esp. in Qing)

nu 奴, *nujia* 奴家 (your slave)

jian 賤 (low); as in *jianzi* 賤子, *jianren* 賤人 (used by women in later empire)

qie 妾 (your slave), used by women

neizi 内子, *neiren* 内人, *jiannei* 賤内 or *shiren* 室人 (the lowly one within),
    husband referring to his wife

waizi 外子 (wife referring to her husband)

Honorific Salutations (Zuncheng 尊稱)

bixia 陛下 (your majesty); see 3.3

dianxia 殿下 (your highness)

gexia 閣下 (your excellency)

zuxia 足下 (beneath the feet); used to rulers in pre-Qin, thereafter between
    those of more or less equal rank

qing 卿 (minister), used by a ruler to his minister

jun 君 (lord, sir, you), could be used by higher to lower or between equals

gong 公 (master); *minggong* 明公 (wise master); mainly used towards elders

xiansheng 先生 (elder born, mister), used especially to teachers

daren 大人 (sir), to official superiors (repl. in 1912 by *xiansheng* 先生 or *jun* 君)

zhangren 丈人, *zhang* 丈 (used to elders or after Jin, usually to fathers-in-law)

zi 子 (master, sir); cf. *fuzi* 夫子, *wuzi* 吾子

xian 賢 (worthy), e.g., *xianzhi* 賢侄 (your nephew), *xiandi* 賢弟 (your brother)

zun 尊 (honorable), e.g., *zungong, zheng* 尊公, 正 (your father, mother, wife)

ling 令 used before a kinship term when referring to someone else's relatives, as
    in *lingzun* 令尊 (your father), *lingtang* 令堂 (your mother), *lingai* 令愛 (your
    daughter), *linglang* 令郎 (your son)

lao 老 (old, term of respect when added to kinship terms), e.g., *laoye* 老爺

dage 大哥, *laoge* 老哥, *age* 阿哥, *laoxiong* 老兄 (elder brother); used by men
    friends of the same generation; *dage* could also be used by a wife to her hus-
    band, who in turn could call her *dajie* 大姐

Note: this is only a tiny selection. *Zhongguo gujin chengwei quanshu* 中國古今
稱謂全書 (Dictionary of Chinese appellations, ancient and modern), Wu Hailin 吳海林, ed., Heilongjiang jiaoyu, 1991, contains 12,000 such expresssions. It
is well indexed, including by *pinyin* and by category; see also *OCCG*, 77–78.

For the Qing, use Yang and Yang, 1988 (50.10.4, *Biographies*). For the late Qing and Republic, try Chen, 1993 (50.10.4, *Biographies*).

In the twentieth century, writers have used *biming* 筆名 (pen names) when in the past they would have used one or another type of *bieming*—for reasons why this was so and for indexes, see 51.6

3.2.5 Self-Deprecatory and Honorific Forms of Address

The basic rule was to use a humble term in referring to oneself (or to one's wife or husband) and to use titles or honorifics to refer to others, especially superiors. Pronouns such as "you" or "he" were avoided. "She" did not exist (38). Table 5 provides only a small selection of the many expressions used.

Young people could refer to themselves by their *ming* when in the company of their elders (to whom they showed normal politeness by invariably calling them by their *zi*, never by the *ming*). Superiors called their juniors while they were still in their youth by their *ming*. Grown people of equal status used each other's *zi* or *hao* (but never to refer to themselves) or they used a title with a suitable honorific. It was taboo to refer to a dead person by his or her *ming*. In addressing a contemporary or senior, it was normal practice to use the family name but always with a prefix or suffix such as similar to the modern "Lao Wang!" 老王 or "Wang *shifu*!" 王師傅. Juniors were often addressed with diminutive *xiao* 小 as in "Xiao Wang!" 小王. Among themselves, family members often used kinship terms rather than names.[14]

3.2.6 Non-Verbal Salutations

Formal non-verbal salutations fell into three main types: genuflection (*guibaili* 跪拜禮), bowing (*jugong* 鞠躬), and cupping of the hands (*gongshou* 拱手). Each dynasty defined various combinations

---

[14] Modern kinship terms took on their present form during the Tang after 1,000 years of transformation, see Han-yi Feng, *The Chinese Kinship System*, *HJAS* 2.2 (1937); rpnt., H-Y Institute Studies 22, 1948, 1967. Includes a "Historical Review of Terms," 64–125. See also Hugh D. R. Baker, *Chinese Family and Kinship*, Col. UP, 1979. For a discussion of Chinese and English kinship terms, see *Kinship Organization in Late Imperial China, 1000–1840*, Patricia B. Ebrey and James L. Watson, eds., UCP, 1986, 4–10; Yuen Ren Chao (Zhao Yuanren 趙元任, 1892–1982), "Chinese Terms of Address," *Language* 32: 217–41 (1956).

of these according to the occasion and rank of the person greeted.
The *locus classicus* is the description of the nine salutations (*jiubai*
九拜) in the *Zhouli* 周禮 (Rites of Zhou, "Chunguan dazhu" 春官
大祝). What came to be called the *koutou* 叩頭 in the Han (from the
Song also called *ketou* 磕頭) was reserved for solemn occasions. It
was not as servile as the nineteenth-century English version "kowtow" suggests because it was introduced at a time when the correct
way of sitting was to kneel (*zuo* 坐) on the floor (37.4.3). The *koutou* was a deep bow from an erect kneeling posture (*changgui* 長跪):
the hands were clasped together and placed on the floor and the
head bowed to the floor behind the hands (sometimes spread out
flat, not clasped). The first three of the nine salutations in the *Zhouli*
were the *qishou* 稽首 (sustained *koutou*, performed before people of
higher status including the ruler), the *dunshou* 頓首 (a slightly more
rapid *koutou*, for people of equal status or belonging to the same
generation), and the *kongshou* 空首 (no-touch *koutou*, the reply offered by higher status people to those below them). The difference
was that for the *qishou* the position was sustained for a while whereas for the *dunshou*, once the head had touched the floor, the upright
position was regained immediately; and for the *kongshou* the head
only rested lightly and briefly on the hands. The number of kneelings and the number of lowerings of the head to the floor depended
on the rank of the person being greeted and the intensity of the occasion. After China shifted from a mat-level to a chair-level culture
(late Tang to Song; 37.4.3) kneeling became much less common and
as a result the *koutou* became more striking (and it could be argued,
more abject).[15]

By the Qing, it was obligatory at imperial audiences to perform
the *sangui jiukou* 三跪九叩 (three kneelings and nine knockings of
the head) to the shouted instructions of a chamberlain—*Gui* 跪
(kneel)! *San koutou* 三叩頭 (three head-knockings)! *Qi* 起 (stand up)!
Then, after repeating this three times, *keju* 可趨 (permission to
withdraw)! The refusal of Western ambassadors to perform this ritual in the nineteenth century became a celebrated diplomatic issue

---

[15] For historical case studies, see *State and Court Ritual in China*, Joseph P.
McDermott, ed., CUP, 1999; Simon King provides late Qing detail in *Quelques
mots sur la politesse chinoise*, Variétés Sinologiques 25, Shanghai, 1906. For other
references, use *Reigaku kankei bunken mokuroku* 禮學關係文獻目錄 (Bibiog-
raphy of ritual-related literature), Saiki Tetsurô 齊木哲郎, comp., Tôhô, 1985.

and turned "kowtow" into a term of derision and ridicule. After 1873, the *koutou* was no longer required for foreign envoys; it was abolished entirely by the Republican government in 1912. Thereafter, only a triple deep bow from the waist was required at formal meetings with the President (since 1949, it has been further simplified to a slight lowering of the head).[16]

The *koutou* was not just a court ritual, it was an integral part of everyday life. It was, for example, customary to request a favor or to beg forgiveness with a *koutou*. It was always used before the ancestors and at new year (*bainian* 拜年). Juniors did a simple one to their elders (or to officials) to congratulate them (*kouzhu* 叩祝), to express gratitude (*kouxie* 叩謝), or to apologize for an offense (*xiezui* 謝罪). It consisted of one or two bows in the kneeling position (*bai* 拜 or *zaibai* 再拜) and three for more solemn occasions (*sanbai* 三拜). The *sanbai* was also adopted in Buddhist ritual as a more elaborate form of *mobai* 膜拜, the normal prostration before the Buddha image. The everyday *koutou* lasted throughout the Republic but fell out of use after 1949, except in some villages where it has been reinvented.[17] Scornful expressions such as *ketouchong* 磕頭蟲 (*ketou* worms), *ketou ru daosuan* 磕頭如搗蒜 (*ketou* like a pestle pounding garlic), or simply *xiangtou* 響頭 were in common use in the Qing for junior officials or anybody else who sought favors or apologized too energetically with rapid or resounding *koutou*.

In the later empire, the normal greeting between those of the same generation was to cup one's hands together at about face level (*gongshou* 拱手); if a slight bow was added it was called *yi* 揖, *zuoyi* 作揖 or *dagong* 大恭; host and guest did the same while seeking to give precedence to the other (*yirang* 揖讓). The norm for the *gongshou* was for the left hand to cover the right. On unfortunate occasions, such as funerals, the right hand covered the left. A woman would move her two loosely cupped hands up and down in front of the lower right part of her chest while simultaneously bowing slightly, a salutation known as the *wanfu* 萬福.

Intimate (same sex) friends would sometimes extend both hands to grasp (*zhi* 執, *wo* 握, *la* 拉) those of the other person. This may

---

[16] Tseng-tsai Wang, "The Audience Question: Foreign Representatives and the Emperor of China, 1858–1873," *Historical Journal* 14: 617–33 (1971).

[17] Andrew Kipnis, "(Re)inventing *Li*: *Koutou* and Subjectification in Rural Shandong," in Zito and Barlow, 1994 (39.3.1), 201–23.

explain why the earliest form of the character for *you* 友 (friend) showed two hands extended (see You, 1994 [16.2], 160–61). By the late nineteenth century, the Western handshake was coming to replace the old double-hand grasp and *woshou* 握手 was redefined to cover the new meaning. Shortly after the establishment of the Republic, the handshake along with bowing and raising the hat, the hand salute, and clapping were promulgated by the government as the correct forms of salutation. The Buddhist greeting, both hands palm to palm in front of the chest (*heshi* 合十, *hezhao* 合爪, or *hezhang* 合掌) was retained.

3.3 Royal, Aristocratic, and Imperial Titles

Leaving aside the mythical *Sanhuang* 三皇 (three sovereigns) and *Wudi* 五帝 (five emperors), from the Shang to the Qin, the normal title of the rulers was *wang* 王, originally meaning, "big man," later "chief," "king" during the Zhou, and "prince" thereafter. They were referred to as Tianzi 天子 (son of heaven) although this expression is not found on the oracle-bone inscriptions, which suggests it may have only come into use from the Zhou.[18] Rulers referred to themselves in the Shang as *yu yiren* 于[余]一人 or *yiren* 一人. These expressions were gradually replaced in the Zhou by *wo* 我 and *wu* 吾 and to a lesser extrent *yu* 余. The Zhou rulers in referring to themselves also used the deprecatory terms *guaren* 寡人 (the bereft), *gu* 孤 (orphan), or *bugu* 不穀 (the unworthy).[19] Informally, a common term was *yi zhangfu* 一丈夫 (the one and only or the lonely fellow). The aristocratic titles of *hou* 侯, *zi* 子, *nan* 男, and *bo* 伯 are traditionally translated as marquis, viscount, baron, and earl. Because the title of king had become so common, the first emperor created the new title of *huangdi* 皇帝 (a combination of the titles of the *sanhuang* and the *wudi*). He also decided that he alone would refer to himself as *zhen* 朕 (previously this had been a common personal pronoun).

---

[18] Qi Wenxin, "An Enquiry into the Original Meaning of the Chinese Character for King," *Chinese Studies in History* 25.2: 3–16 (1991). For a different view arguing that *wang* 王 meant cap, see James Hsu, 1995 (2.3.1), 50–58. Both views stress the importance of height to express authority.

[19] Xia Xianpei 夏先培, *Zuozhuan jiaoji chengwei yanjiu* 左轉交際稱謂研究 (Research on the salutations used in the *Zuozhuan*), Hunan shifan daxue, 1999. A meticulous study backed with statistics.

Others had to call him *bixia* 陛下, and court historians in writing of his actions were to use the simple word *shang* 上. It is not recorded that he used a modest term to refer to himself. On the contrary, two years before his death in 210, he decided to call himself *zhenren* 真人 (the sage) rather than *zhen* 朕. Apart from this change, the first emperor's innovations were to last until 1912. Later rulers continued to use the old expressions *gu*, *gua* and *bugu*, but *gua* fell out of use after the Han (3.2.5).[20] The Qin and Han titles of *huang taizi* 皇太子 (crown prince), *huanghou* 皇后 (the emperor's principal consort), and *huang taihou* 皇太后 (the emperor's mother) were used for the remainder of Chinese imperial history.

From the Shang dynasty to the Sui, rulers were normally referred to in later records by their posthumous title (*shihao* 諡號). The Zhou titles were short, e.g., Zhou <u>Liwang</u> 周厲王. By the Han they were getting longer (from the reign of Han Huidi 漢惠帝, the word filial [*xiao* 孝] was normally added) and so they were customarily abbreviated to a two character appellation preceded by the dynasty. Thus, Han Wudi 漢武帝 instead of his full title Han Xiaowu huangdi 漢孝武皇帝. Starting from the reign of Empress Wu of the Tang, who adopted the title *xianmu shenhuang* 聖母神皇 (sage mother, sovereign divine), fine-sounding honorific titles came into use. These became longer and longer and were retained in the posthumous title (the longest, that of Nurhaci, has 29 characters).[21] Perhaps for this reason temple names (*miaohao* 廟號) replaced posthumous titles as the normal way of referring to emperors from the Tang to the Yuan, e.g., Tang <u>Gaozu</u> 唐高祖 or Tang <u>Taizong</u> 唐太宗 (unless there were special reasons, the dynastic founder alone had *zu* 祖 [progenitor] in his temple name; his successors had *zong* 宗 [ancestor]).

From the beginning of the Ming it became customary to use one era name for the whole reign and to refer to emperors by this name

[20] Evelyn Rawski discusses "The Language of Rank," in idem, *The Last Emperors: A Social History of Qing Imperial Institutions*, UCP, 1998, 49–51.

[21] The posthumous names of the Shang rulers were all taken from the *Tiangan* 天干 (5.2). For later history, see *Lidai renwu shihao fengjue suoyin* 歷代人物諡號封爵索引 (An index of posthumous and conferred titles), Yang Zhenfang 楊震方 and Shui Laiyou 水賚佑, comps., Shanghai guji, 1996. See also Wang Shoukuan 汪受寬, *Shifa yanjiu* 諡法研究 (Research on the system of posthumous titles), Shanghai guji, 1996.

(*nianhao* 年號); thus Zhu Yijun 朱翊鈞, the thirteenth emperor of the Ming, is today usually known as the Wanli emperor (Wanli *huangdi* 萬曆皇帝) rather than Ming Shenzong 明神宗 (the temple name), or the emperor Xian (Xiandi 顯帝, the abbreviated posthumous title). Occasionally, emperors are mistakenly referred to in translation as if the reign name was their own name, for example, "the emperor Wanli." It is less misleading to put it the other way round: "the Wanli emperor." Era names and reign names are discussed in 5.4.1.

The emperor had many other names, titles, and forms of address that he himself or his family and court used during the course of his lifetime.[22] Apart from the temple name and posthumous and honorific titles, every emperor also had a tomb name (*linghao* 陵號), e.g., Dingling 定陵 is the tomb name of the Wanli 萬曆 emperor. Use of the characters in the emperor's personal name (and often, too, of that of the empress) became taboo upon his death (Qin, Han) and upon his accession thereafter. There are several convenient listings.[23]

3.4   Biographical Dictionaries

There are enormous amounts of biographical materials available. The various indexes to them include data on over 250,000 people

[22] For tables of China's rulers with, for example, their names and also families of empresses and names of offspring, see *Zhongguo diwang huanghou qin-wang gongzhu shixilu* 中國帝王皇后親王公主世系錄 (Genealogical records of Chinese emperors and kings, empresses, princes, and princesses), Bai Yang 柏楊, ed., 2 vols., Youyi, 1982. Ann Paludan provides short biographies of the 157 emperors who ruled from the Qin to the Qing and gives their dates, and also their immediate relatives in *Chronicle of the Chinese Emperors*, Thames and Hudson, 1998. Unfortunately, there is a confusion between the different types of imperial names in this otherwise attractive entry-level book.

[23] For example, *Lidai bihuizi huidian* 歷代避諱字匯典 (Collection of historical taboo characters of successive periods), Wang Yankun 王彥坤, ed., Zhongzhou guji, 1997; the classic work is Chen Yuan 陳垣, *Shihui juli* 史諱舉例 (Examples of historical taboo names), Beijing, 1928; rev. edition, Kexue, 1958; rpnt., Shanghai shudian, 1998. B. J. Mansvelt Beck shows that the taboo took effect on an emperor's death in the Qin and Han: "The First Emperor's Taboo Character and the Reign of King Xiaowen," *TP* 73: 68–85 (1987). The practice reached its height in the Tang and Song; see *Sui Tang Wudai shehui shenghuoshi* 隋唐五代社會生活史 (46.5.1), 560–87; and *Liao Song Xixia Jin shehui shenghuoshi* 遼宋西夏社會生活史 (47.4.2), 352–65.

who lived from the Shang to the Qing. Despite this wealth of detail, unmatched in any other historical tradition, there is as yet no satisfactory Chinese dictionary of national biography. The nearest is the *Ershiwushi renming da cidian* 二十五史人名大辭典, which summarizes and indexes the biographical materials in the Standard Histories and also includes dates of birth and death (see 22.2, *Indexes*).[24] If you know when the person you are looking for lived, the best starting place are those biographical works covering individual periods (13.3 for the pre-Qin; part V thereafter) or particular categories of people, such as artists (38.1.4) or Buddhist monks (29.5.3). For a full listing consult the entry "biographical dictionaries" in the subject index at the end of the manual. The main English-language biographical references are:

Qin, Former Han and Xin Dynasties Biographical Dictionary, Michael Loewe, forthcoming, Brill. Planned to include some 5,000–6,000 entries (44.6.2, *Biographies*).

Later Han Biographical Dictionary, Rafe de Crespigny, forthcoming, Brill. Planned to include some 5,000–6,000 entries (44.6.2, *Biographies*).

Sung Biographies, Herbert Franke, ed., 4 vols., Steiner, 1976. Includes 441 people (47.4.2, *Biographies*).

In the Service of the Khan: Eminent Personalities of the Early Mongol Yuan Period (1200–1300), Igor de Rachewiltz, Hok-lam Chan, Hsiao Ch'i-

---

[24] The *Ershiwushi renming da cidian* replaces earlier works such as the *Zhongguo renming da cidian* 中國人名大辭典 (Cyclopaedia of Chinese biographical names), Zang Lihe 臧勵龢, ed. in chief, Shangwu, 1921; frequently reprinted. The editors managed to include brief biographical entries (mainly drawn from the biographies in the Standard Histories) for some 40,000 people. Neither exact dates nor sources are given, and it is none too reliable. The arrangement is by stroke count. There is a four-corner index and an appendix of alternative names of the personalities included in the body of the dictionary arranged by stroke count (*Yiming biao* 異名表, 1–34).

The *Zhongguo wenxuejia da cidian* 中國文學家大辭典 (Encyclopaedic dictionary of Chinese writers), Shangwu, 1934; HK, 1961; Taibei, 1962, gives more details than Zang (1921), including dates, but contains notices of only about 6,000 literati and is not reliable.

A Chinese Biographical Dictionary, Herbert A. Giles, comp., Kelly and Walsh, 1898. Biographical sketches of about 2,500 people—full of inaccuracies, and the selection leaves much to be desired.

ch'ing, and Peter W. Grier, eds., Harrassowitz, 1993. Includes extensive biographies of 37 people (48.5.4, *Biographies*).

DMB. Dictionary of Ming Biography, 1368-1644, 2 vols., Luther Carrington Goodrich and Chaoying Fang (Fang Zhaoying 房兆楹), eds.,
Col. UP, 1976. The *DMB* contains some 659 biographies with bibliographic notes. Has name, book title, and subject indexes (49.5.1, *Biographies*).

ECCP. Eminent Chinese of the Ch'ing Period, Arthur W. Hummel, ed., 2
vols., Washington, DC: Government Printing Office, 1943-44; 1
volume, rpnt., SMC, 1991. The *ECCP* includes authoritative biographies (written by 50 scholars) of over 800 leading officials, writers,
and personalities active during the Qing. There are detailed name,
book title, and subject indexes (50.10.4, *Biographies*).

Biographical Dictionary of Republican China, Howard L. Boorman, ed.,
Richard C. Howard, associate ed., 5 vols., Col. UP, 1967-71. The 5th
vol. is a personal-name index compiled by Janet Krompart, Col. UP,
1979. Includes biographies of 600 leading personalities active in the
years 1911-49. There is some overlap with *ECCP* because almost all
the subjects of this dictionary were born at the end of the Qing and
some had already made their mark before the establishment of the
Republic. The editors have included cross-references to *ECCP*.

Biographical Dictionary of Chinese Communism, 1921-1965, Donald W.
Klein and Anne B. Clark, eds., 2 vols., HUP, 1971. Contains 433
main biographies. Data on some 700 additional persons are provided
in the text and 450 more in the appendixes (51.5).

A quick way of finding someone's dates is to look in one of the
references giving the birth and death dates of famous people; the
most comprehensive is the *Ershiwushi renming da cidian*.[25]

Note that there is no hard and fast rule as to where to classify
people whose lives straddled two dynasties: *ECCP* includes dozens
who died before the Qing even started, but has no separate biographical notices for those dying after 1912. *DMB* does not include

---

[25] See also the earlier *Lidai renwu nianli beizhuan zongbiao* 歷代人物年里
碑傳綜表 (Table of dates and places of birth, dates of death [with epitaphs and
biographical sketches referenced] of historical personalities), Jiang Liangfu 姜
亮夫, comp., Shangwu, 1937; rev. edition, Zhonghua, 1959; HK, 1961; Taibei,
1963. This includes the dates of some 12,000 people who lived between antiquity and 1919. The table is arranged chronologically, and there is also a surname index.

figures with entries in *ECCP*. In old China people were conventionally classified under the dynasty in which they were born even if
they lived many years into the succeeding one. For example, Yuan
Haowen 元好問 (1190–1257) is normally referred to as a Jin poet
although the last 23 years of his life, during which he wrote much
of his work, were spent in the Yuan. This convention is, however,
not always followed. Wang Wei 王禕 (1323–74) spent 45 out of his
51 years under the Yuan, but was classified as a Ming figure because
of his work for the founder of that dynasty. The conclusion is that
in searching for biographical details, as for other sources, cast the
net across the dynastic divides.

3.5   Genealogies, Family Instructions, and Wills

3.5.1   Genealogies

Throughout Chinese history the genealogies (*pudie* 譜牒) or descent lines (*xipu* 系譜, *shibiao* 世表) of royal houses were kept. The
earliest extant traces of genealogical records are those of the Shang
kings, which can be reconstructed from the oracle-bone inscriptions
and later written sources, notably the *Shiji*. Sima Qian used pre-Qin
pudie and the descent lines of Warring States kingdoms (and aristocratic houses) for his own chapters on *benji* 本紀 (basic annals) and
the genealogical lines of early rulers ("Sandai shibiao" 三代世表;
"Shi'er zhuhou nianbiao" 十二諸侯年表) and *shijia* 世家 (hereditary
houses). Few of these early sources were extant even in the Han.
None survive today. One source used by Sima Qian, the *Shiben*
世本, compiled by Liu Xiang 劉向 (ca. 77–ca. 6 BC), is itself an archive of Warring States descent lines. It was lost in the Song, but
partially reconstructed by Qing scholars, eight of whose efforts
have been republished: *Shiben bazhong* 世本八種, Shangwu, 1957.

There were many officially commissioned *pudie* in the Tang.
Only one survives today.[26]

After the Five Dynasties, the *pudie* ceased to have political significance, and many were lost. The Song court established a Yudie-

---

[26] *Yuanhe xingzuan* 元和姓纂, Lin Bao 林寶, comp., 812; annotated edition
by Cen Zhongmian 岑仲勉, *Yuanhe xingzuan si jiaoji* 元和姓纂四校記, *SYSJK*
Special Issue 29, 1948, 1973. It was recovered by the *Siku* editors from the
Yongle dadian 永樂大典.

suo 玉牒所 to compile the imperial genealogy (*Yudie* 玉牒). A draft
of the years 1218 and 1219 survives in the collected works of the
chief compiler, Liu Kezhuang 劉克莊 (1187–1269). The Qing Yu-
dieguan 玉牒館 compiled *Zongshi yudie* 宗室玉牒 (Imperial clan genealogies) every 10 years starting from 1661. They are preserved in
the Yishiguan 一史官 (50.1.2) and in the Shenyang Provincial Archives (50.1.5). They total 2,600 massive volumes (also available on
microfilm, see 50.2.1).[27]

From the Han to the Tang the genealogical records (*pudie* 譜牒)
of the powerful families (*shizu* 士族) became established as a recognized historical genre. After the revival of clan and family institutions in the Northern Song, the well-to-do began compiling clan
(family) genealogies *zupu* 族譜 (*jiapu* 家譜). This trend was encouraged by the Qing court. *Zupu* have survived in considerable numbers, mainly dating from the Republic and late Qing and mainly
from south China. Many of the descent lines in the later genealogies
are traced back to the Tang and Song. Apart from family and clan
trees, they also include biographical details of all kinds, family
covenants and family instructions, and details of commonly held
property such as charitable estates. The *jiapu* are an essential source
for family history, biography, local history, and micro-demography
(7.2).[28] Many were destroyed during the Cultural Revolution. A
number of reprints and excerpts have been published. The Shanghai
Library has a major collection and has established a special genealogical reading room. The main collections and catalogs are as follows:

---

[27] For a description of the Qing *Yudie*, see James Lee, Cameron Campbell,
and Wang Feng, "The Last Emperors: An Introduction to the Demography of
the Qing Imperial Lineage," in Roger Schofield and David Reher, eds., *Old and
New Methods in Historical Demography*, OUP, 1993, 361–82.

[28] Other terms included *zongpu* 宗譜 and *jiasheng* 家乘 (lit. "family history"). See the general introductions by Joanna M. Meskill, "The Chinese Genealogy as a Research Source," in *Family and Kinship in China*, Maurice Freeman, ed., SUP, 1970; and by Otto B. van der Sprenkel, "Genealogical Registers," in Leslie et al., eds., 1973 (20.3), 83–98. See also Ted A. Telford, "Survey
of Social Demographic Data in Chinese Genealogies, *LIC* 7.2: 118–48 (1986),
and by the same author, "Patching the Holes in Chinese Genealogies," *LIC*
11.2: 116–35 (1990). See also 7.2 for further references to micro-demographical
studies based on *zupu*.

Zhongguo jiapu zonghe mulu 中國家譜綜合目錄 (Union catalog of Chinese genealogies), Zhonghua, 1997. Catalogs 14,761 genealogies compiled before 1949 held in 400 Chinese collections.

The largest collection by far in the United States (and in the world) is held on microfilm in the Genealogical Society of Utah (GSU) Family History Library. It contains more than 7,000 printed (woodblock or lead type) editions of genealogies and in addition 9,000 manuscript genealogies, mainly from private owners in Taiwan and Hong Kong. The holdings are described in Melvin P. Thatcher, "Selected Sources for Late Imperial China on Microfilm at the Genealogical Society of Utah," *LIC* 19.2: 111–29 (1998). The printed genealogies contain more data of potential interest to the historian of late imperial China. The GSU also has nearly 5,000 local gazetteers on microfilm and various late Qing census and land taxation data from the Shenyang archives. GSU holdings may be viewed in any of its 2,000 libraries or reading rooms (family history centers) in more than 40 countries.[29]

Note the following catalogs of important collections both inside and outside China (listed alphabetically):

Fujian: *Fujian zupu* 福建族譜 (Fujian genealogies), Chen Zhiping 陳制平, ed., Fujian renmin, 1996.

Guangdong: the provincial library (Zhongshan library) has a catalog of its holdings of 390 Guangdong genealogies: *Guancang Guangdong zupu mulu* 館藏廣東族譜目錄), 1986.

Hong Kong: Luo Xianglin 羅香林, *Zhongguo zupu yanjiu* 中國族譜研究 (Studies on Chinese genealogies), HKCUP, 1971, includes a list of holdings of the Chinese University of Hong Kong.

Huangshan: the municipal museum holds a rich collection of 170 genealogies of local Xin'an 新安 (modern Huangshan, Anhui) families, see Zhai Tunjian 翟屯建, "Huangshanshi bowuguan cang shanben jiapu shuyao" 黃山市博物館藏善本家譜述要 (Brief introduction to the rare genealogies held in the Huangshan municipal museum), *Wenxian* 文獻 3: 113–34 (1996).

---

[29] The earlier catalog of the GSU is now out of date but still useful for its annotations: *Chinese Genealogies at the Genealogical Society of Utah: An Annotated Bibliography*, Ted A. Telford et al., eds., Taibei, 1983; rpnt., Tôhô, 1988. It lists 3,105 genealogies then held on microfilm at the GSU. There are locality and name indexes.

Japan: Taga Akigorô 多賀秋五郎, *Sôfu no kenkyû: shiryôhen* 族譜の研究
史料編 (An analytical study of genealogical books: source materials),
Tôyô bunko, 1960; and the same author's *Chûgoku sôfu no kenkyû* 中
國族譜の研究 (Studies on Chinese genealogies), 2 vols., Tokyo, 1980–
82. Vol. 2 contains detailed listings of (1) 1,276 genealogies in Japanese collections; (2) 1,247 genealogies held by Columbia, Harvard,
Library of Congress, Berkeley, Stanford, and Chicago; (3) 873 genealogies held by six institutions in China, Hong Kong, and Taiwan. In
each case call numbers are indicated. There are surname and title indexes, but no locality index, chronological index, or institution index
(unlike the 1960 volume).

Taiwanqu zupu mulu 臺灣區族譜目錄 (Catalog of Chinese genealogies in
Taiwan), Zhao Zhenji 趙振績 and Chen Meigui 陳美桂, eds., Taiwansheng gexing lishi yuanyuan fazhan yanjiu xuehui 臺灣省各姓
歷史淵源發展研究學會 (Society for the study of the historical origins and development of surnames in Taiwan province), Taiwanqu
xingpu yanjiushe 臺灣區姓譜研究社, 1987. Union catalog of 10,613
genealogies (mainly Taiwanese) held in Taiwan. Note the innovative
selection *Min-Tai guanxi zupu ziliao xuanbian* 閩臺關係族譜資料選
編 (Selected genealogical materials on Fujian-Taiwan relations),
Zhuang Weiji 莊爲璣 and Wang Lianmao 王連茂, comps., Fujian
renmin, 1984.

The Center for the Study of Genealogy (Taiyuan zupu yanjiu
zhongxin 太原族譜研究中心) was established in Taiyuan under the
aegis of the Shanxi Shekeyuan 山西社科院 (Shanxi Academy of Social Sciences) in 1990. It collects *zupu* and puts out an annual journal: *Zhongguo pudie xue yanjiu* 中國譜牒學研究 (published by Shumu wenxian).

3.5.2   Family Instructions

Family instructions (*jiaxun* 家訓, *jiagui* 家規, *jiayue* 家約) are an
important source for family and clan education and organization.
They were either printed separately or also commonly in genealogies.[30] The first extant *jiaxun* is by Yan Zhitui 顏之推 (531–91). It

---

[30] For general studies, see Liu [Wang] Hui-chen, *The Traditional Chinese
Clan Rules*, Col. UP, 1959; also Liu, "An Analysis of Chinese Clan Rules: Confucian Theories in Action," in *Confucianism in Action*, Arthur F. Wright
(1913–76) and David Nivison, eds., SUP, 1959, 63–96; Patricia B. Ebrey, *Confucianism and Family Rituals in Imperial China: A Social History of Writing About*
Footnote continued on next page

is entitled simply *Yan shi jiaxun* 顏氏家訓. There is a translation into English.[31]

3.5.3 Wills

In Europe (and America) one of the main sources for biography and family history, not to speak of social and economic history, are the last wills and testaments of individuals. They have survived in huge quantities, dating back in some cases to the twelfth and thirteenth centuries. Apart from the standard homilies addressed to descendants, they deal with the division of property. In China, property was also divided in wills or household division documents but at the most not more than 1,000 are extant from all of Chinese history up to the twentieth century. The earliest to survive dates from AD 5. It was excavated from a tomb in Jiangsu.[32] It was called a *xianling* 先令 ("command of the seniors"). The normal term in later periods is *yizhu* 遺囑, if the parents had passed away or *fenjiadan* 分家單, if they were still alive when it was drawn up.[33] In Taiwan, the phrase in *jiushu* 闔書. The division of worldly goods should be distinguished

---

Rituals, PUP, 1991; Charlotte Furth, "The Patriarch's Legacy: Household Instructions and the Transmission of Orthodox Values," in *Orthodoxy in Late Imperial China*, K. C. Liu, ed., UCP, 1990, 125–46.

[31] Teng Ssu-yü, *Family Instructions for the Yen Clan*, Brill, 1968. ICS *Concordance 7*. For a Song example, see Patricia Buckley Ebrey, *Family and Property in Sung China: Yuan Ts'ai's Precepts for Social Life*, PUP, 1984; Patricia B. Ebrey, *Chu Hsi's Family Rituals*, PUP, 1991. D. C. Twitchett, "Documents on the Clan Administration: 1. The Rules of Administration of the Charitable Estate of the Fan Clan," *AM* 8: 1–35 (1960); Linda Walters, "Charitable Estates as an Aspect of Statecraft in Southern Sung China," in *Ordering the World: Approaches to State and Society in Sung Dynasty China*, Robert P. Hymes and Conrad Schirokauer, eds., UCP, 1993, 255–79.

[32] Bret Hinsch, "Women, Kinship, and Property as Seen in a Han Dynasty Will," *TP* 84.1–3 (1998). Hinsch bases his article on the transcription and commentary provided in an article by Chen Ping 陳平 and Wang Qinjin 王勤金 in *Wenwu* 1987. 1.

[33] David Wakefield, *Fenjia: Household Division and Inheritance in Qing and Republican China*, UHP, 1998. Appendix 5 provides a list of different terms from all over China for household division. The Huizhou merchant wills (50.7.2). Other evidence on property division comes from documents preserved in Taiwan or from Japanese colonial research—in Taiwan (*Taiwan shihô* 臺灣私法, 51.11.2) or in north China (*Chûgoku nôson kankô chôsa* 中國農村慣行調查, 51.11.1).

from testaments in the sense of final instructions (*yixun* 遺訓, *yiling* 遺令) or last words (*yiyan* 遺言, *yishu* 遺書). For a collection of 289 such last testaments from all periods of Chinese history, see Zhou Wu 周武, *Zhongguo yishu jingxuan* 中國遺書精選.[34]

3.6   *Diaries, Autobiographies, and Letters*

Diaries, letters, and autobiographies, not to speak of poems, post-faces, and prefaces are all important biographical sources. Note that many authors not infrequently talk about themselves or the reasons that they wrote what they did in postfaces or prefaces.[35]

3.6.1   *Diaries* (Riji 日記)

Diaries usually include information about the weather or the social comings and goings of an individual. They are not filled with private revelations (for Republican diaries, see 51.5.4). If diaries were published separately, they were usually classified in the Philosophers' branch (*Zibu* 子部) under miscellaneous writers (*zajia* 雜家).[36]

---

[34] *Zhongguo yishu jingxuan* (A selection of Chinese last testaments), Huadong shifan daxue, 1994. The editor gathered these testamentary writings from all sorts of scattered biographical sources as well as collected works. He provides explanations and linguistic notes. See also Albert E. Dien, "Instructions for the Grave: The Case of Yan Zhitui," *Cahiers d'Extrême Orient*, 8: 41–58 (1995).

[35] Until the Song, authors placed their last words on completion of a work in a postface (*xu* 序) in the last bundle or scroll. With the advent of printing and the possibility for the first time of the whole work circulating in a single text or collection, authors began to put their last words at the beginning in a preface (for which the old word *xu* 序, or 叙, was now used), while *ba* 跋 was retained for colophon or postface. Both words had many synonyms: *tiji* 題記 or *qianyan* 前言 for *xu*; and *tiba* 題跋, *houxu* 後序, *bawei* 跋尾 or *houji* 後記 for *ba*.

[36] Arthur Waley translated excerpts from the diaries of Lin Zexu, which cover the years 1812 to 1845, in *The Opium War Through Chinese Eyes*, Allen and Unwin, 1958. Zhang Dechang 張德昌 tabulates the personal expenditures of Li Ciming 李慈銘 over the years 1854–94 in *Qingji yige jingguan de shenghuo* 清季一個京官的生活, HKCUP, 1970. The main source for the study was Li's diaries, *Yuemantang riji* 越縵堂日記 (Diary of Yuemantang), Shanghai, Shangwu, 1920.

For selections and references to several hundred diaries, see:

Mingren zizhuanwen chao 明人自傳文鈔 (Excerpts from the autobiographical works of Ming writers), Du Lianzhe 杜聯喆, ed., Yiwen yinshuguan, 1977. Contains 180 Ming autobiographical excerpts.

Qingdai riji huichao 清代日記匯抄 (Collection of excerpts from Qing diaries), Shanghai renmin, 1982.

Zhongguo jindaishi wenxian bibei shumu 中國近代史文獻必備書目 lists over 200 diaries written between 1840 and 1919 (50.10.1).

3.6.2 Autobiographies (Zizhuan 自傳)

Autobiographies may sometimes be found in a writer's collected works. On autobiography as a genre, see:

Pei-yi Wu, *The Confucian's Progress: Autobiographical Writings in Traditional China*, PUP, 1990.

For a huge survey of all forms of autobiographical writings, see:

Wolfgang Bauer, *Das Antlitz Chinas: Der autobiographische Selbstdarstellung in der chinesischen Literatur von ihren Anfänges bis Heute*, Hauser, 1990.

3.6.3 Letters (Shu 書)

Shu 書 was the usual word for both official communications and private letters in early China. In order to distinguish the two, terms such as *shangshu* 上書 or *zoushu* 奏書 for the former (26.2) and *shujian* 書簡, *shuzha* 書札 and many others (of which *chidu* 尺牘 was one of the most common) came into circulation in the Han for the latter (see 18.1 for the origin of the term *chidu*). The expression *shuxin* 書信 began to come into use in the Nan-Bei Chao, but replaced *chidu* only in the twentieth century. *Shu* 書 remained in use for most of Chinese history. Traces of military or civilian reports in the form of letters are found in the oracle bones (*heji* 137 and 5511). Several letters are quoted in the *Zuozhuan* (the earliest dating from 617 BC). The earliest extant private letter so far discovered dates from the Qin (44.4.1, Shuihudi). Considerable numbers of private letters have been found in Han tombs; the best preserved is on silk. It was found near Dunhuang (44.4.3). Letters of famous individuals were often included in their collected works (originals of some famous officials of the late Qing have survived). For a selection from 35 famous letters from all periods of Chinese history translated into

English (with Chinese originals in annex), see *Renditions*, 41 and 42, 1994. The earliest extant manual of letter writing dates from the Western Jin. More than 100 such manuals were found among the Dunhuang manuscripts.[37] Liu Xie 劉勰 (ca. AD 465–522) includes a chapter on (official) espistolary writing in *Wenxin diaolong* 文心雕龍 (30.4). A Yuan manual of letter writing has been photographically reproduced: *Xinbian shiwen leiyao qizha qingqian* 新編事文類要啓扎青錢.[38]

Despite repeated prohibitions, officials no doubt used the government postal system to send their private letters. Otherwise, family members, servants, or friends were requested to deliver them. On how private letters circulated in the Ming, see Timothy Brook, "The Transmission of Private Documents," in *CHC*, vol. 8, 639–41.

3.7 Commemorative Writings

The most important types of commemorative writings were those connected with the ancestral cult. These included epitaphs on tombstones (*mubei* 墓碑), which were carved on stelae and erected on the tomb (*mubiao* 墓表), or on the path or avenue leading to it (*shendaobei* 神道碑).[39] Starting from the end of the Later Han there were frequent regulations banning the use of *mubei*. Eventually they were reduced in size and buried in the grave (a practice already in existence judging from a buried epitaph dated AD 73; see *Kaogu* 1992.3). At first this new type of epitaph was called various names, including *muji* 墓記, *fengji* 封記, *shenzuo* 神座, and *muzhi* 墓誌. Eventually, it came to be known as *muzhi* 墓誌 (also *muzhiming* 墓誌銘 or *kuangming* 壙銘). *Muzhi* is sometimes translated into English as "tomb tablet" or "tomb epitaph" to distinguish it from tombstone (*mubei*).

---

[37] *Tang Wudai shuyi yanjiu* 唐五代書儀研究 (Researches on letter-writing manuals of the Tang and Five Dynasties), Zhou Yiliang 周一良, ed., Shehui kexue, 1996.

[38] *Xinbian shiwen leiyao qizha qingqian* 新編事文類要啓扎青錢 (Newly edited forms of correspondence as good as ready cash arranged by categories), Koten kenkyûkai, 1963.

[39] Ann Paludan, *The Chinese Spirit Road: The Classical Tradition of Stone Statuary*, YUP, 1991. Construction works have turned up huge quantities of commemorative and other types of stelae, many of which have been transcribed and published (17.3).

Tomb tablet is the expression used in the manual. About 7,000 *muzhi* have been indexed. Similar inscriptions were also deposited in the ancestral temple (*miaozhi* 廟誌). In addition, there were funeral orations (*jiwen* 祭文, *diaowen* 吊文), eulogies to the dead (*lei* 誄), elegies (*aici* 哀辭), and funerary odes (*song* 頌, *zansong* 贊頌).

Tomb-Tablet Indexes

Collections by place: *Xin Zhongguo chutu muzhi* 新中國出土墓誌 (Tomb tablets excavated in New China) is a series containing inscriptions discovered since 1949, arranged by province, of which the first volume to appear was *Henan* 河南, vol. 1, parts 1 and 2, Wenwu, 1994. It includes illustrations of 461 tomb tablets from the fourth to twentieth centuries, with annotated transcriptions, many published for the first time. There is a chronological index.

Hedong chutu muzhi lu 河東出土墓誌錄 (Record of excavated tomb tablets from Shanxi), Chen Jiyu 陳繼瑜, ed., Shanxi renmin, 1997.

Luoyang chutu lidai muzhi jisheng 洛陽出土歷代墓誌輯繩 (Collected historical tomb tablets from Luoyang), Shehui kexue, 1991. Includes 815 *muzhi*.

Luoyang xinhuo muzhi 洛陽新獲墓誌 (Newly discovered tomb tablets from Luoyang), Li Xianqi 李獻奇 and Guo Yinqiang 郭引強, eds., Wenwu, 1996.

Jiangxi chutu muzhi xuanbian 江西出土墓誌選編 (Selection of tomb tablets excavated in Jiangxi), Chen Baiquan 陳柏泉, ed., Jiangxi jiaoyu, 1991. The editor has added biographical notes on the individuals and appended 40 tomb contracts (for the afterlife). On this latter type of document, see Ina Asani, *Religiöse Landverträge aus der Song-Zeit*, Edition Forum, 1993; Valerie Hansen, "Why Bury Contracts in Tombs?" *Cahiers d'Extrême-Asie* 8: 59–66 (1995).

Collections by period: Part V of the manual contains references to published collections of tomb tablets dating from individual dynasties, for example, transcriptions of well over 5,000 Sui, Tang, and Wudai funerary inscriptions held in collections all over China (46.5).

1949–1989 Sishi nian chutu muzhi mulu 四十年出土墓誌目錄 (Catalog of tomb tablets unearthed during the past 40 years), Rong Lihua 榮麗華, ed.; Wang Shimin 王世民, rev., Wenwu, 1993. This index lists 1,467 stelae and includes references to reports and an index of names appearing on the inscriptions.

Collections of individual libraries, most important, Guotu 國圖, which has published an index of its holdings of rubbings of 4,638 funerary inscriptions from the Former Han to 1949: *Beijing tushuguan cang muzhi tapian mulu* 北京圖書館藏墓誌拓片目錄, Xu Ziqiang 徐自强, Zhonghua, 1990. The *Qian Tangzhizhai* 千唐誌齋 in Xin'an county 新安縣 near Luoyang is the only museum dedicated to ancient tomb tablets, of which it has 1,413, the greater number (1,209) dating from the Tang (46.5).

For two indexes edited by Mao Hanguang 毛漢光 of rubbings of stone inscriptions held at the Shiyusuo, see

Zhongyang yanjiuyuan Lishiyuyan yanjiusuo cang 中央研究院歷史語言研究所藏, *Lidai muzhiming tapian mulu fu suoyin* 歷代墓誌銘拓片目錄附索引, Shiyusuo, 1985 (25,000 tomb tablets and inscriptions)

Zhongyang yanjiuyuan Lishiyuyan yanjiusuo cang 中央研究院歷史語言研究所藏, *Lidai beizhiming tazhiming zazhiming tapian mulu* 歷代碑誌銘塔誌銘雜誌銘拓片目錄 (stele, pagoda, and miscellaneous epitaphs), Shiyusuo, 1987.

Biographies were prepared not only for tomb tablets, but also for family records or the family history (*jiazhuan* 家傳), or to substantiate claims for the subject's inclusion in officially compiled works, such as the local gazetteer, or, for senior officials, the Veritable Records of a reign, or even the Standard History of a dynasty, and also to make the case for the bestowal of posthumous titles and honors. Such claims or assessments were put in the standard form of accounts of conduct (*xingzhuang* 行狀, also called *zhuang* 狀, *xingshi* 行實, or *xingshu* 行述). It was upon these that the biographies in official historical works were usually based.

The classification and models for all these types of writing began to take shape during the Eastern Han, although their origins may be sought in the commemorative writings cast on bronze vessels in the Shang and Zhou. After the Han dynasty, ritual and social biographies are often found in the collected works (*bieji* 別集) of their authors or in the chronological biographies (*nianpu* 年譜) of their subjects. They were also included in literary anthologies. Special collections of commemorative writings have survived in great numbers from later periods.

Not surprisingly, the ritual and social biographies paint a somewhat stereotyped picture, since they were intended as a record of merit (*jigong* 記功) lauding the virtues and achievements of their subjects for the instruction of later generations. Despite this drawback, they provide a huge quantity of basic biographic material on many thousands of members of central and local elites in all periods of Chinese history from the Han down to the twentieth century.

There are some excellent introductory studies on the nature and methods of the different types of Chinese biographical writing, as well as some case studies probing the weaknesses of the sources.[40]

A major problem for the would-be biographer is that most of the biographical sources emphasize the moral, literary, scholarly, and official achievements of their subjects while drawing a veil of silence over their private lives, business interests, or financial dealings. In this sense they are not unlike the bland obituaries of civil servants and other public figures that used to appear in establishment newspapers in the West until quite recently.

The traditional biographical sources do not distort. They simply reflect the basic attitude that self-revelation, whether in action or in words, even in diaries, was not to be encouraged. Attainment lay in the fulfillment of one's familial and social roles. Not surprisingly, some of the best modern biographies have drawn on their subject's poetry or painting to try to get behind the social mask. See, for example, F. W. Mote, *The Poet Kao Ch'i, 1336–1374*, PUP, 1962; Arthur Waley (1889–1968), *Yuan Mei: Eighteenth Century Chinese Poet*, Macmillan, 1956; Patrick Hanan, *The Invention of Li Yu*, HUP, 1988; Jonathan D. Spence, *Emperor of China: Self-portrait of K'ang-hsi*, Knopf, 1974; David S. Nivison, *The Life and Thought of Chang Hsüeh-ch'eng (1738–1801)*, SUP, 1966.

---

[40] Brian Moloughney discusses many of the earlier studies of Chinese biographical writing in "From Biographical History to Historical Biography: A Transformation in Chinese Historical Writing," *East Asian History* 4: 1–30 (1992). See also D. C. Twitchett, "Chinese Biographical Writing,'" in *HCJ*, 95–114; and by the same author, "Problems of Chinese Biography," and Arthur F. Wright, "Values, Roles and Personalities," in *Confucian Personalities*, Wright and Twitchett, eds., SUP, 1962, 24–42 and 3–23, respectively; David S. Nivison, "Traditional Chinese Biography," *JAS* 21: 451–63 (1962); Robert des Rotours, *Les inscriptions funeraires de Ts'ouei Mien (673–739), de sa femme née Wang (685–734) et de Ts'ouei Yeou-fou (721–780)*, Maisonneuve, 1975; Wang Gungwu, "The Rebel Reformer and Modern Chinese Biography," in his *The Chineseness of China: Selected Essays*, HKCUP, 1991, 187–206; Kenneth DeWoskin, "Famous Chinese Childhoods," in *Chinese Views on Childhood*, Anne Behnke Kinney, ed., HUP, 1995, 57–78; Anne Behnke Kinney, "The Theme of the Precocious Child in Early Chinese Literature," *TP* 81.1–3: 1–24 (1995). On Buddhist biography and hagiography, see 29.5, *Biography*. See also the studies in note 41.

3.8   Biographies

3.8.1   Historical Biographies

Biographies included in official historical works were termed *shizhuan* 史傳. All other forms of biographical writing were lumped together in catalogs as *zazhuan* 雜傳. From the Song this began to be replaced with the term *zhuanji* 傳記. Biographies attached to genealogies were called *jiazhuan* 家傳. Apart from authorized biographies (the *shizhuan* and *jiazhuan*), less formal biographies were classified as *biezhuan* 別傳 and *waizhuan* 外傳, of which the latter, just like the *waishi* 外史, verged on fiction. The category *xiaozhuan* 小傳 (brief lives) was also fairly common. Most prestigious of all were the biographies included in the grouped biographies (*liezhuan* 列傳), which had been included in the Standard Histories ever since the *Shiji*. They were put in their final form by each new dynasty for its predecessor. It was also highly prestigious to have your obituary included in the Veritable Records.[41]

For the most part, *liezhuan* were based on the various categories of commemorative and social writings introduced in 3.7. For senior officials they were based on the obituaries in the Veritable Records. Although official historians were expected to take a less eulogistic view of their subject, *liezhuan* were sometimes selected to form a group of exemplary lives of an age to illustrate some larger moral pattern or theme such as chastity of widows, filial conduct, or loyalty. Senior officials of a dynasty or a particular reign were also put together (in chronological rather than moralistic groupings). The standards of historical criticism applied to the biographies were not the same as those applied to other types of historical writing; thus again and again the same clichés (often drawn from a famous literary model) were used to round out the major stages of a subject's

---

[41] Twitchett (1992), 62–83; Herbert Franke, "Some Remarks on the Interpretation of Chinese Dynastic Histories," *Oriens* 3: 113–22 (1950); Hans H. Frankel, "Objektivität und Parteilichkeit in der offiziellen chinesischen Geschichtsschreibung vom 3 bis 11 Jahrhundert," *OE* 5: 133–44 (1958); James T. C. Liu, "Some Classifications of Bureaucrats in Chinese Historiography," in *The Confucian Persuasion*, SUP, Arthur F. Wright, ed., 1959, 165–81; Liu Ts'un-yan, "Men of Letters in the Light of Chinese Historiography," *BMFEA* 37: 137–65 (1965); Hans H. Frankel, "T'ang Literati: A Composite Biography," in Wright and Twitchett (1962), 65–83.

life, which in the end appears two-dimensional, more ideal than real. At times fiction took over altogether, as has been shown, for example, not only in the earlier Standard Histories, but in the later ones as well.

Liezhuan account for over half the space in the Standard Histories and contain individual biographies of nearly 30,000 people. In addition, the Standard Histories contain biographical materials on several thousand more people. Both the biographies and the biographical materials are summarized and indexed in *Ershiwushi renming da cidian* 二十五史人名大辭典 (22.2, *Indexes*).

There are plenty of other official biographies and biographical materials extant from the later empire. The biographies in the Ming Veritable Records have been excerpted in the series *Ming shilu leizuan* 明實錄類纂 (49.1). The mass of Qing biographical sources have not yet been fully exploited. They include those in the Veritable Records and in the Court Diaries (*qijuzhu* 起居注; see 50.4); official CVs in the archives (50.2.4) and in the biographical archives of the Guoshi Guan 國史館 (National History Office).

3.8.2 Chronological Biography

From the Song onward, the application of annals style to biographical materials produced a more rigorous form of biographical writing than the ritual and social biographies and historical biographies discussed above. This new form was called *nianpu* 年譜 (chronological biography). These trace the subject's life, year by year, in great detail, particularly for personalities of the late Ming, Qing, or later, for whose lives the source materials are more copious than for previous periods. An example is the recently compiled *nianpu* of the Ming loyalist, philosopher, writer, and painter Huang Daozhou 黃道周 (1585–1646).[42] The preliminaries include a study of the 32 alternative names used by Huang and an outline of his paternal and maternal ancestors (1–49). There follows a strictly chronological account of his activities in each year of his life (50–367). The second volume contains an annotated bibliography of Huang's writings, inscriptions, paintings, and calligraphy (369–768). *Nianpu* are available for over 4,000 outstanding historical figures up to the end of

---

[42] *Huang Daozhou jinian zhushu hua kao* 黃道周紀念著述畫考, Hou Zhen-ping 侯真平, ed., 2 vols., Xiamen daxue, 1996.

the Qing.[43] The genre continued in use during the Republican period and *nianpu* are still produced today.

3.8.3   Biographies in Local Gazetteers

Local gazetteers contain considerable numbers of biographies, usually grouped as in the Standard Histories. They also sometimes contain additional biographical materials such as epitaphs. In recent years more and more gazetteer indexes have been compiled, sometimes for biographies of people who lived in a particular period, increasingly for biographies of those from a particular region, province, or city. Biographies of people from a particular place are not necessarily published in a gazetteer (see below, *Particular Places*).

Particular Periods

Songdai renwu ziliao suoyin 宋代人物資料索引 (Index to materials on Song figures), see 47.4.2, *Biographies*.

Mingdai difangzhi zhuanji suoyin 明代地方誌傳記索引 (Index of people with biographies in Ming local gazetteers), 2 vols., Taibei, 1986. Includes holdings in Taiwan and Japan and published material, thus expanding *Nihon genson Mindai chihôshi denki sakuin kô* 日本現存明代地方志傳記索引稿 (Draft index of people with biographies in Ming local gazetteers [extant in Japanese collections]), Yamane Yukio 山根幸夫, ed., Tôyô bunko, Mindai kenkyû shitsu, 1964. References to biographies of some 30,000 people in 299 Ming gazetteers.

Particular Places

Beijing: *Beijing Tianjin difangzhi renwu zhuanji suoyin* 北京天津地方志人物傳記索引, Gao Xiufang 高秀芳 et al., eds., Beijing daxue, 1987. Indexes the biographies in 73 editions of local gazetteers of counties presently attached to Beijing and Tianjin. Each of the 14,608 entries

---

[43] *Zhongguo lidai renwu nianpu kaolu* 中國歷代人物年譜考錄 (Catalog of chronological biographies of historical personalities), Xie Wei 謝巍, Zhonghua, 1992. Includes carefully arranged notes on 6,259 *nianpu* of 4,010 people. The author spent a lifetime collecting *nianpu* and has included the holdings of all major libraries in China and abroad. There are convenient indexes of personalities and authors arranged by *pinyin* and notes on editions and provenance of each *nianpu*. Replaces all previous *nianpu* catalogs. Note also Wang Deyi 王德毅, *Zhongguo mingren nianpu zongmu* 中國名人年譜總目 (Comprehensive catalog of *nianpu* of famous Chinese personalities), Huashi, 1978; rev. ed., Xin wenfeng, 1999. Includes details of 1,715 *nianpu*.

gives name, alternative name(s), dynasty, native place, and biographical citations.

Guangdong: *Guangdong difangzhi zhuanji suoyin* 廣東地方志傳記索引, Pan Mingshen 潘銘燊, 2 vols., HKCUP, 1989. Indexes the biographies of 10,222 persons in 11 Qing gazetteers.

Guangxi: *Guangxi difangzhi zhuanji renming suoyin* 廣西地方志傳記人名索引, Guangxi renmin, 1997.

Jiangsu: *Ming Qing Jiangsu wenren nianbiao* 明清江蘇文人年表, Zhang Huijian 張慧劍, comp., Shanghai guji, 1986. Contains the names, dates, and works of 4,379 Ming and Qing (up to 1840) literati from Jiangsu arranged as a chronological table.

Shanxi: *Shanxi tongzhi renwu zhuan suoyin* 山西通志人物傳索引, Chi Xiuyun 池秀雲, Taiyuan, 1984. Indexes 15,808 people.

Northeast: *Dongbei fangzhi renwu zhuanji ziliao suoyin* 東北方志人物傳記資料索引 (Indexes to biographical materials in northeastern gazetteers): (*Jilin juan* 吉林卷), Jilinsheng tushuguan 吉林省圖書館, eds., Jilin wenshi, 1989; (*Liaoning juan* 遼寧卷), Liaoningsheng tushuguan 遼寧省圖書館, eds., Liaoning renmin, 1991; (*Heilongjiang juan* 黑龍江卷), Heilongjiangsheng tushuguan 黑龍江省圖書館, eds., Heilongjiang renmin, 1989.

3.8.4   *Biographical Collections*

Far more extensive than the biographies in the Standard Histories and in the local gazetteers are the very large numbers of ritual, commemorative, and "unofficial biographies" (*biezhuan* 別傳); that is, those not included in an official historical work. They are usually contained in the collected works (*bieji* 別集) of their authors or in special biographical collections. The great bulk date from the last thousand years of Chinese history and are relatively well indexed (see appropriate sections of Part V for titles). Unfortunately the same is not true of the periods before the Song. For these earlier centuries the student should look first through the standard biographical indexes for each period, including indexes of stone inscriptions and tomb tablets (listed in Part V). Next, the collected works of individual authors as well as the great literary anthologies should be checked (many of these latter include commemorative biographical writings as a category).

Large numbers of privately compiled collections of biographies of famous people are also extant. Frequently the organizing principle was the inclusion of all famous people living in a certain region or locality; other collections group the famous men of an age or of a certain type. For this last category a considerable number of modern biographical dictionaries have been compiled. If you know what the individual you are looking was or did, then it is usually quicker to check one of these special references, for example, for military men (Chapter 28), doctors (Chapter 36), non-Han peoples (40.1), women (Chapter 39), artists, craftsmen, and musicians (38.3), writers and poets (Chapter 30), philosophers (Chapter 33), or Daoist and Buddhist monks and nuns (29.4 and 29.5).

To give an idea of the number of biographical collections available today: the section on biographies in the *Siku* (sub-branch seven of the History branch) lists 460 collections, while the much more comprehensive *Zhongguo congshu zonglu* 中國叢書綜錄 contains references to over 2,000 biographical collections under 18 different categories. Fortunately the most important of these have been indexed in standard reference works such as the total of 199 biographical collections indexed in *H-Y Index* 34 (Song), 35 (Liao, Jin and Yuan), 24 (Ming), and 9 (Qing), but not always. More comprehensive indexes are listed in the individual sections of Part V.

3.9   Portraits

The comic-book style faces on the prehistoric petroglyphs are closer to their contemporary cousins on the other continents than to their dynastic descendents.[44] The range of expression of later prehistoric representations of the human face in China is astonishing. Two quite different types of features are shown on the prehistoric jades and again on the rare depictions of humans on bronzes. In one the eyes are slanted and often have striated eyebrows. In the other, the eyes are depicted as deep round hollows. The former are found in the south and West, the latter at Shang centers in Henan such as Anyang.[45]

---

[44] There is a good selection in Song Yaoliang 宋耀良, *Zhongguo shiqian shenge renmian yanhua* 中國史前神格人面岩畫 (Mythical humans in China's prehistoric petroglyphs), HK: Sanlian, 1992.

[45] Jessica Rawson, "Some Examples of Human or Human-like Faces on Shang and Western Zhou Bronzes," in *Proceedings of the International Conference on 'Chinese Archaeology Enters the Twenty-first Century,* Kexue, 1998, 124–

Footnote continued on next page

Animal masks and other disguises were used by shamans (spirit mediums, *wu* 巫), doctors (*yi* 毉), and exorcists (until the Warring States often one and the same person) for the transformation rituals and dances which in early China were an essential part of ancestor worship, the expulsion of evil, fertility rites, propitiation of the gods, and all the other festivities and ceremonies of the ritual year.[46] Masks were also worn in battle (to strike awe and to rally supporters) and for hunting (as a disguise). Some of the early characters depict a person wearing a mask (e.g., the oracle bone form of *yu* 虞 and the bronze script forms of *hei* 黑 and *ji* 冀). By the Song dynasty, masks of gods and humans had begun to be used alongside animal masks. Burial masks (*fumian* 覆面) of jade and precious metals have been found in tombs from the Neolithic to the Liao dynasty. Masks are still used in exorcist drama (*nuoxi* 儺戲) and in Chinese opera. The stylized painted faces of Peking opera therefore come at the end of a long evolution.[47]

From the fifth century BC to the later empire, it was a common practice to bury figurines (*yong* 俑) in tombs.[48] These have survived in large numbers and often have expressive, life-like, non-stylized, albeit generalized, features. But these are exceptional. In many ways the aims of portrait painters and carvers of imperial China were not so different from the authors of biographies: their purpose was spiritual, bureaucratic, or social rather than individual.[49] Good examples are the portrayal of children with their rosy cheeks, smiling faces, and fat little bodies or the ideal images of Confucius as an an-

28; Wu Hung contrasts eyeless figurines with the eyes-on-stalks bronze figures of Sanxingdui in "All About the Eyes: Two Groups of Sculptures from the Sanxingdui Culture," *Orientations* 28.8: 58–66 (1997).

[46] See Chapter 36, note 2.

[47] Li Jinshan 李錦山 and Li Guangyu 李光雨 examine masks from prehistoric times to the Han in *Zhongguo gudai mianju yanjiu* 中國古代面具研究 (Research on ancient Chinese masks), Shandong daxue, 1994; Xue Ruolin 薛若郱 has edited a collection of ritual masks: *Zhongguo wunuo mianju yishu* 中國巫儺面具藝術 (The art of Chinese ritual masks), 2 vols., SMC, 1996. Vol. 2 contains a summary in English.

[48] Ann Paludan, *Chinese Tomb Figurines*, HK: OUP, 1994.

[49] Michael Siggerstedt, "Forms of Fate: An Investigation of the Relationship Between Formal Portraiture, Especially Ancestor Portraits, and Physiognomy (*xiangshu*) in China," *International Colloquium on Chinese Art History, 1991: Proceedings, Painting and Calligraphy*, 2 vols., Taibei, 1992, 713–48.

cient sage embodying all those qualities society wished him to stand for, but with no shred of evidence upon which to base a likeness (he is invariably shown as an immensely old sage, not unlike a Daoist hermit).

Yang Xiaoneng 楊曉能, *Sculpture of Xia and Shang China*, HK: Tai Dao Publishing [1988]. This contains illustrations of not only the monumental Shang funerary bronzes, but also a large number of lesser known, minor pieces of a surprising domesticity. For a general introduction to sculpture in China from the Shang to the present, including Buddhist sculpture, see "Sculpture for Tombs and Temples," in *The British Museum Book of Chinese Art*, Jessica Rawson, ed., British Museum, 1992.

On portrait painting in general, see Audrey Spiro, *Contemplating the Ancients: Aesthetic and Social Issues in Early Chinese Portraiture*, UCP, 1990; and Shan Guoqiang 單國強, "Xiaoxianghua lishi gaishu" 肖像畫歷史概述 (Outline of the history of portrait painting), *Gugong bowuyuan yuankan*, 1997.2: 59–73. On portrait painting in the Ming, see "Man," in Craig Clunas, *Pictures and Visuality in Early Modern China*, Reaktion, 1997, 88–101. Many more portraits survive from the Qing; see Richard Vinograd, *Boundaries of the Self: Chinese Portraits, 1600–1900*, CUP, 1992. Check also exhibition catalogs.

Guotu 國圖 has published 10 volumes of rubbings of portraits in its collection of stone inscriptions.[50] For an index to 4,353 illustrations in a wide variety of historical sources in every conceivable medium, see *Zhongguo lishi renwu tuxiang suoyin* 中國歷史人物圖象索引.[51] Note that there are many portraits among the 7,000 illustrations contained in *Zhongguo gudaishi cankao tulu* 中國古代史參考圖錄 (8.3.2). For missionary and embassy painters, see 42.4.1. Photographic portraits date from the 1850s (42.4.2).

---

[50] *Beijing tushuguan cang huaxiang taben huibian* 北京圖書館藏畫像拓本匯編, 10 vols., Shumu wenxian, 1993.

[51] *Zhongguo lishi renwu tuxiang suoyin* (Index to images of Chinese historical personages), Qu Guanqun 瞿冠群 et al., eds., Jiangsu jiaoyu, 1994.

4

Geography

This chapter is concerned with domestic geography; for works on border areas, the coasts, and countries outside of China, see Chapter 41. Environmental history, including climate change, shifts in river courses, lakes and coasts, desertification and deforestation, and their interaction with economic and social life, are introduced in 35.4. Hydrographic works and water control are the subject of 35.3.

Toponyms carry a lot of history in them and are worth studying for that alone (4.1). More than is generally realized they were often based on the names used by the original non-Han occupants. In imperial times toponyms frequently changed, as did regional and local administrative units (4.2). There are place-name dictionaries (4.3.1) and historical maps (4.3.2) to help trace these changes. The discussion of toponyms begins with that of Zhongguo 中國 itself (Box 2).

The Chinese state and Chinese scholars produced all kinds of geographical works, for military and administrative purposes, for historical studies and for everyday life. The remainder of the chapter covers the following sources and subjects: cartography (4.4); comprehensive geographical works (4.5), monographs in the Standard Histories (4.5.2), comprehensive gazetteers (4.5.3), and geographical studies (4.5.4); local gazetteers and how to find them (4.6); descriptions of cities (4.7) and modern studies (4.7.1); merchant route books and manuals (50.7.4); diaries of travel inside China (4.8); bibliographies and textbooks of historical and economic geography (4.9).

Works on geography (*dili* 地理) were placed in the History branch of the traditional fourfold bibliographical classification (*Sibu* 四部, on which see 9.3).

Box 2: *Zhongguo* 中國

It was only in the nineteenth century that *Zhongguo* 中國 emerged as the name for the country (it appears in a formal document for the first time in the title of the chief Manchu negotiator at the Treaty of Nerchinsk, 1689, and was adopted as the abbreviation of Zhonghua minguo 中華民國 in the early twentieth century).

During the Shang, the name for the royal cultic center, the earliest capital, was *Shang* 商, *Zhongshang* 中商, *Dayishang* 大邑商, or *Tianyishang* 天邑商. This was extended to mean the royal domain. The area indirectly ruled through royal relatives and senior officials was called *sifang* 四方 (the four quarters) or *situ* 四土. Beyond that lay the peoples outside Shang rule, the *duofang* 多方.

During the Western Zhou, *Zhongguo* 中國 was used in the sense of *guozhong* 國中 (inside the kingdom, *guonei* 國內), hence, royal domain (*guo* 國 referred to a city and its surrounding area, traditionally translated as "state" or "statelet," as opposed to the area where the feudal lords had their lands, still called *sifang*). Several centuries after the Eastern Zhou was established at Luoyi 雒邑 (modern Luoyang) in 770, *Zhongguo* came to refer either to Luoyang or to the area around it (what came to be known in the early twentieth century as the Central Plain, Zhongyuan 中原). Because of the weakness of the Zhou, *Zhongguo* was also used at this time to refer to between two and six of the feudal states in the middle and lower reaches of the Yellow River. States outside this area, such as Chu 楚 (central Yangzi) or Qin (upper Yellow R.), were not regarded as being one of the Zhongguo. The expression is also used in the classics as a cultural concept to differentiate the Huaxia from the barbarians. Other expressions used during the Zhou were *Zhongtu* 中土, *Zhongzhou* 中州, *Zhongxia* 中夏, *Fangxia* 方夏, *Quxia* 區夏, *Youxia* 有夏, or *Tianxia* 天下. Later, there were at least a dozen other ways of referring to what we now call "China" (on the origins of this word, see 42.1), e.g., *Shenzhou* 神州, *Jiuzhou* 九州, or *Chixian* 赤縣.

In the Wei and Jin periods, *Zhongguo* 中國 and *Huaxia* 華夏 were abbreviated to form *Zhonghua* 中華, an expression that came into general use during the Nan-Bei Chao. It referred to either the area inhabited by the Zhonghua as opposed to the surrounding barbarian lands, or simply to the Zhongyuan (Central Plain).

It is sometimes implied that the Chinese were unique in regarding their country as central. Nothing could be further from the truth: the ancient Greeks, Romans, Indians, Japanese, Incas, Mayas, and Aztecs all saw their countries as the center of the world—but only the Chinese came to use the concept for the name.

4.1 Toponyms

Formally, Chinese toponyms usually have two elements. First, a specific name; second, a general term indicating the geographical feature, settlement, construction, or administrative unit (as in Lu-shan 盧山, Wangzhuang 王莊, Wanfosi 萬佛寺, or Zhongguo 中國). In ancient texts (just as in the modern spoken language) place names were often abbreviated by dropping off the general term, thus Cao 曹 for Caoyang 曹陽, Yi 易 for Yiyang 易陽 (or Shanghai 上海 for Shanghaishi 上海市).[1]

Chinese toponyms are formed in five main ways. The two most common consist of a noun or adjective plus general term (Yangpu 楊鋪 or Qinghai 清海). Many are composed of a general term followed by a direction word or vice-versa: Shandong 山東 (east of the mountains) and Dongshan 東山 (the eastern mountains). Finally, a general term is often linked to a number as in Sichuan 四川 or Wu-daokou 五道口. The names of rivers and mountains are among the oldest and also the slowest to change.[2]

Often different general terms are used in different parts of the country. From the Shang to the Tang, *shui* 水 and *chuan* 川 were the two most common generics for river. He 河 was used for the Yellow River since the Shang, and Jiang 江 for the Changjiang since the Zhou. Starting from the Tang, *he* 河 became a common generic for river in the north and *jiang* 江 in the south, and *shui* 水 for the provinces in between.[3] Since the Yuan, the word for lane in the north has been *hutong* 胡同; in the south, it is variations of *xiang* 巷, for example, *xiangdao* 巷道, *xiaoxiang* 小巷, or *xiangzi* 巷子. In Wu dialect it is *long* 弄 or *lilong* 里弄 (*longtang* 弄堂 in Shanghai). In the north, villages with periodic markets often have *ji* 集 or *shi* 市 in their names; in the southeast and in Hunan the word is *xu* 墟.

---

[1] In some non-Han languages, the general term precedes the specific name, e.g., in Dai, *meng* 勐 (the Chinese transcription of *Muang*, town) occurs first in place names such as Mengla 勐臘 or Menghai 勐海. In such cases the name can be abbreviated by dropping off the first part.

[2] Li Rulong 李如龍, *Hanyu dimingxue lungao* 漢語地名學論稿 (Draft discussion of Chinese place-name studies), Shanghai jiaoyu, 1998.

[3] Zhang Hongming 張洪明, "Chinese Etyma for River," *JCL* 26.1: 1–47 (1997). For the various names of the Changjiang and Yellow rivers in history, see 35.3.2.

Non-Han languages were the source for many toponyms outside the homelands of the Huaxia in the Central Plains. The newly arrived Huaxia (Han) settlers would ask the name of a place from the indigenous peoples and then choose characters to represent the sounds. For example, the name of Dunhuang 敦煌 (founded 111 BC), Gansu, was probably taken from the early Altaic word Dawan ("continuous mountain range"), the place name given to the nearby mountains by the Rongdi 戎狄;[4] the Han name for the Mekong (Lancang 瀾滄) is derived from the original Dai name of Lanzang (million elephants). Typically, traditional commentators (and not a few modern ones too) ignore the substrata and interpret toponyms on the basis of fanciful meanings attributed to the characters (a form of folk etymology known as *wangwen shengyi* 望文生義; see 2.2.2). Thus the name Wuxi 無錫 is linked to stories based on the meaning of the characters ("no tin"). In fact, "Wuxi" was probably a transcription of the sounds of the original Yue 越 name in whose language the sound transcribed as *wu* 無 was a proper-name prefix (cf. Yu-Yue 于越, or *wu* 蕪, *wu* 烏, and *yu* 余 in other Yue toponyms, or You-Xia 有夏 in Box 2).[5]

See 40.1 for the similar problem of identifying transcriptions of non-Han ethnonyms. Tracing the origins of toponyms in more recent centuries is not so difficult because the pronunciation of Chinese is closer to that of today—for example:

Gobi: Gebi 戈壁 (transcription of *gov*, the Mongolian for desert).

Hutong 胡同 (the name for the lanes in Beijing, Tianjin, and the cities of the northeast; probably from *khôtagh* (also transcribed as *gudum* or *hottôk*), the Mongolian for water well.

Zhan 站 (from Mongolian *jamci*, post station; represented in Chinese as *zhanchi* 站赤[醲]). Found in many places named after Mongolian post stations. Not infrequently such names were subsequently

---

[4] See Qian Boquan 錢伯泉 in *Dunhuang yanjiu* 1: 44–53, 1994.

[5] Zhou Zhenhe 周振鶴 and You Rujie 游汝杰, *Fangyan yu Zhongguo wenhua* 方言與中國文化 (Dialects and Chinese culture), Shanghai renmin, 4th prnt. with revisions, 1997, 173–89. Niu Ruchen 牛如辰, *Zhongguo diming youlai cidian* 中國地名由來詞典 (Dictionary of the origins of Chinese place names), Zhongyang minzu daxue, 1999, contains 2,800 brief entries with the geographic location, date of establishment, and the main traditional and modern explanations of the origins of the names of towns, rivers, lakes and abbreviated place names.

sinicized by using the older Chinese words for post station (*zhi* 置, *yi* 驛). *Zhan* itself survives in modern words such as *jiayouzhan* 加油站 (gasoline station) or *huochezhan* 火車站 (railroad station).

Buildings and constructions of all sorts (e.g., *cheng* 城, *tai* 臺, *lou* 樓, *qiao* 橋) are one of the most common sources of generics in toponyms. Already in the Shang, the names of tall buildings, for example, *gao* 高, *jing* 京, *ting* 亭, *guo* 郭, and *song* 宋, were used as toponyms; another example, perhaps, of the belief (held by many other ancient peoples) that high places are the points were humans can gain privileged access to the gods.[6] Emperors started building their tombs shortly after acceding to the throne. A common practice in the early empire was to found a new county town at the tomb site and populate it with conscript laborers and craftsmen. Such imperial mausoleum counties are identified with the character *ling* 陵 (Liu Bang is at Changlingxian 長陵縣; Han Wudi at Maolingxian 茂陵縣).

Cities were not infrequently named after the era name in which they were founded (e.g., Shaoxing 紹興 in Zhejiang, after the Shaoxing era, 1131–62). Names with characters symbolizing good fortune were very popular in the later empire (Changchun 長春, Jinshan 金山, Longjing 龍井, and so on). Not surprisingly, the most common first characters in county names are for propitious qualities such as *xin* 新 (new, 39 counties); *nan* 南 (south, 38); *ping* 平 (flat or quelled, 31), *an* 安 (peaceful, 31); *yong* 永 (everlasting, 30); *jian* 堅 (firm, 30); *wu* 武 (valiant, 25); *dong* 東 (east, 25) and *ning* 寧 (tranquil, 25). Note that *yang* 陽 in the names of places near a mountain usually indicates that the place is to the south of the mountain (e.g., Guiyang 貴陽), but in places near a river, north of the river (e.g. Huaiyang 淮陽) because these are the positions that catch the sun (first pointed out in the *Guliang zhuan* 穀梁傳 under the 28th year of Xi gong 僖公 (632 BC). Yin 陰 is used in the opposite sense (e.g., Huaiyin 淮陰 is to the south of the river and Mengyin 蒙陰 is to the north of the mountain). For obvious reasons there are many more toponyms with *yang* 陽 in them than *yin* 陰. Note also that *you* 右 (right) and *zuo* 左 (left) in place names often refer to west and east, respectively (on the basis that when you face

---

[6] Zheng Huisheng 鄭慧生, *Jiagu puci yanjiu* 甲骨卜辭研究 (Researches on oracle-bone script), Henan daxue, 1998, 22–27.

south your right side faces west and your left side, east. Thus, Jiangyou 江右 is one of the alternative names for Jiangxi 江西 (Table 6).

Cities (and temples and other institutions) changed names much
more frequently than mountains or rivers. This was partly because
cities tended to change their names when they were reclassified in
the administrative hierarchy (a frequent occurrence) or when they
were rebuilt having been destroyed by fire or war (an equally common occurrence). A new name (or the revival of a previous one)
was intended to bring better fortune. Other reasons were more political. During the reign of Wang Mang 王莽 (AD 9–23), 75 percent
of the commandery, princedom, and county names were changed.
To take another example, in 756, forces in Hebei loyal to the emperor and opposed to An Lushan 安祿山 changed the names of
towns there—Lucheng 鹿城 to Shulu 束鹿 (tying up Lu, i.e., An
Lushan), Luquan 鹿泉 to Huolu 獲鹿 (capturing Lu), and Fangshan
房山 to Pingshan 平山 (quelling Shan, i.e., An Lushan); see *Jiu
Tangshu*, "Benji" 本紀. After An Lushan's death, *an* 安 was removed
from place names. Another reason for place-name changes was that
new dynasties frequently ordered them in order to observe the taboos on using the emperor's or crown prince's name. Finally, note
that many places had popular names as well as formal names, for
example, the Juesheng 覺生 temple in Beijing is better known as the
Big Bell temple (Da zhong si 大鐘寺).

The names of the provinces (Table 6) are usually derived from
topography (Henan 河南); administrative history (Sichuan 四川);
pre-existing non-Han names (Xizang 西藏); major cities (Jiangsu 江
蘇) or they are statements of imperial policy (Ningxia 寧夏). All of
the provinces (and most cities, regions, and counties) have simplified
names, and sometimes several. These are usually a single character
taken from the modern name or from the ancient kingdom in
which the province is situated or from both. Thus Jing 京, Jin 津,
Hu 滬 (or Shen 申), and Yu 渝 for Beijing, Tianjin, Shanghai, and
Chongqing. Single-character province and city names were not used
only in literature, they are still part of everyday life, appearing, for
example, on automobile registration plates. In the spoken language,
they are usually linked with another word to form a compound
(Chuanbei 川北 and Minnan 閩南 for northern Sichuan and southern Fujian, for example). Many of the provinces, especially the
older ones, also have several alternative names, for example, Shanxi
is known as San Jin 三晉; Sichuan, as Shu 蜀 or Ba-Shu 巴蜀.

Table 6: The Origins of the Names of the Provinces

Province Name (Origin of Meaning); Simplified Name, also Alternative Name

---

Anhui 安徽 (<u>An</u>qing 安慶 + <u>Hui</u>zhou 徽州); Wan 皖

Fujian 福建 (<u>Fu</u>zhou 福州 + <u>Jian</u>ning 建寧); Min 閩, also Ba Min 八閩

Gansu 甘肅 (<u>Gan</u>zhou 甘州 + <u>Su</u>zhou 肅州); Gan 甘, also Long 隴

Guangdong 廣東 (The enlarged territories to the [south] east); Yue 粵,
    also Nanhai 南海, Lingnan 嶺南, or Yuedong 越東

Guangxi 廣西 (The enlarged territories to the [south] west); Gui 桂

Guizhou 貴州 (possibly derived from the name of the Tang prefecture Juzhou
    矩州) the formal change from Ju to Gui was made in the Yuan; Qian 黔,
    also Gui 貴

Hainan 海南 (Hainan Isl., Hainan *dao* 海南島); Hai 海, also Zhuyai 珠崖

Hebei 河北 (N. of the Yellow River); Ji 冀, also Zhili 直隸

Heilongjiang 黑龍江 (named after the river Heilong); Hei 黑

Henan 河南 (S. of the Yellow River); Yu 豫, also Zhongzhou 中州

Hubei 湖北 (N. of the [Dongting] Lake 洞庭湖); E 鄂, also Jing 荊

Hunan 湖南 (S. of the [Dongting] Lake 洞庭湖); Xiang 湘

Jiangsu 江蘇 (<u>Jiang</u>ning 江寧 + <u>Su</u>zhou 蘇州); Su 蘇

Jiangxi 江西 (from the Tang name <u>Jiang</u>nan <u>xi</u>dao 江南西道, the western cir-
    cuit south of the Yangzi); Gan 贛, also Yuzhang 豫章; Jiangyou 江右

Jilin 吉林 (Manchu *Jilin* [along] *wula* [the big river, i.e., the Songhua]); Ji 吉

Liaoning 遼寧 (Peaceful territories of the Liao River); Liao 遼

Nei-Menggu 內蒙古 (Mongolian *Mongol*); Nei-Meng 內蒙

Ningxia 寧夏 (Peaceful Xia [the ancient kingdom of Xixia]); Ning 寧

Qinghai 青海 (tr. of Mongolian *Kokonor*, Blue Lake); Qing 青

Shaanxi 陝西 (W. of Shaanzhou 陝州); Shan 陝, also Qin 秦, Guanzhong 關中

Shandong 山東 (E. of the [Taihang 太行] Mts.); Lu 魯, also Qi-Lu 齊魯

Shanxi 山西 (W. of the [Taihang 太行] Mts.); Jin 濟, also San Jin 三濟

Sichuan 四川 (named after the four administrative regions of Tang Sichuan,
    by later convention sometimes associated with the rivers Changjiang 長江,
    Minjiang 岷江, Tuojiang 沱江, Jialingjiang 嘉陵江); Chuan 川, also Shu 蜀,
    Ba-Shu 巴蜀, or Ba 巴

Taiwan 臺灣 known as Daoyi 島夷 (Warring States), Yizhou 夷州 (Sanguo),
    Liuqiu 琉球 (Sui–Yuan), Xiao Liuqiu 小琉球 (from 1373), and Taiwan
    (since the Ming); possibly from S. Min pronunciation of the Ta-hui (Ta-
    youan 大員, the people who lived near Tainan, the main settlement in the
    Ming); Tai 臺 (Ilha Formosa, from Portugese "the beautiful island")

Xinjiang 新疆 (The new frontier), 1884 (previously Xiyu 西域); Xin 新

Xizang 西藏 (from the administrative unit founded by the Yuan, dBus gTsang,
    itself based on the gTsang-bo River [see 41.2.2]); Zang 藏

Yunnan 雲南 (S. of the Yunling 雲嶺 Mts.); Dian 滇, also Yun 雲

Zhejiang 浙江 (Zhejiang was the old name for the Qiantang River 錢塘江);
    Zhe 浙, also Wu-Yue 吳越 or Wu 吳

Romanization of Chinese Toponyms

Europeans first came to China in modern times via the south and therefore they recorded many Chinese toponyms (as well as personal and other names) according to Cantonese pronunciation: "Hong Kong" for Xianggang 香港, "Kiangnan" for Jiangnan 江南, and "Canton" for Guangdong 廣東 (presumably a transcription derived from the Cantonese pronunciation of the province of Guangdong 廣東, not from its capital of Guangzhou 廣州). These were the transcriptions incorporated into the *China Postal Atlas*, 1903 (51.14). In addition, this work also reflects the French system of romanization (based on the Nanjing pronunciation of Mandarin), for example, "Tsinan" for Jinan 濟南, and the British system (Wade-Giles), based on the Beijing pronunciation of Mandarin, for the names of smaller places. Other dialects also affected the romanizations used in the Post Office system, which continued to influence Chinese names in English (and many other languages, including for example, Japanese and Thai) until the 1970s. Thereafter the tendency has been to use *pinyin* based on modern standard pronunciation (e.g., Beijing 北京 instead of Post Office Cantonese, "Peking").

4.2   Administrative Units in Different Dynasties

One of the main problems for the central government throughout most of Chinese history was how to control threats to its authority at the regional level. Many dynasties were brought down by regional warlords, but bit by bit layers of centrally appointed supervision or centrally controlled regional government were installed. The result was that the center became ever stronger. New terms were constantly applied to what gradually evolved into the provincial governments. At the same time many of the older terms were pushed down the administrative hierarchy. *Zhou* 州, for example, began as the highest-level regional unit in the Zhou 周 period and was even used in many synonyms for China (Box 2); from the Sui it was demoted to the second-highest regional unit (prefecture); by the Qing it had become the second-lowest level (department); today it is used only for self-governing administrative units in non-Han areas. Other terms, for example *xian* 縣, underwent a similar process of debasement, covering ever smaller units as new organs of control were added above them.

At the top and in the center, the symbolic and sometimes effective head of the entire system, the emperor, resided in the palace (*da'nei* 大內, *jincheng* 禁城), the heart of the government structure in the capital (*jing* 京 or *du* 都 as in Beijing 北京 or Shangdu 上都). In most dynasties it was normal to have at least one secondary capital, and on several occasions, more than one.[7]

The lowest level to which the center appointed an official was the county (*xian* 縣, sometimes called district). It was governed by a magistrate (*xianling* 縣令 or *xianzhang* 縣長 in the Qin and Han; *xianling* to the Song and thereafter *zhixian* 知縣). Below the counties were various systems of locally regulated control and supervision down to the villages (*li* 里, *cun* 村) and urban wards (*fang* 坊). The Qin introduced regional government after it destroyed the last remaining independent, hereditary kingdoms and set up a total of 36 (later expanded to 48) commanderies (*jun* 郡), each responsible for between five and 20 counties (of which in all there were about 1,000). The Han began by following the same system in about half the empire, but in the other half installed hereditary princedoms (*wangguo* 王國) at the commandery level and marquisates (*houguo* 侯國) the size of counties. Gradually these were brought under central control, and by the end of the Later Han there were nearly 100 *jun*-level units (responsible for a total of 1,500 counties). To control the *jun*, 13 regional inspectorates (*zhou* 州) were established. Out of these eventually developed the provinces of the later empire.

The *zhou-jun-xian* structure was retained by the smaller dynasties during the period of disunion. From the Tang, the term *jun* disappears and is replaced by *zhou* 州 (prefectures headed by prefects *cishi* 刺史). Above these, itinerant regional surveillance commissioners (*anchashi* 按察使) were appointed. Their unit of operation was the circuit (*dao* 道) of which there were 10 to 15. From 977, the *dao* were termed *lu* 路, and from the Yuan (by which time they were beginning to become more like a permanent provincial administration), at first they were called *xingzhong shusheng* 行中書省 (branch secretariats), or *xingsheng* 行省 for short. As a consequence, the Song *lu* were downgraded to prefectural level. The *xingsheng* of

[7] The clearest outline in English of the main administrative units at the center and in the provinces in each dynasty, as well as brief descriptions of military and personnel administration may be found in the Introduction to *DOTIC*, 3–96.

the Yuan became the familiar provinces (*sheng* 省) of the Ming and Qing of which there were between 13 and 18 in China proper. The provincial yamens in the Ming supervised *fu* 府 (prefectures); under which in some cases came *zhou* 州 (subprefectures); and at the bottom some 1,500 *xian* 縣 (counties).

In the Qing, the provincial governors-general or viceroys were called *zongdu* 總督 and the governors, *xunfu* 巡撫. The territorial hierarchy below the province was *fu-ting-zhou-xian* 府廳州縣 (prefectures headed by prefects, *zhifu* 知府; subprefectures headed by subprefectural magistrates, *tongzhi* 同知; departments headed by department magistrates, *zhizhou* 知州; and counties headed by county magistrates, *zhixian* 知縣). There were many other provincial posts, both territorial and functional, for example, the circuit intendants (*daotai* 道臺; the "taotai" of treaty port sources).

At various periods particularly sensitive areas were directly administered. For example, the metropolitan region surrounding the capital since the earliest historical records to the present day has always been administered by the central government. Special units were established to administer and control non-Han regions and to secure the frontiers (in the Qing, the subprefectures, *ting* 廳, were used for these functions). Starting in the Han, throughout the five centuries of the Xiongnu threat, the Western Regions (Xiyu 西域) were kept directly subordinate to the center (44.4.3).

4.3 How to Identify Historical Places

There are four main problems in identifying places referred to in historical sources. The first is that one place could have many names (*tongdi yiming* 同地異名; *yidi duoming* 一地多名). Thus, the city we know today as "Beijing" (Northern Capital) had at least a dozen different names and many different sites in the course of its history—

Ji 薊 (Shang)
Yanguo ducheng 燕國都城 (W. Zhou)
Jicheng 薊城 (E. Zhou)
Ji 薊 (Former Han)
Youzhou 幽州 (Later Han)
Youzhou 幽州, Zhuojun 涿郡 (Sui)
Zhuozhou 涿州 (Tang)
Nanjing 南京 (Liao, 938–1012)
Yanjing 燕京 (Liao, 1012–1123)
Yanshan fu 燕山府 (1123–24)

Nanjing 南京 (Jin, 1125–53)
Zhongdu 中都 (Jin, 1153–1215)
Yanjing 燕京 (1215–64)
Zhongdu 中都 (Yuan, 1264–72)
Dadu 大都 (Yuan, 1272–1368)
Beiping 北平 (Ming, 1368–1403)
Beijing 北京 (Ming, 1403–1927)
Jingshi 京師 (Ming, 1420 to 1927)
Beiping 北平 (1928–49)
Beijing 北京 (1949–)

The second problem is that one name was often used for many places (*tongming yidi* 同名異地; *yiming duodi* 一名多地), for example, Beijing 北京 was the name for nine capital cities between the third and fifteenth centuries before it was applied to the capital we now know by this name. The third problem, how to understand the many different terms used for administrative units at different times, has already been discussed (4.2). The fourth problem is that the administrative boundaries of places frequently shifted. These are conveniently traced in historical atlases and special tables (4.3.2).

Chinese scholars spent a great deal of time compiling reference tools in all branches of historical studies, not least in historical geography. Modern place-name references and historical atlases are based on their labors.[8]

4.3.1   Place-Name Dictionaries

The *Zhonghua renmin gongheguo diming da cidian* 中華人民共和國地名大辭典 is the most comprehensive modern place-name dictionary. It supersedes all previous such dictionaries, including those specializing in historical place-names. It contains 180,000 toponyms of human settlements (from cities to streets and villages), ancient monuments, and natural features (both large and small). All county towns are identified by finding coordinates. There is a great deal of information about places as of end 1994 (including the pronunciation of every name in *pinyin*), but it also gives more details of the changes in a place's administrative status, affiliation, and changes of name since its first appearance until the present than can be found even in the largest historical place-name dictionaries. Perhaps because it was based on detailed on-the-spot investigations as well as book research it not infrequently gives information not found in other references, for example the ancient and modern etymologies of toponyms and rare pronunciations.[9]

---

[8] See Sun Donghu 孫冬虎 and Li Ruwen 李汝雯, *Zhongguo diming xueshi* 中國地名學史 (History of chinese place-name studies), Zhongguo huanjing kexue, 1997.

[9] *Zhonghua renmin gongheguo da diming cidian* (The People's Republic of China place-name dictionary), Cui Naifu 崔乃夫, ed. in chief, Shangwu, 3 vols., 1998–2000. An enlargement and revision of the 32-vol. version published under the same title in 1984–99. The United States Board on Geographic

Footnote continued on next page

Although the *Zhongguo lishi diming da cidian* 中國歷史地名大
辭典 is a historical place-name dictionary containing 60,000 entries
giving the original name and subsequent history of some 90,000 toponyms, by comparison with the *Zhonghua renmin gongheguo diming
da cidian*, the coverage and the information are skimpy. For example, it lists Zaoqiang 棗強 county as having been founded in the
Former Han, while the latter is more precise and gives the date 126
BC. It has administrative and name changes from earliest times to
1949; the latter continues up to 1994.[10]

The volume on historical geography of the *Zhongguo lishi da cidian* 中國歷史大辭典 is broader in scope than a historical place-
name dictionary, covering in 9,640 entries not only historical toponyms (including some found on oracle-bone and bronze inscriptions), but also famous geographers from earliest times to 1911 and
their works.[11]

For some purposes more detailed and accurate information can
be found in specialized historical place-name dictionaries and studies
than in even the largest comprehensive works. References are given
in the appropriate sections of the manual, for example, for the
Western Regions (Xiyu 西域), see 41.3.1; for Southeast Asia, 41.5.1,
and for Taiwan, 51.10.

For an annual handbook incorporating the latest administrative
boundary changes, see *Zhonghua renmin gongheguo xingzheng quhua
jiance* 中華人民共和國行政區劃簡冊, Ditu.

Names, *Mainland China*, 2 vols., Washington, DC: Government Printing Office, 1968, includes 108,000 names.

[10] *Zhongguo lishi diming da cidian* (Dictionary of Chinese historical toponyms), Wei Songshan 魏嵩山, ed. in chief, Guangdong jiaoyu, 1995. Before this
the largest historical place-name dictionary was edited under the direction of
Zang Lihe 臧勵龢, *Zhongguo gujin diming da cidian* 中國古今地名大辭典 (Dictionary of Chinese toponyms, ancient and modern), Shangwu, 1931; 11th rpnt.,
1982. It contains 40,000 historical toponyms and is none too accurate.

[11] *Lishi dili* 歷史地理, Tan Qixiang 譚其驤 editorial chairman, Shanghai ci-
shu, 1996. The work was compiled by historical geographers at Fudan and
Hangzhou universities and at the Shekeyuan. One of the best volumes of the
Zhongguo lishi da cidian, on which see 8.4.

4.3.2   Historical Atlases

The problem of changing territorial and administrative boundaries is a troublesome one; for example, statistics about a circuit (provincial level unit) in the Tang dynasty are difficult to compare with similar statistics for a region in the Han or a province in the Ming since the boundaries may have changed. One solution is to check that the same counties were included, but there is no guarantee that their borders were the same, and it is a laborious business because more often than not the names changed as well. But it can be done. *Zhongguo lidai xingzheng quhua* 中國歷代行政區劃 lists the names of all administrative units, including all counties in every period from 221 BC to the end of 1991.[12] The many works tabling boundary changes in specific periods are listed in the relevant sections of Part V. Note that local gazetteers usually contain tables of administrative changes (*yan'ge biao* 沿革表) that show, for example, when the area of a former locality (*xiang* 鄉) was upgraded to a county (*xian* 縣) and was therefore no longer included in the area of the county to which it had been attached previously.

The most accurate maps of historical changes in China's external frontiers, internal administrative boundaries, and toponyms available is the *Zhongguo lishi dituji* 中國歷史地圖集. This eight-volume work covers from the earliest times to 1840 in 304 historical maps (plus a large number of inset maps).[13] Work on it began in 1954 and had proceeded far enough for an restricted circulation edition to be put out in 1974. This was then corrected and the new archaeological discoveries taken into account before publication began in 1982. The *Lishi dituji* is a summation of many centuries of detailed scholarship.[14] It starts off where the previous largest map showing changing boundaries and toponyms, that of Yang Shoujing

---

[12] *Zhongguo lidai xingzheng quhua* (Chinese historical administrative boundaries), Zhang Minggeng 張明庚 and Zhang Mingju 張明聚, eds. and comps., Zhongguo Huaqiao, 1996.

[13] *Zhongguo lishi dituji* (Collection of historical maps of China), Tan Qixiang 譚其驤 (1911–91), ed. in chief, 8 vols., 2nd rev. edition, Zhonghua ditu xueshe, 1974–76; rpnt., Ditu, 1985; HK: Sanlian, 1991–92.

[14] Six volumes of detailed additional materials that were too bulky to be published in the *Zhongguo lishi dituji* are being separately published under the title *Zhongguo lishi dituji shiwen huibian* 中國歷史地圖集釋文匯編. To date, only vol. 5 on the northeast, has appeared; Zhongyang minzu xueyuan, 1988.

楊守敬, left off.[15] The final map of the volume on the Qing shows
China in 1908. A total of 70,000 toponyms are included. Each volume is indexed. The relevant volume for each period is listed in Part
V. There is a one-volume, concise version with 33 maps, including
two new ones (of the Republic in 1926 and 1946): *Jianming Zhongguo lishi dituji* 簡明中國歷史地圖集.[16] For the years 1900–49, see

*China Postal Atlas Showing the Postal Establishments and Postal Routes in
    Each Province* (51.14.2, *Historical Atlases*), for 1903, 1908, 1919, 1936.

Zhonghua minguo xin ditu 中華民國新地圖 (51.14.2, *Historical Atlases*),
    1934.

For a one-volume historical atlas that shows military campaigns
as well as administrative changes, see *Zhongguo gudai lishi dituji* 中
國古代歷史地圖集.[17] More detailed historical atlases are available,
for example for the Taipings (28.3, *Taiping Heavenly Kingdom*), the
Xinhai Revolution (28.4) or the campaigns of the years 1919–49
(51.14.2, *Historical Atlases* and 4.4.3, *Modern Military Maps*). For an
innovative way of presenting history using maps, see Blunden and
Elvin, *Cultural Atlas of China* (8.1).

Detailed maps of a province, prefecture, or county in a given period are available in most local gazetteers (4.6). In recent years historical atlases of individual provinces have begun to appear, for example *Guangdong lishi dituji* 廣東歷史地圖集.[18] City maps and
plans are dealt with in 4.7.

---

[15] *Lidai yudi yan'getu* 歷代輿地沿革圖 (Maps of geographical changes in
different periods), 42 *ce* (Shanghai, 1906–11; 10 vols., Lianjing, 1975; vol. 11,
place-name index, 1982). Tables of administrative boundary and place-name
changes were compiled on an empire-wide scale, especially in the Qing, culminating in the work of Yang. Part of the information in this work is reproduced
in map form, but not accurately, in Norton Ginsburg, *An Historical Atlas of
China* (new edition, UChP, 1966). This does not include small places (county
towns and below). It has a good index but it was produced at a time when the
printing of characters in Western books, even in indexes, was cumbersome.
There are no characters on the maps.

[16] *Jianming Zhongguo lishi dituji* (Concise atlas of Chinese history), Gu
Naifu 顧乃福, ed., Ditu, 1991.

[17] *Zhongguo gudai lishi dituji* (Collection of historical maps of China), Liaoning jiaoyu, 1992.

[18] *Guangdong lishi dituji* (Collection of historical maps of Guangdong),
Shenzhen: Guangdong sheng ditu, 1995.

4.4   Cartography

4.4.1   History

There are plenty of references to maps in pre-Qin works, but the earliest discovered so far date from the late Warring States. They have a good claim to be the most detailed, oldest maps in the world. Archaeologists have also discovered a handful of maps and plans drawn on wood or silk dating from the Qin and Han. We know from the early literature that they were used primarily for military, fiscal, and administrative purposes, and secondarily for general information for settlement and travel. Another use was to place a map or a plan in tombs showing the main buildings with which the dead person was associated. Sometimes these were drawn as murals or on silk. The modern phrase *bantu* 版圖 meaning domain or territory is derived from the pre-Qin practice of drawing maps on wooden tablets.

The best introduction to ancient Chinese maps, including recent archaeological discoveries, is the three-volume *Zhongguo gudai dituji* 中國古代地圖集. These large volumes contain over 650 reproductions both in color and in black and white. There are scholarly notes in both Chinese and English concerning each map as well as longer papers on various aspects of cartography in each period.[19]

For a short introduction, see Richard J. Smith, *Chinese Maps: Images of All Under Heaven*, HK: OUP, 1996. The author discusses representations of barbarians in histories and encyclopaedias and discusses maps as marking the boundary between the self and the other. The earliest maps and plans so far discovered are briefly described below.

Warring States: Pingshan xian, Hebei 河北平山縣: Architectural blueprint (drawn to scale) of the mausoleum of the King of Zhongshan, 中山國兆域圖. Dated to 323–315 BC. Made of bronze with the lines for the scales and the characters for the names, distances, and orders of the king inlaid in gold and silver. The oldest map or plan excavated to date. Discovered in 1977; illustrated with transcriptions and

---

[19] *Zhongguo gudai dituji* (A collection of ancient Chinese maps), vol. 1, *Zhanguo zhi Yuandai* 戰國至元代 (Warring States to Yuan dynasty), Wenwu, 1990, 1999; vol. 2, *Mingdai* 明代 (Ming dynasty), Wenwu, 1995; vol. 3, *Qingdai* 清代 (Qing dynasty), Wenwu, 1997.

commentary by Sun Zhongming 孫仲明 in *Zhongguo gudai dituji*, vol. 1, "Papers," 1–3 (English summary: "Notes on the Plates," 17). See also 13.2.3 on this tomb and 44.5.1, item 1 for a Han Zhongshan royal tomb.

Qin: Tianshuishi Fangmatan 天水市放馬灘, Gansu: seven maps on four wooden tablets discovered in a late Qin tomb in 1986 (*Wenwu* 1989.2; 1989.12); fragment of one map on paper from a Former Han tomb. Four of the maps on wooden tablets are topographic; two show administrative details; and the remaining two show products and forest resources. The board maps date from about 230 BC. The one on paper from the Former Han. The maps are clearly illustrated with a brief scholarly commentary in *Zhongguo gudai dituji*, vol. 1, Plates 4–19. See also Hsu Mei-ling, "The Qin Maps: A Clue to Later Chinese Cartographic Development," *Imago Mundi* 48: 90–100 (1993).

Han: Mawangdui, near Changsha 長沙馬王堆: three silk maps discovered in Mawangdui tomb 3 (168 BC). None of these maps bore names, but they are now referred to as (1) the *dixing tu* 地形圖 (Topographical map, 96 × 96 cm), which shows the southern part of the kingdom of Changsha (covering northern Guangdong, northeastern Guangxi, and southern Hunan) on a scale of roughly 1:180,000; depicts with remarkable accuracy physical features such as mountains and rivers, towns, villages, and roads; (2) the *zhujun tu* 駐軍圖 (Garrison map, 98 × 78 cm), which is on a larger scale (1:80,000 to 1:100,000) and shows part of the area covered by the topographical map, with garrisons, strongholds, a castle, and lines of march. It dates from about 181 BC, the time when Han armies were sent south to subdue the kingdom of Nanyue; (3) the *chengyi tu* 城邑圖 (City map 52 × 52 cm), which is the oldest extant city map in the world. It may be of Linxiang 臨湘 (Changsha) and shows the city wall, streets, pavilions, and so forth. Each of these three maps was based on surveying and uses standard symbols (e.g., a circle for villages and a square for towns), and color-coding (e.g., red-dotted lines for roads, green lines for rivers, and red triangles for castles). For reproductions with transcriptions, reconstruction of the toponyms and symbols, and scholarly commentary, see *Zhongguo gudai dituji*, vol. 1, Plates 20–29; "Papers," 4–17.

Few traces survive of the innovations in mapping made between the Han and the Song. The main ones are credited to Pei Xiu 裴秀 (AD 224–71) and to Jia Dan 賈耽 (729–805). Pei introduced the system of indicating distances using a grid, and he also made the first historical map showing changes in toponyms and boundaries (*Jinshu* 晉書, *juan* 35, "Pei Xiu zhuan"). None of his maps survive, although the six principles he propounded are known. In the Tang, Jia is said to have used the grid system of Pei to draw a huge map entitled *Hainei Huayitu* 海內華夷圖 (Map of the Hua and barbarian territories within the seas). It was on the scale of one *cun* 寸 (inch) to one hundred *li* 里 (Chinese miles; see Tables 15 and 16, section 7.3). Old toponyms were shown in black; their current ones in red. This convention is still occasionally used (*Jiu Tangshu* 舊唐書, *juan* 138, "Jia Dan zhuan" 賈耽傳).[20]

Two maps carved on opposite sides of a stele in 1136 have survived (they may be seen in the Beilin 碑林 at Xi'an; see 17.3). The first is the *Huayitu* 華夷圖 (Map of the Hua and barbarian territories). It was based on and named after Jia's *Hainei Huayitu* 海內華夷圖. It was drawn between 1117 and 1125. The other is a map of waterways, the *Yujitu* 禹迹圖 (Map of the tracks of Yu). It is the earliest extant map using a grid system. The map was probably drawn between 1081 and 1094 (see the illustrations and notes in *Zhongguo gudai dituji*, vol. 1). See also another three Song maps carved on stone held in the Suzhou Museum of Inscribed Stelae (17.3, *Collections of Stelae*).

After the mariner's compass came into use in the Song (37.4.1), navigational maps were drawn indicating compass courses. They were called *zhenlutu* 針路圖, *zhenjing* 針經, or *zhenshu* 針書 (needle guides). The earliest to survive shows the seventh voyage of Zheng He 鄭和 (1371–1434) to Ceylon (1430). It is partly reproduced in *Zhongguo gudai dituji*, 168–71.

An important step was made in the thirteenth century by Zhu Siben 朱思本 (1273–1337). He produced a new map of the empire (*Yuditu* 輿地圖) using the grid system and showing the Mongol conquests. Zhu's map has not survived, but a manuscript copy of it formed the basis for extant Ming maps.[21] The concept of measuring

---

[20] See *Mathematics and the Sciences of the Heavens and the Earth* (*SCC*, vol. 3); also *Zhongguo cehuishi* 中國測繪史 (History of Chinese surveying and mapping), 2 vols., Cehui, 1995; Lu Liangzhi 盧良志, *Zhongguo dituxueshi* 中國地圖學史 (History of Chinese cartography), Cehui, 1984.

[21] See Walter Fuchs, *The "Mongol Atlas" of China by Chu Ssu-pen and the Kuang yü t'u with 48 Facsimile Maps Dating from 1555*, MS Monograph 8, Catholic Univ., Beiping, 1946. Luo Hongxian 羅洪先 (1504–64), *Guang yutu* 廣輿圖

Footnote continued on next page

height based on the sea level was proposed by Guo Shoujing 郭守敬
(1231–1316).

A new stage in the development of Chinese mapping came in
the eighteenth century when the Jesuits by imperial command conducted trigonometric surveys between 1708 and 1718 and drew a
complete series of maps of China and its neighbors. These far surpass their earlier efforts of the seventeenth century, and they remained the basis for all maps of China, both in China and abroad,
down to the early twentieth century. The results were printed in
various editions and with differing titles between 1717 and 1721.[22]
The scale for the earlier editions was 1:1,400,000, but as the area
covered grew larger, the scale was reduced to 1:2,000,000. These
maps were printed in several publications in China, including in the
imperially commissioned encyclopaedia, the *Gujin tushu jicheng*
(31.2). In Europe, the 1721 woodblock edition was revised and published by Jean-Baptiste du Halde to accompany his *Description géo-
graphique, historique, politique, et physique de l'Empire de la Chine*,
Paris, 1735, and by his cartographer, J-B. D'Anville, as an atlas,
Nouvelle Atlas de la Chine, The Hague, 1737.

By order of the Qianlong emperor a new survey was undertaken
in 1756–59, and the original was revised to include his conquests,
notably what was later to be called Xinjiang.[23] These maps were
held in secret at the Neifu until used as the basis for printing the *Da
Qing wannian yitong tianxia yutu* 大清萬年一統天下輿圖 during
the Tongzhi reign.

Many maps of individual counties and provinces as well as plans
of cities and towns are found in Ming-Qing gazetteers (4.7), while
the comprehensive gazetteers of the empire from the Ming on also
contain maps (4.5.3). The first extant frontier maps (after the stone-

---

(Expanded edition of the *Yutu*), 1541, was one of the first works to be based on
Zhu's "Mongol Atlas." It was printed in 1555. *Zhongguo gudai dituji*, vol. 2,
contains an important, annotated collection of 248 Ming maps with excellent
color reproductions and notes in Chinese and English on every map and research articles by the editors.

[22] *Huangyu quan lantu* 皇輿全[覽]圖 (Comprehensive atlas of the imperial
territory of the Kangxi reign), 1718.

[23] Walter Fuchs, *Der Jesuiten-Atlas der Kanghsi-Zeit, seine Entstehungs-
geschichte nebst Namensindices für die Karten der Mandjurei, Mongolei, Ostturke-
stan und Tibet; mit Wiedergabe der Jesuiten-Karten in Original Grösse*, MS Monograph 4, 1943.

carved twelfth-century *Huayitu*), as well as route maps used by officials and merchants, also date from the Ming (50.7.4).

The Yishiguan 一史館 has over 7,000 Qing maps, some of them
over 400 square feet in area. Most use a grid system and were drawn
to accompany specific reports of campaigns or border relations.
Most are not available to the public (50.1.1.V). The *Zhongguo gudai
dituji* (*Qingdai*), contains reproductions of 212 Qing maps, the largest published selection available.

4.4.2   Reproductions and Collections

Apart from *Zhongguo gudai dituji* 中國古代地圖集 (4.4.1), note

Zhonghua gu ditu zhenpin xuanji 中華古地圖珍品選集 (A selection of
original ancient Chinese maps), Harbin ditu, 1998. Reproductions of
166 maps from the Warring States to the end of the Qing, see

Treasures of Map: A Collection of Maps in Ancient China, Science Press,
1998.

Zhongguo gu dituji 中國古地圖集 (A collection of China's ancient maps),
see Liu Zhenwei 劉鎮偉, ed., Zhongguo shijieyu, 1995. A selection of
100 rare maps (mainly Qing) from the Dalian Library (based on the
South Manchuria Railway Co. Library).

Li Xiaocong 李孝聰, *A Descriptive Catalogue of Pre–1900 Chinese Maps
Seen in Europe*, Guoji wenhua, 1996. Bilingual catalog of old Chinese
maps in European collections.

4.4.3   Modern Military Maps

United States Army maps based on Landsat data are available on the
scale of 1:200,000 with toponyms in English and Chinese. 1:100,000
maps also exist.

Soviet army maps based on original satellite surveys conducted
in the 1980's to the scale of 1:25,000 are available.

A number of national sheet maps were made by the military
authorities in the early Republic on the scale of 1:50,000 and
1:100,000, but the quality is uneven. The most accurate and detailed
maps of China in the first half of the twentieth century were made
by the survey department of the Japanese army:

Chûgoku hondo chizu 中國本土地圖 *Chûgoku hondo chizu*, 1:25,000, 4
vols., Kagaku shoin, 1989–92; separate index vol., 1993. 1:50,000, 5
vols., Kagaku shoin, 1994; separate index vol., 1994. Manchuria, 2

vols., Kagaku shoin, 1985. These maps were reprinted from copies held in the American Geographical Society Collection at the Golda Meir Library, University of Wisconsin-Milwaukee.

There is also an index of the holdings of maps of China in major collections in Japan:

Chûgoku hondo chizu mokuroku 中國本土地圖目錄, Nunome Chôfû 布目潮渢 and Matsuda Kôichi 松田孝一, eds., 1967; rev. and enlarged edition, 1987.

4.5   Comprehensive Geographical Works

4.5.1   Early Works

The earliest extant work covering the whole of China, as it then was, is the *Shanhaijing* 山海經 (Classic of mountains and seas), a mythogeography, parts of which were written in the Warring States period and part in the Han and Jin (29.1). The *Shangshu* 尚書 (Venerated documents) contains an early geographical work, the "Yu-gong" 禹貢 (The tribute of Yu), which describes the nine regions of China and their products.[24] The third important early geographic work, the *Shuijing*, is dealt with under water control (35.3.2).

4.5.2   Monographs on Geography in the Standard Histories

Most pre-Han geographical works as well as those from the Han to the Tang have been lost. Up to the Tang, therefore, the study of Chinese historical geography (including the study of toponyms, changing boundaries, local products, and population) has to be based mainly on the early works (4.5.1), together with the summaries found in the *dilizhi* 地理志 (also called *junguozhi* 郡國志, *zhou-junzhi* 州郡志, or *dixingzhi* 地形志 [monographs on administrative geography]) in the Standard Histories of the Former Han, Later

---

[24] *The Book of Documents*, Bernhard Karlgren, tr., *BMFEA* 22: 1–81 (1950), includes the Chinese text along with his annotated translation. The complete text with extensive commentary and explanations is included in Gu Jiegang 顧頡剛, *Zhongguo gudai dili mingzhu xuandu* 中國古代地理名著選讀 (Selected readings from famous ancient Chinese geographical works), vol. 1, Kexue, 1959.

Han, Jin, Southern Qi, Wei, and Sui, the sections on foreign peoples (Table 36, 41.4), and the monographs on rivers and canals in the *Shiji* 史記 and the *Hanshu* 漢書 (35.3.2). These should also be supplemented with the monographs on financial administration (22.3).

The *dilizhi* reflect much the same origins as were suggested for early Chinese maps; they contain information useful for tax gatherers (hearth and head counts; land under cultivation statistics) and administrators (names of administrative units, changes of toponyms over time, distances between places, main topographical features).

The *Hanshu* was the first to include a monograph on administrative geography (*juan* 28).[25] It is somewhat broader in scope than the monographs in the other Standard Histories, including historical introductions to the regions of China (quoting extensively from the "Yugong"), population figures (the census of AD 2) and the names and numbers of the counties in each province and fief, land under cultivation, and brief economic profiles of each region (following *Shiji, juan* 129).

After the *Hanshu*, 18 of the Standard Histories included monographs on administrative geography. They follow much the same pattern as the monograph in the *Hanshu*, but are more narrowly focused on administrative matters. The Zhonghua Shuju has published place-name indexes to each of the Standard Histories. These cover all toponyms, including those in the monographs on administrative geography. In addition indexes are available to some of the monographs on administrative geography (for titles for each period, see Part V). Failing these, the comprehensive indexes to the Standard Histories can be used (22.2). Even without an index it is not difficult to locate places in the monographs since their arrangement follows standard administrative hierarchies (4.2). In order to check changes in toponyms (often recorded in the monographs) a modern place-name dictionary such as *Zhongguo lishi dili da cidian* (1995), which is based on the monographs, should be used (4.3.1).

After the Tang many more geographical works (including maps) are extant, and the monographs in the later Standard Histories become only one of many sources for Chinese historical geography. Later sources include the comprehensive gazetteers of the Empire,

[25] See Nancy Lee Swann, "An Analysis of Structure of the Treatise on Geography," in *Food & Money in Ancient China*, PUP, 1950, 71–75.

which contain similar information to the monographs (see below); the local gazetteers, which are filled with much greater detail (4.6); and the geographical chapters of the encyclopaedic histories of institutions (Chapter 26), not to speak of the many private geographical works, travel books, and scholarly studies that have survived in great numbers.

4.5.3   Comprehensive Gazetteers

Very few geographic works from the Han to the Tang have survived.[26] The earliest extant geographical work covering the whole empire was compiled in the ninth century by Li Jifu 李吉甫 (758-814), *Yuanhe junxian tuzhi* 元和郡縣圖志.[27]

The next extant comprehensive geography was written by Yue Shi 樂史 to explain the geography of China and her neighbors newly unified under the emperor Taizong: *Taiping huanyu ji* [*zhi*] 太平寰宇記[志] (Gazetteer of the world during the Taiping period, 976-83); late tenth century.[28] This was an influential work in that it set the trend toward the inclusion of biographies, literary works, etc., in geographical works, a trend that was taken up in the local gazetteers. It was highly praised by the *Siku* editors. Yue's gazetteer is largely based on Tang works, and it is therefore an important source for Tang geography. There is an index available.[29] Other important comprehensive Song geographical works are listed in 47.2.

Only fragments of the enormous *Da Yuan yitongzhi* 大元一統志 (Gazetteer of the unified Great Yuan), rev. version, end of thirteenth century, are extant (35 or so *juan* out of 1,000). The title and

[26] *Han-Tang fangzhi jiyi* 漢唐方志輯佚 (Recovered fragments of Han and Tang gazetteers), Liu Weiyi 劉緯毅, comp., Beijing tushuguan, 1997. See also *Han-Tang dili shu chao* 漢唐地理書抄, Wang Mo 王謨 (*jinshi* 1778), Zhonghua, 1961, which gathers together fragments of lost geographic works.

[27] *Yuanhe junxian tuzhi* (Maps and gazetteer of the provinces and counties in the Yuanhe period, 806-14), 2 vols., Zhonghua, 1983, 1995. The maps in this work were lost in the Song, as were also *juan* 19, 20, 23-26, and parts of *juan* 5, 18, and 25, but the work is still an important supplement to the monographs on administrative geography in the Old and New Standard Histories of the Tang. It is indexed along with these works in Hiraoka (1956).

[28] *Taiping huanyu ji*, 3 vols., Wenhai, 1980.

[29] *Taiping huanyu ji suoyin* 太平寰宇記索引, Wang Hui 王恢, comp., Wenhai, 1975.

arrangement of this work were followed, however, in the Ming and again in the Qing.

The comprehensive gazetteers of the empire are easy to use since they, like the monographs on administrative geography in the Standard Histories, are arranged according to well-established administrative hierarchies (4.2). Three were compiled during the Qing with the title provided by Kangxi, *Da Qing yitongzhi* 大清一統志. The third, the *Jiaqing chongxiu yitongzhi* 嘉慶重修一統志, was the largest and most accurate (see 50.5.1 for details).

4.5.4   Empire-wide Geographical Studies

The two outstanding Qing works on historical geography are:

Gu Yanwu 顧炎武 (1613–82), *Tianxia junguo libing shu* 天下郡國利病書 (The characteristics of each province in the empire).

Gu Zuyu 顧祖禹 (1631–92), *Dushi fangyu jiyao* 讀史方輿紀要 (Essentials of geography for reading history).[30]

Gu Yanwu was acknowledged as the founder of what was later termed the Hanxuepai 漢學派 (School of Han learning; see 50.6.4). Gu used the characteristic mode of the Hanxue scholars, *kaozheng* 考證 (evidential research), in all of his studies (as displayed, for example, in his notes, *Rizhilu* 日知錄, 50.6.3), including geography.[31] Emphasizing the effect of topography on political and economic developments, the *Tianxia junguo libing shu* is the most important study of historical and natural geography and local conditions throughout China to have been written up to that time. Gu mentions no less than 6,192 battles in his examination of "the strategic advantages and disadvantages of the topography of each province"

---

[30] The *Tianxia junguo libing shu*, which included many maps, was written between 1639 and 1662 and printed for the first time in 1811; there are many modern editions, and an old manuscript version was included in *Sibu congkan* 四部叢刊, 3rd series.

The *Dushi fangyu jiyao* was written between the 1630s and the 1660s and first printed in 1811; many modern editions, including a punctuated six-volume edition, Zhonghua, 1955; rpnt. 1957, and an indexed edition in 12 vols., Shanghai guji, 1991.

[31] See Chao-ying Fang's masterly profile of Gu and the Hanxuepai in *ECCP* (421–26) or the biography by Willard J. Peterson, "The Life of Ku Yen-wu (1613–1682)," *HJAS* 28: 114–56 (1966); 29: 201–47 (1969).

(the literal translation of his title). In it he combines book learning and on-the-spot investigation.

Like Gu Yanwu, Gu Zuyu (no relation) was influenced as a young man by the collapse of the Ming and resentment at the Manchu conquest. He concentrated all his life on historical geography and is remembered for having identified the historical names of 30,000 places.[32] He also assisted in the compilation of the *Da Qing yitongzhi.* Both Gu Yanwu and Gu Zuyu stimulated the use of local gazetteers in historical and geographical writing. The new interest soon gained imperial sponsorship (more gazetteers were compiled in the Qing than in all previous periods put together).

4.6   Local Gazetteers

Local gazetteers (*difangzhi* 地方志 or *fangzhi* 方志 for short), sometimes also called local histories are called local to differentiate them from the various kinds of comprehensive gazetteers (*zongzhi* 總志) discussed in 4.5.3. Gazetteers are usually subdivided into the gazetteers of provinces (*tongzhi* 通志), prefectures (*fuzhi* 府志), sub-prefectures (*zhouzhi* 州志), and counties (*xianzhi* 縣志). In addition, there are a number of gazetteers for market towns (*xiangzhenzhi* 鄉鎮志), garrisons (*weisuozhi* 衞所志 or *weizhi* 衞志), academies (*shuyuanzhi* 書院志), temples and shrines (*simiaozhi* 寺廟志), and mountains and rivers (*shanshuizhi* 山水志).

The gazetteers were often compiled by members of the local elite and were produced under the sponsorship of the local officials. Altogether about 8,000 local gazetteers are extant, in a staggering total of 125,000 *juan*. They form one of the most important sources for the study of Chinese history in the past one thousand years, since they contain copious materials on local administration, local economies, local cultures, local dialects, local officials, and local dignitaries—materials that often cannot be found elsewhere.

By the Qing they contained materials arranged in all or some of the categories set out in Table 7.

---

[32] For an index to the toponyms identified by Gu Yanwu, see Aoyama Sadao 青山定雄, *Dokushi hôyo kiyô sakuin Shina rekidai chimei yôran* 讀史方輿紀要索引支那歷代地名要覽, Tôhô bunka gakuin, Tôkyô kenkyûjo, 1933; rev. edition, 4th prnt., Shôshin, 1974.

Table 7: The Contents of Local Gazetteers

Preface and general rules (*fanli* 凡例) with compilers and editorial policy

Maps of the county, city plans, etc. (*yutu* 輿圖, *tukao* 圖考)

Changing borders, tables of changing administrative units included in the county, prefecture, etc. (*jiangyu* 疆域, *yan'ge* 沿革)

Main topographical features, rivers, mountains, etc. (*shanchuan* 山川)

Famous places, ruins, views (*mingsheng* 名勝, *guji* 古蹟)

Official buildings, city walls and moats, government offices (*gongshu* 公署, *chengchi* 城池, *jianzhi* 建置)

Passes, fords, and bridges (*guanjin qiaoliang* 關津橋梁)

Water conservancy, canals and rivers, hydraulics, irrigation works (*hefang* 河防, *hequ* 河渠, *shuili* 水利)

Chronicle of natural and manmade disasters or omens: floods, droughts, hail, snow, locusts; uprisings, soldiers, high prices, low prices, etc. (*zaiyi* 災異, *xiangyi* 祥異, *bing* 兵)

Academies (*shuyuan* 書院)

Schools (*xuexiao* 學校)

Buddhist and Daoist temples (*siguan* 寺觀)

Officeholders (*zhiguan* 職官)

Examinations and names of successful candidates (*xuanju* 選舉)

Fiscal information: household and head counts (*hukou* 戶口), land and other taxes (*fushui* 賦稅, *tianfu* 田賦)

Granary reserves (*cangchu* 倉儲)

Markets, tolls, and barriers (*shizhen* 市鎮)

Products and crops (*wuchan* 物產, including dialect words)

Customs and festivals (*fengsu* 風俗)

Biographies of dignitaries, upright officials, chaste women, etc. (*renwu* 人物, *minghuan* 名宦, *lienü* 列女)

Military institutions and military men (*bingzhi* 兵制, *bingyi* 兵役, *junzhi* 軍制); *bingshi* 兵事 (military events)

Biographies of technicians, including doctors; Buddhist and Daoist monks (*fangji* 方技, *shilao* 釋老)

Inscriptions and tombs (*jinshi* 金石, *lingmu* 陵墓)

Bibliographies and choice excerpts (*yiwen* 藝文)

Miscellaneous topics and records (*zalu* 雜錄)

Usually the longest sections in the local gazetteers were the different categories of biographies, followed by various forms of fiscal information and tables of officeholders. Indexes to biographies in local gazetteers are listed in 3.8.4.

In origin, local gazetteers derived from the practice of keeping basic information on local conditions, population, and revenue and submitting these together with maps and plans to the central government. At the same time they also derive from the practice, which became widespread in the third century AD, of collecting biographies of local worthies and their writings in order to celebrate local achievements. Many elements of the later gazetteers were in earlier periods copied and circulated as separate works (for example, the records of local customs [*fengsu zhuan* 風俗傳] or the maps and records of rivers and mountains [*shanchuan tuji* 山川圖記]). The local gazetteer as a work in its own right combining all these elements emerged in the Song (sometimes with the earlier name *tujing* 圖經, the forerunner of the *zongzhi* 總志 first compiled in the Sui). On the earlier types of gazetteer (down to the Yuan), see Zhang Guogan 張國淦 (1876–1959), *Zhongguo gu fangzhi kao* 中國古方志考.[33] This is an annotated bibliography of well over 2,000 gazetteer-style works compiled to the end of the Yuan, about 99 percent of which are no longer extant. Titles are arranged by *zongzhi* 總志 and by *fangzhi* 方志, with the latter grouped by modern provinces. There is a stroke-count title index.

Nearly 200 local gazetteers are known to have been compiled in the Song (mainly in the Southern Song and therefore for localities in south China), of which only about 30 survive. Yuan scholars are known to have compiled 60, of which only 11 are extant. Thereafter, the number of available local gazetteers increases enormously; altogether 900 are extant mainly from the late Ming out of an unknown number compiled (49.8), while more than 5,600 Qing local gazetteers are extant. Approximately 650 were compiled during the Republican period, and many more are being compiled today (with the emphasis on present conditions rather than on history).

The stimulus for gazetteer compilation in the Qing came in part from the practical school of geo-military and geo-historical Ming loyalists (the Zhexi group), whose influence was still felt long after the trend in scholarship had turned to critical philological studies (4.5.4). Official orders in 1672 and 1729 that every province compile a gazetteer also greatly stimulated local gazetteer production.

---

[33] *Zhongguo gu fangzhi kao* (Critical notes on old Chinese gazetteers), Shanghai: Zhonghua, 1962. See also Aoyama (1963).

A great many Qing scholars, historians, and local officials took part in the compilation of local gazetteers, and there arose for the first time the phenomenon almost of the professional gazetteer-compiler. These trends were summed up by the historian Zhang Xuecheng 章學誠 (1738–1801), who was the first to discuss gazetteers as an important branch of historical writing on a par with the National Histories (*Guoshi* 國史).[34] He also suggested that local archives should be kept and that the editing and compilation of the gazetteers should be in the hands of specialists.

The provincial gazetteers were compiled usually by summarizing the information in the prefectural gazetteers, which were in turn abridged from previous editions and from the individual county gazetteers. Not surprisingly, they vary greatly in quality.

As a general rule, richer areas could afford to pay better editors and produced a superior product to that published by poorer areas. So south China is better covered than the north. Gazetteers for the northwest and the northeast are particularly weak.

The author of a monumental study of rural China in the nineteenth century, Kung-chüan Hsiao (Xiao Gongquan 蕭公權), warns about the uneven quality of the gazetteers,

> The local gentry and in some instances the local officials who dictated the actual contents, as well as the editorial policies of the works sponsored by them, were too often not above prejudice or selfishness. The fact that any single gazetteer was written by a number of persons whose scholarly qualifications were not uniformly high and who frequently executed their assignments with poor coordination and inadequate supervision, points to the possibility of unintentional errors and omissions, even where willful misrepresentation was not practiced. A well-known Chinese historian [Mao Qiling 毛奇齡, 1623–1716] went so far as to say that local gazetteers were among those categories of writings to which credence could not be lent. Most of the gazetteers contain sections dealing with geographical and related matters. Even there the data are too often inadequate and inaccurate. In many instances later editions of a gazetteer reproduced entries from editions compiled decades or centuries earlier without

[34] On Zhang's writing on gazetteers and on the interesting gazetteers written by him, see David S. Nivison, *The Life and Thought of Chang Hsüeh-ch'eng (1738–1801)*, SUP, 1966, and in greater detail, Chu Shi-chia (Zhu Shijia 朱士嘉), "Chang Hsueh-ch'eng and His Contributions to Local Historiography," Ph.D., Columbia Univ., 1950.

making necessary provisions to reflect whatever changes may have taken place during the interval and without warning the reader of the fact. Occasionally, in small or remote localities, a dearth of reliable information prevented even the most conscientious compilers from producing satisfactory records.[35]

For a good introduction to local gazetteers (with bibliography), see Pierre-Etienne Will "Chinese Local Gazetteers: An Historical and Practical Introduction," *Notes de recherche du Centre Chine*, No. 3, Paris: Centre de Recherches et de Documentation sur la Chine Contemporaine, 1992. See also Timothy Brook, *Geographical Sources of Ming-Qing History*, Michigan Monographs in Chinese Studies No. 58, Ann Arbor, 1988.

Modern historians and scholars have combed the local gazetteers and collected excerpts on all kinds of topics, for example, on population,[36] on local customs,[37] on celestial phenomena,[38] or on coal mining.[39]

How to Find Local Gazetteers

The quickest way of finding out what gazetteers are extant for a particular county, prefecture, or province is to consult one of the two available union catalogs: *Zhongguo difangzhi lianhe mulu* 中國地方志聯合目錄[40] or *Zhongguo difangzhi zongmu tiyao* 中國地方志

---

[35] Kung-ch'üan Hsiao, *Rural China: Imperial Control in China in the Nineteenth Century*, UWP, 1960, 1967, Preface, vii–viii.

[36] Ping-ti Ho, *Studies on the Population of China, 1368–1953*, HUP, 1959.

[37] *Zhongguo difangzhi minsu ziliao huibian* 中國地方志民俗資料匯編 (29.3).

[38] *Zhongguo gudai tianxiang jilu zongji* 中國古代天象記錄總集 (5.1.2).

[39] Qi Shouhua 祁守華, *Zhongguo difangzhi meitan shiliao xuanji* 中國地方志煤炭史料選輯 (Collected historical materials on coal from Chinese local gazetteers), Meitan gongye, 1990. Contains records from over 937 coal-producing areas from various periods of Chinese history.

[40] *Zhongguo difangzhi lianhe mulu* (Union catalog of Chinese local gazetteers), edited at Zhongguo kexueyuan, Beijing tianwentai 中國科學院北京天文臺 (Chinese Academy of Sciences, Beijing Observatory), Zhuang Weifeng 莊威鳳, Zhu Shijia 朱士嘉, and Feng Baolin 馮寶琳, eds. in chief, Zhonghua, 1985. Based on Zhu Shijia (1962). This lists and gives brief bibliographic notes on 8,264 local gazetteers edited before 1949 held in 191 Chinese libraries and in Taiwan. There is a title index as well as an index of some 10,000 authors and compilers. Both indexes are arranged by stroke count. It was compiled as part

Footnote continued on next page

總目提要, which is the larger of the two and contains more comprehensive notes on each of the 8,557 gazetteers it lists.[41] There are also more detailed studies of local gazetteers and "union catalogs" for individual provinces or regions.

Since gazetteers were usually compiled by committees of local officials and scholars, they are referred to by title (sometimes preceded by reign name to distinguish editions) except when the compiler was a well-known writer. The most convenient form of citation for gazetteers is title followed by date of compilation.

After finding the titles and compilers of gazetteers for a given locality or period, it is necessary to locate the libraries that hold them. The *Zhongguo difangzhi lianhe mulu* shows which of the major Chinese libraries holds each of the 8,264 gazetteers listed. But often you will be able to find the gazetteer you are looking for in one of the many multivolume collections of facsimile reprints of local gazetteers. Indeed, the reprints of rare gazetteers (and their wide availability on microfilm), and the huge compilations of Ming and Qing gazetteers, have made the published catalogs of the holdings of original gazetteers by individual collections, both in China and elsewhere, somewhat out-of-date.[42]

The gazetteers of a province or region are frequently reprinted in special collectanea, for example,

Taiwan fangzhi 臺灣方志 (Taiwan gazetteers), 1,110 vols., Chengwen. Series A, 1–102 (440 vols.); series B, 103–345 (666 vols.). Series A covers from 1696 to 1893; series B, the Japanese occupation (1894–1942).

---

of a huge project that listed celestial phenomena recorded in the Standard Histories, Veritable Records, and local gazetteers (5.1). The net was cast wide enough to include all works functioning as gazetteers, so it includes, for example, geographical surveys and local investigation reports.

[41] *Zhongguo difangzhi zongmu tiyao* (Chinese local histories: a comprehensive annotated catalog), Jin Enhui 金恩輝 and Hu Shuzhao 胡述兆, eds., 3 vols., Sino-American Publishers, 1996. Contains notes on 8,557 titles compiled up to 1949.

[42] *Zhongguo fangzhi congshu* 中國方志叢書, Chengwen, 1,370 titles, 1966–93. The Cambridge University Library Chinese collection online catalog contains detailed entries for each title in this series indicating, for example, the edition from which the reproduction was taken. *Zhongguo difangzhi jicheng*, 中國地方志集成, Jiangsu guji, 1993.

Note also the reprints of historical materials on a particular province or region, which often contain many dozens of gazetteers (or excerpts from them), for example,

Zhongguo de xibei wenxian congshu 中國的西北文獻叢書 (Collectanea of documents on northwest China:), 203 vols., Lanzhou, 1990.

Yunnan shiliao conkan 雲南史料叢刊 (Collection of historical materials on Yunnan), Fang Guoyu 方國瑜, ed. in chief, 10 vols., Yunnan daxue, 1998. Excerpts on Yunnan from all the Histories and Yunnan gazetteers are reproduced, punctuated and annotated, with the flow of sources expanding to many other genres as we approach modern times. Collections such as these can be a most useful starting point for the study of local history.

Riben cang Zhongguo hanjian difangzhi congkan 日本藏中國罕見地方志叢刊 (Reprint series of [31] rare gazetteers held in Japanese collections), Shumu wenxian, 1990–92.

In 1982, a series of catalogs and studies of gazetteers for each province was begun under the general editorship of the Committee for Gazetteer Compilation of Jilin: *Zhongguo difangzhi xianglun congshu* 中國地方志詳論叢書. Some of these contain more information than can be found in the two union catalogs. Examples of titles published to date include:

Guangdong fangzhi yaolu 廣東方志要錄, Li Xian 李獻, ed., Guangdong-sheng fangzhi bianzuan weiyuanhui bangongshi, 1988.

Liaoning difangzhi lunlüe, 遼寧地方志論略, 1982; rev. and enl., Chen Jia 陳加 et al., Liaoning tushuguan, 1986.

Shanghai fangzhi ziliao kaolu 上海方志資料考錄, Shanghai shifan daxue tushuguan, eds., Shanghai shudian, 1987. Detailed catalog of gazetteers on Shanghai compiled between the Song and 1984.

Shaoxing difang wenxian kaolu 紹興地方文獻考錄, Chen Qiaoyi 陳橋驛, ed., Zhejiang renmin, 1983.

Zhejiang fangzhi kaolu 浙江方志考錄, Hong Huanchun 洪煥椿 (1920–), ed., 1958; rev. and enl. under new title, *Zhejiang fangzhi kao* 浙江方志考, Zhejiang renmin, 1984, in which the author lists and describes about 1,800 gazetteers, including lost ones, for this province alone. There is a title index.

There are also comprehensive catalogs of gazetteers for most provinces and other administrative units, often compiled by the provincial or local library; for example:

Hebeisheng difangzhi zonglu chugao 河北省地方志總錄初稿, 1982 (includes gazetteers of Beijing and Tianjin).

Dongbei difangzhi zonglu 東北地方志總錄, Guo Jun 郭君 and Sun Renkui 孫仁奎, eds., in *Zhongguo fangzhixue gailun* 中國方志學概論 (Survey of the study of Chinese local histories), Heilongjiang renmin, 1984.

Hu'nansheng difangzhi zonghe mulu 湖南省地方志綜合目錄, 1987.

Shanghai difangzhi mulu 上海地方志目錄, 1979.

Sichuansheng difangzhi lianhe mulu 四川省地方志聯合目錄, Sichuansheng zhongxin tushuguan, ed. and published, Chengdu, 1982.

In recent years more and more indexes have been compiled for gazetteers, especially for the gazetteer biographies for a period or province (3.8.4). Some of the larger gazetteers should soon be available on computer disk.

In 1934 the Commercial Press reprinted six late Qing provincial gazetteers with (four-corner) indexes attached:

Guangdong tongzhi 廣東通志, 1884
Hubei tongzhi 湖北通志, 1911
Hu'nan tongzhi 湖南通志, 1885
Jifu tongzhi 畿輔通志 (Metropolitan region), 1906
Shandong tongzhi 山東通志, 1911
Zhejiang tongzhi 浙江通志, 1736

There are a number of published catalogs of holdings of local gazetteers in collections outside of China. These, too, have been outdated by the reprint collections for the practical purpose of locating a gazetteer.[43]

---

[43] *Catalog des monographies locales chinoises dans les bibliothèques d'Europe*, Yves Hervouet, comp., Mouton, 1957. Lists 1,434 gazetteers in 17 European collections. *A Catalogue of Chinese Local Histories in the Library of Congress*, Chu Shih Chia (Zhu Shijia 朱士嘉), comp., Washington, DC: Government Printing Office, 1942, Xinwenfeng, 1985. *Nihon shûyô toshokan kenkyûjo shozô Chûgoku chihôshi sôgo mokuroku* 日本主要圖書館研究所所藏中國地方志綜合目錄 (Union catalog of Chinese local gazetteers in fourteen major libraries and research institutes in Japan), Tôyô bunko, 1969. *Zhonghua minguo Taiwan diqu gongcang fangzhi mulu* 中華民國臺灣地區公藏方志目錄 (Catalog of local gazetteers in the Republic of China [Taiwan District] public collections), Wang Deyi 王德毅, comp., Hanxue yanjiu ziliao ji fuwu zhongxin, 1985.

Individuals and local institutions often compile collections of local data and historical materials or catalogs of these. Such compilations are not necessarily intended for historians, and their value is often rather limited. Modern gazetteers, on the other hand, may contain material of interest to the historian, for example, the thorough inventory and glossaries of non-Han languages contained in vol. 59 of the Yunnan Gazetteer (*Yunnan shengzhi* 雲南省志 [Yunnan renmin, 1998]).

4.7   Cities

4.7.1   City Planning and Maps

Dozens of Neolithic and Bronze Age settlements (some of them major cities) have been discovered and some excavated (Chapters 12 and 13). All of the capitals of the principal Warring States kingdoms have also been found and reported on, as have the imperial capitals of Qin and Former Han near Chang'an.[44]

The earliest city plan discovered so far is on silk and dates from the Former Han. It is probably of Changsha and was discovered in Mawangdui tomb 3 (4.4.1, item 3). The influence of cosmology is most clearly seen in the layout of capital cities. Other settlements tend more to reflect topography.[45]

Local gazetteers are a major source for the history of cities and towns from the Song onward, including for schematic plans and maps. Ye Xiaojun 葉驍軍 in *Zhongguo ducheng lishi tulu* 中國都城 歷史圖錄 has included many plans of capital cities as well as illus-

---

[44] For a history of city planning which takes full account of archaeological discoveries, see He Yeju 賀業鉅, *Zhongguo gudai chengshi guihuashi* 中國古代城 市規劃史 (A history of ancient Chinese city planning), Zhongguo jianzhu gongye, 1996. The first 300 pages cover the pre-Qin period. See also Nancy Shatzman Steinhardt, *Chinese Imperial City Planning*, UHP, 1990, one quarter of which despite the title is pre-Han; Shen Chen, "Early Urbanization in the Eastern Zhou in China (770–221 BC): An Archaeological View," *Antiquity* 68.261: 724–44 (1994); *China's Buried Kingdoms*, Alexandria, Va.: Time-Life Books, 1993.

[45] Paul Wheatley, *The Pivot of the Four Quarters*, Aldine, 1971; Arthur F. Wright, "The Cosmology of the Chinese City," in *The City in Late Imperial China*, G. William Skinner, ed., SUP, 1977; SMC, 1995, 33–73. See section 49.4.2 for a description of the Forbidden City in the Ming and Qing.

trations of artifacts in this four-volume collection.[46] There is a 90-page bibliography of books and articles on Chinese capitals at the end of vol. 4, as well as a table of all the dozens of capitals from the Xia dynasty to the present day, including even the capitals of minor kingdoms (for example, the five successive capitals of the kingdom of Nan Zhao 南詔, the last of which, Yangjumie 陽苴咩, was on the site of modern Dali 大理, Yunnan). Where possible the dates are given.

The most detailed city plan known to have survived from the later empire is of Beijing in the mid-eighteenth century, *Qianlong jingcheng quantu* 乾隆京城全圖.[47] Illustrations of this and redrawings of many other historical maps of Beijing are reproduced in Hou Renzhi 侯仁之, *Beijing lishi dituji* 北京歷史地圖集.[48]

The largest, most detailed, and best-produced collection of modern historical maps of a Chinese city is *Xi'an lishi dituji* 西安歷史地

[46] *Zhongguo ducheng lishi tulu* (An atlas of historical capitals of China), 4 vols., Lanzhou daxue, 1986–87. Vol. 1 covers from the Xia to the end of the Warring States; vol. 2, from Qin to the end of the Tang; vol. 3, from Song to the end of the Qing; vol. 4, the Republican period. The table of capitals has been corrected and enlarged in *Zhongguo lidai ducheng* 中國歷代都城 (Historical capitals of China), Li Jieping 李潔萍, ed., Heilongjiang renmin, 1994, 407–18.

[47] Beijing Yanshan, 1994. The first study was put out by the Palace Museum: *Qianlongchao jingcheng quantu fangxiang gongdian kao* 乾隆朝京城全圖坊巷宮殿考 (A study of the Qianlong period map of the streets and wards of the capital), Gugong wenxianguan et al., eds., Beida fashang xueyuan, 1936. The first modern print was under the title *Kenryô keisei zenzu fu kaisetsu sakuin* 乾隆京城全圖附解説索引 (Complete map of the capital in the Qianlong period with explanations and index), 1940, reprinted from a manuscript copy kept in the Imperial Household Archive with notes and an index by Imanishi Shunjû 今西 春秋. Also reprinted by the Palace Museum under the title *Qing Neiwufu cang Jingcheng quantu* 清内務府藏京城全圖, Beijing, 1940.

[48] *Beijing lishi dituji* (Collection of historical maps of Beijing), Beijing, 1988; 2nd collection, 1997. For a scholarly examination of the linguistic and historical origins of Beijing street names, see Zhang Qingchang 張清常, *Beijing jiexiang mingcheng shihua shehui yuyanxue de zai tansuo* 北京街巷名稱史話社會語言學的再探索 (Historical discussion of Beijing street and lane names: Another socio-linguistic exploration), Beijing yuyan wenhua daxue, 1997. Indexed. A follow-up to the author's *Hutong ji qita shehui yuyanxue de tansuo* 胡同及其他社會語言學的探索 (On the *hutong* and other essays: a socio-linguistic exploration), Beijing yuyan xueyuan, 1990.

圖集.[49] The first of the 89 maps shows the Xi'an area at the time of Lantian Man 藍田人, and the last is of Xi'an in 1995. Pride of place is reserved for maps of Xi'an in the Zhou, Han, and Tang. There is extensive commentary and illustrations of artifacts found in the city in each period. There are also collections of historical maps of many other cities, for example, *Wuhan lishi dituji* 武漢歷史地圖集 (Collection of maps on the history of Wuhan), Zhongguo ditu, 1998. This contains more than 100 maps of the three Wuhan cities from the Song to the People's Republic.

4.7.2   City Life

There are many fascinating, detailed, and more informal accounts of cities and city life (usually in the capitals) than can be found in the local gazetteers. They were classified either in the geography section of the History branch or among the miscellaneous notes (*biji* 筆記) in the Philosophers' or one of the other branches. Six of the better-known titles are:

N. Wei Luoyang: *Luoyang qielan ji* 洛陽伽藍記 (45.2)
Tang Chang'an and Luoyang: *Liang jing xinji* 兩京新記 (46.2)
N. Song Kaifeng: *Dongjing menghua lu* 東京夢華錄 (47.2, *Biji*)
Ming Beijing: *Dijing jingwulüe* 帝京景物略 (49.2, *Local Gazetteers*)
Ming Beijing: *Chunming mengyu lu* 春明夢餘錄 (49.2, *Biji*)
Qing Beijing: *Rixia jiuwenkao* 日下舊聞考 (50.6.1)

The most famous painting of city life is the Northern Song scroll *Qingming shanghetu* 清明上河圖 (Traveling upstream at the Qingming festival [in Kaifeng]; see Zhou Baozhu, 1997, 4.7.3). There are many other such genre paintings of market scenes, see *CAAD* 2.2: 148–49 (1997); on the earliest (Qin and Han pictorial stone carvings), see Wang (1994) and Sun (1991) in secion 44.4.2.

4.7.3   Modern Studies of Urban History

There are increasing numbers of histories written of individual cities, usually of the capitals, for which there are more sources. For example,

[49] *Xi'an lishi dituji* (The historical atlas of Xi'an), Shi Nianhai 史念海 (1912–), ed. in chief, Xi'an ditu, 1996

Paul Wheatley, *The Pivot of the Four Quarters* (4.7.1)

Hans Bielenstein, "Lo-yang in Later Han Times," *BMFEA* 48 (1976), 1–142

Ho Ping-ti, "Loyang, A.D. 495–534: A Study of the Physical and Socio-Economic Planning of a Metropolitan Area," *HJAS* 26: 52–101 (1966)

William Jenner, *Memories of Loyang* (45.2)

Li Tingxian 李廷先, *Tangdai Yangzhou shigao* 唐代揚州史稿 (Draft history of Yangzhou in the Tang), Jiangsu guji, 1992

Songdai dongjing yanjiu 宋代東京研究 (Researches on the eastern capital in the Song dynasty), Zhou Baozhu 周寶珠, ed., Henan daxue, 1992

Zhou Baozhu 周寶珠, '*Qingming shanghetu*' *yu Qingming shanghe xue* 清明上河圖與清明上河學 (Traveling upstream at the Qingming festival [in Kaifeng] and *Qingming shanghe* studies), Henan daxue, 1997

Jacques Gernet, *Daily Life in China on the Eve of the Mongol Invasion, 1250–1276*, Allen and Unwin, 1962, SUP, 1970

H. C. Kiang, "The Birth of the Commercial Street: Kaifeng and Yangzhou," in *Streets: Critical Perspectives on Public Space*, Zeynep Celik et al., eds., UCP, 1994, 45-56

Qingxiang Jiang and Guoliang Xiao, "Glimpses of the Urban Economy in Bianjing, Capital of the Northern Song Dynasty," *Social Sciences in China* 4: 145-176 (1981)

R. Stewart Johnston, "The Ancient City of Suzhou: Town Planning in the Song Dynasty," *Town Planning Review* 54.2: 194–222 (1983)

Frederick W. Mote, "A Millennium of Chinese Urban History: Form, Time and Space Concepts in Soochow," *Rice University Studies* 59.4: 35–65 (1973)

Frederick W. Mote, "The Transformation of Nanking, 1350–1400," in G. William Skinner, ed., *The City in Late Imperial China*, SUP, 1977, 101–53

Han Dacheng 韓大成, *Mingdai chengshi yanjiu* 明代城市研究 (Researches on Ming dynasty towns), Renmin daxue, 1991

Shanghai: From Market Town to Treaty Port, 1074–1858, Linda Cook Johnson, ed., SUP, 1995

Mark Elvin, "Market Towns and Waterways: The County of Shanghai from 1840 to 1910," in the author's *Another History: Essays on China from a European Perspective*, Wild Peony, 1996, 101–39 (originally appeared in 1977)

William T. Rowe, *Hankow: Commerce and Society in a Chinese City,
1791–1889*, SUP, 1984; vol. 2, *Hankow: Conflict and Community in a
Chinese City, 1796–1895*, SUP, 1989

Not infrequently the primary sources for a given city are assembled.[50] Studies of the economic or demographic history of a particular town are beginning to appear.[51] Urban social life (apart from the life of the emperor and his court) is only just beginning to be studied in detail—see, for example, the studies of consumption patterns, leisure tastes, and pursuits of the urban literati in Ming and Qing China cited in 50.7.4. A history of hoodlums and vagabonds can reveal one aspect of city life because they usually gathered in the cities.[52] The maintenance of security at night was a constant preoccupation of officials (6.3). Much detail can be gleaned from Ming-Qing vernacular fiction, for example, the action of *Jin Ping Mei* 金瓶梅 is set in a busy local town, Linqing 林清, on the Grand Canal in Shandong (34.3).

For an overview of recent secondary studies, see Frederick W. Mote, "Urban History in Late Imperial China," *Ming Studies* 34: 61–76 (1995).

A great deal of work has been done on marketing systems linking small economic towns and cities, much of it drawn from local gazetteers.[53]

There is an association for the study of ancient Chinese cities, Zhongguo gudu xuehui 中國古都學會. Four volumes of the association's collected essays have appeared: *Zhongguo gudu yanjiu* 中國古都研究, Zhejiang renmin, 1985–89.

[50] *Yandu guji kao* 燕都古籍考 (Examination of the ancient written sources on Beijing), Wang Canchi 王燦熾, ed., Jinghua, 1995, 1996, contains thorough notes and brief summaries of 151 primary sources on Beijing from the earliest times to 1912. Arrangement is by period.

[51] See, for example, Sun Jian 孫健, *Beijing gudai jingjishi* 北京古代經濟史 (Economic history of Beijing in ancient times), Beijing Yanshan, 1996, or *Beijing lishi renkou dili* 北京歷史人口地理 (7.3).

[52] See Chen Baoliang 陳寶良, *Zhongguo liumang shi* 中國流氓史 (A history of vagabonds in China), Shehui kexue, 1993.

[53] *The City in Late Imperial China*, G. William Skinner, ed., SUP, 1977. On Skinner's application of central place theory to Chinese local and regional history, see the debate in *JAS* vols. 46 (1986) and 49 (1990). Linda Cook Johnson, ed., *Cities of Jiangnan in Late Imperial China*, SUNY, 1993.

Republican cities, especially Shanghai, have attracted a lot of attention; see, for example,

The Chinese City Between Two Worlds, Mark Elvin and G. William Skinner, eds., SUP, 1974.

Remaking the Chinese City: Modernity and National Identity, 1900–1950, Joseph Esherick, ed., Curzon, 2000.

Victor F. S. Sit, *Beijing: The Nature and Planning of a Chinese Capital City*, Wiley, 1995.

David Strand, *Rickshaw Beijing: City People and Policy in the 1920s*, SUP, 1989.

Han-chao Lu, *Beyond the Neon Lights: Everyday Shanghai in the Early Twentieth Century*, UCP, 1999.

Leo Ou-fan Lee, *Shanghai Modern: The Flowering of a New Urban Culture in China, 1930–1945*, HUP, 1999.

4.8 Travel Inside China

For a comprehensive history of travel both for business and pleasure and at home and abroad, see Zhang Bigong 章必功, *Zhongguo lüyoushi* 中國旅遊史. For travel in the Qin and Han, see Wang Zijin 王子今, *Qin Han jiaotong shigao* 秦漢交通史稿.[54]

Records of journeys and excursions (*youji* 遊記), often in chronological diary form with the personal observations of the writer, were established as a literary sub-genre in the Tang by Liu Zongyuan 柳宗元 (773–819) in his *Yongzhou baji* 永州八記, and by Li Ao 李翱 (772–841) in his *Lainan lu* 來南錄.[55] Frequently the travel was to take up a new bureaucratic post (or, as in the case of Liu, to go into exile), to return to the capital, or to fulfill a foreign mission (for foreign travel of all sorts, including embassy diaries, see 41.5.2, *Travel Abroad*). For an anthology in English of Chinese travel literature (*youji wenxue* 遊記文學) from ancient times to the present

---

[54] *Zhongguo lüyoushi* (History of Chinese travel), Yunnan renmin, 1992, 1995; *Qin Han jiaotong shigao* (Draft history of travel in the Qin and Han), Dangxiao, 1995.

[55] Liu Zongyuan, *Yongzhou baji* (Eight records of Yongzhou [southern Hunan]), and Li Ao, *Lainan lu*, which briefly records a journey from Luoyang to Guangdong in 819. On the *Yongzhou baji*, see William H. Nienhauser, Jr., *Liu Tsung-yuan*, Twayne, 1973, 66–79.

century, see *Inscribed Landscapes: Travel Writing from Imperial China*, Richard E. Strassberg, tr. and introduced, UCP, 1994. There are many such anthologies in Chinese, sometimes arranged geographically by province, sometimes chronologically, and sometimes containing poetry as well as prose. See, for example:

Zhongguo mingsheng shici da cidian 中國名勝詩詞大辭典 (Dictionary of Chinese poems on scenic and historical sites), Yang Gang 楊鋼, comp., Wuhan daxue, 1992.

For studies of a very common form of travel, the pilgrimage, see *Pilgrims and Sacred Sites in China*, Susan Naquin and Chün-fang Yü, eds., UCP, 1992, especially "Introduction: Pilgrimage in China," ibid, 1–38. Note that going on a pilgrimage was referred to as *chao-shan jinxiang* 朝山進香 (paying respects to the mountain and presenting incense). For the monk pilgrims who journeyed west to "seek the dharma" (*qiufa* 求法), see 41.5.1.

Several of the most famous Chinese travel diaries or records of excursions have been translated. Four are listed here:

On the Road in Twelfth-Century China: The Travel Diaries of Fan Chengda (1126–1193), James M. Hargett, tr., introduced and annotated, Steiner, 1989. In his *Canluan lu* 驂鸞錄 (Register of mounting a simurgh), Fan Chengda 范成大 recorded a four-month journey from his birthplace in Suzhou to take up a post in Guilin in 1171–72; the second Fan diary translated, the *Lanpeilu* 攬轡錄 (Register of grasping the carriage reins), records the author's journey on an ambassadorial mission from the Southern Song capital of Lin'an (Hangzhou) to the Jin capital of Zhongdu (Beijing) in 1170–71.

South China in the Twelfth Century: A Translation of Lu Yu's Travel Diaries, July 3–December 6, 1170, Chun-shu Chang and Joan Smythe, trs., HKCUP, 1981. A fully annotated translation of Lu You 陸游 (1125–1210), *Ru Shu ji* 入蜀記 (Record of entering Sichuan).

Learning from Mt. Hua: A Chinese Physician's Illustrated Travel Record and Painting Theory, Kathlyn Maureen Liscomb, tr., CUP, 1993. Translation of the travel journal of Wang Lü 王履 (d. early Ming).

The Travel Diaries of Hsu Hsia-k'o, Li Chi, ed., HKCUP, 1974. Xu Hongzu 徐弘祖 (known by his *hao* as Xu Xiake 徐霞客, 1587–1641) was the best known of those who traveled inside China in the later empire. Between the years 1607 and 1640 he went on seventeen trips culminating in a four-year exploration of Guangxi, Guizhou, and Yunnan. He left behind lengthy diaries of his travels, amounting to

404,000 characters, of which the greater part is devoted to his last great exploration in the southwest. Xu not only climbed all the sacred mountains of China, but also explored the sources of major rivers and made geographical and geological investigations despite the many hardships and mishaps along the way. Li Ji has translated and annotated those sections of the diaries covering the sacred mountains. There is an appendix containing a short biography by Chun-shu Chang, 223–31. The Ding Wenjiang edition contains a full chronological biography, 1–67.[56] The clearest and most detailed maps of all Xu's routes are in *Xu Xiake lüxing luxian kaocha tuji* 徐霞客旅行路綫 考察圖輯 (Atlas of Xu Xiake's travels), Chu Shaotang 褚紹唐, ed. in chief, Zhongguo ditu, 1991. Note the useful *Xu Xiake youji renming diming suoyin* 徐霞客遊記人名地名索引 (Personal and place-name index to the *Travel Diaries of Xu Xiake*), Feng Junian 馮菊年 and Xiao Qi 蕭琪, comps., Shanghai guji, 1993.

Some twenty to thirty merchant manuals and route books are extant from the late sixteenth to the late nineteenth century, no doubt reflecting the upsurge of trade and travel at this time (50.7.4). Encyclopaedias for daily use of the Ming and Qing also not infrequently contain similar travel information (31.3).

4.9   Bibliography

Zhongguo lishi dilixue lunzhu suoyin (1900–1980) 中國歷史地理學論著索 引 (Index of articles and books on Chinese historical geography, 1900–80), Du Yu 杜瑜 and Zhu Lingling 朱玲玲, comps., Shumu wenxian, 1986. Bibliography of secondary scholarship on Chinese historical geography, both Chinese and Japanese. In it are indexed 15,000 articles and 2,600 books. An appendix gives Japanese contributions (3,000 articles and 500 books).

Chûgoku shûrakushi no kenkyû [zôho] 中國聚落史の研究[增補] (Studies on Chinese settlements [rev. and enl.], Tôdaishi kenkyûkai 唐代史研 究會, comp., Tôsui shobô, 1988; rev., 1990. Bibliography of secondary works in Chinese and Japanese on the history of individual Chinese towns (in all periods, not just the Tang). The listing itself (Part 2) is culled from 20 previous bibliographies and studies.

---

[56] Ting Wen-chiang (Ding Wenjiang 丁文江), *Xu Xiake [Xu Hongzu] youji* 徐霞客遊記 (The travel diaries of Xu Xiake [Xu Hongzu]), 1928; rpnt., Shanghai guji, 1980; Zhonghua, 1988, 1996.

5

Chronology

This chapter focuses on the different methods of recording dates in Chinese history and how to convert these to the Western calendar. No attempt is made to present the adjustments in the Chinese calendars introduced in different periods. This is a complex subject (particularly for the pre-Qin period), which belongs to the history of Chinese astronomy and calendrical sciences.

After a glance at official calendars, popular almanacs, and the sources for the history of Chinese astronomy (5.1), the chapter turns to the recording of days and the *ganzhi* 干支 cycle (5.2), months (5.3), and years (5.4), including regnal years (5.4.1), the 60-year cycle (5.4.2), the Republican calendar (5.4.3), and the division of the year into seasons punctuated with festivals and vacations (5.5). Next comes date conversion (5.6), including the conversion of dates in special calendars such as the Buddhist, Muslim, Dai, or Yi, Tibetan calendars (5.7). There are also short sections on the Korean, Japanese, and Vietnamese calendars (5.8) and on chronological tables of events (5.9). Divisions of the day are the subject of Chapter 6.

Works on astronomy and mathematics (*tianwen suanfa* 天文算法) were placed in the Philosophers' branch of the traditional fourfold bibliographical classification (*Sibu* 四部, see 9.3).

5.1 Calendars, Almanacs, and Astronomical Sources

5.1.1 Official Calendars

A lunisolar calendar (*yinyangli* 陰陽曆) has been used in China since at least the Shang dynasty. After this was abolished in 1911, it was referred to as the *jiuli* 舊曆 the old calendar) or (misleadingly) as the moon calendar (*yinli* 陰曆). After 1949, it was also called the farmer's calendar (*nongli* 農曆). Nowadays all these terms are in use, as well as *Zhongli* 中曆 (Chinese calendar) or *Xiali* 夏曆 (the Xia calendar). The old calendar is still used for certain purposes today. It is essentially the same as the last great revision, the *Shixianli* 時憲曆, devised at the end of the Ming and introduced by the Qing in 1645 (29.7.1).

During the Spring and Autumn and Warring States periods, three main lunisolar calendars were in use at different times: the Xia, Yin (Shang), and Zhou calendars.[1] Each started the year in a different solar month: the Zhou calendar began in the first month (*ziyue* 子月, i.e., in the month on or just before the winter solstice). The Yin or Shang calendar began in the second month (*chouyue* 丑月, i.e., beginning with the first new moon after the winter solstice); and the Xia began in the third month (*yinyue* 寅月, i.e., beginning with the second new moon after the winter solstice). During the Warring States, each kingdom based its calendar with minor variations on one of these three calendars. In general, the states in the middle Yellow River used the Xia calendar, and the remainder used that of the Zhou. Classical works tend to use either the Xia or the Zhou calendar, but if they contain material from different regions (e.g., the *Shijing*), they tend to use more than one. Since 12 lunar months fall short of the solar year by about 11 days, extra months (*runyue* 閏月) were intercalated since at least the Shang dynasty to close the gap. By the seventh century BC, seven intercalations were made every 19 years.[2]

Already by the end of the Warring States, the calendar was remarkably accurate. At the Qin unification, the tenth month (*haiyue* 亥月) was adopted as the beginning of the year (it had been in use in Qin since at least 265 BC). This was continued by the Han until 104 BC, when it was replaced with the Xia calendar. With few exceptions,[3] this remained the basis for all subsequent calendars until 1912 when the Gregorian calendar was promulgated and the old New Year's Day was renamed the Spring Festival (the winter solstice remained in the eleventh month).

---

[1] On the different calendars used in pre-Qin times, see Zhang Peiyu (1987) and the other references cited in 13.3, *Chronology*.

[2] A *zhang* 章 cycle in Chinese (called a Metonic cycle in English after the Greek astronomer Meton, who lived in the fifth century BC).

[3] The main exceptions were the years AD 9–23 and 237–39 (Yin calendar); 689–700 and 761–62 (Zhou calendar).

The annual task of establishing and promulgating the calendar (*zhili* 治曆, *shouli* 授曆) was the exclusive prerogative of the ruler. Each dynasty announced its own calendar, and some dynasties reformed the calendar several times. The work was done by the astronomical bureau, whose duties until the Han were assured by the court historians (who also conducted divination). Right up to the end of the empire, the bureau also had the function of keeping the time (Chapter 6).

The main purpose of premodern Chinese astronomy, however, was not to set the calendar or indeed to regulate the farming year, important though those these tasks were. The main purpose was to predict and interpret heavenly signs, both periodic and nonperiodic, especially to predict eclipses and the movement of the planets for astrological divination. If this responsibility was carried out accurately, it demonstrated the emperor's right to rule.[4] The imperial monopoly on astronomy and the setting of the calendar was enforced by laws forbidding people to possess astronomical instruments, maps of the heavens or esoteric books; to study astronomy privately, or to publish calendars. Infringement was punished by two years of penal servitude.[5]

5.1.2   Popular Almanacs

Chinese traditional society was above all one in which the highest importance was attached to choosing the right time and the right place for activities both high and low, solemn and trivial. The selection was done using myriad mantic arts. The first glimpse we have is in the oracle bones. Much later, despite the prohibitions, popular almanacs (*rishu* 日書, *lipu* 曆譜, *lishu* 曆書, *tongshu* 通書, and so forth) circulated in huge quantities. The earliest extant ones are the dozen or so that have been unearthed in the form of bamboo-strip manuscripts from Warring States, Qin, and Han tombs. The phrase used at that time was *rishu* because their main purpose was for prognostication, typically for choosing an auspicious day for impor-

---

[4] Wolfram Eberhard, "The Political Function of Astronomy and Astronomers in Han China," in *Chinese Thought and Institutions*, J. K. Fairbank, ed., UChP, 1957, 1967, 33–70.

[5] See, for example, Article 110 in *The T'ang Code: Vol. II, Specific Articles*, Wallace Johnson, tr., PUP, 1997.

tant activities. At first they were relatively simple. By the Song dynasty they had become increasingly elaborate with a wealth of information not only on lucky and unlucky days and hours but also on festivals, birthdays of legendary figures, and mantic lore of all kinds. The earliest known almanac is written on silk and dated to 300 BC (19.1.3). The first extant printed almanac dates from the Tang, the *Qianfu sinian lishu* 乾符四年曆書 (The almanac of 877; see 18.4). Popular almanacs should be distinguished from the official calendar (popularly known as *lao huangli* 老皇曆; see 5.1.1) and agricultural calendars (*yueling* 月令; 35.1.1).[6]

5.1.3   Sources for the History of Chinese Astronomy

Chinese records of eclipses, comets, and other celestial phenomena are more complete and continuous than those found in any other culture. There are many such records on the oracle bones. Modern astronomers have calculated the possible dates on which these observations could have been made, although there is no means as yet of situating them in an absolute chronology.[7] Later, for the Spring and Autumn period, it is possible to check the accuracy of the records: 33 out of the 37 solar eclipses recorded in the *Zuozhuan* have been verified.

A huge effort was made in the 1970s and 1980s by historians of science to collect all references to such phenomena from the Standard Histories, local gazetteers, and the Veritable Records of the Ming and Qing. More than 10,000 records of eclipses, sunspots, comets, meteors, etc., were excerpted and edited by Zhuang Weifeng 莊威鳳 and Wang Lixing 王立興 for publication in *Zhongguo*

---

[6] For research on Qin and Han almanacs and prognostication texts, see 6.4; 44.3.2.1–3. On Qing almanacs, see Richard J. Smith, *Chinese Almanacs*, OUP, 1992, and for a translation of a modern Cantonese almanac, see Martin Palmer, *T'ung Shu: The Ancient Chinese Almanac*, Rider and Co., 1986. *Wannianshu* 萬年書 (multiannual almanac), *wannianli* 萬年曆 (perpetual calendar), *rixianshu* 日憲書 (book of constant conformity with the heavens) were common terms for almanacs in the later empire.

[7] The main astronomical, calendrical, and meteorological records on the oracle bones are included in *Jiaguwen heji* 甲骨文合集 and indexed in *Jiaguwen tongjian* 甲骨文通檢, vol. 3 (15.5, *Concordances*). Noel Barnard, "Astronomical Data from Ancient Chinese Records: The Requirements of Historical Research Methodology," *East Asian History* 6: 47–74 (1993).

gudai tianxiang jilu zongji 中國古代天象記錄總集.[8] As part of the same scholarly effort, historians of astronomy at Peking Observatory compiled *Zhongguo tianwen shiliao huibian* 中國天文史料匯編. It was excerpted from the same sources and covered those who wrote on astronomy.[9] All the Standard Histories contain treatises on astronomy (with the exception of the *Liaoshi*) and most also contain treatises on the calendar.[10] There is a punctuated edition of these monographs: *Lidai tianwen lüli deng zhi huibian* 歷代天文律曆等志匯編.[11]

For a comprehensive reader on the early history and development of Chinese astronomy and the calendar, see Zheng Huisheng 鄭慧生, *Gudai tianwen lifa yanjiu* 古代天文曆法研究.[12] The sources excerpted cover a broad range, including the oracle bones and new epigraphic and archaeological materials and ancient texts down to the Han dynasty. Each is given in the original and translated into Modern Chinese. The book also contains a substantial introduction that concentrates on the background to the differences between the Xia, Shang, and Zhou calendars as well as 16 of the author's research articles on early Chinese astronomy and calendars.

On the history of Chinese astronomy, see

Mathematics and the Sciences of the Heavens and the Earth (SCC, vol. 3). Still the single best introduction in a Western language.

Christopher Cullen, *Astronomy and Mathematics in Ancient China: The Zhoubi suanjing* [周髀算經], CUP, 1996, 1–170.

Nathan Sivin, *Cosmos and Computation in Early Chinese Mathematical Astronomy*, in Sivin (1995), originally in TP 55: 1–73 (1969).

---

[8] *Zhongguo gudai tianxiang jilu zongji* (Comprehensive collection of records of celestial phenomena in ancient China), Jiangsu kexue jishu, 1988.

[9] *Zhongguo tianwen shiliao huibian* (Historical materials on Chinese astronomy), Kexue, 1989.

[10] See Beijing Tianwentai (1975–76) and Chen Zunwei, vol. 3, 1984, 1336–1586. For a brief history, see Cui Zhenhua 崔振華, *Zhongguo gudai lifa yan'ge* 中國古代曆法沿革 (The evolution of the ancient Chinese calendar), Xinhua, 1992.

[11] *Lidai tianwen lüli deng zhi huibian* (Collection of treatises on harmonics and the calendar from the Standard Histories), 10 vols., Zhonghua, 1975–76.

[12] *Gudai tianwen lifa yanjiu* (Research on ancient astronomy and the calendar), Henan daxue, 1995.

Sun Xiaochun and Jacob Kristemaker, *The Chinese Sky During the Han: The Constellations Reconstructed and Their Cultural Background Explored*, Brill, 1997.

Chen Zungui 陳遵嬀, *Zhongguo tianwenxueshi* 中國天文學史 (A history of Chinese astronomy), 4 vols., Shanghai renmin, 1980-89; rpnt., Mingwen, 1984-89.

For illustrations and articles on the history of astronomical instruments, including those newly excavated, see the following:

Zhongguo gudai tianwen wenwu tuji 中國古代天文文物圖集 (Collected illustrations of ancient astronomical artifacts), Kaogusuo, eds., Wenwu, 1980.

Zhongguo gudai tianwen wenwu tulu lunwenji 中國古代天文文物圖錄論文集 (Collected articles and illustrations of ancient astronomical artifacts), Kaogusuo, eds., Wenwu, 1980.

Zhongguo gudai tianwen wenwu lunji 中國古代天文文物論集 (Collected articles on ancient astronomical artifacts), Wenwu, 1988.

Zhongguo tianwenxueshi wenji 中國天文學史文集 (Collected articles on the history of Chinese astronomy), 6 vols., Kexue, 1978-94. This series contains over 60 research articles, many on non-Han calendars used within China.

Kejishi wenji 科技史文集 (Papers on the history of science and technology), vols. 1 (1978), 6 (1980), and 10 (1983) were special issues devoted to the history of astronomy.

Ziran kexueshi yanjiu 自然科學史研究 (see Chapter 37) frequently carries articles on the history of astronomy.

5.2   *The* Ganzhi 干支 *Cycle*

The *ganzhi* 干支 cycle is one of the two basic counting systems in Chinese culture, the other being decimal (7.1). The cycle was formed by combining two sets of counters, one denary and the other duodenary to form 60 unique combinations. The denary cycle is called the 10 stems (*shigan* 十干) and the duodenary, the 12 branches (the *shi'erzhi* 十二支). Table 8 shows not only the 10 *gan* and the 12 *zhi* but also how they were combined to form the first of the cycle's six sets of 10 combinations. It starts with *jiazi* 甲子 and ends with *guiyou* 癸酉. The next set of 10 begins with *jia* 甲 coupled with the next branch, the 11th (*xu* 戌) to form *jiaxu* 甲戌. It ends with *guiwei*

Table 8: The Tiangan 天干 *and the* Dizhi 地支

Gan 干	jia 甲	yi 乙	bing 丙	ding 丁	wu 戊	ji 己	geng 庚	xin 辛	ren 壬	gui 癸		
Zhi 支	zi 子	chou 丑	yin 寅	mao 卯	chen 辰	si 巳	wu 午	wei 未	shen 申	you 酉	xu 戌	hai 亥

癸未 before beginning the third set with *jiashen* 甲申 (see Table 9). In this way no single character is repeated in any one of the six sets of 10 combinations and no combination is repeated in the complete cycle of 60.

The 10 *gan* appear already on the oracle bones in the Shang (1200–1045 BC) as a way of enumerating the 10-day "week" (*xun* 旬), normally in combination with the 12 *zhi* (known then as *chen* 辰). In the early Zhou they were called the 10 *ri* 日. They were also used to count six successive *xun* each with its own unique name to form a cycle of 60 days. *Ganzhi* day dates are found on thousands of oracle-bone inscriptions. A number of complete tables of the cycle are also recorded, presumably to serve as a calendar or the result of scribal practice. The best-preserved table dates from the last reigns of the Shang (*Heji* #37986). It is reproduced in most oracle-bone script readers (15.5) and is arranged as shown in Table 9. During the millennium following the Shang, the *ganzhi* were gradually extended to count the other units of time including years (5.4.2), months (5.3), and hours (Tables 10 and 11, Chapter 6). Although used as general counters as in *jia* 甲, *yi* 乙, *bing* 丙, *ding* 丁 (1, 2, 3, 4 or a, b, c, d), they were not used for mathematical calculations.[13]

---

[13] It is tempting to connect the 10 *ri* with the legend of the 10 suns. The 10 *ri* (*gan*) appear in the names attributed (probably at a later date) to the Xia rulers. They were also used as the posthumous names of deceased Shang rulers (although how the names were selected is a matter of controversy). After the Han, the 10 *ri* came to be known by their present name, the *tiangan* 天干 (heavenly stems) or *gan* for short. The second set, the 12 *chen* were from the same time referred to as the *dizhi* 地支 (earthly branches) or *zhi* for short. Before the Han, the *ganzhi* were known as *richen* 日辰. During the Han they were also called *muzi* 母子. The first reference to the term *ganzhi* is in *Bohu tong* 白虎通 (Comprehensive discussions in the White Tiger Hall), "Xingming pian" 姓名篇 (Names).

Table 9: The Ganzhi 干支 *Cycle*

51. 甲寅	41. 甲辰	31. 甲午	21. 甲申	11. 甲戌	1. 甲子
52. 乙卯	42. 乙巳	32. 乙未	22. 乙酉	12. 乙亥	2. 乙丑
53. 丙辰	43. 丙午	33. 丙申	23. 丙戌	13. 丙子	3. 丙寅
54. 丁巳	44. 丁未	34. 丁酉	24. 丁亥	14. 丁丑	4. 丁卯
55. 戊午	45. 戊申	35. 戊戌	25. 戊子	15. 戊寅	5. 戊辰
56. 己未	46. 己酉	36. 己亥	26. 己丑	16. 己卯	6. 己巳
57. 庚申	47. 庚戌	37. 庚子	27. 庚寅	17. 庚辰	7. 庚午
58. 辛酉	48. 辛亥	38. 辛丑	28. 辛卯	18. 辛巳	8. 辛未
59. 壬戌	49. 壬子	39. 壬寅	31. 壬辰	19. 壬午	9. 壬申
60. 癸亥	50. 癸丑	40. 癸卯	30. 癸巳	20. 癸未	10. 癸酉

Nobody knows the origin of the *ganzhi*, but there are many theories. For example, until quite recently, the superficial similarity of the *ganzhi* cycle with the Babylonian base-60 system was taken as one of the "proofs" for the Western origin of early Chinese civilization. But the proof does not work because the *ganzhi* are different from the Babylonian system in both concept and function. In Sumerian-Babylonian mathematics a decimal system was used for counting up to 60, thereafter the cycle began again. The *ganzhi* were derived by combining two separate cyclical systems, not from a base-60 numeral system.[14] Another theory is that in pre-Shang times there was a 10-month solar calendar with each month having 36 days.[15] Later this was combined with a 12-month lunar calendar with each month having 30 days. The tradition linking the *gan* (*ri*) with the sun or heaven and the *zhi* (*chen*) with the moon or the earth is at least as old as the Shang. What better way to unite the two calendrical systems than by combining them in a cycle equivalent to their lowest common multiple (60)? Possibly the two systems (of which the 10 *gan* is the earlier) were combined when two tribes joined their forces. There is no direct evidence to support such theories (base-10 and base-12 numeral systems existed somewhat uneasily throughout Chinese history, for example in the two mutually incompatible systems of counting the hours; 6.5). There

[14] Terrien de Lacouperie (1845–94), who taught at University College, London, in the 1880s was one of the earliest to argue for a Babylonian origin of the *ganzhi*; see Chen Cheng-yih, *Early Chinese Work in Natural Science*, HKUP, 1996, 187–90.

[15] Ye and Tian (1998), 229–58 (full reference at 7.1.2).

are many other hypotheses, including that the *ganzhi* were Austro-asiatic in origin or that they represented Shang consonants.[16] Another hypothesis is that the scribes devised a way of naming and grouping the days to fit the requirements of the complex cycle of ritual sacrifices by the Shang kings to their ancestors. Possible schedules have been worked out by modern scholars.[17] Given the central role of periodic ancestral sacrifices at the Shang court and given the close connection between the origins of the characters and divination, a magico-religious calendrical origin of the *ganzhi* would seem most likely.

In oracle-bone script, none of the 22 *ganzhi* resembles another, which confirms their use to accurately distinguish the different ancestral rituals at the core of state power (just as alteration-proof numbers are more secure than common numerals whose single straight lines can easily be miswritten whether by accident or by design; see 7.1.1). The *ganzhi* were changed only once in the course of 3,500 years: temporarily when the Taipings used three new *zhi* as part of their calendar reform.

The *ganzhi* were among the most frequently used characters, not only because they were used for naming days and years as well as counting the hours and times of the day, but because they were used for counting and classifying in general. They appear as side elements in many other characters (one-third of them are used as classifiers); they also supply one of the most common suffixes (*zi* 子) and appear in many common compounds (e.g., *zhongwu* 中午, midday).

---

[16] An Austroasiatic origin for the *zhi* has been proposed on the basis that 6 out of 12 of them resemble Austroasiatic words for the animals they represent but not one appears to be a Chinese animal name; see Jerry Norman, "A Note on the Origin of the Chinese Duodenary Cycle," in *Linguistics of the Sino-Tibetan Area*, Graham Thurgood et al., eds., ANU, 1985, 85–89. Edwin Pulley-blank believes that the *ganzhi* represented the 22 consonants of the Chinese language at the time of the invention of the script: "The *Ganzhi* as Phonograms and Their Application to the Calendar," *EC* 16: 39–80 (1991), and "The *Ganzhi* as Phonograms," *Early China News* 8: 29–30 (1995). Gordon Whittaker summarizes other speculations in *Calendar and Script in Proto-historical China and Mesoamerica: A Comparative Study of Day Names and Their Signs*, Holos, 1990.

[17] Chang Yuzhi 常玉芝, *Shangdai zhouji zhidu* 商代周祭制度 (The Shang dynasty system of weekly sacrifices), Shehui kexue, 1987; Mizukami Shizuo 水上静夫, *Eto no Kanji gaku* 干支の漢字學 (A study of the Chinese characters of the *ganzhi*), Taishu, 1998.

5.3 Months

The Chinese based their calendar, as did most other ancient civilizations, on observation of the rising and setting of the sun; the phases of the moon, and the movements of the stars, especially the pole star (hence day = *ri* 日; month = *yue* 月, and year = *sui* 歲).

Already in the Shang adjustments were made in the calendar to reconcile the differences between earthly rotations, revolutions of the moon round the earth, and revolutions of the earth round the sun. The twelve lunisolar months were reckoned to contain either 29 or 30 days; an intercallary month was inserted either at the end of the year or when needed during the year. From the Spring and Autumn period months were also named with the 12 *zhi*.[18] Thus the *Chunqiu* records a total solar eclipse on what is the earliest absolute day date in Chinese history: the beginning of the second month of the third year of the reign of Duke Yin (posthumous title) of Lu, i.e., February 22, 720 BC, in the Western (Gregorian) calendar.[19] It is an absolute date because the eclipse has been corroborated by modern astronomical calculations (according to Zhang Peiyu, 1990, its magnitude was 0.50 and it could have been observed at Luoyang at 7.21 AM). From this day onward all Chinese days can be precisely identified up to the present time.

During the pre-Qin period, various other naming systems were used for the months, including the 12 half-tones of the Chinese musical scale, 12 trees and flowers, and the 12 animal signs. Toward the end of the Warring States, the Five Phases were correlated with the months in an elaborate scheme.

From the Later Han, however, in everyday life, it was numbers that were used for naming months and days of the month, although in official documents and records where accuracy was required, including horoscopes, the *ganzhi* tended to be used.

In addition, there were a large number of special terms for particular months and special days, some of which first appeared on the Shang oracle bones and many of which are still in use. For example:

---

[18] See also Marc Kalinowski, "The Use of the Twenty-eight 'Xiu' as a Day Count in Early China," *Chinese Science* 13: 55–81 (1997).

[19] *Yingong Sannian: chun wang eryue jisi ri you shi zhi* 隱公三年春王二月己巳日有食之 (*Chunqiu Gongyangzhuan* 春秋公羊傳, *Yingong sannian* 隱公三年).

Zhengyue 正月 (the first month of the year, which had at least 15 other names in the course of Chinese history); *layue* 臘月 (the last month of the year).

The four phases of the moon: *shuoyue* 朔月 (new moon), *shangxian* 上弦 (first quarter), *wangyue* 望月 (full moon), *xiaxian* 下弦 (last quarter).

Dayue 大月 (large month) is a lunar month of 30 days (or a solar month of 31 days); *xiaoyue* 小月 (small month) is a lunar month of 29 days (or a solar month of 30 days).

The month is divided into three 10-day periods, *sanxun* 三旬 (or *sanhuan* 三浣), referred to as *shangxun* 上旬, *zhongxun* 中旬, *xiaxun* 下旬.

Chuxi 除夕 (New Year's Eve); *yuandan* 元旦 (New Year's Day); *yuanxiao* 元宵 is the night of the fifteenth of the first lunar month (i.e., the eve of the Lantern Festival); *nianye* 年夜 (evening of the last day of the year).

The first 10 days of each of the lunar months are known as *chuyi* 初一, *chu'er* 初二 ... *chushi* 初十.

Shuo 朔 is the first day of the lunar month, *wang* 望 is the fifteenth day of "small" months and the sixteenth day of "large" months, and *hui* 晦, the last day of both the large and small months.

The first, second, and third month of each season was named using the ranking words *meng* 孟, *zhong* 仲, *ji* 季 (3.2), e.g., *mengchun* 孟春, *zhongchun* 仲春, and *jichun* 季春.

5.4   Years

Four main words were used for year in early China. All had different origins, but came to be used interchangeably: *sui* 歲, *nian* 年, *zai* 載, and *si* 祀.[20]

Absolute year dates in Chinese history begin in 841 BC: *Xi Zhou gonghe yuan nian* 西周共和元年 (the first year of the *gonghe* interregnum of Western Zhou). From then on Chinese chronology is on

---

[20] *Sui* 歲 originally meant Jupiter or a cycle of 12 years; in the Eastern Zhou, it was also used to mean a completed cycle of the four seasons, or full harvest, hence year; *nian* 年 originally meant *ren* 稔, a rich harvest or harvest year; *zai* 載 could mean to start and came to be used for the renewal of all things at springtime, hence year; *si* 祀 originally meant annual sacrifice, and in the Shang was also used to mean year. Already in the Warring States *nian* was normally used before numbers and referred to the calendar year; *sui* was used after numbers to count an individual's age (years including year of birth).

firm ground in an unbroken record up to the present (for the situation before 841, see 13.3, *Chronology*).

5.4.1   Regnal Years, Era Names, and Reign Names

The most common and the earliest method of recording years was by eponymous dating, that is by taking the year of accession of the ruler as year one (*jiyuan* 紀元), the year after as year two, and so on successively. This system began in the Shang and continued with certain important modifications until 1911 (for Republican dating, see 5.4.3). Before the mid-fourth century BC, the first year of the new reign began in the same year as the previous ruler's death; after the mid-fourth century, it began on the first day of the New Year following the previous ruler's death, a practice that continued until the end of the Qing.[21]

The first modification to the reign period came during the Warring States when two rulers restarted the cycle from the first year (*yuannian* 元年) during the course of their reign, a practice referred to as *gengyuan* 更元 or *gaiyuan* 改元.[22] The next change was in the reign of Han Wendi 漢文帝, when the year was set to the beginning (*geng yuannian*) upon the adoption of a new calendar in 163 BC. His successor, Jingdi 景帝, after being on the throne six years, did the same in 149, and again after six years, in 143 BC. The next emperor, Han Wudi 漢武帝, followed suit, switching the year count back to the beginning every six years, six times in succession (the six-year gap between *gaiyuan* is a reflection of the Former Han belief that six was a particularly lucky number, a belief inherited from the Qin). Each new six-year period was simply numbered successively as *yuannian*, *eryuan* 二元, *sanyuan* 三元 and so on. By the time the system had reached *wuyuan sannian* 五元三年 (114 BC), it was found so inconvenient that an official proposed retrospectively re-

---

[21] For names of rulers and listings of *nianhao*, see A. C. Moule (1873–1957), *The Rulers of China, 221 BC–AD 1949*, Praeger, 1957. For more thorough imperial genealogical information, including families of empresses and names of offspring, see 3.3.

[22] When Duke Hui of Wei (魏惠公) assumed the title of king and all the pretensions of that title in 334 BC, he started the year count from the beginning (*gaiyuan*), and 334 was termed *houyuan yuannian* (後元元年); likewise, when Duke Huiwen of Qin 秦惠文公 usurped the title of king in 324 BC, the year count was changed to *gengyuan yuannian* 更元元年.

naming each "beginning" with single, mainly astronomical, characters (Jianyuan 建元, Yuanguang 元光, Yuanshuo 元朔). Han Wudi
accepted this proposal only in 110 BC after six years had gone by
since the previous *gaiyuan*. Having just conducted the *feng* 封 rites
at Taishan, he named the new era Yuanfeng 元封. This is usually
regarded as the first era name (*nianhao* 年號) in Chinese history
(according to the *Shiji*, the first reign name was Yuanding 元鼎
[116–111 BC]. However, it was only adopted retrospectively in 113
BC; see *CHC*, vol. 1, 155–56). Six years later in 104 BC, the Han inaugurated a new calendar (Taichu 太初), and the era name was
changed mainly every four years (within reigns) up to the end of the
Former Han.

Thereafter, no particular interval for *gaiyuan* was observed. Instead, new eras were frequently inaugurated to mark a new beginning for political reasons, often on the occasion of an auspicious astronomical sign or splendid event such as a military victory, and
always as an affirmation of the sovereignty of the ruler. Altogether
more than 800 era names were used in Chinese history. Not only
the emperors themselves but also leaders of non-Han and rebel governments adopted *nianhao*, as did the rulers of the kingdoms in Japan, Korea, and Vietnam.

Copper coins also bore the *nianhao* of the ruler (7.4.1).

With only a few exceptions, *nianhao* were composed of two
characters, for example, the much-used Jianyuan 建元 (establishing
the beginning) or Yong'an 永安 (eternal peace). The most frequently used word was *tian* 天 (heaven). From the beginning of the Ming
until the end of the Qing normally only one era name was used for
the whole reign. As a result era names become synonymous with
reign names. For most purposes era names and reign names need not
be translated.[23]

---

[23] For other points of view, see Edward H. Schafer, "Chinese Reign
Names—Words or Nonsense Syllables," *Wennti Papers* 1: 33–40 (1954); Mary
C. Wright, "What's in a Reign Name: The Uses of History and Philology," *JAS*
18.1: 103–6 (1958); Also Schafer, "Reply to Readers' Comments," *Wennti Pa-
pers* 2: 75–77 (1954). See also Arthur F. Wright and E. Fagan, "Era Names and
Zeitgeist," *Etudes asiatiques* 5: 113–21 (1951).

5.4.2   A Cycle of Cathay

The *ganzhi* were used for counting a 60-year cycle (*liushi huajia* 六十花甲 or *liushi jiazi* 六十甲子) from at least the Former Han and during the reign of Wang Mang 王莽. In AD 85 government orders made their use official. Later they were extrapolated backward to count years from the beginning of Chinese history. In treaty port English, the 60-year cycle was often called "a cycle of Cathay."

Between the Han and the Qing there are 25 cycles with the same *ganzhi*. Confusion is avoided because during the whole of imperial China, only one reign period lasted for more than 60 years (Kangxi). Moreover, the dynasty is either known from the context or is given, and era names are also usually written as part of a date. For example, *Yuan Zhongtong ernian xinyou* 元中統二年辛酉 refers to the *xinyou* year, the second year since the adoption of the era name Zhongtong by the Yuan emperor Shizu (Khubilai), i.e., 1261.

Apart from regnal years and *ganzhi*, the names of the 12 annual stations of Jupiter began to be used to count years in 365 BC. They were in turn replaced by the stations of Taisui 太歲 (the God of Time in later popular almanacs), an invisible counter-orbital correlate of Jupiter (*xingsui jinian* 星歲紀年). This method continued in use during the Warring States, the Qin, and the Former Han until replaced by the *ganzhi* in AD 54. It was occasionally used by literati in later periods.[24]

A popular way of counting years was by using the 12 Animals (*shengxiao* 生肖), each of which was associated with one of the 12 Taisui and one of the 12 earthly branches, *dizhi*. The practice was in common use by the Qin dynasty in the form in which it has continued to this day. The Chinese animal signs do not, however, correspond to the 12 signs of the Western zodiac.[25]

[24] See Liu Tan 劉坦, *Zhongguo gudai zhi xingsui jinian* 中國古代之星歲紀年 (Ephemeris years in ancient China), Kexue, 1957.

[25] The classic study is Édouard Chavannes (1865-1918), "Le Cycle turc des douze animaux," *TP* 7: 51-122 (1906). One of the earliest pictures of mythical creatures associated with the 12 months is on the Chu Silk Manuscript dating from the third century BC (18.2). See Liu Xinfang 劉信芳, "Zhongguo zuizao de wuhou liyue ming" 中國最早的物候曆月明 (The earliest names for Chinese signs for the months), *Zhonghua wenshi luncong*, 53: 75-107 (1994).

Table 10: The Twelve Animal Signs

Zhi 支	Animal signs shengxiao 生肖	Zhi 支 (cont.'d)	Animal signs (cont.'d)
zi 子	shu 鼠 rat	wu 午	ma 馬 horse
chou 丑	niu 牛 ox	wei 未	yang 羊 sheep
yin 寅	hu 虎 tiger	shen 申	hou 猴 monkey
mao 卯	tu 兔 rabbit	you 酉	ji 鷄 cock
chen 辰	long 龍 dragon	xu 戌	quan 犬 dog
si 巳	she 蛇 snake	hai 亥	zhu 猪 pig

Finding the equivalent year in the Western calendar is relatively easy. Most dictionaries and encyclopaedias such as the *Hanyu da cidian* or the *Cihai* contain tables of dynasties, names of emperors, accession dates, and era names and cyclical characters. In addition, dozens of chronological tables (*nianbiao* 年表) are available, for example, Fang Shiming 方詩銘, *Zhongguo lishi jinian biao* 中國歷史紀年表, which is short but accurate (it was published as an appendix to the 1979 edition of the *Cihai*).[26] Chronological tables of the Warring States kingdoms and rebel dynasties are clearly indicated, as well as dates of accession and dates of adoption of *nianhao*. It covers 841 BC to AD 1911.

Zhongguo lishi niandai jianbiao 中國歷史年代簡表 is useful for looking up years and *nianhao* of all the main dynasties.[27] It is convenient because of its small size, but it does not have clear tables of complicated periods such as the Warring States and does not indicate the difference between accession and the adoption of the *nianhao*. It covers from 841 BC to AD 1911 and has an index of *nianhao*.

5.4.3 Republican Dating

Between 1903 and 1911 a number of Republican newspapers and revolutionaries used a dating system based on the years since the birth of the Yellow Emperor (Huangdi 黃帝). Because there was no

---

[26] *Zhongguo lishi jinian biao* (Tables of Chinese historical periods), Shanghai renmin, 1976; Shanghai cishu, 1980.

[27] *Zhongguo lishi niandai jianbiao* (Simplified tables of Chinese historical periods), Wenwu, 1973; 2nd ed., 1994; 12th prnt., 1998.

agreement as to when the Yellow Emperor was born, different papers carried different years (*Minbao* 民報 reckoned 1905 as 4603 while *Jiangsu* 江蘇 counted it as 4396).[28] On January 2 1912, the provisional president of the provisional government, Sun Yatsen brought the confusion to an end by decreeing that the 12th day of the 11th lunar month of the year of the Yellow Emperor 4609 was new year's eve 1911 according to the solar (Gregorian) calendar and that January 1st 1912 was the first day of the Republic, which would henceforth use the solar calendar and would count years successively from 1912. Thus 1913 is *Minguo er nian* 民國二年, 1914 is *Minguo san nian* 民國三年, and *Minguo 89* is the year 2000.[29]

After 1949, the People's Republic adopted the Western (Gregorian) calendar, but in Taiwan years are still officially counted by the *Minguo* method. Japan alone retains the reign name count.

5.5 Seasons, Festivals, and Vacations

5.5.1 Seasons

The year was divided according to the seasons (*shi* 時), which were accurately measured in ancient China. The oracle bones record spring and autumn (*chun* 春 and *qiu* 秋, also later used together as a compound meaning "time" and, later still, "year"). In the Chunqiu period, if not before, a more detailed system of four seasons (*sishi* 四時) developed based on the two solstices (*erzhi* 二至) and the two equinoxes (*erfen* 二分). The year itself was measured from winter solstice to winter solstice.

By the Former Han, each season was divided into six climatic periods (*qi* 氣) of fifteen days each (in treaty port English, "calendrical fortnights"). The 24 *qi* alternated between *zhongqi* 中氣 (the odd-numbered *qi* in Table 11, customarily translated as "medial *qi*") and *jieqi* 節氣 (the even-numbered joints, as of a bamboo, usually

---

[28] Comprehensive chronological concordances include a table of alternative Yellow Emperor years in use between 1903 and 1911; see, for example, *Xinbian Zhongguo sanqian nian liri jiansuobiao* 新編中國三千年曆日檢索表 (5.6, item 1), 344.

[29] Despite the simplicity of the *Minguo* system and its similarity with reckoning *nianhao* or counting years of age in *sui*, it is astonishing how often *Minguo* dates are miscalculated, especially in Chinese secondary sources (e.g., *Minguo er nian* 民國二年 is mistakenly given as 1914 instead of 1913).

translated as "nodal *qi* "). The system as a whole was known as the 24 *jieqi* 節氣.

The eight main climatic periods at the beginning and middle of each season were known as the *bajie* 八節.

Table 11: The Jieqi 節氣 System

	Jieqi	*Translation*	*Western Calendar*	*Chinese Calendar*
1	*Dongzhi* 冬至	Winter Solstice	22 or 23 Dec.	十一中
2	*Xiaohan* 小寒	Slight Cold	6 or 7 Jan.	十二節
3	*Dahan* 大寒	Great Cold	21 or 22 Jan.	十二中
4	*Lichun* 立春	Start of Spring	4 or 5 Feb.	正月節
5	*Yushui* 雨水	Rain Water	19 or 20 Feb.	正月中
6	*Jingzhe* 驚蟄	Waking of Insects	6 or 7 March	二月節
7	*Chunfen* 春分	Spring Equinox	21 or 22 March	二月中
8	*Qingming* 清明	Pure Brightness	5 or 6 Apr.	三 etc.
9	*Guyu* 穀雨	Grain Rain	20 or 21 Apr.	
10	*Lixia* 立夏	Start of Summer	6 or 7 May	四
11	*Xiaoman* 小滿	Forming of Grain	21 or 22 May	
12	*Mangzhong* 芒種	Grain in Ear	6 or 7 June	五
13	*Xiazhi* 夏至	Summer Solstice	22 or 23 June	
14	*Xiaoshu* 小暑	Slight Heat	7 or 8 July	六
15	*Dashu* 大暑	Great Heat	23 or 24 July	
16	*Liqiu* 立秋	Start of Autumn	8 or 9 Aug.	七
17	*Chushu* 處暑	Limit of Heat	23 or 24 Aug.	
18	*Bailu* 白露	White Dew	8 or 9 Sept.	八
19	*Qiufen* 秋分	Autumn Equinox	23 or 24 Sept.	
20	*Hanlu* 寒露	Cold Dew	9 or 10 Oct.	九
21	*Shuangjiang* 霜降	Frost's Descent	24 or 25 Oct.	
22	*Lidong* 立冬	Start of Winter	8 or 9 Nov.	十
23	*Xiaoxue* 小雪	Slight Snow	23 or 24 Nov.	
24	*Daxue* 大雪	Great Snow	7 or 8 Dec.	十一

Note: Bold figures indicate the *bajie* 八節. Spring, summer, autumn, and winter start at 4, 10, 16, and 22.

From AD 520, a more refined system of dividing each *qi* into three periods of five days known as the 72 *hou* 候 was made part of the official calendar. On the phenological basis for the *jieqi* and the *hou*, and subsequent adjustments to them to take account of the shift of the center of farming to the different climatic conditions of southern China, see 35.1.1.

Both *qihou* 氣候 and *shihou* 時候 were normally used in the sense of "climate." *Shihou* was used in the sense of "time" only from about the Song.

The *jieqi* system was adopted in Korea, Japan, and Vietnam with the same terms for the four seasons and their subdivisions.

5.5.2   Festivals

Festivals (*jieri* 節日) in China, as elsewhere, served to celebrate, commemorate, reenact, or preview great events whether agricultural, religious, social, or political. The timing of the earliest festivals was set by the seasons of the year and by the food production cycle of north China. There was thus a direct connection between the main *jieqi* 節氣 and the *jieri* 節日. The festivals were linked to the worship of the soil, of fertility, and of the ancestors. The ordering of the annual festivals that took place in the Han dynasty remained basically unaltered for the next 1,000 years. The changes were in the form of additions and adaptations from Buddhism (and to a lesser extent, Daoism). Long after the Han, there were no fixed dates, only rough times according to season. Gradually the practice developed of holding the main festivals on odd days of odd-numbered months (these being considered male and lucky). The imperial government sought to truncate and adapt the festivals and also influenced them by fixing the civil calendar and announcing the dates of the main festival days. In addition to the better known festivals there were many others, both national and local, and a huge number of special days marking the birth of various gods.[30]

As the center of gravity of Chinese life shifted in the Song, many of the festivals were adapted once again, this time to the different customs and climate of the south. An obvious example is the association of Qu Yuan 屈原 and dragon-boat racing with the Duanwu 端午 festival. The main festivals of today are the direct descendants of those of the Song. By the Ming and Qing, the three

---

[30] For the annual festivals observed in the Han, see Derk Bodde, *Festivals in Classical China: New Year and Other Annual Observations During the Han Dynasty, 206 BC–AD 220*, PUP, 1975.

On the Hungry Ghost Festival (7/15), see Stephen F. Teiser, *The Ghost Festival in Medieval China*, PUP, 1988; on a festival for warding off epidemics, see Paul R. Katz, *Demon Hordes and Burning Boats: The Cult of Marshall Wen in Late Imperial Chekiang*, SUNY, 1995.

main festivals of the year were known as the *san dajie* 三大節 (marked with an asterisk in Box 3).

Box 3: Seven Main Annual Festivals in Late Imperial China

1/1*	*yuandan* 元旦 (Lunar New Year; *chunjie* 春節, Spring Festival)
1/15	*yuanxiao jie* 元宵節 (Lantern Festival)
3/early	*qingming jie* 清明節 (Grave-sweeping Festival)
5/5*	*duanwu jie* 端午節 (Dragon Boat or Double Fifth Festival)
8/15*	*zhongqiu jie* 中秋節 (Mid-autumn or Moon Festival)
12/23	Zao Wangye 竃王爺 (Kitchen God); 12/24 in the south
12/29	*chuxi* 除夕 (Lunar New Year's Eve); or on 12/30

The literati not infrequently recorded their observations of annual festivals (*suishi* 歲時, *shiling* 時令) usually chronologically arranged for each of the 12 months of the year. They also recorded popular customs (*fengsu* 風俗, *fengtu ji* 風土紀). Such works were either printed separately for a locality or region or were included as a chapter or two of the local gazetteer or put in their *biji* (miscellaneous notes, see Chapter 31).[31] The earliest extant example is the *Fengsu tongyi* 風俗通義 (*ICS Concordance* 43). A Northern Song example is found in the second part of Meng Yuanlao 孟元老 (fl. 1110–60), *Dongjing menghua lu* 東京夢華錄, which is a *suishi ji* for the capital (see 47.2, under *Biji*). A late Qing example of the genre was translated by Derk Bodde, *Annual Customs and Festivals in Beijing as Recorded in the Yen-ching Sui-shi-chi* [燕京歲時記], Henri Vetch, 1936; SMC, rpnt., 1977, 1994.

5.5.3 Vacations

The main festivals in traditional China extended over many days, sometimes for up to a month in winter (the slack farming season). Officially, the total varied from dynasty to dynasty, and the practice in the countryside and in the administrative centers must also have been very different. In the Tang, the official total of festival days

---

[31] See, for example, Weipang Chao's translation of the description of the dragon-boat festival in Hunan by Yang Sichang 楊嗣昌 (1588–1641) "The Dragon Boat Race in Wuling, Hunan," *Folklore Studies* 2: 1–18 (1943). Also translated in *Chinese Civilization: A Sourcebook* (8.1), 208–10.

was 53 with a maximum of seven days off for any one festival. Periods of up to three years mourning were laid down at the death of a parent. Other periods of leave were granted for important family occasions such as the coming of age of a son. On official holidays and office hours as well as business and working hours, see Liensheng Yang, "Schedules of Work and Rest in Traditional China."[32] Yang shows that official days of rest were gradually reduced from one every five days in the Han to one in 10 in the Tang to the Yuan and none in the Ming and Qing.

5.6 Date Conversion

Several calendrical concordances (*libiao* 曆表 or *liri duizhaobiao* 曆日對照表) are available. They give year, month, and day in cyclical characters and their equivalent in the Western calendar (using the modern Gregorian calendar even for pre-1582 dates). A good concordance will also indicate intercalations, *jieqi* (climatic periods, see Table 11), *nianhao*, and Julian calendar days and much else besides. Some concordances also record dates in the Buddhist, Muslim, Yi, Dai, and other calendars (5.7). Before using any of the concordances, it is essential to read the compiler's introductory remarks to find out what conventions have been followed, for example, how to allow for the zero year between 1 BC and AD 1 in the Western calendar, which of the pre-Qin calendars has been used for calculating pre-Qin dates and where the intercalary months have been inserted. Three of the most comprehensive and accurate are:

1. *Xinbian Zhongguo sanqian nian liri jiansuobiao* 新編中國三千年曆日檢索表 (New search tables for 3,000 years of Chinese calendar days), Xu Xiqi 徐錫祺, ed., Renmin jiaoyu, 1992. This gives the cyclical characters for the year, *nianhao*, and first day of each month (Chinese calendar) from 1500 BC to AD 2050 (between 1500 and 723 BC, the year is given starting with the month containing the winter solstice and ending with the thirteenth month). From 722 BC, to AD 53, the *xingci* 星次 name is indicated and, from 402 BC, also the *sui* 歲 name. After AD 53, these were no longer used. Intercalary months are indicated throughout. There are additional columns for the rulers and reign names of Japan (660 BC–AD 1990), as well as for the differ-

---

[32] *HJAS* 18: 301–25 (1955), rpnt. in his *Studies in Chinese Institutional History*, Harvard-Yenching, 1961, 3rd prnt., 1969; Hongqiao, 1975, 18–42.

ent Korean (207–111 BC; 57 BC–AD 1910) and Vietnamese (208–109
BC; AD 544–1945) kingdoms. From 1500 BC to AD 616, each page has
12 years; from 616 to 2050, there are 10 years to a page (to fit in the
Muslim calendar starting in 622). There are separate tables for the
chronologies of the Spring and Autumn and Warring States duke-
doms and kingdoms, as well as for the later independent kingdoms in
China, including Rouran 柔然 (464–520), Karakhoja (Qoco, Gaochang 高昌, 531–640), Bohai 渤海 (698–925), Nanzhao 南詔 (649–
902), Dali 大理 (937–1254), Tufan 吐蕃 (Tibet, 815–?), Northern
Liao 北遼 (1122–23), Western Liao 西遼 (1124–1211), and the Taiping 太平 (1851–68). One of the appendixes gives the three different
Yellow Emperor dating systems used between 1903 and 1911. The
archeoastronomer Zhang Peiyu (the author of item 3 below) provides a table of calculated winter solstice dates between 1500 BC and
AD 2050 (305–16). The appendixes give detailed and useful supplementary information often lacking from earlier calendrical concordances, e.g., tables of the different names used for the months; festivals in the Buddhist, Daoist, Muslim, and Christian calendars; minor
festivals in the Chinese calendar; a table of different terms for dividing the day according to 14 different sources; a list of 94 calendars
promulgated between the third century BC and AD 1852 (including
some that were not implemented); brief notes on 30 different era systems, including the Christian, Muslim, Japanese, Korean, Buddhist,
Burmese, Jewish, Zoroastrian, Coptic, Egyptian, Babylonian, Olym-
pian, Roman, Seleucid, Byzantine, Nepalese, and Saptashi; and a table
of the dates of adoption of the Gregorian calendar by 26 selected
countries. There are separate indexes (*pinyin*, stroke-count, and four-
corner) of era and reign names, both for China and for independent
kingdoms and neighboring states.

2. *Zhongguoshi liri he Zhong Xi liri duizhao biao* 中國史曆日和中西曆
    日對照表 (Chinese historical calendar days and a calendrical concor-
    dance of Chinese and Western days), Fang Shiming 方詩銘 and Fang
    Xiaofen 方小芬, eds., Shanghai cishu, 1987. The compilers have
    made good use of earlier calendrical concordances, the mistakes in
    eight of which are noted at the dates where they occur. They have
    also taken into account recent archaeological discoveries. Through-
    out all the tables, the format is the same: four years to the page with
    the first day of each of the three 10-day periods (*xun* 旬) of each lunar
    month shown (there is a table listing the 60 *ganzhi* on page 880 to as-
    sist finding the *ganzhi* for other days). Part I covers the years 841 to 1
    BC with the date (year, month, day) in the Chinese calendar and the
    ganzhi equivalents. Appendixes contain a daily concordance for the
    Yin calendar covering 1384 to 1112 BC; for the Western Zhou calen-

dar for the years 1111 to 842 and for the Former Han (Yin) calendar for the years 206–105 BC. Part II is arranged in the same way for the years AD 1 to 1949, but adds the Western calendar month and day equivalents. The dates of accession and adoption of *nianhao* are noted. The Taiping calendar is given. An appendix covers the years 1949 to 2000 with the Western calendar as the base. There is an index of *nianhao* by stroke count.[33]

3. *Sanqian wubai nian liri tianxiang* 三千五百年曆日天象 (3,500-year calendar of heavenly phenomena), Zhang Peiyu 張培瑜, comp., Henan jiaoyu, 1990; rpnt., Dajia, 1997. This enormous calendar cum astronomical table was compiled by a historian of Chinese astronomy. It is divided into two main parts. The first begins with a table of intercalary months for the Spring and Autumn period (722–480 BC). This is followed by a table of intercalary days for the years 221 BC to AD 2050. There are six years to a page, showing the first day of every month and the dates of each of the eight nodal climatic periods (*bajie* 八節). From 104 BC, all 24 of the climatic periods are given). The second part (astronomical) has tables showing the date and time in hours and minutes of the new and full moons for every month from 1500 BC to AD 2000; the date and time of the beginning of the eight nodal periods; the magnitude and different times at which the midpoint of solar eclipses could have been seen from 13 of the main cities of China from 1500 BC to AD 2500. Appendixes show the differences in intercalations used during the Three Kingdoms, the Nan-Bei Chao, and the Song, Liao, and Jin; and lunar eclipses as they would have been seen from Anyang during the years 1500–1000 BC. There is an index of era and reign names.[34]

There are many calendrical concordances for particular periods that are usually more detailed than those covering the whole sweep of Chinese history (see under *Chronology* in 13.3, 44.6, 46.5, 49.5, and 50.10.4).

---

[33] One of the earlier tables corrected by Fang and Fang is Dong Zuobin 董作賓, *Zhongguo nianli zongpu* 中國年曆總譜 (Chronological tables of Chinese history), 2 vols., HKUP, 1960. Vol. 1 contains tables up to 1 BC and vol. 2 contains tables from AD 1 to 2000.

[34] For computer-generated maps of China for the extrapolated positions from which each solar eclipse could have been seen in China between 1500 BC and AD 1900, see F. R. Stephenson and M. A. Houlden, *Atlas of Historical Eclipse Maps in East Asia*, CUP, 1986; and F. R. Stephenson, *Historical Eclipses and Earth's Rotation*, CUP, 1997.

5.7 Buddhist, Muslim, Dai, Yi, and Tibetan Calendars

The Buddhist era (*Buddhasakaraj*) begins in 543 BC (the year in which the Buddha attained nirvana) and counts consecutively from then on: so the year 2340 is 1796 (which, following the Chinese calendar, began on the ninth of the second lunar month).

The Muslim calendar (Huili 回曆) is a lunar calendar. It begins with the day after the Flight (Hegira) of Mohammed to Medina, July 16, AD 622, and counts consecutively from then on. Because years in the Muslim calendar are shorter than in the Western or Chinese calendar, the year of Mohammed 1211 (which began on the seventh of the seventh lunar month) is 1796. The Muslim calendar is included in standard chronological concordances (see 5.5).[35]

The Dai calendar (Daili 傣曆) starts on the first day of the seventh month (March 21) AD 638, and counts consecutively from then on, so the year 1,158 (which began on the sixth of the seventh Dai month, i.e., April 12) is 1796.

The Yi 彝 used two different calendars, one a 12-month lunar calendar, the other a 10-month solar calendar in both of which they counted years according to their own system. So 1796 is the Southwest Year (which began on the nineteenth [pig day] of the first Yi month).

Various calendars based on Chinese and Indian models were used in Tibet until the adoption in 1027 of a cycle of sixty based on the Five Phases (metal, wood, water, fire, and earth) and the twelve animals. This dating system was extended backward to the foundation of the first Tibetan kingdom in 627. The year 1796 is the fire dragon year (following the Chinese calendar, it began on the ninth of the second lunar month).

Calendrical Concordances

Zhongguo minzushi renwu cidian 中國民族史人物辭典 (40.4, *Biographies*) contains a 150-page chronological concordance of non-Han dynasties

---

[35] Two pioneering works often encountered in Western libraries are Dong Zuobin (1960) and *Zhong-Xi Huishi rili* 中西回史日曆 (A comparative daily calendar for Chinese, Western, and Islamic history, AD 1 to 1940), Chen Yuan 陳垣, comp., Yanjing daxue, 1926; rev. edition, Zhonghua, 1962. Both have been superseded by the references at the end of this section.

and regimes that ruled in China, as well as their genealogical tables, 617–805.

Zhonghua tongshi da lidian 中華通史大曆典 (Comprehensive concordance of calendrical tables of Chinese history), Wang Kefu 王可夫 and Li Min 李民, eds., 3 vols., Sichuan minzu, 1996. This is the most detailed concordance matching the main ethnic calendars with the Chinese and Western calendars. In the course of 4,600 pages and three large volumes, it tabulates each day individually (from 1500 BC). There is a great deal of supplementary information, including notes on the major events each year for the years 717 BC to AD 1990. Intercalary months and Julian days are given throughout, as well as a finding code for the *ganzhi* characters for the first day of every month.[36] In addition, the tables show for the legendary years 2674 to 1501 BC: *ganzhi*; traditional rulers; estimates from Dong Zuobin, the *Zhushu jinian*, and other sources; 1500 to 841 BC: traditional rulers; estimations of dates by various scholars; Zhou fiefs and their capitals; temple and posthumous names; 840 BC to AD 2000: rulers (including rulers of kingdoms and fiefs); capitals; temple and posthumous names; calculated days of the month and days of the week. Muslim dates are added from 622, and Tibetan dates are added from 1027. There is table comparing dates in the Western, Taiping, Dai, two Yi, and Russian calendars for the years 1804–2000 (the Russian calendar is not shown from March 1918, when the Western calendar was introduced in the newly established Soviet Republic). Appendixes contain very full tables of the rulers of each dynasty, including those of lesser kingdoms and usurpers and leaders of armed uprisings. There are also annotated lists of tribes and non-Han peoples active in each dynasty with the names of all their rulers when known.

Gong Nong Hui Dai Yi Zang Fo he Rulüeri duizhao biao 公農回傣彝藏佛和儒略日對照表 (Comparative calendar for Western, Chinese, Muslim, Hui, Dai, Yi, Tibetan, Buddhist calendars, and Julian day numbers, AD 622 to 2050), Wang Huanchun 王煥春 et al., comps., Kexue, 1991. A convenient calendrical concordance especially for the period 1840 to the present. The years 622 to 1839 are tabulated in the seven different calendars of the title (taking the Western calendar as the ba-

---

[36] The Julian day calendar system of astronomical dates counts day 1 as starting from noon of Jan. 1st, 4713 BC, a date that precedes all civil calendars. Conversion into Julian days enables comparison between different calendrical systems. Do not confuse Julian days *Rulüeri* 儒略日 with the Julian calendar, *Rulüeli* 儒略曆. Julian days were invented in 1582 when the Julian calendar was replaced with the Gregorian.

sis) plus the day on which New Year's Day fell in the Chinese, Muslim, Yi, and Dai calendars. The main part shows day equivalents (six months to a page) in the Western, Chinese, Muslim, and Dai calendars between 1840 and 2050. In addition, the Western calendar equivalents for New Year's Day in the Yi 10-month solar calendar are shown. Julian day calendar dates are given throughout. Given the clear layout, conversion from any one of the calendars to another is easily done for the modern period. *Ganzhi* characters, *jieqi*, and days of the week are also shown. Appendix 1 gives chronological tables of Chinese, Japanese, Korean, and Vietnamese reign names from 1516 to 1949 (478–91).

5.8   Japanese, Korean, and Vietnamese Calendars

Japanese-style dating works in a similar manner to the Chinese system. Lists of emperors' accession dates and era names (*nengô*) can be found in most Japanese-English dictionaries and the calendrical concordances introduced in 5.5. Japan switched from its lunisolar calendar to the Gregorian calendar on January 1, 1873. A seven-day week was introduced at the same time.[37]

Korea adopted the Chinese calendar in the seventh century and used the era names (*yanho*) of its emperors for dating. From the seventeenth to the nineteenth centuries Qing *nianhao* were used on official documents. Some, however, continued to use the era name of the last Ming emperor, Chongzhen 崇禎 (Sungjong) up to the beginning of the twentieth century. From 1894 to 1896, years were dated from the foundation of the Chosŏn dynasty (thus 1896 was called *Kaeguk* 開國 505). From 1896 to 1910, Korean reign titles were used. Thereafter, from 1911 to 1946, Japanese era names were

---

[37] The most popular pocket-sized Japanese chronological table giving Chinese, Japanese and Korean equivalents to the Western calendar is the long-lived *Tôhô nenpyô* 東方年表 (Chronological tables of Oriental history), Fujishima Tatsurô 藤島達郎 and Nogami Shunjô 野上俊静, comps., Heirakuji, 1955; 3rd rpnt., 1996. A large-format edition was issued in 1996. This table covers dynasties that ruled in China, Korea and Japan (including the kingdom of Bohai and Manchukuo), but not Warring States kingdoms or rebel dynasties. It manages to indicate graphically when there is a difference between the date of adoption of a *nianhao* and the date of accession. Dates covered are 660 BC to AD 1995. There is an index of rulers arranged chronologically as well as an index of *nianhao* arranged by country.

imposed. After the foundation of the two Koreas in 1948, the Gregorian calendar was used (it had been introduced in 1910). The Korean calendar (*Tan'gi* 檀紀, based on the accession of the mythical founder, Tan'gun 檀君 in 2333 BC), was occasionally used between 1897 and 1910 and again from 1948 to 1961 (to convert to Western years subtract 2,333; e.g., 4332 is 1999).

Until 1306, the Vietnamese used the Chinese calendar and Chinese *nianhao*. After 1306, they used the Chinese calendar and their own *niên-hiêu*. From 1644 to 1812 they continued to use the Ming calendar. In 1812, they finally moved to the Qing calendar for lunar reckoning, having inaugurated the Western calendar for certain official purposes at the beginning of the Gia Long period in 1802.[38]

There are a number of tables comparing year dates in the calendars of China, Japan, Korea, and Vietnam.[39]

5.9   Events

Events such as wars, revolutions, reforms, incidents, and movements in Chinese history are usually referred to by four-character mnemonics, often using reign names or cyclical dates, for example:

Jingkang zhi luan 靖康之亂 (Fall of the Northern Song, 1126)
Wuxu bianfa 戊戌變法 (Reform movement of 1898)
Jiawu zhanzheng 甲午戰爭 (Sino-Japanese war, 1894–95)
Xinhai geming 辛亥革命 (1911 Revolution)

Because of a desire to be modern and also because of a declining familiarity with the cyclical dates, after the May Fourth Movement,

[38] Hguyen Ba Trac 阮伯卓, *Hoang Viet Giap Ty Nien Bieu* 皇越甲子年表, Hanoi, 1925; expanded and improved version, National Education Minstry, Saigon, 1963.

[39] *Zhongguo Riben Chaoxian Yuenan siguo lishi niandai duizhaobiao* 中國日本朝鮮越南四國歷史年代對照表 (Comparative table of the historical periods of China, Japan, Korea, and Vietnam), compiled and published by Shanxisheng tushuguan 山西省圖書館, 1979. Covers 660 BC to AD 1918. Many Western libraries may still have older works, such as Mathias Chang, *Synchronismes chinois: Chronologie complète et concordance avec l'ère chrétienne de toutes les dates concernant l'histoire de l'Extrême-Orient (Chine, Japon, Corée, Annam, Mongolie, etc.), (2375 av. J.C.–1904 apr. J.C.)*, Variétés Sinologiques 24, Shanghai, 1905; rpnt., Taipei, 1967.

events are normally referred to by an abbreviation of their newstyle
dates, not by the cyclical characters, as in

Wusi yundong 五四運動 (May Fourth Movement, 4-5-1919)
Wusa yundong 五卅運動 (May Thirtieth Movement, 30-5-1925)
Qiqi shibian 七七事變 (Marco Polo bridge incident, 7-7-1937)

Equally common is the use of four-character descriptive phrases
(sometimes, as in the first example from the *Shujing*, ancient ones),

Pan Geng qian Yin 盤庚遷殷 (Pan Geng moves the capital to Yin)
Shang yang bianfa 商鞅變法 (Shang Yang reforms, 356 BC)
Chu Han zhanzheng 楚漢戰爭 (Chu-Han war, 206–201 BC)
Zhong Fa zhanzheng 中法戰爭 (Sino-French war, 1883–85)

Important events in modern history often have more than one
mnemonic, for example, *Lugouqiao shibian* 蘆溝橋事變 or *Qiqi shibian* 七七事變 (Marco Polo bridge incident); *Bayi qiyi* 八一起義 or
Nanchang qiyi 南昌起義 (Autumn harvest uprising, 1-8-1927). Particularly famous events can eventually acquire two-character abbreviations, for example, *Wusi* 五四 for the May Fourth Movement.

One of the largest of the many chronological tables of important events listed year by year is *Zhongguo lishi dashi biannian* 中國
歷史大事編年.[40]

Even the best Western chronological tables of events tend to pay
scant attention to China and the other countries of East Asia. Use a
Chinese publication such as *Zhongwai lishi nianbiao gongyuan qian
5000 nian–gongyuan 1918 nian* 中外歷史年表公元前 5000 年–公元
1918 年, which is one of the most comprehensive chronological tables of important events in China and the rest of the world.[41]

There are numerous chronological tables for special subjects
whose range at the best is broader than any available work in a
Western language. Take, for example, the *Shijie zhexueshi nianbiao*
世界哲學史年表, whose tables include not only all the main phi-

---

[40] *Zhongguo lishi dashi biannian* (Chronicle of main events in Chinese history), Zhang Xikong 張習孔 et al., eds., 5 vols., Beijing, 1987, 1988.

[41] *Zhongwai lishi nianbiao gongyuan qian 5000 nian–gongyuan 1918 nian*
(Chronological tables of Chinese and world history, 5000 BC to AD 1918), Qi
Sihe 齊思和, Liu Qige 劉啓戈, Nie Chongqi 聶崇岐, and Jian Bozan 翦伯贊,
comps., Zhonghua, 1958; 4th prnt., 1985.

losophers in the Western tradition, but also those in the Arabic, Chinese, Japanese, and Korean traditions. Apart from arranging year by year all world philosophers, including their works and their births and deaths, these tables add reference events under most years. The entries start with the birth of Thales in 624 BC and end in 1945. There is an index of names of non-Chinese philosophers with transcriptions into Chinese and another index by names in Chinese arranged by stroke count.[42]

Chronological tables of events for specific periods are listed in the appropriate section of Part V.

---

[42] *Shijie zhexueshi nianbiao* (Chronological tables of the history of world philosophy), Ma Cai 馬采 and Chen Yun 陳雲, comps., Shehui kexue, 1992.

6

Telling the Time

How days were divided into smaller units of time during different periods of Chinese history is a subject that attracted the attention of the leading Qing historians. They based their researches on historical and literary sources. Modern scholars have been able to add new evidence unearthed by archaeology and exploration, and have also reconstructed some of the main time-keeping instruments, such as the various types of water clock.[1]

Introduction

Three ways of dividing the day into smaller units were used in China before the introduction of the Western 24-hour system and mechanical clocks in the early seventeenth century (6.7):

1. Unequal divisions of the day (*shi* 時), mainly based on the position of the sun, but also set by daily routines such as mealtimes. The earliest evidence is on the Shang oracle bones. Time-telling would have been done by observing the position of the sun or of a shadow (6.1).

2. Ten watches; five during the daytime hours, five at night. The number of watches remained the same throughout the year; so they, too, were of unequal duration. The night watches were shorter, for example, in the summer than in the winter. The first evidence is from the Spring and Autumn period (6.2 and 6.3).

3. Twelve equal two-hour units based on the sun at noon (6.4). This was an absolute system, since the length of the hours was always the same. The hours were named after the 12 *chen* 辰 (mansions of the zodiac) and also after 12 of the ancient periods of the day (the *shi* of

---

[1] For the Han clepsydra, see the references cited in section 6.2; also Joseph Needham, Wang Ling, and Derek Price, *Heavenly Clockwork: The Great Astronomical Clocks of Medieval China–A Missing Link in Horological Research*, CUP, 1960; rev. edition, 1986.

method 1). This system was in use by the end of the Warring States. It was officially promulgated during the Former Han, a time of improvements in the instruments for measuring time and of major calendrical reform. The double "hours" were for many centuries called *chen* or *shi* and, from the Song, also *ke* 刻. Today the term is *shichen* 時辰.

All three methods were in use together from at least the third century BC. After the Han, officials increasingly kept time by the *chen* during the day; officials as well as ordinary people in the towns and cities were kept aware of the time by the drum and gong beats of the watch patrols. But in the villages, as well as in the towns and cities, the position of the sun (or of a shadow) during the day and the stars and moon at night remained, as they had been at least since the Shang, the normal way of indicating the passage from one division of the day to the next (the many ways of referring to the time during the empire are the subject of 6.6). Different ways of trying to make the 10 watches fit with the 12 *chen* are outlined in 6.5.

The main instrument used for measuring time until the seventeenth century was the water clock (clepsydra), which counted 100 *ke* 刻 (eighths) every 24 hours (6.2). In addition, all sorts of other instruments were used for measuring the continuous passage of time (or for measuring lapsed time), such as incense sticks or coils, incense seals (*xiangyin* 香印), moondials (*yuegui* 月晷), sand clocks, and graduated candles (*kezhu* 刻烛). Sundials (*rigui* 日晷) were for the day. Typically, perpetual lamps (*changdeng* 長燈), lit with a wick floating in a sea of oil or butter, were used in temples and tombs.[2]

---

[2] For the history of time keeping in imperial China from the Han to the Ming, see Wang Lixing 王立興, "Jishi zhidu kao" 記時制度考 (An examination of the methods of recording the time), *Zhongguo tianwenxueshi wenji* 中國天文學史文集 (Collected articles on the history of Chinese astronomy), Kexue, vol. 4, 1988, 1–47. The author was joint editor in chief of the major collection of records of celestial phenomena in imperial China and bases his analysis on them (*Zhongguo gudai tianxiang jilu zongji* 中國古代天象記錄總集; 5.1.2). For a collection of 2,500 time-related words and expressions used in Chinese historical sources, see Wang Haifen 王海棻, *Jishi cidian* 記時詞典 (Dictionary of recording time), Anhui jiaoyu, 1999. For the larger context, see David S. Landes, *Revolution in Time*, Belknap Press of HUP, 1985; rev. and enl., 2000.

6.1　Divisions of the Day in the Shang and Zhou

日出而作日入而息 (When the sun comes out, work; when the sun goes down, rest), *Zhouli* 周禮 (Rites of Zhou)

No doubt the earliest division of the day in China was into three unequal periods: morning, afternoon, and night, as measured by sunrise, noon, and sunset. By the Shang, there is evidence on the oracle bones that the hours of light were divided into a number of unequal units (*shi* 時), but a trace of the basic threefold division remained, in that the night was still regarded as basically one unit (*xi* 夕). The daylight units were measured by the position of the sun and also based on the two mealtimes—*dashi* 大食 at about 0800–0900 and *xiaoshi* 小食 at about 1600–1700 (Box 4). There were 10 main time divisions dividing the day into nine periods.[3]

Box 4: Shang Time

1. *nong* 農 (pre-dawn; later *liming* 黎明)
2. *ming* 明, *dan* 旦 (dawn), *zhao* 朝 (early morning), *dacai* 大采 (great brightness)
3. *dashi* 大食 (main meal)
4. *zhongri* 中日 or *rizhong* 日中 (midday)
5. *ze* 昃 (early afternoon; lit. the sun past the meridian)
6. *xiaoshi* 小食 or *guo* 郭, *guoxi* 郭兮 (supper)
7. *hun* 昏 (dusk), *mo* 莫 or *xiaocai* 小采 (small brightness), *mu* 暮 (nightfall)
8. *shu* [?] 杭 (a brand; early evening time)
9. *zhu* 住 (sleep)
10. *su* 夙 (the period before the sun has risen)

---

[3] Altogether there are at least 26 different terms for times of the day on the oracle bones. But there is no agreement as to how many time periods they demarcate because the inscriptions from each period use slightly different terms and there are variants in each period; see Chang Yuzhi 常玉芝, *Yin-Shang lifa yanjiu* 殷商曆法研究 (Research on the Yin-Shang calendar), Jilin wenshi, 1998, 135–80. Chang suggests (citing *Guoyu* 國語, "Luyu 魯語") that different terms may have been used by different social ranks. For a comprehensive summary of the views of Chang and previous scholars, see *Jiaguxue yibai nian* 甲骨學一百年 (15.5), 665–70.

It was a seasonal system since the length of the time periods varied with the length of the day. Several of the periods seem to have fallen at the same or similar times to the daylight periods in common use in the Warring States and later fixed in the Former Han as beginning at 0700 and thereafter continuing at two-hour intervals until 1900 hours. The Shang diviners based their calendar and divisions of the day on close observation of the sun and the moon and the stars. No Shang instrument for measuring time has as yet been deciphered on the oracle bones and none has ever been unearthed, so there is no means of knowing how accurately they fixed the beginning and ending of the daily divisions. No doubt the most common method was by observing the length and direction of the shadow of the sun or the position of the sunbeams. There are references to the use in the Zhou of a stone stele placed in front of a wall. The sun shone through a special hole cut at the top of the stele marking the hours on the wall behind. The Mongolians also used the sunbeams (6.5.3) much as did the early American settlers with their noon mark.

In the Zhou period, a similar way of dividing the day seems to have been used as in the Shang. This was continued into the Spring and Autumn and Warring States periods, whose texts contain many scattered references to the by then familiar divisions of the day. The first evidence for a standardized naming system dates from the end of the third century BC (6.4). By that time the clepsydra (water clock) was used to measure segments of the night.

From the Shang through to the Former Han, the day (daytime, *zhou* 晝 plus nighttime, *ye* 夜) was reckoned to begin at dawn and continue through to the pre-dawn of the next day. In the Han, the idea of the day beginning at midnight (*yeban* 夜半) was introduced, but in daily life the old practice of counting the dawn as the beginning of the day continued. This is a matter on which there is still considerable scholar disagreement, although few consider the likelihood that different practices were followed, for example, by astronomers, the law, or the peasants.[4]

---

[4] For the differing views, see *Jiaguxue yibai nian* (15.5), 670–72.

6.2   The 100-Unit System

The earliest mechanical method of measuring the passage of time
was to divide the day and night into 100 equal units (*baike* 百刻). It
was probably introduced during the Warring States period. The instrument used was a simple clepsydra consisting of a water jar with
a small hole at the bottom. A measuring rod (*loujian* 漏箭) with a
float at its base was slotted through the lid of the jar to indicate the
time as it dropped with the water level. The first reference is in the
Zhouli, which mentions (in the context of military logistics) a jar-
filling official (*qiehu shi* 挈壺氏) charged with several functions, including setting up a water clock to time maneuvers and short, fixed
periods such as the length of the night watches or the wakes at funerals.[5] The military origin of the instrument is also suggested by
the use of the word for arrow for the measuring rod.

The measure used for the 100-unit system was linear in origin.
The Han clepsydras were about 23 centimeters in height, allowing
the insertion of a float stick the same length as a standard Han ruler,
divided into 10 *cun* and subdivided into 100 *fen*. By the Han, one
float stick was used for the daylight hours, another for nighttime.
Altogether 100 units were carved (*ke* 刻) onto the two float sticks,
hence the name *ke* 刻 (translated as "quarters" 2,000 years later
when the Western hour with its four parts was introduced to
China). From early days the practice developed of subdividing each
ke at first into 100 *fen* 分 and later into 60 *fen*. Expressions like *cun-
yin* 寸陰 (an inch of shadow),[6] meaning a short period of time, were

[5] *Zhouli*, "Xiaguan sima" 夏官司馬, 4. In the Qin and Han and in later dynasties, the official was called a *shuaigeng ling* [alt. *leigeng ling*] 率更令 (director
of the watches). Outflow clepsydras were used in ancient Babylon and Egypt
from the sixteenth century BC, and much later in Greece, and in Rome. The
Greeks designed a clepsydra capable of running non-stop for 24 hours in the
fourth century BC. Julius Caesar mentions his army's use of a clepsydra to
measure the length of the British night in *De bello gallico* (v. 13).

[6] The expression first appears in the *Huainanzi*, "Nandaoxun" 南道訓:
"The ancients did not value a span (*chi* 尺) of jade, but an inch of shadow, because time is difficult to get and easy to lose." The earliest known hand-held
device for measuring the length of the shadow of the sun (gnomon, *guibiao* 圭
表) dates from the Later Han. It has a 15-inch measure divided into 150 subunits. See Che Yixiong 車一雄, Xu Zhentao 徐振韜, and You Zhenyao 尤振
堯, "Yizheng Dong Han mu chutu tong guibiao de chubu yanjiu" 儀征東漢墓
Footnote continued on next page

derived from the instrument used to set the clepsydras since at least the seventh century BC, the shadow gnomon whose rule was also measured in decimal units (*cun* 寸). The Han sundials (*rigui* 日晷) or gnomon chronometers (*ribiao* 日表) had 69 radial lines carved on two-thirds of their surface, making a total of 68 segments, each segment taking up one-hundredth of the dial. The 100 units measured by the clepsydra were identical to the time measured by one segment on the sundial, i.e., about 14.4 modern minutes.[7]

The first extant clepsydras are three from the Han dynasty that were recently unearthed (two more are known from illustrations).[8] The earliest of the three dates from some time before 113 BC. All except one are single-chamber, outflow clepsydras in which the float stick sank as the water dripped out. The exception is the "chancellor's office clepsydra" (only illustrations have survived). It appears to have had two holes in the lid (one for water inflow and one for the float stick) and is therefore presumed to have been a two-chamber clepsydra capable of running continuously with constant refills to keep it going. At first it served as an inflow-type with the water dripping from a top chamber (which has not survived), then continued as an outflow-type after the spout was unblocked and the water was allowed to drip from it while the top chamber was filled again. In the Later Han and again in the Eastern Jin, more chambers were added to avoid the uneven water pressure of the old single- or double-chamber clepsydra and to enable the last chamber to serve as a more accurate inflow-type clepsydra (with the measuring rod rising as the water dripped in). The clepsydra was filled at dawn and at dusk. In winter, the water was heated in order to prevent it from freezing.

出土銅圭表的初步研究 (Preliminary research on a bronze gnomon excavated from an Eastern Han tomb), in *Zhongguo gudai tianwen wenwu lunji* (1988), 156–61.

[7] See Yan Linshan 閻林山 and Quan Hejun 全和鈞, "Lun woguo de baike jishi zhi" 論我國的百刻計時制 (On China's 100-quarter system of keeping time), *Kejishi wenji* 6: 1–6 (1980). The earliest gnomon chronometers to have been unearthed are three dating from the Former Han, one of which is on display at the Historical Museum in Beijing, another at the Royal Ontario Museum, Toronto, Canada.

[8] Chen Meidong 陳美東, "Shilun Xi Han louhu de ruogan wenti" 試論西漢漏壺的若干問題 (Preliminary discussion of some questions surrounding the Han clepsydras), in *Zhongguo gudai tianwen wenwu lunji* (1988), 137–44.

Officials at the Bureau of Astronomy in the capital from Han times to the early twentieth century were charged with the maintenance of the bureau's clepsydras, and the keeping and announcing of the hours (*shoushi* 授時, *baoshi* 報時). In most dynasties, after the sounding of the hour, its name was displayed on a tablet, either at the palace gates or at the drum tower or both.

Because there were always five watch periods (*gengci* 更次) during the night and five during the day, the length of the watch depended on the time of the year and on the place. In the pre-Qin, simple indicators were adopted as to the relative lengths of day and night according to the season. The formulation of summer (60:40), winter (40:60), spring and autumn (50:50) was gradually refined to eight adjustments (at the *bajie* nodal points). Then, in 130 BC, a more precise regulation was introduced, and the length of the float sticks had to be changed (*gaijian* 改箭) every 9 days (calculated on the basis that the length of the day varied by 20 *ke* over the 180 days between the winter and summer solstices). In AD 34, a second set of more precise rules was introduced requiring that a night float stick with an extra *ke* and a day stick with one less *ke* had to be used every 7.5 days. In 102, the 9-day rule was finally abolished, and a new regulation introduced to change the float sticks for every 2.4° declination of the sun. In 443, the regulation was made easier to apply by stipulating once again that the changes had to be made at each half-season (i.e., every 7.5 days), both for the day float stick and for the night one. The system therefore required 48 float sticks with different numbers of *ke* on each, but with the total on each night stick and its corresponding day stick always coming to 100. With minor modifications this method remained in use until the beginning of the Qing. One of the duties of the Bureau of Astronomy in drawing up the calendar was to calculate detailed tables of sunrise and sunset and the corresponding times of the night watches for each of the 24 climatic seasons (*jieqi* 節氣). These tables were published with the calendar.

In the history of Chinese time systems, just as in other spheres, it is worth asking the question to what extent were the regulations put into practice in different historical periods and in different places. During the Warring States, each kingdom no doubt kept its own time, just as it kept its own calendar. Strangely enough, time was one of the few measurements that the first emperor of the Qin and his chancellor did not unify, but from the Han standardization

onward, successive dynasties made every effort to apply the regulations and for three good reasons: astrological, security, and administrative. Accurate timekeeping was directly related to the precise recording and interpreting of celestial events. Second, the public announcement of the hours and an efficient watch system were basic
to the security of the imperial palace and the area immediately surrounding it, as well as to the offices of the central administration,
and of the capital itself. Dark, unlighted streets were considered so
dangerous that throughout Chinese history, just as in medieval
Europe, a night curfew was imposed (6.3). It was the same throughout the empire, where we know that in the provincial and county
towns, efforts were made to keep the time and to enforce the curfew, as also by the army, whether on garrison duty at the border or
on campaign. The third reason for accurate timekeeping was administrative: the wheels of the imperial bureaucracy required precise
timing. How precise is revealed on the bamboo documents (*jiandu*
簡牘) discovered at the northwestern border and elsewhere.[9] These
show that from the Han the exact time of the dispatch and arrival of
documents even in remote outposts was meticulously recorded
down to fractions of an hour "so as to expedite a reply" (compare
ancient Greece and Rome, where such accurate records were not
kept except for astronomical observations). Office hours had also to
be maintained. In some dynasties failure to arrive on time was pun-
ishable with a beating.

Nor was careful timekeeping limited to the civil and military
administrations at the capital city, in the provincial and county
towns and at the border. Simple clepsydras were used in the countryside: several poets wrote about the farm clepsydras (*tianlou* 田漏)
in the eleventh century, including Wang Anshi, who also noted the
use of drums and clepsydras in Sichuan to call villagers together and
to set the rhythm for their collective work in the fields. Early in the
fourteenth century, a county magistrate in north China compiled a
farming manual that contains instructions on how to set up a field
clepsydra "in order to time the work," i.e., to measure lapsed time,
like an hourglass.[10]

---

[9] Michael Loewe, *Records of Han Administration*, 2 vols., CUP, 1967, vol. 1
(44.4.3).

[10] For Song and Yuan references to clepsydras, see "Nongqi tupu" 農器圖
譜 14, in *Dong Lu Wangshi nongshu yizhu* 東魯王氏農書譯注 (Mr. Wang's of

Footnote continued on next page

But there were enormous practical difficulties. Even in the capital itself, as early as 762 the Tang official in charge of the security of the palace and the city memorialized that there was a gap of at least a *ke* between the announcement of the first night watch at the palace and the drum signaling its start in the suburbs.

Ever since the Warring States, the regulations stipulated different ways to adjust the watches to the different seasons. Given a recognized margin of error of at least 40 minutes in making these adjustments as well as the fact that local administrations, in many cases at different latitudes from the capital, had to set their own time and taking into account that the clepsydras, even after the Song improvements, cannot have been all that accurate, the empire must have been a huge patchwork quilt of local, idiorhythmic time zones even at the best of times.

Despite all the temporal and regional variations over 2,000 years, the general pattern for the announcement of time and the night watch patrols from the Han to the beginning of the Qing was maintained, in some cases right up to the 1930s.

During the day a drum was sounded five times: at dawn; at main mealtime (*xiagu* 下鼓, 13 *ke* after the lifting of the night curfew), at midday (*wugu* 午鼓 or *shigu* 市鼓), at the afternoon meal (*bugu* 晡鼓, 13 *ke* before the curfew drum), and at dusk. From at least the Tang, the official drum signaling the change of the hours was echoed in each ward or at every street corner. By the Song, the morning and afternoon meal drums had fallen into disuse except in the army. By the later empire, the 12-*chen* system had replaced the five day watches in most places, and only the dawn, noon, and dusk drums were sounded.

6.3   The Night Watch

In the pre-Qin, every kingdom, and under the empire, every dynasty, enforced a strict curfew (*yan'geng* 嚴更, *yanye* 嚴夜, or *jinye* 禁夜), especially in the capital. The potential danger came not only from bandits, thieves, and other disturbers of law and order, but also from the constant risk of accidental fires. The curfew began at nightfall (about 45 minutes after the first night watch was sounded

---

Eastern Lu [Wang Zhen 王禎] *Agricultural Treatise* translated [into Modern Chinese] with notes), Miao Qiyu 繆啓愉, tr., Shanghai guji, 1994, 709–10.

at dusk) and was announced by the dusk barriers drum (*muguan gu* 暮關鼓, *mugu* 暮鼓).[11] Thereafter, the city gates and the ward and street barriers were closed, and nobody was allowed to move about the town except the civil or military watch patrols. Exceptions were made in the summer months, when people were allowed to try and escape the heat indoors by sitting or sleeping outside, but only in their own street or ward. Exceptions for the pregnant or sick could be made throughout the year. There were strict prohibitions against climbing the city walls at night. During the curfew, no lighted fires were allowed (the night watch also performed the function of a fire patrol, part of its duties being to report those who kept a fire burning at night). Anyone found outside without an official lantern was challenged, "who goes there?" (*shei shei* 誰誰?). The curfew was lifted just before dawn by the beating of the dawn barriers drum (*xiaoguan gu* 曉關鼓).[12]

The responsibility for the night watch patrols in the capital was in the hands of the official, usually military, in charge of security. In the county towns and villages it was the local magistrate. Implementation was carried out by the various local self-governing units set up in different periods. In certain dynasties, for example, in the Southern Song, much of the system appears to have broken down. But it was reinstated on the foundation of the Yuan, and it was implemented during the Ming and the Qing.

The night was divided into five watches (*wuye* 五夜, *wugeng* 五更, or *wugu* 五鼓. From the Han, each watch period (*gengci* 更次) was subdivided into five smaller units called *dian* 點 (or *chou* 籌 or *chang* 唱).[13]

---

[11] In the Tang, 800 drumbeats were stipulated. In later dynasties, the number varied. By the Qing, showing the influence of Buddhism, it was 108.

[12] During the Tang, it was 3,000 drumbeats (to wake people up). The practice of blowing a trumpet or horn was also widespread. In the Southern Song capital at Hangzhou, it was the monks who woke people with clappers and announced the weather. From the Ming onward, a dawn cannon (*mingpao* 明炮) was fired at Nanjing, a practice that continued up to the 1930s.

[13] At first, the watches were counted using the *gan* characters (*jiaye* 甲夜, *yiye* 乙夜, *bingye* 丙夜 ...), but later numbers became more widespread (*chugeng* 初更, *ergeng* 二更, *sangeng* 三更 ...). For imaginative ways of keeping the watch operative in a county town and its surrounding villages in the 1670s, see Huang Liuhong 黃六鴻, *Fuhui quanshu* 福惠全書 as tr. by Djang Chu (27.6), 486–94.

In the capital and larger cities, the watch was sounded at the drum or bell tower (*gulou* 鼓樓, *zhonglou* 鐘樓) and in the wards in smaller cities, outside the yamens, or at the post station, or watch towers (*genglou* 更樓); in even smaller places, simply by the night watchmen on their rounds.[14] The time of the start of the first watch varied from about 1700 in winter to about 2000 (modern times) in the summer depending on the time of sunset.

The regulations laid down the number of drumbeats or bell tolls for each watch; local practice gave rise to different rhythms. By the end of the Qing, in Beijing, 108 drumbeats were sounded from the massive drum tower to the north of the palace at each of the five watches until the fifth watch (*wugeng* or *lianggeng* 亮更). The drumbeats were the signal for the 60-ton bell at the nearby bell tower to be tolled. This continued until 1924. Beijingers can still remember the characteristic pattern of "18 fast beats; 18 slow beats; 18 neither fast nor slow," which were repeated to make 108 beats in all.[15]

In large cities the clepsydra (*genglou* 更漏) was normally kept on the drum tower (*gulou* 鼓樓). In well-to-do private households as on the watch towers, the time was also measured with incense sticks (*gengxiang* 更香), one for each watch.

The watchmen sounded the changing of each watch (*gaigeng* 改更) with a drumbeat (*genggu* 更鼓) and the fifths of each watch with a clapper made of bamboo or wood (*tuo* 橐), or with a bell (*zhong* 鐘 or *zheng* 鉦), or gong (*luo* 鑼), or with a chanted phrase

---

[14] Referred to in the *Zhouli* and in the earlier dynasties as *siwu shi* 司寤氏 and by the later empire more commonly as *gengfu* 更夫, *gengren* 更人, or *jiren* 鷄人. At the end of the eighteenth century, the draftsman attached to the Macartney embassy, William Alexander, sketched a watchman with his bamboo rattle, probably in Canton, and recorded that "the barricades at the end of each street are kept shut [at night]," *Views of 18ᵗʰ-Century China*, Studio Editions, 1988, plate iv.

[15] The drum tower in Beijing still stands and is open to the public. It is a huge structure, 50 meters high. It was first built in 1272 and named the *qizheng lou* 齊整樓, "mustering for duty tower," because the morning drum was the signal for all government employees to assemble for the start of the workday. It housed 24 drums (2 meters high), one for each of the 24 seasons. Today only one remains, its skin slashed to shreds by the allied forces at the time of the Boxers. The bronze clepsydra (dating from the Song), fell out of use early in the Qing when official time switched to the Western twenty-four hour system.

(*chang* 唱). Thereafter they remained in touch throughout the night by beating their bamboo clappers, striking their gongs, or calling out to one another.

When Du Fu 杜甫 (712–770) wrote the lines that every school-child has had to learn since then, he was evoking ideal conditions, 好雨知時節，當春乃發生；隨風潛入夜，潤物細無聲 (A good rain knows its season, it brings things to life right in spring. It enters the night, unseen with the breeze; it moistens things gently and without sound).[16] Neither the poet nor anybody else could have spent a quiet night in a Chinese city, in Chengdu in the eighth century (where these lines were written) or at any other time or place, either in town, on the outskirts or in the countryside. Quite apart from all the noises of a pre-industrial age, people were more likely to have been woken by the cacophony of drums, gongs, bells, trumpets, rattles, and the night watchmen's chant. These may have made Chinese cities and villages more secure, but this practice also made them very noisy places, a fact remarked upon by most visitors to China (from Ennin and Sulaiman in the ninth century to Marco Polo in the thirteenth, Magalhaes in the seventeenth, and Macartney in the eighteenth). The conventional image is of the poet lying awake in the depths of the night (*gengshen* 更深) as the moon slowly glides past his window. It is a lonely and silent scene, save for occasional evocative sounds such as the snatch of a song, the notes of a lute, the sighing of a cassia in the breeze, the whisper of the spring rain, or the distant tolling of a bell. These single isolated sounds emphasize the overall silence. The poet's object in using such topoi was to trigger in his reader a refined and literary mood. It was not his intention to describe a particular, and therefore noisy, reality.[17]

6.4   The 12 Double-Hour System

From the Warring States, if not before, the 12 *dizhi* were correlated not only with the 12 stations of Jupiter but also with the 12 directions. The positions of the sun were correlated with the cardinal points (*sifang* 四方), and so sunrise, noon, sunset, and midnight

---

[16] Translation from *An Anthology of Chinese Literature, Beginnings to 1911*, ed. and tr. by Stephen Owen, Norton, 1996, 427.

[17] Qian Zhongshu, "Using Sound to Emphasize Silence," in *Limited Views: Essays on Ideas and Letters*, selected and tr. by Ronald Egan, HUP, 1998, 185–88.

were associated with the *dizhi* characters for E, S, W, and N, respectively, i.e., *mao* 卯, *wu* 午, *you* 酉, and *zi* 子 (Table 12). To this day the directions in Chinese follow the sun in this way (*dong* 東, *nan* 南, *xi* 西, *bei* 北). As a result, we refer, for example, to the Nan-Bei Chao 南北朝, not as we do in English to the "Northern and Southern Dynasties."

The first extant enumeration of the 12 periods of the day correlated with the 12 *chen* (named using the *dizhi*) is found in two popular almanacs dating from about 217 BC. Almanac 2 lists the *chen*, and almanac 1 has the first known list of the 12 animal signs linked to the 12 *chen* in almost the form still in use today. The almanacs were used for choosing lucky and avoiding unlucky days and hours. They were written on bamboo strips and discovered in 1975 at Yunmeng 雲夢 in the former kingdom of Chu in the central Yangzi region. Almanac 2 divides the day into 16, not 12, divisions. This may reflect a local Chu tradition or it may be further evidence that two systems of dividing the day coexisted from the Qin into the Han.[18]

In any event, it is likely that for several centuries two or more variants of naming the periods of the day co-existed in different parts of China (just as different calendars were used in the different kingdoms of the Warring States). The various existing terms for the divisions of day and night were standardized in the *chen* system introduced as part of the Taichu 太初 calendar reform in 104 BC. Alternative descriptive terms for the divisions of the day, many of them variants, had been widespread since the Shang, and many more developed over the centuries. A small selection are given in Table 12. Several of the old terms are still in use today, although often with slightly different meanings, e.g., *zaochen* 早晨, *zhongwu* 中午, and *bangwan* 傍晚. Many alternative terms, some of them ancient, have been retained in the dialects.

---

[18] Yu Haoliang 于豪亮, "Qinjian 'rishu' jishi jiyue zhu wenti" 秦簡日書 記時記月諸問題 (Questions relating to the recording of time and of months in the Qin and Han almanacs on bamboo strips) in *Yunmeng Qin Hanjian yanjiu* 雲夢秦漢簡研究 (Researches on the Qin and Han bamboo strips found at Yunmeng), Zhonghua, 1981, 351–57; Liu Lexian 劉樂賢, "Shuihudi Qinjian rishu yanjiu ershinian" 睡虎地秦簡日書研究二十年 (Twenty years of research on the Qin bamboo almanacs from Shuihudi), *Zhongguoshi yanjiu dongtai*, 10: 2–10 (1996). For further references, see 44.3.2.1 and 44.3.2.2.

Table 12: Chinese Hours in Imperial Times (12 chen 辰)

Chen 辰	Compass (Solstices; Months)	Descriptive Terms (English Translation)	Animal Signs for Hours	Modern Time (Night Watch; approx.)
zi 子	NORTH (Winter solstice; 11th month)	*yeban* 夜半 (midnight) (*wuye* 午夜) (*yewu* 夜午) (*ziye* 子夜) (*yefen* 夜分) (*zhongye* 中夜) (*yezhong* 夜中) (*binggeng* 丙更)	*shu* 鼠 rat	2300–0100 (*sangeng* 三更)
chou 丑	NNE	*jiming* 鶏鳴 (cock crow) (*huangji* 荒鶏)	*niu* 牛 ox	0100–0300 (*sigeng* 四更)
yin 寅	ENE	*pingdan* 平旦 (dawn) (*pingming* 平明) (*danming* 旦明) (*liming* 黎明) (*zaodan* 早旦) (*ridan* 日旦) (*zaochen* 早晨) (*zaozhao* 早朝) (*meishuang* 昧爽)	*hu* 虎 tiger	0300–0500 (*wugeng* 五更)
mao 卯	EAST (Spring equinox; 2nd month)	*richu* 日出 (sunrise) (*dianmao* 點卯) (*rishang* 日上) (*risheng* 日生) (*rishi* 日始) (*rixi* 日晞) (*xuri* 旭日)	*tu* 兔 rabbit	0500–0700
chen 辰	ESE	*shishi* 食時 (breakfast time) (*zaoshi* 早食) (*yanshi* 宴食)	*long* 龍 dragon	0700– 0900
si 巳	SSE	*gezhong* 隔中 (forenoon) (*yuzhong* 禺中) (*riyu* 日禺) (*riyuzhong* 日禺中)	*she* 蛇 snake	0900–1100
wu 午	SOUTH (Summer solstice; 5th month)	*rizhong* 日中 (noon) (*rizheng* 日正) (*riwu* 日午) (*rigao* 日高) (*zhongwu* 中午) (*tingwu* 亭午)	*ma* 馬 horse	1100–1300

Chen 辰	Compass (Solstices; Months)	Descriptive Terms (English Translation)	Animal Signs for Hours	Modern Time (Night Watch; approx.)
wei 未	SSW	ridie 日昳 (afternoon) (rice 日側) (rize 日昃) (rize 日仄)	yang 羊 sheep	1300–1500
shen 申	WSW	bushi 晡時 (supper time) (pushi 鋪食) (rixi 日夕) (xishi 夕食)	hou 猴 monkey	1500–1700
you 酉	WEST (Autumn equinox; 8th month)	riru 日入 (sundown) (rimo 日没) (richen 日沉) (rixi 日西) (riluo 日落) (riwan 日晚) (bangwan 傍晚)	ji 鷄 chicken	1700–1900
xu 戌	WNW	huanghun 黄昏 (sunset) (rimu 日暮) (rixun 日曛) (xunhuang 曛黄)	quan 犬 dog	1900–2100 (chugeng 初更)
hai 亥	NNW	rending 人定 (bedtime) (yinye 黟夜)	zhu 猪 pig	2100–2300 (ergeng 二更)

On the whole, the Han reformed system seems to have become the normative system by the beginning of the first century AD among officials. By the Tang dynasty, the 16 chen had disappeared, and the 12 chen were being taught in rhyming couplets to far-off peoples at the edge of the empire, as evidenced by several of the popular songs found in the Dunhuang temple library.

Since the Zhou, the day had been reckoned from midnight (yeban 夜半) to midnight, that is halfway through the first double-hour, which began at 2300.

From the Han, the division of the chen into two made a total of 24 small hours. The first was named chu 初; the second, zheng 正; and the end, mo 末. Thus shenchu 申出 (or bushichu 晡時初) meant 1500; shenzheng 申正 (or bushizheng 晡時正), 1600; and shenmo 申末 (or bushimo 晡時末), 1600–1700.

Another simplification was to use the 24 points of the compass to name each of the 24 hours (Table 13). This method was used for recording the times of celestial phenomena during the Wei, Jin, and

Nan-Bei Chao. By the Tang it had been forgotten and was only used by geomancers for selecting the grave site. By the Ming, the system had come back into use for recording the time, but the 24-hour cycle usually began not at *zichu*, but at *zizheng* (2400). Thereafter it was a simple matter to adapt this system to the 24-hour Western clock.

Table 13: The Compass Names for the 24 Hours

renshi 壬時	2300		*bingshi* 丙時	1100
zishi 子時	2400		*wushi* 午時	1200
guishi 癸時	0100		*dingshi* 丁時	1300
choushi 丑時	0200		*weishi* 未時	1400
genshi 艮時	0300		*kunshi* 坤時	1500
yinshi 寅時	0400		*shenshi* 申時	1600
jiashi 甲時	0500		*gengshi* 庚時	1700
maoshi 卯時	0600		*youshi* 酉時	1800
yishi 乙時	0700		*xinshi* 辛時	1900
chenshi 辰時	0800		*xushi* 戌時	2000
xunshi 巽時	0900		*qianshi* 乾時	2100
sishi 巳時	1000		*haishi* 亥時	2200

From the third century, it became common to divide the *chen* into "quarters" by adding *shao* 少 [*xiao* 小], *ban* 半 and *tai* 太 [*da* 大] after the hour, e.g., *shenshichu ban* for 1630 and *shenshichu tai* for 1645.

6.5   Using the 100-ke with the 12-Chen

One complication with the different systems of telling the time was that the 12 *chen* could not be divided into an equal number of *ke* (there being 100 *ke*, each *chen* lasted 9.3 *ke*). The *chen* themselves before the Tang were divided into 10 *fen* of 12 minutes each (one *ke* lasted 14.4 minutes). Clearly the 100-*ke* and the 12-*chen* were two systems of completely different origin. Not surprisingly, they coincided only four times in 24 hours (at midnight, 0600, midday and 1800). Efforts to resolve these problems by changing the number of *ke* to 120 (so every *chen* had exactly 10 *ke*), 96 (one *chen* equals eight *ke*) or 108 (one *chen* equals nine *ke*) failed on at least four separate occasions between 5 BC and AD 544. The grounds for refusal were not always the same, but the main argument was the conservative one: the 100-*ke* system had been used since time immemorial and therefore should not be tampered with. In the meantime, as in many other traditional societies, the different timekeeping systems ran in parallel and instead of reform, various compromises were found to make them work more easily together, each dynasty announcing a new system at the promulgation of its calendar.

From the Sui, it became common to place the odd one-third *ke* in every regular *chen* at the end of each *chen*. It was called a *xiaoke* 小刻. Another practice, again starting in the Sui, was to divide the *ke* into 60 *fen*, so that each *chen* had eight *ke* 20 *fen*. From the Han, and increasingly from the Tang, the *chen* were divided into two small hours (*xiaoshi* 小時), each of which had four regular *ke* of 14.4 minutes and 1 small *ke* of 2.4 minutes (popularly inserted at the beginning of the full hour, but officially placed at the end). In the Song, a clock was constructed that measured 96 intervals.[19] The practice also developed of showing both the 12 *chen* and the 100 *ke* on the clepsydra float stick. Thereafter the double-hour began to be called not only *shi*, but also *ke*. Eventually, 96 quarters (of 15 minutes each) replaced the 100 *ke* (of 14.4 minutes each) when the Western system was introduced by the Qing (6.4).

The difference between the 100-*ke* and the 12-*chen* systems has led some scholars to suppose that the 100-*ke*, which was the older of the two, was indigenous, while the 12-*chen* were imported from Babylon. If this were indeed the case, it might help explain the refusal to adapt the Chinese system to the imported one. But there is no evidence one way or the other. Most cultures have used vestiges of several different counting systems as a matter of custom, and some continue to do so to this day, however inconvenient this may be.[20] A more likely explanation is that the 100-*ke* system was origi-

---

[19] Needham, Wang, and Price (1986), 206–15, corrects accounts of Su Song's clock in *Mechanical Engineering* (*SCC*, vol. 4, part 2), 461. For reasons unexplained, Needham is a proponent of the Babylonian origin of the 12 *shi-chen* system (perhaps following Guo Moruo, the only senior Chinese scholar to do so).

[20] For example, in most parts of the world, units of time and angle measure inherited from a sexagesimal system coexist uneasily with a decimal system (and in America, they coexist with a third base unit system, the duodecimal, for linear measure). Thus it is not surprising that the Chinese used two systems of measuring time based on two of the different systems they used for counting, the decimal and the duodecimal.

nally used for measuring the lapse of a fixed length of time, like the five watches of the day or night or a military patrol. It was not originally intended to measure continuous stretches of time since it was not until the Han that an instrument capable of doing so became available.

The history of time keeping in China, as in other spheres, is a history of the official announcement and often official implementation of a new system while ordinary people continued to use previous ones to which they were accustomed. So in the Qing all official time records used the Western system but ordinary people (and the writers of novels) continued to use the 100-*ke* and 12-*chen* as they had developed in the Ming.

The main difficulty in understanding references to the time in Chinese sources is that there was no standard way of referring to it; dozens of terms were used, based on the three main systems of telling the time. Another difficulty is that it is not always clear whether the time phrase refers to a point in time or to a period of time. There were also special terms for special uses, such as recording the exact time of an eclipse or the hour of birth. Table 13 lists the names of the 24 hours, and 6.6, different ways of referring to the time.

6.6   Telling the Time (Han to Qing)

6.6.1   Alternative Expressions

There were no strict rules on how to tell the time, but to take as an example the ninth double-hour, *shen* (1500–1700), it could be called:

bushishen 晡時申
shenshi 申時 (from the Ming, this could also mean 1600)
shenke 申刻 (the expression becomes common from the eleventh century when the clepsydra float stick also had *chen* carved on; from the Ming, this could also mean 1600)
shen paishi 申牌時 (1500–1700 hours; lit. the "shen [hour] as displayed on the hour tablets" [at the drum tower or on street corners]. This was a common way of referring to the hour in novels)
bushi 晡時
houshi 猴時 (the hour of the monkey)

and subdivided for greater accuracy, e.g.:

shenshichu 申時初 (*shenchu* 申初): 1500

shenshizheng 申時正 (*shenzheng* 申正): 1600
shenshimo 申時末 (*shenmo* 申末): 1600–1700

with further subdivisions up to the Tang, e.g.:

shen liuke 申六刻: 1626, approximately
shenshichu erke 申時初二刻: 1528 (and 48 seconds)
shenshichu liangge xiaofen 申時初兩個小分: 1520 (a *xiaofen* was 10 minutes)

and further subdivisions after the Tang, e.g.:

shenshichusanke 申時初三刻 (*shenchusanke* 申初三刻): 1543
shenshizhengsanke 申時正三刻 (*shenzhengsanke* 申正三刻): 1645

6.6.2   Gengdian 更點 (*Watch Hours*)

The night hours in the earlier dynasties up to the Tang were usually referred to by the watch (*wugeng*) count (as were daylight hours):

yelou shangshui shike 夜漏上水十刻: 2 hours 24.4 minutes after the filling of the night clepsydra (or *yelou shang shike* 夜漏上十刻); later could be simplified to *sangeng* 三更

yelou weijin sanke 夜漏未盡三刻: 45.2 minutes before the end of the nightwatch

Note the expressions *ye* 夜少半 (before midnight) in contrast to *ye daban* 夜大半 (after midnight).

In order to convert nightwatch times to absolute times, you need to know the season of the year and where the reading was made. Instead of going through the monographs on the calendar in the Standard Histories (not all of which preserve full nightwatch tables), a good shortcut is to use the charts for converting watch hours to absolute hours in Wang Lixing (1988).

   After the Tang, it became common to refer to the night hours using the *chen* system.

6.6.3   Other Ways of Measuring the Passage of Time

Outside the house, in the fields or on the road, as in other peasant societies all over the world, to the question What time is it? the answer would most likely have been "Look at the sun." To the question How long does it take to the next village? the answer would have been, "The time it takes to eat a bowl of rice (or [hot, cold] meal);" "The time taken to burn a stick of incense;" "The time taken to smoke a pipe," or some such phrase. At this level, China was until the twentieth century a task-discipline rather than a time-discipline society.

One way of telling the time or of anticipating changes in the weather was to observe the behaviour of animals and birds; for example, by looking at the eyes of a cat. According to a late Qing writer on cats quoting a Tang source, at dawn and dusk, a cat's pupils are round like a mirror; at midmorning and midafternoon, they are elliptical like the stone of a date, and at midnight and noon, they are a slit.[21]

6.6.4 Horoscope Hours

Horoscopes required the *shengchen bazi* 生辰八字 or just *bazi* 八字 (the Eight Characters), that is, the *ganzhi* for the year, month, day, and hour of birth, so a *gan* character was added to the *zhi* name of the hour according to the *ganzhi* for the day of birth (there were mnemonics to assist in this task). Population records sometimes give the hour of birth, in which case the *chen* hour was used.

6.6.5 Neighboring Countries

The Chinese systems of telling the time continue to leave their mark in East Asia. Many countries there, including Korea, Japan, and Vietnam, adopted the 12 Chinese double-hours and still today use some of their names to describe different parts of the day and night.[22] In Mongolia, the Chinese double-hours were introduced after the Yuan, although most Mongols continued to judge the time from the position of the sunbeams shining through the *toono* (the hole at the apex of the *ger* [*yurta*]). For example, at midday the sun shone on the uppermost part of the wall of the *ger* opposite the door (which was always aligned with the south). It was under this

[21] Huang Han 黄漢, *Maoyuan* 猫苑 (Garden of cats), 1853, *juan* 1: 8b. Huang quotes the ninth-century *Youyang zazu* 酉陽雜俎 (46.2) as saying that at dawn and dusk a cat's eyes are round and at noon they are like a vertical line. For further references, see T. H. Barrett, *The Religious Associations of the Chinese Cat*, SOAS, 1998.

[22] For a book-length comparison of the variations on telling the time in Japan, China, and Korea, see Saitô Kuniji 齋藤國治, *Kodai no jikoku seido* 古代の時刻制度, Yûzankaku, 1995.

position that the head of the family sat, as he still sits today, at mealtimes and when receiving guests (the first reference to this practice goes back to the Han dynasty. The Mongols also use observations of the routines of animals, such as the marmot, to indicate the time. In Thailand, the words for telling the time in use today reflect a system of Chinese origin, e.g., *thum* (drum sound) for the night hours and *mong* (gong sound) for the daylight hours.

6.7   Qing Reforms

It was Matteo Ricci (Li Madou 利瑪竇), 1552–1610, who introduced the first self-chiming clock (*ziming zhong* 自鳴鐘) to China in 1585. It was considered a great novelty. When he finally managed to reach Peking, in 1601, he presented two to the Wanli emperor.[23] On his death, Ricci became in some parts of China the tutelary deity of clocks and was known popularly as Li Madou pusa 利瑪竇菩薩 (the Bodhisattva Matteo Ricci).

The government abandoned the 100-*ke* system and switched to Western 24-hour time in 1670. Thenceforward each hour officially had four quarters and 60 minutes (*fen* 分) and each minute, 60 seconds (*miao* 秒). But ordinary people continued to rely on the sun or to use the 100-*ke* system, and some Qing scholars continued to argue in favor of retaining the old system.[24]

The Kangxi emperor was an enthusiastic user of the new timepieces. He had a horological manufactory and repair works set up in the palace. It was closed down in 1796 by the Jiaqing emperor, who also banned the import of Western clocks and watches. By this time mechanical clocks (*chenzhong* 辰鐘) were being made in the main Chinese commercial centers. The old practice of naming 24 "small hours" (*xiaoshi* 小時) came into greater use (the word itself has been

[23] One of the criteria for selecting Jesuits for the Far Eastern mission was their horological skill. From the eighteenth century, European embassies took their cue from the Jesuits and brought clocks as presents for the emperors. The Palace Museum in Beijing has a collection of 1,000 magnificently elaborate timepieces presented to the court from the seventeenth century. Two hundred are on display.

[24] See Catherine Jami, "Western Devices for Measuring Time and Space," in *Time and Space in Chinese Culture*, Chun-chieh Huang and Erik Zürcher, eds., Brill, 1995, 169–200.

retained to this day for "hour"), but Western clocks remained a novelty for the rich, a gift or a toy rather than an essential instrument, because there was no felt need for the accurate measurement of time to the last minute or fraction of a minute at least in daily life.[25] It was not until cheap Western clocks and watches became available in the late nineteenth and early twentieth century that old habits began to change and the *chen* double-hours and the 100 *ke* were finally abandoned.

[25] "Why Are the Memorials Late?" Landes (1983), 37–52. The phrase is from the last line of a poem written by the Kangxi emperor in praise of Western clocks.

7

Statistics

No other country has such a wealth of extant historical statistics covering two millennia. Most important are the population statistics (7.2). Other records were also gathered on a regular basis, for example, of astronomical phenomena (5.1.1), or from the Qin, rainfall and crop conditions, and from the Tang, crop prices. Records of examination pass results were also kept and have been used for detailed studies of social mobility in the later empire.

Statistics of all sorts from the earliest periods mainly survive in summarized form in provincial or national totals. Larger quantities of more detailed statistical records from lower levels of the reporting chain are extant from the later empire, especially from the Qing. Land and price statistics in contracts and other private records have survived in smaller numbers, also usually from the last centuries of the empire.

In interpreting Chinese historical statistics, the first essential is to understand what the numbers mean and do not mean in the sources (7.1). In order to appraise their reliability it is necessary to find out why and how they were reported. Population records are a case in point; very often the figures reported in government documents refer to fiscal units converted at varying rates from actual units (7.2). Temporal and regional variations in weights and measures also have to be taken into account (7.3). The chapter ends with a short section on money and prices (7.4–5).

7.1 Numbers and Orders of Magnitude

Base 10 was the main way of counting in China. A sexagenary cycle was also used for recording dates and time (5.2). Both systems are recorded on the oracle bones, and further evidence comes from two extant ivory rulers dated to the Shang. They are neatly divided into units of tens and hundreds (7.3).

There were separate characters in the oracle-bone script for 13 numbers (the nine digits and 10, 100, 1,000, and 10,000). They are recognizably the same as those in use today. In addition, 20 joined characters (*hewen* 合文) have been deciphered for certain multiples of 10, 100, 1,000 and 10,000.[1] The largest number in the oracle-bone script is 30,000 (*sanwan* 三萬).

Table 14: Big Numbers

Numbers	Pre-Qin	Post-Qin	Modern
100,000 (10^5)	*yi* 億		*shiwan* 十萬
1,000,000 (10^6)	*zhao* 兆	*baiwan* 百萬	*baiwan* 百萬
10,000,000 (10^7)	*jing* 經[京]	*jing* 經[京]	*qianwan* 千萬
100,000,000 (10^8)	*yi* 億	*yi* 億	*yi* 億 (萬萬)[2]
1,000,000,000 (10^9)	*zhao* 兆	*zhao* 兆	*zhao* 兆 (*shiyi* 十億)

Very large numbers begin to appear in Zhou texts—*yi* 億, *zhao* 兆, *jing* 經 (京), for example, and many others for even larger ones— but there is some uncertainty as to what they mean, especially in Han and pre-Qin texts, since they could go up by tens (Table 14), by 10,000s or by each unit multiplied by itself. Sometimes this is indicated (as with *juwan* 巨萬 or *dawan* 大萬 meaning 10^8, as distinct from 10^4). Moreover, as with the later mega-numbers in Daoist and Buddhist scriptures, really big numbers are often not intended to be taken literally (7.1.2).

---

[1] *Hewen* are mostly special names, numbers, or dates and common phrases for ritual offerings found in pre-Qin texts. They are usually read as two words, e.g. *wu* 物 was originally a *hewen* joining *niu* 牛 and *wu* 勿 meaning "colored ox." It was later borrowed for the word meaning "thing." The oracle-bone *hewen* numerals for 20, 30, and 40 (*nian* 廿, *sa* 卅, and *xi* 卌) were exceptional in that they came to be pronounced as single words (as the result of eliding the initials of *er*, *san*, and *si* with the final of *shi*); see Redouane Djamouri, "L'emploi des signes numériques dans les inscriptions Shang," *Extrême-Orient, Extrême-Occident* 16: 13–42 (1993); Zhao Cheng 趙誠, "Shuci he liangci" 數詞 和量詞 (Numbers and measure words) in *Jiaguwen jianming cidian–buci fenlei duben* 甲骨文簡明詞典–卜辭分類讀本 (Concise dictionary of oracle-bone characters: A topically arranged reader), 253–59; see 15.5.

For references on the history of Chinese mathematics, see 37.1.

[2] *Wanwan* 萬萬 from the end of the Qing and during the Republic was often used instead of *yi* 億.

7.1.1   Numbers in Literary Chinese

Cardinal Numbers (jishuci 基數詞)

Numbers can appear either before or after the noun in Literary Chinese. They were used without counters, for example, *Li you zui san* 李有罪三 (Li had three offenses; in MC, *Li you santiao zui-zhuang* 李有三條罪狀. If the number is linked to a verb, it often goes before the verb, whereas in MC it comes after. Number one is frequently left out: *lu shang you hu* 爐上有壺 (MC: *lu shang you yiba hu* 爐上有一把壺).

You 有 (or 又) is often used between digits, especially in pre-Qin texts, for example, *wushi you liu* 五十有六 is 56 and *bai you liu* 百有六 is 106. The word for zero (*ling* 零, 0, *dan* 單, or *ling* 另) was introduced to China in the Southern Song. Thereafter it replaced *you* 有 when used as in the second example (106).

All the numbers have many derived meanings and connotations. *Yi* 一 (one), for example, can be used to mean the same as in *yiyang* 一樣, the whole as in *yi beizi* 一輩子, and independent as in *yiyi gu-xing* 一意孤行 (to insist on doing things one's own way); *shi* 十 can mean completely as in *shifen* 十分 (fully) or *shizu* 十足 (downright).

There were many alternative ways of writing numbers, perhaps the most important were the counting-rod numerals (one is one vertical rod; four is four rods, a method identical to the Babylonian, Egyptian, and Roman counting systems). Counting-rod numerals are the only parts of the Chinese script written horizontally from left to right (18.1). Commercial numerals were similar to these and gradually evolved into the following set (known as *Suzhou mazi* 蘇州碼子, Suzhou business characters): 〡 〢 〣 ✕ ✨ 上 〦 〧 〨 〩. They are still in use today for making a quick count.

The set of alteration-proof forms of 13 numbers (*changshu* 長數) for accounting or commercial transactions in use today dates from the Tang (壹, 貳, 叁, 肆, 伍, 陸, 柒[漆], 捌, 玖, 拾); plus *bai* 佰, *qian* 仟, *qianbai* 仟佰, and *baiwan* 佰萬 for 100, 1,000, 100,000, and 1 million. Half were borrowed for their sound (4, 6, 7, 8, 9, 10, 100), the remainder had been in use since the pre-Qin. There were commonly used in government documents (hence another name for them, *guanzi* 官字).

Many trades used their own ways of writing alteration-proof numbers, for example, silversmiths counted from 1 to 10 using 戔, 衣, 寸, 許, 丁, 木, 才, 奇, 長, 田. The same trade in different provinces often used different characters corresponding to the local dialect.

The use of *yao* 幺 (very small) as an alternative for 1 in a series of numbers has been growing for many centuries, but it crept into the script (in telegraphic communications) only at the end of the Qing. It is now normal in spoken Chinese in most parts of China, especially in the north.

Ordinal Numbers (xushuci 序數詞)

Cardinal numbers in Classical Chinese were also used as ordinal numbers. In Literary Chinese, words such as *di* 第 or *qi* 其 were placed before cardinal numbers to indicate the order of things in a series. The *ganzhi* 干支 were used as ordinal numbers as well as many different series, for example, *bo* 伯 (*meng* 孟), *zhong* 仲, *shu* 叔, and *ji* 季 for eldest, second, third, and youngest brother (3.2), or for naming the months (3.1).[3]

Fractions (fenshu 分數)

The following expressions may have been derived from telling the time on the clepsydra (6.4); at least from the Han they were used for the "natural" fractions:

taiban 太半 [*daban* 大半] (two-thirds)
zhongban 中半 (average half; one-half)
xiaoban 小半 [*shaoban* 少半] (one-third)
ruoban 弱半 (one-quarter).

Sometimes *ban* was left out and *da* 大 [*tai* 太] and *xiao* 小 [*shao* 少] were used alone (in modern Chinese *daban* 大半 simply means the greater part or likely and *xiaoban* 小半 means a little bit).

Percentages are expressed without indication following the numbers 10, 100, 1,000, or 10,000, e.g., *shi liu qi* 什[十]六七 means about 60 or 70 percent, not 16 or 17. Note that the earliest meaning of *wanyi* 萬一 was one ten-thousandth.

San fen er 三分二 in MC is *san fen zhi er* 三分之二 (two-thirds). A number before *fen* 分 indicates percentage; for example, *liufen* 六

---

[3] Other ranking series included the Five Phases (Box 7, 22.3.3): wood, fire, earth, metal, water (*mu* 木, *huo* 火, *tu* 土, *jin* 金, *shui* 水); the seasons: spring, summer, autumn, winter (*chun* 春, *xia* 夏, *qiu* 秋, *dong* 冬); or flowers and trees: plum, lotus, bamboo, chrysanthemum (*mei* 梅, *lan* 蘭, *zhu* 竹, *ju* 菊).

分 is 60 percent. It can also indicate fractions of one as in *liushan sanshui yitian* 六山三水一田 (6/10 mountain; 3/10 water, and 1/10 paddy field). The standard mathematical terms for subunits (i.e., *qiang* 强, *ruo* 弱, *ban* 半) are placed after the number, e.g., *wufen ruo* 五分弱 (less than 50 percent).

Yi 一 and *ban* 半 are often used together to indicate a few, or small amount, as in *yishi banke* 一時半刻 (a short time). Three and two are similarly used, *sanyan liangyu* 三言兩語 (a few words).

In multiplication, the smaller number usually comes first, as in *wu qi sanshiwu* 五七三十五 (5 × 7 = 35).

The names for very small numbers used in mathematics and in contracts were derived from the smallest linear measures, which appear in the late Warring States. After the Tang and Song they were also used for weights and area measures (Table 16). Units less than the *wei* 微 were not named systematically. Along with the other small numbers, they were often (and still are) used in the sense of minutely small (e.g., *haoli* 毫厘 or *huwei* 忽微). They are used for translating the international system micro units (Table 15).

Table 15: Very Small Numbers

1 Unit	Equals	International System Prefixes
		(to show modern use of characters)
wei 微	10 *xian* 纖	
hu 忽	10 *wei* 微	*weiwei* 微微 (10^{-12} pico-)
si 絲	10 *hu* 忽	*haowei* 毫微 (10^{-9} nano-)
hao 毫[毛]	10 *si* 絲 (pre-Song: *miao* 秒)	*wei* 微 (10^{-6} micro-)
li 厘[釐]	10 *hao* 毫	*hao* 毫 (10^{-3} milli-)
fen 分	10 *li* 厘	*li* 厘 (10^{-2} centi-)
qian 錢	10 *fen* 分	*fen* 分 (10^{-1} deci-)

7.1.2 Approximate, Hyperbolic, and Auspicious Numbers

Approximate numbers (*yueshu* 約數) are expressed in various ways. *Wu liu ren* 五六人 means about five or six people. Sometimes the particles *ke* 可, *gai* 蓋, or the expression *wulü* 無慮 is used before the number or *xu* 許, *suo* 所, or *yu* 余 after it—for example, *wushi you liu xu* 五十有六許 (about 56); *shiren suo* 十人所 (*shiren zuoyou* 十人左右, about 10 people); or *wulü wushi* 無慮五十 (about 50).

The numbers 10, 100, 1,000, and 10,000 are frequently used to indicate orders of magnitude, not exact numbers. In this usage they are called *xushu* 虛數 (hyperbolic numbers) and are similar to round numbers in English in the plural ("dozens," "tens of thousands," or "hundreds"). Thus the *Wanli changcheng* 萬里長城 is not 10,000 *li*, and there are not 1,000 Buddhas in the *Qianfodong* 千佛洞 just as there are not 10,000 in the *Wanfosi* 萬佛寺. *Qianjin* 千金 as used by Sima Qian may have meant 1,000 catties of gold, but it soon acquired the metaphoric sense of valuable as also did *wanjin* 萬金. Many other numbers were used as *xushu*, for example, 30, 300, or 3,000 or 18, 36, and 72. When used in a compound expression the number often need not be translated as in "the Yue" or "all the Yue" for Baiyue 百越, not "the hundred Yue;" "general merchandise" for *baihuo* 百貨, not "100 goods;" the *Myriad Family Names* (it actually contains 438) for the *Baijiaxing* 百家姓, not the *Hundred Family Names*.

The numbers 3, 9, and 12 are often used to mean several, many, and a lot (characters like *sen* 森 or *yan* 焱 may be traces of a primitive system of counting when more than two was a lot). An expression such as *ma you sanfen longxing* 馬有三分龍性 means "several horses have the spirit of a dragon." Eight, too is used for many as in *babeizi* 八輩子 (many generations).

At least from the Eastern Zhou, odd numbers were regarded as heavenly; even, as earthly.[4] Later, the terms *yin* 陰 (even) and *yang* 陽 (odd) were used (the ancient Greeks also believed that odd numbers were male and even ones, female). The number 72 had a special meaning since it was the result of multiplying 8 and 9, the highest male and female digits. It also featured in everyday life in that the calendar itself was made up of 72 *hou* 候 (periods of five days, see 5.5.1). The belief in the power of mystical numbers was at its strongest in the pre-Qin and Han. Numbers appearing in works written during these centuries (e.g., in the *Shiji*) should therefore be used with extreme caution.

Numbers continued to permeate all areas of Chinese life up to the end of the empire and even later, especially for choosing lucky days and telling fortunes. The senior male digit *jiu* 九 (nine) is associated with authority, power, and longevity. So, all doors in the Forbidden City have nine rows of nine nails; the only exception is the Donghuamen 東華門, the gate from which the coffins of the

[4] Ye Shuxian 葉舒憲 and Tian Daxian 天大憲, *Zhongguo gudai shenmi shuzi* 中國古代神秘數字 (Mystical numbers in ancient China), Shehui kexue wenxian, 1998. Each chapter examines a number or group of numbers using a social anthropological approach.

emperors and their consorts were taken out for burial. It has eight rows of eight nails. Even today, numerological considerations still weigh heavily in everyday life.[5]

Numbers were often used for expressing numerological correspondences and affinities as well as for numerical mnemonics. There are an enormous number of these in Literary Chinese and an equally large number of different ones in the vernacular. The numbers one and three permeate the language more than any other (see the special dictionary of numerical phrases, 2.7, item 9).

Numbers are sometimes still used as a code based on their sounds as in *wu qi yi* 五七一 (*wu [zhuang] qiyi* 武裝起義, armed uprising).

7.1.3   Wrong Numbers

In every dynasty there were a range of punishments laid down in the codes for scribes who miscopied characters, especially numbers.[6] Nevertheless misprints and wrongly copied numbers are legion, especially on excavated local documents such as contracts or tax records. The copyist often wrote two for three; eight for six, or eight for one, or vice-versa in all these cases.

For an overview of the problems with Chinese historical statistics, see L. S. Yang (Yang Liansheng 楊聯陞), "Numbers and Units

---

[5] For example, the choice of automobile registration plates or telephone numbers—and even the dates for important events, like marriage or setting out on a long journey. Such beliefs are especially strong in south China: *si* 四 (four) is unlucky because of the similarity to *si* 死 (death), so the number 4,421 is particularly unfortunate (*sisi eryi* 死死而矣). Eight (*ba* 八) is considered fortunate because of its closeness in Cantonese pronunciation to *fa* 發 (as in *facai* 發財, get rich). So, when Canton telephone numbers moved to eight digits in 1996, as a special dispensation, the Canton area code had an eight added.

[6] The Qin laws discovered in 1975 specify various fines for wrongly recorded tax accounts and also state that "when they fail to report stalwart youths (*aotong* 驁童), as well as when they are careless in registering the disabled, the village chief and the elders are liable to the redeemable punishment of shaving off the beard," Hulsewé, 1985, 115–16 (27.2).

Hong Mai 洪邁 (1123–1202) tells the story of five Song woodblock-engravers who met an even worse fate: they were struck by lightning after changing the texts of prescriptions in a medical book they had been engraving; see Susan Cherniack, "Book Culture and Textual Transmission in Sung China," *HJAS* 54.1 (1994), 5–6.

in Chinese Economic History," in his *Studies in Chinese Institutional History*, HUP, 1963, 75–84. Yang warns against (1) copyists' errors, (2) hyperbolic numbers, (3) under- and over-reporting depending on the matter reported on, and (4) regional variations in units. See also Peng Zeyi 彭澤益 (1916–94), "Quantification Problems in the Study of Chinese Economic History," *SSC* 7.3: 63–88 (1986). Derk Bodde has a brief discussion of some difficulties with the statistics in the *Shiji* in his chapter in the *CHC*, and Fang Chao-ying examines similar problems for the Qing in "A Technique for Estimating the Numerical Strength of the Early Manchu Military Forces."[7]

7.1.4 Misleading Statistics

Exaggerated and misleading statistics in modern statements about the Chinese past are another category against which the student should be on guard. They may not always be wrong, but they are misleading. Some common examples include:

The length of Chinese history (5,000 years is a common figure). A strange claim when the first written records date from 1200 BC and even if the historicity of the Xia is accepted, the length would only come to about 4,000 years (see Introduction, *The Dynasties*).

The total number of Chinese characters. Figures of 60,000 or even over 100,000 are given. On examination this turns out to include dead characters, graphic variants, Japanese characters, dialect characters, and any number of other types of character long since forgotten (see 1.3.1).

The large number and huge variation of strokes in the characters. While it is true that the number of strokes in a single character can range between one and 36, there are very few characters at the extremes—there is only one character with 36 strokes and only three characters with one stroke. Most cluster in the range of 6–12 strokes.

The number of ancient books. The number of extant works written before modern publishing began in the 1890s is sometimes said to be between 70,000 and 100,000. The weakness of such statements is that "works" may cover anything from a slim volume of poems to a huge collection of thousands of memorials. Such statistics are therefore practically meaningless (see 9.1, where a more realistic figure of between 40,000 and 50,000 is suggested).

[7] "The State and Empire of Ch'in," *CHC*, vol. 1, 98–102. The Fang article is in *HJAS* 13.1: 192–214 (1950).

The size of library collections. It often turns out that Chinese *ce* are counted as one volume which gives the impression that the collection is far larger than it is. Another practice is to count each work in a collectanea separately. The number of works in the Buddhist Tripitaka, for example, is sometimes given as over 4,000 although the titles include anything from a brief recipe for toothache to a major life of Sakyamuni.

The number of Qing documents. Archives sometimes give huge figures when the definition of a "document" turns out to include everything from huge memorials to a fragment; from a single edict to a book summarizing at length a year of reports (see 50.1.2).

7.2   Population

7.2.1   Registration and Policy

Throughout Chinese history, governments have attached enormous importance to registering the population. Taxes, tribute, and labor and military services were based on population counts. The registration of the population also served as the basis for social control and security. Families were grouped together and made responsible for registering their numbers and keeping a watch on each other and reporting any crimes. Travel was controlled. The earliest references to such a system go back to the Warring States: "A strong country knows thirteen kinds of statistical [information]: the number of granaries and treasury within its borders, the number of able-bodied men and women, the number of old and of weak people, the number of officials and great officers, the number of those making a livelihood by talking, the number of useful people, the number of horses and of oxen, and the quantity of fodder and of straw" (*Shangjunshu* 商君書, "Jingnei pian" 境內篇, Duyvendak, 1963, 203 [Table 26, 19.2]. See also *Zhouli*, "Qiuguan" 秋官).

Traces of the system in action have been found on Qin documents (19.1.1 and 44.4.1), but the first actual registers to survive in manuscript form (on bamboo strips) date from the Han, as does the first extant census in the world, which was taken by Han officials in AD 2. Each register (made up of several bamboo strips) recorded one household (*hu* 戶), listing the head of the household (*huzhu* 戶主), his wife and adult children (*danan* 大男 and *danü* 大女), and the total number of dependents (mouths, *kou* 口). The registers often recorded much else, including health, domicile, occupation, and wealth. Population was referred to as *hukou* 戶口 (households and mouths) or *dingkou* 丁口 (adults and mouths); *renkou* 人口 is the modern word.

From the Western Jin to the end of the Tang the entire population was divided into five age groups each slightly differently defined according to the period. The five groups were *huang* 黃 (infant, 1–3 years old); *xiao* 小 (child, 4–15 or 17); *zhong* 中 (youth, 11–24, also called *banding* 半丁, *ciding* 次丁, *zhongnan* 中男, *zhongnü* 中女); *ding* 丁 (adult, from 16–60 or 66, also called *zhengding* 正丁, *rending* 人丁, *dingnan* 丁男, *nanding* 男丁, *dingnü* 丁女, *zhuangding* 壯丁); and *lao* 老 (the aged, above 55, or 60 or 66).

From the Tang to the Qing only the adult population was eligible for taxes and services and therefore only the age of entry into adulthood and old age were promulgated (roughly ages 20 and 60 respectively). Population figures (and indeed statistics of all sorts) were reported in summary form to the capital. In imperial times it was these summaries that were typically printed in historical works such as the Standard Histories (in the monographs on financial administration) and in government compendia. In the later empire they also survive in local gazetteers and, in the Qing, sometimes in their original form.

Zhongguo lidai hukou tiandi tianfu tongji 中國歷代戶口田地田賦統計 is a large-scale handbook of Chinese historical statistics, containing 215 printed tables of China's population, acreage, and land-tax statistics from the Former Han to the end of the Qing.[8] The data in the tables were drawn from nearly 300 traditional primary sources, including the Standard Histories, encyclopaedic works on government, and local gazetteers. The author was well aware of the pitfalls in traditional Chinese statistics and added copious notes.

One problem of China's historical population statistics is that very often a unit such as *ding* 丁 (adult) refers to a tax or labor service unit, not to an actual person (see, for example, 7.2.2., Ho, 1959, 101–35). Another problem is that there are few alternative figures with which to check the accuracy of the summary of the population counts in official works such as the Standard Histories or even the

---

[8] *Zhongguo lidai hukou tiandi tianfu tongji* (Chinese historical population, land, and land-tax statistics), Liang Fangzhong 梁方仲 (1908–70), Shangwu, 1980; 4th rpnt., 1993; for similar compendia on the late Qing and Republican periods, see 51.4.2.

local gazetteers. Sometimes there is even internal inconsistency within one set of figures. [9]

Other sources for the study of historical demography include data culled from household registers and from Ming and Qing genealogies (3.5).[10] For these and other late Qing and twentieth-century sources on Chinese population, see "Chinese Population Sources, 1700-2000," Appendix in James Z. Lee and Wang Feng, *One Quarter of Humanity: Malthusian Mythology and Chinese Realities, 1700–2000*, HUP, 1999, 149–57.

The most detailed although hardly the most typical records are those of the Qing imperial household.[11] For a study based on local banner household registers from Liaoning in the late Qing, see James Lee and Cameron Campbell, *Fate and Fortune in Rural China: Social Organization and Population Behavior in Liaoning, 1774–1883*, CUP, 1997. Appendix A sets out the sources and methods used in this important study.

For overall surveys, see

Wang Yuesheng 王躍生, *Zhongguo renkou de shengshuai yu duice* 中國人口的盛衰與對策 (The rise and fall of China's population and policy measures), Shehui kexue wenxian, 1995.

Hans Bielenstein, "Chinese Historical Demography, AD 2–1982," *BMFEA* 59: 1–288 (1987). Updates an earlier survey by Michel Cartier and Pierre-Etienne Will, "Demographie et institutions en Chine: Contribution à l'analyse des recensements de l'époque imperiale (2 ap. J.C.–1750)," *Annales de demographie historique* 1971: 161–245.

Ge Jianxiong 葛劍雄, *Zhongguo renkou fazhanshi* 中國人口發展史 *Zhongguo renkou fazhanshi* (A history of the development of China's population), Fujian renmin, 1991.

---

[9] G. William Skinner, "Sichuan's Population in the 19th Century: Lessons for Disaggregated Data," *LIC* 8.1: 1–79 (1987), shows that the sums of the county figures are overestimates. Arthur P. Wolf and Chieh-shih Huang in *Marriage and Adoption in China, 1845–1945*, SUP, 1980, use Japanese imperial figures to check traditional Chinese head counts.

[10] On the genealogies, see Ted A. Telford, "Survey of Social Demographic Data in Chinese Genealogies," *LIC* 7.2: 118–48 (1986).

[11] *Qingdai huangzu renkou xingwei yu shehui huanjing* 清代皇族人口行爲與社會環境 (The behavior and social background of the Qing royal clan), Li Zhongqing 李中清 and Guo Songyi 郭松義, eds., Beijing daxue, 1994.

Archaeologists and historians have recently made some interesting estimates of China's population and land use patterns at the dawn of history based on the analysis of burial sites; see Song Zhenhao 宋鎮豪, 1994 (Chapter 36). Thereafter, there are a number of studies of the population of China in different historical periods:

7.2.2 Demographic Studies

Hans Bielenstein, "The Census of China During the Period 2–742 AD," *BMFEA* 19: 125–63 (1947).

Robert M. Hartwell (1932–96), "Demographic, Political and Social Transformations in China, 750–1550," *HJAS* 42.2: 365–442 (1982).

Ping-ti Ho (He Bingdi 何炳棣), "An Estimate of the Total Population in Sung-Chin China," in *Etudes Song in memoriam Etienne Balazs*, I (1970).

Ping-ti Ho, *Studies on the Population of China 1368–1953*, HUP, 1959. The classic study of population in late imperial China; see also Perkins, 1969 (35.1.2).

Chinese Historical Micro-Demography, Stevan Harrell, ed., UCP, 1995.

Ts'ui-jung Liu (Liu Cuirong 劉翠溶), "The Demography of Two Chinese Clans in Hsiao-shen, Chekiang, 1650–1850," in *Family and Population in East Asian History*, Susan B. Hanley and Arthur P. Wolf, eds., SUP, 1985, 13–61; Ts'ui also has two chapters in Harrell (1995).

Liu Cuirong 劉翠溶, *Ming Qing shiqi jiazu renkou yu shehui jingji bianqian* 明清時期家族人口與社會經濟變遷 (Lineage population and socio-economic changes in the Ming and Qing periods), 2 vols., Nangang: Institute of Economics, Academia Sinica, 1992.

For further references, see William Lavely, James Lee, and Wang Feng, "Chinese Demography: The State of the Field," *JAS* 49.4: 807–34 (1990).

Studies of the historical demography of individual towns have begun to appear; see, for example,

Han Guanghui, 韓光輝 *Beijing lishi renkou dili* 北京歷史人口地理 (The historical geography of Beijing's population), Beijing daxue, 1996.

7.2.3   Internal Migration

Populations moved in and out and within the China area (and what are now its neighboring countries) for tens of thousands of years during prehistoric times. Forced migrations may have begun in the Shang and Zhou but the earliest recorded migrations only date from the fourth century BC. One of the first was into Sichuan, when up to 50,000 Qin people were settled there following the conquest of the kingdom of Shu 蜀 in 316 BC. Shu loyalists fled south and eventually 60,000 of them settled in what is today the northern part of Vietnam. About 4,000 criminals from the north, along with their families were settled by Qin in Sichuan in 238 (see von Glahn 1987 and Sun 1997 in the list that follows).

Even small numbers of migrants could have a big impact on the place they settled if they came with advanced techniques. For an overview, see James Lee, "Migration and Expansion in Chinese History," in *Human Migration*, William McNeill and Ruth Adams, eds., IUP, 1977, 20–47. The best detailed study of migration is by Ge Jianxiong 葛劍雄, Cao Shuji 曹樹基, and Wu Songdi 吳松第, *Zhongguo yiminshi* 中國移民史 (History of migrants in China), 6 vols., Fuzhou renmin, 1997. For pioneering studies of the Han colonization of the south, including case studies of specific regions or provinces, see Chi (1936), 29.5.3, and the following selection,

Herold J. Wiens, *The Han Chinese Expansion in South China*, Westview, 1967 (first published in 1952).

Edward H. Schafer, *The Vermilion Bird: T'ang Images of the South*, UCP, 1967, 1985.

Edward H. Schafer, *Shore of Pearls*, UCP, 1969. Hainan in the Tang.

Zheng Xuemeng 鄭學檬, *Zhongguo gudai jingji zhongxin nanyi he Tang Song Jiangnan jingji yanjiu* 中國古代經濟重心南移和唐宋江南經濟研究 (Studies on the southward movement of ancient China's center of economic gravity and the economy of south China in the Tang and Song), Yuelu, 1996.

Li Bozhong 李伯重, *Tangdai Jiangnan nongye de fazhan* 唐代江南農業的發展 (The development of agriculture in south China in the Tang), Nongye, 1990.

Richard von Glahn, *The Country of Streams and Grottoes: Expansion, Settlement, and the Civilizing of the Sichuan Frontier in Song Times*, Council on East Asia Studies, Harvard University, 1987.

Sun Xiaofen 孫曉芬, *Qingdai qianqi de yimin tian Sichuan* 清代前期的移民填四川 (The filling up of Sichuan by migrants in the early Qing), Sichuan daxue, 1997. Inmigration to Sichuan throughout Chinese history influenced the development of the Sichuan dialect, see Cui Rongchang 崔榮昌, *Sichuan fangyan yu Ba Shu wenhua* 四川方言與巴蜀文化 (The Sichuan dialect and Ba-Shu culture), Sichuan daxue, 1996.

Li Bozhong, *Agricultural Development in the Yangzi Delta, 1620–1850*, Macmillan, 1998. This is based on many of his more detailed studies.

Hugh R. Clark, *Community, Trade and Networks: Southern Fujian Province from the 3rd to the 13th Centuries*, CUP, 1991.

Hans Bielenstein, "The Chinese Colonization of Fukien Until the End of the T'ang," in *Studia serica Bernhard Karlgren dedicata*, Ejnar Munksgaard, 1959, 98–122.

Edward H. Schafer, *The Empire of Min*, Tuttle, 1954.

Development and Decline of Fukien Province in the 17th and 18th Centuries, E. B. Vermeer, ed., Brill, 1990.

Johanna Menzell Meskill, *A Chinese Pioneer Family: The Lins of Wu-feng, Taiwan, 1729–1895*, PUP, 1979. A fascinating study of how newly-arrived settlers in Taiwan built up the family wealth and power. Based on interviews and a wide range of manuscript sources, including family and local documents and records. Compare with the next item.

Wufeng Linjia zhi diaocha yu yanjiu 霧峰林家之調查與研究 (Investigation and research on the Lin family of Wufeng), Wang Shiqing 王世慶 et al., eds., Taibei: Lin Penyuan Zhonghua wenhua jiaoyu jijinhui, 1991.

J. Shepherd, *Statecraft and Political Economy on the Taiwan Frontier, 1600–1800*, SUP, 1993; SMC, 1996.

Taiwan Hanren yiminshi yanjiu shumu 臺灣漢人移民史研究書目 (Bibliography of research on the history of Han migration to Taiwan), Zhang Yanxian 張炎憲, ed. in chief, 1989.

For Chinese expansion overseas, see 41.5.2.

7.2.4   *Population in the Republican Period*

After 1850, internal warfare and bureaucratic inefficiency led to the breakdown of the old system of population registers. Efforts were made in 1909–11 to make a new count and a sampling of 16 provinces was made the basis of estimates in 1925–34, but these did not produce reliable figures. The first modern census was taken in 1953 and the second in 1964. Even then, the prime minister admitted that the official population figure of 600 million could be wrong by a factor of 10 percent (i.e., plus or minus 60 million people). For further details of the dismal basis for demographic studies of the Republic, see Jiang Tao 蔣濤, *Zhongguo jindai renkou shi* 中國近代人口史 (Modern Chinese population history), Zhejiang renmin, 1993.

7.3   Weights and Measures

The ability to measure with accuracy goes back many thousands of years as suggested by the precision of much of the geometric ornamentation on Neolithic pottery vessels and jade carvings.[12] The first instruments for measuring that have been preserved are one bone and two ivory measures. They have been dated to the Shang. The bone one is about 17 cm (6½ ins) long. It is divided into ten equal units. The ivory ones are about 16 cm long and are divided into tens and hundredths (later *cun* 寸 and *fen* 分). A number of words connected with measuring are recorded in oracle-bone script, for example, *cheng* 程 (to weigh), *liang* 量 (to measure), *dou* 斗 (a measurement), *sheng* 升 (a measurement), *jin* 斤 (ax; later used for catty), *xun* 尋 (8 *chi*), and possibly *jiang* 彊[疆] (to demarcate fields; a character no doubt connected with the practice of using a bow to measure land [cf. *yin* 引 and *gong* 弓, land measures that first appear in later Zhou sources and were still in use in the Qing]).

At the end of the Spring and Autumn and beginning of the Warring States, the rulers defined and unified the weights and measures in their kingdoms as a means of systematizing tax collection, controlling markets, winning supporters, and consolidating power. Many used two sets. It was said that good rulers used long weights to make loans and to distribute grain and short ones to recuperate loans and to collect taxes. This method was used to attract followers by several members of the Tian 田 (Chen 陳) family of Qi 齊 in the fifth to fourth centuries BC (*Zuozhuan*, "Shaogong sannian 昭公三年"; the same technique is credited to "White duke" Sheng 白公勝 of Chu 楚 at the beginning of the fifth century BC; see *Huainanzi* 淮

---

[12] Keightley, 1994–95 (7.3.3); Poor, 1995 (7.3.3).

南子, "Renjian xun" 人間訓). On gaining power, however, they made the long measures the official ones, no doubt in order to collect more taxes (Table 16). Most rulers distributed physical models of the approved units, often with the values inscribed on them (17.2.3). The system introduced by the chancellor of Qin, Shang Yang 商鞅 (361–38 BC), six years before his death. It was later used as the basis for the Qin standardization in 221 BC (Hulsewé, 1981 [7.3.3]).

Shang Yang's inscribed bronze peck (*fangsheng* 方升) can be seen in the Shanghai Museum (Ma Chengyuan, 1972 [7.3.3]). Many of the official measures used during the Warring States were shared by most of the kingdoms even before the Qin unification of weights and measures (Table 16). As time went by, more and more of the Warring States adopted base-10 units. The most common exceptions were 24 *shu* 銖 (scruples) to 1 *liang* 兩 (ounce) and 16 *liang* 兩 to 1 *jin* 斤 (catty). A Warring States balance was excavated in Hunan in 1954. The ounce weights (as their name implies) went up in doubles—1: 2: 4: 8. Another common exception to base-10 measures was 1 *mu* 畝 (Chinese acre) equals 240 square *bu* 步.

From the Qin, each imperial dynasty (and most kingdoms in periods of disunion) continued to promulgate standard measures. Over time there was a tendency for these measures to increase in size, most notably during the Nan-Bei Chao. New dynasties endeavored to bring order to the system but bowed to reality and in the event continued the well-established practice of using a dual system of long and short measures. Thus the Sui introduced, and the Tang continued, short measures based on the standard Han ones while at the same time carrying on with the long measures which had come into general use during the intervening period of disunion. From the Song, the Tang long measures became the new standard, but there were also officially recognized short measures.[13]

---

[13] Tang long measures were called *dachi* 大尺, *dasheng* 大升, and *dajin* 大斤 (1 *dachi* 大尺 [approx. 30 cm] = 1.2 *xiaochi* 小尺; 1 *dasheng* 大升 = 3 *xiaosheng* 小升; 1 *dajin* 大斤 = 3 *xiaojin* 小斤). Song short measures included the *shengsheng* 省升, *shenghu* 省斛, and *shengbai* 省陌 (equivalent to 4/5, 83%, and 77% of the regular units); see Yang, 1963 (7.3.3), 81–83. In the Han, it was customary to distinguish the weight of husked grain as, for example, *dashi* 大石 and unhusked grain as *xiaoshi* 小石. The ratio of husked to unhusked grain was 5:3; see Yang, 1963 (7.1.3), 81–83 and Loewe, 1961 (7.3.3).

Table 16: Weights and Measures: Pre-Qin

	1 Unit	(Treaty Port English Translation) Equals
L e n g t h	cun 寸 zhi 咫 chi 尺 zhang 丈 ren 仞 xun 尋 chang 常 suo 索	(inch) 10 *fen* 分 8 *cun* 寸 (foot) 10 *cun* 寸 (1 Zhanguo *chi* = 9 inches; see Table 18) 10 *chi* 尺 8 *chi* 尺 in Zhou; 7 *chi* in Han; 5.6 *chi* at end Later Han (height measure; arm span reaching up and down; approx. 2 yd = 1 *bu*; see *Area*) 7–8 *chi* 尺 (width measure; arm span reaching horizontally) 2 *xun* 尋 10 *xun* 尋

C a p a c i t y	sheng 升
	dou 斗
	hu 斛
	
	Qi 齊
	dou 斗
	ou 區
	fu 釜
	zhong 鐘
		(peck) 10 *ge* 合 (Zhanguo *sheng* = 5.7–7.7 fl oz; see Table 18)
		(pint) 10 *sheng* 升
		(bushel) 10 *dou* 斗
		In addition to the above three measures, many others were in use by the different kingdoms during the Warring States; the best-known system is that of Qi 齊
		
		Tian of Qi family units *Qi public units*
		   5 *sheng* 升 4 *sheng* 升
		   5 *dou* 斗 4 *dou* 斗
		   5 *ou* 區 4 *ou* 區
		   10 *fu* 釜 10 *fu* 釜

W e i g h t	shu 銖 zi 錙 liang 兩 jin 斤 jun 鈞 shi 石 gu 鼓	(scruple) 10 *lei* 累 (1 *lei* = 10 *shu* 黍 [grains]) 6 *shu* 銖 (ounce) 24 *shu* 銖 (or 4 *zi* 錙) (catty) 16 *liang* 兩 (1 Zhanguo *jin* = 8.8–11 oz; see Table 18) (picul) 30 *jin* 斤 (picul) 4 *jun* 鈞 (= 120 *jin*) 4 *shi* 石 In addition to the above measures, many others were in use by the different kingdoms during the Warring States; e.g., Wei 魏 and Han 韓: 1 *yi* 鎰 (315 gm) = 20 *liang* 兩.
A r e a	bu 步 gong 弓 mu 畝 li 里 she 舍	*Land area and distance measures were used interchangeably* (double pace) 8 *chi* 尺 = 2 yd; see Table 18 (6 *chi* 尺 in Qin 秦 from 350 BC) (bow) same as *bu* 步 (acre) 100 square *bu* 步 (or *gong* 弓); from Warring States increased to 240 square *bu* 步 (or *gong* 弓) Land area measure or distance measure of 300 *bu* 步 An army march of 30 *li* was called a *she*

Note: Only a selection of the main units are included. *Sources*: 7.3.3

Table 17: Weights and Measures: Qin–Qing

	1 Unit	(Treaty Port English Translation) Equals
L **e** **n** **g** **t** **h**	fen 分 cun 寸 chi 尺 zhang 丈 yin 引 li 里	for units below the *fen*, see Table 15 (inch) 10 *fen* 分 (foot) 10 *cun* 寸 (by Qing, 1 *chi* = 12.5 inches; see Table 18) 10 *chi* 尺 10 *zhang* 丈 see under *Area*
C **a** **p** **a** **c** **i** **t** **y**	chao 抄 shao 勺 ge 合 sheng 升 dou 斗 fu 釜 hu 斛 shi 石 yu 庾	10 *cuo* 撮 (pinch) 10 *chao* 抄 10 *shao* 勺; also 2 *yue* 龠 (peck) 10 *ge* 合 (by Qing, 1 *sheng* = 35 fl oz; see Table 18) (pint) 10 *sheng* 升 4 *dou* 斗 (not used after Ming) (bushel) 10 *dou* 斗 (5 *dou* after S. Song) (bushel) 10 *dou* 斗 (since N. Song); 2 *hu* 斛 (since S. Song) 16 *dou* 斗 (not used after Ming)
W **e** **i** **g** **h** **t**	shu 銖 liang 兩 jin 斤 jun 鈞 shi 石	for units below *qian* 錢 introduced in the Tang, see Table 15 (scruple); replaced by *qian* 錢 (mace) in 621 (ounce) 24 *shu* 銖 or 4 *zi* 錙 (since 621, 1 *liang* = 10 *qian* 錢) (catty) 16 *liang* 兩 (picul) 30 *jin* 斤 (not used after Ming) (picul) 4 *jun* 鈞 (= 120 *jin*)

A
r
e
a
 	
&
 	
D
i
s
t
a
n
c
e
	
	bu 步
	
	gong 弓
	
	mu 畝
	qing 頃
	li 里
		Land area and distance measures were used interchangeably
		for units below *mu* 畝 introduced in the Song, see Table 15
		(double pace); 6 *chi* 尺 (Qin–Tang); 5–6 *chi* 尺 (Tang–Qing);
		  by Qing 1 *bu* = 5 *chi* = 1 yd 2 ft 2.5 in; see Table 19
		  Also used as land area measure (abolished in 1928)
		(bow) same as *bu* 步; by Qing used mainly as land area meas-
		  ure; abolished in 1915; the fork-like measuring bow was
		  called a *gongbu* 弓步 or *bugong* 步弓 ("Qingzhang" 清丈
		  (Cadastral survey) in Djang, 1954 (27.6), 241–50
		(1/6 acre) 240 square *bu* 步 (or *gong* 弓)
		100 *mu* 畝
		("Chinese mile"). Up to the early Qing, usually land area
		  measure; as a measure of distance, it was supposed to
		  have been 1/10 of one double-hour's walking on level
		  ground; from the Song, it was officially 360 *bu* 步 (or
		  gong) = 1/3 mile (in the Yuan, exceptionally, it was 240
		  bu). From the Qing, no longer used as an area measure.

Note: Only a selection of the main units are included. The treaty port English translations are often preceded by "Chinese" as in "Chinese mile" (*li* 里), "Chinese ounce" (*liang* 兩) etc. *Sources*: 7.3.3

Table 18: Weights and Measures: Conversion of Historic Values

Period	1 chi 尺 = cm (in)	1 sheng 升 = ml (fl oz)	1 jin 斤 = gm (oz)
Shang 商	16 (6.2)	–	–
Zhanguo 戰國	23.1 (9) [Qin 秦]	169–226 (5.7–7.7)	250–315 (8.8–11)
Qin, Han 秦漢	23.1 (9)	200 (6.8)	220–253 (7.7–8.6)
Tang 唐	30.3 (11.8)	[600] (20)	661 (23)
Song 宋	31.6 (12.3)	[585] (19.8)	633 (22)
Yuan 元	–	[836] (28.4)	633 (22)
Ming 明	32 (12.5)	987 (33.6)	590 (20.7)
Qing 清	32 (12.5)	1035 (35)	596.8 (20.9)
Republic 民國	33.33 (13)	1000 (34)	500 (17.5)

Source: Qiu (1992), 520. Figures are based on actual weights and measures (those in square brackets are taken from literary sources).

Many of the special standard measures used in different trades were officially recognized or condoned. For example, apart from the official foot-rule, there were (to name but three of the most famous ones) the carpenter's foot-rule (*Banchi* 班尺 after Lu Ban 魯班), the tailor's foot-rule (*caichi* 裁尺), and the surveyor's foot-rule (*liangdichi* 量地尺).[14]

Some of the other customary measures included the *gui* 軌 (axle) for road width (1 *gui* = 8 *chi* 尺); the *duan* 端 for cloth; the *juan* 卷 and *pi* 匹[疋] for bolts of silk;[15] and from the Song, various package measures (e.g., *bao* 包 and *dai* 袋) or certificates (*yin* 引) for handling large quantities of monopoly salt and tea (ordinary weights were used for retail transactions). Note the difference between *maozhong* 毛重 (gross weight) and *jingzhong* 淨重 (net weight). For apothecary measures, see Table 15 and Chapter 36, *Medical Terms*.

Because of the enormous number of different definitions of the actual weights and measures in use (often set by the county magistrate or by the local gilds), in estimating the value of any given unit encountered in a document, it is necessary to take into account the period, the purpose (e.g., taxation or market transaction), and the

[14] See "Foot-rules and Measuring Systems," in Ruitenbeek, 1993 (37.2), 90–98. Each dynasty used slightly different foot-rules, for those of the Song, for example, see Hans Ulrich Vogel, 1999 (7.3.3).

[15] In pre-Qin, 2 *juan* 卷 = 1 *pi* 匹, so the *pi* was sometimes called a *liang* 兩. The *duan* 端 was normally 1.8 x 50 or 1.6 x 60 *chi* 尺; the *pi* 匹[疋] was normally 1.8 x 40 *chi* 尺.

type of commodity involved. To give a sense of the variation of measures, take the example of Mianhu 棉湖, a small market town to the west of Shantou 山頭 in Guangdong. One observer there noted in 1889 that 1 catty (*jin* 斤) of ducks and dried cuttle fish weighed 40 ounces (*liang* 兩); the pork and salt fish catty weighed 32 ounces; the sweet potato catty, 28 ounces; the tea and tobacco catty, 18 ounces; the vegetables, charcoal, and fruit catty, 16 ounces; and the hemp and flax catty, 15 ounces.[16] Another variable was the place. The same survey reveals that in the late Qing not only was the Hangzhou white sugar picul (*shi* 石) different from the Hangzhou brown sugar picul, but both were different from the Fuzhou white and brown sugar piculs. Such variation was not something special to the late Qing, but typical of Chinese historical weights and measures.

The chaotic mosaic of official and private practices in defining and using weights and measures was further complicated in the late Qing with the arrival of Western metrological systems.[17] In 1858, the government decreed that the customs foot-rule (*guanchi* 關尺) and the customs weights (*guanping* 關平) were to be expressed in terms of the official Qing units (the *yingzaochi* 營造尺 [construction foot-rule] and the *kuping* 庫平 [Treasury weights]). In practice, either the British imperial system or the French metric system was used in the treaty ports. Note that in the late Qing it became a common practice to write *cun* 寸, *chi* 尺, *li* 里 and other weights and measures with the mouth classifier for English units. They were read either with their normal pronunciation or as *Yingcun* 英寸, *Yingchi* 英尺, *Yingli* 英里, and so forth.

Successive Chinese administrations throughout the twentieth century endeavored to bring metrological order by making the metric system the legal standard for the whole country. In 1908, the

---

[16] Morse, 1890 (7.3.3).

[17] The convertion rates were arbitrarily set at 1 Haikwan tael (*guanjin* 關斤) = 1.3 lb avoirdupois (under the British Treaty) and 604.53 gm (under the French Treaty); see Morse, 1921 (7.3.3), 190–94. The *yingzaozhi* 營造尺 (also called Board of Works foot-rule, *buchi* 部尺), as its name implies, was set by the Board of Works. It was 32 cm long. The *kuping* 庫平 were so called because the Qing official balance weights (*fama* 砝碼) resembled those stored in the treasury. *Kuping liang* 庫平兩 (Treasury tael or ounce) had been in circulation for decades before the term "*kuping*" was made official in a 1908 decree.

Qing court reconfirmed the old standards, stipulating that they were to be adapted to the metric system. In 1915, the Beijing government decreed that the metric system was to be used alongside the old units, but the new law remained a dead letter. In 1930, the Nanjing government accepted a proposal to link existing measures to the metric system by the so-called one-two-three system:

> 1 *shisheng* 市升 (market peck) = 1 *gongsheng* 公升 (liter)
> 2 *shijin* 市斤 (market catty) = 1 *gongjin* 公斤 (kilogram)
> 3 *shichi* 市尺 (market foot) = 1 *gongchi* 公尺 (meter)

There was little headway. The metric system was again promulgated in 1959. Finally, in 1984 the State Council ordered that it be used as the sole legal system throughout the country after 1990. This is now the case, but the market system remains widespread. So, most dictionaries still have tables of the "non-legal" market measures.

7.3.1   The Terminology of Weights and Measures

The *Shuowen* 説文 mentions that Chinese linear and capacity measures are based on parts of the human body (*yi ren zhi ti wei fa* 以人之體爲法). In this respect they are similar to those in most other cultures—for example, *cun* 寸 (the width of a thumb), *chi* 尺 (a span, *zha* 拃), the distance between the tips of the extended thumb and forefinger (customarily and perversely translated as "foot"), *zhang* 丈 (the height of an adult), *yi* 溢[鎰] and *ju* 掬 (one and two handfuls), *kui* 跬 (single pace), and *bu* 步 (double pace, the basic unit for measuring land); silk threads and wool hairs were used for minutely small linear measures of less than one *cun* 寸 (Table 15); and food vessels or ladles gave their names for the capacity measures (*dou* 斗 [豆], *fu* 釜, and *sheng* 升). Most of these terms remained in use throughout Chinese history both for the metrological instrument and for the unit, although the values continually changed. Many are still in use today, albeit redefined as in the names of the prefixes for very small numbers such as pico- (*weiwei* 微微; see Table 15).

The current term *duliangheng* 度量衡 (weights and measures) first appears in the "Shundian" 舜典 chapter of the *Shangshu* 尚書 (Table 26, 19.2): *Tong lü du liang heng* 同律度量衡 ([Shun] unified the harmonics, the linear measures, the capacity measures, and the balances [weights]). The passage probably dates from the Han. It refers to the important Han dynasty standard for weights and measures, the *huangzhong* 黃鐘, the pitchpipe that was used to produce the primary note of the ancient Chinese duodecatonic (12-note) scale.[18] According to the *Hanshu* ("Lüli zhi" 律曆志) and other sources, the exact length required to produce this note was calculated by counting grains of black broomcorn millet, each of which represented one *fen* 分 (one-tenth of an inch). This length and volume was then used to calculate standard weights and measures; in fact, as recorded in the *Hanshu*, 100 grains of millet laid vertically (or 90 laid oblong) do measure 23 cm (the length of the Han *chi* 尺). Hence the name "millet ruler" (*shuchi* 黍尺) for the foot-rule. Ten grains of millet formed the weight measure *lei* 累[絫] or *shulei* 黍累, 1/10 of a *shu* 銖; see Table 15.

From the Warring States to the Han, the instrument for weighing things was the *heng* 衡 or equal-arm balance (*tianping* 天平). Weights were often called *quan* 權 (modern *fama* 砝碼). From the Later Han, a more accurate "steelyard" with unequal arms gradually came into use. It was greatly improved in the late tenth century with the introduction of the *dengzi* 戥[等]子 steelyard. It used the base-10 system as set out in Table 15.[19]

Many of the most frequently used weights and measures came to be written in early imperial times with characters of only a few strokes (e.g., *cun* 寸, *chi* 尺, *zhang* 丈 for linear measurement; *sheng* 升, *dou* 斗, and *shi* 石 for capacity, and *liang* 兩, *jin* 斤, and *shi* 石 for weight). Therefore, to avoid confusion and falsification, just as with numbers, alteration-proof characters were often used for such units (e.g., *sheng* 勝 for 升). Given that weights and measures were drawn from everyday life, it is hardly surprising that eleven of them appear as significs (16.3).

Many linear, capacity, weight, area, and volume units were used interchangeably, often with no indication other than the context.[20]

---

[18] Vogel, 1993 (7.3.3); Wu Chengluo 吳承洛, 1957 (7.3.3), 17–54. The key passage in the *Hanshu* is translated in Dubs, 1938 (44.1), 276–80.

[19] Guo Zhengzhong, 1993–94 (7.3.3).

[20] For example, the *shi* 石 began as a unit of weight but was also used as a capacity measure (probably starting from the Han). By the Southern Song, the practice of measuring grains, especially rice, by weight became gradually more widespread and as a result units of weight began to be used for capacity measures. Thus the Sichuan usage of *dan* 擔 (carrying-pole load = 1 *shi* 石, weight) spread as an alternative to *shi* 石 and *shi* 石 itself began to be pronounced *dan*. By the Qing, *dan* 擔 was used for both weight and capacity and *dan* 擔 and *shi*

Footnote continued on next page

Volume and area (including land area) units were measured using linear measures. Only the context differentiates them. *Fang* 方 (square) was used since earliest times to indicate area as in *fang liubai chi* 方六百尺 (600 *chi* square), but it was only after the introduction of Western concepts in the late Ming by the Jesuits and officials such as Xu Guangqi 徐光啓 that *fang* was used to indicate a square measure (e.g., *liubai fangchi* 六百方尺, 600 square *chi*). By the end of the Qing, volume measures began to be distinguished from units of area by using *lifang* 立方 (*lifangchi* 立方尺: cubic *chi* 尺). For building units, see 37.4.2.

7.3.2   Note on Cultivated-Land Statistics

During the Zhou, a *mu* 畝 was defined as being 100 *bu* 步 (*bu bai wei mu* 步百爲畝), i.e., 100 square *bu*. A 240-*bu mu* was introduced in 350 BC in Qin and was gradually extended to the rest of the country by conquest and after the unification, by decree. During the Former Han until 104 BC, both the 100-*bu* and the 240-*bu mu* were in use. Between 104 BC and 1911, the 240-bu *mu* was the standard (the statistics of cultivated land in the *Hanshu* "Dilizhi" are however in 100-*bu mu*).[21] In theory, one *mu* could have been a strip 240 *bu* long and one *bu* wide or a plot of land 16 x 15 *bu*. In both cases it would have been 240 square *mu*. Over the centuries, the size of the official *mu* changed depending on the definition of the length of a *bu* (6 *chi* 尺 from Zhou to Sui and 5 *chi* thereafter; see Table 17) and also on the gradually increasing length of a *chi*. The resultant increase in the size of the official *mu* are set out in Table 19. In practice, the actual size of a *mu* also varied widely according to the time, the place, and the type of land.

The 100-*bu mu* of the early Zhou was sometimes referred to as the *xiaomu* 小畝 and the 240-*bu mu* as the *damu* 大畝.[22] Today the

---

石 were used interchangeably. In 1928, 石 (pronounced *dan*) was reserved exclusively for the capacity measure and *dan* 擔 for the unit of weight. In 1959, the same distinction was confirmed.

By the later empire, rice and grain were usually sold wholesale by weight as also were fluids. The grain tribute continued to be assessed using measures of capacity, but it was collected by weight at fixed conversion rates (when not commuted to cash); see Morse (1921), 190–94.

[21] Wu Hui, 1985 (7.3.3).

[22] Ochi Shigeaki 約智重明, 1977 (7.3.3).

100-*bu mu* is sometimes called the Zhou *mu* 周畝. During the Ming and Qing *damu* and *xiaomu* were used in a different sense. The *damu* was a fiscal unit and was in some places up to 8–10 times larger than a regular 240-*bu mu* (called *xiaomu*). Total land acreage figures denominated in *mu* 畝 in the Ming and Qing (and earlier periods) often underestimate the actual land (as do the population figures) since they were used for tax assessment purposes (or calculating labor service obligations) as well as for measuring property for sale and inheritance. On the other hand, statistics of military land were notoriously over estimated because owners could claim exemptions.[23]

From the Song, subdivisions of a *mu* were normally calculated using the very small numbers in Table 15, e.g., *yimu sifen sanli sihao* 一畝四分三厘四毫 (3.434 *mu*). Ten *mu* would have been written in a contract as *yishi mu zheng* 壹拾畝整 (ten *mu* exactly).

Table 19: The Mu 畝: *Conversion of Historic Values*

Period	1 *mu* 畝 = m²	*mu* 畝 per acre	*mu* 畝 per hectare
Early Zhou 周	192	21	52
350–104 BC	461 (or 192)	9 (or 21)	22 (or 52)
Han to Tang	457–523	9–8	22–19
Song	573	7	17
Yuan	840	5	12
Ming	640	6	16
Qing	706	6	14
Republic	666	6	15

Sources: 7.3.3.

Many regions and provinces had special names for "their" *mu* 畝 (e.g., *kah* [*jia*] 甲 in Taiwan.[24] Elsewhere, land area units were sometimes based on calculations roughly equivalent to 1 *mu*, e.g., in the New Territories of Hong Kong the *douzhong* 斗種 was the area planted with one peck of rice seed (equal to 0.134 acres). *Shang* 垧

[23] On the distinction between fiscal and actual *mu* 畝, see, for example, Ping-ti Ho, 1959 (7.2.2), 101–35 and contra Ho, Kang Chao, 1986 (7.2.2).

[24] *Kah* (*jia* 甲) is from "*akker*," a unit of measure used by the seventeenth century Dutch administration. It appears in Taiwanese place names to this day.

was used as an area measure in the northeast (about 15 *mu*) and in the northwest (3 to 5 *mu*). Non-Han peoples also used their own methods and units for measuring land area, for example, the *shuang* 雙 in Yunnan was the area ploughed by two oxen in one day, the equivalent of 5 *mu* 畝, the amount supposed to be cultivable in one day by one family. The *shuang* 雙 was subdivided into 4 *jiao* 角 (= 2 *ji* 己 = 2 *fa* 乏). It appears in Yunnanese place names such as Xi-shuang ban'na 西雙版納. Manchu banner land was reckoned in *shang* 晌[垧] (= 6 *mu* 畝), *sheng* 繩 (= 4 *shang*) and *suo* 所 (= 180 *mu* of orchard or vegetable land).

7.3.3   Sources and Studies

Details of the official measures of each dynasty are included in the monographs on harmonics and the calendar or on financial administration in the Standard Histories (Table 31, Chapter 22) and in institutional works such as the *huiyao* 會要 (25.1), the *tongkao* 通考 (25.2), or the *huidian* 會典 (27.5). Mathematical textbooks often give details of how to calculate different unofficial measures. So do scholars in their *biji* 筆記 (Chapter 31); see, for example, Gu Yanwu 顧炎武, *Rizhilu* 日知錄, *juan* 10–11; or Yu Zhengxie 俞正燮, *Guisi leigao* 癸巳類稿 and *Guisi cungao* 癸巳存稿 (50.6.3). Note the *Bibliography of Works on Historical Metrology Relating to China*, Hans Ulrich Vogel, Zhengzhong Guo, and Qiu Guangming, comps., forthcoming.[25] Hundreds of actual measures have survived, the earliest dating back to the third century BC. They provide an essential means of checking the information in written sources (see item one in the following list).

Qiu Guangming 丘光明, *Zhongguo lidai duliangheng kao* 中國歷代度量衡考 (Research on weights and measures through the ages in China), Kexue, 1992. This is an illustrated catalog of 1,481 extant metrological instruments (most of them recently excavated) dating from the Shang to the end of the Qing (plus 26 from the Republic). Introduc-

---

[25] Earlier studies were mainly based on literary evidence; see Wu Chengluo 吳承洛, *Zhongguo dulianghengshi* 中國度量衡史 (A history of Chinese weights and measures), 1937, rev., ed., Shangwu, 1957, 1993; Yang Kuan 楊寬, *Zhongguo lidai chidu kao* 中國歷代尺度考 (Historical study of the Chinese foot-rule), 1938; rpnt., Shangwu, 1955, 1957. These studies have now been superseded by Liang (1980), Qiu (1992), and Guo (1993).

tions and annotations are based on careful measurements of the artifacts, as well as on written sources.

Qiu Guangming 丘光明, *Zhongguo gudai duliangheng* 中國古代度量衡 (Weights and measures in ancient China), Shangwu, 1996.

Duliangheng 度量衡 (Weights and measures) in the series *Zhongguo kexue jishu shi* 中國科學技術史 (History of science and technology in China), Lu Jiaxi 盧嘉錫, ed. in chief, 30 vols, Kexue, 1998- .

Liang Fangzhong 梁方仲, "Zhongguo lidai duliangheng zhi bianqian ji qi shidai tezheng" 中國歷代度量衡之變遷及其時代特征 (The changes in China's historical weights and measures and the characteristics of each period), 521–39. Appendix to Liang, 1980 (7.2.1) summarizing a lifetime's study of China's economic history.

Hanyu da cidian 漢語大詞典 has useful tables on historical changes of weights and measures and their modern equivalents in volume 13. The compiler, Wang Guanying 王冠英, made good use of recent archaeological discoveries.

Wu Hui 吳慧, *Zhongguo lidai liangshi muchan yanjiu* 中國歷代糧食畝產 研究 (Research on the output of crops per *mu* in successive periods), Nongye, 1985.

David N. Keightley, "A Measure of Man in Early China: In Search of the Neolithic Inch," *Chinese Science* 12: 16–38 (1994–95).

Robert Poor, "The Circle and the Square: Measure and Ritual in Ancient China," *MS* 43: 159–210 (1995).

Ochi Shigeaki 約智重明, "Ichiho hihyakuyonjû-ho sei o megutte" 一畝 二百四十步制をめぐつて (On the 240-*bu mu* system), *Tôhôgakuhô* 53: 21–35 (1977).

Ma Chengyuan 馬承源, "Shang Yang fangsheng he Zhanguo liangzhi" 商 鞅方升和戰國量制 (Shang Yang's square peck and the capacity measures of the Warring States), *Wenwu* 6 (1972), 17–24.

A. F. P. Hulsewé, "Weights and Measures in Ch'in Law," in *State and Law in East Asia: Festschrift for Karl Bolger*, Dieter Eikemeier and Herbert Franke, eds., Harrassowitz, 1981, 25–39.

Hans Ulrich Vogel, "Aspects of Metrosophy and Metrology During the Han Period," *Extrême-Orient, Extrême-Occident* 16: 135–52 (1993).

Michael Loewe, "The Measurement of Grain During the Han Dynasty," *TP* 49: 64–95 (1961).

Zhengzhong Guo, "The *Deng* Steelyards of the Song Dynasty (960-1279)," *Cahiers de Métrologie*, tomes 11–12: 297–306 (1993–94).

Guo Zhengzhong 郭正忠, *Zhongguo quanheng duliang san zhi shisi shiji* 中國權衡度量三至十四世紀 (Chinese weights and measures: third to fourteenth centuries), Shehui kexue, 1993.

Hans Ulrich Vogel, "History of Length Measures During the Song Period (960–1279): Some Reflections on the State of the Field and Research Prospects," in *Acta Metrologiae Historicae* 5, Harald Witthöft, ed., Scripta Mercaturae Verlag, 1999, 153–72.

Wen Renjun (聞人軍) and James M. Hargett, "The Measures *Li* and *Mou* During the Song, Liao, and Jin Dynasties, *Bulletin of Sung-Yuan Studies* 21: 8–30 (1989).

Hosea B. Morse, "Currency and Measures in China," *JNCBRAS*, new series XXIV: 46–135 (1890). Contains summaries prepared by Morse of the replies to a circular sent to its members by the China Branch of the Royal Asiatic Society in January 1889.

Hosea Ballou Morse, *The Trade and Administration of China*, 3rd rev. edition, Kelly and Walsh, 1921, 190–94.

On traditional cultivated-land statistics, see:

Liang Fangzhong, 1980 (7.2.1)

Perkins, 1969 (7.2.1), Appendix B (but discount those of his calculations based on Wu Chengluo [1957], many of whose estimations have been called into question).

Kang Chao, "Measuring the Area of Cultivated Land," in Kang, 1986 (4.9), 64–87; *CHC*, vol. 8, 127–28; 439–53.

Zhao Gang 趙岡 et al., *Qingdai liangshi muchanliang yanjiu* 清代糧食畝產量研究 (Research on acreage productivity in the Qing), Nongye, 1995.

He Bingdi 何炳棣, *Zhongguo lidai tudi shuzi kaoshi* 中國歷代土地數字考釋 (Research on Chinese historical land statistics), Lianjing, 1995. This is a revised version of the author's earlier work *Zhongguo gujin tudi shuzi de kaoshi he pingjia* 中國古今土地數字的考釋和評價 (Land statistics in ancient and modern China: research, interpretation, and evaluation), Shehui kexue, 1988, a subject already touched on in Ping-ti Ho, 1959 (7.2.2), 101–35.

Pierre Hoang, *Notions techniques sur la propriété en Chine avec un choix d'actes et de documents officiels*, Variétées Sinologiques 11; Shanghai, 1897.

Swetz, 1992 (37.4).

Zhongguo cehuishi 中國測繪史 (4.4).

7.4   Money

7.4.1   Money

Specie such as iron, copper, silver, or gold, or commodity money such as grain, were denominated in units of weight, thus, for example, the *liang* 兩 in late imperial China was both the "Chinese ounce" as well as the tael (ounce of silver). Not only were the names of the basic Qin and Han bronze coins, the *banliang* 半兩 and the *shu* 銖 derived from the weights, so, too, probably were their forms; see *Bronze (2)*.

Main Monetary Units

These notes are mainly based on Yang (1952), von Glahn (1996), and *Zhongguo qianbi da cidian*; see 7.4.2. Coins, metals, and units are arranged in chronological order according to their importance in each period.

Cowry Shells

Cowry shells were used for money in the Shang and Western Zhou, no doubt against a background of barter exchange and alongside the use of other precious objects for commodity money such as jade and pearls (*zhuyu* 珠玉), tortoise shells and cowries (*guibei* 龜貝), dogs and horses (*quanma* 犬馬), leather (*pibi* 皮幣), hemp and silk (*bubo* 布帛), grains (*gu* 穀) and precious metals (*jin* 金). Many of these objects, including cowries, were also used for gifts (*bi* 幣) and ornaments. This presumably was the use of the cowries that have been excavated in recent decades from many of the most famous prehistoric culture sites. The value attached to the cowry shells, particularly to their ventrical side, may have been connected to fertility rites or beliefs. Later in the Zhou, bronze and iron cowry coins were also cast. Cowry shells were counted in double strings called *peng* 玤 (the *guwen* 古文 form of 朋). Dozens of characters connected with money were given the cowry-shell classifier already during the Zhou. Many are still in use, for example, expensive and cheap (*gui* 貴 and *jian* 賤); buy and sell (*mai* 買 and *mai* 賣); and to trade, to lend, and to present as tribute (*mao* 貿, *dai* 貸, and *gong* 貢). Cowries remained in use in Yunnan until the later empire; see Hans Ulrich Vogel, "Cowry Trade and Its Role in the Economy of Yunnan from the Ninth to the Mid-Seventeenth Century," *JESHO* 36: 211–52; 301–53 (1993).

Bronze (1)

Bu 布 (spade money); fifth to third centuries BC

Dao 刀 (knife money); fifth to third centuries BC

These coins were modeled after spades and knives. They usually had the place of manufacture or weight cast on them (17.2.4).

Commodity Money

Silk (and hemp cloth as well as grain and other precious commodities, such as those mentioned under *Cowry Shells*) had been in use for transactions since archaic times. They returned in the period of disunion between the Han and the Tang, second only to the reintroduced bronze cash coins. They remained in use because taxation in kind formed the bulk of government revenue except in the Southern Song and the Yuan. It was only from the sixteenth century that it was replaced by taxes payable in silver.

Iron

Iron cash were important at certain periods and in certain places, e.g., in southern China during the Five Dynasties or in Sichuan during the Song.

Bronze (2)

Yuanqian 圓錢 (also called *yuanjin* 圓金), round bronze coins. They replaced spade and knife money (see *Bronze, 1*) from the mid-Warring States period. The form is usually said to be derived from a *bi* 璧 (jade disc) or a wagon wheel. It is perhaps just as likely to be taken from the small round bronze weights with a hole in the middle, for example, the *shu* 銖[朱] (after which bronze coins were later named). Like the *shu*, they also had a round hole in the middle (useful for stringing as had also been the practice with the cowries). The first bronze round coins appear in the state of Wei 魏. The place of casting and the denomination (weight) are usually on the face of the coins. They were soon copied in other states, including Qin, which began casting them in 336 BC. The earliest tomb of known date from which the characteristic Qin coin, the *banliang* 半兩 (half ounce, i.e., 12 *shu*) has been excavated is at Qing-chuan 青川 in Sichuan (see 19.1.2). Seven *banliang* coins each with a square hole were found here. The tomb dates from 306 BC, six years after the Qin began the conquest of Sichuan. Excavations show that the new coin also spread to other parts of China in the wake of the Qin armies. When Qin unified the currency in 221 BC the *banliang* became the official coin of the empire thus ensuring that the round coin with the square hole (*fangkongqian* 方孔錢, *kongfangxiong* 孔方兄, or *fanxiong* 方兄) became the characteristic small coin of China and its neighbors. The work that bears one of the chancellors of Qin's name, the *Lüshi chunqiu* 呂氏春秋 (Table 26, 19.2), explains that the round rim signifies heaven and the square hole, the earth ("Yuandao pian" 圓道篇). It is more likely that the square hole was introduced to prevent coins slipping in the mold and that the cosmological explanation came later. The *banliang* was replaced in 118 BC (when the Han introduced the five *shu* 銖 coin). The *shu* was eventually replaced in the Tang by the *qian* 錢, which remained the basic unit until the early twentieth century (originally the *jian* 錢 was a type of bronze-tipped spade; later it was used for "cash" and also for the unit of weight, the *qian* 錢 [mace]; see Table 16. *Qian* 錢 also replaced the Zhou word for coin, *quan* 泉. In English, the coin is often called "copper cash" [cash is from the Sanskrit, *kârsha* via Portuguese *cas, casse, caxa*]). Starting sporadically from the mid-fourth century, and systematically from the eighth century, bronze coins bore the *nianhao* of the ruler either with the four characters *nianhao yuanbao* 年號元寶 (original treasure of such and such era) or *nianhao tongbao* 年號通寶 (circulating treasure of such and such era).[26] Cash were reckoned in *wen* 文 (sapek or sapeca after the Portuguese) and in short, full, and standard strings of 1,000 cash. The strings were called normally *guan* 貫, *suo* 索, or *min* 緡 before the Song and *diao* 吊 or *chuan* 串 in the Ming and Qing. They were defined differently at different times according to how many cash were in the string (e.g., *jiuba* 九八 or *jiuliu* 九六 were strings of 980 or 960 cash, respectively). From the Tang, the government normally defined how many cash could be accepted in short strings (*chubai* 除陌, *shengbai* 省陌) and full strings (*zubai* 足陌). The *bandiaozi* 半吊子 was a string of 500 cash (also used to refer to incomplete people). In 1898, copper coins were issued without a hole in the middle. They were valued at 10 of the old cash. There was an oversupply in the early Republic.

Gold

Jin 金 (used for gold, copper, and metal in general). Was also used to mean catty (*jin* 斤) in Han and earlier texts. In later times, it frequently meant *liang* 兩 (ounce), especially in literary sources.

Silver

Yin 銀 (silver). Uncoined silver ingots (along with bronze coins) were the main money in late imperial China. Prior to that silver played a minor role. There were only two recorded government issues of silver currency: the first in the reign of Han Wudi (called *baijin* 白金, white metal) and in the Jin dynasty. The monetary use of silver became more common in the Tang. But the real change in its importance came only after the imports

---

[26] In the Ming and Qing only the expression *tongbao* was used on coins since *yuanbao* had come to mean a shoe-shaped ingot of silver. See Yang (1952), 24–25 (7.4.2).

from the New World in the Ming and Qing.[27] The normal way of referring to silver by weight was in taels (ounces), e.g., *shiliang yinzi* 十兩銀子
(ten taels of silver). Inscribed silver ingots were called *ding* 錠. From the
Yuan, *yuanbao* 元寶 was also used to refer to the shoe-shaped ingots of
silver (Yuan *baochao* 元寶鈔 was a paper note issued in the Yuan with
silver as its reserve, hence the transfer of the name). Silver ingots were
also called *matiyin* 馬蹄銀 (horse-shoe silver).

Tael 兩; by the late Qing, there were more than 170 currency taels in
China. The differences were in both weight and fineness. Those taels
which attained a certain standard of fineness were called sycee (from the
Cantonese pronunciation of *xisi* 細絲 in *xisi wenyin* 紋銀, fine silk-
pattern silver). The three main taels were the *Kuping* 庫平 (Treasury),
Caoping 漕平 (Tribute), and *Haikwan* 海關 or *Guanping* 關平 (Customs)
taels. The customs tael was in use 1842–1933. Taels were mainly used as a
silver-based unit of account; ordinary payments were in silver dollars.

Dollars (*fanyin* 番銀, *fanbing* 番餅, *yangqian* 洋錢, etc.). The Spanish Carolus dollar was introduced to Fujian and Guangdong via the Philippines in the sixteenth century. By the end of the nineteenth century it
had spread all over China but was overtaken by the Mexican dollar,
which was joined by the British Hong Kong dollar (issued 1866–68); the
American Trade dollar (1873–87), and the Japanese yen (1871–97). From
the late nineteenth century, the 7.2 mace silver dollar became the most
common dollar. It was known as the *longyang* 龍洋 (dragon dollar) from
the design on its reverse. Two other dollars circulated extensively during
the Republic, the Yuan Shikai dollar (1914) or *Yuantou* 袁頭 and the Sun
Yatsen dollar or *Suntou* 孫頭 (1933–34). No more silver dollars were issued after 1935.

Paper

Feiqian 飛錢 (flying money). Tang tea merchants wishing to transfer
safely the profits from selling their wares at the capital Chang'an back to
their home provinces in the south bought vouchers (*feiqian* 飛錢) from
the liaison offices maintained by the provincial governments in the capital. The vouchers guaranteed payment in cash on presentation of the
voucher back in the province.

Jiaozi 交子 (exchange medium). First appeared in Chengdu in the
early eleventh century. In return for depositing iron cash, the deposit
houses issued receipts which were used for financial transactions. In 1107,
26,852,006 strings (one note per string) were outstanding. The name was

---

[27] William Atwell, "Ming China and the Emerging World Economy, c.
1470–1650," *CHC*, vol. 8, 376–416.

changed in the same year to *qianyin* 錢引 (cash voucher) and the area of circulation extended to the Yellow and Huai River valleys. Denominations were in strings (*huizi* 會子). Local officials began issuing *huizi* against commodity reserves. Other credit instruments were tea and salt vouchers (*chayin* 茶引 and *yanyin* 鹽引). The first printed paper money and trademarks also appeared in the Song (*Ji'nan Liujia gongfu zhenpu* 濟南劉家功夫針鋪 [Fine needles made by the Liu family of Jinan]. The design shows a rabbit kissing a needle. It was printed from a copperplate).

The Yuan was the high point of paper currency in China. In the Ming and Qing, silver and bronze were important. Paper money was not revived until the nineteenth century under Western influence.

7.4.2   Secondary Sources on Money

The best introduction to the terminology remains item 1 (supplemented and updated by items 2 and 3; for analysis, see item 4; for quotes from the sources, item 2, 3 and 5, and for a translation of the chapters on food and money in the *Shiji* and *Hanshu*, see Swann, 1950 (41.4, *Translations from the* Hanshu).

L. S. Yang (Yang Liansheng 楊聯陞), *Money and Credit in China: A Short History*, HUP, 1952. In just over one hundred pages Yang covers from antiquity to the end of the Qing: coins, gold and silver, paper money, traditional credit institutions, old-style and modern banks, and loans and interest rates.

Zhongguo qianbi da cidian 中國錢幣大辭典 (Dictionary of Chinese numismatics), 10 vols., Zhonghua, 1995– . This huge work supersedes all previous histories of Chinese coins. It includes archaeological discoveries made since 1949. Each volume is indexed and contains reproductions of coins and molds; transcriptions of the characters found on the coins; tables of denominations (with alternative and simplified characters) and tables of typical weights with their modern equivalents.

Zhongguo lidai huobi daxi 中國歷代貨幣大繫 (Collection of Chinese historical currency), Wang Qingzheng 汪慶正, ed. in chief, 12 large folio vols., Shanghai renmin and Shanghai guji, 1988– . The first volume (1988) is on the pre-Qin.

Richard von Glahn, *Fountain of Fortune: Money and Monetary Policy in China, Tenth to Seventeenth Centuries*, UCP, 1996. Focuses on the transition from a coin to a silver economy in the late imperial period, but also covers wider ground, examining "what money meant to the Chinese themselves, how it was incorporated into economic thought and fiscal policy (which, for all interests and purposes, were virtually identical in imperial China), and how the state and market interacted through a medium vital to both," 12.

Peng Xinwei 彭信威 (1907–65), *A Monetary History of China*, Edward H. Kaplan, tr., Western Washington UP, 2 vols., 1994 (*Zhongguo qianbishi* 中國錢幣史, 2 vols., 1954; 3rd ed., Shanghai renmin, 1965. Detailed, factual history with many quotations from the original sources by a scholarly ex-banker.

Frank H. H. King, *Money and Monetary Policy in China, 1845–1895*, HUP, 1965.

Zhongguo guchao tuji 中國古鈔圖輯 (Selected illustrations of Chinese paper money), Nei-Menggu qianbi yanjiuhui 內蒙古錢幣研究會 and *Zhongguo qianbi* 中國錢幣, editorial dept., comps., Zhongguo jinrong, 1992. This is a well-illustrated bilingual account of the history of paper money.

The Chinese Numismatic Society publishes *Zhongguo qianbi* 中國錢幣 (China numismatics; 1983– , quarterly), which carries news of the discovery of ancient coins and articles on monetary history.

7.5   Prices

For a systematic survey of Chinese price history based on original sources, see Tan Wenxi 譚文熙, *Zhongguo wujiashi* 中國物價史.[28] The author examines in each period of the empire and the republic the concept of price; changing prices as reflected in contemporary data, and government price policy. For the pre-Qin there are almost no price data, but many of the classical thinkers commented on prices and governments sought by various means to control the market. Prices of commodities in the early empire are occasionally recorded in traditional written sources, on stone inscriptions, or on newly discovered documents such as those on the bamboo strips. Specialized works on mathematics also sometimes include problems based on real data and questions using prices.[29]

[28] *Zhongguo wujiashi* (A history of Chinese prices), Hubei renmin, 1994.

[29] Pre-Qin prices are assembled in *Zhongguo qianbi da cidian* (7.4.2), vol. 1, page 5. Qin and Han commodity prices on the *Hanjian* are excerpted in *Zhongguo gudai shehui jingjishi ziliao* 中國古代社會經濟史資料 (Materials on ancient Chinese socioeconomic history), Lishisuo, eds., 1st collection, Fujian renmin, 1985, 1–98. The *Jiuzhang suanshu* 九章算術 (37.1), for example, records 68

Footnote continued on next page

The most extensive price records in imperial times are of crops. Grain price reporting connected with the operation of the ever-normal granaries (*changping cang* 常平倉) was in place at least from the Tang dynasty, although no records are extant. The Qing system was inherited from the Ming and installed during the reign of Kangxi. Reports were made every 10 days and summarized at provincial level for forwarding to the capital.[30] Tens of thousands of the reports have been preserved in the Qing archives and are available today on microfilm.[31] They cover each of the 28 provinces from Kangxi to 1911. The reports were secretly held at the palace and used not only for the granary system, but also as a sort of early warning of trouble. Occasional finds of them have been published, but this is the first time they have been made available in full.

There are fairly extensive price records for salt and other government monopolies, and for palace construction and maintenance, and court consumption.

For sources on prices and inflation in the Republic, see 51.4.5.

prices for 27 different products; see Song Jie 宋傑, *Jiuzhang suanshu yu Handai shehui jingji* 九章算術與漢代社會經濟 (The *Jiuzhang suanshu* and the social economy of the Han), Shoudu shifan daxue, 1993.

[30] On the grain-price reporting system as it was practiced in the Qing, see Wang Yejian 王業鍵, "Qingdai de liangjia chenbao zhidu" 清代的糧價陳報制度 On the grain price reporting system of the Qing dynasty), *Taibei gugong jikan* 13.1 (1978) and the works cited in Wang Yejian and Huang Yingjue 黃瑩珏, "Qing zhongye dongnan yanhai de liangshi zuowu fenbu liangshi gongxu ji liangjia fenxi" 清中葉東南沿海的糧食作物分部糧食供需及糧價分析 (The distribution of grain crops, grain supply, and an analysis of grain prices on the southeast coast of China in the mid-Qing), *SJ* 70.2: 238–88 (1999). Also, Hansheng Chuan and Richard A. Kraus, *Mid-Ch'ing Rice Markets and Trade: An Essay in Price History*, East Asian Research Center, HUP, 1975; Robert B. Marks, "Rice Prices, Food Supply, and Market Structure in Eighteenth-Century South China," *LIC* 12.2 (1991); Kishimoto Mio 岸本美緒, *Shindai Chûgoku no bukka to keizai hendô* 清代中國の物價と經濟變動 (Commodity prices in Qing China and trends in the economy), Kenbun, 1997.

[31] *Gongzhong liangjiadan* 宮中糧價單 (Grain-price reports in the palace archives), Yishiguan, comps., 328 reels, 1990 (see 50.2.1).

8

Guides and Encyclopaedias

This chapter introduces surveys (8.1), guides (sinological and historical, 8.2–3), and encyclopaedias that cover the whole or most of Chinese history (8.4). Chapters 43–51 cover guides and primary sources to individual periods.

8.1 Surveys

The best single-volume survey of Chinese history is Jacques Gernet, *A History of Chinese Civilization*.[1] The following are three of the best illustrated overviews in English (plus two excellent surveys covering between them from the Tang to the present and one source book):

Caroline Blunden and Mark Elvin, *Cultural Atlas of China*, Facts on File (Checkmark Books), 1983; rev. edition, 1998. Innovative maps and many illustrations match the fascinating text.

Patricia Buckley Ebrey, *The Cambridge Illustrated History of China*, CUP, 1996.

A Journey into China's Antiquity, National Museum of Chinese History, eds., Morning Glory, 1997–98. Comprehensive and up-to-date illustrations (including recent archaeological discoveries), plus authoritative explanations. The series is based on the main exhibits of the Museum of Chinese History (after the re-organization that took place from 1988). Also in Chinese, French, German, and Japanese:

> Vol. 1, *Palaeolithic–Spring and Autumn Period*
> Vol. 2, *Warring States–Northern and Southern Dynasties*

[1] J. R. Foster and Charles Hartman, trs., CUP, 1982; NY: CUP, 2nd edition, 1996 (originally published in French, 1972). The English edition of 1996 was based on the revised French edition of 1990 with important improvements, including overall additons, corrections, and changes, and an index with Chinese characters.

Vol. 3, *Sui Tang–Song*
Vol. 4, *Yuan, Ming, and Qing*

An earlier, much longer Chinese version has many more illustrations but they are rather poor black-and-white reproductions and are based on the museum's collections before the 1988 reorganization: *Zhongguo gudaishi cankao tulu* 中國古代史參考圖錄 (Reference illustrations for ancient Chinese history), Zhongguo lishi bowuguan 中國歷史博物館, ed., 9 vols., Shanghai jiaoyu, 1989–91.

F. W. Mote, *Imperial China: 900–1800* (41.3.1).

Jonathan D. Spence, *The Search for Modern China* (50.10.3).

Chinese Civilization: A Sourcebook, Patricia Buckley Ebrey, ed., 1981; 2nd ed., rev. and expanded, Free Press, 1993. Excellent selection of translated and commented excerpts from original sources arranged by topics and periods. Note also the literary anthologies, e.g., Mair (1994) and Owen (1996), 30.4.

8.2 Sinological Guides

For an introduction to reference works on many aspects of Chinese studies (sinology) covering most periods from the first emperor to about 1990, see Harriet S. Zurndorfer, *China Bibliography: A Research Guide to Reference Works About China Past and Present*, Brill, 1995; 2nd prnt. (paperback), UHP, 1999. The author comments on a total of 1,250 books and journals—650 in Chinese, 600 in Western languages (mainly English), and 23 in Japanese. Among the subjects left out or with only limited coverage are the main genres of historical writing (annalistic and dynastic) and reference works on agriculture, archaeology, the arts, Buddhism, the Classics, Daoism, the law, the Manchus, the missionaries, the pre-Qin, medicine, and the military. The names of authors, compilers, or editors are frequently not given. Titles are not translated although the contents of works are described. The names of publishers are not indicated. The Wade-Giles system of romanization is used.

For the twentieth century, by far the most detailed bibliography is James H. Cole, *Twentieth-Century China: An Annotated Bibliography of Reference Works in Chinese, Japanese, and Western Languages*, vol. 1, 2000; vol. 2, 2001. For other references, see 51.14.1.

Although not as up-to-date as Zurndoffer or Cole, Teng Ssu-yü (Deng Siyu 鄧嗣禹, 1905–88) and Knight Biggerstaff, *An Annotated Bibliography of Selected Chinese Reference Works*, 3rd rev. ed., H-Y Institute, 1971, contains fuller descriptions of earlier works. Teng and Biggerstaff cover Chinese studies in general and arrange Chinese reference works of all periods up to about 1940 under the following categories: (1) bibliographies, (2) encyclopaedias, (3) dictionaries, (4) geographical works, (5) biographical works, (6) tables, (7) yearbooks, (8) sinological indexes.

There are large numbers of Chinese guides to modern reference works for students of Chinese literature and history. For example:

Zhongwen gongjushu jichu 中文工具書基礎 (Basic Chinese reference books), Zhu Tianjun 朱天俊 and Li Guoxin 李國新, eds., Beijing tushuguan, 1998. Contains the essentials and has reliable explanations. Replaces earlier versions by the same authors of 1987 (Shumu wenxian) and 1991 (Beijing daxue).

Wenshizhe gongjushu jianjie 文史哲工具書簡介 (A brief introduction to reference works for literature, history, and philosophy), Chinese Dept. and History Dept., Nanjing University Library, eds., Tianjin jiaoyu, 1980. More bibliographic in approach. The compilers note different editions of primary sources from first appearance to the present day. There is a stroke-count index.

Zhongguo lishi gongjushu zhinan 中國歷史工具書指南 (A guide to reference books for Chinese history), Lin Tiesen 林鐵森, Beijing daxue, 1992. Written specifically for students of Chinese history; also includes some Western and Japanese reference books. With a full *pinyin* index it is convenient to use, but has no references published after mid-1990.

8.3   Historical Guides

8.3.1   Chinese

As China becomes more modern and as a result (at least in the early stages), more cut off from its history, Chinese students need guidebooks to help them in their studies, especially of ancient history. Since the 1980s, a large number have been published. The space allotted to primary sources, secondary scholarship, and research problems differs in each. Some concentrate on a single period, others cover all of Chinese history. Some cover a particular type of history (for example social or revolutionary, see items 4 and 5, repectively). Guides devoted to individual periods are introduced in 43.2. Some good readers are mentioned in 1.3.5.

Zhongguoshi yanjiu zhinan 中國史研究指南 (Guide to research on Chinese history), Gao Mingshi 高明士, ed., 5 vols., Lianjing, 1990. One of the most comprehensive guides. It is a translation into Chinese of the leading Japanese guide to Chinese history (Yamane, 1983; see 8.3.2). The editor, Gao Mingshi, has added the contributions of Taiwan and Hong Kong scholars, and thus the guide covers secondary scholarship in all languages (as of the early 1980s) for every period of Chinese history as well as Chinese primary sources. About two-thirds of the guide goes to secondary scholarship and one-third to primary sources and reference works. Secondary Western scholarship is only partially included. Just after this translation was published in 1990, Yamane and his team produced an update to their guide. There is a second Chinese translation of Yamane, this time of the updated version, Tian Renlong 田人隆, tr. *Zhongguoshi yanjiu rumen* 中國史研究入門, 2 vols., Shehuikexue wenxian, 1994.

Zhongguo gudaishi shiliaoxue 中國古代史史料學 (The study of the primary source materials for ancient Chinese history), Chen Gaohua 陳高華 and Chen Zhichao 陳智超 et al., Beijing, 1983; 6th prnt., 1991. Straightforward introduction to primary sources arranged by period from the Shang to the mid-Qing. Each chapter was written by a specialist from the Lishisuo (not to be confused with the next item, which has an identical title but is arranged by genre, not by period). There is little attempt to include either reference books or secondary scholarship.

Zhongguo gudaishi shiliaoxue 中國古代史史料學 (The study of the primary source materials for ancient Chinese history), An Zuozhang 安作璋, ed., Fujian renmin, 1994, 1998. Arrangement is by type of primary source (to the end of the Qing), not by period. There is no attempt to include either reference books or secondary scholarship.

Zhongguo shehuishi yanjiu gaishu 中國社會史研究概述 (Introduction to research on Chinese social history), Feng Erkang 馮爾康 et al., eds., Tianjin jiaoyu, 1988; rpnt., Taibei, 1989. Covers primary sources on social history arranged by traditional categories as well as modern Chinese research on social history arranged by dynasty up to 1985.

Zhongguo xiandai gemingshi shiliaoxue 中國現代革命史史料學 (51.9.2).

8.3.2   *Japanese Historical Guides*

There are several Japanese guides to the study of Chinese history written for Japanese students. One of the more recent was edited by a team of Tokyo historians led by Yamane Yukio 山根幸夫, *Chûgokushi kenkyû nyûmon* 中國史研究入門. The handbook is arranged by period. Vol. 1 covers from earliest times to the end of the Yuan; vol. 2, from the Ming up to the 1980s.[2] Each chapter is written by one or more specialists and includes lengthy discussions of the secondary scholarship on selected themes. The emphasis is on Japanese and Chinese scholarship, but English- and other Western- language work is included. There are also annotated bibliographies of selected primary sources. About two-thirds of the guide is devoted to secondary scholarship and one third to primary sources and reference works. The index includes titles of primary sources. The second edition includes a new essay at the end of each volume summarizing publications that appeared after the first edition, between 1982 and 1991 (vol. 1) and between 1982 and 1994 (vol. 2). Compare the coverage in Yamane with another recent guide produced mainly by historians at Kyoto. Despite the interest of the topically arranged chapters in the Kyoto handbook, the Tokyo guide is more thorough and up-to-date:

Ajia rekishi kenkyû nyûmon アジア歴史研究入門 (Handbook for research into Asian history), Shimada Kenji 嶋田虔次, ed. in chief, 5 vols., Dôhôsha, 1983-4; vol. 6 (index), 1987. China is covered in vols. 1-3. Detailed bibliographical essays by specialists cover both primary and secondary sources (in all languages). Vol. 3 is topically arranged and covers catalogs, historical geography, archaeology, the history of thought, science and technology, customs, and women. A separate, sixth volume contains a comprehensive author-title index to the entire work.

8.4   Historical Encyclopaedias

8.4.1   English

China: A Cultural and Historical Dictionary, Michael Dillon, ed., Curzon, 1998. Contains about 1,500 entries covering from earliest times to the present day.

---

[2] *Chûgokushi kenkyû nyûmon* (Handbook for research on Chinese history), 2 vols., Yamakawa, 1983; rev. and enl. ed., vol. 1, 1991, 1996; vol. 2, rev. and enl., 1995. Supersedes *Tôyô shiryô shûsei* 東洋史料集成 (Bibliography of primary and secondary sources for Oriental history), Heibonsha, 1956; 3rd prnt., 1992.

8.4.2 Chinese

There are two main Chinese encyclopaedias of Chinese history:

Zhongguo da baike quanshu 中國大百科全書 (The great Chinese ency-
clopaedia), 74 vols., 1980–94; among which *Zhongguo lishi* 中國歷史
(Chinese history), 3 vols., Da baike quanshu, 1992; 3rd prnt., 1995.
The fairly long articles were written by China's leading historians.
Coverage is from earliest times to 1949. Arrangement is by *pinyin*.
There is also a detailed *pinyin* index. Although there are only about
2,000 articles in the three history volumes, it is easier to separate the
wheat from the chaff than in the 60,000 very short articles of the
Zhongguo lishi da cidian (next item). Well illustrated. There is an
overall, alphabetically arranged index in one volume to the entire encyclopaedia, which is useful if you are looking up, for example
Chang'an, and want to find references, not only in the history volumes, but also in the separate volumes on archaeology, literature, and
many others. The entire *Zhongguo da baike quanshu* is available on 24
CD-ROMs. There is also a CD-ROM version of the simplified version of the encyclopaedia (1994), which contains 8,000 entries and
five million characters.

Zhongguo lishi da cidian 中國歷史大辭典 (The great encyclopaedia of
Chinese history), 14 vols., Shanghai cishu, 1983– . The eight chronological volumes on the customary periods from pre-Qin through
Qing contain short factual entries of basic information on events,
people, reign names, emperors, institutions, laws, regulations, and
book titles. Arrangement is by stroke count. The entire series contains over 12,000 double-column pages with a total of 60,000 entries.
If the editors had added a little more detail and a *pinyin* index to each
volume (as well as to the whole series), it would be both more useful
and more convenient to use. The chronological vols. are as follows:

Pre-Qin (1996)	Song (1984)
Qin, Han (1990)	Liao, Xia Jin, Yuan (1986)
Wei, Jin, Nan-Bei Chao (1997)	Ming (1995)
Sui, Tang, Wudai (1995)	Qing, vol. 1, 1644–1840; vol. 2, 1840–1912 (1992)

In addition, there are five separate volumes on:

1. Historiography (*Shixueshi* 史學史, 1983). Not a study of historiography but a somewhat skimpily annotated bibliography of traditional historical works arranged by book title (stroke-count index).
2. Historical geography (*Lishi dili* 歷史地理, 1996); over 9,000 entries.
   One of the best pocket-size introductions not only to historical

toponyms, but also to famous geographers from earliest times to
1911 and their works (4.5.3).

3. Ethnic history (*Minzushi* 民族史, 1995).
4. Intellectual history (*Sixiangshi* 思想史, 1989).
5. History of science and technology (*Kejishi* 科技史, forthcoming).

Both the *Zhongguo da baike quanshu* (*Zhongguo lishi*) and the *Zhong-guo lishi da cidian* are strong on historical personages, book titles, and other facts that would normally feature in an old-fashioned index of names, places, and titles, but not on generic terms or concepts. Thus, for example, if you want to look up a subject such as "price history," you will not find it. Even something as concrete as the "navy" merits not a single entry, but you will find references to individual admirals—if you know their names.

8.4.3 Japanese

There are a number of excellent historical encyclopaedias and historical dictionaries containing short articles on all aspects of Asian history, personalities, periods, places, institutions, and events in a readily accessible form. A recent one is *Tôyôshi jiten* 東洋史辞典.[3] Larger but already 30 years old is *Ajia rekishi jiten* アジア歴史事典.[4] Its entries are comprehensive and easy to locate; arrangement is by Japanese syllabary. Vol. 10 contains tables and indexes, including a stroke-count index and a shorter Wade-Giles index.

---

[3] *Tôyôshi jiten* (Dictionary of Oriental history), rev. edition, Sôgensha, 1980.

[4] *Ajia rekishi jiten* (Encyclopaedia of Asian history), 10 vols., Heibonsha, 1959–62, 1984. *Ajia rekishi jiten* replaced the same publisher's prewar historical encyclopaedia, *Tôyô rekishi daijiten* 東洋歴史大辞典 (Encyclopaedia of Oriental history), 9 vols., Heibonsha, 1937–39. This is now superseded, but the articles indicate the level reached by the meticulous, textually based studies of Chinese history in Japan before the war.

9

Locating Books

This chapter concentrates on books produced in imperial China (book production from bamboo strips to printing is discussed in Chapter 18, pre-Qin excavated and transmitted texts are the subject of Chapter 19, and tools for locating Republican era books are introduced in 51.2). The chapter begins with a summary of the different ways of finding out what books were circulating in any period from the Han to the Qing.

Chinese libraries have existed for at least 2,500 years (9.2). Various classification schemes were used. It was in the Han that the four main categories of Classics, History, Philosophy, and Belles-lettres began to take shape (9.3). The largest collections were normally those of the emperor. Six of the imperial library catalogs are included in the Standard Histories (9.4). Book catalogs (*mulu* 目錄) were placed in the History branch of the traditional fourfold bibliographical classification (*Sibu* 四部, 9.3). The largest library of all was the especially commissioned collection of the Qianlong emperor, the *Siku quanshu* 四庫全書 (9.5). Works were often published in *congshu* 叢書 (series or collectanea, 9.6) and the practice continues. One way of tracing old books and finding what they contain is to use modern annotated bibliographies of primary sources (9.7).

Throughout Chinese history there have been large numbers of rare, lost, recovered, forged, and banned books (9.8). This complicates the often tricky problem of alternative and difficult book titles (9.9). The index and the concordance were unknown in old China. Now many works have been indexed (9.10).

9.1   Overview: How to Locate a Work

Nobody knows exactly how many pre-twentieth-century Chinese works have survived. An estimate in the range of 40,000 to 50,000 is probably not too far wrong, but this includes such a wide range of different titles from the flimsiest collection of poetry to major philosophical works that it is a practically meaningless statistic. Most of the works that have survived date from the later empire, because before the widespread use of printing in the Song, books usually circulated only in a few manuscript copies and were therefore easily lost. There are a number of ways to find out what books were circulating in a given period (including the titles of those that have not survived). There are also shortcuts to finding out what the contents of a book are, and there are published catalogs to locate the whereabouts in modern libraries of those books that have survived. Many old Chinese books have been indexed, and there are an increasing number available on CD-ROM or computer disk that enables rapid subject searches. Note that books were very often dated at the end of the preface or in the colophon; sometimes, too, by the dedication or presentation to the emperor, and sometimes by the date of printing.

Dynastic bibliographies were included in many of the Standard Histories. They were normally based on the catalog of the imperial library of a given period. They were usually not annotated. Some have survived, and many have been reconstructed later. Both categories have been enlarged to include all books known to have circulated in a given period. Thus they include the titles of books written in a dynasty plus those that survived from previous dynasties. Altogether, the dynastic bibliographies contain the titles of at least 40,000 separate works (the majority of which have long since been lost). There is a combined index available in the *H-Y Index* 10 (9.4).

Annotated catalogs, usually of a particular library, are the quickest shortcut to the contents of a source without having to read through hundreds of pages of thousands of separate titles. The largest annotated catalog ever compiled in China before modern times was that for the Qianlong emperor's library, the *Siku quanshu zongmu tiyao* 四庫全書總目提要 (*Siku zongmu* 四庫總目 for short), 9.5. This catalog has now been superseded (unless you are specializing in Qing intellectual history) by a modern annotated catalog, the *Siku da cidian* 四庫大辭典 that was modeled after, and to a considerable extent based on, the *Siku zongmu*. Your starting point should be *Siku da cidian*, which contains abstracts of over 20,000 separate works and is by far the largest annotated catalog of traditional Chinese sources available (9.7).

It has been a common practice in China ever since the Song, to reprint separate books together in a *congshu* 叢書 (series, collectanea). A *congshu* can contain anything from a few dozen to a few thousand books. There are two union catalogs available, the first covers *congshu* containing traditional works (*Zhongguo congshu zonglu* 中國叢書綜錄); the second lists *congshu* published between 1902 and 1949 containing modern works (*Zhongguo jindai xiandai congshu mulu* 中國近代現代叢書目錄); see 9.6.

Having found what you are looking for or stumbled across an unexpected title, you will want to check if a modern index is available, because old Chinese books were almost never indexed (9.10).

Major libraries are increasingly putting their catalogs on CD-ROM and also online for Internet searches (11.6). But very often older works are the last to be entered and few libraries have converted all their cards to one system of romanization, hence printed library catalogs are still essential to locate books, especially old ones.

A few of the best collections have excellent published catalogs, notably those of Guotu 國圖 (National Library), Jinbun (the Research Institute for Humanistic Studies at Kyoto University), and Tôbunken (the Institute for Oriental Culture at Tokyo University), on whose collections, see 11.2.

An essential way of keeping up-to-date with reprints and new works is to skim through the catalogs of publishers and bookstores. There are not all that many specializing in Chinese history (see 11.5 for a brief introduction).

Despite the large numbers of different book titles in circulation and the large number of books that have survived, only a handful of references are essential:

1. To find a title in the dynastic bibliographies, use the *Yiwenzhi ershi zhong zonghe yinde* 藝文志二十種綜合引得 (Combined indices to 20 dynastic bibliographies), *H-Y Index* 10 (9.4).

2. To check if there is an alternative title or if there is another book with the same title, use *Tongshu yiming tongjian* 同書異名通檢, which lists books with more than one title, or *Tongming yishu tongjian* 同名異書通檢, which lists books having the same title (9.9).

3. To help find the meaning of a difficult title: *Zhongguo gujin shuming shiyi cidian* 中國古今書名釋義辭典 (9.9).

4. To find the contents of a work: *Siku da cidian* 四庫大辭典 (9.7).

5. To find a title in a *congshu*, or author, or a *congshu*: *Zhongguo congshu zonglu* 中國叢書綜錄 and *Zhongguo jindai xiandai congshu mulu* 中國近代現代叢書目錄 (9.6).

6. Check the published catalogs of the Jinbun and Tôbunken, two of the world's leading collections of Chinese books (11.3).

7. Browse the bookstores specializing in old Chinese books and their reprints (11.5).

8. Browse the international databases of Chinese libraries (11.6).

9.2   Chinese Libraries

Books and documents in China have been collected by the royal court and government offices; private individuals; academies and temples. Modern public libraries were opened for the first time at the end of the nineteenth century. The earliest repositories may have been those of the royal ancestral temple. The first libraries for which there is any evidence date from the Spring and Autumn period. Not much is known about them except that they were primarily official archives (*cefu* 冊府[策府], or generically, *gufu* 故府; see 20.1). The first imperial library as such, the Mige 秘閣, was established in the palace for Han Wudi (140–88 BC), and it was for this collection that Liu Xiang 劉向 developed his influential library classification scheme, the *Qilüe* 七略 (9.3). He did the collating and editorial work in the Tianluge 天祿閣. There were other palace collections in the Han, most famously the Lantai 蘭臺. It was here that the author of the *Hanshu* 漢書, Ban Gu (AD 32–92), worked (44.1). Later dynasties built up their own collections (and continued the tradition of calling the imperial library and archives the Mige, until the Northern Song, when it became known as the Mishusheng 秘書省). An official was appointed as imperial librarian in AD 159 with the title Mishujian 秘書監. The imperial library catalogs of six dynasties were published in the Standard Histories of those dynasties (9.4).[1]

---

[1] Jean-Pierre Drège, *Les bibliothèques en Chine aux temps des manuscrits jusqu'au Xe siècle*, EFEO and Maisonneuve, 1991; John Winkelman, "The imperial library in Southern Sung China, 1127–1279: A Study of the Organization and Operation of the Scholarly Agencies of the Central Government," American Philosophical Society, *Transactions*, n.s. 64.8 (1974).

Academies in China were called *shuyuan* 書院. The term dates from the Tang and referred at first to an official office for collecting and collating books (the term used for schools since the Han was *xuetang* 學堂). Later private *shuyuan* were set up. *Shuyuan* book collections grew after printing (in which they were actively engaged) became more common in the Song. By this time they had become schools, some of which were famous centers for the teaching of *Lixue* 理學 (Neo-Confucianism). Their libraries held anything from 10,000 to 100,000 *juan*, which came from various sources, including public and private donations. During the golden age of the *shuyuan* in the Ming and the Qing, their collections grew, and catalogs of individual *shuyuan* libraries were published.[2] The Ming also saw the rise of prefectural and county school libraries.[3] In the late Qing educational reforms, *shuyuan* were renamed with the old term *xuetang* 學堂. After the 1911 revolution they gained their modern name *xuexiao* 學校 (a long-forgotten Chinese word reimported from the Japanese). Despite the upheavals of the warlord period and of the Japanese invasion and the following civil war, a considerable number of public libraries were built up in the Republic.[4]

Private libraries had been in existence since at least the Han, if not before, but only the very rich could afford them because of the rarity and high price of books. There were 20 or 30 book collectors in the Tang, but private collections became more common only during the Song. The first extant private library catalog dates from ca. 1151:

Chao Gongwu 晁公武 (ca. 1105–80), *Junzhai dushu zhi* 郡齋讀書志 (Record of reading books at the Commandery Study), *Sibu congkan*, 3rd series. Contains annotations on 1,468 books, many of which were

---

[2] All extant catalogs of *shuyuan* and much other information will be found in *Zhongguo shuyuan cidian* 中國書院辭典 (A dictionary of academies in China), Ji Xiaofeng 季嘯鳳, ed. in chief, Zhejiang jiaoyu, 1996. Contains brief articles on over 1,500 *shuyuan* by province; biographies of people connected with them; and primary and secondary sources. A listing in appendix contains the names of 7,300 known *shuyuan* and their founders. There is a *pinyin* index.

[3] Timothy Brook, "Edifying Knowledge: The Building of School Libraries in Ming China," *LIC* 17.1: 93–119 (1996).

[4] Their development is discussed briefly by Sharon Chien Liu in *Libraries and Librarianship in China*, Greenwood, 1998, 4–15. See also Roger Pelissier, *Les bibliothèques en Chine pendant la première moitié de XXe siècle*, Mouton, 1971.

bought by the author when a magistrate at Rongzhou 崇州 in Si-chuan (hence the title of the catalog). For further references to the book trade and collecting in the Song, see 18.4.

More than 500 private libraries flourished in the Qing, both of individual book collectors and academies.[5] Two Qing guides for book collectors have been translated into English by Achilles Fang (1910–95).[6]

The oldest extant private library building is the Tianyige 天一閣 (Yin 鄞 district; modern Ningbo). It was built in the early early 1560s by Fan Qin 范欽 to house his private collection (one of the most famous of the age).[7] The first modern public library (*tushuguan* 圖書館) was the Hunan gongli tushuguan 湖南公立圖書館 (1905).

---

[5] Cheuk-woon Taam (Tan Zhuoyuan 譚卓垣), *The Development of Chinese Libraries Under the Ch'ing Dynasty, 1644–1911*, Shanghai: Shangwu, 1935; rpnt., CMC, 1977; Nancy Lee Swann, "Seven Intimate Library Owners," *HJAS* 1: 363–90 (1936). On the private libraries of Hangzhou in the eighteenth century, see Wu Han 吳晗, *Jiang-Zhe cangshujia shilüe* 江浙藏書家史略 (Brief history of the book collectors of Jiangsu and Zhejiang), Zhonghua, 1981; contains the biographies of 900 book collectors active from earliest times to 1911 in these provinces. Wang Shaozeng 王紹曾 and Sha Jiasun 沙嘉孫, *Shandong cangshujia shilüe* 山東藏書家史略 (Brief history of the book collectors of Shandong), Shandong daxue, 1992, does the same for 559 collectors from Shandong. *Lidai cangshujia cidian* 歷代藏書家辭典 (Dictionary of book collectors in successive dynasties), Liang Zhan 梁戰 and Guo Qunyi 郭群一, eds., Shanxi renmin, 1991, contains brief biographies of 3,400 book collectors, printers, copyists, collators, and woodblock-carvers from all over China. The series *Qingren shumu tiba congkan* 清人書目題跋叢刊 (Qing book catalog annotations), 10 vols., Zhonghua, 1990–93, reprints the most famous Qing book catalogs. *Zhongguo mulu xuejia cidian* 中國目錄學家辭典 (Dictionary of Chinese bibliographers), Shen Chang 申暢 et al., comps., Henan renmin, 1988, contains biographies and details of the contributions of 2,200 bibliographers up to 1949.

[6] "Bookman's Decalogue (*Ts'ang-shu shih-yüeh* 藏書十約) Yeh Tê-hui 葉德輝 (1864–1927)," Achilles Fang, tr., *HJAS* 13: 132–73 (1950); also "Bookman's Manual," *HJAS* 14: 215–60 (1951), a translation of Sun Congtian 孫從添 (1702–22), *Cangshu jiyao* 藏書紀要; both titles, Gudian wenxue, 1957.

[7] *Xinbian Tianyige shumu* 新編天一閣書目 (Newly edited *Tianyige* catalogs), Luo Zhaoping 駱兆平, ed. in chief, Zhonghua, 1996. The history of the Tianyige is told in Ulrich Stackmann, *Die Geschichte der chinesischen Bibliothek Tian Yi Ge vom 16. Jahrhundert bis in die Gegenwart*, Steiner, 1990.

The first recorded book market was in Luoyang in the Former Han. In the Song, the markets shifted to the woodblock printing centers. These were in Jianyang 建陽 (north Fujian), Hangzhou, and Sichuan. In the Ming and Qing, the book trade moved to Jiangsu and Zhejiang. The main markets were there as well in the capitals, Nanjing and Beijing.[8]

. For excerpts from the prefaces, colophons, and postfaces of both public and private book catalogs from the Han to the Qing, as well as tables of contents and the comments of the *Siku zongmu* editors on each catalog, see *Zhongguo lidai tushu zhulu wenxuan* 中國歷代圖書著錄文選.[9]

Just as with archives, book collections, especially imperial libraries, led a precarious existence. In the 2,058 years between Xiang Yu's destruction of the Qin libraries (20.1) and the Taiping Rebellion, the imperial collections were deliberately and totally destroyed by fire on at least 14 occasions (an average of once every 150 years). Each time the buildings were rebuilt and the collections replenished, an interesting illustration of the fact that Chinese imperial institutions and culture did not simply continue, but had to be periodically reconstituted. Quite apart from deliberate acts of destruction, there were the depredations brought about by insects, floods, and accidental fires, and the losses caused by neglect. For private collectors, there was the increasing likelihood that their books would be destroyed for political reasons (9.8.4).

During the nineteenth century, the dispersal and destruction of Chinese printed books and manuscripts continued on a massive scale; the Taipings simply followed a well-established tradition, burning libraries, especially in Jiangsu and Zhejiang, where most of the main private collections were located. Foreign troops joined in

---

[8] Lai Xinxia 來新夏, *Zhongguo gudai tushu shiyeshi* 中國古代圖書事業史 (A history of the book trade in ancient China), Shanghai renmin, 1990, 1991. Good general introduction, covering the collection, storage, editing, production, and circulation of books in each period. For references to the history of printing in China, see 18.4.

[9] *Zhongguo lidai tushu zhulu wenxuan* (Selection from historical records of Chinese book catalogs), Yuan Yongqiu 袁咏秋 and Zeng Jiguang 曾季光, comps., Beijing daxue, 1995. This contains the prefaces of the main public and private library catalogs from the Qin to the Qing, plus in many cases, their tables of contents.

the destruction and looting on several occasions (notably during the Anglo-French expedition in 1860 and the Boxer uprising in 1900). In the first half of the twentieth century, the destruction and dispersal continued. Thousands of the manuscripts, bamboo strips, and oracle bones newly discovered at Dunhuang, Anyang, and elsewhere were sold for export. Famous collections were requisitioned or sold. Connoisseurs would buy books at Beijing's traditional book and antiques street, Liulichang 琉璃廠, not by the title, or even by the shelf, but by the wall, to be dispatched directly to the shipping agent by trucks. Many Japanese and Western individuals and institutes built up their collections during these chaotic years. The last major movement of books took place in late 1948 and early 1949 when the Guomindang shipped to Taiwan large numbers of rare books (plus about 7 percent of the Qing central archives, 50.1.3).

9.3   Classification

Bibliography is the most important requirement for study. It is here that you must start and only then will you be able to find your way (目錄之蜓中第一緊要事必從此問途方能得其門而入), Wang Mingsheng 王鳴盛, *Shiqishi shangque* 十七史商榷, *juan* 1 (22.2, *Studies*)

How knowledge was categorized is a good indicator of what was considered important and how Chinese priorities differed from our own. Also, to find sources produced or preserved in the old historical traditions it is, of course, necessary to know where a given type of source would be classified.

The Confucian *Six Classics* dealt with six broadly separate categories: philosophy (*Yi* 易, Book of changes); government (*Shu* 書, Documents); literature (*Shi* 詩, Songs); society (*Li* 禮, Rites); history (*Chunqiu* 春秋, Spring and Autumn annals); and the arts (*Yue* 樂, Book of music).

The first bibliographic classification (known as the *Qilüe* 七略, Seven epitomes) was devised by Liu Xiang 劉向 (ca. 77–ca. 6 BC) as an annotated catalog for the imperial library at the end of the Former Han. It was modified by his son Liu Xin 劉歆 (d. AD 23). Apart from a general summary, they used six categories: classics, philosophy, poetry, military writers, mathematics and sciences (including astronomy, the calendar, and divination), and medicine (including the arts of the bedchamber). The *Qilüe* itself has not survived, but it was used as the basis of the "Yiwenzhi" 藝文志 in the *Hanshu* (9.4).[10] A number of imperial librarians in the following centuries began to use a fourfold division, classifying all forms of literature into *sibu* 四部 (four branches), namely Classics (*jing* 經), History (*shi* 史), Philosophers (*zi* 子), and Belles-lettres (*ji* 集). This became the norm at the beginning of the Tang with the compilation of the dynastic catalog in the Standard History of the Sui.[11] During the Tang, the four branches were stored in four separate palace depositories (*siku* 四庫), so *siku* was used interchangeably with *sibu*. Color coding was used to distinguish the branches: yellow for Classics (the color symbolizing the center and the emperor); white for History; purple (*zi* 紫) for Philosophy; red for Belles-lettres. Tags were used for silk books and scrolls; later, colored covers or title slips were used for printed books. The phrase *siku quanshu* 四庫全書, or *siku* for short, was also used to mean "all books." In the Qing, it was taken as the title of the most famous of China's imperial library collections, the *Siku quanshu* (imperial library or complete library in four branches of literature, 9.5). In broad outline, these are the classifications still used in library catalogs of old Chinese books today. The first and fourth of the four branches of the *Siku quanshu* (Classics and Belles-lettres) present few difficulties as to their contents (Chapters 19 and 30). The subcategories in the history branch are shown in Table 20 (numbers in brackets after each entry in the lefthand column refer to chapter and section numbers in the manual). Within the History branch, many different classification systems were used in different periods. In broad outline, however, most were similar to that employed by the *Siku* editors. The various changes in the subcategories are traced in *Zhongguo shibu mulu xue* 中國史部目錄學 (A study of classifications of the History branch), Zheng Hesheng 鄭鶴聲, Shangwu, 1930; rev. edition, 1956.

---

[10] In general, private libraries followed the same classification as that in the imperial catalogs. The different early bibliographic classifications are outlined in J.-P. Drège, *Les bibliothèques en Chine* (1991).

[11] *Suishu jingjizhi* 隋書經籍志, 629–36, Shangwu, 1955–57.

Table 20: The History Branch in the Siku *Classification*

Standard Histories (Chapter 22)	*zhengshi* 正史
Annals (21)	*biannian* 編年
Topically arranged histories (23)	*jishi benmo* 紀事本末
Unofficial histories (20.4)	*bieshi* 別史
Miscellaneous histories (24)	*zashi* 雜史
Edicts and memorials (26.1–2)	*zhaoling zouyi* 詔令奏議
Biographical works (3.7–8)	*zhuanji* 傳記
Historical excerpts (20.4)	*shichao* 史抄
Contemporary records (20.4)	*zaiji* 載記
Regulation of time (5, 6, 35.1.1)	*shiling* 時令
Geography (4 and 41)	*dili* 地理
Government offices (22.3.6; 25.3)	*zhiguan* 職官
Government institutions (25; 27.5)	*zhengshu* 政書
Bibliography; epigraphy (9 and 17)	*mulu* 目錄
Historiography (20.3)	*shiping* 史評

The third branch of the *Siku*, Philosophers, also contains many works essential to the historian (Table 21; numbers in brackets after each entry in the lefthand column refer to chapter and section numbers in the manual).

Table 21: The Philosophers' Branch in the Siku *Classification*

Confucian writers (Chapters 19, 33)	*Rujia* 儒家
Military experts (28)	*bingjia* 兵家
Legal writers (19, 27, and 33)	*fajia* 法家
Writers on agriculture (35)	*nongjia* 農家
Writers on medicine (36)	*yijia* 醫家
Astronomy and math (5, 37)	*tianwen suanfa* 天文算法
Mantic arts (36, 37)	*shushu* 術數
The fine arts (38)	*yishu* 藝術
Manuals, e.g., on cooking (35.2.6)	*pulu* 譜錄
Miscellaneous writers (33)	*zajia* 雜家
Encyclopaedias (31)	*leishu* 類書
Essays; miscellaneous works (34.3)	*xiaoshuo* 小説
Buddhists (29.5)	*Shijia* 釋家
Daoists (29.4)	*Daojia* 道家

Note that it is unwise to assume that works will necessarily be where you would expect to find them. Take the example of agriculture. Many books classified under Agriculture (subbranch four of Philosophy) cannot be considered agricultural works, while conversely a great many books connected with agriculture are found in other branches, as well as in other subbranches of Philosophy (e.g., *pulu* 譜錄).

9.4 Dynastic Bibliographies

The simplest way to find what books were circulating in different periods is to check through one of the many library catalogs that have survived. Those of the imperial library were usually printed with, or as a supplement to, the Standard Histories as *yiwenzhi* 藝文志 or *jingjizhi* 經籍志 (dynastic bibliographies). Catalogs of private collections were also printed.

Items one and five of Table 22 give the nearest approximation to a complete summary of the books available at a particular time, i.e., the end of the Former Han and the beginning of the Tang. Item six is the first extant catalog to be arranged in strict four-branch categories. Since it was intended to show the splendor of the Kaiyuan period (713-741), no later works were included.

During the 1950s the Shangwu Press brought out a uniform edition of the *yiwenzhi* with Qing supplements printed with each one.[12] This edition has the added advantage of being indexed. The most complete collection of dynastic bibliographies and supplements can be found in the six volumes of corrections and additions to the monographs and tables in the Standard Histories published with the Kaiming shudian edition of the *Twenty-five Histories*, under the title *Ershiwushi bubian* 二十五史補編 (22.2).

H-Y Index 10 is an index to the contents of seven dynastic bibliographies, eight supplements, four banned book lists, and one private library catalog shown in Table 22.[13]

[12] *Shishi yiwen jingjizhi* 十史藝文經籍志 (Dynastic bibliographies in 10 Standard Histories), Shangwu, 1955-9; rpnt., Shijie, 1963. Arrangement is by four-corner index. Each volume has an author-title index.

[13] *Yiwenzhi ershi zhong zonghe yinde* 藝文志二十種綜合引得 (Combined indices to twenty dynastic bibliographies), *H-Y Index* 10, 4 vols., Beiping, 1933.

Table 22: Dynastic Bibliographies

Title	Period Compiled	No. of titles
1. *Hanshu* 漢書 "Yiwenzhi" 藝文志	Han	596
2. *Hou Hanshu* 後漢書 "Yiwenzhi" 藝文志	Qing	
3. *Sanguo* 三國 "Yiwenzhi" 藝文志	Qing	
4. *Bu Jinshu* 補晉書 "Yiwenzhi" 藝文志	Qing	
5. *Suishu* 隋書 "Jingjizhi" 經籍志	Tang	6,520
6. *Jiu Tangshu* 舊唐書 "Jingjizhi" 經籍志	Later Jin	3,062
7. *Xin Tangshu* 新唐書 "Yiwenzhi" 藝文志	Song	3,277
8. *Bu Wudaishi* 補五代史 "Yiwenzhi" 藝文志	Qing	
9. *Songshi* 宋史 "Yiwenzhi" 藝文志	Yuan	9,819
10. *Songshi* 宋史 "Yiwenzhibu fubian" 藝文志補附編	Qing	
11. *Bu Liao Jin Yuan* 補遼金元 "Yiwenzhi" 藝文志	Qing	
12. *Bu sanshi* 補三史 "Yiwenzhi" 藝文志	Qing	
13. *Bu Yuanshi* 補元史 "Yiwenzhi" 藝文志	Qing	
14. *Mingshi* 明史 "Yiwenzhi" 藝文志	Qing	
15. *Jinshu zongmu* 禁書總目	Qing	
16. *Quanhui shumu* 全毀書目	Qing	
17. *Chouhui shumu* 抽毀書目	Qing	
18. *Wei'ai shumu* 違礙書目	Qing	
19. *Zhengfang Mingji yishumu* 徵訪明季遺書目	Rep.	
20. *Qingshigao* 清史稿 "Yiwenzhi" 藝文志	Rep.	54,880

Note: Items 15–18 are lists of forbidden books (7.2.4). They were compiled during the Qing and reprinted in *Sibu congkan*, 1st series, vol. 42, Shangwu, 1937; rpnt., Zhonghua, 1985. The count for item 20 is taken from *Qingshigao yiwenzhi shiyi* 清史稿藝文志拾遺 (see below under *Recent Editions and Studies*).

Several of the *Shitong* 十通 (25.2) contain important bibliographies, for example "Yiwenlüe" 藝文略 in Zheng Qiao 鄭樵, *Tongzhi* 通志, and the "Jingji kao" 經籍考 in Ma Duanlin 馬端臨, *Wenxian tongkao* 文獻通考; see *Wenxian tongkao Jingji kao* 文獻通考經籍考 (The "Study of Bibliography" in *Wenxian tongkao*), 2 vols., Huadong shifan daxue, 1985.

Recent Editions and Studies

Hanshu yiwenzhi tongshi 漢書藝文志通釋 (Comprehensive study of the *Hanshu yiwenzhi*), Zhang Shunhui 張舜徽, Hubei jiaoyu, 1990

Zuisho keisekishi shôkô 隋書經籍志詳考 (Detailed investigation of the *Suishu* dynastic bibliography), Kôzen Hiroshi 興膳宏 and Kawai Kôzô 川合康三, ed., Kyûko, 1995. Adds biographical notes on the authors and bibliographical comments to their works; also supplements the original by filling in contemporary works on Buddhism and Daoism. Indexes of authors and titles. Based on the Zhonghua punctuated edition.

Qingshigao yiwenzhi shiyi 清史稿藝文志拾遺 (Supplement to the dynastic bibliography of the *Qingshigao*), Wang Shaozeng 王紹曾, vol. 1 (*shi* 史, *zi* 子), Zhonghua, 1997; vol. 2 (*jing* 經, *ji* 集); vol. 3 (index), forthcoming. The count is 20,071 titles in *Qingshigao yiwenzhi ji bubian* 清史稿藝文志及補編 (The dynastic bibliography of the *Qingshigao* with additions), Wu Zuocheng 武作成, 2 vols., Zhonghua, 1982. Vol. 2 is a four-corner index with a stroke-count finding index.

The *Siku jingji tiyao suoyin* 四庫經籍提要索引 indexes titles (vol. 1) and authors (vol. 2) of the bibliographies in four of the *Shitong*, in the *Siku zongmu* itself, and in four of its continuations and supplements. Arrangement is by stroke count. There are author-title and stroke-count indexes.[14] The *Shitong* bibliographies are also fully indexed in a four-corner index (vol. 21 of the original Shangwu edition of the *Shitong*, 1937).

Many dynastic bibliographies and library catalogs were reprinted in *Shumu congbian* 書目叢編, 1st series, Guangwen, 1967.

9.5   *The Imperial Catalog*

Both in China and in Japan there is a long tradition of annotated library catalogs, which in China began at least in the Han and reached its height many centuries later with the carefully annotated catalog of the imperial library, the *Siku quanshu zongmu tiyao* 四庫全書總目提要 (*Siku zongmu* for short).

In 1771, at the command of the emperor, more than 350 eminent scholars began the work of collecting a definitive imperial li-

---

[14] *Siku jingji tiyao suoyin* (Index to the *Siku zongmu* and other bibliographies), 2 vols., Guoli zhongyang tushuguan, comp., and published, 1994. The works indexed are the *Jingjizhi* of the *Wenxian tongkao*, the *Xu Wenxiantongkao*, the *Qingchao wenxian tongkao*, and the *Qingchao xu Wenxian tongkao* (see Table 33, 25.2); *Siku zongmu*; *Xuxiu Siku quanshu tiyao*; *Siku zongmu buzheng*; *Siku zongmu bianzheng*; and the *Siku weishou shumu tiyao*.

brary. They reviewed and annotated over 10,000 books and manuscripts from imperial collections, from collections all over the empire, and from the *Yongle dadian* 永樂大典 (the previous largest collection compiled for an emperor; see 31.1). Some 3,000 works judged to be anti-Manchu were destroyed (the Qing dynasty saw more literary purges, more people imprisoned, and more books proscribed and burned than any other dynasty in Chinese history, a striking contrast with the contemporaneous Enlightenment in Europe). From the remaining 10,585 titles, 3,461 were selected for the imperial library, the *Siku quanshu* 四庫全書. All 2.3 million pages were transcribed by hand. The copyists (of whom there were 3,826) were not paid in cash but rewarded with official posts after they had transcribed a given number of words within a set time. Four copies were made for the use of the emperor in his palaces in the Forbidden City (Zijincheng 紫禁城), the Old Summer Palace (Yuanming yuan 圓明園), the secondary capital of Shengjing 盛京 (Shenyang 沈陽), and the summer retreat at Rehe 熱河 (Chengde 承德). The books were stored in specially constructed library buildings modeled after the Tianyige in Ningbo. In 1782, another three copies were ordered for deposit in Hangzhou, Zhenjiang, and Yangzhou. Unlike the four sets in the north, the emperor commanded that those in the south should be open to the public. Copies of the imperially commissioned encyclopaedia, the *Gujin tushu jicheng* 古今圖書集成 (31.2), were deposited in each of the seven libraries. Two of the *Siku quanshu* library buildings are still standing today, the *Wenyuange* 文淵閣 (Erudite Literature Pavilion, 1776) in the Forbidden City, and the Wenlange 文瀾閣 (Billowing Literature Pavilion, 1783) in Hangzhou, now part of the Zhejiang Provincial Museum. As to the books themselves, four of the seven copies are extant.[15]

[15] The copies of the *Siku quanshu* in the temples at Zhenjiang and Yangzhou were destroyed during the Taiping Rebellion. The copy in the Yuanming Yuan was largely burned by British troops during the Anglo-French attack on Beijing in 1860, although some volumes have since shown up in the sale rooms. The four remaining copies are in the Guotu (the Rehe copy), the Gansu Provincial Library (the Shenyang palace copy briefly captured by the Soviet Army in 1945), the Zhejiang Provincial Library (Hangzhou), and the Palace Museum, Taibei. It is this last copy, that of the Wenyuan ge 文淵閣, the first to be transcribed and the best preserved, which has been printed in photo-facsimile, see next note. For a detailed study of the compilation of the *Siku* and

Footnote continued on next page

The master copy (*Wenyuange*) was photolithographically printed in 1,500 volumes in the 1980s.[16] It is now also available in a
number of CD-ROM editions. Some of these have been entered
from the originals using OCRs; others have been entered in modern
type by hand. The former are known as *tuxingban* 圖形版. They
are cheaper and less flexible to use; the latter are called *quanwenban*
全文版 and are preferable.

All the works not included in the library, but listed by title in
the catalog (*cunmu* 存目), are reprinted from the best available editions in reduced size in the photo-facsimile collection *Siku quanshu
cunmu congshu* 四庫全書存目叢書.[17] Finally, in order to complete
the *Siku quanshu*, not only all those titles left out, but also newly
discovered, or written between the eighteenth century and 1911, are
printed in the *Xuxiu Siku quanshu* 續修四庫全書 (*Siku quanshu* continued), 1,200 vols., Qi-Lu, 1994– . *Xuxiu Siku quanshu zongmu* 續修
四庫全書縱目, Qi-Lu, 1998, includes subject, author, and title indexes to the 33,000 works in the *Xuxiu Siku quanshu* (see 9.7).

The editors of the *Siku quanshu*, under the chief editorship of Ji
Yun 紀昀 (1724–1805), compiled an annotated catalog of all 3,461
books included in the library (*cunshu* 存書), together with brief
notes on the 6,793 works listed by title (*cunmu* 存目). Work began
in 1773. The first draft was ready by 1781, and the final draft was

---

the political and scholarly background, see R. Kent Guy, *The Emperor's Four
Treasuries: Scholars and the State in the Late Ch'ien-lung Era*, Council on East
Asian Studies, Harvard University, 1987. For the basic sources, see *Zuanxiu
Siku quanshu dang'an* 纂修四庫全書檔案 (Archives on the editing of the *Siku
quanshu*), 10 vols., Yishiguan, eds., Shanghai guji, 1997.

[16] *Yingyin Wenyuange Siku quanshu* 影印文淵閣四庫全書 (Photofacsimile
reprint of the Wenyuan Pavilion copy of the *Siku quanshu*), Taibei: Shangwu,
1983–86. Shanghai guji reprinted this in a reduced-size edition, 1,500 vols.,
1987. There is a four-corner author-title index. Note also *Wenyuange siku quanshu shuming ji zhuzhe xingming suoyin* 文淵閣四庫全書書名及著者姓名索引
(Author-title index to the Wenyuange *Siku quanshu*), Taibei: Shangwu, 1986;
Siku quanshu wenji pianmu fenlei suoyin 四庫全書文集篇目分類索引 (Index to
the entries on *wenji* by category), 5 vols., Taibei: Shangwu, 1989; *Siku quanshu
zhuanji ziliao suoyin* 四庫全書傳記資料索引 (Index to *Siku quanshu* biographical materials), 2 vols., Taibei: Shangwu, 1991; with a third vol. index to *zihao*
字號, Taibei: Shangwu, 1990.

[17] *Siku quanshu cunmu congshu* (Collectanea of works mentioned in the
cunmu catalog), Qi-Lu, 1994– . There is a separate volume for the index to the
table of contents (1997).

completed in 1798. The full title of the catalog is *Qinding Siku quanshu zongmu tiyao* 欽定四庫全書總目提要.[18] An entire industry of additions, comments, and corrections to the *Siku zongmu* began almost as soon as it was printed. These have now been incorporated into the revised Zhonghua edition (1997), which makes it the most authoritative one. It is also by far the most convenient to use because it is set in a clear type, is fully punctuated, and has an author-title index with a *pinyin* first-character finding index.[19]

The *Siku quanshu jianming mulu* 四庫全書簡明目錄 by Ji Yun 紀昀 includes brief summaries of the *Siku zongmu* annotations.[20] For information on different editions of the works in the *Jianming mulu*, use the bibliographic notes largely prepared by Shao Yichen 邵懿辰 (1810–61), *Zengding Siku quanshu jianming mulu biaozhu* 增訂四庫全書簡明目錄標注.[21]

The *Siku zongmu* is the largest book catalog to have been compiled in traditional China. It is also the most important, (1) because of the high quality of the annotations, which give information on the nature and style of each work, including its table of contents in whole or in part, a brief biographical sketch of the author (on first appearance), and an evaluation, and (2) because it is the most com-

[18] *Qinding Siku quanshu zongmu tiyao* or *Siku quanshu zongmu* 四庫全書總目 (Annotated catalog of the imperial library by command), 200 *zhuan*, Ji Yun, 1781; palace edition (*dianben* 殿本), 1789; Zhejiang edition, 1795; Canton edition, 1868; 2 vols., Zhonghua, 1965 (based on the Zhejiang edition); 5th prnt., 1995. Note *H-Y Index 7* (an author-title index to the *Siku zongmu*, 2 vols., Beiping, 1932).

[19] *Siku quanshu zongmu tiyao, zhengli ben* 整理本 (rearranged edition), Lu Guangming 盧光明 et al., eds., 2 vols., Zhonghua, 1997 (based on the palace edition). This edition incorporates the most important scholarship on the *Siku zongmu*, especially the corrections and additions of Yu Jiaxi 余嘉錫 (1883–1955), Hu Yujin 胡玉縉 (d. 1940), Wang Xinfu 王欣夫, Li Yumin 李裕民, and Cui Fuzhang 崔富章. Editions and present whereabouts of over 90 percent of the *cunmu* titles are indicated. Simplified characters are used except in places that could cause ambiguity.

[20] *Siku quanshu jianming mulu* (Simplified annotated catalog of the imperial library), Hangzhou, 1782; 2 vols., Shanghai guji, 1985, 1996. There is a four-corner author-title index with stroke-count finding index.

[21] *Zengding Siku quanshu jianming mulu biaozhu* (Marginal notes to the simplified annotated catalog of the imperial library), posthumously published in 1911; rev. and enlarged edition, Zhonghua, 1959. There is a four-corner and stroke-count index.

prehensive by far. But it is limited by the political constraints on the compilers, who were obliged to leave out many works, for example, of all those writers suspected of retaining sympathies with the Ming. Unless there is a special reason to use the *Siku zongmu*, your first reference should therefore be the *Siku da cidian* (9.7).[22]

9.6 Congshu 叢書

Since printing became common in the Song, Chinese works often have been preserved in *congshu* 叢書. These are collections of independent works published together to prevent their loss or to gain them wider circulation. Publishers today in Europe and America would call a *congshu* a reprint series or a library. The phrase is often translated as *collectanea*. Chinese publishers today continue to issue huge *congshu* of both pre-1912 and Republican sources.

There are over 2,000 *congshu*, containing a total of about 40,000 individual works written before 1912. The indispensable index to these is the *Zhongguo congshu zonglu* 中國叢書綜錄, which covers holdings in 41 major Chinese libraries as of the first half of the 1950s. At an early stage of tracing a work, you should consult this catalog.[23] Vol. 1 (*zongmu* 總目) lists *congshu* by title. Arrangement is by the four traditional bibliographic categories (*Sibu* 四部). The titles of individual works contained in each *congshu* are shown. Altogether 2,086 *congshu* are listed in this way. An appendix shows which of the 41 libraries holds each of the *congshu* (including over 700 alternative editions). Vol. 2 (*zimu* 子目) is arranged by the title of the 38,891 individual works contained in the *congshu*. Bibliographic details are given. Because many titles appear in several *congshu*, the total number of entries comes to about 70,000. Arrangement is by the four branches, further divided into subcategories

---

[22] Frederick Mote, "Reflections on the First Complete Reprinting of the *Ssu-k'u Ch'üan-shu*," *Gest Library Journal* 1.2: 26–50 (1987); Hung-lam Chu, "High Ch'ing Intellectual Bias as Reflected in the Imperial Catalogue," *Gest Library Journal* 1.2: 51–66 (1987).

[23] *Zhongguo congshu zonglu* (Bibliography of Chinese collectanea), Shanghai tushuguan 上海圖書館 (Shanghai municipal library), comp., 3 vols., Shanghai guji, 1959–62; reprinted with corrections, 1982–83; reduced-size edition, but clear print on good quality paper, 1986, 1993. The entire work comes to 2,938 double-column and 791 triple-column, pages.

based on those in the *Siku quanshu*. Vol. 3 contains a four-corner title index and author index to vol. 2 (it also contains a *pinyin* and stroke-count finding index). Note the *Daozang* 道藏 is included (1,500 works; see 29.4), but not the Buddhist Canon, *Da zangjing* 大藏經 (3,500 works; see 29.5).

The *Zhongguo congshu zonglu* has been supplemented and corrected by a number of later works:

Zhongguo congshu mulu ji zimu suoyin huibian 中國叢書目錄及子目索引匯編, Nanjing daxue tushuguan and Nanjing daxue lishixi ziliao shi, comps., Nanjing daxue, 1982. This lists the contents of 977 traditional *congshu* omitted from the *Congshu zonglu*. There is a *congshu* title index and an index to the titles of the individual works contained in each *congshu*. Unlike the *Zhongguo congshu zonglu*, it lacks a table of contents.

Zhongguo congshu zonglu buzheng 中國叢書綜錄補正 (Corrections to the *Zhongguo congshu zonglu*), Yang Haiqing 陽海清 and Jiang Xiaoda 蔣校達, comps., Jiangsu guangling, 1984. This not only makes corrections to the *Congshu zonglu*, but also gives lists of reprints of *congshu* between 1960 and 1982 as well as a useful index of alternative titles of *congshu*.

Chûgoku sôsho sôroku mishû Nichizô shomokukô 中國叢書總錄未收日藏書目稿, Li Ruiqing 李銳清, comp., Jinbun, 1995. Lists 852 titles in Japanese collections not included in the *Congshu zonglu*. For tracing original *congshu* in Japan, use the *Kanseki sôsho shozai mokuroku* 漢籍叢書所在目錄 (Catalog of whereabouts of Chinese *collectanea*), Tôyô bunko, 1965. It lists the whereabouts and contents of 1,990 *congshu* in seven Japanese collections.

Zhongguo jindai xiandai congshu mulu 中國近代現代叢書目錄 (Catalog of late Qing, early Republican Chinese collectanea), Shanghai tushuguan, comp., 1979; HK: Shangwu, 1980. Lists 5,549 *congshu* published 1902–49 plus the 30,940 titles they contain. There is an index: *Zhongguo jindai xiandai congshu mulu suoyin* 中國近代現代叢書目錄索引 (Index to *Zhongguo jindai xiandai congshu mulu*), Shanghai tushuguan, comp., 2 vols., 1982. Vol. 1 is a title index and vol. 2 contains an author index to individual works in the *congshu* and an index to the *congshu* editors.

Taiwan ge tushuguan xiancun congshu zimu suoyin 臺灣各圖書館現存叢書子目索引 (Author-title index to *congshu* in Taiwan libraries), Wang Baoxian 王寶先, comp., 3 vols., part 1, 2 vols., title index; part 2, author index, CMC, 1975–77. This is an index to the works included in over 1,500 *congshu* held by 10 libraries in Taiwan. Arrangement is by stroke-count.

During the 1920s and 1930s many pre-1912 original sources and historical works were collected together and published in huge *congshu*. The quickest way of finding the titles and authors of any such series is to consult *Zhongguo congshu zonglu*, which lists the titles of the *Sibu congkan*, for example (285–97). Each *congshu* was usually issued with an annotated catalog. For ease of reference they are listed here alphabetically by title:

Congshu jicheng 叢書集成. Over 4,100 titles taken from 100 previous *congshu*. The editors deliberately included works left out of the *Sibu congkan* and *Sibu beiyao*. The original intention was to print 4,000 volumes numbered 1 to 4,000. Because of the outbreak of the war, only 3,467 volumes were published. The series is mainly in movable type, and as a result there are many typesetting errors. The complete series of over 4,100 titles has been reprinted.[24] The *Baibu congshu jicheng* 百部叢書集成 is a re-creation of the *Congshu jicheng*, 1ˢᵗ series, Yiwen yinshuguan, 1965–70. It contains 4,144 titles, all reproduced from the original *congshu* and done in traditional format. The same publisher also put out *Congshu jicheng xubian*, 1970–71. It contains 774 titles in 1557 *ce* in 176 cases.

Guoxue jiben congshu 國學基本叢書 (Basic sinological series), 400 titles, Shangwu, 1929–41, 100 titles reprinted during the 1950s. Typeset and punctuated editions of titles considered essential for the study of Chinese culture.

Sibu beiyao 四部備要. Contains many of the same titles as in *Sibu congkan*, but Zhonghua turned around its rival's, Shangwu's, claims, and advertised that the ancestor of its owner, Lufei Chi 陸費墀, had been chief collator of the *Siku quanshu*. The Zhonghua editors had carried on this glorious family tradition and corrected the errors in old editions before the typesetting (using the characteristic "imitation Song-style type face" [*fang Songti* 仿宋體]). The publisher offered purchas-

---

[24] *Congshu jicheng chubian* (Collected collectanea, 1ˢᵗ series), 3,467 vols., Shangwu, 1935–7; Zhonghua, 1983, 1996 (including those titles not included in the original 1ˢᵗ series). *Congshu jicheng chubian mulu* 叢書集成初編目錄 (Index to the 1ˢᵗ series of the Collected collectanea), Shangwu, 1935, 1983. This in fact indexes the projected 4,107 titles. Also reprinted under the title *Congshu jicheng xinbian*, 129 vols., Xinwenfeng, 1986. A separate volume contains a table of contents arranged by modern categories as well as author-title indexes.

ers one dollar for every wrong character they could spot. Zhonghua had to pay out thousands of dollars, but was able to publish a second edition in 100 Western-style volumes with plenty of corrections in 1937. It is this edition that Zhonghua still re-issues to this day.[25]

Sibu congkan 四部叢刊.[26] Large *congshu* of the main works of the Chinese scholarly tradition photolithographed from the earliest available editions issued in three series over a seventeen-year period (1919–36). Arrangement, as the title suggests, is by the four branches, *jing*, *shi*, *zi* and *ji*. In its advertisements, the publisher, Shangwu, emphasized that it had managed to avoid typesetting errors (found in next item) by using photolithography. The *Bona* 百衲 edition of the Standard Histories (22.2) was included as a supplement. A separate annotated catalog was issued for the first series; thereafter the notes were published after each title.

Siku quanshu zhenben chuji 四庫全書珍本初集 (First collection of rare works from the *Siku quanshu*), Shangwu, 1934–5; 231 rare editions in 1,960 *ce*. Note two collectanea of the *Siku quanshu* published in the 1990s: *Siku quanshu cunmu congshu* 四庫全書存目叢書 and *Xuxiu Siku quanshu* 續修四庫全書 (9.5).

Wanyou wenku 萬有文庫, Wang Yunwu 王雲五, ed in chief, Shangwu, 2 collections, 1935–37. Includes more than 1,000 titles in 4,340 *ce*. The *Shitong* 十通 was printed in 20 Western-style volumes with a new index (volume 21) and was included in the reference books attached to the 2nd series.

Despite the typesetting errors in items one and three, works in these series are handy to use and were usually taken from good annotated editions. Therefore the old advice to students was to use and quote from editions in major *congshu* series, since these are readily accessible. Nevertheless, there are now so many excellent editions of indi-

---

[25] *Sibu beiyao* (Essentials of the four branches of literature), 336 titles in 2,500 *ce*, Zhonghua, 1920–33; corrected edition in 100 Western-style vols., 1935; rpnt., Taibei: Zhonghua, 1966–75; Zhonghua, 1990. *Sibu beiyao shumu tiyao* 四部備要書目提要 (Annotated catalog to the *Sibu beiyao*), Zhonghua, 1936; William C. Ju, *A Guide to the Ssu-pu pei-yao*, Taibei, 1971, is an index to the Taibei reprint giving author, title, and subject.

[26] *Sibu congkan* (The four branches of literature collection), 3 series (*chubian* 初編, 1919–22; rpnt., 1929; *xubian* 續編, 1934; and *sanbian* 三編, 1936), containing 504 titles in 3,112 *ce*, Shangwu, 1919–36. See Karl Lo, *A Guide to the Ssu-pu Ts'ung-k'an*, Univ. of Kansas Press, 1965; and review by Elling O. Eide, *HJAS* 27: 266–86 (1967).

vidual works, punctuated, annotated, and with "translations" into Modern Chinese, that the advice is no longer as forceful as when this was not the case.

9.7 Modern Annotated Bibliographies

At the end of the Qing and in the early days of the Republic, several scholars proposed updating and enlarging the *Siku zongmu* by including works deliberately left out for political reasons and by adding all the books printed in the intervening years. Eventually, the Japanese Committee for Oriental Culture (Tôhô bunka jimu iinkai 東方文化事務委員會) decided to use part of the Boxer Indemnity Funds to edit a continuation to the *Siku zongmu* in its institute, the Beiping Renwen kexue yanjiusuo 北平人文科學研究所. Hashikawa Tokio 橋川時雄 (1895–1982), the dean of the Institute, was put in charge of the project on the Japanese side, while the president of the Renwen and author of the *New History of the Yuan*, Ke Shaomin 柯 劭忞 (1850–1933), took the lead on the Chinese side. Altogether, some 71 Chinese scholars participated in the project, including many of the leading historians, gazetteer compilers, and bibliophiles of the day.[27] The work started in 1928 with the drawing up of a list of those books left out of the *Siku quanshu* as well as those written between 1750 and 1911. The list of 32,000 titles was agreed upon by 1931. During the next three years, 32,960 abstracts were drafted (a few more titles had been added to the list). Next the slow work of checking and editing the drafts began. By 1940, they had completed 20,319 (the breakdown was Classics: 3,878 titles; History: 8,363; Philosophy: 5,082; and Belles-lettres: 2,996). The abstracts covered works not included in the *Siku zongmu*, especially by Ming and early Qing authors (the *Siku quanshu* did not include the works of contemporaries), Buddhist and Daoist works, as well as books, including 2,000 gazetteers, written between 1750 and 1911. The work

[27] In addition to Ke Shaomin, the group included other senior Chinese historians and bibliophiles such as Wang Shunan 王樹楠 (1851–1936), Luo Zhenyu 羅振玉 (1866–1940), Hu Yujin 胡玉縉 (d. 1940), and Yu Shaosong 余 紹宋 (1883–1949), as well as recently graduated students such as Xiang Da 向達 (1900–1966), Xie Guozhen 謝國楨 (1901–82), Wang Zhongmin 王重民 (1903– 75), Luo Fuyi 羅福頤 (1905–), and Tan Qixiang 譚其驤 (1911–91), many of whom later became well-known scholars.

of typing and mimeographing the abstracts began. Since the funds
were low, only 10,080 were ready by the end of the war. The bulky
draft was sent to the Tôhô bunka gakuin kenkyûjo 東方文化學院
研究所 in Kyoto (51.11.1). The Renwen mimeograph was eventually published 30 years later in Taibei in 13 volumes with a total of
8,000 pages.[28]

The original notes and abstracts in Beijing, along with the Renwen library, were inherited in 1949 by the Chinese Academy of Sciences, which began putting them in order in 1983. In 1993 the notes
on the works in the first of the four branches, Classics, was published. It includes annotations on 1,928 works from the Classics
branch not included in the *Siku zongmu*, but as little more than a
reprint of the original notes it was badly received.[29] At about the
same time the decision was taken to re-edit the typed Renwen draft
and combine it in a single work with a re-edited *Siku zongmu*. One
hundred and seventy-five specialists worked on this new annotated
bibliography. The title chosen for it was *Siku da cidian*.[30] It is the
largest annotated bibliography of Chinese books available. It is also
easy to use, and so should be the first reference for finding primary
sources from all branches of Chinese literature, for getting a short
summary of their contents, and for searching out editions. It covers
the works in the *Siku zongmu* plus another 10,070 appearing from
mainly the late Ming to the early twentieth century, giving a total
of more than 20,000 works. The *Siku da cidian* abstracts include basic information on the author (at first appearance), contents of the
book, date of printing, and subsequent editions up to the 1980s. Arrangement is by the same main categories as in the *Siku zongmu*:
Classics, History, Philosophers, and Belles-lettres. There is a four-

---

[28] *Xuxiu Siku quanshu zongmu tiyao* 續修四庫全書總目提要 (Revised continuation of the annotated catalog of the imperial library), Wang Yunwu 王雲
五, ed. in chief, 13 vols., Taibei: Shangwu, 1971–72. A draft reprint was issued
in 1996: *Xuxiu Siku quanshu zongmu tiyao gaoben* 續修四庫全書總目提要稿本
(Draft revised continuation of the annotated catalog of the imperial library),
Library of the Academy of Sciences, eds., 38 vols., Pengyou and Qi-Lu, 1996.

[29] *Xuxiu Siku quanshu zongmu tiyao: jingbu* 續修四庫全書總目提要經部
(Revised continuation of the annotated catalog of the imperial library: Classics), 2 vols., Zhonghua, 1993.

[30] *Siku da cidian* 四庫大辭典 (Large dictionary of Chinese books), Li Xueqin 李學勤 and Lü Wenyu 呂文郁, eds. in chief, 2 vols., Jilin daxue, 1996.

corner title index with *pinyin* and stroke-count finding indexes attached to it.

There are many other modern Chinese encyclopaedic dictionaries of primary sources, arranged in the form of annotated bibliographies according to the four *Sibu* branches, but even the largest cover only a fraction of the works described in the *Siku da cidian*.

Zhongguo dang'an wenxian cidian 中國檔案文獻辭典, 1994 (Box 6, Chapter 20) contains annotations on 3,985 publications of documentary and archival sources (including modern publications) from the pre-Qin to the People's Republic.

Japanese Annotated Guides to Primary Sources

There are some thorough Japanese annotated bibliographies of Chinese primary historical sources.[31] The most recent, *Chûgoku shiseki kaidai jiten* 中國史籍解題辭典, was edited by a team of 15 Japanese historians working under the editorship of Yamane Yukio 山根幸夫 and Kanda Nobuo 神田信夫.[32] It contains brief summaries of some 1,650 primary sources from the earliest times to the end of the Qing. It is arranged by titles according to Japanese syllabary, but there is a *pinyin* title index, and the contributors have used *kanji* as much as possible in their notes to help those who do not read Japanese. This replaces all earlier such Japanese works. It is particularly useful for indicating Japanese indexes to Chinese primary sources, but it is neither as large nor as comprehensive as the *Siku da cidian* (which includes abstracts of 5,000 works in the History branch alone); nor are the notes as informative.

Western Annotated Guides to Primary Sources

The only guide to primary sources of all periods in English was the pioneering work by Alexander Wylie (1815–87), *Notes on Chinese Literature*, Kelly and Walsh, 1867; rpnt., Paragon, 1964. It is not re-

---

[31] Katsura Isoo (Koson) 桂五十郎 (湖村), *Kanseki kaidai* 漢籍解題 (Annotated bibliography of Chinese works), 1st ed., Tokyo, 1905, and many later editions. Of more use are the similar works compiled by historians, of which the best prewar example was the *Kokushi Tôyôshi Seiyôshi shiseki kaidai* 國史東洋史西洋史史籍解題 (Annotated bibliography of Japanese, Oriental, and Occidental history), Endô Motoo 遠藤元男 et al., eds., Heibonsha, 1936.

[32] Yamane Yukio and Kanda Nobuo, eds., *Chûgoku shiseki kaidai jiten* (Dictionary of annotations of Chinese historical sources), Ryôgen, 1989.

liable. There are, however, excellent guides to the primary sources of particular periods—for example, *ECT* or *A Sung Bibliography*. They are listed in Part V.

9.8   Rare, Lost, Recovered, Forged, and Banned Books

9.8.1   Rare Books

Rare books (*shanben* 善本) are normally defined as fine editions printed or copied in the Ming or earlier. For China itself, there is a union catalog of 60,000 rare books held by 781 public libraries and institutions in China (not including private collections; not including Taiwan, for which see item 2):

Zhongguo guji shanben shumu 中國古籍善本書目 (The China union catalog of rare books), Zhongguo guji shanben shumu bianji weiyuanhui, comp., Shanghai guji, *jingbu* 經部, 1986, 1989; *congbu* 叢部, 1989, 1990; *jibu* 集部, 1989, 1998; *shibu* 史部, 1991, 1993; *zibu* 子部, 1994. Each *bu* (branch) was issued in a separate *han* (case) containing *ce* in traditional thread binding (first date), then reissued in modern binding (second date). The whole set was reprinted in 1998. There are indexes indicating which institutions hold each item. Comprehensive author-title indexes are to be published separately in 2001.

Taiwan gongcang shanben shuming suoyin 臺灣公藏善本書目 (Catalog of titles of rare books in Taiwan public collections), Guoli zhongyang tushuguan, comp., 2 vols., Taibei, 1971. Has stroke-count index. Indicates which library holds each item. There is a personal-name index also compiled by the National Central Library: *Taiwan gongcang shanben shumu renming suoyin* 臺灣公藏善本書目人名索引, Taibei, 1972. Lists the main public holdings of *shanben* in Taiwan.

Other rare book catalogs are listed in Chapter 11.

Wang Zhongmin 王重民, *Zhongguo shanben shu tiyao* 中國善本書提要 (Notes and annotations on Chinese rare books), Shanghai, 1983. Detailed, heavily annotated catalog of over 4,200 rare books inspected by the author, mainly at the Guotu 國圖 (but also at Peking University Library and the Library of Congress). It corrects errors in previous catalogs and indicates which library holds each item. There is an author-title index, and an index of woodblock carvers and of publishers. It has been updated in the same author's *Zhongguo shanben shu tiyao bubian* 中國善本書提要補編, Shumu wenxian, 1991, 1998, in which he adds annotations on a further 770 historical and 10 philosophical works.

Guji banben tiji suoyin 古籍版本題記索引 (Index to bibliographic notes
on rare books), Luo Weiguo 羅偉國 and Hu Ping 胡平, eds., Shanghai shudian, 1991. Index to bibliographic notes on rare books as
found in 102 public and private library catalogs, collections of colophons, and reading notes that appeared from the Song to the 1960s.
Has four-corner index with stroke-count and *pinyin* finding indexes.

Libraries fortunate enough to hold *shanben* not only compile special
catalogs of such works but also publish facsimile reproductions or
make them available on microfilm (Chapter 11).

The Chinese Rare Books Project (CRBP) is in the process of establishing an online, international union catalog of Chinese rare
books. The headquarters is at Princeton University, New Jersey
(Department of East Asian Studies). By the end of the first quarter
1998, the project had created more than 12,000 full bibliographic
records for Chinese rare books held in North America, China, and
Europe. Access is through the RLG Web site.

9.8.2   Lost and Recovered Books

Over the centuries many books were lost, either because of some
catastrophe, such as fire or pillage, or because they were banned, or
simply because fashions and interests changed and a book was no
longer copied or collected and so failed to be transmitted. Small
wonder that only 85 of the 600 works in the *Hanshu* dynastic bibliography have survived, some of them only in part. Likewise, 86
percent of the titles in the *Suishu* bibliography have been lost. The
losses declined after printing became more widespread in the Song
and more copies were made. But those works that were still made
only in one or two manuscript copies (such as the *Yongle dadian* 永
樂大典 or the Veritable Records from the Tang to the Yuan) had a
low survival rate.

Later scholars, particularly in the Qing, used much ingenuity in
trying to recover such "lost" texts (*yishu* 逸[遺,佚]書), often excerpt
by excerpt or quotation by quotation from compilations such as *leishu*. Sometimes they succeeded in recovering the whole text (as with
the *Jiu Wudaishi* 舊五代史, which was one of the 385 works recovered from the *Yongle dadian* 永樂大典 by the *Siku* editors). Sometimes it was possible only to recover fragments of the lost work.
Such "recovered," "reconstituted texts" or *rifacimenti* are called *jiben*
輯本 or *jiyishu* 輯逸[佚]書. For a catalog of *jiben*, see *Gu yishu jiben*

mulu (fu kaozheng) 古佚書輯本目錄附考證.[33] A union catalog is forthcoming: *Zhongguo guji yishu jiben zongmu* 中國古籍佚書輯本總目 (Comprehensive catalog of ancient Chinese recovered books).

9.8.3   Forged Books

Controversy between the supporters of each version of the classics has been a major intellectual debate from the Han to the Qing and early Republic with accusations of forgery, some justified, freely exchanged.[34] Plenty of other kinds of forgery took place and continue to this day.[35] The techniques for proving a forgery were referred to as *bianwei* 辯偽. Textual criticism (*jiaokan* 校勘, 19.2) focused on the correction and authentication of the texts of the classics.

9.8.4   Banned Books

Banned books (*jinshu* 禁書) have been a feature of Chinese political and intellectual life from the Warring States to the present day. For an introduction to the subject covering the Qin to the Qing, see *Zhongguo jinshu daguan* 中國禁書大觀. This contains a discussion of the reasons for banning books, based on 220 outstanding examples (including everything from the *Lunyu* and the

---

[33] *Gu yishu jiben mulu (fu kaozheng)* (Catalog of ancient recovered editions with scholarly apparatus), Sun Qizhi 孫啓治 and Chen Jianhua 陳建華, eds., Zhonghua, 1997. Has author-title indexes.

[34] *ECT* contains notes on the authenticity and textual history of 64 Han and pre-Han works. The latest summary of the many aspects and degrees of forgery, misrepresentation, and misattribution found in 1,200 titles is *Zhongguo weishu zongkao* 中國偽書綜考 (Comprehensive study of forged books in China), Deng Ruiquan 鄧瑞全 and Wang Kuanying 王冠英, eds. in chief, Huangshan, 1998. This replaces the earlier Zhang Xincheng 張心澂, *Weishu tongkao* 偽書通考 (General study of forged books), 2 vols., Shangwu, 1939, 1954; rev. edition, 1957, and Zheng Liangshu 鄭良樹, *Xu Weishu tongkao* 續偽書通考 (General study of forged books, continued), 3 vols., Xuesheng, 1984.

[35] In 1996, there came word of the discovery of an original 82-*juan* version of *Sunzi bingfa* (28.2) on bamboo strips, allegedly discovered in Xi'an in 1895. The owner and his sons had painstakingly copied it onto paper, so the story went; however, during the Cultural Revolution, the Red Guards had destroyed all but one of the bamboo strips (Yang Caiyu 楊才玉, *Shoucang* 收藏, 8, 1996). Indeed the *Hanshu* "Yiwenzhi" records the original *Sunzi* as having had 82 *juan*, but the Xi'an version was quickly shown to have been a fake.

Shijing to the *Diamond Sutra* and the *Dream of the Red Chamber*). The book concludes with a list of 4,000 titles that the editors claim is a complete one of all the books banned in different periods up to the end of the Qing.[36] Note that four of the main earlier lists are indexed in *H-Y Index* 10 (see Table 22).

9.9 Alternative and Difficult Book Titles

A problem encountered throughout Chinese history is the use of more than one title for the same book, caused in the early days by the fact that books circulated as manuscripts in different versions with no fixed title or author (19.2). After the introduction of printing, new titles were often invented by publishers as a sales technique. Another reason why the titles of books changed was convenience. An enormous number were abbreviated. The more famous the work, the shorter the abbreviation (only a handful of the most ancient Confucian classics were customarily known by one-word abbreviated titles, e.g., *Shu* 書, *Shi* 詩, *Yi* 易; see 19.2.1. Most well-known works circulated with disyllabic abbreviations, e.g., *Zuozhuan* 左傳, *Sanzhuan* 三傳, *Lunyu* 論語, *Shiji* 史紀, *Shuowen* 說文). Another reason why titles changed was the need to distinguish two books. Often a reign period or dynastic name was added later.[37] Yet another reason why titles changed was the need to avoid using characters in the title that had subsequently become taboo.

If you have doubts about a title, check

Tongshu yiming tongjian 同書異名通檢 (General investigation into books published under more than one title), Du Xinfu 杜信孚, comp.; rev. and enl. ed., Jiangsu renmin, 1982. Lists 6,000 books with different titles.

---

[36] Zhongguo jinshu daguan (Overview of Chinese banned books), An Pingqiu 安平秋 and Zhang Peiheng 章培恒, eds., Shanghai wenhua, 1990; 4th prnt., 1991. See also Hok-lam Chan, *Control of Publishing in China Past and Present*, ANUP, 1983.

[37] For example, the Song digest of laws known today as *Song xingtong* 宋刑通 began with the title *Song Jianlong chongxiang ding xingtong* 宋建隆重詳定刑通. This was abbreviated to *Chongding xingtong* 重定刑通 or simply *Xingtong* 刑通. But at that point it became necessary to differentiate it from the *Xingtong* 刑通 compiled in the Later Zhou period, and so it acquired its present title of *Song xingtong* 宋刑通.

Tongming yishu tongjian 同名異書通檢 (General investigation into different books having the same title), Du Xinfu 杜信孚 and Mao Junyi 毛俊儀, eds., Jiangsu renmin, 1982. Lists 3,500 different books with others having the same title.

In choosing the title for a book, Chinese writers liked to use classical allusions, sometimes taken from the name of the study in which they wrote, sometimes not, but usually as a means of expressing a personal point of view or whim. It is not always easy to understand the allusion fully unless it is explained in the preface. A good reference book such as the *Siku da cidian* will often give the author's reasons for choosing a particular title, but not always. Take an easy example, the title of a *biji* written by Lu Can 陸粲, *Gengji bian* 庚己編. If you did not know that the author lived at the beginning of the sixteenth century, you might not have guessed that it probably means "Written between 1510 and 1519" (i.e., between *Ming Zhengde gengwu nian* 明正德庚午年 and *Ming Zhengde jimao nian* 明正德己卯年). To take a more difficult example, a *biji* written by Zhu Guozhen 朱國禎 (1558–1632), *Yongchuang xiaopin* 湧幢小品. The original titles were *Xi Hong* 希洪 and later *Fang Hong xiaopin* 倣洪小品 (that is "A modest work in imitation of Hong [Mai's *Rongzhai suibi*]"). On reflection, Zhu decided that it would be presumptuous to compare his work with the famous Song *biji*, so he chose the present title based on the name of his study, "Trifles from the erectable study." Unless you read his preface, you could hardly guess the meaning (49.2, *Biji*). When all else fails, or even before, check *Zhongguo gujin shuming shiyi cidian* 中國古今書名釋義辭典.[38] This has explanations of 3,200 difficult book titles (including the above two), from the earliest times to 1966. Arrangement is by stroke count. There is also a stroke-count table of contents.

In order to find out if a source is extant and if so, in what library, the student should look through the published library catalogs of the major collections of Chinese books in China, Japan, and the West (Chapter 11). For recently published Chinese books, there are databases available on CD-ROM, for example, in China, the *Zhongguo guojia shumu guangpan* 中國國家書目光盤, 1988– . It is updated twice a year.

---

[38] *Zhongguo gujin shuming shiyi cidian* (Dictionary for clearing up doubts about book titles), Zhao Chuanren 趙傳仁 et al., eds., Shandong youyi, 1992.

9.10   Indexes and Concordances

As an aid to literary composition, Chinese scholars compiled what amounted to general indexes of the phrases and quotable quotes in the classical and literary canon (see, for example, the *Peiwen yunfu*; 2.2.1). Such works were normally arranged by rhyme and sometimes by classifier. Encyclopaedias such as the *Taiping yulan* (31.1) also served as detailed subject indexes to the contents of previously published books. Individual works, however, were usually not indexed, although sometimes there was a table of contents at the end of the last scroll (or at the end of sections) as well as a postface. When printing became common in the Song dynasty, the table of contents moved to the front of the book, as did the postface (henceforward, preface; see 3.6).

The main reason why individual books were usually not indexed was no doubt that the most widespread works, such as the Confucian classics, were learned by heart. A good scholar did not need time-saving devices.

Indeed, Jia Sixie 賈思勰, the author of the *Qimin yaoshu* 齊民要術 (35.1.2), felt that he had to apologize for cluttering up his text with tables of contents (*mulu* 目錄) at the head of each *juan*. The most famous table of contents (because it was the first large-scale one for a major work) was that to the *Zizhi tongjian* 資治通鑑 (21.3). To put things in perspective, it is worth remembering that indexes to individual books began appearing in Europe only during the centuries after printing was introduced, and even then they remained something of a rarity. The first modern indexes were introduced in the nineteenth century and in some countries, such as France, the index is still seen as more of an indulgence to be avoided than as a necessity.

Because of the lack of indexes in Chinese books, a great deal of time and effort can be saved by using the indexes and concordances compiled in the twentieth century, not only for the classics, but also for many other Chinese printed sources. Particularly convenient are the growing number that are computer generated and available on CD-ROM. One of the early translations for "index" was *tongjian* 通檢; next came the loanword *yinde* 引得 (from index). Today the word most commonly used is *suoyin* 索引. It covers both indexes and concordances (indexes of all or of a selection of the words in a work).

The most important set of concordances for classical works is the *ICS Ancient Chinese Texts Concordance Series* conceived by D.C. Lau (Liu Dianjue 劉殿爵) and produced at the Institute of Chinese Studies (ICS) at the Chinese University of Hong Kong. The *ICS* is based on a database of the entire corpus of Classical Chinese (9 million characters), the oracle-bone inscriptions (1 million characters), the bronze inscriptions (0.2 million characters), nine bamboo and silk manuscripts (1.2 million characters), as well as all works dating from the end of the Han to AD 589.[39] The database is not yet completed, but most of the transmitted texts are already available online. In book form, the Han and pre-Han concordances comes to 65 volumes. The series covering the Han to Sui texts comes to 27 volumes.[40] Most have been published. The original texts (for the most part taken from *Sibu congkan* editions) are included. Finding a character or phrase in the text is rapidly done because the concordance is arranged by *pinyin*. There are character frequency counts and indexes by stroke count. All volumes will be available on individual discs or on five CD-ROM. The software allows searches across the entire corpus. By their comprehensiveness, accuracy, and ease of use, the *ICS* concordances surpass all previous indexes and concordances of the classics and pre-Sui texts. They have the added advantage that revised editions can be easily issued in the form of corrected disks. References are made throughout the manual to the appropriate *ICS* concordance.

As soon as all major transmitted pre-Sui texts and Han and pre-Han excavated texts are on an easily available computer database, it will be possible to analyze Classical Chinese and its transition to Middle Chinese with a degree of accuracy not previously possible.

[39] *Xian-Qin liang Han guji zhuzi suoyin congkan,* 先秦兩漢古籍逐字索引叢刊, Liu Dianjue 劉殿爵, Chen Fangzheng 陳方正, series eds.; He Zhihua 何志華, executive ed., and He Guojie 何國杰, director of computing; 1st series, HK: Shangwu, 1992; 2nd and 3rd series, HK: Shangwu, 1994–98. The title of the computer database is *Han da guji ziliaoku xian-Qin liang Han chuanshi guji* 漢達古籍資料庫先秦兩漢傳世古籍 ([Chinese ancient texts, CHANT] database, Han and Pre-Han traditional Chinese texts), published by the Gu wenxian ziliaoku zhongxin 古文獻資料庫中心 (CHANT Center), ICS, the Chinese University of Hong Kong. Distributed by HK: Shangwu.

[40] *Wei Jin Nan-Bei Chao guji zhuzi suoyin congkan* 魏晉南北朝古籍逐字索引叢刊, Liu Dianjue 劉殿爵, Chen Fangzheng 陳方正, He Zhihua 何志華, eds., 24 vols. in three series, HKCUP, 1999– .

Many more computer-based indexes and concordances are becoming available, including the entire corpus of the Standard Histories (22.2) and parts of the Daoist and Buddhist Canons (29.4 and 29.5).

The most important precomputer series of indexes and concordances for post-Han works is the *Harvard-Yenching Institute Sinological Index Series*, compiled under the general editorship of William Hung (Hong Ye 洪業, 1893–1980).[41] The series consists of two separately numbered groups; the first entitled Indices (*yinde* 引得, 41 works) and the second, Supplements (*yinde tekan* 引得特刊, 23 works). The Supplements include a number of concordances with complete texts as well as other materials. Under the direction of Nie Chongqi 聶崇岐, the Centre Franco-Chinois d'Etudes Sinologiques (aided by the staff of the *H-Y Index Series*, who had been forced by the war to leave Yenching in 1942) published 13 volumes of indexes, Beiping, 1943–48. Of the total, 77 works covered by the *H-Y* and *CFC* concordance series, 25 classical works have now been superseded by the *ICS* concordance series. That still leaves 52 useful *H-Y* and *CFC* concordances and indexes of works from later periods. These are referred to in the appropriate sections.[42]

A large number of indexes and concordances are compiled in Japan. These are usually produced by members of a seminar or study group collectively as a working aid (appearing under the senior

[41] William Hung, gen. ed., *Hafo-Yanjing xueshe yinde bianzuan chu* 哈佛燕京學社引得編纂處 (Harvard-Yenching Institute Sinological Index Series), 69 volumes, Yenching University, Beiping, 1931–50; rpnt., Zhonghua, 1960, 1966; CMC, Taibei, 1965–69; Shanghai guji, 1983–88. See Susan Chan Egan, *A Latterday Confucian: Reminiscences of William Hung (1893–1980)*, Harvard East Asian Monograph, 131, 1980.

[42] Every character is assigned a number in the *H-Y Index Series* according to the unique and complicated *guixie* system based on the shapes of the five characters in the phrase *Zhongguozi guixie* (中國字庋擷) and the nine strokes and graphemes in the characters *gui* 庋 (put in) and *xie* 擷 (pull out) combined with the four-corner system number (note that *xie* 擷 is deliberately written with *mi* 糸 instead of *ji* 吉 as the middle element). Fortunately there is no need to learn this unique character classification and coding system (devised by William Hung) because each of the H-Y indexes and concordances also includes a Wade-Giles and stroke-count index. In the Shanghai guji reprint of the series *pinyin* is used instead of Wade-Giles. Shanghai guji also printed a separate table converting characters in *pinyin* and the four-corner system to *guixie*: *Yinde jianzi biao* 引得檢字表, Chen Bingren 陳秉仁, comp., Shanghai guji, 1993.

member's name). As a rule a preliminary mimeographed version is circulated for a number of years before a revised printed edition is produced.

Two hundred and eighty-two precomputer indexes and concordances of Chinese texts from antiquity to 1900 are meticulously annotated in David L. McMullen, *Concordances and Indexes to Chinese Texts*, CMC, 1975.

Note that there are many different kinds of index and concordance, usually called in their titles *suoyin*. Apart from author-title, place-names or subject indexes, concordances of the words in a text are very useful. A full concordance of every character (such as the *ICS zhuzi suoyin* 逐字索引) is much more useful than a concordance of the head characters of words or of the first characters of a sentence. Thus, for example, if you look up *yayan* 雅言 in the *Shisanjing zhushu suoyin* 十三經注疏索引 (19.2.1), you will not find it under *ya* 雅 but under *zi* 子 because this is the first character of the phrase in which it occurs. All the *ICS* concordances are full-character indexes; some of the *H-Y* and *CFC* indexes and many of the Japanese indexes are not.

10

Locating Secondary Sources

This chapter surveys comprehensive bibliographies of secondary scholarship on Chinese history (10.1); followed by:

Chinese-language bibliographies and journals (10.2)
Japanese-language bibliographies and journals (10.3)
Western-language bibliographies and journals (10.4)

10.1 Comprehensive Bibliographies

At an early stage of research it is useful to find out what other historians are writing in your field, and also what has been written about it in the past. Computerized library catalogs can be useful, but their very comprehensiveness is a mixed blessing and they do not cover journal articles where most research first appears. So, it quickly pays to turn to the many specialized bibliographies available.

These can cover a single subject, a single period, a single type of historical source, or the works of a particular scholar; many such selective bibliographies, as well as specialist journals, are listed in the appropriate section of the manual. Here the focus is on those bibliographies that cover the entire sweep of Chinese history. Those covering recent scholarship are listed first, followed by comprehensive bibliographies of past scholarship.

The most convenient way of gaining an overview of the entire field of Chinese studies in different languages is through the articles and review pages devoted to Chinese history in the main historical journals that are listed in this section.

Apart from these, there are four annual reviews. The first two cover research on Asian studies, including Chinese history. They are comprehensive, but unannotated and appear with a delay of several years. The next two specialize in Chinese studies and are annotated. Each has particular strengths and weaknesses which makes it worthwhile to consult all four.

1. *Bibliography of Asian Studies*, published by the Association of Asian Studies (under various titles since 1936 and under the present title since 1956), gives a comprehensive listing of books and articles on China (as well as the rest of Asia) in Western languages, mainly English. The volume covering publications in 1991 appeared in 1997. It contained over 37,000 entries (for reviews rather than listings, see the *Journal of Asian Studies* itself). The BAS is available online via library subscription for the years 1971–1991 (plus numerous citations from more recent years, including all articles in the 100 most-used journals in Asian studies). Approximately 420,000 citations are included. For the years before 1970, see 10.4.1.

2. *Tôyôgaku kenkyû bunken ruimoku* 東洋學研究文獻類目 (Annual bibliography of Oriental studies; between 1934 and 1964, the title was *Tôyôgaku bunken ruimoku*). For recent Japanese, Chinese, and Korean scholarship, these are the most comprehensive of the annual bibliographies. They are compiled at the Jinbun (Western works, including Russian, are also listed). Books and articles are arranged according to language and further subdivided within each language group according to subject categories; full author indexes make this bibliography very easy to use. A unique feature is that it includes author's reviews, listed under work reviewed and also indexed by the author of the review. Note also the Tôhô Gakkai's *Books and Articles on Oriental Subjects* (10.3.2).

3. *Revue bibliographique de sinologie* (also titled, since 1997, *Review of Bibliography in Sinology*), Paris (1957– , annual; 1st series, 15 vols., covering the years 1955–70, Paris, 1957–82; 2nd series, covering the years 1983 to the present, Paris, 1983–). The *RBS* is a selective annotated bibliography covering books and articles in Chinese, Japanese, and European languages on all periods of Chinese history, including (since the 1997 issue) current affairs. *RBS* 2nd series comes out rapidly, usually no more than a year after the year covered. Each book and article is briefly reviewed (either in French or in English). There are also (since the 1986 issue) occasional bibliographic essays on chosen topics. Has subject and author indexes.

4. *China Review International*, University of Hawaii (1993–). This quarterly review is strong on new English-language scholarship on all aspects of Chinese studies.

The annual bibliographies and even journal reviews inevitably appear some time after the publication of articles and books. A more immediate way to keep up-to-date is to attend the annual conferences of the learned society or association covering your field of interest. The most important comprehensive Western one is the Association of Asian Studies. If you cannot attend the annual meeting, the abstracts are published (1992–).[1] The European Association of Chinese Studies (EACS) meets annually.

Another way of keeping up-to-date is to skim through the catalogs of publishers and bookstores. There are not all that many specializing in Chinese history. In America and Europe, only a handful of university presses have developed a tradition of publishing studies on Chinese history (11.5).

10.2   Chinese Secondary Sources and Journals

10.2.1   Recent Scholarship

For Chinese historical scholarship of the previous 12 months, use the following:

1. *Zhongguo lishixue nianjian* 中國歷史學年鑑.[2] The survey carries essays on trends in selected fields, reports on conferences and on recent archaeological discoveries, and bibliographies of books and articles. Except for 1979, the year covered is that previous to the one in the title. Publication comes 12–24 months after the year surveyed. Contents are based on the society's quarterly *Shixue qingbao* 史學情報.

2. *Zhongguoshi yanjiu dongtai* 中國史研究動態,[3] carries articles on recent trends in the field of Chinese history arranged in the form of brief state-of-the-field essays and book reviews. It is available on CD-ROM (item 3 below).

3. *Zhongguo xueshu qikan (guangpanban)* 中國學術期刊(光盤版). The database includes articles appearing in many hundreds of scholarly and university journals. Coverage of science and technology journals

---

[1] Association for Asian Studies, Inc., *Abstracts of the [year] Annual Meeting*, Association for Asian Studies, 1992– .

[2] *Zhongguo lishixue nianjian* (Annual survey of Chinese historical studies), Chinese History Society, Zhongguo shixuehui 中國史學會, ed., Sanlian, 1980– .

[3] *Zhongguoshi yanjiu dongtai* (Developments in Chinese Historical Research), Shekeyuan, Lishisuo, ed., monthly, 1978– .

is much better than the humanities, but there are about a dozen historical and archaeological journals on disc F (*Wenshizhe* 文史哲). Those included are marked with an asterisk in the lists of archaeological journals in 12.3 and of historical journals in 10.2.3.[4]

4. *Fuyin baokan ziliao* 復印報刊資料.[5] The main divisions of interest to the historian of China are: K-1, *Lishixue* 歷史學; K-2, *Zhongguo gudaishi* 中國古代史; K-3, *Zhongguo jindaishi* 中國近代史; K-21, *Xian Qin Qin Han shi* 先秦秦漢史; K-22, *Wei Jin Nan Bei Chao Sui Tang shi* 魏晉南北朝隋唐史; K-23, *Song Liao Jin Yuan shi* 宋遼金元史; K-24, *Ming Qing shi* 明清史. Reprints entire articles.

5. *Quanguo baokan suoyin* 全國報刊索引.[6] Monthly. Indexes some 20,000 articles appearing in 150 important newspapers and 6,700 periodicals. Divided into social sciences and natural sciences. Since 1993 available online.

6. *Zhongguo shehui kexue wenxian tilu* 中國社會科學文獻提錄.[7] Contains summaries of articles on social science subjects, including history and archaeology.

7. *Taiwan diqu Hanxue lunzhu xuanmu* 臺灣地區漢學論著選目.[8] See also the quarterly *Hanxue yanjiu tongxun* 漢學研究通訊.

For details, both biographic and bibliographic, on about 3,450 Chinese historians active in the twentieth century (including 110 working in Taiwan), see

[4] *Zhongguo xueshu qikan [guangpanban]* (Chinese academic journal CD publication), produced at Qinghua daxue guangpan guojia gongcheng yanjiu zhongxin 清華大學光盤國家工程研究中心 (Qinghua University reseach center for the national CD-ROM project), Qinghua daxue, 1996– .

[5] *Fuyin baokan ziliao* (Photocopied journal materials), Renmin daxue, bimonthly, 1978– (and since 1985 for separate periods). Available on CD-ROM; also online.

[6] *Quanguo baokan suoyin* (1973– , bimonthly. Appeared under title *Quanguo zhuyao qikan ziliao suoyin* 全國主要期刊資料索引, 1955–56; *Quanguo zhuyao baokan ziliao suoyin* 全國主要報刊資料索引, 1956–66; ceased publication 1966–73), Shanghai tushuguan. Available on CD-ROM.

[7] *Zhongguo shehui kexue wenxian tilu* (Abstracts of articles on Chinese social sciences), separate bimonthly issues on "history" and "archeology," Zhongguo shehui kexue wenxian tilu Editorial Department, ed., 1985– .

[8] *Taiwan diqu Hanxue lunzhu xuanmu* (Selected bibliography of Chinese studies in Taiwan), Hanxue yanjiu zhongxin 漢學研究中心, comp., Taibei, 1982– .

Zhongguo dangdai lishixue xuezhe cidian 中國當代歷史學學者辭典 (Dictionary of contemporary Chinese historical scholars), Xibei daxue, 1993.

10.2.2   Doctoral Dissertations

Ph.Ds were granted in China after 1980. Details can be found in the Boshi lunwen ziliaoshi 博士論文資料室 of the National Library of China (11.1). For Western doctoral dissertations, see 10.4.2.

For catalogs of Ph.Ds written in Taiwan, see

Quanguo boyinshi lunwen mulu 全國博士論文目錄 (Ph.D and MA theses catalog), Guoli Zhengzhi daxue shehui kexue ziliao zhongxin, 6 vols., 1977–92. Covers Ph.D and MA theses in Taiwan in all subjects for the years 1949–90. Arranged by subject. Before 1989, the title was *Quanguo boyinshi lunwen fenlei mulu* 全國博士論文分類目錄.

Hanxue yanjiu tongxun 漢學研究通訊 (10.2.5) contains information on Ph.D theses in Chinese studies in Taiwan.

10.2.3   Previous Scholarship

To locate Chinese historical monographs and books, check *Bashi nian lai shixue shumu* 八十年來史學書目 *1900–1980*.[9] It contains citations of over 12,400 Chinese books (including Chinese translations) published from 1900 to 1980 on China, world history, and archaeology. Arrangement is by subject. There is an author index.

For an index of 20,000 books and articles on socioeconomic history appearing in China, Taiwan, and Hong Kong between 1900 and 1984, see *Zhongguo shehui jingjishi lunzhu mulu* 中國社會經濟史論著目錄.[10]

See also E-tu Zen Sun and J. de Francis, *Bibliography of Chinese Social History: A Selected and Critical List of Chinese Periodical Sources*, YUP, 1952. It lists and annotates 176 articles in Chinese on social history appearing mainly during the 1930s. Richard C. How-

---

[9] *Bashi nian lai shixue shumu 1900–1980* (Bibliography of historical books published in China during the past 80 years), Lishisuo, comp., Shehui kexue, 1984.

[10] *Zhongguo shehui jingjishi lunzhu mulu* (Catalog of books and articles on Chinese social and economic history), Shekeyuan, Jingjishizu 經濟史組 (Economic history group of CASS), comp., Qi-Lu, 1988.

ard, *Index to Learned Chinese Periodicals*, G. K. Hall, 1962, indexes 14 journals by journal and by subject.

Between 1900 and 1976, over 100,000 articles on Chinese history appeared in Chinese journals and newspapers. They are indexed in the three-part *Zhongguo shixue lunwen suoyin* 中國史學論文索引.[11] The arrangement of all three parts is by extremely detailed subject categories as well as by period (earliest times to up to 1949). These volumes now largely supersede earlier bibliographies.[12]

Articles in collected essays (either by an individual or institution) often get left out of the bibliographies of journal articles and books. This gap can be made good with *1,522 zhong xueshu lunwenji shixue lunwen fenlei suoyin* 種學術論文集史學論文分類索引.[13]

[11] *Zhongguo shixue lunwen suoyin* (Index to Chinese historical articles), compiled by members of the Lishisuo and Beijing daxue Lishixi 北京大學歷史系. Part 1 covers 1900–37 (2 vols., Kexue, 1957; rpnt., HK: Sanlian, 1980); part 2 covers 1937 to 1949 (2 vols., Sanlian, 1980); part 3 covers 1949 to 1976 (3 vols., HK: Zhonghua, 1995).

[12] See also Yu Ping-kuen (Yu Bingquan) 余秉權, *Chinese History: Index to Learned Articles, 1902–1962* (*Zhongguo shixue lunwen yinde* 中國史學論文引得), HKUP, 1963; Taibei, 1968. Index of 10,325 articles in 355 journals (found in Hong Kong libraries) appearing between 1902 and 1962 and written by 3,392 authors. This should be used in conjunction with the same author's expansion: *Chinese History: Index to Learned Articles, 1905–64* (H-Y Library, 1970) in which many more journals (found in European and American libraries) not included in the first volume were indexed. There is no duplication between the two volumes. The arrangement of both volumes is by stroke count of authors' names; there is also a Wade-Giles index and a subject index.

There are a very large number of indexes of secondary articles on Chinese history. The most useful are those covering a specific period or problem. They are listed in the relevant chapters of the manual.

[13] *1,522 zhong xueshu lunwenji shixue lunwen fenlei suoyin* (Index to historical articles by category in 1,522 scholarly collections), Zhou Xun 周迅 and Li Fan 李凡, comps., Shumu wenxian, 1990. Contains 34,146 articles and books published in scholarly collections between 1911 and 1986. To a certain extent this is supplemented by *Jianguo yilai Zhongguo shixue lunwenji pianmu suoyin chubian* 建國以來中國史學論文集篇目索引初編, Zhang Haihui 張海惠 and Wang Yuzhi 王玉芝, comps., Zhonghua, 1992. Indexes over 15,000 chapters and articles appearing in over 1,000 collections of scholarly writings on Chinese history published between 1949 and 1984 (not including those in Hong Kong and Taiwan). There is a clear arrangement by subject category and by period. The titles of the collections are listed and there is also an author index.

Supplement the above bibliographies by looking through one of the bibliographic guides listed in 8.1, or use the *Tôyôgaku kenkyû bunken ruimoku* or the *Revue bibliographique de sinologie*.[14]

The single best bibliographic introduction to scholarship on Chinese history in Taiwan and Hong Kong since 1949 is *Zhongguo lishi zhinan* 中國歷史指南, 1990 (8.2). For a book-length introduction to Chinese historical studies in Hong Kong, see

Dangdai Xianggang shixue yanjiu 當代香港史學研究 *Dangdai Xianggang shixue yanjiu* (Contemporary historical research in Hong Kong), Zhou Zhuirong 周佳榮 et al., comp., HK: Sanlian, 1994.

10.2.4   Main Chinese-Language Historical Journals

The abstract, excerpt, and reprint journals listed under 10.2.1 are the best way of keeping up-to-date with the many dozens of Chinese journals publishing historical research. The following list is only a small selection of 58 of the main historical journals and journals of interest to the historian. Those marked with an asterisk are available on Qinghua University's *Zhongguo xueshu qikan (guangpanban)* 中國學術期刊[光盤版] (10.2.1). Dozens of universities publish scholarly journals covering the humanities and social sciences. Such *xuebao* 學報 or *xuekan* 學刊 are far too numerous to list here despite the fact that they often carry articles of interest to the historian. Publishers or editors are only given in the following list if the journal is not listed in another section of the manual. For archaeological journals, see 12.3.

Beichao yanjiu 北朝研究 (45.5.2).

**Beijing daxue xuebao* 北京大學學報 (1955– , bimonthly).

Chongji xuebao 崇基學報 (1960– , semiannual), Chung Chi College, Chinese University of Hong Kong, Shatin.

---

[14] See also Albert L. Feuerwerker and S. Cheng, *Chinese Communist Studies of Modern Chinese History*, HUP, 1961, in which some 500 books on Chinese history published in China between 1949 and 1959 are discussed under various broad subject headings. ("Modern" includes several works on the Ming.) Also consult *Modern Chinese Society, 1644–1970: An Analytical Bibliography*, vol. 2, *Publications in Chinese*, G. W. Skinner and W. Hsieh, eds., SUP, 1973. A critical, thoroughly arranged, annotated bibliography of Chinese publications.

Chongji lishixue jikan 崇基歷史學季刊 (1961– , semiannual), Chung Chi College, Chinese University of Hong Kong, Shatin.

Dang'an yu lishi 檔案與歷史 (51.14.2).

Dunhuang Tulufan yanjiu 敦煌吐魯番研究 (46.3.5).

*Dunhuang yanjiu 敦煌研究 (46.3.5).

Dunhuangxue jikan 敦煌學輯刊 (46.3.5).

Gugong bowuyuan yuankan 故宮博物院院刊 (1978– , quarterly), Beijing.

Guoxue jikan 國學季刊 (1923–52, quarterly). Beijing daxue's journal of sinological studies.

Guji zhengli yu yanjiu 古籍整理與研究 (1986– , irregular), Quanguo gaodeng yuanxiao guji zhengli yu yanjiu gongzuo weiyuanhui 全國高等院校古籍整理與研究工作委員會.

Gujin nongye 古今農業 (35.1).

Guwenzi yanjiu 古文字研究 (13.3).

Hongloumeng xuekan 紅樓夢學刊 (34.3).

Jianduxue yanjiu 簡牘學研究 (18.1).

Jindai Zhongguo 近代中國 (51.14.2).

Jindaishi yanjiu 近代史研究 (51.14.2).

Kang Ri zhanzheng yanjiu 抗日戰爭研究 (51.14.2).

Lishi dang'an 歷史檔案 (1981– , quarterly).

Lishi dili 歷史地理 (1983– , irregular; no. 15, 1999), Fudan daxue.

*Lishi yanjiu 歷史研究 (1954–66; 1974– , quarterly). This used to be the most important Chinese historical journal. Since the proliferation of new and specialized journals in the 1980s and 1990s, it has lost its leading position. It is edited at the Lishisuo. It has been weighted toward pre-1911 Chinese history. There is an index of articles for the issues 1954–83.

Mingshi yanjiu 明史研究 (49.5.2).

Mingshi yanjiu zhuankan 明史研究專刊 (49.5.2).

Mingshi ziliao congkan 明史資料叢刊 (49.5.2).

Minguo dang'an 民國檔案 (51.14.2).

Minzu yanjiu 民族研究 (40.4).

Minzu yanjiu dongtai 民族研究動態 (40.4).

Minzu yuwen 民族語文 (40.4).

Qinghua daxue xuebao (zhexue shehui kexueban) 清華大學學報哲學社會科學版 (1955– , quarterly).

Qinghua xuebao 清華學報 (10.2.4).

Qingshi yanjiu 清史研究 (50.10.4).

Republican China (51.14.2).

Shijie zongjiao yanjiu 世界宗教研究 (29.2).

*Shixueshi yanjiu 史學史研究 (1979- , quarterly), Shifan daxue, Beijing. For the years 1979-81, the title was *Shixueshi ziliao* 史學史資料.

Sichuan dang'an shiliao 四川檔案史料 (51.14.2).

Songshi yanjiu tongxun 宋史研究通訊 (47.4).

Tang yanjiu 唐研究 (46.5.2).

Wenshi 文史 (1962-65, irregular), 4 vols., *Xinjianshe* 新建設, eds.; vol. 5 (1978- , irregular), Zhonghua shuju, ed., Zhonghua; rpnt., 1998.

Wenxian 文獻 (1979- , trimesterly), Shumu wenxian chubanshe, Beijing.

Xianggang Zhongguo Jindaishi xuehui huikan 香港中國近代史學會會刊 (51.14.2).

Xinya xuebao 新亞學報 (1955- , irregular), Xinya xueyuan, Chinese University of Hong Kong, Shatin.

Yanjing xuebao 燕京學報 (1927-51, quarterly; new series, 1995- , annual), Yanjing yanjiuyuan, Beijing. The old series, *Yenching Journal of Chinese Studies*, was one of the four leading sinological (as well as historical) journals of the Republican era (the other three were Beida's *Guoxue jikan* 國學季刊, Qinghua's *Qinghua xuebao* 清華學報 and Academia Sinica's *Zhongyang yanjiuyuan Lishi yuyan yanjiusuo jikan* (10.2.4). The *Yanjing xuebao* was edited and published at the H-Y Institute for Chinese Studies at Yenching University, Beiping, which opened in 1928. Its editors included Rong Geng 容庚, Gu Jiegang 顧頡剛, Hong Ye 洪業 (William Hung), Qi Sihe 齊思和 (1907-81), and Wu Shichang 吳世昌 (1908-86). The journal also published a distinguished monograph series (23 vols.). The institute published the *H-Y Index Series* (see 9.10). For the titles of other major journals of this period plus a sampling of their contents, see E-tu Zen Sun and John de Francis (1952); and Richard C. Howard (1962).

Zhonggong dangshi yanjiu 中共黨史研究 (51.14.2).

Zhongguo jingjishi yanjiu 中國經濟史研究 (1986- , quarterly), Shekeyuan, Jingji yanjiusuo (Institute of Economic Research), Beijing.

Zhongguo keji shiliao 中國科技史料 (37.3).

Zhongguo lishi bowuguan guankan 中國歷史博物館館刊 (1979- , annual), Zhongguo lishi bowuguan, Beijing.

Zhongguo lishi dili luncong 中國歷史地理論叢 (1987- , trimesterly), Shaanxi shifan daxue.

Zhongguo Mingshi xuehui tongxun 中國明史學會通訊 (49.5.2).

*Zhongguo nongshi 中國農史 (35.1).

Zhongguo shehui jingjishi yanjiu 中國社會經濟史研究 (1982– , quarterly), Xiamen daxue, Lishixi.

Zhongguo shehui kexue 中國社會科學 (1979– , bimonthly), Shekeyuan. Articles from the research institutes of the Shekeyuan, including the Lishisuo (a selection of the best articles appear in translation in *Social Sciences in China*).

Zhongguo wenhua yanjiusuo xuebao 中國文化研究中心學報 (*Journal of Chinese Studies: Annual*), 1992– , annual. Previous title (1970–92): *Xianggang Zhongwen daxue Zhongguo wenhua yanjiu zhongxin xuebao* 香港中文大學中國文化研究中心學報 (*Journal of the Institute of Chinese Studies of the Chinese University of Hong Kong*).

*Zhongguoshi yanjiu 中國史研究 (1979– , monthly), Lishisuo.

*Zhongguoshi yanjiu dongtai 中國史研究動態 (1978– , monthly), Lishisuo.

*Zhongguo zhexue nianjian 中國哲學年鑑 (1982– , annual), Shekeyuan, Zhexue yanjiusuo (Philosophy Research Institute), Beijing.

Zhonghua wenshi luncong 中華文史論叢 (1962– , annual), Shanghai guji chubanshe, Shanghai.

Ziran kexueshi yanjiu 自然科學史研究 (37.3).

*Zongjiaoxue yanjiu 宗教學研究 (29.2).

10.2.5 Taiwan

For journals specializing in the history of Taiwan, see 51.10.

Dalu zazhi 大陸雜志 (1950– , semimonthly).

Gugong jikan 故宮集刊 (1966.7–1983, quarterly; thereafter changed name to *Gugong xueshu jikan*).

Gugong wenwu yuekan 故宮文物月刊 (1983– , monthly), National Palace Museum, Taibei.

Gugong wenxian 故宮文獻 (1969.12–1973.12, monthly).

Gugong xueshu jikan 故宮學術季刊 (1983– , quarterly).

Guoshiguan guankan 國史館館刊 (51.14.2).

Hanxue yanjiu 漢學研究 (1983– , quarterly), Zhongyang tushuguan.

Hanxue yanjiu tongxun 漢學研究通訊 (1983– , quarterly), Zhongyang tushuguan, Taibei. Contains information on Ph.D theses in Chinese studies in Taiwan.

Jiandu xuebao 簡牘學報 (18.1).

Jindai Zhongguoshi yanjiu tongxun 近代中國史研究通訊 (51.14.2).

Jindai Zhongguo funüshi yanjiu 近代中國婦女史研究 (39.4).

Jindai Zhongguoshi yanjiu tongxun (1986–, semiannual), Jinshisuo.

Kaogu renlei xuekan 考古人類學刊 (12.3, *Journals*).

Koushu lishi qikan 口述歷史期刊 (51.5.9).

Mingshi yanjiu zhuankan 明史研究專刊 (49.5.2).

Minzuxue yanjiusuo jikan 民族學研究所季刊 (40.4).

National Palace Museum Bulletin (1966– , bimonthly), Gugong bowu-yuan, Taibei.

Qinghua xuebao 清華學報 (1915–19; new series, 1924–47; 2nd series, quar-terly 1956–). Mainly contains articles by Chinese scholars working in Taiwan and the United States on all aspects of Chinese culture.

Shihuo yuekan 食貨月刊 (1971–88, monthly). Specialized in economic and social history (as did its forerunner, the *Shihuo banyuekan* 食貨半月刊, 1934–37, rpnt. Daian, 1965; Shanghai shudian, 1982).

SJ: *Shiyusuo jikan* 史語所季刊 (short for *Zhongyang yanjiuyuan Lishi yuyan yanjiusuo jikan* 中央研究院歷史語言研究所集刊 [Bulletin of the Institute of History and Philology, Academia Sinica]), Nangang, 1928– , quarterly. In some of the earlier Western literature the acro-nyms *BIHP* or *CYYY* are used. The leader of the four main sinologi-cal journals of the Republican era (for the other three, see 10.2.3, *Yanjing xuebao*). The *SJ* continues to carry important articles. Vols. 1–22 (1928–49) were reprinted by Zhonghua in 1987. For an index to all the articles (and their authors) published in vols. 1–66 (1928–90), see *Zhongyang yanjiuyuan Lishi yuyan yanjiusuo chubanpin mulu* 中央研究院歷史語言研究所出版品目錄, 1995.

Taiwan shiliao yanjiu 臺灣史料研究 (51.10).

Taiwan daxue xuebao 臺灣大學學報 (1974– , quarterly; index for the years 1974 to 1998 is in volume 22 (1998).

Taiwanshi yanjiu 臺灣史研究 (51.10).

Tangdai xuehui huikan 唐代學會會刊 (46.5).

Zhongguo lishi xuehui shixue jikan 中國歷史學會史學季刊, Taibei (1970– , quarterly).

Zhongyang yanjiuyuan Jindaishi yanjiusuo jikan 中央研究員近代史研究所季刊 (51.14.2).

10.2.6   Catalogs of Chinese Periodical Holdings

Most major libraries and universities in China have published cata-logs of their holdings of contemporary periodicals. For holdings of late Qing and Republican periodicals, see the union catalogs and other lists in section 51.3.5. For union catalogs of journals held in Taiwan collections, see

Zhonghua minguo zhongwen qikan lianhe mulu 中華民國中文期刊聯合目錄 (Union catalog of periodicals in the Republic of China), Guoli zhongyang tushuguan, comp., 2nd ed., 2 vols., Taibei, 1982. Union catalog of Chinese periodicals giving holding information on 8,397 titles in 155 libraries in Taiwan as of December 1981. Arranged by stroke count. Has title index arranged by subject, Wade-Giles title index, and subject index.

Taiwan diqu xiancang dalu qikan lianhe mulu (xiuding ben) 臺灣地區現藏大陸期刊聯合目錄(修訂本) (Revised union catalog of mainland periodicals currently held in the Taiwan region), Xingzhengyuan dalu weiyuanhui, comp., 1997. Lists 3,490 titles held in 27 Taiwan collections (the original was published in 1994).

Zhonghua minguo zhongwen qikan lunwen fenlei suoyin 中華民國中文期刊論文分類索引 (Subject index of Chinese periodicals in the Republic of China), Guoli Taiwan daxue tushuguan, 1960–82. Covers Taiwan periodicals from the late 1940s to 1981. Discontinued because the contents were covered in the National Central Library, *Zhonghua minguo qikan lunwen suoyin* (1970–84, monthly; 1984– , quarterly; discontinued, 1993).

Zhongyang yanjiuyuan Zhong Ri Han wen qikan guancang lianhe mulu 中央研究院中日韓文期刊館藏聯合目錄 (Union catalog of Academia Sinica library's holdings of Chinese, Japanese, and Korean serials), Zhongyang yanjiuyuan, Taibei, 1996. Well-indexed catalog of the Academia Sinica's holdings of journals: 2,431 from Taiwan; 1,763 mainland and Hong Kong; 526 Japanese; and 85 Korean.

Hong Kong

Periodicals and Newspapers in East Asian Languages in the Fung Ping Shan (Feng Pingshan 馮平山) *Library of the University of Hong Kong*, Fung Ping Shan Library Serials Section, comp., HKCUP, 1990.

Western and Japanese

Note that in order to locate Chinese journals in Western and Japanese libraries, online catalogs are replacing older catalogs and lists such as:

Union List of Chinese Periodicals in American Libraries, Zug, Switzerland: Xerox, Inter Documentation Co., 1968. This is a printing of the microfilm of the Library of Congress "Union Card File of Oriental Vernacular Series (Chinese)."

A Bibliography of Chinese Newspapers and Periodicals in European Libraries, CUP, 1975. Covers 102 collections, including holdings of libraries in Central and Eastern Europe and Russia.

Inventaire des périodiques chinois dans les bibliothèques françaises, Michel Cartier, ed., Institut des Hautes Études Chinoises, Collège de France, 1984. Lists holdings of Chinese-language journals in French libraries.

Union List of Current Chinese Serials in the UK, China Library Group.

Chûgokubun zasshi shinbun sôgo mokuroku 中國文雜誌新聞總合目錄 (A union catalog of holdings of Chinese periodicals and newspapers), Ajia keizai kenkyûjo, 1985. Lists holdings of about 10,000 Chinese serials dating from the end of the Qing to the present in 40 Japanese collections.

10.3   Japanese Secondary Sources and Journals

In Japan there are closely knit schools of historical interpretation that frequently trace their affiliations to an acknowledged leader, often of a previous generation. Thus the historians of China currently at Tôdai and other leading universities connected with Tôdai are the direct descendants in the fourth generation of the founder of the Tokyo school, Shiratori Kurakichi 白鳥庫吉 (1865–1942). This has implications not only for approaches and interpretations, but also for jobs.[15]

Almost all Japanese academic writing on Chinese history appears first in journal articles. Authors frequently later assemble their articles and publish them as books. The standard form of the title of such works is *Nani nani no kenkyû* (collected studies on such and such; sometimes mistranslated as a study of such and such).

Festschrift volumes (*kinen ronbunshû* 紀念論文集) with contributions by pupils and friends are usually published to commemorate a distinguished scholar's sixtieth or seventieth birthday (*kanreki kinen* 還曆紀念 or *koki kinen* 古稀紀念) or as a memorial (*tsuito kinen* 追悼紀念). These frequently contain a short account of his life

---

[15] On Shiratori Kurakichi, see Stefan Tanaka, *Japan's Orient*, UCP, 1993, and on Naitô Konan (1866–1934), the founder of the Kyoto school, see Joshua A. Fogel, *Politics and Modernity: The Case of Naitô Konan*, HUP, 1984.

and a bibliography of his works. *Chûgokushi kenkyû nyûmon* 中國史研究入門 (8.3.2), lists 75 out of a total of no fewer than 700 such collections published on Oriental studies between the first year of Meiji and 1995.

There are two main types of bibliography available to help locate present and past work on a given subject or period. The first is usually in the form of an analytic bibliographic essay and includes the evaluations of the author. This type is called "academic trends" (*gakkai dôkô* 學界動向) or "history of research" (*kenkyûshi* 研究史) and serves to give the context of a given piece of research as well as the present state of the field. The second type is in the form of a straightforward, unannotated bibliography that attempts to list all publications on a given subject or period. This type is called "bibliography of secondary literature" (*bunken mokuroku* 文獻目錄). In Chinese history the usual arrangement in both types of bibliography is by dynasty, by neighboring peoples, and by special subject. In this section only the most important bibliographies covering the whole of Chinese history are given. Thus for works examining Japanese scholarship on the Qing, turn to 50.10.4.

10.3.1   *Japanese Academic-Trends Bibliographies*

Meiji igo ni okeru rekishigaku no hattatsu 明治以後における歴史學の發達 contains bibliographic essays on Chinese history arranged by dynasty and by neighboring peoples (395–625). The standard reference for the years ca. 1870 and 1926.[16]

John Timothy Wixted, *Japanese Scholars of China: A Bibliographical Handbook*, Mellen, 1992, concentrates on the older generations of Japanese historians of China.[17]

For postwar trends several works are available. Most reliable is the annual summary of the previous year's historical writing which

---

[16] *Meiji igo ni okeru rekishigaku no hattatsu* (The development of historical studies since the Meiji period), Rekishi kyôiku kenkyûkai 歴史教育研究會, ed., Tokyo, 1933. Originally appeared in *Rekishi kyôiku*, vol. 7; vol. 9 (1932).

[17] For the years up to the 1950s, see *Japanese Studies on Japan and the Far East: A Short Biographical and Bibliographical Introduction*, Teng Ssu-yü, comp., with the collaboration of Masuda Kenji and Kaneda Hiromitsu, HKUP, 1961; K. H. Kim, *Japanese Perspectives on China's Early Modernization: A Bibliographical Survey*, CCS, 1974, studies trends up to the early 1970s.

has appeared in the May issue (no. 5) of *Shigaku zasshi* since vol. 60 (1950) under the tile "Nihon ni okeru rekishi gakkai no kaiko to genjô" 日本における歴史學界の回顧と現狀. It covers all periods. It has also been published in book form for the years 1949–85 under the title *Nihon rekishi gakkai no kaiko to genjô* 日本歴史學界の回顧と現狀.[18] Several journals (e.g., *EC*, *JSYS*, or *LIC*) publish translations of the *Shigaku zasshi* section on the period they cover.

The quinquennial volume of trends in Japanese historical writing that is published for the International Conference of Historical Sciences has English-language summaries: *Nihon ni okeru rekishigaku no hattatsu to genjô* 日本における歴史學の發達と現狀. It has been published every five years since 1959 by Tôkyô daigaku shuppansha or Yamakawa shuppansha. Yamane's guide, although not strictly speaking an academic-trends bibliography, contains annotated bibliographies giving major works in Japanese (and other languages) on all periods of Chinese history. For bibliographies on Japan-China relations, see 42.5 and 51.11.

10.3.2   Unannotated Bibliographies

In Japan, major publishing houses compete with one another to bring out multivolume histories of the world (including China) or of China itself. These works usually contain thorough bibliographies focused on Japanese scholarship. For example, *Sekai rekishi taikei* 世界歴史大系 (Outlines of world history), 5 vols., Yamakawa, 1996–2000; *Chûgoku shigaku no kihon mondai* 中國史學の基本問題 (Basic issues in Chinese historiography), 4 vols., Kyûko, 1997–99. Such multivolume works are usually edited by the leading scholars of the day and contain essays by younger specialists. For past scholarship, check a retrospective bibliography such as *Nihon ni okeru Tôyôshi ronbun mokuroku* 日本における東洋史論文目錄 (English title: *Japanese Studies on Asian History: A Catalogue of Articles on Asia [Excluding Japan]*).[19]

---

[18] *Nihon rekishi gakkai no kaiko to genjô*, Shigakkai, ed., 25 vols., Yamakawa, 1987 (vols. 12–15 cover Chinese history from the Shang to the contemporary period).

[19] (*Nihon ni okeru*) *Tôyôshi ronbun mokuroku*, Tôyôshi ronbun mokuroku henshû iinkai, ed., 4 vols., Nippon gakujutsu shinkôkai, 1964-67. This lists all articles appearing in no fewer than 1,885 journals, periodicals, and collective

Footnote continued on next page

Books and Articles on Oriental Subjects has appeared annually since 1956. There is always a long section on China.[20]

Both *Shigaku zasshi* and *Tôyôshi kenkyû* list the contents of other Japanese journals regularly throughout the year and thus provide a convenient way of keeping up-to-date with work as it is published (often in out-of-the-way journals).

An unannotated bibliography on Chinese economic history may be found in the annual bibliography of books and articles on Chinese economic history published by the journal *Keizaishi kenkyû*. The title since 1960 is *Keizaishi bunken kaidai* 經濟史文獻解題.[21]

10.3.3 Main Japanese Historical Journals

Those journals marked with an asterisk are indexed in the *Bibliography of Asian Studies*.

*AA. Acta Asiatica (1960– , trimesterly to 1991, thereafter semiannual). Reprints English translations of Japanese articles on Chinese history, mainly by well-established scholars. From time to time an entire issue is devoted to the Japanese scholarship on a particular period or problem of Chinese history, e.g., *Sources of Manchu History* (*AA* 53, 1988); *Viewpoints on T'ang China* (*AA* 55, 1988); *Recent Trends in Mongolian, Tibetan and Vietnamese Studies* (*AA* 76, 1999).

*Annals of the Institute for Research in Humanities (1989– , annual), Jinbun, Kyoto University. From 1957–88, the title was *Zinbun*. Mainly carries English translations of articles appearing in *Tôhô gakuhô*.

---

publications between ca. 1880 and 1962. The arrangement is by journal, all articles in each issue being listed in turn. The fourth volume is an author index. The very wide coverage of this bibliography (which also includes an author's reviews) effectively puts out of business all previous unannotated, general bibliographies of Japanese studies of Chinese history and more than makes up for the lack of arrangement by subject categories.

[20] Tôhô gakkai (The Institute of Oriental Culture), *Books and Articles on Oriental Subjects*, Tokyo, 1956– . Each year covers the scholarship of the preceding year. It is less comprehensive, but comes out more quickly, than the Jinbun's *Tôyôgaku kenkyû bunken ruimoku* (10.1).

[21] The years 1933–38 were covered annually in the journal from vol. 11 (1934); after the war in book form under the title *Keizaishi nenkan* 經濟史年鑑, 3 vols. (Osaka), covering the years 1951–55 and under the title *Keizaishi bunken* 經濟史文獻 from 1956 to 1959.

Chûgoku shutsudo shiryô kenkyûkai kaihô 中國出土資料研究會會報 (18.1, Journals).

*MTB. Memoirs of the Research Department of the Tôyô Bunko (1926– , annual since 1955). Reprints translations of scholarly articles on Chinese historical geography and Chinese history by senior historians of the Tokyo school (English-language equivalent of the Tôyô bunko's *Tôyô gakuhô*).

Rekishigaku kenkyû 歷史學研究 (1933– , monthly). Establishment Marxist historical journal.

Shigaku zasshi 史學雜誌 (1889– , monthly), Shigakkai, Tokyo University. The leading establishment historical journal in Japan; articles on all periods of history of all countries. Important annual bibliographic retrospect. The first 100 volumes (1889–1991) are indexed in *Shigaku zasshi sômokuroku* 史學雜誌總目錄, Yamakawa, 1993. It lists the tables of contents and provides an author index. Since 1983, the annual volume has English-language abstracts.

Tôyô bunka kenkyûjo kiyô 東洋文化研究所紀要 (1943– , trimesterly), Tôbunken, Tokyo University. Contains important articles on Chinese history and also on South and Southeast Asia.

Tôhô gaku 東方學 (1951– , semiannual), Tôhô gakkai, Tokyo.

Tôhô gakuhô 東方學報 (1931– , annual), Jinbun, Kyoto University.

Tôyô gakuhô 東洋學報 (1910– , quarterly), Tôyô bunko, Tokyo. Scholarly contributions on Chinese history before the twentieth century. There is a comprehensive index covering issues 1 to 75 (1910–93): *Tôyô gakuhô sômokuroku* 東洋學報總目錄, Tôyô bunko, 1994.

Tôyôshi kenkyû 東洋史研究 (1935– , quarterly). Carries many important articles on Chinese history, mainly before the twentieth century.

There are a great many other historical journals as well as the journals of many dozens of university history and other departments, all of which carry articles on Chinese history. There are also many specialist journals on a particular period or subject.

In order to locate Japanese-language periodicals and journals in Western collections, check the standard catalogs of periodicals but note the following:

National Union List of Current Japanese Serials in East Asian Libraries of North America, Committee on East Asian Libraries, AAS, 1992.

"Union Card File of Oriental Vernacular Series (Japanese)," Library of Congress, Washington, DC, 1965. Should be in each library whose collection is included.

Check-list of Japanese Periodicals Held in British University and Research Libraries, S. M. Mandahl and P. W. Carnell, comps., Sheffield Univ. Press, 1971.

For names and addresses of Japanese scholars working on Chinese history, consult UNESCO Center for East Asian Cultural Studies, *Directory of Asian Studies in Japan*, Tôyô bunko, 1996.

10.4   Western Secondary Sources and Journals

10.4.1   Bibliography

The study of Chinese history in Europe began with the work of the Jesuit sinologists (29.7.1). It reached its peak in the first half of the twentieth century with French sinology. The center shifted from Europe to the United States with the development of area studies there in the 1950s. These have gradually enlarged their focus to take in the whole sweep of Chinese history.[22]

For names and addresses of many of those working in the field of Chinese history, see the Association of Asian Studies, *Membership Directory* (obtainable from 1021 East Huron Street, Ann Arbor, MI 48104 USA). The European Association of Chinese Studies publishes a quarterly newspaper entitled *EACS Newsletter*, which is also available on the Internet. Note that the *Guide to Asian Studies in Europe*, International Institute for Asian Studies, ed., Curzon, 1998, lists 5,000 European Asianists; 1,200 institutes and university departments; and 300 museums, organizations, and newsletters.

[22] Harriet S. Zurndorfer, "A Brief History of Chinese Studies and Sinology," in *China Bibliography*, Brill, 1994, 4–44; Arthur F. Wright, "The Study of Chinese Civilization," *Journal of the History of Ideas* 2: 233–55 (1960). Herbert Franke summarizes the state of Western sinology of the pre–WWII era in *Sinologie*, Bern, 1951; Alain Thote profiles the founder of modern French sinology in "At the Source of Modern French Sinology: Édouard Chavannes," *Orientations* 28.6: 42–47. Paul A. Cohen includes an assessment of the influence of John King Fairbank (1907–91), the key figure in the development of China studies in the United States in the second half of the twentieth century, in his *Discovering History in China: American Historical Writing on the Recent Chinese Past*, Col. UP, 1984.

The standard bibliography of 70,000 Western-language works (both books and articles) on China up to 1921 was compiled by Henri Cordier, who, although he knew no Chinese, certainly knew the European and treaty port publications on China extremely well: *Bibliotheca sinica: dictionnaire bibliographique des ouvrages relatifs à l'empire chinoise.*[23] There is a useful but not entirely reliable *Author Index to the Bibliotheca Sinica of Henri Cordier*, East Asiatic Library, Columbia University, 1953. It was added to volume 5 of the 1966 Taibei reprint.

Four bibliographies bring Cordier up to the 1970s:

T'ung-li Yuan, *China in Western Literature: A Continuation of Cordier's Bibliotheca Sinica*, YUP, 1958. Covers 18,000 books (not articles) appearing between 1921 and 1956; arrangement by subject category and contains author indexes.

John Lust: *Index Sinicus, A Catalogue of Articles Relating to China in Periodicals and Other Collective Publications, 1920–1955*, Heffer, 1964. Covers 19,734 articles, reviews, and obituary notices appearing between 1920 and 1955; arrangement by subject category and contains author indexes.

Books and articles on China in Western languages appearing between 1941 and 1970 (and therefore bringing Yuan and Lust up to 1970) are listed in *Cumulative Bibliography of Asian Studies, 1941–1965, Subject Bibliography*, 4 vols., G. K. Hall, 1970–71; *Author Bibliography*, 4 vols., 1969; *Cumulative Bibliography of Asian Studies, 1966–1970, Subject Bibliography*, 3 vols., 1972; *Author Bibliography*, 3 vols., 1973. This bibliography is based on the annual *Bibliography of Asian Studies*, which appears as a separate publication of the *Journal of Asian Studies* at year's end (10.1, item 1). Also available on Internet by subscription through AAS.

Modern Chinese Society, 1644–1970: An Analytical Bibliography, vol. 1, *Publications in Western Languages*, G. W. Skinner and E. A. Winckler, eds., SUP, 1973. Covers secondary works on the later empire.

---

[23] *Bibliotheca sinica*, 1893–95; rev. edition, 4 vols., Paris: Guilmoto, 1904–8; 4 vols., plus 1-vol. supplement, Paris: Geuthner, 1922–4; rpnt., Beiping, 1938; Taibei, 1966; New York: B. Franklin, 1968. See also John Lust, *Western Books on China Published up to 1850 in the Library of the School of Oriental and African Studies, University of London: A Descriptive Catalogue*, London: Bamboo Publishers, 1987. Contains citations to 1,283 items, arranged by subject.

The *Bibliography of Asian Studies* or *RBS* should be used as a first reference for Western-language works appearing after 1970.

In addition, there are a number of selective, annotated bibliographies of Western works on all aspects of Chinese history and civilization available:

China: A Critical Bibliography, Charles O. Hucker (1919–94), ed., UAP, 1962. Brief and clear annotations on 2,285 mainly English-language books on China. Partially updated in *Premodern China, A Bibliographical Introduction*, Chun-shu Chang, comp., CCS, Univ. of Michigan, 1971.

China: New Edition, Charles W. Hayford, comp., *World Bibliographical Series* 35, Clio Press, 1997. Contains carefully and wittily annotated entries on 1,502 book titles (with references to a further 700) on all aspects of China. Replaces the earlier volume on China in this series by Peter P. Cheng (Clio, 1983, 1988). Covers books mainly published in the 1980s and 1990s (and almost all in English) therefore continues previous items. Well indexed.

American Historical Association Guide to Historical Literature, Mary Beth Norton, ed., 2 vols., OUP, 1995. Provides a selective and up-to-date bibliography. The chapters on Chinese history contain 750 works on the periods from the Shang to 1911, each entry with a short characterization of its content and value by a team of scholars. The chapter on China up to 1644 was edited by Patricia Buckley Ebrey and that on China after 1644 by James H. Cole. There are author and subject indexes. The *Guide* has the advantage of being regularly updated.

10.4.2   Doctoral Dissertations

For over 2,500 doctoral dissertations written in Western languages between 1976 and 1990 dealing in one way or another with China before 1800, consult Shulman (1998), the first item below; to check theses written 1945–75, use the publications listed in items two and three. For Chinese doctoral dissertations, see 10.2.2.

Doctoral Dissertations on China and on Inner Asia, 1976–1990: An Annotated Bibliography of Studies in Western Languages, Frank Joseph Shulman, comp. and edited, with contributions by Patricia Polansky and Anna Leon Shulman, Greenwood Press, 1998. This is a multidisciplinary, classified, cross-referenced, and indexed guide to 10,293 dissertations in Western languages that in whole or in part are concerned with China, Mongolia, Tibet, Taiwan, Hong Kong, Macao, and the overseas Chinese communities. Encompasses studies not only

in every major discipline of the humanities, the social and behavioral ·
sciences, but also in education, law, medicine, architecture, the natural sciences, and engineering. The typical entry not only contains references to the thesis itself but also citations to one or more published
thesis abstracts, statements indicating availability of copies, descriptive annotations, and bibliographical citations to one or more books
and/or occasional papers published by the author that either constitute his published dissertation or are derived from his research. Indexes by author, by degree-awarding institution, and by subject.

*Doctoral Dissertations on China: A Bibliography of Studies in Western Lan-
guages, 1945–1970*, L. H. D. Gordon and F. J. Shulman, eds., UWP,
1972.

Doctoral Dissertations on China, 1971–1975, UWP, 1978.

10.4.3   Russian Studies of China

The standard bibliography of early Russian-language publications
on China (including Chinese history) is P. E. Skatchkov, *Bibliogra-
fiya kitaya* (Systematic bibliography of books and journal articles on
China in Russian published between 1730 and 1957), Nauka, 1960;
AMS, 1975. The 1960 edition revised and supplemented the original
edition of 1932. The 19,551 entries are arranged under 25 broad subject categories. What amounts to an updated version (on filing
cards) is available in the Sinological Department of the Institute of
Scientific Information on Social Science (INION) of the Russian
Academy of Sciences.

For a brief overview of present-day Russian sinology and Rus-
sian sources on Chinese history, see *Russia*, European Association of
Chinese Studies, ed., 1996. See also the older C. Kiriloff, "Russian
Sources," in Leslie et al., 1973 (20.3), 188–202. See also T'ung-li
Yuan, *Russian Works on China, 1918–1960, in American Libraries*,
YUP, 1961; and Gilbert Rozman, ed., *Soviet Studies of Premodern
China: Assessments of Recent Scholarship*, CCS, Univ. of Michigan,
1984. Fourteen signed bibliographical essays cover history (inclu-
ding archaeology) and literature from antiquity through to the
Qing. There is an index of Soviet specialists on Asia as well as a gen-
eral index.

Note that the *Annual Bibliography of Oriental Studies* (Kyoto)
and the *Bibliography of Asian Studies* both list recent publications in
Russian on Chinese history, as does the *Revue bibliographique de sinologie*, which is less comprehensive but provides brief reviews.

For a "bio-bibliographic dictionary" of 3,000 Soviet Orientalists, see *Biobibliograficheskiy slovar' otechestvennykh vostokovedovs 1917*, S. D. Miliband, comp., 2 vols., Nauka, 1995.

10.4.4   Main Western-Language Journals

To locate Western-language journals, check the standard catalogs such as *Union List of Periodicals* (for the United States and Canada) and the *British Union Catalogue of Periodicals*. Efforts are being made to create a database of sinological (and Chinese-language) periodicals in major European libraries under the auspices of European Association of Chinese Studies.

The following list of 50 journals is by no means exhaustive. It includes only some of the main sinological and historical journals (all of which are indexed in the *Bibliography of Asian Studies*). Note in particular the journals of the various societies for the study of particular periods (*EC*, *TS*, *JSYS*, *MS*, and *LIC*). Similar societies with their own journals exist in China, Japan, and Taiwan. Note also that the reproach leveled at the Royal Asiatic Society of his day by Herbert Giles applies as well to the journals of the older Asiatic and Oriental societies—while nominally inclusive of East Asia, they are really Middle Eastern or Indian in their sympathies.

AA   *Acta Asiatica* (see 10.3.3).

ArtA   *Artibus Asiae* (1925– , semiannual), Zurich and Washington. Scholarly international journal.

ArtsA   *Arts Asiatique* (1954– , semiannual), Musée Guimet and Musée Cernuschi, Paris. Scholarly French journal.

AM   *Asia Major* (3rd series, 1988–96, semiannual; 1996–97, annual; 1998– , semiannual). Started out as leading German sinological journal (old series, Leipzig, 1923–33) before moving to London, where it became main the main British journal of sinology (new series, 1949–75). After a gap, it reopened in the United States, where it was edited and published at Princeton University 1988–98; since 1998 it has been edited at Academia Sinica, Taibei.

AO   *Archív Orientální* (1929– , quarterly), Prague. Index for 1929–92 in vol. 64.4 (1996).

AS   *Asiatische Studien/Études asiatiques* (1947– , quarterly), Bern.

BEFEO   *Bulletin de l'École française d'Extrême-Orient* (1901– , annual). Edited at Hanoi until 1955, then Saigon (1956.1) en route for

Paris (1956.2–). Although it has always concentrated on Indo-China, it not infrequently has important articles on Chinese history.

BMFEA   *Bulletin of the Museum of Far Eastern Antiquities* (1929– , annual), Stockholm. Contains important articles by Karlgren and his pupils. The museum was founded by J. G. Andersson, the discoverer of the Yangshao culture in 1925. Karlgren was the director from 1939 to 1959.

BSEI   *Bulletin de la Société des études indochinoises* (1883–1925; n.s., 1932–75, quarterly), Saigon; see comment on *BEFEO*.

BSOAS   *Bulletin of the School of Oriental and African Studies* (1917– , trimesterly), SOAS, University of London. Carries occasional important articles and reviews on Chinese history and linguistics.

CA   *Cahiers d'Extrême-Asie* (1985– , annual). Bilingual journal of the École française d'Extrême-Orient, Kyoto Section. Specializes mainly in the history of Daoism and Buddhism.

CAAD   *China Archaeology and Art Digest* (1996– , quarterly). Indispensable way of keeping up-to-date with dozens of art and archaeological journals to few of which Western and many libraries even in China have subscriptions (see 12.3).

CAJ   *Central Asiatic Journal* (1976– , semiannual), Harrassowitz.

CLEAR   *Chinese Literature: Essays Articles Reviews* (1978– , annual). Ed. at University of Wisconsin.

CQ   *China Quarterly, The* (1960– , quarterly), Congress for Cultural Freedom, 1960–76; Contemporary China Institute, SOAS, University of London, 1976– . Although devoted to contemporary China, there are also articles on modern Chinese history and reviews of historical works. Articles and reviews are indexed at the end of the fourth issue each year.

Crec   *Chinese Recorder*, 1867–1941, articles on China and missionary activities. Successor of the following item.

CR   *Chinese Repository*, 20 vols., Canton, 1832–51. Well-informed articles by the pioneer Protestant missionaries.

CS   *Chinese Science* (vols. 1–10, 1975–92, irregular; vol. 11– , 1993–94, annual). Edited at CCS, UCLA.

CSH   *Chinese Studies in History* (1962– , annual). Translations into English of important Chinese articles on history. M. E. Sharp, Armonk, New York.

CSWT   *Ch'ing-shih wen-t'i*; see *LIC*.

EAH   *East Asian History* (1991– , semiannual), Canberra (from 1970 to 1990, the title was *Papers on Far Eastern History*).

EC   *Early China* (1975– , annual). Publication of the Society for the Study of Pre-Han China (University of California, Berkeley). Now named the Society for the Study of Early China (SSEC). From 1969 to 1975 was called the society's *Newsletter*. See 13.3 *Societies and Yearbooks* for more on this journal.

EMC   *Early Medieval China* (1994– , irregular annual). Published at Western Michigan University in Kalamazoo, Michigan. All aspects of Han to Tang with special emphasis on the Six Dynasties period. There have been many efforts to start a journal for this period. None have lasted long: *Newsletter of Nan-Pei-Ch'ao Studies*, CMC, 1977–78; *Nan-Pei-Ch'ao Studies* (1979–81); *Newsletter* of the *Early Medieval China Group* (1988).

ÉtC   *Études chinoises* (1983– , semiannual), Paris.

HJAS   *Harvard Journal of Asiatic Studies* (1936– , semiannual), Cambridge, Mass. The main journal in the United States for classical studies of China, Korea, and Japan.

JA   *Journal asiatique* (1922– , semiannual), Paris. Covers the whole of Asia, with focus on the ancient Near East; articles on Chinese history are less frequent than in the past.

JAOS   *Journal of the American Oriental Society* (1849– , quarterly), New Haven, Connecticut. Covers (with increasing difficulty) the entire "Orient."

JAH   *Journal of Asian History* (1966– , semiannual), Harrassowitz, Wiesbaden. Specializes in Inner Asian history.

JAS   *Journal of Asian Studies* (1941–55, quarterly under the title *Far Eastern Quarterly*), Journal of the Association for Asian Studies (AAS), Ann Arbor, Michigan. It covers North, South, and East Asia and publishes many important articles and reviews on China. The focus is on modern China, and the reviews are mainly limited to books in English (and to a certain extent, other Western languages and occasionally in Chinese). Nevertheless this is the main Western journal devoted to Asian studies. It carries important essays on the state of the field of secondary scholarship in particular areas of Chinese historical studies. It is also the one journal in which nearly all US publishers of scholarly books on East Asia advertise, thus making it a convenient way to keep up to date. The *JAS* is available in full text from 1941 (*FEQ*) to 1993 at the JSTOR website.

JASHK   *Journal of the Archaeological Society of Hong Kong* (1970– , annual), Hong Kong.

JCL   *Journal of Chinese Linguistics* (1973– , semiannual), University of California, Berkeley.

JCR   *Journal of Chinese Religions* (1983– , annual), Indiana University. From 1976 to 1983, the title was *Journal of the Society for the Study of Chinese Religions*; from 1998, also incorporates *Taoist Resources*.

JESHO   *Journal of the Economic and Social History of the Orient* (1957– , quarterly), Leiden. Attempts to cover the entire "Orient," and inevitably leaves some countries underrepresented. This has normally been the case for China and Japan. An index volume (1997) covers *JESHO* vols. 1–39 (1957–96).

JOS   *Journal of Oriental Studies* (1954– , semiannual), Hong Kong University. Articles in English or Chinese.

JOSoc   *Journal of the Oriental Society* (1968– , annual), Sydney.

JRAS   *Journal of the Royal Asiatic Society* (1834– , quarterly), London. Divided according to the various branches of the RAS, e.g., North China Branch (1858–1948: *JNCBRAS*); Malayan Branch, Hong Kong Branch. The *JNCBRAS* in particular is worth looking through. The *JRAS* is still published in London, but the articles are mainly on the ancient Near East or parts of Asia other than China.

JSYS   *Journal of Sung-Yuan Studies* (1989– , semiannual), Albany, New York. Started as *Sung Studies Newsletter*, 1969–80; changed title to *Bulletin of Sung-Yuan Studies*, 1980–8; adopted present title in 1989).

LIC   *Late Imperial China* (1985– , semiannual), Society for Qing Studies, California Institute of Technology, Pasadena, California. Started in 1965 under the title *Ch'ing-shih wen-t'i*.

MingS   *Ming Studies* (1975– , annual), University of Minnesota.

MTB   *Memoirs of the Research Department of the Tôyô Bunko* (10.3.3).

MS   *Monumenta Serica* (1935– , annual). German Catholic sinological journal. Edited in Beijing (1935–48); Tokyo (1954–56); Nagoya (1957–62); Los Angeles (1963–71); since 1972 at Sankta Augusta, Germany. Index to vols. 1–35 (1935–83) available.

NN   *NAN NÜ: Men, Women and Gender in Early and Imperial China*, 1999– . Leiden.

NGNVO   *Deutsche Gesellschaft für Natur und Völkerkunde Ostasiens, Nachrichten* (1926–); also *Mitteilungen* (1873–). Currently edited (since 1951, semiannual) at Hamburg.

OE   *Oriens Extremus* (1954– , semiannual), Hamburg.

Orientations (1970– , bimonthly), Hong Kong; see 38.1.4, *Journals.*

OS   *Oriens vostok* (1991– , bimonthly). Formerly *Narody Azii i Af-
            riki* (Peoples of Asia and Africa, 1961–90). Edited at the Insti-
            tute of Oriental Studies of the Russian Academy of Sciences,
            Moscow.

PCH   *Papers on Chinese History* (1991– , annual), Harvard University.
            Graduate student papers.

PV   *Peterburgskoye vostokovedenye* (St. Petersburg Journal of Orien-
            tal Studies), 1992– , irregular; Institute of Oriental Studies of
            the Russian Academy of Sciences, St. Petersburg branch.

PEW   *Philosophy East and West* (1951– , quarterly), UHP.

PDV   *Problemy dalnego vostoka* (Problems of the Far East), incorpo-
            rating *Sovetskoye vostokovedenye* (Soviet Oriental Studies), 20
            vols. (former Sinological Institute, Moscow), 1940–59.

RBS   *Revue bibliographique de sinologie/Review of Bibliography in Si-
            nology*, Paris (1957– , annual); see 10.1.

Rends   *Renditions: A Chinese-English Translation Magazine* (1974– ,
            semiannual); Chinese University of Hong Kong; translated ex-
            cerpts on literary genres or particular themes; see 30.4.

SL   *Sinologica* (1947–72), Basel.

SSC   *Social Sciences in China* (1980– , quarterly); see 10.2.3.

SJ   Chinese acronym (*Shiyusuo jikan*) for the *Zhongyang yanjiu-
            yuan Lishi yuyan yanjiusuo jikan* 中央研究院歷史語言研究所
            集刊. Has occasional articles in English. Other acronyms used:
            BIHP or *CYYY* (10.2.4).

TP   *T'oung Pao* (1890– , semiannual), The Hague and Paris. Leading
            sinological journal in Europe.

TR   *Taoist Resources* (1988–); see *Journal of Chinese Religions.*

TS   *T'ang Studies* (1982– , annual). Edited at Boulder, Colorado.
            Journal of the T'ang Studies Society.

11

Libraries

The present chapter introduces the most important libraries and collections of Chinese books in China (11.1), Taiwan (11.2), Japan (11.3), and the United States, Europe, and Russia (11.4). It concludes with a brief introduction to gaining access to these collections using the Internet (11.6) and a word on publishers and bookstores for Chinese historical works (11.5).

Note that the usefulness of a library for research depends as much on the nature and quality of its collections and the ease of access to them as on the total quantity of the books it contains.

11.1 China

Only the four main libraries in China are given here.

1. Guojia tushuguan 國家圖書館 (National Library of China), or Guotu 國圖 for short (from 1949 to 1999 it was called Beijing tushuguan 北京圖書館, Peking Library). The largest library in China, with a collection of over 20 million volumes (of which 45 percent are Chinese). It is open to the public free of charge with no special formalities. Three books at a time may be called from the stacks for reading on the premises. Guotu was founded in 1909 as the Jingshi tushuguan 京師圖書館 (Capital library), situated in Guanghua temple.[1] It opened for readers in 1912. It was endowed with part of the book collections from the Grand Secretariat (Neige 內閣), the Hanlinyuan 翰林院 (Hanlin academy), and the Guozijian 國子監 (Imperial academy), which in-

---

[1] In 1917 it moved to the site of the 國子監 (Imperial academy), southern school. In 1928 it was renamed the Guoli Beiping tushuguan 國立北平圖書館 (National Library of Peiping); in 1931 it moved to new premises near Beihai. In 1983 it moved to its present location near the Zizhu yuan 紫竹園 (Purple Bamboo Park).

cluded portions of the imperial libraries of the Southern Song and Ming. In 1917 it acquired the copy of the *Siku quanshu* previously deposited in the palace at Chengde and a number of Qing private collections. Today the library possesses probably the finest collection of Chinese rare editions in the world.[2] There is a major *shanben* reprint series.[3] In addition, Guotu has the single largest collection of oracle-bone inscriptions in the world (over 34,500) and also more than 100,000 rubbings of stone inscriptions. Guotu has on deposit copies of all doctoral theses defended in China since 1949. It has put 400,000 of its post-1975 acquisitions into an online catalog and it is also in the process of putting its post-1949 holdings online. Printed catalog:

Beijing tushuguan putong guji zongmu 北京圖書館普通古籍總目 (A comprehensive catalog of ordinary, old Chinese books), 15 vols., Shumu wenxian, 1990–97. Subject catalog of old Chinese books (mainly those published before 1911, but not including *shanben*; see item 2 below). Each volume covers a separate subject category. Vol. 3 covers history, and vol. 4, geography. There are four-corner author-title indexes in each volume. The total number of titles listed comes to about 200,000.

2. Shanghai tushuguan 上海圖書館 (Shanghai Library), or Shangtu 上圖 for short. The second largest library in China. Has a collection of over 10 million books. It resides in a splendid new building with user-friendly reading rooms (ancient texts; genealogy, etc.) and includes other important collections previously housed separately, e.g., the Shanghai baokan tushuguan 上海報刊圖書館 (Shanghai Newspapers and Periodicals Library) and the Shanghaishi lishi wenxian tushuguan 上海市歷史文獻圖書館 (Shanghai Library of Historical Documents).

3. Nanjing tushuguan 南京圖書館 (Nanjing Library), or Nantu 南圖 for short, has a collection of 2.5 million volumes including the old Jiangsu shengli guoxue tushuguan 江蘇省立國學圖書館

---

[2] *Beijing tushuguan guji shanben shumu* 北京圖書館古籍善本書目 (Catalog of rare editions in the Beijing Library), 5 vols., Shumu wenxian, 1989. Lists 11,000 titles of rare editions collected since 1949.

[3] *Beijing tushuguan guji zhenben congkan* 北京圖書館古籍珍本叢刊, 117 vols., Shumu wenxian, 1988–91.

(Jiangsu Provincial Sinological Library), which published one of the few general catalogs of a major Chinese collection:

Jiangsu shengli guoxue tushuguan zongmu 江蘇省立國學圖書館總目, 44 *juan*; *bubian*, 12 *juan*, Nanking, 1933-6; 1937 rpnt., 15 vols., Taibei, 1970.

4. Shehui kexueyuan tushuguan 社會科學院圖書館 (Library of the Shekeyuan, the Chinese Academy of Social Sciences, CASS), or Sheketu 社科圖 for short, is divided among the various institutes of the Academy. Altogether it contains 2.5 million volumes. The Academy inherited the 470,000 *ce* collection of Chinese books that had been built up by the Beiping renwen kexue yanjiusuo (9.7), including a considerable number of rare editions. Holdings of rare editions were increased after 1949. There is a published *shanben* catalog with 8,496 entries.[4] For the Kaogusuo collection, see 13.3.

There are many other important libraries in China, mainly in the older universities, starting with Peking University, and in some of the provincial capitals (these latter often go back a long way and have important collections).[5] Historical archival holdings are listed in Table 29, Chapter 20, and 50.1. There is only one copyright deposit library for all publications (including periodicals) since 1950: Zhonggu banben tushuguan 中國版本圖書館 (Copyright deposit library of Chinese publications), Beijing. The library had five different names before receiving the present one in 1983. The staff of the library edit *Quanguo zong shumu* 全國總書目 (11.1.1).

To locate a library in China, use *Zhongguo tushuguan he qingbao jigou minglu daquan* 中國圖書館和情報機構名錄大全 (Directory of Chinese libraries and information agencies), Xin Ximeng 辛希孟 et al., comps., Dongbei daxue, 1995. It lists a total of 15,697 libraries and information agencies.

---

[4] *Zhongguo kexueyuan tushuguan cang Zhongwen guji shanben shumu* 中國科學院圖書館藏中文古籍善本書目, Kexue, 1994.

[5] The largest university library is that of Peking University. There are several catalogs of its rare books, the most recent of which is *Beijing daxue tushuguan cang gu shanben shumu* 北京大學圖書館藏古善本書目, Beijing daxue, 1999. Peking University also publishes a reprint series of its rare editions: *Beijing daxue tushuguan shanben congkan* 北京大學圖書館善本叢刊, vols. 1-80, 1997.

Hong Kong

There is an efficient online service linking university library catalogs in Hong Kong, enabling searches in all the collections simultaneously. The largest academic library is that of the University of
Hong Kong.

11.1.1   Cumulative Catalogs of Modern Chinese Books

For catalogs of books published during the Republican period, see
51.2

Quanguo zong shumu 全國總書目 (National book catalog), Zhongguo
   banben tushuguan 中國版本圖書館 (11.1), ed., Zhonghua, 1956–65;
   not issued, 1966–69; annual, 1970– . As of 2000, all volumes up to
   and including 1998 had been published. A catalog of this title was edited and published by Zhonghua in 1956. It covered the years 1949–
   54; a second volume covered 1955.

Quanguo neibu faxing tushu zongmu 全國內部發行圖書總目, 1949–86
   (National catalog of internal distribution books), Li Paoguang 李泡
   光, ed., Zhongguo banben tushuguan, ed., Zhonghua, 1988. Includes
   17,754 first editions and 547 revised editions; see Flemming Chris-
   tiansen, "The *Neibu* Bibliography: A Review Article," *CCP Research
   Newsletter* 4: 1319 (1989).

11.1.2   Union Catalogs of Modern Chinese Books

Zhongguo congshu zonglu 中國叢書綜錄 (Bibliography of Chinese collectanea); see 9.6.

Zhongguo guji shanben shumu 中國古籍善本書目 (The China union catalog of rare books); see 9.8.1.

Zhongguo difangzhi lianhe mulu 中國地方志聯合目錄 (Union catalog of
   Chinese local gazetteers); see 4.6, *How to Find Local Gazetteers.*

Zhongguo difangzhi zongmu tiyao 中國地方志總目提要 (Chinese local
   histories: a comprehensive annotated catalog); see 4.6, *How to Find
   Local Gazetteers.*

Zhongguo jiapu zonghe mulu 中國家譜綜合目錄 (Union catalog of Chinese genealogies); see 3.5.1.

Quanguo Zhongyi tushu lianhe mulu 全國中醫圖書聯合目錄 (National
   union catalog of works of traditional Chinese medicine); see Chapter
   36, *Bibliography.*

1833–1949 quanguo Zhongwen qikan lianhe mulu zengdingben 1833–1949
全國中文期刊聯合目錄增訂本 (Revised national union catalog of
Chinese periodicals, 1833–1949); see 10.2.5.

Increasingly provinces are publishing union catalogs—for example, *Sichuansheng difangzhi lianhe mulu* 四川省地方志聯合目錄 (A
union catalog of Sichuan province local gazetteers); see 4.6.

11.2 Taiwan

1. Guoli zhongyang tushuguan 國立中央圖書館 (National Central
   Library), also known as Guojia tushuguan 國家圖書館. Includes
   12,000 rare books (including from the former National Central
   Library [founded 1928, opened 1933, 1940], and the former
   Northeastern University.[6] Splendidly housed; online catalog. Excellent reference rooms including the Hanxue yanjiu zhongxin
   漢學研究中心 (Center for Chinese studies), which holds reference works, periodicals and other materials relating to mainland
   China. The Center also publishes a Sinological journal, *Hanxue
   yanjiu* 漢學研究 and a very useful newsletter, *Hanxue yanjiu
   tongxun* 漢學研究通訊 (10.2.4)

2. Guoli zhongyang tushuguan, Taiwan fenguan 國立中央圖書館
   臺灣分館 (National Central Library, Taiwan Branch). Based on
   the Taiwan sôtokufu toshoshitsu 臺灣總督督撫圖書室 (1915)
   and the Nanhô shiriôkan 南方資料館. Important holdings and
   publications on Taiwan history.

3. Guoli gugong bowuyuan 國立故宮博物院 (Library of the National Palace Museum). Includes many *shanben* plus important
   archival holdings representing 5–10 percent of the Qing palace
   records and Grand Council archives (50.1.3). Superb reference
   rooms and catalogs.

4. Fu Sinian tushuguan 傅斯年圖書館 (Fu Sinian Library), Zhongyang yanjiuyuan 中央研究院 (Academia Sinica), Nangang 南港,
   Taibei. The library of the Shiyusuo. It contains important collec-

---

[6] *Guojia tushuguan shanben shuzhi chugao* 國家圖書館善本書志初稿 (Draft
catalog of rare books in the national library), 4 vols., 1996–99. Follows the
same order as *Guoli zhongyang tushuguan shanben shumu* 國立中央圖書館
善本書目, 3 vols., Taibei, 1957–58; 2nd rev. edition, 4 vols., 1967; 2nd ed., 1986.

tions, built up in the 1930s, of oracle bones, Ming-Qing state papers, Han wooden slips, and folk songs. It is well cataloged and maintained as a first-class research library.

5. Guo Tingyi tushuguan 郭廷以圖書館 (Guo Tingyi Library), Library of the Jindaishi yanjiusuo 近代史研究所 (Institute of Modern History), Academia Sinica. Holds late Qing and early Republican archives, including on foreign affairs (1861–1926) and economics (1903–1950s); see 50.1.3 and 50.2.7 for catalogs. The Jinshisuo conducts a number of projects, including an important oral history one on the Republican period (51.5.9). It also publishes various journals (10.2.4).

6. Guoli Taiwan daxue tushuguan 國立臺灣大學圖書館 (National Taiwan University Library). Various collections attached to different departments and research institutes. Holds the only Qing local archive to survive in Taiwan, those of Tamsui (Danshui) 淡水 (50.3).

To locate or contact a library in Taiwan, use *Zhonghua minguo Hanxue jigou lu* 中華民國漢學機構錄.[7] It gives details of 88 institutes, university departments, museums, and libraries. For each is listed the address, phone number, director's name, and detailed description (both in English and Chinese). It has institutional name indexes arranged by stroke count and alphabetically by the English translation of name. For archives in Taiwan, see 51.1.3. Note the following union catalogs for Taiwan library collections:

Taiwan ge tushuguan xiancun congshu zimu suoyin 臺灣各圖書館現存叢書子目索引 (Author-title indexes to *congshu* in Taiwan libraries); see 9.6.

Zhonghua minguo Taiwan diqu gongcang fangzhi mulu 中華民國臺灣地區公藏方志目錄 (Catalog of local gazetteers in the Republic of China [Taiwan District] public collections); see 4.6.

Zhonghua minguo Zhongwen qikan lianhe mulu 中華民國中文期刊聯合目錄 (Union catalog of periodicals in the Republic of China); see 10.2.6.

---

[7] *Zhonghua minguo Hanxue jigou lu* (Directory of institutes of Chinese studies in the Republic of China), Guoli zhongyang tushuguan, ed., Taibei, 1987

Zhonghua minguo tushu lianhe mulu 中華民國圖書聯合目錄, 4 vols., 1974–82.

Zhonghua minguo chuban tushu mulu 中華民國出版圖書目錄 (Chinese national bibliography), 1950–92, monthly; 1992–94, quarterly; from 1994 published on CD ROM as *Zhonghua minguo chuban tushu mulu guangpan xitong* 中華民國出版圖書目錄光盤系統 (*SinoCat*), Guojia tushuguan. This annual publication covers the holdings of the National central library (which since the 1930s has in principle received a copy of all books published in the Republic of China). Prior to 1960, it appeared under various titles. The library also publishes this catalog in the form of a collection of the annual catalogs every five years under the title *Zhonghua minguo chuban tushu mulu leibian* 中華民國出版圖書目錄類編 (Chinese national bibliography by categories).

Taiwanqu zupu mulu 臺灣區族譜目錄 (Catalog of Chinese genealogies in Taiwan); see 3.5.1.

11.3 Japan

Japan is the only country in which dozens of literary and historical sources that were lost in China have been preserved. Chinese books began to be imported into Japan after Shôtoku Taishi 聖德太子 (574–622) sent an embassy to the Sui in 607. In the Edo period, Chinese literary, historical, and philosophical works, and also practical manuals—for example, on medicine or law or geography—were imported in large numbers through the Chinese trading station at Nagasaki.

Work has begun on a union catalog of Chinese books in Japan. Anything published after 1965 in Japanese can now be looked up on CD-ROM (J-BISC). There is also an online interlibrary catalog system, *Toshokan jôhô kensaku shisutemu* 圖書館情報檢索システム (Online Public Access Catalog, OPAC).

Nihon ni okeru Kanseki no shûshû: Kanseki kankei mokuroku shûsei 日本における漢籍の蒐集漢籍關係目錄集成 is a bibliography of published catalogs of Chinese books in Japan. It includes 3,100 catalogs from the late nineteenth century to 1980.[8]

---

[8] *Nihon ni okeru Kanseki no shûshû: Kanseki kankei mokuroku shûsei* (Collections of Chinese books in Japan: a catalog of catalogs of Chinese books in public and private collections), Tôyô bunko, 1961; rev. and enl., Kyûko, 1982.

Footnote continued on next page

Tokyo

1. Tôyô bunko 東洋文庫 (Oriental Library). Originally established by Iwasaki Hisaya 岩崎久彌 (1865–1955) in 1917, since 1948 it has been a branch of the National Diet Library. The Tôyô bunko contains one of the largest collections of old Chinese books in Japan, including important holdings on twentieth century China. Has functioned as a focus of research on Chinese history. It is open to the public. There is not as yet a published catalog of its overall holdings of old Chinese books, but there is a separate one for the History branch:

> *Tôyô bunko shozô Kanseki bunrui mokuroku shibu* 東洋文庫所藏漢籍 分類目錄史部 (Classified catalog of the Tôyô bunko holdings of Chinese books, History branch), Tôyô bunko, 1986. It has a title index. The Tôyô bunko has also published catalogs in the same series for its holdings in the *Congshu* (1967), Classics (1978), and Philosophy (1993) categories.

2. Tôyô bunka kenkyûjo 東洋文化研究所 (The Institute for Oriental Culture) at Tôdai 東大 (Tokyo University). The Tôbunken was established in 1929 and took its present form in 1948. The Chinese section has an excellent collection of books with important holdings in social and economic history. The collection includes the holdings of the Institute's first main collection, the 45,000 volumes of Ôki Kan'ichi 大木幹一 (rich in Qing legal, economic, and administrative history), also many other collections left it by scholars such as Matsumoto Tadao 松本忠雄, Nagasawa Kikuya 長澤規矩也, and Niida Noboru 仁井田陞. Published catalogs:

> *Tôkyô daigaku Tôyô bunka kenkyûjo Kanseki bunrui mokuroku* 東京 大學東洋文化研究所漢籍分類目錄 (Classified catalog of Chinese books in Tôbunken), 2 vols., 1973–75; reduced-size edition with corrections, 1 vol., 1981; rpnt., with corrections, Kyûko,

---

Arrangement is by place. On the exchanges of books between China and Japan, see the volume *Dianji* 典籍 (books) in the series *Zhong-Ri wenhua jiaoliushi daxi* 中日文化交流史大系, Wang Yong 王勇 and Ôba Osamu 大庭脩, eds., Zhejiang renmin, 1996.

For an account of how some of the most important collections of Chinese books in Japan were built up, see Yu-ying Brown, "The Origins and Characteristics of Chinese Collections in Japan," *JOS*, 31.1: 19–31 (1983).

1996. Altogether the titles of 200,000 volumes are listed; there are author-title indexes. Arrangement is by six branches (the traditional four plus *Sôsho* 叢書 collectanea, and *Xingaku* 新學 modern studies).

Tôyô bunka kenkyûjo shozô Chûgoku tochi monjo mokuroku kaisetsu 東洋文化研究所所藏中國土地文書目錄解說 (Annotated catalog of Chinese land documents); see 51.4.4.

Tôkyô daigaku sôgo toshokan Kanseki mokuroku 東京大學綜合圖書館漢籍目錄 (Catalog of Tokyo University Library's collection of old Chinese books), Tôkyô daigaku, 1995. Collection built up since the near-complete destruction by the Taishô earthquake. Includes a title index by stroke count of the first character.

Gendai Chûgokusho bunrui mokuroku 現代中國書分類目錄 (Classified catalog of modern Chinese books), 2 vols., Uchiyama, 1996. Works published between 1912 and 1990. See also the earlier *Gendai Chûgoku kankei Chûgokugo bunken sôgô mokuroku* (see *Combined and Union Catalogs*, below).

Other important libraries in Tokyo (in alphabetic order):

3. Kokuritsu kokkai toshokan 國立國會圖書館 (National Diet Library). Open to the public without special formalities. Has excellent catalog (including online) and good, research-oriented reading rooms. Published catalogs:

Kokuritsu kokkai toshokan Kanseki mokuroku 國立國會圖書館漢籍目錄 (Catalog of Chinese books in the National Diet Library), Kokkai toshokan, 1987. Indexed in:

Kokuritsu kokkai toshokan Kanseki mokuroku sakuin 國立國會圖書館漢籍目錄索引 (Index to catalog of Chinese books in the National Diet Library), 2 vols., Kokkai toshokan, 1995.

Kokuritsu kokkai toshokan: Chûgokugo Chôsengo zasshi shinbun mokuroku 國立國會圖書館中國語朝鮮語雜誌新聞目錄 (An index of journals and newspapers in Chinese and Korean in the National Diet Library), Kokkai toshokan, 1993. Important collection.

4. Kunaichô shoryôbu 宮內廳書陵部 (Imperial Household Library). Published catalog:

Wa-Kan tosho bunrui mokuroku 和漢圖書分類目錄 (Classified catalog of Japanese and Chinese books), 2 vols., plus index, plus one-volume continuation (1952–55).

5. Naikaku bunko 內閣文庫 (Cabinet Library). Founded in 1884 on the basis of the Tokugawa government library. It holds 175,000 old Chinese books. Published catalog:

   Naikaku bunko Kanseki bunrui mokuroku 內閣文庫漢籍分類目錄 (Classified catalog of old Chinese books in the Naikaku bunko), Tokyo, 1956; rev. edition, 1971. Includes title index.

6. Seikadô bunko 靜嘉堂文庫. Founded by Iwasaki Yanosuke 岩崎彌之助 (1851–1908) and his son, Iwasaki Koyata 岩崎小彌太 (1879–1945), in 1893. Has been a branch of the National Diet Library since 1948. The collection has a huge number of rare books of which the core is the Bi Song lou 丽宋樓 library of Lu Xinyuan 陸心源 (1834–94), one of the four finest private collections of the Qing. It was purchased in 1907. The lexicographer Morohashi Tetsuji 諸橋轍次 was appointed curator in 1921 and held this post until 1955. One of his first jobs was to edit the catalog. The observant user of Morohashi's great dictionary, the *Dai Kan-Wa jiten* (2.3), will notice that the decorations on the endpapers are from works held in the Seikadô. Published catalog of old Chinese books:

   Seikadô bunko Kanseki bunrui mokuroku 靜嘉堂文庫漢籍分類目錄 (Classified catalog of old Chinese books in the Seikadô bunko), Tokyo, 1930.

   Seikadô bunko Sô-Gen pan zuroku 靜嘉堂文庫宋元版圖錄 (Illustrated catalog of Song and Yuan printed books in the Seikadô bunko), 2 vols., Kyûko, 1992. Vol. 1 contains illustrations; vol. 2, notes.

7. Sonkeikaku bunko 尊經閣文庫. Published catalog:

   Sonkeikaku bunko Kanseki bunrui mokuroku 尊經閣文庫漢籍分類目錄索引 (Classified catalog of old Chinese books in the Sonkeikaku bunko), Tokyo, 1934 (*mokuroku*), 1935 (*sakuin*).

Kyoto

Jinbun kagaku kenkyûjo 京都大學人文科學研究所 (Research Institute for Humanistic Studies), Kyôdai (Kyoto University). The Chinese section of the Jinbun contains the major sinological library in the Kansai region. Published catalog:

Kyôto daigaku Jinbun kagaku kenkyûjo Kanseki bunrui mokuroku 京都大學人文科學研究所漢籍分類目錄 (Classified catalog of old

Chinese books in the Jinbun), 2 vols., 1964–65. Collectanea arranged by subject.

Kyôto daigaku Jinbun kagaku kenkyûjo Kanseki mokuroku 京都大學人文科學研究所漢籍目錄 (Catalog of Chinese books in the Jinbun), 2 vols., 1979–80; reduced-size edition, 1981.

Tenri University 天理大學. Situated in Tenri (close to Kyoto), it has an excellent Chinese collection and a distinguished series of published catalogs.

Nagoya

Hôsa Bunko 蓬左文庫. Housed as a unit in the Nagoya city library. Published catalog:

Nagoya shi Hôsa bunko Kanseki bunrui mokuroku 名古屋市蓬左文庫漢籍分類目錄 (Classified catalog of old Chinese books in the Hôsa bunko), Nagoya, 1975.

Combined and Union Catalogs

Note the following union catalogs of the holdings of Chinese works in important Japanese libraries:

Chûgoku chihôshi sôgo mokuroku 中國地方志綜合目錄 (Union catalog of Chinese local gazetteers); see 4.6.

Gendai Chûgoku kankei Chûgokugo bunken sôgô mokuroku 現代中國關係中國語文獻總合目錄 (Union catalog of Chinese documentation on modern China), Ajia keizai kenkyûjo, comp. and published, 8 vols., 1967–68; supplement, 1969–70. Holdings of 25 Japanese libraries (of which 3 in the supplement) of Chinese books published between 1912 and 1965.

Kanseki sôsho shozai mokuroku 漢籍叢書所在目錄 (Catalog of whereabouts of Chinese *congshu*); see 9.6.

Nihon genson Genjin bunshû mokuroku 日本現存元人文集目錄 (Catalog of collected works by Yuan authors extant in Japanese libraries); see 48.5.2, *Bieji*.

Nihon genson Mindai chihôshi mokuroku 日本現存明代地方志目錄 (Catalog of Ming gazetteers in Japanese collections); see 3.8.4.

Nihon genson Sôjin bunshû mokuroku 日本現存宋人文集目錄 (Catalog of collected works of Song authors); see 47.2, *Bieji*.

Chûgokubun zasshi shinbun sôgo mokuroku 中國文新聞雜誌總合目錄 (A union catalog of holdings of Chinese periodicals and newspapers),

Ajia keizai kenkyûjo, 1986. Holdings of 40 Japanese collections of 10,000 titles from end Qing to 1985. Replaces *Nihon shuyô kenkyû kikan toshokan shozô Chûgokubun shinbun zasshi sôgo mokuroku* 日本主要研究機關圖書館所藏中國文新聞雜誌總合目錄 (1959).

Nihonbun Chûgokubun Chôsenbun nado chikuji kankôbutsu mokuroku 日本文中國文朝鮮文等逐次刊行物目錄 (Catalog of periodicals in Japanese, Chinese, and Korean), Tôyô bunko, 1963.

Tokushu bunko shozô maikurofuirumu rengô mokuroku 特殊文庫所藏マイクロフィルム連合目錄 (Union index of microfilms of Japanese, Chinese, Korean, Manchu, Mongolian, Vietnamese, and Tibetan books and manuscripts preserved in specialist libraries), Kokuritsu kokkai toshokan, 1967.

Zôtei Nihon genson Minjin bunshû mokuroku 增訂日本現存明人文集目錄 (Catalog of collected works of Ming writers extant in Japan); see 49.2, *Bieji*.

11.4 The United States, Europe, and Russia

11.4.1 The United States

The major collections of Chinese sources, both ancient and modern, outside of China and Japan are in the United States. Note that in counting the number of books in Chinese collections it is common practice to count the number of volumes (*ce* or sometimes *juan*) rather than titles. The 11 main Chinese libraries in the United States by order of size of holdings (as of June 1996) are:

1. Library of Congress, Washington, DC, founded 1861 (718,000 vols). Although the largest collection of Chinese and Japanese books in the United States, it is not open stack and not research-oriented. There is, however, an online catalog, a printed version of which is published annually.[9] For a history, see Shu Chao Hu, *The Development of the Chinese Collection in the Library of Congress*, Westview, 1979. There are a number of published cata-

---

[9] This massive four-volume work is surprisingly detailed in some areas, less so in others. For example, there are 22 entries under "Chinese Cabbage," including alternative spellings and different Latin names for different varieties. By comparison, under "China History," all the dynasties are listed along the following rather more simple and unexpected lines, "Sung: Dynasty; Anecdotes, Humor."

logs of the huge Chinese and Japanese collections, including those of *shanben* (the largest collection outside of China);[10] of local gazetteers (the largest collection in the United States);[11] of periodicals;[12] and of newspapers.[13] Has large holdings of SMRC materials (51.11.3). General catalog: Library of Congress, Washington, DC: *Far Eastern Languages Catalog*, 22 vols., G. K. Hall, 1972.

2. Harvard: Harvard-Yenching Library (494,000 vols). Leading university research library for East Asia in the United States. Published catalog: *Catalogs of the Harvard-Yenching Library: Chinese Catalog*; *Author-Title*, vols., 1–28; *Subject*, vols., 29–38; *Serial Records*, vol. 39, Garland, 1986. For a catalog of 1,431 Song to Ming editions in the library, see *An Annotated Catalog of Chinese Rare Books in the Harvard-Yenching Library*, Shanghai cishu, 1998.

3. Princeton University (380,000 vols). *A Catalogue of the Chinese Rare Books in the Gest Collection of the Princeton University Library*, Ch'ü Wanli, comp., Taibei: Yiwen, 1974; Lianjing rpnt., 1984 (includes *shanben* to the end of the Qianlong period).

4. Yale University (378,000 vols).

5. University of California, Berkeley (330,000 vols). Published catalog: *East Asiatic Library, University of California, Berkeley, Author-Title Catalog*, 13 vols.; *Subject Catalog*, 6 vols., G. K.

[10] Wang Chung-min, *A Descriptive Catalog of Rare Chinese Books in the Library of Congress*, 2 vols., Library of Congress, Washington, DC, 1957.

[11] Chu Shih Chia, *A Catalog of Chinese Local Histories in the Library of Congress*, Washington, DC, 1942; rpnt., Zhonghua, 1991.

[12] Han Chu Huang and David H. G. Hsu, *Chinese Periodicals in the Library of Congress, A Bibliography*, Library of Congress, Washington, DC, 1988. Revised and expanded edition of 1978 original. Provides holdings information on over 8,000 periodicals published 1864–1986. Arranged alphabetically by title. Gives call numbers.

[13] Han-chu Huang and Hseo-chin Jen, *Chinese Newspapers in the Library of Congress: A Bibliography*, Washington, DC, 1985. Provides holdings information on some 1,200 newspapers published from the 1870s to the early 1980s. Arranged alphabetically by title. Has localities index and stroke-count index for first character in title.

Hall, 1968; *Author Catalog: First Supplement*, 2 vols., G. K. Hall, 1973; *Subject Catalog: First Supplement*, 2 vols., G. K. Hall, 1973.

6. University of Chicago (327,000 vols). *Catalogs of the Far Eastern Library, University of Chicago, Illinois: Author-Title Catalog of the Chinese Collection*, 18 vols., G. K. Hall, 1973; *First Supplement*, 4 vols., G. K. Hall, 1981.

7. Columbia University. C. V. Starr East Asian Library (305,000 vols). See 51.5.9, *USA*. For the Columbia Oral History Project.

8. University of Michigan (303,000 vols). *Catalogs of the Asia Library, University of Michigan, Ann Arbor: Chinese Catalog, Japanese Catalog*, 25 vols., G. K. Hall, 1978.

9. Cornell University (302,000 vols). *The Catalog of the Wason Collection on China and the Chinese, Cornell University Libraries*, Part I, *Serials Catalog*, Center for Chinese Research Materials, 1978; Part II, *Catalog of Monographs in Chinese, Japanese, and Western Languages*, 7 vols., 1980. *Supplement*, 1 vol., 1985.

10. Hoover Institution, Stanford University (222,000 vols). *The Library Catalogs of the Hoover Institution on War, Revolution, and Peace, Stanford University, Catalog of the Chinese Collection*, 13 vols., G. K. Hall, 1969; *First Supplement*, 2 vols., 1972. *Catalog of the Japanese Collection*, 7 vols., G. K. Hall, 1969. Both the Chinese and Japanese catalogs include subject entries. Concentrates on twentieth century China.

11. University of Washington (220,000 vols).

Note that the Library of the University of British Columbia, Vancouver, contains 226,000 vols. of Chinese books.

For further details, consult *A Guide to East Asian Collections in North America*, Thomas H. Lee, comp., Greenwood, 1992.

11.4.2   Europe

See John T. Ma, *Chinese Collections in Europe: Survey of Their Technical and Readers' Service*, Zug, 1985, for one-page entries on 60 European Chinese collections, including names of librarians and telephone numbers. Some of the main libraries and published catalogs are listed below. Most sinological libraries in Europe are in the process of converting their catalogs to computer and in doing so are taking the opportunity to convert from earlier systems of romanization to *Hanyu pinyin*. The European Association of Sinological Librarians meets every year, usually just before the meeting of the European Association of Chinese Studies. The EACS has published national or regional surveys of Chinese studies that include details of sinological libraries: Italy (1984); France (1988); Germany (1990); the Nordic countries (1994); Russia and the CIS countries (1996); Central Europe (1996); the United Kingdom (1997).

France

1. Institut des Hautes Études Chinoises, Collège de France. Main research library on China in France (300,000 vols.). Founded by Paul Pelliot and Marcel Granet in the early 1920s.

2. Bibliothèque Nationale de France, Département des manuscrits orientaux, Paris (46.3.1).

Germany

Staatsbibliothek preussischer Kulturbesitz Berlin: Katalog der ostasien Abteilung, 19 vols., Osnabrück: Biblio Verlag, 1983–85. Contains about 80,000 cards for the Chinese collection.

UK

1. London: *School of Oriental and African Studies, University of London, Library Catalogue*, 28 vols. (of which the *Chinese catalogue* occupies vols. 23–27), G. K. Hall, 1963. Same title, *First supplement*, 1968; *Second supplement*, 1973; *Third supplement*, 1973–78.

2. British Library; large collection of English-language treaty port newspapers.

3. Cambridge University: University Library. Online catalog of 45,000 titles in the Chinese collection. Also the Needham Research Institute, East Asian History of Science Library.

4. Oxford University.

11.4.3   Russia

The three main sinological libraries in Russia are:

1. Russian State Library (formerly the Lenin Library), Moscow.

2. The Institute of Oriental Studies of the Russian Academy of Sciences, St. Petersburg branch (formerly the Institute of the Peoples of Asia under the Academy of Social Sciences, Leningrad Branch).

The collection began as the Asiatic Museum in 1818; it holds the S. F. Oldenburg collection of Dunhuang manuscripts (46.3).

3. Oriental Faculty of St. Petersburg University (formerly the collections of the Sinological Institute, Leningrad University).

Union catalogs of Chinese books and periodicals in Russia were previously published by the former Lenin Library.[14]

11.5   Publishers and Bookstores

In China itself, many publishers who do reprints of traditional historical sources and publish historical scholarship now keep up-to-date lists or catalogs.[15] Larger publishers specializing in history (for example, Zhonghua and Shanghai guji) publish retrospective, annotated catalogs in book form.[16] Zhonghua publishes a quarterly (*Shupin* 書品, 1986–). It contains scholarly reviews of its own new books as well as short articles on literary and historical subjects. In the 1980s many *guji* 古籍 (ancient texts) publishers were set up in the provinces. They mainly publish local history works and those of an antiquarian interest.

The rule in China is that if you see a book, buy it, because it will not be there when you next go shopping, and stores and publishers do not keep stocks. Many of the publishers have their own retail outlets. Several have Web sites and accept direct orders over the internet. Because of the poor distribution of academic books, ordering directly from the publisher is often more rewarding than browsing the large general bookstores, although the bookstore scene is changing so fast it is unwise to generalize.

[14] Consult *Soviet Studies of Premodern China*, Gilbert Rozman, ed., CCS, Univ. of Michigan, 1984.

[15] Zhonghua shuju, Shanghai guji chubanshe (from 1958 to 1978 the Shanghai branch of Zhonghua Shuju), Zhonghua shudian, Zhongguo shudian, Zhongzhou guji, and many others. See *Directory of Publishers in China*, Jin Sheng 金聲, ed. in chief, FLP, 1992; rev. edition, 1996. There are 547 publishers listed with their addresses and telephone and fax numbers.

[16] *Zhonghua shuju tushu mulu 1949–1991*, 中華書局圖書目錄 (Catalog of books published by the Zhonghua shuju, 1949–91), Zhonghua, 1993; *Shanghai guji chubanshe sishi zhounian* 上海古籍出版社四十周年, 1956–1996 (The fortieth anniversary of the Shanghai guji chubanshe, 1956–96), Shanghai guji, 1996.

In Taibei several publishers specialize in printing academic books on Chinese history and reprints or Taiwan editions of works in Western languages. They usually have their own retail outlets, for example, Lexue shuju 樂學書局 (Lexis), Nantian shuju 南天書局 (SMC), Shangwu yinsuguan 商務印刷館 (Taiwan), or Xuesheng shuju 學生書局. Many publishers maintain catalogs of their books. The Shiyusuo, the Jinshisuo and other institutes of the Academia Sinica (Zhongyang yanjiuyuan 中央研究院) also regularly publish updated catalogs of their publications as does the Palace Museum.

For those who enjoy browsing the Web, there are several online bookstores specializing in Chinese-language books, for example, Dragon Source bookstore in Canada (www.dragonsource.com). One of the store's specialities is the provision of access to articles from Chinese scholarly journals, including *Lishi yanjiu* 歷史研究.

In America and Europe, only a handful of publishers have developed a list on Chinese history. They include the university presses of California, Columbia, Harvard, Stanford, Princeton, the State University of New York, Michigan, Oxford, and Cambridge, and such specialist publishers as M. E. Sharpe or E. J. Brill. The Harvard University Asia Center, the University of Michigan Center for Chinese Studies, and the Centers for Chinese Studies at the University of California, Berkeley, and UC, Los Angeles, all publish special series on China.

In Japan, there are over 20 bookstores specializing in Chinese books. Most are in Tokyo and Kyoto. Several have Web sites and accept direct orders over the internet. A stroll through the half dozen in Kanda's Jinbochô 神田神保町 (including one whose Shanghai branch was much patronized by Lu Xun in the 1930s) can reveal Chinese works that you might otherwise have missed or been unable to find in China. Several of these stores also publish book review magazines of Chinese books. Two of these reviews, those of Tôhô and Uchiyama, even include a section of dozens of forthcoming titles from Chinese publishers as well as lists of recent and forthcoming Japanese and Western works on China. Bookstores specializing in Chinese books include the following:

Tôhô shoten 東方書店 (monthly book magazine: *Tôhô* 東方 [Eastern Book Review], 1975–). Branches in Kyoto and Osaka.

Uchiyama shoten 內山書店 (monthly book magazine: *Chûgoku tosho* 中國圖書, 1988–).

Yamamoto shoten 山本書店. Specializes in Japanese sinology.

Tôfuku shoten 東豊書店 (just next to Yoyogi JNR station). Huge stock of scholarly books from both China and Taiwan.

Rinrôkaku 琳琅閣. Publishes extensive lists of rare and old books on China twice a year.

Ryôgen shoten 燎原書店. Stocks both mainland and Taiwan publications; specializes in medical texts (monthly journal: *Ryôgen*, 1992–).

Taishûkan shoten 大修館書店, Tokyo. Publishes the *Dai Kan-Wa jiten* and many other reference works (monthly journal: *Shinika* しにか, 1990–).

Kaifû shoten 海風書店, Tokyo. Carries mainly pirated editions of mainland publications.

Kyûko shoin 汲古書院. Publishing scholarly books on China (monthly magazine with news about books on China: *Kyûko* 汲古).

Chûbun shuppansha 中文出版社, Kyoto. Carries mainly pirated editions of mainland publications.

Hôyû shoten 朋友書店, Kyoto. Has a comprehensive collection of sinological works with the emphasis on scholarly works from China (monthly list, *Hôyû* 朋友). Publishes a number of important Japanese scholarly works on China.

For guides to the bookstores of Tokyo and Kyoto, see:

Tokyo Book Map, Shoseki jôhôsha, annual. Contains brief descriptions of 400 bookstores in Tokyo libraries.

Kyôto koshoten meguri 京都古書店巡り (A tour of Kyoto antique bookstores), Kyoto, 1995, 1996. Carries information on nearly 100 old bookstores in Kyoto (including about 10 stocking exclusively Chinese books).

11.6   *International Databases and Online Access*

For rapid access to library holdings of Chinese books, the wave of the future is the international database. At present there are two. The RLIN (Research Libraries Information Network) database is run by the Research Libraries Group (RLG), supported by a consortium of American university libraries and located in California. The OCLC (Online Computer Library Center) database is maintained by an organization of that name in Ohio. Since the mid-1980s, most East Asian libraries in North America have begun to

enter their bibliographical records on one or other of these databases, which in turn have begun to incorporate each other's records.
As a result, either of them can offer access to the holdings of dozens
of East Asian libraries (including all the major ones) and display
them in full Chinese, Japanese, and Korean script as well as romanization. And both are increasing their coverage of East Asian libraries in Asia, Europe, and Australia. Already they contain hundreds
of thousands of publications—mostly rather recent ones, but also
several major collections of Chinese rare books—and they are growing fast (for the RLG database of Chinese rare books, see 9.8.1).

There are two problems. First, these are not open websites but
proprietary databases accessible only to paying subscribers armed
with a password. But because they can be consulted at almost any
university library (though not always with Chinese, Japanese, and
Korean script), they are widely available. The second problem is
that no major East Asian library has yet converted all its old records
to machine-readable form and entered them in the databases, and so
their coverage is fractional at best. In this respect Harvard-Yenching
is the leader: it has about half of its Chinese, Japanese, and Korean
records online already and will complete the job early this century.

A growing number of East Asian libraries have home pages on
the Internet that allow access to their online catalogs. The best of
them also offer descriptions of special collections, locally produced
bibliographies and study aids, and an overview of sinological resources at the particular university. They also provide links to the
home pages of other libraries and research organizations and to
other sources of sinological information that are proliferating all
over the world. These include important indexes and databases,
home pages devoted to particular areas of study and to individual
texts, and a plethora of other information: for example you can
search the 25 Histories full-text database (22.2) through the home
page of the Harvard-Yenching. Elsewhere you can search the catalogs of entire library systems from UC to Kyôdai.

Probably the most convenient gateway to this cyberworld in the
United States is the home page of the Council on East Asian Librar-
ies (CEAL) of the Association for Asian Studies. Another is the
Asian Studies World Wide Web Virtual Library, based at the Aus-
tralian National University but with outposts around the world.
The China branch of this resource is the Internet Guide for Chinese
Studies. Once you succeed in contacting one sinological site, you

should be able to contact them all, as they are mostly linked to one another, and you can spend weeks exploring them. If you lack the time for serendipity, you can contact the Virtual Library at ANU and subscribe to a mailing list that describes and evaluates websites.

Many of the innovations and new services are discussed in the pages of the *Journal of East Asian Libraries* (CEAL, trimesterly) and in the *Bulletin of the International Association of Oriental Libraries* (1971– , quarterly).

II

PRE-QIN SOURCES

12

Archaeology

Archaeology in the twentieth century has transformed our understanding of the prehistory of China and many of the steps leading much later to the emergence of civilization there and its subsequent development. Archaeology has also enriched our understanding of the history of imperial China. New discoveries are made almost every day, new techniques are being applied, and new interpretations are appearing. The chapter sketches the development of modern Chinese archaeology (12.1), suggests ways of keeping up-to-date with recent work (12.2), and lists a number of essential research tools (12.3). Pre-Qin sources are introduced in Chapter 13 (Neolithic and early Bronze Age cultures), Chapters 14 to 17 (proto forms of writing and epigraphy), and Chapters 18 to 19 (manuscripts and texts). Some of the main archaeological discoveries of sites and objects from imperial China are detailed in brief sections in each chapter of Part V.

12.1 *Chinese Archaeology in the Twentieth Century*

The first use of the term *kaogu* 考古 is credited to Li Daoyuan 酈道元, d. 527, in his *Shuijingzhu* 水經注 (35.3.1). It was used in the general sense of "the investigation of ancient things," chiefly inscriptions. *Jinshi* 金石 (the study of bronze and stone inscriptions), since at least the Song, primarily took the form of collecting and classifying antique bronze vessels and stone inscriptions and deciphering them (Chapter 17). Sometimes these studies led to the correction or verification of the written record as found in transmitted texts, but not to the questioning of the historical account found therein. Both *jinshi* and *kaogu* remained one of the many activities of antiquarian scholars and calligraphers. Neither developed into a separate branch of study actively searching for new material evidence of the past. Indeed, it would have been considered not only unnecessary to do so, but also a sacrilege to search in places like tombs (one of the main sources of data for the modern archaeologist). Tombs were not studied by scholars but robbed by criminals.[1]

Given this tradition, it is no surprise to find that Chinese archaeology was ushered in at the beginning of the twentieth century by the discovery of inscriptions (those on the Shang oracle bones; 15.2). Other inscriptional sources—on wood, bamboo, and paper— were also discovered in the early years of the century, mainly in the northwest of China by foreign explorers (44.4). At about this time, the old terms *jinshi* and *kaogu* were both modernized by adding *xue* 學 to form *jinshixue* 金石學 (epigraphy) and *kaoguxue* 考古學 (archaeology).

The 1920s and 1930s saw the first modern archaeological digs and important discoveries, including "Peking Man" (13.1) and the late Neolithic cultures of Yangshao and Longshan. The decipherment of the oracle bones got under way and the first excavations began in 1928 at the place where they were found, the Shang cult center near Anyang 安陽 in northern Henan (13.2.2). From 1929, the work was led by Li Ji 李濟 (1896–1979), one of the pioneers of modern Chinese archaeology and the first Chinese archaeologist to conduct field work (in Shanxi in 1926 at a Yangshao site).[2]

The next period of discovery was in the 1950s and early 1960s. Planned excavation concentrated on the traditional core area, the Yellow River valley and on ancient capitals such as Luoyang. One of the most notable (and controversial) excavations was the first opening of an imperial tomb by archaeologists, that of the Ming Wanli 萬曆 emperor, the Dingling 定陵.[3] The work here and elsewhere was interrupted by the Anti-Rightist campaign (1957). There

---

[1] Yin Shaohu 殷嘯虎 and Yao Ziming 姚子明, *Daomushi* 盜墓史 (History of tomb robbery), Shanghai wenyi, 1997.

[2] For an evaluation of Li Ji's work, see Hsü Cho-yün, "Commemorating the Tenth Anniversary of Mr. Li Chi's Death," *Chinese Studies in History* 18.1: 11–17, 71 (1994).

[3] The leader of the excavation team characterizes the conditions in which the Dingling excavation took place (long before the Cultural Revolution) as "interference by political movements, damage done unwittingly and, chiefly, the lack of knowledge and responsibility of the people involved" (Yue Nan and Yang Shi, *The Dead Suffered Too: The Excavation of a Ming Tomb*, FLP, 1996, 276).

was also a hiatus and much destruction during the Cultural Revolution (1966–72). Excavation reports were delayed (up to 30 years in some cases), and archaeological journals suspended for several years. Nevertheless some extremely important discoveries were made during the first half of the 1970s, for example, the bamboo and silk manuscripts at Mawangdui, Shuihudi, Yinqueshan, Wuwei, and Juyan (19.1.3; Chapter 36; 44.4). Some of the finds have become household words—perhaps the best-known example being the 7,000 warriors of the terracotta "underground army" found in 1974 in the guard chambers to the tomb of the first emperor, Qin Shihuangdi 秦始皇帝 (presaging who knows what splendors in the as yet unexcavated inner tomb). The pace of discovery and research gathered momentum in the late 1970s, the volume of excavated sites is now without precedent, and techniques of dating have greatly improved (12.3, *Dating Techniques*).

Although the most spectacular archaeological finds have come from prehistoric and ancient China, archaeology, below ground, above ground, and under water, has also contributed much to later Chinese history. Take the example of the discovery (and equally important, the conservation) of tomb frescoes and tomb brick paintings. These have survived from every period from the Han through to the Ming. They are fresh and life-like and more detailed and down to earth (in the case of the brick paintings) than most of the surviving paintings or written descriptions from the scholar's brush. Archaeological finds such as these are introduced in the appropriate sections of the manual. To locate excavated inscriptions and texts, see Table 29, Chapter 20.

Excavation has concentrated on cities (especially capital cities, their walls, and their palaces), Buddhist temples, workshops (for example, kilns and foundries), imperial mausolea and more ordinary tombs, and on the artifacts from all of these. The choice of site has been either deliberate and based on a desire to supplement or vindicate the historical record (e.g., searching for Xia, Shang, and Zhou capitals), or it has been a random choice based on accidental discoveries usually made during major construction or civil engineering projects. This salvage archaeology, as it is called, has taken place all over the country. It has had the effect of extending archaeology to regions and places far from the old centers of concentration in the upper and middle reaches of the Yellow River, and has led to the discovery of numerous previously unknown Neolithic and Bronze

Age cultures from all over the China area. Nobody disputes the importance of the Yellow River region, but it is no longer possible to maintain that it was the sole locus of Neolithic and Bronze Age cultures in the China area. Thus the "Zhou interpretation of history," which held that the Chinese people descended in a single direct line from the Three Sovereigns and the Five Emperors through the Three Dynasties, the Xia, Shang, and Zhou, and that they came from one core region, the middle and lower reaches of the Yellow River, is no longer tenable. The Zhou interpretation was used for self-legitimation, not as a description of reality.[4]

Already in 1933, the May Fourth intellectual, Fu Sinian 傅斯年 (1896–1950), the first and longtime director of the Shiyusuo, published an influential paper arguing on the basis of his analysis of the Zhou texts that the prehistory of north China was deeply influenced by the interactions and struggles between two main groups of peoples: the Xia 夏 to the west (in the middle Yellow River valley) and the Yi 夷 to the east (in the lower Yellow River region).[5]

The Yi-Xia thesis appeared to be substantiated by the striking evidence of two separate traditions suggested by the first excavations of the Yangshao 仰韶 (middle Yellow River) culture with its characterisitic red painted pottery and the Longshan 龍山 culture to the east (Lower Yellow River), often distinguished by its shiny black pottery.[6] The thesis remained the accepted one until the 1960s when

[4] Jessica Rawson, "Statesmen or Barbarians? The Western Zhou as Seen through their Bronzes," *Proceedings of the British Academy*, 75: 71–95 (1989); Robert W. Bagley, "Changjiang Bronzes and Shang Archaeology," *International Colloquium on Chinese Art History, Proceedings, Antiquities*, Part I, Taibei, 1992, 209–55.

[5] Fu Sinian, "Yi-Xia dongxi shuo" 夷夏東西說, in *Qingzhu Cai Yuanpei xiansheng liushiwu sui lunwenji* 慶祝蔡元培先生六十五歲論文集 (Papers presented to Mr. Ts'ai Yuan P'ei on his sixty-fifth birthday), Shiyusuo, 1933.

[6] The Swedish archaeologist J. Gunnar Andersson (1874–1960) recounts in his memoirs how his search for prehistoric fossils led him to Henan and eventually to Yangshao village, where in 1920 he found some shards of painted pottery; see *Children of the Yellow Earth*, Kegan Paul, 1934; rpnt., MIT, 1973. The subsequent excavations conducted at Yangshao by Andersson led to the identification of the first archaeological culture in China.
Longshan was discovered by Wu Jinding 吳金鼎 (1901–48) in 1928 in a Shandong village of that name at the Chengziyai 城子崖 site and identified in 1930–31.

the sequence occupation of the Miaodigou 廟底溝 site in Henan appeared to show that a branch of the Longshan culture had grown out of Yangshao. This apparent substantiation of the traditional view—that the Central Plain was the single nuclear area from which later Chinese civilization gradually radiated out to the barbarian areas—did not last long. By the mid-1970s enough evidence had accumulated from the rest of China to create an infinitely more diverse and varied picture with evidence of many flourishing regional Neolithic and early Bronze Age cultures. As a result, monogenesis is now out and multiple origins are in. The new "regional systems and cultural types theory" as it was called (*quxi leixing lilun* 區系類型理論) was proposed in 1979 by one of the leading archaeologists of his generation, Su Bingqi 蘇秉琦 (1909–97), and published in *Wenwu* 1981.5. In one sense, therefore, modern Chinese archaeologists have gone back two generations to the Doubting Antiquity School (Yigupai 疑古派) in that they reject many of the old accounts of the origins of the Chinese people and Chinese civilization.[7] But instead of foreshortening Chinese prehistory, they have lengthened it and changed its definition. In this sense they are said to belong to a new school, the Believing in Antiquity School (Xingupai 信古派).

Despite the recognition of diversity and despite the huge increase in the inventory of excavated sites and artifacts, Chinese archaeology continues to take a culture-historical and teleological approach, according to which everything that took place within the China area in prehistory is interpreted as a factor leading to the birth of Chinese civilization.[8] The current consensus sees this hap-

[7] The Doubting Antiquity School began during the May Fourth Movement. It was initiated by Hu Shi 胡適 (1891–1962) and led by his pupil Gu Jiegang 顧頡剛 (1893–1980) and other historians. They began from 1920 onward by rejecting many previously revered classics as later forgeries and soon cast doubt on the entire Zhou (Confucian) view of early Chinese history as being a series of later accretions of myth. See section 29.1–2.

[8] Lothar von Falkenhausen, "On the Historiographical Orientation of Chinese Archaeology," *Antiquity* 67.257: 839–49; also idem, "The Regionalist Paradigm in Chinese Archaeology," in *Nationalism, Politics, and the Practice of Archaeology*, Philip Kohl and Clare Fawcett, eds., CUP, 1995, 198–217. For a good overview of prehistory which gets away from archaeology as the anachronistic extension into prehistory of modern nationalistic concerns, see Gina L. Barnes, *China, Korea and Japan, the Rise of Civilization in East Asia*, Thames and Hudson, 1993; Charles Higham rightly views south China and mainland

Footnote continued on next page

pening following the emergence of a "Chinese interaction sphere," in which the main regional cultures become joined together in archaeological terms by 3000 BC. According to this view, from then on the sphere may properly be called China, which makes the country 5,000 years old.[9] Direct diffusion from "outside" the borders of what is in effect the area of modern China projected back into the remote past is automatically rejected. On the other hand, paradoxically, diffusion inside the China area itself is taken for granted in accounts of the role of the Shang and later dynasties. Since anything which happened outside the borders is regarded as largely irrelevant, external influences are downplayed, and comparisons with Neolithic and Bronze Age cultures from other parts of the world, including those of China's neighbors, are often limited to citing generic similarities as laid down in the Marxist classics (see Introduction, *Periodization*). Even the extent to which China shared common characteristics with other ancient city-state or territorial state systems, for example, those of the Sumerians, Egyptians, or Aztecs, is largely unexplored. There are increasing signs that these narrow confines are being breached; nevertheless, archaeology (a costly interpretative discipline that almost entirely depends on state support) remains the handmaid of nationalism.

From the sixteenth to the early twentieth centuries, many, but by no means all, Western scholars believed that key elements of early civilization in China (for example, astronomy, crops, metallurgy, pottery, writing, or music), if not the Chinese people themselves, had their origins in ancient Egypt, the ancient middle-East, or India. The recent discoveries of copious traces of early man and of numerous indigenous prehistoric cultures clearly antecedent to

---

Southeast Asia as one huge region in his *The Bronze Age of Southeast Asia*, CUP, 1996. See also, *Ancient Chinese Culture of South China and Neighbouring Regions*, Centre for Chinese Archaeology and Art, ICS, and Chinese Univ. of Hong Kong, eds., HKCUP, 1994.

[9] This is also the view of Kwang-chih Chang (Zhang Guangzhi 張光志); see his "China on the Eve of the Historical Period," *CHAC*, chapter 1, 37–73, upon which I have drawn heavily in the above account. K. C. Chang introduced several generations of Western students to Chinese archaeology, including myself, in his continuously revised *The Archaeology of Ancient China* (12.1, *References*). See also *Zhongguo gudai wenming yu guojia xingcheng yanjiu* 中國古代文明與國家形成研究 (Research on the formation of the ancient Chinese culture and nation), Li Xueqin 李學勤, ed. in chief, Yunnan renmin, 1997.

what came later within the area of present-day China has led to the abandonment of such simplistic diffusion theories. A more nuanced view is now gaining ground. It allows that some elements of Bronze Age culture may have been stimulated by outside contacts—if not by direct importation, then by stimulus diffusion.[10] As Edwin Pulleyblank puts it after reviewing previous theories and the most recent evidence, "the arrival of Indo-Europeans, with their horse culture, in the northwestern frontier zone [of China] about four thousand years ago must have been indirectly very important in the formation of Chinese civilization; [but] the content of that civilization ... mainly grew out of indigenous traditions ...."[11]

Given the pace of economic and societal change in China today, the desire of localities and regions to establish local cultural traditions, and the need felt by a new generation of wealthy collectors to authenticate their acquisitions, the next decades will no doubt see not only many new discoveries but also new analyses of both civilization in China and of Chinese civilization itself.

References

Kwang-chih Chang, "Traditional Historiography and Antiquarianism," and "Modern and Contemporary Archaeology" in his *The Archaeology of Ancient China*, 1986, (13.1) 4–21.

[10] An Zhimin 安志敏, "Shilun Zhongguo de zaoqi tongqi" 試論中國的早期銅器 (Preliminary discussion of China's early copper and bronze artifacts), *Kaogu* 12: 1110–19 (1993), in which the author argues that metallurgy could have come from further West to northwest China, from where it was later transmitted to the Central Plain. In a later article he stresses the role of the northwest as an early cultural intermediary between west Asia and China; see his "Talimu pendi ji qi zhouwei de qingtong wenhua yicun" 塔里木盆地及其周圍的青銅文化遗存 (Remains of bronze cultures in the Tarim Basin and adjacent regions), *Kaogu* 12: 70–77 (1996).

[11] "Early Contacts Between Indo-Europeans and Chinese," *International Review of Chinese Linguistics*, 1.1: 1–24 (1996). See also the same author's "The Chinese and Their Neighbours in Prehistoric and Early Historic Times," in *The Origins of Chinese Civilization*, David N. Keightley, ed., UCP, 1983. (1983), 411–66. Most Western scholars believe that the war chariot was introduced into China from Central Asia around 1500–1200 BC (see note 2, Chapter 28). This is at about the time from which the first Chinese writing survives, although there is no evidence that it was imported and considerable evidence that it developed indigenously (Chapters 14–15). On prehistoric routes to Inner Asia and the West via what was much later called the "Silk Road," see 41.3.1.

Chen Xingcan 陳星燦, *Zhongguo shiqian kaoguxueshi yanjiu* 中國史前考古學史研究 (Research on the history of Chinese prehistoric archaeology, 1895 to 1949), Sanlian, 1997. Monographic overview of the development of prehistoric archaeology in China between 1895 and 1949.

Zhonghua renmin gongheguo zhongda kaogu faxian 中華人民共和國重大考古發現 (Great archaeological discoveries of the People's Republic of China), Su Bai 宿白, ed. in chief, Wenwu, 1999. This lavishly illustrated scholarly volume contains brief overviews of the prehistoric and historical periods between the Paleolithic and the Ming with references to the main archaeological reports. Individual archaeologists then introduce 122 of the most important sites discovered between 1949 and 1999. There are color photographs of each site and some of the main objects excavated.

Kaoguxue 考古學 (Archaeology) in *Zhongguo da baike quanshu* 中國大百科全書 (The great Chinese encyclopaedia), Da baike quanshu, 1986. A good first reference on Chinese archaeology of all periods up to 1984. The articles contain material covering not only China, but also world archaeology, including short entries on the ancient cultures of the nation-states bordering modern China and biographies of 40 of China's leading archaeologists of the first and second generations. Arrangement is by *pinyin*; there is a *pinyin* index as well as a thematic table of contents. There are more than 250 color plates.

Mianshang dadi de qiusuo: 20 shiji de Zhongguo kaoguxue 面向大地的求索20史記的中國考古學 (The exploration of the earth: Chinese archaeology of the twentieth century), Zhi Yuan 知原, ed. in chief, Wenwu, 1999. Popular account, includes biographies of China's leading archaeologists of the third generation.

Zhongguo wenwu jinghua da cidian 中國文物精華大辭典 (The large dictionary of the best of Chinese cultural relics), 4 vols., Guojia wenwuju 國家文物局, ed., Shanghai cishu and HK: Shangwu, 1996. "Dictionary" of 5,500 of the finest recently excavated *objets d'art*. Each treasure has a color photograph and a brief description. Arrangement is by material; for example, vol. 1 contains annotated photographs of metal, silver, jade, and stone *objets*.

Zhongguo kaogu wenwu zhi mei 中國考古文物之美 (The best of the archaeological finds in China), 10 vols., Wenwu, 1994, 1995. The 10 major archaeological discoveries of the 1970s and 1980s are presented in this superb series arranged as a pictorial record of the excavations and inventory of the findings.

Mysteries of Ancient China: New Discoveries from the Early Dynasties, Jessica Rawson, ed., British Museum, 1996. The catalog of a major exhibition held in several European countries in 1995 and 1996 provides a reliable overview of many of the main discoveries made of Neolithic to Han dynasty objects between the mid-1970s and the mid-1990s.

Recent discoveries are conveniently listed by province in the *Annual Surveys* of the Archaeological Association and (in lesser detail) of the History Association, or in more detail in the retrospective and other bibliographies published by provincial archaeological institutes and museums (see 12.2 for details).

12.2 The Current Archaeological Scene

There are 50 archaeological institutes and 17 university departments of archaeology in China with over 1,500 full-time archaeologists. There are national associations for ancient history and archaeology (see 13.3 for pre-Qin associations), and there are usually annual conferences on a specific theme. These are good occasions for exchanging news and views long before they get into the research publications, let alone written up in book form. Each province's Wenkaosuo 文考所 (Cultural relics and archaeology institute) manages provincial associations of cultural relics and archaeology. Some of the larger cities also have their own archaeological departments. The general trend since the 1980s is for these provincial and local institutes to gain more control over their agendas than was the case when Guo Moruo 郭沫若 (1892–1978) was the all-powerful president of the Academy of Sciences during the first 25 years of the People's Republic.

Since the early 1990s, several hundred major new excavations have been undertaken every year. After the excavation a short preliminary report is usually published in one of the archaeological journals (12.3). A few years later this is followed by a full report containing an account of the excavation; a factual and illustrated inventory of the site and the objects found there and analytical studies. Dozens of such reports have been published annually, and the archaeological journals (of which there are now well over 100) have carried 4,000 to 5,000 specialist reports and research articles every year. An ever larger number of studies of the archaeology of individual provinces are being published. In Henan, for example, between 1978 and 1999, 2,214 excavation projects were undertaken and 21,000 ancient tombs were excavated (for Henan archaeological publications, see 12.3, *Bibliographies*).

New branches of archaeology have been and are being developed. What might be called the archaeology of everyday life has made good use of newly unearthed objects to interpret ancient terms and institutions and situate them in their historical and social contexts.[12] Art archaeology (*meishu kaogu* 美術考古) concentrates on the aesthetics of recovered objects.[13] The archaeology of cave temples and grottos (*shikusi kaogu* 石窟寺考古) examines the Buddhist cliff and cave sanctuaries and sculptures, such as those at Dunhuang or Longmen (45.4).[14] Other new branches are often linked to a discipline—for example, astroarchaeology (Chapter 6), the archaeology of science (Chapter 37), the archaeology of music (38.2), the archaeology of agriculture (Chapter 35), the archaeology of religion (Chapter 29), ethnoarchaeology (Chapter 40), zooarcheology, and geoarchaeology.

Foreign archaeologists worked in China during the early part of the twentieth century and in the 1920s and 1930s. Between 1949 and the late 1970s, they were not permitted to do so. During the 1980s, foreign scholarly exchanges started up again and in 1991 joint archaeological excavations began. For a review with selected bibliography, see Robert E. Murrowchick, "The State of Sino-Foreign Collaborative Archaeology in China," *Orientations* 28.6: 26–33 (1997).

Not surprisingly, general books on Chinese history do not always reflect the state of the field. Indeed, because of the volume of discoveries, and the decline of funding for research and publication, even within the archaeological profession itself there are often considerable delays. At the best of times, the process from discovery to

[12] For example, Sun Ji 孫機, *Zhongguo gu yufu luncong* 中國古輿服論叢 (Collected papers on ancient Chinese carriages and dress), Wenwu, 1993; Yang Hong 楊泓 and Sun Ji 孫機, *Xunchang de jingzhi* 尋常的精致 (The fineness of the ordinary), Liaoning jiaoyu, 1996.

[13] Yang Hong 楊泓, *Meishu kaogu ban shiji Zhongguo meishu kaogu fazhanshi* 美術考古半世紀中國美術考古發展史 (Half a century of art archaeology: A history of the development of Chinese art archaeology), Wenwu, 1997.

[14] Su Bai 徐白, *Zhongguo shikusi yanjiu* 石窟寺考古研究 (Research on Chinese grotto temples), 1996. The same scholar contributed the summary article on this branch of Chinese archaeology to the archaeology volume of the great Chinese encyclopaedia, 1986 (12.1), 698–99.

excavation to report to analysis can be lengthy, especially if the site is a large and complex one.

A convenient way of keeping up-to-date is to subscribe to the following two publications. The first reports recent discoveries, the second summarizes what is in the archaeological journals:

Zhongguo wenwubao 中國文物報 (1985–87, weekly with title *Wenwubao*), Henan Wenhuaju; (1987–97, weekly; 1998– , twice weekly), Guojia Wenwuju 國家文物局 (State Bureau of Cultural Relics), Beijing. This newspaper carries articles about all kinds of archaeological, museum, and cultural news in more detail than the ordinary press and more rapidly than the archaeological journals. The years 1985–97 are available on CD-ROM.

CAAD: China Archaeology and Art Digest (1996– , quarterly or semi-annual), Bruce Gordon Doar and Susan Dewar, eds., HK: Art Text. This publication includes fairly full English summaries of articles in dozens of Chinese archaeological journals, many appearing in the same year as the publication of *CAAD*. There are also translations of longer articles on selected themes. An indispensable way of keeping up-to-date with many journals, to all of which no Western library, and few even in China, have subscriptions.

Societies and Yearbooks

Zhongguo kaogu xuehui 中國考古學會 (The Archaeological Society of China) was founded in its present form in 1979. Holds annual meetings. The proceedings are published in *Zhongguo kaogu xuehui nianhui lunwenji* 中國考古學會年會論文集, 1980– . The society publishes the following yearbook:

Zhongguo kaoguxue nianjian 中國考古學年鑑 (Yearbook of Chinese archaeology), Zhongguo kaoguxuehui, eds., Wenwu, 1983– . Covers activities and publications of each year, including state-of-the-field essays arranged by period and by subject; brief descriptions of new archaeological discoveries by province (200–300 pages); archaeological exhibitions and conferences; international scholarly exchanges; publications by subject and by province; details of the work of university and other archaeological departments; obituaries. Appears two or three years after the year covered.

Journals

Only a selection of the most important archaeological journals is given below. Those marked with an asterisk are available on the CD-ROM *Zhongguo xueshu qikan (guangpanban)* 中國學術期刊 (光

盤版); see 10.2.1 for details. See also 38.1.4 for art journals, many of which carry articles on archaeological subjects.[15]

Journal of the Archaeological Society of Hong Kong (1970- , annual), Hong Kong.

Kaogu 考古 (Archaeology); appeared first under the title: *Kaogu tongxun* 考古通訊, 1955–58; thereafter under the present title, 1958–66; did not appear 1966–71; 1972–82, bimonthly; 1983- , monthly), Kaogusuo. Each year the December issue has an index by subject for the current year. All issues between 1955 and the end of 1996 (containing nearly 8,000 articles and 16,000 archaeological drawings) are available on CD-ROM: *Kaogu zazhi tuwen shujuku guangpan* 考古雜志圖文數據庫光盤 (CD-ROM database of illustrations and text from the journal *Kaogu*), 7 discs, 1997. There is a printed index to the first 200 issues, *Kaogu 200 qi zongmu suoyin 1955.1–1984.5* 考古 200 期總目索引, Kexue, 1984.

Kaogu renlei xuekan 考古人類學刊 (1953- , semiannual), Guoli Taiwan daxue.

Kaogu xuebao 考古學報 (Acta Archaeologica Sinica, 1978- , quarterly), Kaogusuo. Began as *Anyang fajue baogao* 安陽發掘報告, 1929–33; then changed to *Tianye kaogu baogao* 田野考古報告 in 1936; issues 2–4 (1947–49) appeared as *Zhongguo kaogu xuebao* 中國考古學報; issue 5 appeared in 1952. In 1953, the present title was adopted; 1953–60 (quarterly); 1962–65 (semiannual); 1960 (latter half), 1961 and 1966–71 did not appear; 1972–77 (semiannual). Has English-language abstracts.

Kaoguxue jikan 考古學季刊 (1981- , irregular, 11 vols., as of 1998), Kaogusuo. Vol. 10 contains an index of the articles in vols. 1–10; vol. 11, Da baike quanshu, 1998.

*Nongye kaogu 農業考古, 1981–90, semiannual; thereafter, quarterly. Edited since 1990.2 by Jiangxi shekeyuan, Lishisuo, Nanchang, Jiangxi.

Tianye kaogu 田野考古 (1990- , semiannual), Taibei.

Wenwu 文物 (1972- , monthly), Wenhuabu, Wenwuju 文化部文物局 (Cultural relics bureau, Ministry of culture), Beijing. Each year, the December issue has an index by subject for the current year. Also,

---

[15] For an annotated list of well over 100 archaeological journals from all over China, see Lothar von Falkenhausen, "Serials on Chinese Archaeology," *EC* 17: 247–95 (1992). *Chinese Archaeology and Art Digest* also lists and annotates over 100 archaeological journals, including the main university journals.

the issues of the previous year are bound together and published with a comprehensive index. There is also an index to the first 500 issues, *Wenwu 500 qi zongmu suoyin* 文物 500 期總目索引, Wenwu, 1998. It covers issues 1950.1–1998.1; arrangement is by topics, and there is also an author index in *pinyin*.

After restarting in 1972, *Wenwu* became one of the main archaeological journals (earlier issues up to 1959 had few articles on archaeology). Unlike *Kaogu*, which is strictly for professional archaeologists, it includes papers on stone inscriptions, rare books, and other cultural relics. Original title, *Wenwu cankao ziliao* 文物參考資料, 1950–58. Present title, 1959–66. 1966.6–1971, ceased publication.

The provincial *wenkaosuo* and the larger provincial museums put out their own journals:

Beifang wenwu 北方文物 (1985– , quarterly), Heilongjiang Wenkaosuo, Harbin

*Dongnan wenhua 東南文化 (1978– , quarterly), Nanjing Museum, Nanjing

Huaxia kaogu 華夏考古 (1987– , quarterly), Henan Wenkaosuo, Zhengzhou, Henan

Jiang-Han kaogu 江漢考古 (1981– , quarterly), Hubei Wenkaosuo

*Kaogu yu wenwu 考古與文物 (1980– , bimonthly), Shaanxi Kaogusuo

Liaohai wenwu xuekan 遼海文物學刊 (1992– , quarterly), Liaoning Wenkaosuo

Nanfang wenwu 南方文物 (1992– , quarterly), Jiangxi Provincial Museum and Wenkaosuo

Sichuan wenwu 四川文物 (1984– , bimonthly), Chengdu

*Zhongyuan wenwu 中原文物 (1978– , quarterly), Henan Provincial Museum, Zhengzhou

12.3   Research Tools and Bibliographies

Note that the fullest archaeological library in China is that of the Kaogusuo 考古所. It contains over 300,000 volumes.

Dating Techniques

Zhongguo kaoguxue zhong tan shisi niandai shuju ji 中國考古學中碳十四年代數據集 (Collection of radiocarbon dates for Chinese archaeology, 1965–91), Wenwu, 1992. Updates of new radiocarbon dates are published in *Kaogu* (for a summary of the different scientific methods for dating and other archaeological purposes, see *Science and the Past*, Sheridan Bowman, ed., British Museum, 1991).

Dictionary

Wenhua kaogu cidian Ying-Han Han-Ying 文化考古詞典英漢漢英 (Dictionary of Culture and Archaeology: English-Chinese; Chinese-English), Han Xinghua 韓興華, ed. in chief, FLP, 1998.

Bibliographies

The best retrospective bibliographical essays on Chinese archaeology during the years 1949–99 is item 1. For more detail on the years 1949–89, see items 2–4.

Xin Zhongguo kaogu wushi nian 新中國考古五十年 (Fifty years of archaeology in new China), Wenwu, 1999. Summarizes archaeological discoveries of the years 1949–99 by province with bibliographical notes. Also covers Hong Kong, Macao, and Taiwan.

Wenwu kaogu gongzuo sanshi nian 1949–1979 文物考古工作三十年 1949–1979 (Thirty years of work on archaeological and cultural relics), Wenwu, 1980. Summarizes archaeological discoveries of the years 1949–79 by province with bibliographical notes.

Xin Zhongguo de kaogu faxian he yanjiu 新中國的考古發現和研究 (Archaeological excavation and studies in new China), Wenwu, 1984. The years 1949–79 also summed up by the Kaogusuo.

Wenwu kaogu gongzuo shinian 1979–1989 文物考古工作十年 1979–1989 (Ten years of work on archaeological and cultural relics), Wenwu, 1991, uses the same format for the years 1979–89.

Revue bibliographique de sinologie (10.1) carries short notices of selected archaeological books and articles and has done so since 1957.

Zhongguo kaoguxue wenxian mulu 1900–1949 中國考古學文獻目錄 1900–1949 (Bibliography of Chinese archaeology, 1900–1949), Wenwu, 1991. Covers Chinese scholarship published up to 1949 in all fields of archaeology.

Zhongguo kaoguxue wenxian mulu 1949–1966 中國考古學文獻目錄 1949–1966 (Bibliography of Chinese archaeology, 1949–1966), Wenwu, 1978. Covers Chinese scholarship published between 1949 and the outbreak of the Cultural Revolution in all fields of archaeology.

Zhongguo kaoguxue wenxian mulu 1971–1982 中國考古學文獻目錄 1971–1982 (Bibliography of Chinese archaeology, 1971–1982), Wenwu, 1998. Covers Chinese scholarship published between 1971–82 in all fields of archaeology.

Chinese Archaeological Abstracts, 4 vols., Institute of Archaeology, Univ. of California at Los Angeles, 1978–85. About 1,200 articles appearing between 1963 and 1981 are summarized in English translation; vol. 1, edited by Richard C. Rudolph, covers articles in *Kaogu xuebao*, *Kaogu*, and *Wenwu*; vols. 2–4, edited by Albert E. Dien, Jeffrey K. Riegel, and Nancy T. Price, cover articles in *Kaogu* and *Wenwu*. Each volume has a comprehensive subject index.

Zhongguo Xinshiqi shidai kaogu wenxian mulu 中國新石器時代考古文獻目錄 (Index of studies of Neolithic archaeology in China), Miao Yajuan 繆雅娟 et al., eds., Kexue, 1993, covers Chinese scholarship published between 1923 and 1989.

University archaeological departments and provincial archaeological societies and museums publish bibliographies covering the secondary archaeological literature on their provinces or regions, often on special occasions, for example, the anniversary of the establishment of a provincial kaogusuo or the anniversary of the discovery of a particular site or culture, for example, *Zhongguo kaoguxue luncong* 中國考古學論叢 (Collected studies on Chinese archaeology), Kexue, 1993, a collection of research articles marking the fortieth anniversary of the Kaogusuo. Note that the archaeologically richest provinces, for example, Henan, are well served with separate bibliographies:

Henan Xinshiqi shidai tianye kaogu wenxian juyao 河南新石器時代田野考古文獻舉要 (Selections from the archaeological fieldwork on the Neolithic in Henan), Zhongzhou guji, 1997. Lists 300 reports published 1923–96 on Neolithic sites excavated in Henan and summarizes 200 of them.

Henan wenbo kaogu wenxian xulu 河南文博考古文獻叙錄 (List of museum and archaeological research in Henan), 2 vols., special publication, *Zhongyuan wenwu*, vol. 1 (1986) covers publications 1913–85; vol. 2 (1996), 1986–95.

Henan kaogu sishi nian 河南考古四十年 (Forty years of Henan archaeology), Henan renmin, 1994. Archaeological activities in Henan, 1952–92.

Luoyang kaogu sishinian 洛陽考古四十年 (Forty years of archaeology in Luoyang), Ye Wansong 葉萬松, ed. in chief, Kexue, 1996.

13

Pre-Qin Archaeology

Pre-Qin covers the period before the Qin unification of China in 221 BC. It traditionally refers to the Xia, Shang, and Zhou dynasties. Modern archaeology has confirmed part of the historical record, but there is no conclusive evidence linking archaeological cultures or sites with the Xia, or with the Shang before Anyang (that is before about 1200 BC). The three dynasties (if the Xia did in fact exist, see below) coexisted with many other statelets, the spectacular traces of some of which have been discovered during the past fifty years.

The main sources for the pre-Qin are of three types: archaeological (Chapter 13), epigraphic (Chapters 14–17), and textual (Chapters 18–19). This chapter begins with an outline of the main Neolithic cultures (13.1). The early Bronze Age (Shang and Zhou) follows (13.2). General research tools are introduced in section 13.3.

Even if only the historically attested Shang and Zhou are included, the pre-Qin still covers a period of well over 1,000 years, which is more than one-third of all Chinese history. It is one of the most exciting and one of the most difficult periods to study. It is exciting because it deals with the beginning of the story—the emergence of early civilization in China. Part of the excitement also comes from the flow of new evidence provided by archaeological discoveries, a flow which has accelerated as more land is churned up in the course of economic development. The combination of the new evidence (*xinzheng* 新證) with the critical reading of transmitted texts using the best traditions of text-critical scholarship (*kaozheng* 考證) has led to much of the best work on Chinese ancient history in the twentieth century. The pioneer was Wang Guowei 王國維 (1877–1927), who used the oracle-bone script to verify the *Shiji* Shang king lists (15.1). However, the new archaeological data, including artifacts, epigraphic sources, and excavated texts are beginning to reveal much richer and more diverse traces of civilization in China than is suggested by the traditional written sources. The new data should be used to piece together their own story, not simply to verify an old one or to satisfy a chauvinistic impulse to modernize the Zhou interpretation of history (12.1).

One reason that the pre-Qin is one of the most difficult periods is the limited number of textual sources, far fewer than for any later period, a shortage already noted for the Shang by Confucius in the fifth century BC (*Lunyu* 論語, iii.9). Texts that did survive were often partly lost or corrupted in oral transmission and had to be painstakingly reconstructed centuries later, mainly in the Han. They were written in Classical Chinese, still recognizable to someone who reads Modern Chinese but nevertheless requiring special training to understand fully (1.3.5). Moreover, however difficult the mastery of Classical Chinese may be, it is easy compared to the skills required to handle the earliest epigraphic sources for the pre-Qin that were written in archaic forms of the language and in scripts that are extremely difficult to read (16.4–5).

References

The Cambridge History of Ancient China, Michael Loewe and Edward L. Shaughnessy, eds., New York: CUP, 1999. The benchmark for pre-Qin history in English. *CHAC* contains 14 chapters by different hands, of which four concentrate on archaeology and four on transmitted texts. It is well illustrated and has a full bibliography. I have relied heavily on *CHAC* in preparing Chapters 12 and 13 for the revised and enlarged edition of the manual.

Kwang-chih Chang, *The Archaeology of Ancient China*, 4th ed., rev. and enl., YUP, 1986. From the Paleolithic to the early Bronze Age. For many years this was the standard book-length survey in English. It is summarized in Chang's chapter in *CHAC*.

13.1   Paleolithic and Neolithic

The first discovery of early man in China took place in 1926 just outside Peking, hence the name "Peking Man" (*H. erectus pekinensis* or *Beijing zhili ren* 北京直立人 ca. 700,000–230,000 BP).[1] Since 1949, another dozen sites of *H. erectus* have been found from different parts of China, some possibly up to one million years older than

---

[1] BP (Before the Present) is used for the time periods before the Neolithic. Jia Lanpo 賈蘭坡 (1908–97) and Huang Weiwen 黃慰文, *The Story of Peking Man*, Yin Zhiqi, tr., FLP and HK: OUP, 1990.

Peking Man. The transition to *H. Sapiens* was completed some 100,000 years ago. More than 40 sites where he lived have been excavated.[2] The shift from the Paleolithic to the Neolithic was coterminous with the end of the last Ice Age and was well under way by 8000 BC. Whether the shift took place as the result of a second radiation out of Africa or whether H. sapiens in China was the local descendant of local Paleolithic hominoids is a matter of continuing controversy. Subsequent developments were rapid. Many thousands of Neolithic sites have been discovered spanning a period stretching from the beginning of the seventh to the end of the third millennium BC. Some 50 of them were large settlements protected with stamped earth walls. The occupants engaged in permanent farming.[3] The eight regions into which archaeologists currently group the Neolithic cultures are shown in Table 23. By about 2000, early Bronze Age cultures were emerging. Rice had long since been the main crop in the south, millet in the north.[4] Domestic animals were raised (pigs and dogs in the south; horses, cattle, and sheep in the north). The farmers used bronze and stone for their implements, as did the warriors for their weapons.

[2] X. Z. Wu (Wu Xinzhi 吳新智) and F. E. Poirier, *Human Evolution in China: A Metric Description of the Fossils and a Review of the Sites*, OUP, 1995. A thorough summary of the evidence with a bibliography of the main works in Chinese and English up to 1993.

[3] Bruce D. Smith, *The Emergence of Agriculture*, New York: Scientific American Library, 1995; Hui-lin Li, "The Domestication of Plants in China: Ecogeographical Considerations," and Te-tzu Chang, "The Origins and Early Cultures of the Cereal Grains and Food Legumes," in *The Origins of Chinese Civilization*, David Keightley, ed., UCP, 1983, 21–64 and 65–94.

[4] *Huaxia kaogu* (1997.1). The proto-paddy fields with irrigation systems that were excavated in 1992–95 by a joint Sino-Japanese team at a Hemudu site (Caoxieshan 草鞋山, near Suzhou) are the oldest so far discovered in any country. Cultivated rice has been excavated from a total of more than 120 Neolithic sites in south China (mainly from the central and lower Yangzi regions) and from about 20 sites in the north. The northern sites date from the late Neolithic (4000–3000 BC) and in some cases, e.g., Jiahu 賈湖 (12.3), possibly earlier; see *CAAD* 3.1: 134–37 (1999). *Antiquity*, vol. 72, no. 178 has a special section on rice domestication, 857–907.

Chinese rice strains probably found their way to Japan directly from the Lower Yangzi region at the beginning of the first millennium BC during the Jômon 繩文 period and to Korea during the Zhou dynasty (*Nongye kaogu*, 1998.1).

Table 23: Neolithic (ca. 8000–2000 BC) and *Early Bronze Age Cultures (ca. 2000–1045 BC)

	ca. BC–BC
1. Northeast (Inner Mongolia, Heilongjiang, Jilin, Liaoning)	
Xinle 新樂	5300–4800
Zhaobaogou 趙寶溝	4500–4000
Hongshan 紅山	3400–2300
*Xiajiadian 夏家店	2000–300
2. Northwest or Upper Yellow River (Shaanxi, Gansu, Qinghai)	
Laoguantai 老官臺 (incl. Gansu Yangshao 甘肅仰韶)	6000–5400
Majiayao 馬家窯	3300–2050
*Qijia 齊家	2300–1800
3. North Central or Central Yellow River (Henan, Hebei, Shanxi, Shaanxi)	
Cishan 磁山, Peiligang 裴李崗, Dadiwan 大地灣	6000–5400
Yangshao 仰韶 ("Painted pottery culture")	5000–3000
*Henan (or Central) Longshan 龍山	2800–2000
*Erlitou 二里頭	1900–1500
4. Lower Yellow River (Shandong, East Henan, Jiangsu, Anhui)	
Qinglian'gang 青蓮岡 (incl. Beixin 北辛)	5400–4000
Dawenkou 大汶口	4300–2200
*Shandong Longshan 山東龍山 ("Black pottery culture")	2400–2000
Yueshi 岳石	1900–1500
5. Southeast or Lower Yangzi (Zhejiang, Jiangsu)	
Hemudu 河姆渡	5000–3400
Majiabang 馬家浜 (incl. Songze 崧澤)	5000–3200
Liangzhu 良渚 (incl. Maqiao 馬橋)	3200–2200
6. South Central or Central Yangzi (Hubei, E. Sichuan, N. Hunan)	
Pengtoushan 彭頭山	7000–5800
Daixi 大溪	4400–3300
Qujialing 屈家嶺	3500–2600
Hubei Longshan 湖北龍山 (Qinglongquan 青龍泉)	2500–2000
7. Southwest or Upper Yangzi (Guizhou, Yunnan, Sichuan)	
Baiyangcun 白陽村	2200–2100
Dalongtan 大龍潭	2100–2000
8. South (Fujian, Guangdong, Guangxi, Taiwan)	
Cord-marked cultures, e.g., Zengpiyan 甑皮岩	7000–5500
Coastal region painted pottery cultural sphere (e.g., Dapenkeng 大坌坑, Shixia 石峽)	4400–1500

Note: Individual cultures are usually named after their place of discovery. Different archaeologists and publications of different date vary widely in their grouping and nomenclature of Neolithic cultures.

The most characteristic artifacts are the pottery vessels whose different styles and colors help differentiate cultures.[5] Some exceptional cultures also produced elaborate jade carving and silk weaving, for example, Hongshan 紅山 in the northeast and Liangzhu 良渚 in the southeast.[6]

The excavation of Neolithic burials has thrown new light on conditions in those days, including the population profile, life ex-

---

[5] The earliest Chinese prehistoric painted pottery comes from the Laoguantai 老官臺 culture (modern Gansu, Qinghai, and Ningxia), 5,000 to 6,000 years BC. An authoritative study is Zhang Mingchuan 張明川, *Zhongguo caitao tupu* 中國彩陶圖譜 (Illustrated catalog of Chinese painted pottery), Wenwu, 1990. This superbly printed work contains a 200-page introduction followed by meticulous, hand-painted illustrations of 2,009 prehistoric pots arranged geographically by place of discovery (there is a finding index for cultures at the end of the book). Appendixes contain a bibliography of research published between 1920 and 1982 (also arranged by province), a table of carbon-14 dates, analysis of chemical composition and firing temperatures of selected pots from the main cultural sites, maps of sites, and a brief introduction to the 72 main cultures which produced painted pottery in prehistoric China. In his introduction the author analyzes the pottery from many different points of view, including the characteristics and technologies used in the main cultures, a systematic study of the symbols (showing, for example, how they moved from pictures to abstract designs), and the style of life reflected in the decorations of the pottery.

[6] Hongshan is characterized by elaborate altars and statues of naked pregnant figurines. They are similar to, but much later than, the "Venus" fertility cult figures of prehistoric Europe (*nüshenyong* 女神俑). *Niuheliang Hongshan wenhua yizhi yu yuqi jingcui* 牛河梁紅山文化遺址與玉器精粹 (Treasures and jades from the Niuheliang Hongshan culture site), Liaoning Kaogusuo, ed., Wenwu, 1997. Other female fertility symbols were found 50 km (30 miles) away at another Hongshan site, Dongshanzui 東山嘴, and also at Houtaizi 後臺子 in Hebei.

The Liangzhu culture (to the west of Hangzhou) is famous for its *yucong* 玉琮 (jade tubes), square on the outside and round in the middle. They were used as burial objects and perhaps also as ritual or dance paraphernalia. The beast-riding emblem found on a few of them is similar to the anthropomorphic splayed animal-mask, the demon devourers of the Shang bronzes, and may have been their stylistic forebear as some have argued. Fragments of silk and lacquer ware have also been found. See Sun Zhixin, "The Liangzhu Culture: Its Discovery and Its Jades," *EC* 18: 1–40 (1993); *Dongfang wenming zhi guang–Liangzhu wenhua faxian 60 zhounian jinian lunwenji* 東方文明之光-良渚文化發現60周年紀念論文集 (The light of Oriental civilization–collected essays in celebration of the 60th anniversary of the discovery of Liangzhu culture), Xu Huping 徐湖平, ed. in chief, Hainan guoji xinwen chuban zhongxin, 1996.

pectancy, diseases, and early religious beliefs of the tribes who inhabited the area of what was later to become China. Enough has been unearthed to justify studies as diverse as prehistoric rock art (14.2), pottery marks and symbols (Chapter 14), masks (3.9), divination (15.3), cooking (35.2.2), and the arts, not to speak of prehistoric pottery and bronze casting.

13.2   Xia, Shang, and Zhou Archaeology

13.2.1   Xia

The historicity of the Xia is now generally accepted in China although no specific evidence predating the Shang that identifies sites or artifacts with a kingdom or people or settlement known as Xia has been unearthed.[7] A number of Bronze Age sites, however, have tentatively been identified as Xia, most important of which are the remains of a palace settlement at Erlitou 二里頭, just east of Luoyang and a few miles to the southwest of the modern city of Yanshi 偃師 in Henan (discovered 1959). Erlitou was the center of a culture covering Henan and adjacent parts of Shaanxi, Shanxi, Hebei, and Hubei during the first half of the second millennium BC.

13.2.2   Shang

There were other early Bronze Age cultures contemporaneous with Erlitou elsewhere in the China area, notably:

Yueshi 岳石 culture, Shandong; Sishui Yinjiacheng 泗水尹家城 site; see *Sishui Yinjiacheng* 泗水尹家城 (The Yinjiacheng site at Sishui), Shandong daxue Lishixi kaogu zhuanye jiaoyan shi, ed., Wenwu, 1990.

Lower Xiajiadian 厦家店, Liaoning; see Sarah Milledge Nelson, *The Archaeology of Northeast China*, Routledge, 1995, ch. 5.

Erlitou appears to be the immediate ancestor of the Erligang 二里崗 culture (centered at modern Zhengzhou), which has been described as the "first great civilization of East Asia." In their desire to trace the ancestral origins of the Chinese state, some even claim that Erli-

---

[7] Bagley, 1992 (12.1); Robert L. Thorp, "Erlitou and the Search for the Xia," *EC* 16: 11–38 (1991); Sarah Allen, "The Myth of the Xia Dynasty," *JRAS* 2: 242–56 (1984); David Nivison and Kevin Pang, "Astronomical Evidence for the *Bamboo Annals*' Chronicle of the Early Xia," *EC* 15: 87–95 (1990).

gang is the site of the early Shang, but there is no evidence to show that it is.[8] Note that dates of discovery are given in brackets (excavations have often continued on and off for many years after the initial discovery):

Erligang 二里崗 culture, 1500–1300 BC?

> Yanshi Shang city 偃師商城 (1983)

> Zhengzhou Shang city 鄭州商城 (1952). Covers 25 sq km (10 sq miles) and has a stamped earth city wall of seven km (4 miles) in circumference; see *Zhengzhou Shangcheng kaogu xin faxian yu yanjiu 1985–1992* 鄭州商城考古新發現與研究 1985–1992 (New archaeological discoveries and research at Zhengzhou Shang city), Henansheng Wenwu yanjiusuo, ed., Zhongzhou guji, 1993, *Zhengzhou Shangdai tongqi jiaocang* 鄭州商代銅器窖藏 (Storage pits containing Shang bronzes at Zhengzhou), Kexue, 1999, and *Henan kaogu sishi nian* (12.3, *Bibliographies*), 181–204.

> Zhengzhou Xiaoshuangqiao 鄭州小雙橋 (1990). 20 km (12 miles) from Zhengzhou.

In addition to Erligang culture, recent years have seen the discovery of a number of other early Bronze Age cultures in other parts of China, sometimes sharing common elements with Erligang, sometimes not. They come after Erligang and before the thirteenth century BC (the transition period preceding Anyang). Three important examples are:

Panlongcheng 盤龍城 (1963), Hubei; see Robert Bagley, "P'an-lung-ch'eng: A Shang City in Hupei," *Artibus Asiae* 39: 165–219 (1977).

Gaocheng, Taixicun 藁城縣臺西村 (1973), Hebei; *Gaocheng Taixi Shang yizhi* 藁城臺西商遺址 (The Shang site at Taixi, Gaocheng), Hebei Wenwu yanjiusuo, ed., 1985; on the pottery graphs found here, see 14.6.

Wucheng 吳城 (1973), Jiangxi; typified by the tomb discovered at Xingan 新干 (1989), Dayangzhou 大陽洲. It is the second richest known early Bronze Age tomb (the richest is that of Fu Hao 婦好, consort

---

[8] The description of Erlitou is that of Robert Bagley in his "Shang Archaeology," *CHAC*, ch. 3, 124–231. Bagley points out that a Shang earlier than Anyang exists in the historical record but has not been epigraphically identified on the ground. Therefore to avoid misunderstandings Anyang should be called Shang and not "late Shang" (personal communication).

of the Shang king Wu Ding 武丁, ca. 1200 BC); see *Xin'gan Shangdai da mu* 新干商代大墓 (A great Shang tomb at Xin'gan), Jiangxi Wenkaosuo, ed., Wenwu, 1997; also Robert Bagley, "An Early Bronze Age Tomb in Jiangxi Province," *Orientations*, July 1993, 20-36; on the pottery graphs found here, see 14.6.

The picture (at least in Henan) becomes clearer at the end of the second millennium BC with the first extant corpus of written evidence (the oracle-bone inscriptions). These confirm part of the account in the *Shiji* (15.1) and are also directly linked to the material remains excavated from the same site, the Shang cult center at Anyang. The excavations began in 1928 and have continued until the present day. The first two items are specifically on Anyang; the remainder on other aspects of the Shang dynasty.

Yinxu de faxian yu yanjiu 殷墟的發現與研究 (The discovery and research on the Yin ruins), Kaogusuo, eds., Kexue, 1994. A well-illustrated and thoroughly documented retrospective of 60 years' work on Anyang. Contains reference to the main Anyang excavation reports.

Li Ji, *Anyang: A Chronicle of the Discovery and Excavations and Reconstructions of the Ancient Capital of the Shang Dynasty*, UWP, 1977. The account of one of China's pioneer archaeologists.

David Keightley, "The Shang: China's First Historical Dynasty," *CHAC*, ch. 4, 232-91. See also *The Origins of Chinese Civilization*, David Keightley, ed., UCP, 1983.

Jiaguxue yibai nian 甲骨學一百年 (15.5), 522-690, contains a summary of the research on all aspects of Shang society and institutions based on the oracle-bone inscriptions discovered at Anyang (and Zhouyuan).

Zhang Zhiheng 張之恒 and Zhou Yuxing 周裕興, *Xia Shang Zhou kaogu* 夏商周考古 (The archaeology of the Xia, Shang, and Zhou), Nanjing daxue, 1995, 1998. A manual of pre-Qin archaeology which includes discoveries announced up to the early 1990s.

K. C. Chang, *Shang Civilization*, YUP, 1980, based on archaeological discoveries available as of the late 1970s.

Song Xinchao 宋新潮, *Yin-Shang wenhua quyu yanjiu* 殷商文化區域研究 (Research on the culture areas in the Yin-Shang period), Shaanxi renmin, 1991. A summary of the evidence of the bronze cultures of the various peoples in the China area and of their interaction.

Recent years have also seen the discovery of regional Early Bronze Age cultures more or less contemporary with Anyang but with distinctive features of their own. One striking example is Sanxingdui 三星堆 on the Chengdu plain, whose elongated bronze figures with mask-like heads with eyes on stalks, straight nose, large mouth and ears, and with gold foil stuck to their puttied and limed features are unlike anything else so far discovered in the China area:

> Sanxingdui 三星堆 sacrificial pits (1986); late Bronze Age culture discovered at Guanghan 廣漢 county, 40 km (25 miles) north of Chengdu, Sichuan. Flourished ca. 1200 BC? See Robert Bagley, "A Shang City in Sichuan Province," *Orientations*, November 1990, 52–67, and idem, "Sacrificial Pits of the Shang Period at Sanxingdui in Guanghan County, Sichuan Province," *Arts Asiatiques* 43: 78–86 (1988); *Sanxingdui jisi keng* 三星堆祭祀坑 (Excavation of the sacrificial pits at Sanxingdui), Sichuan Wenkaosuo, ed., Wenwu, 1999; also *Sanxingdui yu Ba-Shu wenhua* 三星堆與巴蜀文化 (Sanxingdui and Ba-Shu culture), Li Shaoming 李紹明, Lin Xiang 林向, and Zhao Dianzeng 趙殿增, eds., Ba-Shu, 1993; *Sanxingdui wenhua* 三星堆文化 (Sanxingdui culture), Qu Xiaoqiang 屈小强, Li Dianyuan 李殿元, et al., eds., Sichuan renmin, 1993, 1994.

The discovery of cultures such as Sanxingdui poses new questions: "Rationalizations that would attach the whole of a large and diverse archaeological record to a royal house attested at one city in north China [i.e., Shang Anyang] have come to look arbitrary and improbable."[9] In other words, the Early Bronze Age in the China area is not limited to the history of the Shang dynasty, and the entire period is wide open to new interpretations.

13.2.3 Zhou

Extensive efforts have been made to fill in the archaeological record of the Western Zhou in north China and to try and provide answers to the question of the origins of the people or peoples who founded the Zhou dynasty, the first from which historical and literary texts have been transmitted (Chapters 18–19).[10] Some of the transmitted texts can now be checked with, and in some cases supplemented by, excavated ones, including inscriptions cast on bronze vessels, of

---

[9] Robert Bagley, *CHAC*, 124.

[10] Jessica Rawson, "Western Zhou Archaeology," *CHAC* ch. 6, 352–449; Cho-yun Hsu (Xu Zhoyun 許倬雲) and Katheryn M. Linduff, *Western Zhou Civilization*, YUP, 1988.

which about 6,000 are extant (17.1). The archaeological record begins with the pre-dynastic site of Zhouyuan.

Zhouyuan 周原 site (named in modern times after a line from the *Shijing*), about 100 km (60 miles) to the west of Xi'an; see Chen Quanfang 陳全方, *Zhouyuan yu Zhou wenhua* 周原與周文化 (Zhouyuan and Zhou culture), Shanghai renmin, 1988.

Despite a great deal of searching, the early Zhou palaces at the capitals of Feng 灃 and Hao 鎬 have not yet been discovered (*CHAC*, 393–97). Later sites of the dynasty itself and of its feudatories have been found, for example:

The capital of Yan 燕 about 30 km (20 miles) south of modern Beijing at Liulihe 琉璃河; see *Liulihe Xi Zhou Yanguo mudi* 琉璃河西周燕國墓地 (The Liulihe Western Zhou burial ground of the kingdom of Yan), Beijingshi Wenwu yanjiusuo, ed., Wenwu, 1995.

Tianma/Qucun 天馬/曲村, site of the cemetery of the first capital of the state of Jin, Shanxi; near Houma 侯馬 (1979); see *Wenwu* 1994.1 and 8; *Wenwu* 1995.7. For the archive of blood covenants inscribed on jade discovered at a later capital of Jin at Houma, see 17.2.1.

Before 841 BC, many of the names and dates of rulers and particular events are known back to the Shang, but no absolute chronology has as yet been agreed upon (see 13.3, *Chronology*). Thus the dating of an important battle such as the Zhou defeat of the Shang has been since the Han dynasty (and remains today) a controversial subject.[11]

Much more evidence survives from the Eastern Zhou, which saw the rise of numerous independent states as China entered the Iron Age. Their higher culture shared many common traits, but retained distinctive elements that in some cases can be traced back to

[11] Various hypotheses place the battle at dates ranging from 1130 BC to 1018 BC with some 40 alternatives in between. For a summary of the background to the problem, see Edward L. Shaughnessy, "Calendar and Chronology," *CHAC, Introduction*, 19–36. For collections of Chinese ancient and modern arguments on the date of the defeat of the Shang and of the Western Zhou kings, see, respectively, *Wu wang ke Shang zhi nian yanjiu* 武王克商之年研究 (Research on the year of King Wu's defeat of the Shang), Beijing shifan daxue, 1997, and *Xi Zhou zhu wang niandai yanjiu* 西周諸王年代研究 (Research on the dates of Western Zhou kings), Guizhou renmin, 1998.

regional Neolithic and Bronze Age cultures and tribes.[12] All the capitals of the Eastern Zhou have now been excavated (for works on their city plans, see 4.7.1). The tombs of Warring States local rulers have also yielded rich treasures (see Wu Hung in *CHAC*, 708–44). To cite but two examples:

Zenghou Yi mu 曾侯乙墓 (The grave of Marquess Yi of Zeng), Hubeisheng bowuguan, ed., 2 vols., Wenwu, 1989.

Cuo Mu—Zhanguo Zhongshanguo zhi mu 瞖墓—戰國中山國國王之墓 (The Cuo tomb: the Warring States tomb of the king of Zhongshan), Hebeisheng Wenwu yanjiusuo, ed., Wenwu, 1996. See also 4.4.1 for the map of the mausoleum discovered in this tomb.

13.3   Research Tools

Different types of special-purpose reference works for pre-Qin archaeology and history are introduced in Chapters 14–19 and in other sections on particular subjects, for example, myth (29.1) or weights and measures (7.3). Below, only a handful of indispensable reference works on pre-Qin history are introduced.

Historical Encyclopaedia

Zhongguo lishi da cidian, Xian-Qinshi juan (Zhanguoqian) 中國歷史大辭典先秦史卷戰國前 (The great encyclopaedia of Chinese history, volume on pre-Qin), Li Xueqin 李學勤, ed. in chief, Meng Shikai 孟世凱 and Qiu Xigui 裘錫圭, deputy eds., Shanghai cishu, 1996. One of the best volumes in this 14-volume encyclopaedia of Chinese history (8.4.2), it contains 5,592 brief entries covering both history and archaeology.

Biographical Dictionary

Zhongguo shanggu renming cihui ji suoyin 中國上古人名詞彙及索引 (Dictionary of archaic Chinese names with index), Pan Ying 潘英, ed.,

---

[12] Lothar von Falkenhausen, "The Waning of the Bronze Age: Material Culture and Social Developments, 770–481 BC," *CHAC*, ch. 7, 450–544; Wu Hung, "The Art and Architecture of the Warring States Period," *CHAC*, ch. 10, 651–744; Li Xueqin 李學勤, *Eastern Zhou and Qin Civilizations*, K. C. Chang, tr., YUP, 1985. The original Chinese edition (1984) was re-issued in a revised version, *Dong Zhou yu Qindai wenming* 東周與秦代文明, Wenwu, 1991.

Mingwen, 1993. Indexes 3,600 personal names found in *Chunqiu*, *Zuozhuan*, *Guoyu*, *Shangshu*, *Guben Zhushu jinian*, *Shijing*, *Lunyu*, and *Yi Zhoushu*.

Official Titles

For official titles in use in China up to the Qin unification, see Zuo Yandong 左言東, *Xian-Qin zhiguan biao* 先秦職官表 (Tables of official posts in the pre-Qin), Shangwu, 1994. Thorough and indexed.

Xi Zhou jinwen guanzhi yanjiu 西周金文官制研究 (Studies on the office system of Western Zhou bronze inscriptions), Zhang Yachu 張亞初 and Liu Yu 劉雨, Zhonghua, 1986. Provides a convenient correlation with the *Zhouli* 周禮. For post-Qin titles and translations, see section 22.3.6, *Official Posts and the Examination System*).

Geography

Zhongguo lishi dituji 中國歷史地圖集, vol. 1, *Yuanshi shehui Xia Shang Xi Zhou Chunqiu Zhanguo shiqi* 原始社會夏商西周春秋戰國時期 (Primitive society, the Xia, Shang, Western Zhou, Chunqiu, and Zhanguo); out of date and gives no references to site reports so it is impossible to know the basis upon which the mapping was done.

Zhongguo shanggu guoming diming cihui ji suoyin 中國上古國名地名辭彙及索引 (Glossary and index of names of states and toponyms in archaic China), Pan Ying 潘英, comp., Taibei: Mingwen, 1986.

David Keightley, "The Environment of Ancient China," *CHAC*, 30–36.

Chronology

A project was included in the ninth five-year plan (1996–2000) to establish an absolute chronology for Chinese history before 841 BC and to write annals-style histories of the Xia, Shang, and Zhou (*Xia-Shang-Zhou duandai gongcheng* 夏商周斷代工程). To get results, it will be necessary to improve archeometric techniques, including specially adapted radiocarbon dating for relatively late artifacts such as those of the Shang. Some of those who describe the project assume that the outlines of Chinese archaic history are well known, all that remains is to establish their chronology. If the project can go beyond such old-fashioned nationalistic assumptions it will provide fascinating new insights. For an outline, see *Early China News*, vol. 9, 1996. Note the following works on pre-Qin chronology:

Chang Yuzhi 常玉芝, *Yin-Shang lifa yanjiu* 殷商曆法研究 (Research on the Yin-Shang calendar), Jilin wenshi, 1998.

Zhongguo xian-Qinshi libiao 中國先秦史曆表 (Calendrical concordance for pre-Qin history), Zhang Peiyu 張培瑜, comp., Qi-Lu, 1987. Extrapolates, using modern astronomical data, the first day and hour of winter equinoxes between 1,500 and 105 BC and gives the corresponding cyclical characters for the days; Part II gives the first day of each month and shows the position of the intercalary months from 722 to 105 BC in eight different calendars in use during these centuries. This allows the reader to choose the calendar equivalents according to the text being read. There are appendixes of technical tables, e.g., catalogs of solar eclipses that could have been seen from Anyang 安陽 between 1300 and 1000 BC, and from Qufu 曲阜 during the Spring and Autumn period.

Xi Zhou (Gonghe) zhi Xi Han lipu 西周 (共和) 至西漢曆譜 (Calendrical tables from the Western Zhou [Gonghe interregnum] to the Western Han), Xu Xiqi 徐錫祺, ed., 2 vols., Beijing kexue jishu, 1997. Preface by Zhang Peiyu.

Shinpen Shiki Tô-Shû nenpyô 新編史記東周年表 (Newly edited *Shiji* Eastern Zhou chronological tables), Hirase Takao 平勢隆郎, comp., Tô-bunken, Tôkyô daigaku, 1995. Revised chronological table from 841 to 221 BC mainly based on comparison of the chronological tables in *Shiji, juan* 14 and 15 (the basic sources on pre-Qin chronology) with copious annotations seeking to correct the discrepancies and errors in them. See also Hirase's

> *Chûgoku kodai kinen no kenkyû tenmon to koyomi no kentô kara* 中國
> 古代紀年の研究天文と曆の檢討から (Studies on the chronology of ancient China—an examination of astronomy and the calendar), Tôbunken, Kyûko, 1996. Contains studies of the dating systems of the Shang, Western Zhou, and Spring and Autumn and Warring States with 150 pages of calendrical tables. For a brief study in English emphasizing the importance of the *Hanshu* 漢書 "Lülizhi" 律曆志 and the connections between the calendar and harmonics, see Hirase's "The Emperor and the Calendar in Ancient China," *MTB* 51: 85–96 (1993).

Some of the complexities of pre-Qin chronology and timekeeping and further references are introduced in Chapters 5 and 6.

Regional Reference Works

Of the many regional "dictionaries" available, three are cited as examples:

Chuguo lishi wenhua cidian 楚國歷史文化辭典 (Dictionary of the history and culture of the state of Chu), Shi Quan 石泉, ed. in chief, Wuhan daxue, 1996; rev., 1998, contains 6,480 entries written by 59 scholars.

Zhongguo wenwu tuji 中國文物圖集 (Collected maps of China's cultural objects), Wenwu, eds. in chief, Zhongguo ditu, 1991– . Archaeological sites by province. The most detailed so far is the one on Shaanxi (1998, 2 vols). Volume 1 contains detailed maps by county of the entire province with illustrations of the most important artifacts. Vol. 2 is a gazetteer with descriptions of every site and artifact.

Textual Sources

ECT: Early Chinese Texts: A Bibliographical Guide, Michael Loewe, ed., *Early China* Special Monograph Series, SSEC and IEAS, 1993, 1999. *ECT* contains short articles by different specialists on the 64 main textual sources for the Han and pre-Qin (19.2).

Indexes and Concordances

ICS: The main corpus of transmitted texts of the pre-Qin and Han are indexed character by character in the *ICS Ancient Chinese Texts Concordance Series*, ICS, Chinese University of Hong Kong. The *ICS* concordances are also available on CD-ROM. For details, see 9.10.

Paleographic Sources

NSECH: New Sources of Early Chinese History: An Introduction to the Reading of Inscriptions and Manuscripts, Edward L. Shaughnessy, ed., SSEC and IEAS, 1997. *NSECH* is a unique guide. It contains eight chapters by different scholars on inscriptions on bronzes, oracle bones, stone, jade, bamboo, wood, and silk, and an introduction by the editor. The authors examine how these sources are read and, second, how they can be used to reconstruct ancient society. With few exceptions, no discoveries made after 1985 and no works published after the end of 1993 are covered.

Corpora Inscriptionum

The main collections of inscriptions and pre-Qin manuscripts are introduced according to the medium on which they were recorded: pottery symbols (Chapter 14); oracle bones (Chapter 15); bronze, stone, bones, coins, jade, seals, and pottery (Chapter 17); bamboo and silk (Chapter 18).

Illustrations

A Journey into China's Antiquity, vol. 1, *Palaeolithic–Spring and Autumn Period*; vol. 2, *Warring States–Northern and Southern Dynasties* (see 8.1 on this authoritative illustrated series).

Qin wuzhi wenhuashi 秦物質文化史 (History of material culture during the Qin), Wang Xueli 王學理 et al., San-Qin, 1994. Excellent introduction to Qin archaeology in the form of an illustrated inventory of Qin artifacts from the earliest times to the fall of the Qin in 206 BC. There is also an extensive summary in English.

Bibliographies

For archaeological bibliographies, see 12.3. In addition to these and the specialized references in Chapters 13 to 19, see the following:

CHAC : *The Cambridge History of Ancient China*, Michael Loewe and Edward L. Shaughnessy, eds., New York: CUP, 1999. Contains a bibliography with 3,000 references on all aspects of pre-Qin history in Chinese, Japanese, and Western languages.

Xian-Qinshi yanjiu gaiyao 先秦史研究概要 (Survey of research on pre-Qin history), Zhu Fenghan 朱鳳瀚 and Xu Yong 徐勇, eds., Tianjin jiaoyu, 1996. Apart from introducing the sources on the Xia, Shang, and Zhou and surveying scholarly debates (1–475), it contains a bibliography of 4,000 references to Chinese secondary sources (up to 1991), arranged by period and by topic (518–764). In addition, there are 50 pages on Japanese scholarship as well as a brief outline of Western work (512–17).

For a much shorter survey, see Li Xueqin 李學勤 and Zheng Chao 鄭超, "Xian-Qin shiqi shiliao jieshao" 先秦時期史料介紹 (Introduction to the sources of pre-Qin history), in *Zhongguo gudaishi daodu* 中國古代史導讀 (A guide to reading ancient Chinese history), Xiao Li 肖黎 and Li Guihai 李桂海, eds., Wenhui, 1991, 1992, 1–76. See also the chapter on the pre-Qin in Yamane Yukio 山根幸夫 (1991), of which Tian Renlong 田人隆 (1994) and Gao Mingshi 高明士 (1990) are Chinese translations (8.2.2).

Xiashi Xia wenhua yanjiu shumu 夏史夏文化研究書目 (Bibliography of books on Xia history and culture), Zhou Hongxiang 周鴻翔, ed., Xianggang daxue 香港大學, Zhongwenxi 中文系, 1990.

Bainian jiaguxue lunzhu mu 百年甲骨學論著目 (15.5, *Bibliography*)

Zhanguo Qin Han shi lunwen suoyin 戰國秦漢史論文索引 (Index of articles on the history of the Warring States, Qin, and Han), Zhang Chuanxi 張傳璽, Hu Zhihong 胡志宏, Chen Keyun 陳柯雲, Liu

Huazhu 劉華祝, Beijing daxue, 1983. This large-scale, unannotated bibliography of secondary scholarship covers articles written between 1900 and 1980 in China, Taiwan, and Hong Kong, including articles appearing in the main archaeological journals. Arrangement is by period and by topic. A continuation covers books published from 1900 to 1990 and articles from 1981 to 1990: *Zhanguo Qin Han shi lunzhu suoyin; xubian lunwen 1981–1990; quanzhu 1900–1990* 戰國秦漢史論著索引, 續編論文 1981–1990, 全著 1900–1990 (Continuation to index of articles and books on the history of the Warring States, Qin and Han; articles, 1981–90; books, 1900–90), Beijing daxue, 1992.

The China volumes of the latest Japanese scholarly, multi-volume history of the world usually contain up-to-date bibliographies of Japanese secondary scholarship—for example:

Sekai rekishi taikei 世界歷史大系 (World history series), *Senshi–Kô-Kan* 先史–后漢 (Prehistory to Later Han), Matsumaru Michio 松丸道雄 (1934–), ed., Yamakawa, forthcoming. Volume 1 of a 5-volume series on China.

Archaeological journals often carry detailed bibliographies of a particular subject or region (12.3). On the textual sources for the pre-Qin, see Chapter 19.

Societies and Yearbooks

Zhongguo shixuehui 中國史學會 (Chinese history society), founded in 1979. The society compiles the *Zhongguo lishixue nianjian* 中國歷史學年鑑.[13] It includes chapters on the state of the field in special subjects; state-of-the-field essays arranged by topic and by period, including the pre-Qin; brief reviews of new (and reprinted) books and monographs; a calendar of the main conferences; brief descriptions of archaeological discoveries arranged by province; obituaries; bibliography of books and articles arranged by period. The yearbook covers Chinese studies of world history as well as Chinese history.

Zhongguo guwenzi yanjiuhui 中國古文字研究會 (Chinese association for the study of pre-Qin scripts), 1979. Since 1986, the association has published the annual journal *Guwenzi yanjiu* 古文字研究, Zhonghua.

---

[13] *Zhongguo lishixue nianjian* (Yearbook of Chinese historical studies), Sanlian, 1980– . Appears about one year after the year covered.

Nihon kôkotsugakkai 日本甲骨學會 (Japanese association for the study of oracle-bone inscriptions). Publishes the journal *Kôkotsugaku* 甲骨學 (irregular, has bibliography of oracle-bone and bronze inscriptions), 1952– .

Xia-Shang xuehui 夏商學會 (Xia-Shang society), founded in 1982. Holds annual meetings.

Zhongguo Xian-Qinshi xuehui 中國先秦史學會 (China pre-Qin history society), founded in 1982.

Zhongguo Yin-Shang wenhua xuehui 中國殷商文化學會 (China Yin-Shang culture society), founded in 1989.

SSEC (The Society for the Study of Early China, University of California, Berkeley). Publishes *Early China* (1975– , annual). This began in 1969 as *Newsletter* of the Society for the Study of Pre-Han China. It is a lively and informative professional journal carrying articles, review articles, and surveys of Chinese and Japanese scholarship (including a translation of the bibliographical review on early China appearing in the May issue of *Shigaku zasshi* 史學雜誌 every year). There is an annual bibliography as well as abstracts of Ph.D. dissertations. The society has published some important monographs and also puts out *Early China News*, which carries information about the profession.

14

Prehistoric Signs and Symbols

There have been many theories about the origin of Chinese characters, including that they developed from knot tying (like Inca Qipu), from notched tallies, from hexagrams, or from the hand of a single inventor. To the extent that some of these theories can provide an interesting hint, and because they convinced many Chinese scholars for over two thousand years, they are briefly examined (14.1). Until the mid-twentieth century, it was quite widely believed that Chinese characters were derived from cuneiform or hieroglyphs (see 12.1, note 4). Since then, the climate of opinion has changed—local invention has replaced diffusion as the archaeologists' default hypothesis, moreover, chance discovery and the archaeologist's spade have turned up some evidence on long-lasting media such as turtle shell, pottery, or jade to support the local invention view. The evidence (14.2–6) predates the Shang oracle-bone inscriptions (Chapter 15) and suggests that the characters had different origins within the China area (14.7).

14.1   Mnemonics

The earliest method of keeping records according to the *Yijing* 易經 (Classic of changes) was by tying knots in string.[1] This technique has been found in many cultures from all over the world from ancient times to the present day and is not unknown to anyone who has ever tied a knot in a handkerchief or used a rosary. In China, according to an ancient commentary on the *Yijing*, large knots were used for important matters, small knots for lesser ones. The system

---

[1] *Yijing*, "Xici," *xia* 系辭下 (Commentary on the appended phrases), ii: "Shanggu jiesheng er zhi" 上古結繩而治 (in archaic times, good government was achieved by knotting string). This is the first known usage of the expression *shanggu*.

could have been further elaborated by using different colored strings and by varying the number and length of the strings and the spaces between the knots. Some of the non-Han peoples in China until recently still used knot tying as a mnemonic, usually for numbers or dates. The only traces to have survived in Han culture are possibly the characters (chiefly numerals), some of whose earliest forms may have been derived from representations of string knots;[2] take, for example, the following oracle or bronze-script characters:

╽	*shi* 十 (ten)	Ʊ	*nian* 廿 (twenty)
卅	*sa* 卅 (thirty)	卌	*xi* 卌 (forty)
⸙	*qian* 千 (thousand)	拜	*peng* 朋 (two strings of five cowries)

Pre-Qin and Han dynasty texts also mention notched tallies (*qi* 契), sometimes linked to the discovery of writing. They were used for recording contract details such as numbers or dates on bamboo or wood. Forty made of bone from a tomb dating from the third millennium were excavated at Liuwan 柳灣, Qinghai, in 1974–75 (*Kaogu xuebao*, 1976.4). They have varying numbers of notches (*chi* 齒), but neither signs nor writing on them. Several of the Han bamboo strips (*Hanjian* 漢簡) are in the form of notched tallies, and they have writing. Tallies were still in use for communication or for counting days by certain non-Han peoples in China until recently. The characters for the digits one to eight resemble notches, but nobody would therefore claim that writing was derived from notching. Writing is a record of the sounds and meanings of words using a coherent system of graphs. The tallies are simply another form of mnemonic.

Early writers (including Xu Shen) mention the *bagua* 八卦 (eight trigrams) in the context of the discovery of writing. This is unlikely. New evidence suggests that the *bagua* derived from a

---

[2] Liu Xie 劉勰 (ca. 465–522) is the earliest to note that the ancient practice of keeping records by tying knots was still in use in his day among non-Han peoples (the Qiang 羌 and the Hu 胡). He also says that peddlers kept records of their cash in a similar way; see *The Literary Mind and the Carving of Dragons* (*Wenxin diaolong* 文心雕龍), 290–91 (30.4). See also Xu Zhongshu 徐中舒 (1898–1991), "Jiesheng yisu kao" 結繩遺俗考 (Investigation of the practice of knot tying), in *Xu Zhongshu lishi lunwen xuanji* 徐中舒歷史論文選輯 (Selected historical papers of Xu Zhongshu), 2 vols., Zhonghua, 1998, 705–12 (originally published in *Shuowen yuekan* 説文月刊, 1944.6).

method of divination based on a game dating back to Neolithic times. One hypothesis is that you guessed three times whether the number of sticks or stalks in a bundle was odd or even. The results of the three guesses were then written in a simple numerical annotation (three evens, three odds, two odds and one even, and so on).[3] Even was written with the ancient character for 6 (like an inverted "v," much later written with a broken line). Odd was, and remains, the character for one, a single straight line. The diviner based his prediction on which of the eight possible combinations of odd and even was scored. It was only in the mid-Zhou that the two basic annotations began to be called *yinxiao [yao]* 陰爻 and *yangxiao [yao]* 陽爻, and that the eight trigrams were combined to form 64 named hexagrams (*gua* 卦), each composed of two trigrams and an associated meaning forming a comprehensive wisdom text based on Yin-yang 陰陽 theory. In short, the trigrams started as numerals of the earliest known Chinese script; they cannot therefore be the origin of it, but are derived from a common source.[4]

For more than two thousand two hundred years the invention of the characters was credited to one of the scribes of the legendary Yellow Emperor, Cang Jie 倉頡. The first surviving mention of him dates from the third century BC. A Later Han writer suggests that he drew his inspiration from the realization that the tracks of birds

[3] Nobody knows for sure the origin of the *bagua*; for the extremely complex post-Han method of casting a hexagram using 50 yarrow stalks and the much simpler method of tossing three coins, see Richard John Lynn, 1994 (Table 26, 19.2), 19–22.

[4] On the earliest evidence of Chinese mathematics, see Wu Wenjun 吳文俊, 1998 (37.1), vol. 1, 115–268. It was Zhang Zhenglang 張政烺 (1914–) who first showed that the *bagua* were recorded in the oracle-bone and bronze scripts in the form of strings of digits (the so-called strange characters, *qizi* 奇字), in which what counted was the alternation of odd and even, not the actual numerals themselves; see his "Shishi Zhouchu qingtongqi mingwen zhong de Yigua" 試釋周初青銅器銘文中的易卦 (Exploratory interpretation of *Yi* hexagrams in early Zhou bronze script), *Kaogu xuebao* 4: 403–15 (1980); Zhang's article is translated by H. Huber et al in *EC* 6: 80–96 (1980–81); see also Li Ling 李零, "Zaoqi bushi de xin faxian" 早期卜筮的新發現 (New discoveries of early milfoil divination), in his *Zhongguo fangshu kao* 中國方術考 (Studies on Chinese divinatory and medical arts), Renmin Zhongguo, 1993, 218–80.

and animals indicate in a consistent way different species and types.[5] There is no reliable evidence that such a person ever existed, although the first known users of the Chinese script were indeed, as the story suggests, court officials, namely, the diviners and scribes of the Shang kings.

14.2   Rock Art

Rock art (*yanhua* 岩畫) in China was first cataloged in the sixth century AD by Li Daoyuan 酈道元 in his *Shuijingzhu* 水經注, which contains descriptions of 20 different sites (35.3.1). Recent years have seen the discovery of many more sites, some prehistoric. The petroglyphs are usually painted or carved onto rocks or cliffs and have been found mainly in the northwest and in Tibet, in the northeast, and along the southeast coast. It is not easy to date them with any accuracy. Many show striking similarities to prehistoric rock art found elsewhere in the world. The main subjects are hunting, fertility and other religious rites, dances, and battles.[6] Zhu Qixiang 朱岐祥 shows that the stylized depictions of men, women, deer, oxen, horses and other animals, snakes, hands, feet, eyes, mountains, and chariots bear a strong resemblance to the oracle-bone and bronze script graphs for the words for these things. The petroglyphs almost certainly provided forms for some of the most common characters (as they did for other early writing systems found elsewhere in the world), but they were not themselves part of a writing system representing words with sounds and meanings.[7] Long after the inven-

---

[5] The Postface to the *Shuowen jiezi* 說文解字 (2.2.1). The first legends about the invention of the Chinese characters are curiously late; see Boltz, 1994 (2.3.2), 129–38.

[6] For a comprehensive study of Chinese rock art that puts it in comparative perspective, see Gai Shanlin, 蓋山林, *Zhongguo yanhuaxue* 中國岩畫學 (The study of Chinese rock art), Shumu wenxian, 1995. For a more popular treatment with many excellent color photographs, see Song Yaoliang 宋耀良, *Zhongguo shiqian shen'ge renmian yanhua* 中國史前神格人面岩畫 (Mythical human faces in China's prehistoric petroglyphs), HK: Sanlian, 1992. Note also Tang Huisheng, "Theory and Methods in Chinese Rock Art Studies," *Rock Art Research* 10.2: 83–90 (1993).

[7] "Lun yanhua yu wenzi de qiyuan" 論岩畫與文字的起源 (On rock art and the origin of writing) in his *Jiaguwen yanjiu* 甲骨文研究 (Research on oracle-bone script), Liren, 1998, 1–22.

tion of Chinese characters, non-literate peoples in China continued to cover rocks and cliffs with petroglyphs. The Han people also continued the old practice, but used characters instead (*moyai* 摩崖; see 17.3).

14.3 Early Turtle Shell and Bone Inscriptions

A small number of symbols carved on turtle shells and bones have been found that appear to predate by several millennia the Shang oracle-bone inscriptions. Among the earliest are those from the Peiligang 裴李崗 site of Jiahu 賈湖 (7000–5800 BC) in northern Henan. There are nine signs on eight separate shells. They are dated to 6000 BC. Two bear a close resemblance to oracle-bone graphs, one for *mu* 目 (eye) and the other for *ri* 日 (sun); of the remainder, two have not been deciphered, and five appear to be numbers. There are also signs (one of which is complex) on several bone flutes from the same site. It is hard to conceive how these few symbols from a primitive Neolithic culture predating the oracle-bone graphs by some 4,000 years can have had any direct connection with the writing system of the Shang. Moreover, unlike the characters in the inscriptions, these early symbols do not usually occur in a series, but singly, one on each shell. They are therefore best considered not as early writing, but as signs or emblems having no connection with the representation of speech.[8] So far, the earliest claim for marks that may well be writing are the characters *liubu* 六卜 incised on both sides of a scapula from a Yueshi 岳石 culture site (1700–1500 BC) in Zibo 淄博 county, Shandong.[9] Next come two bones from Erligang, Zhengzhou, possibly dating from the mid-Shang. One has only one character; the other has 10 that await interpretation, unless indeed, as has been suggested, they have no meaning, being merely 10 graphs incised for exercise.[10]

[8] *Wuyang Jiahu* 舞陽賈湖 (Wuyang Jiahu), Henan Wenkaosuo, ed., 2 vols., Kexue, 1999, vol. 2, 984–91; color plates 47–48.

[9] *Zhongguo wenwu bao* 中國文物報 535: 1 (1997.18.5).

[10] *Zhengzhou Erligang* 鄭州二里崗, Kexue, 1959, plate 30.

14.4 Pottery Pictographs

The main medium on which Neolithic symbols have been found is pottery. Pottery symbols (*taoqi fuhao* 陶器符號 or *taofu* 陶符 for short) have been found at sites all over China. They date from the early Neolithic right down to the third century BC. They can be divided into three kinds—pictographs (this section), marks (14.5), and early characters (14.6). The pictographs are like graphic signs (not unlike some of those found in rock art). Sometimes they are composed of separate components. The earliest discovered so far are three on Jiahu shards, two of which are similar to many later finds: ⊕ ☼ .[11] Sixteen vessels or shards have also been found at Dawenkou 大汶口 sites in Shandong. Each has one symbol engraved on it. One is a radiating sun as large as that of Jiahu and also placed on the upper part of the vase. Of the six different motifs, the two most common are 🌿 and ⤳ . The first appears to be the sun above what looks like a crescent moon or a three- or five-pointed altar or mountain; the second is an ax. They date from between 4200 and 2600 BC.[12] Two dozen other examples of the first symbol have been found at other sites in Shandong, Anhui, Zhejiang, and Hubei. They are similar to the sacred bird emblems found on half a dozen or so Liangzhu jades. We know that the *yangniao* 陽鳥 (sun-bird) was the talisman or totem of the peoples who inhabited the lower Yangzi region.[13] This suggests that Liangzhu symbols, and possibly also those from Dawenkou, may have served the same function as the clan emblems on early bronzes. On the other hand, non-Han potters in Yunnan in modern times have been observed putting a circle above what looks like a crescent resting on a five-pointed object in a design similar to that on the Dawenkou ceramics. When asked its

[11] *Wuyang Jiahu* 舞陽賈湖, vol. 1, 207; vol. 2, 984–991.

[12] Wang Zhenzhong 王震中, "Shilun taowen A (🌿), B (⤳) yu dahuo xing yu huozheng" 試論陶文與大火星與火正 (Preliminary discussion of the pottery symbols Dahuo and Huozheng), *Kaogu yu wenwu* 1997.5.

[13] The sun-bird was said to live inside the sun; it may have been connected with sun worship. The bird in shamanistic ritual symbolized the soul or the instrument for carrying it into heaven. Wu Hung (Wu Hong 巫鴻), "Bird Motifs in Eastern Yi Art," *Orientations* 16,10: 30–41 (1985); Hayashi Minao 林巳奈夫, "Liangzhu wenhua he Dawenkou wenhua zhong de tuxiang jihao" 良渚文化和大汶口文化中的圖像記號 (The pictographs and signs in the Liangzhu and Dawenkou cultures), *Dongnan wenhua*, 1991.3 and 4.

meaning, one potter replied that it showed that he had made the pot under the light of the sun and the moon; another said the mark showed the sun and the moon and a mountain and that storing grain in a pot like this would bring luck—a salutary warning, perhaps, against overinterpreting.[14]

Plenty of other symbols of fish (from the west) and birds (from the east) have been found painted on prehistoric pottery from sites all over China.[15] The bird-eating-fish design (*niaoxianyu tu'an* 鳥銜魚圖案) is a good example. The best known is on a Yangshao vase from Yancun 閻村 in Henan. It shows a cormorant holding a carp in its beak with a stone ax to the right (illustrated in Chang, 1986 [12.1], 137). This is often interpreted as a funerary vase (when discovered it held the bones of an adult) for the leader of the tribe (the cormorant) who had used his power (the ax) to conquer his enemy (the carp). Others have compared various examples of the design, down to those found in Later Han tombs, and have argued that it is a sexual symbol expressing transmigration sorcery. Before jumping to a conclusion, all known examples of a design should be compared, and the date and time taken into account. It should not be assumed that only one interpretation is correct. It is quite possible that the designs held different meanings and that these may have changed over time. Some of the pictures on the prehistoric pottery developed into more abstract forms along similar lines to the earliest characters. But thereafter they become ever more abstract, ending up as pure design elements or patterns whose earlier meanings had probably long since been forgotten.

[14] Wang Hengjie 王恒杰, "Cong minzuxue faxian de xin cailiao kan Dawenkou wenhua taozun de *wenzi*," 從民族學發現的新材料看大汶口文化陶尊的'文字' (The 'writing' on the Dawenkou *zun* as seen from the point of view of new materials from ethnographic studies), *Kaogu*, 1991.12.

[15] For a wide-ranging summary, see Lu Sixian 陸思賢, *Shenhua kaogu* 神話考古 (The archaeology of myths), Wenwu, 1995; see also David N. Keightley, "Art, Ancestors, and the Origin of Writing in China," *Representations* 56: 68–95 (1996). A modern theory has the characters derived from pictures of fish heads (based on the designs found on Neolithic pottery), see *Zhongguo Hanzi wenhua daguan* 中國漢字文化大觀 (The culture of Chinese characters), He Jiuying 何九盈 et al., eds., Beijing daxue, 1995.

14.5   Pottery Marks

The second type of pottery symbol is nearly always composed of geometric marks, consisting of simple straight lines or curves; some resemble the oracle-bone or bronze characters for numbers; some, notched tallies, for example, 彡 . About half consist of a single vertical line. Particular marks are usually found in the same place and on the same type of pot. There are a total of about 100 separate types of mark. At a rough estimate one in every 30 or 40 pottery vessels had a single mark incised with a sharp object, often before the firing took place and usually at the rim.[16] Several hundred shards with such marks have been found. Some scholars have gathered together all known pottery marks to try to show that they formed a set of numerals. Such demonstrations are not convincing because they throw together single graphs from regions far apart in both space and time and removed from their contexts. The weakness of such an approach is illustrated by John DeFrancis who shows that the proofreaders' marks as listed in Webster's *Dictionary* bear a striking resemblance to 19 of the pottery symbols.[17] A similar flaw undermines claims that the Olmec of ancient North America used an oracle-bone style script or that the Hunanese female script (*nüshu* 女書, see 39.1) is related to pottery marks.[18]

Nobody knows the function of the pottery marks. Some have speculated that they represent the tribal owners of the pottery, numbers representing dates, or the hallmarks of their makers. This last may be nearer the truth. Dai 傣 potters in Yunnan have been observed scratching a distinguishing symbol, perhaps a number, on their pots with a fingernail before putting them into a shared kiln in

---

[16] There were, for example, a total of 500,000 shards unearthed at Banpo 半坡 (of which 113 had a mark of one of 27 different types).

[17] See his "Chinese Prehistoric Symbols and American Proof Readers' Marks," *JCL* 19.1: 116–21 (1991).

[18] Li Jinglin 李荆林, *Nüshu yu shiqian taowen yanjiu* 女書與史前陶文研究 (Research on female script and prehistoric pottery script), Zhuhai, 1995. A careful and imaginative reconstruction of the early history of the *nüshu* comparing it with pottery symbols and early pottery script (with illustrations from more than 50 prehistoric sites) and both with the oracle-bone and bronze scripts as well with some of the oldest non-Han scripts and rock art symbols.

order to identify theirs from those of other potters.[19] But one thing is clear. The pottery marks predate the earliest known Chinese characters by several millennia and then continue in use to the end of the Zhou (from which time characters were used to identify the maker, date, and use of pottery and much later, porcelain vessels). During all this time, they remained as they had been when they first appeared, limited in form, and limited in number, essentially without development. The characters, on the other hand, from their first appearance in the Shang, went through many changes during these centuries. Some were discarded, and new ones developed. Overall, their numbers rose from 4,000 to 9,000. The conclusion is inescapable: much later than their first appearance the pottery marks may have been one of the sources on which the devisers of the script drew for character forms, but they themselves existed apart from and uninfluenced by the development of the· characters (14.7).

14.6   Multiple Pottery Symbols and Characters

Only a few shards of prehistoric pottery bearing multiple symbols have been found. They include

One shard with four graphs and four symbols from a Longshan site found at Longqiuzhuang, Gaoyou city 高郵龍虬莊 in Jiangsu (early third millennium, excavated in 1993). See *Longqiuzhuang* 龍虬莊, Ke-xue, 1999, color plate 9; Rao Zongyi 饒宗頤, "Tan Gaoyou Longqiuzhuang taopian de kehua wen" 談高郵龍虬莊陶片的刻畫文 (Discussion of the incised symbols on a pottery shard from Longqiu village, Gaoyou), *Dongnan wenhua* 4: 11–12 (1996).

One Longshan shard with two or three groups of symbols from Jingyanggang, Yanggu county 陽榖縣景陽崗, in Shandong (dated to about 2300 BC and excavated in 1995; see *Wenwubao* 1/14 1998).

One Longshan shard with 11 symbols arranged vertically in five columns from Dinggongcun, Zouping county 鄒平縣丁公村, in Shandong (dated to about 2100 BC and excavated in 1991–92; *Kaogu* 1993.4 for a discussion favoring this to be writing and *Zhongyuan wenwu* 1996.2

---

[19] Wang Ningsheng 汪寧生, "Cong yuanshi jishi dao wenzi faming" 從原始記事到文字發明 (From primitive ways of recording to the invention of characters), *Kaogu xuebao*, 1981.1.

for an article by Cao Dingyun 曹定雲 who thinks it is a fake). If it is writing, as Li Xueqin points out, then it is the first known example of graphs being arranged from top to bottom and from right to left.

One Liangzhu pot with nine graphs vertically on one of the feet in the Harvard University Art Museums. Liangzhu pottery marks and symbols, including those on the Harvard pot, are reproduced with a bibliography by Qian Yuzhi 錢玉趾 in *Dongfang wenming zhi guang—Liangzhu wenhua faxian 60 zhounian jinian lunwenji* 東方文明之光一良渚文化發現60周年紀念論文集 (13.2), 454–61.

Four shards (with between four and 12 graphs each arranged horizontally) from among several excavated in 1973 from Wuchengcun 吳城村 in Jiangxi (mid-second millennium BC).

There is considerable controversy about all these pieces. Many believe that the multiple pottery graphs on them are a form of writing. Most are of the opinion that the writing is not related to the Shang oracle-bone script but could be the script of the peoples of the areas in which the shards were found, possibly Yue 越 in the south and Yi 夷 in Shandong. Although they may look like early writing, there is no way to prove that they have any connection to speech since we do not know enough about the early language of the Yue and Yi.

The Wucheng shards are particularly interesting. The site is that of a regional early Bronze Age culture (13.2.2). Other shards have been found here from two later phases extending to the end of the Shang and Western Zhou. They bear graphs similar to the early period Anyang oracle-bone characters, but the inscriptions are shorter than those on the first-phase shards.

A few isolated prehistoric pottery marks are tantalizingly similar to early oracle-bone characters, for example, those found at a Neolithic site at Fengbu Shuangtun 蜂埠雙墩 in Anhui (5000–4000 BC) or at a Daixi culture site at Yangjiawan, Yichang 宜昌揚家灣, in Hubei (4400–3300 BC).[20] As we approach the Shang, more pottery graphs similar to those on the oracle-bone inscriptions begin to appear, for example, those at Taixicun, Gaocheng county 藁城縣臺

---

[20] Xu Dali 徐大力, "Fengbu Shuangtun xinshiqi yizhi taoqi kehua chulun" 蜂埠雙墩新石器遺址陶器刻劃初論 (Preliminary discussion of incised pottery marks from a Neolithic site at Fengbu Shuangtun), *Wenwu yanjiu* 文物研究 5, Qi-Lu, 1989, and *Kaogu* 1987.8 for the Yangjiawan marks.

西村, in Henan (13.2.2; *Wenwu* 1974.8)[21] and those found at An-yang itself.[22] Several thousand shards bearing what are clearly pot-tery characters (*taowen* 陶文) have survived from the sites of at least 30 Spring and Autumn and Warring States cities, but by that time there is plenty of other epigraphic evidence for the development of Chinese characters (17.1–2).

Most of the early pottery characters are difficult to read. Some are similar to the Shang bronze characters, which are more archaic or at least more pictographic than those on the oracle bones.[23]

14.7 · Conclusions

Mainly on the basis of pottery pictographs and marks on some of Andersson's Yangshao finds at Xindian 辛店 (Gansu), the influen-tial paleographer Tang Lan 唐蘭 (1900–78) proposed in the 1930s that Chinese characters had a history of at least 4,000 to 5,000 years.[24] After the publication of more evidence in the 1950s and 1960s, mainly from the Yangshao site at Banpo 半坡 and the Long-shan site at Dawenkou 大汶口, scholars both inside China and out

---

[21] Gao Ming 高明, *Gu taowen huibian* 古陶文彙編 (Collection of ancient pottery script), Zhonghua, 1990, contains exceptionally clear rubbings and transcriptions of 2,602 pre-Qin and Qin pottery shards with inscriptions on them discovered up to 1987, including 114 shards from Shang sites with what he believes are 145 characters, and 46 from the Western Zhou with 73 charac-ters. The companion volume, Gao Ming and Ge Yinghui 葛英會, *Gu taowenzi zheng* 古陶文字徵 (Inquiry into ancient pottery characters), Zhonghua, 1991, is an annotated listing of the various forms (drawn by hand) of 1,823 different pottery characters, mainly as found on the shards illustrated in Gao (1990). For a similar listing of 1,700 pottery characters with 9,000 examples, see Xu Gufu 徐谷甫 and Wang Tinglin 王廷林, *Gu taozi hui* 古陶字彙 (Lexicon of ancient pottery characters), Shanghai shudian, 1994, 1996. This has the advantage that all the characters are reproductions of rubbings rather than drawings. There is a stroke-count index.

[22] Eighty-two shards with writing on them (out of a total of 25,000 shards) were found at Xiaotun 小屯, during the excavations there in 1928–36. Fifteen of the 82 have between two and three marks in a row.

[23] Zhu Qixiang 朱歧祥, "Lun taofu he taowen" 論陶符和陶文 (On pottery symbols and pottery writing), in his *Jiaguwen yanjiu* 甲骨文研究 (Research on oracle-bone script), Liren, 1998, 23–31.

[24] Tang Lan, *Guwenzixue daolun* 古文字學導論 (Introduction to the study of pre-Qin Chinese scripts), 1934; rev. ed., 1936, 47a; rpnt., Qi-Lu, 1981, 399.

again began claiming that the characters had a 6,000-year history.[25] In recent years, most have been more cautious in their judgment, preferring to wait until more direct evidence is available and to use a stricter definition of what constitutes the difference between isolated marks and symbols and a writing system representing speech.[26]

Just as with the two other ancient (and earlier) writing systems, Mesopotamian cuneiform and Egyptian hieroglyphic, writing in China was able to draw on ancient traditions of pictorial recording (*tuhua jishi* 圖畫記事) and of geometric symbols, neither of which traditions had direct connections with the spoken language. It may also be, as several scholars have suggested, that pictorial symbols (e.g., on prehistoric rock art and pottery) are the ancestors of pictographic characters, while mnemonics such as notched tallies or knot tying and geometric patterns on painted pottery and incised symbols (such as those on prehistoric pottery) are the forerunners of the indicative characters symbolizing concepts such as numbers (16.2).[27]

[25] Li Xiaoding 李孝定 (1918–), *Hanzi de qiyuan yu yanbian luncong* 漢字的起源與演變論叢 (Articles on the origin and development of Chinese characters), Lianjing, 1986 (the first article appeared in 1969). Guo Moruo, the leading Marxist paleographer and historian of ancient China lent his influence to the view that the pottery pictographs were a direct forerunner of Chinese characters, which *therefore* [my emphasis] could be said to have a 6,000-year history: "Gudai wenzi zhi bianzheng de fazhan" 古代文字之辯證的發展 (The dialectic development of ancient Chinese writing), *Kaogu xuebao* 1: 1–13 (1972). This view was rapidly espoused by other leading scholars in both China and abroad, including Tang Lan 唐蘭, Yu Xingwu 于省吾 (1896–1984), *Wenwu*, 1973.2; Ping-ti Ho (He Bingdi 何炳棣), *The Cradle of the East: An Enquiry into the Indigenous Origins of Techniques and Ideas of Neolithic and Early Historic China, 5000–1000 BC*, HKCUP and UChP, 1975. Cheung Kwong-yue (Zhang Guangyu 張光裕) also tends toward the same view: "Recent Archaeological Evidence Relating to the Origin of Chinese Characters," in *The Origins of Chinese Civilization*, David N. Keightley, ed., UCP, 1983, 323–91.

[26] Rao Zongyi 饒宗頤 compares the pottery symbols found in China with those from the Indus valley and the ancient Near East: *Fuhao chuwen yu zimu— Hanzi shu* 符號初文與字母—漢字樹 (Symbols, early writing, and letters—the tree of Chinese characters), HK: Shangwu, 1998. See also Gao Ming 高明 (1926–), "Lüetan gudai taoqi fuhao, taoqi tuxiang he taoqi wenzi" 略談古代陶器符號陶器圖像和陶器文字 (Brief discussion of ancient pottery marks, pictures, and characters), *Xueshu jilin* 學術集林, vol. 2, Shanghai yuandong, 1994, 73–100.

[27] For a recent statement of this view, see Zhu Minshen 祝敏申, *The Shuowen jiezi: The Dawn of Studies of the Ancient Characters*, Fudan University

Footnote continued on next page

That is to say, the characters may not have had one origin—different types of character may have derived from different traditions of keeping records and have come from different archaeological cultures.

As with the Egyptian hieroglyphs, the reason that so little prior evidence of gestation of the Shang script has been unearthed is presumably that writing was recorded mainly on perishable materials (indeed, at least one source suggests that inscriptions on bronze and stone were used because the ancient kings feared that their records on bamboo and silk would rot or be eaten by insects).[28]

The evidence for a wider use of writing in the early Bronze Age than that found on the Shang oracle-bone inscriptions comes from the brief inscriptions on bronze vessels (including bronze seals) dating from the same period and from pottery writing, some of which may be slightly earlier (14.5). In addition, there are fragmentary examples of Shang writing on stone and jade. There are traces of brush writing on Shang pottery and on some of the later oracle bones, and it is believed that the divination records were initially written on a material such as bamboo (15.3).[29]

There are plenty of references on the oracle bones to *ce* 冊 and *dian* 典, which appear to have been the records of important sacrifi-

---

Press, 1998, 33. While this may have been the case in a general sense, in practice, only a tiny number of the graphs in Shang oracle-bone script appear to be directly derived from geometric symbols, for example, 㐅 十 (standing for "5" and "7," respectively), see Lin Xiao'an 林小安, "Zhongguo wenzi de qiyuan zhi wojian" 中國文字的起源之我見 (My view of the origin of Chinese characters), *Quantong wenhua yu xiandaihua* 3: 86–90 (1993); idem, "Yinqi benyi lungao" 殷契本義論稿 (Draft discussion of etyma in oracle-bone script), *Chutu wenxian yanjiu* 出土文獻研究 (Research on excavated documents), vol. 5, Kexue, 1999, 6–24.

[28] Mozi 墨子 (468–376 BC), *Mozi, juan* 8, "Mingguixia" 明鬼下. This is one of several passages in which the *Mozi* discusses the use of writing to record good or bad conduct for the benefit of later generations.

[29] Jiang Hongyi 蔣紅毅 et al., "Shilun Yindai jiance de shiyong" 試論殷代簡冊的使用 (Examination of the use of bamboo documents in the Yin), *Yindu xuekan* 2: 11–14 (1992); also Li Xueqin (1985), 414–33.

Wang Yunzhi 王蘊智, *Yin-Zhou guwen tongyuan fenhua xianxiang tansuo* 殷周古文同源分化現象探索 (2.3.2) argues that in origin *dian* 典 and *ce* 冊 were the same word (represented by the same character) meaning "the records of important rituals"—for example, those conducted before the king went to war.

cial rituals. In the later oracle-bone inscriptions, the phrase *zuoce* 作
册 is usually taken to mean "recorder" or "scribe." There is also a
reference in the *Shangshu* saying that "the Yin ancestors had *ce* and
dian." It is generally assumed that the Spring and Autumn sense of
ce (bamboo writing strips; record) and *dian* (collection of *ce*; important documents) already existed in the Shang.

Another indication of a wider use of writing in the Shang comes
from an analysis of the oracle-bone characters themselves. Some of
the characters are compounds whose component parts are found
neither on the oracle-bone inscriptions nor on the Shang bronze inscriptions. This suggests that the inscriptions contain only part of a
larger Shang lexicon recorded on other media, including, presumably, bamboo and possibly even silk.

Bamboo is suggested as the original medium for writing by the
arrangement of the characters from top to bottom in vertical columns on some of the pottery inscriptions (14.6), on late-period oracle-bone inscriptions (15.4) and on bronze inscriptions (17.1). It is
also an arrangement which helps explain the forms of the characters
for long-bodied animals, birds, and fishes in the oracle-bone script.
The elephant, horse, tiger, dog, pig, bird, swallow, fish, locust,
snake, dragon, and phoenix, for example, are all shown looking
sideways with their tails (or fins) at the bottom of the character and
the head at the top. Had the script first been written on a medium
other than thin strips of bamboo there would have been no need to
write such long characters vertically (18.1).[30]

If the huge volume of archaeological discoveries going on today
succeeds in unearthing precursors of the Shang oracle-bone script,
they will almost certainly be on nonperishable materials such as
stone, pottery, or bone. But we should not expect that they will
necessarily lead in a direct line backward from the oracle bones discovered at Anyang. The pottery pictographs from Jiahu and Dawenkou in the east, the pottery graphs from Liangzhu in the southeast, and Wucheng in the south may well represent traces of early
writing systems that died out or were absorbed into the earliest
forms of what later became Chinese characters.

---

[30] You Shunzhao 游順釗 (Shun-chiu Yao), "La verticalisation en écriture
chinoise archaique, excursion au-delà des six principes," *Ecritures archaiques,*
systèmes, et déchiffrement, Centre de Recherches Linguistiques sur l'Asie Orientale, 1995, 197–212.

The Shang kings extended their influence if not their direct rule over a considerable number of different peoples and tribes in lowland north China as well as further south. In doing so, they created the conditions and the need to unify into a single writing system what may well have been a number of mnemonic methods and proto writing systems developed by the peoples over whom they ruled or with whom they came into contact through war or trade.

Later history is filled with examples of rulers ordering the creation of new writing systems. In China and its neighbors, it was not uncommon for conquerors or founders of dynasties to do so. It is true of Songtsen Gampo, who sponsored the development of three different Tibetan scripts based on north Indian examples in the early seventh century. It is also true of the Khitan (920), the Tangut (early eleventh century), the Jurchen (early twelfth century), the Mongols (*hPhags-pa*, 1269), the Vietnamese (*Chữnôm*, fourteenth century), and the Manchu (*Manju*, 1599, a modified form of *hPhags-pa*), not to speak of the Koreans (*Hangûl*, 1446). But it could be argued that by the time these scripts were promulgated the knowledge of different writing systems was widespread, and many of them were derived from existing models.

The fact that the first known users of the Chinese script were the diviners and scribes of the Shang kings has led some scholars to hypothesize that they were the first developers of the script.[31] One of the arguments for the timing that this implies is that the oracle-bone script dates from the beginning of the reign of Wu Ding 武丁 (ca. 1200 BC), some years after the establishment of the Shang cult center at Yin (Anyang). This suggests that there had not been much advance in the script since the one or two known examples on bone or on pottery dated to several centuries before.[32] If this is correct, it suggests that it is unlikely that archaeology will ever turn up examples of pre-Anyang script. In this context, it may be significant that the earliest bronze vessels with writing on them were those found buried in the tomb of one of Wu Ding's principal consorts, Fu Hao

---

[31] Xu Zhongshu 徐中舒 and Tang Jiahong 唐嘉弘, "Guanyu Xiadai wenzi de wenti" 關于夏代文字的問題 (On the problem of Chinese characters in the Xia dynasty), *Xiashi luncong* 夏史論叢, Qi-Lu, 1985, 127, 140.

[32] Li Xueqin 李學勤 and Peng Yushang 彭裕商, *Yinxu jiagu fenqi yanjiu* 殷墟甲骨分期研究 (Researches on the periodization of Yinxu oracle bones), Shanghai guji, 1996, 410.

婦好. Most of the inscriptions simply bear the two characters of her name.

The oracle-bone script seems to have the capacity to transcribe speech. Comparison with the evolution of cuneiform in the Near East suggests that this capacity only comes at the end of a long development, to be measured perhaps in centuries. But the first oracle-bone inscriptions may still be close to the stage when the writing system first reached the capacity to transcribe speech, because by the standard of the inscriptions only a few centuries later, they are unstandardized.[33] For example, the forms, the size, and the position of the characters were not fixed, and the proportion of pictographic characters was much greater than it later became. The origin of the characters as a system of writing is therefore most likely to have been around 1500–1100 BC.

If divination was the first extensive use of the characters, this suggests a religious and political origin of Chinese writing rather than an economic one, as with the writing in ancient Mesopotamia.[34] It is a difficult theory to either prove or disprove because, as outlined above, the Shang almost certainly used writing for other purposes on other media, most of which have not survived.

[33] I am grateful to Robert Bagley for helping me formulate this paragraph more clearly. For a comparative framework which suggests a relatively short gestation period, see Boltz (1994) and idem, "Language and Writing," *CHAC*, chapter 2, 74–123.

[34] K. C. Chang, "Writing as the Path to Authority," *Art, Myth and Ritual: The Path to Political Authority in Ancient China*, HUP, 1983, 81–94. On the other hand, Xu Shen seems to suggest an economic origin when he says that after the invention of writing the hundred craftsmen were regulated and the myriad ranks were brought under surveillance (Boltz, 1994, 135). For a comparative view, see Nicholas Postgate, Tao Wang, and Toby Wilkinson, "The Evidence for Early Writing: Utilitarian or Ceremonial?" *Antiquity* 69: 459–80 (1995).

15

Oracle-Bone Inscriptions

15.1 Significance of the Oracle Bones

The fascination of the oracle-bone inscriptions is that they provide the first glimpse of the Chinese language and of Chinese characters centuries before the previously known earliest evidence from the Zhou period. They also provide a glimpse of Huaxia civilization before the Zhou version of Chinese history, before the Confucian classics, before the Qin unification, and before the Han consolidation of the institutions of the early empire.[1]

Until the oracle-bone script was deciphered, very little was known about the Shang other than what was contained in the account of the lineage of the Shang royal house in *Shiji, juan* 3 ("Yin benji" 殷本紀), written 1,000 years after the dynasty had ended, largely on the basis of records that have long been lost. The decipherment confirmed the credibility of the account in the *Shiji*. It also dealt a severe blow to the skeptical approach to the reliability of early Chinese texts taken by the Yigupai 疑古派 (Doubting Antiquity School); see 12.1. The oracle bones provide a great deal of new information about the Shang period, including astronomy and the calendar, climate, animals and plants, farming, local kingdoms, toponyms, military expeditions, sacrifices, personalities, the royal house, and religious beliefs. The discovery of the oracle bones also led to the rediscovery and eventual excavation of the long-lost Shang cult center of Yin.

---

[1] "Oracle-bone script" (*jiaguwen* 甲骨文 or *jiawen* 甲文) is short for *guijia shougu wenzi* 龜甲獸骨文字 (turtle-shell and animal-bone script). In the early twentieth century, it was also called *qiwen* 契文 (incised script), *Yinxu shuqi* 殷墟書契 (Yin ruins inscriptions; *Yinqi* 殷契 for short), *zhenbu wenzi* 貞卜文字 (oracular script; *buci* 卜辭 for short), or *Yinxu buci* 殷墟卜辭 (Yin ruins oracular script). Yinxu 殷墟 is the name given since the Han to the last Shang cult center of Yin after its destruction.

The chapter continues with the discovery of the oracle-bone inscriptions (15.2). The earliest traces of pyromancy are briefly examined (15.3) before turning to the inscriptions themselves (15.4) and the guides, readers, research tools, and reference works to assist in their decipherment and understanding (15.5).

15.2   The Discovery of the Oracle Bones

The first oracle-bone inscriptions to be recognized as such were unearthed at the very end of the nineteenth century from the buried ruins of the Shang cult center of Yin 殷, in the modern village of Xiaotun 小屯, three km (2 miles) to the northwest of Anyang in the northernmost part of Henan province. The discovery of the bones was accidental and, unusually in China, unanticipated.

In the course of Chinese history, divination and fortune-telling have been omnipresent. Scapulimancy and plastromancy (divination using shoulder blades and turtle shells, respectively) were widespread from the Neolithic to the Western Zhou. As might be expected, there are many references to the earlier use of turtle shells for divination in Han and pre-Qin texts, but no scholar appears to have suspected that a Shang royal archive of these records might have been preserved, indeed Sima Qian 司馬遷 reports the rumor that the Xia and Shang deliberately threw away the shells after the divination (although the Zhou stored theirs). He makes no mention of any writing on the shells (*Shiji* 史記, *juan* 128).

During the Sui and the Tang, many people were buried at Anyang and some of the oracle bones were disturbed, but the grave diggers did not realize what they had found and reinterred them.

The modern discovery of the bones was made by peasants digging in the fields around Anyang toward the end of the nineteenth century. Not realizing the value of their discovery, they used them as "dragon bones" (*longgu* 龍骨) for grinding into a tonic infusion or for poultices.[2] An antiques dealer from Weixian in Shandong spotted them while buying bronzes in the neighborhood. He sold

---

[2] "Dragon bones" and "dragon teeth" had been used in Chinese medicine for centuries. They were Tertiary and Pleistocene period fossils. Since the late nineteenth century, paleontologists, archaeologists, and geologists often began their searches at famous sites of dragon-bone deposits. The trail which eventually led to the discovery of Peking Man in 1926 began in this way.

some in Tianjin in 1899 and also to Wang Yirong 王懿榮 (1845–1900), a well-known scholar and collector in Beijing who was at that time the chancellor of the Imperial Academy (Guozijian *jijiu* 國子監祭酒). Wang was the first to realize that the writing on the oracle bones was similar to that on ancient bronze inscriptions, of which he was an expert collector.[3]

He asked his house guest Liu E 劉鶚 (1857–1909) to help him identify the inscriptions on the bones as Shang script. A few months after his discovery, Wang committed suicide by taking poison and throwing himself into a well the day after the allied troops entered Beijing (he had shortly before reluctantly accepted the appointment as leader of the Boxer defense forces). His son sold the bones in 1902 to Liu, who published the first collection of rubbings of the inscriptions in 1903 under the title *Tieyun canggui* 鐵雲藏龜 (The turtles collected by Tieyun [Liu's studio name]), 6 *ce*, 1903.

Word spread, and antique dealers bought up more bones in Anyang but deliberately concealed where they were buying them. It was not until 1908 that a scholar named Luo Zhenyu 羅振玉 (1866–1940), who had first seen an oracle-bone rubbing in his friend Liu E's house in 1902, found out the real source and realized that this was the site of the last capital of the Shang. Meanwhile, the peasants continued to search for bones to sell to the dealers. By the time archaeological excavations began at Anyang in 1928, a large number of oracle bones had already been sold, many to foreign collectors.

---

[3] Li Xueqin 李學勤, Preface to *Wang Yirong ji* 王懿榮集 (Selection of Wang Yirong's writings), Lü Weida 呂偉達, ed. in chief, Qi-Lu, 1999, 1–9; Jean A. Lefeuvre, "Les inscriptions des Shang sur carapaces de tortue et sur os; aperçu historique et bibliographique de la découverte et des premires études," *TP* 61: 1–82 (1975). A second story about the discovery of the oracle bones began to circulate in the 1930s, according to which Wang Yirong, suffering from the ague, consulted one of the imperial physicians, who gave him a prescription requiring the use of "dragon bones." Wang sent a servant to an old pharmacy dating from the Ming, the Darentang 達仁堂, outside the Xuanwu gate 玄武門, to get the medicine. On opening the package, he found to his astonishment that some of the dragon bones had strange writing on them, so he immediately sent the servant back to buy up the remaining stock. This is an unlikely story for various reasons, not the least being that there was no Darentang pharmacy outside the Xuanwu gate or indeed anywhere in Beijing. There was, however, a pharmacy of this name in Tianjin.

At first there was a suspicion of forgery. But thanks to the efforts of a small but outstanding group of scholars, a specialized field of oracle-bone script studies developed. The four who created the new field were Luo Zhenyu; his pupil Wang Guowei 王國維 (1877–1927), considered by many to be the most outstanding Chinese classical scholar of the twentieth century;[4] Dong Zuobin 董作賓 (1895–1963);[5] and Guo Moruo.[6]

Wang used the oracle bones in 1917 to authenticate the names of the last nine Shang rulers as found in the *Shiji* king lists. He also made major contributions to Shang chronology. Dong was the first to propose systematic criteria for dating the oracle bones and also to make a detailed study of the Shang calendar. Guo not only interpreted the inscriptions but also used them to write the first Marxist accounts of ancient China.

The main scholars of the next generation were Hu Houxuan 胡厚宣 (1911–95), and Yu Xingwu 于省吾 (1896–1984), both pupils of Dong Zuobin. They in turn trained the current generation of Chinese oracle-bone specialists.

15.3   Pyromancy

Scapulimancy began to emerge in China during the late Yangshao period (the earliest traces to be discovered so far date from about 4000 BC). During the Longshan culture (2900–2000 BC), this method of divination (the generic term is *pyromancy*) was gradually spreading over the rest of north China and into Korea. By the time of the Erlitou culture (1900–1500 BC), just before the Shang, it was becoming more widespread. Traces of prehistoric pyromancy have been found at 59 sites in eight provinces (usually on the shoulder blades of oxen, sheep, deer, pigs, and occasionally humans). They are less well prepared than those of the Shang. Several bear signs and symbols, but not characters (14.3).[7] Turtles were worshipped for their

[4] Joey Bonner, *Wang Kuo-wei: An Intellectual Biography*, HUP, 1986.

[5] *Jiaguxue wushi nian* 甲骨學五十年 (incompletely translated under the title *Fifty Years of Studies in Oracle Inscriptions*, Tôyô bunko, 1964).

[6] The first part of Guo Moruo's life is told in David Tod Roy, *Kuo Mo-jo: The Early Years*, HUP, 1971.

[7] On the pre-Anyang evidence of scapulimancy, see *Jiaguxue yibai nian* 甲骨學一百年 (15.5), 220–230.

magical properties. Their plastrons are quite commonly found in Neolithic tombs, but they were not normally used for pyromancy. Then, in the Shang, they too began to be used for divination (because the plastron rather than the carapace was usually used, the term is plastromancy). The application of scapulimancy to the divine medium of the turtle shell ushered in the golden age of oracle-bone divination (ca. 1200–1045 BC).

The shells were first cleaned, and then a small, oval-shaped hollow was prepared on the rough side, into which a red-hot bronze point or a heated brand of chaste wood (*jing* 荆) was inserted. This caused a fissure on the smooth side from which branched out horizontal cracks (of which *bu* 卜 may be a graphic representation). These cracks were the omen (*buzhao* 卜兆) that the diviner interpreted as either auspicious or inauspicious responses to the "charge" (main question) he had posed. To take one example: if the king goes hunting on such and such a date, will he get a good bag? After the divination, in order to sort out which cracks belonged to which questions, the practice developed of incising the matter inquired about on the shell or bone with a bronze burin or knife. Occasionally a brush appears to have been used first. Quite possibly the initial records were written on some perishable material such as bamboo before being summarized for posterity on the oracle bones (14.5).[8]

Many of the questions were more elaborate and often contain three or four elements: the time of the divination and the name of the diviner; the question inquired about; and the judgment of the oracle and in some cases the outcome of the action. A few of the inscriptions simply record events. The king seems not to have taken the smallest decision without consulting the oracle, especially as regards picking an auspicious day or time for religious sacrifices or ancestor worship or for his actions, including matters related to birth and marriage, illness or death, hunting, the weather, agriculture (especially the state of the harvest), appointments and dismissals, and military campaigns.

---

[8] David N. Keightley, "Were the Shang Kings Literate? Who Read the Shang Texts and Why? Reflections on Early Chinese Literacy and Scribal Practice," Paper presented to the panel "Literacy in Ancient China," Center for Chinese Studies, Berkeley, 1997.

After the Shang and early Zhou, plastromancy continued in use, with the text of the divination at times written on bamboo strips, but by the Spring and Autumn period, the *Liji* 禮記 criticized the Shang people for attaching more importance to ghosts than to the rites (*Yinren ... xian gui er hou li* 殷人 ... 先鬼而後禮). In the Warring States there were others who faulted the use of turtle shells for divination as being non-rational or inconsistent. Plastromancy did not developed into an abstract system linked to a wisdom text, and by the end of the Han, it had been almost totally replaced by the methods of divination descended from yarrow or milfoil stalk (*Achillea millefolium*) and later enshrined in the *Yijing*.[9] There were, however, manuals still circulating in the Han dynasty on the subject of turtle-shell divination, one of which was the basis for much of "Guice liezhuan" 龜策列傳 (Biographies of the turtle-shell diviners), *Shiji, juan* 128.

The enshrining of Confucianism as the official orthodoxy in the Han spelled the beginning of the end of the use of the turtle for divination, which from the golden days of the Shang had relied on court sponsorship. Some of the Han successor courts continued to practice the old arts, and there was a brief revival at the beginning of the Tang, but thereafter they all but died out except among some of the non-Han peoples who continued, but with scapulimancy.[10] In the Shang and Zhou, the turtle had been a rare item presented to the northern courts as tribute by the peoples of the Yangzi valley and on occasion used as money. By the later empire the Chinese cultural center of gravity had long since shifted to the south, and the turtle had lost its rarity value. It remained a symbol of longevity; it served

---

[9] See Michael Loewe, "Divination by Shells, Bones and Stalks During the Han Period," in Loewe, *Divination, Mythology and Monarchy in Han China*, CUP, 1994, 160–90. See also Léon Vandermeersch, "De la tortue à l'achillée," in *Divination et Rationalité*, J. Vernant et al., eds., Seuil, 1974, 29–51.

[10] *Zhongguo gudai guibu wenhua* 中國古代龜卜文化 (The culture of turtle divination in ancient China), Liu Yujian 劉玉建, Guangxi shifan daxue, 1992, 1993, assembles literary and historical references to turtle divination from the earliest times to its last revival in the early Tang. Even to this day some non-Han peoples in China practice various forms of scapulimancy. It was also practised in other parts of the world. In Scotland up to the eighteenth century, it was called "sleinanachd" or, in English, "reading the speal-bone." The blade-bone of a well-scraped shoulder of mutton rather than the carapace of a turtle was used.

as an ingredient in tonic dishes and potions, but in day-to-day language it was mainly used as a coarse scolding word for cuckold or penis.[11]

15.4 The Oracle-Bone Inscriptions

Of the total published corpus of approximately 155,000 oracle-bone inscriptions, 99.7 percent date from the Shang and were found or excavated at or near the main Shang palace and temple complex in Xiaotun village. Less than 0.001 percent date from the early Shang or from other Shang cities. Less than 0.2 percent come from Western Zhou sites. The finds took place haphazardly from the end of the nineteenth century to 1928, by which time about 100,000 fragments bearing inscriptions had fallen into the hands of private collectors. Thereafter, systematic archaeological excavations conducted at Anyang between 1928 and 1937 by the Shiyusuo and by the Henan Provincial Museum (1929–30) turned up a total of 28,575 inscriptions. In 1940–41, excavations were made by archaeologists from Keio and Tokyo Universities, and several thousand more were found. By 1941, 96 percent of all oracle-bone inscriptions known today had been unearthed.[12] Since 1950, the Kaogusuo has continued excavations at Anyang. A total of about 6,275 pieces with inscriptions had been excavated as of 1999. The major finds were

---

[11] Cuckold: *guizi* 龜子, *gui'er* 龜兒, *gui sunzi* 龜孫子 or *wangba* 王[忘]八, *wangbadan* 王[忘]八蛋 (cuckold's egg); penis: *gui* 龜 or *guitou* 龜頭. *Guitou* was also used for brothelkeeper in Mandarin. In Modern Chinese it is the term for glans penis.

[12] Today, there are 129,487 inscribed oracle bones in Chinese collections (at least 99,194 in China, possibly more; 30,204 in Taiwan and 89 in Hong Kong); and about 26,700 are held in 12 other countries around the world, mainly in Japan (12,443), Canada (7,802), the United Kingdom (3,355) and the United States (1,882). These figures may not be entirely accurate, as they are based on counts taken from dozens of publications of oracle-bone fragments from collections all over the world. There must be a significant number of duplicates and forgeries included in the total, although not nearly as many as the forgeries of ancient bronzes, which for centuries have been highly prized collectors' items. The most thorough count of mainland collections is in Hu Houxuan, "Dalu xiancang zhi jiagu wenzi" 大陸現藏之甲骨文字, *SYSJK* 67.4: 815–76 (1996). This article also includes lists of rubbings and charts showing to where the early collections were dispersed.

5,335 pieces at Nandi, Xiaotun, in 1973–77 and 579 inscribed pieces (of which more than 300 are intact, some with over 200 characters on them) excavated in 1991 at Huayuanzhuang 花園莊, just south of Xiaotun, Anyang.[13]

Of particular interest was the discovery in 1977–79 of 296 Zhou oracle-bone inscriptions, 280 of which were from a cache of approximately 17,000 pieces (mainly turtle shells) from the excavations at a predynastic Zhou palace at the early Zhou cultic center of Qiyi 岐邑 (Zhouyuan, see 13.2.3). They seem to confirm that the Zhou practiced and recorded oracle-bone divination widely.[14] In addition to the Zhouyuan finds, about 20 inscribed pieces have been found at other Western Zhou sites, mainly in Shaanxi and also near Beijing. The content is much the same as the Shang inscriptions but the characters are smaller, sometimes so minute that you need a magnifying glass to see them.

Most of the Shang oracle-bone inscriptions are on fragments and are very short, some only one character. The longest is not much more than 200 characters. If the fragments were excavated from one pit, they can often be rejoined into whole-plastron inscriptions. The characters are often in rough forms (unlike the bronze characters, which are more carefully written in ornate, formal, archaic scripts). Sometimes they point to the right, sometimes to the left. At times they are vertical, sometimes horizontal. The writing is usually recorded on segments of the shell, each segment arranged from top to bottom (and vice-versa on the scapula). Within each segment, the characters on late-period oracle bones are usually incised in columns from top to bottom and from right to left, although sometimes in rows from left to right, depending on the contours and the position on the bone or shell. The vertical strokes were incised before the horizontal ones. In a few cases a single inscription covers several bones or shells. In all, the oracle bones discovered to date contain a

[13] The total number of pieces discovered at Huayuanzhuang was 1,583. They date from the early Wu Ding reign and are mainly concerned with sacrifices, hunting, the weather, and exorcizing illness. The divinations were conducted for a prince, not the king; see Liu Yiman 劉一曼 and Cao Dingyun 曹定雲, *Kaogu* 1993. 6; *Kaogu xuebao* 3: 251–310 (1999).

[14] For a thorough summary, see *Jiaguxue yibai nian* 甲骨學一百年 (15.5), 281–334; see also Edward L. Shaughnessy, "Zhouyuan Oracle-Bone Inscriptions: Entering the Research Stage?" *EC* 12: 146–63; 182–94 (1985–87).

total of about one million characters, of which about 4,000 are different characters (if alternative forms were included, it would bring the total to about 5,000).

The meanings of about 1,200 to 1,500 characters have been deciphered in a manner that meets with general acceptance by *jiaguwen* scholars. Opinions differ over the interpretation of several hundred more. A further 1,500 characters can be identified and transcribed into Han chancery or regular script forms (a step known as *liding* 隸定, *ligu* 隸古, or *lishi* 隸釋), but their meanings and pronunciation are not known (many are performing the functions of names of people or places). The remainder have not yet been deciphered in ways that are generally accepted. The oracle-bone script contains much of the core vocabulary of Chinese. It is composed mainly of nouns (1.2.3 and 16.3). From time to time fanciful interpretations of individual characters are made. These should be treated with the utmost skepticism, especially when the new interpretation is used to fit a character into a particular scheme or theory of history.

Before their use as historical sources, the oracle-bone inscriptions have to be dated. Oracle-bone divination started in the reign of Wu Ding 武丁 (ca. 1200–1189 BC) about 30 years after the capital was moved to Yin, reached its height not long thereafter, and continued another 120 years until the end of the dynasty (ca. 1045 BC). Dating of the inscriptions is impossible so long as there is no absolute chronology for any period before 841 BC (13.3). Relative dating or sorting into periods can be done on the basis of the internal stylistic evidence contained on the inscriptions themselves and by using various archaeological criteria. Dong Zuobin's pioneer 1933 study establishing five main periods has been modified by later scholars, but his approach and his findings still set the framework for a debate that is by no means ended.[15]

---

[15] For a survey of the different theories on the dating of the oracle bones from the 1930s to the late 1990s, see *Jiaguxue yibai nian* 甲骨學一百年 (15.5), 124–93. Dong's key study was "Jiaguwen duandai yanjiu" 甲骨文斷代研究 (Researches on the periodization of the oracle bones), *SYSJK* special issue, 1.1: 323–424 (1933); later modifications were incorporated in his *Yin lipu* 殷曆譜 (Manual of the Yin calendar), 2 vols., Nanqi, Sichuan: Shiyusuo, special publication, 1945, 1992. Dong's periodization and later interpretations up to 1970 are introduced in "Dating the Inscriptions: Relative Chronology," Chapter 4 of Keightley, *Sources* (1978), 91–133. Edward L. Shaughnessy, "Recent Approaches

Footnote continued on next page

In China there are about 150 *jiaguwen* scholars; in Japan about 50, in Korea some 20; and in the rest of the world no more than a handful. The toughest task of the *jiaguwen* scholar is the elucidation of individual characters. The task has become harder and harder, as the least controversial ones were done first. During more than 40 years of study Yu Xingwu, one of the leading scholars of the second generation, claimed to have provided fresh interpretations of something less than 300 oracle-bone characters (see 15.5; Yu Xingwu, 1979). Some manage no more than a handful; most, none.

15.5   Research Tools

For advice on studying Classical Chinese, see 1.3.5, and on ancient Chinese scripts, including *jiaguwen*, 16.5.

David N. Keightley, "Shang Oracle-Bone Inscriptions," in *NSECH*, 15–56. The best short introduction in English.

David N. Keightley, *Sources of Shang History: The Oracle-Bone Inscriptions of Bronze-Age China*, UCP, 1978; paperback rpnt. with minor revisions, 1985. This is the standard work in English.

There is one essential overview:

Jiaguxue yibai nian 甲骨學一百年 (One hundred years of oracle-bone studies), Wang Yuxin 王宇信 and Yang Shengnan 楊升南, eds. in chief, Shehui kexue wenxian, 1999. This is the most up-to-date and comprehensive account available in any language. It was prepared by leading oracle-bone scholars in China at the Lishisuo (in addition to the editors, the authors were Meng Shikai 孟世凱, Song Zhenhao 宋鎮豪, and Chang Yuzhi 常玉芝). Chapters cover the process of discovery and excavation, sorting, dating and publication, different theories of periodization, divination markings, Zhou oracle bones, main achievements of previous scholars, and research on particular topics relating to Shang history (the single longest section, 250 pages, of this huge book). *Jiaguxue yibai nian* replaces the previous best summary in Chinese, that of Chen Mengjia 陳夢家 (1911–66).[16]

---

to Oracle-Bone Periodization: A Review," *EC*, 8: 1–13 (1982–83), chiefly analyzes the impact of the Nandi finds on periodization.

[16] *Yinxu buci zongshu* 殷墟卜辭綜述 (Comprehensive account of the divinatory inscriptions from Yinxu), Kexue, 1956, 1988; Zhonghua, 1992.

Shima Kunio 島邦男 (1907–77), *Inkyo bokuji kenkyû* 殷墟卜辭研究, Chû-gokugaku kenkyûkai, 1958. Chinese tr.: *Yinxu buci yanjiu* 殷墟卜辭研究, Wen Tianhe 文天河 and Li Xiaolin 李孝林, trs., Dingwen, 1975. Important overview by leading Japanese scholar.

The following are entry-level introductions:

Zhao Cheng 趙誠, *Jiaguwen jianming cidian—buci fenlei duben* 甲骨文簡明詞典—卜辭分類讀本 (Concise dictionary of oracle-bone characters: a topically arranged reader), Zhonghua, 1988; 3rd prnt., 1996. Departs from the conventional arrangement by inscriptions and instead examines the lexemes (usually characters) in 26 semantic fields (e.g., sacrifices, plants, time), with readings presented as examples of usage. There is a stroke-count index of the 2,000 different characters introduced.

Ma Rusen 馬如森, *Yinxu jiaguwen yinlun* 殷墟甲骨文引論 (Introduction to the oracle-bone script from the wastes of Yin), Dongbei shifan daxue, 1993. Contains a small dictionary that illustrates and defines 1,056 oracle-bone characters (255–683). *Shuowen* definitions are given, plus examples of usage. There is a *pinyin* index and also an introduction to oracle-bone studies, 1–254.

Li Pu 李圃, *Jiaguwen wenzixue* 甲骨文文字學 (The study of oracle-bone script), Xuelin, 1995; 3rd prnt., 1997. Good introductory textbook containing a thorough analysis of the construction of the oracle-bone characters, including the 348 basic graphical units from which they were formed. The same author has also compiled a reader, *Jiaguwen xuanzhu* 甲骨文選注 (Selected oracle-bone inscriptions with notes), Shanghai guji, 1989, 1993. This provides tracings of 60 pieces with transcriptions and translations into Modern Chinese.

Gao Ming 高明, *Zhongguo guwenzixue tonglun* 中國古文字學通論 (General introduction to the study of Chinese paleography), Wenwu, 1987; new rev. edition, Beijing daxue, 1996, 1997, includes extensive readings of oracle-bone inscriptions (225–332), including those from Zhouyuan. Based on the author's lectures at Peking University.

The detailed interpretations of individual characters by leading scholars can serve as advanced introductions. For example:

Tang Lan 唐蘭, *Yinxu wenzi ji* 殷墟文字記 (Notes on Yinxu script), Peking University, 1934. Mimeograph of the author's lecture notes; published edition, rev. with index, Zhonghua, 1981. Contains analysis of 74 difficult characters.

Yu Xingwu 于省吾, *Jiagu wenzi shilin* 甲骨文字釋林 (Forest.of interpretations of oracle-bone characters), Zhonghua, 1979; 3rd rpnt., 1993. Collected and revised analysis of 190 individual characters. Meticulous scholarship that has stood the test of time.

Kaizuka Shigeki 貝塚茂樹 (1904–87) and Itô Michiharu 伊藤道治, *Kôkotsu moji kenkyû* 甲骨文字研究 (Studies on the oracle-bone characters), *Zuhan* 圖版 (rubbings), *Honbunhen* (本文篇), Dôhôsha, 1980. This is the revised and renamed version of *Kyôto daigaku Jinbun kagaku kenkyûjo shozô kôkotsu monji* 京都大學人文科學研究所所藏甲骨文字 (The oracle-bone inscriptions of the Institute for Humanistic Studies, Kyoto University), *Zuhan* 圖版 (rubbings), *Honbunhen* (本文篇), and Index, 3 vols., Jinbun, 1959, 1960, and 1968. Exemplary presentation and analysis of the Jinbun's collection of 3,426 oraclebone inscriptions.

Corpora Inscriptionum

The most comprehensive printed corpus is the *Jiaguwen heji* and its supplement *Jiaguwen heji bubian* (next two items). The 20 volumes of these two works contain a total of 55,406 inscriptions, including recombined inscriptions (*zhuihe* 綴合). A large part of these inscriptions will soon be available on the Internet and in the form of a computer database. The work has been done at the ICS of the Chinese University of Hong Kong.

Jiaguwen heji 甲骨文合集 (Collected oracle-bone writings), Guo Moruo, ed., Hu Houxuan, ed. in chief, 13 large folio vols., Zhonghua, 1979–82; 3rd prnt., 1998.[17] The *Heji* contains 41,956 photographs of rubbings and lithographs of most of the main oracle-bone inscriptions discovered between 1899 and 1970. It is arranged under three subject categories (class and country, society and production, thought and culture) and 19 subcategories, which are set out in chronological order. Before the publication of the massive volumes of the *Heji*, illustrations of the oracle bones were scattered in more than 150 separate publications containing rubbings, drawings, or photographs. There were also many scattered pieces in private collections. It was the chief editor, Hu Houxuan, who made it his lifetime work to bring together all this material from public and private collections, to examine individual inscriptions, and to weed out the fakes. In the process

---

[17] The *Heji* and Part I of the *Xiaotun Nandi jiagu* 小屯南地甲骨 collections (see below) were reprinted in Taibei under the title: *Shang-Zhou jiaguwen zongji* 商周甲骨文總集, 16 vols., Yiwen, 1984.

he also visited many of the major foreign collections. It was Hu who proposed the *Heji* project already in 1956.[18] He guided the team that started the editorial work in 1961 and, despite interruptions from political campaigns, continued on it for the next 20 years. The *Heji* should be used with its separate volume of transcriptions (next item) and its supplement, *Heji bubian* (second item below).

Jiaguwen heji shiwen 甲骨文合集釋文 (Transcriptions of *Jiaguwen heji*), Hu Houxuan, ed. in chief, Wang Yuxin 王宇信 et al., eds., Shehui kexue, 1999.

Jiaguwen heji bubian 甲骨文合集補編 (Supplement to *Jiaguwen heji*), Peng Bangjiong 彭邦炯 et al., eds., 7 vols., Yuwen, 1999. Contains rubbings and transcriptions of inscriptions not included in the *Heji* or discovered after the *Heji*. In all, 13,450 inscriptions are included. The *Bubian* also corrects errors in the *Heji*, including left out, wrongly combined, and incorrectly periodized inscriptions. Annexes include not only transcriptions but also provenance and recombined tables and a listing of 316 inscriptions found elsewhere than at Anyang (mainly the Zhou oracle-bone inscriptions; see 15.4).

A selection of the most important catalogs of collections are listed below by date of publication. For a full list of 116 catalogs plus another 100 publications of scattered pieces, see *Bainian jiaguxue lunzhu mu* 百年甲骨學論著目 (see under *Bibliography* at end of this section), items 552–770.

The Menzies Collection of Shang Dynasty Oracle Bones, vol. 1, *A Catalogue*, Chin-hsiung Hsu (Xu Jinxiong 許進雄), ed., Royal Ontario Museum, 1972. The museum's collection of 8,700 pieces is the second largest outside of China after the 12,400 in Japanese collections.

The Menzies Collection of Shang Dynasty Oracle Bones, vol. 2, *The Text*, Chin-hsiung Hsu (Xu Jinxiong 許進雄), ed., Royal Ontario Museum, 1977.

Oracle Bones from the White and Other Collections, Chin-hsiung Hsu (Xu Jinxiong 許進雄), ed., Royal Ontario Museum, 1979 (1,915 inscriptions).

---

[18] Hu took the term *heji* from the most comprehensive collection of the works of Liang Qichao 梁啓超 (1873–1929), *Yinbingshi heji* 飲冰室合集, 40 vols., Zhonghua, 1936. It has the sense of a careful assemblage and collation of already published materials.

Tôkyô daigaku Tôyô bunka kenkyûjo shozô kôkotsu monji 東京大學東洋文化研究所所藏甲骨文字 (Oracle-bone script in the Institute of Oriental Studies, Tokyo University), Matsumaru Michio 松丸道雄, comp., 1979 (1,315 inscriptions).

Collections d'inscriptions oraculaires en France, Jean A. Lefeuvre, ed., Variétés sinologiques, New Series, 70, Institut Ricci, 1985. Contains photographs, transcriptions, and translations of 64 pieces held in France.

Xiaotun Nandi jiagu 小屯南地甲骨 (Oracle bones from Nandi, Xiaotun), Kaogusuo, eds., 2 parts in 5 large folio vols., with a supplement, Zhonghua, 1980, 1983; vol. 5 is an index. This work contains illustrations (Part I) and transcriptions (Part II) of 4,589 of the oracle bones discovered at Nandi in 1973 and another 23 in its neighborhood between 1975 and 1977. For a detailed review, see David N. Keightley, "Sources of Shang History: Two Major Oracle-Bone Collections Published in the People's Republic of China," *JAOS* 110.1: 39–59 (1990). Use Cai Fangpei, Edward L. Shaughnessy, and James F. Shaughnessy, Jr., *A Concordance of the Xiaotun Nandi Oracle-Bone Inscriptions*, *EC* Special Monograph Series, no. 1, Chicago, 1988.

Tenri daigaku fuzoku Tenri sankôkan zô kôkotsu monji 天理大學附屬天理參考館藏甲骨文字 (Oracle-bone inscriptions stored in the Tenri reference library attached to Tenri University), Itô Michiharu 伊藤道治, ed., 1987.

Yingguo suocang jiagu ji 英國所藏甲骨集 (Oracle-bone collections in Great Britain), Qi Wenxin 齊文心, Sarah Allen, and Li Xueqin 李學勤, eds., part 1 (rubbings), 2 vols., Zhonghua, 1985; part 2 (transcriptions, studies, and index), 2 vols., Zhonghua, 1992 (2,674 inscriptions).

Several Collections of Oracular Inscriptions in Germany, Switzerland, the Netherlands, Belgium, Jean A. Lefeuvre, ed., Variétés sinologiques, New Series, 77, Institut Ricci, 1997. For a review of this (plus Lefeuvre, 1985) dealing with the methodology of decipherment, see Takashima Ken'ichi, "*Several Collections of Oracular Inscriptions in Germany, Switzerland, the Netherlands, Belgium*: A Review in Metatheories," *TP* (1998).

The following collection was published before the *Heji*. It remains important, not least because of the editor's comments and a number of studies and translations made of it:

Xiaotun Di'erben Yinxu wenzi bingbian 小屯第二本殷墟文字丙編 (Xiaotun, vol. 2, Yinxu inscriptions, Part 3), 3 vols., 6 *ce*, Zhang Bingquan

張秉權, ed., Shiyusuo, 1957–72, 1992–97. Referred to as *Yinxu wenzi bingbian* or *Bingbian*, for short. These volumes contain 632 complete recombined (*zhuihe* 綴合) plastrons (made possible because the fragments were excavated from one pit).

Takashima Ken'ichi 高嶋謙一 (1939–), *Commentaries to Fascicle Three of Inscriptions from the Yin Ruins: Palaeographical and Linguistic Studies*, forthcoming. These are notes to the translations in the following item.

Translations of Fascicle Three of Inscriptions from the Yin Ruins, Paul L-M. Serruys and Takashima Ken'ichi, trs., forthcoming.

Takashima Ken'ichi, *Yinxu wenzi bingbian tongjian* 殷墟文字丙編 通檢 (A concordance to fascicle three of inscriptions from the Yin ruins), Shiyusuo, 1985.

For works on the two most important finds of recent years, Huayuan-zhuang and Zhouyuan, see 15.4.

Language and Dictionaries

On the language of the oracle-bone inscriptions, see:

Paul L-M. Serruys, "The Language of the Shang Oracle-Bone Inscriptions," *TP* 60: 12–120 (1974); "Basic Problems Underlying the Process of Identification of the Chinese Graphs of the Shang Oracular Inscriptions," *SJ* 53: 455–94 (1982); "Notes on the Grammar of the Oracular Inscriptions of Shang," in *Contributions to Sino-Tibetan Studies*, John McCoy and Timothy Light, eds., Brill, 1986, 203–57.

Itô Michiharu 伊藤道治 and Takashima Ken'ichi 高嶋謙一, *Studies in Early Chinese Civilization, Religion, Society, Language and Palaeography*, Hirakata, Osaka: Kansai Gaidai University Publications, 2 vols., 1996. Vol. I contains the text; vol. II, the tables, notes, bibliography, and index. The chapters written by Itô are translated from his book *Chûgoku kodai ôchô no keisei* 中國古代王朝の形成 (The form of the ancient Chinese royal court), Sôbunsha, 1975, 1–133; those by Takashima are based on his articles on the language. There is also a lengthy bibliography of Japanese secondary scholarship on the Shang up to the 1980s.

Zhao Cheng 趙誠 mainly concentrates on the language in *Jiagu wenzixue gangyao* 甲骨文字學綱要 (Introduction to the study of oracle-bone script), Shangwu, 1993.

Jiaguwen zidian 甲骨文字典 (Dictionary of oracle-bone characters), Xu Zhongshu 徐中舒 et al., eds., Sichuan cishu, 1988; 4th prnt., 1995.

The best *jiaguwen* dictionary available; not always reliable.[19] Arrangement is by *Shuowen* classifiers. An analysis of the form of each character (*jiezi* 解字) is provided. This is followed by an explanation of the meaning (*shiyi* 釋義), with an example of usage both in oracle-bone script and in modern characters. Most individual oracle-bone characters are included, even when their meanings or identifications are not known, so the total of head characters comes to 2,938. There is a stroke-count index of characters in their *kaiti* forms at the front.

Zhang Yujin 張玉金, *Jiaguwen xuci cidian* 甲骨文虛詞辭典 (Dictionary of oracle-bone particles), Zhonghua, 1994. A study of the particles found on the oracle-bone inscriptions arranged in dictionary form.

Collected Interpretations

There are two main works that assemble the different interpretations by modern scholars of the oracle-bone characters. They largely, but not entirely, supersede the similar work of Li Xiaoding (1965). The more comprehensive of the two is the first:

Kôkotsu moji jishaku sôran 甲骨文字字釋綜覽 (Synthetic index for interpretation of oracle-bone characters), Matsumaru Michio 松丸道雄 and Takashima Ken'ichi 高嶋謙一, eds., Tôbunken, 1993, Tokyô daigaku, 1994. This gives regular-script equivalents as found in the interpretations drawn from works published between 1904 and 1988 by 471 scholars in Chinese, Japanese, English, German, French, Russian, and Korean (the list of these works, which is appendixed, amounts to a full bibliography of interpretations of oracle-bone characters up to 1988). In addition, the *Sôran* shows the different forms of the oracle-bone characters and also contains cross-references to the standard reference works as of 1988 (*Jiagu wenbian, Inkyo bokuji sôrui, Jiagu wenzi jishi, Jiaguwen zidian*).

Jiagu wenzi gulin 甲骨文字詁林 (Collected commentaries on the oracle-bone characters), Yu Xingwu 于省吾, ed. in chief, Yao Xiaosui 姚孝遂 (1926–95) and Xiao Ding 肖丁 (Zhao Cheng 趙誠), gen. eds., 4 vols., Zhonghua, 1996. The authors have assembled the interpreta-

---

[19] The *Jiaguwen zidian* attempts to combine the strengths of Li Xiaoding 李孝定, *Jiagu wenzi jishi* 甲骨文字集釋 (Collected explanations of the oracle-bone characters), 16 vols., Shiyusuo, special publication 50 (1965); rpnt., 8 vols., 1970, 1991; and *Jiaguwen bian* 甲骨文編 (Compilation of oracle-bone characters), Sun Haibo 孫海波 (1910–72), ed. in chief, 1934 (which contained 2,116 characters); rev. edition, Zhonghua, 1965 (which contained 4,672 characters); rpnt., 1982, 1989, 1997.

tions of 3,691 oracle-bone characters by the leading Chinese authorities (as of the end of 1989). The interpretations are arranged chronologically in the order in which they were written. For the most part contributions not written in Chinese are not included. There is neither a name nor a title index. Unfortunately, this huge work (it runs to over 3,700 pages) is reproduced from handwriting and is not always very clear.

Concordances

Yinxu jiagu keci leizuan 殷墟甲骨刻辭類纂 (Concordance of Yin inscribed oracle bones), Yao Xiaosui 姚孝遂 and Xiao Ding 肖丁, eds. in chief, 3 large folio vols., Zhonghua, 1989, 3rd prnt., 1998. The most comprehensive concordance. The *Leizuan* lists some 200,000 phrases and sentences in which the 1,473 head characters included occur. It also indicates *Heji* numbers. It thus not only shows the different contexts in which each character was used but can also serve as an index to the *Heji*. Vol. 3 contains a *pinyin* index in addition to classifier and stroke-count indexes. It is handwritten, but clearly printed and easy to read. However, *Leizuan* does not treat key words consistently as pointed out by Qiu Xigui in his review in *Shupin* 1: 4–14 and 2: 2–9 (1990) and by David N. Keightley in *JAOS* 117.3: 507–24 (1997). By the simple fact that all excerpts are given in both direct (oracle-bone) and in modern (*kaishu*) character transcription, the *Leizuan* largely supersedes the previous standard concordance, Shima Kunio 島邦男 (1907–77), *Inkyo bokuji sôrui* 殷墟卜辭綜類 (Comprehensive classification of the oracle-bone inscriptions from the ruins of Yin), Kyûko, 1967; 2nd rev. edition, 1971. Moreover, the *Leizuan* includes the important finds since Shima's work was compiled.[20]

Jiaguwen tongjian 甲骨文通檢 (A concordance to oracle-bone inscriptions), Rao Zongyi 饒宗頤, ed., 5 vols. to date, HKCUP, 1989–99. This is a concordance to *Heji* and eight other collections arranged by categories, which, if they fit your research, is useful. Vol. 1 covers

---

[20] The *Leizuan* is based on *Yinxu jiagu keci moshi zongji* 殷墟甲骨刻辭摹釋總集 (Comprehensive copies and transcriptions [into *kaishu*] of inscribed oracle bones from Yinxu), Yao Xiaosui 姚孝遂 and Xiao Ding 肖丁, eds. in chief, 2 large folio vols., Zhonghua, 1988, 3rd prnt., 1998. This contains copies, transcriptions, and an index of some 50,000 oracle-bone inscriptions found in *Heji* (1979–82), *Tunnan* (1980–83), *Yingguo* (1985–91), *Tôkyô* (1979), and *Huaiteshi* (1979). The transcriptions are handwritten and clearly readable in a standardized oracle-bone script and in *kaishu*. They follow the order of the plates.

former kings, predynastic ancestors, and diviners; vol. 2, toponyms; vol. 3, astronomy and the weather; vol. 4, official posts and people; vol. 5, hunting. There is a finding list at the beginning of each volume in regular script, but the characters in the body of the work are in oracle-bone script. All references to each character or phrase are indicated by finding number in the *Heji* and supplementary collections.

Bibliography

Bainian jiaguxue lunzhu mu 百年甲骨學論著目 (Bibliography of books and articles of 100 years of oracle-bone studies), Song Zhenhao 宋鎮豪, ed. in chief, Yuwen, 1999. Supersedes all previous oracle-bone bibliographies. Contains 10,946 entries arranged by nine subjects: discovery, comprehensive accounts, published inscriptions, research on the inscriptions (divination, periodization, characters, grammar, collation, and recombined fragments *zhuihe* 綴合), 21 special topics (e.g., the state, society, history, inheritance lines, rituals, official posts, punishments, the military, lineages, geography, the economy), study tools, book reviews, miscellaneous, and biographies of oracle-bone specialists. An appendix lists works on other objects excavated at Yinxu and studies of oracle bones found elsewhere than at Yinxu (notably those found at Zhou Yuan). There is a chronological index and an author-title index.

Specialized journals (many of which contain articles and reviews of oracle-bone scholarship) are listed along with yearbooks and other bibliographical references for early Chinese history in 12.3 and 13.3.

16

The Characters:

Evolution and Structure

There is plenty of new evidence to trace the evolution of the different ways of writing the characters during the thousand years between the oracle-bone script and the emergence of Han chancery
script (16.1). Characters were constructed in three main ways (16.2).
A huge number of them are classified under surprisingly few significs (16.3). One of the main difficulties in reading any transmitted
text written in the Han or before is the amount of orthographic
variation, a situation that improves thereafter but remains a hazard,
especially in manuscript sources (16.4). The chapter ends with some
brief advice on studying ancient scripts (16.5).

16.1   Evolution of Scripts

The first special terms for the different scripts or character forms
(*zixing* 字形) date from the Later Han, notably those in the *Shuowen jiezi* 説文解字 (2.2.1).[1] These terms can now be elaborated and
in some cases corrected using the writing on the oracle-bone and
bronze inscriptions and on other excavated artifacts and texts. The
new picture that emerges is summarized in Table 24.

---

[1] Zhan Jinxin 詹鄞鑫, *Hanzi shuolüe* 漢字説略 (Outline of Chinese characters), Hongye, 1995, 55–150; Qiu Xigui 裘錫圭, *Wenzixue gaiyao* 文字學概要
(Essentials of paleography), Shangwu, 1988; 4th prnt., 1998, 40–96. For an English translation of Qiu (rev. edition, Wanjuanlou, 1994), see *Chinese Writing*,
Gilbert L. Mattos and Jerry Norman, trs., *Early China* Special Monograph Series 4, SSEC and IEAS, 1999.

Table 24: Main Script Forms

Form of Script (tr.), origin	Period of Use
Jiaguwen 甲骨文 (Oracle bone, Chapter 15)	Shang; W. Zhou
Jinwen 金文 (Bronze, Chapter 17)	Shang; Zhou
Zhouwen 籀文 (Large seal)	E. Zhou
Zhuanwen 篆文 (Seal)[2]	Warring States, W. Han
Lishu 隸書 (Chancery), cursive *zhuanwen*[3]	4th c. BC (Qin)–4th AD
Caoshu 草書 (Cursive), cursive *lishu*[4]	Han
Xingshu 行書 (Running), cursive *lishu/caoshu*	E. Han (matures 4th c.)
Kaishu 楷書 (Model), from *xingshu*[5]	4th c. (matures 5th–6th c.)

The history of Chinese scripts can be broadly divided into two stages: *guwen* 古文 (the first four rows of Table 24), which was in use from the Shang to Qin, and *jinwen* 今文, or *likai* 隸楷, from the

[2] The term *zhuanwen* is first used in the *Shuowen*. It may simply have meant "carved script," but it is conventionally translated into English as "seal script." It is sometimes referred to as *xiaozhuan* 小篆 (small seal script) to distinguish it from *dazhuan* 大篆 (large seal script or *zhouwen* 籀文), the script found on Eastern Zhou bronzes.

During the Spring and Autumn and Warring States periods, a number of aesthetic forms of seal script were used mainly in the Yangzi kingdoms of Chu 楚, Yue 越, and Ba 巴 on bronze weapons as well as on insignia and seals, for which they are still popular to this day. They were known as *chongshu* 蟲書 (insect script) and briefly became official during the reign of Wang Mang under the name *niaochongshu* 鳥蟲書 (birds and insect script). It was used on flags and pennants. *Kedou* 蝌蚪 (tadpole) script was another variety of seal script. It was named after its appearance: heavy strokes at the top tapering off at the bottom.

[3] *Lishu* 隸書 (literally, script of the common people). It began as a carelessly written form of small seal script used in the chancelleries.

[4] Han *caoshu* was termed *zhangcao* 章草 in the fourth century to distinguish it from *jincao* 今草 of that time. Wang Fang-yü (Wang Fangyu 王方宇), *Introduction to Chinese Cursive Script*, Far Eastern Publications, YUP, 1958; 7th prnt., 1972.

[5] *Kaishu* or *kaiti* after its emergence in the fourth century was used in parallel with *lishu* during the Wei and Jin before becoming the predominant style from the Nan-Bei Chao. *Kaishu* is also called *zhenshu* 真書 (true script) or *zhengshu* 正書 (correct script). Variations on *kaishu* for block-printed books from the Song were based on the differing *kaishu* styles of famous calligraphers. In the later empire *zhengkai* 正楷 (correct model script) and *caoshu* 草書 were the two most common script forms.

Han to the present (the last four rows). The late Warring States to the early Han marks a transitional stage between the two. Modern typefaces are based on *kaishu*.[6]

Needless to say, the different scripts did not follow one after the other in orderly fashion, each growing from the previous one in a linear progression. They evolved over several centuries and often overlapped. A clear-cut profile of each of the main scripts was established only long afterwards when fine examples were taken as calligraphic models.

During the Warring States, two main scripts began to develop from *zhouwen* 籀文, namely *zhuanwen* 篆文 and *lishu* 隸書.[7] The first was more formal; the second was a cursive in day-to-day use by clerks and scribes, especially in the state of Qin. On the advice of his chancellor Li Si 李斯 (apart from his other accomplishments, a noted philologist and calligrapher), the first emperor standardized the characters (*shu tong wenzi* 書同文字). He made *Qinzhuan* 秦篆 (the Qin variety of seal script) the official standard for the whole country and suppressed the variant characters of the scripts of the six states (*liuguo wenzi* 六國文字). *Qinli* 秦隸 (Qin chancery script) continued in informal use in Qin. The unification laid the groundwork for an even bigger change, the shift from seal to chancery script.

This shift took place gradually with *lishu* 隸書 (variously translated as chancery, official, or clerk's script) emerging in the Later Han as the standard. It was referred to as *jinwen* 今文 or *jinzi* 今字 (contemporary or modern script) to distinguish it from pre-Qin scripts, especially the *liuguo wenzi*, which were termed *guwen* 古文

---

[6] As relative terms, *guwen* 古文 and *jinwen* 今文 have changed their meanings many times. The second main usage refers to the Old and the New Text traditions (*guwen* and *jinwen*) and the schools of classical learning based on each (19.2); in addition, *guwen* is used for the *wenyan* style of writing introduced in the Tang by writers such as Han Yu 韓愈 (768–824) in contrast to the ornate *pianwen* 駢文 parallel prose of the Six Dynasties. *Guwen* is also sometimes used as a synonym for *Gudai Hanyu* embracing all forms of Classical and Literary Chinese before modern times (although, strictly speaking, not *pianwen*).

[7] *Zhanguo guwen zidian: Zhanguo wenzi shengxi* 戰國古文字典戰國文字聲系 (Dictionary of Warring States characters according to rhyme groups), He Linyi 何林義, ed., 2 vols., Zhonghua, 1999, illustrated with copious graphic variants; gives oracle-bone usage, quotes the *Shuowen*, and provides definitions.

or *guzi* 古字 (ancient scripts). Today, the term *guwen* is still used, but it has been extended to cover all pre-Qin scripts, including the oracle-bone script (which was no longer known in the Han).

The change to *lishu* (described since the late Tang as *libian* 隸變) was the biggest transformation of the Chinese writing system that has ever taken place. The old curvaceous *guwen* characters, many still clearly pictographic in inspiration, were finally replaced by *lishu* composed of geometric strokes in abstract patterns more easily and quickly written by brush.[8] A student today without special training would find it hard to read any of the *guwen* scripts. On the other hand *jinwen* (*lishu*) is sufficiently close to today's characters (Table 25) as to be recognizable.

Table 25: Modern Movable Typefaces

Kaiti 楷體 (devised for Shangwu)[9]	Since 1909
Songti 宋體[10]	Since early 20th c.
Fang-Songti 仿宋體[11]	Since 1916
Heiti 黑體 (bold typeface used for headlines)	Since early 20th c.
Jiantizi 簡體字 (Simplified characters)	1956; 1964 (rev., 1986)

16.2   Structure

Analysis of the structure of a character has always been used as a way of providing clues to its original and later meanings and also as a technique for committing it to memory (1.3.2). The earliest evidence dates from the Spring and Autumn period, but the first systematic analysis came only after the shift to chancery script had been completed. One of the effects of the shift was that the struc-

[8] Zhao Ping'an 趙平安, *Libian yanjiu* 隸變研究 (Research on the change to chancery script), Hebei daxue, 1993.

[9] Based on a Ming woodblock typeface. Also called *Zhengkai* 正楷. The typeface used in the manual is *Kaiti*.

[10] *Songti* 宋體 or (*jiangti* 匠體) was a Ming development of a Southern Song woodblock typeface. Hence its Japanese name *Minchôtai* 明朝體.

[11] *Fang-Songti* was based on the Wuyingdian (Qing imperial printing office) re-creation of Northern Song woodblock typeface. Hence its Japanese name, *Sôchôtai* 宋朝體.

tural elements of the characters became much less clear than they had been in small seal script. It was this that led Xu Shen 許慎 to compile the *Shuowen* 説文. As a member of the Old Text school (19.2), his aim was to produce a standard for writing the characters and to define their correct meanings based on his analysis of the small seal script (which he believed was the earliest form of the characters). In this way he felt orthographic and semantic confusion could be avoided and the link with old traditions as expressed in the *guwen* texts reestablished (prerequisites for good government). Not surprisingly, the *Shuowen* and all later philological works were placed in the Classics bibliographic classification (Table 26, 19.2).

The basis of Xu's analysis was the *liushu* 六書 (six types of character composition theory).[12] His theory remained in use from the Later Han until the twentieth century, even though the definition and boundaries between the six categories are not entirely clear:[13]

> *zhishi* 指事 (indicative), e.g., *shang* 上 (up) and *xia* 下 (down) or the numbers *yi* 一, *er* 二, *san* 三, *shi* 十, *nian* 廿, *sa* 卅[14]
>
> *xiangxing* 象形 (pictographic), e.g., *ri* 日 (sun) and *yue* 月 (moon)

---

[12] Xu's six categories should not be confused with *liushu* 六書, *liuti* 六體, or *liuwen* 六文, meaning the "six calligraphic scripts" variously defined from the Han onward.

[13] The phrase *liushu* 六書 appears in the *Zhouli* without explanation. Apart from tradition, the reason that Xu chose to retain six categories was influenced by the prevailing fashion in the Han, inherited from the Qin, to regard six as a particularly fortunate number. See Zhao Cheng 趙誠, *Jiagu wenzixue gangyao* 甲骨文字學綱要, 140–56.

Dai Zhen 戴震 (1723–77) modified the *liushu* to "four ways of constructing characters, two ways of using them," an approach many still use. Various new analyses were put forward in the 1930s, including a threefold division proposed by Tang Lan 唐蘭: pictographs (*xiangxing* 象形), ideographs (*xiangyi* 象意), and picto-phonetic compounds (*xingsheng* 形聲). This was in turn modified by Chen Mengjia 陳夢家, who replaced *xiangyi* with *jiajie* 假借 (phonetic loans). Tang and Chen and later philologists were able to challenge Xu on the basis of newly discovered pre-Qin epigraphic sources not available in the Han.

[14] *Shi* 十, *nian* 廿, and *sa* 卅 in their oracle-bone script forms are simply 一, 二, and 三 written vertically, but in the bronze script they probably recall the knots in strings which may earlier have been used as a mnemonic in the conduct of government business (14.1). In both cases, they are considered *zhishizi*. The other numerals (四, 五, 六, 七, 八, 九) probably began as *zhishizi* before acquiring their present phonetic loan characters (an example of the fluidity in matching characters to words in the early stages of Chinese orthography).

huiyi 會意 (associative), e.g., *lin* 林 (wood) and *sen* 森 (forest)
xingsheng 形聲 (picto-phonetic), e.g., *song* 松 (see below)
zhuanzhu 轉注 (notative), e.g., *she* 蛇 (snake; originally *she* 它)
jiajie 假借 (loan characters), e.g., *wo* 我, *ru* 汝 (see below)

The title of the *Shuowen* reflects exactly the basic distinction drawn by Xu between single-component and compound characters, *wen* 文 and *zi* 字 (e.g., *shui* 水 and *he* 河). It is a distinction that is followed to this day (*dutizi* 獨體字 and *hetizi* 合體字); it was also the first work to arrange the characters in groups according to their significs (those components that gave a clue as to their meaning), hence called classifiers (often also called "radicals"), *bushou* 部首 (16.3). Until Xu's day the commonly used words for writing were *ming* 名, *shu* 書, or *wen* 文. His use of *wenzi* 文字 (first attested on the Liangya inscription of 219 BC), ensured that it became the standard word for script.

Despite the modern discovery of new and earlier forms of writing on artifacts and in excavated texts, Xu's work is still the single most important historical source on ancient Chinese characters and on the written language as it had developed up to his day. It is used as the basis for most modern analyses of the structure of the characters, which are frequently divided into three categories: (1) the form indicates the word and hence the sound; (2) a character is used for its phonetic properties; and (3) the character combines (1) and (2).[15]

Type-1 characters, *xingyizi* 形義字, are those in which the form indicates or symbolizes the meaning of words (*yixing biaoyi* 以形表義), usually for objects from everyday life. *Xingyizi* include Xu Shen's *zhishi*, *xiangxing*, and *huiyi* categories.

Pre-classical Chinese contains some 1,000 words represented by *xingyizi* (including about 300 that have not been deciphered), but that was about the limit as to how many words for things, let alone concepts, could be represented by characters derived from pictures, signs, or associations (Modern Chinese includes about 500 frequently used *xingyizi*). One interesting but very small subset of the *xingyizi* were those characters which may have been based on sign lan-

---

[15] This threefold classification is based on Qiu, 1996 (16.1). Boltz's three stages (zodiographic, multivalent, and determinative) are almost identical; see Boltz, 1994 (2.3.2); also Yin Binyong 尹斌庸, *Modern Chinese Characters*, John S. Rohsenow, tr., Sinolingua, 1994.

guage.[16] Later, ingenious ways were found of forming new characters based on the *xingyizi*, but the most important way was to borrow them.[17]

Type-2 characters, *yinyizi* 音義字 (that is, *jieyin biaoyi* 借音表義), are phonetic loans, formed according to a method used by other writing systems of the ancient world (the so-called rebus principle whereby, for example, pictures of a cat and a log are borrowed for their sounds for the word pronounced "catalog"). Thus the word for "don't" (pronounced *wu* in Modern Chinese) was represented by *mu* 母. The character was borrowed for its sound irrespective of its original meaning of "mother."[18] *Yinyizi* were fairly common on oracle-bone and bronze inscriptions when the development of new characters could hardly keep pace with the language, especially the requirement to find characters for proper nouns and abstract words such as numbers (*jia* 甲, *yi* 乙, *bing* 丙, *ding* 丁), pronouns (*wo* 我, *ru* 汝, *zhen* 朕), or particles (*wu* 毋, *wu* 勿, *bu* 不, *fo* 弗, *yi* 以, *yu* 于, *qi* 其).

In order to avoid the confusion arising when a character was borrowed to represent different words, small changes were made, for example, by adding strokes, dots, and circles either singly or in combination (thus *wu* was written 毋 to distinguish it from 母; *shao* 少 [few] was written with an extra stroke to distinguish it from *xiao*

---

[16] "Liuge gu Hanzi beihou de chuantong shoushi" 六個古漢字背后的傳統手勢 (Traditional gestures behind six ancient characters), in You Shunzhao 游順釗 (Shun-chiu Yao), *Shijue yuyanxue lunji* 視覺語言學論集 (Collected essays on visual language studies), Yuyan, 1994, 151–71.

[17] Xu Jinxiong 許進雄 examines the forms, basic meanings, and sounds of 830 type-1 characters and gives the *Shuowen* definitions, examples of usage, and the number of *xieshengzi* in which the components feature: *Guwen xiesheng zigen* 古文諧聲字根 (The constituent roots of ancient Chinese phonetic compound characters), Taibei: Shangwu, 1995.

[18] Traditionally *yinyizi* are termed *jiajiezi* 假借字 (loan or borrowed characters). Those which were formed for words with no previous characters are mainly found on the oracle-bones and bronze inscriptions. Those which were borrowed for words with existing characters are called *tongjiazi* 通假字 (alternative characters). They became increasingly common in the Warring States, the Qin, and the Han for reasons explained in 16.4.4. See E. G. Pulleyblank, "*Jiajie* and *Xiesheng*," in *Studies on Chinese Historical Syntax and Morphology: Linguistic Essays in Honor of Mei Tsu-lin*, Alain Peyraube and Sun Chaofen, eds., École des Hautes Etudes en Sciences Sociales, Centre de Recherches Linguistiques sur l'Asie Orientale, Paris, 1999, 145–63.

小 [small]; when *lao* 老 [old] took the meaning of father, the pronunciation changed to *ku* and the character was altered to *kao* 考, later borrowed for *kao* [examine] as in *kaozheng* 考證). But as the number of characters grew, it became difficult to memorize all such small changes. Eventually, the practice developed of adding a second component, the signific or determinative, in order to distinguish different words written with the same or a similar character. Likewise, a phonetic was often added to characters having the same or similar forms. This led to the third type.

Type-3 characters, *xingshengzi* 形聲字, are compounds usually of two parts, one of which, the signific (*xingfu* 形符), gives a clue to the meaning by suggesting in which broad category of things a word should be classified in (as with *mu* 木 "tree" in *song* 松 "pine"). It thus helps distinguish homophones. The other part, the phonetic (*shengfu*), gives a hint of the sound (as with *gong* 公 in *song* 松) and sometimes of the meaning (2.3.2).[19] *Xingshengzi* became the principal way of avoiding ambiguity and also of forming new characters. As a result, today most characters are of this type. As the name indicates, *xingshengzi* were typically formed by combining existing characters of types 1 and 2.

Only about 25 percent of the oracle-bone characters that have been deciphered to date are *xingshengzi* 形聲字 (of the remainder, more than half are *xingyizi* 形義字). About 40 percent of the bronze characters are *xingshengzi*; by the beginning of the second century AD, 80–85 percent of the small seal characters were *xingshengzi* and *xingyizi* had declined to less than 15 percent.[20] Ninety-nine percent of all new characters invented from the Han to the present day have been *xingsheng* compounds.

Although the relative number of Type-1 characters (*xingyizi*) declined during the Zhou as other types (especially Type-3 charac-

---

[19] *Xingshengzi* 形聲字 (picto-phonetic characters) are also called *xieshengzi* 諧聲字 (phonetic compound characters). *Xingfu* 形符 are also known as *xingpang* 形旁 or *yifu* 意符; *shengfu* 聲符 are sometimes referred to as *shengpang* 聲旁 or *yinpang* 音旁.

From the Han, the significs may properly be termed classifiers because from then on they were used as the basis of a system for organizing characters into groups according to semantic classifiers, *bushou* 部首 (radicals); see 16.3.

[20] Li Guoying 李國英, *Xiaozhuan xingshengzi yanjiu* 小篆形聲字研究 (Research on small seal *xingsheng* characters), Beijing shifan daxue, 1996.

ters, *xingshengzi*) were formed, they are still among the most frequently used for three main reasons: as the first to be developed, they represent the words for basic things and concepts; second, arising from this, almost all significs were originally *xingyizi*, so *xingyizi* appear as one of the components in almost every character in the script; third, nearly all classifiers as well as a large number of phonetic indicators are *xingyizi*. Another reason is that one type of *xingyizi*, the *huiyizi* 會意字, continued to be invented in small numbers throughout Chinese history. For example, fire is *huo* 火; two fires are scorching hot, *yan* 炎; three are flames, *yan* 焱.

16.3   Significs and Classifiers

Philologists have counted about 150 significs in use from the oracle-bone script to the centuries before the Qin unification. Many more have since been invented, but the original 150 are still in use today in thousands of the most frequently used characters. Almost without exception they are type-1 characters (the original form indicates the meaning). Words such as *shan* 山 (mountain), *shui* 水 (water), *niu* 牛 (ox), *ma* 馬 (horse), and numerals did not change their meaning from the Shang to the present day. For these reasons the Shang lexical heritage survives in Modern Chinese to an extent that may not always be fully recognized.

The core significs cover (1) man and parts of the body (the single most complete category);[21] (2) animals, insects, reptiles, and their pelts and skins;[22] (3) trees, plants, wine, and food;[23] (4) housing, clothing, utensils, equipment, and weapons;[24] (5) the sun, the moon, topography, and the elements;[25] (6) gods and divination;[26] (7) metrological units.[27] As time went by, more and more words with extended meanings were placed in these categories. For example, the characters for mouth, ears, nose, eyes, tongue, heart, hands, and feet were not used only for parts of the body but also as significs in words related to eating, talking, hearing, smell, sight, taste, emo-

---

[21] 人 儿 大 兒 尸 士 女 男 父 老 子 民 臣 首 頁 面 耳 目 口 自 鼻 彡 身 手 又 足 勺 骨 肉 血 力

[22] 馬 牛 羊 犬 豕 隹 豸 虎 鹿 鳥 蟲 魚 黽 龜 龍 羽 毛 角 革

[23] 木 竹 艸 禾 食 米 酉 鹵

[24] 門 戶 京 瓦 穴 衣 巾 糸 革 帛 章 舟 車 斤 耒 网 工 鼎 鬲 豆 壺 斗 皿 缶 爵 聿 弓 矢 干 戈 刀 矛 殳

[25] 日 月 風 雨 山 阜 厂 川 田 里 邑 行 金 玉 石 土 水 火

[26] 巫 卜 示 鬼

[27] 寸 工 弓 斗 斤 石 里 厘 角 鼓 龠 (7.3.1)

tions, and actions using the hands and feet. Characters were associated now with one signific, now with another as a result of similarities of meaning or of form between the significs. After several centuries of experimentation, most characters eventually came to be placed under very few classifiers (significs) in dictionaries. Even today, the 85,568 characters in the *Zhonghua zihai* 中華字海 (Table 1, Chapter 1) are classified under just 200 significs. This clearly indicates that the significs can be only very broad indicators of category.[28]

All the classifiers in use today have customary descriptions. The easiest to remember are those that are also independent single-component characters. They are simply listed with an indication of their position in the character, e.g., *shanzitou* 山字頭 (as in *yan* 岩); *yanzipang* 言字旁 (as in *shuo* 說); *xinzidi* 心字底 (as in *ying* 應). Classifiers that cannot stand alone have their own nicknames, such as *liangdianshui* 兩點水 and *sandianshui* 三點水 (as in *bing* 冰 and *he* 河). These ways of referring to classifiers are listed in the appendixes of most good dictionaries. They are worth remembering because they are used in everyday life (to identify *ru* 汝 during a telephone call, you would say *sandianshui, yige nü zi* 三點水一個女字).

---

[28] The characters classified under the Five Phases—*shui* 水 (water), *mu* 木 (wood), *jin* 金 (metal), *tu* 土 (earth), and *huo* 火 (fire)—account for 20 percent of the total 10,000 characters in the modern dictionary *Xinhua zidian* 新華字典. If you add three more of the most frequently used classifiers, the characters *kou* 口 (mouth), *shou* 手 (hand), and *cao* 艹 (grass or flower), these eight alone account for over one-third of all the characters in the dictionary; another 18 classifiers account for a second third. The same proportions hold for the *Kangxi zidian* 康熙字典, in which approximately two-thirds of the characters are listed under and contain the 25 most frequent classifiers. The remaining characters are scattered in small numbers under the other 150 classifiers.

On the graphic development of the characters, including a long section on the pre-Qin development of the classifiers, see Gao Ming 高明, *Zhongguo guwenzixue tonglun* 中國古文字學通論 (General introduction to the study of Chinese paleography), Wenwu, 1987; new rev. edition, Beijing daxue, 1996, 1997. He uses hundreds of drawings and includes 200 pages of annotated, illustrated readings of ancient script (*guwenzi* 古文字) forms. It should be read together with the same author's tabulated comparison of 3,056 characters in the different *guwen* scripts, *Guwenzi leibian* 古文字類編 (Ancient Chinese characters arranged by type), Zhonghua, 1980, Tôhô, 1987; 5th print., 1990. Both works are exceptionally clearly printed.

16.4 *Variants*

One of the main difficulties in reading Classical Chinese is that the same character could be written in many different ways: there were graphic variants (*yitizi* 異體字, 16.4.1); a later way of writing a character often differed from an earlier way (*gujinzi* 古今字, 16.4.2); and variants with fewer strokes than the official ones were in popular use from the earliest times to the present day (*suzi* 俗字, 16.4.3). Another type of difficulty is that one character could be used to represent two or more words with the same pronunciation (*tongjiazi* 通假字, 16.4.4), moreover, one character could have two or more different pronunciations (16.4.5). Finally, foreign loanwords were written with all sorts of different characters (usually approximating the original sound, see 1.2.6). There were also many special characters, for example, those which were unique to a particular area. They are called dialect characters (*fangyanzi* 方言字), e.g., *mou* 冇 for *meiyou* 没有 in modern Cantonese. There were also special characters for particular trades, *hangyu wenzi* 行語文字 (for example, *dangzi* 當字, pawnshop writing; see 7.1.2); magical and riddle characters,[29] and many others. It was forbidden to use such characters in official documents.

Most of these variants arose because at the formative stages of the writing system communication between different centers of learning was poor and standardization of the characters was difficult during the two millennia before the invention of printing (and not easily achieved after that).

As time went by, graphic variants declined: there are sometimes up to 50 different ways of writing a single character in the oracle-bone script, the golden age of *yitizi*. By the Han chancery script, their number was falling, largely as the result of official efforts to standardize the characters. The Zhou began the effort that was continued when the first emperor decreed that the Qin small seal script was to be the standard for the whole country. Significant advances were made during the Han with the editing of authorized editions of the classics in *lishu* for the imperial library and the carving of

---

[29] Ireneus Laszlo Legeza, *Tao Magic: The Secret Language of Diagrams and Calligraphy*, Thames and Hudson, 1975, 1987; Liu Xiaoming 劉曉明, *Zhongguo fuzhou wenhua daguan* 中國符咒文化大觀 (Overview of the culture of Chinese charms and spells), Baihuazhou wenyi, 1995.

some of them on stone in the Later Han. Inclusion in the *Shuowen* was taken as the basis for recognition as a *zhengzi* 正字 (standard form of character) as opposed to *suzi* 俗字 (vulgar character). The *Shuowen* lists graphic variants for no less than 12 percent of the characters it contains, a practice followed in many later dictionaries and character primers. Tang scholars and the court worked on a standard form of *kaishu* to replace the chaotic variations that had developed during the Nan-Bei Chao. The examination system required candidates to use the standard forms of the characters. Indeed, one of the most popular Tang character primers was written to help scholars avoid common variants and vulgar characters.[30] When printing became widespread in the Song, it too helped standardize the characters, but there were still many variants and a large gap between printed and handwritten forms. In this respect, it is worth remembering that orthographic variation in Europe was common even within a single printed work until the early seventeenth century. In China, different ways of writing and printing the characters continued into the twentieth century.

16.4.1 *Graphic Variants*

There was a huge amount of graphic variation in all the scripts (the sound in the standard Chinese of the day and the meaning were the same, only the form was different). The old terms for graphic variants are *chongwen* 重文 or *huoti* 或體, the modern one, *yitizi* 異體字.[31] In a different context, these are what we would call alternative spellings. *Yitizi* developed in many ways:

1. Characters for the same word were formed using more than one of the three main ways of forming characters, e.g., *jian* 奸 is a type-3 character, which was also written as a type-1 character with three *nü* 女 together: 姦.

---

[30] *Ganlu zishu* 干祿字書 (Character primer for office seekers), Yan Yuansun 顏元孫 (?–714).

[31] *Yitizi zidian* 異體字字典 (Dictionary of graphic variants), Li Pu 李圃, ed. in chief, Xuelin, 1997, contains nearly 10,000 head characters and 50,000 variants of them drawn from 151 dictionaries and epigraphical works from the Shang dynasty to the present day. Arrangement is by *Shuowen* classifiers. There is a stroke-count index of head characters, and modern pronunciations are shown in *pinyin*.

2. Different significs (typically with closely related meanings) were as-signed at different periods (or in different texts) to the same character, especially before the standardization in Qin and Han, e.g., *yong* 咏 either with *kou* 口 or *yan* 言 as signific (咏 or 詠).

3. The same character, but with a different phonetic, e.g., *gu* 菰, with either 孤 or 姑 as phonetic.

4. The same character, but with the signific or phonetic put in different positions, e.g., *lüe* 略 with the 田 either at the left (略) or on top (畧).

5. Variant ways of writing a component part, e.g., *mu* 畝 written either with 久 or 厶 as the right-hand component (畝 or 𤱔).

6. Sometimes a *sutizi* 俗體字 became an *yitizi*, e.g., 吴 was used for 吳.

7. Previous ways of writing a character were held over long after the in-troduction of a major script reform. For example, *tu* 徒 (the *lishu* form of *tu* 徒) continued in use for centuries after *kaishu* had replaced *lishu*.

A special reason for creating graphic variants was the need to avoid taboo words, such as the personal name of the emperor (3.3). One way in which scribes did so was to drop a stroke as with *xuan* 玄 for *xuan* 玄 or *zhao* 炤 for *zhao* 照 (compare part-spelling of four-letter words in English).

Large character dictionaries include *yitizi* (a) whose "correct" character, *zhengzi* 正字 (b), is normally indicated by the formula, *yitizi* (a) *tong* 同 *zhengzi* (b).

In 1955, the authorities forbade the use of 1,055 graphic variants (except in reprints of classical texts and other scholarly works, in-cluding dictionaries of Classical Chinese). Twenty-eight characters were reinstated in three subsequent revisions (the last in 1988), thus reducing the total proscribed graphic variants to 1,027.

Quite apart from graphic variants, characters were frequently written by mistake for another (*wuzi* 誤字, *huaizi* 壞字, *ezi* 訛字). As such they are regarded as textual errors resulting from the mis-takes of copyists or as ill-advised attempts to improve a text.[32]

Manuscripts also often contain large numbers of wrongly writ-ten, that is to say, non-existent, characters (*cuozi* 錯字).

[32] Susan Cherniack discusses textual errors and lists six common types of them in the appendix to "Book Culture and Textual Transmission in Sung China," *HJAS* 54.1: 5–125 (1994), 102–25.

16.4.2   Ancient and Modern Characters (gujinzi 古今字)

If a word was written with a type-1 or type-2 character (normally invented in the pre-Qin period) and later with a type-3 character (usually to distinguish one of its meanings), or if a type-3 character was later modified for the same reason, the pair was termed *gujinzi* 古今字 (ancient and modern characters), a description that has been in use since the Later Han. The modern term is *qubiezi* 區別字 (differentiated characters). For example, *yao* 腰 (waist) is a *jinzi* because it had a signific added later to differentiate it from the original character (*yao* 要, waist), which in the interim had acquired the following additional meanings in Classical Chinese (also in the first tone): binding, stop midway, invite, coerce, seek, overlooked, hold back, verify. Sometimes for a period of centuries both the old and new forms of a character were in use interchangeably, but this was exceptional. A good dictionary such as the *Hanyu da cidian* will indicate the earlier form of a differentiated character: thus one of the entries for *yao* 要 reads, "*yao de guzi*" 腰的古字. Normally the pronunciation and meanings of *gujinzi* were closely related. Indeed, the *jinzi* is often a reliable indication of the root meaning or etymon (*benyi* 本義) of the *guzi* (thus we can know that the etymon of *yao* 要 is waist). Likewise, with *zhang* 丈 and *zhang* 杖 and *liang* 兩 and *liang* 輛. Both pairs are *gujinzi* 古今字. *Zhang* 杖 (walking stick) is the etymon of the one and *liang* 輛 (two-wheeled chariot) of the other.[33]

16.4.3   Correct and Vulgar Characters (zhengsuzi 正俗字)

Characters have been written in simplified ways ever since they first appeared on the oracle-bone script, often by dropping one or other component, typically the classifier when these became common, the context making the meaning clear. Many Han and post-Han simplified characters were based on *xingshu* or *caoshu* forms.

After the Qin and Han script reforms, the distinction was drawn between *zhengzi* 正字 (standard characters), which were to be

[33] Lin Xiao'an 林小安, "Yinqi liushu yanjiu (yi)" 殷契六書研究 (一) (Research on the *liushu* in the oracle-bone script), *Chutu wenxian yanjiu* 出土文獻研究 (Research on excavated documents), vol. 3, Zhonghua, 1998, 6–20; "Yinqi benyi lungao" 殷契本義論稿 (Draft discussion of basic meaning in oracle-bone script), *Chutu wenxian yanjiu*, vol. 5, Kexue, 1999, 6–24.

used in official writing, and *suzi* 俗字 (vulgar characters), which were banned but remained in everyday use. At the end of the nineteenth century, pioneer script reformers made efforts to make the *suzi* more respectable and they were renamed "simplified characters" (*jiantizi* 簡體字) as opposed to the *zhengzi*, renamed *fantizi* 繁體字 (complex characters).

A list of simplified characters was first made official in August 1935. The Harvard-Yenching Institute was quick off the mark in deciding to publish a dictionary of them, but by the time it was out, the government had withdrawn the list in February 1936.[34] A selection of *jiantizi* was finally made official on a national scale in 1956 (an enlarged list was gazetted in 1964).[35]

Plans to extend the list of simplified characters during the Cultural Revolution were shelved immediately after it was over, and only minor adjustments have since appeared (in 1986). Today, the core number of simplified characters is 535 out of a total of 2,233 (for example, *ma* 马 is one of the 535 core characters and also appears in its role as a classifier in many of the characters in the full list). Of the 535, one-third were already in circulation in pre-Qin and Han times; 40 percent date from between the Han and 1911. The Republic saw 12 percent invented, and 20 percent were devised since 1949.

16.4.4 Alternative Characters (tongjiazi 通假字)

In Classical Chinese the same character can be used for different words. This can be the result of a type-1 character being used as a phonetic loan to stand for a word with no previous character (type-2 character, *jiajiezi* 假借字).[36]

A character (often type 3) can also be used to represent words that already have a character (*benzi* 本字). The second character has

---

[34] Rong Geng 容庚 (1894–1983), *Jianti zidian* 簡體字典 (Dictionary of simplified characters), H-Y Institute, 1936.

[35] Li Leyi 李樂毅, *Jianhuazi yuan* 簡化字源 (The origins of simplified Chinese characters), Sinolingua, 1996; Yin (1966), 56–61.

[36] The definition of the same pronunciation is if the initial (*sheng* 聲), the rhyme (*yun* 韵), and tone (*diao* 調) are identical; similar refers to when two of these conditions are met, the sounds belonging to that period of the language in which the borrowing took place (normally Old Chinese).

the same or a similar pronunciation to the first, but the meaning is different. For example, *shi* 矢 (arrow) was often used in place of *shi* 屎 (excrement), and *zao* 蚤 (flea) for *zao* 早 (early). Such alternative characters (*tongjiazi* 通假字) are distinguished from wrongly used characters (*biezi* 別字, *baizi* 白字) by the fact that they were recognized as alternatives (the conventional term means "generally used borrowed characters"). A character can have several *tongjiazi*, and one *tongjiazi* can serve for several different characters (*shi* 矢, for example, also stood for *shi* 誓). *Tongjiazi* were not normally used interchangeably (矢 for 屎 or 誓, but never 屎 or 誓 for 矢), but this sometimes occurs (*ce* 策 for *ce* 冊 and vice-versa). *Tongjiazi* were already widespread on the Zhou bronzes and became increasingly so in the Warring States, Qin, and Han. They appear in all types of words, including in personal names and toponyms. These were the centuries that saw the biggest changes that have ever taken place in the writing system, including the rapid increase of picto-phonetic compound characters. But during these centuries there was no uniform standard for the writing system; so it is understandable that a scribe might prefer a character with which he was more familiar—in other words, one whose pronunciation was closer to the local language in his kingdom or region. There was also a tendency to choose characters with fewer strokes.[37] More than 15,000 different *tongjiazi* have been counted. This does not include the large numbers found on new epigraphic sources such as bamboo strips and silk manuscripts. After the Tang and Song, new alternative characters tended to be regarded as *biezi* (wrongly used characters), but established *tongjiazi* continued in use until the script reforms of the twentieth century and have been retained in old texts to this day.[38]

[37] Zhao Ping'an (1993), 136–50. This study is based on the analysis of excavated manuscripts on bamboo and silk and also takes into account earlier work based on transmitted texts; for example, Bernhard Karlgren, *Loan Characters in Pre-Han Texts*, MFEA, 1967; originally appeared in *BMFEA* 35: 1–128 (1960).

[38] There are also specialized works, such as *Guzi tongjia huidian* 古字通假 會典 (Collection of ancient alternative characters), Gao Heng 高亨 comp., Dong Zhi'an 董治安, readied for publication, Qi-Lu, 1989, 1997, which contains no fewer than 16,000 examples of *tongjiazi*, almost all from Han and pre-Han works, but not including new epigraphic sources. The compilers reached such a huge number by including *gujin*, *yiti*, and *jianti* characters. Others using a stricter definition are on a more modest scale, e.g., *Gu Hanyu duoyong tongjia zidian* 古漢語多用通假字典 (Multi-use dictionary of *tongjiazi*), Zhang Jun 張

Footnote continued on next page

Characters that appear to have been "borrowed" not so much for their sound, but for their similarity of form are generally regarded as *biezi*. For example, *yi* 已 instead of *ji* 己 or *wu* 戊 instead of *shu* 戌. *Biezi* and *suzi* are common in *baihua* fiction.

Had the use of *tongjiazi* continued to grow, thus downplaying the semantic component of characters, Chinese writing might have developed into a syllabic system. That it did not was because Old Chinese was mainly monosyllabic: every character normally stood for a syllable, and each syllable was a word with meaning. As William Boltz puts it, "if a language does not have syllables without meaning, why should its speakers include in their writing system a way to write such syllables?" (Boltz, 1994, 171; see 2.3.2 for full reference). *Tongjiazi* are a pitfall for the unwary. If you come across an apparently meaningless character in a phrase, especially in a pre-Qin text, it may be a *tongjiazi*. To confirm it, check any good dictionary. The formula under the entry of the borrowed character (e.g., 蚤) is "通[早]," or "(古)同[早]." *Tongjiazi* are normally pronounced according to the *benzi* they replace, thus *tuo* not *shui* for 税 (通 [脱]).

16.4.5 Different Pronunciations

About 20 percent of the characters in Classical Chinese (and 10–15 percent in *Putonghua*) have more than one reading. This is especially true of frequently used characters. The modern term is polyphonic characters, *duoyinzi* 多音字 or *poyinzi* 破音字.[39]

The changes in pronunciation or in tone can indicate different meanings and sometimes also different parts of speech (1.2.2).

軍 and Liu Naishu 劉乃叔, eds. in chief, Dongbei shifan daxue, 1991, contains 1,300 *tongjiazi* and indicates both ancient and modern pronunciation as well as giving definitions.

[39] For a convenient dictionary of polyphonic characters, see *Shiyong sucha duoyin zi cidian* 實用速查多音字詞典 (Practical quick reference polyphonic character dictionary of compounds and phrases), Jiang Xue 江雪 and Chen Lin 陳琳, eds. in chief, Changchun, 1995, 1996. This includes 2,600 polyphonic characters both ancient and modern. They are indexed in *pinyin* under all readings and (an unusual feature) with copious examples of each character's different readings in compounds and phrases whether at the beginning, middle, or end.

Both in standard Chinese and in the dialects, there were often literary readings (*wendu* 文讀) and vernacular pronunciations (*baidu* 白讀) for the same character, for example, *ji* 給 (*wen*) as in *jiyu* 給予 (render, give) and *gei* 給 (*bai*) as in *gei ta* 給他 or *xue* 血 (*wen*) and *xie* 血 (*bai*). Literary readings are sometimes retained in standard spoken Chinese in words that are in no sense literary, for example, *peiji* 配給 (ration) or *xuehong* 血紅 (blood-red).

When polyphonic characters (*duoyinzi* 多音字) have the same meaning, they are simply variant reading characters (*yiduzi* 異讀字) whose origins no doubt lie in changes in pronunciation over time and in different dialects and the differences between literary and vernacular pronunciations. It is possible that different pronunciations were most commonly given to characters that had no phonetic indicator (*shengfu* 聲符) or to borrowed characters (*jiajie*).

Polyphonic characters have been retained in the modern standard language when the change in pronunciation indicates a change in meaning. But when the change is simply a variant reading, they have generally been discarded except in a small number of cases where it is customary to use the old pronunciations.[40]

16.5   On Studying the Ancient Scripts

The historian of ancient China Li Xueqin 李學勤 offers advice to the beginner. He emphasizes the analysis of the form of a character as the starting point (begin with the *Shuowen* and then move to newly excavated documents, preferably near in place and time to the one you are analyzing); trace the development of the character to its later forms (including its sound and meaning); check the result by testing your interpretation in the original context. A good knowledge of Old Chinese is essential, not least to help spot alternative and phonetic loan characters. Finally, the student will not get far without a good knowledge of modern archaeology and of the literature close in time to the inscription being studied.[41]

---

[40] The modern list of received pronunciations is *Putonghua yiduci shenyinbiao* 普通話異讀詞審音表 (List of authorized pronunciations for heterophonic words in Putonghua), Beijing, 1985.

[41] Li Xueqin, *Guwenzixue chuji* 古文字學初級 (First steps in paleography), Zhonghua, 1985; 3rd prnt., 1997, 67–72.

The paleographer Qiu Xigui 裘錫圭 advises Chinese students against trying to jump straight into ancient scripts such as the oracle-bone or bronze inscriptions, simply relying on dictionaries. They should first get a good grounding in Classical Chinese by reading as much as possible (1.3.5). Then do what Sima Qian 司馬遷, Sima Guang 司馬光, and countless other Chinese historians began by doing: read the *Chunqiu sanzhuan* 春秋三傳 (21.1). A knowledge of the context, as provided by archaeology and ancient history, is also essential, as is a thorough acquaintance with the *Shuowen* (16.2).[42]

Another Beida paleographer, Gao Ming 高明, emphasizes four techniques for analyzing the meanings of ancient characters (which also apply to the study of Classical Chinese). Compare the evolution of the forms of characters as they appear on different media and in different periods (not only as they appear in the *Shuowen*); compare the usage of characters in inscriptions with those found in contemporary texts; analyze the development and use of the components of the characters; and finally, examine the institutional context in which the characters appear.[43]

The historian and paleographer Xu Zhongshu 徐中舒 notes that the six types of characters composition theory (*liushu* 六書) was a late rationalization. In practice, the form, sound, and meaning of characters went through a complex process of construction and adaptation before reaching acceptance and standardization. He stresses the importance therefore of investigating both the linguistic and the graphic etymologies of characters (*yuyuan* 語源 and *ziyuan* 字源) and in doing so, the need to make the interconnections between groups of characters placed in their historic context. He takes as his examples the two words for dog (*quan* 犬 and *gou* 狗) and a number of characters in origin connected with the most common form of

---

[42] Qiu Xigui, "On the Methods of Studying Ancient Chinese Script," *Yuwen daobao* 語文導報, 1985.10; reprinted in the author's *Guwenzi luncong* 古文字論叢 (Collected papers on ancient characters), Zhonghua, 1992, 652-60, tr. by Gilbert L. Mattos in *EC* 11-12: 301-16 (1985-87).

[43] Gao Ming (1996), 167-72; see also Edward L. Shaughnessy, "How to Read a Western Zhou Bronze Inscription," in *Sources of Western Zhou History: Inscribed Bronze Vessels*, UCP, 1991, Chapter 3, 63-105.

housing in the Shang, loess cave dwelling (*xue* 穴), showing as he does so the mistaken interpretations in the *Shuowen*.[44]

For reference works and readers on the oracle-bone script, see 15.5. For a description of epigraphic sources on other media such as bronze, stone, or jade, see Chapter 17. General introductions to the different types of *guwen* usually contain annotated readings. One of the best is Gao Ming (1996). Another is *Shang-Zhou guwenzi duben* 商周古文字讀本. It contains selected, annotated readings of oracle-bone, bronze, stone drum, jade, and pottery inscriptions.[45]

[44] Xu Zhongshu, "Zenmeyang kaoshi guwenzi" 怎么樣考釋古文字 (How to interprate the ancient scripts), in *Xu Zhongshu lishi lunwen xuanji* 徐中舒歷史論文選輯 (Selected historical papers of Xu Zhongshu), 2 vols., Zhonghua, 1998, 1433–42.

[45] *Shang-Zhou guwenzi duben* (Reader of ancient characters from the Shang and Zhou), Liu Xiang 劉翔 et al., comps., Yuwen, 1989, 3rd print., 1996.

17

Epigraphy

Most inscriptions were cast in bronze (17.1) or carved on stone (17.3). In addition, they were recorded on all sorts of other materials and objects, including bone (Chapter 15 and 44.3.1), turtle shell (Chapter 15), jade, seals, coins, brick, and pottery (17.2).

The antiquarian study of inscriptions dug up from the earth, particularly those on auspicious and valuable objects such as ancient bronze vessels or stone tablets, began in earnest in the Song dynasty, which first saw the use of the old phrase *jinshi* 金石 "(cast in) bronze and (carved on) stone" in this new sense.[1] It was mainly pursued by collectors and calligraphers. More than 500 ancient bronzes were dug up in the Northern Song. They were categorized and printed with illustrations and transcriptions in works such as *Kaogu lu* 考古錄, Lü Dalin 呂大臨 (1046–92), comp., preface, 1092; and in the catalog of the emperor Huizong's collection of 839 bronzes, *Bogutu* 博古圖, Wang Fu 王黼 (1079–1126), ed., 1123. They not only categorized the bronze vessels according to formal criteria, but they also began the arduous task of reconstructing the forms and the meanings of the ancient characters found on some of them.

Today, for the most part, it is only these transcriptions which survive.[2] In the Qing, the Qianlong emperor sponsored the publication of three works on the massive imperial collections of bronze

---

[1] See Edward L. Shaughnessy, "Introduction," in *NSECH*, 1–14. For a general history of epigraphy, see Zhu Jianxin 朱劍心 *Jinshixue* 金石學 (The study of inscriptions on bronze and stone), Shanghai: Shangwu, 1955; rpnt., Wenwu, 1981.

Guides and research tools to particular epigraphic materials are listed at the end of 17.1, 17.2, and 17.3.

[2] See Noel Barnard, "Records of Discoveries of Bronze Vessels in Literary Sources and Some Pertinent Remarks on Aspects of Chinese Historiography," *Journal of the Institute of Chinese Studies of the University of Hong Kong*, 6.1: 455–546 (1973).

vessels. This stimulated scholars to begin their own collections and to apply text-critical methods to the study of the inscriptions (*jinshi* 金石), which flourished as never before. Modern historians use them as independent checks on the record found in received texts.

Collections of epigraphy of particular periods or regions have been printed for many centuries. Today modern collections of newly unearthed bronze and stone inscriptions are also published in book form, often by region.

Note that the *Zhongguo kaoguxue nianjian* 中國考古學年鑑 (Yearbook of Chinese archaeology) includes over 30 double-column pages at the end indexing the inscriptions discovered the previous year, arranged by material, period, and place.

17.1   Bronze Inscriptions

A very large number of elaborately decorated bronze vessels, bells, tools, and weapons are extant today.[3] Only about 12,000 have inscriptions (*jinwen* 金文 or *zhongdingwen* 鐘鼎文, "the writing on bells and caldrons," so called since these were the most prestigious bronzes and therefore those upon which inscriptions were most frequently cast). The writing on the inscriptions is normally arranged in columns from top to bottom reading from right to left. Of the total of inscribed bronzes, about one-quarter date from the Yin-Shang period, half from the Zhou and one-quarter from the Qin and Han. The nature of the inscriptions in each period is dif-

---

[3] For introductions, see Jessica Rawson, *Chinese Bronzes: Art and Ritual*, British Museum, 1987; Ma Chengyuan 馬承源, *Zhongguo qingtongqi quanji* 中國青銅器全集, 16 vols., Wenwu, 1996–98. *The Art of the Houma Foundry*, Institute of Archaeology of Shanxi Province, eds., PUP and FLP, 1996, describes the workings and shows the remains of the largest Bronze Age foundry ever discovered in the world. On whether the bronze decorations have an iconographic meaning and if so, what, see *The Problem of Meaning in Early Chinese Ritual Bronzes*, Roderick Whitfield, ed., University of London, Percival David Foundation, SOAS, 1993. For an inventory of bronze vessels of every kind up to and including the Warring States, see *Gudai Zhongguo qingtongqi* 古代中國青銅器, Zhu Fenghan 朱鳳瀚, comp., Nankai daxue, 1995. Note Hayashi Minao 林巳奈夫, *In-Shû jidai seidôki sôran* 殷周時代青銅器綜覽 (Comprehensive studies on the bronze vessels of the Yin and Zhou), vols. 1 and 2 (Yin and Zhou), Tokyo, 1984, 1986; vol. 3 (Spring and Autumn and Warring States periods), Yoshikawa, 1989.

ferent. The Shang ones start at the same time as the oracle-bone inscriptions (Wu Ding 武丁 reign). They contain only two or three characters recording the name of the maker and an ancestor, often with a generation tag (*jiming jinwen* 記名金文). Some are emblems in the form of a single pictograph, probably representing a clan or lineage, or its settlement. Functionally such identifications may have been similar to the single marks found on prehistoric pottery vessels.

The form of the writing on the early bronzes reflects the medium: the strokes are thicker than those on the oracle-bone inscriptions. The bronze characters are also more pictographic than the oracle-bone characters, that by comparison appear schematic and simpler. Most of the Shang bronze inscriptions have been found in the vicinity of the Shang cult center at Anyang. At the very end of the Shang, bronze inscriptions of 30 or 40 characters began to appear. The total vocabulary of the Shang bronzes does not contain more than 300 characters (far less than that contained on the Shang oracle-bone inscriptions (15.4).

Gradually, in the Western Zhou the inscriptions grew longer and the forms of the characters became simpler and more standardized. The longest inscription (497 characters) is that on the Maogong *ding* 毛公鼎, which is similar to a passage in the *Shangshu* 尚書 (Venerated documents).[4]

It is probable that the bronze inscriptions are secondary sources summarized from longer texts recorded on perishable materials such as bamboo.[5]

Bronze characters are called *jinwen* 金文 because *jin* 金 was used interchangeably with *tong* 銅 (bronze) in Old Chinese. A total of about 4,000 separate bronze characters have been distinguished, of which 2,500 have been deciphered.

---

[4] The authenticity of the Maogong *ding* (currently in the Palace Museum, Taibei) has been challenged, but it is now generally regarded as dating from the late Western Zhou. It was discovered ca. 1840 at Qiyi, the cultic center of the Zhou, 90 km (56 miles) to the west of modern Xi'an; see Shaughnessy, 1991 (listed under *Guides and Readers* below), 75, and on the question of authenticity of the bronzes in general, *id.*, 43–62.

[5] Lothar von Falkenhausen, "Issues in Western Zhou Studies," *EC* 18: 161–67 (1993).

The bronzes are prized collectors' items not only in China but also in Japan and in the West, where from time to time sumptuous exhibitions are held of Shang and Zhou bronzes, introduced in monographic exhibition catalogs.[6] Collectors, too, publish scholarly catalogs.[7]

Many of the bronze inscriptions have been published in collections of rubbings or transcriptions by scholars both traditional and modern (17.1, *Corpus Inscriptionum*).

Note the large number of bronze weights and capacity measures, several of which are inscribed with regulations. The earliest extant ones date from the Warring States.[8]

The most prestigious bronze vessels, the caldrons, were used in ancestral sacrifices. As with the other vessels, heroic deeds and honors were recorded on them. Different ranks of the nobility were entitled to use different numbers of caldrons and other vessels and different sacrificial foods. The same applied to burials. The system as set out in the *Zhouli* and other ritual texts has been largely confirmed by late Zhou archaeological finds. By that time, the king alone was entitled to use nine caldrons (*jiuding* 九鼎). These became the symbol of the ruler and of legitimate succession. The sacrificial bronze vessels were not only used by him as an expression of his power but also by lesser lords as a sign of their status and influence. The word for caldron also meant "huge" or "solemn" (it is also a cognate of *zheng* 政, "to rule"). Symbolic *ding* 鼎 were not used for everyday cooking, for which different vessels with different names were used. Most of the inscriptions record gifts bestowed by the monarch following some other kind of record such as orders of appointment to office, military campaigns, covenants, treaties or

[6] See, for example, *The Great Bronze Age of China*, Wen C. Fong, ed., Metropolitan Museum, and Thames and Hudson, 1980.

[7] There are a large number of important monographic catalogs of bronze collections; see, for example, Robert Bagley, *Shang Ritual Bronzes in the Arthur M. Sackler Collections*; Jessica Rawson, *Western Zhou Bronzes from the Arthur M. Sackler Collections*; Jenny F. So, *Eastern Zhou Ritual Bronzes from the Arthur M. Sackler Collections*, Arthur M. Sackler Museum and HUP, 1987; 2 vols., 1990; and 1995, respectively.

[8] For illustrations, rubbings, and transcriptions, see Qiu Guangming 丘光明, *Zhongguo lidai duliangheng kao* 中國歷代度量衡考 (Research on weights and measures through the ages in China), Kexue, 1992.

ceremonial events. The arrangement of the writing on the Zhou bronzes is more strict than on the oracle bones. The characters run from top to bottom in vertical rows reading from right to left. The characters themselves are in great seal script. By the Warring States, the inscriptions once again became shorter, mainly recording the owners and the makers of the implements on which they were cast.

When the Western Zhou had left the scene, bronze vessels gradually lost their importance as the principal way of expressing status and power, although there are some remarkable Eastern Zhou ones. By the Han, stone stelae and monuments had become the main media for proclaiming political messages and for recording commemorative inscriptions of all sorts. Thus bronze inscriptions, or the rubbings taken from them, are important sources mainly for the earlier Zhou, while stone inscriptions are vital supplementary sources for the Qin, the Han, and all subsequent periods.

Guides and Readers

The best short introductions to the Zhou bronze inscriptions with examples of how to read them as historical sources are:

Edward L. Shaughnessy, "Western Zhou Bronze Inscriptions," and Gilbert L. Mattos, "Eastern Zhou Bronze Inscriptions," both in *NSECH*, 57–84 and 85–124, respectively.

Edward L. Shaughnessy, *Sources of Western Zhou History: Inscribed Bronze Vessels*, UCP, 1991. The standard introduction in English; also contains advice on reading the inscriptions. For guidance in studying the ancient scripts (including bronze script), see 16.5.

On Shang bronze inscriptions as historical sources, see K. C. Chang, "Bronzes" in *Shang Civilization*, YUP, 1980, 20–31. Note also the use made of bronze inscriptions in Li Xueqin 李學勤, *Eastern Zhou and Qin Civilizations*, K. C. Chang, tr., YUP, 1985.

Corpora Inscriptionum

Note: it is important to use rubbings reproduced to the actual size of the originals, not in reduced size, which can alter the appearance.

Yin-Zhou jinwen jicheng 殷周金文集成 (Complete collection of Yin Zhou bronze epigraphy), *Kaoguxue* special publication, 18 folio vols., Zhonghua, 1984–95, includes 11,984 inscription rubbings. There are transcriptions, explanations, and an index. Arrangement is by 51 different vessel types (including five kinds of military weapons and tallies). Shorter inscriptions come first; longest, last. The largest number of inscriptions are found on caldrons (1,858). Work on this collection from conception in 1956 to the publication of the final volume took almost forty years. A supplementary volume of inscriptions not accepted for inclusion (either because they are illegible or because they are suspected of being forgeries) is forthcoming.

Shang-Zhou qingtongqi mingwen xuan 商周青銅器銘文選 (Selected inscriptions from Shang and Zhou bronze vessels), Ma Chengyuan 馬承原 et al., eds., 4 vols., Wenwu, 1986–91. Contains rubbings and transcriptions of 925 inscriptions conveniently arranged by topic and by period. Vol. 5 (forthcoming) is to contain an index to vols. 1–4.

Sandai jijin wencun 三代吉金文存 (Collection of bronze inscriptions from the three dynasties), Luo Zhenyu 羅振玉, ed., 1937; 3 vols., Zhonghua, 1983; 3rd prnt., 1992. To identify the bronzes in this first important modern collection of rubbings (from 4,800 vessels), use *Sandai jijin wencun zhulubiao* 三代吉金文存著錄表, Zhou Fagao 周法高 et al., Xuesheng, 1977. For a list of "Major Catalogs of Inscribed Western Zhou Bronze Vessels," see Shaughnessy (1991), 289–92.

Examples of collections and studies of bronze inscriptions from particular provinces or ancient kingdoms:

Shaanxi chutu Shang-Zhou qingtongqi 陝西出土商周青銅器 (Excavated vessels of Shaanxi from the Shang and Zhou), 4 vols., Wenwu, 1978–82 (includes photographs of the vessels and rubbings of the inscriptions).

Hubei chutu Shang-Zhou wenzi jizheng 湖北出土商周文字輯證 (Collected texts and studies of Shang-Zhou excavated scripts from Hubei), Huang Xiquan 黃錫全, ed., Wuhan daxue, 1992. Rubbings, transcriptions and explanations of nearly 1,700 inscriptions.

Dictionaries, Concordances, and Interpretations

Jinwen changyong zidian 金文常用字典 (Dictionary of frequently used bronze characters), Chen Chusheng 陳初生, comp., Shaanxi renmin, 1987. A good beginner's dictionary with examples of graphical variants and explanations of 1,000 frequently used bronze characters.

Kinbun tsûshaku 金文通釋 (Comprehensive interpretations of bronze inscriptions), Shirakawa Shizuka 白川靜, *Hakutsuru bijutsukanshi* 白鶴美術館志, nos. 1–56, 1962–84. The single most important work interpreting the bronze inscriptions and also introducing the main alternative opinions.

Jinwen gulin 金文詁林 (Etymological dictionary of ancient Chinese bronze inscriptions), Zhou Fagao 周法高 (1915–94), ed. in chief, Zhang Risheng 張日升 et al., comps., 16 vols., HKCUP, 1974–75, with supplements, *Jinwen gulin futu* 金文詁林附圖, HKCUP, 1977 (references are based on Luo, 1937); *Jinwen gulin bu* 金文詁林補 (Corrections and additions to the *Jinwen gulin*), 8 vols., Shiyusuo, 1982, 1997. Li Xiaoding 李孝定, *Jinwen gulin duhouji* 金文詁林讀後記 (Notes on reading the *Jinwen gulin*), Shiyusuo, 1982, 1992. A concordance plus repertory of scholarly interpretations of bronze characters (including many of those by Shirakawa).

Jinwen bian 金文編 (A compilation of bronze characters), Rong Geng 容庚, ed., Yi'an tang 貽安堂, 1925; 2nd ed., rev. and expanded, Shangwu, 1939; 3rd ed., rev. and expanded, Kexue, 1959; 4th ed., rev. by Zhang Zhenlin 張振林 and Ma Guoquan 馬國權, 1985; 5th prnt., Zhonghua, 1996; Chen Hanping 陳漢平, *Jinwen bian dingbu* 金文編訂補 (Revisions to the *Jinwen bian*), Shehui kexue, 1993. A concordance to bronze characters of the Shang and Zhou. The 1985 revised edition is still considered the best listing.

Biographies

Jinwen renming huibian 金文人名匯編 (Collection of personal names in bronze inscriptions), Wu Zhenfeng 吳鎮烽, comp., Zhonghua, 1987. Contains the names of 5,228 people found on the bronze inscriptions dating from the Shang to 221 BC discovered up to June 1985. The names recorded are normally those who commissioned the casting of the vessel. It is difficult to judge when the same name on two bronzes refers to the same or to two people. For this reason scholars sometimes reach very different conclusions on the date of a bronze.

Bibliography

For a bibliography of secondary sources in Chinese (up to 1982) on bronze (and many other ancient inscriptional materials), see *Qingtongqi lunwen suoyin* 青銅器論文索引, Sun Zhichu 孫稚雛, comp., Zhonghua, 1986. For more recent bibliographies, see 12.3.

17.2   Jade, Seal, Coin, and Pottery Inscriptions

17.2.1   Jade Inscriptions

The earliest extant writing on jade is found on Shang jade objects recording origin, ownership or an event; see Li Xueqin, "Jade and Stone Epigraphy from the Shang and Early Zhou Periods," in *Chi-*

nese Jades, Rosemary E. Scott, ed., University of London, Percival
David Foundation, SOAS, 1997, 99–104.

The first long texts on jade record blood covenants (*mengshu* 盟
書, *zaishu* 載書). There have been several finds, all from the ancient
kingdom of Jin 晉. They probably date from the fifth century BC.
The first were found in Wenxian 溫縣, Henan, in the 1930s but
have been lost. More turned up in 1942. Eleven of these narrow oblong tablets are now in the Kaogusuo (*Kaogu* 1966.5). The first major find (5,000 tablets), was made at Houma 侯馬, Shanxi, in 1965–
66 (*Wenwu*, 1975.5, and *Guwenzi yanjiu*, vol. 1, 1979). For photographs of 200 examples and transcriptions of the 656 legible inscriptions (kept in the Shanxi provincial museum), see *Houma mengshu*
侯馬盟書.[9] The second major find (10,000 tablets or fragments) was
made in 1980–82, at Wenxian, Henan. They are held in the Henan
provincial museum at Zhengzhou (*Wenwu* 1983.3). They have not
yet been published.[10] A separate cache of 50 jade strips in the same
shape as bamboo strips was found in 1950 at Huixian 輝縣, Henan.
They were ready for use but had not yet been written on.

The best introduction in English to the covenant texts is Susan
Weld, "The Covenant Texts from Houma and Wenxian," *NSECH*
(1997), 125–60.

In later Chinese history, jade remained in use as a material for
inscribed objects of special ceremonial importance or value, for example, the imperial seal, *yuxi* 玉璽, or the records of accession of an
emperor.

17.2.2   Seal Inscriptions

Pre-Qin seals (*guxi* 古璽) were mainly used on clay. Letters or bundles were tied up with string and sealed with clay, upon which a seal
was impressed (like sealing wax in the West). Many such clay seal
impressions have survived from imperial times, some from the pre-

---

[9] *Houma mengshu* (Jade covenant inscriptions from Houma), Shanxisheng
wenwu gongzuo weiyuanhui 山西省文物工作委員會, ed., Wenwu, 1976. This
work also includes a listing of all the characters in the inscriptions and their
variants, as well as a list of proper names occurring in the texts.

[10] On the role of blood covenants in Zhou interstate relations and inter-
lineage struggles, see Mark Edward Lewis, *Sanctioned Violence in Early China*,
SUNY, 1990, 43–52. For additional readings, see Gao (1996), 418–30.

Qin and a few seals, perhaps, even from the Shang.[11] Red-ink seals appear from the Qin and Han. Seals were cut either in relief (*yang-wen* 陽文) in order to produce a positive imprint of the characters, or incised in intaglio (*yinwen* 陰文) to create a negative imprint. In both cases they were cut in a mirror image, as were the molds used in casting characters in bronze, and as much later were the wood-blocks for printing.

17.2.3 Pottery Inscriptions

Pottery inscriptions (*taowen* 陶文 is the modern word) were utilitarian or informal. Most are found on shards, bricks, and tiles. They are usually very short. Among the rare exceptions is a Qin letter of investiture (*washu* 瓦書) of 119 characters dated 334 BC,[12] and the imperial decree on weights and measures of 221 BC (40 characters long), which was inscribed on all bronze and pottery weights and measures.[13] The characters on the pottery measures are stamped on in ten sets of four characters, presumably using a bronze seal in a kind of primitive "printing." Several complete measures have been unearthed in Shandong and fragments from elsewhere.[14] *Taowen* also include the symbols and records (sometimes graffiti) left by builders, craftsmen, convicts, and corvée laborers. As the least prestigious type of inscription, writing on pottery has received the least

---

[11] *Gu fengni jicheng* 古封泥集成 (Collection of ancient clay seal impressions), Shanghai shudian, 1994, 1996. For a short history of seals, see Wang Tingqia 王廷洽, *Zhongguo yinzhangshi* 中國印章史 (History of Chinese seals), Huadong shifan daxue, 1996. For a repertory of seal characters, see Luo Fuyi 羅福頤 (1905–81), *Guxi wenbian* 古璽文編 (A repertory of ancient seal characters), Wenwu, 1981. Based on the author's earlier work of 1930; 2nd rpnt., 1994. It contains 2,773 characters. See also the same author's *Guxi huibian* 古璽匯編 (Ancient seals), Wenwu, 1981, 1994, which contains beautifully executed impressions of 5,708 Warring States seals, mainly official ones. It is a useful supplementary source on local government.

[12] Yuan Zhongyi 袁仲一, *Qindai taowen* 秦代陶文 (Qin dynasty pottery script), San-Qin, 1987. Transcription and discussion of the *washu* 瓦書 on pages 75–84. There is a much clearer rubbing in Gao Ming, 1990 (14.6), 513.

[13] The imperial decree has been found on pottery capacity measures, both complete and fragmentary. For a transcription with notes, see *Shang-Zhou guwenzi duben* 商周古文字讀本 (Reader of ancient characters from the Shang and Zhou), Liu Xiang 劉翔 et al., comps., Yuwen, 1989, 3rd prnt., 1996, 174–75.

[14] Yuan Zhongyi (1987), 418–31; Gao Ming, 1990 (14.6), 517–24.

attention from collectors and scholars (the first collection was begun only in 1872).[15] Yet prehistoric pottery symbols and markings,
as we saw in Chapter 14, may yet hold one of the keys to the origins of Chinese characters. *Taowen* is often exceedingly difficult to
read because it was written by illiterate craftsmen who freely invented their own variants of the ancient scripts. Of a total of about
2,000 different pre-Qin pottery characters, about two-thirds have
been deciphered. Another reason why *taowen* inscriptions were ig-
nored until recently is their shortness.

17.2.4   Coin Inscriptions

Starting from the Warring States, coin inscriptions (*quanwen* 泉文,
qianwen 錢文, *huobiwen* 貨幣文) record the place they were cast or
the denomination; from the fourth century AD, the era name was
also recorded. On the history of Chinese coins, see 7.4.1.[16]

17.3   Stone Inscriptions

Stone has been used as an artistic medium or to keep records for
longer than any other material in China. There are plentiful examples of prehistoric rock art from many regions with carved or painted pictographic symbols (14.2). Examples of pre-Qin inscriptions on
stone using characters are few and far between. There are about a
dozen from the Former Han; 160 from the Later Han; and several
hundred from Wei, Jin, Nan-Bei Chao, and Sui. Thereafter the
numbers go up steeply: 4,000 to 5,000 tomb tablets from the Tang
alone (46.4) and many thousands from late imperial China.

There are many different types of inscription. In imperial times,
the most common form of stone inscription is the stele (*bei* 碑), an
upright slab of stone with the characters carved in intaglio. Stele
were used for commemorating talented writers and upright officials,
for inscribing poems or statues, portraits, pictures, and maps. Also,
as any traveler in China knows, there is hardly a famous mountain

---

[15] By Chen Jieqi 陳介祺 (1813–84), a scholar and famous collector of antiques from Weixian, Shandong.

[16] For a repertory of the characters found on pre-Qin coins, see *Xian-Qin
huobi wenbian* 先秦貨幣文編, Shang Chengzuo 商承祚 (1902–91) et al., eds.,
Shumu wenxian, 1983.

or scenic spot whose cliffs and rocks do not carry the calligraphy of emperors, statesmen, and poets. Stone inscriptions were also used for more prosaic functions, such as marking the boundaries of fields (*jiebei* 界碑 or *sizhi* 四至); the details of ownership and construction; contracts and the names of contributors to public buildings such as temples, bridges, pagodas, or wells; and many other matters of great interest to the student of Chinese social and economic history, for example, guild rules.

It was in the Han that stone replaced wood for tombstones and tomb inscriptions (*mubei* 墓碑 and *muzhi* 墓誌), which are basic sources for Chinese biographical studies. The *muzhi* were usually placed in the tomb. Transcriptions of some 7,000 have been published and indexed (3.7).

Stone was also used for recording the classics of Confucianism, Buddhism, and Daoism.

Of the more than 100,000 stone inscriptions extant today, only about 30,000 have had rubbings made or have been transcribed or published. Fewer still have been studied.

Tomb inscriptions and literary stelae from the Han to the Tang have been much studied, but those from later dynasties, including those with an economic interest, did not come within the purview of the literati collectors of inscriptions, who were interested more in ancient calligraphic models than in the economic and social history of the later dynasties. In the twentieth century, too, historians have been slow to use this type of material. There have been some notable exceptions, however (see 50.7.6 for published collections of stelae of an economic interest, especially those dating from the Ming and Qing).

In general, most stone inscriptions from Shaanxi and the Central Plains date from the Sui and Tang (and to a lesser extent from the Han and Jin); those from the northeast date from the Liao and Jin; those from the northwest and the southeast contain materials relative to the non-Han peoples; those from the southeast date from the Ming and Qing.

The few pre-Qin stone inscriptions so far discovered were all carved on rocks and stones in their natural state and hence termed *keshi* 刻石 rather than *shike* 石刻. Most famous are the 10 *jie* 碣 (drum-stones) of Qin (763 BC). They were discovered in the Tang dynasty in Shaanxi province and are today preserved in the Palace Museum. Each round-topped stone has a 70-character poem inscribed on it. Of the total of 700 characters, only 272 are still legible, but from rubbings made in the Song dynasty 501 characters have been preserved. They record in a script similar to Qin great seal the hunting and military expeditions of the Qin monarchs in a language similar to that of the *Shijing*.[17]

The first emperor made five inspection tours or progresses and altogether had seven stone inscriptions carved extolling his accomplishments and his wise policies (the texts are in *Shiji*, *juan* 5). They are said to have been written by his chancellor, Li Si 李斯. Fragments of two of them have survived. One (the Langye 琅邪 inscription, 219 BC) is in the National Museum of Chinese History, Beijing. Subsequent emperors followed the same practice, but used specially made stelae rather than natural rock faces. One of the most famous is the 13-meter-high stele on Mt. Tai in the Tang emperor Xuanzong's own hand recording his conduct of sacrifices there in 725. It can still be seen on the mountain to this day. Monumentally large stelae, their base one of several varieties of stone turtle (*guifu* 龜趺), mark the Qianlong emperor's visits wherever he went, especially in the temples and historical sites around Beijing.

Throughout Chinese history, the prehistoric practice of leaving a record on natural rocks and stones continued. Important visitors, for example, left their mark in the shape of an inscription naming the place, or mountain, or grotto. This type of inscription is called *moyai* 摩崖. Subsequent less exalted or distinguished travelers, in addition to acquiring rubbings of the inscriptions, would seek to have their own comments and poems inscribed beneath or alongside the famous one or they would erect a stele. Not all found this urge to leave one's mark an improvement on the scenery. As one late Ming official observed, "It is disgusting to see inscribed stone tablets cluttering the foothills. ... The law provides regular punishments for those who rob mountains or open mines. Why is it that it does not prohibit the defiling and defacing of the spirit of the mountain by vulgar scholars?"[18] The writer of these words was no doubt well intentioned, but he was also misinformed in that at least since the early third century AD the erection of private stelae epitaphs was

---

[17] Gilbert L. Mattos, *The Stone Drums of Ch'in*, Steyler, 1988.

[18] *The Travel Diaries of Hsu Hsia-k'o* [Xu Xiake 徐霞客 (1586–1641)], Li Chi, ed., HKCUP, 1974, 62 (see 4.7, *Ming*); see also the comments of the author of *Wu zazu* 五雜組 as quoted in Oertling, 1997 (49.2, *Biji*).

forbidden.[19] *Moyai* are most numerous at the traditional scenic spots: for example, in the foothills around Hangzhou or Guilin, or along the paths right up to the summit of sacred mountains such as Taishan or Huashan. Even some of the large flat rocks along the banks of the upper reaches of the Yangzi have been carved, not only with records of high-water marks, but also with poems, in some cases since the first century AD (but those extant today date mainly from the Tang or post-Tang). All over China there were always many passersby who simply had carved for them that "So and so [of such and such rank] was here on such and such date."

When Confucianism was made the official state doctrine in the Later Han and seven classics were selected (19.2), the complete text of 200,000 characters was inscribed onto 46 stelae each 2.5 meters high and 1 meter broad. It took eight years to carve them. They were placed outside the instruction hall of the Imperial Academy in Luoyang for everyone to see and copy. Only fragments remain today because they were soon broken or destroyed, but the practice of inscribing *shijing* 石經 (stone classics) continued.[20] Three classics were carved in three scripts (*guwen*, seal, and chancery) in 241. No trace survives. The best-preserved *shijing* were made on the occasion that the seven classics were increased to twelve. The carving of the *Kaicheng shijing* 開成石經 took four years and was completed in 837. The entire set is in the Forest of Stelae (Beilin 碑林), at Xi'an (see the list of *Collections of Stelae* below). Subsequently three other *shijing* were inscribed, of these 85 stelae of the *Taixue shijing* (1131) and the *Qianlong shijing* (1794) have survived. This last was carved for display at the Imperial Academy in Beijing. It is now housed next door, behind the Confucian Temple. The set of 190 stelae contains just over 630,000 characters. The temple also has a copy made in the Qianlong period of two of the stone drums of Qin, as well as

---

[19] Kenneth K. S. Ch'en, "Inscribed Stelae During the Wei, Chin, and Nan-ch'ao," in *Studia Asiatica*, Laurence G. Thompson, ed., CMC, 1975, 75–84. In the Tang "officials who improperly set up stone monuments" were punished with one year of penal servitude; see *The T'ang Code: Vol. II, Specific Articles*, Wallace Johnson, tr., PUP, 1997, 102–4.

[20] In 1980, 96 fragments were discovered on the site of the old academy, and more turned up later (*Zhongyuan wenwu*, 1988.2). The first *shijing* were probably those inscribed in *guwen* 古文 on the orders of Wang Mang in AD 1. They included the *Yi*, the *Shu*, the *Shi*, and the *Zuozhuan*.

the originals of most of the 198 stelae upon which were carved the
names, native places, and academies of the 50,000 people who passed
the *jinshi* 進士 degree during the five centuries between the beginning of the Yuan and the end of the Qing.

The Buddhist and Daoist scriptures were also carved on stelae
and on rocks. The largest collection of Buddhist *shijing* in the
world, 14,278 stelae, is stored in caves on Stone Scripture Mt., Fangshan county, southwest of Beijing (29.5).

The monumental *shijing* served two main purposes. The first
was practical, especially in the early empire before the invention of
printing: to establish standard texts of works, which otherwise circulated in many different versions and on less sturdy media, and to
enable comparison of the different script forms of characters and
also to fix standard forms for them, since most existed in a bewildering number of graphic variants. Accurate copies could easily be
made by taking a rubbing. The second aim was to show esteem and
devotion to canonical texts.

Guides and Research Tools

Zhao Chao 趙超, *Zhongguo gudai shike gailun* 中國古代石刻概論 (General introduction to ancient Chinese stone inscriptions), Wenwu,
1997. A reliable introduction to all forms of stone inscription. There
is a long chapter on the language of the inscriptions, including the set
phrases which more and more characterized tomb tablets and memo-
rial-stele inscriptions from the Tang on. There is also a chapter on
how to distinguish fakes. Many thousands of alternative and unorthodox characters were used on the stone carvings. See

Bei biezi xinbian 碑別字新編 (New edition of *Wrongly used characters
on stelae*), Qin Gong 秦公, ed., Wenwu, 1985. Assembles 12,844
alternative and unorthodox stelae characters.

Guang Bei biezi 廣碑別字 (Enlarged *Bei biezi*), Qin Gong 秦公 and
Liu Daxin 劉大新, eds., Guoji wenhua, 1995, 1997. Adds a further 3,450 alternative and unorthodox stelae characters to those
in the previous item.

Shike tiba suoyin 石刻題跋索引 (Index to colophons on stone inscriptions), Yang Dianxun 楊殿珣, comp., Shangwu, 1940; enlarged edition, with index, 1957; rev., 1980; 2nd rpnt., 1995. Indexes the colophons on stone inscriptions in 137 collections of inscriptions from
the earliest times to the Yuan. Arranged by category (tombstones,
tomb tablets, inscribed classics, etc.). There is a four-corner index.

Published Collections of Stone Rubbings

Stone inscriptions such as *moyai* were written not only by powerful political figures but also by renowned calligraphers, as were the *shijing*. Rubbings were taken as models for handwriting and circulated in bound sets, an early form of printing.[21] Thanks to this practice and thanks to *jinshixue*, a vast number of rubbings and transcriptions have survived, in special collections, arranged by style, period, medium, subject matter, or place (often in local gazetteers), in collected works and other such sources. References to several of these collections are listed in the appropriate sections of the manual (especially in Part V). Many libraries have published collections of stone rubbings. The largest collection of books of rubbings is held at Guotu 國圖:

Beijing tushuguan cang Zhongguo lidai shike taben huibian 北京圖書館藏 中國歷代石刻拓本匯編 (Collection of rubbings of Chinese stone inscriptions held in the Beijing tushuguan), 101 vols., Zhongzhou guji, 1989–91. Altogether, these 101 volumes contain over 20,000 rubbings (about one-fifth of the library's collection). They date from 475 BC to AD 1949, and include 2,182 funerary inscriptions, 270 epitaphs, and 172 inscriptions related to guilds. The collection is arranged by period, which, incidentally, gives a good indication of the enormous amount of inscriptions that have survived from the Tang and the Ming and Qing. There are 195 inscriptions from the Warring States up to and including the Han; 1,182 from the period between the end of the Han and the Sui dynasty; 5,000 from the Sui, Tang and Five Dynasties; 1,500 from the Song; 567 from the Liao, Jin and Xixia;

---

[21] Examples of the work of famous calligraphers were also inscribed onto stone blocks, from which rubbings were taken and bound together as *tie* 帖. They were used for collecting and also for calligraphic practice. Casual writings (including letters) on small pieces of silk or paper came into vogue in the third century. They too were used as calligraphic models. *Two Chinese Treatises on Calligraphy*, introduced, tr., and annotated by Chang Ch'ung-ho and Hans H. Frankel, YUP, 1995, presents the original texts and English translations of the seventh-century calligrapher Sun Guoting 孫過庭, *Shupu* 書譜 (Treatise on calligraphy), and Jiang Kui 姜夔 (1163–1203), *Xu Shupu* 續書譜 (Sequel to *Shupu*). *Zhongguo beitie yishu lun* 中國碑帖藝術論 (On the art of China's stone-carved calligraphy), Jiang Wenguang 蔣文光 and Zhang Juying 張菊英, Zhongguo gongren, 1995, not only discusses the making of the copybooks, but gives a straightforward account of China's heritage of stone inscriptions as well. Zeng Yigong 曾毅公, *Shike kaogong lu* 石刻考工錄, Shumu wenxian, 1987, contains the names of nearly 1,800 stone carvers from the Han to the Qing.

500 from the Yuan; 2,000 from the Ming; and 9,000 from the Qing. The last volume contains place and inscription indexes.

Shike shiliao xinbian 石刻史料新編 (Newly edited historical materials on stone inscriptions), 90 vols., Xinwenfeng, 1977, 1979, 1986. A collectanea of many of the important early collections of stone inscriptions, including the earlier *Shike shiliao congshu* 石刻史料叢書 (Collectanea of historical materials on stone inscriptions), Yan Gengwang 嚴耕望, ed., 420 ce in 60 cases, Yiwen, 1966. For indexes to authors and compilers in the *Shike shiliao xinbian*, see *Annotated Bibliography to the Shike shiliao xinbian*, Dieter Kuhn and Helga Stahl, comps., Forum, 1991.

Collections of inscriptions from a particular place were also published separately and continue to be—for example:

Dali congshu 大理叢書 (The Dali series), Zhang Shufang 張樹芳, ed., 10 vols., Shekeyuan, 1993. Inscriptions from Dali, Yunnan. Vol. 10 contains transcriptions.

Sichuan lidai beike 四川歷代碑刻 (Historical stone inscriptions from Sichuan), Gao Wen 高文 et al., eds., Sichuan daxue, 1990.

Yunnan gudai shike congkao 雲南古代石刻叢考 (Investigation into ancient stone inscriptions from Yunnan), Sun Taichu 孫太初, comp., Wenwu, 1983. Contains 17 important inscriptions dating from the Han to the Qing.

Collections of Stelae

Major collections of stone inscriptions can be seen at:

Beijing shike yishu bowuguan 北京石刻藝術博物館 (Beijing Art Museum of Stone Carving). Housed at the Zhenjue temple 真覺寺 (also known as Wutasi 五塔寺, Five Pagoda Temple). Contains 1,500 stelae, of which 400 are on display.

Beijing, Yunjusi 雲居寺 (29.5).

Hangzhou beilin 杭州碑林 (Forest of Stelae, Hangzhou). Contains seven of the Confucian classics from the Taixue *shijing*.

Luoyang shike yishu bowuguan 洛陽石刻藝術博物館 (Luoyang Art Museum of Stone Carving). Has the largest collection of tomb tablets in China (more than 5,000), from which rubbings of those dating from the Sui, Tang, and Five Dynasties have been published (see 46.6 for details).

Qian-Tangzhi zhai 千唐誌齋, in Xin'an county 新安縣 near Luoyang, is the only museum dedicated to ancient tomb inscriptions, of which it has 1,413. The greater number (1,209) date from the Tang (see 46.4 for details).

Nanmen beilin 南門碑林, Gaoxiong 高雄, Taiwan.

Qufu 曲阜 at the Kongmiao 孔廟 (Confucian Temple); 6,000–7,000 inscriptions.

Suzhou beike bowuguan 蘇州碑刻博物館 (Suzhou Museum of Inscribed Stelae) contains a special gallery with 226 inscriptions of an economic interest from the later empire. The museum is housed in the buildings of the Confucian School established by the Song man of letters Fan Zhongyan 范仲淹 in 1034. It also contains four unique Song dynasty maps, including the earliest stone-carved star map in the world (dating from 942) and a stone map of Pingjiang 平江 (Suzhou). See Chen Meidong 陳美東, *Zhongguo gu xingtu* (China's ancient star maps), Jilin jiaoyu, 1996.

Xi'an beilin bowuguan 西安碑林博物館 (Museum of the Forest of Stelae, Xi'an) housed in the old Confucian Temple. Founded in 1087. The most famous of the *beilin* because it has the largest collection of early stone inscriptions, including the Kaicheng *shijing* 開成石經, the earliest extant version of the Confucian classics on stone.

Xichang dizhen beilin 西昌地震碑林 (Xichang Earthquake Museum), Sichuan. A unique collection containing 89 stelae and 20 stone rubbings of inscriptions related to the major earthquakes in Xichang of 1536, 1732, and 1850.

Apart from such special collections as these, all major historical museums, temples, and ancient buildings and monuments in China have copious examples of stelae of every kind, and construction work continues to turn up large quantities of them.

18

From Bamboo Strips to
Printed Books

Chinese manuscript and book production has gone through six main stages:

Manuscripts written on bamboo strips and wooden tablets: Shang to Later Han (18.1)

Manuscripts written on silk: Warring States to Later Han (18.2)

Manuscripts written on paper: Later Han to Five Dynasties (18.3)

Woodblock-printing: seventh to nineteenth centuries (18.4)

Introduction of Western printing machinery: late nineteenth century to 1949 (18.5)

18.1   Manuscripts on Bamboo and Wood

"[Those who are righteous are praised in their own times,] but their deeds should also be written on bamboo and silk, inscribed on bronze and stone, and incised onto vessels in order to pass them down to later generations" 又書其事於竹帛鏤之金石琢之盤盂傳遺後世子孫, Mozi 墨子 (468–376 BC), *Mozi*, *juan* 27, "Tianzhi zhong" 天志中.

A much handier and a cheaper medium for keeping records than shells, bones, jade, bronze, or stone was bamboo or wood. The evidence that writing on bamboo had already begun at least during the later Shang is summarized in 14.7. Thereafter, bamboo and wooden documents and other writings (*diance* 典册, *jiance* 簡策) continued in use until the third and fourth centuries AD. This makes them a longer-serving medium for writing than paper.

Up until at least the time of Confucius, texts were mainly official records and documents not for circulation or general use. They were usually written on strips (*jian* 簡) either of bamboo (*zhujian* 竹簡) or of wood (*mujian* 木簡). The strips normally held one, or sometimes two or more, rows of characters. No doubt the very first use of the bamboo strips was for very short texts. The writer would hold the top end of the strip in the left hand with the other end resting against his waist to steady it. He would then write vertically down the length of the strip using his right hand to hold the brush. When the individual strips were bound together they were called a *ce* 冊. They were either fastened together with a single thread at the head of the strips (*pian* 篇) or bound together in a bundle (*juan* 卷), usually with two, or for longer strips, three threads.[1]

Later, it became more practical for long texts to bind the strips before writing on them, although even as late as the Han the binding was still sometimes done after the writing (for example, for lists of funerary objects). The writer would lay the bundle out horizontally before him to write on, starting from the right-hand strip. The characters were written with a brush and ink vertically down the strips following the grain, usually on the inside surface. After they were tied together, the strips were rolled up (from the left to the right, as picture scrolls are to this day, so that the last strip with writing functioned as the spindle of the bundle and the beginning of the text, on the first strip, was the first to be unrolled). This way of writing and storing the strip bundles helps explain why old Chinese records started at what for us today is the end. It was an arrangement that was retained when books began to be printed in the seventh century AD and it lasted until the 1950s. The only exception to this order of writing was counting-rod numerals, which were written horizontally from left to right (7.1.1).

Reading was a weighty matter; the first emperor is commended for his industriousness in getting through a large number of official

---

[1] Tsuen-hsuin Tsien (Qian Cunxun 錢存訓), *Written on Bamboo and Silk: The Beginnings of Chinese Books and Inscriptions*, UChP, 1962. An elegant and beautifully illustrated study on Chinese writing and writing materials before the invention of paper and printing; still the best introduction in English. There is a revised and updated edition: *Zhongguo gudai shushi* 中國古代書史, HKCUP, 1975. References such as *Chuban cidian* 出版詞典 (A dictionary of publishing), Shanghai cishu, 1992, contain short, up-to-date entries on all aspects of printing and publishing from the earliest times to the present day, including the history of old books and information relating to inscriptions and writing.

documents every day, not in terms of the numbers of bundles or strips, but in terms of their weight (in this case according to the *Shiji*, one *shi* 石 a day [equivalent to about 27 kilo or 60 lb]). Collections were measured by the cartload, a practice that continued to the third century AD. Hence the expression *xuefu wuche* 學富五車 (a learned man; literally, "to have five cartloads of learning"). Because of the weight of the bamboo strips, texts did not circulate widely, and if they did, it must have been in a few bundles rather than as complete works.[2] A small number of copies were written for rulers and nobles on silk, which was less bulky than the strips, but much more expensive (18.2).

Apart from writing on bamboo and wooden strips, shorter documents, or those such as maps, which required a larger surface, were written on tablets, usually of wood (*du* 牘, *mudu* 木牘, *bandu* 版牘, *chidu* 尺牘, *gu* 觚, *ban* 板, or *fang* 方). They came into general use in the Han. The tablets were usually broader and shorter than the strips and could accommodate a short document with several rows of characters. For letters, two tablets were often notched into each other face-to-face and then tied together. The top tablet was used to record the addressee and the sender. Wooden tablets were also used as the table of contents of a bamboo record.

Both the strips and the tablets varied in length according to the type of document. By the Han there were regulations that government laws should be written on strips of 3 *chi* 尺 (1 *chi* was by that time about 23 cm); the Confucian classics on 2.4 *chi* strips; and correspondence on tablets 1 *chi* 尺 long (hence the old name for a letter, *chidu* 尺牘). In practice, we know from excavated strips that there was considerable variation in length.[3]

There were many words and compounds for different types of writing. *Jiance* 簡策[冊], along with *jiandu* 簡牘 (strips and tablets), was one of the most common early ones. Others were *dianji* 典籍,

---

[2] The *Shiji* 史記 numbers 130 *pian* 篇 and has a total of 530,000 characters. If each strip contained 60 characters, the *Shiji* would have totaled 8,833 strips arranged into about 150–300 bundles (assuming 30–60 strips per bundle). Like other works of history or literature, the *Shiji* would also have been written on silk. Indeed, the 130 *pian* 篇 into which it is divided may refer to the number of silk rolls or to groups of rolls (or possibly sections).

[3] See Michael Loewe, "Wood and Bamboo Administrative Documents of the Han Period," in *NSECH*, 161–92.

jiance boshu 簡册帛書 or *zhubo* 竹帛, "documents on bamboo and silk" (*jianbo* 簡帛 is the modern term), *shuji* 書籍, *shuce* 書册, or *bandu* 版牘. *Dianji* came to mean writing in general (perhaps even "books") only after the Han. The principal meaning of the modern word for books, *tushu* 圖書, was "maps and documents" from its first appearance in the Zhou until after the Han.

Much of the vocabulary for books and publishing in use today reflects the bamboo and wooden origins of Chinese writing: the word for book or volume (*ce* 册), for example, is often explained as a pictograph of two vertical bamboo or wooden strips held together with threads. Other such words include *dian* 典 (a pictograph of *ce* being placed on a stand); *ji* 籍 (2-foot bamboo strip), as in *dianji* 典籍 (classics); and *pian* 篇 (swatch of bamboo or wooden strips secured with a thread), as in the modern usage *yipian wenzhang* 一篇文章 (an article). The old word for "namecard" was *ci* 刺 because the name was carved on a bamboo or wooden strip. *Shan* 删, as in modern *shanchu* 删除 (to delete), originally meant to scrape the strips clean with a paring knife to ready them for writing on again, as also did *xiao* 削 and *kan* 刊, as in modern *kanwu* 刊誤, to cut out errors. Later *kan* also took on the meaning of carve, as on a wooden block for printing; hence eventually the modern word for publication, *kanwu* 刊物. Population registers were originally called *huang-ji* 黄籍, probably after the color of the bamboo strips on which they were written. In the Ming and Qing the tradition was maintained by recording the population registers in thread-bound fascicles, with yellow covers (*huangce* 黄册, yellow registers).

18.2   *Manuscripts on Silk*

After bamboo and wood, silk was the most commonly used writing material from at least the Warring States to the Tang (as suggested by the expression *zhubo* 竹帛 "documents on bamboo and silk"; see the quotation at the beginning of this chapter). Because of the expense, silk was less widely used than bamboo. The arrangement of the characters on the silk follows the same order as on the bamboo strips. Works on silk were counted by the *juan* 卷 (rolled up sections; scroll). *Juan* could also refer to works written on bamboo. Several books, as well as documents and maps, written on silk dating from the Warring States and Han periods have been excavated (most importantly at Mawangdui; see 19.1.3).

18.3 Manuscripts on Paper

Paper of a quality good enough to write on was produced in the second century AD and gradually came into general use during the third and fourth centuries, replacing bamboo, wooden tablets, and silk as it did so. Traditionally the discovery is credited to Cai Lun 蔡倫 (d. AD 121), but descriptions of paper making using silk waste and scraps of paper made from fibers predating his birth have been found.[4] The earliest fragment of paper found so far is of a map. It was excavated from a Former Han tomb (4.4.1).

In AD 404, the self-appointed emperor of Chu, Huan Xuan 桓玄 (369–404) ordered that paper should be used instead of bamboo strips and wooden tablets. It is one sign of the beginning of the age of paper. Handwritten editions written up to the end of the Tang are usually referred to as *xieben* 寫本; after the that, as *chaoben* 抄本.

A single book would consist of several scrolls. The scrolls were made by pasting together sheets of paper. Looking something up in a reference work would have taken a lot of time, but would have been a much less cumbersome affair than handling heavy bundles of bamboo. Books could also now be carried by hand rather than transported by cart. Literary culture with authors of individual works and different audiences of readers now became a feature of Chinese life.

Over 42,000 manuscripts written on paper dating from the early fifth to eleventh century were discovered in the secret temple library at Dunhuang and at Turpan at the beginning of the twentieth century (46.3).

Gradually scrolls were replaced in the ninth century by "sutra" binding (*jingzhe zhuang* 經折裝) in which the leaves were folded flat

---

[4] The authority in English on the history of paper and printed books in China is Tsuen-Hsuin Tsien, *Paper and Printing* (*SCC*, vol. 5, part 1). The authoritative work in Chinese is the volume by Pan Jixing 潘吉星, *Zaozhi yu yinshua* 造紙與印刷 in the series *Zhongguo kexue jishu shi*, Kexue, 1998. For further references, see notes 16 and 20. See also Thomas F. Carter, *The Invention of Printing in China and its Spread Westward*, Col. UP, 1925; rev. edition, 1931; 2nd rev. edition, L. C. Goodrich, Ronald Press, 1955. See also Denis Twitchett, *Printing and Publishing in Medieval China*, London: Wynkyn de Worde Society, 1983. For the wider context, see 9.2 on *Early Chinese Libraries*; and note Lai Xinxia 來新夏, *Zhongguo gudai tushu shiyeshi* 中國古代圖書事業史 (A history of the book trade in ancient China), Shanghai renmin, 1990, 1991.

rather than rolled up. This may have begun in imitation of the palm-leaf books of Buddhist scriptures imported from India.[5] It had the advantage that it was now possible to turn to a reference without unfolding the entire document. The next step was that the first and last leaves were pasted onto a single large sheet so the sheets were more secure (xuanfeng zhuang 旋風裝 "whirlwind binding"). The book opened like an accordion with both covers placed face downwards on the table. With the spread of printing, it became convenient to fold printed sheets into two to form pairs of facing pages that were bound together by pasting the backs of the folds (tenth-century hudie zhuang 蝴蝶裝 "butterfly binding"). The disadvantage was that every two pages the reader encountered two blank pages. By the thirteenth century this had been overcome by pasting together the edges of the pages so the reader encountered no blank pages (baobei zhuang 包背裝 "wrapped-back binding"). In the late Ming, early Qing, thread stitching replaced pasting or paper for the binding to produce the familiar thread-bound ce 冊 (fascicle) with soft covers (xianzhuang 綫裝). To protect these Chinese "paperbacks" and to make it easier to pull out a particular ce from a pile, sets of ce were boxed together in a protective case (han 函 or tao 套).

18.4   Woodblock Printing

Seals (yin 印) were in use at least from the Shang (17.2.2). They were used for a sort of primitive printing on pottery as early as the third century BC. Wooden seals with up to 120 characters are mentioned in written sources in the Nan-Bei Chao. Seal-like stamps were used for one of the earliest uses of printing—the reproduction of hundreds of identical Buddha images (qianfo xiang 千佛象). It is fitting, therefore, that seals gave their name to printing (yinshua 印刷). Books of paper rubbings taken from stone blocks incised with characters were made from the fourth century AD. This was a further step toward the invention of printing using wooden blocks (banben 版本), which started in the early seventh century using fine-grained woods such as jujube or pear tree.[6]

[5] Edward Martinique, Chinese Traditional Bookbinding, CMC, 1983; Tsien (1987), 227–33.

[6] Tsien (1987), 136–39; see 17.2.3 for seal-stamped pottery.

The earliest example of printing in the world is a single scrap of a *dhâranî* (Buddhist spell) miniature scroll in Sanskrit, which was found in 1974 in a tomb in Xi'an. It has been dated to 650–70. Another similar example was found in a stupa in 1966 in Pulguk-sa temple 佛國寺, Kyongju 慶州, the ancient capital of the Korean kingdom of Silla 新羅. It was probably printed in China sometime at the beginning of the eighth century. The oldest known *banben* is a printed manuscript of portions of the Lotus Sutra (*Miaofa lianhua jing* 妙法蓮花經) discovered at Turpan in 1906 (Calligraphy Museum, Tokyo). The earliest extant dated *banben* is a Diamond Sutra (*Jingang bore boluomi jing* 金剛般若波羅密經) of 868 found at Dunhuang in 1907. It is in the form of a 14-foot-long illustrated scroll (British Museum, London, which also houses the first extant printed almanac in the world, the *Qianfu sinian lishu* 乾符四年曆書, Almanac of 877). Buddhism remained an important stimulus for printing.[7] However, before long other types of demand were being met as woodblock printing (*diaoban yinshua* 雕版印刷) spread out from the capitals in the late Tang to centers in Sichuan and Huainan. The *Jiujing* 九經 (Nine classics) were printed in the tenth century. The *Shisanjing* 十三經 (Thirteen classics) and the *Shiqishi* 十七史 (Seventeen Histories) were printed in the Song along with many other kinds of literature.[8] The first printed paper money and trademarks also appeared in the Song (7.4.1).

Movable-type printing (*huozi yinshua* 活字印刷) was invented by Bi Sheng 畢升 in the eleventh century using clay, but the invention was only rarely put to use. The earliest extant example of mov-

---

[7] The Tripitaka was printed on at least six separate occasions during the Song, starting in 971 with the *Kaibao zangshu* 開寶藏書 (Kaibao Tripitaka) in 1,076 ce. It took 10 years to cut the 130,000 blocks for this edition. It was not surpassed in size until the two Ming Chinese Tripitaka and the Ming Tibetan Tripitaka (29.5).

[8] It took 67 years to collate the Standard Histories and to cut the blocks for the first official printing of the *Shiqishi* 十七史 (*Seventeen Histories*, see 22.1). The work was done at Chengdu. On Song printing, the book trade, and book collecting, see Sören Edgren, "Southern Song Printing at Hangzhou," *BMFEA* 61: 1–212 (1989); Susan Cherniack, "Book Culture and Textual Transmission in Song China," *HJAS* 54.1: 5–125 (1994); Thomas H. C. Lee, "Books and Bookworms in Song China: Book Collection and the Appreciation of Books," *JSY* 25: 193–218 (1995); Lucille Chia, "The Development of the Jianyang Book Trade, Song-Yuan," *LIC* 17.1: 10–48 (1996).

able type is a late twelfth-century Buddhist work in Xixia wooden-type characters discovered in 1991. The technique was systematized by Wang Zhen 王槙, a Yuan local magistrate, who printed the now lost Shengde gazetteer using the technique. He added a short description and illustration of movable woodblock printing at the end of his agricultural treatise, the Nongshu 農書 (35.1.2, Fourteenth Century). His description is translated in Carter (1955, 162–66). The technique became quite common in the Ming and widespread in the Qing. The Ming also saw considerable use of metal movable type (pioneered with tin and copper in the late Song and Yuan) and multi-color printing (replacing the earlier hand coloring and multiple block coloring).[9]

During the Qing, the authorities printed books on a scale never before seen in China. The main government printing office, the Wuying dian (武英殿), used a specially engraved set of movable copper type to print in 1727 the 852,408 pages of the Gujin tushu jicheng 古今圖書集成 (Imperial encyclopaedia; see 31.2). The two copper type fonts were melted down for coins at the beginning of the Qianlong reign. When the question arose of printing selected works assembled for the Siku quanshu 四庫全書 (The imperial library, 1789), the emperor decided in favor of movable wood type (9.5), partly on the grounds that it was cheaper. Indeed it was not until the early twentieth century that woodblocks (the main method) and movable wood type were replaced by metallic type printing.[10]

18.5   Introduction of Modern Typography

As with the introduction of printing in the Tang, the impetus for adopting more efficient techniques in the early nineteenth century

[9] For a thorough catalog of known woodblock publishers, both official and private, see Yang Shengxin 楊繩信, Zhongguo banke zonglu 中國版刻綜錄 (Catalog of Chinese woodblock publishers), Shaanxi renmin, 1983, 1987. Hiromitsu Kobayashi and Samantha Sabin provide a case study of Ming printing in "The Great Age of Anhui Printing," in Shadows of Mt. Huang: Chinese Painting and Printing of the Anhui School, Berkeley: University Art Museum, 1981.

[10] There is a detailed account of the printing of the Tushu jicheng, see Richard C. Rudolph, A Chinese Printing Manual, 1776, Ward Ritchie Press, 1954. See also Shiow-jyu Lu Shaw, The Imperial Printing of Early Ch'ing China, 1644–1805, CMC, 1983.

was religious. In this case, it was the desire of Christian missionaries
to propagate the faith more quickly and economically than could be
done with woodblock printing that led them to introduce metallic-
type printing. From 1815 to 1844 it was a capital crime to print
books on Christianity in China, so the missionaries set up their
printing presses in Southeast Asia (50.8.3). The publication of the
Edict of Tolerance in 1844 enabled the missionaries to preach and
print in China. Different methods of manufacturing metal type
were tried before the application of the electrotype process in 1859
revolutionized the production of Chinese matrices. The innovator
was an Irish American named William Gamble (Gan Bu'er 甘布爾,
1830–86), who came to China as head of the American Presbyterian
Mission Press (APMP) in 1858. With certain modifications Gamble's electrotype process for Chinese matrices (*diandu Zhongwen zi-
mo* 電鍍中文字模) remained in use until the advent of computer
generated fonts in the 1970s. Thanks to Gamble's invention, the
APMP was able to supply complete Chinese fonts to printers in
other parts of China (including to the leading Shanghai newspaper,
Shenbao) and, indeed, all over the world. Gamble also conducted the
first systematic frequency counts of Chinese characters and ascer-
tained that only 5,150 different characters were needed for most
purposes. Using this finding he was able to design a type-case for
compositors with the characters arranged in sets according to their
frequency and Kangxi classifier. This enabled composition to be
done much more quickly than previously. APMP's division of the
fonts into seven type sizes is still in use today as well as in Japan (to
which Gamble introduced the new techniques during a brief stop-
over on his return to America in 1869). The organization of the
APMP into three departments, namely editing, printing, and distribution was adopted by the first modern Chinese publisher, the
Commercial Press in 1902 (51.2). It was taken as the model by other
leading Chinese twentieth-century publishers.[11]

Other printing innovations included the following:

1872 Automatic inking (introduced by *Shenbao*; enabled printing of a
few hundred sheets per hour—previously hand inking had produced a few hundred sheets per day)

---

[11] Wu Kwang-Tsing, "The Development of Typography in China During
the Nineteenth Century," *Library Quarterly* 22: 288–301 (1952).

1872 *Shenbao* starts to use movable lead type (a few 100 sheets per hour)

1874 Photolithography used for the first time

1876 Lithography introduced by Ernest Major (50.8.3, *Shanghai*)

1882 First Chinese operated lithographic publisher, Tongwen shuju

1884 Movable lead type used to print a photolithographic edition of *Tushu jicheng* and a lithographic edition of the Palace edition of the *24 Histories*.

1898 First European-style rotary press (introduced from Japan)

1908 Shangwu introduces leaden type (1,500 pages per hour)

1912 *Shenbao* introduces first double rotary press

1916 *Shenbao* introduces first cylinder press (8,000 sheets per hour)

1919 Shangwu introduces first Miehle press in China (black and white, duo tone, or color printing; 2,000 sheets per hour)

1922 Shangwu introduces first German cylinder press in China (8,000 recto-verso sheets per hour)

For the history of Chinese publishing and printing in the modern period (to 1949), see the following:

Zhongguo da baike quanshu 中國大百科全書 (The great Chinese encyclopaedia), *Xinwen chuban juan* 新聞出版卷 (Newspaper and publishing volume), Da baike quanshu, 1992; 3rd prnt., 1998; see 51.3.5 for evaluation.

Zhongguo jindai chuban shiliao 中國近代出版史料 (Historical materials on modern Chinese publishing), Zhang Jinglu 張靜廬, ed., 2 vols., Shanghai Qunlian, 1953–54; Zhonghua, 1957. Covers 1840–1919.

Zhongguo xiandai chuban shiliao 中國現代出版史料 (Historical materials on modern Chinese publishing), Zhang Jinglu 張靜廬, ed., 4 parts, 5 vols., Zhonghua, 1954–59. Covers 1919–1949.

Zhongguo chuban shiliao (*bubian*) 中國出版史料(補編) (Additional historical materials on Chinese publishing), Zhonghua, 1957. Covers 1840–1949.

19

Excavated and Transmitted

Texts

Pre-Qin written sources are rare. They are of two main types: excavated (19.1) and transmitted (19.2).[1] The pre-Qin transmitted texts are listed in Table 26, 19.2. The Confucian classics are briefly introduced at the end of the Chapter (19.3), including how they were classified (19.3.1).

19.1   Excavated Texts on Bamboo, Wood, and Silk

Excavated written sources fall into two broad categories: inscriptions and brush-written texts and documents. Inscriptions carved on bone and turtle shell, on bronze and stone, and on jade and pottery are introduced in section 3.7 and Chapters 14 to 17. Excavated texts and documents written on bamboo, wood, and silk are the subject of this Chapter (19.1). The use of these materials for writing was discussed in the previous Chapter (18.1–2).[2]

All the classics of the Spring and Autumn and Warring States periods were originally written in the form of what are conventionally called "bamboo records" (or on silk). How long and which ones were handed down by word of mouth before being written down is not known. Warring States bamboo writings were discovered twice during the Han, once during the Jin, and once during the Qi. Sev-

---

[1] Depending on the context and emphasis, scholars sometimes refer to excavated texts as discovered texts, epigraphic sources, or paleographic materials. Transmitted texts are often referred to as received texts or traditional texts.

[2] Manuscripts and texts written on paper dating from the Tang and later periods have also been excavated or discovered, chiefly from Dunhuang (46.3.3), Turpan (46.3.4), and Kharakoto (48.5.3).

eral of the classics written in ancient script (*guwen* 古文) on bamboo strips were found in 168 BC hidden in the wall of Confucius's house at Qufu, Shandong.[3] More *guwen* bamboo strips were found in a tomb in 73 BC. Several tens of cartloads of strips were discovered in AD 279 in the tomb of King Xiang of Wei 魏襄王 (died 296 BC) at Jixian 汲縣 in Henan. They were stored in the imperial library and transcribed from the Warring States original scripts (according to one source, tadpole script) to chancery script, but were later lost except for portions of the *Zhushu jinian* 竹書紀年 (Bamboo annals) and the *Mu tianzi zhuan* 穆天子傳 (Travels of Prince Mu). More *guwen* strips were found in a Chu tomb in Xiangyang 襄陽 in AD 479.

Half a dozen minor discoveries are recorded up to the Song, but all have been lost. The first finds in modern times were not from tombs, but were made by Western and Japanese archaeologists and explorers at the beginning of the twentieth century in the northwest among the ruins of the frontier posts of the empire along the Silk Roads. Most of these military border documents dealt with administrative matters and dated from the Han, hence the name *Hanjian* 漢簡. The main finds and publications are listed in the chapter on Han dynasty sources (44.4).

The oldest documents and writings on silk and bamboo strips were not found in the northwest, but in tombs in the kingdom of Chu 楚 (central Yangzi). The main finds are listed in section 19.1.1. They date back to the Warring States and Former Han and include classical works and shorter documents. The texts placed in the tombs were not only classics, but also practical works that the occupant (depending on his status and special interests or skills) was expected to need in the afterlife, including almanacs; mathematical, astronomical, and divinatory texts; maps, laws, and regulations; and letters. Most tombs also include inventory lists of the funerary objects that were placed in them. The Chu bamboo strips were preserved by the humidity (as were some important finds of Qin and Former Han *jiandu* in the area). The Han *jiandu* border administrative documents, on the other hand, are usually of wood and were

---

[3] For the significance of these ancient-text editions, see Michael Nylan, "The *ku wen* Documents in Han Times," *TP* 81.1–3: 25–50 (1995).

saved by the arid climate. There are also finds from Wu, Wei, and Jin. They come both from the northwest and from the south.

Altogether, over 180,000 *jiandu* were discovered in the twentieth century (of which 130,000 were found between 1975 and 1999). Some 8,500 date from the Warring States; 2,500 from the Qin; 70,000 from the Former Han; 800 from the Later Han; 92,000 from Wu; and 603 from the Wei and Jin.

There are dozens of different publications containing photographs and transcriptions of the *jiandu*, but there is as yet no *corpus inscriptionum*, nor is there likely to be one because of the disparate nature of the subject matter recorded on the *jiandu*. In addition, new discoveries are constantly being made, and many of those that have been excavated are still being prepared for publication. The reasons for delays in publication, which are not uncommon, are varied. In some cases the strips were found by peasants, and the negotiation of their purchase has been a protracted one. In a few cases they have been stored in small county museums. After they are brought to light, the strips, which are often out of order, stuck together, or fragmented, need to be treated, sorted, reassembled, analyzed, and transcribed. Once this has been done, reading them is by no means an easy matter, especially the earlier ones. The Chu strips are in Chu Warring States small seal. The Qin ones are in Qin small seal and early Qin chancery script. The Han strips are mainly in chancery script, and the Three Kingdoms strips are on the cusp between chancery and regular script. All the strips contain numerous graphic variants and wrong characters, especially those which were everyday administrative records rather than more carefully written texts. Despite intensive studies of the different scripts found on *jiandu* and on *boshu* 帛書 (silk manuscripts), there are still a large number of characters that have not been identified.

Once the *jiandu* have been sorted, they are transcribed and published in a preliminary form in one of the archaeological journals, usually *Wenwu*. The official excavation reports come some years later and sometimes include more authoritative transcriptions and photographs. Finally, separate studies are published for the more important finds with transcriptions and notes. Historians comb the new sources for the information they contain on particular aspects of early history ranging from local administration to popular beliefs and for checking received texts.

Quite apart from the historical and literary interest of the *jiandu*, they provide copious insights for paleographers (they have been used, for example, to show the extent to which borrowed characters were written in different localities and also that *lishu* 隸書 was in use at an earlier date than had hitherto been known; see 16.1).

There are several guides to the *jiandu* and bibliographies of secondary scholarship on them, for example:

Li Junming 李均明 and Liu Jun 劉軍, *Jiandu wenshu xue* 簡牘文書學 (The study of documents on bamboo and wood), Guangxi jiaoyu, 1999. A systematic and detailed introduction to the study of the jiandu.

Hu Pingsheng 胡平生, "Yi ce zhi daxiao wei shu de zunbei—jiandu zhidu xintan" 以策之大小爲書之尊卑—簡牘制度新探 (Judging the importance of a document on the basis of the size of the strips—a new investigation of the system of bamboo strips and wooden tablets), *Wenwu* 2000.3.

Ben shiji yilai chutu jianbo gaishu ziliao lunzhu mulu pian 本世紀以來出土簡帛概述資料論著目錄篇 (General introduction to bamboo and silk books excavated in this century: materials, studies and index), Pian Yuqian 駢宇騫 and Duan Shu'an 段書安, comps., Wanjuanlou, 1998. Briefly describes 50 of the main discoveries of the twentieth century (1901–96) and lists studies of them.

"Qin Han jiandu yu boshu yanjiu wenxian mulu" 秦漢簡牘與帛書研究文獻目錄, Xing Yitian 邢義田, *Qin Han shi lungao* 秦漢史論稿, Dongda tushu gongsi, 1987, 569–635.

"Chûgoku kantoku kenkyû bunken mokuroku, 1903–1997 中國漢簡牘研究文獻目錄," Manida Akira 間田明, comp., *Kankan no kiso teki kenkyû* 漢簡の基礎的研究 (Basic research on *Hanjian*), Ôba Osamu 大庭脩, ed., Shibunkaku, 1999, 125–212.

Ôba Osamu 大庭脩, *Kankan kenkyû* 漢簡研究 (Researches on *Hanjian*), Hôyû, 1992.

Ôba Osamu 大庭脩, ed., *Kankan kenkyû no genjô to tenbô* 漢簡研究の現狀と展望 (Present state and prospects of research on bamboo documents), Kansai daigaku, 1993.

The *jianbo* also provide models for the calligrapher. Modern *jianbo* character exercise books are available. There are several compilations showing the forms of characters and their variants, for example:

Jiandu boshu zidian 簡牘帛書字典 (Dictionary of bamboo and silk characters), Chen Jiangong 陳建貢 and Xu Min 徐敏, comps., Shanghai shuhua, 1991. Not a dictionary in the conventional sense, but rather a listing of the different ways in which each bamboo character was written as a means of understanding their forms (*jiexing* 解形) and modern equivalents.

Collections of Articles and Journals

Chutu wenxian yanjiu 出土文獻研究 (Research on excavated texts), Wenwu yanjiusuo, ed., 5 collections, Wenwu (vols. 1-2), Zhonghua (vols. 3-4), and Kexue (vol. 5), 1985-99. Articles on oracle-bone, bronze, bamboo, wood, and silk excavated texts.

Jianbo yanjiu 簡帛研究, vols. 1-3, Shekeyuan, Jianbo yanjiu zhongxin 簡帛研究中心 (Center for research on bamboo and silk books). Three collections of more recent articles: Falü, 1993, 1996; Sheke, 1998.

Jiandu xuebao 簡牘學報, Taibei (1970- , annual)

Jianduxue yanjiu 簡牘學研究, Lanzhou (1996- , irregular)

Chûgoku shutsudo shiryô kenkyûkai kaihô 中國出土資料研究會會報 (The journal of the society for the study of Chinese excavated texts), Tôkyô daigaku bungakubu, irregular.

The *jiandu* are referred to either by the period from which they date or by the place in which they were found, or both; for example, *Zhanguojian* 戰國簡 (Warring States bamboo strips), *Chujian* 楚簡 (Bamboo strips from the kingdom of Chu), *Qinjian* 秦簡, *Hanjian* 漢簡, *Juyan Hanjian* 居延漢簡, and so forth.

Modern findings of Warring States *jiandu* are listed alphabetically in 19.1.1 (Chu *jiandu*) and 19.1.2 (non-Chu *jiandu*). Post-Qin unification and Han *Jiandu* are listed in 44.4. Three Kingdoms and Jin *jiandu* in 45.3. In the lists below, the following distinctions are made:

Bamboo strips (*zhujian* 竹簡)
Wooden strips (*mujian* 木簡)
Bamboo and wooden strips (*jiandu* 簡牘)
Bamboo tablets (*zhudu* 竹牘)
Wooden tablets (*mudu* 木牘)

19.1.1 *Warring States* Chujian 楚簡

The origins of the central Yangzi state of Chu can be traced back to the Shang and Western Zhou. It had not only a distinctive high culture but also a spectacularly successful history of military expansion. Between the tenth and third centuries BC it absorbed a total of 61 kingdoms, thus becoming the largest power in the Warring States period, before eventually being destroyed by Qin in 223 BC. For over 400 years, from the end of the eighth (or the very beginning of the seventh) century to 278 BC, the capital was situated at Ying 郢, the site of which during the Warring States period was located at or near the city of Ji'nan 記南, Jiangling 江陵 county, Hubei. On Chu archaeology and history, note the following:

Defining Chu: Image and Reality in Ancient China, Constance A. Cook and John S. Major, eds., Curzon, 2000.

Chuxue *wenku* 楚學文庫 (Chu studies collection), Chu wenhua yanjiuhui 楚文化研究會 (Chu culture society), ed., 18 vols., Hubei jiaoyu, 1993–96. The best series on all aspects of Chu history and culture.

Chu kaogu wenhua da shiji 楚考古文化大事記 (Main events in Chu archaeology), Wenwu, 1984, an index to Chu archaeological finds up to 1982 (see also the literature on Mawangdui silk books, 19.1.3).

Guo Dewei 郭德維, *Chudu Ji'nan cheng fuyuan yanjiu* 楚都記南城復員研究 (Research on the restoration of the Chu capital of Ji'nan), Wenwu, 1999.

Over 7,000 Chu strips, with a total of 40,000 legible characters, have been discovered at 30 separate sites. In addition, Chu silk manuscripts with a total of about 1,000 characters have been discovered (19.1.3). Most of the finds have been from tombs around the ancient capital of Ying and later from around Changsha:

Li Yunfu 李運富, *Chuguo jianbo wenzi gouxing xitong yanjiu* 楚國簡帛文字構形系統研究 (Systemic studies of the forms of Chu bamboo and silk characters), Qi-Lu, 1997. Contains a thorough description of the excavated manuscripts and also lists nearly 400 studies of them.

For compendia of Chu-style characters, see:

Chuxi jianbo wenzi bian 楚系簡帛文字編 (Compilation of Chu-style *jiandu* and silk manuscript characters), Teng Rensheng 滕壬生, comp., Hubei jiaoyu, 1995, and for corrections, see Li Ling 李零, "Du *Chuxi jianbo wenzi bian"* 讀'楚系簡帛文字編', *Chutu wenxian yanjiu* 5, 139–62 (1999).

Zhanguo Chu zhujian huibian 戰國楚竹簡匯編 (Glossary of Chu Warring States bamboo strips), Shang Chengzuo 商承祚, ed., Qi-Lu, 1995.

Note that the journal *Jiang-Han kaogu* 江漢考古 (12.3, *Journals*) carries many articles on the *Chujian*. The following is a list of the main finds of *Chujian* (by name of site). The most important finds are marked with an asterisk:

*Baoshan 包山, Jingmen 荆門, Hubei: 278 strips containing 12,472 characters. Excavated from tomb 2 in 1986 and 1987. The texts date from 323 to 292 BC. They are among the earliest yet discovered and include records of events, legal works, divinatory texts, and lists of burial articles. For archaeological report, see *Baoshan Chumu* 包山楚墓 (Chu tomb at Baoshan), Wenwu, 1991; for transcriptions, see *Baoshan Chujian* 包山楚簡 (Chu bamboo strips from Baoshan), Wenwu, 1991; for listing of characters, see *Baoshan Chujian wenzibian* 包山楚簡文字編 (Compilation of characters found on Chu bamboo strips from Baoshan), Wenwu, 1996; for research, see Chen Wei 陳偉, *Baoshan Chujian chutan* 包山楚簡初探 (Preliminary investigations of the Chu bamboo strips from Baoshan), Wuhan daxue, 1996; Li Ling 李零, "Formulaic Structure of Chu Divinatory Bamboo Slips," *EC* 15: 71–86 (1990). *Jianghan kaogu* 1993.4; *Huaxia kaogu* 1994.2; *Wenwu* 1996.12; *Nanfang wenwu* 1996.2 (on the legal texts).

Changtaiguan 長臺關, Xinyang 信陽, Henan: 2 sets; the first (119 strips) is part of a book relating to the Duke of Zhou; the second (29 strips) is a list of burial articles. Excavated in 1957 from tomb 1. See *Xinyang Chumu* 信陽楚墓 (The Chu graves at Xinyang), Henan Wenwu yanjiuso, ed., Wenwu, 1986.

Deshan Xiyangpo 德山夕陽坡, Changde 常德, Hunan: 2 strips with a total of 54 characters recording events. Excavated in 1984 (tomb 2).

Fanjiapo 范家坡, Jiangling 江陵, Hubei: 1 strip from tomb 7, not yet published. Excavated in 1993.

*Guodian 郭店, Jingmen 荆門, Hubei: 804 strips in tomb 1, of which 730 with writing on them, amounting to a total of over 13,000 characters. The single largest find from a Chu tomb. The strips record two Daoist works (one of which is the earliest known copy of about two-fifths of the modern *Laozi*, the fifth to have been unearthed to date) and several Confucian works. These are some of the earliest *jiandu* ever found. The texts are largely the same as the transmitted texts, but the order of the chapters is sometimes different. The strips are clearly reproduced and transcribed (with annotations by Qiu Xigui) in *Guodian Chumu zhujian* 郭店楚墓竹簡 (The bamboo strips from the Chu tomb at Guodian), Jingmenshi bowuguan, ed., Wenwu, 1998. See also Cui Renyi 崔仁義, *Jingmen Guodian Chujian Laozi yanjiu* 荊門郭店楚簡老子研究 (Studies of the Guodian bamboo strip *Laozi*), Kexue, 1998. Excavated in 1993; *Wenwu* 1997.7.

*Jiudian 九店, Jiangling 江陵, Hubei: Total of 130 readable bamboo strips containing the earliest extant almanacs and prognostication texts. *Jiangling Jiudian Dong Zhou mu* 江陵九店東周墓 (The Eastern Zhou tombs at Jiudian, Jiangling), Kexue, 1995. See 5.1.2 on the almanacs of the Warring States, Qin, and Han. Tombs 56, 411, and 621 excavated in 1981 and 1989.

Jiuli 九里, Linfeng 臨澧, Hunan: 10 strips excavated in 1980. Not published.

Mashan 馬山, Jiangling 江陵, Hubei: 1 strip from tomb 1 with 8 characters recording events. Also many textiles, including woven and embroidered silks (illustrated in Rawson, 1996 [12.1], 144–49). Excavated in 1982; *Wenwu* 1982.10.

Qinjiazui 秦家嘴, Jiangling 江陵, Hubei: divination and sacrificial records. Tomb 1 contains 7 strips and wooden tablets; tomb 13 contains 18 damaged strips; tomb 99 contains 16 damaged strips. Excavated in 1986; *Jiang-Han kaogu* 1988.2.

*Shanghai bowuguan 上海博物館 bought 1,437 *Chujian* from Hong Kong in 1994. The strips relate to fourth century BC religious and intellectual life and include the earliest known text of the *Yijing*. To be published by Wenwu in 2000.

Shibancun 石板村, Cili 慈利, Hunan: 800–1,000 strips and wooden tablets badly damaged (broken into more than 4,000) recording historical events, mainly war between Wu and Yue (tomb 36). Not yet published. Excavated in 1987; *Wenwu* 1990.9.

Tengdian 藤店, Jiangling 江陵, Hubei: 24 badly damaged *zhujian* and *mudu* with only a total of 47 decipherable characters. Excavated from tomb 1 in 1973; *Wenwu* 1973.9.

Tianxingguan 天星觀, Jiangling 江陵, Hubei: Over 70 *zhujian* and *mudu* containing records of events, divination and sacrificial records, and lists of burial articles in a tomb; ca. 340 BC. Excavated in 1978; *Kaogu xuebao* 1982.1.

*Wangshan 望山, Jiangling 江陵, Hubei: 207 strips and wooden tablets in tomb 1 with records of events and divination and sacrificial records:

Wangshan Chujian 望山楚簡, Hubei Kaogusuo 湖北考古所 and Bei-da Zhongwenxi 北大中文系, ed., Zhonghua, 1995. Includes illustrations of the originals, transcriptions, translations into Modern Chinese, and meticulous annotations and introductions. Excavated in 1965.

Wangshan 望山, Jiangling 江陵, Hubei: 66 strips with lists of burial articles. *Wangshan Chujian* (1995). Also contains tools for preparing bamboo strips, including a chopper, two splitting knives, and a paring knife for scraping off old inscriptions (illustrated in Rawson, *Mysteries*, 1996, 151). Excavated in 1966 from tomb 2.

Wulipai 五里牌, Changsha, Hunan: 37 damaged strips with lists of burial articles. Excavated from tomb 406 in 1951; *Kexue tongbao* 1952.3.

Yangjiawan 楊家灣, Changsha, Hunan: 72 strips, of which 54 have writing. Excavated in 1954 from tomb 6; *Wenwu cankao ziliao* 1954.12.

Yangtianhu 仰天湖, Changsha, Hunan: 43 *jiandu* with lists of burial articles. Excavated in 1953 from tomb 25. See Rao Zongyi 饒宗頤, *Zhanguo Chujian jianzheng* 戰國楚簡箋證 (Critical commentary on the Warring states *Chujian*), Shanghai chubanshe, 1957.

Zenghou Yi mu 曾侯乙墓, Suizhou 隨州, Hubei: Over 240 *zhujian* with 6,696 characters written on them were found in the tomb dating from 433 BC of Marquis Yi of Zeng. Lists of burial articles. Excavated in 1978; see 13.2.3 for excavation report.

Zhuanwachang 磚瓦廠, Jiangling 江陵, Hubei: 6 strips from tomb 370 with divination and sacrificial records. Excavated in 1992.

Zhulüguan 竹律管, Jiangling 江陵, Yutaishan 玉臺山, Hubei: 4 strips with 38 characters of musical texts. Excavated in 1986.

19.1.2 *Warring States* Jiandu 戰國簡牘: *Non-Chu*

*Fangmatan 放馬灘, Tianshuishi 天水市, Gansu: 470 Qin bamboo strips with eight maps (seven on wooden tablets and a fragment of one on paper) and 2 almanacs dating from the end of the Warring States (see 4.4.1 for details of the maps). *Qin Han jiandu lunwenji* 秦漢簡牘論文集, Gansu renmin, 1989; *Wenwu* 1990.4. Excavated from a Qin tomb in 1986.

*Haojiaping 郝家坪, Qingchuan 青川 county, Sichuan: 2 wooden tablets, 1 on land law (dated to 306 BC), the second indecipherable; see *Wenwu* 1982.1; *Kaogu* 1988.8. Also 7 *banliang* bronze coins; see 7.4.1, *Bronze (2)*. Excavated from tomb 50 in 1979–80 (27.2).

19.1.3   Silk Manuscripts

Several books, as well as documents and maps, written on silk dating from the Warring States and Han periods have been excavated. The earliest was stolen from a Chu tomb at Zidanku 子彈庫, near Changsha, in 1942 and is now held in the Arthur M. Sackler Museum in Washington, DC. It contained 900 characters and colored illustrations of the gods of the 12 months in the margins. Exposure to the light has made it dark and illegible. It is dated to ca. 300 BC.[4]

Most famous of the silk manuscripts are the dozen dating from the late Warring States and the Han excavated in 1973 from Mawangdui 馬王堆 Former Han tomb 3 (168 BC), near Changsha. They contain over 120,000 characters and include two copies of Laozi 老子.[5] They were written at the transition point between

---

[4] See Noel Barnard, *The Ch'u Silk Manuscript—Translation and Commentary*, ANUP, 1973. Over 75 books and articles have been published on this silk manuscript. For a bibliography of studies on the tomb, see Li Meilu 李梅鹿, *Mawangdui Hanmu yanjiu mulu* 馬王堆漢墓研究目錄, Hunansheng bowuguan, 1992, and for a brief bibliography of the texts, Li Ling 李零, *Zhongguo fangshu kao* 中國方術考 (Studies on Chinese divinatory and medical arts), Renmin Zhongguo, 1993, 167–85. See also the same author's *Changsha Zidanku Zhanguo Chu boshu yanjiu* 長沙子彈庫戰國楚帛書研究 (Research on the Chu silk manuscript from Zidankui, Changsha), Zhonghua, 1985; and *Zhujian boshu lunwen ji* 竹簡帛書論文集 (Collected articles on the books written on bamboo and silk), Zheng Liangshu 鄭良樹, ed., Zhonghua, 1982. For a listing of the characters in the manuscript, see *Changsha Chu boshu wenzibian* 長沙楚帛書文字編 (Compilation of the characters in the Changsha Chu silk manuscript), Zeng Xiantong 曾憲通, comp., Zhonghua, 1993, and for the larger context of Chu-style characters as found on the Chu bamboo strips, see Teng Rensheng (19.1.1).

[5] For transcriptions, see *Mawangdui Hanmu boshu* 馬王堆漢墓帛書 (The silk books from the Han tomb at Mawangdui), Mawangdui Hanmu boshu zhengli xiaozu 馬王堆漢墓帛書整理小組, ed., 6 vols., Wenwu, 1980– . Vol. 1 contains the *Laozi* A and B texts; vol. 2, the *Yijing* 易經 (Classic of changes), not yet published; vol. 3 (titles added by the editors), the *Chunqiu shiyu* 春秋事語 (Deeds and words of the Spring and Autumn) and the *Zhanguo zonghengjia shu* 戰國縱橫家書 (Book of Warring States strategists), 1983; vol. 4, reproductions as well as transcriptions of all the writings relating to medicine (1985); vols. 5 (astrology) and 6 (occult texts), forthcoming. The tomb also contained three tricolored maps on silk (4.4). *Mawangdui Hanmu wenwu* 馬王堆漢墓文物 (The cultural relics unearthed from the Han tombs at Mawangdui), Hunan, 1992, contains transcriptions of some of the silk texts not yet published in the *Mawangdui Hanmu boshu* series. Medical texts, including a silk painting

Footnote continued on next page

small seal and chancery scripts. There are several more works written on silk, including fragments of texts, which have been excavated
from tombs elsewhere, but await publication.

The discoveries of manuscripts written on bamboo and silk have
enabled comparison of the transmitted texts of literary works,
which passed through many editorial hands over the centuries, with
these older versions, sometimes untouched since their entombment
in the Han or earlier.[6] In some cases lost works have been recovered, and in other cases hitherto unknown works have been discovered.[7]

19.2   Main Transmitted Texts and Their Translations

The pre-Qin transmitted texts are referred to today as "books" with
"titles" and in some cases "authors." This is misleading insofar as it
implies that they were the deliberate creations of a single person.
Whether they began as the sayings of a school of thought, as anthologies of poetry, as collections of documents, or as court chronicles, they all had one thing in common: most had no fixed titles and
no known authors. They were, rather, the work of many hands that
compiled them over several centuries on the basis of oral traditions,
during which they were transmitted in different versions with only
extremely limited circulation and access (scholars went to texts, not
vice versa). Eventually, each was edited into a more definitive form
(sometimes in the late Warring States, often during the Former
Han). It was only then that they acquired the titles (and "authors")
by which they were known in succeeding centuries right up to our
own day (Table 26).

---

showing 44 people doing *daoyin* 導引 (stretching and breathing) exercises, have
been separately published (Chapter 36). Robin D. S. Yates translates some of
the philosophical texts in *Five Lost Classics: Tao, Huang-Lao and Yin-Yang in
Han China*, Ballantine, 1996. See also *The Four Political Treatises of the Yellow
Emperor*, Leo Chang and Yu Feng, trs., UHP, 1998.

  [6] William Boltz discusses manuscripts of transmitted texts on bamboo and
silk in *NSECH* (1997), 253–84.

  [7] Portions of *Sunzi bingfa* 孫子兵法 (Sunzi: art of war) and the previously
lost *Sun Bin bingfa* 孫臏兵法 (Sun Bin: art of war) were found in 1972 in a
Former Han tomb at Yinqueshan, Linyi county, Shandong (28.2).

Table 26: Main Textual Sources for Pre-Qin History

Note: A plus ("+") indicates the period(s) to which a work is dated. An arrow ("⇦") indicates that it contains material about an earlier period. ICS refers to the number of the concordance in the *ICS Ancient Chinese Texts Concordance Series* (9.10).

All the main pre-Qin and Han historical works are included in the table, but not all the philosophical works (for which, see also 19.2 and Chapter 33).

Col. 1: 西周 (Western Zhou)   *Col. 2:* 春秋 (Spring and Autumn)
Col. 3: 戰國 (Warring States)   *Col. 4:* 漢代 (Han)

Title of book (*translation*), translator, publisher	周	春	戰	漢	*ICS*
Shangshu 尚書 (*Book of Documents*, Bernhard Karlgren, Elanders, 1950; also Karlgren, *Glosses on the Book of Documents*, Elanders, 1970; first issued in *BMFEA*, 20: 39–315 [1948] and 21: 63–206 [1949]). See Shaughnessy in *ECT*, 376–89.	+	+	+ ⇦		28
Yi Zhoushu [逸]周書 [Remaining] Zhou documents); originally entitled *Zhoushiji*, also called *Jizhong Zhoushu* 汲冢周書 (Ji tomb *Zhoushu*). Compilation of recorded comments and documents similar to those in the *Shangshu* dating from different periods. See Shaughnessy in *ECT*, 229–33. Later classified as a *bieshi* 別史 or *zashi* 雜史; see 20.4.	+	+	+ ⇦		12
Yijing 易經 (*The Classic of Changes: A New Translation of the I Ching as Interpreted by Wang Bi*, tr. by Richard John Lynn, Col. UP, 1994 [also available on CD-ROM]; *I Ching, The Classic of Changes: The First English Translation of the Newly Discovered Second-Century B.C. Mawangdui Texts*, Edward L. Shaughnessy, Ballantine, 1996). See Shaughnessy in *ECT*, 216–28.	+				27

Table continues

Table 26—Continued

Title of book (*translation*), translator, publisher	周	春	戰	漢	ICS
Shijing 詩經 (*Book of Odes [Songs]: Chinese Text, Transcription and Translation*, Bernhard Karlgren, *BMFEA*, 14, 16 and 18 [1942, 1944 and 1946]; issued as a book, MFEA, 1950). See Loewe in *ECT*, 415–23.	+	+	+		29
Chunqiu 春秋 (*The Chinese Classics, The Ch'un Ts'ew with The Tso Chuen*, James Legge (1815–97), vol. 4, Parts 1 and 2, OUP, 1893–94); for the length of the *Chunqiu* and its commentaries, see Table 27, 19.2; for editions, studies, and other translations of the *Chunqiu* and its three commentaries, see 21.1.	+	+	+⇦		30–32
Zhanguoce 戰國策 (*Chan-kuo-ts'e*), Liu Xiang 劉向, comp.; J. I. Crump, tr., Clarendon, 1970; rev. with index, CCS, Univ. of Michigan, 1996; 3 vols.; Shanghai guji, 1978, also contains transcription of Mawangdui version. See 21.1 and Tsuenhsuin Tsien in *ECT*, 1–11.			+		1
Lunyu 論語 (*Confucius, the Analects [Lun yü]*), D. C. Lau, HKCUP, 1979; 3rd rpnt., 1992. Bilingual text. *The Original Analects: Sayings of Confucius and His Successors*, E. Bruce Brooks and A. Taeko Brooks, Col. UP, 1997, attempts to show the text gradually taking shape during the centuries after the death of Confucius (551–479 BC). See Cheng in *ECT*, 313–23.			+		33
Mengzi 孟子 (*Meng tzu*), D. C. Lau, 2 vols., HKCUP, 1979, 1984. See Lau in *ECT*, 331–36.			+⇦		34
Mozi 墨子 (*The Ethical and Political Works of Mo Tzu*), Yipao Mei, Probsthain, 1929; rpnt., Hyperion Press, 1973, tr. of Chapters 1–39 and 46–50; See Graham in *ECT*, 336–41.			+		54

Table continues

Table 26—Continued

Title of book (*translation*), translator, publisher	周	春	戰	漢	ICS
Shangjunshu 商君書 (*Le livre du prince Shang*), Jean Levi, tr., Flammarion, 1981; *The Book of Lord Shang*, J. J. L. Duyvendak, tr., Probsthain, 1928; UChP, 1963. See Levi in *ECT*, 368–75.		+			3
Han Feizi 韓非子 (*The complete works of Han Fei Tzu*), W. K. Liao, vol. 1, Probsthain, 1939, 1959; vol. 2, 1959. See Levi in *ECT*, 115–24.			+		56
Guanzi 管子 (*Guanzi*), W. Allyn Rickett, 2 vols., PUP, 1985 and 1998. Annotated, indexed translation. See Rickett in *ECT*, 244–51.			+		55
Laozi 老子 (*Chinese Classics, Tao Te Ching*), D. C. Lau, HKCUP, 1963, 1982, 2nd ed., 1989, 1996. Bilingual text. Part I (tr. of Wang Bi text); part II (tr. of Mawangdui texts). See Boltz in *ECT*, 269–92.			+		43
Zhuangzi 莊子 (*The Complete Works of Chuang-tzu*), putative author: Zhuang Zhou 莊周, ca. 370–301 BC; Burton Watson, Col. UP, 1968, 1996; A. C. Graham, *Chuang-tzu: The Inner Chapters*, Allen and Unwin, 1981. See Roth in *ECT*, 56–66.			+		57
Bingshu 兵書 (Military manuals): *Sun-tzu: The Art of Warfare: The First English Translation Incorporating the Yin-ch'üeh-shan Texts*, Roger T. Ames, Ballantine, 1993; see below under "Excavated texts" and also 28.2.			+		11
Guoyu 國語 (Discourses of the states), discourses from eight of the Warring States, authorship traditionally attributed to Zuo Qiuming 左丘明 (or Zuoqiu Ming), 5th c., but more likely by several hands, possibly edited by Zuo. Regarded as a *waizhuan* 外傳 (informal commentary) on the *Chunqiu*. See Chang et al. in *ECT*, 263–68.			+ ⇦		53

Table continues

Table 26—Continued

Title of book (*translation*), translator, publisher	周	春	戰	漢	*ICS*
Zhushu jinian 竹書紀年 (Bamboo annals), in *The Chinese Classics*, James Legge, vol. 3, OUP, 1865, *Prolegomena*, Chapter 4, 108–76. Edward L. Shaughnessy, "On the Authenticity of the *Bamboo Annals*," *HJAS* 46.1: 149–80 (1986). See also Nivison in *ECT*, 39–47.			+ ⇦		48
Shiben 世本 (Basics of hereditary lines), Liu Xiang 劉向; archive of Warring States descent lines; see *Shiben bazhong* 世本八種, Shangwu, 1957 (3.5).			+ ⇦		47
Yili 儀禮 (*The I li, or Book of Etiquette and Ceremonial*), John Steele, 2 vols., Probsthain, 1917; Taibei rpnt., 1972. For a recently discovered *jiandu* version, see 46.3, item 7. See Boltz in *ECT*, 234–43.			+ ⇦		24
Zhouli 周禮 (*Le Tcheou-li ou Rites des Tcheou*), Édouard Biot, Imprimerie Nationale, 3 vols., 1851. See Boltz in *ECT*, 24–32.			+ ⇦		13
Liji 禮記 (*Li Ki*), James Legge, in *Sacred Books of the East*, Max Müller, ed., vols., xxvii–xxviii, OUP, 1879–91, rpnt., 1926, 1967. See Riegel in *ECT*, 293–97.			+ ⇦		2
Chuci 楚辭 (*The Songs of the South*), David Hawkes, OUP, 1959; rev., Penguin, 1985. See Hawkes in *ECT*, 48–55.			+ ⇦		59
Mu tianzi zhuan 穆天子傳 (*Le Mu Tianzi zhuan: traduction annotée: étude critique*, Rémi Mathieu, Collège de France, 1978). See the same scholar's contribution in *ECT*, 342–46. Note Deborah Lynn Porter, *From Deluge to Discourse: Myth, History, and the Generation of Chinese Fiction*, SUNY, 1996.			+ ⇦		22

Table continues

Table 26—Continued

Title of book (*translation*), translator, publisher	周	春	戰	漢	*ICS*
Shanhaijing 山海經 (*The Classic of Mountains and Seas*, Anne Birrel, Penguin, 1999). See Fracasso in *ECT*, 357–67.			+ ⇦		22
Xunzi 荀子 (*Xunzi: A Translation and Study of the Complete Works*), John Knoblock, 3 vols., SUP, 1988–94. See Loewe in *ECT*, 178–88.			+ ⇦		45
Lüshi chunqiu 呂氏春秋, ca. 239 BC (*The Annals of Lü Buwei*), John Knoblock and Jeffrey Riegel, trs., SUP, 2000; see also *Frühling und Herbst des Lü Bu We*, Richard Wilhelm (1873–1930), tr., Diederichs, 1928; rpnt., 1971. See Carson and Loewe in *ECT*, 324–30.			+ ⇦		23
Yanzi chunqiu 晏子春秋 (Spring and Autumn of Yan Ying). See Durrant in *ECT*, 483–89.			+ ⇦		15
Excavated pre-Qin texts: a number have been unearthed from Warring States and Han tombs, notably the *Yili, Shijing, Yijing, Sun Bin*, and *Sunzi bingfa*; see 18.2 and Boltz in *NSECH*.			+		
A number of Warring States maps have been unearthed; see 4.4.			+		
A number of Warring States and Qin legal works have been unearthed; see 18.1.3 and 27.1.			+		
For pre-Qin medical works, see Chapter 36.			+		
Title of book (*translation*), translator, publisher	周	春	戰	漢	*ICS*
A number of pre-Qin almanacs have been unearthed; see 5.1.2, 6.4, 44.3.2.1, 44.3.2.2.			+		
A pre-Qin mathematical text (*Suanshu shu* 算術書) has recently been unearthed (44.3.2.2).			+		

Table continues

Table 26—Continued

Title of book (*translation*), translator, publisher	周	春	戰	漢	ICS
Jiuzhang suanshu 九章算術 (Nine chapters on the mathematical arts). See Cullen in *ECT*, 16–23, and 37.1.				+ ⇦	62
Zhoubi suanjing 周髀算經 (The Zhou gnomon), tr. In Christopher Cullen, *Astronomy and Mathematics in Ancient China: The* Zhoubi Suanjing, CUP, 1996. See Cullen in *ECT*, 33–38.				+ ⇦	62
Chunqiu fanlu 春秋繁露, Dong Zhongshu 董仲舒 (179?–104? BC); see Sarah A. Queen, *From Chronicle to Canon*, CUP, 1996, also Davidson and Loewe in *ECT*, 77–87.				+ ⇦	21
Lunheng 論衡 (Doctrines evaluated), Wang Chong 王充 (AD 27–ca. 100): *Lun Heng*, Alfred Forke, 2 vols., Kelly and Walsh, 1907, 1911; Paragon rpnt., 1962. See Pokora and Loewe in *ECT*, 309–12. Note *Lunheng suoyin* 論衡索引, Cheng Xiangqing 程湘清 et al., comps., Zhonghua, 1994. A complete concordance with *pinyin*, stroke-count, classifier, and four-corner indexes. Arrangement is by *pinyin*. The text is printed at the end.				+ ⇦	41
Huainanzi 淮南子: John S. Major, *Heaven and Earth in Early Han Thought: Chapters Three, Four and Five of the Huainanzi*, SUNY, 1993; Harold D. Roth, *The Textual History of the Huai-nan Tzu*, MUP, 1992. See Le Blanc in *ECT*, 189–95.				+ ⇦	9
Fengsu tongyi 風俗通義 (Comprehensive meaning of customs), Ying Shao 應劭 (ca. 140–ca. 206): observations of Later Han cults and beliefs. See Nylan in *ECT*, 105–12.				+ ⇦	42
Shuowen jiezi 説文解字 (Explaining single-component graphs and analyzing compound characters), Xu Shen 許慎; see 2.2.1 and 16.2.				+ ⇦	63

Table continues

Table 26—Continued

Title of book (*translation*), translator, publisher	周	春	戰	漢	*ICS*
Chu-Han Chunqiu 楚漢春秋, Lu Jia 陸賈 (ca. 240–170), a high official under Liu Bang, who recorded in chronicle form the rise to power of Xiang Yu 項羽 and Liu Bang 劉邦 and the reigns of Huidi 惠帝 and Wendi 文帝. Used as a source by Sima Qian 司馬遷. Exists today only in a recovered edition (*jiben* 輯本).				+	
Shiji 史記 (Records of the historian); see 44.1. See *Nianwushi quanwen ziliaoku* 廿五史全文資料庫 (25 Histories full-text database), Shiyusuo, 1988; see 22.1.				+ ⇦	DB
Hanshu 漢書 (History of the Former Han); see 44.1. Available on computer database: *Nianwushi quanwen ziliaoku* 廿五史全文資料庫 (25 Histories full-text database), Shiyusuo, 1988. See 22.1 for further details.				+ ⇦	DB
Yuejue shu 越絕書 (Yue's destruction of Wu). Compiled in Later Han. See Schuessler and Loewe in *ECT*, 490–93.				+ ⇦	17
Wu-Yue chunqiu 吳越春秋 (The annals of Wu and Yue). Compiled in Later Han by various hands. See Lagerwey in *ECT*, 473–76.				+ ⇦	16

The work of an editor in ancient China was more arduous than that of most editors today. First, he had to collate the bamboo or wooden strips in a coherent order into bundles (18.1). If, as often happened, the threads had perished, he had to put the strips back into order. If there were missing strips (*tuojian* 脫簡), or broken strips, missing characters (*tuozi* 脫字) would have to be replaced, a common cause of confusion and variant readings. Sometimes a previous editor had put the strips in the wrong order (*cuojian* 錯簡) or had been tempted to add material at the end of a bundle if there were blank strips left, thus creating a puzzle for future editors. Next, he had to assign to each bundle a heading (or, as we would say, a chapter title). This was often chosen from the key characters in the first sentence of the first strip in each bundle.[8] Finally, the bundles had to be arranged into a coherent order. In the course of his work, the editor often had to compare various editions, usually with the aim of producing a single reliable text, but in some cases recognizing the validity of several versions of a single work. Another task was to chose the title from one of several available alternatives or to invent one and, in some cases, to attribute an author.[9] One thing he did not have to do was to correct the punctuation, since there was none (1.3.4).

During the Former Han, much of the editorial work was handled by the court archivists, historians, or librarians, who on three occasions were charged with gathering together books from all over the empire and putting into order the imperial collection.[10] This was a formidable task after the depredations of the Qin, and it was one that came to be surrounded with the greatest academic controversy in Chinese history (that between the Old and the New Text traditions, see 19.3).

Ever since the Han, textual criticism as applied to the classical canon (broadly the pre-Qin and principal Han texts) has been one of the main activities and achievements of Chinese scholarship.[11]

---

[8] For example, Chapter 1 of the *Lunyu* is entitled *Xue'er* 學而 after the opening characters of the first sentence, 子曰, 學而時習之.

[9] In later Chinese history, many works continued to have alternative titles, but for different reasons (9.9). For a comprehensive survey of how works were assembled, see Mark Edward Lewis, *Writing and Authority in Early China*, Suny Press, 1999. For a brief account of two individual works, see "The Problem of Authorship" and "The Nature of the Work," in *Laozi* 老子 (*Chinese Classics, Tao Te Ching*, D. C. Lau, tr., HKCUP, 1963, 1982; 2nd ed., 1989, 1996), Appendix I and II; John Makeham, "The Formation of *Lunyu* as a Book," *MS* 44 (1996), 1–24.

[10] The three occasions were at the beginning of the dynasty in about 200 BC, in 124 BC, and again in 26 BC.

[11] Textual criticism was called *choujiao* 讎校 or *jiaochou* 校讎 in the Han and *jiaokan* 校勘 beginning in the Six Dynasties. The modern term is *jiaokanxue* 校勘學. Other terms for collating and editing used in book titles include *jiaozhu* 校注 or *jiaoshi* 校釋 (i.e., *jiaokan zhushi* 校勘注釋, collated and annotated); *jiaoding* 校訂 (i.e., *jiaokan dingzheng* 校勘訂正, collated and corrected); *jiaobu* (校補, collated and enlarged); *jiaodian* 校點 (collated and punctuated). The marks and colors used for collating texts are discussed in Susan Cherniack, "Book Culture and Textual Transmission in Sung China," *HJAS* 54.1: 5–125 (1994), 88–102. For an introduction, see, for example, Song Ziran 宋子然,

Footnote continued on next page

The advances in textual criticism made by Qing *kaozheng* 考證 scholars were very great (50.6.4). Although concentrating on the texts of the classics, they also did much important work on later sources as well. Students should make sure, therefore, especially if working on an earlier text, that they have checked the Qing (and later) scholarship on it. Throughout the manual every effort has been made to draw attention to the best modern editions and reprints, which are by definition those that take account of, or are based on, the relevant Qing scholarship.

After the collapse of the Chinese empire, modern scholars have continued the work in a more skeptical spirit and with the added advantage in some cases of being able to compare the transmitted texts with newly discovered Han and Warring States manuscripts on bamboo and silk. The result of all these efforts is that most of the early texts are now available in critical, annotated editions, although some of the old controversies have still not been resolved. Given the above, it is hardly surprising that few, if any, translations of pre-Qin works can be regarded as definitive, although some have been translated hundreds of times.[12]

The best scholarly introduction to the philological minefield of the main textual sources of the pre-Qin (and Han) is *ECT*.[13] It contains short articles by different specialists on 64 of them. The authors outline the content, date of composition and authenticity, text history and editions, translations, studies, Japanese editions, research aids, indexes, and concordances.

If you want to look something up in the main pre-Qin and Han sources, the most convenient way is to use the Institute of Chinese Studies, *ICS Ancient Chinese Texts Concordance Series*. This contains the full texts with punctuation added as well as character frequency counts and indexes by *pinyin* and stroke-count. The *ICS* series is

---

Zhongguo gushu jiaodufa 中國古書校讀法 (Techniques for the collation and reading of old Chinese books), Ba-Shu, 1995.

[12] For an instructive comparison of nine translations of one of the Confucian classics into Western languages, see David S. Nivison, "On Translating Mencius," in *The Ways of Confucianism*, edited with an introduction by Bryan W. Van Norden, Open Court, 1996, 175–201. Nivison favors the Lau translation (Table 26).

[13] *Early Chinese Texts: A Bibliographical Guide*, Michael Loewe, ed., *Early China* Special Monograph Series, SSEC and IEAS, 1993, 1999. Liaoning jiaoyu published a Chinese translation in 1997.

available not only in book form and disc, but also on a single CD-ROM, making it a most convenient and authoritative research tool (for more on the *ICS* concordances as well as other indexes, see 9.10).

One of the first ancient works that appears to have been conceived from start to finish as a complete "book" is credited to Lü Buwei 呂不韋, the *Lüshi chunqiu* 呂氏春秋 (Table 26, 19.2). It is an anthology of excerpts on many subjects apparently written by several scholars employed by Lü (who served at the end of his life as chancellor of Qin). Subsequent Chinese history was to see not only an enormous number of such encyclopaedic compilations but also books whose authorship was credited to senior officials, emperors, or famous scholars, although their contribution to the actual writing may have been nil (a practice that is not unknown to this day). By the Han, the practice of a single author or compiler planning a book before beginning to compose it was becoming the norm for the first time. But even so, one of China's most famous books, whose authorship has never been in doubt, had no fixed title. Sima Qian may have indicated a title in his Postface (*Shiji, juan* 130), but it was only two centuries after his death that his work came to be known by the generic term *Shiji* (Historical record; see 44.1).

It follows from this that a pre-Qin text should be handled with extreme caution, with regard to both the text itself and its interpretation. For a start, it is vital to establish as far as possible which parts of it were written when and by whom (or by what school).

Some are nearly contemporaneous with the period they describe. Many contain materials written at different times, sometimes stretching over several centuries. Some were written later about an earlier period. Some were written as historical works (mainly court annals) or as compilations of official documents; others are classified as literature or philosophy but contain material of interest to historians. It is not unlikely that the list of pre-Qin texts will grow longer as archaeology continues to turn up excavated texts (*chutu wenxian* 出土文獻), not only of transmitted works (*chuanshi wenxian* 傳世文獻) but also of hitherto unknown works (for example, those found in Baoshan 包山, tomb 2 or Shuihudi 睡虎地, tomb 11 [19.1.1–1.3]).

For overall introductions to the main thinkers and schools of thought as reflected in the pre-Qin and Han texts, start with Frederick W. Mote, *Intellectual Foundations of China*, 2nd ed., McGraw-

Hill, 1988, or with Angus Graham (1919–91), *Disputers of the Tao*, Open Court, 1989, or with Nivison and Harper in *CHAC*.[14] Thereafter, go directly to one of the main schools, thinkers, or texts.

19.3   The Confucian Classics

Four hundred years after the death of Confucius, Han Wudi 漢武帝 (140–88 BC) adopted the policy of *bachu bojia duzun rushu* 罷黜百家獨尊儒術 (ban the hundred schools; recognize only the Confucians). The Confucian works were made state doctrine, and their mastery, the entry to officialdom. The *Wujing* 五經 (Five classics) selected were the six mentioned by Confucius (minus the *Yue* 樂 [Music], which had been lost when the first emperor of Qin ordered the burning of the books). They were known for short as the *Shi* 詩 (The songs); the *Shu* 書 (The documents); the *Li* 禮 (The rites); the *Yi* 易 (The changes); and the *Chunqiu* 春秋 (The Spring and Autumn annals).

In the Eastern Han, the *Xiaojing* 孝經 (The classic of filial piety) and the *Lunyu* 論語 (Analects) were added to make the *Qijing* 七經 (Seven classics). During the Tang, the number eventually rose to 12 (the *Li* and the *Chunqiu* were each split into three constituent parts, and the *Erya* 爾雅 was added). These were the *Shi'erjing* 十二經 (Twelve classics) inscribed on stelae and placed in the Imperial Academy in Chang'an, where they remain to this day. In the Song dynasty, the *Mengzi* 孟子 was added to make the *Shisanjing* 十三經 (Thirteen classics), as set out in Table 27.

The *Shisanjing* are for the most part very short; altogether they are only slightly longer than the *Shiji* (about 1.5 percent the length of the Standard Histories). They contain 589,283 characters (of which 6,544 are different characters, including 1,500 personal names). Nevertheless, just to write 589,283 characters would have taken 9,821 strips (assuming 60 characters per strip). This would have made 300–500 bundles. Small wonder that the emphasis was on memorization: until the age of paper, manuscripts could circulate only with difficulty.

---

[14] David Shepherd Nivison, "The Classical Philosophical Writings," *CHAC*, chapter 11, 745–812; Donald Harper, "Warring States Natural Philosophy and Occult Thought," *CHAC*, chapter 12, 813–85.

The word *jing* 經 was added to the titles only in the Former Han when the Confucian classics were first made official. The original meaning of the word was the warp (vertical threads) on a loom. It was used in the extended sense of basic or long-lasting, and of books it meant those that have high and permanent authority, as in the *Laozi* 老子 (*Daodejing* 道德經) or the *Shanhaijing* 山海經 (Classic of mountains and seas). Later it was also used in a Buddhist context for "sutra." When it appears in titles it is normally translated "Classic of ...."

Table 27: The Shisanjing 十三經 (*Thirteen Classics*)

	Title	Zishu 字數	ICS
1.	*Yijing* 易經 (Classic of changes) or *Zhouyi* 周易 (Zhou changes)	24,000	27
2.	*Shangshu* 尚書 (Venerated documents) or *Shujing* 書經 (Classic of documents)	25,700	28
3.	*Shijing* 詩經 (Classic of poetry)	39,200	29
4.	*Zhouli* 周禮 (Rites of Zhou)	45,800	13
5.	*Yili* 儀禮 (Etiquette and rites)	57,800	24
6.	*Liji* 禮記 (Records of ritual)	99,000	2
7.	*Chunqiu Zuoshizhuan* 春秋左氏傳 (Spring and Autumn annals, Zuo's tradition)	178,000[15]	30
8.	*Gongyangzhuan* 公羊傳 (Gongyang's tradition)		31
9.	*Guliang zhuan* 穀梁傳 (Guliang's tradition)		32
10.	*Lunyu* 論語 (Analects)	12,000	33
11.	*Xiaojing* 孝經 (The classic of filial piety)	1,799	35
12.	*Erya* 爾雅 (*Erya*)	10,900	35
13.	*Mengzi* 孟子 (The Mencius)	34,000	34

Note: the figures after each Classic refer to the total characters it contains; *ICS* numbers (right-hand column) refer to the *ICS* concordances (9.10).

The term *Sishu* 四書 (Four books) dates from the Song, when Zhu Xi 朱熹 in 1190 edited in one book four texts chosen from the Confucian classics. Thereafter, every Chinese examination candidate, if not schoolchild, had to remember them by heart (the *Sishu* were *Daxue* 大學, *Zhongyong* 中庸, *Lunyu* 論語, and *Mengzi* 孟子).

[15] The *Chunqiujing* itself has 16,771 characters; the *Gongyang zhuan* and *Guliang zhuan* have 27,590 and 23,293, respectively.

The *Daxue* and *Zhongyong* are both short chapters of the *Liji*. The subject matter and brevity of the *Xiaojing* made it the ideal basic textbook for children, not only in China but also in Korea, Japan, and Vietnam.[16]

Many of the classics had alternative titles for the reasons explained at the beginning of this chapter. For example, the original title of the *Zhouli* 周禮 was *Zhouguan* 周官. It was later known as the *Zhouguan jing* 周官經. It gained its present title only in the Eastern Han. The *Shangshu* 尚書 was originally called the *Shu* 書 and also *Shujing* 書經, which is still often used.

After the "burning of the books" by the first emperor in 213 BC and the destruction of the copies kept in the Qin academy in 207, many attempts were made to restore the pre-Qin classics (only the Qin historical records and works on medicine, divination, agriculture, and forestry had been exempted). The two main rival schools in the Han were based on the Old and the New Text traditions (*guwen* 古文 and *jinwen* 今文). *Guwen* in this context referred to the discovery in the Han of classics written in Warring States seal script that differed from the versions of them written in the contemporary Han chancery script (in this context, *jinwen*); see 16.1 on the different scripts, and 18.1 on the discoveries of the *guwen* texts. The controversy was revived again in the Qing (18.1).

By the eighteenth century a huge body of commentary had accumulated amounting to more than 100 times the length of the *Shisanjing* (The *Siku quanshu zongmu* lists 3,900 works in the Classics branch [*jingbu* 經部, see 19.2.1] in more than 50,000 *juan*. The classics themselves contain only 416 *juan*). The earliest commentaries, for example, the *Zuozhuan* 左傳, had a tendency to become part of the classical canon. From the Later Han, the terms *zhu* 注 or *jian* 箋 were used for commentary (along with other expressions such as *gu* 詁 or *zhuan* 傳). From the Tang, commentaries on the classics, or on the Han commentaries, were termed *shu* 疏 (subcommentary). Large numbers of collected commentaries were also published (*jizhu* 集注, *jijie* 集解, *jishi* 集釋, *jiyi* 集義). In Han and pre-Han works, the texts and commentaries circulated separately. From the Later Han commentaries began to be incorporated as interlinear

---

[16] On Zhu Xi's choice, see Daniel K. Gardner, *Chu Hsi and the* Ta-hsüeh: *Neo-Confucian Reflection on the Confucian Canon*, HUP, 1986.

notes, and from the Song, subcommentaries too were incorporated (hence the new expression *zhushu* 注疏).[17]

19.3.1   Classification of the Classics

There are plenty of modern editions that give the original text (often with the scholarly annotations of the modern editors). There are also numerous translations into Modern Chinese. If you use one of these, make sure to choose one that gives the original text in full characters, not in their simplified form. Texts of all the classics are printed together with their concordances in the *ICS* series. Different editions are available for each of the Confucian classics. They have also been printed and edited together as the *Shisanjing* 十三經 many times and with many of the commentaries and subcommentaries added by scholars down the ages.[18]

The Classics branch (*jingbu* 經部) ranked first in the traditional Chinese bibliographic classification (9.3). By the eighteenth century, it comprised 10 subbranches as shown in Table 28:

Table 28: The Classics Branch in the Siku *Classification*

Yi 易 (The changes)
Shu 書 (The documents)
Shi 詩 (The songs)
Li 禮 (The rites)
Chunqiu 春秋 (Spring and Autumn annals)
Xiao 孝經 (Classic of filial piety)
Wujing zongyi 五經總義 (Commentaries on the *Wujing*)
Sishu 四書 (The four books)
Yue 樂 (The music)
Xiaoxue 小學 (The study of the characters)

[17] John B. Henderson, *Scripture, Canon, Commentary: A Comparison of Confucian and Western Exegesis*, PUP, 1991; Daniel K. Gardner, "Confucian Commentary and Chinese Intellectual History," *JAS* 57.2: 397–422 (1998).

[18] *Shisanjing zhushu* 十三經注疏, Ruan Yuan 阮元, ed., 1815; Kaiming (with index), 1934; Zhonghua, 2 vols., with corrections, 1957; 4th prnt., 1980; separate index: *Shisanjing zhushu suoyin* 十三經注疏索引, Zhonghua, 1983; 5th prnt., 1996. Indexes phrases by their first character.

19.3.2   Dictionaries of Individual Works

In addition to the specialized dictionaries for ancient Chinese scripts *guwenzi* (Chapters 15 to 17) and the dictionaries of Classical Chinese discussed in Chapter 2, note the sometimes useful dictionaries of a particular work of the classical period that are intended for readers who are not specialists and are therefore useful for beginners. Some examples follow:

Shijing baike cidian 詩經百科詞典 (Encyclopaedic dictionary of the *Shijing*), Chi Wenling 遲文泠, ed. in chief, 3 vols., Liaonong renmin, 1998. Vol. 1 contains the poems plus translation into modern Chinese and commentary; vol. 2 is an 800-page dictionary of the language of the poems; vol. 3 has illustrations and commentary on plants, birds, animals, insects, and objects; a gazetteer of places and people, and a 300-page annotated bibliography of ancient and modern research. Compare vol. 2 with the handy *Shijing cidian* 詩經詞典 (Dictionary of the *Shijing*), Xiang Xi 向熹, comp., Sichuan renmin, 1986; Introduction by Wang Li 王力; 2nd ed., rev. and enlarged, 1997. Arrangement is by *pinyin*. See also W. A. C. H. Dobson, *The Language of the Book of Songs*, University of Toronto Press, 1968.

Shikyô kenkyû bunken mokuroku 詩經研究文獻目錄 (Index to scholarship on the *Shijing*), Matsuyama Yoshihiro 村山吉廣 and Eguchi Masayoshi 江口尚純, eds., Kyûko, 1992. Covers scholarship in Chinese written 1900–90 and in Japanese 1868–1990.

Chunqiu Zuozhuan cidian 春秋左傳詞典 (21.1).

Xian-Qin yaoji cidian 先秦要籍辭典 (Dictionary of some important pre-Qin sources), Wang Shishun 王世舜, ed. in chief, Xueyuan, 1997. Dictionary in three parts of the language of the *Liezi* 列子, *Shangjunshu* 商君書, and *Chunqiu Gongyangzhuan* 春秋公羊傳. Altogether 8,207 terms are defined.

Lao-Zhuang cidian 老莊辭典 (Dictionary of *Laozi* and *Zhuangzi*), Dong Zhian 董治安, ed. in chief, Shandong jiaoyu, 1993, 1995.

III

HISTORICAL GENRES

20

Primary and Secondary Sources

In a country such as China with a long tradition of historical writing and compilation, the distinction between a primary and a secondary source is not an easy one to make. Various Qing archives survived the collapse of the empire (20.1), and discoveries of earlier archives were made in the twentieth century, but "original" documents up to the Qing are typically preserved in whole or in part in compiled sources (Box 6). Far fewer private records survive than official documents (20.5). The connections between history and literature remained close (20.2), as did the connections with politics, even after the development of history as a separate branch of scholarship (20.3). Not all Chinese historical writing was done by officials. There was also a strong tradition of private historical writing (20.4). Note that to the modern historian, creative literature itself can be a useful type of historical source (Chapters 30 and 34).

Part III deals with eleven of the fifteen categories listed in the History branch in the *Sibu* classification (Table 20, 9.3). The other four categories are covered in Part I: biographical writing (Chapter 3); time and the calendar (Chapters 5 and 6); geography (Chapter 4) and bibliography (Chapter 8). Part III also deals with two types of historical source classified by the *Siku* editors in the Philosophers' branch (Table 21, 9.3), namely military experts (Chapter 28) and legal writers (Chapter 27, also Chapters 19 and 33). Primary sources of the Republic are dealt with in Chapter 51.

Introduction

The earlier the period, the fewer the primary sources from the bottom of the pile listed in Box 5. In other words, more survives from each succeeding dynasty than from its predecessor: by the Qing, more survives than from all previous periods put together and the same is also true of the Republic. Some notable exceptions to this rule are the archaeological discoveries from earlier periods not matched later on, but these remain exceptions, albeit important ones.

After the Qin and even more so after the Han, traditional historical sources become more plentiful, but for the most part they survive only in excerpted or condensed form (Box 6).

Thus the earlier Standard Histories down to the Tang are based on materials that have long since been lost, and as a result they are vital sources for the period. The reverse holds true for the post-Song Standard Histories, because many of the sources upon which they were based are still extant. This is even more true by the Ming and the Qing, for which periods sources such as the Court Diaries or the Veritable Records, not to speak of over 6,000 local gazetteers and historical, documentary, genealogical, and literary sources of all kinds, have survived in enormous quantities (Chapters 49 and 50).

Box 5: The Sources for Chinese History

Standard Histories
National Histories
Veritable Records
Court Diaries, Records of Current Government, Daily Calendars
Collections of important documents, statutes, laws
Encyclopaedic compilations of primary materials
Edicts, memorials, and other documents of the central government
Local official records (land and household registers, routine reports),
Local gazetteers, occasional finds from local archives
Nonofficial historical writings and inscriptions
Creative literature
Newspapers (late Qing, Republic)
Individual, family and business records
Archaeological artifacts

20.1 Archives

Governments in China have kept archives ever since they began to use writing. The earliest court documents to have survived are the Shang oracle-bone inscriptions. During the Spring and Autumn period, interstate treaties were kept in special archives called *meng fu* 盟府 (state treaty archive). Books and other documents were stored in *cefu* 冊府[策府]. The practice continued in the Warring States period. We know that the different kingdoms kept archives containing maps of their territories, population registers, records of their ruling houses, treaties, and other documents. Some of these archives were destroyed (as recommended by Mencius) to prevent their falling into enemy hands. Many more were destroyed by order of the first Qin emperor. The Qin imperial library itself and the Qin academy (which preserved unique copies of the burned books) were razed to the ground by Xiang Yu 項羽 (233–202 BC) when he captured the capital, Xianyang 咸陽, in 207. The *tuji* 圖籍 (military maps and population registers) in the Qin chancellor's archive, however, were captured by Xiao He 蕭何 (d. 196 BC), who moved them to archives that he had especially constructed on the grounds of the Weiyang palace (未央宮). For security against fire and thieves, water from a nearby canal was diverted to flow under and around one of the buildings, hence its name, the Shique 石渠閣 (Stone Canal Pavilion). This eventually housed not only the main Han central archive, but also part of the Han imperial library. It was here that the *Five Classics* were edited (19.2). Two hundred years later, the archive was deliberately destroyed during the fighting at the end of the Former Han. The site of the Weiyang palace, including the Shique, was excavated in the 1980s and can be visited today.[1]

The widespread use of paper from the Tang and printing from the Song led to the proliferation of archives. From the Song the most common classification system for documents was to arrange them chronologically divided into eight categories named after the first eight characters of the *Qianziwen* 千字文: *tian* 天, *di* 地, *yuan* 元 (or *xuan* 玄), *huang* 黃, *yu* 宇, *zhou* 宙, *hong* 洪, *huang* 荒. The inventor of the system was the Northern Song official Zhou Zhan 周湛. This continued to be the most common system until the early Republic.

---

[1] The site of the Shiquge (and of the Tianluge 天祿閣 and Qilinge 麒麟閣, the other two archives cum libraries built by Xiao He) is in the protected grounds of the Han capital about 2.5 km (1.5 miles) northwest of modern Xi'an. All that remains of the three are parts of their *terre pisé* (*hangtu* 夯土) foundations. A primary school exists on the site of the Tianluge. One decorated, circular tile-end from the Shiquge survives. It bears the inscription *Shiqu qianqiu* 石渠千秋 (The Stone Canal Pavilion lasts for ever).

Box 6: Documents Preserved in Compilations

The earliest compilation of what purport to be selected historical documents is the *Shangshu* 尚書 (Venerated documents), parts of which were written in the Western Zhou. From that time to this day, large numbers of compilations were made of every conceivable subject: of edicts and memorials; of laws and regulations of bureaus and organs of central, provincial, and local governments; of poetry and verse; of genres and styles; of people and places. Many of the most important of these are referred to in the appropriate sections throughout the manual.

A convenient, annotated inventory has been compiled of compilations containing archival materials and excerpts, including modern publications (both books and journal articles) of archive documents and of materials extracted from them: *Zhongguo dang'an wenxian cidian* 中國檔案文獻辭典 (Dictionary of archival literature), Zhu Jinfu 朱金甫, ed. in chief, Zhongguo renshi, 1994. Contains annotations on 3,985 compilations of documents from the pre-Qin to 1949 (and 70 post-1949). Of the total, 1,800 were published before 1949, 1,900 from 1949 to 1991. There are about 600 entries from the pre-Qin to the end of the Ming, 1,700 from the Qing, and 1,600 from the Republican period. The notes give details of the contents, editions, and premodern compilers and the circumstances of compilation. Arrangement is chronological by period, and there is also a stroke-count index of titles.

To give an idea of the coverage in this useful work, and of the huge increase in availability of original documents from the Qing as opposed to earlier periods, there are entries on only 55 collections from the 320 years of the Song (including the main collected works of individual authors and statesmen containing documents such as edicts and memorials) as compared with 75 published collections of documents from the 13 years of the Yongzheng reign, including contemporary eighteenth-century collections, later Qing collections, and modern publications from the central and local archives.

By the Han an elaborate tradition of governmental compilation and history writing based on the archives had developed. As time went by this was continuously expanded. It is the compendia and books produced in this tradition that have survived in astonishing numbers from early imperial China, not usually the original archives. Considerable quantities of original documents have, however, survived from local archives (see Table 29).

Table 29: Archives and Other Collections of Original Documents

---

The Shang oracle-bone inscriptions (Chapter 15)

Excerpts from documents cast on bronze vessels, 11th–3rd century BC (17.1)

Documents on jade from the state treaty archive (*mengfu* 盟府) of the kingdom of Jin (17.2.1)

Documents and books, mainly on bamboo strips, mainly private, from the Warring States kingdom of Chu (19.1.1)

Warring States bamboo and wooden documents, non-Chu (19.1.2)

Silk documents and books from Mawangdui 馬王堆 tomb (19.1.3; Chap. 36)

Maps on silk, mainly from the kingdom of Chu (4.4.1)

Bone chits (*guqian* 骨簽) from the Former Han (44.3)

Qin documents from tombs (44.4.1)

Han documents from tombs (44.4.2)

Part of Donghai commandery archive (Later Han), Jiangsu (44.4.3)

Han documents and maps, many from local archives at the northwest border, mostly public, but some private (44.4.3)

Wu documents mainly from the commandery archive at Changsha (45.3)

Documents on bamboo strips from Wei, Jin, Nan-Bei Chao (45.3)

Manuscript documents from 4th–14th century from tombs and ruined cities near Turpan, Xinjiang (46.3)

Manuscripts, mainly religious, but also some private and secular ones, temple library, Dunhuang, 5th–11th century (46.3)

Xixia documents in the Tangut script, 11th–13th century (48.3)

Buddhist scriptures carved on stelae from all periods (17.2)

A small part of the Ming central archives (49.3)

About ten million documents (mainly late Qing) from the central archives and Shenyang archives (50.1–2)

Documents from Ba county archive, Sichuan, 18th–19th century (50.3)

Documents (19,281) from the Danshui subprefecture and Xinzhu county archives, Taiwan, 18th–19th century (50.3)

About 2.4 million documents in the Lhasa archives (50.3)

Documents from the 19th century Canton provincial archive (50.3)

Documents from various late Qing provincial archives (50.3)

The very efficiency with which the official historians produced excerpts, compilations, and historical works based on the original documents led to an attitude after the Song that attached more value to the printed book than to the original manuscript documents. Another important reason why more manuscripts have not survived is that until the twentieth century it was cheaper to copy books by hand than to print them, so printed books, not manuscripts, were collector's items. In addition, it was expensive to keep documents in good condition. Special buildings had to be constructed, and their contents regularly aired. From the Tang, government documents were divided between those that were for long storage (*changliu* 常留) and those that could be destroyed after three years. Archives and libraries were constantly burning down by accident, and at times of warfare, as during the previous centuries, they continued to be deliberately destroyed (the imperial collections went up in flames on at least a dozen occasions in the course of Chinese history). Quite apart from the depredations of fire and war, storage space had to be found for the new documents that the bureaucracy continuously produced. So, once the summaries or histories were written, even long-storage documents became superfluous and were often destroyed. For all these reasons, it is hardly surprising that in imperial China's 2,200 years of record keeping, with the outstanding exception of a part of the Qing central archives, only very few archives, either at the center or in the provinces, have survived. They did so by accident and were opened or discovered only in the twentieth century. So exceptional have these discoveries been that in many cases they have led to specialized fields of study, for example,

> *Jiaguxue* 甲骨學 (Chapter 15)
> *Jianduxue* 簡牘學 (18.1 and 44.3)
> *Dunhuangxue* 敦煌學 (46.3)
> *Huizhouxue* 徽州學 (50.7.2)
> *Ming Qing dang'anxue* 明清檔案學 (49.3 and 50.1–3)

The value to the historian of the new archival sources varies as much as the materials themselves. At their best, they open the possibility of constructing a view of Chinese history unmediated by the efforts of Confucian historians, official compilers, or modern theoreticians. They can often provide local detail on implementation and practice not found in the historical record.

For the earliest periods, the archaeological finds of books and archival sources are transforming ancient Chinese history because few textual sources were transmitted. At the end of the empire, the Qing central archives, because of their huge size, offer the chance of a closer look at decision making and historical events in general than is possible for any other period. They have not yet been fully utilized. Needless to say, all the different archives present two challenges in common: first, understanding the system that produced the documents and for what purposes; second, decipherment.

20.2   History and Literature

The relation between literature (*wen* 文) and history (*shi* 史) was a close one. In the earliest days the two were almost the same.[2] Even after the development of history as a separate genre, great value was placed on literary expression and a cultivated style. As Liu Zhiji 劉知幾 put it, "To be effective, history must borrow from literature" (*Shi zhi wei wu bi jie yu wen* 史之為務必借于文, Shitong, "Xushi" 叙事 [Narrating the facts]). Compare the comment of Zhang Xuecheng 章學誠 expressed one thousand years later, "there is no good historical writing without a polished style (*Liang shi mo bu gong wen* 良史莫不工文, *Wenshi tongyi*, "Shide" 史德 [The historian's virtue]). The title of Zhang's own work reflects the close connection between *wen* 文 and *shi* 史. The work of Liu and Zhang is the subject of the next section.

20.3   Historiography

History was written by officials for officials—Etienne Balazs

One of the unique features of Chinese historical studies is that a very large number of the primary sources were works produced in or preserved by a conscious tradition of historical writing and compilation, often by officials. The two most famous works of historical criticism (*shiping* 史評) were by Liu Zhiji and Zhang Xuecheng:

Liu Zhiji 劉知幾 (661–721), *Shitong* 史通 (Generalities on history), 710.[3]

---

[2] Note that *shi* 史 only came to mean "history" in the Tang; see 21.1, note 1. On the overlap between early historical and literary narrative, see David Derwei Wang, "Fictional History/Historical Fiction," in *Studies in Language and Literature* I (1985), 64–74; Anthony C. Yu, "History, Fiction and the Reading of Chinese Narrative," in *Chinese Literature: Essays, Articles, Reviews* X (1988), 1–19; Andrew H. Plaks, "Toward a Critical Theory of Chinese Narrative," in Plaks, *Chinese Narrative: Critical and Theoretical Essays*, PUP, 1977, 309–52; Sheldon Hsiao-peng Lu, *From Historicity to Fictionality: The Chinese Poetics of Narrative*, SUP, 1994; Henri Maspero (1883–1945), "Historical Romance in History," in *China in Antiquity*, Frank A. Kierman, Jr., tr., Univ. of Massachusetts Press, 1978, 357–65; and David Johnson, "Epic and History in Early China: The Matter of Wu Tzu-hsu," *JAS* 40.2: 255–71 (1981).

[3] Liu's work is discussed by Edwin G. Pulleyblank, "Chinese Historical Criticism: Liu Chih-chi and Ssu-ma Kuang," in *HCJ*, 135–66; and by David

Footnote continued on next page

Zhang Xuecheng 章學誠 (1738–1801), *Wenshi tongyi* 文史通義 (General meaning of historiography), 1832, Shanghai guji, 1993.[4]

Note also *Wenxin diaolong* 文心雕龍 (30.4).

Because of the long and sophisticated historiographical tradition in China, instead of working from official archives or private documents (as in post-Rankean European historiography), the modern student of Chinese history is liable to be handling historical works compiled by Chinese historians continuously over the last 3,000 years. In order to be able to assess the qualities and the biases of these works, clearly some knowledge of the aims and methods of the historians and compilers who produced them is essential.[5]

Furthermore, in order to be able to start looking for primary sources on the topic of his choice, the student of Chinese history will also need to know how traditional historians organized their materials and classified different types of sources. This is a subject discussed in 9.3.[6]

The characteristics of traditional Chinese historical writing from the Han onward were as follows: (1) Chinese historians were typically Confucian literati, but more significantly, they were also offi-

---

McMullen, "History," in *State and Scholarship in Tang China*, CUP, 1988, 159–205. See also Guy Gagnon, *Concordance Combinée du Shitong et du Shitong xiaofan*, 2 vols., Maisonneuve, 1977. For a translation, see Stuart H. Sargent, "Liu Chih-chi, *Understanding History*: The Narration of Events," in *Renditions* 15: 27–35 (1981).

[4] On Zhang's work, see David S. Nivison, *The Life and Thought of Chang Hsüeh-ch'eng (1738–1801)*, SUP, 1966.

[5] Denis Twitchett, "The T'ang Historian," in *The Historian, His Readers, and the Passage of Time, The Fu Ssu-nien Memorial Lectures, 1996*, Institute of History and Philology, Academia Sinica, 1997, 57–77.

[6] Denis Twitchett, *The Writing of Official History Under the T'ang*, CUP, 1992, analyzes the process of official historical writing and compilation at a formative period. *HCJ* contains 11 papers on different aspects of Chinese traditional historical writing and still forms the best interpretive introduction to the subject in a Western language. *Essays on the Sources for Chinese History*, Donald Daniel Leslie, Colin Mackerras, and Wang Gungwu, eds., ANU, 1973; Univ. of South Carolina Press, 1975, has some excellent chapters which are cited in the appropriate chapters of this manual. Han Yu-shan, *Elements of Chinese Historiography*, W. M. Hawley, 1955, contains a lot of basic information. Charles S. Gardner (1900–66), *Chinese Traditional Historiography*, HUP, 1938; rev. edition, 1961, provides a brief overview.

cials. Their primary focus was on politics, defined as the affairs of state, which meant the record of imperial government. In common with officials in other societies, the final record that they compiled was based on official documents and encoded into bureaucratic (Confucian) categories. These were usually far removed from actual transcripts of conversations or events. From this follow the second, third, and fourth characteristics of traditional historical writing: (2) its many close connections with government and the orthodox ideology, as seen in the theory of *zhengtong* 正統 (legitimate succession), which official historians traced in an effort to legitimize new dynasties,[7] and also as seen in the compilation of compendia of historical precedents as a guide to official action; (3) its strong moral didacticism, with the historian's duty being to bestow *baobian* 褒貶 (praise and blame), using Confucian moral tenets as the yardstick; (4) its ruthless excision of anything judged in conflict with the above two concerns (thus not only a focus on the elite and its ideology but also a particularly narrow focus on that elite). Additional characteristics of China's traditional historical writing are: (5) its early elevation to the status of an activity differentiated from other branches of writing, to which great importance was attached for two millennia of continuous historical production (6); its development into many well-defined genres and subgenres; (7) its scholarly attention to such ancillary disciplines as historical geography, the calendar, cataloging, ancient scripts, and artifacts; and (8) its development of a philosophy of history.[8]

---

[7] L. S. Yang (Yang Liansheng 楊聯陞), "Toward a Study of Dynastic Configurations in Chinese History," in his *Studies in Chinese Institutional History*, HUP, 1963, 1–17 (orig. in *HJAS* 17: 329–45 (1954)); Rao Zongyi 饒宗頤, *Zhongguo shixue shang zhi zhengtong lun* 中國史學上之正統論 (The theory of legitimate succession in Chinese historiography), HKCUP, 1977; rpnt., Shanghai yuandong, 1996. Anthology of 170 excerpts on the theme preceded by a lengthy introduction. See also Box 7, 22.3.3.

[8] For an overview of Chinese historiography arranged by themes (for example, "talking straight and making a point by indirection," or "the advantages and disadvantages of national, informal, and family histories"), see Qu Lindong 瞿林東, *Zhongguo gudai shixue piping zongheng* 中國古代史學批評縱橫 (An evaluation of historical criticism in ancient China), Zhonghua, 1994. For a bibliography of Chinese writing on historiography between 1900 and 1985, see *Zhongguo shixueshi yanjiu shuyao* 中國史學史研究述要, Yang Yixiang 楊翼驤 et al., eds., Tianjin jiaoyu, 1996.

20.4   Private Historical Writing

In addition to official historical writing, a large number of historical works were written privately (*sishi* 私史). Often they followed the main forms of the official histories, including annals, topically arranged histories, and so forth (Table 20, 9.3). Indeed, many of the most distinguished works in the official historical canon were written by or credited to private individuals, for example, the *Zuozhuan* 左傳 or the *Shiji* 史記. Private historical writing also took many other forms, including scholarly commentaries, studies of primary sources, and informal jottings (*biji* 筆記). There were special terms to distinguish privately written histories from official ones, e.g., *bieshi* 別史, *zashi* 雜史, and *yeshi* 野史.

The definition of *bieshi* (lit. "separate history") changed over time. In general it was applied to nonofficial works that were not in annals or annals-biography form (*jizhuanti* 紀傳體). Sometimes it was used interchangeably with *zashi*, but normally the distinction between the two was that *bieshi* were considered more serious works, lying somewhere between *zhengshi* 正史 on the one hand and *zashi* on the other.

Zashi (Chapter 24) were often in the form of *biji* (Chapter 31).

Baishi 稗史 was a term sometimes used in book catalogs in the sense of record of folkways, otherwise just as another word for nonofficial history.

The general expression *yeshi* 野史 was not used as a category in book catalogs. In ordinary language it meant nonofficial histories written about the dynasty of the day (private history, as opposed to official history). *Yeshi* flourished in the Nan-Bei Chao, in the Song, and in the Ming. From the Qing onward, they typically recount in a semifictional way life at the court.[9]

Waishi 外史 (informal history) was normally used in the titles of fictional narratives, the most famous example being the eighteenth-century satire *Rulin waishi* 儒林外史 (*The Scholars*).[10]

---

[9] For an annotated catalog of a selected 2,000 *yeshi*, see *Zhonghua yeshi cidian* 中華野史辭典 (Dictionary of Chinese *yeshi*), Lao Tie 老鐵, ed. in chief, Daxiang, 1998. There is a *pinyin* index.

[10] Harold Kahn, *Monarchy in the Emperor's Eyes*, Univ. of Massachusetts Press, 1971, 1978, contains a perceptive study of official and unofficial historiography of the later empire.

Shichao 史抄 (historical excerpts) began to be published in the Song. They consist of quotations usually culled from the Standard Histories.

Zaiji 載記 (contemporary records) are the histories of states not regarded as legitimate; see, for example, *Wu-Yue chunqiu* 吳越春秋 (Table 26, 19.2), *Shiliuguo chunqiu* 十六國春秋 (45.2), or *Manshu* 蠻書 (41.5.1, *Tang*).

Bieshi 別史, *zaiji* 載記, or *baishi* 白史 were also often classified as *zashi* 雜史.

20.5   Private Documents

Until recently, few archives and records (as distinct from historical and literary compositions) of private individuals and businesses were known to have survived, but more have been turning up in recent years. The largest finds from the early years of Chinese history are from archaeological excavations of tombs. In addition, a considerable number of private documents were found among the documents on bamboo strips and wooden tablets. They date from the Warring States to the Tang. More private documents have survived from the late Ming and Qing, notably the Huizhou documents and the Sichuan Zigong salt works archive (the latter is strictly speaking not a private archive, 50.7).

Note the minor part played by family and kin, or business and other association, records. Although such nonofficial records and private documents were voluminous, few if any have escaped the ravages of time and fire (with the outstanding exception of several thousand genealogies from the Ming and Qing), because Chinese historians were primarily concerned to establish and to preserve the official record. Moreover, China had no corporations independent from the state as there were in Europe, each with its own private archive.

Although the literary output of China's elite has survived in very large quantities and although this includes private diaries, letters (3.6), notebooks (Chapter 31), and other such writings, the only major nonliterary type of documents to have survived are chance finds such as those among (or on the back of) the Dunhuang and Turpan manuscripts (46.3) and in miscellaneous writings and on inscriptions. Contracts, land deeds, accounts, and litigation of all kinds did not come within the purview of the traditional Chinese historian, and the owners of such documents usually guarded them jealously from prying eyes. Moreover, in the 1930s and 1940s, the burning of land deeds and IOUs was used as a way of mobilizing the peasantry. For these reasons, only scattered examples of this type of private document have been utilized or published. How many are still extant is unknown, but a great many must have been destroyed in the upheavals during the nineteenth and twentieth centuries.

21

Annals

The earliest and one of the most important methods of arranging historical materials throughout Chinese history began as a bare catalog of court events arranged chronologically: e.g., "on such and such a year, month, day, King X of Y went on a hunt." Much of the writing on the oracle bones (Chapter 15), which predates the first extant historical work by many centuries, concerns divinations regarding single events and actions, but the relations between court scapulimancy and the origins of a continuous process of record keeping are obscure. The court chronicler in early China was an important official charged with astronomical as well as archival functions; he played a key part in the arrangement, timing, conduct, and recording of royal ancestor worship and sacrificial rites and other ceremonies. He may also have had remonstrance functions, in light of his duties of keeping records of models worthy of emulation and of portents heralding disaster.[1]

In later Chinese history, the bare catalog of events at court was greatly expanded, and elaborate composite chronicles of events throughout the empire began to appear, either written privately or under official sponsorship (although always with the major focus on the court and central government).

---

[1] The scribes (*shi* 史) at the courts of Shang and early Zhou drafted documents to present to the spirits of the ancestors; see Shirakawa, "Shaku shi 釋史 (interpreting *shi*)," Shirakawa, 1955 (17.1), vol. 1, 1–66. In the Western Zhou, *chunqiu* 春秋 meant "year" and was used as one of the generic terms for "historical annals." There are seven Warring States works with *chunqiu* in the title. Between the Han and the Sui, the word *shi* 史 was not applied to works of history, which were called *shu* 書 or *ji* 記. It was only during the Tang that *shi* came to be used in its modern sense.

21.1   Chunqiu 春秋

The earliest extant example of a historical work in the annals style is
the *Chunqiu* 春秋 (Spring and Autumn annals), the court chronicle
of the state of Lu. It is only 17,000 characters long, but covers 242
years (722–481 BC), which works out at 70 characters per year; so
events are tersely recorded. The longest entry is only 47 characters.
The average is 10. The shortest is just one character under the year
715 BC: "*Ming*" 螟 (pests).[2] Editorship was traditionally and implau-
sibly attributed to Confucius. The *Chunqiu*'s title was later used to
name the period 770–476 (see Introduction, "The Dynasties").

The longest of the three commentaries on the *Chunqiu* to have
survived, the *Zuozhuan* 左傳 (Zuo's tradition), is much fuller and
more lively than the *Chunqiu* itself. It also contains a far richer text
than the other two commentaries on the *Chunqiu*.[3] For this reason
it is the prime source on the years it covers (805–453 BC).[4]

---

[2] Because of the connection with Confucius, who also came from Lu, the
Lu chunqiu 魯春秋 became one of the classics and the only one of the early
chronicles to survive. The most convenient edition of the *Chunqiu* and its three
commentaries is included in *ICS Concordances* 30–32. See also the older *H-Y
Index*, Supplement 17. The best annotated edition is *Chunqiu Zuozhuan zhu*
春秋左傳注, Yang Bojun 楊伯峻 (1909–91), ed., Zhonghua, 1981; rev., 1990.
See also *Baihua Zuozhuan* 白話左傳, Yang Bojun and Xu Ti 徐提, trs., Yelu,
1993.

For a dictionary of the language, as well as a place name and personal-name
index, see *Chunqiu Zuozhuan cidian* 春秋左傳詞典 (Dictionary of the *Chunqiu
and Zuozhuan*), Yang Bojun 楊伯峻 and Xu Ti 徐提, eds., Zhonghua, 1985.

[3] See Göran Malmqvist, "Studies on the *Gongyang* and *Guuliang* commentaries," *BMFEA* 43: 67–222 (1971); 47: 19–69 (1975); 49: 33–215 (1977).

[4] The first recorded title (in *Hanshu* 30 "Yiwenzhi," Zhonghua, 1,713) is
Zuoshizhuan 左氏傳. It is usually referred to simply as the *Zuozhuan*. On the
nature of the narrative and speeches in the *Zuozhuan*, see David Schaberg,
"Remonstrance in Eastern Zhou Historiography," *EC* 22: 133–79 (1997) and
the same author's, "Foundations of Chinese Historiography: Literary Repre-
sentation in *Zuozhuan* and *Guoyu*," Ph.D., Harvard University, 1996; Yuri
Pines, "Intellectual Change in the *Chunqiu* Period: The Reliability of the
Speeches in the *Zuo Zhuan* as Sources of *Chunqiu* Intellectual History," *EC* 22:
77–132 (1997). Compare the rhetoric in the *Zhanguoce*, on which see J. I.
Crump, Jr., *Intrigues: Studies of the Chan-kuo Ts'e*, MUP, 1964, 47–75. Note
Bernhard Karlgren, "Glosses on the *Tso chuan*," *BMFEA* (1969–70); for other
references, see Anne Cheng in *ECHBG*, 67–76.

Footnote continued on next page

Another important early chronicle (mainly of the state of Wei) is the *Zhushu jinian* 竹書紀念 (Table 26, 19.2).

21.2   Annalistic Sources and Veritable Records

Annalistic writing was one of the main methods of arrangement adopted by Sima Qian in the *Shiji* (in the Basic Annals section), and it remained an integral part of the Standard Histories thereafter (see Chapter 22). Xun Yue 荀悅 (148–209), *Hanji* 漢紀 was based on the *Hanshu*. It is the first annals of a single dynasty. From the Tang, the official writing of annalistic history had become standardized into the following types:

1. *Qijuzhu* 起居注 (Court Diaries), sometimes translated as diaries of activity and repose, imperial diaries or audience records. They record the decisions and actions of the emperor in the conduct of government business, normally as this occurred in formal sessions of the imperial court each morning. In periods when the emperor conducted the government informally or secretly, the *qijuzhu* were weak or nonexistent; the *qijuzhu* began in the Later Han and continued on and off until 1911. They were in no sense intended for publication. Only a tiny fraction survive up to the Qing, from which time the greater part, both in Chinese and Manchu, are extant in 12,000 *ce*.[5]

2. *Shizhengji* 時政記 (Records of Current Government) were in some periods confidential records compiled under the authority of ministers.

3. *Rili* 日曆 (Daily Calendars) were a condensation, arranged day by day, of the first two.

Only fragments of the Court Diaries, the Records of Current Government, and the Daily Calendars have survived from before the Qing.

For a full translation, see James Legge in *The Chinese Classics*, vol. 4 in 2 parts, HKUP, 1960; Séraphin Couvreur, *Tch'ouen ts'iou et Tso tschouan*, 3 vols., Ho-kien fu, 1914; rpnt., Cathasia, 1951, and for excerpts, Burton Watson, *The "Tso chuan": Selections from China's Oldest Narrative History*, Col. UP, 1989;

[5] The Chinese versions of the following reigns have been printed: Kangxi, Yongzheng, Daoguang, Xianfeng, Tongzhi, and Guangxu (see 50.2.2 for details). The *Neige Manwen qijuzhu* 內閣滿文起居注 (Manchu versions of the *qijuzhu*) are available on microfilm at the Yishiguan in Beijing (50.2.1).

Given that the Court Diaries were composed almost immediately after the event, and were usually secret, they tend to be more reliable than other officially compiled sources, for example, the Veritable Records, or even more so, the Standard Histories, which were compiled only after the downfall of a dynasty by its successor and therefore often came several hundred years after the event.

All three of the above were used as the chief source for the annalistic Veritable Records (*Shilu* 實錄), of which there was one for each emperor, as well as for the less detailed National Histories (*Guoshi* 國史), which were compiled in some periods for each reign. The keeping of Veritable Records began in the Nan-Bei Chao and continued until 1911. Less than 1 percent of the Veritable Records survive from before the Ming (a small part of the year 805 from the Tang and portions of the years 983 and 996 from the Song).

The Veritable Records of the Ming and Qing covering the years 1368 to 1911 are extant in over 7,500 *juan*. They form an extremely important source for the Ming and for the Qing, but they were compiled only after the end of each reign, so they could come at some distance from what happened at the beginning of a long reign, and always with the risk of strong influence from participants (or their successors) in the events recorded. Despite these drawbacks, the Veritable Records contain an extraordinarily detailed record, unequaled for any comparable period in any country. Many edicts, memorials and other documents, as well as day-to-day events, are preserved in them.[6] They constitute the single most important source for the last 500 years of Chinese history.

---

[6] On the process of the compilation of the Tang Veritable Records (and of the other sources of the Standard Histories), see Denis Twitchett, *The Writing of Official History Under the T'ang*, CUP, 1992, 119–59; L. S. Yang (Yang Liansheng 楊聯陞), "The Organization of Chinese Official Historiography: Principles and Methods of the Standard Histories from the T'ang Through the Ming Dynasty," in *HCJ*, 44–59; rpnt. in Yang's *Excursions in Sinology*, HUP, 1969, 96–111; Wolfgang Franke examines the compilation of the Ming Veritable Records in *ISMH*, 29–33. For editions of the Ming and Qing *shilu*, see 49.1 and 50.4, respectively.

21.3   Zizhi tongjian 資治通鑑

Although many annals and chronicles (not to mention Veritable Records) were written during and after the Han, it was not until the Song that a major step forward took place in this genre with the compilation of the *Zizhi tongjian* 資治通鑑 (Comprehensive mirror for aid in government) by Sima Guang 司馬光 (1019–86). This magisterially carries the history of China from 403 BC in continuous chronicle form over the following 1,362 years down to AD 959. In the catholicity of sources consulted, many since lost, in its discussion of disputed points where there was a divergence of evidence (*kaoyi* 考異), as well as in its huge table of contents (running to 74 pages in the Zhonghua edition), it marked an important new level for the chronicle form as well as for general historical methodology. It had an enormous influence on later Chinese historical writing, either directly or through its many abbreviations, continuations, and adaptations.[7] It remains an extraordinarily useful first reference for a quick and reliable coverage of events at a particular time.

In writing it, Sima Guang was assisted by two outstanding young scholars: Fan Zuyu 范祖禹 (1041–98), who prepared the first draft on the Tang, and Liu Shu 劉恕 (1032–78), who prepared the draft on the Wei, Jin, and Nan-Bei Chao. Liu Ban 劉攽 (1023–89), helped on the Han period. Sima Guang's son did the proofreading.

The best modern edition of the *Tongjian* is the punctuated, movable-type one prepared by a team of 12 editors led by Wang Chongwu 王崇武, Nie Chongqi 聶崇岐, and Gu Jiegang 顧頡剛. The text used was a Qing reprint of the Yuan dynasty edition of *Zizhi tongjian* by Hu Sanxing 胡三省 (1230–1302). Hu incorporated the *kaoyi* 考異 into the text as notes (they had originally been printed separately). Many of the sources quoted in them have since been lost. Hu also provided his own comments and corrections separately (appendix to vol. 20 of the Zhonghua edition, 1–190). The Zhonghua editors have incorporated the textual notes of Zhang

---

[7] On the compilation of Sima Guang's great work, see Edwin G. Pulleyblank, "Chinese Historical Criticism: Liu Chih-chi and Ssu-ma Kuang," in *HCJ*, 135–66; also Zhang Xu 張須, *Tong jian xue* 通鑑學 (*Tongjian* studies), Shanghai: Kaiming shudian, 1948; rev., 1957; rev. and exp., Anhui renmin, 1981.

Juan 54 to 78 of the *Zizhi tongjian*, covering the last years of the Han and the Three Kingdoms, have been translated into English (45.2).

Yu 章鈺 (1865–1937), which were taken from the most important Song, Yuan, and Ming editions and added these and other Song commentaries in bracketed notes in the main text.[8]

Many adaptations and summaries of this massive 294-chapter chronicle were made. The most popular of all was a highly moralistic one entitled *Zizhi tongjian gangmu* 資治通鑑綱目. It was devised by Zhu Xi 朱熹 (1130–1200) and written by his pupils.[9] The *Siku* editors classified it under historiography (*shiping* 史評), nevertheless; because of Zhu Xi's name, it was the *Gangmu* that was read in the Ming and Qing rather than the much longer and more rigorous *Tongjian*.[10] But it is the *Tongjian* itself and the full continuations of it that are of interest to the modern historian.[11] The most important of these cover the Song and are listed in 47.1 and 47.2.

There is a dictionary to help find one's way around the *Tongjian*: *Zizhi tongjian da cidian* 資治通鑑大辭典 (Great dictionary of the *Zizhi tongjian*), Shi Ding 施丁 and Shen Zhihua 深志華, eds. in chief, Jilin renmin, 1994.

Also indexes:

Shiji tsûgan sakuin 資治通鑑索引, Saeki Tomi 佐伯富, ed., Tôyôshi kenkyûkai, 1961.

Shiji tsûgan Kochû chimei sakuin 資治通鑑胡注地名索引, Araki Toshikazu 荒木敏一 and Yoneda Kenjirô 米田賢次郎 comps., Jinbun, 1967. An index to the toponyms in Hu Sanxing's notes.

---

[8] Sima Guang 司馬光, *Zizhi tongjian* 資治通鑑, Guji, 1956; 9th rpnt., 20 vols., Zhonghua, 1995; convenient and readable, two-volume, reduced-size reprint (four pages to the page with original page numbers indicated), 1997.

[9] Conrad Schirokauer, "Chu Hsi's Sense of History," in *Ordering the World: Approaches to State and Society in Sung Dynasty China*, Robert P. Hymes and Conrad Schirokauer, eds., UCP, 1993, 193–220.

[10] J. A. M. de Moyriac de Mailla's *Histoire générale de la Chine, ou annales de cet empire; traduites du Tong-Kien Kang-Mou*, 13 vols., Paris: Pierres et Clousier, 1777–85; rpnt., Taibei, 1968, is an abridged translation from the Manchu version of Zhu Xi's *Zizhi tongjian gangmu* (Summary of the comprehensive mirror for aid in government) and its later continuations. It was the largest general history of China available in a Western language for two centuries (until the publication of the *CHC*), and it was used by many later textbook writers.

[11] For example, Bi Yuan 畢沅 (1730–97) et al., *Xu Zizhi tongjian* 續資治通鑑, 12 vols., Beijing, 1957; 6th rpnt., 1988. Replaces the other continuations compiled in the Qing and covers the years 960–1370.

22

Standard Histories

The first great innovation in historical writing and departure from the early annals style was the work of Sima Tan 司馬談 (d. 110 BC) and his son, Sima Qian 司馬遷 (ca. 145–86 BC), court astronomers and librarians during the second and at the beginning of the first century BC (44.2). They wrote what many centuries later was chosen as the first of the *zhengshi* 正史 (Standard Histories). Eventually there was one History for each legitimate dynasty. In all, 24 were written over 1,832 years. They comprise just under 40,000,000 characters, of which 13,966 are different ones.

Zhengshi 正史 recalls the term *zhengtong* 正統 (legitimate succession); see 20.3. Therefore, *zhengshi* 正史 is translated as "Standard Histories" throughout the manual (two other terms sometimes encountered are "Official Histories" or "Dynastic Histories;" the first is perhaps closer than the second to the sense of legitimate, canonical or orthodox implied by *zhengtong*).

22.1 Structure, Contents, and Titles

The *Shiji* 史記 is a history of China from the Yellow Emperor down to Han Wudi arranged in a manner which, with certain adaptations, was to set the form for a new way of writing history that came to be known as *jizhuanti* 紀傳體 (annals-biography) after its two most important parts. It was to be used in all of the Histories, which became known in the eighteenth century as the *Ershisishi* 二十四史 (The 24 histories).

The *Shiji* contains 130 chapters (*juan* 卷) divided into 12 *benji* 本紀 (basic annals, i.e., a chronological account of the ruler and his government), 10 *biao* 表 (tables), 8 *shu* 書 (monographs), 30 *shijia* 世家 (hereditary houses), and 70 *liezhuan* 列傳 (grouped biographies or memoirs). The two main innovations of Sima Qian were the monographs (*shu* 書) and the memoirs (*liezhuan* 列傳). The monographs (in later Standard Histories usually called *zhi* 志 and sometimes translated as "treatises") cover the historical evolution of selected institutions such as rituals, the calendar, astronomy, or political economy (with the emphasis on taxation and coinage). The memoirs are groups of biographies or profiles of both famous and (some) less famous people (as well as foreign peoples) of each age. These two sections of the *Shiji*, together with the older-style basic annals (*benji* 本紀), which carried on the court annals tradition, became the three major elements of the *jizhuan* genre of history writing. In the Chinese historiographical tradition, the basic annals were considered the core and the biographies as illustrations of the core. The monographs were entirely left out of eight of the earlier Standard Histories. They were considered to belong to a separate tradition of institutional history writing. The other sections of the *Shiji*, the *biao* and the *shijia* (which cover the history of the major pre-Han states) were incorporated only sporadically or not at all in the later Standard Histories.

The most important difference between all the Standard Histories from the *Hanshu* 漢書 onward and the *Shiji* was that they covered only one dynasty and made no attempt to cover the vast sweep of history (3,000 years) embraced by the *Shiji*. The generic term is *duandaishi* 斷代史; as distinct from works such as the *Shiji*, which are called *tongshi* 通史 (general histories). Only the monographs continued to cover periods of time extending earlier than the dynasty in question (see Table 31 for a list of the different topics covered in the monographs in each of the Standard Histories). Another important difference between the earlier and later Standard Histories is that before the Tang, eight of what later were recognized as Standard Histories were written by private individuals, and another seven were commissioned from one or two individuals. After the Tang reorganization of the Bureau of Historiography, the Standard Histories (with some notable exceptions) tended to become more and more standardized as they became the final step in a cumulative process of compilation by committees of official historians (which History fell into which category of authorial composition is indicated in Table 30).

Table 30: The Standard Histories

One asterisk indicates that the work was written by a private individual. Two asterisks indicate that the work was commissioned from one or two individuals. Standard Histories that were officially compiled (marked with three asterisks) had a nominal editor-in-chief (whose name is listed in the table), but they were the work of many hands at the Historiography Bureau. They based themselves on materials compiled by the bureau of the previous dynasty. The numbering from 1–24 in the left-hand column is the same order as that in the *Siku quanshu zongmu*. With the exception of the *Nanshi* and the *Beishi*, it follows the chronological order of the dynasties. The numbering in brackets in the left-hand column (1–26) shows the order according to the dates of compilation.

Title	Author, editor (dates)	Compiled (presented or printed)	Period covered
*1 (1). *Shiji* 史記 (Records of the historian)	Sima Tan 司馬談 (ca. 180–110 BC) and Sima Qian 司馬遷 (ca. 145–86 BC)	104–87 (91) BC	Yellow Emperor to 95 BC
**2 (2). [*Qian*] *Hanshu* [前] 漢書 (History of the Former Han)	Ban Gu 班固 (AD 32–92)	AD 58–76 (92)	206 BC – AD 24
*3 (4). *Hou Hanshu* 後漢書 (History of the Later Han)	Fan Ye 范曄 (398–445)	3rd–5th centuries (445)	25–220
*4 (3). *Sanguozhi* 三國志 (Record of the Three Kingdoms)	Chen Shou 陳壽 (233–97)	285–97 (297)	Wei 221–65; Shu 221–64; Wu 222–80
***5 (13). *Jinshu* 晉書 (History of the Jin)	Fang Xuanling 房玄齡 (578–648)	644 (646)	265–419
**6 (5). *Songshu* 宋書 (History of the Song)	Shen Yue 沈約 (441–513)	492–493	420–78
*7 (6). *Nan Qishu* 南齊書 (History of Southern Qi)	Xiao Zixian 蕭子顯 (489–537)	(537)	479–502
**8 (8). *Liangshu* 梁書 (History of the Liang)	Yao Cha 姚察 (533–606) and Yao Silian 姚思廉 (d. 637)	628–35 (636)	502–56

Table continues

Table 30—continued

Title	Author, editor (dates)	Compiled (presented or printed)	Period covered
**9 (9). *Chenshu* 陳書 (History of the Chen)	Yao Cha 姚察 (533–606) and Yao Silian 姚思廉 (d. 637)	622–29 (636)	557–89
**10 (7). *Weishu* 魏書 (History of the Wei)	Wei Shou 魏收 (506–72)	551–54 (554)	386–550
**11 (10). *Bei Qishu* 北齊書 (History of the Northern Qi)	Li Delin 李德林 (530–90) and Li Boyao 李百藥 (565–648)	627–36 (636)	550–77
***12 (11). *Zhoushu* 周書 (History of the Zhou)	Linghu Defen 令狐德棻 (583–661)	ca. 629 (636)	557–81
***13 (12). *Suishu* 隋書 (History of the Sui)	Wei Zheng 魏徵 (580–643)	629–36 (636)	581–617
*14 (14). *Nanshi* 南史 (History of the Southern Dynasties)	Li Yanshou 李延壽 (fl. 618–76)	630–50 (659)	420–589
*15 (15). *Beishi* 北史 (History of the Northern Dynasties)	Li Yanshou 李延壽 (fl. 618–76)	630–50 (659)	368–618
***16 (16). *Jiu Tangshu* 舊唐書 (Old History of the Tang)	Liu Xu 劉煦 (887–946)	940–945 (945)	618–906
**17 (18). *Xin Tangshu* 新唐書 (New History of the Tang)	Ouyang Xiu 歐陽修 (1007–72) and Song Qi 宋祁 (998–1061)	1043–60 (1060)	618–906
***18 (17). *Jiu Wudaishi* 舊五代史 (Old History of the Five Dynasties)	Xue Juzheng 薛居正 (912–81)	973–74 (974)	907–60
*19 (19). *Xin Wudaishi* 新五代史 (New History of the Five Dynasties). Original title: *Wudai shiji* 五代史記	Ouyang Xiu 歐陽修 (1007–72)	1044–60 (1072)	907–60

Table continues

Table 30—continued

Title	Author, editor (dates)	Compiled (presented or printed)	Period covered
***20 (22). *Songshi* 宋史 (History of the Song)	Tuotuo (Toghto 脱脱) (1313–55)	1343–45 (1345)	960–1279
***21 (20). *Liaoshi* 遼史 (History of the Liao)	Same as *Songshi*	1343–44 (1344)	916–1125
***22 (21). *Jinshi* 金史 (History of the Jin)	Same as *Songshi*	1343–44 (1344)	1115–1234
***23 (23). *Yuanshi* 元史 (History of the Yuan)	Song Lian 宋濂 (1310–81)	1369–70 (1370)	1206–1369
***24 (24). *Mingshi* 明史 (History of the Ming)	Zhang Tingyu 張廷玉 (1672–1755)	1678–1735 (1739)	1368–1644
*25 (25). *Xin Yuanshi* 新元史 (New History of the Yuan)	Ke Shaomin 柯劭忞 (1850–1933)	1890–1920 (1920)	1206–1367
***26 (26). *Qingshigao* 清史稿 (Draft History of the Qing)	Zhao Erxun 趙爾巽 (1844–1927)	1914–27 (1927)	1644–1911

The concept of a single Standard History for each successive dynasty emerged only very gradually. The term *zhengshi* 正史 itself was used for the first time in the Liang dynasty in AD 523 and incorporated into the *Suishu* "Jingjizhi" 隋書經籍志 (History of the Sui, monograph on bibliography) as a category distinct from *bashi* 霸史 (histories of dynasties not recognized as legitimate) or from *bieshi* 別史 (not officially recognized history). As such it was applied to important historical works mainly in the *jizhuan* (and to some extent in the *biannian*) genres, and it continued to be used in this sense until the Qing. The present usage to refer to the 24 (or 25, or 26) Standard Histories became the norm only after the compilation of the *Siku quanshu* 四庫全書 in the eighteenth century (9.5).

Until the Tang, the usual reference was to the *Sanshi* 三史 (The three histories): that is the *Shiji*, the *Hanshu*, and the *Hou Hanshu* 後漢書 (replacing the *Dongguan Hanji* 東觀漢記; 44.2, *History*). From the Tang, the *Sanguozhi* 三國志 was added to make the *Sishi* 四史 (The four histories), or *Qian sishi* 前四史 (The first four histories), terms still in use. During the Tang, six new Standard Histories of different kingdoms of the preceding period were compiled by the Bureau of Historiography. Together with three privately written works, this made a total of 13 works recognized as the main histories of China up to the end of the dynasty. They were referred to as the *Shisandai shi* 十三代史 (The Histories of thirteen dynasties). During the Northern Song, the *Nanshi* 南史 and *Beishi* 北史, which had been privately compiled in the Tang, were added to the Standard Histories, as were the newly compiled *Xin Tangshu* 新唐書 and *Xin Wudaishi* 新五代史. This brought the total to 17 (*Shiqishi* 十七史). Thereafter new ones were added as they were officially compiled. At the end of the fourteenth century, there were 21. The completion of the *Mingshi* 明史 in 1735 raised the number to 22, to which were added at the time of the compilation of the *Siku quanshu* the recovered editions of the *Jiu Tangshu* 舊唐書 and the *Jiu Wudaishi* 舊五代史. The number now stood at 24, and the phrase *Ershisishi* 二十四史 (The 24 Histories) was coined on the completion of the palace edition in 1775 (22.2). The number rose to 25 after the official addition of the *Xin Yuanshi* 新元史 in 1921. The *Qingshigao* 清史稿 has not been officially included in the Standard Histories, but it is in the old tradition and is therefore included in Table 30 to bring the total to 26.[1]

Although varying greatly in quality and length, the Standard Histories constitute a monumental *oeuvre*, the importance of which can hardly be exaggerated. They provide remarkably accurate coverage of over 2,000 years of Chinese history (from the official, Confucian standpoint, as seen from the imperial court), and they include historical profiles of the rulers, events, leading personalities, major institutions, and administrative boundaries of each dynasty, as well as a considerable quantity of detailed information on the peoples of East, Inner, and Southeast Asia. The value of the earlier Standard Histories is greatly enhanced by the fact that many of the sources upon which they were based have since been lost, and alternative

---

[1] *Zhongguo jizhuanti wenxian yanjiu* 中國紀傳體文獻研究 (Research on Chinese annals-biography literature), Wang Jingui 王錦貴, ed., Beijing daxue, 1996. *Chûgoku seishi kenkyû bunken mokuroku* 中國正史研究文獻目錄 (Bibliography of research on Chinese Standard Histories), Kokusho kankôkai 國書刊行會, ed., Kokusho kankôkai, 1977. Covers books and articles in Japanese, Chinese, and Korean from 1868 to 1977. Arranged by Standard History.

sources are lacking. For these reasons the scissors-and-paste methods of some of their editors should be regarded as an asset.

A huge literature exists on the Standard Histories, especially on the first four, which are regarded as monuments of literary and historical excellence. A fraction of this literature is listed in the appropriate chapters of Part V. The following section notes various reference tools for the Standard Histories as a whole.

22.2 Editions and Research Tools

Editions

The best modern edition is the Zhonghua shuju punctuated, collated edition (*dianjiao ben* 點校本), *Ershisishi* 二十四史, 241 vols., Zhonghua, 1962–75. It uses complex characters throughout. There are numerous later reprints, including a convenient and readable reduced-size one (four pages to the page with original page numbers indicated), 20 vols., 1997; there is also a two-volume personal-name index to this edition. For a reprint of the *Qingshigao* in a similar format, see 50.4.

Editorial work on the Zhonghua edition began in 1958 at the request of Mao Zedong 毛澤東 (1893–1976). Senior historians were assigned to the task and worked full-time on it. The best previous editions and commentaries were consulted, and modern punctuation and paragraphing added. It took more than twenty years to complete the editing. This was not just a scholarly task. On at least one occasion, a question of punctuation, and hence interpretation, had to be referred to the prime minister, Zhou Enlai 周恩來 (1898–1976), whose decision in this case was surely the right one.[2] Each History has a brief introduction, both on textual matters and on the authors. This edition is not only the standard one, it is also the most handy, in that the entire set is now available in database form, searches and printouts from which are available on request from the Harvard-Yenching Library (and also from the East Asian Library at

[2] Before committing suicide by hanging himself from the branch of a tree on Coal Hill, the Chongzhen 崇禎 emperor (Ming) is recorded as having written on the flap of his jacket the following phrase: 任賊分裂毋傷百姓一人 (*Mingshi* 明史, *juan* 24). The punctuator feared that if he put the period where it should go after the first four characters, he would be accused of helping to place the emperor in a flattering light.

the University of Washington) free of charge. Access can be made through the home pages of these libraries on the Internet.[3]

Before the *Zhonghua*, the most commonly used uniform edition of the Standard Histories was the *Bona* edition:

Bona ben ershisishi 百衲本二十四史, 820 *ce*, *Sibu conkan* series, Shangwu, 1930–37; 24 vols., 1958; Taibei rpnt., 1965. The title means "hundred patches edition," referring to the fact that each History was patched together from the best Song and Yuan editions.

Other commonly used editions of the Standard Histories are the many reprints of the 1739–75 *Wuying dianben* 武英殿本 (palace edition), *Ershisishi* 二十四史 (The 24 Histories), *dianben* for short:

Tongwen shuju 同文書局, *Ershisishi* 二十四史, 711 *ce*, Shanghai, 1894.

Wuzhou shuju 五洲書局, *Ershisishi* 二十四史, 524 *ce*, 1869–78.

Kaiming shudian 開明書店, *Ershiwushi* 二十五史, 9 vols., Shanghai, 1935, which added the *Xin Yuanshi*. References are listed at the end of each History to the most important of the very large number of corrections and supplements produced by traditional scholars. These were printed separately, see *Ershiwushi bubian*.

Annotations and comments on the Standard Histories from 245 works of traditional scholarship (mainly Qing) are brought together in two massive collections, the first published in the 1930s as a supplement to the Kaiming edition and the second appearing sixty years later. The two do not overlap:

Ershiwushi bubian 二十五史補編 *Ershiwushi bubian* (Supplements to the 25 Histories), 6 vols., Kaiming, 1936–37; rpnt., Zhonghua, 1955, 1986.

Ershisishi dingbian 二十四史訂編 (Supplements to the 24 Histories), Xu Shu 徐蜀, comp., 12 vols., Shumu wenxian, 1996.

---

[3] Ten people worked for three years in Taibei at the Shiyusuo, keying the Zhonghua edition of the Standard Histories plus the *Qingshigao* into a computer. The resultant *Nianwushi quanwen ziliaoku* 廿五史全文資料庫 (25 Histories full text database), 1988, is now available on CD-ROM from the Shiyusuo and on the Internet by subscription. See the Web Site of Academia Sinica Computing Center (Zhongyang yanjiuyuan Jisuan zhongxin 中央研究院計算中心 for details of the Academy's expanding database of ancient texts.

Studies

During the Qing, the practice of carefully reading and comparing the Standard Histories gave rise to three brilliant studies that combine textual acuity with a keen sense of the significance of the historical topics that they selected for attention:

Wang Mingsheng 王鳴盛 (1722–97), *Shiqishi shangque* 十七史商榷 (A critical study of the seventeen histories), 1787; 2 vols., punctuated edition, Shangwu, 1937, 1959. Covers the 17 Standard Histories listed in Table 30 up to the *Xin Wudaishi*, but not including the *Jiu Tangshu* and the *Jiu Wudaishi*. It is indexed in *CZS*.

Zhao Yi 趙翼 (1727–1814), *Nian'er shi zhaji* 廿二史劄記 (Critical notes on the 22 Histories), 1799. Covers the 24 Standard Histories up to and including the *Mingshi* and including the *Jiu Tangshi* and the *Jiu Wudaishi*, which the author preferred not to allude to in his title. Use *Nian'er shi zhaji jiaozheng* 廿二史劄記校證, Wang Shumin 王樹民, ed., 2 vols., Zhonghua, 1984, and note also the critical edition by Du Weiyun 杜維運, Huashi, 1977. Of the three Qing studies of the Standard Histories, this is the most interesting from the point of view of analytic insights, as opposed to philological expertise. Indexed in *CZS*.

Qian Daxin 錢大昕 (1728–1804), *Nian'er shi kaoyi* 廿二史考異 (Discrepancies in the 22 Histories), 1782; 2 vols., punctuated edition, Shangwu, 1937; rpnt., Shijie shuju, 1939; rpnt., Zhongguo shudian, 1987, 1990. Covers the Standard Histories up to and including the *Yuanshi* except for the *Jiu Tangshi* and the *Jiu Wudaishi*.

The best modern book-length study of the process of compilation that went into the production of a Standard History is Twitchett (1992). He takes the Tang dynasty as his period and the writing of the basic annals and monographs in the *Jiu Tangshu* as his examples (20.3).[4]

---

[4] Note also L. S. Yang, *Excursions*, 1969 (21.2), and the same scholar's "A Theory About the Titles of the Twenty-four Dynastic Histories," also in Yang (1969), 87–93 (orig. in *HJAS* 10: 41–47 (1947). See also Herbert Franke, "Some Remarks on the Interpretation of Chinese Dynastic Histories," *Oriens* 3: 113–22 (1950).

Indexes and Concordances

Indexes and concordances are indispensable in looking up names of people and places, official titles, book titles, and special terms. Apart from using the 25 Histories full text database (22.2) or the indexes to individual Standard Histories or to parts of them (see Part V), note that there are a number of dictionaries or indexes that cover certain parts of all the Standard Histories. An essential one is *Ershiwushi renming da cidian* 二十五史人名大辭典.[5] This biographical dictionary summarizes and indexes all the nearly 30,000 biographies in the 25 Standard Histories as well as biographical materials on the several thousand more people found in other sections of the Histories. It also includes dates of birth and death and identifies ancient toponyms. Earlier personal-name indexes (including those published by Zhonghua and Shanghai guji) do not carry the same amount of information.[6] The edition indexed is the Zhonghua (by page number, but *juan* references are also given, so it can be used with other editions). There are also indexes available to the monographs on bibliography, financial administration, law, official posts (22.3), and foreign peoples (Table 36, 41.4).

Translations

An indispensable aid for locating translations from the first 19 Standard Histories (excluding those for the first three) is Hans H. Frankel, *Catalogue of Translations from the Chinese Dynastic Histories for the Period 220–960*, UCP, 1957; rpnt., Greenwood, 1974. There have been a considerable number of translations since this catalog was compiled (see 41.4, note 17).

---

[5] *Ershiwushi renming da cidian* (Dictionary of personal names in the 25 Histories), Huang Huixian 黃惠賢, ed. in chief, 2 vols., Zhongzhou, 1997.

[6] *Ershisishi jizhuan renming suoyin* 二十四史紀傳人名索引 (Index to personal names in the annals and biographies sections of the 24 Histories), Zhang Chenshi 張忱石 and Wu Shuping 吳樹平, comps., Zhonghua, 1980, 1985; *Ershiwushi jizhuan renming suoyin* 二十五史紀傳人名索引 (Index to personal names in the annals and biographies sections of the 24 Histories), Shanghai guji, 1990. Zhonghua also issued separate full biographical indexes to all of the 24 Standard Histories. They were published in reduced format in two volumes in 1998. They have now been superseded by the *Ershiwushi renming da cidian*. In their day the Zhonghua indexes replaced the earlier *Ershiwushi renming suoyin* 二十五史人名索引 (Biographical index to the 25 Histories), Kaiming, 1935; Shanghai: Zhonghua, 1956.

Excerpts

Particular sections from all the Standard Histories are published together, for example, the monographs on a given subject or the *lunzan* 論贊 (comments placed at the end of each chapter intended to express the personal view of the compilers).[7]

So have the sections on non-Han peoples (41.1 and Table 36, 41.4).

Even references to the sea have even been excerpted: *Ershisishi de haiyang ziliao* 二十四史的海洋資料.[8]

22.3 Monographs in the Standard Histories

For a table of all the monographs in all the Histories, see Table 31.

22.3.1 Administrative Geography (see 4.5.2)

22.3.2 Astronomy and the Calendar

For a punctuated uniform edition of the *tianwen lülizhi* 天文律曆志 (monographs on astronomy and the calendar), see *Lidai tianwen lüli deng zhi huibian* 歷代天文律曆等志彙編 (5.1.2).

22.3.3 Official Posts and the Examination System

Sixteen of the Standard Histories contain *baiguanzhi* 百官志 or *zhiguanzhi* 職官志 (monographs on official posts); eight have *xuanjuzhi* 選舉志 (monographs on the examination system; see Table 31). Note the summaries of the organization of the bureaucracy discussed in 25.3.1 and in specific periods in Chapter 12 (pre-Qin) and in Part V. Reference works and translations are also listed in each chapter of Part V under *Research Tools, Official Titles and Office Holders*. Note also Table 34, *The Qing Examination System* (25.3).

---

[7] *Zhengshi lunzan* 正史論贊 (Authors' comments in the Standard Histories), Song Xi 宋晞, ed., 5 vols., Taibei, 1954–60.

[8] *Ershisishi de haiyang ziliao* (Materials in the 24 Histories on the oceans), Liu Pei 劉佩 et al., eds., Haiyang, 1995.

Table 31: Monographs in the Standard Histories

History:	1	2	3	4	5	6	7	8	9	10	11	12	13	14	15	16	17	18	19	20	21	22	23	24	25	26
Ritual	X	X	X		X	X	X			X			X			X	X	X		X	X	X	X	X	X	X
Music	X	X			X	X	X			X			X			X	X	X		X	X	X	X	X	X	X
Harmonics	X	X	X	X						X			X				X									
Calendar	X	X	X	X						X			X			X	X	X		X	X	X	X	X	X	X
Astronomy	X	X	X		X	X	X			X			X			X	X	X	X	X	X	X	X	X	X	X
Sacrifices	X	X	X																				X			
Rivers and canals	X	X																		X		X	X	X	X	X
Financial admin.	X	X			X					X			X			X	X	X		X	X	X	X	X	X	X
Law		X			X					X			X			X	X	X		X	X	X	X	X	X	X
Omens, anomalies		X	X		X	X	X									X	X	X		X		X	X	X	X	X
Admin. Geography	X	X			X	X	X			X			X			X	X	X	X	X	X	X	X	X	X	X
Bibliographies	X															X	X			X				X		X
Official posts				X		X	X	X		X			X			X	X	X		X	X	X	X	X	X	X
Carriages and dress				X		X		X								X	X			X		X	X	X	X	X
Auspicious influences					X	X				X																
Buddhists, Daoists										X													X			
Imperial guards																X				X	X	X				
Exam system																X	X			X		X	X	X	X	X
Army																	X			X	X	X	X	X	X	X
Border guards																				X						
Militia																				X						
Communications																										X
Foreign relations																										X

1. *Shiji* 史記
2. *Hanshu* 漢書
3. *Hou Hanshu* 後漢書
4. *Sanguozhi* 三國志
5. *Jinshu* 晉書
6. *Songshu* 宋書
7. *Nan Qishu* 南齊書
8. *Liangshu* 梁書
9. *Chenshu* 陳書
10. *Weishu* 魏書
11. *Bei Qishu* 北齊書
12. *Zhoushu* 周書
13. *Suishu* 隋書
14. *Nanshi* 南史
15. *Beishi* 北史
16. *Jiu Tangshu* 舊唐書
17. *Xin Tangshu* 新唐書
18. *Jiu Wudaishi* 舊五代史
19. *Xin Wudaishi* 新五代史
20. *Songshi* 宋史
21. *Liaoshi* 遼史
22. *Jinshi* 金史
23. *Yuanshi* 元史
24. *Mingshi* 明史
25. *Xin Yuanshi* 新元史
26. *Qingshigao* 清史稿

22.3.4 The Five-Phases

Fourteen of the Standard Histories contain monographs on Five-Phases (*wuxing* 五行) theory (Box 7).

Box 7: Five-Phases Theory (Wuxing 五行)

From the Warring States to the Nan-Bei Chao, it was considered vital to identify correctly the pattern of the rise and fall of dynasties and to identify each dynasty with the right one of the Five Phases (also translated as Five Agents or Five Elements). At first these were ordered in a mutually overcoming cycle (*xiangke* 相克) in which each element successively overcomes the next one: water, fire, metal, wood, earth (*shui* 水, *huo* 火, *jin* 金, *mu* 木, *tu* 土). Then in the Han dynasty, the order was changed to a "mutually producing" cycle (*xiangsheng* 相生) in which each element produces its successor: wood, fire, earth, metal, water (*mu* 木, *huo* 火, *tu* 土, *jin* 金, *shui* 水). The debate on the legitimacy of the Northern Wei dynasty turned on the choice of the right element; the same applied to the debate on the legitimacy of the Jin (Chapter 48). Thereafter, political legitimacy used other symbols, although the Five Phases continued to be a popular means of ranking people and things (for example, in the choice of the characters for siblings; see 3.2).[9]

22.3.5 Financial Administration

Fifteen of the Standard Histories contain *shihuozhi* 食貨志 (monographs on financial administration). They constitute the single most important source on the economic institutions (and economy in general) of each period, and as a result they have been relatively intensively studied, translated, and indexed. The texts of the *shihuozhi*

---

[9] John Lee, "From Five Elements to Five Agents: Wu-hsing in Chinese History," in *Sages and Filial Sons*, Julia Ching and R. W. L. Guisso, eds., HKCUP, 1991, 163–78; John B. Henderson, *The Development and Decline of Chinese Cosmology*, Col. UP, 1984; A. C. Graham, "Yin-Yang and the Nature of Correlative Thinking," Institute of East Asian Philosophy, University of Singapore, Occasional Paper, 1986; also Graham, "The Cosmologists," in *Disputers of the Tao* (19.2), 315–70; *Zhongguo gudai siwei moshi yu yinyang wuxing shuo tanyuan* 中國古代思維模式與陰陽五行說探源 (The origins of Chinese correlative thinking and *yin-yang* Five-Phases theories), Ai Lan 艾蘭 et al., eds., Jiangsu guji, 1998.

have been published together several times.[10] The major studies and translations of individual *shihuozhi* are listed in Part V. Note that several conveniently print the original text along with the notes and supplementary matter.

The standard combined index to the *shihuozhi* is in *H-Y Index* 32. For a dictionary of special terms in them, see Hoshi Ayao 星斌夫, *Chûgoku shakai keizaishi goi* 中國社會經濟史語彙.[11] The brief explanations are based on the major Japanese studies and translations of the *shihuozhi* as well as on 18 other important contributions of Japanese scholars to Chinese socioeconomic history.

22.3.6 Rivers and Canals

Seven of the Histories contain *hequzhi* 河渠志 (monographs on rivers and canals): the *Shiji*, the *Hanshu, Songshi, Jinshi, Yuanshi, Mingshi*, and *Qingshigao*.[12]

22.3.7 Law

The 15 *xingfazhi* 刑法志 (monographs on law) have been annotated and published together several times, recently also with translations into Modern Chinese.[13] Studies and translations of individual monographs on law are listed in the appropriate chapters of Part V. See Chapter 27 for more detailed sources on law than can be found in the monographs.

---

[10] For a convenient punctuated and annotated edition, see *Lidai shihuozhi zhushi* 歷代食貨志注釋, Wang Leiming 王雷鳴, tr. and ed., 5 vols., Nongye, 1985–93. See also *Zhongguo lidai shihuozhi zhengbian* 中國歷代食貨志正編, Chengwen, 1971.

[11] *Chûgoku shakai keizaishi goi* (Glossary of Chinese socioeconomic history), Tôyô bunko, 1966; rev. edition, Kôbundô, 1976; continuation (*zokuhen* 曾編), Kôbundô, 1975; third collection (*sanhen* 三編), Kôbundô, 1988. The *zokuhen* and *sanhen* are drawn from more than 50 Japanese studies published between 1965 and 1983.

[12] *Ershiwushi hequzhi zhushi* 二十五史河渠志注釋 (Monographs on rivers and canals in the 25 Histories, with annotations), Zhou Kuiyi 周魁一 et al., eds., Zhongguo shudian, 1990.

[13] See, for example, *Xingfazhi zhushi* 刑法志注釋 (Monographs on law, with annotations), Jilin renmin, 1994.

22.3.8 *Carriages and Dress*

Eleven of the Histories contain monographs on carriages and dress (*yufu zhi* 輿服志). These set out the regulations and customs regarding official attire and vehicles. For a detailed, illustrated commentary on the monographs in the two Tang histories, see 46.1.

23

Topically Arranged Histories

Until the Song, the two main forms of historical writing were *Bian-nianti* 編年體 (annals) and *jizhuanti* 紀傳體 (annals-biographies, see Chapters 21 and 22). The disadvantage of these two forms was that in order to find out about one person or one event, the reader had either to search through many different entries in the rigid chronological frame of the annals or to bring together information often scattered in the different parts of the composite Standard Histories. These difficulties were partially resolved when a Song scholar named Yuan Shu 袁樞 (1131–1205) rearranged all the chronological entries in Sima Guang's *Zizhi tongjian* into 239 topical entries and thus broke out of the strict annals framework.

Yuan Shu called his rearrangement *Tongjian jishi benmo* 通鑑紀事本末.[1] He is generally credited with having developed the third major type of Chinese historical writing, *jishi benmoti* 紀事本末體 (from beginning to ending of events or topically arranged style). There were many imitators, especially in the Qing, when *fanglüe* 方略 (official histories of campaigns), became particularly popular (28.2), but for the most part, writers in this style only rearranged existing works (as had Yuan); they did not add new materials or interpretations. The single outstanding exception was Gu Yingtai 谷應泰 (d. 1689), who wrote his *Mingshi jishi benmo* 明史紀事本末 before the *Mingshi* had been compiled and thus made an important contribution to Ming history (49.1).

The Zhonghua Shuju published many of the main *jishi benmo* titles in punctuated, collated editions in the 1970s and 1980s and reissued them in 1997 in a reduced-type edition, *Lidai jishi benmoti* 歷代記事本末體, 2 vols.:

---

[1] *Tongjian jishi benmo* (The comprehensive mirror for aid in government, topically arranged), 1173; punctuated edition, 12 vols., Zhonghua, 1964, 1986.

Tongjian jishi benmo 通鑑紀事本末 (see previous page)

Zuozhuan jishi benmo 左傳紀事本末 (The *Zuozhuan* topically arranged), Gao Shiqi 高士奇 (1645–1703), ed., 1690

Songshi jishi benmo 宋史紀事本末 (The *Songshi* topically arranged), Chen Bangchan 陳邦瞻 (1557–1602), 1605

Liaoshi jishi benmo 遼史紀事本末 (The *Liaoshi* topically arranged), Chen Bangchan 陳邦瞻, 1606

Jinshi jishi benmo 金史紀事本末 (The *Jinshi* topically arranged), Chen Bangchan 陳邦瞻, 1606

Yuanshi jishi benmo 元史紀事本末 (The *Yuanshi* topically arranged), Chen Bangchan 陳邦瞻, 1606

Mingshi jishi benmo 明史紀事本末 (49.1)

Sanfan jishi benmo 三蕃紀事本末 (The three feudatories topically arranged), Yang Lurong 楊陸榮 (dates not known), 1717

24

Miscellaneous Histories

Zashi 雜史 (miscellaneous histories) is a residual bibliographical category, not a style of historical writing.

The definition of *zashi* changed after its introduction in the Tang, but in general, it included all those historical works not fitting into the official categories and considered less serious than the *bieshi* 別史 (20.4). Many were also sometimes classified under *biji* 筆記 (miscellaneous notes, Chapter 31) or in the *zajia* 雜家 (miscellaneous writers), one of the subbranches of the Philosophers' branch. *Zashi* usually do not cover a whole dynasty, but rather a single event or a reign period or a particular institution. Records of Chinese embassies to neighboring states were often classified as *zashi*. On the whole *zashi* are an extremely valuable type of source. Their wide scope is illustrated in the range of subjects covered in the examples given below.

A number of Han and pre-Qin works were cataloged as *zashi* (for details, see Table 26, 19.2):

> *Yi Zhoushu* 逸周書
> *Guoyu* 國語
> *Zhanguoce* 戰國策
> *Yuejueshu* 越絕書
> *Wu-Yue chunqiu* 吳越春秋
> *Chu-Han chunqiu* 楚漢春秋

Han to Tang

Gushi kao 古史考 (Investigation of ancient history), Qiao Zhou 譙周 (201–70). Exists today only in a recovered edition contained in various *congshu*.

Diwang shiji 帝王世紀 (Record of the lives of the emperors and kings), Huangfu Mi 皇甫謐 (215–82), Zhonghua, 1964. Ancient history using sources long since lost.

Fengsu tongyi 風俗通義 (5.5.2)

Shishuo xinyu 世説新語 (45.2).

Tang

Zhenguan zhengyao 貞觀政要 (Essentials of government of the Zhenguan era), Wu Jing 吳兢 (670–749), Shanghai guji, 1978, 1999. Contains documents of senior officials of the Zhenguan period (627–49).

An Lushan shiji 安祿山事蹟 (46.2).

Dongguan zouji 東觀奏記 (Record of events from the Eastern Library), 891, Pei Tingyu 裴庭裕. Reminiscences of the Xuanzong 宣宗 court. The writer was a Hanlin scholar and one of those who attempted to compile the *Xuanzong shilu*. An important source for the later Tang.

Tang to Yuan

Nan Tang jinshi 南唐近事 (Recent events in Nan Tang), Zheng Wenbao 鄭文寶 (953–1013). Recounts the events of 937–75.

Zhushi 麈史 (Chats on historical matters), Wang Dechen 王得臣 (1036–1116). Has details on the institutions of Northern Song (indexed in CZZS).

Qingxi kougui 青溪寇軌 (Traces of the bandits of Qingxi), Fang Shao 方勺 (1066–?). An independent account of the Fang La 方臘 rebellion, differing from that found in the *Songshi* 宋史 (Qingxi was the place in Zhejiang in which the rebellion occurred).

Beishou wenjian lu 北狩聞見錄 (Record of experiences in northern captivity), Cao Xun 曹勛 (1098–1174). Records the capture of Emperor Huizong 徽宗 by the Jin after the fall of Kaifeng in 1127.

Chaoye leiyao 朝野類要 (Important affairs at court and in country), Zhao Sheng 趙陞, 1234. Defines terms from many areas of official life. See Stephen Yu, *Chaoye leiyao yinde* 朝野類要引得 (Index to the important affairs at court and in the country), CMC, 1974 (also in CZS).

Xiangyang shoucheng lu 襄陽守城錄 (Record of the defense of Xiangyang), Zhao Wannian 趙萬年, 1207. Diary of the siege by the Jurchen of Xiangyang from 1206/11 to 1207/2; see Herbert Franke, "Siege and Defense of Towns in Medieval China," in *Chinese Ways in Warfare*, Frank A. Kierman and John K. Fairbank, eds., HUP, 1973.

Ru'nan yishi 汝南遺事 (48.4).

Menggu bishi 蒙古秘史 (48.5.1).

Gengshen waishi 庚申外史 (48.5.2).

Zhanchi 站赤 (The postal relay system); recovered from the *Yongle dadian*, *juan* 19,416–19,426. Originally in *Jingshi dadian* 經世大典 and *Yuan dianzhang* 元典章. It was used as the basis for the coverage of this subject in the *Yuanshi*, *juan* 101. Describes the workings of the Yuan horse-relay system, 1229–30. *Zhanchi* is a loanword from the Mongolian *jamci* (4.1).

Changchun zhenren xiyouji 長春真人西遊記 (41.5.1, *Song*).

Ming and Qing

Beizheng lu 北征錄 (Record of the northern offensive), Jin Youzi 金幼孜 (1368–1431). Record in diary form of the Yongle emperor's first Mongolian campaign in 1410 and and second one in 1414 (*Beizheng houlu* 北征後錄), Wenhai, *Zhongguo fangzhi congshu* 中國方志叢書 edition.

Xiyuan wenjianlu 西園聞見錄 (Heard and seen by Xiyuan), Zhang Xuan 張萱 (1558–1641), 1632; H-Y Institute, Beiping, 1940. Notes on the words and deeds of hundreds of Ming personalities. Includes gossip and observations of institutions at the end of the sixteenth century. Xiyuan was Zhang's *hao* (*DMB*, 78–79).

Chunming mengyu lu 春明夢餘錄 (see 49.2, *Biji*).

Fu'an dongyiji 赴安東夷記 (Record of pacification of the eastern barbarians), 1520, Ma Wensheng 馬文昇 (1426–1510). One of the earliest descriptions of Liaodong 遼東 (1478).

Jiajing ping Wo zhiyi jilüe 嘉靖平倭祗役紀略 (Record of pacification of the pirates in the Jiajing era), Zhao Wenhua 趙文華 (?–1557), 1555; Yangzhou guji, 1959. See Kwan-wai So, *Japanese Piracy in Ming China During the Sixteenth Century*, Michigan State University Press, 1975.

Jiajing dongnan ping Wo tonglu 嘉靖東南平倭通錄 (Complete record of pacification of the southeast pirates in the Jiajing era), Xu Xueju 徐學聚 (*jinshi* 1583). Excerpts from the author's *Guochao dianhui* 國朝典彙 (Collection on the statutes of the dynasty) section on Japan, 1552–54; *Zhongguo lishi yanjiu ziliao congshu* 中國歷史研究資料叢書 edition, 1947.

Wanli wugonglu 萬曆武功錄 (Record of military affairs of the Wanli era), Qu Jiusi 瞿九思 (*jinshi* 1573). Biographies of the Wanli emperor's military opponents.

Guochu qunxiong shilüe 國初群雄事略 (Brief lives of the heroes at the beginning of the dynasty), Qian Qianyi 錢謙益 (1582–1664). Compilation of records on the rise of military leaders in the late Yuan and early Ming.

Qizhen liangchao bofulu 啓禎兩朝剝膚錄 (Record of the calamities in the Tianqi 天啓 and Chongzhen 崇禎 reigns), Wu Yingji 吳應箕 (1594-1645). Chronicles the political struggles of 1624-28.

Liehuang xiaoshi 烈皇小識 (Brief notes on the Chongzhen 崇禎 emperor), Wen Bing 文秉 (1609-69); *Zhongguo lishi yanjiu ziliao congshu* 中國歷史研究資料叢書 edition, 1947.

Mingji beilüe 明季北略 (Brief account of the late Ming in the north) and *Mingji nanlüe* 明季南略 (Brief account of the late Ming in the south), Ji Liuqi 計六奇 (1622-87?), Zhonghua, 1984. A history of the end of the Ming in *jishi benmo* style; the former covers the years 1595-1644; the latter, 1644-65.

Dongnan jishi 東南紀事 (Record of events in the southeast) and *Xi'nan jishi* 西南紀事 (Record of events in the southwest), Shao Tingcai 邵廷采 (1648-1711). Deals with the Southern Ming regime; *Zhongguo lishi yanjiu ziliao congshu* 中國歷史研究資料叢書 edition, 1946.

Suikou jilüe 綏寇紀略 (Record of insurrections), Wu Weiye 吳偉業 (1609-71). Recounts the insurrections at the end of the Ming.

Menggu yuanliu 蒙古源流 (Origins and development of the Mongols), comp. in the early eighteenth century. The original Mongolian title is *Erdeni-yin tobci*; completed in 1662 by Sayang Secen (b. 1604), Nei Menggu renmin, 1980.

25

Government Institutions

Very large quantities of official documents of all sorts were stored, collected, and compiled under each dynasty. Some of the resulting printed collections are still extant. Broadest in coverage are the *Huiyao* 會要 (collection of important documents). They flourished under the Song. In the Ming and Qing their place was taken by the *Huidian* 會典 (collected statutes; 49.2 and 50.5.2). The terms *huiyao* and *huidian* were derived from the same four-character phrase, *huiyao dianzhang* 會要典章 (digest of regulations of government offices). They trace the history of institutions of a given dynasty using excerpts from contemporary documents (25.1) and were intended as a guide to bureaucratic practice.

Other collections trace the history of governmental institutions over many dynasties. They served as repositories of precedents. The ten most famous are known as the *Shitong* 十通 (The ten encyclopaedic histories of institutions, 25.2). The *Huiyao*, *Huidian*, and the *Shitong* are listed as *Zhengshu* 政書 (works relating to government) in the History branch of the Sibu classification along with the codes, statutes, and other works of law (Chapter 27).

25.1 Huiyao 會要

The first *Huiyao* was compiled during the Tang and formed the basis of the *Tang huiyao* 唐會要 (Important documents of the Tang), Wang Pu 王溥 (922–82). Wang also compiled the *Wudai huiyao* 五代會要 (Important documents of the Five Dynasties). These two and the *Song huiyao* 宋會要 (Important documents of the Song) were all compiled during the period to which they refer (or shortly thereafter) and, as a consequence, only they contain large amounts of primary materials not found in other sources. Of the other nine *huiyao*, two were compiled in the Song and the remainder in the Qing (see Table 32).

Table 32: Huiyao 會要

Chunqiu huiyao 春秋會要, Yao Yanqu 姚彥渠 (Qing), punctuated edition, Zhonghua, 1955. Records gathered from existing sources under 98 subheadings.

Qiguo kao 七國考, Dong Yue 董說 (1620–86), punctuated edition, Zhonghua, 1956. Covers 14 subjects, including official posts, cities, palaces, music, clothing, weapons, laws, disasters of the Seven Kingdoms of the Warring States period.

Qin huiyao dingbu 秦會要訂補, Sun Kai 孫楷 (1871–1907), 1904; corrections by Xu Fu 徐復, punctuated edition, Zhonghua, 1959. Contains 336 entries covering the standard categories.

Xi Han huiyao 西漢會要, Xu Tianlin 徐天麟 (twelfth–thirteenth centuries), 1211; punctuated edition, Zhonghua, 1955; Shanghai guji, 1977. The author used the *Tang huiyao* as his model. Sources are indicated.

Dong Han huiyao 東漢會要, Xu Tianlin, 1226; punctuated edition, Zhonghua, 1955; Shanghai guji, punctuated edition, 1978.

Sanguo huiyao 三國會要, Yang Chen 楊晨 (late Qing), 1899; punctuated edition, Zhonghua, 1956. Since the Standard Histories of the Three Kingdoms have no monographs, this work is useful in rearranging under subject categories information scattered in many sources.

Gaoben Jin huiyao 稿本晉會要 (Draft of the *Jin huiyao*), Wang Zhaoyong 汪兆鏞 (1861–1939), punctuated edition, Shumu wenxuan, 1988. Similar categories to previous *huiyao* with the addition of inscriptions, the classics, and main events.

Nanchao Song huiyao 南朝宋會要, *Nanchao Qi huiyao* 南朝齊會要, *Nanchao Liang huiyao* 南朝梁會要, *Nanchao Chen huiyao* 南朝陳會要, Zhu Mingpan 朱銘盤 (1852–93), punctuated edition, Shanghai guji, 1984–86. These are useful sources on the institutions of these Southern Dynasties.

Tang huiyao 唐會要, 3 vols., Zhonghua, 1956; 3rd rpnt., 1998; name index: *Tang huiyao renming suoyin* 唐會要人名索引, Zhang Chenshi 張忱石, ed. in chief, Zhonghua, 1991, 1999.

Wudai huiyao 五代會要, Shanghai guji, 1978.

Song huiyao jigao 宋會要輯稿 (see 25.1).

Ming huiyao 明會要, Long Wenbin 龍文彬 (1821– ?), 1887; typeset, punctuated edition, Zhonghua, 1956; Shijie shuju, 2 vols., 1963.

Of the three most important *huiyao*, the third and by far the largest is the *Song huiyao jigao* 宋會要輯稿 (so called because it was recovered from the *Yongle dadian* 永樂大典 [Yongle encyclopaedia] in the early nineteenth century by Xu Song 徐松, 1781–1848). It was printed for the first time only in 1936.[1] The materials in the *Song huiyao* were taken from sources no longer extant such as the *Rili* 日曆 (Daily calendar). It is the largest collection of Song documents extant and the most important of the *Huiyao*. It has been intensively studied and indexed by historians of the Song (47.2). The special compiling office for *huiyao* in the Song, the Huiyaosuo 會要所 was not established in later dynasties.

The *Huiyao* for pre-Tang periods and for the Ming were mainly compiled during the Qing. Although the sources on which they were based are often still extant today, they have a certain use in that the material they contain is organized systematically to cover the institutions of a particular dynasty—political, economic, military, and cultural. It is, therefore, often easier to find things in them than in the sources from which they were taken.

All the *Huiyao* were published in a uniform, punctuated edition in 1959. It was reissued in 1998.

For compendia containing similar information on governmental institutions, laws and regulations, see:

Administrative Law (27.5)
Encyclopaedic Histories of Institutions (25.2)
Monographs in the Standard Histories (22.3)

25.2   Shitong 十通

The *Shitong* (The ten encyclopaedic histories of institutions) cover much the same subjects as the monographs in the Standard Histories (22.3). They were also written for the same purposes, that is, as guides and reference works to the administration and institutions of past periods for scholars and officials. In scope, however, they are often wider than the monographs; furthermore, the authors of the three most famous of them covered much longer periods and left

---

[1] *Song huiyao jigao* 宋會要輯稿, photolithographic reproduction, 200 *ce*, Beiping tushuguan, 1936; reduced-size, facsimile reproduction, 8 vols., Zhonghua, 1957, 1987; Shanghai guji, 1986; Xinwenfeng, 1976.

the mark of their own individual views. The work that was to set the model was Du You 杜佑 (735–812), *Tongdian* 通典. It lays greater emphasis on administration (Du had been chancellor three times) than on ritual as compared to the monographs in the Standard Histories up to that time. Du based it on *Zhengdian* 政典 (Governmental institutes), a work by Liu Zhi 劉秩, the son of the historian Liu Zhiji 劉知幾. The *Tongdian* is divided into nine main sections covering (1) food and money, (2) the examination system, (3) official titles, (4) rites, (5) music, (6) the army, (7) punishments, (8) provincial administration, and (9) border defense. The value of the *Tongdian* lies not only in its assembling of many disparate sources under clear subject headings, but also in the fact that many of the sources used have since been lost.[2]

The two other most famous such works are Zheng Qiao 鄭樵 (1104–62), *Tongzhi* 通志,[3] and Ma Duanlin 馬端臨 (1254–1323) *Wenxian tongkao* 文獻通考.[4] The three were often published together and are usually referred to as the *Santong* 三通.

The following is a list of the main section headings of the *Wenxian tongkao*, which gives some idea of the scope of the subjects covered: (1) land taxes, (2) currency, (3) population, (4) services and corvée, (5) customs and tolls, (6) official markets and purchases, (7) local tribute, (8) national expenditure, (9) examinations and promotions, (10) schools, (11) government posts, (12) imperial sacrifices, (13) minor sacrifices, (14) imperial ancestral temple, (15) other temples and shrines, (16) court rites, (17) posthumous titles, (18) music, (19) the army, (20) penal law, (21) bibliography, (22) calligraphy, (23) imperial genealogy, (24) nobility, (25) the sun, the moon and the five planets, (26) freaks of nature, (27) geography, (28) foreign countries.

Six continuations were compiled during the eighteenth century and published together under the title *Jiutong* 九通. Although lacking the individual editorial touch and broad chronological sweep of

[2] *Tongdian* (Encyclopaedic history of institutions), AD 801; 5 vols., punctuated edition, Zhonghua, 1988; 3rd prnt., 1996.

[3] *Tongzhi* (Comprehensive treatise on institutions), 1149; Zhonghua, 1987, rpnt., 1990.

[4] *Wenxian tongkao* (General history of institutions and critical examination of documents and studies), 1224; Zhonghua, 1986.

the *Santong*, these six (plus a Ming and a late Qing one) are well-arranged collections of sources (Table 33).

Table 33: Shitong 十通

---

1. Du You 杜佑, *Tongdian* 通典, 801; punctuated edition, 5 vols., Zhonghua, 1988. Earliest times to 755; important for pre-Tang institutions.

2. Zheng Qiao 鄭樵, *Tongzhi* 通志, 1149; Shangwu, 1935; rpnt., Zhonghua, 1990 (in *Shitong*); the 20 monographs (*lüe* 略) are the most original part. They were reprinted separately in *Sibu beiyao* under the title *Tongzhi lüe* 通志略, and thereafter many times, for example, by Shanghai guji in 1993 and by Zhonghua in 1995. They cover from earliest times to the end of the Tang. The "Yiwen lüe" 藝文略 is the most detailed bibliographic scheme devised in pre-modern China.

3. Ma Duanlin 馬端臨, *Wenxian tongkao* 文獻通考, 1224; Shangwu, Shanghai, 1936. Earliest times to 1204; especially important for the Song; also contains a major bibliography, the "Jingjikao" 經籍考.

   Wang Qi 王圻, *Xu Wenxian tongkao* 續文獻通考, 1586. Not included in either *Jiutong* or *Shitong* editions; original edition only. Covers the years 907–1586; especially important for the Ming. Not superseded by no. 8.

4. *Xu Tongdian* 續通典. From 756 to end of the Ming.

5. *Qingchao Tongdian* 清朝通典. From 1644 to 1785 (original title: *Qinding huangchao tongdian* 欽定皇朝通典).

6. *Xu Tongzhi* 續通志. Monographs cover from 907 to 1644.

7. *Qingchao Tongzhi* 清朝通志. From 1644 to 1785 (original title: *Qinding huangchao tongzhi* 欽定皇朝通志).

8. *Xu Wenxian tongkao* 續文獻通考. From 1224 to 1644 (does not supersede Wang Qi).

9. *Qingchao Wenxian tongkao* 清朝文獻通考. From 1644 to 1785 (original title: *Qinding huangchao wenxian tongkao* 欽定皇朝文獻通考).

10. *Qingchao xu Wenxian tongkao* 清朝續文獻通考 (1921), Liu Jinzao 劉錦藻. From 1786 to 1911 (original title: *Huangchao xu Wenxian tongkao* 皇朝續文獻通考). Highest quality of the Qing continuations.

Note: Nos. 4–9 were compiled under imperial sponsorship in the eighteenth century.

Wang Qi 王圻, *Xu Wenxian tongkao* 續文獻通考 (1586) was not included in either the *Jiutong* or *Shitong* editions. It contains some sections not found in the others, notably on clans and on Daoists and Buddhists, Liu Jinzao 劉錦藻, *Qingchao xu Wenxian tongkao* 清朝續文獻通考 (1921) contains sections on posts and communications, industry, constitutional government, and external relations. Detailed tables of section and subsection headings to seven of the *Tong* (including Wang Qi) are available.[5]

The best modern edition was published by Shangwu under the tile *Shitong* 十通. It has an index (vol. 21), essential for works with a combined total of over 20,000 triple pages.[6]

Given the fact that in Chinese history different names and titles were often used for the same institution or office in different periods and that likewise, an institution or office might change its functions but keep the same name or title, and given the added advantage that the *Shitong* are indexed, they are often used as a first step in sorting out the functions of institutions and offices at different points in time.

25.3 Degree Holders and Official Titles

25.3.1 Degree Holders

Examination lists of successful candidates for the *jinshi* 進士 degree were kept from 622 to the end of the Qing. These lists (*dengke lu* 登科錄) are useful for finding place of origin, paternal background, and approximate dates of individuals (and hence, for example, which local gazetteer to search for further details). Similar official registers (*timing lu* 題名錄) or directories of officials (*jinshen quanshu* 縉紳全書) were also kept for other degrees (sometimes to be found in local gazetteers), and for candidates of the same year.

---

[5] *Bunken tsûkô goshu sômokuroku fu Tsûten Tsûshi* 文獻通考五種總目錄附通典通志 (General index to the *Santong* and to the four continuations of the *Wenxian tongkao*), Tôyôshi kenkyûkai, 1954.

[6] *Shitong* (The ten *Tong*), 21 vols., Shangwu, 1935–37; Xinxing, reduced-size version, 24 vols., 1963; Beijing neibu, 1965; Zhejiang guji, 1988; Taibei: Shangwu 3rd rpnt., 1994.

None of the Tang lists is extant, but an early nineteenth-century scholar, Xu Song 徐松, managed to piece together references to 3,326 successful candidates (including also those in the Five Dynasties).[7] There are also reconstructed lists of Hanlin members in the Tang. *Jinshi* lists for only three years of the Song and the Yuan have survived, namely those for 1148, 1256, and 1333.[8] From the Ming through the Qing complete lists have survived.[9] Most are available on microfilm either through the Family History Library of the Genealogical Society of Utah or directly from the Yishiguan in Beijing. See Table 34 for an outline of the examination system and its different degrees in the Qing dynasty. Note that Many of the terms for graduates at different levels had been in use since ancient times, but with different meanings. Thus *xiucai* 秀才, for example, simply meant a learned person in the Han and in the Tang it was applied to somebody who had passed the imperial examination. The imperial examination system was abolished in 1905 (see Franke, 1960; 25.3.2).

25.3.2   *Additional References*

Ichisada Miyazaki, *China's Examination Hell: The Civil Service Examinations of Imperial China*, Conrad Schirokauer, tr. from Japanese original (1963), Weatherhill, 1976; YUP, 1981.

Wolfgang Franke, *Reform and Abolition of the Traditional Chinese Examinatiion System*, HUP, 1960.

---

[7] *Dengkeji kao* 登科記考, 1838; rpnt., 3 vols., Zhonghua, 1984. There is a short supplement with corrections and additions by Cen Zhongmian 岑仲勉. There is also a name index to this work as well as to the short supplement: *Tōkaki kô sakuin ichi, ni* 登科記考索引 一, 二, Jinbun, 1949.

[8] See Edward A. Kracke, "Family vs. Merit in Chinese Civil Service Examinations Under the Empire," *HJAS* 10: 103-23 (1947); reprinted in John L. Bishop, ed., *Studies of Governmental Institutions in Chinese History*, HUP, 1968, 171-94.

[9] *Ming Qing jinshi timing beilu suoyin* 明清進士題名碑錄索引 (Index to Ming-Qing stele lists of *jinshi* degrees), Zhu Baojiong 朱保炯 and Xie Peilin 謝沛霖, eds., 3 vols., Shanghai guji, 1980; Taibei: Wenshizhe, 1982, gives the names of the 51,624 *jinshi* of the Ming and the Qing. Arranged by name. Gives native place, date of degree, and quality of degree (i.e., rank in that year's class). There is a *pinyin* index. Vol. 3 also lists those who passed by date, rank, and category and most usefully, also indicates where biographical sources on them may be found.

Table 34: The Qing Examination System

Exam type	Tongshi 童試 juvenile (preliminary test to qualify for the *xiang-shi*)	Xiangshi 鄉試 provincial	Huishi 會試 metropolitan	Dianshi 殿試 palace
Time	annual	triennial; usually in the 8th month	triennial; 3rd month of the year after the *xiangshi*	triennial; after the *huishi* on 21/4
Place	*xian* 縣, *fu* 府, and *xueyuan* 學院	provincial capitals; Beijing and Nanjing	Beijing and Nanjing	Beijing Taihedian 太和殿
Those eligible	*tongsheng* 童生	*xiucai* 秀才 (flourishing talents) and *jiansheng* 監生 (students of the Imperial Academy)	*juren* 舉人 (recommended men)	*gongshi* 貢士 (tribute students)
Content of exam	Classics; Histories; Imperial Rescript; *baguwen* 八股文 (eight-legged essays); poetry composition.	same content	same content	*cewen* 策問 (questions on policy)
Degree	*shengyuan* 生員 (also *xiangsheng* 庠生); popularly referred to as *xiucai* 秀才	*juren* 舉人 (recommended man; graduate). Popularly referred to as *xiaoqing* 孝廉; first ranked: *jieyuan* 解元. *Juren* 舉人 were eligible to serve as county magistrates or directors of county schools (*zhixian* 知縣 or *jiaozhi* 教職)	*gongshi* 貢士; first ranked: *jieyuan* 解元 or *huiyuan* 會元; second: *yayuan* 亞元 or *yakui* 亞魁; top five: *jingkui* 經魁 sixth: *bangyuan* 榜元; the last: *dianbang* 殿梆	*jinshi* 進士 (presented scholar; doctor); *jinshi* were popularly known as *laohuban* 老虎班 (tiger class); first ranked: *zhuangyuan* 狀元; second: *bangyan* 榜眼; third: *tanhua* 探花

Note: The above in outline was the imperial examination system (*kejuzhi* 科舉制) of the Qing as it had emerged after many centuries of evolution since the first competitive public examinations for public service began in the Sui (622). The Ming system was broadly the same as that of the Qing.

Benjamin Elman, "Changes in Confucian Civil Service Exams from the Ming to the Ch'ing Dynasties," in Elman and Woodside, 1994 (1.3.2), 111–49.

Ping-ti Ho (He Bingdi 何炳棣), *The Ladder of Success in Imperial China: Aspects of Social Mobility, 1368–1911*, Col. UP, 1962.

Edward A. Kracke, "Family vs. Merit in the Examination System," "Sponsorship and the Selection of Talent," in *The Chinese Civil Service*, Johanna Menzel, ed., Heath, 1963, 1-8; 84-91.

Thomas H. C. Lee, *Education in Traditional China: A History*, Brill, 1999. Includes the development of schools and the examination system, family education, student movements, and contains an extensive bibliography.

Etienne Zi (Xu 徐), SJ, *Pratique des examens littéraires en Chine*, Variétés sinologiques 5, 1894; rpnt., Ch'eng-wen, 1971. Detailed, factual account of the system as practiced in the late Qing. Contains an index of over 500 terms connected with the examination system.

Etienne Zi (Sui), SJ, *Pratique des examens militaires en Chine*, Variétés sinologiques 6, 1894; rpnt., Ch'eng-wen, 1971. See comments on previous item.

Adam Yuen-cheng Liu, *The Hanlin Academy*, 1644–1850, Archon Books, Shoestring, 1981.

25.3.3   Official Titles

All officials (*guan* 官) on the organization tables of the imperial government were assigned a rank in a system known from AD 220 as the Nine Ranks (*jiupin* 九品). The most senior was rank one. Each rank was further subdivided into upper (*zheng* 正) and lower (*cong* 從) grades (*deng* 等, also translated as classes or degrees). Thus the supervisor of the imperial secret service in the Ming, whose official post was eunuch director of the Directorate of Ceremonial (*Sili jian taijian* 司禮監太監), was ranked as *zheng sipin* 正四品 (Rank 4, upper grade, conventionally translated "4a"). In some periods and for some posts the 18 grades were further divided into upper (*shang* 上) and lower (*xia* 下) echelons. If this is the case, write 4a1 or 4a2.

The starting point is Charles O. Hucker, *A Dictionary of Official Titles in Imperial China*, SUP, 1985; SMC rpnt., 1988. It is the single best introduction in English to central and provincial administration in all periods of Chinese imperial history. As an added bonus, the Introduction gives an account of governmental organization from the Zhou to the Qing. *DOTIC* lists 8,291 titles, arranged alphabetically by Wade-Giles. Changing titles for the same function or office are indicated, but it is weak on alternative names of official posts (*zhiguan bieming* 職官別名). These were often derived from abbreviated titles, commonly found in everyday correspondence and writing; see second entry below. There is an index to the English translations of the titles, plus a character index. If you cannot find a title in *DOTIC*, then either try an even larger comprehensive dictionary or one of the more specialized references for individual periods or for alternative titles:

Zhongguo lidai guanzhi da cidian 中國歷代官制大辭典 (Large dictionary of Chinese official titles in different periods), Lü Zongli 呂宗力, ed. in chief, Beijing, 1994, 1995. Has 21,659 entries from all periods up to 1911. It also has something missing in *DOTIC*, namely tables of the ranking systems used in each period, "Lidai zhiguan pinwei biao" 歷代職官品位表, 871–915.

Zhongguo lidai zhiguan bieming cidian 中國歷代職官別名辭典 (Dictionary of alternative official titles), Gong Yanming 龔延明, ed., Shanghai cishu, 1999. Contains over 10,000 alternative titles.

Zhongguo jindai guanzhi cidian 中國近代官制詞典 (Dictionary of official titles in the modern period), Qiu Yuanyou 邱遠猷, Shumu wenxian, 1991.

Sixteen of the Standard Histories contain *baiguanzhi* 百官志 or *zhiguanzhi* 職官志 (monographs on official posts); eight have *xuanjuzhi* 選舉志 (monographs on the examination system; see Chapter 22, Table 31). These are summaries of the organization of the bureaucracy in specific periods. Specialized references and translations for individual periods are listed in Part II (pre-Qin) and in each chapter of Part V under *Research Tools, Official Titles, and Office Holders*.

Throughout Chinese history summaries of official posts of all periods were also compiled. The most complete was made in the Qing and served as the basis for modern dictionaries or directories of official posts such as *DOTIC* and Lü (1994):

Lidai zhiguan biao 歷代職官表 (Tables of official posts from the earliest times to the nineteenth century), Huang Benji 黃本驥, comp., with introduction and glossary by Qu Tuiyuan 瞿蛻園, Zhonghua, 1965. Huang produced his original table as a simplified version of the imperially sponsored work of the same title that had been compiled by Ji Yun 紀昀 and others in 1782.

26

Official Communications

Since the beginning of the empire, there have been strict regulations as to the type of document to be used depending on the occasion, the addressee, and the rank of the person whose name or seal was to appear on it. There have also been punishments for violation of name taboos and orthographic errors in documents, especially those submitted to the emperor.

By far the most numerous types of document were those from the top down (26.1), notably from the ruler to his officials or to the people. One modern study lists 175 terms for top-down documents (edicts, *zhaoling* 詔令, became the generic term for these imperial commands); 64 for bottom-up (memorials *zoushu* 奏書, *zouyi* 奏議, 26.2) and only 28 for documents between equal-ranking officials or offices (26.3).

The names for different documents were often derived from the materials upon which they were originally written. Thus the *zha* 札 (small wooden tablet) came to mean "note" or "document."

Terms changed substantially over the dynasties and the same term was also used for different types of document. Introductions to the different types of document are given in Box 8 at the end of this chapter.

26.1 *Edicts*

Tens of thousands of original documents have survived from the Ming and earlier dynasties, and many more have been excerpted in whole or in part in various collections, historical works, and official compilations. Approximately fourteen million original documents survive from the Qing. They are one of the most important basic materials used by historians in the past as well as today.

Most common of all were the proclamations or edicts (*zhao* 詔) of the ruler or his commands (*ling* 令). There were many different terms for edict apart from *zhao*, which during the Warring States had grown out of the expression *gao* 告 or *gao* 誥, meaning to call together to hear an announcement or proclamation. The first emperor standardized the terms for his edicts to *zhao* 詔 (or *zhaoshu* 詔書) and *zhi* 制 (particularly important pronouncements). These terms continued in use until 1911.

During the Han, edicts were composed in an elegant style unmatched in later history. There were many varieties: secret edicts (*mizhao* 密詔) or personally written edicts (*qinzhao* 親詔), for example. They were also called *zhaoce* 詔策[冊], reflecting the material (*jiandu* 簡牘) on which the edicts were written. *Ce* 冊 (or *ceshu* 冊書 before the Han and *ce* 策, *ceshu* 策書, or *ceming* 策命 after the Han) is as old a term as *zhao* 詔 and in imperial times was used for different types of enfeoffment, investiture, or appointment instruments such as letters patent. By the Qing, the material used, for example, gold, silver, jade or paper, depended on the quality of the person being invested with a title or office. *Chi* 敕 was another term for documents of appointment, as in the expression *chiming* 敕命, which by the Qing was used for the letter of appointment of officials below grade 6. *Chi* was also used for rescript, as in *chizhi* 敕旨. It became a formal term in this sense during the Song. There were many other terms for imperial decrees, such as *shengyu* 聖諭 or *shengzhi* 聖旨, as well as instructions from the emperor, such as *xun* 訓 (or *shengxun* 聖訓), *yu* 諭, or *jiao* 教. By the Ming, *yu* had become *yuzhi* 諭旨 (imperial rescript) and continued in use in this sense in the Qing. *Shangyu* 上諭 in the Qing normally refers to the "Sacred Edict" or 16 maxims of the Kangxi emperor. In the Ming, the emperor expressed his endorsement of a proposal with a *pida* 批答, which by the Qing was called a *zhupi* 硃批 (vermilion comment, from the color of the special ink reserved for use by the emperor).

Senior officials addressing an instruction to a subordinate in the Qing used a *yutie* 諭帖. To inform a wider public they used (as they still do today) a *gaoshi* 告示 or *bugao* 布告 (announcement), which the Qianlong emperor ordered "should be written in a style that women and children can understand." Other official communications to subordinates or inferior offices were called *zha* 劄 (or *zhawen* 劄文; informally *zha* 札 was also used), *pai* 牌, or *feng* 封.

The practice of collecting together memorable edicts or imperial instructions (*shengxun* 聖訓) of a particular reign or dynasty began

early, but the first large surviving collections were made during the
Song, the most famous being the *Tang da zhaoling ji* 唐大詔令集
(46.2). Other collections of edicts are listed in the appropriate chapters of Part V. Many collections of Qing edicts and imperial instructions were published during the Qing, and tens of thousands of
Qing edicts from the central Qing archives have been published in
the course of the twentieth century and the process continues (50.2).

26.2   *Memorials*

Memorials (*zouyi* 奏議) were of many different types and were
called by many different names in different periods. The earliest
term was *shu* 書, which the first emperor had renamed *zou* 奏, although people continued to use *shu* 書 or *shu* 疏 (or *shangshu* 上書,
shangshu 上疏, *zoushu* 奏書). In the Han, a *zhang* 章 was used to
make clear one's gratitude; a *zou* 奏 was used for reporting an investigation or to impeach; a *biao* 表 was used to express feelings; and an
yi 議 was to voice a contrary opinion. Other terms included *ce* 策 (a
policy proposal). All could be used with *zou* 奏 prefixed to indicate
they were directed to the emperor. A remonstrance was termed a
boyi 駁議, or less formally, an *yi* 議 (opinion). These distinctions
were not strictly adhered to in subsequent dynasties, during the
course of which additional terms were developed.

By the Ming, in theory, anybody (including non-officials) could
submit a *zouben* 奏本 (personal memorial) to the emperor. *Tiben*
題本 (usually translated as "routine memorials") were reserved for
official matters. The Qing continued the Ming system, but the
Kangxi emperor introduced secret palace memorials (*zouzhe* 奏摺,
literally, "memorials written on folded paper"). The personal memorials (*zouben*) were abolished in 1748. The *tiben* gradually faded
in importance until they, too, were abolished in 1901.[1]

---

[1] Silas Hsiu-liang Wu, "Transmission of Ming Memorials," *TP* 54: 275–87
(1968); Timothy Brook, "The Transmission of State Documents," in his chapter "Communications and Commerce," in *CHC*, vol. 8, 637–39; Silas Wu, "The
Memorial Systems of the Ch'ing Dynasty," *HJAS* 27: 7–75 (1967); Beatrice S.
Bartlett, *Monarchs and Ministers: The Grand Council in Mid-Ch'ing China, 1723–
1820*, UCP, 1991. Further references to the Ming and Qing memorial systems
are given in Chapters 49 and 50.

The emperor would often add brief remarks to a memorial such as *zhidao le* 知道了 (as we would say, "noted"). Frequently, he just put a circle to show the same (*hua quan'er* 畫圈兒). This implied neither approval nor disapproval, merely that he had taken note.

The codes and statutes stipulated what terms could be used by officials of what rank to approve which documents.

Memorials and other bottom-up documents, form one of the basic sources of Chinese history, flowing in and up to all levels of the bureaucracy on all subjects. Many of the types of historical writing and documents so far discussed either quote from them in whole or in part or were based upon them.

As in all branches of Chinese historiography, the further back the period, the fewer such basic sources survive intact. Instead we have them in excerpted or adapted form in the Standard Histories or other compilations; the originals have long since been lost. If they have survived, it is among the newly discovered documents (such as those on bamboo strips, *jiandu* 簡牘) or more usually, in an author's collected works (*bieji* 別集, 30.3). During the Ming it became common practice for the first time to publish collections of memorials (either of an individual, or of a given period or on a given subject). This practice was continued in the Qing. In the twentieth century, the Qing central archives were opened, and selections of memorials and other documents began to be edited and published from them. At a conservative estimate, something on the order of four million late Qing memorials have yet to be published (50.1–2).

There is no easy way of tracing memorials on a particular subject or by a given author before the Ming.

The earliest comprehensive collection of memorials from all periods was the imperially sponsored *Lidai mingchen zouyi* 歷代名臣奏議, Huang Huai 黃淮 (1367–1449) et al., comps., 1416. It includes 8,000 memorials. The Shanghai guji edition has an author index.[2]

The surest way of finding memorials by pre-Ming officials is first to check through their biographies and then to check through their collected works. The memorials of eminent officials were often collected and published together.

---

[2] *Lidai mingchen zouyi* (Memorials of leading officials of each period), 1416; 5 vols., Shanghai guji, 1989.

26.3 Lateral Communications

One of the earliest terms for lateral communications was *yi* 移 (or *yishu* 移書), with *yi* 移 changing to *yi* 遺 (or *yishu* 遺書) in the Warring States. Other expressions used later, included *guan* 關 (*guanwen* 關文). *Zi* 咨 (*ziwen* 咨文 or *zicheng* 咨呈) was reserved for communications between high-ranking offices or officials at the same level (for example, during the Ming, for communications between ranking officials of the Six Boards). Documents between offices were sent in the form of a *zhihui* 知會 (*zhaohui* 照會 during the Qing). The Grand Council used *jiaopian* 交片 for its everyday lateral communications.

Mengshu 盟書 was used for a covenant or treaty between two states (or two families). *Die* 牒 (*diewen* 牒文, *diecheng* 牒呈) began as a synonym for *zha* 札 (from the name of the wooden tablet on which it was originally written). It later came to mean note or record. Today it is still used, as in *tongdie* 通牒 (diplomatic note) or *zuihou tongdie* 最後通牒 (ultimatum). *Ci* 刺 (or *ye* 謁) was a name-card. *Han* 函 (*hanwen* 函文) by the Ming meant letter, both in public and private life, although in the former use, it was a letter signed by an individual official. The generic term for private letters was *chidu* 尺牘 or *shuxin* 書信 (3.6).

26.4 Official and Unofficial Gazettes

Ever since the Tang, selected memorials and edicts were distributed in the capital and to the provinces in gazette form called *Jinzou yuan zhuangbao* 進奏院狀報 (Report of the capital liaison office) (also *baozhuang* 報狀 or *zabao* 雜報).[3] One is referred to in Sun Qiao 孫樵, *Jingwei ji* 經緯集 (Collection of main points), 724–26. The first known fragment to survive is dated about 876 and is 47 columns long. The only other fragment dates from about 887 and is 60 col-

---

[3] The Jinzou yuan 進奏院 in the Tang were the capital liaison offices of provincial officials, also referred to as liaison hostels (*di* 邸, *dishe* 邸社). In the Song they became formalized as the Memorial Office, charged *inter alia* with transmitting government documents between the center and the circuit authorities (*DOTIC*, 1156). In the Yuan, Ming, and Qing official gazettes were issued by the transmission offices called, respectively, Tongzheng yuan 通政院, Tongzheng si 通政司, and Titang guan 提塘官.

umns long (over 2,000 characters). Both were found at Dunhuang in the early years of the century; the first is in the Bibliothèque Nationale de France in Paris, the second, is in the British Library. In the Northern Song, the official gazettes began to be called *dibao* 邸報 (also *dichao* 邸抄, *chaobao* 抄報, *baozhuang* 報狀, or *chumu* 除目; from the mid-Ming, the term *jingbao* 京報 came into use). The only gazettes to survive from before the late Qing are copies of two short runs of late Ming gazettes (50.).[4]

From the Song, individuals began to publish unofficial gazettes (called *xiaobao* 小報 or *xinwen* 新聞). They were usually written by junior officials at the Jinzou yuan and sometimes contained news not deemed fit to print in the official gazettes. They were frequently forbidden by the government, which sought to control the supply of information, especially when things were going wrong (the late Ming minister of war, Chen Xinjia 陳新甲 was executed in 1642 when a copy of his draft of a peace probe to the Manchus appeared in the official gazette). In the late Qing it became more and more common for private printing houses (*baofang* 報房) to publish both official and unofficial gazettes (whose contents were almost identical). The last *Jingbao* appeared in 1900. Already by that time, the new printing technology encouraged the publication of more than 60 new official periodicals (*guanbao* 官報). Thereafter, twentieth-century Chinese governments continued to issue official news, using not only gazettes, but also newspapers and many other means. These are best considered as part of the history of modern Chinese journalism (on which, see sections 50.8 and 51.3).

---

[4] *Wanli dichao* 萬曆邸抄 (Wanli excerpts from the capital gazette), Taibei: Guoli zhongyang tushuguan, 1963, covers 1573.1 to 1617.6 in slightly over 38,000 characters; the late Ming *Hongguang dichao* 弘光邸抄 are presumed to be the basis of *Hongguang shilu chao* 弘光實錄抄 (published in *Jiashen chuanxin lu* 甲申傳信錄, Shanghai shudian, 1982); see Yin Yungong 尹韵公, *Zhongguo Mingdai xinwen chuanboshi* 中國明代新聞傳播史 (History of news dissemination in the Ming dynasty), Chongqing, 1990, 1997.

Box 8: Introductions to Documentary Chinese

Wang Guihai 汪桂海, *Handai guan wenshu zhidu* 漢代官文書制度 (The documentary system of Han dynasty officials), Guangxi jiaoyu, 1999. Takes into account both documentary and *Hanjian* evidence.

Gujin gongwen wenzhong huishi 古今公文文種匯釋 (Collected explanations of the different types of official correspondence, ancient and modern), Liang Qinghai 梁清海 et al., eds., Sichuan daxue, 1992. Examples are given of the most important types of document with summary translations into Modern Chinese. The first two-thirds of the book are on documents up to 1911; the last third is on documents from 1912 to the present day.

Lishi wenshu yongyu cidian Ming Qing Minguo bufen 歷史文書用語辭典明清民國部分 (Dictionary of terms in official despatches, Ming, Qing, and Republican, periods), Liu Wenjie 劉文傑, ed., Sichuan renmin, 1988.

A list of the many terms used for edicts and memorials is given with brief annotations in E. D. Edwards, "A Classified Guide to the Thirteen Classes of Chinese Prose," *BSOAS* 12: 777–88 (1948).

For general introductions to literary Chinese, see 1.3.5. For documentary Chinese of individual periods, see Part V (especially the Qing, 50.10.2).

27

Law

Law in China was promulgated by the ruler and administered by his officials. There was no independent judiciary. The emperor was both law giver and supreme judge. Both the criminal codes and the administrative regulations included civil and economic laws. But there was no separate civil law code. From the Han, the laws became permeated with Confucian morality, which embodied the rites (*li* 禮) or customary law. For example, the punishment for lack of filial piety (a Confucian virtue) was unusually severe.[1]

After introducing the different forms of law, the present chapter then deals with pre-Qin law (27.1), Qin law (27.2), Han law (27.3), criminal law in the Tang and after (27.4), administrative law in the Tang and after (27.5), guides and handbooks for local magistrates and clerks (27.6), and law in the Republic (27.7).

Note that official works relating to law are usually listed as *zhengshu* 政書 in the History branch of the *Sibu* classification (Table 20, 9.3); unofficial legal works tend to appear in the *fajia* 法家 section of the Philosophers' branch (Table 21, 9.3).

Introduction

Penal law was set out in the codes (*lü* 律), which prescribed the action to be taken and the punishments to be inflicted for all infringements of the laws. Fragments of law codes have survived from as early as the Warring States (27.1), but the first complete one dates from the Tang. It formed the basis of all subsequent codes for the remainder of Chinese history (27.4), as also for China's neighbors.[2]

---

[1] T'ung-tsu Ch'ü, *Law and Society in Traditional China*, Mouton, 1961 (English version of Chinese original of 1947), 267–79.

[2] For an outline, see Geoffrey MacCormack, *Traditional Chinese Penal Law*, Edinburgh UP, 1991; R. P. Peerenboom, "The Victim in Chinese Crimin-

Footnote continued on next page

The most general form of codified administrative law was found in the *ling* 令 (statutes or commands), which were promulgated in most dynasties down to the *Da Mingling* 大明令 (Great Ming statutes), 1368 (27.5).

The division between the two types of law, penal and administrative (the *lü* and the *ling*) was not hard and fast, although it became much more so after the Tang. Both were modified or supplemented in the *ge* 格 (regulations), and their implementation was defined in the *shi* 式 (ordinances). They were also altered, expanded, and applied in the light of particular precedents or substatutes (*li* 例, *zeli* 則例, *shili* 事例), the most important of which are introduced below.

From the Tang dates the practice of compiling comprehensive handbooks on the structure and functions of the bureaucracy, referred to in what follows as *huidian* 會典 (collected statutes), ultimately modeled on the *Zhouli* 周禮 (Rites of Zhou).

The *lüling geshi* 律令格式, the edicts (*chi* 敕), and other decisions of the emperor, together with the precedents, are the basic sources for Chinese legal and institutional history. They are also important sources for all the many different areas of Chinese society with which they deal, either in the generalized terms of the codes, the statutes and other compendia of administrative law, or in the more detailed commentaries, precedents, cases, and handbooks that frequently illustrate the actual working of the law in concrete terms as it touched everyday life—for example, in laws of inheritance or divorce, or the laws and regulations governing ownership and contract (50.7.5).

On the different kinds of primary sources, both epigraphic and textual, for the history of Chinese law from the Zhou dynasty to the present day, see *Chûgoku hôseishi kihon shiryô no kenkyû* 中國法制史基本資料の研究. It contains 28 chapters, each written by a specialist (hereafter abbreviated as *CHKSK*).[3]

---

al Theory and Practice: A Historical Survey," *Journal of Chinese Law* 7.1: 63–110 (1993). For translations, see *Chinese Law Past and Present: A Bibliography of Enactments and Commentaries in English Text*, Lin Fushun, comp., Col. UP, 1966.

[3] *CHKSK* (Chinese legal history, studies on basic source materials), Shiga Shûzô 滋賀秀三, ed., Tôkyô daigaku, 1993, 1994; *Law and the State in Traditional East Asia: Six Studies on the Sources of East Asian Law*, Brian E. McKnight,

Footnote continued on next page

Zhongguo zhenxi falü dianji jicheng 中國珍稀法律典籍集成 is a major collection of rare and important works of Chinese law from the oracle bones to the Qing. It is typeset, clearly printed, and carefully annotated (hereafter abbreviated as *ZZFDJ*).[4]

27.1   Pre-Qin Law

The first code is traditionally supposed to have been promulgated at the beginning of the fourth century BC (Li Kui 李悝, *Fajing* 法經 [Canon of Laws]), but considerable doubt is attached to the later descriptions of this work.[5] There are also scattered references to the laws and to the punishments of the Xia and the Shang dynasties in early texts such as the *Shangshu* and the *Shiji*. These can now be supplemented with excavated sources. Oracle-bone and bronze inscriptions relating to punishments as well as laws, regulations and contracts are transcribed, punctuated, collated, and translated into Modern Chinese in *Jiaguwen jinwen jiandu falü wenxian* 甲骨文金文簡牘法律文獻.[6]

27.2   Qin Law

The study of Qin and Han law and regulations has been transformed by the discovery of laws, regulations and case books on

---

ed., UHP, 1987; *Zhongguo fazhishi shumu* 中國法制史書目 (Bibliography of the history of Chinese law), Zhang Weiren 張偉仁, ed. in chief, 3 vols., Lishi yuyan yanjiusuo, *zhuankan* 67, 1976. Based on holdings in Taiwan libraries.

[4] *Zhongguo zhenxi falü dianji jicheng* (Collection of rare works of Chinese law), Liu Hainian 劉海年 and Yang Yifan 楊一凡, series eds., 14 vols., Kexue, 1994.

[5] See Timoteus Pokora, "The Canon of Laws of Li K'uei: A Double Falsification?" *Archiv Orientalni* 27: 96–121 (1959). Herrlee G. Creel, "Legal Institutions and Procedures During the Chou Dynasty," in *Essays on China's Legal Tradition*, Jerome A. Cohen, R. Randle Edwards, and Fu-mei Chang Chen, eds., PUP, 1980, 26–55. Yongping Liu, *Origins of Chinese Law*, HK: OUP, 1998.

[6] *Jiaguwen jinwen jiandu falü wenxian* (Texts on law from oracle-bone and bronze inscriptions and bamboo MSS), Yang Shengnan 楊陞南, ed.; oracle-bone inscriptions (1–229); bronze inscriptions (231–362). This is vol. 1 of series 1 of *ZZFDJ*. *CHKSK*, Chapter 1, has a bibliography of secondary literature on Western Zhou laws cast on bronze vessels.

bamboo and wooden strips. For an introduction to these new sources, see A. F. P. Hulsewé , "Qin and Han Legal Manuscripts."[7] The earliest legal document so far discovered on bamboo or wood dates from 309 BC. It was found on a single wooden tablet at Hao-jiaping 郝家坪, Qingchuan 青川 county, near the border with Gansu in Sichuan. On the front is recorded the setting of a Qin statute on land law and on the back, various related matters (19.1.2). By far the most important breakthrough in the study of pre-Han law came in 1975–76 with the discovery at Shuihudi in Hubei of 612 legible bamboo strips mainly recording fragments of the long-lost Qin code and other legal or administrative works. They were found in the coffin of a Qin local judicial official named Xi 喜 (262–217 BC). Along with the Haojiaping land law, they are transcribed, punctuated, collated, translated into Modern Chinese, and annotated in *Jia-guwen jinwen jiandu falü wenxian* (367–695).[8]

---

[7] In *NSECH*, 193–221. The author does not cover the important finds of Qin law made since the late 1980s, notably those excavated from Yunmeng, Longgang (see 44.4.1).

[8] This collection contains the best text of the Shuihudi legal works including *Qinlü shibazhong* 秦律十八種, *Xiaolü* 效律, *Falü dawen* 法律答問, and *Fengzhenshi* 封診式. It also includes the *Shoufa shouling deng shisan pian* 守法守令等十三篇 discovered at Yinqueshan 銀雀山 (44.4.1). For a translation and studies of the Shuihudi texts, see A. F. P. Hulsewé, *Remnants of Ch'in Law: An Annotated Translation of the Ch'in Legal and Administrative Rules of the 3rd Century BC Discovered in Yün-meng Prefecture, Hu-pei Province, in 1975*, Brill, 1985; by the same author, "The Influence of the Legalist Government of Qin on the Economy as Reflected in the Texts Discovered in Yunmeng County," in *The Scope of State Power in China*, Stuart R. Schram, ed., London: SOAS and HKCUP, 1985, 211–36; Katrina C. D. McLeod and Robin D. S. Yates, "Forms of Ch'in Law: An Annotated Translation of the *Feng-chen shih*," *HJAS* 41.1: 111–63 (1981); Chen Gongrou 陳公柔, "Yunmeng Qinmu chutu *Falü dawen* jiance kaoshu" 雲夢秦墓出土法律答問簡册考述 (Study of the bamboo documents *Falü dawen* unearthed at Yunmeng), *Yanjing xuebao*, new series, 2: 171–212 (1996); A. F. P. Hulsewé, "The Legalists and the Laws of Ch'in," in *Leyden Studies in Sinology*, W. L. Idema, ed., Brill, 1981, 1–22; see also Li Jing 栗勁, *Qin lü tonglun* 秦律通論 (Introduction to Qin law), Shandong renmin, 1985.

27.3   Han Law

The basic source on Han law is the "Xingfazhi" 刑法志 in the *Han-shu*, the first Standard History to contain such a monograph.[9] This should be supplemented with the growing body of Han legal texts and documents excavated from tombs (44.4.2) or found at the posts along the Silk Roads (44.4.3). *Handai tunshu yijian falü zhi* 漢代屯戍遺簡法律志[10] has transcriptions of texts excerpted from published collections of *Hanjian* including the new Juyan documents. The texts are arranged under three headings: laws, edicts, and punishments (1–304); judicial documents (305–425); other documents (427–607). There are copious annotations.

A pioneering attempt was made by Cheng Shude 程樹德 (1877–1944) in *Jiuchao lü kao* 九朝律考 to reconstruct the codes promulgated from the Han through to the Sui.[11] He uses the four monographs on law and the five monographs on official posts in the Standard Histories of these years as well as many other contemporary sources.

See Table 31 (22.3) for a list of the Standard Histories containing monographs on law and the chapters of Part V for studies and translations of them.

27.4   Penal Codes

During the Tang there were four main types of codified law, all of which had been inherited from the past. In addition to the *lü* 律 and

---

[9] Note the following studies of A. F. P. Hulsewé, "Ch'in and Han Law," in the *CHC*, vol. 1, 520–44; "Introductory Studies," in *Remnants of Han Law*, Brill, 1955, 1–307; "The *Shuo-wen* Dictionary as a Source for Ancient Chinese Law," in *Studia serica Bernhard Karlgren dedicata*, Sören Egerod and Else Glahn, eds., Copenhagen: Munksgaard, 1959, 239–58. See also Ôba Osamu 大庭脩, *Shin Kan hôseishi no kenkyû* 秦漢法制史の研究 (Research on the legal institutions of the Qin and Han), Sôbunsha, 1982, 1985. Chinese version published by Shanghai renmin, 1991.

[10] *Handai tunshu yijian falü zhi* (Collection of legal documents from the Han border posts), Li Junming 李均明 and Liu Jun 劉軍, eds. Kexue, 1994. This is the second volume of series 1 of *ZZFDJ*.

[11] *Jiuchao lü kao* (A study of the penal statutes of nine dynasties), Changsha: Shangwu, 1927; Shanghai: Shangwu, 1934, 1955; Zhonghua, 1963; Taibei: Shangwu, 1965; Shanghai shudian, 1989.

the *ling* 令, there were the *ge* 格 (regulations) and the *shi* 式 (ordinances).[12] The *Tanglü shuyi* 唐律疏議 (Tang code with commentary), 635, was the basis of all Chinese law codes down to the Qing.[13] It was also taken as the model for the codes of Japan, Korea, and Vietnam.[14] For a complete, annotated translation with introduction, see Wallace Johnson, *The T'ang Code: Vol. I, General Principles*, PUP, 1979; *The T'ang Code: Vol. II, Specific Articles*, PUP, 1997.[15] On the application of the code, see Wallace Johnson and Denis Twitchett, "Criminal Procedures in T'ang China," *AM* 3rd series, 6.2: 113–46 (1993); and Denis Twitchett, "The Implementation of Law in Early T'ang China," *Civiltà Veneziana: Studi* 34: 57–84 (1978). A large amount of detailed research has been done using the fragments of laws discovered at Dunhuang and further to the west around Turpan.[16]

[12] Shiga Shûzô, "A Basic History of T'ang Legislative Forms," *AM* 3rd series. V.2: 97–127 (1992).

[13] Brian E. McKnight, "T'ang Law and Later Law: The Roots of Continuity," *JAOS* 115.3: 410–20 (1995). The text is in *Tanglü shuyi jianjie* 唐律疏議箋解 (Analysis of the articles in the Tang code and annotations on the commentaries), Liu Junwen 劉俊文, ed., 2 vols., Zhonghua, 1996. Contains an index to special terms used in the annotations, 2112–2148. For a translation of the code into Japanese, see *Tôritsu sogi* 唐律疏議, vols. 5–7 of *Yakuchû Nihon ritsuryô* 譯注日本律令, Shiga Shûzô 滋賀秀三 et al., trs., Tôkyôdô, 1975, and see also Niida Noboru, *Tô-Sô hôritsu monjo no kenkyû* 唐宋法律文書の研究 (Studies on legal works of the Tang and Song dynasties), Tokyo, 1937.

[14] For a study and translation of the Lê Dynasty code, which was modeled closely after the Tang code, see Nguyen Ngoc Huy et al., *The Lê Code: Law in Traditional Vietnam. A Comparative Sino-Vietnamese Legal Study with Historical-Juridical Analysis and Annotations*, 3 vols., Athens: Ohio UP, 1987.

[15] Also Zhuang Weisi 莊爲斯, *Tanglü shuyi yinde* 唐律疏議引得 (Concordance to the Tang code with commentary), Wenhai, 1964.

[16] Legal texts from Dunhuang and Turpan are punctuated and collated in *Dunhuang fazhi wenshu* 敦煌法制文書 (Dunhuang legal documents), Tang Geng'ou 唐耕耦, ed. in chief, and in *Tulufan chutu falü wenxian* 吐魯番出土法律文獻 (Legal texts excavated at Turpan), Wu Zhen 吳震, ed. in chief, 1st series, vols. 3 and 4 of *ZZFDJ*.

ZZFDJ, Vol. 3 (Dunhuang) is a massive collection (1,630 pages) containing punctuated transcriptions of over 500 Dunhuang legal documents arranged according to subject matter. There are lengthy notes and summaries. Vol. 4 (Turpan) contains punctuated transcriptions of 63 fragments of laws, cases, and judgments as well as 415 legal documents. For other references, see the section on Dunhuang and Turpan (46.3).

The *Song huiyao jigao* 宋會要輯稿, "Xingfa" 刑法 section (*ce* 164–71), is an important source for Song legal history, as is also the *Song xingtong* 宋刑統 (Song repertory of penal law), 963, which was largely based on the Tang code and in use throughout the dynasty.[17]

Several collections of cases survive from the Song. They were intended to provide examples to assist county magistrates in reaching judicial decisions. The *Minggong shupan qingmingji* 名公書判清明集 (1260–65) was only rediscovered in the 1980s.[18] It contains a wealth of socioeconomic detail in the form of judgments and cases. It has been described as the most important new source on the Southern Song to have been found in the last century. About half the collection has been translated into English.[19] Another such collection, the *Tangyin bishi* 棠陰比事 (1211), has also been translated.[20] It cites cases from the whole of Chinese history up to that time.

None of the Liao or Jin codes are extant, although parts can be reconstructed on the basis of detailed studies of documents such as the monographs on law in the *Liaoshi* and *Jinshi*.[21] For the Xixia

[17] For an evaluation and a study of the editions and secondary scholarship, see Okano Makoto 岡野誠, "*Sô keitô*" 宋刑統, in *CHKSK*, 281–318.

[18] *Minggong shupan qingmingji* (Collection of enlightened judgments by celebrated judges), 14 *juan*, 1260–65; punctuated and collated edition of Song and Ming editions in *Zhongguo gudai shehui jingjishi ziliao* 中國古代社會經濟史資料, Wang Zengyu 王曾瑜, Chen Zhichao 陳智超, and Wu Tai 吳泰, eds., 1st collection, Fujian renmin, 1985; reprinted as *Minggong shupan qingmingji* 名公書判清明集, Zhonghua, 1987. This replaces the earlier photoreprint of a 1 *juan* fragment of a Song edition reprinted by the Koten kenkyûkai in 1964. For an evaluation and a study of the editions and secondary scholarship, see Takahashi Yoshirô 高橋芳郎, "Meikô shohan Seimeishô," 名公書判清明集, in *CHKSK*, 361–82.

[19] *The Enlightened Judgments: Ch'ing-ming Chi: The Sung Dynasty Collection*, Brian E. McKnight and James T. C. Liu, trs., SUNY, 1999.

[20] R. H. van Gulik (1910–67), *T'ang-yin pi-shih, Parallel Cases from Under the Peartree: A 13th Century Manual of Jurisprudence and Detection*, Brill, 1956.

[21] Herbert Franke, "The 'Treatise on Punishments' in the Liao History," *Central Asiatic Journal* 27: 9–38 (1983); and the same author's, "The Legal System of the Chin Dynasty," in *Collected Studies on Sung History Dedicated to Professor James T. C. Liu in Celebration of His Seventieth Birthday*, Tsuyoshi Kinugawa, ed., Dôhôsha, 1989, 387–409; and "Jurchen Customary Law and the Chinese Law of the Chin Dynasty," *State and Law in East Asia: Festschrift for Karl Bünger*, Dieter Eikemeier and Herbert Franke, eds., Harrassowitz, 1981, 215–

Footnote continued on next page

code, see 48.3. The Yuan never established a formal code. On Yuan law, see the monograph on law in the *Yuanshi* and the *Zhiyuan xinge* 至元新格 (48.5.2).[22]

The first version of the *Da Minglü* 大明律 (Great Ming code), 1373–74, was largely based on the Tang code as it had been transmitted down to the Yuan. The third version (1397), however, was completely revised and marks an important break from the 600-year tradition set by the Tang code. Its title was *Gengding Da Minglü* 更訂大明律, but it is usually referred to as the *Da Minglü* 大明律, or simply the *Minglü* 明律. It contained 460 articles covering general principles, personnel, revenue, rites, war, justice, and public works (see John D. Langlois, Jr., "Ming Law," in *CHC*, vol. 8, 172–220). Like the Tang code, it was extremely influential in Korea, Japan, and Vietnam. Many annotated editions were issued in these countries. A very large number of editions of the 1397 version are extant; most include the itemized substatutes. After the 1585 edition, they were made an integral part of the code, hence the title, *Minglü jijie fuli* 明律集解附例.[23]

Recently reprinted from a unique manuscript copy are the extremely detailed (5,000-page) substatutes, regulations, etc., used in the actual implementation of the code in the late fifteenth and early sixteenth centuries:

Huang Ming tiaofa shilei zuan 皇明條法事類纂, Dai Jin 戴金, comp., 1531–33; typeset, punctuated edition, Yang Yifan 楊一凡, ed. in chief, 2nd series, vols. 4–6, *ZZFDJ* (based on the manuscript copy held in Tokyo University library that was earlier photolithographically reproduced by the Koten kenkyûkai, 2 vols., 1966–67; rpnt., Wenhai, 1985. The *ZZFDJ* edition is more convenient to use).

---

33. Ye Qianzhao 葉潛昭, *Jinlü zhi yanjiu* 金律之研究 (Researches on the Jin penal code), Taibei: Shangwu, 1972.

[22] Paul Ratchnevsky, *Un Code des Yuan*, vol. 1, Leroux, 1937; vol. 2, PUF, 1972; vol. 3 (with Françoise Aubin), *Index*, PUF, 1977; vol. 4, Collège de France: Institut des Hautes Etudes Chinoises, 1985. This is an annotated translation with a long introduction (vol. 1) and index (vol. 3) of the monograph on law in the *Yuanshi* (*juan* 102–5).

[23] See *ISMH*, 185–87, for an annotated list of 12 editions; rpnt. in *Huang Ming zhishu* 皇明制書, Zhang Lu 張鹵, ed., 1579; 2 vols., Koten kenkyûkai, 1966–67, vol. 2, 23–172; for a modern edition, see *Da Minglü*, Huai Xiaofeng 懷

Footnote continued on next page

Collections of itemized substatutes (*tiaoli* 條例) have survived in greater numbers from the Qing (50.5.2).

The early version of the Qing code (1646) reached its final form in the expanded *Da Qing lüli* 大清律例 (Great Qing code with substatutes), 1740.[24] It was one of the first works studied and translated into English in the nineteenth century, albeit fairly freely.[25] An important new translation has recently been published, *The Great Qing Code*, William C. Jones, tr., Clarendon, 1993. An introduction gives the legal background. The Jones translation replaces all previous ones into either English or French.[26] It is based on the text of the code in the modern, punctuated edition of *Du li cunyi* 讀例存疑 (1905), a commentary on the code and its substatutes by one of the last presidents of the Board of Punishments, Xue Yunsheng 薛允昇 (1820–1901).[27]

For a translation from the largest Qing casebook, *Xing'an huilan* 刑案匯覽 (The conspectus of penal cases), see Bodde and Morris (1967). The *Xing'an huilan* (1834, 1886) and its continuation have been reprinted: 11 vols., Taibei, 1968; and 10 vols., Taibei, 1970. For an interesting study of murder and adultery and the influence of Confucian morality, see M. J. Meijer, *Murder and Adultery in Late Imperial China: A Study of Law and Morality*, Brill, 1991.

效鋒, ed., Liao-Shen, 1990; for Japanese studies, see Satô Kuninori 佐藤邦憲 in *CHKSK*, 435–72.

[24] For editions and extensive introductions to different aspects of the Qing code and penal law in the Qing, see Derk Bodde and Clarence Morris, *Law in Imperial China, Exemplified by 190 Ch'ing Dynasty Cases Translated from the "Hsing-an hui-lan" with Historical, Social, and Juridical Commentaries*, HUP, 1967; *Civil Law in Qing and Republican China*, Kathryn Bernhardt and Philip C. C. Huang, eds., SUP, 1994; Zheng Qin, "Pursuing Perfection: Formation of the Qing code," *Modern China* 21.3: 310–344 (1995); Sybille Van der Sprenkel, *Legal Institutions in Manchu China: A Sociological Analysis*, Athlone Press, 1962.

[25] George T. Staunton, *Ta Tsing Leu Lee*, 1810; Ch'eng-wen, 1967. For a translation of the Nguyen code (1812), see P. L. F. Philastre, *Le Code annamite*, 2 vols., 1875; 2nd ed., 1909; rpnt., Ch'eng-wen, 1967. The Ngyuen code was identical with the Qing code of 1740 save for 38 articles left out.

[26] Guy Boulais, *Manuel du Code chinois*, 2 vols., Variétés sinologiques 55, Shanghai, 1924; rpnt., Taibei, 1957. Leaves out portions of the original without indication, but does include translations of the substatutes and also has the Chinese text on each page.

[27] *Du li cunyi* 讀例存疑, Huang Jingjia 黄靜嘉, ed., 5 vols., CMC, 1970.

On Qing legal training, see Weijen Chang, "Legal Education in Ch'ing China," in Elman and Woodside, 1994 (1.3.2), 229–39.

27.5　Administrative Law

Although the monographs on official posts, examinations, and law in the Tang and post-Tang Standard Histories contain useful overviews of administrative law, they are not mentioned in this section, which outlines instead the much more detailed sources that are increasingly available in the later dynasties.

None of the statutes of the Tang are extant, but no fewer than 715 of the original 1,546 articles were reconstructed from other Chinese and Japanese sources in an important work by Niida Noboru 仁井田陞 (1904–66).[28]

Fragmentary remains of the regulations and ordinances of the Tang have been preserved in other compilations and in their original form among the manuscripts discovered at Dunhuang and other sites in northwest China (46.3). For an English translation of one of these fragments as well as a useful brief introduction to the different types of Tang administrative law, see Denis Twitchett, "The Fragment of the T'ang Ordinances of the Department of Waterways Discovered at Tun-Huang," *AM* 6.1: 23–79 (1957).

The earliest extant collection of administrative law was the *Tang liudian* 唐六典 (Compendium of administrative law of the six divisions of the Tang bureaucracy).[29] It is based on all the different types

---

[28] Niida's famous work of scholarship is the *Tôryô shûi* 唐令拾遺 (Collected vestiges of the Tang statutes); Tokyo, 1933; 3rd rpnt. (reduced- size), 1993; rev. edition, Tôkyô daigaku, 1997; Chinese translation of original edition: *Tangling shiyi* 唐令拾遺, Changchun, 1989. For an evaluation and a study of the reconstructions of the *Tangling* and secondary scholarship, see Ikeda On 池田温, "*Tôrei*" 唐令, in *CHKSK*, 203–39.

[29] *Da Tang liudian* 大唐六典, 738; the best Song edition was preserved in Japan and edited by Konoe Iehiro 近衛家熙, *Kôtei Dai Tô rikuten* 考訂大唐六典, 1724; facs., *Da Tang liudian* 大唐六典, Wenhai, 1962, 1974. For an introduction, see Wang Chao, "The Six Codes of the Tang Dynasty: China's Earliest Administrative Code," *Social Sciences in China* 2: 113–50 (1986); and Robert des Rotours, "Le T'ang Lieou tien d'écrit-il exactement les institutions en usage sous la dynastie des Tang?" *JA* 263: 183–201 (1975). On the Japanese scholarship, see Okamura Ikuzô 奥村郁三, "*Dai Tô rikuten*" 大唐六典 in *CHKSK*, 263–80.

of administrative law as these were applied in all branches of the bureaucracy in the early eighth century.

During the Song, the division between penal and administrative
law was made even more sharp by separating out the codes (lü 律)
and their commentaries, substatutes, etc., and referring to administrative law under the fourfold division of edicts, statutes, regulations, and ordinances (chiling geshi 敕令格式). Definitions of these
four terms (as in other periods) were not strict, and it would be a
mistake to suppose that they represent exclusive categories.[30]

None of the Song statutes (inherited from the Tang) are extant,
but part of the most important compendium of Song administrative
law, the Qingyuan tiaofa shilei 慶元條法事類 of 1203, has been preserved and in it about two-thirds of the Qingyuan Statutes.[31] The
reason for making such a compilation is explained in the Songshi:
"As few literati are proficient in law, if they just try and read up on
it at the last moment, they are often cheated by the clerks. Now if
we compile a work by categories, literati officials can see all the pertinent laws when the need arises, and then the clerks cannot
cheat."[32]

Many of the edicts, statutes, ordinances, regulations, and substatutes of the Song, as of other periods, were excerpted or quoted
in compilations such as the Song huiyao 宋會要 (Collections of im

[30] Brian E. McKnight, "From Statute to Precedent: An Introduction to
Song Law and Its Transformation," in Law and the State in Traditional East
Asia: Six Studies on the Sources of East Asian Law, Brian E. McKnight, ed., UHP,
1987, 111–31.

[31] Qingyuan tiaofa shilei (Compendium of administrative law of the
Qingyuan period [1195–1200] arranged by categories), 80 juan (of which only
30 survive), 1203, Koten kenkyûkai photoprint of Seikadô Library copy,
1960. For an evaluation and a study of the editions and secondary scholarship,
see Kawamura Yasushi 川村康 "Keigen jôhô jirui to Sôdai no hôden" 慶元條法
事類と宋代の法典, in CHKSK, 331–60. There is a glossary to this important
text: Keigen jôhô jirui goi shûran 慶元條法事類語彙輯覽, Umehara Kaoru 梅
原郁, comp., Jinbun, 1990.

[32] Songshi quanwen xu Zizhi tongjian, ch. 26, as quoted in Chikusa Masaaki,
"Introduction to the Study of Five Dynasties and Sung History," Kenneth
Chase, tr., in Research Tools for the Study of Sung History (47.4.2), 134. See also
Brian E. McKnight, "Mandarins as Legal Experts: Professional Learning in
Sung China," in de Bary and Chaffee, 1989 (1.3.2), 493–516.

portant documents of the Song); see 25.1 and 47.1–2 for further references.

The main compendium of administrative law in the Yuan was the *Yuan dianzhang* 元典章 (Collection of statutes and substatutes of the Yuan), 1303; revised and expanded edition, 1322. See 48.5.1 for comments on this work.

The *Da Mingling* 大明令 (Great Ming statutes), 1368, is the first complete set to have survived.[33] They have been translated by Edward Farmer.[34] The Ming did not revive the Song practice of compiling important documents relating to government institutions and precedents in *huiyao*, but produced similar collections called *huidian* 會典 (collected statutes; 49.2). Several Ming handbooks of rules and regulations printed by individual branches of the administration are also extant.

During the Qing dynasty, no *ling* 令 were promulgated, but the Ming model of issuing detailed *huidian* 會典 (collected statutes) was followed. There were five editions of such compendia of administrative regulations, all of which were entitled *Da Qing huidian* 大清會典 (Collected statutes of the great Qing). Each also was published with supplementary precedents and regulations (*shili* 事例). A very large number of other works of early Qing administrative law as well as many editions of the regulations and substatutes of individual departments of the bureaucracy are extant (on these *buli* 部例, *zeli* 則例, as well as the *huidian*; see 50.5.2).

One of the unique features of Qing administrative law is that collections of provincial substatutes and cases (*shengli* 省例) relating only to a single province were printed. In addition, provincial yamens from the eighteenth century began issuing the regulations that they received from the central government in works usually called *dingli* 定例 (established regulations) or *tiaoli* 條例 (itemized regulations or substatutes), some of which have survived (50.5.2).

---

[33] The *Da Mingling* was included in vol. 1 of *Huang Ming zhishu*. The *Da Mingling* is much shorter than the previous ones are known to have been and was soon supplemented by such works as the *Zhusi zhizhang, Xian'gang shilei* 諸司職掌憲綱事類 (Handbook of government posts, Regulations for the censorate), 1371, and other similar works all included in the *Huang Ming zhishu*.

[34] Edward L. Farmer, *Zhu Yuanzhang and Early Ming Legislation: The Reordering of Chinese Society Following the Era of Mongol Rule*, Brill, 1995.

Detailed references to earlier fragments of statutes and compendia of administrative law as well as to the complete works of the later empire are given in Part V.

27.6   Guides and Handbooks

Handbooks (*guanzhen* 官箴) for local officials and clerks contain a great deal of interesting supplementary material on the operation of the bureaucracy at the local level.[35] Fragments of such a Qin guide are translated and annotated in Hulsewé (1985). Other fragments have since been excavated (44.4.2-3). Many more have survived from the Song.

Official Handbooks and Anthologies of Imperial China: A Descriptive and Critical Bibliography, Pierre-Etienne Will, ed., forthcoming. To include not only *guanzhen*, but also a range of manuals and tools for local officials and clerks as well as *gongdu* 公牘 (anthologies of administrative documents published to provide examples and models for administrators). When completed this fully annotated catalog with many hundreds of entries will replace previous more general catalogs such as Ma, 1935 (50.5.2), Zhang, 1976 (Chapter 27, *Introduction*).

Note that some of the authors of the legal handbooks also worked on the various central and local itemized substatutes of the Code and administrative regulations (50.2.3).

There are several indexes and collectanea of the handbooks available, for example, the first three items.

Sô-Gen kanshin sôgô sakuin 宋元官箴綜合索引 (Combined index to Song and Yuan *guanzhen*), Akagi Ryûji 赤城隆治 and Satake Yasuhiko 佐竹靖彦, comps., Kyûko, 1987.

Zhiyuan cuoyao 職源撮要. A late twelfth-century work on the Song bureaucracy and its origins; *Shokugen satsuyô sakuin* 職源撮要索引 (Index to the *Zhiyuan suoyao*), Tôyôshi kenkyûkai, 1956.

---

[35] On the administrative handbooks, see Etienne Balazs, "A Handbook of Local Administrative Practice of 1793," in *Political Theory and Administrative Reality in Traditional China*, SOAS, 1965, 50–75 (tr. mainly from Wang Huizu 王輝祖 [1731–1897], *Xuezhi yishuo* 學治臆説, 1793; rpnt. many times in the nineteenth century; incl. in *Guanzhenshu jicheng*). Also, Van der Sprenkel, 1962

Footnote continued on next page

Guanzhenshu jicheng 官箴書集成 (Collectanea of *guanzhen*), 10 vols., Huangshan, 1998. Reprint of 101 of titles (Tang, 1; Song, 5; Yuan, 2; Ming, 17; Qing, 73; Republic, 3).

Qingdai zhouxian gushi 清代州縣故事 (Informal materials on local government under the Qing dynasty), Cai Shenzhi 蔡申之, comp., HKCUP, 1968. Contains excerpts from many types of handbooks for local officials and secretaries.

There is an annotated translation of the important handbook by Huang Liuhong 黃六鴻, *Fuhui quanshu* 福惠全書, 1694: Djang Chu (Zhang Chu 章楚), *A Complete Book Concerning Happiness and Benevolence: A Manual for Local Magistrates in Seventeenth-Century China*, AUP, 1984.

Apart from such general guides to local administration, from the Qing there are also extant some practical handbooks containing regulations and procedures for secretarial assistants in charge of finance under the local magistrates (*qiangu* 錢穀). Some of them were printed, but they usually circulated in manuscript. The most famous one was Wang Youhuai, 王又槐, *Qiangu beiyao* 錢穀備要 (Essentials for financial secretaries), 1793.[36]

Handbooks of jurisprudence are also extant. They were written for magistrates as well as for the secretarial assistants in charge of legal matters (*xingming* 刑名). Many survive from the later empire.[37]

A Song handbook of forensic medicine for coroners, the *Xiyuanlu* 洗冤錄 (Manual of forensic medicine), 1247, by Song Ci 宋慈 (1186–1249) has been translated by Brian E. McKnight under the title *The Washing Away of Wrongs*.[38]

(27.4), 137–50; T'ung-tsu Ch'ü in his *Local Government in China Under the Ch'ing*, HUP, 1962, drew heavily on this type of source.

[36] Pierre-Etienne Will, "Administrative Handbooks Concerned with Fiscal Matters (*qiangu* 錢穀)," *Caizheng yu jindai lishi* 財政與近代歷史 (*Public Finance in Modern History*), Jinshisuo, 1999, 847–63.

[37] Langlois, *CHC*, vol. 8, contains in Appendix A the titles of extant Ming commentaries on the code and handbooks of jurisprudence (211–13). Appendix B (by Thomas J. Nimick) contains notes on over 20 Ming handbooks for local magistrates (214–20). Philip C. C. Huang, "From the Perspective of Magistrates' Handbooks," in *Civil Justice in China: Representation and Practice in the Qing*, SUP, 1996, 198–222.

[38] CCS, UMP, 1981. For a modern Chinese edition, see *Xiyuan jilu jiaoyi* 洗冤集錄校譯, Yang Fengkun 楊奉琨, ed., Qunzhong, 1980. The *Xiyuan jilu* was constantly revised and enlarged over the centuries; an official edition was

Footnote continued on next page

Ch'ing Administrative Terms: A Translation of the Terminology of the Six Boards with Explanatory Notes, E-tu Zen Sun (Ren Yidu 任以 都, tr., HUP, 1961, is another example of this type of source; it is useful for understanding and translating administrative terminology. It was originally written for Manchu officials to help them find their way around the Six Boards of the Qing government in Beijing and has often been reprinted: *Liubu chengyu* 六部成語, 1742.

27.7   Law in the Republic

During the Republic a modern Western legal code and system (borrowed from the German and Swiss models via Japan) was grafted onto the system inherited from the late Qing. Reform of the Qing system had already begun at the end of the dynasty. A new civil code was promulgated in 1929–31 (see Bernhardt and Huang, 1994, 1–12; cited below).

The Provisional Criminal Code of the Republic of China, The Commission on Extraterritoriality, Beijing, 1923.

The Civil Code of the Republic of China, Kelly and Walsh, 1930; rpnt., University Publications of America, 1976.

The Code of Civil Procedure of the Republic of China, Kuei Yu, tr., Commercial Press, 1935.

The Code of Criminal Procedure of the Republic of China, Shanghai: Municipal Goal Printing Department, 1935.

Civil Law in Qing and Republican China, Kathryn Bernhardt and Philip C. C. Huang, eds., SUP, 1994; SMC, 1997.

---

issued by the Board of Punishments in 1694 (*Lüliguan jiaozheng Xiyuanlu* 律例 館校正洗冤錄). Herbert Giles translated a version dating from 1843, "The *Hsi Yuan Lu* (洗冤錄) or Instructions to Coroners," *The China Review* 3: 30–172 (1874–75); rpnt. in the *Proceedings of the Royal Society of Medicine* 17: 59–107 (1924); rpnt. together with McKnight (1981), Taibei, 1982. See also Gwei-djen Lu and Joseph Needham, "A History of Forensic Medicine in China," *Medical History* 32: 357–400 (1988).

28

War

28.1 Army Administration

Studies on pre-Qin military affairs are able to use newly discovered epigraphic sources and archaeological artifacts to supplement transmitted texts.[1] Among the most striking examples are the two dozen or more Bronze Age war chariots excavated from tombs all over north China,[2] the 7,000 lifesize figures of warriors found guarding the first emperor's tomb,[3] and the Han border documents on wooden strips, which are mainly concerned with army administra-

---

[1] See "General Introduction and Historical Overview," in Ralph D. Sawyer, *Sun Tzu: Art of War*; also Raimund Theodor Kolb, *Die Infanterie im alten China: Ein Beitrag zur Militärgeschichte der Vor-Zhan-Guo-Zeit*, Mainz: Philipp von Zabern, 1991. These and other recent Western works are evaluated by Edward L. Shaughnessy, "Military Histories of Early China: A Review Article," *EC* 21 (1997), 159–82. See also *Jiaguxue yibai nian* 甲骨學一百年 (15.5), 490–505; Chen Enlin 陳恩林, *Xian-Qin junshi zhidu yanjiu* 先秦軍事制度研究, Jilin wenshi, 1992; Gao Rui 高鋭, *Zhongguo shanggu junshishi* 中國上古軍事史 (A history of Chinese military affairs in archaic times), Junshi kexue, 1995. Includes maps, chronology, and illustrations.

[2] Liancheng Lu , "Chariot and Horse Burials in Ancient China," *Antiquity* 67: 824–38 (1993); for the widespread view that the war chariot originated in Central Asia and was later adopted in China, Mesopotamia, and the Caucasus, see Edward Shaughnessy "Historic Perspectives on the Introduction of the Chariot into China," *HJAS* 48: 189–237 (1988), and *CHAC*, passim.

[3] Each of the three pits in which the terracotta warriors were buried was intended to show different aspects of the Qin army's order of battle. Pit 1 shows the battle formation; pit 2, the barracks, and pit 3, the command tent. Much therefore can be learned from these of Qin's successful military organization and tactics; see Wang Xueli 王學理, *Qin Shihuang bingmayong bowuguan* 秦俑專題研究 (Special studies on the Qin terracotta figures), San-Qin, 1994. Has an extensive summary in English, 615–52; *Qin yongxue yanjiu* 秦俑學研究 (Research on the Qin terracotta figures), Qin shihuang bingmayong bowu guan, ed., Shaanxi renmin jiaoyu, 1996. Collection of over 200 research papers.

tion (44.4.3). For imperial China, the Standard Histories are a good starting point; eight of them have monographs on *bingwei* 兵衛,[4] *yiwei* 儀衛 (imperial guards),[5] or *yingwei* 營衛 (border guards).[6] Other monographs in the Standard Histories (for example, on law or on financial administration) also deal with the army.[7] In the Qing more specialized sources become available, such as the histories of campaigns (*fanglüe* 方略) and archive documents (28.2).

For a brief but innovative introduction to ancient military language, see Zhu Liangcai 諸良才, *Zhongguo gudai junyu yanjiu daolun* 中古代軍語研究導論 (Guide to research on ancient military language), Zhejiang jiaoyu, 1998.

28.2   The Art of War (to 1840)

There is a very large group of writings which in the old catalogs was grouped under the general heading of Military Experts (*bingjia* 兵家), a subbranch of the Philosphers' branch (*zibu* 子部) in the fourfold bibliographic classification (9.3). For a modern heavily annotated catalog, see Xu Baolin 許保林, *Zhongguo bingshu zhijianlu* 中國兵書知見錄.[8] This arranges 3,380 works by period, including collected biographies of famous generals, histories of imperial and other campaigns, techniques of warfare (including weapons), strategy and tactics (cavalry and infantry), and accounts of sieges (tech-

---

[4] *Xin Tangshu* (whose monograph on the army is the subject of a scholarly study and translation by Robert des Rotours; see 46.1); also those in the *Songshi, Liaoshi, Jinshi, Yuanshi, Xin Yuanshi, Mingshi, Qingshigao.*

[5] *Xin Tangshu*; also *Songshi, Liaoshi, Jinshi*, and *Mingshi.*

[6] *Liaoshi.*

[7] *Zhongguo junshi jingjishi* 中國軍事經濟史 (Economic history of Chinese military affairs), Zhang Zhenlong 張振龍, ed. in chief, Lantian, 1990. The first 400 pages cover from earliest times to the Taiping. The sources used are the obvious ones: monographs on the army and on financial administration from the Standard Histories and encyclopaedias of government.

[8] *Zhongguo bingshu zhijianlu* (Record of Chinese works on warfare), Jiefangjun, 1988. Liu Shenning 劉申寧, *Zhongguo bingshu zongmu* 中國兵書總目 (Comprehensive catalog of Chinese works on warfare), Guofang daxue, 1990, 1993, lists the location of no fewer than 4,221 works on the military found in 161 libraries and collections in China and nine in the rest of the world. Arrangement is by period. There is a stroke-count index.

niques of city defense). Altogether 2,308 extant works are discussed. References to modern research are given.

The most famous Chinese work on strategy and tactics, Sun Wu 孫武, *Sunzi bingfa* 孫子兵法 (Sunzi: the art of war) dates from the Spring and Autumn period. It has been translated into Western languages almost as many times as Laozi's *Daodejing* (Napoleon is said to have carried on his campaigns the first European translation of *Sunzi*, that done by the Jesuit Jean-Joseph Marie Amiot [1718–93], Paris, 1772). There are several new translations, plus also of the recently discovered manual by his descendant Sun Bin (*Sun Bin bingfa* 孫臏兵法), which also dates from the Warring States. The *Sunzi* 孫子 and three other militarists are in *ICS Concordance* 11.[9]

There is a collectanea of 220 traditional works on warfare: *Zhongguo bingshu jicheng* 中國兵書集成.[10]

For heavily annotated chronological tables of all known battles in Chinese history from the earliest days to 1911, see

Lidai zhanzheng nianbiao 歷代戰爭年表 (Tables of Chinese historic battles), 2 vols., Jiefangjun, 1985–86. The tables are annexed as a supplementary volume to the general history, *Zhongguo junshishi* 中國軍事史 (History of Chinese military affairs), 6 vols., Jiefangjun, 1983–91. Each volume covers the history of a different topic, e.g., military institutions (vol. 3); strategists (vol. 5). An even more thorough coverage is in *Zhongguo junshi tongshi* 中國軍事通史 (General

---

[9] *Bingshu sizhong zhuzi suoyin* 兵書四種逐字索引 (Concordance to four military manuals), *ICS Concordance* 11, HK: Shangwu, 1992. Apart from *Sunzi*, the three other manuals are *Weiliaozi* 尉繚子, *Wuzi* 吳子, and *Simafa* 司馬法. On the text and editions of *Sunzi bingfa*, see Gawlikowski and Loewe in *ECHBG*, 446–455. Note Roger T. Ames, *Sun-tzu: The Art of Warfare. The First English Translation Incorporating the Yin-ch'üeh shan Texts*, Ballantine, 1993. The text of Sun Bin had been lost since the end of the Han and was rediscovered written on bamboo strips along with *Sunzi* in a tomb excavated in Shandong in 1972. D. C. Lau and Roger T. Ames have translated it: *Sun Bin: the Art of Warfare*, Ballantine, 1996.

Ralph D. Sawyer, *The Seven Military Classics of China*, Westview, 1993, not only translates these works but has much interesting commentary. For the historical background to the military manuals of the Warring States period, see Mark Edward Lewis, *Sanctioned Violence in Early China*, SUNY, 1990, Chapter 3, 97–135.

[10] *Zhongguo bingshu jicheng* (Collectanea of Chinese books on war), 50 vols., Jiefangjun and Liao-Shen, 1987– .

history of the Chinese military), Zhu Dawei 朱大渭 and Zhang Wen-
qiang 張文強, eds. in chief, 17 vols., Junshi kexue, 1998.

There are several dictionaries of Chinese military history. One is
Zhongguo gudai junshi da cidian 中國古代軍事大辭典[11]

On Chinese strategic culture, see Alastair Iain Johnson, *Cultural
Realism: Strategic Culture and Grand Strategy in Chinese History*,
PUP, 1995; and on the role of defensive border walls, see Arthur
Waldron, *The Great Wall of China: From History to Myth*, CUP,
1990; paperback, 1992.

For a thorough survey of military technology and weapons
from the Stone Age to the invention of gunpowder, see Yang Hong,
Weapons in Ancient China, Kexue, 1992 (part English translation of
Chinese original, Yang Hong 楊泓, *Zhongguo gu bingqi luncong* 中
國古兵器論叢 [Collected articles on ancient Chinese weapons],
Wenwu, 1980; enl., 1985); Herbert Franke, "Sources on Chinese
Military Technology and History" in *Chinese Ways in Warfare*,
Frank A. Kierman and John K. Fairbank, eds., HUP, 1973, 195–
201, and the two *SCC* volumes investigating military technology.[12]

For a study of strategic geography, see Zhang Xiaosheng 張曉
生 *Bingjia bizheng zhi di* 兵家必爭之地,[13] and on the history of the
Chinese navy (apart from the Ming and the late Qing, a relatively
neglected subject), see Zhang Tieniu 張鐵牛, *Zhongguo gudai haijunshi* 中國古代海軍史.[14]

There are a few histories of military campaigns in Western languages such as Herbert Franke, *Studien und Texte zur Kriegsgeschi-
chte der südlichen Sungzeit*, Harrassowitz, 1987.

Many of the Qing *fanglüe* 方略 (Histories of imperial campaigns) have been reprinted in a special collectanea: *Zhongguo fanglüe*

[11] *Zhongguo gudai junshi da cidian* (Great dictionary of military affairs in
ancient China), Wang Zheyue 王者悅, ed., Guofang daxue, 1991.

[12] *Military Technology: Missiles and Sieges* (*SCC*, vol. 5, part 6); *Military
Technology: The Gunpowder Epic* (vol. 5, Part 7).

[13] *Bingjia bizheng zhi di* (Land for which the strategist must fight), Jiefangjun, 1987.

[14] *Zhongguo gudai haijunshi* (History of China's navy in ancient times),
Bayi, 1993; Also, *Ershisishi de haiyang ziliao* 二十四史的海洋資料 (Materials on
the seas and oceans in the 24 histories), Liu Pei 劉佩 et al., eds., Haiyang, 1995.

congshu 中國方略叢書, 1ˢᵗ and 2ⁿᵈ series, Taibei, 1968–71.[15] The historian and geographer Wei Yuan 魏源 (1794–1856) compiled a general study of Qing military campaigns from the rise of the Manchu to the eve of the Opium War. It was entitled *Shengwuji* 聖武記.[16] He wrote in the Preface, "[The book] is some 400 *juan* in length, so the gentry only stare at it with glazed eyes. Meanwhile the old generals are gradually fading away. How then will later generations be instructed? It is for this reason that I compiled this work."

28.3 *Post-1840 Wars*

Copious materials from the archives on foreign encroachments and wars in the nineteenth century have been published, starting with the Opium War:

Opium War

Yapian zhanzheng dang'an shiliao 鴉片戰爭檔案史料 (Historical materials from the archives on the Opium War), Yishiguan, ed., 7 vols., Shanghai renmin and Tianjin guji, 1987–92.

Yapian zhanzheng zai Zhejiang 鴉片戰爭在浙江 (The Opium War in Zhejiang), Yishiguan, ed., Zhejiang renmin, 1991.

Yapian zhanzheng zai Zhoushan shiliao xuanbian 鴉片戰爭在舟山史料選編 (Selected historical materials from the archives on the Opium War in Zhoushan), Yishiguan and Zhoushanshi Shekelian 舟山市社科連, eds., Zhejiang renmin, 1992.

Yapian zhanzheng wenxueji 鴉片戰爭文學集 (Collection of literary materials for the study of the Opium War), 2 vols., Zhonghua, 1957.

Lin Zexu xin'gao 林則徐信稿 (Draft letters of Lin Zexu), Huang Zede 黃澤德, ed., Fujian renmin, 1985.

Lin Zexuji (zougao riji gongdu) 林則徐集 (奏稿日記公牘) (Lin Zexu collection: draft memorials, diary, public documents), Zhongshan daxue lishixi, ed., 4 vols., Zhonghua, 1962–65. Of which the fourth vol. is *Lin Zexu zougao gongdu riji bubian* 林則徐奏稿公牘日記補編 (Addit-

---

[15] See "The Office of Military Archives," in Beatrice Bartlett, *Monarchs and Ministers: The Grand Council in Mid-Ch'ing China, 1723–1820*, UCP, 1991, 225–28.

[16] *Shengwuji* (Record of the campaigns of the holy warriors), 1842; Zhonghua, 1984.

ions to Lin Zexu's draft memorials, public documents, and diary),
Chen Xiqi 陳錫祺, ed. in chief, Zhongshan daxue, 1985.

Zhejiang yapian zhanzheng shiliao 浙江鴉片戰爭史料 (Historical materials on the Opium War in Zhejiang), Yishiguan and Ningboshi shehui
kexuejie lianhehui, eds., Ningbo, 1997.

Di'erci Yapian zhanzheng 第二次鴉片戰爭 (The second Opium War), 6
vols., Gugong Ming-Qing dang'anbu, ed., Shanghai renmin, 1978–79.
In the series *Zhongguo jindaishi ziliao congkan* 中國近代史資料叢刊.

For other materials on foreign wars in the nineteenth century, see
50.2.7. For warlords and the military in the twentieth, see 51.7 and
51.9.3.

28.3   Uprisings (Han–1911)

In the 1950s, historical judgments were reversed and the study of
court politics and culture was pushed into the background as the
new regime officially proclaimed that "peasant uprisings were the
major driving force of the development of China's feudal society."
Accordingly, "peasant uprisings" (*nongmin qiyi* 農民起義) became a
top priority for historians and a large number of studies with sup-
porting source materials were published.[17] As most soldiers fighting
for or against any traditional state were generally peasants, the category "peasant uprising" can cover a wide range of disturbance.
There is hardly a "peasant uprising" of any size in Chinese history
for which there is not now a volume or several volumes of source
materials and also a large secondary literature on individual rebellions and peasant uprisings (several of which are listed below).

Qin Han—Nan-Bei Chao

Qin Han nongmin zhanzheng shiliao huibian 秦漢農民戰爭史料彙編
(Collection of historical materials on peasant wars in the Qin and
Han), An Zuozhang 安作璋, ed., Zhonghua, 1982.

Wei Jin Nan-Bei Chao nongmin zhanzheng shiliao huibian 魏晉南北朝農
民戰爭史料彙編 (Collection of historical materials on peasant wars

---

[17] James P. Harrison, *The Communists and Chinese Peasant Rebellions: A Study
in the Rewriting of History*, Atheneum, 1968.

in the Wei, Jin, Nan-Bei Chao), Zhang Zexian 張澤咸 and Zhu Da-wei 朱大渭, eds., 2 vols., Zhonghua, 1980. Contains excerpts from Standard Histories, *biji*, and funeral tablets.

Sui—Tang

Suimo nongmin zhanzheng shiliao huibian 隋末農民戰爭史料彙編 (Collection of historical materials on peasant wars at the end of the Sui), Wang Yongxing 王永興, ed., Zhonghua, 1980. Contains excerpts from the Standard Histories and the *Tong jian*.

Tang Wudai nongmin zhanzheng shiliao huibian 唐五代農民戰爭史料彙編 (Collection of historical materials on peasant wars in the Tang and Five Dynasties), Zhang Zexian 張澤咸, ed., 2 vols., Zhonghua, 1979. Contains excerpts from Standard Histories, *biji*, funeral inscriptions, and *wenji*.

Song—Yuan

Liang Song nongmin zhanzheng shiliao huibian 兩宋農民戰爭史料彙編 (Collection of historical materials on peasant wars in the two Songs), He Zhuqi 何竹淇, ed., 4 vols., Zhonghua, 1976.

Songdai sanci nongmin qiyi shiliao huibian 宋代三次農民起義史料彙編 (Collection of historical materials on the three peasant uprisings in the Song), Su Jinyuan 蘇金源 and Li Chunpu 李春圃, eds., Zhonghua, 1963.

Yuandai nongmin zhanzheng shiliao huibian 元代農民戰爭史料彙編 (Collection of historical materials on peasant wars in the Yuan), part 1, Yang Na 楊訥 and Chen Gaohua 陳高華, eds., Zhonghua, 1985. Covers uprisings between 1234 and 1350; part 2, Yang Po 楊伯 and Chen Gaohua 陳高華, eds., 2 vols., 1985, includes excerpts from 187 sources; part 3, Chen Gaohua 陳高華, ed., 1985.

Ming—Qing

For the Ming, and even more so for the Qing, there are the rich resources of the archives.[18] For example:

---

[18] Susan Naquin, "True Confessions: Criminal Interrogations as Sources for Ch'ing History," *National Palace Museum Bulletin* 11.1: 1–17 (1976); and the same author's *Millenarian Rebellion in China: The Eight Trigrams Uprising of 1813*, YUP, 1976. Based on documents relating to cases involving religious rebels (*jiaofei an* 教誹案) and their confessions (*gongci* 供詞).

Mingmo nongmin qiyi shiliao 明末農民起義史料 (Historical materials on peasant uprisings at the end of the Ming), Zheng Tianting 鄭天挺 et al., eds., Kaiming, 1952. Contains 220 documents dating from 1627 to 1648 dealing with the uprising of Li Zicheng. See James B. Parsons, *The Peasant Rebellions of the Late Ming Dynasty*, UAP, 1970.

Qingdai qianqi Miaomin qiyi dang'an shiliao huibian 清代前期苗民起義檔案史料彙編 (Archival historical materials on the Miao people's armed uprisings in the early Qing dynasty), Yishiguan and Guizhousheng dang'an, eds., 3 vols., Guangming ribao, 1987. The Miao are perhaps more familiar by the Vietnamese name of Hmong or Mong.

Kangxi Qianlong shiqi chengxiang renmin fankang douzheng ziliao 康熙乾隆時期城鄉人民反抗斗爭資料 (Materials on uprisings by city and country folk during the Kangxi and Qianlong periods), Zhongguo renmin daxue, Qingshi yanjiusuo et al., eds., 2 vols., Zhonghua, 1979.

Bailianjiao (1796–1804)

Qing zhongqi wusheng Bailianjiao qiyi ziliao 清中期五省白蓮教起義資料 (Materials on the White Lotus uprising in five provinces in the Qing), Lishisuo, ed., 5 vols., Jiangsu renmin, 1981–82.

Taiping Heavenly Kingdom (1851–64)

Wang Qingcheng 王慶成, "Taiping tianguo de wenxian de xingcheng he yanmo 太平天國文獻的形成和漂没" (The appearance and disappearance of Taiping heavenly kingdom documents) chapter 1 of idem, *Taiping tianguo de wenxian he lishi: Haiwai xin wenxian kanbu he wenxian shishi yanjiu* 太平天國的文獻和歷史海外新文獻刊布和文獻時事研究 (The sources and history of the Taiping heavenly kingdom: publication of new documents and research on them), Shehui kexue wenxian, 1993, 1–59. This chapter contains an overall evaluation of the primary sources produced by and about the Taipings.

Qing zhengfu zhenya Taiping tianguo dang'an shiliao 清政府鎮壓太平天國檔案史料 (Historical materials from the archives on the Qing government's suppression of the Taiping heavenly kingdom), Yishiguan, ed., 20 vols., Shehui kexue wenxian and Guangming ribao, 1990–94; 6 vols., Sheke wenxian, 1996; rpnt., 26 vols., Sheke wenxian, 1999.

Taiping tianguo 太平天國 (Taiping heavenly kingdom), Wang Zhongmin 王重民, Xiang Da 向達, and Zhongguo shixuehui, eds., 8 vols., Shenzhou guogangshe, 1952–53; Shanghai renmin, 1957. Important collection of Taiping historical materials. In the series *Zhongguo jindaishi ziliao congkan* 中國近代史資料叢刊.

Taiping tianguo cidian 太平天國辭典 (Dictionary of the Taiping heavenly kingdom), Guo Yisheng 郭毅生, ed. in chief, Shuhu kexue, 1995.

Taiping tianguo ciyu huishi 太平天國詞語匯釋 (Glossary of Taiping vocabulary), Shi Shi 史式 and Wu Liangzuo 吳良祚, comps., Guangxi renmin, 1993. Special expressions used in Taiping documents, including religious, dialect, spoken language, new characters, and neologisms. There is a *pinyin* index. Replaces earlier work by Shi Shi published by Sichuan renmin, 1984.

Taiping tianguo lishi dituji 太平天國歷史地圖集 (Collection of maps on the history of the Taiping heavenly kingdom), Guo Yisheng 郭毅生, ed., Ditu, 1989. Contains 132 maps giving details of Taiping campaigns. There is a commentary, photographs and reproductions of some of the maps used by the Taipings.

Taiping tianguo shiliao 太平天國史料 (Historical materials on the Taiping heavenly kingdom), Jin Yufu 金毓黻 et al., comps., Kaiming, 1950; rev. ed., Zhonghua, 1959.

Taiping tianguo wenshu huibian 太平天國文書彙編 (Collection of despatches of the Taiping heavenly kingdom), Taiping tianguo lishi bowuguan, ed., Zhonghua, 1979. 418 Taiping documents.

Taiping tianguo yinshu 太平天國印書 (Facsimile reproductions of Taiping heavenly kingdom publications), Taiping tianguo lishi bowuguan, comp., 20 vols., 1961; Jiangsu renmin, 1979.

Taiping tianguo ziliao huibian 太平天國資料彙編 (Collection of materials on the Taiping heavenly kingdom), Taiping tianguo lishi bowuguan, ed., 2 parts in 3 vols., Zhonghua, 1979–80. General descriptions and by province.

Tianfu tianxiong shengzhi 天父天兄聖旨 (The sacred declarations of the Heavenly Father and Elder Brother), Wang Qingcheng 王慶成, ed., Liaoning renmin, 1986. From the early period of the movement, from which few materials survive, hence their value.

Yanjiu Taiping tianguoshi zhushu zongmu 研究太平天國史著述總目 (Comprehensive catalog of research and materials on Taiping history), Jiang Bingzheng 姜秉正, ed., Shumu wenxian, 1984. Includes Chinese and foreign-language materials on the Taipings appearing between 1850 and 1981. There is an author index.

Zhongguo dang'an wenxian cidian 中國檔案文獻辭典, 1994 (Box 6, Chapter 20) contains descriptions of a further 17 published collections of source materials on the Taipings.

Ssu-yü Teng, *Historiography of the Taiping Rebellion*, Harvard East Asian monographs, HUP, 1962.

Franz Michael and Chung-li Chang, *The Taiping Rebellion: History and Documents*, 3 vols., UWP, 1966–71.

Vincent Shih, *The Taiping Ideology, Its Sources, Interpretations and Influences*, UWP, 1967.

Jonathan D. Spence, *God's Chinese Son: The Taiping Heavenly Kingdom of Hong Xiuquan*, Norton, 1996. Contains an extensive and up-to-date bibliography of Chinese and Western sources.

Nian (1851–68)

Nianjun 捻軍 (The Nian army), Zhongguoshi xuehui, 6 vols., Shanghai renmin, 1957. In the series *Zhongguo jindaishi ziliao congkan* 中國近代史資料叢刊. See Ssu-yü Teng, *The Nien Army and Their Guerrilla Warfare, 1851–1868*, Mouton, 1961; Elizabeth Perry, *Chinese Perspectives on the Nien Rebellion*, Sharpe, 1981.

Xiaodao (1853–55)

Fujian Shanghai Xiaodaohui dang'an shiliao huibian 福建上海小刀會檔案史料彙編 (Collection of historical materials on the Small Sword Society in Fujian and Shanghai), Yishiguan and Shanghai shifan daxue, eds., Fujian renmin, 1993.

Much of the Qing archival material has been put on microfilm (50.2.1).

Muslim (Second Half of Nineteenth Century)

There were a large number of major Muslim uprisings in the nineteenth century: in Yunnan, 1856–73; in Shaanxi and Gansu, 1862–78; in northern Xinjiang, 1873–78; and in the Gansu and Qinghai border regions, 1895; see, for example:

Huimin qiyi 回民起義 (The Muslim uprisings), Bai Shouyi 白壽彝, ed., 4 vols., Shenzhou guoguangshe, 1953. In the series *Zhongguo jindaishi ziliao congkan* 中國近代史資料叢刊. See Wen-djang Chu, *The Moslem Rebellon in North-West China, 1862–1878: A Study of Government Minority Policy*, Mouton, 1966.

Yihetuan (1898–1900)

Yihetuan 義和團 (The Boxers, lit. "militia united in righteousness"), Zhongguoshi xuehui, ed., 4 vols., Shanghai renmin, 1957. In the series *Zhongguo jindaishi ziliao congkan* 中國近代史資料叢刊. See Paul A. Cohen, *History in Three Keys: The Boxers as Event, Experience, and Myth*, Col. UP, 1997, and for a useful reference, *Yihetuan da cidian* 義和團大辭典 (Dictionary of the Boxers), Miao Yizhong 廖一中, ed. in chief, Shehui kexue, 1995. Contains 1,447 entries.

Yihetuan yundong shiliao congbian 義和團運動史料叢編 (Collection of historical materials on the Yihetuan movement), Beijing daxue lishixi, Zhongguo jindaishi jiaoyanshi, ed., 2 vols., Zhonghua, 1964.

Yihetuan dang'an shiliao 義和團檔案史料 (Historical materials on the Yihetuan from the archives), Guojia dang'anju, Ming-Qing dang'anguan, ed., 2 vols., Zhonghua, 1959, 1979.

Dongbei Yihetuan dang'an shiliao 東北義和團檔案史料 (Archival historical materials on the Yihetuan in the northeast), Liaoning shehui kexueyuan, ed., Liaoning renmin, 1981.

Shandong Yihetuan anjuan 山東義和團案卷 (Archival files on Yihetuan cases in Shandong), Shekeyuan, Jindaishi yanjiusuo, eds., 2 vols., Qi-Lu, 1980.

Sichuan jiao'an yu Yihequan 四川教案與義和拳 (Missionary cases in Sichuan and the Yihetuan), Sichuansheng Dang'anguan, ed., Sichuan renmin, 1985.

Yihetuan yuanliu shiliao 義和團源流史料 (Historical materials on the origins of the Yihetuan), Lu Jingqi 陸景琪 et al., eds., Renmin daxue, 1980.

Bibliography

Protest and Crime in China: A Bibliography of Secret Associations, Popular Uprisings, Peasant Rebellions, Ssu-yü Teng, comp., Garland, 1981, lists nearly 4,000 citations to books and articles (1,275 of them are in Western languages and 2,725 in Chinese and Japanese). It is arranged alphabetically by author, with cross-references to titles, and has a subject index.

Frederic Wakeman, Jr., "Rebellion and Revolution: The Study of Popular Movements in Chinese History," *JAS* 36.2: 201–327 (1977).

Popular Movements and Secret Societies in China, 1840–1950, Jean Chesneaux, ed., SUP, 1972, "Bibliography," 279–88.

On warfare in the first half of the twentieth century, see 51.7–9.

IV

OTHER PRIMARY SOURCES

29

Myth and Religion

This chapter covers myth (29.1), religion in general (29.2), popular beliefs (29.3), Daoist works (29.4), and Buddhist works (29.5), including those of Tibetan Buddhism (29.5.1). There are also short sections on Islam (29.6) and Christianity and Judaism (29.7). Sources on the religions of the non-Han peoples are discussed in Chapter 40.

29.1 Myth

Myths (*shenhua* 神話) are the basis for understanding of any society for three main reasons: (1) they reveal the values and beliefs not only of the earliest peoples who lived in that society, but also of later generations who codified and passed down the elaborate mythology that generations of children learned from their mothers and wet nurses;[1] (2) an understanding of myth is essential in decoding symbols and art motifs (which can themselves provide in all periods, especially in the earliest ones for which other sources may be lacking, important keys to the understanding of values and beliefs);[2] (3) the relationship of myth and history, of fiction and fact, lie at the heart of our understanding of the credibility of the earliest written records.

Sorting out what was genuinely an ancient myth from later inventions is no easy matter. In China, the work began in the twentieth century with the Yigupai 疑古派 (Doubting Antiquity School)

---

[1] On myth, I have drawn heavily on Anne M. Birrell, "Review Article: Studies in Chinese Myth Since 1970: An Appraisal," Parts I and II, *History of Religions*, 39.4: 380–93 (1994); 39.5: 70–94 (1994). See also Whalen Lai, "Recent PRC Scholarship on Chinese Myths," *Asian Folklore Studies* 53.1: 151–63 (1994).

[2] K. C. Chang, *Art, Myth and Ritual: The Path to Political Authority in Ancient China*, HUP, 1983.

led by Gu Jiegang 顧頡剛. Gu argued that China's earliest history was based on myths, with each successive layer adding more and more spurious detail to remoter and remoter ages in the past (*cenglei de zaocheng de Zhongguo gushi* 層累地造成的中國古史). He believed that these later accretions could be stripped away (thus reducing the length of China's history from 5,000 to 3,000 years) and analyzed as mythology.[3]

The first modern study of China's early myths using the findings of archaeologists was made by Xu Xusheng 徐旭生, *Zhongguo gushi de chuanshuo shidai* 中國古史的傳說時代.[4]

The best introductions to Chinese mythology in English are Anne M. Birrell, *Chinese Mythology: An Introduction*, Johns Hopkins Univ. Press, 1993, and Derk Bodde, "Myths of Ancient China" in *Mythologies of the Ancient World*, S. N. Kramer, ed., Doubleday, 1961, 369–408. The contributions of Japanese studies of Chinese mythology are summarized in Wang Xiaolian 王孝廉, *Zhongguo de shenhua yu chuanshuo* 中國的神話與傳說 (Chinese myths and legends), Lianjing, 1977.

Interpretations of Chinese society were until recently influenced by Confucian orthodoxy, which paid little attention to popular religious beliefs. Not a few scholars even claimed that the Chinese were basically not a religious people and had no creation myths. Nothing could be further from the truth.

In "A Classification of Shang and Chou Myths," K. C. Chang examines the schemes proposed by previous scholars (up to 1961) and offers his own: (1) nature myths; (2) the world of gods and its

---

[3] The most influential works of the Yigupai were published in the series *Gushibian* 古史辨 (Debates on ancient history), 7 vols., 1926–41; several reprints, including Shanghai guji, 1982. In the *Preface* to vol. 1 of *Gushibian*, the young Gu wrote an account of his life up to that time (he was 33 in 1926). It has been translated under the title *The Autobiography of a Chinese Historian*, Arthur W. Hummel, tr., Brill, 1931; Taibei, 1966 and 1972. On Gu, see Laurence A. Schneider, *Ku Chieh-kang and China's New History: Nationalism and the Quest for Authoritative Traditions*, UCP, 1976.

[4] *Zhongguo gushi de chuanshuo shidai* (The legendary period of ancient Chinese history), 1943; rev. edition, Kexue, 1960, rpnt., Wenwu, 1985. The first Western study was Marcel Granet, *Danses et légendes de la Chine ancienne*, 3rd ed., corrected and annotated by Rémi Mathieu, PUF, 1994 (1926).

separation from the world of humans; (3) natural calamities and human saviors; and (4) heroes and their descendants.[5]

The corpus of ancient Chinese myths is scattered in the written texts of the sixth to first centuries BC. These have been collected in Yuan Ke 袁珂 (1916–), *Shenhua xuanyi baiti* 神話選議百題 and in Yuan Ke and Zhou Ming 周明, eds., *Zhongguo shenhua ziliao cuibian* 中國神話資料萃編[6] (see also Yuan [1998] cited below).

Some of the main mythological texts have been translated, for example, the *Shanhaijing* 山海經 (Classic of mountains and seas), a mythogeography, parts of which were written in the Warring States period and part in the Han.[7] In the words of Ann Birrell, it "constitutes a fabulous bestiary, a botanical thesaurus, a dictionary of natural science, a catalog of geological substances and rare jewels, a guide to portents and omens, a register of medical ailments, an apothecary's handbook, and a medley of folkloric and ethnological material."[8] The *Huainanzi* has been partly translated into English (Table 26, 19.2). Another important later source on myths, the fourth-century AD *Bowu zhi* 博物志 (The treatise on research into nature), has been fully translated.[9]

The interpretation of the evidence found in ancient tombs and other archaeological artifacts have provided powerful stimuli to the

---

[5] K. C. Chang, *Early Chinese Civilization: Anthropological Perspectives*, HUP, 1976, 149–73. Also Chang (1983).

[6] *Shenhua xuanyi baiti* (One hundred topics in Chinese mythology: an anthology with notes and translation), Shanghai guji, 1980, and in Yuan Ke and Zhou Ming, eds., *Zhongguo shenhua ziliao cuibian* (A source book of Chinese myth texts), Sichuan sheng Shekeyuan, 1985. Michael Puett argues that the textual narratives assembled by Yuan Ke are part of a Warring States debate, not traces of an oral mythology as Yuan advocates; see "Early Chinese Creation Narratives," *HJAS* 58.2: 425–79 (1998).

[7] See Rémi Mathieu, *Étude sur la mythologie et l'ethnologie de la Chine ancienne*, 2 vols., Collège de France, Institut des Hautes Etudes Chinoises, 1983, for an annotated translation (vol. 1) and index (vol. 2). *ICS Concordance* 23 replaces the earlier *CFC Index* 9. The best modern, annotated edition is Yuan Ke 袁珂, *Shanhaijing jiaozhu* 山海經校注 (*Shanhaijing*, collated and annotated), Shanghai guji, 1980, 1983; Yuan Ke, *Shanhaijing jiaoyi* 山海經校譯 (The *Shanhaijing*, collated and translated), Shanghai guji, 1985.

[8] Anne M. Birrell (1994), 387.

[9] Roger Greatrex, *The Bowu Zhi: An Annotated Translation*, Stockholm: Orientalska Studier, 1987. ICS *Concordance* 21, forthcoming.

study of ancient Chinese myths.[10] Ethnographic evidence drawn from the study of the beliefs of China's minority peoples is also sometimes used as a means of tracing the origin and meaning of Han myths.[11]

There are several dictionaries of Chinese mythology. The earliest, by E. T. C. Werner, mixes myths and legends from all periods.[12] More to the point is Wolfgang Münke, *Mythologie der chinesischen Antike*, Frankfort: Peter Lang, 1998, and the more detailed:

Zhongguo shenhua da cidian 中國神話大辭典 (Dictionary of Chinese mythology), Yuan Ke 袁柯, ed., Sichuan cishu, 1998. The first part of this dictionary consists of 3,006 entries covering Han mythology (1–680) and is drawn from the earlier *Zhongguo shenhua chuanshuo cidian* 中國神話傳說辭典 (A dictionary of Chinese myth and legend), Yuan Ke, ed., Shanghai cishu, 1985; the second part covers the myths of 56 ethnic minorities (680–1051). There are detailed tables of contents arranged by stroke count, theme, and ethnic minority (1–120).

29.2 Religion

To the extent that historians are concerned with questions of value and belief, they cannot afford to ignore the history of Chinese religion in all its many forms—popular or elite, public or private, formal

---

[10] For a wide-ranging summary of archaeological and pictographic evidence bearing on primitive beliefs, using insights from anthropology, astronomy and history, see Lu Sixian 陸思賢, *Shenhua kaogu* 神話考古 (The archaeology of myths), Wenwu, 1995. This work is more rigorous than the rapidly expanding number of fascinating but surely fanciful interpretations of the patterns and symbols on Neolithic utensils.

[11] See, for example, Xiao Bing 蕭兵, *Chuci yu shenhua* 楚辭與神話 (Myth and the *Songs of Chu*), Jiangsu guji, 1986. The author finds traces of ancient myths in the cultures of many of today's minority peoples in south China.

[12] *A Dictionary of Chinese Mythology*, Kelly and Walsh, 1932; Taibei, 1961. A collection of popular beliefs in late nineteenth- and early twentieth-century China, but useless for earlier periods. The same could be said of Henri Doré, *Recherches sur les superstitions en Chine*, 18 vols., Shanghai, 1911–38; English tr. by M. Kennelly, *Researches into Chinese Superstitions*, 5 vols., T'usewei Press, 1914–18; rpnt., Taibei, 5 vols., 1966–67. This was based on data originally published by the Jesuit scholar Pierre Hoang (Huang Bolu 黃伯祿) under the title *Jishuo quanzhen* 集說詮真, Shanghai, 1879; continuation, 1880, 1884.

or informal, common or esoteric, home-grown or imported, secret or open.

In China itself, as the this-worldly influence of the Confucian state ideology and examination system for officials fades ever further into the past, and after the failure of the state ideologies that succeeded it, there is a growing appreciation of the importance of religions, both as systems of belief and as a body of ritual and practice embedded in every nook and cranny of daily life. For the same reasons, the earlier Western interpretations of Chinese history and culture based on the self-view of Confucian officials that theirs was an entirely rationalistic view of the world is now also increasingly questioned.[13]

Archaeology is providing huge amounts of new data from tombs, on oracle bones, and in medical and mantic texts on silk and bamboo on early religious beliefs and practices, particularly in the pre-Qin period.[14]

One interesting trend is the reinterpretation of the major pre-Qin classics using anthropological analysis, an approach pioneered by Marcel Granet (1884–1940) in the 1920s. The difference today is that there is much more information available from the archaeological record. See, for example, the titles in the series *Zhongguo wenhua de renleixue poyi* 中國文化的人類學破譯 (An anthropological interpretation of Chinese culture), Ye Shuxian 葉舒憲, Xiao Bing 蕭兵, and Wang Jianhui 王建輝, eds.:

Ye Shuxian 葉舒憲, *Shijing de wenhua chanshi* 詩經的文化闡釋 (A cultural hermeneutics of the *Shijing*), Hubei renmin, 1994, 1996.

Xiao Bing 蕭兵, *Chuci de wenhua poyi* 楚辭的文化破譯 (A cultural interpretation of the *Chuci*), Hubei renmin, 1991, 1997.

Xiao Bing 蕭兵 and Ye Shuxian 葉舒憲, *Laozi de wenhua jiedu* 老子的文化解讀 (A cultural interpretation of the *Laozi*), Hubei renmin, 1994, 1996.

Ye Shuxian 葉舒憲, *Zhuangzi de wenhua jiexi* 莊子的文化解析 (A cultural analysis of the *Zhuangzi*), Hubei renmin, 1997.

---

[13] Stephen F. Teiser, "The Spirits of Chinese Religion," in *Religions of China in Practice*, Donald S. Lopez, Jr., ed., PUP, 1996, 3–37.

[14] For a convenient and original summary, see Mu-chou Poo, *In Search of Personal Welfare: A View of Ancient Chinese Religion*, SUNY, 1998.

Zang Kehe 臧克和, *Shuowen jiezi de wenhua shuojie* 說文解字的文化説解 (A cultural interpretation of the *Shuowen jiezi*), Hubei renmin, 1995, 1996.

Xiao Bing 蕭兵, *Zhongyong de wenhua xingcha* 中庸的文化省察 (A cultural perspective on the doctrine of the mean), Hubei renmin, 1997.

Wang Zijin 王子今, *Shiji de wenhua poyi* 史記的文化破譯 (A cultural interpretation of the *Shiji*), Hubei renmin, 1997.

Bibliographies

For publications in Western languages, note the series compiled by Laurence G. Thompson. It covers publications appearing from the eighteenth century to 1995:

Chinese Religion in Western Languages: A Comprehensive and Classified Bibliography of Publications in English, French, and German Through 1980, UAP, 1985. Expanded version of 1976 original.

Chinese Religions: Publications in Western Languages, 1981 Through 1990, Association for Asian Studies Monograph, 1993.

Chinese Religions: Publications in Western Languages Volume 3, 1991 Through 1995, Association for Asian Studies Monograph, 1998.

For surveys of the field of Han and pre-Qin religion, see Daniel L. Overmyer with David N. Keightley, Edward L. Shaughnessy, Constance A. Cook, and Donald Harper, "Chinese Religions: The State of the Field, Part I, Early Religious Traditions: The Neolithic Period Through the Han Dynasty (ca. 4000 B.C.E. to 220 C.E.)," *JAS* 54.1: 124–60 (1995).

For state-of-the-field essays on religion in imperial China, see Daniel L. Overmyer with Gary Arbuckle, Dru C. Gladney, John R. McRae, Rodney L. Taylor, Stephen F. Teiser, and Franciscus Verellen, "Living Religious Traditions: Taoism, Confucianism, Buddhism, Islam and Popular Religion," *JAS* 54.2: 314–95 (1995).

Alvin P. Cohen, "A Bibliography of Written Contributions to the Study of Chinese Folk Religion," *Journal of the American Academy of Religion* 43.2: 238–65 (June 1975). Western-language books and articles, arranged alphabetically by author. There is no index.

Zong Li 宗力 and Liu Qun 劉群, *Zhongguo minjian zhushen* 中國民間諸神 (Chinese popular deities), Shijiazhuang, Hebei renmin, 1987. Contains information on over 200 folk deities, cited from primary sources. For example, the section on the city god (*chenghuang* 城隍),

194–206, consists of quotations from 24 sources, beginning with the *Liji*, plus an essay by the editors. There is no index.

Chûgoku bunka jinruigaku bunken kaidai 中國文化人類學文獻解題 (An annotated bibliography of anthropological studies of China), Suenari Michio 末成道男 et al., eds., Tôkyô daigaku, 1995. Contains annotations on 600 books in all languages on Chinese anthropology, including the study of Chinese religion. There is an author index.

Anthologies

Religions of China in Practice, Donald S. Lopez, Jr., ed., PUP, 1996. One of the purposes of this excellent anthology is "to demonstrate that the 'three religions' of China—Confucianism, Daoism, and Buddhism (with a fourth, popular religion, sometimes added)—are not discrete, mutually exclusive traditions, but instead overlap and interact with each other" (xi). Accordingly, the selection of translated excerpts by 29 scholars includes ritual manuals, hagiographical and autobiographical works, folktales, and many other texts not usually found in anthologies of Chinese religion.

Journals

Journal of Chinese Religions (10.4.4)

Tôhô shûkyô 東方宗教 (Eastern religions), Nippon Dôkyô Gakkai 日本道教學會 (Japan society for Taoistic research), 1951– .

Shijie zongjiao yanjiu 世界宗教研究 (Studies in world religions), *Shijie zongjiao yanjiusuo* 世界宗教研究所 (Institute for the study of world religions), Shekeyuan, 1979– .

Cahiers d'Extrême-Asie (10.4.4)

Calendars

Buddhist and Muslim calendars were different from the ordinary Chinese calendar (see 5.7).

29.3   Popular Religion

Popular religion is defined as those everyday beliefs held in common by most members of society. Its definition changed over time as some elements may have fallen out of favor with one section of the population or another. It is a catch-all category for a huge range of beliefs and activities including animism; mountain cults;[15] totemism; festivals (5.5.2); the cult of the dead (ancestor worship); divination (Chapter 15; 44.4.1, *Shuihudi*); the interpretation of dreams and other practices to secure good fortune and to avoid bad luck;[16] magic and techniques to protect against ghosts, including spellcasting and exorcism;[17] the search for immortality;[18] geomancy (37.4); and belief in functional gods.[19] It found expression in mythologies (29.1), folklore (34.1), and all kinds of ritual and devotional practices.[20] The extent of these is hinted at in encyclopaedic studies such as *Zhonghua shenmi wenhua* 中華神秘文化, in which there are chapters on all of the above plus Yinyang 陰陽 and *bagua* 八卦, climate, sacrifices, shamans (spirit mediums), Daoism, Buddhism, and sexual and medicinal exercises.[21]

Research into popular religion uses archaeological data (for example, on divination, sacrifices, or burial practices) transmitted philosophical and religious texts as well as folk literature (34.2) and folk

---

[15] The Shang kings sacrificed to Mt. Yue 岳 (Huoshan 霍山 in southeast Shanxi). By imperial times, the main cult mountain was Taishan; see Édouard Chavannes (1865–1918), *Le T'ai chan: Essai de monographie d'un culte chinois*, Annales du Musée Guimet 28, Leroux, 1910 (described by Michael Loewe as "modern Western sinology's first great original achievement," *CHAC*, 3); see also Pei-yi Wu, "An Ambivalent Pilgrim to T'ai Shan in the Seventeenth Century," in Naquin and Yü, 1992 (4.8), 65–88, and Kiyohiko Munakata, *Sacred Mountains in Chinese Art*, Univ. of Illinois Press, 1991.

[16] Wolfgang Bauer, *China and the Search for Happiness*, tr. from the German by Michael Shaw, New York: Seabury Press, 1979; Richard J. Smith, *Fortune-Tellers and Philosophers: Divination in Traditional Chinese Society*, Westview, 1991.

[17] Donald Harper, "A Chinese Demonography of the Third Century BC," *HJAS* 45: 459–98 (1985).

[18] *SCC*, vol. 5, parts 3 and 5 (see Chapter 37); Michael Loewe, *Ways to Paradise: The Chinese Quest for Immortality*, Allen and Unwin, 1979; Ngo Van Xuyet, *Divination, magie, et politique dans la Chine ancienne: Essai suivi de la traduction des "Biographies des Magiciens" tirées de l'Histoire des Hans postérieurs*, PUF, 1976.

[19] See, for example, Valerie Hansen, *Changing Gods in Medieval China, 1127–1276*, PUP, 1990; or *Unruly Gods: Divinity and Society in China*, Meir Shahar and Robert P. Weller, eds., UHP, 1996.

[20] *Religion and Ritual in Chinese Society*, Arthur P. Wolf, ed., SUP, 1974.

[21] *Zhonghua shenmi wenhua* (Chinese mystic culture), Wang Yude 王玉德 et al., eds., Hunan, 1993.

art; specialist texts, such as those of the *fangshu* 方術 (mystical and magical arts); other transmitted texts such as observations of literati[22] or local gazetteers;[23] and finally, the all too few reports based on ethnographic, anthropological, and sociological field research, for example, that done in the 1930s by the group from the Catholic University in Beijing led by W. A. Grootaers, whose inventories of temples, shrines, and cult units are unique; see his

"Les temples villageois de la région au sudest de Tat'ong (Chansi Nord), leurs inscriptions et leur histoire," *Folklore Studies* 4: 161–212 (1945).

"Temples and History of Wanch'üan (Chahar): The Geographic Method Applied to Folklore," *MS* 13: 209–315 (1948).

"Rural Temples Around Hsüan-hua (South Chahar), Their Iconography and Their History," *Folklore Studies* 10.2: 1–116 (1951).

The Sanctuaries in a North-China City. A Complete Survey of the Cultic Buildings in the City of Hsüan-hua (Chahar), William A. Grootaers, Li Shih-yü, and Wang Fu-shih, comps., Mélanges chinois et bouddhiques, vol. 26, Bruxelles: Institut des Hautes Études Chinoises, 1995.

Chinese and Japanese articles and books are on Chinese popular religion 1900–84 (in some instances, 1987) are referenced in *Min Shin shûkyôshi kenkyû bunken mokuroku* 明清宗教史研究文獻目錄 (Bibliography of research on religion in the Ming and Qing), special issue no. 4 of *Shihô* 史報, Tsukuba: Tôyôshi kenkyûshitsu 東洋史研究室, 1989.

29.4 Daoism

The *Daodejing* 道德經 and the *Zhuangzi* 莊子 had become the classics of a Daoist religion by the end of the Eastern Han.[24] The religion spread rapidly in the Wei, Jin, and Nan-Bei Chao and many

---

[22] Ying Shao 應劭 (ca. AD 140–206), *Fengsu tongyi jiaoshi* 風俗通義 校釋 (Explanations of social customs), Wu Shuping 吳樹平, collated and translated into Modern Chinese, Tianjin renmin, 1980; Zhonghua, 1981. Indexed in *CFC Index* 3, 2 vols., 1943.

[23] *Zhongguo difangzhi minsu ziliao huibian* 中國地方志民俗資料匯編 (34.1).

[24] Isabelle Robinet, *Taoism: Growth of a Religion*, Phyllis Brooks, tr., SUP, 1997.

new Daoist works were written. Their main repository (and a quantity of other works considered unorthodox) is the *Daozang* 道藏, which has grown over the centuries since it began to be put together in the fifth century AD.[25] By the Ming, this huge collection (like a Daoist *congshu*) contained 1,500 works from both philosophical and religious Daoism (*Daojia* 道家 and *Daojiao* 道教). It contains materials not found elsewhere and is an important supplement to the various categories of Confucian historical and biographical writing.[26]

For annotated catalogs, see *Daozang tiyao* 道藏提要,[27] and Kristofer Schipper and Franciscus Verellen, *Handbook of the Taoist Canon*, UChP, forthcoming.

For an index, see *Daozang suoyin* 道藏索引, Shanghai shudian, 1996, which indexes five different editions, or the older *Combined Indices to the Authors and Titles of Books in Two Collections of Taoist Literature*, Weng Dujian 翁獨健, comp., H-Y Index 25; *Concordance du Tao-tsang: Titres des ouvrages*, Kristofer Schipper, comp., EFEO, 1975. Indexes all characters in the titles of all texts in the *Daozang*.

There is now a comprehensive catalog of Daoist works among the Dunhuang manuscripts.[28]

---

[25] See Stephen R. Bokenkamp, "Taoist Literature, Part I: Through the T'ang Dynasty," in *ICTCL*, vol. 1, 138–52; Judith Magee Boltz, "Part II: Five Dynasties to Ming," in *ICTCL*, vol. 1, 152–74. Both authors have also published book-length studies: Stephen R. Bokenkamp, *Early Daoist Scriptures*, UCP, 1997; Judith M. Boltz, *A Survey of the Taoist Literature: Tenth to Seventeenth Centuries*, IEAS, 1987; corrected rpnt., 1995.

[26] The only existing version of the *Daozang* today was the one compiled between 1436 and 1449 with an additional portion added in 1606: *Zhengtong Daozang* 正統道藏 (Daoist canon compiled during the Zhengtong era) plus Wanli 萬曆 continuation. It survives in a 1920s reprint: *Daozang* 道藏, 1120 ce, Shangwu, 1923–26; rpnt., Yiwen, 1962; rpnt., Xinwenfeng, 60 ce, 1977 (includes as index: Schipper, 1975); *Daozang* 道藏, 30 vols., Wenwu, 1985; *Zangwai daoshu* 藏外道書, Hu Daojing 胡道靜 et al., eds., 36 vols., Ba-Shu, 1992–94.

On the various versions of the *Daozang* from the post-Han, see Chen Guofu 陳國符 (1915–), *Daozang yuanliu kao* 道藏源流考, rev. and enlarged edition of 1949 original, 2 vols., Zhonghua, 1963; Mingwen, 1983.

[27] *Daozang tiyao* (Descriptive notes on the *Daozang*), Ren Jiyu 任繼愈, ed. in chief, Shehui kexue, 1991; 2nd rev. edition, 1995. Indexed.

[28] Ôfuchi Ninji 大淵忍爾, comp., vol. 1, *Tonkô Dôkyô mokuroku hen* 敦煌道經目錄編 (Catalog of Daoist scriptures from Dunhuang); vol. 2, *Zurokuhen* 圖錄編 (Plates), Fukutake, 1978, 1979.

Dictionaries

A good test of Daoist dictionaries is to see if they cover both the *Daojia* 道家 and *Daojiao* 道教. Do they include book titles that survive only in the *Daozang*? Do they include temples? Do the definitions simply quote examples of usage or do they in addition use modern scholarship and language to define the meaning?

Daojiao da cidian 道教大辭典 (Dictionary of the Daoist religion), Zhongguo Daojiao xiehui 中國道教協會, eds., 1994; rpnt., Huaxia, 1995. A large-scale, scholarly work based on Daoist texts.

Zhonghua Daojiao da cidian 中華道教大辭典, Hu Fuchen 胡孚琛, ed., Shehui kexue, 1995.

Bibliographies

Franciscus Verellen, "Taoism," in *JAS* 54.2: 322–46 (1995).

Anna K. Seidel (1938–91), "Chronicle of Taoist Studies in the West, 1950–90," *Cahiers d'Extrême-Asie*, 5: 223–347 (1989–90).

John Lagerwey in "Entre taoïsme et culture populaire" reviews recent work, *BEFEO* (1996), 438–61.

Julian F. Pas, *A Historical Dictionary of Taoism*, Scarecrow, 1998. Note the same author's earlier *Select Bibliography on Taoism*, SUNY, 1988; 2nd enlarged ed., Saskatoon China Pavilion, 1997; SMC, 1997, which contains Western-language books and articles, arranged by subject. There is an author index.

Biographies

Chen Yuan 陳垣, *Daojia jinshi lüe* 道家金石略 (Daoist figures on bronze and stone inscriptions), Wenwu, 1988; posthumously published. Contains 1,538 inscriptions with biographical materials of Daoist figures from 133 BC to AD 1655, mostly from the Jin and Yuan. There is no index.

Journals

Taoist Resources (1988–98, irregular); from 1998, incorporated into *Journal of Chinese Religions*.

Daojia wenhua yanjiu 道家文化研究, Zhonghua (1981–).

29.5   Buddhism

Buddhism (*Fojiao* 佛教, *Shijiao* 釋教) was introduced into China in the Later Han and spread rapidly during the period of disunion after the fall of the dynasty.[29] The new religion had a massive impact on all aspects of Chinese life. Many aspects of Indian culture entered China with it and left a lasting impression, including even on the development of the language itself (1.1.2 and 1.2.6).

The main repository of all branches of Buddhist scriptures as well as historical writings is the *San zangjing* 三藏經 (Tripitaka), so called because it contains the three main categories of the scriptures—*sûtra* (*jing* 經), *vinaya* (*lü* 律, law) and *sâstra* (*lun* 論, treatise). Other names for the Tripitaka include *Da zangjing* 大藏經, *Zangjing* 藏經, and *Yiqiejing* 一切經 (Buddhist Canon). The Tripitaka accumulated over a 2,000-year period. In form it is like an enormous *congshu*. There are at least 23 different editions, each one larger than the last. The most recent one contains over 3,500 titles (including all categories of writings). The *Taishô* Tripitaka is the one most used by scholars who also complain of the many mistakes that it contains.[30] There is a full concordance for each section: *Taishô shinshû Daizôkyô sakuin* 大正新修大藏經索引, 44 vols., Tokyo, 1975–88. It is arranged by detailed subject categories, and it is well indexed. Use vols. 1-55 with *H-Y Index* 11 and the general index, *Répertoire du Canon bouddhique sino-japonais, Edition de Taishô*.[31] To look up the whereabouts of a work or sutra in all major editions of the Tripitaka up to the Taishô edition, use the handy *Ershi'er zhong Da zangjing tongjian* 二十二種大藏經通檢.[32] It is indexed by *pinyin*, by

---

[29] Erik Zürcher, *The Buddhist Conquest of China*, 2 vols., Brill, 1959, 1972.

[30] *Taishô shinshû Daizôkyô* 大正新修大藏經 (The Tripitaka, new compilation of the Taishô era), compiled under the direction of Takakusu Junjirô 高楠順次郎 (1866-1945) and Watanabe Kaikyoku 渡邊海旭 (1872-1932), Tokyo: Issaikyô kankôkai 一切經刊行會, vols. 1-85, 1924-34; Bekkan: Shôwa hôbô sômokuroku 別卷紹和法實總目錄 (Appendix: Shôwa era catalog of the jewel of law), vols., 1-3, Issaikyô kankôkai and Daizô shuppan, 1924-34.

[31] Fascicule Annexe du *Hôbôgirin*, 2nd rev. and enl. ed., Paul Demiéville (1894–1979), Hubert Durt, Anna Seidel, eds., Maisonneuve and Tokyo: Maison Franco-Japonaise, 1978. The *Hôbôgirin* is the EFEO encyclopaedia of Buddhism; see below under *Dictionaries*.

[32] *Ershi'er zhong Da zangjing tongjian* (Index to 22 editions of the Buddhist Canon), Tong Wei 童瑋, comp., Zhonghua, 1997.

stroke count, and by Sanskrit and English titles; there are Chinese and English summaries of a total of 4,175 titles. Each title is translated, and the names of the translators and the dates of translation are given.

The *Zhonghua Da zangjing (Hanwen bufen)* 中華大藏經 (漢文部分) began publication by Zhonghua in 1984 and was completed in 1997. It contains 106 large volumes, and it is now the main repository of Chinese Buddhist texts. The texts have been reproduced from original woodblock editions (unlike the typeset *Taishô* Tripitaka).

The Buddhist (and Daoist) scriptures were not only printed, they were also carved on stelae and on rocks. The largest collection of Buddhist stone inscriptions (*shijing* 石經) in the world is stored in caves on the Mountain of Stone Scriptures at and near the temple of Yunzhu, Fangshan county, 70 km (45 miles) southwest of Beijing. The collection numbers 14,278 stelae and took 1,000 years to carve.[33]

For tracing manuscripts of Buddhist scriptures throughout the world in Sanskrit and Pâli, in Chinese, Tibetan, Mongolian, Manchu, Korean, and Japanese as well as in the languages of Inner Asia, use *Bibliographical Sources for Buddhist Studies: From the Viewpoint of Buddhist Philology*, Yasuhiro Sueki, comp., Tokyo: International Institute for Buddhist Studies, 1998; *Addenda 1*, 1999. This unique bibliography provides not only details of catalogs of Buddhist collections but also references to the secondary literature on particular scholars, texts, and book reviews.

Sources for the institutional history of Buddhism in Chinese society are not necessarily included in the Tripitaka, for example, the monograph on Buddhists and Daoists in the *Weishu* 魏書; the tem-

---

[33] The carving of the Buddhist scriptures began at the Yunjusi on the Shijingshan (房山縣石經山雲居寺) at the beginning of the seventh century and continued on and off until the early Qing. The 14,278 stelae record 3,400 volumes of scriptures and 6,051 explanatory notes in a total of about 22.5 million characters. Many of them were carved in the Liao dynasty based on the *Qidan zang* 契丹藏 (Khitan Canon). The *Fangshan shijing tiji huibian* 房山石經題記匯編 (Collected inscriptions of Fangshan stone sutras), 22 vols., Shumu wenxian, 1987, contains reproductions of rubbings of the Liao and Jin scriptures and some of the Ming ones. The temple was well restored in 1998–99.

ple gazetteers, and also the extensive sections on temples found in most local gazetteers (4.6).

Note that the Dunhuang documents (46.3) are an important source for Tang and pre-Tang Buddhism.[34] The classic study on the economic role of Buddhism, in which the author used many of the documents in the Pelliot collection, is Jacques Gernet, *Buddhism in Chinese Society: An Economic History from the Fifth to the Tenth Centuries*.[35]

Unfortunately there is no guide to Buddhist historiography, but see Chen Yuan 陳垣 (1880–1971), *Zhongguo Fojiao shiji gailun* 中國佛教史籍概論, which not only outlines the Buddhist record but also corrects errors in the *Siku tiyao*.[36]

On Buddhism in the Republic, start with Holmes Welch, *The Practice of Chinese Buddhism, 1900–1950*, HUP, 1967.

For a guide to the language, see *Reading Buddhism Through Chinese: An Introductory Grammar and Reader*, Stephen Hodge, Curzon, 2000.

The *Electronic Buddhist Text Initiative* (*EBTI*) was founded to coordinate the various projects involving the computer reading of Buddhist texts in all languages and in all traditions.

On the *baojuan* 寶卷, a form of popular religious literature (chiefly Buddhist), see Daniel Overmyer, *Precious Volumes: An Introduction to Chinese Sectarian Scriptures from the Sixteenth and Seventeenth Centuries*, HUP, 1999; Che Xilun 車錫倫, *Zhongguo baojuan zongmu* 中國寶卷總目, Zhongyuan yanjiuyuan, 1998.

29.5.1 Tibetan Buddhism

The main non-Han tradition of Buddhism in the China area is found in Tibet. The Tibetan Tripitaka is divided into two main parts, the *Tanjur* or commentaries (*bsTan'gyur* in Tibetan; *Dan zhu'er* 丹珠爾 in Chinese) and the *Kanjur* or main text (*bKa'gyur* or

---

[34] Makita Tairyô 牧田諦亮, *Tonkô to Chûgoku Bukkyô* 敦煌と中國佛教, *Kôza Tonkô*, vol. 7, Daitô, 1984.

[35] Translated from the original French (*Les aspects économiques du bouddhisme dans la société chinoise du Ve au Xe siècle*, Saigon: EFEO, 1956) by Franciscus Verellen, Col. UP, 1995. Contains new material and references.

[36] *Zhongguo Fojiao shiji gailun* (A survey of Chinese Buddhist historical books), Kexue, 1955; Zhonghua, 1962.

Ganzhu'er 甘珠兒). They were first assembled in the fourteenth century. The *Tanjur* is currently being collated and published based on the Derge (sDebGe) edition: *Zhonghua Da zangjing Danzhu'er Duikanben (Zangwen)* 中華大藏經丹珠爾對勘本[藏文].[37] It contains annotations and works written over the course of 1,000 years on philosophy, literature, art, language, astronomy, medicine, and much else besides. The new edition is projected to fill 120 volumes with an average of about 1.5 million words per volume. About 100 monks and scholars are working on it in Chengdu. It will have a full author-title catalog. After the remaining 110 volumes are published, work will begin on the *Kanjur*. Another edition has recently been published: *The Tibetan Tripitaka, Taipei Edition*, A. W. Barber, ed. in chief, 72 vols., SMC, 1991.

The two most important collections of rare Tibetan Buddhist works are held at the Sakya monastery in Shigaze and the Yonghegong 雍和宮 (Lama Temple) in Beijing (into which were assembled the libraries of the 28 Lama temples of Beijing in the early 1950s). There are large collections of Tibetan texts in the United States thanks to the activities of the Library of Congress office in New Delhi. For introductions to Tibetan Buddhism, see

Donald S. Lopez, Jr., *Prisoners of Shangri-la: Tibetan Buddhism and the West*, UChP, 1998.

Religions of Tibet in Practice, Donald S. Lopez, Jr., ed., PUP, 1997.
Thirty-six chapters with an introduction and translated texts.

Guiseppe Tucci, *The Religions of Tibet*, Routledge, 1980.

29.5.2   *Zen Canonical Texts on CD-ROM*

One day, the entire Tripitaka will be available on CD-ROM or online. The work has already begun in centers in China, Korea, Japan, and North America; see, for example, Urs App, "Reference Works for Ch'an Research: A Selective, Annotated Survey," *Cahiers d'Extrême-Asie* 7: 357–409 (1993–94), and *ZenBase CD 1*, Kyoto, International Research Institute for Zen Buddhism, 1995. This contains many basic Zen texts as well as a bibliography of 20,000 books held

---

[37] *Zhonghua Da zangjing Danzhu'er Duikanben (Zangwen)* (The Tibetan collated edition of the Chinese Tripitaka: *Tanjur*), Zhongguo Zangxue, 10 vols., 1989–98.

at Hanazono University, built up by Yanagida Seizan 柳田聖山. On Zen research, see *Zengaku kenkyû nyûmon* 禪學研究入門.[38]

29.5.3 Research Tools

Dictionaries

Bussho kaisetsu daijiten 佛書解説大辭典 (Great dictionary of Buddhist works with explanations), Ono Genmyô 小野玄妙 (1883–1939), ed., 12 vols. Daitô shuppansha, 1933–36, 1966; Chinese tr., Xinwenfeng, 1983. This is the basic comprehensive reference on Buddhist works.

Hôbôgirin (法寶義林). *Dictionnaire encyclopédique du Bouddhisme d'après les sources chinoises et japonaises*, fascicules I–VIII, Académie des Inscriptions et Belles-Lettres, Institut de France, 1927–99. This huge terminological encyclopaedia of Buddhist history and culture in China and Japan began under the guidance of Paul Demiéville. The first eight volumes cover the letters A–D. They took 72 years to compile. As the current editor, Hubert Durt, has remarked, "Great works take time." The articles are mainly written in French although some are in English. The *Hôbôgirin* covers Chinese, Japanese, Sanskrit, and Pâli sources (but not Tibetan).[39]

A Dictionary of Chinese Buddhist Terms: With Sanskrit and English Equivalents and a Sanskrit-Pali Index, William Edward Soothill and Lewis Hodous, eds., Kegan Paul, 1937; rpnt., Xinwenfeng, 1982; 3rd prnt., 1998; Curzon, 1995. Awaiting the completion of the *Hôbôgirin*, this early work is all that is available in a Western language.

The Encyclopedia of Religion, Mircea Eliade, ed. in chief, New York: Macmillan, 15 vols., 1987. Contains articles on Buddhism in East Asia, including in China, and explanations of the main doctrinal terms.

Fojiao da cidian 佛教大辭典 (Dictionary of Buddhist phrases), Wu Rujun 吳汝鈞, ed., Taibei: Foguang, 1992; Shangwu International, 3rd prnt., 1995. The central focus is on Indian and Chinese Buddhist thought. A handy reference: the Sanskrit, Pâli, or Tibetan originals of the phrases explained are given and indexed.

---

[38] *Zengaku kenkyû nyûmon* (Introduction to research in Zen studies), Tanaka Ryôshô 田中良昭, Daitô, 1994.

[39] *Index des caractères chinois dans les fasc. I–V du Hôbôgirin*, Antonino Forte, comp., Fascicule Annexe 2 du *Hôbôgirin*, Maisonneuve and Tokyo: Maison Franco-Japonaise, 1984.

Fojiao wenhua cidian 佛教文化辭典 (Dictionary of Buddhist culture), Zhang Zhijiang 張治江, ed. in chief, Changchun, 1992.

Foxue da cidian 佛學大辭典 (The great Buddhist dictionary), Ding Fubao 丁福保 (1874–1952), ed., 16 vols., Yixue, 1922; Wenwu, 1984; 2 vols., Taibei, 1986; Shanghai guji, 1991. Based on the first edition of Oda Tokunô 織田得能 (1860–1911), *Bukkyô dai jiten* 佛教大辭典, 1917; enlarged ed., Okura shoten, 1929; Daizô, 1954. Contains over 30,000 entries.

Mochizuki Bukkyô dai jiten 望月佛教大辭典 (The Mochizuki large Buddhist dictionary), Mochizuki Shinkô 望月信亨, ed., 6 vols., 1932–33; 10 vols., Tokyo: Sekai seiten kankô kyôkai 世界聖典刊行協會, 1957–68. The best dictionary. Indexes of Chinese, Japanese, and Tibetan Buddhist terms.

Biographies

On Buddhist biography and hagiography, see John Kieschnick, *The Eminent Monk: Buddhist Ideals in Medieval Chinese Historiography*, UHP, 1997; also Arthur F. Wright, "Biography and Hagiography, Huichien's [Hui Jiao 慧皎, 497–544] *Lives of Eminent Monks* [*Gaoseng zhuan* 高僧傳]," in Wright, *Studies in Chinese Buddhism*, Yale, 1990, 73–111 (first published in 1954). Note *Ryô Kôsôden sakuin* 梁高僧傳索引, (Index to the Liang *Gaoseng zhuan*), Makita Tairyô 牧田諦亮, ed., Heirakuji, 1972.

The best single work for finding the dates and also for locating biographical materials on Buddhist monks is Chen Yuan 陳垣, *Shishi yinian lu* 釋氏疑年錄 (Record of dubious dates of Buddhist monks), Shangwu, 1939; Zhonghua, 1964; Jiangsu guangling guji, 1991. It includes materials on 28,000 monks from the fourth to the seventeenth century. Based on 700 sources, it gives the monk's name, place-name, temple name, and dates of birth and death, native place, secular name (*suxing* 俗姓), and references to sources.[40]

Zhongguo Foxue renming cidian 中國佛學人名辭典 (Biographical dictionary of Chinese Buddhist names), Mingfu 明復, ed., Fangchou, 1974; Zhonghua, 1988. Contains 5,326 detailed factual biographies of Chi-

---

[40] Compare Chen's entries and coverage with Zhang Zhizhe 張志哲, *Zhongguo Fojiao renwu da cidian* 中國佛教人物大辭典 (Dictionary of Chinese Buddhist personalities), Zhonghua, 1993. It gives biographies of over 14,000 people in 12,300 entries from the Han to the present with personal data and activities. There is a four-corner index.

nese Buddhist monks and monks who came to China from the Han
dynasty to the present. Based on Chen (1939).

Anthology

In addition to Lopez, 1996 (29.2), see *Buddhism in Practice*, Donald S.
Lopez, Jr., ed., PUP, 1995. Contains readings on Buddhism in India,
China, Tibet, and Southeast Asia.

State of the Field

John R. McRae, "Buddhism," in *JAS* 54.2: 354–71 (1995).

29.6　Islam

Islam (*Huijiao* 回教; *Qingzhenjao* 清真教) was introduced into Chi-
na at the end of the Sui and the beginning of the Tang, no doubt by
Arab merchants who settled in great ports such as Guangzhou and
Quanzhou (42.3.2). Many more Muslims came to China during the
Yuan dynasty, some by choice, some moved forcibly by their Mon-
gol conquerors. The Muslims were Muslims in China until the
Yuan. By the Ming they had become transformed into Chinese
Muslims and had produced the greatest admiral and explorer in
Chinese history (Zheng He 鄭和; original name, Ma He 馬和).

The first extant copies of the Koran (*Gulanjing* 古蘭經) in
China date to 1318. They are handwritten. The first introductions
in Chinese to Islam are from the seventeenth century. The first
translations of the Koran into Chinese were made in the nineteenth
century. There were several large-scale Muslim uprisings in the
nineteenth century (28.3). There are currently in China over 14 million Muslims. Note the following studies and references:

Donald Daniel Leslie, *Islam in Traditional China: A Short History to 1800*,
Canberra College of Advanced Education, 1986.

Morris Rossabi, "Islam in China," in *The Encyclopedia of Religion*, Mircea
Eliade, ed., Macmillan, 1987, vol. 7, 377–90.

Zhongguo Yisilan baike quanshu 中國伊斯蘭百科全書 (Chinese encyclopaedia of Islam), Sichuan cishu, 1994.

Donald Daniel Leslie, "Living with the Chinese: The Muslim Expansion
in China, T'ang to Ming," in *Chinese Ideas About Nature and Society:
Studies in Honour of Derk Bodde*, Charles Le Blanc and Susan Blader,
eds., HKUP, 1987, 175–94.

Jianping Wang, *Concord and Conflict: The Hui Communities of Yunnan Society in a Historical Perspective*, Univ. of Lund, 1996.

Pu Shougeng 蒲壽庚 (42.2, *Thirteenth Century*), for a case study of the acculturation of a single family.

Bibliography

Dru C. Gladney, "Islam," in *JAS* 54.2: 371–77 (1995).

Donald Daniel Leslie, "Islam in China to 1800: A Bibliography," *Abr-Nahrain* 16: 16–48 (1976).

Islam in China: A Critical Bibliography, Raphael Israeli, comp., Greenwood, 1994, contains Western language works to 1992.

29.7   Christianity and Judaism

Nestorianism (*Jingjiao* 景教) is the first form of Christianity to have left a trace in China. There was a Nestorian community from the seventh century in Chang'an, the Tang capital. The so-called Nestorian monument, dated 781, can be seen to this day in the Museum of the Forest of Stelae, Xi'an. It is written in Syriac and Chinese.[41] Nestorians are also mentioned in the Yuan dynasty (Khubilai's mother, Sorghagtani Beki, was one). Other Christian visitors to China up to the Jesuits in the late sixteenth century are introduced in 42.2.

29.7.1   The Jesuits

Tianzhujiao 天主教 was one of the terms selected for Catholicism by the early Jesuit missionaries (*Yesuhui chuanjiaoshi* 耶穌會傳教士). Despite (or maybe because) of the fact that it was a familiar Buddhist term meaning the Lord of devas, Devendra, it became the standard translation. The Jesuits were the first full-time professional observers to report on China to Europe. Other religious orders were active in missionary work in China and Japan, notably the

---

[41] Paul Pelliot, *L'Inscription nestorienne de Si-ngan-fou, Oeuvres posthumes de Paul Pelliot*, ed. with supplements by Antonino Forte, ISEAS and Collège de France, 1996; "Christianity in China," in Ian Gillanen and Hans-Joachim Klinkeit, *Christianity in Asia Before 1500*, Curzon, 1999; A. C. Moule, *Christians in China Before the Year 1550*, Macmillan, 1930.

Franciscans,[42] but the Jesuits were the most influential. Much of their scholarly work went into letters and reports whose influence on the Western image of China was large. In many respects it is still felt today.[43]

On being assigned to proselytizing missions in distant countries, including China, the Jesuits took a vow never to return, which in part explains why they made such efforts to study the language and customs of the country of their mission.[44] They rose higher in the imperial bureaucracy than any other Westerners before or since. The reformers of the astronomical system of China in the late Ming and early Qing, Adam Schall von Bell and Ferdinand Verbiest, were the *de facto* managers of the Bureau of Astronomy. Ignaz Koegler was the first to be formally appointed Director of the Board in 1725. This was ironically the very year in which the Jesuits lost their case in Rome in the Rites Controversy, which eventually lead to the dissolution of the Jesuit order in 1773 (on which, see *The Chinese Rites Controversy: Its History and Meaning*, David E. Mungello, ed., Steiner, 1994). Nevertheless, Jesuits continued as directors of astronomy until the early nineteenth century. By that time, 456 Jesuits had worked in China in the "old mission." The Vincentians were authorized by the pope to take the place of the Jesuits. The new Jesuit mission began in the nineteenth century, by which time the Protestant missionaries (and other Catholic missions) were also active (37.7.3).[45]

For the study of the Chinese Christian Churches, including the Catholic Church, see 29.7.4.

---

[42] See *Sinica Franciscana: Relationes et Epistolas*, 10 vols. in 15 parts, 1929–97, Madrid.

[43] For an evaluation of the key to their understanding of China and of their influence in the West, see Paul Rule, *K'ung-tzu or Confucius? The Jesuit Interpretation of Confucianism*, Sydney: Allen and Unwin, 1986; Lionel M. Jensen, *Manufacturing Confucianism*, DUP, 1997; Thomas A. Wilson, *Genealogy of the Way: The Construction and Uses of the Confucian Tradition in Late Imperial China*, SUP, 1995.

[44] David E. Mungello, *Curious Land: Jesuit Accommodation and the Origins of Sinology*, Steiner, 1985; UHP, 1989.

[45] Willard Peterson, "Learning from Heaven: The Introduction of Christianity and of Western Ideas into Late Ming China," chapter 12 of *CHC*, vol. 8, 789–839.

The four leading Jesuits in the old China mission were Matteo Ricci, Johann Adam Schall von Bell, Ferdinand Verbiest, and Antoine Gaubil:[46]

Matteo Ricci (Li Madou 利瑪竇, 1552–1610): *Fonti Ricciane: Documenti originali concernenti Matteo Ricci e la storia delle prime relazioni tra l'Europa e la Cina (1579–1615)*, Pasquale d'Elia, ed., 3 vols., Libreria dellò Stato, Rome: 1942–49. The history of the Jesuit mission in China by its founder, with copious notes and Chinese characters. The text was completed after the death of Ricci by the Belgian Jesuit Nicolas Trigault (1577–1628) and published under the title *De Christiana Expeditione apud Sinas*, 1615; translated into English under the title *China in the Sixteenth Century: The Journals of Matthew Ricci: 1583–1610*, Louis J. Gallagher, tr., Random House, 1967. See also Jonathan Spence, *The Memory Palace of Matteo Ricci*, Penguin, 1984.

Johann Adam Schall von Bell (Tang Ruowang 湯若望, 1592–1666); German Jesuit astronomer and scientist. Senior official in the Bureau of Astronomy, 1645–66: *Lettres et mémoires d'Adam Schall, S.J.: Relation historique*, Henri Bernard and Paul Bornet, eds. and trs., Tianjin: Mission de Sienhsien, 1942; Alfons Väth, *Johann Adam Schall von Bell, S.J.*, Steyler, 1991; *Western Learning and Christianity in China: The Contribution and Impact of Johann Adam Schall von Bell, S.J. (1592–1666)*, 2 vols., Steyler, 1998.

Ferdinand Verbiest (Nan Huairen 南懷仁, 1623–88); Belgian Jesuit astronomer. Manager of the Bureau of Astronomy, 1669–88: *A Journey of the Emperor of China into East Tartary in the Year 1682*, Collins, 1686; *Correspondance de Ferdinand Verbiest de la Compagnie de Jésus (1623–1688)*, Henri Josson and Louis Willaert, eds., Brussels: Palais des Acadamies, 1938; *Ferdinand Verbiest, S.J. (1623–1688): Jesuit Missionary, Scientist, Engineer, and Diplomat*, John W. Wiket, ed., Steyler, 1994. Contains assessments of Verbiest as missionary, scientist, ballistics engineer, official, and diplomat. Verbiest was promoted to the brevet rank of vice-minister of the right in the Board of Works in 1682. This was in recognition of his casting of 130 canon and writing a treatise on gunnery, not for his contributions to astronomy.

---

[46] For a complete listing of all the Jesuits in the China mission, see Joseph Dehergne, *Répertoire des Jésuites de Chine de 1552 à 1800*, Bibliotheca Instituti Historici SI, vol. 37, Rome and Paris: Institutum Historicum and Letouzey & Ané, 1973.

Antoine Gaubil (Song Junrong 宋君荣, 1689–1759); learned French Jesuit, historian, and astronomer: *Le P. Antoine Gaubil, S.J.: Correspondance de Pekin 1722–1759*, René Simon, ed., Librairie Droz, 1970. Preface by Paul Demiéville; appendixes by Joseph Dehergne.

Jesuit letters: *Lettres édifiantes et curieuses écrites des missions étrangéres par quelques missionnaires de la Compagnie de Jésus*, 34 vols. Paris, 1702–76; new edition, 1780–83 (vols. 16 to 20 contain the letters from the China mission). There is a sampling of these in *Lettres édifiantes et curieuses de Chine par les missionnaires jésuites 1702–1776*, I. Vissière and J.-L. Vissière, eds., Garnier-Flammarion, 1979.

Jesuit reports: *Mémoires concernant l'histoire, les sciences, les arts, les moeurs, les usages, etc. des Chinois*, 15 vols., Paris, 1776–96.

The old Jesuit cemetery (Zhalan 栅欄) in Beijing contains 83 tombstones, including those of Matteo Ricci, Verbiest, and Schall. It can be visited. The cemetery stands today on the grounds of the Beijing Party School. For a study of its history from the opening (1610) through the Cultural Revolution, when the stelae of Ricci and his colleagues were saved by the staff who buried them, see *Departed, Yet Present, Zhalan, The Oldest Christian Cemetery in Beijing*, Edward J. Malatesta, SJ, and Gao Zhiyu, eds., Instituto Cultural de Macau and Ricci Institute, University of San Francisco, 1995. Following a decision taken by the Standing Committee of the Politburo, the stelae were eventually re-erected and restored in 1979 (some had been smashed in 1900). The study contains photographs of each of the tombstones in the cemetery and transcriptions of the brief inscriptions on them in Latin and Chinese and, in some cases, also in Manchu.

Bibliographies

There are five main bibliographies of Jesuit writings, the first two are general ones covering the Jesuit missions worldwide, the other three are specific to the China mission. Each is arranged differently, so they are complementary:

Robert Streit and Johannes Dindinger, *Bibliotheca Missionum*, vols 4, 5 and 7, Aachen: Franziskus Xaverius Missionsverein, 1928–31. Chronological arrangement, covers Jesuit missions worldwide, including China.

Carlos Sommervogel, *Bibliothèque de la compagnie de Jésus*, 12 vols., Brussels, 1890–1932; rpnt., Louvain, 1960. Arranged by name, covers Jesuit missions worldwide, including China.

Louis Pfister (1833–91), *Notices biographiques et bibliographiques sur les Jésuites de l'ancienne mission en Chine, 1552–1773*, 2 vols., Variétés sinologiques, 59–60, Shanghai: Imprimerie de la Mission Catholique, 1932–34; rpnt., CMC, 1976. Arranged by name. This has been translated into Chinese and at the same time extensively corrected by Geng Sheng 耿昇, *Zai Hua Yesu huishi liezhuan ji shumu bubian* 在華耶穌會士列傳及書目補編, 2 vols., Zhonghua, 1995.

Henri Cordier, *Bibliotheca sinica* (10.4.1).

Erik Zürcher, Nicolas Standaert and Adrianus Dudink, *Bibliography of the Jesuit Mission in China, ca. 1580–ca. 1680*, Leiden Univ., 1991. Covers secondary literature in European languages on the first century of the Jesuit mission.

The Jesuits also translated many European works, both religious and scientific, into Chinese (37.2).

Among the many aspects of European science, culture, and faith that the Jesuits introduced to the Manchu court was Baroque music: for a CD of music by the Lazarist missionary to China Teodorico Pedrini (1671–1746) and the Jesuit Joseph-Marie Amiot (1718–93), see *Teodorico Pedrini, Baroque Concert at the Forbidden City*, Auvidis-Astrée, 1996.

29.7.2   Judaism in China

The first sources that mention Judaism in China relate to worshippers in Kaifeng from the Northern Song onward. The sources include four Ming and Qing stelae from the Kaifeng synagogue, local gazetteers, the *Yuanshi*, and the observations of some of the early travelers to China,[47] as well as of Matteo Ricci and other Jesuits.[48] At that time a common name for Judaism was *Tiaojinjiao* 挑筋教 (the sect that plucks out the sinews).[49] Today it is called *Youtaijiao* 猶太教.

The Jews of China, Jonathan Goldstein, ed.; vol. 1, *Historical and Com-*

---

[47] For example, Marco Polo or Abû Zaid, *Record of Observations in India and China* (see 42.2, *Ninth Century*).

[48] Joseph Dehergne and Donald Daniel Leslie, *Juifs de Chine à travers la correspondance inédite des jésuites du 17ᵉ siècle*, Institutum Historicum SI and Les Belles Lettres, 1980.

[49] After the Kashrut regulation that forbids the eating of the thigh muscle on the hip socket.

parative Perspectives; vol. 2, *A Source Book and Research Guide*,
Sharpe, 1999.

Michael Pollak, *The Jews of Dynastic China: A Critical Bibliography*, Cin-
cinnati, Ohio: Hebrew Union College Press in association with the
Sino-Judaic Institute, Menlo Park, California, 1993. See also the same
author's *Mandarins, Jews, and Missionaries: The Jewish Experience in the
Chinese Empire*, Philadelphia: Jewish Publication Society of America,
1980.

Yang Haijun, "Eighty Years of Research on Jews in China," *Social Sciences in China*," 1: 83–94 (1996).

29.7.3   The Protestants in China

The first Protestant missionary to arrive in China was Robert Morrison in 1807 (Box 1, Chapter 2). It took nearly 60 years for their
numbers to reach 112 (in 1865). In 1890, there were 1,296; in 1905,
3,445; by the 1920s, there were over 10,000 throughout the country.
They were active in proseletyzing and good works, and the necessary adjuncts—teaching, translating, editing, printing, publishing
(18.5), and journalism (50.8). They were also pioneers in the introduction of Western medicine, science and technology (37.2),
women's schools,[50] and scholarly analysis of China and the Chinese
language.[51] The "new" branch of Christianity, Protestantism, was
called *Jidu xinjiao* 基督新教 or simply *Xinjiao* 新教 to distinguish it
from Catholicism. In the nineteenth century those Protestant missionaries that wrote about the current scene in China, and there
were many that did, often tended to take a more critical view than
had the Catholic missionaries in the two previous centuries. There
are several reasons why this was so. To old industrial countries in
Europe, and to even to relative newcomers like the United States
and Japan, at the end of the nineteenth century non-industrial countries like China appeared extremely backward. And this was a time

---

[50] The first modern girls' school was founded by an Anglican missionary in
Ningbo in 1845. By 1866, the total number of students enrolled in girls' schools
established by missionaries was 576, and in 1877, 2,064. The first group of Chinese women who refused to bind their feet came from such schools, as did
China's first women teachers to found their own schools, and the first group of
professional women.

[51] Paul A. Cohen, "Christian Missions and Their Impact to 1900," *CHC*,
vol. 10, 543–90; 611–14.

when China too was beginning to weaken. But perhaps most important for the individual Protestant missionary (or businessman) was that he or she typically operated far from the court and the educated elite. They deliberately led less privileged lives than had the Jesuits (or official embassies). As a consequence they saw a much more impoverished and illiterate side of Chinese life. Finally, the publication in the second half of the nineteenth century in popular Western and Japanese journals of photographs of starving beggars, public executions, and humiliating punishment of prisoners was instrumental in de-romanticizing the image of China (42.3.2). The coup de grace was the news of the murder of missionaries, antimissionary riots, and the siege of the legations during the Boxer Uprising.

There are several guides to missionary archives—for example, those listed in "Suggestions for Additional Reading," in *Christian Missions in China: Evangelists of What?* Jessie G. Lutz, ed., Boston: Heath, 1965. See also:

Alexander Wylie, *Memorials of Protestant missionaries to the Chinese: giving a list of their publications, and obituary notices of the deceased,* American Presbyterian Mission Press, 1867. Covers 1807–67.

Christianity in China: A Scholar's Guide to Resources in the Libraries and Archives of the United States, Archie R. Crouch et al., eds., M. E. Sharpe, 1989 (an earlier and much smaller version appeared in 1983).

China and the Christian Colleges, 1850–1950, Jessie G. Lutz, ed., Corn. UP, 1971.

A Guide to the Archives and Records of the Protestant Christian Missions from the British Isles to China, Leslie R. Marchant, comp., Univ. of West Australia Press, 1966. Does not include the personal papers of missionaries.

A Guide to Archival Resources on Canadian Missionaries in East Asia, 1890–1960, Peter M. Mitchell, comp., Univ. of Toronto-York, 1988.

The Missionary Enterprise in China and America, John King Fairbank, ed., HUP, 1974.

Christianity in China: Early Protestant Missionary Writings, Susan Wilson Barnett and John King Fairbank, eds., HUP, 1985.

Note the collections of Chinese sources on missionary cases *jiao'an* 教案 and the bibliography by Wu Shengde 吳盛德 and Chen Zenghui 陳增輝 (50.2.6).

29.7.4   *The Chinese Christian Churches*

Unlike the history of Chinese Jews, Chinese Christianity remains under-researched. For an overview of the Christian enterprise in China in the seventeenth century as seen from the Chinese point of view, see

Jacques Gernet, *China and the Christian Impact: A Conflict of Cultures*, Janet Lloyd, tr., CUP, 1985.

For a study of one particular group of early Chinese Christians, see

David E. Mungello, *The Forgotten Christians of Hangzhou*, UHP, 1994.

For the Chinese Catholic Church in the nineteenth and twentieth centuries, see

Historiography of the Chinese Catholic Church: Nineteenth and Twentieth Centuries, Jerome Heyndrickx, ed., Leuven: Ferdinand Verbiest Foundation, 1994.

30

Literary Anthologies and
Collected Works

Very large literary anthologies (*zongji* 總集) are extant from the sixth century onward. They contain memorials, letters, and commemorative biographies by different hands as well as many other types of source material useful to the historian. By the Tang, the practice of collecting together the prose and poetry of individual authors (called *bieji* 別集 to distinguish them from the *zongji*) was widespread, and several have survived. After the Tang many hundreds of individual collected works (also called *wenji* 文集) are extant, and the importance of the general anthologies for the historian declines as a result. This chapter examines the three most important general anthologies of Tang and pre-Tang prose literature (30.1); three examples of the massive poetry anthologies compiled (30.2); and reference tools for getting at the collected works of individual authors in the post-Tang period (30.3). It concludes with some useful reference tools for traditonal literature as a whole (30.4). Popular literature and modern literature are covered in Chapter 34 (guides to modern literature are in 34.4).

Both *zongji* and *bieji* are usually listed in the Belles-lettres branch (*jibu* 集部) of the *Sibu* classification (9.3).

30.1 *Anthologies and Collections of Prose*

Wenxuan 文選 (Anthology of literature), compiled by Xiao Tong 蕭統, Crown Prince Zhaoming of Liang 梁昭明太子 (501–31). Divided into poetry and prose, with the 761 prose excerpts further subdivided into 37 genres. Writings from the late Zhou to the Liang. A model for later anthologies; a textbook for examination candidates and a mine for compilers of dictionaries. A scholarly English-language translation is in progress. Three volumes of the projected eight-volume annotated translation by David R. Knechtges have been pub-lished under the title *Selections of Refined Literature. Volume One: Rhapsodies on Metropolises and Capitals*; *Volume Two: Rhapsodies on Sacrifices, Hunting, Travel, Sightseeing, Palaces and Halls, Rivers and Seas*; *Volume Three: Rhapsodies on Natural Phenomena, Birds and Animals, Aspirations and Feelings, Sorrowful Laments, Literature, Music, and Passions*, PUP, 1982; 1987; 1996.[1]

Quan shanggu Sandai Qin Han Sanguo Liuchao wen 全上古三代秦漢三國六朝文 (Complete collection of prose literature from remote an-tiquity, the Three Dynasties, the Qin and Han, the Three Kingdoms, and the Six Dynasties), Yan Kejun 嚴可均 (1762–1843), comp.; com-pleted 1836; printed, Guangya shuju, 1893; rpnt., 4 vols., Zhonghua, 1951; 6th prnt., 1996. Yan was not invited to join the editing of the *Quan Tangwen* (next item), and so he spent the following 27 years (1808–36) working on this huge collection (746 *juan*) of pre-Tang works of 3,497 writers. The contents were garnered from inscrip-tions and texts preserved in other works, not from obvious sources.[2]

Quan Tangwen 全唐文 (Complete prose literature of the Tang), Dong Hao 董浩 (1740–1818), comp., 1814; 11 vols., Zhonghua, 1983; 3rd prnt., 1996; 4 vols., Shanghai guji, 1990. Contains 18,400 literary compositions of 3,042 named Tang authors (plus those of several hundred anonymous writers active in the Tang). There are supple-ments[3] and indexes available.[4] A single large volume of excerpts of in-

---

[1] Note Shiba Rokurô 斯波六郎, *Monzen sakuin* 文選索引 (A concordance to *Wenxuan*), *T'ang Civilization Reference Series*, 4 vols., Jinbun, 1957–59; Chûmon, 1995. This supersedes *H-Y Index* 25 to authors, titles, and works quoted in the anthology; Chinese translation, Shanghai guji, 3 vols., 1997.

[2] *H-Y Index* 8 is an index to authors; *Quan shanggu Sandai Qin Han Sanguo Liuchao wen pianming mulu ji zuozhe suoyin* 全上古三代秦漢三國六朝文篇名目錄及作者索引, Zhonghua, 1958 (with corrections); 6th rpnt., 1995; Cheng-wen, 1966. It includes an index to the table of contents as well as to the authors.

[3] *Quan Tangwen buyi* 全唐文補遺 (Supplements to the *Quan Tangwen*), Wu Gang 吳鋼 et al., eds., 5 vols., San-Qin, 1994–98.

[4] *Quan Tangwen pianming mulu ji zuozhe suoyin* 全唐文篇名目錄及作者索引, Ma Xuchuan 馬緒傳, comp., Zhonghua, 1985. Also the *T'ang Civiliza-tion Reference Series*, vols. 3 and 10: *Tôdai no sanbun sakka* 唐代の散文作家 (Tang prose authors), Hiraoka Takeo 平岡武夫 et al., eds., Jinbun, 1954; Dôhô-sha, 1977. Gives alternative names, floruit of author, and reference to his works in *Quan Tangwen* and its continuations; *Tôdai no sanbun sakuhin* 唐代の散文作品 (Tang prose works), Hiraoka Takeo et al., eds., Jinbun, 1960; Dôhôsha,

Footnote continued on next page

terest to the political and economic historian has been published: *Quan Tangwen zhengzhi jingji ziliao huibian* 全唐文政治經濟資料彙編 (Collection of political and economic materials from the *Quan Tangwen*), Li Jiping 李季平, ed. in chief, San-Qin, 1992. There are other such collections of excerpts—for example, historical materials on Tibet: *Quan Tangwen Quan Tangshi Tufan shiliao* 全唐文全唐詩吐蕃史料, Fan Xuezong 范學宗 et al., eds., Xizang renmin, 1988.

Quan Songwen 全宋文 (47.2, *Collections of Song Prose and Poetry*)

30.2   Collections of Poetry

"*Du qi shi zhi qi ren*" 讀其詩知其人 (Know a man by his poetry), traditional saying.

A huge amount of poetry was written during the course of Chinese history, much to mark particular occasions. So poetry is an essential source for biography and atmosphere. Some forms of poetry (the Yuan *qu* 曲) are good sources for the colloquial language.[5] Of the many hundreds of poetry collections, and leaving aside the *Shijing* 詩經, six examples are given below.

Yuefu shiji 樂府詩集 (Collection of Music Bureau poems), Guo Maoqian 郭茂倩, comp., 12th century (on the *yuefu*, see 34.2).

Yutai xinyong 玉臺新咏 (New songs from a jade terrace), Xu Ling 徐陵 (507–83), comp., ca. 545. Famous collection of 656 palace-style poems mainly written during the Southern Dynasties. Anne M. Birrell, *New Songs from Jade Terrace*, Allen and Unwin, 1982; rev. edition, Penguin 1986. A complete annotated translation into English.[6]

Xian-Qin Han Wei Jin Nan-Bei Chao shi 先秦漢魏晉南北朝詩, 3 vols., Zhonghua, 1983; 3rd prnt., 1995. A large collection of poetry up to

---

1977. Indexes the works in *Tôdai no sanbun sakka* and gives the personal names found in the titles of the prose works. See also *Quan Tangwen zhiguan congkao* 全唐文職官叢考 (Comprehensive study of officials in the *Quan Tangwen*), Chen Guocan 陳國燦 and Liu Jianming 劉建明, eds., Wuhan daxue, 1997.

[5] Zhang Xiang 張相, *Shi ci qu yuci huishi* 詩辭曲語詞匯釋 (Collected explications of the language of the *shi*, *ci*, and *qu*), 2 vols., Zhonghua, 1953, 1978. Contains carefully researched definitions with copious examples of usage of 600 terms.

[6] *Gyokudai shin'ei sakuin* 玉臺新咏索引, Obi Kôichi 小尾郊一 and Takashi Sadao 高志貞夫, comps., Yamamoto, 1976.

the Sui arranged chronologically with short biographies of each poet.
There is an index available.[7]

Tangshi jishi 唐詩記事, Ji Yougong 計有功 (*jinshi* 1121), comp. Ji's
words are quoted at the head of this section. This anthology of Tang
poetry is one of the earliest large-scale ones. In it he assembles the
work of 1,100 poets together with anecdotes about the occasion for
the writing of the poem. Many other poetry anthologies followed
this "*jishi* 記事" style. Three have *H-Y Indexes*:

Tangshi jishi zhuzhe yinde 唐詩記事著者引得, *H-Y Index* 18
Songshi jishi zhuzhe yinde 宋詩記事著者引得, *H-Y Index* 19
Yuanshi jishi zhuzhe yinde 元詩記事著者引得, *H-Y Index* 20

Quan Tangshi 全唐詩, Peng Dingqiu 彭定求 (1645–1719) et al., comps.,
1705. The largest general anthology of Tang poetry. It contains
48,900 poems by 2,200 Tang authors. There is a database of the *Quan
Tangshi* at the Shekeyuan computer office. It has been used to gener-
ate a multi-volume concordance on every character.[8] In addition,
modern publishers of the *Quan Tangshi* usually include author-title
indexes.[9] Personal names appearing in the titles, prefaces, and annotations to the poems have also been indexed.[10] Finally, there is an index
to occasional poetry in the *Quan Tangshi* (partings, gifts, visits, banquets, and so forth).[11]

---

[7] *Xian-Qin Han Wei Jin Nan-Bei Chao shi zuozhe pianmu suoyin* 先秦漢魏
晉南北朝詩作者篇目索引, Chang Zhenguo 常振國 et al., comps., Zhonghua,
1988.

[8] *Quan Tangshi suoyin* 全唐詩索引, Luan Guiming 欒貴明, ed., Zhonghua
and Xiandai, 1991– . Arrangement is by individual poets. There is a Zhonghua
typeset edition of the *Quan Tangshi* in 25 *ce*, 1960; 5th prnt., 1992.

[9] *Quan Tangshi suoyin* 全唐詩索引, Shi Cheng 史成, ed., Shanghai guji,
1990; *Quan Tangshi zuozhe suoyin* 全唐詩作者索引, Zhang Chenshi, 張忱石,
ed., Zhonghua, 1983. There is a Chinese translation of the Jinbun's *T'ang Civilization Reference Series* index 4 (Tang poets, 1960): *Tangdai de shiren* 唐代的詩
人, Shanghai guji, 1991; indexes 11 and 12 (Tang poetry, 1964 and 1965): *Tangdai de shipian* 唐代的詩篇, 2 vols., Shanghai guji, 1990. Indexes 50,000 poems
from all main collections of Tang poetry and includes lists of persons to whom
poems were addressed as well an index of Five Dynasty poets.

[10] *Quan Tangshi renming kao* 全唐詩人名考, Wu Ruyu 吳汝煜 and Hu Ke-
xian 胡可先, comp., Jiangsu jiaoyu, 1990. Sometimes a brief biography is supplied. There is a *pinyin* index at the end.

[11] Wu Ruyu 吳汝煜, *Tang-Wudai ren jiaowangshi suoyin* 唐五代人交往詩
索引, Shanghai guji, 1993.

There have been numerous supplements to the *Quan Tangshi* incorporating poems found in the twentieth century at Dunhuang or on tomb tablets, for example. Five supplements were incorporated into *Quan Tangshi bubian* 全唐詩補編, Chen Shangjun 陳尚君, ed., Zhonghua, 1992. This in turn was absorbed into the 15-volume text and indexes of the 1999 Zhonghua simplified-character edition.

For an indexed catalog of anthologies of Tang poetry from the Tang to 1985, see

Tangshi shulu 唐詩書錄, Chen Bohai 陳伯海 and Zhu Yi'an 朱易安, eds., Qi-Lu, 1988.

There are large poetry anthologies for most of the subsequent dynasties, for example,

Quan Songshi 全宋詩 (47.2, *Collections of Song Prose and Poetry*).

If you want to find what poetry has been written about a place, try

Zhongguo gudian shici diming cidian 中國古典詩詞地名詞典 (Dictionary of place names in ancient Chinese poetry), Wei Songshan 魏嵩山, ed., Jiangxi jiaoyu, 1989. Contains 18,000 entries.

30.3   Collected Works

Collected works of individual authors (*bieji* 別集 is the classificatory term used by the *Siku* editors) usually contain several of the following categories of writing: (1) prefaces to the collection; (2) memorials and other official writings; (3) congratulatory poetry for public occasions; (4) prefaces; (5) commentary on events and diaries; (6) letters; (7) commemorative biographies for tombstones, tomb tablets, encomia, and accounts of conduct; (8) poems; (9) family instructions; and (10) miscellaneous. Collected works do not necessarily include all the works of an author.

Of 904 *bieji* known to have been in existence in the Sui, 467 have been lost, as also have been most of the Tang *bieji*. Thanks to the invention of printing, about 750 survive from the Song; about 1,500 from the Ming, and at least 5,000 from the Qing.

The titles of *bieji* normally begin with the author's name, alternative name, studio name, nickname, or place of origin followed by the term *wenji* 文集, *ji* 集 or *quanji* 全集. But many other such descriptive terms were used. They are worth noting in order to be able to quickly spot a *bieji*. Alternative terms included simply *gao* 稿 (draft or manuscript [mss]), or

leigao 類稿 (classified mss)
shenggao 剩稿 (remaining drafts)
weiding gao 未定稿 (unedited mss)
wenchao 文鈔 (literary excerpts)
wencun 文存 (extant works)

wen'gao 文稿 (draft literary works)
wenhui 文匯 (literary collectanea)
yigao 遺稿 (bequeathed drafts or mss)
yiji 遺集 (bequeathed collection)
yishu 遺書 (literary remains)

Titles of an author's collected works are usually mentioned in his biography. Note that occasionally a part of the collected works of a particularly famous author will have an index or concordance made especially for it. Otherwise, there are reference works to help locate an author's collected works and also to use them rapidly. Some are catalogs, others detailed subject indexes. References to some of the main ones are given below. Details and more indexes are given in Part V in the chapters indicated after each title below:

Tang

Tang ji xulu 唐集敘錄 (46.2, *Bieji*)

Song

Xiancun Songren bieji banben mulu 現存宋人別集版本目錄 (47.2, *Bieji*)

Yuan

Yuanren wenji pianmu fenlei suoyin 元人文集篇目分類索引 (48.5.2)

Ming

ISMH lists *bieji* if they contain three or more memorials (49.5.1)

Qing

Qingren wenji bielu 清人文集別錄 (50.6.2)

Qingren shiwenji shulu 清人詩文集書錄 (50.6.2)

30.4   Guides and Modern Anthologies

The first comprehensive study of literary criticism in China was *Wenxin diaolong* 文心雕龍 by the scholar and monk, Liu Xie 劉勰 (ca. 465–522). Liu includes a thorough discussion of literary genres, including historical writings, edicts, memorials, dispatches, and letters. There is a bilingual Chinese-English edition: Vincent Yu-chung Shih, *The Literary Mind and the Carving of Dragons: A Study of Thought and Pattern in Chinese Literature*, HKCUP, 1983. This supersedes Shih's original translation published without Chinese text by Col. UP, 1959. Shih traces the history of literary criticism in China up to Liu, whose life and work he also examines.

The best available modern introduction and reference in English to traditional Chinese literature up to the late Qing is the *Indiana Companion to Traditional Chinese Literature (ICTCL)*. It contains over a dozen longer essays on important genres and more than 550 entries on individual authors, works, schools, and terms. Editions, references, translations, and studies are indicated. The second volume contains 60 new entries and also updates the bibliographies in the first volume with a 300-page listing of secondary literature covering the years 1984–96 and in some cases 1997–98. There are separate name, title, and subject indexes to both volumes. Wade-Giles romanization is used.[12]

For a smaller scale guide than the *ICTCL*, which nevertheless provides much detail from earliest times to 1990, see Wilt Idema and Lloyd Haft, *A Guide to Chinese Literature*, CCS, Univ. of Michigan, 1998. Pithy and handy. The selective bibliography in the paperback edition (pp. 303–351) is shorter than in the hardcover edition but is adequate for an introductory handbook.

For a comprehensive, well-indexed, Chinese encyclopaedic dictionary of literature (33,000 entries), see *Zhongguo wenxue da cidian* 中國文學大詞典.[13] Vol. 1 contains a stroke-count and a *pinyin* index.

Two excellent and very different one-volume anthologies of Chinese literature in English translation are:

The Columbia Anthology of Traditional Chinese Literature, Victor Mair, ed., Col. UP, 1994. Four hundred translations by many hands. Belles-

---

[12] William H. Nienhauser, Jr., ed. and compiler; Charles Hartman, associate ed. for poetry; Y. W. Ma, associate ed. for fiction; Stephen H. West, associate ed. for drama, IUP, vol. 1, 1986; rev. rpnt., SMC; 1988 (this corrects many of the printing mistakes; 700 are listed at the end of vol. 2); vol. 2, William H. Nienhauser, Charles Hartman, and Scott W. Galer, associate eds., IUP, 1998; SMC, 1999.

[13] *Zhongguo wenxue da cidian*, Ma Liangchun 馬良春 and Li Futian 李福田, eds. in chief, 8 vols., Tianjin renmin, 1991.

lettres are well represented, but in addition almost anything written in Chinese during the last 3,200 years is sampled from divination records to philosophical texts to anonymous folk ballads and marginal doodles of copyists. There is no index.

An Anthology of Chinese Literature, Beginnings to 1911, ed. and tr. by Stephen Owen, Norton, 1996. The editor has not only done all the translations himself but has also provided up-to-date introductions to each major period of history and style of writing. Particularly interesting for anyone trying to understand the possibilities and constraints of the different genres of Chinese literature. Well indexed.

For a reader of Chinese theories of literature, use *Readings in Chinese Literary Thought*, ed. and tr. by Stephen Owen, HUP, 1992. For guides to modern Chinese literature (1900–1949) and anthologies, see 34.4.

Note the journal *Renditions* (7.4.2). It contains translations from Chinese into English with issues often grouped around a theme—for example, "letters" or "classical prose." The Chinese text is usually printed after the translations.

There are a large number of Chinese dictionaries of the language found in various genres of literature as well as dictionaries of the language of specific periods and of individual works. Those covering *baihua* literature from the Tang to the Qing, especially vernacular fiction and specific periods, are listed in 34.3, *Dictionaries*.

For a bibliography of modern scholarship on Chinese literature of all periods, see the following two items. To give an idea of the scale, volume 7 (on Qing literature) contains 14,854 entries in the main part and 7,733 entries in the continuation.

Zhongguo wenxue lunzhu jimu zhengpian 中國文學論著集目正篇 (Catalog of books and articles on Chinese literature: main section), Guoli Bianyiguan, ed., 7 vols., Wunan, 1996. Covers publications, 1912–81.

Zhongguo wenxue lunzhu jimu xupian 中國文學論著集目續篇 (Catalog of books and articles on Chinese literature: continuation), Guoli Bianyiguan, ed., 7 vols., Wunan, 1996. Covers publications, 1982–90.

31

Leishu 類書

After a short introduction to *leishu* 類書 as a genre, the discussion turns to general *leishu* (31.1); the largest surviving general *leishu*, the *Gujin tushu jicheng* 古今圖書集成 or Imperial Encyclopaedia (31.2); and the *riyong leishu* or encyclopaedias for daily use (31.3).[1]

Introduction

Many different kinds of *leishu* 類書 (lit., "classified matters" or "classified books," customarily translated as "encyclopaedia") were compiled for many different purposes. Unlike a modern encyclopaedia, the *leishu* typically consist of large numbers of excerpts from primary sources rather than specially written articles. The arrangement is usually by subject or by rhyme. If by subject, the overall categories are Heaven (astronomy, heavenly portents); Earth (geography, antiquity); Man (emperors, officials, prominent individuals); Events (government, economy, culture); Arts and Sciences (animals, plants, manmade objects, including technology, agriculture, and medicine). The genre began as a reader of moral and political precedent to assist the emperor and his officials in government; it soon developed in other directions. Some *leishu* were intended as elementary primers or as the sum total of knowledge necessary to pass the examinations to become an official. Some covered a particular branch of literature (history or belles-lettres, for example), others covered all

[1] On the *leishu*, see Michael Loewe, *The Origins and Development of Chinese Encyclopedias*, London: China Society Occasional Paper 25, 1987; also Ssu-yü Teng (Deng Siyu 鄧嗣禹) and Knight Biggerstaff, *An Annotated Bibliography of Selected Chinese Reference Works*, 3rd rev. ed., H-Y Institute, 1971, 83–96. Zhang Dihua 張滌華, *Leishu liubie* 類書流別 (On the different types of *leishu*), 1943; rev. edition, Shangwu, 1958, contains the important primary sources on the compilation of *leishu* as well as an exhaustive list of over 400 lost and extant *leishu* from all periods.

branches. Some were more literary and lexicographical and served as aids to composition, as vast repositories of well-turned phrases either general in application or devoted to specific models, such as letter writing or document drafting. By the later empire the tendency to include all existing human knowledge led to the compilation of monumental imperially sponsored *leishu* in which whole works, rather than excerpts, were copied into different categories.

Also in the later empire, with the spreading of written knowledge to strata outside the literati, *riyong leishu* 日用類書 (Encyclopaedias for daily use) began to be compiled, summarizing practical information for townsfolk and others not primarily concerned with mastering the Confucian heritage (23.4).

The historical value of the *leishu* is threefold:

1. Works that have long since been lost have often been preserved in whole or in part in the *leishu*. For example, the *Yiwen leiju* 藝文類聚 (see item 2 in the list below) has excerpts from 1,400 books written before the seventh century, of which only 140 are extant today. The *Yongle dadian* 永樂大典 (beginning of the fifteenth century) contained no fewer than 385 complete books that had been lost by the eighteenth century. This has enabled scholars to recover works (or parts of them) that would otherwise have been completely lost (9.8.2).

2. The *leishu* not only provide a unique view of how Confucian education and knowledge were actually transmitted, they also provide a useful shortcut to materials on any given, traditionally defined subject.

3. The *riyong leishu* 日用類書 contain important materials on culture and attitudes of strata below the Confucian elite.

Besides these reasons, there are specific ones why particular categories of *leishu* are still useful as works of reference. Thus the *Shitong* 十通 (25.2) provide easily accessible sources on all branches of the government, while some of the great encyclopaedias compiled as aids to literary composition are still useful for placing characters or phrases in the contexts in which they were used at different periods.

31.1 General Encyclopaedias

About 600 *leishu* were compiled between the Wei (early third century AD) and the eighteenth century. Of these, 200 are extant today, and 10–20 are still used by historians. Seven of the most important are introduced here (the order is chronological):

Yiwen leiju 藝文類聚 (Collection of literature arranged by categories), Ouyang Xun 歐陽詢 et al., comps., 100 *juan*, 604; *Yiwen leiju*, punctuated with corrections, 2 vols., Zhonghua, 1965; rpnt., Shanghai guji, 4 vols., 1982, has new index at end. Divided into 47 sections and many subsections. Criticised by the *Siku* editors as "of uneven quality and unsuitable categories." Nevertheless, the *Yiwen leiju* covers all subjects and contains many quotations from works long since lost. It also cites its sources.[2]

Beitang shuchao 北堂書鈔 (Excerpts from books in the Northern Hall), Yu Shinan 虞世南 (558–638), comp., ca. 630; 2 vols., Xinxing, 1978 (reprint of an 1888 collated edition); Zhonghua, punctuated edition, 1982. The earliest extant *leishu*. Divided into nineteen sections and many subsections. Deals mainly with government. Has quotations from many pre-Sui works long since lost. There is an index available.[3]

Chuxue ji 初學記 (Writings for elementary instruction), Xu Jian 徐堅 et al., comps., 713–42; 3 vols., Zhonghua, 1962, 3rd prnt., 1985. Background knowledge for beginning students. Divided into 23 main categories and 313 subcategories. Largely drawn from pre-Tang sources. There is an index available.[4]

Taiping yulan 太平御覽 (Imperially reviewed encyclopaedia of the Taiping era), Li Fang 李昉 (925–96) et al., comps., 984; 4 vols., Zhonghua reprint of *Sibu congkan* 3rd series, 1960; 5th prnt., 1995. Important for Tang and Five Dynasties history. It took Li and 10 other scholars 10 years to compile the *Taiping yulan*, and two years were needed to cut the woodblocks and do the printing. Divided into 55 main sections and 5,363 subsections. Quotations from over 1,690 sources, 70 of which have since been lost. *H-Y Index* 23.[5]

---

[2] Nakatsuhama Wataru 中津濱涉, *Geibun ruijû insho sakuin* 藝文類聚引書索引 (Index to books quoted in the *Yiwen leiju*), rev. edition, Chûbun, 1974.

[3] Yamada Hideo 山田英雄, *Hokudô shoshô insho sakuin* 北堂書鈔引書索引 (Index to the books quoted in the *Beitang shuchao*), Nagoya: Saika shorin, 1973.

[4] *Chuxue ji suoyin* 初學記索引, Xu Yimin 許逸民 comp., Zhonghua, 1980. Has a four-corner as well as a stroke-count index.

[5] See J. W. Haeger, "The Significance of Confusion: The Origins of the *T'ai-p'ing yü-lan*," *JAOS* 88.3: 401–10 (1968).

Cefu yuangui 册府元龜 (Outstanding models from the storehouse of literature), Wang Qinruo 王欽若 et al., eds., completed in 1013; photoreprint of Song edition, 4 vols., Zhonghua, 1989; photoreprint of 1642 ed., 12 vols., Zhonghua, 1960; 4th prnt., 1994. The Song edition is more reliable. Divided into 31 main sections and 1,104 subsections, covers from earliest times to the end of the Five Dynasties (960). Sources were mainly the Standard Histories and, when not, often from works since lost. Particularly important for Tang and Five Dynasty history. There is an index to the names, titles, and technical terms in the sections on foreign countries and diplomatic affairs.[6]

Yuhai 玉海 (Ocean of jade), Wang Yinglin 王應麟 (1223–96), comp., Yuan edition, 1330–40; photoreprint, Huawen, 1964; Zhejiang shuju, 1883; 6 vols., Jiangsu guji, 1987. Clumsily arranged but contains much important material for Song history, including quotations from the lost Song *Shilu*, National Histories, and Daily Records. There is an index to the table of contents.[7] Wang Yinglin was also the author of a large number of scholarly and pedagogical works, including *Xiaoxue ganzhu* 小學紺珠 (Purple pearls for the beginner), 1299, on which see 2.7, and possibly the *Sanzijing* 三字經 (*Three Character Classic*); see 1.3.2.[8]

Yongle dadian 永樂大典 (Yongle encyclopaedia), 22,877 *juan* plus 60 *juan* index and preface; 11,095 *ce*, completed in 1408. The largest *leishu* ever compiled in China, with an estimated total of 370 million characters (compare the Standard Histories, which contain a total of 40 million characters). Seven to eight thousand works from the Spring and Autumn period to the early Ming were copied into this imperially sponsored attempt to save for posterity the sum total of all Chinese written knowledge. Under the general editorship of Yao Guangxiao 姚廣孝, 2,169 scholars worked four years on the project. When it was completed, there was no money in the treasury to print it. A second manuscript copy was completed in 1567. The original manu-

---

[6] *Sappu genki Hôshibu Gaishinbu sakuin* 册府元龜奉使部外臣部索引, Utsunomiya Kiyoyoshi 宇都宮清吉 and Naitô Shigenobu 內藤戊申, eds., Tôhô bunka kenkyûjo, 1938; with Wade-Giles index appended.

[7] *Gyokkai mokuroku* 玉海目錄, Yoshida Tora 吉田寅 and Tanada Naohiko 棚田直彦, eds., Kyôiku daigaku bungakubu, Tôyôshigaku kenkyûshitsu, Ajiashi kenkyûkai, 2 vols., 1957, 1958.

[8] Hoyt Cleveland Tillman, "Encyclopaedias, Polymaths, and Tao-hsüeh Confucians: Preliminary Reflections with Special Reference to Chang Ju-yü," *Journal of Sung Yuan Studies* 22: 89–108 (1990–92), compares Zheng Qiao 鄭樵, Zhang Ruyu 章如愚, and Wang Yinglin 王應麟.

script was almost entirely lost by the end of the Ming. The eighteenth-century editors of the *Siku quanshu* took 385 works from the copy and also used it in making annotations to works not included in the Imperial Library. A number of late Qing scholars also recovered lost works from it. By the eighteenth century, about 10 percent of the *Yongle dadian* copy itself had been lost. The Anglo-French forces took a considerable amount as souvenirs in 1860. By 1875, only 5,000 *ce* remained, less than half the complete work. By 1894, the number had dwindled to 800 *ce*. During the occupation of Beijing in 1900 at the time of the Boxers, allied soldiers and officials took several hundred *ce*, and many more were destroyed during the looting. By 1900, only 60 *ce* were left. The painstaking work of tracking down the dispersed *ce* that had escaped destruction has gone on for over 60 years. Different fragments were published between 1926 and 1983. Finally all of these (amounting to 3.5 percent of the original) have now been photolithographically reproduced as a set of 797 *juan*: *Yongle dadian*; Zhonghua, 10 folio vols., 1959; 3rd prnt., 1994; also Zhonghua, 1986, 222 *ce* in 22 *han*. There is a separate index: *Yongle dadian suoyin* 永樂大典索引, Luan Guiming 欒貴明, comp., Zuojia, 1997.

31.2   The Imperial Encyclopaedia

Qinding Gujin tushu jicheng 欽定古今圖書集成 (Imperially approved synthesis of books and illustrations past and present), Chen Menglei 陳夢雷 et al., comps., 10,000 *juan* plus 40 *juan* index, engraved movable copper type edition, Beijing: Neifu 內府, 1726–28. By far the largest of the *leishu* to have been printed. It numbers 100 million characters on 852,408 pages and is divided into six main categories, 32 sections, and 10,000 subsections as shown in Table 35.

Under each of the 6,109 subsections are sources gathered from the Zhou to the seventeenth century arranged under the following eight headings: (1) orthodox writings, especially the classics, (2) other Confucian writings, (3) biographies, (4) literary works, (5) felicitous phrases and sentences, (6) historical works, (7) indirect reports, and (8) anecdotes and myths.

There is an excellent index to the translated titles of the subsections. It provides a convenient first entry point into this vast work: Lionel Giles (1875–1958), *Index to the Chinese Encyclopaedia* and has been used to make Table 35.[9]

---

[9] British Museum, 1911; rpnt., Ch'eng-wen, 1969.

Table 35: The Imperial Encyclopaedia 古今圖書集成

Section (*dian* 典) number	Number of Chapters (*juan* 卷)	Subsections (*bu* 部)
Category I. Celestial Matters (*lixiang* 曆象)		
1 The Heavens (*qianxiang* 乾象)	21	100
2 The Year (*suigong* 歲功)	43	116
3 Calendrical Sciences (*lifa* 曆法)	6	140
4 Strange Phenomena (*shuzheng* 庶徵)	50	188
Category II. Geography (*fangyu* 方輿)		
5 The Earth (*kunyu* 坤輿)	21	140
6 Political Divisions (*zhifang* 職方)	223	544
7 Mountains and Rivers (*shanchuan* 山川)	401	320
8 Foreign Countries (*bianyi* 邊裔)	542	140
Category III. Human Relationships (*minglun* 明倫)		
9 The Emperor (*huangji* 皇極)	31	300
10 The Imperial Household (*gongwei* 宮闈)	15	140
11 The Government Service (*guanchang* 官常)	65	800
12 Family Relationships (*jiafan* 家範)	31	116
13 Social Intercourse (*jiaoyi* 交誼)	37	120
14 Clan and Family Names (*shizu* 氏族)	694	640
15 Man and His Attributes (*renshi* 人事)	97	112
16 Womankind (*guiyuan* 閨媛)	17	376
Category IV. Arts and Sciences (*bowu* 博物)		
17 Arts and Occupations (*yishu* 藝術)	43	824
18 Religion (*shenyi* 神異)	70	320
19 The Animal Kingdom (*qinchong* 禽蟲)	317	192
20 The Vegetable Kingdom (*caomu* 草木)	700	320
Category V. Confucianism and Literature (*lixue* 理學)		
21 Canonical and Other Literature (*jingji* 經籍)	66	500
22 The Conduct of Life (*xuexing* 學行)	96	300
23 Branches of Literature (*wenxue* 文學)	49	260
24 Characters and Writing (*zixue* 字學)	24	160

Table continues

Table 35—Continued

Section (*dian* 典) number	Number of	
	Chapters (*juan* 卷)	Subsections (*bu* 部)
Category VI. Political Economy (*jingji* 經濟)		
25 The Examination System (*xuanju* 選舉)	29	136
26 The Official Career (*quanheng* 銓衡)	12	120
27 Foods and Traded Goods (*shihuo* 食貨)	83	360
28 Ceremonies (*liyi* 禮儀)	70	348
29 Music (*yuelü* 樂律)	46	136
30 Military Administration (*rongzheng* 戎政)	30	300
31 Law and Punishment (*xiangxing* 詳刑)	26	180
32 Industries and Manufactures (*kaogong* 考工)	154	252
Totals	6,109	10,000

Modern editions are available, including on CD-ROM. The most detailed index is that prepared for the 1985 Zhonghua and Ba-Shu edition, *Gujin tushu jicheng suoyin* 古今圖書集成索引.[10] It not only indexes the whereabouts of the subsections, but also contains separate indexes of illustrations, biographies, the political division section, and the entries in the animal and vegetable kingdoms sections. The index also includes various additional notes on, for example, the sources of the *Tushu jicheng*. Note also the index of Ming personalities (49.5.2).

The *Tushu jicheng* (as it is usually called) has frequently been used not only as a shortcut, but as the main and sometimes only route to primary sources. To use it this way is to risk becoming circumscribed by the biases of the eighteenth-century editors.

31.3 Encyclopaedias for Daily Use

From the Song, and increasingly from the Yuan and the Ming, encyclopaedias were compiled for a more popular audience than the emperor, the officials, and the literati. Such works as *Shilin guangji*

[10] It accompanies the facsimile reproduction of the original edition, Shanghai: Zhonghua, 1934; rpnt., 82 vols., Zhonghua and Ba-Shu, 1985.

事林廣記, *Wanbao quanshu* 萬寶全書, or *Wanyong zhengzong* 萬用
正宗 were issued in innumerable editions by the pulp publishers of
Fujian and Jiangnan.[11] Their arrangement followed the literati *leishu*. There were sections on Heaven, Earth, and Man, but the contents of these sections were concerned with current practical matters (e.g., advice to merchants and trade routes) rather than providing literary and historical models from the past. Many also contained sections on popular superstitions with instructions, for example, on how to select lucky days for different kinds of activity.
Examples of such popular almanacs include *Jujia biyong shilei quanshu* 居家必用事類全書 (Guide to domestic operations), Yuan; or
Duoneng bishi 多能鄙事 (Various arts in everyday life), Ming. Many
include brief outlines of the bureaucracy and the main administrative divisions of the empire.

These *riyong leishu* 日用類書 (encyclopaedias for daily use) form
an important source on popular religion and everyday attitudes, social practices, law, and the economy not found in other extant
sources. They have been intensively studied in Japan where many
copies found their way in the Ming and Qing. Note, for example,
the work of Sakai Tadao 酒井忠夫 on popular education, of Niida
Noboru 仁井田陞 on contracts, and of Ogawa Yôichi 小川陽一 on
vernacular novels,

Sakai Tadao, "Mindai no nichiyô ruisho to shomin kyôiku" 明代の日用
類書と庶民教育 (Encyclopaedias for daily use and popular education
in the Ming dynasty), in Hayashi Tomoharu 林友春, ed., *Kinsei Chûgoku kyôikushi kenkyû* 近世中國教育史研究, Kokudo, 1958, 26–154.

Tadao Sakai, "Confucianism and Popular Educational Works," in *Self
and Society in Ming Thought*, William T. de Bary, ed., Col. UP, 1970,
331–66.

Niida Noboru, "Gen Min jidai no mura no kiyaku to kosaku shôsho nado, nichiyô hyakka zensho no rui nijûshu no naka kara" 元明時代
の村の規約と小作證書等日用百科全書の類二十種の中から (Yuan

---

[11] *Shilin guangji* (Wide gleanings of miscellaneous matters), Chen Yuanjing
陳元靚 (end of Song), ed., 1322; rpnt. in 6 vols., Zhonghua, 1963; Chûbun,
1988. *Wanbao quanshu* (Complete book of 10,000 treasures). *Wanyong zhengzong* (The all-purpose correct way), early sixteenth century; Six of these works
have been photographically reproduced in *Chûgoku nichiyô ruisho shûsei* 中國日
用類書集成 (Collection of Chinese encyclopaedias for everyday use), Sakai Tadao 酒井忠夫 et al., eds., 14 vols., Kyûko, 1998.

and Ming village regulations and wage laborer contracts as seen in 20 encyclopaedias for daily use), in his *Chûgoku hôseishi kenkyû* 中國法制史研究 (Collected papers on Chinese legal history), vol. 3, Tôbunken, 1962; 2nd ed., rev., 1980, 741–831.

Ogawa Yôichi, *Nichiyô ruisho ni yoru Min-Shin shôsetsu no kenkyû* 日用類書による明清小説の研究 (Researches on Ming-Qing novels using everyday encyclopaedias), Kenbun, 1995.

Certain miscellaneous notes, for example, *Wu zazu* 五雜俎 (49.2, *Biji*), are not dissimilar in content to the *riyong leishu*.

Biji 筆記

As Yuan Mei 袁枚 (1716–98) observed of reading notes, when they have reached a certain bulk, "one is reluctant to keep them and equally reluctant to throw them away."[1] The solution was to publish them, sometimes more or less as they were written, often meticulously rearranged according to topic, often maintaining a "notes and queries" form.

If *biji* covered only reading notes, the category would be easy enough to understand. But it was used in other ways, to include, for example, short stories or to record anecdote and gossip. Reflecting the width of the definition, *biji* were classified under different *Sibu* categories, including *zashi* 雜史 or *dili* 地理 of the History branch, and the *zajia* 雜家 or *xiaoshuo* 小說 of the Philosophers' branch. They were often included in *congshu* 叢書.

The practice of writing *biji* had already begun after the Han dynasty, but it became widespread only in the Tang and the Song. The *biji* 筆記 ("miscellanies" or "random notes" as they are sometimes called in English) often started as reading notes to which, fortunately, sometimes the author added his direct observations. Not a few were written in retirement and take the form of recollections of official and court life. They cover as wide a range of subjects as the individual interests and tastes of their authors. Some are purely fictional. Some are on scholastic points of history or philology; others simply record the flux of city life, including theatrical and other divertissements, local customs, and practical guidebook-style advice. They often relate anecdotes, gossip, and rumor—subjects considered unfit for more formal works but not infrequently essential for social history. The *biji* are therefore a useful corrective to the Standard Histories and other works of Confucian historiography and an im-

---

[1] Arthur Waley, *Yuan Mei: Eighteenth Century Chinese Poet*, Macmillan, 1956, 112–16.

portant supplement to an author's *bieji* in which they were not normally included until long after his death. The quality and reliability of the *biji* are as varied as their subject matter.[2] Students of any post-Han period should make sure that they have found out the most important *biji* and glanced over them. It is often surprising what these works contain. Fifty of the most famous *biji* are listed in the relevant chapters of Part V.

In their titles, in addition to the terms *biji* and *suibi* 隨筆, many others were used, for example,

bitan 筆談 (brush talk)	*suowen* 瑣聞 (trifles overheard)
congtan 叢談 (collected chats)	*zalu* 雜錄 (miscellaneous records)
conghua 叢話 (collected talk)	*zhaji* 札記 (simplified notes)
jianwenlu 見聞錄 (record of things seen and heard)	*suilu* 隨錄 (miscellaneous records)
jiuwen 舊聞 (things heard long ago)	*xinyu* 新語 (new talk)
kehua 客話 (the talk of guests)	*zazhi* 雜誌 (miscellaneous notes)
suichao 隨鈔 (miscellaneous excerpts)	*zhaji* 劄記 (classified notes)

There are many collectanea of *biji* devoted to a single region. There are also a large number of collectanea that contain only *biji* novels, for example, *Biji xiaoshuo daguan* 筆記小説大觀, many editions; e.g., 16 vols., Zhejiang guji, 1995. It contains over 200 fictional and other *biji* from the Tang and Song. Note the Yuan collection *Shuofu* 説郛 (48.5.2, *Biji*).

Zhonghua published 106 *biji* in excellent punctuated, annotated editions in the 1950s in three series of "historical materials *biji*" They were reprinted in the 1980s and again in 1997:

Tang Song shiliao biji congkan 唐宋史料筆記叢刊 (40 titles)
Yuan Ming shiliao biji congkan 元明史料筆記叢刊 (24 titles)
Qingdai shiliao biji congkan 清代史料筆記叢刊 (42 titles)

There are a number of indexes to the key terms in *biji*. The two compiled under the direction of Saeki Tomi index the chapter headings, key words, and important nouns found in 130 *biji*:

---

[2] For a general introduction to *biji* of all periods, see Liu Yeqiu 劉葉秋, *Lidai biji gaishu* 歷代筆記概述, Zhonghua, 1980.

CZS. Chûgoku zuihitsu sakuin 中國隨筆索引 (Index to Chinese *suibi*), Saeki Tomi 佐伯富 ed., Nihon gakujutsu shinkôkai, 1954.

CZZS. Chûgoku zuihitsu zatcho sakuin 中國隨筆雜著索引 (Index to Chinese *suibi* and miscellaneous works), Tôyôshi kenkyûkai, 1960.

Umehara Kaoru 梅原郁 has indexed the five main *biji* on life in the two Song capitals (47.2).

Chidu 尺牘 or *shujian* 書簡 (letters) and *daobi* 刀筆 (notes), can contain information on matters such as land prices (see, for example, Ronald C. Egan, "Su Shih's 'Notes' as a Historical and Literary Source," *HJAS* 50.2: 561–88 (1990).

33

Philosophical Works

Works listed under Philosophers in the *Imperial Catalog* cover a broad range including miscellaneous and incidental works:

The Philosophers' Branch in the Siku *Classification*

Confucian writers (Chapters 19, 33)	*Rujia* 儒家
Military experts (28)	*bingjia* 兵家
Legal writers (19, 27, and 33)	*fajia* 法家
Writers on agriculture (35)	*nongjia* 農家
Writers on medicine (36)	*yijia* 醫家
Astronomy and math (5, 37)	*tianwen suanfa* 天文算法
Mantic arts (36, 37)	*shushu* 術數
The fine arts (38)	*yishu* 藝術
Manuals, e.g., on cooking (35.2.6)	*pulu* 譜錄
Miscellaneous writers (33)	*zajia* 雜家
Encyclopaedias (29)	*leishu* 類書
Essays; miscellaneous works (34.3)	*xiaoshuo* 小說
Buddhists (29.5)	*Shijia* 釋家
Daoists (29.4)	*Daojia* 道家

Note: the numbers in brackets following each entry in the lefthand column refer to chapter and section numbers in the manual.

For the philosophers of the pre-Qin and Han, see Table 26, 19.2, and for studies of the pre-Qin philosophers, see 19.3. For histories of Chinese philosophy in English, see

Kung-chuan Hsiao (Xiao Gongquan 蕭公權), *A History of Chinese Political Thought, Volume 1: From the Beginnings to the Sixth Century* A.D, F. W. Mote, tr. (from the Chinese original, 1945–46), PUP, 1979.

Fung Yu-lan (Feng Youlan 馮友蘭, 1895–1990), *A History of Chinese Philosophy*, Derk Bodde, tr. (from the Chinese original, 1931, 1934), 1937; PUP, 1952; vol. 2, 1953, 1983.

For critical examinations of the lives and teachings of the later Confucian philosophers, see the three *Xue'an* 學案 collections. There are a number of indexes available, including a combined one (item 5 below):

Song Yuan xue'an 宋元學案 (Major schools of Song and Yuan Confucians). The author, Huang Zongxi 黃宗羲 (1610–95), left this work uncompleted (it was modelled on his *Mingru xue'an*); finally completed and printed for the first time in 1838; 4 vols., Zhonghua, 1986, 1990. Use *Song Yuan lixue jia zhushu shengzu nianbiao* 宋元理學家著書生卒年表 (Chronological table of bibliographical and biographical data of the Sung and Yuan Confucian philosophers), Mai Zhonggui 麥仲貴, comp., HKCUP, 1968; *Sô-Gen gakuan Sô-Gen gakuan hoi jinmei ji gô betsumei sakuin* 宋元學案宋元學案補遺人名字號別名索引 (Name index to *Song-Yuan xue'an* and its continuation), Kinugawa Tsuyoshi 衣川強, comp., Jinbun, 1974. For an English translation of Huang's *Mingyi daifang lu* 明夷待訪錄, 1662, see *Waiting for the Dawn: A Plan for the Prince*, Wm. Theodore de Bary (1918–), Col. UP, 1993.

Mingru xue'an 明儒學案 (Records of Ming scholars), Huang Zongxi, 1700; 2 vols., Zhonghua, 1985. This has been partly translated in *The Records of Ming Scholars by Huang Tsung-hsi*, Julia Ching and Chaoying Fang, eds., UHP, 1987.

Qingru xue'an 清儒學案 (Records of Qing scholars), Xu Shichang 徐世昌, comp., 1940; Zhongguo shudian rpnt., 1985.

Ming Qing ruxuejia zhushu shengzu nianbiao 明清儒學家著述生卒年表 (Chronological table of bibliographical and biographical data of the Ming and Qing Confucian philosophers), Mai Zhonggui 麥仲貴, comp., Xuesheng, 1977.

Song Yuan Ming Qing sichao xue'an suoyin 宋元明清四朝學案索引 (Index to the *xue'an* of the Song, Yuan, Ming, and Qing dynasties), Chen Tiefan 陳鐵凡, comp., Yiwen, 1974.

Dictionaries

Zhongguo ruxue cidian 中國儒學辭典 (Dictionary of Confucianism), Zhao Jihui 趙吉惠 and Guo Houan 郭厚安, eds., Liaoning renmin, 1988. Contains over 2,200 signed entries, arranged in five sections: biographies, texts, academies, schools of thought, and philosophical terms. Has stroke-count index of names, titles, and terms.

Zhongguo zhexue da cidian 中國哲學大辭典 (Large dictionary of Chinese philosophy), Fang Keli 方克立, ed., Shehui kexue, 1994, covers philosophers, their works, and their concepts. Arrangement is by stroke count. There is a useful index of key concepts arranged by categories, i.e., schools of thought, personalities, works, concepts, and the philosophy of the non-Han peoples. There is a *pinyin* index.

Translations and Excerpts

Sources of Chinese Tradition, William Theodore de Bary, Wing-tsit Chan and Burton Watson, comps., Col. UP, 1960; new edition, William Theodore de Bary and Irene Bloom, comps., 2 vols., Col. UP, 1999. A huge selection of excerpts (translated by many leading scholars) of primary sources on Chinese intellectual and religious traditions from the Shang to modern times. The arrangement is chronological. Eminently browsable and also useful as a first reference thanks to full indexes—the best reader of its kind by far. The second edition improves on the already excellent original edition. It does so by expanding the range of selections. Due emphasis is given to both practical reflections on government and economic and social questions as to the moral and spiritual life. The authoritative introductions to the excerpts have been completely rewritten. Volume 1 covers to the end of the Ming. Volume 2 starts in the mid seventeenth century. There is a glossary of the 69 key terms used in traditional Chinese thought (vol. 1, 925–27), most of which typically also feature as part of the core vocabulary of the everyday language. *Pinyin* is used throughout.

A Source Book in Chinese Philosophy, Wing-tsit Chan, PUP, 1963; 4th prnt., 1973.

Reflections on Things at Hand: The Neo-Confucian Anthology, Wing-tsit Chan, tr., Col. UP, 1967. Translation of *Jin silu* 近思錄 by Zhu Xi 朱熹, 1130–1200, and Lü Zuqian 呂祖謙, 1137–81.

Neo-Confucian Terms Explained (The Pei-hsi tzu-i 北溪字義 *by Ch'en Ch'un* [Chen Chun 陳淳], *1159–1237)*, Wing-tsit Chan, tr., ed., and introduced, Col. UP, 1988.

Bibliography

Guide to Chinese Philosophy, Boston, Charles Wei-hsin Wu and Wing-tsit Chan, comps., 1978. An annotated bibliography of Western-language books and articles.

"Chinese Philosophy: A Philosophical Essay on the State of the Art," Lin Tongqi, Henry Rosemont, Jr., and Roger T. Ames, *JAS* 54.3: 727–58 (1995), especially pages 745–58, where the authors argue that Chinese philosophy has suffered in translation from the use of Western words and terms already freighted with their own meanings. To avoid this problem, they suggest using transliterations of Chinese concepts with explanations on first appearance.

Zhongguo zhexueshi lunwen suoyin 中國哲學史論文索引 (An index of articles on the history of Chinese philosophy), Fang Keli 方克立 et al., comps., 4 vols., Shehui kexue, 1986–91. Articles written in China between 1950 and 1985.

Journals

Philosophy East and West (1951– , quarterly), University of Hawaii

Journal of Chinese Philosophy (1973– , quarterly), University of Hawaii

There is an annual survey edited by the Shekeyuan, Zhexue yanjiu suo 哲學研究所 (Philosophy institute), *Zhongguo zhexue nianjian* 中國哲學年鑑, Shanghai: Zhongguo baike quanshu, 1982–90; Beijing: Zhexue yanjiu zazhishe, 1991–). It includes coverage of current research on Chinese philosophy.

34

Popular Literature

34.1 Folklore Studies

The Chinese literati recorded oral sources on legends, cults, popular beliefs and popular arts, festivals and customs, and language in their miscellaneous and literary writings and sometimes in the gazetteers, but on the whole their interest was occasional rather than systematic. Note, for example, the type of sources from which Du Wenlan 杜文瀾 (1815–81) drew his enormous *Gu yaoyan* 古謠諺;[1] and likewise note that Zhang Yuan 張援 based his *Tianjian shi xuan* 田間詩選 mainly on works of scholarly poets.[2]

For an annotated bibliography of 325 primary sources on the history of popular customs, see

Zhongguo minsu shiji juyao 中國民俗史籍舉要 (Annotated bibliography of historical works on Chinese popular customs), Liu Deren 劉德仁 et al., eds., Sichuan minzu, 1992. There is a comprehensive table of contents in lieu of an index.

Note also *Zhongguo difangzhi minsu ziliao huibian* 中國地方志民俗資料匯編 (Collection of materials from Chinese gazetteers on popular customs), Ding Shiliang 丁世良 and Zhao Xiaozhong 趙曉鐘, eds., 11 vols., Shumu wenxian, 1989–95. The vols. on Huabei, Dongbei, and Xibei were published in 1989, Zhongnan and Xinan (both 2 vols.) followed in 1991, and Huadong in 1995. The series was reprinted by Beijing tushuguan chubanshe in 1997. The first 11 volumes contain 5,500 pages of extracts from local gazetteers arranged under seven headings: rites, festivals, living conditions, popular literature and art, language, creeds, and others. There is a place-name index. Future volumes will cover the south.

---

[1] *Gu yaoyan* (Ancient songs and sayings), Zhou Shaoliang 周紹良, ed. in chief, Zhonghua, 1958, 1984.

[2] *Tianjian shi xuan* (Selection of poems from the fields), Shangwu, 1931.

Early research on folklore and religion in China was usually the work of the missionaries, but not always. See, for example, the first two major studies of the Dutch student interpreter and later sinologist Jan Jakob Maria de Groot (1854–1921):

Les Fêtes annuellement célébrées à Emoui [Amoy], étude concernant la religion populaire des chinois, 2 vols., Batavia, 1881 (in Dutch); Annales du Musée Guimet, vols. 11–12, 1886 (in French); rpnt., Leroux, 1977.

The Religious System of China, 6 vols., Brill, 1892–1910; rpnt., SMC, 1982.

After the May Fourth Movement there developed considerable interest among Chinese researchers into folklore collection and anthropological studies. Special societies were set up and journals, reports and collectanea were published; see Chang-tai Hung, *Going to the People: Chinese Intellectuals and Folk Literature, 1918–1937*, HUP, 1985; and also Laurence A. Schneider, "The Folk Studies Movement and Its Populist Milieu," and "Popular Culture as a Modern Alternative," in *Ku Chieh-kang and China's New History*, UCP, 1971, 121–52 and 153–87. Many of the publications of this period have recently been reprinted in Taiwan, where the original folk song and folk literature collections of the Shiyusuo are located.

A handful of Western folklorists and anthropologists also began field studies in this period (to 1949); see Morton Fried, "Community Studies in China," *FEQ* 14: 11–36 (1954–55). Some specialized in popular religion (29.3).

During the 1950s and 1960s in China, extensive oral history projects were launched, and considerable attention was also paid to the recording of legends and popular tales. See Yen Chung-chiang, "Folklore Research in Communist China," *Folklore Studies* 26.2: 1–67 (1967).

Note the following works:

Nai-tung Ting, *A Type Index of Classical Folktales in the Oral Tradition and Major Works of Non-religious Chinese Literature*, Academia Scientiarum Fennica FF Communications XCIV3 No. 223 (1978), Helsinki.

Chinese Fairy Tales and Folk Tales, Wolfram Eberhard, tr., Dutton, 1938 and 1958; also the same scholar's *Folktales of China*, UChP, 1965.

Legend, Lore and Religion in China: Essays in Honor of Wolfram Eberhard on his 70th Birthday, Sarah Allen and Alvin P. Cohen, eds., CMC, 1979. ·

34.2 Popular Literature

Popular literature consisted principally of mythology (29.1); legends; folk songs (and poems); short stories (and later novels); local operas and plays; and *chante-fables*. There were also many other forms, such as jokes and riddles (see the essays on "Popular Literature" in *ICTCL*, vol. 1, 75–92).

The *Shijing* 詩經 (Classic of poetry) contains 305 folk and ritual odes that have been used as primary sources for the popular beliefs and customs of the Zhou period.

In the second century the government set up an agency called the Yuefu 樂府 (Music Bureau) to collect popular tunes. Some of the ballads, love songs, and laments that were collected have survived, and contain important materials for the study of the popular culture of the Han.[3]

After the Han, it may well have been the influence of Buddhism that led to the creation of a vernacular literature in China.[4] The earliest translations of the Buddhist texts are more in vernacular than *wenyan*, as are the popular stories on Buddhist themes (*bianwen* 變文) and secular ballads found at Dunhuang.[5] After the Tang, ver-

---

[3] See the extensive article on *Yuefu* by Ying-hsiung Chou in *ICTCL*, vol. 1, 961–65; also, Anne M. Birrell, *Popular Songs and Ballads of Han China*, Unwin Hyman, 1988; rev. edition, UHP, 1993; Michael Loewe, "The Office of Music, c. 114–7 BC," *BSOAS* 36 (1973), 340–51.

[4] Victor H. Mair, "Buddhism and the Rise of the Written Vernacular in East Asia: The Making of National Languages," *JAS* 53.3: 707–51 (1994). Mair has translated one of the earliest examples of non-Buddhist written vernacular. It is embedded in a poem by Ren Fang 任昉 (459–508), "Memorial of Indictment against Liu Cheng," see *The Columbia Anthology of Traditional Chinese Literature* (30.4), 542–47; see also Mair, "Reflections on Book Language and the Vernacular Prompted by a Passage in the *History of the Sui*," in *Studies on Chinese Historical Syntax and Morphology: Linguistic Essays in Honor of Mei Tsu-lin*, Alain Peyraube and Sun Chaofen, eds., École des Hautes Etudes en Sciences Sociales, Centre de Recherches Linguistiques sur l'Asie Orientale, Paris, 1999, 119–31. He notes that the few passages of anything approaching vernacular in Literary Chinese texts are often in contexts related to northern barbarians.

[5] *Bianwen* means transformation texts (hagiography was transformed into playlets and picture books); see Victor H. Mair, *Painting and Performance: Chinese Picture Recitation and Its Indian Genesis*, UHP, 1988, 1996; Arthur Waley, *Ballads and Stories from Tun-huang*, Allen and Unwin, 1960. *Dunhuang bianwen*

Footnote continued on next page

nacular literature spread more widely, probably aided by the use of printing, more schools, and a wealthy urban class looking for amusement. See, for example, the late tenth-century *Taiping guangji* 太平廣記, which contains sociological and mythological materials in the form of quotations from 485 titles, 240 of which have since been lost. The contents include fictional sources considered improper for inclusion in the *Taiping yulan* 太平御覽 (31.1).[6]

One of the most important of the new types of popular literature to emerge in the Song was the novel, which was rewritten in many different versions, from a storyteller's prompt book to finished literary product (34.3).

The main sources for the study of popular culture divide into four types: (1) vestiges of popular literature and legends in the elite literature; (2) extant works of popular literature (from the late Tang), including stories, dramas, and local operas; (3) the records and direct observations of literati of "manners and customs," temples, cults, and festivals; (4) popular tracts, devotional and other works of religion (Chapter 33).

While the four types of source have by no means been fully utilized by modern historians, it would be misleading to suggest that the sources for the study of oral traditions and "popular culture" are rich, for they are not. As has already been pointed out, the recorders in traditional China were the Confucian literati who had scant respect for oral traditions. Nevertheless, these sources can to some extent be checked with and filled out using the reports and field studies of modern folklore researchers and anthropologists (see 29.2, *Bibliography*).

On popular literature, the pioneering study was

Zheng Zhenduo 鄭振鐸 (1898–1958), *Zhongguo suwenxueshi* 中國俗文學史 (History of Chinese popular literature), 2 vols., Shanghai, 1938; rpnt., Dongfang, 1996.

---

jiaozhu 敦煌變文校注 (Collated and annotated ballads from Dunhuang), Huang Zheng 黃徵 and Zhang Yongquan 張涌泉, eds., Zhonghua, 1997.

[6] *Taiping guangji* 太平廣記 (Wide gleanings made in the Taiping era), Li Fang 李昉 (925–96) et al., comps., 1,000 *juan*, 984; 10 vols., Zhonghua, 1961; 6th prnt., 1996. The most complete of several indexes is *Taiping guangji suoyin* 太平廣記索引 (Index to the *Taiping guangj*), Wang Xiumei 王秀梅 and Wang Hongbing 王泓冰, comps., Zhonghua, 1996. *H-Y Index* 15 is a title index.

34.3   Fiction and Drama

Chinese popular novels (*tongsu xiaoshuo* 通俗小説 or *baihua xiao-shuo* 白話小説) were not included in the *Sibu* classification. They can be of great interest to the historian.[7]

On the early history of Chinese fiction, see Robert Hegel, "Traditional Chinese Fiction: The State of the Field," *JAS* 53: 394–426 (1994); William H. Neinhauser, Jr., "The Origins of Chinese Fiction," *MS* 38: 191–219 (1988–89), and the references cited in 20.5 on narrative in early historical and fictional sources.[8]

The thirteenth to fifteenth centuries were the golden age of the drama combining singing, acrobatics, and speech. The two main traditions were the *Yuanqu* 元曲 and the *Nanxi* 南戲, from the north and the south, respectively. See Wilt Idema and Stephen H. West, *Chinese Theater, 1100–1450: A Source Book*, Steiner, 1982; and James I. Crump, *Chinese Theater in the Days of Kublai Khan*, CCS, Univ. of Michigan, 1990. See also 38.2 on music.

Plot Summaries

Zhongguo tongsu xiaoshuo zongmu tiyao 中國通俗小説總目提要 (Annotated catalog of Chinese popular fiction), Ouyang Jian 歐陽健 and Xiao Xiangkai 蕭相愷, eds., Academy of Social Sciences, Jiangsu, Center for Ming-Qing Fiction, eds., Zhongguo wenlian, 1990. contains plot summaries including chapter headings of all the 1,164 extant popular novels from the earliest surviving Song novel to the late Qing. It also includes brief biographies of the authors, when known, as well as publishing histories. It is more complete than any previous bibliography.

Inventaire analytique et critique du conte chinois en langue vulgaire, André Lévy and Michel Cartier, eds. in chief, 4 vols., Collège de France, 1978–91, is less comprehensive.

---

[7] On the novels and stories as historical sources, see H. F. Schurmann, "On Social Themes in Sung Tales," *HJAS* 20: 239–61 (1957); Jaroslav Prusek, "Les Contes chinoises du Moyen Age comme source de l'histoire économique et sociale sous les dynasties des Song et des Yuan," in *Chinese History and Literature*, Prague, 1970, 467–94.

[8] For an outline, see Lu Xun, *A Brief History of Chinese Fiction*, tr. by Yang Hsien-yi and Gladys Yang, FLP, 1959.

Bibliographies

For a bibliography listing both studies and translations into English, see Winston Yang, Peter Li, and Nathan K. Mao, *Classical Chinese Fiction: A Guide to Its Study and Appreciation, Essays and Bibliographies*, G. K. Hall, 1978. This includes both *wenyan* and *baihua* fiction and largely replaces the older *Chinese Fiction: A Bibliography of Books and Articles in Chinese and English*, Li Tien-yi, YUP, 1968. For earlier translations into English and other European languages (up to 1950), see Martha Davidson, *A List of Published Translations from Chinese into English, French and German, Vol. 1, Literature Exclusive of Poetry, Vol. 2, Poetry*, YUP, 1953, 1957.

Manuel D. Lopez, *Chinese Drama: An Annotated Bibliography of Commentary, Criticism, and Plays in English Translation*, Scarecrow, 1992.

Note the cumulative bibliography of works in all languages on all aspects of Chinese literature published at the end of each issue of *Chûgoku bungakuhô* 中國文學報, Jinbun, 1954– .

Dictionaries

Zhongguo huaben xiaoshuo suyu cidian 中國話本小説俗語辭典 (A dictionary of colloquial terms and expressions in Chinese vernacular fiction), Tian Zongyao 田宗堯, comp., rev. and enlarged edition of the same author's 1983 work, Xinwenfeng, 1985 (see 2.5.2 for details of this and other bilingual dictionaries of the colloquial language).

Jindai Hanyu cidian 近代漢語辭典, Xu Shaofeng 許少峰, comp., Tuanjie, 1997. Covers the language of vernacular literature from the late Tang to the end of the Qing. All 25,000 entries include examples of usage with references cited. Arrangement is by *pinyin* with every phrase spelled out in full.

Jindai Hanyu duandai yuyan cidian xilie 近代漢語斷代語言詞典系列 (Single-period dictionaries of early Mandarin series). There are separate volumes on Tang-Wudai, Song, and Yuan (for details, see 46.5.2, 47.4.2, and 48.5.4).

Jindai Hanyu cidian 近代漢語辭典, Gao Wenda 高文達, ed. in chief, Zhishi, 1992. A smaller dictionary (13,000 entries) of a similar nature to item 2.

Shi ci qu xiaoshuo yuci dadian 詩詞曲小説語詞大典 (*Shi ci qu xiaoshuo yuci dadian*, Wang Guiyuan 王貴元 and Ye Guigang 葉桂剛, eds. in chief, Qunyan, 1993. Contains more than 20,000 entries explaining terms drawn from poetry and *baihua* literature from the Tang to the Qing.

Zhongguo gudai xiaoshuo renwu cidian 中國古代小説人物辭典 (Dictionary of personalities in old Chinese fiction), Miao Zhuang 苗壯, ed., Qi-Lu, 1991. Includes 1,700 persons, arranged according to genres.

There are now also any number of "dictionaries" of the language found in individual works (examples of these are given in the appropriate chapters). Here are some examples of dictionaries of the language (which in most cases also include the principal characters and places) of China's six greatest *baihua* novels. The best English translation is indicated:

Hongloumeng 紅樓夢 (Dream of the red chamber), Cao Xueqin 曹雪芹, 1760: *Hongloumeng yuyan cidian* 紅樓夢語言辭典 (Dictionary of the language of *Hongloumeng*), Zhou Dingyi 周定一, ed. in chief, Shangwu, 1995. The first part (1–1194) covers Chapters 1–80. The second part, Chapters 81–120 (1195–1445). According to the editor's foreword, the language of both parts of the novel is basically eighteenth-century Beijing dialect with some influence of Nanjing dialect, but more from the language of the northeast (which heavily influenced Beijing dialect at this time). The foreword is dated 1988. The study of the novel and its social and economic background is known as *Hongxue* 紅學; a field that brings together almost all of the methods and sources that historians use for the period. There are several *Hongxue* journals, notably *Hongloumeng xuekan* 紅樓夢學刊 (1979– , quarterly). As of 1999.5, it had published 1,600 articles on the novel totaling 21 million words.

English translation: David Hawkes and John Minford, *The Story of the Stone*, 5 vols., Penguin Books, 1973–86.

Jin Ping Mei 金瓶梅 (Gold, Vase, Plum or The plum in the golden vase), anon, ca. 1618: *Jin Ping Mei cidian* 金瓶梅詞典 (Dictionary of *Jin Ping Mei*), Bai Weiguo 白維國, ed., Zhonghua, 1991, 1994. Concentrates on difficult phrases from the spoken language rather than encyclopaedic coverage of personal names and toponyms, and so forth.

Annotated English translation: David Tod Roy, *The Plum in the Golden Vase or Chin P'ing Mei*, Vol. 1, *The Gathering*, PUP, 1993.

Rulin waishi 儒林外史 (The scholars), Wu Jingzi 吳敬梓 (1701–54): *Rulin waishi cidian* 儒林外史辭典 (Dictionary of *Rulin waishi*), Chen Meilin 陳美林, ed. in chief, Nanjing daxue, 1994.

English translation by Yang Hsien-yi and Gladys Yang, *The Scholars*, FLP, 1957.

Sanguozhi yanyi 三國志演義 (Romance of the Three Kingdoms), attrib. to Luo Guanzhong 羅貫中 (born ca. 1315): *Sanguozhi yanyi cidian* 三

國志演義辭典 (Dictionary of the *Sanguozhi yanyi*), Zhang Shunhui 張舜徽 et al., eds., Shandong jiaoyu, 1992.

Annotated English translation with afterword: Moss Roberts, *Three Kingdoms: A Historical Novel*, 3 vols. FLP and UCP, 1991.

Shuihu zhuan 水滸傳 (Water margin, or Outlaws of the marsh) *Shuihu cidian* 水滸詞典 (Dictionary of *Shuihuzhuan*), Hu Zhu'an 胡竹安, ed., Hanyu da cidian, 1989. Concentrates on difficult phrases from the spoken language rather than attempting an encyclopaedic coverage of personal names and toponyms, and so forth.

English translation: Sidney Shapiro, *Outlaws of the Marsh*, 3 vols., FLP, 1980. See also Richard G. Irwin, *The Evolution of a Chinese Novel, Shui-hu-chuan* [*Shuihuzhuan* 水滸傳], H-Y Institute, 1953.

Xiyouji 西遊記 (Journey to the west; or Monkey), attrib. to Wu Cheng-en 吳承恩 (ca. 1500–1582), 1592: *Xiyouji cidian* 西遊記辭典 (Dictionary of *Xiyouji*), Zeng Shangyan 曾上炎, Henan renmin, 1994.

English translations: *Journey to the West*, William J. F. Jenner, tr., 2 vols., FLP, 1982–84; *The Journey to the West*, Anthony C. Yu, tr., 4 vols., UChP, 1977–83. See 41.5.1 for the original *Xiyuji* from which the story is derived.

Guides and Studies of the Novel

How to Read the Chinese Novel, David L. Rolston, ed., PUP, 1990.

C. T. Hsia, *The Classic Chinese Novel: A Critical Introduction*, Col. UP, 1968; rpnt., Corn. UP, 1996.

Andrew H. Plaks, *The Four Masterworks of the Ming Novel: Ssu-ta Ch'i-shu*, PUP, 1987.

Note also the studies comparing narrative in historical writing and in the novel cited in section 20.2.

34.4   Twentieth-Century Literature to 1949

See 51.6.

35

Agriculture, Food, and the Environment

Early farmers timed their tasks on the basis of periodic changes in natural and celestial phenomena (*Almanacs*, 35.1.1). From the Han, comprehensive agricultural treatises (*nongshu* 農書) on all aspects of agriculture, as well as specialized works on everything from crop systems to locust control, from pigeon raising to horse breeding, from irrigation to tea cultivation, gradually became an established genre (35.1.2). Some 260 such treatises are extant (out of a total of 650 known titles), mainly from the later empire. Some quote from previous works; others are based on the experience and observation of their authors; some were officially sponsored (to popularize a new crop or technique, for example); and many were written by private authors (usually retired officials), discussing the agriculture of a single county, locality, or estate. Most of the comprehensive agricultural treatises contain chapters on general principles of agriculture, crop types, the farming year, tools (often with illustrations) and side occupations. Taken as a whole, the *nongshu* are an important source for the history of Chinese agriculture and agricultural techniques, and taken singly, some of them are good sources for the organization of agriculture in particular places at specific times.

The history of Chinese cooking can be traced using the *nongshu*, cookbooks, dietary treatises, and *materia medica*. Much of what is commonly thought typical of Chinese food today is relatively recent in origin (35.2). Food production would have been impossible without water control (35.3). The chapter ends with a short section on the history of the environment and natural disasters (35.4). Medicine, disease, and sex, all closely linked to the subjects of this chapter, are dealt with in Chapter 36.

35.1 Agricultural Calendars and Agricultural Treatises

35.1.1 Agricultural Calendars

The earliest records relating to harvests and agriculture are scattered among the divinatory texts recorded on the oracle-bones.[1] We know from later sources that pre-Qin farmers judged the changing seasons by closely observing natural phenomena that occur periodically such as hibernation, migration, and blossoming. In addition to phenology (the relation of climate to periodic biologic activity), they also noted those changes in the weather and of celestial phenomena that took place at regular intervals. These observations, called *wuhou* 物候, were collected together and eventually written down arranged by season and by month in agricultural calendars. Several pre-Qin calendars, or fragments, survive. The earliest phenological one has been preserved in the *Shijing*:

Shijing 詩經 (Classic of poetry), "Binfeng" 豳風, "Qiyue," 七月 (Odes of Bin, seventh month). A rhyming seasonal calendar, it gives in verse form the different farming and household tasks and seasonal sights and sounds: "In June the crickets start to skip out; in July they live in the fields; in August they live under the eaves; in September in the room they keep; in October under the bed they sleep," *The Book of Poetry*, Wang Rongpei and Ren Xiuhua, tr. and annotated, Liaoning jiaoyu, 1995, 616–17. Also translated slightly differently by Jeffrey Riegel in *The Columbia Anthology of Traditional Chinese Literature* (30.4), 158–60. A controversy has raged for centuries as to which calendar the poem is based on (and hence which months are referred to).

Other pre-Qin works with important chapters or fragments on the farming year include the following (bibliographic references in Table 26, 19.2):

---

[1] Peng Bangjiong 彭邦炯, *Jiaguwen nongye ziliao kaobian yu yanjiu* 甲骨文農業資料考辨與研究 (Verification and research on agricultural materials in the oracle-bone inscriptions), Jilin wenshi, 1997. Part 1 reproduces 614 inscriptions with references to agriculture grouped by subject; part 2 contains transcriptions and commentary on each inscription; this is followed by a study of Shang agriculture which includes inventories of excavated crops, tools and place names; the appendix contains a bibliography of secondary literature on Shang agriculture.

Lüshi chunqiu 呂氏春秋 (ca. 239 BC), "Shi'er ji" 十二季. Connects phe-nological observations with the 12 seasons (months).

Liji 禮記, "Yueling" 月令 (Monthly ordinances). Combines farming ad-vice with the type of information that was later included in popular encyclopaedias (23.4). The strictly farming features of the agricultural calendars were usually incorporated into the later *nongshu*; the calen-drical information went into popular almanacs (5.1.2). The heavenly phenomena were revised to fit the Tang calendar at the time of the carving of the Kaicheng stone classics in 837 (17.3).

"Xia xiaozheng" 夏小正. Similar to the "Yueling"; survived in a Han col-lection of mainly Warring States ritual texts similar to the *Liji* known as the *Da Dai liji* 大戴禮記; later circulated as a separate work. See Benedykt Grynpas, *Les écrits de Tai l'Ancien et le petit cal-endrier des Hia*, Paris, 1972.

"Shize xun" 時則訓 (On times and seasons), *juan* 5 of the *Huainanzi* 淮南子 (presented to the emperor in 139 BC). Includes the 24 *jieqi* more or less in the form in which they are still in use in the countryside today. See "The Treatise on Seasonal Rules," in Major, 1993 (Table 26, 19.2), 217–68.

Yi Zhoushu 逸周書 (different *pian* date from different times), "Shixun jie" 時訓解 (Interpretations of times and seasons). Includes the phe-nological basis for the system of 72 *hou*.

In the Former Han, phenological characteristics associated with each of 24 seasons (*jieqi* 節氣) were standardized into a system that has been used to the present day. The 72 minor periods of five days each (*hou* 候) were incorporated into the calendar in AD 520 (5.5.1).

Farmers and peasants strictly followed the traditional times as fixed with reference to the *jieqi* for planting, harvesting, pruning, and all the other main tasks of the farming year. Later, as the terri-tory of China expanded to cover an area where the flowering, for example, of the peach, occurred nearly four months earlier in the south than in the north, adjustments were made to the phenological observations to fit them to different regions.[2] These adjustments of-ten featured in local *nongshu*, but many centuries passed before

---

[2] The first early modern thermometers and hydrometers were introduced by the Jesuit scientist Ferdinand Verbiest in 1673 (29.7.1); see "Rexue" 熱學 (Thermodynamics) in Lu Jiaxi 盧嘉錫 and Lu Yongxiang 路甬祥 (1998; Chap-ter 37, *Introduction*), 136–45.

anybody openly criticized the practice of publishing official calendars for the whole of the country based on observations originally made in the Chang'an-Luoyang region during the Han. The first to do so was the geographer Liu Xianting 劉獻廷 (1658–95), who made the point out that different places had different 72 *hou*. The Taiping calendar, however, was the first to include revised phenological observations (made in Nanjing); See Cao Wanru 曹婉如 in *Ancient China's Technology and Science*, FLP, 1987, 229–35.

35.1.2 Agricultural Treatises

When reading agricultural treatises, as with other Chinese sources, it is essential to distinguish between what was based on the author's direct experience or contemporary information and what was simply quoted, repeated, or culled from previous writers, with or without acknowledgment.[3]

First Century AD

Fan Shengzhi shu 范勝之書 (Fan Shengzhi's work on agriculture). See Shih Sheng-han (Shi Shenghan 石聲漢, 1907–71), *On "Fan Sheng-chih shu,"* Science Press, 1959, 1963. Only fragments survive (3,500 characters preserved in encyclopaedias and in the next item). Based on farming in Guanzhong 關中 (Shaanxi).

Second Century

Cui Shi 崔寔, *Simin yueling* 四民月令 (Monthly ordinances for the four classes [scholars, farmers, artisans, and merchants]); *Simin yueling ji-shi* 四民月令集釋 (Collected annotations on the *Simin yueling*), Miao Qiyu 繆啓愉, Nongye, 1981. Includes translation into Modern Chinese. An important source for the economic history of the Later Han. Only fragments survive (preserved in *Qimin yaoshu*, see below). Consists of instructions in the form of an agricultural calendar based on private-estate management. One of the earliest in this style, the forerunner of which is the "Yueling" (Monthly observances) sections of the *Liji*, the *Lüshi chunqiu*, and the *Huainanzi*. Agricultural calendars have remained popular to this day. Most later agricultural treatises contained a calendrical section or diagram setting out the

---

[3] On both the early agricultural calendars as well as the *nongshu*, see "Sources," in SCC, vol. 6, part 2, 47–93. This includes a comparison of the Chinese sources with Greek, Roman, and European agricultural works (85–93).

main tasks of the farming year. See Patricia Buckley Ebrey, "Estate and Family Management in the Later Han as Seen in the *Monthly Instructions for the Four Classes of People*," *JESHO* 17: 173–205 (1974).

Sixth Century

Jia Sixie 賈思勰 (b. end of fifth century in Shandong), *Qimin yaoshu* 齊民要術 (Techniques essential for the subsistence of common people); for the original text punctuated, annotated, and put into Modern Chinese, see *Qimin yaoshu jiaoshi* 齊民要術校釋, Miao Qiyu 繆啓愉, ed., Nongye, 1982. ICS *Concordance* 8, forthcoming. The first complete extant comprehensive agricultural treatise. Although half the book is in the form of quotations from previous works (which have thereby been preserved), the rest is based on Jia Sixie's experience of farming in Shandong. He also has much material on eating and drinking habits during the Northern Wei. His notes on different methods of preparing everyday food are the first such descriptions to survive and can be used as recipes. See *SCC*, vol. 6, part 2, 55–59 (also includes a translation of the table of contents); see also Shih Shenghan, *A Preliminary Survey of the Book* Ch'i Min Yao Shu: *An Agricultural Encyclopaedia of the 6th Century*, Kexue, 1958; 2nd ed., with corrections, 1962; Amano Motonosuke, "Dry Farming and the *Chi-min yao-shu*," in *Silver Jubilee Volume of the Zinbun-Kagaku-Kenkyusyo*, 1954, 451–66.

Tenth Century

Han E 韓鄂, *Sishi zuanyao* 四時纂要 (Essentials of the four seasons); *Sishi zuanyao jiaoshi* 四時纂要校釋, Miao Qiyu 繆啓愉, ed., Nongye, 1981 (based on the Japanese photoreprint by Yamamoto, 1961). This is the only farming manual to survive from the seventh to tenth centuries. It was lost in China, but found in Japan in 1960 preserved in a Korean woodblock edition of 1590.

Eleventh Century

Chen Fu 陳敷 (1076–1154), *Nongshu* 農書 (agricultural treatise), 1149. Based on paddy rice farming and sericulture in southern China.

Thirteenth Century

Nongsang jiyao 農桑輯要 (Essentials of agriculture and sericulture), 1273; *Yuanke Nongsang jiyao* 元刻農桑輯要, Miao Qiyu 繆啓愉, ed., Nongye, 1988. Comprehensive, imperially sponsored. The earliest official agricultural treatise to have survived. Mainly quotations from previous works, some of which have been lost. See *SCC*, vol. 6, part 2, 71–72 (also includes a translation of the table of contents).

Fourteenth Century

Nongsang yishi cuoyao 農桑衣食撮要 (Essentials of agriculture, sericulture, clothing, and food), compiled by a Uighur official, Lu Mingshan 魯明善. Important because written as an actual handbook for magistrates in their role as agricultural instructors. Arranged in agricultural calendar style.

Wang Zhen 王禎, *Nongshu* 農書 (Agricultural treatise), Preface dated 1313, but probably written slightly earlier; *Dong Lu Wangshi nongshu yizhu* 東魯王氏農書譯注 (Mr. Wang of Eastern Lu's agricultural treatise, translated [into Modern Chinese] with notes), *Zhongguo gudai keji mingzhu yizhu congshu* 中國古代科技名著譯注叢書 (Collectanea of annotated famous Chinese works on science and technology done into Modern Chinese), Miao Qiyu 繆啟愉, ed., Shanghai guji, 1994. Wang's *Nongshu* is important because it was based on the author's observations as a county magistrate in Anhui and Jiangxi, and travels in north China. The first two sections (on agriculture, sericulture, and crops) are mainly based on previous works. The author, however, draws attention to differences in northern and southern agriculture. The third section, "Nongqi Tupu" 農器圖譜 (Illustrations of agricultural implements), is unique and takes up most of the book. The drawings of all the main farming implements in use at that time are annotated. Compare these to the implements in use in the first part of the twentieth century as shown in *China at Work*.[4] Many are the same. See *SCC*, vol. 6, part 2, 59–64 (also includes a translation of the table of contents). In order to print the *Nongshu*, Wang developed the use of movable type using wood (18.4).

Seventeenth Century

Nongzheng quanshu 農政全書 (Comprehensive treatise on agricultural administration), Xu Guangqi 徐光啓 (1562–1633), comp., 1639; *Nongzheng quanshu jiaozhu* 農政全書校注 (Collated and annotated *Comprehensive Treatise on Agriculture*), Shi Shenghan 石聲漢, ed., 3 vols., Shanghai guji, 1979. Important because it summed up the state of the art; it was highly popular in Tokugawa Japan. Xu was friendly with some of the Jesuit scholars and has included excerpts from European works on hydraulics. See *SCC*, vol. 6, part 2, 64–70 (also includes a translation of the table of contents).

---

[4] Rudolph P. Hommel, *China at Work: An Illustrated Record of the Primitive Industries of China's Masses, Whose Life is Toil, and Thus an Account of Chinese Civilization*, New York: John Day & Company, 1937; MIT Press, 1969.

Tiangong kaiwu 天工開物 (Chapter 37).

Bu Nongshu 補農書 (Addendum to [Mr Shen's] *Nongshu* of 1643), Zhang Lüxiang 張履祥 (1611–74). Chen Hengli 陳恒力 (1911–78), *Bu Nongshu yanjiu* 補農書研究 (Studies on the *Bu Nongshu*), Zhonghua, 1958; Nongye, 1961. The same scholar also published a punctuated, annotated edition with translation into Modern Chinese: *Bu Nongshu jiaoshi* 補農書校釋, Chen Hengli 陳恒力 and Wang Da 王達, eds., Nongye, 1983. *Bu Nongshu* is important because it contains advice on how to run a single estate in Tongxiang 桐鄉, Zhejiang.

Zhang Ying 張英, *Hengchan suoyan* 恒產瑣言 (Fragmentary remarks on real estate), ca. 1697. Written for the benefit of his heirs (as were many other such treatises that were more in the form of family instructions than farming manuals). Translated in Hilary J. Beattie, *Land and Lineage in China—A Study of T'ung-ch'eng County, Anhwei, in the Ming and Ch'ing Dynasties*, CUP, 1979, Appendix III, 140–51. Also by Clara Yu in *Chinese Civilization: A Sourcebook* (8.1), 287–91.

Eighteenth Century

Shoushi tongkao 授時通考 (Comprehensive study of the farming year), imperially sponsored and distributed, 1747, Nongye, 1963. Almost entirely culled from previous works. See *SCC*, vol. 6, part 2, 72–74 (also includes a translation of the table of contents).

Gengzhi tu 耕織圖 (Pictures of plowing and weaving [agriculture and sericulture]), imperially sponsored. Expanded from a Song original dating from 1210. The China Agriculture Museum in Beijing has reproduced pictures from this plus many other similar collections in *Zhongguo gudai gengzhitu* 中國古代耕織圖 (Farming and weaving pictures in ancient China), Wang Chaosheng 王潮生, ed. in chief, Nongye, 1995. The explanatory text is in Chinese and English. For a German translation, see *Kêng tschi tu: Ackerbau und Seidengewinnung in China, ein kaiserliches Lehr- und Mahn-buch*, Otto Franke, tr., Hamburg: L. Friederichsen & Co., 1913.

Nineteenth Century

Yang Xiuyuan 楊秀元, *Nongyan zhushi* 農言著實 (Practical advice on farming), in *Qin-Jin nongyan* 秦晉農言 (Shaanxi and Shanxi farm manuals), Zhonghua, 1957.

35.1.3 Research Tools

In addition to the agricultural treatises, local gazetteers and the monographs on financial administration in the Standard Histories also contain information on Chinese agricultural history.

The best introduction to the history of Chinese agriculture in English is the substantial, well-illustrated work by Francesca Bray, *Agriculture* (*SCC*, vol. 6, part 2), CUP, 1984.

The Nongye chubanshe in Beijing has published a number of important studies and reference works on the history of Chinese agriculture:

Zhongguo nongye baike quanshu: Nongye lishijuan 中國農業百科全書農業 歷史卷 (Encyclopaedia of Chinese agriculture, volume on agricultural history), Nongye, 1995. Contains articles on the history of each of the main Chinese crops, animal husbandry, irrigation, techniques, implements, land taxes, disaster relief, and agricultural treatises (an annex lists 650 titles arranged in 11 categories). There are also articles on the agricultural history of each dynasty, the different regions of China, and the main non-Han peoples both in China and abroad. The title of each of the 500 articles in the encyclopaedia is translated into English and there is also an English index. This is an excellent work of reference with over 150 color plates and numerous black and white illustrations. The other 30 vols. of this encyclopaedia all contain articles on the historical background to their subject.

Zhongguo nongye kexue jishu shigao 中國農業科學技術史稿 (Draft history of Chinese agricultural science and technology), Liang Jiamian 梁家勉, ed. in chief, Nongye, 1989, 1992. Covers from the Neolithic to the end of the Han in 240 pages and thoroughly incorporates the findings of archaeology. It also contains a further 240 pages carrying the story to the end of the Qing. Appendix I summarizes the main innovations in agricultural technology in each period and in each field, appendix II gives the Latin and English names for all plants mentioned in the text, and Appendix III is a bibliography of 750 primary and secondary sources used.

Zhongguo gudai nongye kejishi tushuo 中國古代農業科技史圖說 (Illustrations with commentary on the history of ancient Chinese agricultural science and technology), Chen Wenhua 陳文華, ed., Nongye, 1991. Based on the historical displays in the Agricultural History Museum in Beijing. It covers crops, implements, animals, and techniques and contains copious illustrations from archaeological reports and *nongshu* from prehistoric times to 1840.

The following studies examine the history of Chinese agriculture from the viewpoint of economists and historians:

Dwight H. Perkins, *Agricultural Development in China*, Aldine, 1969.

Kang Chao (Zhao Gang 趙岡), *Man and Land in Chinese History, An Economic Analysis*, SUP, 1986.

Gang Deng, *Development Versus Stagnation: Technological Continuity and Agricultural Progress in Pre-modern China*, Greenwood, 1993.

Mark Elvin, *The Pattern of the Chinese Past*, SUP, 1973.

Liu Ts'ui-jung (Liu Cuirong 劉翠溶), "Agricultural Change and Population Growth: A Brief Survey in the Case of China in Historical Perspective," *Academia Sinica Economic Papers* 14.1: 29–68 (1986).

Botanical Names

The problem of botanical names in Chinese sources is the same as in many other fields—homonymy and synonymy, that is the same name was often used for different plants (*tongming yiwu* 同名異物) and the same plant was often called different names (*tongwu yiming* 同物異名). For a rather simplistic introduction, see "Botanical Linguistics," *SCC*, vol. 6, part 1, 117–42. To identify and check the English names of plants and flowers in Chinese works, in addition to the references cited under *Studies* above, use one of the many concordances such as

Yangshi yuanyi zhiwu da mingdian 楊氏園藝植物大名典 (Yang's compendium of horticulture and plant names), Yang Gongyi 楊恭毅, comp., 9 vols., Taibei: Zhongguo huahui zazhishe 中國花卉雜志社, 1984. It contains color photographs of the trees, flowers, and plants, and the compiler indicates their Chinese, English, Latin, French, and German names as well as giving a synopsis of their history and their alternative names in Chinese.

Xinbian La Han Ying zhiwu mingcheng 新編拉漢英植物名稱 (Latin, Chinese, and English plant names, newly edited), Zhongkeyuan Zhiwu yanjiusuo, comp., Hangkong gongye, 1996. Gives the Chinese and English equivalents of 55,800 plant names in Latin. It is alphabetically arranged by Latin name and also contains Chinese and English indexes.

Since the leaves, seeds, and other parts of a huge variety of plants and flowers were used in Chinese medicine, medical dictionaries can also be helpful (Chapter 36, *Medical Terms*).

There are also numerous specialized studies identifying the terminology found in the classics and other early works, see, for example,

Shijing 詩經: Wu Houyan 吳厚炎, *Shijing caomu huikao* 詩經草木匯考 (Investigation of the vegetation in the *Shijing*), Guizhou renmin, 1992.

Michael E. Carr, *A Linguistic Study of the Flora and Fauna Sections of the Erh ya*, Ph.D., University of Arizona, 1972.

Bibliography

Wang Yuhu 王毓瑚 (1907–80), *Zhongguo nongxue shulu* 中國農學書錄, is the basic bibliographic guide to all types of *nongshu* from all periods. The author arranges all known agricultural treatises (whether lost or extant) according to broad categories with bibliographic notes and summaries of the contents of each: *Zhongguo nongxue shulu* (Annotated catalog of Chinese agricultural treatises), Nongye, 1964; rev. edition, 1979. Wang's work was reprinted and introduced by Amano Motonosuke 天野元之助, *Chûgoku nôgaku shoroku* 中國農學書錄 (Annotated catalog of Chinese agricultural treatises), Ryûkei, 1975, and commented in the same author's *Chûgoku konôsho kô* 中國古農書考 (Researches on ancient Chinese agricultural works), Ryûkei, 1975. Amano's introduction formed the basis of the revised edition of Wang Yuhu (1979). See also Amano's *Chûgoku nôgyôshi kenkyû* 中國農業史研究 (Researches into Chinese agricultural history), Ochanomizu shobô, 1962; expanded edition, 1979. Amano (1975) was translated into Chinese under the same title and published by Nongye, 1992.

William Y. Chen, *An Annotated Bibliography of Chinese Agriculture*, CMC, 1993, provides brief notes in English on 542 traditional works on agriculture (both lost and extant).

For 19,255 articles (including book reviews) on Chinese agricultural history published in China (as well as in Taiwan, Hong Kong, and, to a certain extent, Japan) between the late Qing and 1991, see *Zhongguo nongshi lunwen mulu suoyin* 中國農史論文目錄索引 (Index to articles on agricultural history), Zhongguo nongye bowuguan, Ziliaoshi 中國農業博物館資料室 (Documentation room, China Agricultural Museum), ed., Linye, 1993. This also includes studies of water control and transport, fertilizer, population, land systems, land taxes, and trade in agricultural produce.

SCC, vol. 6, part 2, contains a full bibliography of primary and secondary sources.

Journals

Gujin nongye 古今農業 (Ancient and modern agriculture of China), 1987– , semiannual (1987–90); thereafter, quarterly (Zhongguo nongye bowuguan 中國農業博物館 (China Agricultural Museum), Beijing.

Nongye kaogu 農業考古 (12.3).

Zhongguo nongshi 中國農史 (Chinese agricultural history), quarterly; since 1981, Nanjing nongye daxue et al., eds., Nanjing.

35.2 Food

35.2.1 Variety and Changes in Chinese Cuisine

There are at least four keys to the richness of the ever-changing Chinese cuisine. The first is the huge and expanding area from which it was able to draw its resources. Eventually, after millennia of expansion, this area included climate zones ranging from the subarctic to the tropical, each providing not only new ingredients, but often also cultures with distinct cooking traditions of their own. Chief among these are what can broadly be described as the northern and southern traditions. The southern traditions were based on rice, fish, fish sauce, domestic animals, vegetables, and tropical fruits; those of the north were characterized by dry-land crops, the meat of wild animals, northern vegetables, including the soybean, and temperate fruits. Different eating habits of the various non-Han peoples within the China area were gradually absorbed into the two great traditions, for example, eating snakes, which was typical of the Yue 越, became part of the southern tradition (later incorporated in the rest of the country in the attenuated form of tonic potions). The interplay of the northern and southern traditions eventually became elaborated into variously defined, but strongly differentiated regional cuisines, the natural complement to the regional cultures and dialect areas whose emergence is one of the main themes of Chinese history.

The second key is the development during the empire of an elaborate tradition of dietary and medicinal cooking (*shiliao* 食療; *shizhi* 食治). Food was seen as the basis of good health, provided the right amounts and combinations were taken. Eating the right ingredients could ensure a long life and potency (*yangsheng* 養生). Food was medicine and medicine, food.

The third key was the number of demands from different patrons or groups for their own specialized cuisines. Such patrons included the court, rich households, and scholar-gourmands. Buddhists and Muslims also elaborated their own cuisines (*sucai* 素菜 and *qingzhen* 清真). Furthermore, by the later empire, there were enough wealthy businessmen and officials living away from their home towns, especially in the capitals, to support restaurants catering to their desire to eat the cuisine they were familiar with (35.2.4).

The fourth key (and it is related to the first two) was the continuous absorption of all sorts of foreign influences, including ingredients, cooking methods, and recipes from the peoples of the steppe (Xiongnu to Manchu), as well as from the rest of Asia, the Americas, Europe, and Japan.

These are the key factors that have made Chinese cuisine the most varied in the world. More than is generally realized, they also ensured that it was constantly changing. As a result, many of what are considered typical features today turn out to have been added relatively recently. To somebody brought up on late twentieth century Chinese cuisine, Ming food would probably still seem familiar, but anything further back, especially pre-Tang would probably be difficult to recognize as "Chinese."[5] It is a question the answer to which is changing rapidly because the contemporary basis of comparison itself is being altered at the beginning of the twenty-first century. Open-door policies, greater wealth, new life-styles, and new influences from Hong Kong, Taiwan, Japan, and the West are all accelerating changes in Chinese cooking methods, ingredients, and eating habits as never before.

[5] Clearly the overall diet would have been very different, but the question here is the taste of a good meal. As an experiment, during a three month period in the Beijing winter of 1999, I asked my chef to prepare dishes on the basis of the cooking methods, ingredients, and occasional recipes found in the early sixth-century farming manual *Qimin yaoshu* 齊民要術 (35.1.2). The ingredients include many grasses and fibrous plants difficult to find today, but not unpleasant to anyone fond of vegetarian cooking. The fermentation of many of the ingredients or their dousing in fermented bean sauce becomes an acquired taste. The absence of sugar, vegetable cooking oil, chili, and tomatoes is hardly missed, and the use of boiling, roasting, or baking is a relief from the oily monotony conferred by stir frying. However, I noticed that most of my Chinese guests felt that what they were eating was foreign, not Chinese.

35.2.2   Pre-Qin Foodstuffs and Cooking

In surveying the history of agriculture and food in China, it is important to bear in mind that certain crops and ingredients may have been indigenous but not widely used, while the same import or a new variety has often been introduced on separate occasions, sometimes centuries apart.[6] Often, too, a related or better strain of a plant was imported, even though it may have already existed for centuries in one or another part of the China area. One conclusion is that diffusion to different parts of China may not always have followed the introduction of a plant or crop, and if it did, only very slowly, at least in the earlier centuries.

Rice cultivation had already spread from the Yangzi valley to the north as far as Shanxi and Henan in the late Neolithic. It possibly predates the main staple in the north, millet (*he* 禾, *gu* 谷, *su* 粟, *ji* 稷, *liang* 粱, *shu* 秫). It is only from sites seven or eight millennia later in the Shang and Western Zhou that wheat (*xiaomai* 小麥) and barley (*damai* 大麥) begin to appear (many have assumed that they were imported from the West).[7]

Cooking was mainly by boiling and steaming; the typical dish was a millet stew with mallow, turnips, reeds, or radish and, for most people, only occasionally deer, rabbit, or dog meat, fish, or fruit. The staple was accompanied by a savory paste (*jiang* 醬, *misô* in Japanese) made from hydrolyzed (fermented) meat, fish, crustaceans, or, most important of all, soybeans.[8]

The soybean is indigenous to northeast China. Its cultivation began in the Zhou period. It was a major source of protein, especially for peasants and laborers. Starting in the Yangzi valley, it was brined and hydrolyzed into the characteristic Chinese flavoring, soy

[6] For discussions of the historical characteristics of Chinese food, see *Food in Chinese History: Anthropological and Historical Perspectives*, K. C. Chang, ed., YUP, 1977; E. N. Anderson, *The Food of China*, YUP, 1988; Wang Renxiang 王仁湘, *Yinshi yu Zhongguo wenhua* 飲食與中國文化 (Food and drink in Chinese culture), Renmin, 1994; 3rd prnt. 1999.

[7] See 13.1, on the earliest evidence for the cultivation of rice and *SCC*, vol. 6, part 2, 440, for a table of the terminology of Chinese millets.

[8] *Zhongguo shiqian yinshishi* 中國史前飲食史 (A history of Chinese prehistoric food and drink), Wang Renxiang 王仁湘, ed. in chief, Qingdao, 1997.

sauce (*jiangyou* 醬油).[9] By the Han, a new process had been discovered; if the production was interrupted half way and the beans dried, they became blackened and delicious. Along with savory pastes (*jiang* 醬) and pickles (*zu* 菹), these fermented soybeans (*chi* 豉) were immensely popular.[10]

The rulers of ancient China attached huge importance to food. The main symbol of royal power was a massive cooking vessel, the *ding* 鼎 (caldron; see 17.1). At the Zhou court (according to the *Zhouli*), there were 21 different official posts with a total staff of 2,300 people involved in cooking and the preparation of food for banquets, ceremonies, rituals, sacrifices, and medicine (compare the late Qing court which was served by only 300 chefs). One of the common words for cooking was *gepeng* 割烹 (to cut and cook), which possibly suggests the early appearance of one important characteristic of the Chinese cuisine, fine cutting of ingredients before cooking.

The *Shijing* 詩經 mentions at least 44 definite or probable food plants and 260 of the common domestic and wild animals, birds, fishes, and insects found in the north during the first millennium BC. The dishes in the southern cuisine are invoked in the other great anthology of ancient poetry, the *Chuci* 楚詞, and also in the "Benwei" 本味 chapter of the *Lüshi chunqiu* 呂氏春秋. Pre-Qin lists of ingredients and descriptions of food rituals are found in the *Liji* 禮記 and the *Yili* 儀禮. Discoveries in tombs of actual foodstuffs have added much to the written sources as well as corroborating them (the difficult problem of the identification of the plants, however, remains; see 35.1.3 *Botanical Names*). Han tomb paintings and carvings of kitchens and feasts round out the general picture. The first recipes which indicate how the food was prepared (at a provin-

---

[9] The origin of "soya" in European and other languages is from either *xiyao* 豉油 or from *shôyu* 醬油 (the Cantonese and Japanese words for *jiangyou* 醬油, respectively). The early generic word was *shu* 菽 (*Glycine max*), later *dou* 豆, and later still, *dadou* 大豆 to distinguish it from post-Han imported pulses.

[10] *Chi* 豉 used to be pronounced *shi*. Other early names for *chi* were *douchi* 豆豉, *daku* 大苦, and *nadou* 納豆 (*nattô* in Japanese). The vocabulary of pre-Qin cooking is minutely examined in the special dictionary *Zhongguo shanggu pengshi zidian* 中國上古烹食字典 (Dictionary of archaic Chinese cooking), Lin Yinsheng 林銀生 et al., eds., Shangye, 1993. In all, 940 words related to food and cooking are analyzed. They are drawn from the *Shuowen* 說文, the *Erya* 爾雅, and the *Fangyan* 方言.

cial court) are on bamboo strips discovered in 1999 at Huxishan 虎溪山, near Changsha (44.4.2). The earliest record of everyday cooking is in the sixth-century *Qimin yaoshu* 齊民要術 (35.1.2).[11]

35.2.3   New Foodstuffs

During the four hundred years of the Han, cooking made great advances. One sign was the appearance of more elaborate cooking stoves. The meat stew and stewing remained popular; other methods of cooking meat included open roasting, deep frying, drying in the sun, mud-baking, boiling, braising, and steaming. The necessity of combining the five flavors (sweet, sour, hot, bitter, and salty) was well established. Thin slicing for eating raw (or pickling) was not uncommon. Noodles were introduced (called *bing* 餅 because they were made from flour and water). Soy beans (in both their *jiang* 醬 and *chi* 豉 forms) remained an important source of protein.

The Han and the centuries up to and including the Tang saw the introduction and spread from Inner Asia of many foodstuffs. Some may have been imported earlier than their appearance in written sources suggests. The first wave was credited to the Former Han emissary, Zhang Qian 張騫 (41.5.1, *Travel Abroad*). They included:

grapes (*putao* 蒲桃[陶], imported from Ferghana; possibly a loan from putative early Persian *budâwa*, a cognate of Greek *botros*? modern *putao* 葡萄)

lucerne [alfalfa] (*musu* 目宿 or *mushu* 木粟, loan from *buksuk*, the name used in Ferghana, from which it was imported to feed the war horses from the same place; modern *musu* 苜蓿)

peas (*hudou* 胡豆, modern *wandou* 豌豆; also later used for broad bean, modern *candou* 蠶豆)

rape (*hucai* 胡菜, modern *youcai* 油菜)

sesame (*huma* 胡麻, modern *zhima* 芝麻)

The names of the imports were either transliterations of the original names, for example:

coriander (*husui* 胡荽, Persian *goswi*; modern *yansui* 芫荽, *xiangcai* 香菜)

fenugreek (*huluba* 葫蘆巴, *kudou* 苦豆, from Arabic *hulba*)

---

[11] David R. Knechtges, "A Literary Feast: Food in Early Chinese Literature," *JAOS* 106: 49–63 (1986).

jasmine (*moli* 茉利, Sanskrit *mallika*; modern *molihua* 茉莉花)

lemon (*limengzi* 黎檬子, Persian *leymun*; modern *ningmeng* 檸檬)

or they were prefixed with the name of the country of origin as in

pomegranate (*anshiliu* 安石榴, after Anxi guo 安息國, Parthia; modern *shiliu* 石榴)

spinach (*boleng* 菠薐, after Nepali *palinga*; modern *bocai* 菠菜)

or they had the prefix "*hu*" 胡 placed before an existing Chinese word as in

black pepper (*hujiao* 胡椒)[12]

cucumber (*hugua* 胡瓜, modern *huanggua* 黃瓜)

walnuts (*hutao* 胡桃, modern *hetao* 核桃; used for desserts, in mediccine, and as a fixative for paintings)

or they had the prefix "*a*" 阿 as in

fig (*azang* 阿馹, modern *wuhuaguo* 無花果)

pistachio (*ayue hunzi* 阿月渾子, *hu zhenzi* 胡榛子)

Frequently these indications of a foreign origin were dropped as the import became domesticated. Sometimes the process was accelerated as when Shile 石勒 (274–333), the king of Later Zhao, is said to have taken exception to the word *hu* 胡 (barbarian) and forbidden its use. There were many other imports between the Han and the Tang, including almonds, apples, coriander, garlic, lettuce (presented as tribute during the Sui), Mediterranean olives, western onions (*Allium cepa*), Persian dates, rock salt, and sugar beet. Each plant or fruit had (and often still has) many alternative names in different parts of China.[13]

---

[12] Beware the assumption that all disyllabic words beginning with *hu* 胡 are loanwords. Sometimes they are. As such, they indicate a barbarian or Xiongnu origin (in the Han) or Inner Asiatic origin (Tang). But *hu* can also be a meaningless prefix (especially in words for plants, birds, and insects and when it predates the meaning of barbarian, e.g., *hudie* 胡蝶); see Zhou Zhenhe 周振鶴 and You Rujie 游汝杰, *Fangyan yu Zhongguo wenhua* 方言與中國文化 (Dialects and Chinese culture), Shanghai renmin, 4th prnt. with revisions, 1997, 139–43.

[13] Berthold Laufer (1874–1934), *Sino-Iranica; Chinese Contributions to the History of Civilization in Ancient Iran; With Special Reference to the History of Cultivated Plants and Products*, Anthropological Series, 15 (3), Chicago: Field Museum of Natural History, 1919; Ch'eng-wen, 1967; Edward H. Schafer, *The Golden Peaches of Samarkand: A Study of T'ang Exotics*, UCP, 1963; paperback,

Footnote continued on next page

During the Nan-Bei Chao, the Chinese had the opportunity to observe and taste the cuisine of the northern kingdoms, those ruled and partly settled by the *wuhu* 五胡 (five barbarians). As early as the Later Han, some of these foodstuffs had become popular. By the Tang, many more of the *hushi* 胡食 (barbarian dishes) had become fashionable and were entering the mainstream. In some cases they probably originated in Persia or Inner Asia but were introduced by the northern kingdoms. They included the following:

dianxin 點心, *dimsum* in Cantonese. First used in the Tang as a verb to mean "put a bit in the stomach," i.e., stave off hunger before main meal; still used in this sense in several dialects; also *dianbu* 點補; compare similar (Yuan) expression *dianji* 點饑; in the Song it came to mean snack (cf. *xiaoshi* 小食). The modern meaning of pastry snack dates from the Ming.

hubao rou 胡爆肉 (clay-baked or mutton haggis)

hubing 胡餅 (sesame buns), a form of spiced wheat bread

huchi 胡豉 (bitter fermented blackened soy beans)

hufan 胡飯 (roasted mutton slices seasoned with pickled cucumber and chopped fresh vegetables rolled in pancakes)

hugeng 胡羹 (sheep stew)

mozhi 貊炙 (whole-roasted lamb or calf)

mantou 饅頭 (steamed bread rolls)[14]

Qiang zhufa 羌煮法 (boiled lamb slices à la Qiang); the forerunner of the northern dish of rinsed lamb (*shuanyangrou* 涮羊肉)

Xi Qiang zhi or *zha* 西羌鮓 (pickled fish slices à la West Qiang)[15]

1985; *Han-Tang yinshi wenhuashi* 漢唐飲食文化史 (History of the culture of food and drink from the Han to the Tang), Li Hu 黎虎, ed., Beijing shifan daxue, 1998.

[14] Zhuge Liang 諸葛亮 is said to have invented the *mantou* during his conquests in the south of China as a substitute for real human heads (used by southerners for sacrifices), hence *mantou* 饅頭 meaning *mantou* 蠻頭 (the head of a southern barbarian). Another theory is that it is a loan from Turkish *mantu*. In the Song, *mantou* were very popular with students. Apart from snacks and as a staple in the north, they were used as a sacrificial food at festivals, see Zhu Wei 朱偉, *Kaochi* 考吃 (Philological researches into eating), Zhonghua, 1997, 61–65.

[15] The main primary source on food and cooking methods in the north during the Nan-Bei Chao is *Qimin yaoshu* 齊民要術 (35.1). For modern studies, see David R. Knechtges, "Gradually Entering the Realm of Delight: Food and Drink in Early Medieval China," *JAOS* 117: 229–39 (1997); Lü Yifei 呂一飛,

Footnote continued on next page

Turning to the south, Guangdong supplied tropical fruits and in some cases their Yue language names with them: *lizhi* 荔枝 (lychee), *pipa* 枇杷 or *lüjüe* 蘆橘 (loquat), *longyan* 龍眼 (longan), *jinjüe* 金橘 (kumquat). Lychee are attested in the literature as early as the Han, when unsuccessful efforts were made to cultivate them in the imperial orchards in Chang'an and Luoyang. For most of the dynasty, they were rushed posthaste to the court as tribute, a practice that continued in later dynasties. The cultivation of such fruits became widespread in the south only in the Tang and Song.[16] From Southeast Asia came spices such as long pepper (*biba* 蓽茇 or *bibo* 蓽撥), betel leaf (*binlang* 檳榔 from Malay *pinang*) and fruits, including several varieties of banana (*bajiao* 芭蕉 from Malay *pisang*, *ganjiao* 甘蕉, *meirenjiao* 美人蕉), coconut (*Yuewang tou* 越王頭, i.e., the head of the king of Yue, modern *yezi* 椰子), star fruit (*yangtao* 洋桃, modern *wulianzi* 五歛子).

From India came the eggplant *qiezi* 茄子 (it had spread to the whole country by the Song, having arriving along with Buddhism during the Han), sugar cane (first mentioned in the Buddhist scriptures; techniques for refining it were imported from India during the early Tang), and cotton (*jibei* 吉貝 or *gubei* 古貝 from Sanskrit *karpâda* or Malay *kapuk*).[17]

Early ripening rice was imported from Champa to join local strains in the eleventh century. Bean curd (*doufu* 豆腐) is first mentioned in the early Song. It was imported into Japan and first appears there in a source of 1183. It was used as a substitute for meat

---

Huzu xisu yu Sui-Tang fengyun 胡族習俗與隋唐風韵 (The customs of the foreign tribes and the fashions of the Sui and Tang), Shumu wenxian, 1996.

[16] The English names for these fruits are usually derived from the Cantonese or Min pronunciation, for example, *laiqi* (not *lizhi*) gives lychee; *lougwat* (not *lüjüe*) gives loquat, and *gemgwat* (not *jinjüe*) gives kumquat. In the twentieth century, the lychee and longan reached China-town restaurants in America, Europe, and Japan before most people in north China had ever seen them, thanks to companies like the Amoy Canning Corporation.

[17] Cotton may have been imported much earlier. It has been found in Former Han tombs. On sugar, see Christian Daniels, *Agro-Industries and Forestry. Agro-Industries: Sugarcane Technology* (SCC, vol. 6, part 3). On imports from India, see Xinru Liu, *Ancient India and Ancient China: Trade and Religious Exchanges, AD 1–600*, New Delhi: OUP, 1988. See also Edward H. Schafer, *The Vermilion Bird: T'ang Images of the South*, UCP, 1967, 1985.

and fish in the Buddhist vegetarian cooking. The first mention of watermelon (*xigua* 西瓜 from Jurchen *xeko*) is also in the Song.

Liquor distillation using sorghum (*gaoliang* 高粱), the base of many of China's most famous spirits, became common only during the twelfth century. The Mongols and other northern rulers may not have introduced the firepot (*huoguo* 火鍋), but they probably helped enhance the popularity of lamb and stewed mutton in Beijing and the north with their own versions of old favorites introduced during the Northern Dynasties over a thousand years before. The first mention of carrot (*huluobo* 胡蘿卜, barbarian radish) is in the Yuan.

New World crops made their way into China from the sixteenth century. They included chili, corn, peanuts, sweet potato, tomato, papaya, pineapple, vanilla, and sweet-sop. Terms for those crops imported via the south are often indicated by the character *fan* 番 (also written *fan* 蕃), another word for aboriginal or barbarian. It had been in use in this sense since the Zhou, became widespread in the Song and was extended to foodstuffs in the Ming (see 41.2.1). Just as with the earlier *hu* 胡, it was often prefixed to an existing plant or fruit name, and then as the import became domesticated, *fan* was dropped—for example, chili (*fanjiao* 番椒, modern *lajiao* 辣椒); corn, maize (*fanmai* 番麥, modern *yumi* 玉米); sweet potato (*fanshu* 番薯 or *fanyu* 番芋, modern *ganshu* 甘薯); tomato (*fanqie* 番茄, modern *xihongshi* 西紅柿); peanuts (*fandou* 番豆, modern *huasheng* 花生); mangoes (*fansuan* 番蒜, modern *mangguo* 芒果).

Portuguese or Spanish food was called *fancai* 番菜; *fancai guan* 番菜館 or *fanguan* 番館 were early terms for Western-style restaurants. *Fanguan* 番館 was also used for foreign-style hotel (compare the use of *fandian* 飯店 for "hotel"). As *fan* was dropped, *xi* 西, *yang* 洋, or *hai* 海 came into greater use to indicate foreign imports. In the southern dialects, however, *fan* is sometimes retained; in Min dialect, for example, *fanjiang* 番姜, *fanke* 番客, and *fanshi* 番柿 are still used for "chili," "Overseas Chinese," and "tomato," respectively.

Two other major characteristics of Chinese cuisine, the bird's nest (*yanwo* 燕窩) and shark's fin (*yuchi* 魚翅), only entered China in the early Ming (they are said to have been brought back from Southeast Asia by Zheng He 鄭和).

Some of what until recently were typical dishes or sweets of the north, for example, the *saqima* 薩齊瑪[薩其馬], are Manchu in origin. The succulent and popular *baizhurou* 白煮肉, *shaguo bairou* 沙鍋白肉, *baipianrou* 白片肉, and other boiled pork recipes may have been derived from the Manchu practice of sacrificing pigs before shaman rituals. The Qing also saw many imported foodstuffs, including agar agar, asparagus, bullfrog, baby corn, cauliflower, Jerusalem artichoke, and kidney bean. The flow of imported foodstuffs has continued to the present day.

In ancient times the main beverage was boiled water, or boiled rice water. Ordinary people on special occasions drank fruit cordials and schnapps; the mighty took millet or rice ale. The leaves of the wild tea tree (*camellia sinensis*; indigenous to Yunnan) were chopped up and mixed with shallot, ginger, dogwood, and other ingredients and boiled as a medicine. Up to the Han, such potions were called *tu* 茶. After the Qin conquest of the Sichuanese kingdoms of Ba and Shu (the main cultivation centers) in 316 BC, tea planting and drinking spread to other parts of south China. Gradually tea began to be drank on its own; the habit spread in the north (and to Japan) thanks to Buddhist monks who used it as a means of both stimulating meditation and of staying awake. Northern nomads acquired the taste for tea early; it was a major item at the border markets from the Tang. The most famous work on tea was written in the late Tang by Lu Yu 陸羽 (?–804): *Chajing* 茶經 (760). He lists other names for tea that had come into use since the Han as *she* 荈, *ming* 茗, and *chuan* 荈.[18] In the Song the leaves were steamed and ground into a powder. Then, instead of boiling, hot water was added and the beverage was whipped into a froth (as is still practiced in the Japanese tea ceremony, a method imported during the Song). Roasting of the leaves spread in the Song and Yuan. It was in the Yuan and Ming that steeping became the main method of preparation and along with it the teapot was introduced for the first time. The inclusion of flower petals with the tea leaves began in the Yuan (the forerunner of Jasmine tea) as also did the drinking of tea as part of a meal or snack (often with the addition of mare, sheep or yak butter to make Mongolian or Tibetan *suyoucha* 酥油茶). Tea was exported

---

[18] Lu Yu, *The Classic of Tea*, Francis Ross Carpenter, tr., Little, Brown, 1974; *Chajing qianshi* 茶經淺釋 (Treatise on tea), Zhang Fangci 張芳賜 et al., tr. with annotations, Yunnan renmin, 1981.

to the West in the seventeenth century, and its cultivation introduced to India and Sri Lanka only in the nineteenth century.[19]

A number of condiments and spices that are today frequently used in Chinese cuisine were all imported, albeit over many centuries, e.g., black pepper (*hujiao* 胡椒), cardamoms (*doukou* 豆蔻), chili (*lajiao* 辣椒), cloves (*dingxiang* 丁香), sesame seeds (*mazi* 麻子), star anise (*bajiao* 八角), and star fruit (*wulianzi* 五斂子). On the other hand, something thought typical of Chinese cooking, monosodium glutamate (MSG), was invented in Japan only in 1905. It was not until the 1930s and 1940s that it began turning up in every Chinese restaurant.

35.2.4 Regional Cuisines

Different eating habits in different regions had no doubt existed since prehistoric times as the result of varied resource bases and of the fact that those belonging to different language groups ordinarily have different food habits; indeed in imperial times there is some correlation between the dialect areas and regional cuisines.[20] But the emergence of restaurants serving regional specialities in the capital and other major cities took place only in the later empire. They were stimulated by guilds and meeting places catering to fellow provincials away from home. These businessmen and officials preferred to eat the dishes to which they were accustomed. They also

---

[19] In most languages the word for tea reflects the route by which it was exported from China. If by the northern overland route, it is derived from the Mandarin pronunciation *cha*, e.g., in Arabic, Persian, Turkish, Italian, Russian, and early English. If, on the other hand, by the southern sea route from Xiamen 厦門 and other ports in Fujian, it reflects the Min dialect pronunciation of 茶 as *te*. The product and this pronunciation of it were introduced to the rest of Europe by the Dutch in the seventeenth century. They called it *thee*, from whence German *Tee*, French *thé*, and English *tea* (to rhyme with obey as in Pope's "Rape of the Lock," 1712, Canto III). This was the first English pronunciation. It coexisted for a century with *tea* (to rhyme with see), the new standard after 1762 (except in Ireland). *Cha* or *chai* was a variant word for tea in English in the early days. *Cha* is now British slang and *chai* is used for Indian spiced tea.

[20] *Juan* 1 of the late Warring States medical classic *Huangdi neijing* (Chapter 36) has a schematic account of different eating habits linked to the five directions and to five-phase theory and correlated with different diseases and medical traditions.

had the opportunity to compare their favorites with those of other regional cuisines, each of which was continuously developed by inventive restaurateurs and cooks who borrowed ideas and techniques from each other. Until the Song only two main cuisines were distinguished, the north (*beishi* 北食) and the south (*nanshi* 南食). In the Northern Song there is mention of restaurants in the capital, Bianliang 汴梁 (modern Kaifeng), specializing in both of these as well as Sichuan dishes (*Chuanfan dian* 川飯店). Some of the dishes in the "*Chuanfan*" eating places had names identical to those still used in Sichuan today, but they cannot have been the same dish. One of the signatures of modern Sichuan cuisine (*Chuancai* 川菜 as it is called today) is the use of the Sichuan indigenous peppercorn (*huajiao* 花椒) mixed with chili to create the famous numbing and hot (*mala* 麻辣) effect. But chili was imported to the province by Hunanese settlers only in the eighteenth century. The first collection of recipes of a regional cuisine is devoted to Sichuan: the *Xingyuan lu* 醒園錄 (late eighteenth century). No dishes using *mala* appear in it. Many of what are today considered typical Sichuanese dishes were introduced only in the nineteenth century. For example, Sichuan hotpot, *huoguo* 火鍋, came in during the Daoguang reign, and *Gongbao jiding* 宮保鷄丁 is said to be the invention of the famous late Qing governor of Sichuan, Ding Baozhen 丁寶楨, 1820–86. Indeed, all the elements that we associate with *Chuancai* today had come together only by the very end of the Qing. National prominence came during WWII when people from the rest of the country moved to the wartime capital of Chongqing.[21]

35.2.5 Cooking and Eating Implements

Chopsticks are one of the defining characteristics of Chinese culture. But even they had a long evolution before reaching their present familiar form and use. Since the Neolithic, small sticks or twigs were probably used as tongs (*jia* 梜) to put pre-heated stones into the cooking pot to heat up the water. Later such sticks were used along with spoons as a cooking utensil for taking morsels of food out of the gruel (the original name for chopsticks, *zhu* 箸, 筯, or 櫡,

---

[21] The *Chengdu tonglan* 成都通覽 (Guide to Chengdu), which appeared in the last years of the Qing, contains most of the ingredients and dishes which are now associated with *Chuancai*.

is a cognate of boil, *zhu* 煮). In other words, they were used for serving, not for eating, for which hands were still employed (along with bone spatulas, *bi* 匕, and later with pottery spoons and ladles, *shao* 勺). It was only in the Former Han that chopsticks began to come into use for lifting tidbits from small bowls into the mouth. Many centuries were to go by before they replaced the use of hands at the table (and the forefinger is still called *shizhi* 食指, the eating finger).[22] Also, until the Song, the spoon continued in use for eating the staple. During the Ming, chopsticks came into normal use for both purposes. They also gained the name *kuaizi* 快子 (the bamboo signific [*zhu* 竹] was only added in the twentieth century [to make 筷子]). One explanation of the switch of name is that *zhu* 箸 was a taboo amongst Wu boatmen because of its similarity with *zhu* 住, stop (see 2.7, *Taboo, linguistic*). *Kuai* (quick) only gradually replaced *zhu*, which is still used as the word for chopsticks in Fujian and in several of the other southern dialects as well as in Japanese and Korean. It was also from the Ming that the characteristic form of the chopsticks, square at the head and round and tapered at the tip, became more and more common.

The *wok* (the English word is from *wog* 鑊 [MC *huo*], Cantonese for *guo* 鍋) may have been introduced during the Han, but it was mainly used for drying grains (as Tibetans prepare their roasted or parched barley meal, *rtsampa* [*zanba* 糌粑], to this day). *Chao* 炒 meaning stir-frying of meats, vegetables, and eggs using a *wok* did not overtake boiling, steaming, open roasting, or deep-frying, and other ways of preparing food for many centuries; indeed it began to become one of the more important cooking methods only in the Ming (which is also the time that *guo* 鍋 began to be used in its present sense). The sixteenth-century novel *Jin Ping Mei* 金瓶梅 includes references to only five or six stir-fry recipes out of a total of more than one hundred.[23] Even by the eighteenth century, *wok*

[22] *Zhongguo zhu wenhua daguan* 中國箸文化大觀 (Grand spectacle of Chinese chopstick culture), Liu Yun 劉雲, ed. in chief, Kexue, 1996. This also contains an interesting chapter tracing the development of the spatula and the spoon in China from Neolithic times. See also Xu Jinxiong 許進雄, *Gushi zatan* 古事雜談 (Random chats on old things), Shangwu, 1997, 123–28.

[23] *Jin Ping Mei fanshi pu* 金瓶梅飯食譜 (Recipes in the *Jin Ping Mei*), Hu Derong 胡德榮, ed., Jingji ribao, 1995.

dishes accounted for only 16 percent of the recipes in the most famous recipe book of the day, *Suiyuan shidan* 隨園食單 (35.2.6).

All sorts of pictures of people eating and drinking have survived.
Together with archaeological finds, they show that from the Han to
the Qing square or oblong tables were used. Small round trays for
snacks (*an* 案) were placed on them or on sitting platforms. Round
tables were manufactured during the Ming, but not used for eating.
Large round tables with chairs, so typical of Chinese restaurants today, were not common until the late nineteenth century (they can
be seen in the illustrations of late Qing novels). Indeed, many other
characteristics of what Americans or Europeans consider typical of
Chinese eating culture turn out on closer inspection to have their
origin in China towns of America or Europe. Take the "lazy Susan"
(the rotating glass server on top of the table). It is an American invention, adopted in Chinese restaurants in San Francisco (along
with fortune cookies) and imported to China from there. Other examples of such reverse imports (if they ever made it to China at all)
would include the following:

chop-suey (from Cantonese *tsap suei*, Mandarin *zasui* 雜碎). Legend has it
that this too was a San Francisco China town invention.

chow (slang for food, possibly from *chao* 炒, also allegedly from *chao*, the
Cantonese pronunciation of *gou* 狗, dog); first appearance in English
(USA), 1906.

chow-mein (from *chaomin*, the Cantonese pronunciation of *chaomian*
炒面, fried noodles), first appearance in English (USA), 1906.

gulurou 咕嚕肉 (sweet and sour pork); the first appearance in the English
language was in the 1950s; the dish was invented in Guangzhou in
the nineteenth century to suit western taste. The bones in an already
existing Cantonese dish, spare ribs sautéd in sweet-sour sauce (*tang-
suan paigu* 糖酸排骨), were found distasteful to foreigners, but they
liked the sauce. So a new dish without the bones was created and
dubbed *gulurou* (complaining meat) or in its more polite form *gu-
laorou* 古老肉 (meat in the ancient style). As a speciality in Cantonese restaurants catering to foreigners this dish is often not mentioned
even in the largest Chinese cooking encyclopaedias.

35.2.6 Bibliography

The history of Chinese food up to the twentieth century can be
traced in the pre-Qin works (35.2), in agricultural treatises (35.1), in

medical works (Chapter 36), and in recipe books and encyclopae-dias, as well as in *biji* and other literary sources. After the Han, rec-ipe books are called *shijing* 食經 (food treatises), and after the Tang, *shipu* 食譜 (recipe manuals) or *shidan* 食單 in the later empire. Most have been lost. One of those to survive, the treatise on diet written for the khan by the Muslim court doctor, the Mongolian Hoshoi (Husihui 忽思慧), *Yinshan zhengyao* 飲膳正要, 1330, has been trans-lated into English.[24]

Literati gourmands, the four most famous of whom were Su Shi 蘇軾 (1037–1101), Ni Zan 倪瓚 (1301–74), Xu Wei 徐渭 (1521–93) and Yuan Mei 袁枚 (1716–98), exerted a considerable influence on the development of a higher cuisine, especially when they compiled their own cookbooks, as did both Ni and Yuan.[25] The main tradi-tional cookbooks are reprinted in the series, *Zhongguo pengren guji congkan* 中國烹飪古籍叢刊 (Collection of ancient works on Chi-nese cooking), Shangye, 1984.

For a bibliography of 300 or so *shijing*, *shipu*, *nongshu*, and other works containing materials on the Chinese diet and recipes in his-torical times, see the appendix to the largest collection of classical Chinese recipes, *Zhongguo gudian shipu* 中國古典食譜, a monumen-tal collection of 3,249 historical recipes selected from a database of 11,000 compiled by the Chinese Classical Nutrition Research Insti-tute (Zhongguo jingdian yingyang yanjiusuo 中國經典營養研究所).[26] Arrangement is according to main ingredient (e.g., the 484 fish recipes are grouped together and listed in alphabetical order). The earliest recipes are from the Zhou dynasty, the latest from the end of the Qing. There is a *pinyin* index. A special feature is that ingre-dients are also indicated by Latin names. The original texts are given, as well as translations into Modern Chinese. Unfortunately there is no index by period. For that, see the *Zhongguo pengren ci-dian* 中國烹飪辭典 (2.7).

---

[24] *Yinshan zhengyao* (Essentials of eating and drinking); presented 1330; *A Soup for the Qan*, Paul D. Buell and Eugene N. Anderson, trs. and introduced, Kegan Paul Intl., 1998.

[25] Ni Zan, *Yunlintang yinshi zhidu ji* 雲林堂飲食制度集 (The food and drink system of Yunlin); Yuan Mei, *Suiyuan shidan* 隨園食單 (The Suiyuan recipes), 1792, Shangye, 1984.

[26] *Zhongguo gudian shipu* (Chinese classical recipes) ed. Liu Daqi 劉大器, Shaanxi lüyou, 1992.

Yan-kit So's *Classic Food of China*, Macmillan, 1992, contains a good introduction and 150 recipes (many of which are those of famous Chinese gourmands). Xiong Sizhi 熊四智 collects a large number of the references in poetry to food and drink from earliest times to the Qing, arranged by period, in *Zhongguo yinshi shiwen dadian* 中國飲食詩文大典 (Dictionary of food and drink in Chinese poetry), Qingdao, 1995. Two books for beginning students explain the characters found in cooking and on menus: Anthony Zee's *Swallowing Clouds*, Simon and Schuster, 1990, and James McCawley's *The Eater's Guide to Chinese Characters*, UChP, 1984.

35.3   *Water Control* (Shuili 水利)

No plant or human can exist without water. But water is rarely where you need it, when you need it, and in the quantities required. Chinese civilization was characterized by small urban elites ruling over large rural populations engaged in intensive agriculture. Therefore one of the great themes of Chinese history is the channeling and control of water—for irrigation, for city drinking supplies; for defense. Rivers, lakes, and canals were also used as a principal means of transport. Finally, water was one of the main conduits for the rapid spread of disease (Chapter 36).

There is a long tradition of Chinese geographical writing on natural river systems and lakes (35.3.1). There is an equally important tradition of practical works on the control of rivers and the digging of canals for many purposes, including irrigation, flood control, and transport, both civil and military (35.3.2). For modern studies of Chinese water control, see 35.3.3

35.3.1   *Geographical Works on River Systems*

The earliest extant work on rivers is the *Shuijing* 水經 (Book of waterways), third century BC. It contains an inventory of 137 rivers and waterways. There is an extensive and important commentary by Li Daoyuan 酈道元 (d. 527) in what amounts to a separate work, the *Shuijingzhu* 水經注, edited ca. AD 515–24. Li greatly expanded the original with detailed comments on 1,252 rivers and waterways, land routes, famous products, antiquities, personalities, and dialects, not to speak of providing the world's first inventory of rock art (14.2). He quotes from well over 400 books, many since lost, and he also records data of 300 stone inscriptions; see the introduction to the *H-Y Index*.[27] Two later examples of the genre are:

Shuidao tigang 水道提綱 (Essentials of waterways), Qi Zhaonan 齊召南, 1703-68; rpnt., 1877–78.

Xiyu shuidaoji 西域水道記 (Record of waterways in the Western Regions), Xu Song 徐松, 1833. Xu wrote copiously on Ili. He was also the scholar who retrieved the *Song huiyao* 宋會要 from the *Yongle dadian* 永樂大典.

35.3.2 Works on Water Control

The monographs on rivers and canals in the Standard Histories contain important materials on irrigation and water control; see *Ershiwushi hequzhi zhushi* 二十五史河渠志注釋 (22.3.6).

See also, for example:

Wuzhong shuili shu 吳中水利書, Dan E 單鍔 (Northern Song). Based on the author's 30 years of investigations of the water control works in the prefectures of Suzhou, Changzhou, and Huzhou, *Congshu jicheng*, 1st series.

Xingshui jingjian 行水金鑑, Fu Zehong 傅澤洪, 1725; describes the river systems of China and their water control works from earliest times to 1721. *Xu Xingshui jingjian* 續行水金鑑 is a continuation covering the years 1721–1820. It was compiled by Yu Zhengxie 俞正燮 (1775–1840).

The Yangzi River had on average a bad flood every 10 years between the Han and the end of the Qing.[28] The lower reaches of the Yellow River had six major, and 20 relatively large, changes of

[27] *Shuijingzhu yinde* 水經注引得 (Index to the *Shuijing* and commentaries), *H-Y Index* 17.

[28] From the Zhou to the Later Han, the Yangzi River was known simply as the Jiang 江. Thereafter, it began to be called the Dajiang 大江 (Big River) or the Changjiang 長江 (Long River). Starting in the Sui, Yangzi jiang 揚子江 was used by poets as the name for the stretch of the river between Yangzhou 揚州 and Zhenjiang 鎮江. From the Ming *yang* 揚 was sometimes also written *yang* 洋. After the Opium War, the English translation of this part of the river (Yangtze Kiang) began to be applied to the whole river, sometimes with the spurious explanation that it meant "Son of the Ocean." Under the Republic, Yangzi jiang 揚子江 became official. Under the People's Republic, the name was changed back to Changjiang 長江.

course in the last 3,000 years; each was the result of different combinations of natural and manmade causes.[29] The destruction and loss of life was enormous. There is much material in the archives on the efforts made under the Qing to cope with such disasters, some of which has been published. See, for example, *Qingdai Huanghe honglao dang'an shiliao* 清代黃河洪澇檔案史料.[30] This is in the archival series: *Jianghe dang'an shiliao congshu* 江河檔案史料叢書 (Collection of historical materials from the archives on rivers), which also includes the archives on the flooding of other rivers, including:

Qingdai Haihe Luanhe honglao dang'an shiliao 清代海河灤河洪澇檔案史料 (Qing dynasty historical materials from the archives on the flooding of the Haihe and Luanhe basins [Hebei]), Zhonghua, 1981. Covers 1736 to 1911.

Qingdai Huaihe honglao dang'an shiliao 清代淮河洪澇檔案史料 (Qing dynasty historical materials from the archives on the flooding of the Huai River), Zhonghua, 1988.

Major Water Control Works

Several of the large-scale water control works of ancient China can still be visited today, for example:

Dujiangyan 都江堰 (60 km [38 miles] northwest of Chengdu), 250 BC; built by Li Bing 李冰 in the kingdom of Shu 蜀 after it had fallen to Qin 秦. The largest irrigation works of ancient China.

Eleven canals were dug in the Warring States extending over a total of 1,000 km (625 miles). The longest was that designed by Zheng Guo 鄭國 in Shaanxi to the north of Xianyang 咸陽. Work began in 246 BC. Parts have been excavated.

Under the Sui, hundreds of thousands of people were mobilized to repair old canals and to dig new ones. The resultant complex of manmade and modified waterways linked the north to the south using the five river systems of the Haihe 海河, Huanghe 黃河, Huaihe 淮河, Changjiang 長江 and Qiantangjiang 錢塘江. The canal was 40 paces

[29] The changes in course are conveniently mapped in Blunden and Elvin, 1998 (8.1), 16. From the Shang, the Yellow River was called simply the He 河; it began to be called by its present name from the Han. See Qu Wanli 屈萬里, "He zi de yiyi yanbian" 河字意義的演變 (Changes in the meaning of the character *he*), *LYYJ* 30:143–55 (1959).

[30] *Qingdai Huanghe honglao dang'an shiliao* (Qing dynasty historical materials from the archives on the flooding of the Yellow River), Zhonghua, 1993.

wide, willow trees were planted on both sides, and granaries were built along the route as well as 40 imperial rest houses. From the Song the entire system was called the Grand Canal (Da yunhe 大運河). In the Yuan, a 1,000-mile canal was cut from the existing canal at Xuzhou north across Shandong via Jizhou 濟州, Linqing 臨清, and Haijin 海津 to Beijing. The distance from the southern terminal Hangzhou to Beijing is about 1,750 km (1,100 miles). By the Ming 4,000,000 piculs of unhusked rice were being shipped up the canal every year under the supervision of 120,000 soldiers. The operation was financed locally as a surcharge on the land tax, of which the grain was the principal payment. The bulk of the grain went to the imperial palace in Beijing and its huge numbers of retainers and dependents; it was also used as a stipend for central government officials. Consult Chapter 5 of Denis Twitchett, *Financial Administration Under the T'ang Dynasty*, CUP, 1963; 2nd rev. edition, 1970; *The Ming Tribute Grain System,* by Hoshi Ayao; Mark Elvin, tr., CCS, Univ. of Michigan, 1969; Harold C. Hinton, *The Grain Tribute System of China*, HUP, 1956, 1970; Jane Kate Leonard, *Controlling from Afar: The Daoguang Emperor's Management of the Grand Canal Crisis, 1824–1826*, CCS, Univ. of Michigan, 1996.

Quite apart from these huge canal and irrigation works, equally impressive is the gradual extension of irrigation (using polders, dykes, storage tanks, drainage channels, and terracing) to individual fields, at first in north China and then, after the Tang, to the whole of the south.

35.3.3   Modern Studies

English-language studies of the development of water control have been made, see, for example:

Karl Wittfogel, *Oriental Despotism*, YUP, 1957. Most would now regard this Marxist study as an overinterpretation.

Ch'ao-ting Chi (Ji Chaoding 冀朝鼎), *Key Economic Areas in Chinese History as Revealed in the Development of Public Works for Water-Control*, Allen and Unwin, 1936; rpnt., Paragon, 1963; Kelley, 1970.

Zhongguo shuili shigao 中國水利史稿 (Draft history of Chinese water control), Shuili dianli xueyuan 水利電力學院 (Water control and hydropower academy), ed., 3 vols., Shuili dianli, 1979 and 1989.

Japanese Studies on the History of Water Control in China: A Selected Bibliography, Mark Elvin, Hiraoka Nishioka, Keiho Tamura, and Joan

Kwek, eds., Institute of Advanced Studies, ANU in conjunction with the Center for East Asian Cultural Studies for UNESCO, Tôyô bunko, 1994. Contains references to 600 Japanese works on water control in its widest sense, covering manmade systems of drainage, irrigation, urban systems of water supply, inland water transport, and defence against floods and tidal incursions, together with the related technology and hydrological and hydraulic theories. For an overview, see Mark Elvin's introduction.

"The Literature on Civil Engineering and Water Conservancy," in *SCC*, vol. 4, part 3, 323–29; also "Hydrographic Books and Descriptions of the Coast," in *SCC*, vol. 3, 514–17.

Societies and Journals

Chûgoku suirishi kenkyû 中國水利史研究, 1970– , annual.

35.4   The Environment and Natural Disasters

35.4.1   Environmental History

Long-term natural processes combined with ever more intensive agriculture, deforestation, and water control (and deliberate acts of destruction at times of war) had huge impacts on the Chinese environment. Environmental history studies these impacts over time and is concerned with "the interface where specifically human systems meet with other natural systems," as Mark Elvin puts it in his introduction to the most thorough collection of studies on various aspects of Chinese environmental history currently available.[31] See also J. R. McNeill's chapter in the same collection, "China's Environmental History in World Perspective,"[32] and Mark Elvin, "Three Thousand Years of Unsustainable Development: China's Environment from Archaic Times to the Present," *East Asian History* 6: 7–46 (1993). Note Georges Métailié, *Consolidated Bibliography of the Environment in China* (Laboratoire d'Ethnologie, Paris), forthcom-

---

[31] *Sediments of Time: Environment and Society in Chinese History*, Mark Elvin and Ts'ui-jung Liu (Liu Cuirong 劉翠溶) eds., CUP, 1998, Introduction, 5. This large collection of studies first appeared in Chinese under the title *Jijian suozhi: Zhongguo huanjingshi lunwenji* 積漸所至中國環境史論文集 (Sediments of time: Collected essays on the history of the Chinese environment), 2 vols., Zhongyang yanjiuyuan, Jingjisuo, 1995.

[32] Elvin and Liu (1998), 31–49.

ing. Recent years have seen more studies of individual environments or rivers or lakes over long periods of time. Many of these are referred to in the chapters in *Sediments of Time*. Studies of the environment in different historical periods in China are mentioned in the appropriate sections of Part II and Part V.

Climate Change

For a comparative view of climate change in history, see

Climate and History: Studies in Past Climates and Their Impact on Man, T. M. L. Wigley et al., eds., CUP, 1981.

The Climate of China and Global Climate: Proceedings of the Beijing International Symposium on Climate, Yu Duzheng et al., eds., Springer, 1988.

On climate change in China, the pioneering work (mainly based on data culled from local gazetteers) was done by Zhu Kezhen 竺可楨, who began publishing on the subject in 1925. For a summary of his work, see his "Zhongguo wuqian nian lai qihou bianqian de chubu yanjiu" 中國五千年來氣候變遷的初步研究 (Preliminary researches on climate change in China over the last 5,000 years), *Kaogu xuebao* 1: 15–38 (1972), and in English in *Cycles* 25: 243–61 (1974).

Later research using different methods has tended to confirm Zhu's findings:

Ren Zhenqiu 任振球, "Zhongguo jin wuqian nian lai qihou de yichangqi ji qi tianwen chengyin tantao" 中國近五千年來氣候的異常期及其天文成因探討 (An enquiry into the abnormal periods in China's climate during the last 5,000 years and contributing astronomical factors), *Nongye kaogu* 1 (1986); Wang Zichun 汪子春 and Gao Jian'guo 高建國, "Zhongguo jin erqian wubai nian lai zhiwu chonghua lishi jilu zhi wuhou yanjiu" 中國近二千五百年來植物重花歷史記錄之物候研究 (Phenological studies on historical records relating to the reflowering of plants in China during the last 2,500 years), *Nongye kaogu* 1982. 1 and 2.

See also:

Zhang Jiacheng and Thomas B. Crowley, "Historical Climate Records in China and the Reconstruction of Past Climates," *Journal of Climate*, 2 (1989).

Zhang Peiyuan, "Extraction of Climate Information from Chinese Historical Writings," *LIC* 14.2: 96–106 (1993).

Quanguo qihou bianhua xueshu taolunhui wenji 全國氣候變化學術討論會文集 (Collected essays from the national symposium on climate change), Institute of Meteorology, comp., Kexue, 1981.

Zhongguo lishi shiqi zhiwu yu dongwu bianqian yanjiu 中國歷史時期植物與動物變遷研究 (Shifts of plants and animals in China in historical times), Wen Huanran 文煥然 et al., eds., Chongqing, 1995. Collection of twenty-two research papers on historical biogeography.

Liu Zhaomin 劉昭民, *Zhongguo lishi shang qihou zhi bianqian* 中國歷史上氣候之變遷 (Climate change in Chinese history), Taibei: Shangwu, 1981; rev., 1991.

Wen Huanran 文煥然, *Zhongguo lishi shiqi dong ban'nian qihou lengnuan bianqian* 中國歷史時期冬半年氣候冷暖變遷 (Wintertime changes in warm and cold in Chinese historical times), Kexue, 1996. Based on a close study of the changing appearance in different parts of China of different animals and plants.

Tianjia wuxing 田家五行 (Peasant proverbs on climate), Lou Yuanli 婁元禮, end of Yuan, beginning of Ming. Weather tips from around the Taihu 太湖 region.

Landscape, Culture, and Power in Chinese Society, Wen-hsin Yeh and Stephen West, eds., IEAS, 1997.

Confucianism and Ecology: The Interaction of Heaven, Earth, and Humans, Mary Evelyn Taylor and John Berthrong, eds., HUP, 1998.

Forests

Christian Daniels and Nicholas K. Menzies, *Agro-Industries and Forestry* (*SCC*, vol. 6, part 3), CUP, 1996.

Nicholas K. Menzies, *Forest and Land Management in Imperial China*, Macmillan, 1994.

35.4.2   *Natural Disasters*

The monographs on omens and anomalies (*wuxingzhi* 五形志) in the Standard Histories and in the local gazetteers report on natural disasters. There are many modern tables and atlases showing droughts, floods, earthquakes, and fires in Chinese history based on these and other sources. Many of the works dealing with climate change and the environment analyze and discuss natural disasters. For the extremes to which hunger could drive people, see Key Ray Chong (Zheng Qilai 鄭麒來), *Cannibalism in China*, Longwood,

1990 (Chinese translation: *Zhongguo gudai de shiren* 中國古代的食
人, Shehui kexue, 1994).

Zhongguo gudai zhongda ziran zaihai he yichang nianbiao zongji 中國古代
重大自然災害和異常年表總集 (A comprehensive table of major nat-
ural disasters in Chinese ancient history), Song Zhenghai 宋正海 ed.,
Guangdong jiaoyu, 1992. Arrangement is chronological by types of
disaster. The sources used are extensive.

Earthquakes and Fires

The first description of an earthquake in Chinese sources is in the
Shijing: "Xiaoya" 小雅, *Shiyue zhijiao* 十月之交. For quakes since
then, see collections and atlases such as the following:

Zhongguo lishi qiang dizhen mulu 中國歷史強地震目錄 (Index of major
Chinese earthquakes in history), Dizhen, 1995. Records 1,034 major
quakes occurring between 2300 BC and AD 1911.

Zhongguo dizhen lishi ziliao huibian 中國地震歷史資料匯編 (Collection
of historical materials on Chinese earthquakes), Xie Yushou 謝毓壽
and Cai Meibiao 蔡美彪 comps., 5 vols., Kexue, 1983–87. Vol. 1 covers up to the end of the Yuan; vol. 2, the Ming; vol. 3, the Qing (2
vols); vol. 5, the Republic.

Zhongguo gujin dizhen zaiqing zonghui 中國古今地震災情總匯 (Comprehensive collection of Chinese ancient and modern earthquake disaster
conditions), Lou Baotang 樓寶棠, ed. in chief, Dizhen, 1996. Has a
good bibliography.

Qingdai dizhen dang'an shiliao 清代地震檔案史料 (Archival materials on
earthquakes in the Qing), Ming-Qing dang'anguan, ed., Zhonghua,
1959.

Xizang dizhen shiliao huibian 西藏地震史料匯編 (Collection of materials
on earthquakes in Tibet), Xizang Dang'anguan et al., eds., 2 vols.,
Xizang renmin, 1982.

Xichang dizhen beilin 西昌地震碑林 (17.3, *Collections of Stelae*)

Zhongguo huozai da dian 中國火災大典 (Grand collection of Chinese
fires), 3 vols., Shanghai kexue jishu, 1998.

Journals

Chinese Environmental History Newsletter (semiannual), Helen Dunstan,
ed., 1994– . School of Asian Studies, University of Sydney, Sydney,
Australia. English-language and Chinese-language versions available
(also online).

36

Medicine

The bones unearthed from Neolithic burial sites show that people died very young and often of disease. In particular they suffered from mouth diseases and decayed teeth as well as intestinal, gynecological, and bone disorders. Infant mortality was high. Women began childbearing at puberty and had reached old age by 30. Average height was quite tall (men between 160 and 170 cm, and women between 150 and 160 cm).

Life expectancy began to increase in the Bronze Age as a result of better living conditions, including settled life in houses that were regularly cleaned; the use of deep wells for clean drinking water; the introduction of regular eating habits (two meals a day); and the use of eating implements that were cleaned after use. Other hygienic practices such as washing and cleaning the teeth; delousing, cutting, and combing the hair; and de-waxing the ears also became more widespread.

Archaeology has unearthed traces of the early use of medicinal plants and berries, the evidence for which increases in Shang tombs. An early form of acupuncture had been practiced from the Neolithic using pointed stone implements called *bian* 砭, which were also made of bone, ivory, or bamboo. Moxibustion came into use at the same time. The medicinal use of liquor was recognized from at least the Shang.

There are over 500 references to diseases on the oracle bones of which 39 are separate ailments, among which parasites and tooth decay were the most common.[1]

---

[1] Song Zhenhao 宋鎮豪, "Yiliao baojian" 醫療保健 (Medicine and health care), Chapter 7 of his *Xia-Shang shehui shenghuoshi* 夏商社會生活史 (History of social life in the Xia and Shang periods), Shehui kexue, 1994, 1996, 407–51; Li Liangsong 李良松, *Jiagu wenhua yu Zhongyi xue* 甲骨文化與中醫學 (Oracle-bone culture and the study of Chinese medicine), Fujian kexue jishu, 1994.

The doctor (medicine man) in Shang times was the medium or shaman because it was believed that diseases were caused by vengeful ancestors and thus were cured by sacrifices, praying, and exorcism (*yi* 醫 was sometimes written 毉, i.e., with *wu* 巫 not *you* 酉).[2]

In historical times, a large number of medical texts were written. Many of these are extant. Quite apart from being the main sources for the history of Chinese medicine, they are naturally also the essential sources for the history of Chinese disease. In the later empire, the local gazetteers supply some details of the course of historical epidemics and pandemics.[3] The history of individual Chinese medical specialties or of particular diseases is as yet in its infancy.

The earliest surviving medical texts are those found written on three silk rolls in an early Han tomb at Mawangdui in Hunan (see 19.1.3). They reflect a more this-worldly, body-centered approach to medicine than that of the Shang. It was an approach that by Zhou times had become the dominant tradition, although exorcism and the use of charms and spells remained a popular form of "alternative" medicine up to the twentieth century and the mainstream among some of the non-Han peoples within China.

The 13 Mawangdui medical manuscripts include:

Maifa 脈法 (Methods of pulse feeling)

Wushi'er bing fang 五十二病方 (Prescriptions for 52 diseases)

Zubi shiyi mai jiujing 足臂十一脈灸經 (Eleven meridians for moxibustion of the arms and feet)

---

[2] David N. Keightley, "Shamanism, Death, and the Ancestors: Religious Mediation in Neolithic and Shang China (ca. 5000–1000 BC)," *Asiatische Studien* 52.3: 763–831 (1998); Shigehisa Kuriyama, "The Imagination of Winds and the Development of the Chinese Conception of the Body," in Zito and Barlow, 1994 (39.3.1), 23–41; Paul U. Unschuld, *Medicine in China: A History of Ideas*, UCP, 1985, 17–28.

[3] For an overview, see Angela Ki Che Leung, "Diseases of the Premodern Period in China," in the *Cambridge World History of Human Disease*, Kenneth Kiple, ed., CUP, 1993, 354–62; for case studies, see, for example, Carol Benedict, *Bubonic Plague in 19ᵗʰ-Century China*, SUP, 1996, which traces an epidemic of bubonic plague that began in Yunnan in the late eighteenth century and spread to the rest of southeast China during the nineteenth century; Kerrie L. MacPherson, "Cholera in China, 1820–1930," and Zhang Yixia and Mark Elvin, "Environment and Tuberculosis in Modern China," Chapters 13 and 14, respectively, of Elvin and Liu, 1998, (35.4.1), 87–519, 520–542.

Yinyang shiyi mai jiujing 陰陽十一脈灸經 (Eleven meridians for moxibustion of the Yin Yang system)[4]

Traditional Chinese medical works were classified under subbranch five of the Philosophers' Branch of the *Sibu*. Below are a handful of the most famous:

Huangdi neijing 皇帝內經 or *Neijing* 內經 for short. Maoshing Ni, *The Yellow Emperor's Classic of Medicine*, Shambhala, 1995. A composite work that reached its present form at the end of the Warring States period in the third century BC, it is divided into two parts, *Suwen* 素問 (Plain questions) and *Zhenjing* 針經 (Classic of acupuncture; renamed *Lingshujing* 靈樞經 [Classic of the numinous pivot] in the eighth century). A third part, the *Taisu* 太素 (Great purity) was added in the seventh century. See Yamada Kenji, "The Formation of the *Huang-ti nei-ching*," *AA* 36: 67–89 (1979).

The *Shanhaijing* 山海經 (see 29.1) has references to 132 drugs, including 28 based on plants, 23 on trees, 16 on animal products, 25 on birds, 30 on fish products, and 5 on minerals.

Shennong bencao jing 神農本草經 (Shennong's classic *materia medica*), compiled in the Qin and Han, is the earliest systematic pharmacology to have survived. It contains instructions on how to prescribe, administer, and process 365 drugs that are divided according to their strength into three categories: superior, common, and inferior.

---

[4] *Early Chinese Medical Literature: The Mawangdui Medical Manuscripts, Translation and Study*, Donald J. Harper, Routledge, Kegan Paul International, 1998. All these works have been collated and transcribed in *Mawangdui Hanmu yishu jiaoshi* 馬王堆漢墓醫書校釋 (Collated and annotated Mawangdui tomb medical works), 2 vols., Chengdu, 1992. Includes translation into Modern Chinese.

For other early texts, see Gao Dalun 高大倫, *Zhangjiashan Hanjian 'maishu' jiaoshi* 張家山漢簡'脈書'校釋 (Collated and annotated edition of the bamboo strip 'Book on the pulse' from Zhangjiashan), Chengdu, 1992. Parts of a maishu (medical book on the pulse) were also discovered at Mawangdui. See also the same author's *Zhangjiashan Hanjian 'yinshu'* 張家山漢簡'引書' (Researches on the bamboo strip 'Book on stretching and contracting' from Zhangjiashan), Ba-Shu, 1995. *Yinshu* were Daoist manuals of breathing exercises (*daoyin* 導引, stretching and contracting). A similar, badly damaged work was found at Mawangdui, as was a silk painting of the exercises. The author situates this type of manual in its historical and medical context and provides an annotated transcription of the text. There is an index of key terms.

Shang hanlun 傷寒論 (Treatise on febrile diseases caused by cold), Zhang Zhongjing 張仲景 (150–219). English tr.: *Treatise on Febrile Diseases Caused by Cold with 500 Cases*, Luo Xiwen, New World Press, 1985. The cases in this edition are mainly taken from the annals of modern medicine.

Jingui yaolüe 金匱要略 (*Jingui* collection of prescriptions), Zhang Zhongjing 張仲景. English tr.: *Synopsis of Prescriptions of the Golden Chamber with 300 Cases*, Luo Xiwen, New World Press, 1995. The cases are mainly taken from the annals of modern medicine.

Zhenjiu jiayijing 針灸甲乙經 (Classic ABC of acupuncture and moxibustion), Huangfu Mi 皇甫謐 (215–82); collated, punctuated, and annotated edition in the series *Zhongyi guji zhengli congshu* 中醫古籍整理叢書 (Collection of re-edited ancient works of Chinese medicine), Renmin weisheng, 1996. Huangfu's work was also called *Huangdi sanbu zhenjiu jiayijing* 黃帝三部針灸甲乙經, or *Jiayijing* 甲乙經 for short.

Maijing 脈經 (Classic of the pulse), Wang Shuhe 王叔和. Drawn from previous works, including *Neijing* 內經. Although pulse feeling was already a well-tried technique of clinical examination, this was the first book-length treatment of the subject.

Beiji qianjin yaofang 備急千金要方 (Prescriptions for emergencies worth a fortune [lit. one thousand catties of gold]), also called *Qianjin yaofang* 千金要方 (Prescriptions worth a fortune), Sun Simiao 孫思邈 (581–682?), Renmin weisheng, 1955. Also by the same author, *Qianjin yifang* 千金翼方 (Supplement to prescriptions worth a fortune), Renmin weisheng, 1955.

Xiaoer yaozheng zhijue 小兒藥證直訣 (Key to therapeutics of children's diseases), Yan Xiaozhong 閻孝忠, ed., 1110. Yan collected the findings of his teacher Qian Yi (ca. 1032–1113).

Sanyin jiyibing zhengfang lun 三因極一病證方論 or *Sanyin jiyibing yuanlun cui* 三因極一病源論粹, or simply *Sanyin fang* 三因方 (Treatise on the three categories of pathogenic factors of diseases), Chen Yan 陳言 (1131–89), 1174; Renmin weisheng, 1955.

Xi yuanlu 洗冤錄 (Manual of forensic medicine), Song Ci 宋慈 (1186–1249), 1247 (27.6).

Xiao'er douzhen fanglun 小兒痘疹方論 (Treatise on smallpox and measles in children), Chen Wenzhong 陳文中 (fl. mid-thirteenth century), 1241.

Xiao'er bingyuan fanglun 小兒病源方論 (Treatise on etiology of children's diseases), Chen Wenzhong 陳文中 (fl. mid-thirteenth century), 1253.

Yinhai jingwei 銀海精微 (Essential subtleties on a silver screen), anon, fifteenth century, attributed (probably falsely) to Sun Simiao 孫思邈. English translation (with original text): *Essential Subtleties on a Silver Screen, The* Yin-hai jing-wei: *A Chinese Classic on Ophthalmology*, Jürgen Kovacs and Paul U. Unschuld, trs. and annotated, UCP, 1998. Includes introductory chapters on the history of ophthalmology in China from the Shang to the Song (6–52) with a section on "India in Chinese Ophthalmology" (43–48); an alphabetical list of drugs as well as Chinese and English indexes of prescriptions mentioned in the *Yinhai jingwei*.

Bencao gangmu 本草綱目 (Collection of *materia medica*), Li Shizhen 李時珍 (1518–93), 1602. The most famous *materia medica* of all. It contains 1,892 varieties, 11,096 prescriptions, and 1,110 illustrations; collated and punctuated edition, Renmin weisheng, 4 vols., 1977. Indicates edibility of each plant. For ease of identification, use *Bencao gangmu caise tupu* 本草綱目彩色圖譜 (Color photo inventory of the *Bencao gangmu*), Shen Liansheng 沈連生, ed. in chief, Huaxia, 1998. The 2,669 photographs are clear, and modern Chinese, Latin, English, and Japanese names are given; in addition there are indexes in these languages. In cases of difficulty of identification, alternative interpretations are included.

Yixue yuanliu lun 醫學源流論 (Treatise on the development of medical studies), Xu Daqun 1693–1771, 1757; see *ECCP*, 323. Tr. and annotated by Paul U. Unschuld in *Forgotten Traditions of Chinese Ancient Medicine: A Chinese View from the Eighteenth Century (The I-hsueh Yan Liu Lun)*, Paradigm, 1990. Essays by a distinguished Chinese physician and scholar who advocated a return to the medical classics.

Nan-ching: The Classic of Difficult Issues, with Commentaries of Chinese and Japanese Authors from the Third Through the Twentieth Century, Paul U. Unschuld, tr. and annotated, UCP, 1986.

Ethnic Medicine

See 40.3.1.

Medical Terms

Ingredients for the medical recipes were weighed on the balance using base-10 units similar to those used for subdivisions of the linear *fen* 分 (Table 15, 7.1.1). There were also older base-4 measures (Wu

Chengluo 吳承洛, 1957, 128–29) and later medical writers mentioned different measures; see "Apothecaries' Measure in the Tang Period," in Nathan Sivin, *Chinese Alchemy: Preliminary Studies*, HUP, 1968, 252–56; and Guo, 1993 (7.3.3), 22–25, 46–49, 81–82.

In order to find translations of medical and biological terms, start with works such as the *Bencao gangmu caise tupu* (see above) and consult Nathan (1968), 272–321, and Jürgen Kovacs, "Linguistic Reflections on the Translation of Chinese Medical Terms," in *Approaches to Traditional Chinese Medical Literature: Proceedings of an International Symposium on Translation Methodologies and Terminologies*, ed. Paul U. Unschuld, Kluwer, 1986. Next, use:

Introductory Readings in Classical Chinese Medicine: Sixty Texts with Vocabulary and Translation, a Guide to Research Aids and a General Glossary, ed. Paul U. Unschuld, Kluwer, 1988.

The same author's *Learn to Read Chinese*, 2 vols., Paradigm, 1994, complements his article on translation mentioned above. Vol. 1 has 64 texts with translation into English; vol. 2, grammatical explanations. For identifying *materia medica*, see

Shiu-ying Hu, *An Enumeration of Chinese Materia Medica*, HKCUP, 1980. Quick reference for identifying 1,700 plants, 135 animals, and 110 minerals and chemicals.

Zhongyao da cidian 中藥大辭典 (Dictionary of traditional Chinese medicine), Jiangsu xinyiyuan 江蘇新醫院, ed., 2 vols., Shanghai kexue jishu, 1986; 10th prnt., 1996. Identifies a huge range of *materia medica* and gives botanical names, with their Latin and alternative Chinese names.

Bibliography

There are a large number of catalogs and guides to the original sources for traditional Chinese medicine. For a union catalog, see the first item in the following list, and for annotated guides to the primary sources, see the remainder:

Quanguo Zhongyi tushu lianhe mulu 全國中醫圖書聯合目錄 (Union catalog of works of traditional Chinese medicine), Beijing tushuguan, 1961; rpnt., Zhongyi guji, 1991.

Zhongguo da baike quanshu 中國大百科全書 (The great Chinese encyclopaedia), *Chuantong yixue* 傳統醫學 (Traditional medicine), Da baike quanshu, 1992, includes many articles on sources.

Zhongguo yiji tiyao 中國醫籍提要, Jilin renmin, 2 vols., rpnt., 1984.

Zhongguo yiji tongkao 中國醫籍通考, Yan Shiyun 嚴世蕓, ed. in chief, 4 vols., Shanghai Zhongyi xueyuan, 1990–93.

Zhongyi guji zhenben tiyao 中醫古籍珍本提要 (Notes on rare works on Chinese medicine), Yu Ying'ao 余瀛鰲 and Fu Jinghua 傅景華 eds., Zhongyi guji, 1992. Contains abstracts of more than 1,000 rare medical works.

Paul U. Unschuld, *Medicine in China: A History of Pharmaceutics*, UCP, 1986. Analyzes contents and structure of traditional Chinese pharmaceutical literature.

Gujin tushu jicheng, yibu quanlu 古今圖書集成, 醫部全錄 (Complete records of the medical section of the *Tushu jicheng*), 12 vols., Renmin weisheng, 1988–91.

For the secondary literature on Chinese medicine, see Nathan S. Sivin, "Science and Medicine in Imperial China: The State of the Field," *JAS* 47.1: 41–90 (1988). See also the same author's "An Introductory [annotated] Bibliography of Traditional Chinese Medicine: Books and Articles in Western Languages," in Sivin, *Medicine, Philosophy and Religion in Ancient China*, Variorum, 1995.

Note the following studies:

Liu Yanchi, *The Essential Book of Traditional Chinese Medicine*, 2 vols., Col. UP, 1988.

Paul U. Unschuld, *Medicine in China: A History of Ideas*, UCP, 1985. An appendix contains 100 pages of translated excerpts from primary sources.

Manfred Pokert, *The Theoretical Foundations of Chinese Medicine: Systems of Correspondence*, MIT Press, 1974.

Lu Gwei-Djen and Joseph Needham, *Celestial Lancets: A History and Rationale of Acupuncture and Moxa*, CUP, 1980. The *SCC* sections on medicine are unfinished, but note *SCC*, vol. 5, part 5 (37.1).

Robert Hymes, "Not Quite Gentlemen? Doctors in Sung and Yuan," *Chinese Science* 8: 9–76 (1987).

Vivien Ng, *Madness in Late Imperial China: From Illness to Deviance*, University of Oklahoma Press, 1990.

Li Zhende 李貞德, "Han-Tang zhi jian yishu zhong de shengchan zhi dao" 漢唐之間醫書中的生產之道 (Childbirth in late antiquity and early medieval China), *SJ* 67.3 (1996), 533–654; "Han-Tang zhi jian qiuzi yifang shitan–jianlun fuke lanshang yu xingbie lunshu" 漢唐之間求子醫方試探兼論婦科濫觴與性別論述 (Reproductive medicine in late antiquity and early medieval China: gender discourse and the birth of gynecology), *SJ* 68.2 (1997), 283–365. Li bases her reconstructions on a close reading of contemporary medical texts.

Charlotte Furth, *A Flourishing Yin: Gender in Chinese Medicine, 960–1665*, UCP, 1998.

Angela K. Leung, "Autour de la naissance: la mère et l'enfant en Chine aux XVIᵉ et XVIIᵉ siècles," *Cahiers internationaux de sociologie* 76: 51–69 (1994).

Charlotte Furth, "Concepts of Pregnancy, Childbirth and Infancy in Ch'ing Dynasty China," *JAS* 46.1: 7–35 (1987).

Note the Zhongguo yishi bowuguan 中國醫史博物館 (Chinese Museum for the History of Medicine) in Zhongguo Zhongyi yanjiuyuan 中國中醫研究院 (Academy for research on traditional Chinese medicine), Beijing.

Sex

The works below (especially the first six) give some idea of the sources available for tracing Chinese sexual practices and attitudes towards sex. They range from sexual manuals and medical works to erotic art works and pornography (for works on female prostitution, see 39.3.3):

Zhonghua xingxue guanzhi–Zhonghua xingyixue zhenji jicheng 中華性學觀止-中華性醫學珍籍集成 (The best of Chinese sexology—a collection of original sources on Chinese traditional medicine sexology), Fen Youping 樊友平 et al., eds., Guangdong renmin, 1997. The first excerpt is from the Mawangdui sex manuscripts; the remainder from 31 medical works.

Robert van Gulik, *Sexual Life in Ancient China: A Preliminary Survey of Chinese Sex and Society from ca. 1500 BC till 1644 AD*, Brill, 1961, 1964. See Charlotte Furth, "Rethinking Van Gulik: Sexuality and Reproduction in Traditional Chinese Medicine," in Christina K. Gilmartin et al., *Engendering China: Women, Culture and the State*," HUP, 1994, 125–46.

Donald J. Harper, "The Sexual Arts of Ancient China as Described in a Manuscript of the Second Century BC," *HJAS* 47.2: 539–93 (1987). See also the chapter on esoteric texts by Harper in *NSECH*, 223–52.

Robert H. Van Gulik, *Erotic Colour Prints of the Ming Period, with an Essay on Chinese Sex Life from the Han to the Ch'ing Dynasty, 206 BC–AD 1644*, 3 vols., privately published, Tokyo, 1951.

Howard S. Levy, *Chinese Sex Jokes in Traditional Times*, Taibei: The Orient Culture Service, 1974.

Howard S. Levy, *Chinese Footbinding: The History of a Curious Erotic Custom*, Rawls, 1966; rpnt. under the title *The Lotus Lovers*, Buffalo, NY: Prometheus, 1992.

Douglas Wile, *Art of the Bedchamber: The Chinese Sexual Yoga Classics Including Women's Solo Meditation Texts*, SUNY, 1992. On Daoist sexual practices with translated excerpts.

Liu Dalin 劉達臨, *Zhongguo gudai xing wenhua* 中國古代性文化 (Sex culture of ancient China), Ningxia renmin, 1993, 1994. A historical survey, with much quotation of original sources.

Zheng Sili 鄭思禮 offers a Freudian analysis: *Zhongguo xing wenhua yige qiannian bujie zhi jie* 中國性文化一個千年不解之結 (The sex culture of China: a thousand-year-old enigma), Zhongguo duiwai fanyi, 1994. Argues that sex, not culture or politics, was the original root of Chinese ritual and ethics.

Zhao Guohua 趙國華, *Shengzhi chongbai wenhua lun* 生殖崇拜文化論 (On fertility rites), Shehui kexue, 1990; 3rd prnt., 1996.

Li Ling 李零, *Zhongguo fangshu kao* 中國方術考 (Studies on Chinese divinatory and medical arts), Renmin Zhongguo, 1993.

Bret Hinsch, *Passions of the Cut Sleeve: The Male Homosexual Tradition in China*, UCP, 1990.

Fang Fu Ruan and Vern L. Bullough, "Lesbianism in China," *Archives of Sexual Behavior* 21.3: 217-26 (1992).

Frank Dikötter, *Sex, Culture, and Modernity in China: Medical Science and the Construction of Sexual Identities in the Early Republican Period*, UHP, 1995.

37

Technology and Science

Technology and science were mainly listed under the Philosophers' branch of the *Siku*. The ordering can give some indication of the priority placed on different technologies in late imperial China: the military (Chapter 29), agriculture and water control (Chapter 35), medicine (Chapter 36), astronomy and mathematics (Chapter 5 and 37.1), divination (Chapter 15), geomancy and the mariner's compass, and architecture (37.4), mining and metallurgy, and printing (18.4). Of these, the four main scientific traditions were calendrical astronomy, medicine, *materia medica*, and mathematics. Each of the four had its own paradigm, classical text(s), and learned group.

Introduction

For a supposedly secular and pragmatic society such as that projected by the Confucian self-image, it is striking that many of the most famous Chinese inventions had their origins in magic and the mantic arts. For example, writing probably grew from the requirements of divination (14.5); printing, from the desire to gain merit by multiplying prayers and chants (18.4); magnetism, geology, and the navigator's compass grew from the geomancer's arts (37.4.1); gunpowder for weapons developed from its use for fireworks to scare off evil spirits; astronomy was closely linked to astrology (5.1); and chemistry grew from alchemy. In the later empire the old inventiveness dried up.

The earliest work with an interest for the historian of Chinese technology is the *Kaogong ji* 考工記 (Record of the scrutiny of crafts). It is part of the *Zhouli* 周禮 (Table 26, 19.2) and dates from the fifth century BC. It contains details of the making, for example, of carriages, weapons, boats, and musical instruments and details on compounding bronze. The most comprehensive work on industrial and agrarian arts is from the later empire: Song Yingxing 宋應星,

Tiangong kaiwu 天工開物 (The exploitation of the works of nature), 1637. It has been translated into English: *T'ien-kung k'ai-wu: Chinese Technology in the Seventeenth Century*, E-tu Zen Sun and Sun Shiou-chuan, trs. and annotated, Pennsylvania State Univ. Press, 1966; Dover, 1997.[1] Song's chapters cover the growing of grains and their preparation; clothing materials; salt technology; sugar technology; ceramics; bronze casting; ships and carts; iron metallurgy; calcination of stones; vegetable oils and fats; paper making; metallurgy of silver, lead, tin, copper, and zinc; military technology; vermilion and ink; yeast; and pearls and gems. The principal manufacturing processes for all these are discussed and illustrated.

Song concluded his preface by warning "An ambitious scholar will undoubtedly toss this book onto his desk and give it no further thought: it is a work that is in no way concerned with the art of advancement in officialdom," Sun and Sun (1966), xiv. He knew what he was saying; despite repeated attempts he himself never succeeded in gaining the *jinshi* degree. Li Shizhen 李時珍 only turned to *materia medica* after failing the imperial exams three times (Chapter 36). Many of China's greatest mathematicians also failed to pass the exams to become officials. It is also worth noting that the reason that we know almost nothing about the inventor of printing with movable type (Bi Sheng 畢昇) is that he was a wealthy craftsman and businessman, not a scholar.[2] Another reason was that his invention had to wait many centuries until it was fully exploited. In the meantime labor intensive woodblock printing continued (18.4). The gap between tinker and thinker was a wide one.

The Standard Histories contain monographs covering astronomy-astrology, the calendar, mathematical harmonics, and unusual phenomena (5.1.2). Archaeologists in recent decades have turned up invaluable evidence of many ancient technologies (see *Bibliography*).

---

[1] There are several excellent modern editions, e.g., *Tiangong kaiwu jiaozhu yu yanjiu* 天工開物校注與研究 (*Tiangong kaiwu* collated and annotated with research), Pan Jixing 潘吉星, ed., Ba-Shu, 1989; rpnt., Shanghai guji, 1993; see also the collection of studies edited by Yabuuchi Kiyoshi 藪内清, *Tenkô kaibutsu no kenkyû* 天工開物の研究, Tokyo, 1953; Chinese tr.: *Tiangong kaiwu yanjiu lunwenji* 天工開物論文集, Shangwu, 1959.

[2] In 1990, a stele dated 1052 was discovered in Hubei. It appears to be that of Bi Sheng. The designs on the stele suggest that he was a Manichaean. However, the attribution to Bi has been challenged; see *CAAD* 2.1: 69–71 (1997).

Many of the scientific classics have been republished photolitho-graphically in the multivolume series *Zhongguo kexue jishu dianji tonghui* 中國科學技術典籍通彙.[3] The advantage of a collection like this is that you have works in the same genre easy to hand. The dis-advantage is that there are many scholarly editions of individual texts available that most would prefer to use.

The best introductions in English to the primary sources for the history of most branches of technology and science in China up to the nineteenth century remain the volumes of *Science and Civil-isation in China* (37.1). On an even larger scale and more up-to-date is the 30-volume series *Zhongguo kexue jishu shi* 中國科學技術史.[4] It also stops in the nineteenth century. The guiding principle found in many works on the history of science and technology is to collect the great "achievements" with scant attention paid to the broader intellectual, social, or historical context, let alone to the "failures." The overall impression of such works is therefore rather like listen-ing to a compact disk of the main themes of classical music divorced from the music itself.

37.1 Science and Civilisation in China

Chinese primary and secondary sources (as well as Western nine-teenth-century sources) on all aspects of traditional technology and science are quoted and discussed throughout the volumes of Joseph Needham (1900–95), *Science and Civilisation in China* (*SCC*), as well as in the various works that grew out of it. Needham conceived the series in 1944, and the first volume appeared ten years later in 1954. The first 17 books appeared under his editorial direction. Although

[3] *Zhongguo kexue jishu dianji tonghui* (General collection of Chinese classi-cal works on sciences and technology), Henan jiaoyu, 1993.

[4] *Zhongguo kexue jishushi* 中國科學技術史 (History of science and technol-ogy in China), Lu Jiaxi 盧嘉錫, ed. in chief, 30 vols., Kexue, 1998– . A good single-volume brief introduction is *Ancient China's Technology and Science*, compiled at the Institute of the History of Natural Science, Chinese Academy of Sciences, FLP, 1983, 1987; Chinese original: *Zhongguo gudai keji chengjiu* 中國古代科技成就, Qingnian, 1978; rev. edition, 1995; 4th prnt., 1996. For a more substantial single-volume introduction, see *Zhongguo gudai kexue shigang* 中國古代科學史綱 (Outline history of Chinese sciences), Lu Jiaxi 盧嘉錫 and Lu Yongxiang 路甬祥, eds., Hebei kexue jishu, 1998. It has a name/title index.

some of Needham's basic assumptions have since been questioned (see below, *Evaluation of SCC*) and research has also advanced, *SCC*, vols. 3–7, remain the best starting point:

Vol. 1, *Introductory Orientations*, CUP, 1954, 1961.

Vol. 2, *History of Scientific Thought* (with Wang Ling 王鈴), CUP, 1956.

Vol. 3, *Mathematics and the Sciences of the Heavens and the Earth* (with Wang Ling), CUP, 1959.

On the earliest of the ten mathematical manuals (*Suanjing shishu* 算經十書) written between the Han and the Tang, the *Zhoubi suanjing* 周髀算經, see Christopher Cullen, *Astronomy and Mathematics in Ancient China: The Zhoubi Suanjing*, CUP, 1996. The most influential of the ten manuals was the Han *Jiuzhang suanshu* 九章算術 (Nine chapters on the mathematical arts). It contains 246 math problems likely to be encountered by government officials and clerks. It has been translated many times; see *Zhongguo gudai shuxue mingzhu Jiuzhang suanshu* 中國古代數學名著九章算術 (Ancient China's famous work on mathematics, the *Jiuzhang suanshu*), Shen Kangshen, 沈康身, ed. in chief, vol. 2 of *Zhongguo shuxueshi daxi* 中國數學史大系 (Collection of works on the history of Chinese mathematics), Wu Wenjun 吳文俊, ed. in chief, Beijing shifan daxue, 1998; for an introductory study of the historical background, see Song Jie 宋杰, *Jiuzhang suanshu yu Handai shehui jingji* 九章算術與漢代社會經濟 (The *Jiuzhang suanshu* and the social economy of the Han), Shoudu shifan daxue, 1994.

In addition to Needham, see Jean-Claude Martzloff, *A History of Chinese Mathematics*, Springer, 1997 (tr. from the French original of 1987), and Li Yan 李儼 and Du Shiran 杜石然, *Chinese Mathematics: A Concise History*, John N. Crossley and Anthony W.-C. Lun, trs., OUP, 1987; *Sous les nombres le monde: matériaux pour l'histoire culturelle du nombre en Chine ancienne*, *Extrême-Orient, Extrême-Occident* 16 (1993), contains articles that give a good indication of the efforts being made to trace the history of Chinese mathematics as it was conceived and used in historical contexts.

Vol. 4, *Physics*, part 1, *Physics and Physical Technology* (with Kenneth Girdwood Robinson and Wang Ling), CUP, 1962.

Vol. 4, *Physics*, part 2, *Mechanical Engineering* (with Kenneth Girdwood Robinson and Wang Ling), CUP, 1965.

Vol. 4, *Physics*, part 3, *Civil Engineering and Nautics* (with Wang Ling and Lu Gwei-Djen [Lu Guizhen 魯桂珍]), CUP, 1971.

Vol. 5, *Chemistry and Chemical Technology*, part 1, Tsien Tsuen-Hsuin (Qian Cunxun 錢存訓), *Paper and Printing*, CUP, 1985. See 18.3–4.

Vol. 5, *Chemistry and Chemical Technology*, part 2 (with Lu Gwei-Djen), *Spagyrical Discovery and Invention: Magisteries of Gold and Immortality*, CUP, 1974.

Vol. 5, *Chemistry and Chemical Technology*, part 3 (with Ho Ping-Yü [He Bingyu 何炳郁] and Lu Gwei-Djen), *Spagyrical Discovery and Invention: Historical Survey, from Cinnabar Elixirs to Synthetic Insulin*, CUP, 1976.

Vol. 5, *Chemistry and Chemical Technology*, part 4 (with Ho Ping-Yü, Lu Gwei-Djen, and Nathan Sivin), *Spagyrical Discovery and Invention: Apparatus, Theories and Gifts*, CUP, 1980.

Vol. 5, *Chemistry and Chemical Technology*, part 5 (with Lu Gwei-Djen), *Spagyrical Discovery and Invention: Historical Physiological Alchemy*, CUP, 1983.

Vol. 5, *Chemistry and Chemical Technology*, part 6 (with Robin Yates, Krzysztof Gawlikowski, Edward McEwen, and Wang Ling), *Military Technology: Missiles and Sieges*, CUP, 1995. See 28.2.

Vol. 5, *Chemistry and Chemical Technology*, part 7 (with Ho Ping-Yü, Lu Gwei-Djen, and Wang Ling), *Military Technology: The Gunpowder Epic*, CUP, 1986. See 28.2.

Vol. 5, *Chemistry and Chemical Technology*, part 9, Dieter Kuhn, *Textile Technology: Spinning and Reeling*, CUP, 1986. Note that considerable amounts of Chinese clothing have survived. Some was even found in Warring States tombs. For a comprehensive introduction, see Zhou Xun 周汛 and Gao Chunming 高春明, *5,000 Years of Chinese Costumes*, HK: Shangwu, 1987; 2nd rpnt., 1988; *Zhongguo fuzhuangshi* 中國服裝史 (History of Chinese clothing), Huang Nengfu 黄能馥, ed. in chief, Lüyou, 1995, 1996; or *Zhongguo yiguan fushi dacidian* 中國衣冠服飾大辭典 (Dictionary of Chinese clothing and costumes), Zhou Xun, comp., Shanghai cishu, 1996. On the clothing of ordinary people, see Gao Chunming, *Zhongguo gudai pingmin fuzhuang* 中國古代平民服裝 (Ancient Chinese vernacular clothing), Shangwu Intl., 1998; Verity Wilson, *Chinese Dress*, Victoria and Albert Museum, 1986. For scholarly catalogs of exhibitions of Qing official clothing, see John E. Vollmer, *Decoding Dragons: Status Garments in Ch'ing Dynasty China*, Museum of Art, Univ. of Oregon, 1980; Julia White and Emma C. Bunker, *Adornment for Eternity: Status and Rank in Chinese Ornament*, Denver and Hong Kong, 1994.

Vol. 5, *Chemistry and Chemical Technology*, part 10, Dieter Kuhn, *Textile Technology: Weaving*, CUP, forthcoming.

Vol. 5, *Chemistry and Chemical Technology*, part 13, Peter Golas, *Mining*, CUP, 1999.

Vol. 6, *Biology and Biological Technology*, part 1 (with Lu Gwei-Djen and Huang Hsing-Tsung [Huang Xingzong 黃興宗]), *Botany*, CUP, 1986.

Vol. 6, *Biology and Biological Technology*, part 2, Francesca Bray, *Agriculture*, CUP, 1984.

Vol. 6, *Biology and Biological Technology*, part 3, Christian Daniels and Nicholas K. Menzies, *Agro-Industries and Forestry*, CUP, 1996.

Vol. 6, *Biology and Biological Technology*, part 5, Huang Hsing-Tsung, *Biochemical Technology*, CUP, 1999.

Vol. 7, part I, *Language and Logic in Traditional China*, Christoph Harbsmeier, CUP, 1998.

See also:

Joseph Needham, *The Development of Iron and Steel Technology in China*, Newcomen Society, 1958 (Compare with Donald B. Wagner, *Iron and Steel in Ancient China*, Brill, 1993).

Lu Gwei-Djen and Joseph Needham, *Celestial Lancets: A History and Rationale of Acupuncture and Moxa*, CUP, 1980.

Joseph Needham, Wang Ling, and Derek Price, *Heavenly Clockwork: The Great Astronomical Clocks of Medieval China—A Missing Link in Horological Research*, CUP, 1960; rev., ed. 1986.

Joseph Needham, Lu Gwei-Djen, John H. Combridge, and John S. Major, *The Hall of Heavenly Records: Korean Astronomical Instruments, 1380–1780*, CUP, 1986.

Explorations in the History of Science and Technology in China, comp. in honor of the 80th birthday of Dr. Joseph Needham, Shanghai Classics Publishing House, 1983.

Evaluation of SCC

At its best *SCC* is a cornucopia. Sometimes the quality or the detail varies, a reflection no doubt of the different approaches taken by the many scholars who contributed to or wrote volumes in the series. Over the years the international scholarly community has had nothing but praise for the industry and insights displayed by Needham and his team of collaborators. He has been especially honored in China for drawing attention to some of the greatest achievements of Chinese civilization, hitherto (apart from the "four great discoveries" of paper, printing, the magnetic compass, and gunpowder) somewhat overlooked. However, while nobody has doubted the importance of his work, several have questioned his teleological approach as embodied in the so-called Needham question: Why did no scientific and technical revolution occur in China, despite its notable early record in technology and science? Nowadays views have changed: some regard the emergence of modern science in Europe as exceptional and depending on particular historical circumstances there. So its non-emergence elsewhere hardly needs explanation.[5] Others see the rise of Europe in the nineteenth century as "one more great shift in the global locus of power within a broader network."[6]

Needham has also been criticized for his overreliance on missionary and treaty port scholarship and for his anachronistic readings of Chinese texts, apparently based on his conviction that technology is the practical application of science, and therefore if the Chinese were good at making something there must have been a scientific theory to underpin it.[7]

Another weakness is his tendency to believe that because something was invented in China, it must have contributed to the similar later discovery in Europe (the reverse is not given such easy acceptance).[8]

Needham always intended that his final volume would take up the "Needham question," whose answer he felt lay in the influence of officialdom (bureaucratic feudalism). SCC, vol. 7, part 2 (the final

---

[5] Nathan Sivin examines the question and cites much of the literature in his "Why the Scientific Revolution Did Not Take Place in China—or Didn't It?" in *Explorations in the History of Science and Technology in China* (1983), 89–106; rpnt. in Sivin (1995). Francesca Bray, "Technology and Culture in Chinese History: An Introduction," *Chinese Science* 12: 13–17 (1995).

[6] Peter C. Perdue, "China in the Early Modern World: Short Cuts, Myths, and Realities," *Education About Asia* 4.1:21–26 (1999).

[7] Francesca Bray, "Eloge," *Isis* 87.2: 312–17 (1996).

[8] For balanced assessments, see *Chinese Science: Explorations of an Ancient Tradition*, Nathan Sivin and Shigeru Nakayama, eds., MIT, 1973, and Mark Elvin, ed., "The Work of Joseph Needham: A Symposium," *Past and Present* 87: 17–53 (1980).

volume in the originally planned series) will contain Needham's "General Conclusions," together with other writings by him constituting his final reflections on the project.[9] Work was begun on the volume by Derk Bodde, who eventually published his findings as a separate book: *Chinese Thought, Society and Science: Intellectual and Social Background of Science and Technology in Pre-modern China*, UHP, 1991.

The Needham History of Science Project is now at the Needham Research Institute, Robinson College, Cambridge University.

37.2 The Transplantation of Modern Science

The transplantation of some European sciences to China had already begun in the late Ming, early Qing. The intermediaries were the Jesuit missionaries and the Chinese scholars who helped them translate many scientific works.[10] These were for use within the existing Chinese context. European astronomy and mathematics, for example, were adopted primarily to improve calculation of the traditional Chinese calendar even if they may have stimulated new thinking among Chinese mathematicians, as has been argued.[11]

In the nineteenth century the main intermediaries were the small number of "secular missionaries" (almost entirely Protestant) and the Chinese scholars they worked with who devoted themselves

[9] Needham's overall views as expressed in articles and speeches were published under the title *The Grand Titration: Science and Society in the East and the West*, George Allen and Unwin, 1969.

[10] See Henri Bernard, "Les Adaptations chinoises d'ouvrages européens: Bibliographie chronologique depuis la venue des Portuguais à Canton jusqu' à la mission française de Pékin (1544-1688)," *MS* 10: 1-54; 309-88 (1945); and part 2, covering 1689-1799, *MS* 19: 349-83 (1960). The earlier translations into Chinese as well as those made in the nineteenth century are analyzed in Tsuenhsuin Tsien, "Western Impact on China Through Translation," *FEQ* 13: 305-27 (1954).

[11] Joanna Waley-Cohen, "China and Western Technology in the Late Eighteenth Century," *American Historical Review* 98: 1525-44 (1993); S-R. Du and Q. Han, "The Contributions of French Jesuits to Chinese Science in the Seventeenth and Eighteenth Centuries," *Impact of Science on Society* 167: 265-75 (1992). The Jesuits only passed on the Copernican heliocentric theory of planetary motion in 1760, two centuries after it had been propounded. Their reason for not doing so was because the theory was banned by the church.

to translating, publishing and teaching modern science. Their work was given an entirely new impulse by the fact that some of the most powerful officials in the empire, leaders of the self-strengthening movement (*ziqiang* 自強 or *yangwu* 洋務), such as Zeng Guofan 曾 國藩 (1811–72), recognized the need for Western knowledge as a means of making China strong (chemistry for explosive shells; mathematics to land them in the right place and to make precision machinery).[12] Many of the missionaries worked for one of the government established translation and educational agencies, such as the Interpreters College in Beijing (Tongwenguan 同文館, 1862–1902) or the similar college in Shanghai, eventually attached to the Kiangnan Arsenal (Jiangnan jiqi zhizaoju fanyiguan 江南機器制造局翻 譯館, 1868–1912).[13] Other foreigners taught at the new military academies, such as the Naval School at Fuzhou (Fuzhou chuanzheng xuetang 福州船政學堂, 1866–).[14] Working together with a Chinese scholar, they used the old translation method, the Westerner approximated the text in spoken Chinese, which his Chinese amenuensis then wrote down in *wenyan*. In this way Alexander Wylie and the leading Chinese mathematician of the day, Li Shanlan 李善蘭 (1810–82) translated chapters 7–15 of Euclid's *Elements* (Ricci and Xu Guangqi had already done chapters 1–6; 29.7.2). Zeng Guofan later contributed the preface. During 30 years, the College published translations of more than 200 works of modern science and the Arsenal published 178 translations. In the process, hundreds of new words had to be coined (1.2.6).

The Protestant missionaries set up polytechnic schools and also pioneered periodicals on science, technology, medicine, and other

[12] Ting-yee Kuo and Kwang-ching Liu, "Self-strengthening: the Pursuit of Western Technology," *CHC*, vol. 10, 491–542.

[13] The Shanghai Tongwenguan 同文館 (1863–) was renamed the Guang fangyanguan 廣方言館 on its incorporation into the Arsenal in 1869. A third interpreters' school was established in Canton (1864–).

[14] The French naval officer, Prosper Marie Giquel (1835–86), for example, was co-director of the Fuzhou Dockyard Naval School; see Steven Liebo, *Transferring Technology to China: Prosper Giquel and the Self-Strengthening Movement*, UCP, 1985. The great scholar and translator, Yan Fu 嚴復 (1854–1921) was a graduate of the school in navigation. But for reasons explained in Benjamin Schwartz (1916–1999), *In Search of Wealth and Power: Yen Fu and the West*, HUP, 1964, Yan chose to translate works of social and political science, not the natural sciences.

new subjects. Several of the most influential of these journals are introduced in 50.8.3. The editor of one of them, the prodigiously productive John Fryer, is an excellent exemplar of the "secular missionary" (he worked for 28 years as a translator at the Arsenal, and there and later translated 129 works in the natural and social sciences into Chinese). Of him it has been said that he "seems to have attached more importance to the strengthening of the Chinese nation than to the conversion of the Chinese people. Fryer's mission was to bring Western learning—especially science—to China." A remark that could be extended to not a few of the other missionaries.[15] Demand for science not only came from the reformers; industry also needed technology and engineers to service it. In the case of medicine, a practical demonstration effect was provided by the establishment of modern clinics and hospitals. The establishment of schools and academies teaching the new knowledge and the organization of societies for its propagation began in the 1880s and 1890s. But for most, Western studies (*xixue* 西學) remained "one more bleak alternative for those whose path to an official career had been blocked" (Schwarz, 1964, p. 25). The change came after the abolition of the imperial examination system in 1905 and the consequent liberation of students from the treadmill of the classical curriculum. During the May Fourth era science and democracy became for a short while the slogans of all those who wanted change. Science and practical studies were emphasized in the schools during the Nanjing decade. The institutionalization of the sciences in newly established professional associations and universities took place for the most part in the same period. National scientific research bodies were established and several universities set up research institutes. Foreign scientists were invited to lecture.

The attendance of Chinese students at European and American universities and military academies began with the small number sent abroad under the sponsorship of self-strengthening officials in the 1870s. Much larger numbers of students were only sent to Japan after the demonstration that Japan had successfully mastered Western studies by defeating the Qing in 1894 and Russia in 1904. In 1905, the leading statesman of the day, Zhang Zhidong 張之洞

---

[15] Paul Cohen, 1978 (29.7.3), 579. For a book-length study, see Adrian Arthur Bennett, *John Fryer: The Introduction of Western Science and Technology into Nineteenth-Century China*, HUP, 1967.

(1837–1909) urged Chinese students to study in Japan rather than in the West. Many went.[16] Despite the smaller numbers who were able to go to America and Europe, most graduated from university there while the majority of those in Japan never got beyond middle school.[17] The first Chinese student graduated from an American university (Yale) in 1854 in liberal arts but the first Chinese Ph.D in mathematics (from Harvard) was not granted until more than 50 years later in 1917 and there were only two more by 1920 (also from Harvard). By the same year, only three postgraduate science degrees had been gained by Chinese students in France (and none in Japan). The numbers increased thereafter.[18] The first four Chinese women to study in the United States all went there in the early 1880s to study medicine and on their return became the first lady doctors.[19]

Given almost constant war and civil unrest, it is remarkable to what degree the modern sciences had been successfully transplanted by the end of the 1930s. The story of how it was done has not yet been told in any detail in English. For a thorough overview in Chinese, see the first item. For a monograph on the establishment of a modern university system, see items two and three. For a rare history of the introduction of one branch of science, in this case chemistry, see the last item.

Ruth Hayhoe, *China's Universities, 1895-1995: A Century of Cultural Conflict*, Garland, 1996.

---

[16] Zhang recommended Japan on the grounds that students could complete their studies more quickly there than in the West—it was closer, cheaper, the language was akin to Chinese, and the courses were more practical than in the West; see his *Quanxue pian* 勸學篇 (Exhortation to study), "Waipian, Youxue" 外篇, 游篇 (External chapter, overseas studies), 1898.

[17] In 1896, 13 Chinese students went to study in Japan; by 1903, there were 1,300 and in 1906, 12,000. The numbers declined to 1,400 in 1912. Moreover, the few who went on to higher education studied liberal arts, law, military affairs, or medicine, not the natural sciences; see Paula Harrell, *Sowing the Seeds of Change: Chinese Students, Japanese Teachers, 1895-1905*, SUP, 1992.

[18] Yung Wing [Rong Hong 容閎, 1828-1912]) was the first graduate. His story is a fascinating one and is well told in *ECCP*, 402-405.

[19] All four girls went to the USA under missionary auspices; see Weili Ye, "*Nüliuxuesheng*: The Story of American-Educated Chinese Women, 1880s–1920s," *Modern China* 20.3: 315-46 (1994).

E-tu Zen Sun, "The Growth of the Academic Community, 1912–1945," *CHC*, vol. 13, 261–420.

Sally Borthwick, *Educational and Social Change in China*, Hoover Institution, 1983.

Peter Burke, *American Science in Modern China, 1876–1936*, CUP, 1980.

Mary Brown Bullock, *An American Transplant: The Rockefeller Foundation and Presbyterian Union Medical College*, UCP, 1980.

James Reardon-Anderson, *The Study of Change: Chemistry in China, 1840–1949*, CUP, 1991.

Zhongguo jin xiandai kexue jishu shi 中國近現代科學技術史 (History of Chinese science and technology in the late Qing and Republican periods), Dong Guangbi 董光璧, ed. in chief, Hunan jiaoyu, 1995.

37.3   Research Tools

Bibliography

Zhongguo gudai kejishi lunwen suoyin 中國古代科技史論文索引, Yan Dunjie 嚴敦傑, ed. in chief, Jiangsu kexue jishu, 1986. Bibliography of articles on the history of science and technology in China written between 1900 and 1982 arranged by subject and by period.

Chinese Studies in the History and Philosophy of Science and Technology, Fan Dainian and Robert S. Cohen, eds. Kluwer, 1996. A broad selection of articles.

Nathan Sivin, *Science in Ancient China: Researches and Reflections*, Variorum, 1995, IX, 1–17. Annotated bibliography of works in English.

Kaoguxue he kejishi 考古學和科技史 (Archaeology and the history of science and technology), Xia Nai 夏鼐 (1910–85), Kexue, 1979. Collection of articles by a leading Chinese archaeologist, written 1960–76.

Keji kaogu luncong 科技考古論叢 (Collected papers on the archaeology of science and technology), Wang Zhenduo 王振鐸, Wenwu, 1989.

Keji kaogu luncong 科技考古論叢 (Collected papers on the archaeology of science), Zhongguo kexue jishu daxue, 1991. Contains 41 papers delivered at the second conference on the archaeology of science.

Note that the bibliographies listed in 10.1 include sections on Science and Technology.

Journals

Chinese Science, vols. 1–10, irregular; from vol. 11 (1993–94), annual. Edited at the University of California at Los Angeles.

Newsletter for the History of Chinese Science, 1988– , annual.

Zhongguo keji shiliao 中國科技史料 (1980– , quarterly), Beijing.

Ziran kexueshi yanjiu 自然科學史研究 (1992– , quarterly), Beijing. From 1958–66, the title was *Kexueshi jikan* 科學史季刊. The present title was adopted in 1967 (annual through 1985; quarterly since 1986).

37.4   Geomancy, Architecture, Furniture, and Gardens

37.4.1   Geomancy and the Mariner's Compass

From the earliest times, as in all other societies, settlements and buildings in the China area were carefully sited in relation to hills and streams, the position of the sun, and local beliefs. In north China, the city or the palace was arranged along a south-north axis so the main entrance faced south. Likewise, ordinary family living spaces were organized round open courtyards with the main entrance facing south (similar to the ancient Greeks and Romans and for the same reasons: to gain the maximum of light and heat from the sun). In the Han these and other early practices were systematized and aligned with the official cosmology. Thereafter, at all levels of society and throughout the remainder of Chinese history geomancy (*fengshui* 風水 or *kanyu* 堪輿) played an essential role in Chinese architecture as a system of rules for siting manmade structures in the landscape (cities, temples, tombs, and houses). To assist him in his task, the geomancer used a schematic representation of heaven and earth with a number of circles indicating the 24 directions (also used on Chinese navigating compasses in the Tang and Song).[20]

[20] See *SCC*, vol. 4, part 1, 249–334; for additional material on the Han diviner's board set against Han ideas of cosmology, see Michael Loewe, *Ways to Paradise: The Chinese Quest for Immortality*, 1979; rpnt., SMC, 1994; on the geomancer's compass, see de Groot, 1892–1910 (34.1), vol. 3, bk. 1, part III, ch. XII, 935–1056. For geomancy as practiced in the Qing, see Richard J. Smith, "The Ways of Wind and Water," in Smith, *Fortune-Tellers and Philosophers: Divination in Traditional Chinese Society*, Westview, 1991, 131–72.

The 24 compass-points (*ershisi fang* 二十四方, *ershisi wei* 二十四位, *ershisi xiang* 二十四向, or, in geomantic parlance, *ershisi shan* 二十四山) were set at 15° intervals. The geomantic compass (*luopan* 羅盤) evolved from the Han diviner's board (*shi* 式, 栻) from which the mariner's compass (*zhinanzhen* 指南針) developed. It was like the geomancer's *luopan* 羅盤 (37.4.1), indeed probably evolved from it, but retained only the essential directional information on its dial (usually the 24 directions). The 24 points were set at 15° intervals. They were indicated with the characters for the 12 earthly branches (*dizhi* 地支), eight of the heavenly stems (*tiangan* 天干), and four of the *bagua* 八卦 from the *Yijing* (the *siwei* 四維, four directions, namely *gen* 艮, *xun* 巽, *kun* 坤, and *qian* 乾) for the inter-cardinal points. Some compasses showed only the eight directions (the four cardinal and inter-cardinal points). At the end of the Qing, the Western 16-point compass card began to come into use.

There is a lack of comparative studies of Chinese geomancy and cosmology as these relate to Chinese architectural practices and traditions, but see:

Stephan Feuchtwang, *An Anthropological Analysis of Chinese Geomancy*, Vientiane: Vithagana, 1974.

Yi-fu Tuan, *Topophilia: A Study of Environmental Perception, Attitudes and Values*, Prentice-Hall, 1974.

Rolf A. Stein, *The World in Miniature: Container Gardens and Dwellings in Far Eastern Religious Thought*, tr. from the French original (1987) by Phyllis Brooks, SUP, 1990. Sums up a lifetime's reflection on the cosmological meanings of miniature gardens, dwelling places, and the world and architecture in religious thought.

"Indian and Chinese 'Foreign Influences'," in Clarence Aasen, *Architecture of Siam: A Cultural History Interpretation*, Kuala Lumpur: OUP, 1998, 18–28.

The House in East and Southeast Asia: Anthropological and Architectural Aspects, K. G. Izikowitz and P. Sorensen, eds., Curzon Press, 1982.

For references on the influence of cosmological beliefs on city planning, see 4.7.1. For an architectural study of geomancy, see:

Zhongguo gudai fengshui yu jianzhu xuanzhi 中國古代風水與建築選址 (Ancient Chinese *fengshui* and the choice of site for buildings), Yi Ding 一丁 et al., Hebei kexue jishu, 1995.

37.4.2   Architecture

There is a large literature on palace construction and expenditures (not cited here), and the regulations of the Qing Board of Works are extant (50.6.2, *Zeli*). There are also more specialized texts on boat building and garden construction. Only a few of the manuals used by Chinese architects have survived; two have been translated:

Klaas Ruitenbeek, *Carpentry and Building in Late Imperial China: A Study of the 15ᵗʰ-Century Carpenter's Manual* Lu Ban jing [魯班經], Brill, 1993.

Frank J. Swetz, *The Sea Island Mathematical Manual, AD 263: Surveying and Mathematics in Ancient China*, Pennsylvania State Univ. Press, 1992.

Yingzao fashi 營造法式 (Treatise on architectural methods), Li Jie 李誠 (? –1110), completed in 1100; prnt., 1103; rpnt., 1145; Wanyou wenku, 1925; Shangwu, 1953. The *Yingzao fashi* was lost in the early sixteenth century and only came to light when a manuscript copy was found in 1919. Li was vice-minister in the Board of Construction and supervisor of the construction and maintenance of government buildings in the capital Bianliang (modern Kaifeng). The work of the architectural historian Liang Sicheng 梁思成 on this important classic has been published: *Yingzao fashi zhushi* 營造法式註釋 (Commentaries and notes on the *Yingzao fashi*), vol. 1, Zhongguo jianzhu gongye, 1983.

Note the illustrated dictionary of architectural terms: *Zhongguo gu jianzhu shuyu cidian* 中國古建築術語辭典, Shanxi renmin, 1996.

Construction of buildings was carried out according to standard dimensions, which were graded according to the different type and size of a building. By the end of the empire, building area was normally measured in square *chi* 尺 or in *jian* 間 (bays). A *jian* was defined as the space between four roof pillars. It varied in size according to the status and wealth of the owner. The ancient *yan* 筵 (mat) measure was still sometimes used for imperial palaces (1 *yan* 筵 = 9 *chi* 尺). The length of a building was called *miankuo* 面闊 and its depth, *jinshen* 進深.

For general outlines of architecture, see the following:

Liang Ssu-ch'eng (Liang Sicheng 梁思成, 1901-72), *A Pictorial History of Chinese Architecture*, Wilma Fairbank, ed., MIT Press, 1984. English version of Chinese original. Based on photographs taken by the author, the pioneer of Chinese architectural history, in the late 1920s and 1930s. The story of his life (and that of his wife Lin Whei-yin), and the conditions under which they worked on Chinese architecture are told in Wilma Fairbank, *Liang and Lin: Partners in Exploring China's Architectural Past*, Univ. of Pennsylvania Press, 1994.

Chinese Academy of Architecture, eds., *Ancient Chinese Architecture*, China Building Industry Press, 1982.

Ronald G. Knapp, *China's Traditional Rural Architecture: A Cultural Geography of the Common House*, UHP, 1986.

Ronald G. Knapp, *China's Vernacular Architecture: House Form and Culture*, UHP, 1989.

Ronald G. Knapp, "Dwellings as Social Templates," in idem, *China's Living Houses: Folk Beliefs, Symbols, and Household Ornamentation*, UHP, 1998, 7–28.

Francesca Bray, "House Form and Meaning," in idem, *Technology and Gender: Fabrics of Power in Late Imperial China*, UCP, 1997, 59–90.

Zhongguo meishu quanji 中國美術全集 (Complete collection of Chinese arts), *Jianzhu yishu pian* 建築藝術篇 (The art of architecture), Jiangong, 6 vols., 1987–88. The same publisher also put out a lavish 10-vol. series: *Zhongguo gu jianzhu daxi* 中國古建築大系 (A grand collection of ancient Chinese architecture), 1993.

37.4.3   Furniture

For most of its recorded history China was a mat-level culture— people sat on the floor (as can still be seen in Japan). The late Tang to the Song saw the gradual transition to a chair-level culture, and furniture was accordingly adjusted upwards and began to take on the forms that we now think of as typically Chinese. Furniture making reached its finest expression during the Ming (thanks in part to the importation of tropical hardwoods from Southeast Asia) and entered a new (and final) period in the Qing characterized by elaborate carving and decoration.

During the two millennia of living at floor mat level (*xidi* 席地), the different ways of sitting (from the formal to the informal) included kneeling; sitting cross-legged (*fuzuo* 跃坐, *panzuo* 盤坐); squatting on the haunches (*ju* 踞, modern *dun* 蹲); or sitting on the buttocks with knees tucked up and spread out in front (*jiju* 箕踞, open like a winnowing fan; also *yang bacha* 仰八叉). There were three main ways of kneeling: with both feet tucked under the buttocks, the buttocks resting on the heels, and the hands resting on the knees (*zuo* 坐; to sit on one's legs Japanese-style, *suwaru*); with the body not resting on the heels but raised slightly above them (*gui* 跪); or with the body erect from the knees (*ji* 跽); this last was the most formal, *zuo*, the least.[21] If erect kneeling was associated with worship or a salutation, it was termed *changgui* 長跪. The *koutou* 叩頭 was a deep bow from this position (3.2.3).

Women knelt or they sat with their feet tucked to the side; monks sat in the lotus position (*chanzuo* 禪座) to meditate (*zuochan* 坐禪). Soldiers normally dropped to one knee before presenting a report to an officer. It showed respect, and it was also an easier position from which to leap to their feet to carry out instructions than kneeling on both knees. Thus soldiers were unaffected by the changes in seating posture in the Tang and Song and continued to report to superior officers from the one-knee crouch position. Archers often knelt on their right knee (to make it easier to steady and aim their crossbows with the left hand holding the bow, the left elbow resting on the left knee, and the right hand holding the trigger. The mausoleum of the first emperor contains 160 lifesize statues of bowman resting in this position, ready to raise their bows and lower their heads to take aim at the slightest sign of trouble).

Sitting was either directly on the floor, on a large low platform (*chuang* 床) used also for sleeping, or on a smaller platform (*xiaochuang* 小床, *ta* 榻) for one or two people. The folding stool (*huchuang* 胡床), probably an import from ancient North Africa via Central Asia, became popular from the Later Han (at first mainly among military officers on campaign). Until the relaxing of manners which took place between the Nan-Bei Chao and the Tang, it was considered impolite and disrespectful for men to sit with their legs spread out in front in the *jiju* position. After the Nan-Bei Chao, largely thanks to the influence of the "barbarians," *jiju* and other

---

[21] Several Shang jade figurines in the *zuo* 坐 position have been excavated; they are reproduced in Cui Yongxue, 1989 (see next page) and in Song Zhenhao, 1994 (Chapter 36), fig. 47 and 49 (*jiju* 箕踞); for the Han, see Sun Ji 孫機, 1991 (44.4.2), chaps. 54–55.

On the different types of kneeling, see Yang Hong 楊泓, "Shuo zuo, ji he qizuo," 說坐跽和跂坐 (On kneeling, erect kneeling, and dangling the feet) in Yang Hong 楊泓 and Sun Ji 孫機, *Xunchang de jingzhi* 尋常的精致 (The fineness of the ordinary), Liaoning jiaoyu, 1996, 3–7; Wang Fengyang 王風陽 (2.5, item 11), 812–13.

forms of informal sitting (*xiaozuo* 小坐) became more common; above all, the use of the chair spread from Buddhist monks, to VIPs, then to the rich and eventually to ordinary folk. People began to sit high (*gaozuo* 高坐) with their legs pendant and feet resting on the floor or on a foot stool (it was frowned upon to leave them dangling or for only the toes to touch the floor).[22] By the later empire, it had even become the norm for senior officials to sit firmly against the chairback (*manzuo* 滿座), often with their legs open (not pressed together or crossed) and hands supported by the arm rests, a posture that would have been considered scandalously disrespectful in the Han or earlier centuries. Juniors were supposed to sit perched on the edge of the chair (*banzuo* 半座) as a sign of respect and were not supposed to cross their legs.

On the introduction and history of the chair, see

Yang Hong 楊泓, "Huchuang" 胡床 (Barbarian stools) in Yang Hong 楊泓 and Sun Ji 孫機, *Wenwu congtan* 文物叢談 (Collected essays on cultural relics), Wenwu, 1991, 254–62.

Charles Patrick FitzGerald, *Barbarian Beds: The Origin of the Chair in China*, London: Cresset Press, 1965.

Cui Yongxue 崔詠雪, *Zhongguo jiajushi: zuoju bian* 中國家具史坐具編 (A history of Chinese furniture: seating furniture), Mingwen, 1989; rev. and enl., 1990, 1994.

The evidence for the history of Chinese furniture up to the Ming is mainly in the form of tomb artifacts or tomb and other paintings. Actual pieces of Tang furniture have been preserved in the Shôsô-in at Nara. The *Liji* 禮記 and later rules of etiquette stipulate correct (and incorrect) seating postures (see, for example, *Libu zeli* 禮部則例, 50.5.2, *Zeli*). On the history of Chinese furniture, see

Craig Clunas, *Chinese Furniture*, Victoria and Albert Museum, 1988; 2nd ed., London: Art Media Resources Ltd., 1997.

Wang Shixiang 王世襄, *Connoisseurship of Chinese Furniture*, Wang Shixin and Lark E. Mason, trs., 2 vols., Joint Publishing (HK), 1990. A one-volume version appeared as *Classical Chinese Furniture*, 1985.

---

[22] A famous monk was named Gaozuo 高座, presumably referring to the characteristic manner in which monks sat on chairs (*gaozuo* 高坐), not the floor.

Tian Jiaqing 田家青, *Classic Chinese Furniture of the Qing Dynasty*, Lark E. Mason and Juliet-Yi Chou, trs., London: Philip Wilson and Joint Publishing (HK), 1996.

Wang Shixiang and Curtis Evarts, *Masterpieces from the Museum of Classical Chinese Furniture*, Chinese Art Foundation, Chicago and San Francisco, 1995. A fine exhibition catalog with authoritative notes and an excellent introduction entitled "A Brief History of Pre-Ming Chinese Furniture," xxii–xxix.

Bibliography

"A History of the Scholarship of Classical Chinese Furniture," *Journal of the Classical Chinese Furniture Society*, 3.2: 58–70 (1993).

Society

The Classical Chinese Furniture Society (Renaissance, California) publishes the quarterly *Journal of the Classical Chinese Furniture Society* (1990–) and maintains the Museum of Classical Chinese Furniture.

37.4.4 Gardens

Stein, 1990 (37.4.1).

Maggie Keswick, *The Chinese Garden: History, Art, and Architecture*, with contributions and conclusion by Charles Jencks, London: Academy Editions, 1978; New York, St. Martin's Press, 1986. Contains a list of selected gardens open to the visitor.

Craig Clunas, *Fruitful Sites: Garden Culture in Ming Dynasty China*, Reaktion, 1996. The work of a historian interested in the social and economic background.

R. Stewart Johnson, *Scholar Gardens of China*, CUP, 1991.

Yuanming yuan 圓明園 (The summer palace), Yishiguan, ed., 2 vols., Shanghai guji, 1991.

38

Calligraphy, Painting, and Music

In addition to their aesthetic appeal, Chinese calligraphy and paint-ing (and the other decorative and useful arts) can also provide the historian unique clues, and often evidence, of behavior, lifestyles, beliefs, and attitudes at every period of Chinese history.[1] This is par-ticularly true of the earlier dynasties for which other sources are scarce or nonexistent (44.4.2).[2] It goes without saying that the arts also provide vital evidence for other fields, such as the history of re-ligion.

38.1 Calligraphy, Painting, and Forgery

38.1.1 Calligraphy

On the early history of Chinese writing, including its close connec-tions to divination, see Chapters 14–17. In the empire, calligraphy (*shufa* 書法) continued to be highly prized. Indeed, it was regarded as more important than painting. Every child who went to school (and many who did not) learned to practice calligraphy by studying the works of famous calligraphers (1.3.2). On the importance of models of calligraphy carved on stone, see 17.3, note 21. There are

---

[1] See the grouped entries on Chinese art in *The Grove Dictionary of Art*, Jane Turner, ed., Macmillan, 1997, vol. 6, 607–925; vol. 7, 1–162. *The British Museum Book of Chinese Art*, Jessica Rawson, ed., British Museum, 1992, has good, select bibliographies, including ones on jades and bronzes; painting, cal-ligraphy and printing; sculpture; the decorative arts (silk and dress; lacquer; ivory carving; jade; gold, silver and jewelery; polychrome, cloisonné and enameled wares; glass; snuff bottles; and miscellaneous); ceramics; and trade in art objects.

[2] M. J. Powers, *Art and Political Expression in Early China*, YUP, 1991.

numerous introductions to calligraphy and reference works available, for example, Tseng Yuho, *A History of Chinese Calligraphy*, HKCUP, 1993. The *Sho no uchû* 書の宇宙 collection is notable for the high quality of the photographs, including close-ups and analytical drawings. It also includes examples of many of the latest inscriptional and manuscript discoveries.[3]

38.1.2   Painting

The earliest known painting in the China area is that found in prehistoric rock art (14.2) and on Neolithic pottery.[4] Fragments of Shang period wall paintings have also been discovered. More evidence of decorative and didactic painting is available from Warring States tombs. We also know that early Chinese texts such as the *Shanhaijing* 山海經 were copiously illustrated. The first known painters date from the Han but the first paintings to have survived are from the Tang.

A number of universities have built up photographic data banks of Chinese painting (for example, at the Tôbunken or Princeton). Based on these, illustrated catalogs in the form of inventories have now been published. The illustrations are small but these works graphically index many thousands of paintings. They make a convenient way of finding out what paintings survive of a particular painter or from a given period. Within China itself, there are catalogs of the main paintings and calligraphic works held in Chinese collections,[5] including in the Palace Museum, Taibei.[6] In addition,

---

[3] *Sho no uchû* (Universe of calligraphy), 24 vols., Nigensha, 1996–98.

[4] *Zhongguo yuanshi yishu* 中國原始藝術 (Chinese primitive art), Wu Shichi 吳詩池, Zijincheng, 1996; Liu Xicheng 劉錫誠, *Zhongguo yuanshi yishu* 中國原始藝術 (Chinese primitive art), Shanghai wenyi, 1998. Wu's book contains fuller references and also distribution tables; Liu has chapters on tatooing, songs, and myth, which are not covered by Wu.

[5] *Zhongguo gudai shuhua tumu* 中國古代書畫圖目 (Illustrated catalog of selected works of ancient Chinese painting and calligraphy), 20 vols., Wenwu, 1986–99.

[6] *Gugong shuhua tulu* 故宮書畫圖錄 (Illustrated catalog of painting and calligraphy in the National Palace Museum), 16 vols., Taibei: Guoli gugong bowuyuan, 1989–96; *Gugong canghua daxi* 故宮藏畫大系 (A panorama of painting in the National Palace Museum), 16 vols., Guoli gugong bowuyuan, 1993–95.

there is a comprehensive, illustrated catalog of all main murals in China.[7]

To find a painting held in a collection outside China, first consult *Chûgoku kaiga sôgô zuroku* 中國繪畫總合圖錄. The text is in Japanese and English.[8]

References such as *Zhongguo gudai shuhua tumu*, the *Gugong shuhua tulu*, Suzuki, or Ogawa, although relatively comprehensive, are not exhaustive. If you are particularly interested in the works of a painter, you should double-check with individual collections.

Many of the texts of Chinese connoisseurship have been translated into English:

W. R. B. Acker, *Some T'ang and Pre-T'ang Texts on Chinese Painting*, 2 vols., Brill, 1954–74.

Susan Bush, *The Chinese Literati on Painting: Su Shih (1037–1101) to Tung Ch'i-ch'ang (1555–1636)*, HUP, 1971.

Susan Bush and Hsio-yen Shih, *Early Chinese Texts on Painting*, HUP, 1985.

Rocks play a central role in Chinese garden design (37.4.4) and as Robert Mowry puts it, "to Chinese artists, rocks are the basic build-

---

[7] *Zhongguo bihua quanji* 中國壁畫全集 (Comprehensive collection of Chinese murals), 34 vols., Tianjin renmin meishu and other provincial art publishers, 1989– .

[8] *Chûgoku kaiga sôgô zuroku* (Comprehensive illustrated catalog of Chinese paintings), Suzuki Kei 鈴木敬 (1905–81), ed., 5 vols., Tôkyô daigaku, 1982–83. Vol. 1 covers Chinese paintings in America and Canada; vol. 2, Southeast Asia and Europe; vols. 3 and 4, Japan; vol. 5 is an index. A new version was published in 1998–2000 edited by Ogawa Hiromitsu 小川裕元. It is based on materials gathered during a second world-wide research carried out in 1990–98. Vol. 1 covers America and Canada; vol. 2 Asia and Europe; vols. 3 and 4, Japan.

See also James Cahill, *An Index of Early Chinese Painters and Paintings: T'ang, Sung and Yuan*, UCP, 1980. This does not include frescoes. See also the lists in vols. 2 and 7 of Osvald Sirén's *Chinese Painting: Leading Masters and Principles*, Lund Humphries, 1958; New York: Hacker Art Books, 1973. James Cahill's studies on Chinese painting from the thirteenth to the seventeenth centuries are the best introductions to these paintings: *Hills Beyond a River: Chinese Painting of the Yuan Dynasty, 1279–1368*, Weatherhill, 1976; *Parting at the Shore: Painting of the Early and Middle Ming Dynasty, 1368–1580*, Univ. Art Museum, Berkeley, 1978; *The Restless Landscape: Chinese Painting of the Late Ming Period*, Weatherhill, 1971; *The Compelling Image: Nature and Style in Seventeenth-Century Chinese Painting*, HUP, 1982.

ing blocks of landscape paintings: magnified in scale, the rocks become mountains; embellished with rivers, trees, and winding paths, the mountains become complete landscapes."

Robert D. Mowry, *Worlds Within Worlds: The Richard Rosenblaum Collection of Scholar's Rocks*, Harvard University Art Museums, 1997.

John Hay, *Kernels of Energy, Bones of Earth: The Rock in Chinese Art*, New York: China House Gallery, China Institute in America, 1985.

Until recently the study of Chinese painting concentrated on aesthetic analysis. Now, its social and economic history is beginning to attract more attention. See, for example,

Craig Clunas, *Art in China*, OUP, 1997.

Patricia Ebrey, *The Cambridge Illustrated History of China*, CUP, 1996.

James Cahill, *The Painter's Practice: How Artists Lived and Worked in Traditional China*, Col. UP, 1994.

Chu-tsing Li and James C. Y. Watt, *The Chinese Scholar's Studio: Artistic Life in the Late Ming Period*, Thames and Hudson and Asia Society Galleries, 1987.

Chu-tsing Li et al., *Artists and Patrons: Some Social and Economic Aspects of Chinese Painting*, Nelson-Atkins Museum of Art, Univ. Press of Kansas and the UWP, 1989 (includes Jason Chi-sheng Kuo, "Huichou Merchants as Art Patrons in the Late Sixteenth and Early Seventeenth Centuries," 177–88).

Shadows of Mt. Huang: Chinese Painting and Printing of the Anhui School, James Cahill, ed., Berkeley: University Art Museum, 1981.

Art and Power in Japan and China, special number of *Asian Cultural Studies*, International Christian Univ. publications III-A, Tokyo, 1989.

38.1.3   Forgery

For a good introduction to the key question of forgery (*weituo* 偽託) in Chinese calligraphy and painting, see

Xu Bangda 徐邦達, *Gu shuhua wei'e kaobian* 古書畫偽訛考辨 (Research into the forgery of ancient calligraphy and painting), 4 vols., Jiangsu guji, 1984. A carefully argued, scholarly work. Vols. 1–2, calligraphy; vol. 3, painting; vol. 4, black and white illustrations.

Zhongguo gujin shuhua zhenwei tudian 中國古今書畫真偽圖典 (Genuine and fake illustrated dictionary of Chinese calligraphy and painting in every dynasty), Yang Renkai 楊仁愷, ed. in chief, Liaoning huabao,

1997. This is based on an exhibition catalog. It contains brief bilingual comments on excellent color reproductions of the originals of many famous calligraphers and painters alongside forgeries of them.

38.1.4   Research Tools

Biographies

The standard English-language biographical dictionaries include painters; for example, vol. 4 of *Sung Biographies* deals with the main painters of the Song (3.4). For a specialized biographical dictionary, see

Zhongguo meishujia renming cidian 中國美術家人名辭典 (Dictionary of Chinese historical personalities in the fine arts), Yu Jianhua 俞劍華, comp., Shanghai renmin meishu, 1981; rev., 1987; 7ᵗʰ prnt., 1996. Contains biographies of 13,000 painters. Note that it was not uncommon for a single Chinese painter to use dozens of alternative names. If you cannot find an alternative name in this dictionary, which includes an appendix of them, then there is also a separate publication.[9]

There are also indexes and biographical dictionaries for specific periods— for example, *Tang-Song huajia renming cidian* 唐宋畫家人名辭典 (Personal-name dictionary of Tang and Song painters), Zhu Zhuyu 朱鑄禹, comp., Zhongguo gudian yishu, 1958; *Song Liao Jin huajia shiliao* 宋遼金畫家史料 (Historical materials on Song, Liao, and Jin painters), Chen Gaohua 陳高華, comp., Wenwu, 1984.

Bibliography

Jerome Silbergeld, "Chinese Painting Studies in the West: A State-of-the-Field Article," *JAS* 46.4: 849–97 (1987).

---

[9] *Zhongguo lidai shuhua zhuanke jia zihao suoyin* 中國歷代書畫篆刻家字號索引 (Index of styles and alternative names of Chinese historical painters and seal cutters), Shang Chengzuo 商承祚 and Huang Hua 黃華, comps., 2 vols., Renmin meishu, 1960. This index contains alternative names of 16,000 painters and seal cutters from the Qin and Han periods to the Republic, and also gives birth and death dates, native place, and so on. It has an index of names. See also Nancy N. Seymour, *Index Dictionary of Chinese Artists, Collectors and Connoisseurs*, Scarecrow, 1988, which contains entries on over 5,000 persons from the Tang onward.

Museums

The imperial collections of paintings and art objects are held in the Palace Museums in Beijing and in Taibei. Numerous catalogs of the holdings are available.[10] The third largest portion of the old palace collections is held by the Liaoning Museum, thanks to the scrolls brought to Shenyang by the last Qing emperor, Puyi.

Apart from the Palace Museums, the best museums are the National Museum of Chinese History in Beijing (8.2, *Illustrations*); the new Shanghai Museum (opened in 1996); the various museums in Xi'an (46.4.1), and the provincial museums in Gansu, Henan, Hubei, Hunan, Liaoning, Shanxi, and Xinjiang. Several major museums have recently been rebuilt (Shaanxi, Shanghai, and Henan). Others are rebuilding. There is a series of large-scale, beautifully illustrated introductions to some of these collections. It is particularly strong on archaeological finds.[11] There are also numerous museums of single archaeological sites well worth the detour, for example, the museum of the first site of the Western Zhou fief of Yan 燕 (Beijing) at Liulihe 琉璃河 or of the tomb of the King of Nan Yue (Nam Việt) in Guangzhou (44.5.1).

For a detailed, comprehensive guide to the museums of China, both large and small (including those in Taiwan, Hong Kong, and Macao), many of which are of great interest to the historian, see *Zhongguo bowuguan zhi* 中國博物館志.[12]

---

[10] *Gugong wenwu dadian* 故宮文物大典 (Antiques canon: the Palace Museum), 4 folio vols., Fujian renmin, Jiangxi renmin, Zhejiang jiaoyu and Zijincheng, 1994; *Zhonghua wuqian nian wenwu jikan* 中華五千年文物季刊 (Five thousand years of Chinese art series), 132 vols., Taibei: Guoli gugong bowuyuan, 1983– .

[11] *Zhongguo bowuguan* 中國博物館 (China's museums), 14 vols., Wenwu and Kodansha, 1991–94.

[12] *Zhongguo bowuguan zhi* (Handbook of Chinese museums), Zhongguo bowuguan xuehui 中國博物館學會 (Chinese Society of Museums), ed., Huaxia, 1995. Arrangement is by province. Information on each museum includes details of the collections, main publications and serials, hours of opening, and average number of visitors per year. An English translation is given for each museum, and there is an English index.

Catalogs and Collections of Illustrations

Some of the most interesting writing on the Chinese arts appears not only in books and journals but also in monographic catalogs of collections or exhibitions, which often have sumptuous illustrations. To take but four examples of major exhibition catalogs of Chinese art:

Mysteries of Ancient China: New Discoveries from the Early Dynasties, Jessica Rawson, ed., British Museum, 1996.

Possessing the Past: Treasures from the National Palace Museum (Taipei), Wen C. Fong and James C. Y. Watt, eds., Metropolitan Museum and the National Palace Museum, 1996.

The Chinese Exhibition: A Commemorative Catalogue of the International Exhibition of Chinese Art, Royal Academy of Arts, November 1935–March 1936, Faber, 1936. This was the most comprehensive exhibition of Chinese art ever held outside China before World War II.

A Descriptive Catalogue of the Chinese Collection, now exhibiting at St George's Place, Hyde Park Corner, London with condensed accounts of the genius, government, history, literature, agriculture, arts, trade, manners, customs & social life of the people of the Celestial Empire, William B. Langdon, ed., London, 1842. This is the first catalog of a Chinese exposition held in the West.

Old Chinese books were often illustrated and in some cases scholars collected illustrations of interesting artifacts, notably Wang Qi 王圻 (*jinshi* 1565), *Sancai tuhui* 三才圖會.[13] This contains maps, plans, and sketches of everyday utensils and portraits.

Works containing illustrations of material culture are found on stone reliefs, brick paintings, and other archaeological artifacts (44.5.2). For an enormous modern collection of illustrations of Chinese painting and artifacts, see *Zhongguo meishu quanji* 中國美術全集. It contains 15,000 plates in 59 folio volumes (vol. 60 is an index).[14] The

---

[13] *Sancai tuhui* (Assembled pictures of the three realms [i.e., heaven, earth and man]), 1607; 3 vols., Shanghai guji, 1988; *Heaven and Earth: Album Leaves from a Ming Encyclopaedia*, Shambhala, 1979, contains 120 plates selected, translated, and annotated by John A. Goodall.

[14] *Zhongguo meishu quanji* (Complete collection of Chinese arts), 60 vols., Wenwu and many other publishers, including Renmin meishu, Gongyi meishu, Zhongguo jianzhu gongye, 1984– . This collection is eventually planned to expand to 400 vols.

first 21 volumes cover all forms of painting. Next come 13 volumes of sculpture, followed by 12 volumes of handicrafts and six volumes each of architecture and calligraphy and seals. Each volume has many hundreds of excellent color plates as well as smaller "inventory-style" black and white photographs with notes. The entire collection is available on CD-ROM. More manageable is the sumptuous "dictionary" of 5,500, mainly recently excavated, art objects, edited by the Wenwuju 文物局 (Cultural relics bureau).[15] Each treasure has a color photograph and a brief description. Arrangement is by material; for example, vol. 1 contains annotated photographs of metal, silver, jade, and stone objects.

Western Painters and Photographers

From the eighteenth century, there were several excellent missionary painters at the Qing court, as well as artists attached as recorders to the first embassies to China (42.4.1). The first photographs to have survived date from the 1850s (42.4.2).

Journals

Artibus Asiae (1925– , semiannual), Zurich and Washington. Scholarly international journal.

Arts Asiatique (1954– , semiannual), Musée Guimet and Musée Cernuschi, Paris. Scholarly French journal.

Gugong bowuyuan yuankan 故宮博物院院刊 (1978– , quarterly), Palace Museum, Beijing

Orientations (1970– , bimonthly), Hong Kong. For collectors and art historians. Has frequent articles publicizing the latest discoveries, often by well-known authorities.

38.2   Music

In Chinese music as in other fields, many features that today seem typical, for example, Peking opera (*jingxi* 京戲) or the *erhu* 二胡 (two-stringed fiddle), took their present form or prominence only at

---

[15] *Zhongguo wenwu jinghua da quan* 中國文物精華大全 (The complete collection of the best of Chinese cultural relics), 4 vols., Wenwu and HK: Shangwu, 1993–95; Cishu, 1995–96 (with the title 中國文物精華大辭典).

the very end of the imperial period (Peking opera) or at the beginning of the twentieth century (the *erhu*).

The earliest and largest collection of musical instruments so far discovered in the world are 23 bone flutes (*gudi* 骨笛) from Jiahu 賈湖, Wuyang 舞陽, in central Henan. The site belongs to the Peiligang culture and dates from 7000–5800 BC.[16] Hunting whistles have also been found: some were made of animal bone (*gushao* 骨哨, ca. 6000 BC from Hemudu), and some were globular pottery flutes or ocarina (*taoxun* 陶塤, ca. 5000 BC from Yangshao sites). They may have been used for dancing as well as for hunting.

Neolithic chime bells as well as stone chimes from Anyang have been unearthed. Later, bronze chime bells became a characteristic of Chinese music and remained so for 2,000 years until the end of the Bronze Age.[17] Several huge sets dating from the Warring States have been unearthed in recent years, the best-known of which is the complete set of 65 found in the tomb of Marquis Yi of Zeng 曾侯乙 (19.1.1):

Lothar von Falkenhausen, *Suspended Music: Chime Bells in the Culture of Bronze Age China*, UCP, 1993.

Music in the Age of Confucius, Jenny F. So, ed., Washington DC: Sackler Gallery, 2000. Scholarly catalog of an exhibition of instruments from the Marquis of Zeng's tomb.

Seventeen of the Standard Histories have monographs on music.[18] Most of the encyclopaedias also have sections on it (Chapter 29).

---

[16] The earliest of the flutes are one with five holes and one with six holes (7000–6600 BC). Eleven date from 6600–6200 BC and have seven holes. Of three dated to 6200–5800 BC, two have seven holes and one, eight. The remainder are damaged; see *Wuyang Jiahu* 舞陽賈湖 (Wuyang Jiahu), Henan Wenkaosuo, ed., 2 vols., Kexue, 1999, vol. 2, 992–1020; color plates 39–40.

[17] Li Chunyi 李純一, *Zhongguo shanggu yueqi zongbian* 中國上古樂器綜編 (An overall survey of archaic Chinese musical instruments), Wenwu, 1996; Chen Cheng-yih (Cheng Zhenyi 程貞一), "Early Chinese Work on Acoustics," in *Early Chinese Work in Natural Science*, HKUP, 1996, 19–112.

[18] See Michael Loewe, "The Office of Music, c. 114–7 BC," *BSOAS* 36 (1973), 340–51; Denis Twitchett, "A Note on the 'Monograph on Music' in *Chiu T'ang shu*," *AM*, 3rd series, 3.1: 51–62 (1990).

For a general introduction to the history of Chinese music, use the articles in the standard reference, *The New Grove Dictionary of Music and Musicians*, vol. 4, Macmillan, 1980, 245–83.

On music in Classical China, see Kenneth J. DeWoskin, *A Song for One or Two: Music and the Concept of Art in Early China*, CCS, Univ. of Michigan, 1982. On the social and ritual uses of music in the later empire, see Joseph Lam, *State Sacrifices and Music in Ming China: Orthodoxy, Creativity and Expressiveness*, SUNY, 1998, and *Harmony and Counterpoint: Ritual Music in Chinese Context*, Bell Yung, Evelyn S. Rawski, and Rubie S. Watson, eds., SUP, 1996. On the discoverer of equal temperament tuning, Zhu Zaiyu 朱載堉 (1536–1611), see Kenneth Robinson, *A Critical Study of Chu Tsai-yu's Contribution to Equal Temperament in Chinese Music*, Steiner, 1980.

Colin P. Mackerras, *The Rise of the Peking Opera, 1770–1870: Social Aspects of the Theatre in Manchu China*, Clarendon, 1972, is a study as broad as the title suggests.

Recordings

Only two pre-Song musical sources are extant in China today. The earlier of the two is a piece for the seven-string zither (*qin* 琴) ascribed to the sixth century.[19] The other is a set of 25 melodies for the four-string lute (*pipa* 琵琶). It was found among the Dunhuang manuscripts and has been dated to the early tenth century. Attempts have been made to reconstruct the sounds of these. Previous literature on the melodies plus new transcriptions and recordings can be found in *Dunhuang guyue* 敦煌古樂.[20] Echoes of the sonorous and slow rhythms of Tang court music and dances can be heard in Japanese *Gagaku* 雅樂 (imperial court music), which was based on Tang music. See Laurence Picken et al., *Music from the Tang Court*, 7 vols., CUP, 1981–97.

[19] Robert Van Gulik, *The Lore of the Chinese Lute: An Essay in Ch'in Ideology*, *MN* Monograph 3, Tokyo, 1940.

[20] *Dunhuang guyue* (Ancient music of Dunhuang), Dunhuang wenyi and Gansu yinxiang, 1992.

Much more Chinese music has survived from the Song and later dynasties.[21] For a CD of Qing court music as it sounded to a Lazarist and a Jesuit missionary, see 29.7.

Ancient Instruments by Province

Zhongguo yinyue wenwu daxi 中國音樂文物大系 (Collection of Chinese musical artifacts), Daxiang, 1995- . The series contains much new material.

Bibliographies

Walter Kaufmann, *Musical References in the Chinese Classics*, Info Coordinators, 1976. Gathers together with translations the references to music in the Confucian classics (bilingual text).

Zhongguo gudai yinyue shumu 中國古代音樂書目 (Catalog of ancient Chinese books on music), first draft, Yinyue, 1961. Lists 1,400 works on Chinese music written before 1840.

Zhongguo yinyue shupuzhi 中國音樂書譜志 (Catalog of Chinese books on music), Renmin yinyue, 1984; rev. edition, 1994. Contains listings of 5,000 works on music from earliest times to 1949. Arrangement is by *pinyin*. There is a title index.

Western-language studies are discussed in François Picard, "La Connaissance et l'étude de la musique chinoise: une histoire brève," *RBS* 13: 265–72 (1996).

Biographies

Zhongguo yinyue wudao xiqu renming cidian 中國音樂舞蹈戲曲人名詞典, Cao Chousheng 曹惆生 (Dictionary of personal names of Chinese musicians, dancers, and actors), ed., Shangwu, 1959. Gives biographical notices of 5,201 persons connected with music, dance, and the theater up the end of the Qing. Arrangement is by stroke count and classifier.

---

[21] Rulan Chao Pian, *Sonq Dynasty Musical Sources and Their Interpretation*, HUP, 1967.

39

Women's Studies

The sources for women's history in the pre-Qin are the same as for any other form of history of those centuries: archaeology, the oracle-bone and bronze inscriptions, and the contemporary sources listed in Table 26, 19.2. Archaeology has unearthed new and fascinating evidence, including prehistoric statues of women possibly used in fertility rites, but there is no consensus as to what light these finds throw on the role of women in society and attitudes towards them. In China the discussion normally turns round the question of the timing of the transition from matriarchal to patriarchal tribes according to the Morgan/Engels scheme.[1] The little evidence there is relates to women at the top of society and often seems to provide insufficient support for the conclusions reached.

There seems to be some evidence that women aristocrats in the Shang had a powerful role in society, at least by comparison with their role in the Zhou period.[2]

The ground becomes slightly more solid for the study of women in Chinese imperial history. The direct primary sources can be divided between works written by women (39.1) and works written for or about them by both men and women (39.2). Modern interest in gender studies has led to a closer study of these sources as well as the re-interpretation of standard primary sources, such as the laws and customs relating to marriage (39.3).

From the end of the nineteenth century, new sources to trace the history of women begin to appear. These include newspapers, magazines, new forms of literature, social surveys and social prob-

---

[1] Zhang Jing 張經, "80 niandai yilai de xian-Qin funüshi yanjiu" 80 年代以來的先秦婦女史研究 (Research on the history of women in the pre-Qin since the 1980s), *Zhongguoshi yanjiu dongtai*, 1998.1: 2–8.

[2] David N. Keightley, "At the Beginning: The Status of Women in Neolithic and Shang China," *MWG* 1.1: 1–63 (1999).

lem analyses. Examples of some outstanding modern studies that use them are listed (39.3.3). The chapter ends with a section on research tools (39.4).

On women's names and how they differed from those of men, see 3.2.3. On family and clan instructions, see 3.5. Some secondary sources on sex are listed in Chapter 36 and on female prostitution, in 39.3.3.

39.1   Works Written by Women

Since women during imperial times were supposed to be educated for wifely tasks such as sewing and embroidery or running a household, they did not attend government schools nor did they sit the official exams (at no time were they eligible for public office). But in the course of Chinese history there were many outstanding women writers (typically of poetry), especially in the later empire.[3]

The most complete bibliography of works written by women is that of Hu Wenkai 胡文楷, *Lidai funü zhuzuo kao* 歷代婦女著作考.[4] In it he provides place of origin, family background, occupation, marital status, and lists of all extant or known works for over 3,600 women writers from the Han to the Qing (mostly Qing).

Note the following anthologies and collections of materials (up to 1912):

Chinese Women Poets: An Anthology of Poetry and Criticism from Ancient Times to 1911, Kang-i Sun Chang and Haun Saussy, eds., SUP, 1999.

Views from the Jade Terrace: Chinese Women Artists, 1300–1912, Marsha Weidner et al., eds., IUP, 1988.

One unusual way in which women communicated with each other in southern Hunan was by using *nüshu* 女書 (women's script). Most of the known texts are marriage congratulations. See 14.5 and:

William W. Chiang, *"We Know the Script: We Have Been Good Friends": Linguistic and Social Analysis of the Women's Script Literacy in Southern Hunan, China*, Lanham: University Press of America, 1995.

---

[3] Sharon Shih-jiuan Hou, "Women's Literature," in *ICTCL*, vol. 1, 175–94; *Writing Women in Late Imperial China*, Ellen Widmer and Kang-i Sun Chang, eds., SUP, 1997.

[4] *Lidai funü zhuzuo kao* (Study of the works of women throughout history), Shangwu, 1957; rev. edition, Shanghai guji, 1985.

39.2 Works Written For and About Women

Many works were written for the ethical and moral instruction of girls and women, starting with elementary-school primers and readers.[5] They normally either took the form of exemplary biographies of virtuous women or sets of rules and admonitions. The models for both these forms were written in the Han, one by a man, one by a woman:

Liu Xiang 劉向 (ca. 77–ca. 6 BC), *Lienüzhuan* 列女傳. Contains the biographies of 125 women famous for their virtue who lived from the earliest times to the Former Han. Liu arranges the biographies into six groups according to the virtues exemplified and one group of pernicious and depraved (*niebi* 孽嬖) negative examples. His work was much imitated and many later collections were made right down to the later empire.[6]

Ban Zhao 班昭 (ca. 48–ca. 116), the most famous woman historian of China, wrote a set of instructions for her daughters, *Nüjie* 女誡 AD 106. It is the earliest text on ideal womanhood. For a translation and commentary on Ban Zhao's most influential work, see Nancy Lee Swann, *Pan Chao, Foremost Woman Scholar of China, First Century A.D.*, Century, 1932; New York: Russell, 1960; her translation (chap. 5), is reprinted in *The Columbia Anthology of Traditional Chinese Literature* (30.4), 534–41. See also Yu-shih Chen, "The Historical Template of Pan Chao's *Nü chieh*," *TP* 82: 229–97 (1996).

---

[5] For example, the *Nü'er jing* 女兒經, the *Nü Lunyu* 女論語, or the *Gailiang Nü'er jing* 改良女兒經. Many of these are collected in *Chuantong nüzi mengdu xinbian* 傳統女子蒙讀新編 (Newly edited traditional primers for girls), Chen Ju 陳駒 et al., eds., Guangxi jiaoyu, 1992.

[6] *Lienüzhuan* (Biographies of famous women) has been translated (except for the introductions to each group of biographies) in *The Position of Women in Early China*, Albert Richard O'Hara, tr., Catholic University of America, 1945; 2nd ed., 1955. There is an index with the original text appended: *Retsujoden sakuin (fu honbun)* 列女傳索引 (附本文), Miyamoto Masaru 宮本勝 and Mihashi Masanobu 三橋正信, comps., Tokyo, 1982. See also Lisa Raphals, *Sharing the Light: Representations of Women and Virtue in Early China*, SUNY, 1998; Katherine Carlitz, "The Social Uses of Female Virtue in Late Ming Editions of *Lienüzhuan*," *LIC* 12.2: 117–48 (1991); Mark Elvin, "Female Virtue and the State in China," in the author's *Another History: Essays on China from a European Perspective*, Wild Peony, 1996, 302–51 (originally appeared in *Past and Present* 104 [1984]).

The *Nüjie* set the model for innumerable such works, some of which were eventually gathered together in the Qing as the *Nü sishu* 女四書 (The four books for women). Apart from the *Nüjie* itself, this contained *Nü lunyu* 女論語 (The Woman's *Lunyu*), Tang; *Neixun* 內訓 (Instructions for the inner quarters), fifteenth century and *Nüfan jielu* 女範捷錄 (A concise account of basic regulations for women), Qing. Illustrations to such didactic works either circulated with them or separately and in both cases served to reinforce the message conveyed by the written word.[7]

Note that women feature explicitly in only one of the Confucian five relations (*wulun* 五倫), namely, that between husband and wife (characterized by *bie* 別, separateness). Despite this the ideal relation between elder sister and younger sister, and between two women friends, was characterized along the same lines as the ideal for elder brother and younger brother, and for two friends, namely by *xu* 序, precedence, and by *xin* 信, trust, respectively.

39.3   Modern Studies

The following is a small selection of the growing number of studies in English of the role of women in different periods of Chinese history. It is not intended as a bibliographic guide to secondary studies of women's history but as a list of outstanding examples of how different primary sources have been used. Each subsection is arranged in rough chronological order:

39.3.1   General Studies

Du Fangqin 杜芳琴, *Nüxing de guannian yanbian* 女性的觀念演變 (The changes in attitudes of women), Henan, Renmin, 1988.

Du Fangqin 杜芳琴, *Zhongguo shehui xingbie de lishi wenhua xunzong* 中國社會性別的歷史文化尋踪 (Tracing the Chinese historical culture of social gender distinction), Tianjin shekeyuan, 1999.

Body, Subject & Power in China, Angela Zito and Tani E. Barlow, eds., UChP, 1994.

---

[7] Julia K. Murray, "Didactic Art for Women: The *Ladies' Classic of Filial Piety*," in *Flowering in the Shadows: Women in the History of Chinese and Japanese Painting*, Marsha Weidner, ed., UHP, 1990, 27–53.

Chen Peng 陳鵬, *Zhongguo hunyin shigao* 中國婚姻史稿 (Draft history of marriage in China), Zhonghua, 1990.

Patricia Buckley Ebrey, "Women, Marriage, and the Family in Chinese History," in *Heritage of China: Contemporary Perspectives on Chinese Civilization*, Paul S. Ropp, ed., UCP, 1990, 197–223.

Marriage and Inequality in Chinese Society, Rubie S. Watson and Patricia Buckley Ebrey, eds., UCP, 1991.

Kathryn Bernhardt, *Women and Property in China, 960–1949*, SUP, 1999.

39.3.2   Imperial China

On women in early China, see the studies cited in 39.1–2. Also:

Chinese Women in the Imperial Past: New Perspectives, Harriet T. Zurndorfer, ed., Brill, 1999.

Lien-sheng Yang, "Women Rulers in Imperial China," *HJAS* 23: 47–61 (1960–61).

Ann-Marie Hsiung, "The Images of Women in Early Chinese Poetry: The *Book of Songs,* Han Ballads and Palace Style Verse of the Liang Dynasty," *Chinese Culture* 35.4: 81–90 (1994).

Deng Xiaonan, "Women in Turfan During the Sixth to Eighth Centuries: A Look at their Activities Outside the Home," *JAS* 58.1: 85–103 (1999).

Julia Ching, "Sung Philosophers on Women," *MS* 42 (1994), 259–74.

Kathryn Bernhardt draws the evidence for "The Inheritance Rights of Daughters: The Song Anomaly?" *Modern China* 21.3: 269–309 (1995), from the Song collection *Minggong shupan qingming ji* 名公書判清明集 (see 27.4 for details).

Patricia Ebrey, *The Inner Quarters: Marriage and the Lives of Chinese Women in the Sung Period*, UCP, 1993. One of the points made in this excellent study is that men could divorce women, but not vice-versa.

Priscilla Ching Chung, *Palace Women in the Northern Sung*, Brill, 1981.

Charlotte Furth, *A Flourishing Yin: Gender in Chinese Medicine, 960–1665*, UCP, 1999.

Karl A. Wittfogel and Feng Chia-sheng, "Position of Women in Liao Society," in Wittfogel and Feng, *History of Chinese Society: Liao (907–1125)*, Philadelphia: American Philosophical Society, *Transactions*, n.s., 26 (1949), 199–202; see 48.2.

Herbert Franke, "Women Under the Dynasties of Conquest," in Franke, *China Under Mongol Rule*, Variorum, 1994, 23–43.

Charlotte Furth, "Poetry and Women's Culture in Late Imperial China," editor's introduction, *LIC* 13.1: 1–8 (1992).

Francesca Bray, *Technology and Gender: Fabrics of Power in Late Imperial China*, UCP, 1997.

Jonathan Spence, *The Death of Woman Wang*, Viking, 1978. Based on a manual for local magistrates (*Fuhui quanshu* 福惠全書, 27.6), local gazetteers and fiction.

Dorothy Ko, *Teachers of the Inner Chamber: Women and Culture in Seventeenth-Century China*, SUP, 1994.

Susan Mann, *Precious Records: Women in China's Long Eighteenth Century*, SUP, 1997.

J-K. T'ien, *Male Anxiety and Female Chastity: A Comparative Study of Ethical Values in Ming-Ch'ing Times*, Brill, 1988.

Women in Baihua 白話 Fiction

Keith McMahon, *Misers, Shrews and Polygamists: Sexuality and Male-Female Relations in Eighteenth-Century Chinese Fiction*, DUP, 1995. A rare study of polygamy in Qing fiction, setting the background out of which more famous novels such as the *Hongloumeng* or *Jin Ping Mei* grew.

Angela K. Leung, "Sexualité et sociabilité dans le *Jin Ping Mei*, roman érotique chinois de la fin du XVIème siècle," *Information sur les sciences sociales* 23.4–5: 653–76 (1984).

Louise P. Edwards, *Men and Women in Qing China: Gender in the Dream of the Red Chamber*, Brill, 1994.

Eugene Cooper and Meng Zheng, "Patterns of Cousin Marriage in Rural Zhejiang and in the *Dream of the Red Chamber*," *JAS* 52.1: 90–106 (1993).

Yenna Wu, *The Chinese Virago: A Literary Theme*, HUP, 1995.

The Chinese Femme Fatale: Stories from the Ming Period, Anne E. McLaren, tr. and introduced, Wild Peony, 1994.

39.3.3   1890s–1949

A special new character was invented for "she" (*ta* 她) in 1917 to translate the word as found in Western works. At the same time, *tuo* 它 was borrowed for "it" (modern *ta*). Hitherto, *ta* 他 had been used for "he," "she," and "it." These innovations, by no coincidence, were introduced as the status of women was beginning to improve after 4,000 years of subordination.[8]

Luo Suwen 羅蘇文, *Nüxing yu jindai Zhongguo shehui* 女性與近代中國社會 (Women and modern Chinese society), Shanghai renmin, 1996. A good overall account of the steps by which women changed their self-regard and improved their status in the late Qing and Republic. An introductory chapter sketches their subordinate position since the earliest times to the nineteenth century. The rest of this sophisticated study then traces women's gradual access to education, to new types of work, the organization of the women's movement, and the roles women began to play and their life styles in the new cities of the eastern coast, notably Shanghai.

Kazuko Ono, *Chinese Women in a Century of Revolution, 1850–1950*, Joshua A. Fogel, ed., SUP, 1989 (Japanese original, 1978). A pioneering collection of studies.

Elizabeth Croll, *Feminism and Socialism in China*, Routledge, 1978; Schocken, 1980. A pioneering overview.

Jane Hunter, *The Gospel of Gentility: American Women Missionaries in Turn-of-the-Century China*, YUP, 1984. The contribution of missionaries, in this case female missionaries, is only now beginning to receive the recognition that for many years it was not granted in China.

Amy D. Dooling and Kristina M. Torgeson, *Writing Women in Modern China: An Anthology of Women's Literature from the Early Twentieth Century*, Col. UP, 1998.

Gender Politics in Modern China: Writing and Feminism, Tani E. Barlow, ed., DUP, 1993.

Gender and Sexuality in Twentieth-Century Chinese Literature and Society, Tonglin Lu, ed., SUNY, 1993.

---

[8] The social derogation of women through the use of language is studied by socio-linguists, for example, Ken Burridge and Ng Bee-chin, "Writing the Female Radical: The Encoding of Women in the Writing System," and by Ben Hodge and Kam Louie in "Gender and the Classification of Chinese Characters," both papers in *Dress, Sex, and Text in Chinese Culture*, Antonia Finnane and Anne McLaren, eds., Monash Asia Institute, 1999, 109–42 and 143–63, respectively.

Catherine Gipoulon, "The Emergence of Women in Politics in China, 1898-1927," *Chinese Studies in History* 1989-90: 46-67.

Janice E Stockard, *Daughters of the Canton Delta: Marriage Patterns and Economic Strategies in South China, 1860-1930*, SUP, 1989.

Emily Honig, *Sisters and Strangers: Women in the Shanghai Cotton Mills, 1919-1949*, SUP, 1986. The type of more detailed study upon which new overviews of the changing status of women in modern China will be more securely based in the future.

Kathryn Bernhardt, "Women and the Law: Divorce in the Republican Period," *Civil Law in Qing and Republican China*, Kathryn Bernhardt and Philip C. C. Huang, eds., SUP, 1994, 187–214.

Zheng Wang, *Women in the Chinese Enlightenment: Oral and Textual Histories*, UCP, 1999. A fascinating study of the genesis of Chinese feminism during the New Culture era based on a study of the journal *Funü zazhi* 婦女雜志 (*The Ladies' Journal*, Commercial Press, 1915–) and on interviews with four participants, including Wang Yiwei 王伊蔚 (1905-93), editor in chief of *Nüsheng* 女聲 (1932-35; 1945-47).

Daughter of Han: The Autobiography of a Chinese Working Woman, Ida Pruitt, from the story told her by Ning Lao Taitai, YUP, 1945; rpnt., SUP, 1967.

Delia Davin, *Woman-Work: Women and the Party in Revolutionary China*, OUP, 1979.

Christina Gilmartin, *Engendering the Chinese Revolution: Radical Women, Communist Politics, and Mass Movements in the 1920s*, UCP, 1995.

Kay Ann Johnson, *Women, the Family and Peasant Revolution in China*, UChP, 1983.

Judith Stacey, *Patriarchy and Socialist Revolution in China*, UCP, 1983.

Patricia Stranahan, *Yan'an Women and the Communist Party*, IEAS, 1983.

Female Prostitution

Xu Jun 徐君 and Yang Hai 楊海, *Jinüshi* 妓女史 (A history of prostitution), Shanghai wenyi, 1995.

Christian Henriot, *Belles de Shanghai: Prostitution et sexualité en Chine aux XIXe–XXe siècle*, CNRS, 1997. Includes bibliographical references (455–493) and index. English tr., CUP, 2000.

Gail Hershatter, *Dangerous Pleasures: Prostitution and Modernity in Twentieth-Century Shanghai*, UCP, 1997.

39.4   Research Tools

Guide to Women's Studies in China, Gail Hershatter, Emily Honig, Susan Mann, and Lisa Rofel, comps. and eds., IEAS, 1999. Has chapters introducing research on women in China, on women's studies centers and special projects in the PRC, on women's studies in Hong Kong, on women's studies and feminism in Taiwan, and on women's studies research centers, publications, and scholars in Taiwan. It also contains a brief list of bibliographic guides to publications on women (with selected bibliography), along with an index classifying each entry by one or more topics.

Bibliographies

Clara Wing-chung Ho, "Toward a Redefinition of the Content of Chinese Women's History: Reflections on Eight Recent Bibliographies," *Nan Nü* 1.1: 145-59 (1999).

Women in China: Current Directions in Historical Scholarship, Richard W. Guisso and Stanley Johannesen, New York: Philo, 1981.

Women in China: Bibliography of Available English Language Materials, Lucie Cheng et al., UCP, 1984. Contains citations to 4,107 items, arranged by subject. Includes pre-1911 coverage. Has author index and "index of Chinese women as subjects."

Zhongguo dalu funü wenxian mulu 中國大陸婦女文獻目錄 (Catalog of women's studies in mainland China), Yin Baoshan 尹寶珊 and Xiong Jingpeng 熊景朋, HK: Chinese University, Yatai yanjiusuo, 1998. Covers works written 1949-94.

Jindai Zhongguo funüshi: Zhongwen ziliao mulu 近代中國婦女史中文資料目錄 (Woman in modern Chinese history: Publications in Chinese), Wang Shuhuai 王樹槐 et al., comps., Jindai yanjiusuo, 1995.

Jindai Zhongguo funüshi: Yingwen ziliao mulu 近代中國婦女史英文資料目錄 (Woman in modern Chinese history: Publications in English), Lucie Cheng et al., comps., Jindai yanjiusuo, 1996. Covers publications 1832-1980.

Jindai Zhongguo funüshi: Riwen ziliao mulu 近代中國婦女史日文資料目錄 (Woman in modern Chinese history: Publications in Japanese), Jindai yanjiusuo, 1995.

Zhongguo funü wenxian conglan 中國婦女文獻叢覽 (Women's studies in China: a selected bibliography and resource guide from ancient times to the present), Qi Wenlei 齊文類, ed., Beijing daxue, 1995. Includes some references to pre-twentieth-century history and some inscriptional materials.

Jindai Zhongguo nüquan yundong shiliao 近代中國女權運動史料, 1842–1911 (Historical materials on the movements for women's rights, 1842–1911), Li Youning 李又寧 and Tan Yufa 譚玉法, eds., 2 vols., Longwen, 1995.

Guandong funü yundong lishi ziliao 廣東婦女運動歷史資料 (Historical materials on the Guangdong women's movement), 8 vols., Guangdong fulian, 1991. The material herein published date from the years 1924–49.

Biographical Dictionaries

Yuan Shaoying 袁韶瑩 and Yang Guizhen 楊瑰珍, *Zhongguo funü mingren cidian* 中國婦女名人辭典 (Dictionary of famous Chinese women), Beifang funü, 1989. Contains entries on some 4,100 women from all periods of Chinese history. Includes alternative names, dates, and publications. Arranged by stroke count of name. Also has stroke-count name index arranged by occupation.

Biographical Dictionary of Chinese Women: The Qing Period, 1644–1911, Lily Xiao Hong Lee and A. D. Stefanowska, eds. in chief; Clara Wing-chung Ho, Qing period ed., Sharpe, 1998; HKUP, 1999. Contains biographies of some 200 women active during the Qing period. As the editors note, this goes some way to redress the imbalance of *ECCP*, which contains nine biographies of women and 800 of men. However, the biographies are much shorter than those in *ECCP* and the reference value is reduced by the failure of the editors to provide a subject, name, or book title index.

Excerpts

Excerpts on women from the *Ming shilu* in the series *Ming shilu leizuan* 明實錄類纂 (Veritable Records of the Ming by category), Li Guoxiang 李國祥 and Yang Chang 楊昶, eds., 1995. Useful if you are researching the history of women in the Ming dynasty.

Journals

Jindai Zhongguo funüshi yanjiu 近代中國婦女史研究 (1993– , annual), Jinshisuo

Nan Nü, Brill, 1999– .

40

Non-Han Peoples
(Inside China)

In the Chinese view, the peoples they encountered—whether the indigenous tribes of the south or the nomad and semi-nomad peoples of the north—were all at a lower level of civilization than themselves. They divided them between those that had submitted and begun the process of acculturation and those that had not (the terms used were the cooked and the raw barbarians, the *shufan* 熟蕃 and the *sheng fan* 生蕃).

Chapter 40 covers the cooked barbarians; Chapter 41 deals with the sources on the raw ones and independent kingdoms and foreign states. Because many of the barbarians started outside China and later settled inside, the distinction is not a hard and fast one (the Mongols or Manchus, for example, both began as tribal confederations that succeeded in conquering China; thereafter, to a greater or lesser extent, they became ethnicities in China). So, chapters 40 and 41 should be read together.

The broad distinction (first proposed by Owen Lattimore) between a frontier of exclusion to the north and a frontier of inclusion to the south is a useful one.[1] The nomadic or semi-nomadic people to the north from the Xiongnu to the Manchus often organized for war and posed a much greater threat to the Han state than the pre-state "savages" or "aborigines" in the south and southeast, who were gradually marginalized to the mountainous areas or absorbed as Han farmers settled in the valleys (7.2.2). Note, however, that the southwest does not fit the definition of an inclusive frontier; it had

[1] Owen Lattimore (1900–89), "The Frontier in History," in his *Studies in Frontier History: Collected Papers, 1928-1958*, OUP, 1962, 477. On Lattimore, see 42.3.

long-lasting independent kingdoms in Tibet, in Nanzhao 南詔 (649–902), and in Dali 大理 (937–1254).

Chapter 40 begins with some comments on the question of ethnicity and the origins of the Chinese people. Next, one of many research problems is discussed, namely, the question of accurately identifying non-Han peoples (40.1). The remainder of the chapter briefly discusses non-Han scripts and languages (40.2), primary sources in non-Han languages and Chinese (40.3), and secondary sources and research tools (40.4).

Introduction

Ethnic consciousness as it is understood today was a late phenomenon in Chinese history. Ethnic terms such as Hanzu 漢族 (Hans), Manzu 滿族 (Manchus), Mengzu 蒙族 (Mongols), and Zangzu 藏族 (Tibetans) entered the language only under Western influence during the nineteenth century. *Minzu* 民族 (ethnicity, nationality) came into Chinese from Japanese *minzoku* 民族 in 1895. The Stalinist generic "national minorities" (*shaoshu minzu* 少數民族) became orthodox in China in the 1950s. It remains so, although the phrase is heard less and less. Not infrequently it is abbreviated to *minzu*. Today, the normal way of referring to an ethnicity, e.g., the Miao 苗, is Miaozu 苗族 (40.3.1, *Anthropology and Ethnology*).

In order to avoid injecting modern political sensitivities into the past, I have used the term "non-Han" or "non-Han peoples" rather than modern terms such as "national minority," "ethnic group," or "ethnicity." Even "non-Han" is obviously anachronistic for the pre-Han period (and for most of the remainder of Chinese history, because as explained in 3.1, "Han" was not a common Chinese ethnonym until quite late in the imperial period). Although "non-Huaxia" would therefore be more appropriate, there is a point beyond which accuracy risks becoming quaint, so I have used it only occasionally. One advantage of the term non-Han is that it accords quite well with the Chinese view, which tended to define "savages" (aborigines) and "barbarians" alike in terms of the qualities they lacked.

One of the most contentious historical debates in China is on the origin of the Chinese people. It was a subject shrouded in myth until the archaeologists and linguists began turning up evidence that for the first time enabled the historians to begin to sort out fact from fantasy and to link tribal peoples and early kingdoms referred to in Zhou texts with archaeological remains. The last word has by no means been written, but the discussion serves as a reminder that the formation of the Chinese (or rather, Huaxia) evolved over millennia with contributions from many different peoples and tribes (12.1). Indeed, recent archaeology has shown that at the dawn of history in East Asia the peoples of the north and the south may also have farmed and have been as "civilized" as the peoples of the Yellow River and Yangzi. As if to underline the diverse origins of Chinese civilization, recent studies have also shown that the peoples of north China are more closely related genetically to their northern neighbors outside present-day China than they are to the peoples in south China. These are in turn more closely related to their southern neighbors in Southeast Asia than they are to the northern Chinese. Possibly reflecting a combination of these millennial differences combined with the influence of migration and invasion in historic times, the dialect map of China today also breaks down into two broad groups: the Mandarin-related dialects of the north and northwest on the one hand, and the dialects of the southeast and south on the other.[2]

In direct contrast to the findings of archaeology and historical genetics, according to the Zhou and Han interpretation of history (the orthodoxy until the twentieth century), the peoples outside the heartland areas of the Xia, Shang, and Zhou were regarded as one or other form of non-settled, nomadic, warlike barbarian or savage, in bipolar contrast to the qualities of the Zhou (later the Han), who saw themselves as settled, civilized, moral, and peaceful. Needless to say, the non-Huaxia were considered to have contributed little or nothing to the genesis of Chinese civilization. They were regarded as potential if not actual enemies and scorned for their uncouth ways. Yet barbarians and savages, it was felt, if they submitted and studied, could become civilized (sinicized) and eventually accepted into the Huaxia melting pot.

Just as the Huaxia organized themselves hierarchically, so too they saw the rest of the world as a hierarchy: Huaxia; barbarians; animals. The Huaxia lived in the *Jiuzhou* (the nine continents; see

[2] Glen Dudbridge, "China's Vernacular Cultures," Inaugural Lecture, Clarendon, 1996.

Box 2); they were surrounded by the *Sihai* 四海 (the four seas), the dwelling place of the barbarians who in turn were surrounded by the *Bahuang* 八荒 (the endless wastes). Within the category barbarian different degrees were recognized according to level of subjugation, proximity, and sinicization (*Hanhua* 漢化 or more correctly, *Huahua* 華化; *laihua* 來華).[3]

40.1   *Han Ethnonyms for the Non-Han*

The earliest terms for barbarians included collective terms such as the *siyi* 四夷[4] or (from the place where they lived) the *sihai* 四海. More prejudiced and informal terms are discussed in 41.2.[5]

Well over 700 non-Han peoples and tribes are mentioned in Chinese sources. It is not easy to trace their history, not only because there are usually no non-Han sources and ethnoarchaeology is in its infancy, but also because the names constantly changed. This

---

[3] For a recent overview, see Ping-ti Ho, "In Defense of Sinicization: A Rebuttal of Evelyn Rawski's 'Reenvisioning the Qing,'" *JAS* 57.1: 123–55 (1998). Rawski's article appeared in *JAS* 55.4: 829–50 (1996). In part she argues that "sinicization—'the thesis that all of the non-Han peoples who have entered the Chinese realm have eventually been assimilated into Chinese culture'—is a twentieth century Han nationalist interpretation of China's past." See also her *The Last Emperors: A Social History of Qing Imperial Institutions*, UCP, 1998, 1–8. For case studies of acculturation, see David B. Honey, *Stripping off Felt and Fur: An Essay on Nomadic Sinification*, Papers on Inner Asia 21, Bloomington, 1992; Jianpang Wang, 1996 (29.6); Ch'en Yuan, 1966 (48.5.4); Jing-shen Tao, 1976 (48.4).

[4] The Siyi 四夷 were the Dong Yi 東夷, Bei Di 北狄, Xi Rong 西戎, and Nan Man 南蠻. Most of these ethnonyms became generics for barbarian (41.2) and were also often used in combination (e.g., Rongdi 戎狄, Yidi 夷狄). Ruth I. Meserve compares Chinese, Graeco-Roman, Persian, Western, and Hebraic concepts of barbarians in "The Inhospitable Land of the Barbarian," *JAH* 16: 51–89 (1982).

[5] The *Erya* defines *sihai* 四海 in the following way: *Jiuyi badi qirong liuman wei zhi sihai* 九夷八狄七戎六蠻謂之四海 (the nine Yi, eight Di, seven Rong, and six Man are called the four seas), *Erya* 爾雅, "Shidi" 釋地. So, one of the meanings of *sihai* was the place where the barbarians lived, hence by extension, the barbarians. The expression *sihai zhinei* 四海之內 was used as a synonym for Zhongguo (the central states) as in the famous expression *Sihai zhi nei jie xiongdi ye* 四海之內皆兄弟也 (all within the four seas are his brothers), *Lunyu*, 12.5 (referring to what the gentleman who has no brothers of his own can expect if he treats people well). *Sihai zhinei* 四海之內 was abbreviated to *hainei* 海內.

is particularly true of the tribes and peoples of the north and west. Typically, when tribal federations were established, new and more bombastic ethnonyms were selected. Thereafter, following defeat and absorbtion they changed their names again (see 41.2.2 for the origins of the historic names by which they are best known).

In order to trace the history of the non-Han peoples, it is necessary to identify them in the Chinese sources. Chinese writers almost invariably represented the names of non-Han peoples (and their personal names), both inside and outside China, using loanwords transcribing the sounds of the non-Han language (*yinyi* 音譯).[6] Many ethnonyms started as day-to-day words in use by members of the same group, such as "us," "our people," "the locals," "the village." Later, when outsiders transcribed these into their languages, they often took on new connotations in those languages.[7] Often different characters (with more or less the same sound) were used before a standard transcription emerged. To find the origin of an ethnonym loan, a certain amount of detective work (sometimes termed linguistic ethnology) is required. For example, to trace the meaning behind the Luo-Yue 駱越[粤] peoples (literally the "white-horse-with-black-mane Yue"), you have to know that the pre-Qin and Han sources stress the importance that this branch of the Yue attached to bronze drums (excavated from Luo-Yue sites from Yunnan to Vietnam).[8] There is no record of them rearing white horses with black manes (*luo* 駱). So, *luo* is clearly used for its sound, at that time pronounced *lak*. In Zhuang (one of the languages of the

---

[6] In the south more than in the north, there is the suspicion that Han officials or travelers did not always bother to record accurately the names of the peoples with whom they came into contact, often preferring to use a generic rather than a specific (thus the Yi 彝 were frequently just called Manzi 蠻子).

[7] *Man* 蠻 (the southern tribes), is probably derived from the word for "I" or "people" in one of the Miao-Yao languages. Liang Min 梁敏 and Zhang Junru 張均如, *Dong-Tai yuzu gailun* 東泰語族概論 (Introduction to Kam-Tai), Shehui kexue, 1996, 8–10. *Man* 蠻 was frequently spuriously glossed as being a cognate of *man* 慢 (slow, lazy); cf. the gloss on *hua* in Huaxia 華夏 (3.1).

[8] Tan Xiaohang 覃曉航, *Lingnan gu Yueren mingcheng wenhua tanyuan* 嶺南古越人名稱文化探源 (Investigation into the origins of the culture of the names of the ancient Yue peoples of Lingnan), Zhongyang minzu daxue, 1994. The author shows how to trace the names of peoples, individuals, things, and general vocabulary that have been transcribed or translated into Chinese characters from Zhuang-Kam 壯侗 languages.

Luo-Yue descendants), there are four words meaning bronze drum, including *la*. This suggests that the meaning of Luo-Yue is "the Bronze-drum Yue." Whether the Luo-Yue themselves chose the ethnonym "Lac" for this reason is another matter altogether. They are presumably the same as the Lac who founded the first Vietnamese kingdom by the Red River near modern Hanoi (Ouluo 甌駱; Âu-Lac in Vietnamese), and there is no lack of different theories as to the meaning of *their* ethnonym.

At the same time as finding characters to fit the sounds of a foreign word or name it is also possible to choose ones with a particular meaning, in the case of non-Han peoples and foreigners, usually a pejorative meaning. It was the practice, for example, to choose characters with an animal or reptile signific for southern non-Han peoples, and many northern peoples were given characters for their names with the dog or leather hides signific. In origin this practice may have derived from the animal totems or tribal emblems typical of these peoples. This is not to deny that in later Chinese history such graphic pejoratives fitted neatly with Han convictions of the superiority of their own culture as compared to the uncultivated, hence animal-like, savages and barbarians. Characters with animal, hides, or other such significs were generally not used in formal correspondence. On and off they were banned by non-Han rulers in China culminating with the Qing. Many were systematically altered during the script reforms of the 1950s (Dada 韃靼, Tartar, is one of the few to have survived. It first appears in the Tang as the name of a Turkic tribe; thereafter it was applied to the Mongols and their successors, the Tartars, and later to the Manchus).

To identify the ethnonyms and personal names and toponyms of non-Han tribes and peoples inside the area of what later became China, the ideal would be to know the pronunciation both in the original language and of the characters used for the transcription into Chinese. Unfortunately, there are usually insufficient records to reconstruct most of the non-Han languages, but for Chinese, it is possible using handbooks on historical phonology (2.5.1). The task becomes easier from the Yuan because Chinese begins to sound as it does today, and transcriptions of non-Han names are therefore easier to recognize.

Non-Han languages were the source for many modern Chinese toponyms, including the names of at least five of the modern provinces (Table 6, 4.1).

40.2　Non-Han Scripts and Languages

The languages of the non-Han peoples fall into the Tibeto-Burman, Kam-Thai, Miao, Turkic, Mongolian, Manchu-Tungusic, Arabic, and Indo-European language families. Some of the non-Han peoples developed their own scripts; some adapted Chinese characters, others had no script at all. Altogether there are some 30 different scripts. The earliest is Karosthi.

Before the dynasties of conquest, especially the Qing, Han scholars showed little or no interest in the languages of non-Han peoples in or around China, or in foreign languages in general. After the Han, the only sustained exception was the interest taken in Sanskrit by those monks who participated in the translation of the texts of Buddhism (1.2.6). Otherwise, occasionally scholars or officials posted or exiled to live in distant outposts of the empire would sometimes note down a few words of the language of the local people (see, for example, the 16 words in Baiman 白蠻 and the six words in Wuman 烏蠻 recorded in the *Manshu* 蠻書, 41.5.1, *Tang*).

The *Liaoshi* 遼史 and the *Jinshi* 金史 contain chapters with glossaries of Khitan and Jurchen, respectively (48.2 and 48.4). In the Southern Song glossaries of Mongolian and other languages into Chinese were officially compiled. The title of one that survives is *Menggu yiyu* 蒙古譯語. Others were compiled in the Ming and Qing for a variety of languages under the generic title *Huayi yiyu* 華夷譯語 (Sino-barbarian glossary). They were arranged according to subject categories. Four survive, the earliest dating from 1389; see Daniel Kane, *The Sino-Jurchen Vocabulary of the Bureau of Interpreters*, IUP, 1989. A large number of Manchu dictionaries, grammars, and glossaries were compiled in the Qing, including:

Yuding Qingwen jian 御定清文鑑 (Authorized mirror for Qing writing, i.e., Manchu), 1673–1708. The final version was entitled *Wuti Qingwen jian* 五體清文鑑 (Five-language Manchu glossary), 1790; Minzu, 1957; rev., 1997. The five languages were Manchu, Tibetan, Mongolian, Uighur, and Chinese. Compare *Qinding Xiyu tongwenzhi* 欽定西域同文志, 1763, which includes Manchu, Chinese, Mongolian, Tibetan, Xinjiang Mongolian, and Uighur. There were also various Manchu-Chinese glossaries of official terms. The best known is the *Liubu chengyu* 六部成語. It has been translated into English (see 27.6).

Several bilingual glossaries were compiled by non-Han peoples, e.g., Tangut-Chinese: *Wenhai* 文海 and *Tongyin* 通音, anon, early twelfth century (48.3); Tibetan-Chinese: *Dingxiang zhang* 丁香帳, Rin-chen bkra-shis 仁欽扎西, comp., 1536; Minzu, 1981.

The best introduction in English to non-Han languages and scripts is S. Robert Ramsey, "The Minority Languages of China," in Ramsey, *The Languages of China*, PUP, 1987; rpnt., with corrections, 1989, 155–332. Supplement with:

Ershi shiji de Zhongguo shaoshu minzu yuyan yanjiu 二十世紀的中國少數民族語言研究 (Research on Chinese national minority languages in the twentieth century), Dai Qingxia 戴慶厦, ed. in chief, Shuhai, 1998.

Zhongguo minzu guwenzi tulu 中國民族古文字圖錄 (Ancient scripts of China's minorities: an illustrated catalog), Shehui kexue, 1990.

Zhongguo minzu guwenzi yanjiu 中國民族古文字研究 (Studies on the ancient scripts of China's minorities), Shehui kexue, 1984.

40.3   Primary Sources

40.3.1   Non-Han Primary Sources

Considerable amounts of non-Han written primary sources have survived. They include Neolithic and later rock pictograms; inscriptions on stone and bronze; and written sources of a religious, calendrical, legal or historical nature. There are also important archives from the Qing, principally in Manchu and Tibetan (see 50.2.6 and 50.3, respectively). For systematic and comprehensive outlines of non-Han sources, see the first item below; the second is a collection of articles (some of which have already appeared elsewhere) on particular works or problems.

Minzu gu wenxian gailan 民族古文獻概覽 (Outline of ancient texts of the minorities), Huang Jianming 黄建明, Zhang Gongjin 張公瑾, et al., eds., Minzu, 1997.

Zhongguo shaoshu minzu guji lun 中國少數民族古籍論 (Essays on the ancient texts of China's national minorities), Li Jinyou 李晉有 et al., Ba-Shu, 1997.

Inscriptions

A number of collections of inscriptions either in Chinese or in non-Han languages have been published—for example,

Guangxi shaoshu minzu diqu shike beiwen ji 廣西少數民族地區石刻碑文集 (Collected stone inscriptions from the national minority areas in Guangxi), Guangxi renmin, 1982.

Tufan jinshi lu 吐蕃金石錄 (Record of Tibetan inscriptions on bronze and stone), Wang Yao 王堯, comp., Wenwu, 1982.

Calendars

On the main non-Han calendars (Dai, Yi, Tibetan, Buddhist, and Muslim) and the concordances to convert them to the Gregorian calendar, see 5.7.

Weights and Measures

Some examples of non-Han terminology are given in 7.3.2.

Archaeology

The archaeology of the non-Han peoples in China is beginning to receive more attention. See, for example,

Minzu kaoguxue jichu 民族考古學基礎 (The basics of ethnoarchaeology), Wang Hengjie 王恒杰 and Zhang Xuehui 張雪慧, Minzu daxue, 1999. Briefly covers theoretical and field work issues before going into details of the ethnoarchaeological state-of the-field for each of the main non-Han peoples.

Li Yangsong 李仰松, *Minzu kaoguxue lunwenji* 民族考古學論文集 (Treatises on ethnoarchaeology), Kexue, 1998. The papers in this collection were used by the author as the basis of his courses in ethnoarchaeology in the archaeology department of Peking University. Li did his field work in 1956–57 studying the Wa 佤 of Yunnan. His technique is to try and solve problems in Chinese prehistory using insights gained from the study of primitive peoples.

Minzu kaoguxue lunwenji 民族考古學論文集 (Collected articles on ethno-archaeology), Wang Ningsheng 王寧生, ed., Wenwu, 1989.

Zhongguo ge minzu yuanshi zongjiao ziliao jicheng kaogu juan 中國各民族原始宗教資料集成考古卷 (A series of source books on the primitive religions of the minorities in China: archaeology), Yu Jinxiu 于錦綉 and Yang Shurong 楊淑荣, eds. in chief, Shehui kexue, 1996.

Zhongguo Xi'nan minzu kaogu 中國西南民族考古 (Archaeology of the minorities of southwest China), Zhang Zengqi 張增祺, Yunnan renmin, 1990.

Hou Shigui 侯石珪, *Xizang kaogu dagang* 西藏考古大綱 (Broad outlines of Tibetan archaeology), Xizang renmin, 1991.

Anthropology and Ethnology

Zhongguo minzuxue yu minsuxue yanjiu lunzhu mulu 1900–94 中國民族學與民俗學研究論著目錄 1900–94 (Bibliography of books and articles on Chinese ethnological and folk studies, 1900–94), 3 vols., Hanxue yanjiu zhongxin, 1997.

James S. Olson, *An Ethnohistorical Dictionary of China*, Greenwood, 1998.

Wang Jianmin 王建民, *Zhongguo minzuxueshi* 中國民族學史 (History of ethnology in China), 2 vols., Yunnan jiaoyu, 1997 and 1999.

Pamela K. Crossley, "Thinking About Ethnicity in Early Modern China," *LIC* 1: 1–34 (1990).

Zhongguo yuanshi zongjiao ziliao congbian 中國原始宗教資料叢編 (Collection of materials on primitive religion), Lü Daji 呂大吉 et al., eds., Shanghai renmin, 1993– . Vol. 6, for example, contains copious materials on the Naxizu 納西族, Qiangzu 羌族, Dulongzu 獨龍族, Lisuzu 傈僳族, and Nuzu 怒族; volumes in the same series include materials on the Manchus, Mongols, and Tibetans (1997) and on the Dai, Hani, and nine other Yunnan non-Han peoples (1997).

Cultural Encounters on China's Ethnic Frontiers, Stevan Harrell, ed., UWP, 1995. Note the editor's introduction "Civilizing Projects and the Reaction to Them," 3–36.

Morris Rossabi, "Chinese Myths About the National Minorities: Khubilai Khan, a Case Study," *Central and Inner Asian Studies* 1: 47–81 (1987).

Medicine

Non-Han peoples have their own traditions of medicine. The most elaborate is that of the Tibetans. It is similar to the Han tradition but incorporates additional elements of its own and from Nepal and India. See, for example:

Tibetan Medical Thangka of the Four Medical Tantras, Byams-pa 'Phrin-las, tr. and comp.; Cai Jingfeng, English tr. and annotator, People's Publishing House of Tibet, 1994. This is a reproduction of the illustrations and text of the eighth-century classic *rGyud-bzhi* as written down in the late seventeenth century.

Mythology

For a dictionary of mythology, see *Zhongguo shenhua da cidian* 中國神話大辭典 (29.1). The last section covers the myths of 56 ethnic minorities (680–1051).

40.3.2 Chinese Primary Sources on Non-Han Peoples

The Standard Histories and the Veritable Records as well as the gazetteers carry important materials on the non-Han peoples. Many have been excerpted, for example:

Ming shilu youguan Yunnan lishi ziliao zhaiyao 明實錄有關雲南歷史資料摘要 (Selected excerpts from the Veritable Records of the Ming on the history of Yunnan), *Yunnansheng shaoshu minzu shehui lishi yanjiusuo* 雲南省少數民族社會歷史研究所, Kunming, 1959.

Qing shilu Yunnan shiliao jiyao 清實錄雲南史料輯要 (Historical materials on Yunnan from the *Qing shilu*), 4 vols., Yunnan: Xinhua shudian, 1986.

Qing shilu Yizu shiliao jiyao 清實錄彝族史料輯要 (Selections from the *Qing shilu* on the Yi people), Yunnan minzu, 1986.

For similar volumes of excerpts on many other provinces, see 50.4, and on Tibet, 41.4.1. The surveys and original documents on the non-Han peoples of Taiwan are particularly rich; see, for example,

Taiwan yuanzhumin shiliao huibian 臺灣原住民史料匯編, Xie Yingcong et al., Nantoushi: Taiwansheng wenxian weiyuanhui, 1995.

Chantal Zheng, *Les Austronésiens de Taïwan: à travers les sources chinoises*, Harmattan, 1995.

There are collections of excerpts from local gazetteers on non-Han peoples, often of a particular province or region, for example,

Hunan difangzhi shaoshu minzu shiliao 湖南地方志少數民族史料 (Historical materials from Hunan local gazetteers on national minorities), Hunansheng shaoshu minzu guji bangongshi, ed., 2 vols., Yuelu, 1991–92.

Archives

A considerable amount has been published, for example,

Heilongjiangsheng shaoshu minzu dang'an shiliao xuanbian 黑龍江省少數民族檔案史料選編 (Selection of historical materials from the Heilongjiang provincial archives on national minorities), Heilongjiang dang'anguan, Heilongjiangsheng, 1985.

Qingdai Xibozu Manwen dang'an shiliao 清代錫伯族滿文檔案史料 (Historical materials from the archives in Manchu on the Xibo people), Yishiguan, ed., 2 vols., Xinjiang renmin, 1987.

Qingdai Xibozu Hanwen dang'an shiliao xuanbian 清代錫伯族漢文檔案史料選編 (Selected historical materials in Chinese from the archives on the Xibo people in the Qing dynasty), Yishiguan, ed., 2 vols., Liaoning minzu, 1989. Contains 647 documents in Manchu; 95 in Chinese.

Bibliographies of Primary Sources in Chinese

Zhongguo minzu gongju wenxian cidian 中國民族工具文獻詞典 (Dictionary of reference works and literature on Chinese minorities), Liu Guanghong 劉光宏, ed. in chief, Gaige, 1995. There is a 160-page stroke-count index.

Nanfang minzu gushi shulu 南方民族古史書錄 (Records from ancient historical works on the southern minorities), Lü Mingzhong 呂名中, ed. in chief, Sichuan minzu, 1989. There is a title index arranged by stroke count. Annotated bibliography of 1,653 primary historical sources and 828 modern reports and studies on the southern minorities.

Zhongguo nanfang minzu shizhi yaoji tijie 中國南方民族史志要籍題解 (Explanatory notes on the main histories and treatises on China's southern minorities), Wu Yongxin 吳永辛, Minzu, 1991. Notes on 120 primary sources, mainly in Chinese.

40.4   Secondary Sources and Research Tools
Encyclopaedias

Zhongguo da baike quanshu 中國大百科全書 (8.4.2) contains a separate volume on *Minzu* 民族 (Ethnic groups), Da baike quanshu, 1995.

Zhongguo lishi da cidian 中國歷史大辭典 (8.4.2) contains a separate volume on *Minzushi* 民族史 (Ethnic history), 1995.

Zhongguo nongye baike quanshu 中國農業百科全書: *Nongye lishijuan* 農業歷史卷 (35.1.1, *Studies*). Includes articles on the agricultural history of the main non-Han peoples.

Biographies

Zhongguo minzushi renwu cidian 中國民族史人物辭典 (Dictionary of personalities in the history of China's nationalities), Gao Wende 高文德, ed. in chief, Shehui kexue, 1990. Contains biographies of 5,500 non-Hans from earliest times to the end of the Qing; also 2,000 cross-references from variant character transcriptions to main entries.

On the naming systems used for family names by 56 non-Han peoples, see Zhang Lianfang 張聯芳, *Zhongguoren de xingming* 中國人的姓名 (The names of Chinese people), Shehui kexue, 1992.

Chen Lianqing 陳連慶, *Zhongguo shaoshu minzu xingshi yanjiu* 中國少數民族姓氏研究 (Research on national-minority names), Jilin wenshi, 1993. Indexed identification of many transliterations of non-Han names into Chinese characters in standard historical sources.

Zhao Fansheng 趙帆聲 *Gushi yinshi* 古史音釋 (Investigation of phonetic loans in the ancient histories), Henan daxue, 1995. Examines foreign loan words in the Standard Histories.

Outline Histories and Studies

Leo J. Moser, *The Chinese Mosaic: The Peoples and Provinces of China*, Westview, 1985. Introductory text; see also Wiens (7.2.2).

Zhongguo minzushi 中國民族史 (The history of Chinese nationalities), Wang Zhonghan 王鍾翰, ed. in chief, Shehui kexue, 1994.

Shaoshu minzu yu Zhongguo wenhua 少數民族與中國文化 (The national minorities and Chinese culture), Tian Jizhou 田繼周 et al., eds., Shanghai renmin, 1996.

Zhongguo minzu guanxishi yanjiu 中國民族關係史研究 (Studies on the history of relations with the nationalities), Weng Dujian 翁獨健, ed., Shehui kexue, 1984, has an extensive bibliography, 525–66.

Zhu Zhuxian 祝注先, *Zhongguo shaoshu minzu shigeshi* 中國少數民族詩歌史 (History of the songs and poetry of China's national minorities), Zhongyang minzu daxue, 1994. Few songs and poems of non-Han peoples survive, but from the Yuan onward the numbers increase as more and more ethnicities began learning Chinese.

Studies of Individual Cultures

There are large numbers of modern histories and studies of particular non-Han peoples and of their cultures. Sometimes the material is presented in the form of dictionaries, as with the first example below:

Xizang lishi wenhua cidian 西藏歷史文化辭典 (Dictionary of historical Tibetan culture), Wang Yao 王堯 and Chen Qingying 陳慶英, eds. in chief, Zhejiang renmin and Xizang renmin, 1998.

Nanzhao wenhua lun 南詔文化論 (Research on Nanzhao culture), Yang Zhonglu 楊仲錄 and Zhang Fusan 張福三, eds., Yunnan renmin, 1991.

Zhongguo gudai beifang minzu wenhuashi: zhuanti wenhua juan 中國古代北方民族文化史專題文化卷 (The ancient cultural history of China's northeastern peoples: special cultural volume), Zhang Bibo 張碧波 and Dong Guoyao 董國堯, eds. in chief, Heilongjiang renmin, 1995.

Bibliographies of Secondary Sources

Guancang Zhongguo minzu yanjiu cankao jianmu 館藏中國民族研究參考簡目 (Reference bibliography to research materials in the library [of the Central Nationalities Academy] on the peoples of China), Zhongyang minzu xueyuan tushuguan 中央民族學院圖書館, eds. and pub., 3 vols., 1985. Contains citations to 6,590 items dating from antiquity to 1949 (vol. 1) and 6,155 items from 1951 to 1977 (vol. 2). Especially valuable for citations to historical materials. Volume 3 is a title index. There is a *pinyin* index.

Zhongguo minzu yu minsuxue yanjiu lunzhu mulu 中國民族與民俗學研究論著目錄 (Bibliography of research on China's ethnology and folklore), 3 vols., CCS, Taibei, 1997.

Zhongguo shaoshu minzu lunzhu suoyin 中國少數民族論著索引 (Articles and books on China's national minorities), Chen Ting 陳廷 and Wang Ying 王應, comps., Xinjiang renmin, 1992, covers 3,088 books and 28,500 articles appearing between 1949 and 1988.

Alain Y. Dessaint, *Minorities of Southwest China: An Introduction to the Yi (Lolo) and Related Peoples and an Annotated Bibliography*, New Haven: HRAF, 1980.

Journals

Minzu yanjiu 民族研究 (1979– , semimonthly), Shehui kexue.

Minzu yanjiu dongtai 民族研究動態 (1983– , quarterly), Shekeyuan, Minzu yanjiusuo 社科院民族研究所 (from 1984 absorbs *Minzu yanjiu tongxun* 民族研究通訊, Zhongguo minzu xuehui 中國民族學會).

Minzu yuwen 民族語文 (1979– , semimonthly), Shekeyuan, Minzu yanjiusuo 社科院民族研究所.

Minzuxue yanjiusuo jikan 民族學研究所季刊 (1956– , trimesterly), Zhongyang yanjiuyuan, Minzuxue yanjiusuo, Taibei.

41

Non-Han Peoples
(Outside China)

Accounts of non-Han peoples outside China are found in the Standard Histories (41.4), in the Veritable Records (41.4.1), and in various other sources, including records of journeys to foreign countries and diplomatic diaries (41.5). Some of the generics for barbarians or foreigners are discussed in 41.1.1; ethnonyms for Tibetans, Uighurs, and Manchus are traced in 41.2.2; and some of the changing meanings of the "West" are presented in 41.2.3. The main routes to and from China are the subject of 41.3. Enemies and innovations for most of Chinese history came overland from the north and northwest (41.3.1). In the late Qing, these land routes were eclipsed by the maritime routes via the southern and east coast ports (41.3.2). Extensive archival sources on negotiations with foreign states are extant only from the Qing (50.2.7). The chapter begins with some remarks on the Chinese world order (41.1).

41.1   The Chinese World Order

From the very earliest centuries of Chinese history, the in-group visualized its relations with out-groups in hierarchical terms with the in-group at the top and center. The definition of the hierarchies and their number changed in each historical period according to the circumstances. The arrangements that governed the relations of the center with the various zones into which the rest of the territory was divided were also extended to the barbarians. The most famous example is the offering of gifts and the acceptance of tribute, expected alike from the Chinese as from the barbarian, from the feudatory to his lord, from the inferior to the superior, from a minor kingdom on the periphery of the empire to the emperor at the center (there are at least 10 different words on the Shang oracle-bone inscriptions for presenting different types of gift or tribute and 16 such words in Zhou texts).[1]

The Han established a system of diplomatic relations and alliances (*heqin* 和親).[2] It was mainly developed to deal with the Xiongnu threat. It was based on the despatch of embassies, letters of credence (*jie* 節), royal marriages, granting of titles, the taking of hostages (*zhi* 質), and the exchange of gifts and tribute (*gong* 貢)—all practices already found during the Warring States period.[3] The conduct of diplomacy was entrusted to permanent and specialized officials at the capital.[4] These officials handled not only relations with non-Han peoples and states, but also the visits of domestic kings and nobles to the capital. The *Yili* stipulates how diplomatic missions were to be received. There was no concept of resident embassies. All ambassadors (*shi* 使) were envoys extraordinary.[5]

Numerous words were used for diplomacy or foreign relations (e.g., *bangjiao* 邦交, *waishi* 外事, *yishi* 夷事, and at the end of the empire, *yangwu* 洋務 and *waiwu* 外務). The expression used today (*waijiao* 外交) is a nineteenth-century neologism. *Waiguo* 外國 (foreign country, abroad) came into use from the Tang to mean states

---

[1] For excerpts from the original sources recording over 3,000 tribute missions from the Zhou to the end of the Qing, with translations into Modern Chinese, see *Zhongguo lidai gongpin daguan* 中國歷代貢品大觀 (Grand collection of historical tribute), Gong Yu 龔予 et al., eds., Shanghai Shekeyuan, 1992. Under the empire, it was the duty of the Board of Rites to manage the tribute missions and to keep lists of them and of the tribute they presented and the presents received from them. These lists were written into the Veritable Records and later summarized in the Standard Histories (see 41.4.1).

[2] Yü Ying-shih, "Han Foreign Relations," *CHC*, vol. 1, 377–462; Li Hu 黎虎, *Han-Tang waijiao zhidushi* 漢唐外交制度史 (A history of diplomatic institutions from the Han to the Tang), Lanzhou daxue, 1998.

[3] For interstate relations during the Warring States period, see Richard L. Walker, *The Multi-State System of Ancient China*, Shoestring Press, 1953.

[4] The *dianke* 佃客 (Chamberlain for dependencies) of the Qin and early Han, superseded in 144 BC by the *da xingling* 大行令 (Director of the messenger office), in turn superseded in 104 BC by the *da honglu* 大鴻臚 (Chamberlain for dependencies).

[5] There is no thorough history of Chinese foreign relations or diplomacy from the Warring States through to modern times. But there are studies of individual periods. Most volumes of the *CHC* contain chapters or sections on foreign relations.

outside China (during the Warring States it had referred to the territory of local lords outside the capital or to another of the Warring States). In general, in the later empire, the Board of Rites supervised peaceful relations with foreigners; the Board of War dealt with military relations.

Different foreign policies and models of how to conduct foreign relations were employed in China in different periods. No one model such as the tributary system fits all the Chinese historical experience.[6] Strategy was adjusted according to the strength of the adversary. Thus tribute (symbolizing a subservient relation) on many occasions was replaced by other forms of diplomacy, including the signing of treaties (implying some degree of equality). When they did encounter a country with a higher civilization such as Rome or India, the Chinese placed it in a different category other than savage or barbarian—but these encounters were at a distance and rare. The three main policy options that emerged first in the Han were diplomatic accommodation; static defense (behind walls) combined with punitive expeditions; offensive conquest.[7] Some of the common terms associated with these strategies were:

Jimi 羈靡 (bridle and halter; loose reign policy)

Yiyi bianhua 以夷變華 (*hua-Hua* 化華; *lai-Hua* 來華; see end of 41.1)

Yiyi zhiyi 以夷制夷 (using barbarians to control barbarians)

Yiyi gongyi 以夷功夷 or *yiyi fayi* 以夷伐夷 (using barbarians to attack barbarians)

Zhengfa 征伐 (attack)

Heqin 和親 (appeasement, often by marrying the daughters of the imperial family to non-Han or foreign princes)

[6] See Jing-shen Tao (Tao Jinsheng 陶晉生), "Foreign Relations in Ancient China," Chapter 1 of *Two Sons of Heaven: Studies in Sung-Liao Relations*, UAP, 1988, 1–9. See also *China Among Equals—The Middle Kingdom and Its Neighbors, 10th–14th Centuries*, Morris Rossabi, ed., UCP, 1983.

[7] Alastair Iain Johnson, *Cultural Realism: Strategic Culture and Grand Strategy in Chinese History*, PUP, 1995, 116–17; Lien-sheng Yang, "Historical Notes on the Chinese World Order," in *The Chinese World Order*, John K. Fairbank, ed., HUP, 1968.

41.2   Naming the Barbarians (2)

41.2.1   Terminology

Many of the names found in Zhou texts for specific barbarian peoples became in time generic terms for "barbarian." This is true of the *siyi* 四夷 (Yi 夷, Rong 戎, Di 狄, and Man 蠻), and also of Hu 胡 and *fan* 蕃 [番] (the same happened with names such as Hun or Vandal in English). Rong 戎 and Di 狄 dropped out of common use after the Nan-Bei Chao. Yi 夷 continued to be used in formal documents such as memorials right up to the end of the empire, for example, Yingyi 嘆夷 (English barbarians). Man 蠻 (southern barbarian) is still part of the language, for example, *yeman* 野蠻 (barbarous) and *fan* 番 still indicates a foreign origin in some of the southern dialects. But none of these generics have influenced the Chinese language as much as *hu* 胡 (the basic meaning is dewlap; hence beard; hence the bearded ones; hence barbarians; hence foreigners). A memory of the strange (barbarous) ways in which the non-Han spoke is reflected in the many expressions beginning with *hu* such as *huche* 胡扯 (talk nonsense), *hushuo* 胡説 (drivel), or *hushuo badao* 胡説八道 (talk rubbish). In addition, the memory of the barbarian's uncouth behavior is recalled in terms such as *huchi haisai* 胡吃海塞 (eat anything and everything), *huchou* 胡臭 (or *huchou* 狐臭; body [armpit] odor), or *hugao* 胡搞 (be promiscuous; mess things up).

The word *fan* (Old Chinese *biuan*) has been in use since the Zhou to mean foreign or feudatory. During the course of Chinese history, it was written with several alternative characters: *fan* 蕃 (luxuriant), *fan* 番 (barbarian, foreign), *fan* 藩 (protecting, feudatory). From about the Tang, and increasingly after the court moved to Hangzhou in the Southern Song, *fan* (OC *piuan*) 蕃[番] was also used to mean southern barbarian or foreigner. Despite this usage, which continued until the Qing, *fan* has not given the standard language nearly as many derogatives as *hu* 胡. This may reflect the more open culture of the Tang, a period when foreign was not necessarily regarded as synonymous with barbarous. Also, *fan* (and *man* 蠻) originally applied to the pre-state aboriginals of the south, who were considered less of a threat than the dreaded northern enemy associated with the *hu* 胡 (Xiongnu). Whatever the reasons may be, expressions beginning with *fan* sound more neutral—for example, *fanbang* 蕃[番]邦 (foreign countries), *zhufan* 諸蕃 (foreigners), *fanshang* 蕃商 (foreign merchants), or *fanbo* 蕃[番]舶 (foreign boats).

From the Han, *hu* 胡 was used in the names of many foodstuffs imported from foreign countries, especially from the Western Regions, often via the Silk Roads; from the Ming, *fan* 蕃[番] was also used in the same way, especially for foodstuffs imported through the southern seaports (35.2.3). *Fan* continued to serve as a general term for foreign as long as Guangzhou was the main gateway for new products, but in the nineteenth century it was replaced by *yang* 洋 or *xi* 西, the more modern terms preferred in Shanghai.

In the pre-Qin, the barbarian peoples were commonly differentiated by the direction in which they lived or sometimes by the color associated with them, as in Dongyi 東夷 or Baidi 白狄. Under the empire, new descriptives came into use as the situation changed, for example, in the south when the indigenous peoples were pushed out of the valleys and into the mountains by the Han settlers they were often referred to as mountain people (*shanren* 山人) or qualified as Shanyue 山越 or Shanman 山蠻.

Derogatory terms for naming the barbarians were also common. The usual practice was to use words such as slave (*nu* 奴), devil (*gui* 鬼), caitiff (*lu* 虜), or robber (*ze* 賊) linked to the old generic terms *hu* 胡, *yi* 夷, *man* 蠻, and *fan* 蕃[番]. Thus the chief enemy of the Qin and Han empires, the Xiongnu, were called 匈奴. The Xiongnu called themselves by a name earlier transcribed into Chinese with the character *hu* 胡. From the Han, they were termed Xiongnu 匈奴 (a transcription of their original ethnonym).[8] Although *nu* 奴 (Old Chinese *na*) is a character frequently used in transcriptions, the fact that it was used for the Xiongnu (and not another character) is no doubt linked to the common tendency to use derogatory characters for non-Han peoples (40.1).

---

[8] Sophia-Karin Psarras, *Han and Xiongnu*, forthcoming. Xiongnu is the same word as Hun; the Southern Xiongnu were referred to as *xwn* (Hun) in letters sent back by Sogdians to their home base that were found in Dunhuang; the so-called White Huns in the Hephthalite empire based in Afganistan in the fifth and sixth centuries were called Huna in India. But how the Xiongnu and the Huns of European history were related has been a matter of controversy ever since Deguignes in the eighteenth century raised the question; personal communication from Edwin G. Pulleyblank.

A list of the most popular derogative terms from all periods of Chinese history would include the following:

nu 奴 (slaves) as in Xiongnu 匈奴; *hunu* 胡奴 (barbarian slaves); *guinu* 鬼奴 (devil slaves); *heinu* 黑奴 (black slaves, Africans); *wonu* 倭奴 (dwarf slaves, Japanese)

lu 虜 (caitiffs) as in Hulu 胡虜 (Xiongnu) or Suolu 索虜 (the unkempt caitiffs, i.e., the Toba)

gui 鬼 (devils) as in *heigui* 黑鬼 (black devils, Africans or Indians); *guinu* 鬼奴 (devil slaves); *guizi* 鬼子 (devils); *heiguinu* 黑鬼奴 (black devil slaves) or *baigui* 白鬼 (white devils); *fangui* 蕃[番]鬼, or the more recent *yangguizi* 洋鬼子 (foreign devils); *guailou* 鬼佬 (Cantonese pronunciation for *guilao*, devil men), the usual Cantonese appellation for the Western barbarians, from *fanguai lou* (*fanguilao* 蕃[番]鬼佬). Foreign women were called *guipo* 鬼婆. *Guihua* 鬼話, devil talk, i.e., English, Dutch, etc.

Facial features, such as the length of the nose, skin color,[9] the color of the eyes, hair styles, hirsuteness, the size of the body, or just general appearance were also used to nickname non-Han peoples—for example,

choulu 丑虜 (ugly caitiff)

biyan wuxu 碧眼烏須 (blue eyes and black beards, i.e., Inner Asians). *Hu* as in *huzi* 胡子 (beard, moustache, whiskers) is an extended meaning of *hu* (barbarian)

wo 倭 (dwarf; reserved almost exclusively for the Japanese in whose language it is pronounced *wa*, as in *wa* 和). It was used originally in the *Hanshu* probably to refer to the inhabitants of Kyûshu and the Korean peninsula. Thereafter to the inhabitants of the Japanese archipelago; *Woguo* 倭國 (dwarfs' country); in official documents Japan was called *Riben* 日本 after the Japanese started using this name in the Tang dynasty; *Wonuguo* 倭奴國 (dwarf slaves' country); *wonu* 倭奴 (dwarf slaves); *Woren* 倭人 (dwarf

[9] Frank Dikötter, *The Discourse of Race in Modern China*, Hurst, 1992. Pages 1–125 cover from earliest times to 1915. Zheng Yan, "Barbarian Images in Han Period Art," *Orientations* 31.6: 50–59 (1998). Qian Zhongshu argues that the distinction between Chinese and barbarian was not of race (ethnos) but rather of culture (ethos); see "The Concepts of 'Chinese' and 'Barbarian,'" in *Limited Views: Essays on Ideas and Letters*, selected and tr. by Ronald Egan, HUP, 1998, 373–81.

men); *wozi* 倭子 (dwarf kids); *wokou* 倭寇 (dwarf pirates) was used from the fourteenth century; Chinese pirates were also tarred with the same brush.

hongmaoyi 紅毛夷 or *hongmaofan* 紅毛番 (red-haired barbarians, i.e., the northern Europeans, particularly the Dutch). The phrase may have been used first to describe the Dutch in Taiwan in the first half of the seventeenth century. It appears in several prominent place names, including for the Dutch forts at Tainan (Hongmaolou 紅毛樓) and Danshui 淡水 (Hongmaocheng 紅毛城). Some Hongmao names are still in use.

chang bizi 長鼻子 or *da bizi* 大鼻子 (the long or big noses; i.e., Europeans and Americans).

Shendu 身毒, early transcription of the Persian for "India"; the characters not only transcribe the sound "Sind" but also literally mean "body poison;" the more neutral transcription Yindu 印度 was introduced by Xuanzang 玄奘 (596–664), see 41.5.1.

41.2.2   *Ethnonyms (2)*

The origins of the ethnonyms (and toponyms) of the Xiongnu, Tangut, and Mongols are discussed in 41.2.1, 48.3, and 48.5, respectively. Those for the Tibetans, Uighurs, and Manchu follow.[10]

Tibetans

When the Tibetan peoples first united and began to call themselves "*Bod-pa" the Chinese referred to them as Fan 蕃 (sometimes incorrectly written Bo).[11] The Tibetan name for their kingdom was based on the same word and transliterated by the Tang as Tufan 吐蕃 (629–824). This, or Xi Fan 西蕃, was used in Chinese sources for

---

[10] See Wang Penglin 王鵬林, "A Linguistic Approach to Inner Asian Ethnonyms," in *The Bronze Age and Early Iron Age of Peoples of Eastern Central Asia* (see 41.3.1), vol. 1, 483–507.

[11] On the possible earliest references to the ethnonym Bod, see Christopher I. Beckwith, *The Tibetan Empire in Central Asia*, PUP, 1987, 3–10. On the unattested pronunciation *bo* for *fan* 蕃, see Paul Pelliot, "Quelques transcriptions chinoises de noms tibétains," *TP* 16: 1–26 (1915); Pulleyblank, 1991 (2.5.1), 19–20. There is also a controversy surrounding the meaning of "*Tu*," which is sometimes explained as derived from the Tibetan assumption of *Da* 大 (as in Da Tang 大唐) and from the Tang turning it into a meaningless word. Others have suggested it might have come from Turpan (Tulufan 吐魯番).

the Tibetans (Tufanren 吐蕃人) and for the vast area in which they lived (Tibet proper as well as parts of modern Qinghai, Gansu, Sichuan, and Yunnan) until the thirteenth century. Tufan is referred to in medieval Arabic sources from the ninth century as "al-Tibbat" from which "Tibet" in English and other Western languages is presumably derived. But it is not the name for Tibet in Chinese itself. The Yuan divided up greater Tibet into separate administrative units and established an Office for the Pacification of central and southern Tibet proper, naming it Wusizang 烏思藏 (from the Tibetan toponyms *dBus* "center," the Lhasa area; and *gTsang* "pure," the old name for the upper Brahmaputra river, whose valley had been the birthplace of Tibetan culture). The Ming used Xifan or the newer Wusizang for Tibet proper. In the Yongzheng period, Wu (seat of the Dalai Lama) was termed Qian-Zang 前藏 and Zang (seat of the Panchen Lama), Hou-Zang 後藏, terms still in use today. The switch to using Xizang 西藏 in official documents took place for the first time in 1663 and was imperially endorsed with the promulgation of the *Qinding Xizang zhangcheng* 欽定西藏章程 (Regulations for Tibet). *Zang* 藏 eventually became the standard Chinese term both for the place (Tibet Autonomous Region, Xizang zizhiqu 西藏自治區) and the people of Tibet (Zangzu 藏族, Tibetans).

Uighurs

Uighur (meaning "united" in that language) is also ultimately derived from a Chinese approximation of the original sounds using characters (Weiwu'er 維吾爾).

Manchus

There are numerous theories as to the origin of the neologism *Manju* (Manzhou 滿洲 in Chinese; Manchu in English).[12] It appears first in the *Jiu Manzhou dang* 舊滿洲檔 (Old Manchu chronicles) in

---

[12] "Cong yuyan lunzheng Nüzhen, Manzhou zhi zucheng" 從語言論證女真, 滿洲之族稱 (Examination of the tribal names of Jurchen and Manchu from the standpoint of language) in *Aixinjueluo shi sandai Manxue lunji* 愛新覺羅氏三代滿學論集 (Collected scholarly articles of three generations of the Aisingoros), Wulaxichun 烏拉西春 et al., Yuanfang, 1996, 381–88. See also Pamela Kyle Crossley, "An Introduction to the Qing Foundation Myth," *LIC* 6.2: 13–23 (1985); Pei Huang, "New Light on the Origin of the Manchus," *HJAS* 50.1: 239–82 (1990).

1613 and was officially adopted in 1635 as part of the political effort to consolidate the newly multi-ethnic confederation founded by Nurhaci (see Box 10, Chapter 50). In Manchu itself the word appears to be derived from the same root as the Mongolian word *baatur* meaning "brave" or "hero." But there is no certainty in the matter.

41.2.3   The Shifting "West"

Directional phrases such as *xifang* 西方 or *xitu* 西土 changed their meaning according to the position of the speaker and to the period. For much of Chinese imperial history, starting in the Han, Xiyu 西域 (the Western Regions) was the standard term for Inner Asia (41.3.1). *Xi* 西 also had a strong Buddhist connotation. Thus *Xiguo* 西國 was India; *Xiyu* 西語, Sanskrit, and *Xifang* 西方 was *pascima digbhâge* "the place where the sun goes down"; *Xifang jile shijie* 西方極樂世界 (Sukhâvatî or paradise). Later, in the nineteenth century, it was *Xifang* that was borrowed for what became the main word for the "West" or "Occident" (replacing the similar neologism, *Xitu* 西土). It also gave one of the many terms for "Westerner" (*Xifang-ren* 西方人).

During the Southern Song, a number of new geographic terms came into circulation. One was *Xiyang* 西洋 for the oceans and seas and countries on the coasts of Southeast Asia. It was still in use in this sense in the Ming (the voyages of Zheng He along these coasts and on through the Indian Ocean were described as going down to the western oceans *xia Xiyang* 下西洋).

There was no general term for Westerners until quite late in Chinese history. There were plenty of foreign traders (*fanke* 蕃客 or *fanmin* 蕃民) from Arabia, Persia, and Africa in Guangzhou during the Tang and in Quanzhou in the Song and Yuan, but not from Europe. The quarters or streets in which they lived were known as the *fanfang* 蕃坊 or *fanxiang* 蕃巷. The same terms were used until the Yuan.[13] In the north, in the Yuan, foreigners were mainly from West or Inner Asia and were called *semu* 色目 (42.1). *Xiyang* 西洋 was extended to cover the place where the Europeans (*Xiyangren* 西洋人) came from in the Ming and early Qing. The term *Da Xiyang*

---

[13] Several hundred tombstones in Quanzhou recording their deaths in ancient Arabic and Persian have been preserved (47.3).

大西洋 (lit. the Greater Western Ocean, i.e., the Atlantic) was coined by the Jesuits and their translators in the early seventeenth century. At first its use was controversial because of the presumption of using *da* 大 (normally reserved as a Chinese dynastic epithet or for the toponyms of respected countries). No connection was drawn between the *Xiyangren* and the people of Da Qin 大秦 (the eastern part of the Rome empire), which is first mentioned in the *Hou Hanshu*.[14]

In the early sixteenth century, Portugal was called Folangji 佛朗機, a term the Chinese took from Muslim traders (from the Persian for Europeans, Firangi, i.e., Franks). A *falangji* also meant a Portuguese cannon (a confusion probably introduced by the third character in the transcription, *ji* 機, "instrument"). At the end of the sixteenth century, Spain was also dubbed Folangji. England was transcribed with many different characters for *Yingjili*, e.g., 英吉利 or 嘆咭唎 (the mouth classifier is frequently used to indicate that the character to which it is attached is used for its sound not for its sense; see the end of section 1.2.6). France was known as Falanxi 法蘭西 from Falanke 法蘭克 (Franks), a variant of the older Folangji 佛朗機. The USA was called Lianhe shengguo 聯合省國, Yameilijia hezhongguo 亞美理駕合眾國, or Meilige heshengguo 美理哥合省國. Russia was called Luocha 羅剎 or Eluosi 俄羅斯 (a transcription of Mongolian "Oros").

These early transcriptions (mainly demotic with many variants at different times and in different parts of China) followed one of the normal courses for loanwords (1.2.6) by eventually becoming standardized in elegant abbreviated Literary Chinese hybrids (based on the first syllable of the name or via Japanese transcription): Yingguo 英國 (England); Faguo 法國 (from Falanke); Deguo 德國 (via Japanese *Doitsu*: Deutschland); Yidali 意大利 (Italia) or Meiguo 美國 (abbreviated from Yameilijia hezhongguo). Unofficially and not infrequently graphic pejoratives were added or substituted, as when France was written Falangxi 法狼西 instead of Falanxi 法蘭西 (the character for wolf being used in the place of that for orchid or

---

[14] D. D. Leslie and K. J. H. Gardner, *The Roman Empire in Chinese Sources*, Rome: Bardi Editore, 1996. The authors cite the copious previous scholarly literature on this subject. Note that Likan 犁靬 appears in the *Shiji* and refers to the Seleucid empire; Fulin 拂菻 is used in Sui and Tang sources for Byzantium.

moral excellence, *lan* 蘭). Countries considered powerful have *guo* 國 in their names, others not.

41.3   Main Routes to and from China

41.3.1   Overland (North and West)

The earliest overland links connecting the two ends of the Eurasian continent probably crossed the steppes of Russian Inner Asia via the grasslands of the Altay (Altun in ancient Turkish, but with the same basic meaning of "gold" as in Mongolian and Kazak).

The routes now known as the Silk Roads were also in use long before historic times, as attested by copious excavations of Paleolithic and Neolithic cultures along them. Even Caucasoid remains have been discovered in modern Xinjiang (the earliest probably dating from about 2000 BC). For a popular treatment of these by an expert in prehistoric and ancient textiles, see Elizabeth Wayland Barber, *The Mummies of Ürümchi*, Norton, 1999, and for a collection of scholarly articles, consult:

The Bronze Age and Early Iron Age of Peoples of Eastern Central Asia, Victor H. Mair, ed., 2 vols., *Journal of Indo-European Studies* Monograph Series 26, 1998.

Apart from specialized studies, exhibition catalogs are an excellent introduction to the archaeology of the steppe, which has provided the main evidence of the prehistoric contacts between China and the peoples of Central and Western Asia in the millennia before the opening of the Silk Roads. See, for example,

Ancient Chinese and Ordos Bronzes, Jessica Rawson and Emma Bunker, eds., Oriental Ceramic Society of Hong Kong, 1990.

Traders and Raiders on China's Northern Frontier, Jenny F. So and Emma C. Bunker, eds., Smithsonian Institution, 1995. Covers from the second millennium BC to the Qing.

For the broad picture of how the pastoral steppe empires of inner Euroasia interacted with the agricultural empires, including China, at their periphery, see

David Christian, *A History of Russia, Central Asia and Mongolia*, vol. 1, *Inner Eurasia from Prehistory to the Mongol Empire*, Blackwell, 1998.

History of the Civilizations of Central Asia, vol. 1, *The Dawn of Civiliza-tions: Earliest Times to 700 BC*, A. H. Dani and V. M. Masson, eds., Paris: UNESCO, 1992; vol. 2, *The Development of Sedentary and No-madic Civilizations*, Janos Harmatta, ed., Paris: UNESCO, 1994; vol. 3, *The Crossroads of Civilizations: AD 250 to 750*, B. A. Litvinsky, ed., Paris: UNESCO, 1996.

Cambridge History of Early Inner Asia, Denis I. Sinor, ed., CUP, 1990.

Out of a vast literature on the interactions of successive Chinese empires with their steppe neighbors to the north, the following handful of references has been chosen. Only overviews are included; studies of individual periods are given in Part V:

Owen Lattimore, *Inner Asian Frontiers of China*, American Geographical Society of New York, 1940; 2nd edition, 1951. Essays by a pioneering scholar who not only read the literature (in Chinese and Mongol) but also traveled the routes (42.3).

Sechin Jagchid and Van Jay Symons, *Peace, War, and Trade Along the Great Wall*, IUP, 1989.

Thomas J. Barfield, *The Perilous Frontier: Nomadic Empires and China, 221 BC to AD 1757*, Blackwell, 1989, 1996.

Nicola Di Cosmo, "Ancient Inner Asian Nomads: Their Economic Basis and Its Significance in Chinese History," *JAS* 53.4: 1092–1126 (1994).

Nicola Di Cosmo, "The Northern Frontier in Pre-Imperial China," *CHAC*, 885–966.

Jaroslav Prusek, *Chinese Statelets and the Northern Barbarians in the Period 1400–300 BC*, Reidel, 1971.

Sophia-Karin Psarras, "Exploring the North: Non-Chinese Cultures of the Late Warring States and Han," *MS* 42: 1–125 (1994).

Christopher I. Beckwith, *The Tibetan Empire in Central Asia*, PUP, 1987.

CHC, Vol. 6, *Alien Regimes and Border States, 907–1368*, Herbert Franke and Denis Twitchett, eds., CUP, 1994.

F. W. Mote, *Imperial China: 900–1800*, HUP, 1999.

Morris Rossabi, *China and Inner Asia from 1368 to the Present Day*, Thames and Hudson, 1975.

The Silk Roads

The first routes recorded in Chinese historical sources are those skirting the Taklamakan desert. They were explored in the Former

Han by Zhang Qian 張騫, who was sent on a mission to seek alliances against the Xiongnu (41.5.1, *Han*). Next, campaigns were launched, starting with those of General Huo Qubing 霍去病. In 121 BC he drove the Xiongnu out of the strategic Hexi corridor (*Hexi zoulang* 河西走廊), the narrow 600 km (375 mile) valley in modern Gansu west of the Yellow River. He then set up a line of frontier walls with guard houses, post stations, and grain stores. A few years later (115–11 BC), four commanderies were established along the corridor (44.4.3). The furthest was at Dunhuang 敦煌, the gateway to what was beginning to be termed the Western Regions (Box 9). Two routes both start from Dunhuang and then make their separate ways through the border passes of Yumenguan 玉門關 and Yangguan 陽關. The northern route connects the oases skirting the northern edges of the Tarim basin and the Taklamakan desert (Turpan, Korla, Kucha, Aksu); the southern route links the oases along the southern rim (Loulan, Cherchen, Khotan, Yarkand). These two sections of the Silk Roads both meet at Kashgar. The route from Chang'an (modern Luoyang) to Dunhuang went via the Hexi corridor (now called the Gansu corridor or panhandle).[15]

The "Tibetan Route" (Tufan *dao* 吐蕃道) branched from the southern oasis silk road across the Qinghai plateau through Lhasa and Nepal to India.

Silk Road References

Sichou zhi lu wenhua da cidian 絲綢之路文化大辭典 (Dictionary of Silk Road culture), Wang Shangshou 王尚壽 and Ji Chengjia 季成家, eds., in chief, Hongqi, 1995. A most informative dictionary on all aspects of the history and cultures of the Silk Roads. Contains 12,500 entries arranged topically on archaeological and textual sources (including 82 foreign sources from Herodotus to the seventeenth century).

---

[15] In 1877, the geographer Ferdinand Baron von Richthofen (1833–1905) termed these routes "die Seidenstrassen" (the silk roads; customarily mistranslated into English as the "Silk Road"). Xinru Liu examines the role of silk as a luxury traded item in China and the rest of Eurasia during the Tang and Song in *Silk and Religion: An Exploration of Material Life and the Thought of People, AD 600–1200*, New Delhi: OUP, 1996.

Box 9: The Western Regions

The term *Xiyu* 西域 (Western Regions) was used in two different senses. Narrowly, it meant the region of what is now the province of Xinjiang 新疆 (equivalent to four times the size of California). In its broadest sense it referred not only to this region but also to huge parts of Inner and West Asia, India, the Levant, and even North Africa. Which definition was used depended on the power of the imperial government. In the Han, Tang, and Qing it was used in a somewhat broad sense. In the Yuan it reached its broadest extent. In other periods, when China lost control of the region, the definition narrowed. The growing importance of the sea route between Europe and Asia in modern times and the simultaneous expansion of imperial Russia and Qing China into Inner Asia led to the decline of the region. The expression *Xiyu* fell out of use at the end of the nineteenth and the beginning of the twentieth centuries with the establishment there of the provinces of Xinjiang, Gansu, Qinghai, and Ningxia.

Xiyu tongshi 西域通史 (Comprehensive history of the Western Regions), Yu Taishan 余太山, ed. in chief, Zhongzhou guji, 1996.

Xiyu fanyishi 西域翻譯史 (History of translation in the Western Regions), Rezhake Maitiniyazi 熱扎克買提擬牙孜, ed. in chief, Xinjiang daxue, 1997.

Xiyu yanjiu shumu 西域研究書目 (Bibliography of research on the Western regions), Chen Yanqi 陳延琪 et al., comps., Xinjiang renmin, 1990. Covers from the Qin to 1989.

One problem of researching the Western Regions is the difficulty of correctly identifying toponyms encountered in Chinese sources. Use references such as:

Xiyu diming 西域地名 (Western Region Toponyms), Feng Chengjun 馮承鈞 (1885–1955), comp., 1930; Zhonghua, 1955; Lu Junling 陸峻嶺, enl., and corrected, 1980.

Hanshu xiyuzhuan dili jiaozhu 漢書西域傳地理校注 (Collated and annotated geographical names in the *Hanshu* chapter on the Western Regions), Cen Zhongmian 岑仲勉, 2 vols., Zhonghua, 1981.

Zhang Liren 張力仁, "Diming yu Hexi de minzu fenbu" 地名與河西的民族的分布 (Toponymy and the distribution of ethnic groups in Hexi), *Zhongguo lishi dili luncong*, 1998.1.

Other Overland Routes

The Southwestern Silk Road (Yongchangdao 永昌道) was another important overland route to the West. It started from Chang'an and led via Chengdu in Sichuan through Yunnan (passing Kunming, Dali, Baoshan [Yongchang], and Tengchong 腾冲) before crossing into northern Burma and thence overland to India (or through southern Burma, to the sea). The Burma Road of WW II (Dian-Mian *gonglu* 滇緬公路) for part of the way followed the same route as the old Southwestern Silk Road.

The route to Korea went either overland through northeast China and over the Yalu river 鴨綠江, or across the bay of Bohai and then overland via the Yalu. The direct sea route went from the port of Dengzhou 登州 in Shandong to the mouth of the Yalu and then along the Korean coast before going inland to the capital of Silla. It was one of many important sea routes to and from China.

41.3.2 Maritime Routes

The main maritime routes from China to the rest of Asia started from the ports of Tianjin 天津, Dengzhou 登州, Shanghai 上海, Ningbo 寧波, Fuzhou 福州, Quanzhou 泉州, and Guangzhou 廣州. Of these, Guangzhou served not only Southeast Asia, but also India, Africa, Arabia, and Europe.[16] A Qin shipyard has been excavated in Guangzhou (Panyu 番禺 as it was then called), the busiest overseas trading port from at least that time until the Southern Song, when it was temporarily overtaken by Quanzhou. Of 56 Chinese monks who went to India or Ceylon to study Buddhism during the Tang, 34 traveled by ship from Guangzhou (the remainder went overland by the Silk Roads in the northwest). From the early Ming there was a prohibition on foreign trade (*haijin* 海禁). In the Qing, after the recapture of Taiwan in 1683, four provinces

---

[16] *Chinese Maritime History*, A. Leung and Shi-yeong Tang, eds., Brill, 1999; *The Maritime Silk Route: 2,000 Years of Trade in the South China System*, produced by the Hong Kong Museum of History, HK: Urban Council, 1996. See also Wang Gungwu, *The Nanhai Trade: The Early History of Chinese Trade in the South China Sea*, Singapore: Times Academic Press, 1998 (1958); Chen Yan 陳炎, *Haishang sichou zhilu yu Zhongwai wenhua jiaoliu* 海上絲綢之路與中外文化交流 (The maritime silk road and Sino-foreign cultural exchanges), Beijing daxue, 1996.

were opened for overseas trade until the southern coast was closed in 1757, except for Guangzhou (a monopoly that it enjoyed until 1842 and again from 1949 to 1979). The trade had always been supervised and taxed by the central authorities, and not infrequently indirectly controlled using authorized Chinese merchants. In the Qing it came to be conducted and guaranteed through a monopoly guild of Cantonese merchants (the *shisan hang* 十三行, known better in English as the *Cohong*, an approximation of the Cantonese pronunciation of *gonghang* 公行, meaning combined merchant companies).

41.4   Accounts of Foreign Peoples

The Histories usually have summaries on foreign peoples at the end of the *liezhuan* 列傳 (Grouped biographies) chapters (Table 36).

Table 36: Non-Han Peoples and Countries in the Standard Histories

1. *Shiji* 史記	Xiongnu 匈奴; Dongyue 東越; Nanyue 南越; Chaoxian 朝鮮; Xi'nanyi 西南夷
2. *Hanshu* 漢書	Xiongnu 匈奴; Xiyu 西域; Xi'nanyi 西南夷; Nanyue 南粵; Minyue 閩粵; Chao-xian 朝鮮
3. *Hou Hanshu* 後漢書	*Siyi* 四夷
4. *Sanguozhi* 三國志	
5. *Jinshu* 晉書	*Siyi* 四夷
6. *Songshu* 宋書	*Siyi* 四夷; *Suolu* 索虜 (the unkempt caitiffs, i.e., the Toba); *Hudi* 胡氐
7. *Nan Qishu* 南齊書	*Weilu* 魏虜
8. *Liangshu* 梁書	*Zhuyi* 諸夷
9. *Chenshu* 陳書	
10. *Weishu* 魏書	
11. *Bei Qishu* 北齊書	
12. *Zhoushu* 周書	*Yicheng* 異域
13. *Suishu* 隋書	Xiyu 西域; *Nanman Beidi* 南蠻北狄; Dongyi 東夷
14. *Nanshi* 南史	*Yimo* 夷貊
15. *Beishi* 北史	*Jianwei fuyong* 僭偽附庸
16. *Jiu Tangshu* 舊唐書	Xiyu 西域; *Nanman Beidi* 南蠻北狄; Dongyi 東夷

Table continues

Table 36—Continued

17. *Xin Tangshu* 新唐書	Xiyu 西域; *Nanman Beidi* 南蠻北狄; Dongyi 東夷
18. *Jiu Wudaishi* 舊五代史	*Waiguo* 外國
19. *Xin Wudaishi* 新五代史	*Siyi fulu* 四夷附錄
20. *Songshi* 宋史	*Waiguo Manyi* 外國蠻夷
21. *Liaoshi* 遼史	*Waiji* 外紀
22. *Jinshi* 金史	*Waiguo* 外國
23. *Yuanshi* 元史	*Waiguo* 外國
24. *Mingshi* 明史	Xiyu 西域; *Waiguo* 外國; *Tusi* 土司
25. *Xin Yuanshi* 新元史	*Waiguo* 外國
26. *Qingshigao* 清史稿	*Tusi fanbu shuguo* 土司藩部屬國

See *Niansan zhong zhengshi ji Qingshi zhong ge zu shiliao huibian* 廿三種正史及清史中各族史料彙編, Rui Yifu 芮逸夫 et al., eds., 5 vols., Shiyu-suo, 1973. All mentions of non-Han peoples in 23 Standard Histories plus the Draft History of the Qing are excerpted. Because of the name-index this collection replaces earlier ones.

In Western sinology there is a long tradition of studies of China's foreign relations based on annotated translations of the *liezhuan*, a practice known as "translating the barbarians." Works on border areas and foreign peoples are also found in many other types of source, including the Veritable Records, geographies, encyclopaedias, biographies of officials who served in or visited a country or territory on diplomatic missions (41.4.1) and in their collected prose or verse.[17]

41.4.1 Translations, Excerpts, and Studies

Below follows a list of some of the main translations and collections of excerpts on foreign peoples, many from the *liezhuan* in the Standard Histories.

---

[17] Hans H. Frankel lists many of the early translations and studies in *Catalogue of Translations from the Chinese Dynastic Histories for the Period 220–960*, UCP, 1957; rpnt. Greenwood, 1974; Ruth Dunnell supplies an extensive list of translations and studies (including many new ones) in "Central Asia," in *American Historical Association Guide to Historical Literature*, Mary Beth Norton, ed., 2 vols., New York: OUP, 1995, 263–83.

CHC: for chapters or sections on foreign relations as well as bibliographic notes, see 41.4.2.

A. F. P. Hulsewé and M. A. N. Loewe, 1979 (44.1, *Translations from the Hanshu*).

Rafe de Crespigny, *Northern Frontier: The Policies and Strategies of the Later Han Empire*, Faculty of Asian Studies, ANU, 1984.

Xiongnu: *Xiongnu shiliao huibian* 匈奴史料彙編 (Collection of historical materials on the Xiongnu), Lin Gan 林幹, 2 vols., Zhonghua, 1988. Includes excerpts from textual sources, archaeological materials, and inscriptions. Volume 1 covers from the Warring States to the third century AD; vol. 2, up to the Tang.

Turks: Édouard Chavannes, *Documents sur les Tou-kiue (Turcs) occidentaux*, 1903; rpnt. Maisonneuve, 1942; Taibei, 1969; "Notes additionelles sur les Tou-kiue (Turcs) occidentaux," *TP* 2nd ser., 5:1–110 (1904); Cen Zhongmian 岑仲勉, *Xi Tujue shiliao buque ji kaozheng* 西突厥史料補缺及考證 (Historical materials on the Western Turks supplemented and corrected), Zhonghua, 1958; *Tujue jishi* 突厥集史, Cen Zhongmian, ed., 2 vols., Zhonghua, 1958. Much of the same material may be found in *Die chinesischen Nachtrichten zur Geschichte der Ost-Türken (T'u-küe)*, Liu Mao-tsai, tr., 2 vols., Harrassowitz, 1958.

Uighurs: Colin Mackerras, *The Uighur Empire According to the T'ang Dynastic Histories*, 2nd ed., ANUP, 1972.

Nanzhao (南詔, 649–902): Charles Backus, *The Nan-chao Kingdom and T'ang China's Southwestern Frontier*, CUP, 1981.

Tuyuhun: Gabriella Molè, *The T'u-yü-hun from the Northern Wei to the Time of the Five Dynasties*, Serie Orientale Roma, 41, 1970.

Cambodia: *Zhongguo gujizhong youguan Jianpuzhai ziliao huibian* 中國古籍中有關柬埔寨資料匯編 (Collection of materials on Cambodia from old Chinese sources), ed. and annotated by Lu Junling 陸峻嶺 and Zhou Shaoquan 周紹泉, Zhonghua, 1986. Note the *Zhenla fengtu ji* 真臘風土記 (Customs of the Khmer), Zhou Daguan 周達觀, 1297; Xia Nai 夏鼐, collated and annotated, Zhonghua, 1981. This is the fullest account of ancient Khmer ways of life in any language. *The Customs of Cambodia*, J. Paul, tr., Siam Society, 1992; translation into English of French tr. by Paul Pelliot, *BEFEO* 2: 123–77 (1902). See also Stephen O. Murray, "A Thirteenth-Century Imperial Ethnography," *Anthropology Today* 10.5: 15–18 (1994).

Japan: *Zhong-Ri guanxishi ziliao huibian* 中日關係史資料匯編 (Collected materials on the history of Sino-Japanese relations), Wang Xiangrong

汪向榮 and Xia Yingyuan 夏應元, eds., Zhonghua, 1984. Includes excerpts from Standard Histories from the Later Han onward and from encyclopaedias on Japan as well as excerpts from Japanese sources. See also Ryusaku Tsunoda, *Japan in the Chinese Dynastic Histories, Later Han Through Ming Dynasties*, South Pasadena, 1951 (for archival documents on Sino-Japanese relations, see 50.2.7).

Laos: *Zhongguo guji zhong youguan Laowo ziliao huibian* 中國古籍中有關老撾資料匯編 (Collection of materials on the kingdoms of Laos from old Chinese sources), Jing Zhenguo 景振國, ed., Zhongzhou guji, 1985. Contains 150 annotated excerpts (33 of which date from before the Ming) on the history of Laos and its precursors; there is a place-name index.

Philippines: *Zhongguo gujizhong youguan Feilübin ziliao huibian* 中國古籍中有關菲律賓資料匯編 (Collection of materials on the Philippines from old Chinese sources), Zhongshan daxue, Dongnan Ya lishi yanjiusuo (Institute for Southeast Asian History, Zhongshan daxue), ed., Zhonghua, 1980. All mentions of the Philippines (Luzon, Sulu) in Chinese sources are excerpted. There are people and place-name indexes as well as a listing of the works from which the excerpts are drawn.

Southeast Asia: *Dongnan Ya gudaishi Zhongwen wenxian tiyao* 東南亞古代史中文文獻提要 (Extracts from Chinese historical sources on Southeast Asian history), Gu Hai 顧海, comp., Xiamen daxue, 1990.

For the Ming and Qing, the Veritable Records are an important source on all aspects of external relations, including tribute missions. See, for example,

Mindai Man-Mô shiryô: Min jitsuroku shô Manshûhen Môkohen 明代滿蒙史料明實錄抄滿洲篇蒙古篇 (Historical materials concerning Manchuria and Mongolia under the Ming selected from the *Ming shilu*), Imanishi Shunju 今西春秋 and Mitamura Taisuke 三村泰助, eds., 17 vols., Kyôto daigaku, 1943-59. There is an itemized index: *Mindai Man-Mô shiryô kômoku sôsakuin* 明代滿蒙史料項目總索引, Kyoto, 1959.

Watanabe Hiroshi, "An Index of Embassies and Tribute Missions from Islamic Countries to Ming China (1368-1644) as Recorded in the *Ming shih-lu* 明實錄 Classified According to Geographic Area," *MTB* 33: 285-347 (1975); see also the volumes of excerpts from the *Ming shilu* cited in 49.1 and from the *Qing shilu* in 50.4.

Henry Serruys, *Sino-Mongol Relations During the Ming II: The Tribute System and Diplomatic Missions (1400–1600)*, Brussels: *Mélanges chinois et bouddhiques* 14, 1967.

Henry Serruys, *The Mongols and Ming China: Customs and History*, Variorum, 1995.

Roger Greatrex, "Tribute Missions from the Sichuan Borderlands to the Imperial Court (1400–1665)," *Acta Orientalia* 58: 75–151 (1997).

Ming shilu Zangzu shiliao 明實錄藏族史料 (Historical materials on the Tibetan people in the *Ming shilu*), Gu Zucheng 顧祖成 et al., eds., Lhasa, Xizang renmin, vols. 1 and 2, 1982; vol. 3, 1985.

Ming Qing shilu zhong zhi Xizang shiliao 明清實錄中之西藏史料 (Historical materials on Tibet from the *Ming* and *Qing shilu*), Luo Xianglin 羅香林, ed., HKCUP, 1981.

Qing shilu Zangzu shiliao xuan 清實錄藏族史料選 (Selection of historical materials on the Tibetan people from the *Qing shilu*), Gu Zucheng 顧祖成 et al., eds., 10 vols., Xizang renmin, 1982, 1993.

Yuan yilai Xizang difang yu zhongyang zhengfu guanxi dang'an shiliao huibian 元以來西藏地方與中央政府關係檔案史料匯編 (Collection of historical materials from the archives on the relationship between the Tibetan area and the central government since the Yuan), Zhongguo Zangxue zhongxin et al., Zhongguo Zangxue, 1994.

Ming shilu zhong zhi Dongnan Ya shiliao 明實錄中之東南亞史料 (Historical materials on Southeast Asia from the Veritable Records of the Ming), Chiu Ling-yeong (Zhao Lingyang 趙令揚) et al., comps., 2 vols., Hsüeh-tsin press, 1968, 1976.

Qing shilu Taiwanshi ziliao xuanji 清實錄臺灣史資料選輯 (Selection of materials from the *Qing shilu* on Taiwan history), Fujian renmin, 1993.

Qing shilu Chaoxian shiliao zhaibian 清實錄朝鮮史料摘編 (Edited excerpts of historical materials from the *Qing shilu* on Korea), Jilin wenshi, 1991.

A considerable amount of material on the border areas has been published from the Qing archives. For sources on foreign countries from the archives, see 50.2.7.

41.4.2 Bibliography

For a full bibliography of primary sources on border areas, see

Deng Yanlin 鄧衍林, *Zhongguo bianjiang tuji lu* 中國邊疆圖籍錄. (Catalog of maps and writings on China's border areas), Shangwu, 1958. Deng's work is arranged by place and it is also indexed; references to maps are included.

There are also bibliographies of particular border areas or regions, for example:

Tibet

For an annotated bibliography of Tibetan sources, see *Tibetan Histories*, Dan Martin, London: Serindia, 1997, which contains notes on 700 Tibetan-language sources from the earliest times (eighth century) onward. The most extensive local archive in China is held in Lhasa (50.3). For a Chinese collection, see

Zangzu shiliaoji 藏族史料集 (Collection of historical materials on the Tibetan people), Chen Xiezhang 陳燮章 et al., comps., 4 vols., Sichuan minzu, 1982–93.

Note the secondary studies in

Zangxue shumu 藏學書目 (Catalog of Chinese publications in Tibetan studies, 1949–1991), FLP, 1994; Continuation (covering publications of 1992–95), FLP, 1997.

For a bibliography of secondary literature on Tibet up to and including 1975, see *Bibliography of Tibetan Studies*, Hallvard Kåre Kuløy and Yoshiro Imaeda, comps., Naritasan Shinshoji, 1986. Contains 11,822 entries.

South

"Descriptions of Southern Regions and Foreign Countries," in *SCC*, vol. 3, 510–14.

Southeast Asia: *Dongnan Ya yanjiu lunwen suoyin (1980–89)* 東南亞研究論文索引 (Index of studies on Southeast Asia), Xiamen daxue, Nanyang yanjiusuo ziliaoshi 厦門大學南洋研究所資料室, comp., Xiamen daxue, 1993.

Dongnan Ya yanjiu shumu huibian 東南亞研究書目彙編 (Collection of bibliographies of research on Southeast Asia), Xiao Xinhuang 蕭新煌 and Lin Shuhui 林淑慧, comps., Zhongyang yanjiuyuan 中央研究院, Dongnan Ya quyu yanjiu jihua 東南亞區域研究計劃, 1995.

Note that for Vietnam until about the tenth century the only major sources are all in Chinese and thereafter, if Vietnamese, then written in Chinese. See the sources cited in Keith Weller Taylor, *The Birth of Vietnam*, UCP, 1983.

Some of the *CHC* volumes have extensive bibliographic essays or notes on the border regions and external relations covering both primary and secondary sources, notably,

"The Liao," "The Hsi Hsia," "The Chin Dynasty," and "A Note on Traditional Sources for Yüan History," *CHC*, vol. 6, 665–726.

"The Ming and Inner Asia," *CHC*, vol. 8, 987–89.

"Sino-Korean Tributary Relations Under the Ming,"*CHC*, vol. 8, 989–91.

"Ming Foreign Relations: Southeast Asia," *CHC*, vol. 8, 992–95.

"Relations with Maritime Europeans, 1514–1662," *CHC*, vol. 8, 995–98.

"The Canton Trade and the Opium War," *CHC*, vol. 10, 599–601.

"The Creation of the Treaty System," *CHC*, vol. 10, 601–3.

"Late Ch'ing Foreign Relations, 1866–1905," *CHC*, vol. 11, 605–8.

"Changing Chinese Views of Western Relations, 1840–95," *CHC*, vol. 11, 608–10.

41.4.3 Transcription Conventions

The conventional systems for transcribing the languages of China's neighbors into English, are

Japanese: the Hepburn system.

Korean: the McCune-Reischauer system; for a full description, see *Korea: A Historical and Cultural Dictionary*, Keith Pratt and Richard Rutt, eds., Curzon, 1999, xiii–xvii.

Manchu: Möllendorf system as adapted by Jerry Norman in *A Concise Manchu-English Lexicon*, UWP, 1978.

Mongolian: Antoine Mostaert, *Dictionnaire Ordos*, vol. 3, *Index des mots du Mongol écrit et du Mongol ancien*, Peiping, 1944; Johnson Reprint Company, New York, 1968. The only deviations from this system are that *q* becomes *kh*; γ becomes *gh*; and the hacek (ˇ) is removed from above *j*, *c*, and *s*, which become *j*, *ch* and *sh*.

Tibetan: Turrell/Wylie, "A Standard System of Tibetan Transcription," *HJAS* 22: 261–67 (1959).

Vietnamese: the standard Quôc-ngu spelling. In non-specialist Western works, it is not uncommon to leave out both sets of diacritics (one for the tones, the other for vowel quality).

41.5   Travel and Sojourn Abroad

41.5.1   Travel Abroad

The first historical record of a Chinese traveler going abroad is of Xu Shi (Fu) 徐市(福), who proposed to the first emperor to obtain the elixir of life from the immortals living in Penglai 蓬萊 (as legend has it, Japan) and in other islands to the East. He received money and young men and women for his mission, but it is not clear that he ever went.[18]

For a comprehensive history of Chinese travelers, see Zhang Bigong 章必功, *Zhongguo lüyoushi* 中國旅遊史 (4.8). A popular anthology of English translations from Chinese travel literature is Jeanette Mirsky: *The Great Chinese Travelers*, Allen and Unwin, 1965. Zhonghua shuju has published 17 of the most famous Chinese overseas travel accounts, each work punctuated and annotated: *Zhongwai jiaotong shiji congkan* 中外交通史籍叢刊 (Collectanea of Chinese historical works on overseas travel), Zhonghua, 1961–96.

Han

The first famous and documented Chinese traveler abroad was Zhang Qian 張騫. He led two expeditions to the Western Regions in the second century BC. Altogether, he spent 11 years abroad, mostly in captivity, married a Xiongnu wife, and had children by her. He was instrumental in opening up the Western Regions and setting Han policy towards its neighbors there. He brought back news of the blood-sweating horses of Ferghana and was also later apocryphally credited with introducing many Inner Asian fruits and other products to China (35.2.3).[19]

[18] *Shiji, juan* 6, "Qin benji" 秦本紀; tr. by Watson, *Qin*, 1993 (44.1).

[19] The principal sources on Zhang Qian are *Shiji, juan* 123, "Dayuan" 大宛 (Ferghana); tr. by Watson, 1993, vol. 2 (44.1), 231–52; and *Hanshu, juan* 61, tr. by Hulsewé, 1979 (44.1); J. R. Gardiner-Garden, "Chang Ch'ien and Central Asian Ethnography," *Papers of Far Eastern History* 33: 23–79 (1986). Also Yingshi Yü, *Trade and Expansion in Han China: A Study in the Structure of Sino-Barbarian Economic Relations*, UCP, 1967, and Yü, chapter 6 in *CHC*, vol. 1.

For a collection of voyages throughout the remainder of Chinese history to the Xiyu, see *Gu Xixingji xuanzhu* 古西行迹選注 (Selected and annotated ancient journeys to the Western regions), Yang Jianxin 楊建新, ed. in chief, Ningxia renmin, 1987, 1996.

Nan-Bei Chao

The travels of Chinese Buddhist pilgrims to India to seek the dharma (*qiufa* 求法), starting with Faxian's 法顯 (ca. 337–422) *Foguo ji* 佛國記, have frequently been translated.[20] See Nancy E. Boulton, "Early Chinese Buddhist Travel Records as a Literary Genre," Ph.D. dissertation, Georgetown University, 1982; and "The Buddhist Pilgrims," *SCC*, vol. 1, *Introductory Orientations*, 207–11, for a brief summary.

Tang

Da Tang Xiyuji 大唐西域記 (Record of the Western Regions), Xuanzang 玄奘 (596–664), 646; use *Da Tang Xiyuji jiaozhu* 大唐西域記校注 (Collated and annotated edition of *Da Tang Xiyuji*), Zhonghua, 1985; 3rd prnt., 1995. Xuanzang's journey to India began in 629 and ended in 644. In all he is reckoned to have covered 25,000 km (15,725 miles). Alexander Leonhard Mayer et al., *Xuanzang's Leben und Werk*, Veröffentlichungen der Societas Uralo-Altaica, vol. 34, 5 parts, Harrassowitz, 1992; Arthur Waley, *The Real Tripitaka*, Allen and Unwin, 1932; *Si-yu-ki: Buddhist Records of the Western World*, Samuel Beal, tr., 2 vols., Trübner, 1884; CMC, 1976; New Delhi: Munshiram Manoharlal, 1983. Sally Hovey Wriggins, *Xuan-zang: A Buddhist Pilgrim on the Silk Road*, with a Foreword by Frederick W. Mote, Westview, 1996. Legends about Xuanzang formed the basis of the novel *Xiyouji* (34.3).

Manshu 蠻書 (The book of the southern barbarians), Fan Chuo 樊綽 (ninth century), Zhonghua, 1962; *The Man Shu: Book of the Southern Barbarians*, G. H. Luce, tr., Southeast Asia Program, Cornell University, 1961. Mainly on the kingdom of Nanzhao (649–902) in modern Yunnan. The best Chinese edition is *Manshu jiaozhu* 蠻書校注 (*Manshu*, collated and annotated), Xiang Da 向達, ed., Zhonghua, 1962. Fan was military and surveillance commissioner of Annam in

[20] *The Travels of Fa-hsien*, Herbert A. Giles, tr., CUP, 1923; rpnt., Routledge, 1956; *A Record of Buddhist Kingdoms*, James Legge, tr. Clarendon, 1886; Dover, 1965.

the late Tang. Text retrieved from the *Yongle dadian* in the eighteenth century.

Song

Changchun zhenren xiyouji 長春真人西遊記 (The western journey of the sage of eternal spring), 1121–23, records in diary form the journey of the Daoist master Qiu Chuji 丘處機, who was invited to visit Chinggis khan (Temüjin) in the Hindu Kush; written by his disciple, Li Zhichang 李志常 (1193–1256). It contains the only eyewitness account of the founder of the Mongolian empire. See *The Travels of an Alchemist: The Journey of the Taoist Ch'ang ch'un from China to the Hindukush at the Summons of Chinghiz Khan. Recorded by His Disciple Li Chih-ch'ang*, Arthur Waley, tr., London, Headley Bros., 1931; Routledge, 1963; SMC, 1991; Paul Ratchnevsky, "The World Conqueror and the Taoist Monk," in *Genghis Khan, His Life and Legacy*, Blackwell, 1991, 134–36.

Song Diplomatic Diaries

There have been many studies and translations of individual diplomatic diaries, starting with Chavannes and continuing to the present. For a bibliography of these mission reports, see Herbert Franke's 1981 article cited below. See also idem, "Sung Embassies: Some General Observations," in Rossabi, 1983 (41.1), 116–48.

Édouard Chavannes, "Voyageur chinois chez les Khitan et les Jurchen," pt. 1, *JA* 9.9: 377–442 (1897); pt. 2, *JA* 9.11: 361–439 (1898); and by the same scholar, "Pei Yuan lou 北轅錄: récit d'un voyage dans le nord par Tcheou Chan 周煇," *TP* 5: 162–92 (1904).

Christian Lamouroux, "De l'étrangeté à la difference: les récits des émissaires Song en pays Liao (XIᵉ s.)," in *Pérégrinations en Asie*, 101-26. Study of the eight extant reports of Song embassies to the Liao.

Herbert Franke, "A Sung Embassy Diary of 1211–12: The *Shih Chin lu* [使金錄] of Ch'eng Cho [Cheng Zhuo 程卓]," *BEFEO* 69: 171–207 (1981).

Erich Haenisch, Yao Ts'ung-wu et al., trs., *Meng-Ta pei-lu* [*Meng Da beilu* 蒙韃備錄] *und Hei-Ta shih-lüeh* [*Hei Da shilüe* 黑韃事略]: *chinesische Gesandtenberichte über die frühen Mongolen, 1221 und 1237*, Harrassowitz, 1980.

James Hargett, "Fan Ch'eng-ta's *Lanpeilu:* A Southern Sung Embassy Account," *Tsing Hua Journal of Chinese Studies* 16.1-2: 119–77 (1984).

Song (others)

Zhufan zhi 諸蕃志, Zhao Rugua 趙汝适, 1242–58: *Chao Ju-Kua: His Work on the Chinese and Arab Trade in the Twelfth and Thirteenth Centuries, Entitled Chu-fan-chi*, Friedrich Hirth and William W. Rockhill, trs., St. Petersburg, 1911; Ch'eng-wen, 1967. Zhao was *shibosi* 市舶司 (superintendent of shipping) at Quanzhou and based his account partly on information obtained from merchants there.

Yuan

Liu Yu 劉郁, *Xi shiji* 西使記 (Record of a mission to the West). The author was on mission to Persia between 1259 and 1263.

Yelü Chucai 耶律楚材 (1190–1244), *Xi youlu* 西遊錄 (Record of a journey to the Western Regions), Zhonghua, 1981. See Igor de Rachewiltz, "The *Hsi-yu lu* by Yeh-lü Ch'u-ts'ai," *MS*: 1–128 (1962).

Wang Dayuan 汪大淵 (ca. 1311– ?), *Daoyi zhilüe* 島夷志略 (Brief record of the island barbarians; also *Daoyizhi* 島夷志), 1350.

Voyager from Xanadu: Rabban Sauma and the First Journey from China to the West, Morris Rossabi, Kodansha Intl., 1993. Rabban was sent by the Ilkhan Arghun to Europe in 1287.

Ming

Yingyai shenglan 瀛涯勝覽, Ma Huan 馬歡. This is the most important account of Zheng He's voyages. Ma Huan was a participant and wrote in the colloquial. *Ying-yai Sheng-lan: The Overall Survey of the Ocean's Shores (1433)*, J. V. G. Mills, tr., Hakluyt Society, 1970; rpnt., White Lotus, 1997. Mills' scholarly translation has a gazetteer of more than 700 names mentioned in the text with their modern equivalents, as well as an index of conventional names of identified places.[21] The translator also describes sources similar to the *Yinghai shenglan*, 55–66. See also J. J. L. Duyvendak, *China's Discovery of Africa*, Probsthain, 1949.

Xingcha shenglan 星槎勝覽, Fei Xin 費信, 1436, is the second-most important account of Zheng He's voyages and was also written by a participant: *Hsing-ch'a Sheng-lan: The Overall Survey of the Star Raft by Fei Hsin*, J. V. G. Mills, tr., rev. and annotated by Roderich Ptak,

---

[21] Note *Gudai Nanhai diming cidian* 古代南海地名詞典 (Dictionary of Nanhai place names), Chen Jiarong 陳佳榮, comp., Zhonghua, 1999 (replaces the author's *Gudai Nanhai diming cihui* 古代南海地名匯釋, Zhonghua, 1986). Has an English index.

Harrassowitz, 1995. This translation is based on the edition of Shen Jiefu 沈節甫, 1617; rpnt., Taibei: Yiwen, 1966.

Xiyang fanguo zhi 西洋番國志 (Gazetteer of the barbarian countries in the western oceans), Gong Zhen 鞏珍, Preface, 1434; Zhonghua, 1961. Supplements the above two accounts.

Zheng He xia Xiyang ziliao huibian 鄭和下西洋資料匯編 (Collection of materials on Zheng He's voyages to the southern seas), Zheng Hesheng 鄭鶴聲 and Zheng Yijun 鄭一鈞, eds., 3 vols., Qi-Lu, 1980–89.

Zhang Xie 張燮 (1574–1640), *Dong Xi yang kao* 東西洋考 (On the eastern and western oceans), 1618; Zhonghua, 1981, is the most comprehensive Ming description of the countries of Southeast Asia.

Xiyu xingchengji 西域行程記 (Record of travels in the western regions), Chen Cheng 陳誠. The author's travels began in 1414 and took him to present-day Samarkand and Herat. See Morris Rossabi, "Two Ming Envoys to Inner Asia," *TP* 62.3: 1–34 (1976), and the same scholar's "A translation of Ch'en Ch'eng's *Hsi-yu fan-kuo chih* [*Xiyu fanguo zhi* 西域番國志]," *Ming Studies* 17: 49–59 (1983).

Qing

Theodore Foss, "The European Sojourn of Philippe Couplet and Michael Shen Fuzung, 1683–92," in Philippe Couplet, S.J. (1623–93), *The Man Who Brought China to Europe*, Jerome Hendrickx, ed., Steyler, 1990.

Fan Shouyi 樊守義 (1682–1753), a Christian convert from Shanxi, accompanied the Kangxi emperor's special envoy to the Vatican, the Jesuit Francesco Provana (1662–1717). They went to Europe in 1707. Fan remained there until 1717 using the name Louis Fan. On the return voyage Provana died (a fragment of his tombstone survives: "Hic jacet P. Josephus Provana Societatis JESU Professus Sacerdos et Missionarius Sinensis"). Fan wrote the earliest Chinese account of Europe based on first-hand acquaintance: *Shenjian lu* 身見錄 (Seen with my own eyes), 1721. He was chiefly impressed by the magnificence of the royal palaces and also by the Vatican Library, St. Peter's, and the other sights of Rome. For a study of John Hu, a near contemporary of Fan, who was in France from 1722 to 1725, see Jonathan D. Spence, *The Question of Hu*, Knopf, 1988.

Haiguo wenjian lu 海國聞見錄 (Record of things seen and heard about the maritime countries), Chen Lunjiong 陳倫炯 (fl. 1730).

Zhouju suozhi 舟車所至 (Places reached by land and by boat), Zheng Guangsu 鄭光祖 (b. 1775), 1843; Zhongguo, 1991. Account of the author's travels in China and Asia, including the Indian Ocean.

Hailu 海錄 (Maritime records), Xie Qinggao 謝清高 (1765–1822). Xie boarded a trading vessel (probably Portuguese) and sailed to America, Europe, and Asia. On losing his eyesight, he returned home and dictated his recollections in 1820 to Yang Bingnan. See Kenneth Ch'en, "*Hai Lu*: Forerunner of Chinese Travel Accounts of Western Countries," *MS* 7: 208–26 (1942). The work indicates how little was known at the beginning of the nineteenth century in China about the West (contrast Japanese knowledge at this time about not only the West, but also China).

Wanli xingchengji 萬里行程記 (Record of a long journey), Qi Yunshi 祁韻士 (1751–1815). Record of Qi's journey from Beijing to Yili.

Shuofang beisheng 朔方備乘 (Historical sources on the northern regions), He Qiutao 何秋濤 (1824–62), 80 *juan*, originally called *Beijiao huibian* 北檄彙編.

After the Opium War, demand for more information about foreign countries led to much more detailed travel accounts and to the publication of collectanea of Chinese and foreign works about travel and world geography such as the *Xiaofanghu zhai yudi congchao* 小方壺齋輿地叢鈔 (Collections of historical writings from the *Xiaofanghu* studio, 1897). The translation of foreign textbooks, including those on geography, also began at this time.

Haiguo tuzhi 海國圖志 (Gazetteer and maps of the maritime world), Wei Yuan 魏源, 50 *juan*, 1844; 60 *juan*, 1847; 100 *juan*, 1852; punctuated and annotated edition, 3 vols., Yelu, 1998. See Jane Kate Leonard, *Wei Yuan and China's Rediscovery of the Maritime World*, HUP, 1984. This work contains many early Western loanwords (1.2.6).

Yinghuan zhilüe 瀛環志略 (A brief description of the ocean circuit), Xu Jiyu 徐繼畬 (1795–1873), 1848. Based on Western geographic works. See Fred Drake, *China Charts the World: Hsü Chi-yü and His Geography of 1848*, HUP, 1975. Xu was much criticized for his progressive ideas and forced to retire in 1852. In 1865 he was recalled to be minister of the Zongli Yamen 總理衙門 and in 1866 made director of the Tongwenguan 同文館, the college for interpreters.

The First Chinese Embassy to the West, Translated from the Journals of Kuo Sung-t'ao, Liu Hsi-hung and Chang Te-yi, J. D. Frodsham, tr., OUP, 1974. Guo Songtao 郭嵩燾 (1818–91) set sail from Shanghai in 1876 to act as minister to England (1877–78) and concurrently to France (1878).

The European Diary of Hsieh Fucheng (1838–94), Helen Hsieh Chien, tr., introduced and annotated by Douglas Howland, St. Martin's Press, 1993. Recounts Hsieh's travels in Europe, the United States, and Asia in the years 1890–94.

See also *Land Without Ghosts: Chinese Impressions of America from the Mid-Nineteenth Century to the Present*, R. David Arkush and Leo O. Lee, tr. and ed., UCP, 1989.

41.5.2   Overseas Chinese

For early Chinese expansion into the ancient kingdoms of Vietnam, see Jennifer Holmgren, *Chinese Colonization of Northern Vietnam: First to Sixth Centuries AD*, ANU, 1980, and the sources cited in Keith Weller Taylor, *The Birth of Vietnam*, UCP, 1983. For later Chinese migration overseas, see:

The Encyclopaedia of Overseas Chinese, Lynn Pan, ed. in chief, Curzon, 1999.

Shijie Huaqiao Huaren cidian 世界華僑華人詞典 (Dictionary of Overseas Chinese), Zhou Nanjing 周南京, ed. in chief, Beijing daxue, 1993.

Huaqiaoshi lunwen ziliao suoyin 華僑史論文資料索引 (Index of articles on the history of the Huaqiao), Guangzhou, 1981. Covers secondary sources published in Chinese, 1895–1980.

Kajin Kakyô kankei bunken mokuroku 華人華僑關係文獻目錄 (Bibliography on overseas Chinese), Fukuzaki Hisakazu 福崎久一, ed., Ajia keizai kenkyû sentâ, 1996. Includes 10,400 holdings of Ajiaken in all major languages.

42

Foreign Accounts of China

Early travelers to China, whether from Japan or Korea, from the Arabic or Persian empires, or from Europe and later from North America, frequently left records of their stay. These make fascinating reading, especially if they can claim some kind of exclusivity such as being the first on the scene. A tiny number from the late Tang to the end of the Republic are introduced in this Chapter. Some were written by monks or merchants, others by adventurers and explorers or by missionaries, diplomats, and officials (42.2–3).[1] Before the twentieth century, the most detailed (and with the highest access) were those written by the Jesuits (29.7.1).

China is featured in official Korean, Ryûkyû, and Vietnamese historical works based on the documentary sources of these countries. Some important items are briefly introduced (42.5).

In the eighteenth century, many closely observed paintings and sketches were made by European painters. The first photographs survive from the 1850s (42.4.2). They were influential in replacing the eighteenth-century image of the Chinese as a civilized people ruled by enlightened despots with images of a cruel, violent, and backward country.

There are a number of references for coping with the frequently encountered problem of knowing a foreign person's name when the only reference is in Chinese characters transcribing an approximation of the original sound.[2] There are also more specialized refer-

---

[1] *Visiteurs de l'empire céleste*, Réunion des Musées Nationaux, 1994, is the well-illustrated and scholarly catalog of an exhibition held at the Musée Guimet in Paris in 1994. It covers foreign visitors to China from the Tang to the Qing. See also the references in notes 3 and 4.

[2] *Jindai lai Hua waiguo renming cidian* 近代來華外國人名詞典 (Dictionary of the names of foreigners who came to China in modern times), Jindaishisuo fanyishi 翻譯室, comp., Shehui kexue, 1981. The brief biographies indicate the subject's main works. The transcriptions are indexed.

ences covering special categories of foreign visitors, for example, Christian missionaries (29.7) or diplomats coming to China (and sent abroad by the Qing) between 1843 and 1911 (50.10.4 *Biographies*). The chapter begins by examining the various terms that outsiders have used for the "Chinese" and "China."

42.1   The "Chinese" and "China"

42.1.1   The "Chinese"

Outsiders (including non-Han peoples living in the China area) usually called the Chinese by the name of the ruling dynasty, as did the Chinese themselves (3.1). For example, during the Qin and the Han, the Xiongnu 匈奴 referred to the people of north China as the men of Qin (*Qinren* 秦人) or men of Han (*Hanren* 漢人).[3] During the Northern Dynasties, Han 漢 was usually used in a pejorative sense for the people of the Southern Dynasties as in terms such as *Hanjia* 漢家, *Han'er* 漢兒, *Hanzi* 漢子, *zei Han* 賊漢, *gou Han* 狗漢, and so forth. Sometimes, the northerners also used the old Zhou expression *daoyi* 島夷 (barbarians living in the islands off the east China coast). In return, the Han used terms such as *Suolu* 索虜 (unkempt caitiffs) or *Hu'er* 胡兒 (barbarian weaklings) to refer to the northerners. *Hu'er* was revived at the end of the empire by the Taipings to refer to the Manchus and in the late Qing, early Republic it was used for foreigners (41.2).

By the end of the Tang, *Hanren* or *Han'er* had lost any pejorative sense and *Hanzi* was no longer used to describe the Han people. Inside China it was used in the sense of "man" or "husband," but it still retained the pejorative sense of contemptible husband (*jian zhangfu* 賤丈夫) right up to the later empire.[4]

Among the Jin 金 elite, *Hanren* 漢人 was used to refer to the Chinese in the south. During the Yuan, conversely, *Hanren* or *Han'er* included all those of whatever ethnic background who had been living in the north in Jin 金 territory, so the phrase included Han Chinese, Manchurians, and Koreans. All those who had lived under the Southern Song were officially called *Nanren* 南人 (unof-

[3] For the origins of the patronym *Zhongguo* 中國, see Box 2, Chapter 4.

[4] Chen Shu 陳述, "Han'er Hanzi shuo" 漢兒漢子説 (On *Han'er* and *Hanzi*), *Shehui kexue zhanxian* 1986.1: 290–97.

ficially, *Manzi* 蠻子, *Nan Manzi* 南蠻子, southern "savages," "barbarians," or *Nanggiat* [*Nanjia* 南家 "southerners"], *Songren* 宋人, or
xin furen 新附人, "men of Song" or "newly submitted people").
Nanren were ranked after Mongols, *Semu* 色目 or *Semuren* 色目人,
and *Hanren*. *Semuren* referred to northwestern peoples, those from
along the Silk Roads in Central and Western Asia as well as from
Europe. The expression is usually translated as "Western Asians" or
"multi-origin people". They were also called *Zhuguoren* 諸國人—
"people from all over."

Southerners referred politely to all those living in north China
as *Beiren* 北人. The expression *Beifanghua* 北方話 (northern speech)
appears for the first time in the Northern Song.[5]

During the Tang, several of the non-Han peoples in south China
as well as foreigners referred to the inhabitants of the Central Plains
(the Huaxia) as *Tangren* 唐人 (men of Tang), a practice that continued well into the Ming. *Tô* or *kara* (唐) in Japanese, or *Tang* 唐 in
Korean, are used to this day in the sense of meaning "Chinese" or
"foreign."[6] *Tangren* was also adopted by overseas Chinese (especially
Cantonese), who still often refer to themselves in this way, as well
as to their Chinatowns as *Tangrenjie* 唐人街, to their (Cantonese)
cuisine as "Tang food" and to old-style Chinese clothing as *Tang-
zhuang* 唐裝. China itself is called *Tangshan* 唐山 by many overseas
Chinese (Guangdong's Tang connection comes from the fact that it
was colonized from the Tang on. So modern Cantonese still shows
traces of the variety of literary Chinese current in the late Tang dynasty; see 1.2.1).

"Seres" (the silk people) may have been intended by some Roman writers to refer to the Chinese. "Silk" possibly came from
Latin *sericus*, itself in turn derived by way of Greek and Persian
from the Old Chinese pronunciation *sie* for *si* 絲. The English word
"Chinese" came from "China" and was used for the first time in the
sixteenth century. "Chinaman" meant a dealer in porcelain in the
eighteenth century; in the late nineteenth century it became the
slightly pejorative term for "Chinese." In Japan, new colonial attitudes also ensured that the old reverence for the Chinese past was

---

[5] Jing-shen Tao (Tao Jinsheng 陶晉生), "Barbarians or Northerners:
Northern Sung Images of the Khitans," in Rossabi, 1983 (41.1), 66–88.

[6] E.g., *Tôbutsu* 唐物 (foreign goods); *karafû* 唐風 (Chinese style); *Tôhon* 唐
本 (books from China); *karamatsu* 唐松 ("Japanese" larch).

overcome with scorn for the Chinese present. Even more derisory terms than "Chinaman" were the outcome (e.g., *chanchan* ちゃんち ゃん, *chankoro* ちゃんころ, or *tombi* とんび, meaning pigtail).

42.1.2 "China"

In the European Middle Ages, China was known in Latin as Cathaya, a name derived via Inner Asia from Qidan 契丹 (Khitan), the founders of the Liao dynasty. From whence came Slavonic, Turkic, and Arabic words for China such as "*Kitaia*" or *Hitai* and, eventually, the English "Cathay." At first Cathay referred to north China only. The south was known as the land of the Manzi 蠻子 or Chin (also Tame or Tameng from Da Ming 大明). Later, Cathay was retained as a poetic name for the whole of China as in Tennyson's (1842) phrase "Better fifty years of Europe than a cycle of Cathay."

The word "China" entered European languages only in the sixteenth and seventeenth centuries (probably via Persian *Chînî*.[7] At first "China" was used mainly to refer to what the Portuguese called "porcelain" (from its resemblance to polished Venus shell or cowrie). In the nineteenth century "China" became the main word for the country from which the porcelain came, that is, China.

Shina 支那 (*Zhina* 支那) began to be used as the "modern" Japanese word for China in the eighteenth century (before that, Kara 唐 [Morokoshi, Tô], Kando 漢土, Min 明, or Shin 清 were among the main ones used). By the late nineteenth century *Zhina* was replacing them all and had become associated with Japan's colonial and imperial policies in China. *Shina* 支那 and *Shinajin* 支那人 (Chinaman) all but fell out of use after 1949 in Japan, as did the same words in Chinese.

---

[7] This was possibly based on Sanskrit *cîna*, which was used in India since at least the Tang to describe China. The old claim that *cîna* was derived from Qin 秦 is unlikely because the pronunciation of Qin in Old Chinese was *dz'ien*. Moreover, Sanskrit toponyms were usually translations of meanings, not transliterations of sounds. It is therefore more likely to have come from *cîna*, the Sanskrit for "thoughtful" or "cultivated." In Chinese, it was transliterated as *Zhina* 支那, 至那, 脂那, *Zhendan* 震旦, 真丹, etc. Joshua Fogel examines "The Sino-Japanese Controversy Over *Shina* as a Toponym for China," in *The Cultural Dilemmas of Sino-Japanese Relations*, Sharpe, 1994, 66–76.

42.2   Travel Accounts and Reports, 850–1900

The main entry points into China for foreign travelers, including for tribute missions, throughout most of Chinese history were the Yumen pass at the western end of the Hexi corridor, the overland route from Korea, and the ports of the eastern and southern coasts, notably Guangzhou (see 41.3).

Ninth and Tenth Centuries

Japanese monk, Ennin 圓仁, who visited Tang China in 840 and spent nine years there, mainly·at Chang'an: *Nit-Tô guhô junrei gyôki* 入唐求法巡禮行記 (Account of a pilgrimage to Tang in search of the law), tr. into English as *Ennin's Diary*, Edwin O. Reischauer, Ronald Press, 1955. See also Reischauer's commentary in *Ennin's Travels in Tang China*, Ronald Press, 1955.[8] The text was rediscovered only in a handwritten copy in the twentieth century.

Arab merchant: *Voyage du marchand arabe Sulayman en Inde et en Chine, rédigé en 851, suivi de remarques par Abu Zayd Hasan (vers 916)*, Gabriel Ferrand, tr., Paris: Editions Boissard, 1922. Also *Relation de la Chine et de l'Inde*, Jean Sauvaget, tr., Maisonneuve, 1949. Abû Zaid (Abu Zayd Hasan) visited Quanzhou just after the Huang Chao uprising, see *The Huang Ch'ao Rebellion*, Howard S. Levy, IEAS, 1961, 110–31. For other Arab sources on China, of which there are many, see the articles on "China" and "Djugrafiya" in the *Encyclopaedia of Islam*, 2nd edition, Lucazs and Brill, 1960– .

Eleventh Century

Japanese Buddhist pilgrim, Jôjin 成尋 (1011–81), *San Tendai Godai sanki* 叁天臺五臺山記 (An account of a pilgrimage to the Tiantai and Wudai Mountains); Charlotte von Verschuer, "Le Voyage de Jin au mont Tiantai," *TP* 77:1–48 (1991). Rare glimpses of everyday life in Song China by a foreigner.

---

[8] There were 19 Japanese embassies to China from the late sixth to early ninth centuries, most of which were of Buddhist monks. Ennin's is the longest and most interesting account to have survived. For a comprehensive study covering Japanese embassies to China, see Charlotte von Verschuer, *Les Relations officielles du Japon avec la Chine aux VIIIe et IXe siècles*, Droz, 1985; also Joshua A. Fogel, "Travel in the Context of East Asia," Chapter 1 of his *The Literature of Travel in the Japanese Rediscovery of China, 1862–1945*, SUP, 1996, 13–33.

Twelfth Century

Arab merchant: *Sharaf Al-Zaman Tahir Marvazi on China, the Turks and India*, V. Minorsky, tr. from the Arabic, Royal Asiatic Society, 1942.

Thirteenth Century

Early European travelers: See Leonardo Olschki, *Marco Polo's Precursors*, Johns Hopkins Univ. Press, 1943.

Papal diplomats and priests: *Cathay and the Way Thither, Being a Collection of Medieval Notices of China*, Henry Yule, tr., London: Haklyut Society, 2 vols., 1866; rev. edition, Henri Cordier, ed., 4 vols., Haklyut Society, 1913-16, Taibei reprint, 1966. Igor de Rachewiltz, *Papal Envoys to the Great Khans*, Allen and Unwin, 1971.

Franciscan diplomats: *The Mongol Mission: Narratives and Letters of the Franciscan Missionaries in Mongolia and China in the Thirteenth and Fourteenth Centuries*, Christopher Dawson, ed., Sheed and Ward, 1955. Also, *The Mission of Friar William of Rubruck*, Peter Jackson and David Morgan, tr., Hakluyt Society, 1990.[9] William was sent by Louis IX of France to the khan. He set out in 1253 and reached the Mongol capital of Karakhorum in 1254. He was a keen observer. Although he never reached China, he records the first description in a European source of the Chinese script, the postal system, the Southern Song empire, and the kingdom of Korea. He also describes divination using the thigh-bone of a sheep (a form of pyromancy) at the Mongol court. While there, he encountered a French goldsmith working for the khan; see Leonardo Olschki, *Guillaume Boucher, A French Artist at the Court of the Khans*, Johns Hopkins Univ. Press, 1946. A predecessor of William's, Odorico of Pordenone contains in his *Recensione* the first mention in a Western language of Cantonese cuisine (snakes) and of foot-binding (see Yule, 1913-16).

Venetian merchant: *The Travels of Marco Polo*, Robert E. Latham, tr., Penguin Books, 1958. For two more scholarly editions, see *The Travels of Marco Polo: The Complete Yule-Cordier Edition*, 2 vols., Dover Publications reissue (1993) of the original Yule translation (1871 and 1875) as annotated by Cordier in 1903 and 1920; *Marco Polo: The Description of the World*, Arthur C. Moule and Paul Pelliot, tr. and annotated, 2 vols., Routledge, 1938, plus Paul Pelliot, *Notes on Marco*

---

[9] Replaces the old study *The Journey of William of Rubruck to the Eastern Parts of the World, 1253-55*, William W. Rockhill, tr., London: Haklyut Society, 1900.

Polo, 3 vols., Imprimerie nationale, Maisonneuve, 1959, 1963, 1973. The third volume contains an index. See also Arthur C. Moule, *Quinsai with Other Notes on Marco Polo*, CUP, 1957. Polo is supposed to have arrived in China in 1275. Whether or not he himself went there (the question is raised in Frances Wood, *Did Marco Polo Go to China?*, Secker and Warburg, 1995), the fact remains that the work with which he is credited was widely circulated and was regarded as containing the sum total of European knowledge of China between the thirteenth and sixteenth centuries and was therefore immensely influential. It may leave out much (foot-binding, tea, chop-sticks, Chinese characters), but it also has many passages that ring true, whether based on what Polo himself had seen or picked up from others.

Kuwabara Jitsuzô, "On P'u Shou-keng 蒲壽庚: A man of the Western regions who was the superintendent of the Trading Ships' Office in Ch'üan-chou toward the end of the Sung dynasty, together with a general sketch of trade with the Arabs in China during the T'ang and Sung eras," *MTB* 2: 1–79 (1928); 7: 1–104 (1935); Luo Xianglin 羅香林, *Pu Shougeng yanjiu* 蒲壽庚研究 (Studies on Pu Shougeng), HK: Zhongguo xueshe, 1959, traces the fate of Pu and his descendants, who successfully acculturated.

Fourteenth Century

Islamic traveler: *Ibn Battuta: Travels in Asia and Africa 1325–54*, H. A. R. Gibb, tr., Routledge, 1929; rev. edition, 3 vols., Cambridge: Hakluyt Society, 1958, 1962, 1971. Ibn Battuta (1304–68) was one of the greatest world travelers before the European voyages of discovery; see Ross E. Dunn, *The Adventures of Ibn Battuta: A Muslim Traveller of the Fourteenth Century*, UCP, 1986.

Fifteenth Century

Shipwrecked Korean official: *Ch'oe Pu's Diary: A Record of Drifting Across the Sea* [*P'yohae-rok* 漂海錄, 1488], John Meskill, ed. and tr., UAP, 1965. Ch'oe Po 崔溥 (1454–1504) was caught in a storm and washed up on the Chinese coast near Ningbo. From there he was sent under escort to Beijing and repatriated overland via the Yalu. Many Koreans who visited China for one reason or another during the following centuries left interesting travel diaries, usually recounting the sights and sounds of Beijing, Shenyang, or Chengde (see *Eighteenth Century*, item 2, for another example); Gari Ledyard, "Korean Travelers in China over Four Hundred Years, 1488–1887," *Occasional Papers on Korea* 2: 1–42 (1974).

Influential fantasy in Europe: *Travels of Sir John Mandeville*, 1499. See John Higgins and Ian Macleod, *Writing East: The Travels of Sir John Mandeville*, Univ. of Pennsylvania Press, 1997, who argue persuasively that it is a compilation of travel writings, first shaped by an unknown redactor, to which Sir John's name was later attached.

Sixteenth Century

Japanese monk: Diary of trips to Ming China, in Makita Tairyô 牧田諦亮, *Sakugen nyû Minki no kenkyû* 策彦入明記の研究, 2 vols., Hôzôkan, 1955, 1959. Sakugen was deputy chief of the Japanese embassy to China in 1539-41 and led the mission of 1547. His diaries were based on these two visits. See also Wang Yi-t'ung, *Official Relations Between China and Japan, 1368-1549*, HUP, 1953.

Shipwrecked Portuguese and Spanish travelers and clerics: *South China in the Sixteenth Century, Being the Narratives of Galiote Pereira, Fr. Gaspar da Cruz, O. P., Fr. Martin de Rada OESA*, Charles R. Boxer, tr., Haklyut Society, Series II, 1953; Kraus, 1967.

Spanish adventurer and missionary: Juan González de Mendoza, *The History of the Great and Mighty Kingdom of China*, Robert Parke, tr., 1588; Sir George Staunton, ed., 2 vols., London: Haklyut Society, 1853-54 (tr. of *Historia de la cosas más notables, ritos y costumbres del gran Reyno de las China*, Rome 1585). González' *History* (based on the works translated in Boxer, *South China*), was influential in Europe as the first circumstantial account of China since Marco Polo.

Seventeenth Century

Rumors at Nagasaki: *Ka-i hentai* 華夷變態, written by members of the Hayashi family (1644-77), 3 vols., Tôyô bunko, 1958-59, describes conditions during the Ming-Qing divide and in the subsequent decades. As the title indicates, the authors' sympathies were with the Ming. It was based on the reports of merchants from China visiting the Chinese trading station at Nagasaki (hence also the title of the continuation, *Kikô shôsetsu* 崎港商説, rpnt., Tôhô, 1981).

Shipwrecked Japanese boat crew: *Dattan hyôryûki* 韃靼漂流記 (An account of being shipwrecked among the Tartars). Takeuchi Tôemon 竹内藤右衛門 and 41 companions drifted onto the northeast China coast in the summer of 1644 and were sent to Shenyang and then to Beijing. In the following year they returned to Japan via Korea. The account of the adventure written by Captain Takeuchi includes much acute observation of the contemporary scene in China. There is a German translation available. See Tatiana A. Pang, "Das *Dattan Hyôryûki*," in *Materialien zur Vorgeschichte den Qing Dynastie*, Giovanni Stary, ed., Harrassowitz, 1996, 69–90; see also Sonoda Kazuki 園田一龜, *Dattan hyôryûki no kenkyû* 韃靼漂流 記の研究 (Researches on the *Record of Castaways in Tartary*), Fengtian: Mantetsu, 1939; Tokyo, 1980.

The Jesuits were the most important foreign observers in China in the seventeenth and eighteenth centuries. Once established, they had plenty of opportunity to travel on cartographic assignment or as diplomatic interpreters. In Beijing itself, their entrée to the emperor was their expertise in the arts and sciences of Europe: music, painting, architecture and, more important, astronomy, horology, mathematics, and ballistics. The four leading Jesuits in the China mission were Matteo Ricci, Johann Adam Schall von Bell, Ferdinand Verbiest, and Antoine Gaubil. Details on them and their works, and of the two main collections of their letters and reports that circulated in Europe, are given in 29.7.1.

Eighteenth Century

The Chronicles of the East India Company: Trading to China, 1638–1834, Hosea Ballou Morse (1855–1934), 3 vols., HUP, 1935.

Korean member of embassy to participate in the celebrations of the Qianlong emperor's 70th birthday in 1780: Pak Chi-won 朴趾源 (1737–1835), *Yorha ilgi* 熱河日記 (Chengde diary). Pak traveled to Rehe 熱河 overland via Shengjing 盛京 and Yanjing 燕京 (modern Shenyang and Beijing) and in his diary compares conditions in Korea unfavorably with what he saw in China. There is a punctuated edition: *Rehe riji* 熱河日記, Shanghai shudian, 1997. Several other Korean scholars wrote similar diaries at this time, for example, Hong Tae-yong 洪大容 (1731–83), *Yon-gi* 燕記 (Yanjing diary).

British diplomat: *An Embassy to China; Being the Journal Kept by Lord Macartney During his Embassy to the Emperor Ch'ien-lung, 1793–1794*, edited with an introduction and notes by J. L. Cranmer-Byng, London: Longmans Green, 1962. See also Sir George Staunton (1781–1859), *Authentic Account of an Embassy from the King of Great Britain to the Emperor of China*, 2 vols. London: W. Bulmer and Co., 1797. Staunton accompanied his father as page to the ambassador, Lord Macartney. He was the only member of the embassy to be able to speak and write some Chinese (having picked it up on the long voyage out). He published a translation of the Qing code into English in 1810 (27.3). For an innovative analysis of the rituals that organized the relations between the British and Chinese, see James L. Hevia, *Cherishing Men from Afar: Qing Guest Ritual and the Macartney Embassy of 1793*, DUP, 1995. For a short historical study of diplomatic audiences, see *Diplomatic Audiences at the Court of China*, William Woodville Rockhill, Luzac, 1905; rpnt., Ch'engwen, 1971. Rockhill (1854–1914) was a US scholar diplomat who before serving as minister to China (1905–1909) represented the US at the congress that negotiated the Boxer settlement and participated on the committee entrusted with proposing the reform of the court ceremonial for the reception of foreign envoys.

Comptroller of the household in the Macartney Embassy: Sir John Barrow (1764–1848), *Travels in China*, London: Cadell and Davies, 1804; rpnt., Ch'engwen, 1972. Barrow absorbed much of the information contained in earlier accounts, including that of the Dutch East India ambassador, Johan Nieuhoff (1673) and Evert Ysbrants Ides, ambassador from the czar of Muscovy (1706).

Nineteenth Century

Nagasaki magistrate, Nakagawa Tadahide 中川忠英 (d. 1830), *Shinzoku kibun* 清俗記聞 (Dictated records of Qing customs), 1799; Dali Press, 1982; annotated Japanese translation, Heibonsha and Tôyô bunko, 2 vols., 1966. Based on discussions with Chinese merchants. Contains rich materials on the manners and customs of Zhejiang, Jiangsu, and Fujian during the Qianlong period; see Bray, 1997, 65–70 (37.1).

Mamiya Rinzô 間宮林藏 visited Heilongjiang twice in 1808–9 and recorded his observations on the customs and trade of the local inhabitants in *Tô-Datsu kikô* 東韃紀行, 1810; Chinese translation under the same title, Shangwu, 1974.

British botanical collector of the Horticultural Society of London: Robert Fortune (1812–80), *Three Years' Wanderings in the Northern Provinces of China, Including a Visit to the Tea, Silk, Cotton Countries: With an Account of the Agriculture and Horticulture of the Chinese, New Plants etc.*, London, 1847; *A Journey to the Tea Countries of China*, 1852; *A Residence Among the Chinese: Inland, on the Coast, and at Sea*, Murray, 1857. Before his departure for China, the Horticultural Society minuted that "Fortune be supplied with fowling piece and pistols, and a Chinese Vocabulary."

British consular interpreter: Thomas Taylor Meadows (1815–68), *The Chinese and Their Rebellions*, London: Smith Elder, 1856; SUP, 1953. See J. K. Fairbank, "Meadows on China: A Centennial Review," *FEQ* 14: 365–71 (1954–55). Meadows' earlier work is still worth reading both on the difficulties of learning the Chinese language and on Chinese officialdom: *Desultory Notes on the Government and People of*

China and on the Chinese Language, London: Wm. H. Allen, 1847; Praeger, 1970.

French missionary zoologist, botanist, and ethnographer: Jean Pierre Armand David (1826–1900), *Journal*, Paris, 1875.

English botanist and plant hunter: E. H. Wilson (1876–1930), *A Naturalist in Western China*, 2 vols., Methuen, 1913; reissued in America as *China: Mother of Gardens*, 1931. Recounts "Chinese" Wilson's three itineraries, mainly in Sichuan in 1903–5, 1907–8 and 1910–11. Wilson worked for the Arnold Arboretum, whose keeper he became. On Fortune, David, Wilson and many of the earlier great plant hunters, see E. H. M. Cox, *Plant Hunting in China: A History of Botanical Exploration in China and the Thibetan Marches*, Collins, 1945; rpnt., OUP, 1987; Stephen A. Spongberg, *A Reunion Of Trees*, HUP, 1990.

French Lazarist missionaries: Evariste-Régis Huc (1813–60) and Joseph Gabet (1808–53), *Travels in Tartary, Thibet, and China, 1844–46*, William Hazlitt, tr. from the French original of 1850, London, 1851; edited with an introduction by Paul Pelliot, Routledge, 2 vols., 1928; Dover rpnt., 1 vol., 1987. Huc followed up on this success with *The Empire of China*, New York: Harper Bros., 2 vols., 1855 (tr. from French original of 1854).

French colonial explorers: *Voyage d'exploration en Indo-Chine effectué pendant les années 1866, 1867, et 1868*, Louis Delaporte, Ernest Doudard de Lagrée, and François Garnier, Paris, 1873; Hachette, 1885. English translation by Walter E. J. Trips, *The Mekong Exploration Commission Report*, 3 vols., White Lotus, 1996–98. See also Milton Osborne, *River Road to China*, Allen and Unwin, 1975, 1996.

Russian explorers: Petr Piassetsky, *Russian Travellers in Mongolia and China*, Jane Gordon-Cummings, tr., London: Chapman and Hall, 1884.

American Protestant missionary who spent the years 1850–64 in Fuzhou: Justus Doolittle (1824–80), *Social Life of the Chinese*, 2 vols., New York: Harper and Bros., 1865; rpnt., Graham Brash, 1986. Based on the author's popular "Jottings About the Chinese" that appeared in the Hong Kong newspaper *The China Mail*, 1861–64.

Western Observers of the Taipings: *Western Reports on the Taiping: A Selection of Documents*, Prescott Clarke and J. S. Gregory, eds., ANU, 1982.

American Presbyterian in Shandong for 50 years: Arthur H. Smith (1845–1932), *Chinese Characteristics*, Shanghai: Kelly and Walsh; rev. and enl. ed., New York: Fleming H. Revell, 1894. This began (as did much nineteenth-century Western commentary on China) as a series of articles in a treaty port newspaper (*The North-China Daily News*, 1889). It soon became the most read book on China and the Chinese—in America and Europe as well as among expatriates in China, a status it retained until the 1920s. In its Japanese translation, Smith's book deeply influenced Lu Xun 魯迅, helping him to formulate his own views on the theory of national character and to make the switch from medicine to writing.[10] Not a few of Smith's "characteristics" make an ironic appearance in Lu Xun's short story "A Qiu zhengzhuan" A Q 正傳 (The true story of Ah Q).

See also Arthur Smith, *Proverbs and Common Sayings from the Chinese*, American Presbyterian Missionary Press, 1914; rpnt., Dover, 1965; Graham Brash, 1988 (under the new title *Pearls of Wisdom*). It contains explanations of 1,900 phrases and proverbs current in the latter part of the nineteenth century. Arrangement is by genre, with a running commentary in the learned but condescending tone of the nineteenth-century Protestant missionary.

American Protestant missionary and chief instructor at the Tongwenguan: W. A. P. Martin (1827–1926), *A Cycle of Cathay: Or, China, South and North, with Personal Reminiscences*, Revell, 1896; 3rd ed., 1900. Martin did his missionary work in Ningbo (1850–63), including a spell of translating for the first US minister to China, William Bradford Reed (1858). In 1864, he moved to Beijing and began teaching English at the Tongwenguan. In 1869, he was appointed chief instructor of the college. He wrote an influential introduction to science (*Gewu rumen* 格物入門, 1868) and he also made several important translations, e.g., of Henry Wheaton's *Elements of International Law*, *Wanguo gongfa* 萬國公法 (Public law of all nations), Beijing: Chongshi guan 崇實館, 1864.

One of the most thorough of the nineteenth-century commercial missions is *La Mission lyonnaise d'exploration commerciale en Chine, 1895–1897*, 2 vols., Lyons: A. Rey et Cie, 1898.

The journals of the influential inspector-general of the Imperial Maritime Customs: Robert Hart (1835–1911), *Entering China's Service: Robert Hart's Journals, 1854–1863*, Katherine F. Bruner, John K. Fairbank, and Richard J. Smith, eds., Council on East Asian Studies, Harvard University, 1986; and *Robert Hart and China's Early Modernization:*

---

[10] Lydia H. Liu, "Lu Xun and Arthur H. Smith," in *Translingual Practice*, SUP, 1995, 51–76.

Robert Hart's Journals, 1863–1866, Richard J. Smith, John K. Fairbank, and Katherine F. Bruner, eds., HUP, 1991.

French consular official (in Ningbo and Fuzhou) and scholar: G. Eugène Simon (1829–96), *La Cité chinoise*, Paris: Nouvelle Revue, 1895; rpnt., Editions Kimé, 1992.

Hobson-Jobson: A Glossary of Colloquial Anglo-Indian Words and Phrases, and of Kindred Terms, Etymological, Historical, Geographical, and Discursive, Henry Yule and A. C. Burnell, eds., 1887; new edition, William Crooke, ed., London: Murray, 1903; rpnt., Routledge, 1994.

Some of the terms in common use in treaty port English were of Chinese origin (for example, cohong, congee, hong, hoppo, likin, or nankeen). *Hobson-Jobson* has many of these plus the much greater number of words that were imported into English from Anglo-Indian, Malay, or Portuguese, such as Bocca Tigris, Bogue, bund, compradore, cash, factory, picul, shroff, or tael. Note also the very small number of treaty port words of Southeast Asian origin that had already entered Chinese many centuries before, e.g., *jiadi* 家底 for Malaysian *kati* (catty), which appears in the *Songshi* 宋史. To identify treaty port renditions of official titles (e.g., Taotai), see 4.2, or check *DOTIC* (22.3.6, *Official Posts and the Examination System*).

Jacques M. Downs puts the early American China trade and traders under the microscope in *The Golden Ghetto: The American Community at Canton and the Shaping of American China Policy, 1784–1844*, Lehigh University Press, 1997; Rhoads Murphy situates the treaty ports in an East Asian perspective in *The Outsiders*, UMP, 1977, Frances Wood examines life in them in *No Dogs and Not Many Chinese*, Murray, 1998, P. D. Coates provides a detailed history of the British consular officials who served in the treaty ports: *The China Consuls*, HK: OUP, 1988, and Susan Schoenbauer Thurin analyzes *Victorian Travellers and the Opening of China, 1842–1907*, Ohio UP.

42.3   Eyewitness Accounts, 1900–49

The numbers of those coming to China and writing about it dramatically increases in the twentieth century. As a result, it is only possible here to cite a tiny fraction of the total. For brief descriptions of most of these titles plus many more, see Charles Hayford, 1997 (10.4.1).

Early Twentieth-Century Explorers

Mark Aurel Stein (1862–1943), *Ruins of Desert Cathay*, 2 vols., Macmillan, 1912. Includes Stein's account of how he purchased a large part of the secret temple library of Dunhuang in the years 1907-8 (46.3). Towards the end of his life, Stein summed up his life's work in *On Ancient Central Asian Tracks*, Macmillan, 1933; Pantheon, 1964. The best popular account of the explorations of Stein, Hedin, Grünwedel, Von Le Coq, Ôtani, and Pelliot is by Peter Hopkirk, *Foreign Devils on the Silk Road*, London: Murray, 1980; OUP, 1984.

Imperial Tutor

Reginald Fleming Johnson (1874-1938), *Twighlight in the Forbidden City*, Gollancz, 1934; rpnt., HK: OUP, 1985. Johnson worked as a Hong Kong official and magistrate at Weihaiwei before being hired to teach Puyi English from 1918 to 1924.

Soviet Political and Military Advisers

Missionaries of Revolution: Soviet Advisers and Nationalist China, 1920- 1927, C. Martin Wilbur and Julie Lien-ying Howe, eds., HUP, 1989. Contains 50 documents on Soviet involvement in Chinese politics. The documents were seized by Chinese police in a raid on the Soviet Embassy in Beijing in 1927 and published by Wilbur and Howe in 1956. A further 30 documents have been added to this second collection.

Dan Jacobs, *Borodin: Stalin's Man in China*, HUP, 1981. Mikhail Borodin (1884-1953) helped Sun Yatsen and Chiang Kaishek reorganize the Nationalist Party along Leninist lines.

Vladimirovna Vishnakova-Akimova, *Two Years in Revolutionary China, 1925-1927*, Steven R. Levine, tr., HUP, 1971.

Otto Braun (1900-74), *A Comintern Agent in China, 1932-1939*, Jeanne Moore, tr. from German original, 1973; SUP, 1982.

Scholars and Writers

Bertrand Russell (1872-1969), *The Problem of China*, Allen, 1922. Russell was guest professor at Beijing University, 1920-21. He also travelled and lectured extensively in the rest of China during these years.

R. H. Tawney (1880-1962), *Land and Labor in China*, Allen, 1932; rpnt., with an introduction by Barrington Moore, Jr., Beacon Books, 1966. Tawney, a British Fabian and economic historian visited China to lecture there in 1931. His analysis of rural problems made more sense than most books after a brief visit by visiting scholars and others.

Wystan Auden (1907-73) and Christopher Isherwood (1904-86), *Journey to a War*, Faber and Faber, 1939. Auden responds to the anti-Japanese war in verse and Isherwood reports in prose.

Military Adviser, Political Adviser, and Diplomat

Joseph W. Stilwell (1883–1946), *The Stilwell Papers*, Theodore H. White, ed., Sloane, 1948; rpnt., Da Capo, 1991. Extracts from Stilwell's private papers, including his journal, covering from Pearl Harbor to October 1944, when he was relieved from his post as chief of staff to Chiang Kaishek and commander of US forces in the China-Burma-India theater. The US military's top China expert in the twentieth century (on and off he had spent 10 years in China before taking up his wartime command there). "Vinegar Joe" had a high opinion of himself, a low opinion of Chiang Kaishek (whom he nicknamed the "peanut"), a high regard for the potential of the ordinary Chinese soldier, and an acerbic, witty way with words. See Barbara W. Tuchman, *Stilwell and the American Experience in China, 1911–1945*, Macmillan, 1971.

Owen Lattimore (1900–89), *China Memoirs: Chiang Kai-shek and the War Against Japan*, University of Tokyo Press, 1990. Lattimore was appointed by President Roosevelt as political adviser to Chiang Kaishek (1941–42). See Robert P. Newman, *Owen Lattimore and "Loss" of China*, UCP, 1992. Lattimore was the leading US Mongolist and historian of China's northern and northwestern frontiers of his generation. He also traveled the nomadic routes and worked as a journalist and editor and is therefore better listed under scholars, writers, journalists, or travelers. His best known work, *Inner Asian Frontiers of China*, is cited in 41.3.1, and his collected papers at the beginning of Chapter 40.

John Leighton Stuart, *Fifty Years in China: The Memoirs of John Leighton Steuart*, Random, 1946; idem, *The Forgotten Ambassador: The Reports of John Leighton Stuart*, Westview, 1981. See Yu-ming Shaw, *An American Missionary in China: John Leighton Steuart and Chinese-American Relations*, HUP, 1992.

Journalists

Peter Rand, *China Hands: The Adventures and Ordeals of the American Journalists Who Joined Forces with the Great Chinese Revolution*, Simon and Schuster, 1995.

Harold Isaacs (1910–), *The Tragedy of the Chinese Revolution*, 1938, rev., 1951, 2nd rev. ed., SUP, 1961. Isaacs, a US journalist, came to Shanghai in the early 1930s and stayed there until 1943. He argued against Stalin's policies in China.

Agnes Smedley (1892–1950), *The Great Road: The Life and Times of Zhu De (1886–1976)*, Monthly Review Press, 1956. Smedley arrived in

China in 1928 as a reporter for the *Frankfurter Zeitung*. She reached Yenan in 1937 and was so deeply impressed by the Red Army, that she only returned to America in 1949. See Janice R. MacKinnon and Steven MacKinnon, *Agnes Smedley: The Life and Times of an American Radical*, UCP, 1988.

Edgar Snow (1905–72), *Red Star Over China*, Gollancz, 1937; rev. ed., Grove, 1968. Unique interviews with Mao Zedong and other Communist leaders in Yenan in 1936. See S. Bernard Thomas, *Season of High Adventure: Edgar Snow in China*, UCP, 1996.

Jack Belden, *China Shakes the World*, Harpers, 1949; rpnt. with an introduction by Owen Lattimore, Monthly Review, 1970.

Theodore White and Annalee Jacoby, *Thunder Out of China*, Sloane, 1946; reissued with a new preface, 1961; rpnt., Da Capo, 1980.

Western Sources: General Bibliographies and Introductions

For a full list of early Western writings on China, including travel accounts, see Henri Cordier, *Bibliotheca sinica* (10.4.1). The second part is devoted to an exhaustive annotated list of "Les Étrangers en Chine, connaissances des peuples étrangers sur la Chine." Volume 3, columns 1917–2091, cover foreign writing on China from Strabo to 1700; the remainder of the volume deals with the eighteenth and nineteenth centuries. The continuations to Cordier and the other standard bibliographies are listed in 10.4.1.

Nineteenth-century non-Chinese sources are introduced in the manual as follows:

treaty port newspapers (50.8.6)
Western archives (51.13)
Western diplomatic documents publication series (51.13.1)

For an entry-level guide for general students to Chinese history from about 1780 to the 1990s, use *The Columbia Guide to Modern Chinese History*, R. Keith Schoppa, ed., Col.UP, 2000. Apart from an outline of the main themes, it contains much useful supplementary information, including thumbnail sketches of Communist base areas from the late 1920s to 1949, major party congresses of both the Guomindang and the Communist Party from their formation in the 1920s to the present, their meeting dates, leaders, and major party decisions. It is well organized for ease of reference. Given the nature of the intended reader, it contains no Chinese characters.

For a more advanced guide to the primary sources, see Andrew J. Nathan, *Modern China, 1840–1972: An Introduction to Sources and Research Aids*, CCS, Univ. of Michigan, 1973. See also

Chûgoku sankô tosho gaido Kingendaishi hen 中國叅考圖書ガイド近現代史編 (China reference guides: modern and contemporary history section), Ichiko Kenji 市古健次, comp., Kyûko, 1997.

Kindai Chûgoku kenkyû annai 近代中國研究案内 (Guide to the study of modern China), Kojima Shinji 小島晋治 and Namiki Yorihisa 並木賴壽, comps., Iwanami, 1993. This guide to modern Chinese history covers 1840 to the present day and is organized into four parts: (1) research trends; (2) secondary sources (Japanese, Chinese and American); (3) short excerpts in Japanese from primary sources; (4) statistical tables and a simple chronology from 1793 to 1949.

42.4   Paintings, Sketches, and Photographs

Many of the earlier European accounts of China are beautifully illustrated as well as extensively introduced in Donald F. Lach's voluminous series, *Asia in the Making of Europe*:

The Century of Discoveries, 2 vols., UChP, 1965 (covers up to 1600).

A Century of Wonder, 2 vols., UChP, 1970 (covers the sixteenth century); Book 2, *The Literary Arts*; Book 3, *The Scholarly Disciplines*, UChP, 1977.

A Century of Advance (with Edwin J. Van Kley), 4 vols., UChP, 1993 (covers up to 1700); Book 1, *Trade, Missions, Literature*; Book 2, *South Asia*; Book 3, *Southeast Asia*; Book 4, *East Asia*.

42.4.1   Paintings and Sketches

Before photographs began to be taken in the 1840s, the only visual representations of China were the sketches and paintings of Jesuit artists such as Giuseppe Castiglione or draftsmen such as William Alexander, who accompanied the early embassies: [11]

---

[11] Michel Beurdeley, *Peintures jesuites en Chine au XVIIIe siècle*, Paris, 1997; Harrie Vanderstappen, "Chinese Art and the Jesuits in Peking," in *East Meets West: The Jesuits in China, 1582–1773*, Charles E. Ronan and Bonnie B. C. Oh, eds., HKCUP, 1988; Mayching Kao, "European Influences in Chinese Art, Sixteenth to Eighteenth Centuries," in *China and Europe: Images and Influences in*

Footnote continued on next page

Giuseppe Castiglione (1688–1766), Dennis Attiret (1702–68), and other Jesuit painters not only made some fascinating paintings of Beijing and the court, they also had a considerable influence on a few Chinese painters. Cécile Beurdeley and Michel Beurdeley, *Giuseppe Castiglione: A Jesuit Painter at the Court of the Chinese Emperors*, Tuttle, 1971; *Orientations* 19.11 (1988) is devoted to Castiglione. *Europa und die Kaiser von China (1240–1816)*, Berliner Festspiele, Insel Verlag, 1985, contains scholarly essays and reproductions of paintings and sketches of Europeans at the court of the Chinese emperors.

William Alexander (1767–1816), the junior draftsman on the Macartney Embassy, filled three volumes of sketches of the everyday life of ordinary people, see *Image of China: William Alexander*, Susan Legouix, ed., Jupiter Books, 1980. In his lifetime he published several books of his prints (e.g., *The Costume of China*, London: William Miller, 1804; simplified version, Graham Brash, 1990). Selections from these and by another artist, George Henry Mason, were published under the title *Views of 18th-Century China*, Studio Editions, 1988. The originals are in the British Library.

British painter: George Chinnery (1774–1853). A student of Joshua Reynolds, Chinnery took up residence in Macao and eventually Hong Kong in order to escape his wife. He painted a large number of rustic, romantic scenes that greatly influenced the early photographers. See Patrick Conner, *George Chinnery, 1774–1852*, Antique Collectors' Club, 1993.

42.4.2 Photographs

The first surviving photographs of China date from the 1850s. The earliest are of the coastal areas around Hong Kong, but from the 1860s photographers began accompanying the troops and from the 1870s, the explorers. Beijing, north China, and the interior provinces in addition to Canton, Shanghai, and Hong Kong were extensively photographed by pioneers such as Felix Beato, Michael Miller, and John Thomson, all of whom de-romanticized the image of China (29.7.3). Their work circulated in stereographic form or was published in individual collections such as John Thomson (1837–1921), *Illustrations of China and Its People*, 4 vols. London, 1873–74. The works of early Chinese photographers are less well known; see

Sixteenth to Eighteenth Centuries, Thomas H. C. Lee, ed., HKCUP, 1991, 251–304.

Hu Zhichuan 胡志川 et al., *Zhongguo sheyingshi* 中國攝影史, *1840–1937* (A history of Chinese photography, 1840–1937), Zhongguo chubanshe, 1990. Several selections of early photographs of China have been published:

The China Century: A Photographic History of the Last Hundred Years, Jonathan D. Spence and Annping Chin, Random House, 1996. Carefully chosen selection of stunning photographs with fine commentary.

James Orange, *The Chater Collection, Pictures Relating to China, Hong Kong and Macao, 1655–1860, with Historical and Descriptive Letterpress*, London: Thornton, Butterworth, 1924.

Imperial China, Photographs, 1850–1912, Pennwick Press, 1978; Scholar Press, 1979. The short account of "Photography in Early China," by Clark Worswick on pages 134–51 is excellent.

The Face of China as Seen by Photographers and Travellers, 1860–1912, with a preface by Luther Carrington Goodrich and historical commentary by Nigel Cameron, London: Aperture Books, 1978.

Thomson's China: Travels and Adventures of a Nineteenth Century Photographer, Introduction and selection by Judith Balmer, HK: OUP, 1993.

Caught in Time: Great Photographic Archives: China, Garnet Publishing, 1993. Photographs taken during the Russian research and trading expedition of 1874–75, now held in the St. Petersburg archives.

Photographs of China During the Boxer Rebellion, taken by James Ricalton, Christopher J. Lucas, ed., Mellen, 1990. The leading photographers of the many who covered the siege of Peking were Yamamoto and Killie.

On the Tracks of Manchu Culture, 1644–1994, Giovanni Stary et al., comps., Harrassowitz, 1995; 200 photographs and a bibliography.

China's Inner Asian Frontier: Photographs of the Wulsin Expedition to Northwest China in 1923, Mary Ellen Alonso, ed.; historical text by Joseph Fletcher; Donald Freeman, design ed., Peabody Museum, HUP, 1979.

Osvald Sirén (1879–), *The Walls and Gates of Peking*, John Lane, 1924. Contains 109 collotypes after photogravures by the author and 50 architectural drawings.

Osvald Sirén, *The Imperial Palaces of Peking*, 3 vols., G. Van Oest: Paris and Brussels, 1926. Contains 274 collotypes after photogravures by the author and 12 architectural drawings

Hedda Morrison, *A Photographer in Old Peking*, HK: OUP, 1985.

Beijing jiuying 北京舊影 (Old photos of Beijing), Renmin meishu, 1989.

Dijing jiuying 帝京舊影 (As dusk fell on the Imperial City), Zhu Chuan-rong 朱傳榮, ed., Zijincheng, 1992. Selections from the photographs made in 1900 by a mission from Tokyo Imperial University.

Jiujing daguan 舊京大觀 (Old Beijing in panorama), Renmin Zhongguo, 1992.

Old Peking: The City and Its People, Haifeng, 1993.

Shanghai: A Century in Photos, 1843–1949, Lynn Pan, ed., Haifeng, 1993.

Note that the Zhongguo zhaopian dang'anguan 中國照片檔案館 (Photography archives of China) is open to researchers (51.1).

One of the outstanding collections of photographs of China in the first half of the twentieth century is in New York at the Sydney D. Gamble Foundation for China Studies. It contains 5,000 photographs taken by Gamble (1890–1968) during the years 1908–32.

42.5   China in East Asian Historical Records

Historical genres in Vietnam and Korea were closely modeled on those of the Chinese. They were mainly written in *wenyan*. Only a small sampling is given here.

Vietnamese Sources

Ðại Việt sử ký toàn thư 大越史記全書, 1479, is the Lê dynastic chronicle from the earliest times up to the late fifth century, with continuations up to the end of the seventeenth century. It contains much material on Vietnam's relations and negotiations with its neighbors, including China, during the Yuan dynasty.[12]

Ðại Nam thực-lục 大南實錄 (The Veritable Records of the Nguyen dynasty 阮朝), 453 *juan*, completed in 1909.

---

[12] On these and other Vietnamese sources, see Keith Weller Taylor, *The Birth of Vietnam*, UCP, 1983; and Alexander Woodside, *Vietnam and the Chinese Model*, HUP, 1971.

Đại Nam liệt truyện 大南列傳 (Biographies of the Nguyen dynasty), 85 *juan*, Yurindô, 1962.

Việt-sử thông-giám cường-mục 越史通鑑綱目 (Outline complete mirror of government of the history of Vietnam), Historical office of the Nguyen dynasty 阮朝國史館, eds., 1856–84, covers from the earliest times to 1789.

Đại Nam hội-điển sú-lệ 大南會典事例 (Statutes and precedents of the Nguyen dynasty).

Korean Sources

Koryŏ-sa 高麗史, Chong In-ji 鄭麟趾 et al., comps., 1454; 3 vols., Asea Munhwasa, 1972. Composed in chronicle form, it has especially full records on Koryo-Liao relations and also on Yuan China.

Nogoltae 老乞大 and *P'ak Tongsa* 朴通事 were primers of Chinese intended for Koryo merchants. They were probably both written in the early fourteenth-century. They contain unique material on the social history of the Yuan capital Dadu (Beijing). On the *Nogoltae*, see Svetlana Dyer, *Grammatical Analysis of the Lao Chi-da, with an English Translation of the Chinese Text*, ANU, 1983.

Chosŏn wangjo sillok 朝鮮皇朝實錄 (or *Yijo sillok* 李朝實錄; Veritable records of the Choson [Yi] dynasty), 1,893 *juan*, 1392–1863. Contains much material on China's relations with its neighbors in northeast Asia. Seoul Imperial University, 1930–32; Seoul University, 1953; Nihon gakushûin and Tôbunken, 50 vols., 1953; jointly published by the Academy of Sciences in China and Korea, 1959.

Chaoxian Lichao shilu zhong de Zhongguo shiliao 朝鮮李朝實錄中的中國史料 (Excerpts on China from the Veritable Records of the Yi dynasty of Korea), Wu Han 吳晗, comp., 12 vols., Shangwu, 1930; Zhonghua, 1980. Important additional sources on the early history of the Manchus.

Mindai Man-Mô shiryô: Richô jitsuroku shô 明代滿蒙史料李朝實錄抄 (Manchurian and Mongolian materials on the Ming dynasty: excerpts from the Yi dynasty Veritable Records), 18 vols., Tôkyô daigaku, Bungakubu, 1954–59.

Simyang changgye 審陽狀啓, in Chinese, 1636; Seoul Imperial University, 1935; covers the years 1637–43; contains information on life in Shenyang and on the activities of the Banner troops.

P'il I-je yugo pyonggyu 畢依齋遺稿拼庚. The author, P'il I-je, went on two embassies to China (1734 and 1750).

Zhong-Han guanxi shiliao jiyao 中韓關係史料輯要, Taibei, 1978, contains Korean accounts of Ming and Qing China.

Ku Han'guk Uegyo munso 舊韓國外交文書 (Old Korean diplomatic documents), Koryo Taehakkyo Asea Munje Yonguso 高麓大學校亞西亞問題研究所, ed., 22 vols., 1965–73; *Ku Han'guk Uegyo pusok munso* 舊韓國外交附屬文書, idem, ed., 8 vols., 1972–74. Documents of Korean foreign policy (in Literary Chinese, except for the last years, 1907–8 before the conduct of Korean foreign policy was finally taken over by the Japanese colonial government).

See also those sources listed under 42.2.

Japanese Sources

See the titles listed in 42.2 and 51.11 (for the modern period), and note the following handbook and bibliography,

Kindai Nit-Chû kankeishi kenkyû nyûmon 近代日中關係史研究入門 (Research guide to the modern history of Japan-China relations), Yamane Yukio et al., ed., 1992; rev. ed., Kyûbun shuppan, 1996.

Kindai Nit-Chû kankeishi ronbun mokuroku 1946–1989 近代日中關係史論文目錄 (Catalog of articles on Japan-China relations in the modern period), Kyûko, 1990, p. 25.

Ryûkyû 琉球 Sources

The Ryûkyû islands (Liuqiu) extend in a chain from south of Japan to Taiwan. After the king of Ryûkyû began presenting tribute to the Yuan in 1372, his territory was referred to as Liuqiu and Taiwan was called Xiao Liuqiu 小琉球; see 51.10. In 1609, Liuqiu (the Ryûkyûs) were brought under the control of the *daimyô* of Satsuma. In 1879, the Ryûkyûs were designated Okinawa Prefecture, a move only accepted by the Qing court in the treaty of Shimonoseki 下關 (1895), which concluded the Sino-Japanese War. Taiwan and the Pescadores were ceded to Japan under the terms of the same treaty.

Rekidai hôan 歷代寶案/*Lidai bao'an* 歷代寶案, 1697, with later continuations; Taiwan daxue, facsimile, 15 vols., 1972. Contains a large number of original documents on Ryûkyû 琉球 relations with the Ming and Qing (covers the years 1424–1867).

Guancang Liuqiu ziliao mulu (Holdings of materials on Liuqiu), Guoli zhongyang tushuguan, Taiwan fenguan 國立中央圖書館臺灣分館, compiled and published, 1989.

Kyûyô 球陽 is a history of Ryûkyû from the founding there of the Chû-zan kingdom 中山國 in the fourteenth century to 1876.

Setoguchi Ruiko 瀬戸口律子, *Liuqiu guanhua keben yanjiu* 琉球官話課本研究 (Studies of Ryûkyû textbooks of Mandarin), HKCUP, 1994. Studies of three handwritten early Qing Okinawan textbooks of Chinese preserved in Tenri University Library. The textbooks are reproduced in an appendix.

V

PRIMARY SOURCES BY PERIOD

43

Introduction: Guides

Part V covers the primary sources for imperial China (221 BC to AD 1911) and for the Republic (1912 to 1949). Imperial China is divided into seven periods from the Qin unification to the fall of the empire at the end of the Qing dynasty (the pre-Qin is the subject of Part II). The Republic is dealt with in Part V, Chapter 51.

Before starting to look for primary sources on Chinese imperial history, it is essential to have developed an understanding of the different types of historical writing, literary genres, and sources of archaeological data discussed in Parts III, IV, and II. It is also essential to know how a certain type of source would have been classified; knowing this helps locate a source in catalogs of old Chinese books (see 9.3 for a discussion of classification and bibliography and 9.1 on locating an individual work). To find out what printed sources were in circulation at a given time and who their authors were, look through the most extensive bibliographies of primary sources, the *yiwenzhi* and their supplements in the Standard Histories (9.4), as well as other official and private catalogs.

Such catalogs do not contain references to the very important new types of documentary sources discovered in the twentieth century such as the documents on bamboo strips and wooden tablets, the Dunhuang manuscripts, the documents of the Huizhou merchants, the Ming-Qing archives, and all the other new sources for imperial history listed in Table 29, Chapter 20.

The arrangement of each chapter of Part V is not identical because the sources available from each period differ greatly. Nevertheless, in general, the pattern followed is to put the basic historical works first followed by examples of other important primary sources. Next come newly discovered documentary sources (archival or excavated) and archaeological artifacts. Because both these categories are less well known, they are treated in greater detail than the traditional primary sources. Each chapter concludes by introducing guides to the primary sources of the period and a selection of research tools, usually under the following heads: language, biography, official titles and officeholders, geography, chronology, bibliographies, societies and journals.

43.1   Western Guides

Introductions to Chinese historiography are discussed in 20.3. Annotated catalogs of primary sources are covered in 9.4, 9.5, and 9.7, and secondary sources in Chapter 11. Guides to sinological reference works are given in 8.1. There are a number of guides to the primary sources and research problems of individual periods. Their focus and scope differ widely. Details are given in the appropriate sections of Part V. Some of the main titles are listed below.

A Handbook for T'ang History (46.5.1)

SB. A Sung Bibliography (47.4.1)

Research Tools for the Study of Sung History (47.4.2)

ISMH. An Introduction to the Sources of Ming History (49.5.1)

Ming History: An Introductory Guide to Research (49.5.1)

Introduction to Ch'ing Documents (50.10.2)

State and Economy in Republican China: A Handbook for Scholars (51.14.1)

The main English-language biographical dictionaries for all periods of Chinese history are listed in 3.4. Those for imperial China and the Republic cover the last thousand years of history. They contain brief information on a large number of individual book titles because they record the main writings of their subjects:

A Biographical Dictionary of the Qin, Former Han, and Xin Periods (44.6.2, *Biographies*)

Later Han Biographical Dictionary (44.6.2, *Biographies*)

Sung Biographies (47.4.2, *Biographies*)

In the Service of the Khan: Eminent Personalities of the Early Mongol Yuan Period (1200–1300) (48.5.4, *Biographies*)

DMB. Dictionary of Ming Biography, 1368–1644 (49.5.2, *Biographies*)

ECCP. Eminent Chinese of the Ch'ing Period (50.10.4, *Biographies*)

Biographical Dictionary of Republican China (51.5)

Biographical Dictionary of Chinese Communism, 1921–1965 (51.5)

A great deal can be learned about what primary (and secondary) sources are available on a given problem or period of Chinese history by looking through the 15 volumes of *CHC—The Cambridge History of China*, John K. Fairbank and Denis Twitchett, general editors, CUP, 1978– :

Vol. 1, *The Ch'in and Han Empires, 221 BC–AD 220*, Denis Twitchett and Michael Loewe, eds., 1986; 3rd rpnt., 1995

Vol. 2, *The Northern and Southern Kingdoms*, Denis Twitchett, ed., 2000

Vol. 3, *Sui and T'ang China, 589–906*, part 1, Denis Twitchett, ed., 1979

Vol. 4, *Sui and T'ang China, 589–906*, part 2, Denis Twitchett, ed., 2000

Vol. 5, *Sung China, 907-1267*, 2000

Vol. 6, *Alien Regimes and Border States, 907–1368*, Herbert Franke and Denis Twitchett, eds., 1994

Vol. 7, *The Ming Dynasty, 1368–1644*, part 1, Frederick W. Mote and Denis Twitchett, eds., CUP, 1988

Vol. 8, *The Ming Dynasty, 1368–1644*, part 2, Denis Twitchett and Frederick W. Mote, eds., 1998

Vol. 9, *Early Ch'ing, 1644–1800*, 2000

Vol. 10, *Late Ch'ing, 1800–1911*, part 1, John K. Fairbank, ed., 1978

Vol. 11, *Late Ch'ing, 1800–1911*, part 2, John K. Fairbank and Kwang-ching Liu, eds., 1980

Vol. 12, *Republican China 1912–1949*, part 1, John K. Fairbank, ed., 1983

Vol. 13, *Republican China 1912–1949*, part 2, John K. Fairbank and Albert Feuerwerker, eds., 1986

Vol. 14, *The People's Republic, part 1: The Emergence of Revolutionary China 1949–1965*, Roderick MacFarquhar and John K. Fairbank, eds., 1987

Vol. 15, *The People's Republic, part 2: Revolutions Within the Revolution 1966–1982*, Roderick MacFarquhar and John K. Fairbank, eds., 1991

In addition to the annotations to each chapter, many of the *CHC* volumes include bibliographic notes, and all have bibliographies. These are not all of the same standard, and some are already showing signs of age. But in general they have the advantage that they cover not only the main primary sources, but also the research tools and secondary scholarship in Western languages as well as in Chinese and Japanese. After checking the *CHC*, turn to the following Chinese and Japanese works.

43.2   Chinese and Japanese Guides

There are numerous guides in Chinese and Japanese covering the whole of Chinese history. Some are arranged by individual period, some by genre. Details are given in 8.2. Four outstanding ones are:

> *Zhongguoshi yanjiu zhinan* 中國史研究指南. Arrangement is by dynasty. Covers both primary and secondary sources. Based on translation of the next item (8.2.2)

> *Chûgokushi kenkyû nyûmon* 中國史研究入門. Arrangement is by dynasty (8.3.2)

> *Zhongguo gudaishi shiliaoxue* 中國古代史史料學. Arrangement is by dynasty (8.2.2)

> *Zhongguo gudaishi shiliaoxue* 中國古代史史料學. Arrangement is by genre (8.2.2)

In addition to these, there are also a number devoted to single periods or types of history. For example, the series *Xueshu yanjiu zhinan* 學術研究指南 (Guides to academic research) published by Tianjin Jiaoyu in the 1980s and 1990s. They emphasize Chinese secondary scholarship. The titles and editors are listed below with section references.

> *Sui Tang Wudai shi yanjiu gaiyao* 隋唐五代史研究概要 (46.5.2)

> *Yuanshixue gaishuo* 元史學概説 (48.5.4)

> *Mingshi yanjiu beilan* 明史研究備覽 (49.5.1)

> *Qingshi shiliaoxue* 清史史料學 (50.10.1). More useful than the Tianjin Jiaoyu volume on the Qing

> *Zhongguo shehuishi yanjiu gaishu* 中國社會史研究概述 (8.2.2)

> *Zhongguo jindai jingjishi yanjiu zongshu* 中國近代經濟史研究綜述 (51.4.2)

> *Zhongguo jindai junshishi yanjiu gailun* 中國近代軍事史研究概論 (51.7)

> *Jindai Zhongwai guanxishi yanjiu gailan* 近代中外關系史研究概覽 (51.12)

The *Zhongguo tongshi* 中國通史, under the editorship of Bai Shouyi 白壽彝 covers from prehistory to 1949. More than 500 historians contributed. The format is to give a basic outline of the main political events and then short biographies of the major figures of an age, followed by short monographic chapters on the arts and sciences and foreign affairs. In a way the format is not unlike that of the Standard Histories. There are also notes on the main primary sources of each period. If the editors or the publishing house decided to add an index volume it would greatly enhance the value of this huge work. However, there are detailed tables of contents:

Zhongguo tongshi 中國通史, 22 vols., Shanghai renmin, 1994–99.

For an introduction to the sources for the history of the Chinese revolution, see Zhang Zhuhong 張注洪, *Zhongguo xiandai gemingshi shiliaoxue* 中國現代革命史史料學 (51.9.2).

44

Qin and Han

221 BC–AD 220

Qin 秦[1]	221–206 BC
Han 漢[2]	202 BC–AD 220
Former Han 前漢 (also called Western Han)	202 BC–AD 23
Xin 新 (Wang Mang 王莽 reign)[3]	AD 9–23
Later Han 後漢 (also called Eastern Han)	AD 25–220

The history of the Qin and Han is based on transmitted texts, excavated texts, and artifacts.

The Han saw the first large-scale histories ever written in China as well as the inauguration of the annals-biography form. Most history writing was the work of private historians, not officials. However, very few Qin and Former Han texts have survived, and only about 10 percent of the works written in the Later Han are extant.

The three main historical sources on the Former and Later Han are the *Shiji* 史記, the *Hanshu* 漢書, and the *Hou Hanshu* 後漢書 (the first three of what later were called the Standard Histories). The *Shiji* is also the main textual source on the Qin (44.1). Three dozen

---

[1] The kingdom of Qin was established in 337 BC. It was named after the place in Shaanxi in which the king's ancestors had been enfeoffed. On the establishment of the empire in 221 BC, the name was retained.

[2] The dynastic name of Han was taken from Liu Bang's title, King of Han, which he had been granted in 206 on taking control of Hanzhong 漢中 (a Qin commandery) and the area further to the southwest, *CHC*, vol. 1, 116.

[3] In AD 9 Wang Mang (45 BC to AD 23) dismissed the imperial heir apparent and declared the beginning of the Xin 新 dynasty with himself as emperor. The name of the dynasty was taken from his title Marquis of Xindu (新都侯), which he had acquired in 16 BC. His reign lasted until AD 23 and is sometimes referred to in English as an interregnum or in Chinese as Xin Han 新漢 or Xin Mang 新莽.

other transmitted texts are listed in 44.2. This is not intended as an exhaustive inventory. There is little or no comment on these well-known sources save to refer to the section in which they are mentioned elsewhere in the manual. Excavated texts and fragments, on the other hand, are given a great deal more attention since most have only recently been discovered, and they have not yet been fully utilized (44.3-4). They are particularly important for economic, social, and legal history (especially of the Qin, for which there are so few contemporary sources). The archaeology of the Qin and Han and stone inscriptions also provide important supplemental evidence (44.5). The chapter ends with a selection of guides, readers, and research tools not mentioned in the preceding sections (44.6).

44.1   Main Historical Works

Shiji 史記, Sima Qian 司馬遷 (145-86 BC), 130 *pian* 篇 (*juan* 卷), 530,000 characters (for the text history and early editions of the *Shiji*, of which there are at least 60, recent editions, translations, research aids and indexes, see A. F. P. Hulsewé in *ECT*, 405-14).

Sima Qian fulfilled the request of his father, Sima Tan 司馬談 (180-110? BC), to complete the project for which he had begun to gather the materials, a history of China from the earliest times to the reign of Han Wudi 漢武帝, a period of 3,000 years. Three-fifths of the work is on the period between the reforms of Shang Yang 商鞅 (d. 338 BC) and Han Wudi (140-88 BC).

Sima Qian, to whom authorship is traditionally solely credited, refers to his work as *Taishigong shu* 太史公書. During the Han, this title was used, or *Taishigong* 太史公, *Taishigong zhuan* 太史公傳, or *Taishigongji* 太史公記 (hence the best known English title, *Records of the Grand Historian*).[4] It was abbreviated in

---

[4] For a study of Sima Qian, see Burton Watson, *Ssu-ma Ch'ien: Grand Historian of China*, Col. UP, 1958; Stephen W. Durrant, *The Cloudy Mirror: Tension and Conflict in the Writings of Sima Qian*, SUNY, 1995; Grant Hardy, *Worlds of Bronze and Bamboo: Sima Qian's Conquest of History*, Col. UP, 1999; Wai-Yee Li "The Idea of Authority in the *Shih-chi* (Records of the Historian)," *HJAS* 54.2: 345-405 (1994); Willard J. Peterson, "Ssu-ma Ch'ien as Cultural

Footnote continued on next page

the second century AD to *Shiji* 史記 (The scribe's record), a generic term in the Han for history books, which suggests that only a century after its completion, Sima Qian's work was regarded as unique.[5]

For a brief description and an evaluation of the historiographical influence of this, the most famous of all Chinese historical works, see 22.1.

Use the Zhonghua punctuated, collated edition, *Shiji*, 10 vols., 1959; rev., 1985; 14th prnt., 1996; reduced-sized, 1997. At each printing typos and errors were corrected, so it is best to use the most recent one. Another much-used edition (with notes in Chinese) is that of Takigawa Kametarô 瀧川龜太郎, *Shiki kaichû kôshô* 史記會注考證, 10 vols., Tôhô bunka gakuin, Tokyo kenkyûjo, 1932–34; rpnt., Beijing: Wenxue guji kanxingshe, 1955; Shanghai guji, 1986.

There are many different types of index to the *Shiji*. The most convenient are those based on the Zhonghua edition.

Nianwushi quanwen ziliaoku 廿五史全文資料庫 (25 Histories full text database), Shiyusuo, 1988. As soon as this database version of the Zhonghua edition becomes more widely and cheaply available, it will supersede all previous indexes not only to the *Shiji*, but also to *Hanshu*, the *Hou Hanshu*, and later Standard Histories (22.1).

Shiji ji zhushi zonghe yinde 史記及注釋綜合引得 (Combined indexes to the *Shiji* and the notes of Pei Yin 裴駰, Sima Zhen 司馬貞, Zhang Shoujie 張守節, and Takigawa Kametarô 瀧川龜太郎), *H-Y Index* 40, 1940; 2nd ed., HUP, 1955. Based on the Tongwen edition.

Shiji suoyin 史記索引 (Index to the *Shiji*), Li Xiaoguang 李曉光 and Li Bo 李波, comps., Zhongguo guangbo dianshi, 1989. Complete index to the Zhonghua (1985) edition. Easier to use than the next item.

Shiji suoyin 史記索引 (Subject index to the *Records of the Grand Historian*), Wong Fook-luen (Huang Fuluan 黃福鑾), ed., HKCUP, 1963. Index by stroke count of terms, names, etc., arranged under

---

Historian," in *The Power of Culture: Studies in Chinese Cultural History*, Willard J. Peterson et al., eds., HKCUP, 1994, 70–79.

[5] Sima Qian uses the title *Shiji* in his work dozens of times as an abbreviation for the *Lieguo shiji* 列國史記, not to refer to his own work.

24 categories, with references to the *Sibu beiyao* and *Bona* editions.

Shiji cidian 史記辭典 (Dictionary of the *Shiji*), Cang Xiuliang 倉修良, ed. in chief, Shandong jiaoyu, 1991, 1994. Includes proper names and definitions of technical terms and phrases.

Shiji renming suoyin 史記人名索引 (Personal-name index to the *Shiji*), Zhong Hua 鍾華, comp., Zhonghua, 1977.

Shiji diming suoyin 史記地名索引 (Place-name index to the *Shiji*), Ji Chao 稽超 et al., comps., Zhonghua, 1990.

Translations from the Shiji

Leaving aside the 10 chapters of Tables (*biao* 表), 111 of the remaining total of 120 chapters of the *Shiji* have been translated in the first three of the following translations:

Les mémoires historiques de Se-ma Ts'ien, Édouard Chavannes, tr., 5 vols., Leroux, 1895–1905. The first 47 chapters of the *Shiji* are translated with an important introduction and supplementary matter in this monument of French sinology. It was reprinted with a sixth volume (*juan* 48–52), edited and completed by Paul Demiéville et al., Maisonneuve, 1967. This contains a full index and bibliography, as well as a list of translations from the *Shiji* into Western languages. The first five volumes were reprinted by Maisonneuve in 1969.

Records of the Grand Historian of China, Burton Watson, rev., tr., 3 vols., Col. UP and *Renditions*, HKCUP, 1993. Vol. 1 (on the Qin) is indexed and vols. 2 and 3 (on the Han, originally published by Col. UP, 1961) also have an index. Translation of 65 chapters (of which 46 are not included in Chavannes); 2 on the Qin, the rest on the Han.

Selections from Records of the Historian, Yang Hsien-yi and Gladys Yang, trs., FLP, 1979, contains 13 chapters translated neither by Chavannes nor Watson.

The Grand Scribe's Records, vol. I, *The Basic Annals of Pre-Han China by Ssu-ma Ch'ien*; vol. II, *The Memoirs of Pre-Han China by Ssu-ma Ch'ien*, William H. Nienhauser, Jr., ed., Tsai-fa Cheng, Zongli Lu (Lü Zongli 呂宗力), William H. Nienhauser, Jr., and Robert Reynolds, trs., IUP, 1994. This new translation of the *Shiji* started out as a translation of those chapters not translated by Chavannes and Watson. It is now attempting the more difficult aim of a full translation replacing previous efforts. Two-thirds of the way still remain before an evaluation is in order. In the meantime, for some of the pitfalls awaiting translators of the *Shiji*, see Michael Loewe's review in *TP* 84: 153–67 (1998).

Syma Cian, Istoriceskie zapiski–Siczi, Rudolph V. Viatkin and V. S. Taskin, trs., Nauka, 6 vols., 1972– .

Bibliographies of the Shiji

Shiji yanjiu de ziliao he lunwen suoyin 史記研究的資料和論文索引 (Index of research materials and articles on the *Shiji*), Zhongkeyuan, Lishisuo, comp., Kexue, 1957. Contains a detailed account of the editions, scholarship, and comments on the *Shiji* down to 1937.

Shiji yanjiu ziliao suoyin he lunwen zhuanzhu tiyao 史記研究資料索引和論文專著提要 (Index of research materials and summaries of articles and books on the *Shiji*), Yang Yanqi 楊燕起 and Yu Zhanghua 俞樟華, comps., Lanzhou daxue, 1989. Continuation of the previous item.

Sima Qian yu Shiji yanjiu lunzhu zhuanti suoyin 司馬遷與史記研究論著專題索引 (Index of articles and books on research on Sima Qian and the *Shiji*), Xu Xinghai 徐興海, ed. in chief, Shaanxi renmin jiaoyu, 1995. Includes references to 236 books and 3,300 articles, mainly written in the 1980s and early 1990s.

Shiki gaku 50 nen 史記學50年, Ikeda Hideo 池田英男, comp., Meitoku, 1996. Covers publications in Japanese and Chinese between 1945 and 1995.

Hanshu 漢書 (Standard History of the Han), Ban Gu 班固 (AD 32–92) et al., 100 *pian* 篇 (120 *juan* 卷); 810,000 characters (for the text's history and early and later editions, translations, research aids and indexes, see A. F. P. Hulsewé in *ECT*, 129–36).

In order to distinguish it from the *Hou Hanshu*, the *Hanshu* is sometimes called the *Qian Hanshu* 前漢書. It covers the Former Han from about 210 BC to AD 23. It is the first Standard History to cover a single dynasty. The arrangement of the *Hanshu* is similar to that of the *Shiji*. It is divided into 12 *benji* 本紀 (basic annals), 8 *biao* 表 (tables), 10 *zhi* 志 (monographs) and 70 *liezhuan* 列傳 (grouped biographies). The section on *shijia* 世家 (hereditary houses) and the biographies of rich merchants were dropped, but some very important new monographs were added, including the first "Yiwenzhi" 藝文志 (dynastic bibliography), "Xingfazhi" 刑法志 (law), "Dilizhi" 地理志 (administrative geography), and "Baiguan gongqing biao" 百官公卿表 (official posts), all of which became familiar features of many of the subsequent Standard Histories. Like Sima Qian, Ban Gu set out to complete a work begun by his father (the *Shiji houzhuan* 史記后傳, which he had begun in order to bring the story to the end of the Former Han).[6] Ban Gu worked for twenty years as a historian in the Lantai 蘭臺, one of the palace libraries. By the time of his execution, he had almost finished. The tables were completed by his sister, Ban Zhao 班昭 (ca. 48–ca. 116),[7] and the monograph on astronomy by Ma Xu 馬續.

Use the Zhonghua punctuated, collated edition, *Hanshu*, 12 vols., 1962; 10th prnt., 1998; reduced-size, 1997. This was based on *Hanshu buzhu* 漢書補注, Wang Xianqian 王先謙 (1842–1918), ed., Changsha: Xushou tang 虛受堂, 1900; Yiwen, 1955. Wang's edition provides the most easily available notice of comments by Qing scholars.

The most convenient indexes are those based on the Zhonghua edition.

Nianwushi quanwen ziliaoku 廿五史全文資料庫 (25 Histories full text database), Shiyusuo, 1988 (see above).

Hanshu ji buzhu zonghe yinde 漢書及補注綜合引得 (Combined indexes to the *Hanshu* and the notes of Yan Shigu 顏師古 (581–645) and Wang Xianqian 王先謙), *H-Y Index* 36. Index of names and terms based on the Tongwen edition.

Hanshu suoyin 漢書索引 (Index to the *Hanshu*), Wong Fook-luen, comp., HKCUP, 1966. Index by stroke count of terms, names, etc., arranged under 25 categories with references to the *Sibu beiyao* and *Bona* editions.

---

[6] For a comparison of the chapters on the Han in the *Hanshu* with those in the *Shiji*, see Yves Hervouet, "La valeur relative des textes du *Che-ki* et du *Han chou*," in *Mélanges de sinologie offerts à Monsieur Paul Demiéville*, Bibliothèque de l'Institut des Hautes Etudes Chinoises, vol. 2, 1974, 55–76. For a book-length treatment of the same subject, see Pak Chai-u 朴宰雨, 'Shiji' 'Hanshu' bijiao yanjiu 史記漢書比較研究 (Comparative research on the *Shiji* and the *Hanshu*), Zhongguo wenxue, 1994. There is a bibliography on pages 389–426.

[7] Nancy Lee Swann, *Pan Chao, Foremost Woman Scholar of China, First Century A.D.*, New York: Century, 1932; Russell, 1960.

Hanshu cidian 漢書辭典 (Dictionary of the *Hanshu*), Cang Xiuliang 倉修良, ed., Shandong jiaoyu, 1994.

Hanshu renming suoyin 漢書人名索引 (Personal-name index to the *Hanshu*), Wei Lianke 魏連科, comp., Zhonghua, 1979.

Hanshu diming suoyin 漢書地名索引 (Place-name index to the *Hanshu*), Chen Jialin 陳家麟, comp., Zhonghua, 1990.

Translations from the Hanshu

The following works translate 31 of the 90 chapters of text in the *Hanshu*:

The History of the Former Han Dynasty, Homer H. Dubs (1892–1969), tr., 3 vols., Baltimore: Waverly Press, 1938–55. Translation with notes of the first 12 chapters (the 12 basic annals) and chapter 99 (on Wang Mang 王莽).

Remnants of Han Law, A. F. P. Hulsewé, tr., vol. 1, Brill, 1955. An annotated translation of the "Xingfazhi" 刑法志 (chapters 22 and 23). Only vol. 1 of this monograph was finished.

Food & Money in Ancient China: The Earliest Economic History of China to A.D. 25, Han shu 24, with Related Texts, Han shu 91 and Shih-chi 129, Nancy Lee Swann, tr., PUP, 1950. Reviewed by L. S. Yang, "Notes on Dr. Swann's *Food and Money in Ancient China*," *HJAS* 15: 507–21 (1952); rpnt. in *Studies in Chinese Institutional History*, HUP, 1963, 85–118. Yang points out the importance of the "Pingzhunshu" 平準書 (*Shiji*) and "Shihuozhi" 食貨志 (*Hanshu*): "Familiarity with certain passages from these chapters may be considered a requirement for every advanced student of Chinese history."

Rhea C. Blue, "The argumentation of the Shih-huo-chih chapters of the Han, Wei and Sui dynastic histories," *HJAS* 11.1 and 2: 1–118 (1948), includes a translation of the prefaces to the treatises on food and money in the *Shiji, Hanshu, Weishu*, and *Suishu*.

Courtier and Commoner in Ancient China: Selections from the History of the Former Han by Pan Ku, Burton Watson, tr., Col. UP, 1974. Translation of 11 chapters (54, 63, 65, 67–68, 71, 74, 78, 92, 97A–B).

China in Central Asia: The Early Stage: 125 BC–AD 23. An Annotated Translation of Chapters 61 and 96 of the History of the Former Han Dynasty, A. F. P. Hulsewé tr., with an Introduction by M. A. N. Loewe, Brill, 1979.

Po Hu T'ung, The Comprehensive Discussions in the White Tiger Hall, Tjan Tjoe Som, tr., vol. 1, Brill, 1949. Partial translation of Chapter 88. The title of the original work is *Bohu tong* 白虎通 (or *Bohu tongyi* 白虎通義). *ICS Concordance* 40. Attributed to Ban Gu; a work of Confucian exegesis.

Hou Hanshu 後漢書 (Standard History of the Later Han), Fan Ye 范曄 (398–445), 120 *juan*, covers the years 25–220 AD.[8]

Of the 90 original *juan*, 10 are annals and 80 biographies. Later, 30 *juan* of monographs were added from another history of the Han written in the third century during the Western Jin by Sima Biao 司馬彪.[9]

Use the Zhonghua punctuated edition, *Hou Hanshu*; 12 vols., 1965; 8th prnt., 1996; reduced-size edition, 1997. The most convenient indexes are those based on this edition:

Nianwushi quanwen ziliaoku 廿五史全文資料庫 (25 Histories full text database), Shiyusuo, 1988 (see above).

Hou Hanshu ji zhushi zonghe yinde 後漢書及注釋綜合引得 (Combined indexes to *Hou Hanshu* and the notes of Liu Zhao 劉昭 and Li Xian 李賢); *H-Y Index* 41. Index of names and terms based on the Tongwen edition.

Hou Hanshu suoyin 後漢書索引 (Index to the *Hou Hanshu*), Wong Fook-luen, comp., HKCUP, 1971. This is an index by stroke count of terms, names, etc., arranged under 25 categories with references to the *Sibu beiyao* and *Bona* editions.

Go-Kansho goi shûsei 後漢書語彙集成 (Glossary of historical terms in *Hou Hanshu*), 3 vols., Jinbun, 1960–62. Indexes some 15,000 names, geographical names, official titles, and technical terms. Mainly based on the *Bona* edition.

Hou Hanshu cidian 後漢書辭典 (Dictionary of *Hou Hanshu*), Zhang Shunhui 張舜徽, ed., Shandong jiaoyu, 1994.

---

[8] Hans Bielenstein, "The Restoration of the Han Dynasty, with Prolegomena on the Historiography of the *Hou Han Shu*," 4 vols., *BMFEA* 26: 1–209 (1954); 31: 1–287 (1959); 39: 1–198 (1967); 51: 1–300 (1979). See esp. 26: 20–81 (1954).

[9] B. J. Mansvelt-Beck, *The Treatises of Later Han: Their Author, Sources, Contents and Place in Chinese Historiography*, Brill, 1990.

Hou Hanshu renming suoyin 後漢書人名索引 (Personal-name index to *Hou Hanshu*), Li Yumin 李裕民, comp., Zhonghua, 1979.

Hou Hanshu diming suoyin 後漢書地名索引 (Place-name index to *Hou Hanshu*), Wang Tianliang 王天良, comp., Zhonghua, 1988.

44.2   Other Textual Sources

History

Sanguozhi 三國志 (for the end of the Han); see 45.1.

Hanji 漢紀 (or *Qian Hanji* 前漢紀), Xun Yue 荀悅 (148–209). This was the first chronicle of a single dynasty. The author rearranged the material in the *Hanshu* (including the tables) in chronological order as well as adding from other sources. The period covered is from 209 BC to AD 22.

Hou Hanji 後漢紀, Yuan Hong 袁宏 (328–76). An annalistic history covering the years 23 to 220. It was based on many sources and was not entirely superseded by the *Hou Hanshu*.

Dongguan Hanji 東觀漢記. Until the Tang this was regarded as the standard work on the Later Han. It was used as a main source by Fan Ye for the *Hou Hanshu*. Sixty percent of it was retrieved from the *Yongle dadian* by the *Siku* editors (*ICS Concordance* 19).

Geography

Huayang guozhi 華陽國志 (45.2)

Shuijingzhu 水經注 (29.3)

Agriculture and the Economy

Simin yueling 四民月令 (35.1)

Fan Shengzhi shu 范勝之書 (35.1)

Yantielun 鹽鐵論, Huan Kuan 桓寬, comp., 1st c. BC. See *Discourses on Salt and Iron: A Debate on State Control of Commerce and Industry in Ancient China: Chapters I–XIX Translated from the Chinese of Huan K'uan with Introduction and Notes*, Esson M. Gale, tr., Brill, 1931; Esson M. Gale, Peter A. Boodberg, and T. C. Lin, "Discourses on Salt and Iron (*Yen T'ieh Lun*: chapters XX–XXVIII)," *JNCBRAS* 65: 73–110 (1934); both reprinted together under the title of the former, Ch'engwen, 1967. *Yantielun jiaozhu* 鹽鐵論校注 (*Yantielun*, collated and annotated), Wang Liqi 王利器, ed., 2 vols., Tianjin guji, 1983. For a concordance, see *ICS Concordance* 26.

and annotated), Wang Liqi 王利器, ed., 2 vols., Tianjin guji, 1983. For a concordance, see *ICS Concordance* 26.

Official Titles and Officeholders

Hanguan liuzhong 漢官六種 (*ICS Concordance* 18). Supplements material in the monographs on official posts in the *Hanshu* and *Hou Hanshu*; note *Index du Han-kouan ts'i-tchong* 漢官七種通檢, Chen Tsu-lung (Chen Zuolong 陳祚龍), comp., Institut des Hautes Etudes Chinoises, Université de Paris, 1962.

Laws and Institutions

For the transmitted and excavated sources on Han dynasty law, see 27.3 and 44.3. Also:

Qin huiyao 秦會要 (Table 32, 25.1)

Xi Han huiyao 西漢會要 (Table 32, 25.1)

Dong Han huiyao 東漢會要 (Table 32, 25.1)

Tongdian 通典 ("Shihuo" 食貨, "Xuanju" 選舉, "Zhiguan" 職官 and "Dian" 典), 25.2

Philosophy and Religion

Note *Liang Han zhuzi yanjiu lunzhu mulu 1912–96* 兩漢諸子研究論著目錄 *1912–96* (Bibliography of books and articles on philosophers of the Former and Later Han, 1912–96), Hanxue yanjiu zhongxin, 1998.

Huainanzi 淮南子 (Table 26, 19.2)

Lunheng 論衡 (Table 26, 19.2)

Chunqiu fanlu 春秋繁露 (Table 26, 19.2)

Taiping jing 太平經. Daoist classic.

Fengsu tongyi 風俗通義 (5.5.2)

Bohu tong 白虎通 (see page 753)

Mathematics

Jiuzhang suanshu 九章算術 (Table 26, 19.2)

Zhoubi suanjing 周髀算經 (Table 26, 19.2)

Medicine

Shennong bencao jing 神農本草經 (39.1)

Shang hanlun 傷寒論 (36)

Jingui yaolüe 金匱要略 (36)

Literature

Yuefu shiji 樂府詩集 (30.2)

Quan shanggu Sandai Qin Han Sanguo Liuchao wen 全上古三代秦漢三國六朝文 (30.1)

Xijing zaji 西京雜記, Liu Xin 劉歆 (d. AD 23). Former Han recovered miscellany on institutions and events linked to Chang'an

Bowu zhi 博物志 (29.1)

Qilüe 七略 (9.3)

Language

Shiming 釋名 (2.2.2)

Shuowen jiezi 説文解字 (2.2.1 and 16.2)

Fangyan 方言 (1.1.1)

Jijiu pian 急就篇 (1.3.2)

44.3   Han Documents on Bone

During the excavations of the Weiyang Palace 未央宮 in Chang'an in 1980–89, archaeologists discovered over 60,000 Former Han "bone chits" or "bone tags" (*guqian* 骨簽), of which 57,000 are inscribed with records containing a total of several 100,000 characters. The material used is mainly ox bone. They are the first and only such massive find of writing on bone since the oracle-bone discoveries (15.4). But the purpose of the *guqian* was completely different. They are inventories of tribute and goods (mainly weapons) manufactured and presented to the Han court throughout almost the entire Former Han period. It is not clear why these inventories were written on bone, but presumably it was desired to have a more lasting record than bamboo, wood, or silk.[10]

---

[10] Many dozens of examples of the *guqian* are transcribed in vol. 1 of the excavation report and there are also 142 photographs in vol. 2 (plates 107–44); see *Han Chang'an cheng Weiyanggong fajue baogao* 漢長安城未央宮發掘報告, Kaogu yanjiusuo, eds., vol. 1, text; vol. 2, plates, Da baike quanshu, 1996.

44.4 Qin and Han Documents on Bamboo and Wood

For a general introduction to documents on bamboo strips and wooden tablets, see *jiandu* 簡牘, 18.1, and for those on silk, 18.2.

The Qin (221–206 BC) and Han (202 BC–AD 220) *jiandu* are especially interesting for the information they contain on administration, especially local administration,[11] the law,[12] the calendars in actual use at a particular period,[13] information on commodity prices (7.5), medicine, the mantic arts, and geography. They can also be used to check transmitted texts or, in some notable cases, to supplement them with large quantities of new historical data.[14] Note that it is on the *jiandu* that some of the few private documents of the Qin and Han have been found.[15]

Below is a list of the main finds of Qin and Han *jiandu* (to date, 2,500 from the Qin; 71,000 from the Former Han; and 800 from the Later Han). The bamboo strips from the Qin come almost entirely from tombs in the south, where the humidity kept them intact for 2,000 years. The Han *jiandu* administrative documents are usually of wood and have been mainly found in the northwest, where it was the arid climate that preserved them (almost 60,000 are from just two of the three Han commanderies and guardposts along the Silk Road in modern Gansu, see 44.4.3). There have also been some important finds of Former Han *jiandu* from tombs in the south. Most Later Han *jiandu* come from the northwest.

The Qin strips are in Qin small seal and early Qin chancery script. The Han strips are mainly in chancery script. All the strips contain large numbers of graphic variants and wrong characters, es-

[11] See Michael Loewe, "Wood and Bamboo Administrative Documents of the Han Period," *NSECH*, 161–92.

[12] See A.F.P. Hulsewé, "Qin and Han Legal Manuscripts," *NSECH*, 193–221. For more on Qin and Han laws, see 27.2 and 27.3.

[13] Yu Zhongxin 俞忠鑫, *Hanjian kaoli* 漢簡考曆 (Calendrical records on the *Hanjian*), Wenjin, 1994. The 12 almanacs discovered on bamboo strips are listed by place of discovery in 19.1.2 and 44.4.1–3; see also 5.1.1 and 6.4.

[14] The most striking example of *jiandu* supplementing existing historical sources are the estimated 90,000 discovered at Zoumalou 走馬樓, near Changsha in 1996; see 45.3.

[15] See, for example, A. F. P. Hulsewé, "Contracts of the Han Period," in *Il diritto in Cina*, L. Lanciotti, ed., Florence: Olschki, 1978, 11–38.

pecially those that were everyday administrative records rather than more carefully written documents.

44.4.1   *Qin* Jiandu 秦簡牘

In the list below, the most important finds are marked with an asterisk. Note also the following distinctions:

> Bamboo strips (*zhujian* 竹簡)
> Wooden strips (*mujian* 木簡)
> Bamboo and wooden strips (*jiandu* 簡牘)
> Bamboo tablets (*zhudu* 竹牘)
> Wooden tablets (*mudu* 木牘)

Guanju 關沮, Shashi 沙市, Hubei: 500 *zhujian* excavated in 1990 (some date from the Han). Shashi is the modern town near the old Chu cities of Ying 郢 (capital; 19.1.1), Ji'nan 紀南, and Jiangling 江陵 [Jingzhou 荊州].

Guanju 關沮, Shashi 沙市, Hubei: 387 *zhujiandu* excavated from tomb 30 at Zhoujiatai 周家臺 in 1993, including a *ganzhi* calendar of the days of the 34th year (213 BC) of the first emperor, solar observations, and medical recipes; *Wenwu* 1999.6.

Longgang 龍崗, Yunmeng 雲夢 county, Hubei (to the north of Dongting Lake just south of the Chu capital): 283 *zhujian* and one wooden tablet dating from the Warring States and (most) from the last years of Qin (excavated from tomb 6 in 1989 and 1991): legal texts on the management of roads, horses, sheep, and cattle and taxation. See *Yunmeng Longgang Qinjian* 雲夢龍崗秦簡 (Qin bamboo strips from Longgang, Yunmeng county), Liu Xinfang 劉信芳 and Liang Gui 梁桂, eds., Kexue, 1997. See also Hu Pingsheng 胡平生, "Yunmeng Longgang Qinjian kaoshi jiaozheng" 雲夢龍崗秦簡考釋校證, *Jianduxue yanjiu*, 1 (1996).

Shuihudi 睡虎地, Yunmeng 雲夢, Hubei: the first Qin *zhujian* ever discovered. 1,155 strips dating from 217 BC were found in tomb 11 (excavation in 1975–76). The tomb is in the western suburbs of the county town; Longgang is a few miles away in the southern suburbs. The strips record 10 works, written at different times from the end of the Warring States to the beginning of the Qin, including a lengthy portion of the lost Qin Code and other fragments of Qin laws and regulations (for references to research on these important texts, see 27.2), mantic texts, and two almanacs. The tomb also contained two letters on wooden strips from two soldiers writing home to their families asking for clothes and money. They are the earliest actual private letters found so far. For archaeological report and transcriptions, see *Yunmeng Shuihudi Qinmu* 雲夢睡虎地秦墓 (The Qin tomb at Shuihudi, Yunmeng), Wenwu, 1981; for transcriptions with commentary, see *Shuihudi Qinmu zhujian* 睡虎地秦墓竹簡 (Bamboo strips from the Qin tomb at Shuihudi), Wenwu, 1978; rev., 1990; transcriptions of the letters are not included (for them, see *Wenwu* 1976.9). For a listing of characters, see *Shuihudi Qinjian wenzibian* 睡虎地秦簡文字編 (Compilation of Qin bamboo strip characters from Shuihudi), Zhang Shouzhong 張守中, comp., Wenwu, 1994; for research, see *Yunmeng Qinjian yanjiu* 雲夢秦簡研究 (Studies on the Qin bamboo strips from Yunmeng), Zhonghua, 1981; Xu Fuchang 徐富昌, *Shuihudi Qinjian yanjiu* 睡虎地秦簡研究 (Studies on the Qin bamboo strips from Shuihudi), Taibei: Wenshizhe, 1993; Wu Fuzhu 吳福助, *Shuihudi Qinjian lunkao* 睡虎地秦簡論考 (Discussion on the Qin bamboo strips from Shuihudi), Wenjin, 1994. Rao Zongyi 饒宗頤 and Zeng Xiantong 曾憲通, *Yunmeng Qinjian rishu yanjiu* 雲夢秦簡日書研究 (Studies on the Qin bamboo almanacs from Yunmeng), HKCUP, 1982 (part 2 contains transcriptions); Motoo Kudô (工藤元男), "The Ch'in Bamboo Strip *Book of Divination (Jih-shu)* and Ch'in Legalism," *AA*, 58 (1990), 24–37; Michael Loewe, "The Almanacs (*jih-shu*) from Shui-hu-ti," *AM* 1.2: 1–28 (1988); Liu Lexian 劉樂賢, *Shuihudi Qinjian rishu yanjiu* 睡虎地秦簡日書研究 (Studies on the Qin bamboo almanacs at Shuihudi), Wenjin, 1994; Mu-chou Poo, "Newly Discovered Daybooks and Everyday Religion," in *In Search of Personal Welfare: A View of Ancient Chinese Religion*, SUNY, 1998, 69–101. See also the references in 6.4.

Yangjiashan 楊家山, Jiangling 江陵, Hubei: 75 *zhujiandu* recording burial articles. Excavated from tomb 135 in 1990. Not yet published; *Wenwu* 1993.8.

Wangjiatai 王家臺, Jiangling 江陵, Hubei: more than 800 *zhujiandu* found in Tomb 15 in 1993, including a copy of the *Xiaolü* 效律 similar to that found at Shuihudi 睡虎地 (27.2), an almanac, *bagua* divinations and records of local disasters (a type of strip not yet found anywhere else); *Wenwu* 1995.1.

44.4.2 *Han* Jiandu 漢簡牘 *from Tombs*

Bajiaolang 八角廊, Dingzhou 定州, Hebei: about 2,500 *zhujian* in the tomb of Liu Xiu 劉修, Prince Huai of Zhongshan 中山懷王 (d. 55 BC). They were burned by robbers at the end of the dynasty, making most of the strips almost illegible. They include the earliest known manuscript of the *Lunyu*, other Confucian works, and an almanac, *Wenwu* 1981.8. About half of the text (7,576 characters on 620 mostly broken strips) of the *Lunyu* has now been deciphered and punctuated and compared with the *jinwen* texts of the *Lunyu*; see *Dingzhou Hanmu zhujian Lunyu* 定州漢墓竹簡論語 (The Dingzhou Han tomb bamboo strip *Lunyu*), Dingzhou Hanmu zhujian zhengli xiaozu, eds., Wenwu, 1997. In addition, 277 strips of the *Wenzi* 文字 have been deciphered; *Wenwu* 1995.12; 1996.1. The tomb was excavated in 1973.

Fenghuangshan 鳳凰山, Jiangling 江陵, Hubei: five Former Han tombs. 575 *jiandu* excavated 1973–75, containing tenant contracts, merchant accounts, and burial lists; *Wenwu* 1974.7; 1976.6. Two of the tombs also included ink pellets and ink stones. Tomb 168 contained the arm of a balance with 18 characters inscribed on it.

Gaotai 高臺, Jiangling 江陵, Hubei: four *mudu* from tomb-18 discovered in 1990.

Huaguoshan 花果山, Lianyungang 連雲港, Jiangsu: Former Han. 13 *zhumu jiandu*.

Liujiaping 劉家坪, Hangu 旱谷, Gansu: 23 *mujian* discovered from Later Han tomb in 1971. See Xue Yingqun, 1991, 44.4.3, *Juyan*.

Luopowan 羅泊灣, Guixian 貴縣, Guangxi: 15 *mujiandu* discovered in 1976.

Mawangdui 馬王堆 *Chujian*, Changsha, Hunan: discovered in 1972 and 1973. Tomb 1 (dating from 186 BC contained 361 *zhujian mudu*, and there were 617 *zhumu jiandu* in tomb 3, mainly medical works and also lists of burial articles. Also the earliest and most complete almanac ever found in China (dating from 129 BC). *Mawangdui Hanmu wenwu* 馬王堆漢墓文物 (The cultural relics unearthed from the Han tombs at Mawangdui), Hunan, 1992; Hunansheng bowuguan, *Changsha Mawangdui yihao Hanmu* 長沙馬王堆一號漢墓 (Han tomb no. 1 from Mawangdui, Changsha), Wenwu, 1973. The important silk books found at Mawangdui are discussed in 19.1.3 and Chapter 36 (medical works).

Shang Sunjiazhai 上孫家寨, Datong 大通, Qinghai: mainly military administration documents. More than 300 *mujian*; excavated in 1978, *Wenwu* 1981.2.

Shuanggudui 雙古堆, Fuyang 阜陽, Anhui. Former Han tomb (165 BC) discovered in 1977. More than 6,000 *zhujian mudu* containing several classics, the texts of which differ significantly from the transmitted texts, including the *Shijing*, the *Yijing*, and the *Chuci*; an almanac; a manual on dogs; a text containing medicinal recipes; and fragments of one of the earliest character primers (the *Cang Jie pian* 倉頡篇, *Wen-*

wu 1983.2; *Jianbo yanjiu*, 2, 1996; see 1.3.2 for further references); and various medical texts; see *Wenwu* 1978.8, 1983.1, 1984.8, 1988.4, 1989.1. Hu Pingsheng 胡平生 and Han Ziqiang 韓自強, *Fuyang Hanjian Shijing yanjiu* 阜陽漢簡詩經研究 (Studies on the Fuyang bamboo strip *Shijing*), Shanghai guji, 1988.

Wanghou 王后, Changsha, Hunan: more than 100 wooden tomb tablets in the "Yuyang" 漁陽 grave.

Weiyanggong 未央宮, Chang'an, Shaanxi: 98 badly burned *mujian* containing medical recipes and descriptions of events (discovered 1980–89): see *Han Chang'an cheng Weiyanggong fajue baogao*, 1996, 238–48, for illustrations and transcriptions.

Yinqueshan 銀雀山, Linyi *xian* 臨沂縣, Shandong: Former Han tombs discovered in 1972. 4,942 *zhujian* in tomb 1 and 32 in tomb 2. One of the most important discoveries of *zhujian* in the twentieth century. Pre-Qin legal texts (27.2), a Han calendar, and portions of *Sunzi bingfa* 孫子兵法 (Sunzi: art of war), the previously lost *Sun Bin bingfa* 孫臏兵法 (Sun Bin: art of war) and other strategic works; see *Yinqueshan Hanmu zhujian* 銀雀山漢墓竹簡 (Silver Sparrow Mt. Han tomb bamboo strips), vol. 1, Wenwu, 1985; Wu Jiulong 吳九龍, *Yinqueshan Hanjian shiwen* 銀雀山漢簡釋文 (Transcriptions of the Han bamboo strips from Silver Sparrow Mt.), Wenwu, 1985. Portions of the *Yanzi chunqiu* 晏子春秋. Also an almanac dating from 174 BC found in tomb 2, *Wenwu* 1974.3.

Yinwan 尹灣 village, Lianyungang 連雲港 city, Jiangsu: Later Han tombs. 23 *mudu* and 133 *Hanjian* from the end of the Former Han from tomb 6 (the owner was Shi Rao 師饒, chief of the Labor Service section of the Donghai commandery 東海郡). The tablets are written on both sides (total more than 40,000 characters). They are the earliest extant traces of a commandery archive and contain details of the administration of Donghai in the last two decades BC. There are also almanacs and funerary texts; a silk funerary shawl, bronze vessels and objects, jade, and pottery. Tomb 2 contained one wooden tablet consisting of a clothes list (the owner was a woman who died somewhat later than Shi Rao). For photographs and transcriptions, excavation report, and maps, see *Yinwan Hanmu jiandu* 尹灣漢墓簡牘 (Wooden tablets and *Hanjian* from the Han tombs at Yinwan), Zhonghua, 1997; see also *Yinwan Hanmu jiandu zonglun* 尹灣漢墓簡牘總論 (Comprehensive studies of the wooden tablets and *Hanjian* from the Han tombs at Yinwan), Kexue, 1999; also *Wenwu* 1996.8, 10; 1997.1. Discovered and excavated in 1993.

Huxishan 虎溪山, Yuanling 沅陵 county, Changsha. Nearly 1,000 strips discovered from the tomb of Marquis Wu Yang 吳陽 of Yuanling (d. 162 BC). The tomb had not been robbed and many intact burial goods were found in it. Discovered in 1999. A nearby tomb is presumed to be that of his wife. The subject matter of the strips may be divided into three types: the earliest records of household head counts and land and labor taxes so far discovered; court recipes (also the earliest discovered); and divinatory texts. The population and tax statistics include some for the whole county. The recipes include instructions on how to prepare the food. Not yet published.

Zhangjiashan 張家山, Jiangling 江陵, Hubei: Former Han tombs. About 1,000 *zhujian*, plus nine *mudu*. Early Han legal texts (tomb 247); two almanacs; medical and mathematical texts (discovered in 1983–84; *Wenwu* 1985.1). Transcriptions and studies of the medical works (on the pulse and on breathing exercises) have been published; Gao Da-lun 高大倫, 1992 and 1995 (see Chapter 36). One of the legal texts is the *Zouyanshu* 奏言書 (Casebooks), which includes two cases from the Spring and Autumn period (*Wenwu* 1993.8, 1995.3; see 27.3 on Han law). The mathematical work (*Suanshu shu* 算術書) is the oldest yet found. It predates the previous earliest known mathematical text, the *Jiuzhang suanshu* 九章算術 (37.1) by about 200 years. It covers many different types of computation couched in the form of practical examples. The total length is 7,000 characters on 180 strips. Publication of this text and about 500 *jian* of the Former Han code (*Hanlü* 漢律) along with the other finds from Zhangjiashan is scheduled for publication in 2000.

44.4.3   *Han* Jiandu 漢簡牘 *Border Documents*

The four commanderies established by Han Wudi in 115–11 BC in the Hexi corridor in what is today the province of Gansu were at Dunhuang 敦煌 (the westernmost), Jiuquan 酒泉, Zhangye 張掖, and Wuwei 武威. Their northern flank was protected by a line of frontier walls armed with guardhouses and post stations. Most *Hanjian* 漢簡 have been discovered here.

Finds of single *Hanjian* in Juyan 居延 (a border county in Zhangye) were reported in the Northern Zhou and again in the Northern Song. The first modern finds of *Hanjian* (dating from the Wei and the Jin) were made at Niya 尼雅 near the ancient buried city of Loulan 樓蘭 (in modern Xinjiang) by the discoverer of the city, the Swedish explorer Sven Hedin in 1899 and 1901 and a few years later by Mark Aurel Stein and Ôtani.[16] The *Hanjian* are listed below under the four main places around and in which they have been found in the twentieth century: Dunhuang 敦煌, Juyan 居延 (or Edsingol), Wuwei 武威, and Loulan 樓蘭.

Dunhuang 敦煌, Gansu. The second largest finds of bamboo and wooden documents from the Han. A total of about 27,400 *muzhu jiandu* were discovered between 1907 and 1992 (some from beacon towers, *fengsui* 烽燧 and some from tombs). Those from Dunhuang itself deal mainly with border administration; the 397 Jiuquan *mudu* include official reports, laws, letters, almanacs, medical and divination texts, and the last testament of Han Wudi, which is not recorded in any other place. A further major find of more than 18,000 wooden tablets and strips was discovered at Xuanquan 懸泉, Dunhuang county, in 1990 and 1992. They include laws and regulations, divination and medical texts, and many documents on the Han postal system. Of the Dunhuang tablets, 2,484 (those discovered between 1907 and 1988) have been published in reproductions and transcribed. The most complete collection of the original materials is contained in *Dunhuang Hanjian* 敦煌漢簡 (Dunhuang *Hanjian*), Gansusheng wenkaosuo, ed., 2 vols., Zhonghua, 1990; vol. 1 contains photographs of 2,484 tablets and strips, and vol. 2 the transcriptions. See also *Dunhuang Hanjian shiwen* 敦煌漢簡釋文 (Transcriptions of Dunhuang *Hanjian*), Wu Rengxiang 吳礽驤 et al., eds., Gansu renmin, 1991, for annotated, punctuated transcriptions. Note Chen Zhi 陳直, *Dunhuang Hanjian pingyi* 敦煌漢簡評議 (A critical study of the Dunhuang *Hanjian*), Tianjin renmin, 1991. Rao Zongyi 饒宗頤, *Dunhuang Hanjian biannian kaozheng* 敦煌漢簡編年考證 (Studies on the chronology of the Dunhuang *Hanjian*), Xinwenfeng, 1995. The

---

[16] Édouard Chavannes, *Les Documents chinois découverts par Aurel Stein dans les sables du Turkestan oriental*, OUP, 1913. A translation with annotations of 991 documents, mainly on wood, brought back by Stein from his first and second expeditions (1906–8). Of the 991 documents and fragments, 720 date from 98 BC to AD 153; 229 are from the Jin and 40 from the Tang; Henri Maspero, *Les documents chinois de la troisième expédition de Sir Aurel Stein en Asie centrale*, British Museum, 1953. Tr. with annotations of 930 manuscripts mainly from Turpan (219 on wood and 711 on paper) from Stein's third expedition (1913–16). There are 84 manuscripts from Dunhuang; see Ôba Osamu 大庭脩, *Dai-Ei hakubutsukan zô Tonkô Kankan* 大英博物館藏敦煌漢簡 (Dunhuang Han bamboo strips in the British Museum), Dôhôsha, 1990.

Xuanquan tablets have not yet been published although some have been exhibited.[17]

Juyan 居延, Gansu and Inner Mongolia. The largest finds of bamboo and wooden documents from the Han. Altogether there are about 32,200 strips and wooden tablets covering the century and a half from 119 BC to AD 167. These documents are mainly from 160 scattered sites along the 350 km (218 miles) of the Han Juyan 居延 and Jianshui 肩水 border defense lines. They include reports of fines and expenses, laws and regulations, and a variety of other documents. The first large finds (10,100 jiandu) were made in 1930 and 1931 by the Sino-Swedish expedition led by Folke Bergman. The collection is housed in Taibei at the Shiyusuo.[18] The second, even larger finds in the Juyan area (19,637 muzhu jiandu) were made during excavations in 1973 and 1974 and sporadically thereafter.[19] They date from 128 BC

---

[17] Zhongguo wenwu jingcui 中國文物精粹 (Gems of China's Cultural Relics), 1997. Item 111 is a full-page photograph of a letter written on silk found at Xuanquan and dated to 32–37 BC. It contains 370 characters and is the longest and best-preserved private letter from the Han dynasty.

[18] Juyan Hanjian jiayi bian 居延漢簡甲乙編 (First and second collections of Han wooden strips from Juyan), Kaogusuo 考古所, ed., vol. 1, photographs; vol. 2, corrected transcriptions, Zhonghua, 1980. The most complete collection of original materials of the 1930s Juyan finds; based on earlier publications, notably those of Lao Gan 勞幹, Shiyusuo, 2 vols., 1957–60; vol. 1 (photographs), rpnt., 1992; vol. 2 (transcriptions and commentary), rpnt., 1997; a supplementary volume, Juyan Hanjian bubian 居延漢簡補編, 1998, contains 33 strips made readable using infrared photography, including Xia Nai's 1945 discovery of 7 mujian in Gansu. Xie Guihua 謝桂華 and Li Junming 李均明, Juyan Hanjian shiwen hejiao 居延漢簡釋文合校 (Collated transcriptions of Juyan documents on wood), 2 vols., Wenwu, 1987, contains corrected transcriptions of the old Juyan materials. For a pioneering study based on these documents, see Michael Loewe, Records of Han Administration; 2 vols., CUP, 1967.

Chen Zhi 陳直, Juyan Hanjian yanjiu 居延漢簡研究 (Researches on the Juyan Hanjian), Tianjin guji, 1986. For a thorough index to toponyms, contents, and research on the old Juyan documents as well as some of the new ones, see Kyoen Kankan sakuin 居延漢簡索引 (Index of Han wooden strips found at Juyan, 1930–31 and 1973–74), Ōba Osamu 大庭脩, ed., Kansai daigaku, 1995.

[19] Juyan xinjian 居延新簡 (New documents on wood from Juyan), Gansu Wenkaosuo, Gansu Provincial Museum, Chinese Culture Research Institute, and Lishisuo, eds., 2 vols., Zhonghua, 1994. This contains photographs and transcriptions of 7,000 Hanjian. Juyan xinjian: jiaqu houguan yu disi sui 居延新簡甲渠候官與第四燧 (New documents on wood from Jiaqu houguan, Juyan

Footnote continued on next page

to AD 32. There is a good introduction to the Juyan *Hanjian*: Xue Yingqun 薛英群, *Juyan Hanjian tonglun* 居延漢簡通論 (Survey of Han dynasty Juyan wooden documents), Gansu jiaoyu, 1991. It covers all the different finds at Juyan from Stein to the 1980s. See also Li Zhenhong 李振宏 and Sun Yingmin 孫英民 et al., *Juyan Hanjian renming biannian* 居延漢簡人名編年 (Personal names on the Juyan *Hanjian* arranged by year), Shehui kexue, 1997. This is a major effort to place in chronological order the Juyan *Hanjian* despite the fact that many of the strips have only partial dates or none at all.

Wuwei 武威, Gansu. There have been seven finds at Wuwei, coming to a total of 622 tablets and strips. Despite the smaller numbers, they are valuable because unlike the finds at Juyan and Dunhuang, they are either transmitted texts or rare medical works, not administrative documents. Four of the most important discoveries from sites at Wuwei were:

(i) Hantanpo 旱灘坡: 92 *mujiandu* discovered in 1972 (78 wooden strips; 14 wooden tablets). Mainly medical texts from the Later Han: *Wuwei handai yijian* 武威漢代醫簡 (Wooden medical documents from Wuwei), Wenwu, 1975. Grass and Han chancery script is used, with an even larger share of *tong jiazi* than usual for this period.

(ii) Mozuizi 磨嘴子: 469 *zhumujian* excavated in 1959 from tomb 6 (dating from the reign of Wang Mang 王莽, AD 9–23), including what had once been complete rolls of strips (total 370) with 20,000 characters of the *Yili* 儀禮 (Etiquette and rites). The text is slightly different from the transmitted version: *Kaogu* 1960.5, 8.

(iii) Mozuizi: finds include 10 strips recording two edicts relating to the rites due those attaining 70 years of age. Discovered in tomb 18 (Later Han) in 1959. *Wuwei Hanjian* 武威漢簡 (Wuwei *Hanjian*), Wenwu, 1964 (although it is not indicated, the principal author was Chen Mengjia 陳夢家).

(iv) Mozuizi: 26 *mujian* were found in 1981 from a Han tomb with the *Wang Zhang zhaoling ce* 王仗詔令冊 (contents similar to the previous item); see *Hanjian yanjiu wenji* 漢簡研究文集 (1984, 1988).

---

and the fourth beacon tower), Gansu Wenkaosuo et al., eds., 2 vols., Wenwu, 1990. Contains photographs to the original size (vol. 2) plus transcriptions (vol. 1) of the 8,409 *Hanjian* (mainly administrative documents) found between 1972 and 1982 at Jiaqu houguan (Juyan).

Loulan 樓蘭, Xinjiang: documents found by Hedin were translated by August Conrady;[20] documents found by Aurel Stein in Loulan in 1906–7 and 1914 were cataloged by Giles and by Ôba along with the Stein Dunhuang documents; in addition, 71 wooden documents dating from 49 to 8 BC were discovered at Loulan in 1930 and 1934 and a further 65 in 1980. They are mainly laws and a copy of the *Lunyu*. Most of the other documents were in other languages such as Turkish, Khotarian, Tibetan, Sanskrit and Karosthi. *Loulan jiandu wenshu jicheng* 樓蘭簡牘文書集成 (Collection of documents on wooden slats and paper from Loulan), Tiandi, 1998. Contains annotated transcriptions of 575 of the Loulan documents in Chinese. See also Lin Meicun 林梅村 and Li Junming 李均明, *Shulehe liuyu chutu Hanjian* 疏勒河流域出土漢簡 (Bamboo strips excavated from the area of Shulehe), Wenwu, 1984. Shulehe 疏勒河 (north of Dunhuang), Xinjiang was the sight of Stein's 1907 discovery 704 wooden slats.

44.5   Archaeology and Inscriptions

44.5.1   Archaeological Sites

The main archaeological sites of post-unification Qin and Han are as follows (detailed descriptions may be found in the *References* after this list):

Xianyang 咸陽 (capital of the first emperor of Qin, east of modern Xi'an).

Donghai xinggong 東海行宮 (Qin palace on the cliffs at modern Suizhong, Liaoning).

Museum of the Terracotta Army guarding the tomb of the first emperor (Qin Shihuang bingmayong bowuguan 秦始皇兵馬俑博物館 at Lintong, 35 km [22 miles] east of modern Xi'an). For research, see 28.1.

The city walls and site of the Former Han capital of Chang'an (just outside modern Xi'an).[21]

Later Han capital (at Luoyang).

---

[20] August Conrady, *Die chinesischen Handschriften und sonstigen Kleinfunde Sven Hedins in Lou-lan*, Stockholm: Generalstatens Litografiska Anstalt, 1920. The documents and fragments mainly date from the Jin.

[21] *Xi'an lishi dituji* 西安歷史地圖集 (Historical atlas of Xi'an), Shi Nianhai 史念海, ed. in chief, Xi'an ditu, 1996.

Baimasi 白馬寺 (White Horse Temple), Luoyang (first Buddhist temple to be established in China).

Sections of the Qin and Han Walls and guard posts and beacon towers extending into the Hexi 河西 corridor.

Non-Han archaeology (mainly artifacts from tombs in the north, northwest and southwest).

The Shaanxi History Museum (Shaanxi lishi bowuguan 陕西歷史博物館) has particularly fine collections.

Imperial Tombs of the Former Han (the 11 are scattered around modern Xi'an); the tomb of Jingdi 景帝 (188–41 BC) has been opened and turned into a museum. It contains the earliest female terracotta warriors so far discovered.

Imperial Tombs of the Later Han (the 12 are scattered around Luoyang).

Mawangdui 馬王堆, Changsha, Hunan: the three tombs of Li Cang 利蒼, the Marquis of Dai 軟 (d. 186 BC), Chancellor of the princedom of Changsha, his wife Xin Zhui 辛追 (d. ca. 168 BC), and probably their son; now in the Hunan Provincial Museum (44.4.2). The 2,100-year-old corpse of Xin Zhui is perfectly preserved with its viscera.

Tombs of Han princes and their wives (34 tombs from the Former Han; five from the Later Han).[22] Over two dozen jade burial suits (three of which are complete) have been unearthed from these tombs. Each suit was made of between several hundred and 5,000 plaques of jade. The plaques were stitched together with gold, silver, or bronze wires or with silk, depending on the rank of the deceased. In form the jade suits were not dissimilar to the early Chinese iron or leather armor worn by the living. They were intended to prevent decay and to protect the wearer in the afterlife. The tombs with the richest finds (and they are spectacular) are the four that were not robbed in the course of the past 2,000 years, namely:

1. Mancheng 滿城, Hebei: the tomb of Liu Sheng 劉勝 (d. 113 BC), Prince Jing of Zhongshan 中山靖王. Can be seen at the original site on a hilltop in Mancheng county. Liu's consort died sometime after her husband. Her tomb can also be seen at the same hilltop site.

---

[22] Huang Zhanyue 黃展岳, "Handai zhuhou wangmu lunshu" 漢代諸侯王墓論述 (On the tombs of princes and marquises of the Han dynasty), *Kaogu xuebao* 128: 11–34 (1998.1).

2. Nan Yue 南越, Guangzhou: tomb of Zhao Mei 趙眜 (also known as Zhao Hu 趙胡), 137–125 BC, the second king of Nan Yue (207–111 BC). His grandfather, Zhao Tuo 趙佗 (?–137 BC; Trieu Da in Vietnamese) was from Hebei. While head of the military forces of the Nanhai 南海 commandery, he had taken his opportunity during the confusion at the fall of the Qin to seize the principality of Ouluo 甌駱 (257–208 BC; Âu-Lac in Vietnamese) and declare himself emperor (*di* 帝) of Nan Yue (Nam Viêt, i.e., Vietnam). The territory extended over modern Guangdong, Guangxi, and North Vietnam. The capital was Panyu 番禺 (outside modern Guangzhou), the main port in the south already by the Qin. Excavations of the harbor and shipyard of Panyu have been made. The magnificent tomb is now in a special museum in Guangzhou: Xi Han Nan Yue wang mu bowuguan 西漢南越王墓博物館.

3. Shuangrushan 雙乳山, Changqing 長清 county, Shandong: the tomb of Liu Hu 劉胡 (d. 98 BC), or Liu Kuan 劉寬 (d. 87 BC), prince of Qibei 齊北; excavated 1995–96 (*Kaogu* 354: 1–15; 1997.3).

44.5.2   Archaeological References

Song Zhimin 宋治民, *Zhanguo Qin Han kaogu* 戰國秦漢考古 (The archaeology of the Warring States, Qin, and Han), Sichuan daxue, 1993. Contains references to the considerable number of reports and monographs on Qin and Han archaeology, including lesser-known ones.

Wang Xueli 王學理 et al., *Qin wuzhi wenhuashi* 秦物質文化史 (History of material culture during the Qin), San-Qin, 1994. Excellent introduction to Qin archaeology in the form of a copiously illustrated survey of Qin artifacts from the earliest times to the fall of the Qin in 206 BC. There is a chronology of the main discoveries and excavations of Qin sites from 1933 to 1992 (397–417). Also an extensive summary in English.

Wang Xueli 王學理, *Xianyang didu ji* 咸陽皇帝都城記 (Notes on the imperial capital Xianyang), San-Qin, 1999. This detailed history of Xianyang with many drawings and illustrations of artifacts amounts almost to a history of the rise of Qin as seen through the fortunes of its last capital.

Wang Zhongshu 王仲殊, *Han Civilization*, K. C. Chang, tr., YUP, 1982.

Handai wuzhi wenhua ziliao tushuo 漢代物質文化資料圖説 (Annotated illustrations on the material culture of the Han dynasty), Sun Ji 孫機, comp., Wenwu, 1991. Almost an illustrated dictionary of Han terminology arranged under 110 topics (transport, clothing, hairstyles, farming, mining, and so forth). Each topic is illustrated with between 5 and 20 line drawings traced from the originals (fully referenced). The notes quote from contemporary Han descriptions of the artifacts and also from the archaeological reports. Large numbers of crudely incised, broken tiles or bricks survive from the Han, especially from Yanshi, on the outskirts of Luoyang (Later Han). They provide a rare direct glimpse at the underside of Han rule.

A Journey into China's Antiquity, vol. 2, *Warring States–Northern and Southern Dynasties* (see 8.1 on this authoritative illustrated series).

The Land Within the Passes, Zou Zongxu, ed.; Susan Whitfield, tr. from Chinese original (1987), Penguin Viking, 1991.

Michèle Pirazzoli-t'Serstevens, *The Han Civilization of China*, Janet Seligman, tr. from the French original (1982), New York: Rizzoli, 1982.

There are a considerable number of works on Han stone reliefs (*huaxiangshi* 畫像石) found on tombs, shrines, and other monuments:

Jean M. James, *A Guide to the Tomb and Shrine Art of the Han Dynasty, 206 B.C.–A.D. 220*, Mellen, 1996.

Wu Hung (Wu Hong 巫鴻), *The Wu Liang Shrine: The Ideology of Early Chinese Pictorial Art*, SUP, 1989.

Édouard Chavannes, *La sculpture sur pierre en Chine au temps des deux dynasties Han*, Leroux, 1893.

Édouard Chavannes, *Mission archéologique en Chine septentrionale*, 4 vols., Leroux, 1910–15.

Zhongguo Handai huaxiangshi huaxiangzhuan wenxian mulu 中國漢代畫像石畫像磚文獻目錄 (Bibliography of works on Han dynasty stone and brick reliefs), Shenzhou bowuguan, eds., Wenwu, 1995. Covers books and articles written between 1900 and 1993.

44.5.3 Stone Inscriptions

Note that the earliest stone inscriptions of any length are from pre-imperial Qin (the stone-drum inscriptions). The fragments of the rock inscriptions, which the first emperor had inscribed, are also the earliest of this type to have survived (17.3).

Qindai taowen 秦代陶文 (Qin dynasty pottery script), Yuan Zhongyi 袁仲一, comp., San-Qin, 1987. Has 1,610 rubbings, which contain in all over 600 characters in rough forms of the Qin small seal script. Very few examples of Qin pottery script have survived from before 361 BC. The excavations of the ante-chambers of the tomb of the first emperor of Qin, however, turned up large quantities of pottery script, including names of corvée laborers who had worked on the tomb, funeral notices scratched onto tiles of those who had died during its construction, and numbers on the statues of warriors and horses to put them in their right places.

Gao Wen 高文, *Hanbei jishi* 漢碑集釋, Henan daxue, 1985, is a study of 59 Han stelae with transcriptions and notes on the authors.

Wang Qingzheng 汪慶正, *Dong Han shike wenzi zongshu* 東漢石刻文字綜述 (General description of the scripts carved on stone in the Later Han), *Shanghai bowuguan guankan*, 1. Collects materials of interest from stelae on economic, military and other topics.

Wu Tianying 吳天穎, "Handai maidi quan kao" 漢代買地券考 (A study of Han land deeds), *Kaogu xuebao*, 1982.1.

Patricia Buckley Ebrey, "Later Han stone inscriptions," *HJAS*, 40: 325–53 (1980).

Hans Bielenstein, "Later Han Inscriptions and Dynastic Biographies: A Historiographical Comparison," in *Proceedings of the International Conference on Sinology, on History and Archaeology*, Nan'gang: Academia Sinica, 1981, 571–86.

Han Wei Nan-Bei Chao muzhi jishi 漢魏南北朝墓誌集釋 (Han, Wei, and Nan-Bei Chao annotated transcriptions and originals of collected tomb tablets), Zhao Wanli 趙萬里, ed., Kexue, 1956; Tianjin guji, 1992.

44.6 Guides and Research Tools

44.6.1 Guides to Sources and Readers

The main Han bibliographical work is the "Yiwenzhi" 藝文志 in the *Hanshu* (9.4).

ECT. Early Chinese Texts: A Bibliographical Guide, Michael Loewe, ed., SSEC and IEAS, 1993. See 13.3.

NSECH. New Sources of Early Chinese History: An Introduction to the Reading of Inscriptions and Manuscripts, Edward L. Shaughnessy, ed., SSEC and IEAS, 1997. See chapters 15 and 16.

CHC, vol. 1, contains brief introductory essays on "The Written Sources and Their Problems," "Archaeology," and "Historical Scholarship," 2–14.

Zhongguo lishi da cidian 中國歷史大辭典 (The great encyclopaedia of Chinese history), 14 vols., Shanghai cishu, 1983– , contains a separate volume on *Qin Han shi* 秦漢史, 1990. See 8.4.2, item 2, for comments on this encyclopaedia.

A. F. P. Hulsewé, "Notes on the Historiography of the Han Period," in *HCJ*, 31–43.

For a shorter and more up-to-date introduction to primary (and secondary sources), see "Qin Han shi bufen" 秦漢史部分 (Section on Qin and Han history) in *Zhongguo gudaishi daodu* 中國古代史導讀 (A guide to reading ancient Chinese history), Xiao Li 肖黎 and Li Guihai 李桂海, gen. eds., Wenhui, 1991, 1992, 77–136.

The History of the Han Dynasty: Selections with a Preface, Kan Lao (Lao Gan 勞幹), ed., 2 vols., Princeton Univ., Chinese Linguistics Project, 1983. Contains annotated readings from Han primary sources with the Chinese texts in volume 2.

T'ung-tsu Ch'ü, *Han Social Structure*, Jack L. Dull, ed., UWP, 1972, arranges translated excerpts from Han primary sources by subject.

Cho-yun Hsü, *Han Agriculture*, Jack L. Dull, ed., UWP, 1980. The first part of the book discusses the topic. The second part (157–320) contains numerous translated excerpts from Han sources arranged by subject.

Clarence Martin Wilbur, *Slavery in China During the Former Han Dynasty*, Chicago: Field Museum of Natural History, *Anthropological Series* 34, 1943. After a thorough introduction to the subject, the author assembles excerpts from Han primary sources in the original and with translations.

Qin Han nongmin zhanzheng shiliao huibian 秦漢農民戰爭史料匯編 (28.3).

44.6.2 *Research Tools*

Different types of special-purpose reference works for Qin and Han history are introduced along with the main primary sources listed in 44.1. Note, too, special-purpose reference works for all of Chinese history, which are also useful for the Qin and Han, for example, on weights and measures (7.3). Below are given a handful of reference works specifically for the Qin and Han.

Biographies

Liang Han bulie zhuan renming yunbian 兩漢不列傳人名韵編 (Index by rhymes of people not included in the *liezhuan* chapters of the *Shiji*, *Hanshu*, and *Hou Hanshu*), Zhuang Dingyi 莊鼎彝, comp., Shangwu, 1935.

A Biographical Dictionary of the Qin, Former Han, and Xin Periods (221 BC–AD 29), Michael Loewe, comp., 2000, Brill. Includes over 6,000 entries.

Later Han Biographical Dictionary, Rafe de Crespigny, comp., forthcoming, Brill. To include some 5,000–6,000 entries.

Official Titles and Officeholders

In addition to *DOTIC*, check Rafe de Crespigny, *Official Titles of the Former Han Dynasty*, ANUP, 1967; and Homer H. Dubs and Rafe de Crespigny, *Official Titles of the Former Han Dynasty: An Index*, ANUP, 1969.

Hans Bielenstein, *The Bureaucracy of Han Times*, CUP, 1980.

Geography

Zhongguo lishi dituji 中國歷史地圖集, vol. 2, *Qin Han shiqi* 秦漢時期 (The Qin and Han periods); see 4.3.2 on this essential series.

Chronology

Zhongguo Xian-Qinshi libiao 中國先秦史曆表 (Calendrical concordance for pre-Qin history), Zhang Peiyu 張培瑜, comp., Qi-Lu, 1987.

Xi Zhou (Gonghe) zhi Xi Han lipu 西周 (共和) 至西漢曆譜, Xu Xiqi 徐錫祺, ed., 2 vols., Beijing kexue jishu, 1997. Preface by Zhang Peiyu.

Further details on these and other references on chronology and timekeeping are given in 5.6.

Indexes and Concordances

ICS Ancient Chinese Texts Concordance Series (for further details, see 9.10).

Bibliographies of Secondary Scholarship

Michael Loewe, "The History of the Early Empires," chapter 1 of Loewe, *Divination, Mythology and Monarchy in Han China*, CUP, 1994. An essay on the state of the field in Qin and Han history arranged by subject categories.

CHC, vol. 1, contains a bibliography of secondary as well as primary sources, 879–920.

Zhanguo Qin Han shi lunwen suoyin 戰國秦漢史論文索引 (for details, see 13.3, *Bibliographies*).

Zhanguo Qin Han shi lunzhu suoyin; xubian lunwen 1981–1990; zhuanzhu 1900–1990 戰國秦漢史論著索引續編論文 1981–1990; 專著 1900–1990 (a large-scale unannotated bibliography of Chinese twentieth-century scholarship on the Qin and Han; for details, see 13.2, *Bibliographies*).

Koga Noboru, "A Brief History of Ch'in and Han Studies in Japan," *AA* 58: 89–119 (1990).

Check also the bibliographies in one of the recent Japanese scholarly histories of China, for example Yamakawa Shuppansha 山川出版社, *Sekai rekishi taikei* 世界歷史大系 (World History Series).

Societies and Journals

The following are just some of the learned societies that publish newsletters and/or collected articles based on conferences.

Qin Han shi yanjiuhui 秦漢史研究會 (Qin, Han history society), Xi'an; founded in 1981.

Xian-Qinshi xuehui 先秦史學會 (Pre-Qin history society), Chengdu; founded in 1982.

The SSEC publishes the important journal *Early China* (13.2).

45

Wei, Jin, Nan-Bei Chao

220–581

Wei 魏, Jin 晉, Nan-Bei Chao 南北朝[1]	220–589
†*Sanguo* 三國 (three kingdoms)	220–280
Wei 魏 (commonly known as Cao Wei 曹魏)	220–265
Han 漢 (commonly known as Shu Han 蜀漢)	221–263
Wu 吳 (commonly known as Sun Wu 孫吳)	222–280
†Jin 晉	265–420
Western Jin 西晉	265–316
Eastern Jin 東晉	317–420
Six Dynasties 六朝[2]	222–589
Sixteen Kingdoms 十六國[3]	304–439
Nan-Bei Chao 南北朝	420–589
†Southern Dynasties 南朝	420–579
†Liu Song 劉宋	420–479
†Qi 齊	479–502

[1] Cao Wei came to be regarded as in the legitimate succession, not Shu Han or Sun Wu, hence the expression Wei, Jin, Nan-Bei Chao.

[2] The Six Dynasties (*Liuchao* 六朝) of the years 222–589 were Wu 吳, Dong Jin 東晉, and the four southern dynasties of Song 宋, Qi 齊, Liang 梁, and Chen 陳. They were grouped together because they all had their capitals in the south at Jiankang 建康 (Nanjing). They are sometimes called the southern Six Dynasties to distinguish them from another definition of the term, the northern Six Dynasties (Wei, Xi Jin, Hou Wei, Bei Qi, Bei Zhou, and Sui). Occasionally, too, the whole period of Wei, Jin, Nan-Bei Chao is also called the Six Dynasties.

[3] Conventional term for the sixteen states established over most of north China and Sichuan between 304 and 439, of which five were Xianbei 鮮卑; three Han 漢; three Xiongnu 匈奴; two Di 氐, and one each Qiang 羌, Jie 羯, and Badi 巴氐. Collectively the non-Han peoples who ruled in the north at this time were known as the "five barbarians" (*wuhu* 五胡). They were not counted in the legitimate succession of dynasties (*zhengtong* 正統), on which see 20.3.

†Liang 梁	502–557
†Chen 陳	557–589
†Northern Dynasties 北朝[4]	386–581
†Northern Wei 北魏[5]	386–534
Eastern Wei 東魏	534–550
Western Wei 西魏	535–556
†Northern Qi 北齊	550–577
†Northern Zhou 北周	557–581

† indicates those dynasties for which a Standard History was compiled.

Few historical sources other than the 11 Standard Histories have survived, which makes gives them added importance (45.1).

This was a period in which the annotation of texts, biography, and geography flourished. Buddhist and Daoist works became widespread, and collected works became an established form.

The discovery in 1996 of documents written on 90,000 bamboo strips dating from the third century marks an important new source for the period (45.3).

45.1   Main Historical Works

Many of the 11 Standard Histories listed below either have incomplete monographs or none at all. Qing scholars did much to make up this gap. Many of their corrections and additions are published in *Ershiwushi bubian* and *Ershisishi dingbian* (22.2).

Works written by a private individual are indicated with a single asterisk. Those officially commissioned from one or two individuals are shown with double asterisks. Finally, those written by official historians are indicated with triple asterisks. In addition to the Standard Histories listed below, use also the *Hou Hanshu* (44.1) and the *Hou Hanji* (44.2) for the beginning of the period and the *Suishu* (46.1) for the end. Use the Zhonghua punctuated editions.

---

[4] The founders and rulers of the Northern Dynasties were all Xianbei 鮮卑 (a non-Han people), with the exception of the Northern Qi whose ruling house was founded by a Han from Bohai 渤海. Another convention is to date the Northern Dynasties to the years 439–581 (from the Wei unification of north China to the establishment of the Sui dynasty).

[5] Also called Tuoba Wei 拓拔魏.

Sanguozhi 三國志* (Records of the Three Kingdoms), Chen Shou 陳壽 (233–97), comp., 285–97.[6]

> *Sanguozhi ji Pei zhu zonghe yinde* 三國志及裴注綜合引得 (Combined indices to the Standard History of the *Sanguozhi* and the notes of Pei Songzhi), *H-Y Index* 33. Indexes proper names, offices, titles, technical terms, and titles of works in the standard commentary. Note the preface by Hong Ye 洪業.

> *Sanguozhi diming suoyin* 三國志地名索引 (Index of geographical names in the *Sanguozhi*), Wang Tianliang 王天良 ed., Zhonghua, 1980.

> Rafe de Crespigny, *The Records of the Three Kingdoms: A Study in the Historiography of the San Kuo Chih*, ANUP, 1970.

Jinshu 晉書*** (Standard History of the Jin), Fang Xuanling 房玄齡 (578–648) et al., comps., 644; covers the years 265–419.

> *Jinshu renming suoyin* 晉書人名索引 (Personal-name index to the *Jinshu*), Zhang Chenshi 張忱石, ed., Zhonghua, 1977. Indexes the biographies in the Zhonghua punctuated edition.

> Lien-sheng Yang, "Notes on the Economic History of the Chin Dynasty," *HJAS* 8: 107–85 (1945–47), rpnt. in *Studies in Chinese Institutional History*, HUP, 1963, 119–97. Includes a translation of the "Shihuozhi" of the *Jinshu*, 137–97.

Southern Kingdoms

Songshu 宋書** (History of the Song), Shen Yue 沈約 (441–513), comp., 492–93; covers the years 420–78.

Nan Qishu 南齊書* (History of the Southern Qi), Xiao Zixian 蕭子顯 (489–537); covers the years 479–502.

Liangshu 梁書** (History of the Liang), Yao Cha 姚察 (533–606) and Yao Silian 姚思廉 (d. 637), comp., 628–35; covers the years 502–56.

---

[6] *Sanguozhi* (History of the Three Kingdoms), 5 vols., Zhonghua, 1962. The *Sanguozhi jizhuyi* 三國志集注譯 (Annotated and translated *Sanguozhi*), Fang Beichen 方北辰, 3 vols., Shanxi renmin, 1996, includes a newly punctuated original text as well as correcting many mistakes in the Zhonghua edition and in the notes of Pei Songzhi 裴松之 (372–451), *Sanguozhi jijie* 三國志集解, Lu Bi 盧弼, ed., Shanghai guji, 1957.

Chenshu 陳書** (History of the Chen), Yao Cha 姚察 (533–606) and Yao Silian 姚思廉 (d. 637), comp., 622–29; covers the years 557–89.

Nanshi 南史* (History of the Southern Dynasties), Li Yanshou 李延壽 (fl. 618–76), comp., 630–50; covers the years 420–589.

> *Nanchao wushi renming suoyin* 南朝五史人名索引 (Personal-name index to the five Standard Histories of the Southern Kingdoms), Zhang Chenshi 張忱石, comp., 2 vols., Zhonghua, 1985. Indexes the biographies in the Zhonghua punctuated editions of the *Song-shu*, *Nan Qishu*, *Liangshu*, *Chenshu*, and the *Nanshi*.

Northern Kingdoms

Weishu 魏書** (History of the Wei), Wei Shou 魏收 (506–72), comp., 551–54; covers the years 386–550.

Bei Qishu 北齊書** (History of the Northern Qi), Li Delin 李德林 (530–90) and Li Boyao 李百藥 (565–648), comp., 627–36; covers the years 550–77.

Zhoushu 周書*** (History of the Zhou), Linghu Defen 令狐德棻 (583–661), comp., ca. 629; covers the years 557–581.

Beishi 北史* (History of the Northern Dynasties), Li Yanshou 李延壽 (fl. 618–76), comp., 630–50; covers the years 368–618.

> *Beichao sishi renming suoyin* 北朝四史人名索引 (Personal-name index to the four Standard Histories of the Northern Kingdoms), Zhang Zhong'an 張仲安 et al., eds., Zhonghua, 1988. Indexes the biographies in the Zhonghua punctuated editions of the *Weishu*, *Bei Qishu*, *Zhoushu*, and *Beishi*.

On the composition of the above 11 Standard Histories (as well as the *Suishu* 隋書), see William Hung, "The T'ang *Kuo-shih kuan* Before 708," *HJAS* 23: 93–107 (1960–61); L. S. Yang, "The Official History of the Chin Period," in Yang (1963), 119–24; J. R. Ware, "Notes on the History of the *Wei shu*," *JAOS* 52: 33–45 (1932).

> *Jiuchao lü kao* 九朝律考 (27.3).

Translations

For earlier translations into Western languages from these Standard Histories, see Hans H. Frankel, *Catalogue of Translations from the Chinese Dynastic Histories for the Period 220–960*, UCP, 1957; rpnt.,

Greenwood, 1974. There have been a considerable number of translations since this catalog was compiled (see 41.4, note 17).

Hans Bielenstein has compiled an annalistic history based on the Standard Histories: "The Six Dynasties, Vol. I," *BMFEA* 68 (1996); Vol. II, *BMFEA* 69 (1997).

45.2   Other Textual Sources

Wudai shizhi 五代史志 (compiled in the Tang as the monograph section of the *Suishu*).

Tongdian 通典 (25.2).

Zizhi tongjian 資治通鑑 (21.3). Many of the chapters covering the Later Han, Wei, Jin, and Nan-Bei Chao have been translated into English, notably chapters 54 to 59 in *Emperor Huan and Emperor Ling, Being the Chronicle of Later Han for the Years 157-189 AD*, Rafe de Crespigny, tr. and annotated, vol. 1, *Text*; vol. 2, *Notes*, Faculty of Asian Studies, ANU, 1989; chapters 59-69 in *To Establish Peace, Being the Chronicle of Later Han for the Years 189-220 AD*, Rafe de Crespigny, tr. and annotated, 2 vols., ANU, 1997; and chapters 69-78 in *The Chronicles of the Three Kingdoms (220-265)*, Achilles Fang, tr. and annotated, 2 vols., HUP, 1952 and 1965. Fang's annotated translation is particularly useful in that the focus is on Sima Guang's sources for this period, thus providing a detailed view of his method of compilation.

Weilüe 魏略 (Brief history of Wei), Yu Huan 魚豢 (third century), privately written in Standard History form.

Huayang guozhi 華陽國志, Chang Qu 常璩 (fl. 265-316), early gazetteerlike history cum topography of Sichuan; the Ba-Shu edition (1984) is punctuated and indexed. *ICS Concordance* 24.

Shiliuguo chunqiu 十六國春秋, Cui Hong 崔鴻, Northern Wei, is based on historical works of the 16 kingdoms.

Jiankang shilu 建康實錄, Xu Song 許嵩, Tang, has details on Jiankang (Nanjing). The Shanghai guji (1987) edition is punctuated.

Shuijingzhu 水經注 (4.4.1).

Wenxuan 文選 (30.1).

Quan shanggu Sandai Qin Han Sanguo Liuchao wen 全上古三代秦漢三國六朝文 (30.1).

Shishuo xinyu 世說新語 (A new account of tales of the world), comp. under the aegis of Liu Yiqing 劉義慶 (403-44). Contains anecdotes about personalities and society, AD 150–420. Also important for recording the contemporary language. English translation: *A New Account of Tales of the World*, Richard B. Mather, tr., Univ. of Minnesota Press, 1976. Note *Shishuo xinyu yizhu* 世說新語譯注 (Shishuo xinyu with annotations and translation into modern Chinese), Zhang Wanqi 張萬起 and Liu Shangci 劉尚慈, eds., Zhonghua, 1998; and *Shishuo xinyu cidian* 世說新語詞典 (Dictionary of *Shishuo xinyu*), Zhang Wanqi, comp., Shangwu, 1993; rpnt., 1998.

Luoyang qielan ji 洛陽伽藍記 (Record of the monasteries of Luoyang), Yang Xuanzhi 楊衒之 (?–555), AD 530; Zhou Zumo 周祖謨 (1914–95), collated and annotated, Kexue, 1958; rev. edition, Zhonghua, 1985. ICS *Concordance* 16, forthcoming. *Qielan* 伽藍 is an abbreviation of the loan-word *sengqie lanmo* 僧伽藍摩 (Sanskrit *sangharama*, Buddhist grove or monastery). More than the title suggests; the earliest substantial account of a Chinese city to survive (in this case, Luoyang, the capital of the Northern Wei). *Memories of Loyang*, tr. with introduction by William Jenner, OUP, 1983. Contains a major study of the short-lived capital (1–138). See also, *A Record of Buddhist Monasteries in Lo-yang*, Yi-t'ung Wang, tr., PUP, 1984; Ho Ping-ti, 1966 (4.7.2).

Qimin yaoshu 齊民要術 (35.1).

Yanshi jiaxun 顏氏家訓 (3.5).

Xian-Qin Han Wei Jin Nan-Bei Chao shi 先秦漢魏晉南北朝詩 (30.2).

Sanguo huiyao 三國會要 and *Gaoben Jin huiyao* 稿本晉會要 are more useful than the *huiyao* for the Southern Dynasties compiled in the late Qing (25.1).

Chuxue ji 初學記 (31.1).

Taiping yulan 太平御覽 (31.1).

Yiwen leiju 藝文類聚 (31.1).

Beitang shuchao 北堂書鈔 (31.1).

Wei Jin Nan-Bei Chao nongmin zhanzheng shiliao huibian 魏晉南北朝農民戰爭史料彙編 (28.3).

45.3 Documents on Bamboo and Wood

A spectacular cache from the kingdom of Wu 吳 (220–80) was discovered at a construction site at Zoumalou 走馬樓, Changsha, in 1996 (*Wenwu* 1999.5; 1999.9). The documents date from 220 to 237. They were probably part of the Changsha commandery archive.

They total more than the number of all previously known *jiandu*. The find includes 2,480 large wooden tablets half a meter in length each with 100 to 160 characters and an estimated 90,000 bamboo strips, each with about 20 characters. Altogether, they contain an estimated total of about 1.5 million legible characters (twice as long as the Standard History of Wu and longer than the *Sanguozhi*). Photographs and transcriptions of the wooden tablets have been published: *Changsha Zoumalou Sanguo Wu jian: Jiahe limin tianjia bie* 長沙走馬樓三國吳簡嘉禾吏民田家莂.[7] The tablets and strips contain records of land and household taxes, and receipts for many other types of tax, rental, legal, and administrative records and official correspondence, and private letters. The bamboo strips are mainly population registers (*huji* 戶籍). The documents were stored in what appears to be an underground grain silo. They survived because water seeped in. It will take many years to sort them. One of the main difficulties is that the tens of thousands of population strips have become out of sequence. Originally each family's register was tied together in a bundle with the family name only on the strip of the head of the household. In the course of time, the strings holding the strips together rotted so it is extremely difficult to establish where the separate strips recording other family members (including wives and children) belong.

Almost the last documents to be written on bamboo and wood date from the Wei and Jin and were first found in small numbers in modern times in Xinjiang at Loulan (44.4.3). Note that *Tulufan chutu wenshu* 吐魯番出土文書 (46.3.1), vols. 2 and 3, contain a considerable number of documents on wood from the Northern Wei.

45.4 Archaeology and Inscriptions

The archaeological record, although not yet as rich as that of the Qin and Han, is nevertheless an essential adjunct to make up for the paucity of historical sources. For an introduction, see Luo Zong-

---

[7] *Changsha Zoumalou Sanguo Wu jian: Jiahe limin tianjia bie* (Wooden tablets from the Three Kingdoms state of Wu found at Zoumalou, Changsha: Jiahe reign period official copies of tallies), Changsha Wenkaosuo, Wenwu yanjiusuo, and Beijing daxue Lishixi, Wenwu, 2 vols., 1999. Vol. 1 contains photographs of the wooden tallies; vol. 2, the transcriptions.

zhen 羅宗真, *Liuchao kaogu* 六朝考古 (Archaeology of the Six Dynasties), Nanjing daxue, 1994.

Archaeological Sites

Traces of the capital cities of the kingdoms of Wei (Yecheng 鄴城), Jin (Luoyang 洛陽), and Wu (Wuchang 武昌) have been excavated at modern Linzhangxian 臨漳縣 (Hebei), Luoyang, and Echengxian 鄂城縣 (Hubei). No trace remains of the Six Dynasties capital of Jianye 建鄴 (Nanjing).

Many tombs of the Three Kingdoms, Jin, and Nan-Bei Chao have been excavated.

The capital of the Xiongnu kingdom of Xiaguo 夏國 or Da-Xia 大夏 (407–31) was called Tongwancheng 統萬城. It has been excavated at modern Jingbianxian 靖邊縣 (Shaanxi).

All three of the great Buddhist cliff grotto carvings began in this period: Mogaoku 莫高窟 (also known as Qianfodong 千佛洞 at Dunhuang, modern Gansu province); Yungang *shiku* 雲岡石窟 (Datong, modern Shanxi), and Longmen *shiku* 龍門石窟 (Luoyang, modern Henan). The carving continued for a thousand years.

A project is underway to publish reproductions of all the Dunhuang paintings: *Dunhuang shiku quanji* 敦煌石窟全集 (The complete collection of the Dunhuang grottoes), Dunhuang yanjiusuo, ed., 28 vols., HK: Shangwu, 1999-2002. There are also many reproductions of selected paintings from Dunhuang. Outstanding is *Caves of the Singing Sands: Dunhuang, Buddhist Art from the Silk Road*, text: Roderick Whitfield; photography: Seigo Otsuka, 2 vols., Textile and Art Publications, 1996.

Buddhist stone figurines from the site of the central Shandong temple of Longxing 龍興 at Qingzhou 青州. About 400 were excavated in 1996 in excellent condition (the original paint and applied gold is still on some of them). They date from the Northern Wei to the Northern Song (529–1026); see *Masterpieces of Buddhist Statuary from Qingzhou City*, Su Bai 徐白, ed. in chief, National Museum of Chinese History, 1999; *CAAD* 3.1: 5-54 (1999). The Longxing temple was visited by Ennin 圓仁 in the ninth century (42.2).

Illustrations

A Journey into China's Antiquity, vol. 2, *Warring States–Northern and Southern Dynasties* (see 8.1 on this authoritative illustrated series).

Stone Inscriptions

Han Wei Nan-Bei Chao muzhi jishi 漢魏南北朝墓誌集釋 (Annotated transcriptions and originals of collected tomb tablets from the Han, Wei, and Nan-Bei Chao), Zhao Wanli 趙萬里, ed., 6 vols., Kexue, 1953–56; Tianjin guji, 1992.

Beichao muzhi yinghua 北朝墓誌英華 (The best of the tomb tablets of the Northern Dynasties), Zhang Boling 張伯齡, ed., San-Qin, 1988.

Liuchao muzhi jianyao 六朝墓誌檢要 (Index to tomb tablets of the Six Dynasties), Wang Zhuanghong 王壯弘 and Ma Chengming 馬成名, comps., Shanghai shuhua, 1985; index with abbreviated summaries of about 1,800 tomb tablets from the Later Han to the Sui.

45.5 Guides and Research Tools

45.5.1 Guides to Sources

Sangokushi kenkyû yôran 三國志研究要覽 (Manual of research on the Three Kingdoms), Nakabayashi Shirô 中林史郎 and Watanabe Yoshihiro 渡邊義浩, eds., Tokyo: Jinbutsu ôraisha 人物未來社, 1996, contains an introduction on doing research on the Three Kingdoms as well as a bibliography of over 5,000 items of Japanese and Chinese secondary scholarship.

Zhongguo lishi da cidian 中國歷史大辭典 (The great encyclopaedia of Chinese history), 14 vols., Shanghai cishu, 1983– , contains a separate volume entitled *Wei Jin Nan-Bei Chao shi* 魏晉南北朝史, 1997. See 8.4.2, item 2 for comments on this encyclopaedia.

Zhu Dawei 朱大渭 et al., *Wei Jin Nan-Bei Chao shehui shenghuoshi* 魏晉南北朝社會生活史 (A history of social life in the Wei, Jin, and Nan-Bei Chao periods), Shehui kexue, 1998. Contains much fascinating material, with references indicated, on housing, clothing, food and drink, travel, marriage and burials, religion and ghosts, festivals, music and dance, education, medicine, and the customs of non-Han peoples in this period.

45.5.2 Research Tools

In addition to the indexes and other research tools listed under individual works above, note the following:

Bibliography

Bibliography in CHC, vol. 2.

Wei Jin Nan-Bei Chao shi lunwen suoyin 魏晉南北朝史論文索引 (上, 中, 下), Wuhan tushuguan, 1982. Includes Japanese scholarship.

Geography

Zhongguo lishi dituji 中國歷史地圖集, vol. 3, *San Guo Xi Jin shiqi* 三國西晉時期 (The Three Kingdoms and Western Jin); vol. 4, *Dong Jin Shiliuguo Nan-Bei Chao shiqi* 東晉十六國南北朝時期 (Eastern Jin, Sixteen Kingdoms, and Nan-Bei Chao); see 4.3.2 on this essential series.

Societies and Journals

Wei Jin Nan-Bei Chao shi xuehui 魏晉南北朝史學會 (Wei, Jin, and Nan-Bei Chao history society) founded in 1984; the headquarters is at the Lishisuo.

Early Medieval China (1994– , irreg. annual). All aspects of Han to Tang with special emphasis on the Six Dynasties period (see 10.4.4 for previous titles.

Beichao yanjiu 北朝研究 (1991– , quarterly), Pingcheng Beichao yanjiuhui 平城北朝研究會 (Taiyuan Northern Dynasty history society), ed., Taiyuan.

46

Sui, Tang, and Five Dynasties

581–979

Sui 隋[1]	581–618
Tang 唐	618–907
Wudai Shiguo 五代十國	902–79
Five Dynasties 五代[2]	907–60
Ten Kingdoms 十國[3]	902–79

The official writing of history came of age in the Tang (21.2), which also saw the first major work on historiography (*Shitong* 史通, 20.3). Legal and institutional sources compiled at central government agencies have survived intact, notably the *Tanglü* and the *Tang liudian* (Chapter 27). Thanks to the preservation of the documents at Dunhuang and Turpan, there is also a rich collection of religious works and popular literature. Among these are preserved a considerable number of documents drafted at distant outposts of the em-

---

[1] The founder of the Sui 隋, Yang Jian 楊監 (541–604) used his previous title (prince of Sui, Sui wang 隨王) to name the new dynasty. It is not known why the scribes used a variant character (Sui 隋 instead of Sui 隨). Later sources suggest the emperor felt the character was inauspicious because it contains *chuo* 辶. They do not explain why he preferred Sui 隋 (its basic meaning is leftover sacrificial meat).

[2] The Five Dynasties were Later Liang 後梁 (907–23), Later Tang 後唐 (Shatuo 沙陀, a Turkic people, 923–36), Later Jin 後晉 (Shatuo, 936–46), Later Han 後漢 (Shatuo, 947–50), and Later Zhou 後周 (951–60).

[3] The Ten Kingdoms were Wu 吳 (902–37), Southern Tang 南唐 (937–75), Wu-Yue 吳越 (907–78), Chu 楚 (907–51), Min 閩 (909–45), Southern Han 南漢 (917–71), Former Shu 前蜀 (903–25), Later Shu 後蜀 (933–65), Jingnan 荊南 (924–63), and Northern Han 北漢 (Shatuo 沙陀, 951–79). Most were conquered by the Song.

pire. Most are documents of local government, but some are of private individuals or of temples. Interesting in themselves, they also provide a means of checking the extent and the manner in which centrally drafted laws and regulations were carried out at the periphery (46.3). The widespread use of paper encouraged individual authors to gather their collected works together. Not surprisingly, more Tang *bieji* are extant than for all of the preceding dynasties put together. Several geographical works are also extant as well as the beginnings of local gazetteers. The Tang is rich in stone inscriptions (at least 6,000 are known to have survived, 46.4.2).

46.1   Main Historical Works

For the sake of convenience of presentation, the Standard Histories are listed first. As was made clear in Chapter 22, they are comprehensive summaries, compiled much after the event from many sources, which may themselves be just as important and often more detailed.

46.1.1   Sui and Tang

Suishu 隋書 (Standard History of the Sui), Wei Zheng 魏徵 (580–643) et al., comps., 629–36; 3 vols., Zhonghua, 1973. Covers the years 581–617.

> *Suishu renming suoyin* 隋書人名索引 (Personal-name index to the *Suishu*), Deng Jingyuan 鄧經元, comp., Zhonghua, 1979.

> Etienne Balazs, "Le Traité économique du *Souei-chou*," *TP* 42.3 and 4 (1953). Translation with notes and introduction of the *Suishu* "Shihuozhi."

> Etienne Balazs, *Le Traité juridique du "Souei-chou,"* Brill, 1954. Annotated translation with introduction to the *Suishu* "Xingfazhi."

Jiu Tangshu 舊唐書 (Old Standard History of the Tang), Liu Xu 劉昫 (887–946) et al., comps., 940–45; 16 vols., Zhonghua, 1975. Covers the years 618–906.

> On the compilation of the *Jiu Tangshu*, see Denis C. Twitchett, *The Writing of Official History Under the T'ang*, CUP, 1992.

> Denis Twitchett, "The Derivation of the Text of the *Shih-huo-chih* of the *Chiu T'ang-shu*," *JOS* 3: 48–62 (1956).

Denis Twitchett, *Financial Administration Under the T'ang Dynasty*, 1963; 2nd rev. edition, CUP, 1970. Introductory matter to (unpublished) translation of the monograph on financial administration in the *Jiu Tangshu*.

Hans H. Frankel, "T'ang Literati: A Composite Biography," in *Confucian Personalities*, Arthur Wright and Denis Twitchett, eds., SUP, 1962, 65-83. A study of the biographical sketches in the "Garden of Letters" (*wenyuan* 文苑) category of the *liezhuan* in the *Jiu Tangshu* (*juan* 190).

Sun Ji 孫機, "Liang Tangshu yu (che) fu zhi jiaoshi gao" 兩唐書與 (車)服志校釋稿 (Draft collated and annotated monographs on carriages and dress of the two *Tangshu*) in *Zhongguo gu yufu luncong* 中國古典服論叢 (Collected papers on ancient Chinese carriages and dress), Wenwu, 1993, 231-365. Illustrated.

Xin Tangshu 新唐書 (New Standard History of the Tang), Ouyang Xiu 歐陽修 (1007-72), Song Qi 宋祁 (998-1061) et al., comps., 1043-60; 10 vols., Zhonghua, 1975. Covers the years 618-906.[4]

Xin-Jiu Tangshu renming suoyin 新舊唐書人名索引 (Personal-name index to the *Xin-Jiu Tangshu*), Zhang Wanqi 張萬起, comp., 3 vols., Shanghai guji, 1986. Index to the Zhonghua edition.

Xin Tangshu zaixiang shixibiao yinde 新唐書宰相世繫表引得 (Index to the genealogical tables of families of chief ministers in the *Xin Tangshu*), H-Y Index 16.

Karl Bünger, *Quellen zur Rechtsgeschichte der T'ang-zeit*, MS Monograph 9, Beijing, 1946; new edition, Steyler, 1996. Annotated translation of the fifth and sixth of the monographs on law, those in the *Jiu Tangshu* (*juan* 50) and *Xin Tangshu* (*juan* 56). Also includes the sections on law in *Tang huiyao* (*juan* 39-40). Original texts included. The 1996 edition contains an introduction by Denis Twitchett and a bibliography on Chinese law.

Etienne Balazs, "Beiträge zur Wirtschaftsgeschichte der T'ang Zeit, 618-906," in *Mitteilungen des Seminars für orientalische Sprachen*

---

[4] The *Jiu Tangshu* is more reliable than the *Xin Tangshu*. The *XTS* has tables and better monographs, but much of the rest of the work was rewritten and contains many errors. For a comparison of the *Jiu* with the *Xin Tangshu*, see des Rotours (1932), 56-71; Twitchett and Goodman, 1986, 32-35 (46.5.1). On the author of the *XTS*, see James T. C. Liu, *Ou-yang Hsiu, an Eleventh-Century Neo-Confucianist*, SUP, 1967.

34: 1–92 (1931); 35: 1–73 (1932); 36: 1–62 (1933). Analytic study of the Tang economy based on the "Shihuozhi" of both the *Jiu Tangshu* and the *Xin Tangshu*.

Robert des Rotours (1891–1980), *Le Traité des examens*, Leroux, 1932; rpnt., CMC, 1976. Annotated translation of the monograph on the examination system in the *Xin Tangshu* (*juan* 44 and 45).

Robert des Rotours, *Traité des fonctionnaires et traité de l'armée*, 2 vols., Brill, 1947–48; rpnt., CMC, 1974. Annotated translation of the monographs on official posts and the army in the *Xin Tangshu* (*juan* 46–50).

Tangshu bingzhi jianzheng 唐書兵志箋正 (Annotations and corrections to the monograph on the army in the *Xin Tangshu*), Tang Changru 唐長孺 (1911–94), Kexue, 1957; new edition, Zhonghua, 1962.

Hiraoka Takeo 平岡武夫, *Tôdai no gyôsei chiri* 唐代の行政地理 (Tang dynasty administrative geography), vol. 2 of *T'ang Civilization Reference Series*, Jinbun, 1954. Indexes the monographs on administrative geography in both the *Jiu* and *Xin Tangshu*; Chinese translation, *Tangdai de xingzheng dili* 唐代的行政地理, Shanghai guji, 1989.

Zizhi tongjian 資治通鑑 is the single most important source for Sui, Tang, and Wudai Shiguo 五代十國 history (21.3).

Tanglü shuyi 唐律疏議 (The Tang Code with commentaries). The first Chinese penal code to survive and of immense importance for both the Tang and later Chinese codes as well as those of China's neighbors, including Japan (27.4).

Tang liudian 唐六典 (27.4)

Tongdian 通典 (25.2)

Tang huiyao 唐會要 (25.1)[5]

Wudai huiyao 五代會要 (25.1)

Cefu yuangui 冊府元龜 contains many Tang documents (31.1)

---

[5] *Tang huiyao renming suoyin* 唐會要人名索引 (Name index to the *Tang huiyao*), Zhang Chenshi 張忱石, ed. in chief, Zhonghua, 1991.

46.1.2   *Wudai Shiguo* 五代十國

The Five Dynasties (and Ten Kingdoms) lasted just 77 years, during which there was much fighting between the many kingdoms and regimes. Few historical sources have survived. Those that do were written in the Song or preserved in Song sources (Chapter 47). There is a good brief introduction to the primary sources for the Five Dynasties in Chikusa Masaaki 竺沙雅章, "Five Dynasties and the Song."[6]

Jiu Wudaishi 舊五代史 (Old Standard History of the Five Dynasties), Xue Juzheng 薛居正 (912–81), 6 vols., Zhonghua, 1976. Covers the years 907–60.

> Wang Gungwu, "The *Chiu Wu-tai Shih* and History-Writing During the Five Dynasties," *AM* 6.1: 1–22 (1957), and on the period in general, the same author's *The Structure of Power in North China During the Five Dynasties*, Kuala Lumpur: Univ. of Malaya Press, 1963.

Xin Wudaishi 新五代史 (New Standard History of the Five Dynasties), Ouyang Xiu 歐陽修 (1007–72), 2 vols., Zhonghua, 1976. Covers the years 907–60.[7]

> *Xin-Jiu Wudaishi renming suoyin* 新舊五代史人名索引 (Personal-name index to the *Xin-Jiu Wudaishi*), Zhang Wanqi 張萬起, comp., Shanghai guji, 1980. The edition indexed is the Zhonghua.

Jiuguo zhi 九國志 (Monographs of nine kingdoms), Lu Zhen 路振 (957–1014); the work was completed in the Song (1064). The tenth kingdom, Northern Chu 北楚, was added by Zhang Tang-ying 張唐英. Recovered from the *Yongle dadian* in the Qing. In *Congshu jicheng*, 1st series.

Nan Tangshu 南唐書 (History of the Southern Tang). There are two works of this title. The first was by Ma Ling 馬令 (completed in 1105); the second was compiled by Lu You 陸游 (1125–1210) in 1184. Both are important sources for the history of the kingdom of Southern Tang.

---

[6] English tr. by Kenneth Chase of Chikusa's chapter in *Ajia rekishi kenkyû nyûmon* アジア歴史研究入門 (8.4) in *Research Tools for the Study of Sung History* (47.4.2), 115–20.

[7] See Liu, 1967 (46.1.1).

Shiguo chunqiu 十國春秋 (Spring and autumn of the ten kingdoms), Wu Renchen 吳任臣, 1669; punctuated and collated edition, 4 vols., Zhonghua, 1983.

46.2 Other Textual Sources

History

Yao Runeng 姚汝能, *An Lushan shiji* 安祿山事蹟 (The deeds of An Lushan), Shanghai guji, 1983. Recounts the events of An Lushan's life (703–57), with details on the rebellion which he started (755–63). For a translation, see *Histoire de Ngan Lou-chan* (*Ngan Lou-chan chetsi*), Robert des Rotours, tr., PUF, 1962. For a study, see Edwin G. Pulleyblank, *The Background of the Rebellion of An Lu Shan*, London: OUP, 1955.

Shitong 史通 (20.3).

Geography

Taiping huanyu ji [*zhi*] 太平寰宇記[志] (Gazetteer of the world during the Taiping period, 976–83), comprehensive geography written by Yue Shi 樂史, late tenth century. Largely based on Tang works and therefore an important source for Tang geography (4.5.3). There is an index available.[8]

Yuanhe junxian tuzhi 元和郡縣圖志 (4.5.3).

Yuanhe xingzuan 元和姓纂 (3.5.1).

Liang jing xinji 兩京新記 (New record of the two capitals; also called *Liang jing ji* 兩京記, *Dong Xi jingji* 東西京記), Wei Shu 韋述 (? – 757), 722. Indexed along with six other texts on the two Tang capitals, Chang'an and Luoyang, plus maps in *Tôdai no Chôan to Rakuyô* 唐代の長安と洛陽 (46. 5.2, *Geography*).

Manshu 蠻書 (41.5.1).

Travel

Da Tang Xiyuji jiaozhu 大唐西域記校注 (41.5.1)

Nit-Tô guhô junrei gyôki 入唐求法巡禮行記 (42.2)

---

[8] *Taiping huanyu ji suoyin* 太平寰宇記索引, Wang Hui 王恢, comp., Wenhai, 1975.

Edicts and Memorials

Tang da zhaoling ji 唐大詔令集 (Collected edicts of the Tang), Song Min-
qiu 宋敏求, comp., 1070; Shangwu, 1959. Indexed in *T'ang Civilization Reference Series*, nos. 3 and 7.

Tôdai shôchoku mokuroku 唐代詔敕目錄 (Catalog of imperial edicts under the Tang arranged in chronological order), Tôyô bunko Tôdaishi
kenkyû iinkai, eds., Tôyô bunko, 1981. Indexes 37 printed sources;
12 collections of epigraphy, and five collections of Dunhuang and
Turpan documents. A number of edicts not included in this collection have been found on recently excavated stone inscriptions
(46.4.2).

Examinations

Dengkeji kao 登科記考 (25.3). See also Table 34, 25.3 and Chapter 27.

Encyclopaedias

Chuxue ji 初學記 (31.1)

Yiwen leiju 藝文類聚 (31.1)

Beitang shuchao 北堂書鈔 (31.1)

Yuhai 玉海 (31.1)

Agriculture

Chajing 茶經 (35.2)

Sishi zuanyao 四時纂要 (35.1)

Bieji 別集

Of 904 collected works of individual authors (*bieji* 別集) known to
have been in existence in the Sui, 467 have been lost. The majority
of Tang *bieji* have also been lost. However, for a catalog of 108 extant Tang collected works, see *Tangji xulu* 唐集敍錄.[9] See also the
large anthologies of Tang prose and poetry such as *Quan Tangwen*
全唐文, *Quan Tangshi* 全唐詩, or *Wenyuan yinghua* 文苑英華 and
Tangwencui 唐文萃 (30.1).

---

[9] *Tangji xulu* (Catalog of Tang collected works), Wan Man 萬曼, ed.,
Zhonghua, 1980.

Biji 筆記

For a repertory of terminology in Tang and Song *biji*, see

Tang-Song biji yuci huishi 唐宋筆記語辭匯釋 (Collected notes on the language of Tang and Song miscellaneous notes), Wang Ying 王瑛, ed., Zhonghua, 1990). Arrangement is by *pinyin* with a stroke-count index (incomplete). There are also many printing mistakes. More useful, including for *biji*, is *Tang-Wudai yuyan cidian* 唐五代語言辭典 (46.5.2, *Language*).

For a name-index to Tang fictional *biji*, see *Tang-Wudai wushi'er zhong biji xiaoshuo renming suoyin* 唐五代五十二種筆記小説人名索引.[10]

There follows a selection of five Tang *biji* (see also *Tang zashi* 唐雜史, Chapter 24) and two later *biji* with Tang materials:

Fengshi wenjian ji 封氏聞見記 (Records of things heard and seen by Mr. Feng), Feng Yan 封演, completed in 800; Shangwu, 1933; punctuated edition, Zhonghua, 1985. *H-Y Index, Supplement 7*. Contains observations made during the second half of the eighth century on military institutions, court life, customs, local sights, and the lives of the famous.

Tang zhiyan 唐摭言 (Picked-up words of Tang), Wang Dingbao 王定保 (870–941), Shanghai guji, 1978. Contains mainly anecdotes about the examination system and Tang literati. For some translated excerpts, see *Chinese Civilization: A Sourcebook* (8.1), 128–31.

Beilizhi 北里志 (Anecdotes of the northern quarter), Sun Qi 孫棨, preface, 884; Zhonghua, 1959; translated in *Courtisanes chinoises à la fin des T'ang*, Robert des Rotours, tr., Paris, 1968. The northern quarter was where the prostitutes gathered (in the reassuringly named Ping-kang *fang* 平康坊 [safe and sound ward]).

Beimeng suoyan 北夢瑣言 (Chit-chat of the northern dreamer [i.e., written at Jiangling 江陵]), Sun Guangxian 孫光憲 (ca. 900–968), punctuated edition, Shanghai guji, 1981. Notes on politics, institutions, and customs at the Tang/Five Dynasties divide.

Youyang zazu 酉陽雜俎 (Miscellany of Youyang mountains), Duan Chengshi 段成式 (ca. 803–63), punctuated edition, Zhonghua, 2nd prnt., 1981. Wide-ranging *biji xiaoshuo*.

[10] *Tang-Wudai wushi'er zhong biji xiaoshuo renming suoyin*, Fang Jiliu 方積六, comp., Zhonghua, 1992.

Taiping guangji 太平廣記 (Wide gleanings from the Taiping era), Li Fang 李昉 (925–96), Zhonghua, 1961; 6th prnt., 1996. Collection of fictional *biji* containing 475 *biji xiaoshuo* from Han to the Five Dynasties (34.1). Title index: *H-Y Index* 15; Zhonghua published an index in 1982; 10th prnt., 1996.

Shuofu 説郛 (48.5.2, Yuan *biji*)

46.3   Dunhuang and Turpan Documents

In 1897, an ex-soldier from the Gansu border army, Wang Yuanlu 王圓籙 [元籙] (1849–1931), found refuge in one of the Mogao 莫高 temple caves at Dunhuang. There he practiced as a Daoist priest in order to make a living. He took an assistant named Yang, who one day early in 1900 discovered by accident a secret chamber, which turned out to be stacked with bundles of ancient manuscripts. Later research shows that the cave had most likely been sealed off in 1035, the year that the Xixia 西夏 occupied Dunhuang.

A few years before the discovery, Mark Aurel Stein (1862–1943), the Hungarian-born British archaeologist and explorer, had heard about the Caves of the Thousand Buddhas at Dunhuang (but not about the manuscripts) from his teacher, the head of the Hungarian geological survey who had been there in 1879. Stein finally visited during his second expedition to Inner Asia in 1907 and then learned of Wang's discovery of "several cartloads" of ancient manuscripts. He persuaded Wang to let him see the secret chamber: "The sight disclosed in the dim light of the priest's oil lamp," he later wrote, "made my eyes wide open. Heaped up in layers, but without any order, there appeared a solid mass of manuscript bundles rising to ten feet from the floor and filling, as subsequent measurement showed, close on five hundred cubic feet."[11]

The collection consisted mainly of Chinese Buddhism manuscripts as well as a much smaller number of Daoist, Manichaean, and Nestorian scriptures.[12] There were also Confucian works and

[11] Aurel Stein, *On Ancient Central Asian Tracks*, 1941; rpnt., Pantheon, 1964, 179.

[12] Manichaeism was an eclectic dualistic religion founded in the third century AD. It remained strong in the Western Regions (Box 9) until the Yuan dynasty. The documents discovered at Turfan (and to a much lesser extent at Dunhuang) are a prime source on the religion; see Samuel N. C. Lieu, *Manich-*

Footnote continued on next page

school primers and some local records, account books, musical scores, astronomical, arithmetical, and medical works, calendars, and popular literature. Some of the documents were in Sanskrit, Sogdian, Tangut, Tufan (Tibetan), Turkic, and Uighur. Stein paid Wang 300 taels (just over 200 1910 US$) for 10,000 manuscripts, which he sent back to the British Museum packed into 24 wooden crates. "The Chinese regard Stein and Pelliot as robbers," wrote the British sinologist Arthur Waley (1889–1968), whose opinion is worth quoting at length since he had no particular ax to grind and he knew both men well and discussed the matter with them:

> I think the best way to understand [the feelings of the Chinese] on the subject is to imagine how we should feel if a Chinese archaeologist were to come to England, discover a cache of medieval manuscripts at a ruined monastery, bribe the custodian to part with them and carry them off to Peking. ... We have to remember that in the nineteenth century archaeology combined with a mild kind of espionage (consisting in little more than map-making) had been carried on extensively in Moslem countries where conversion to Islam had long ago completely divorced the inhabitants from their remote past. ... Stein was of course aware that the Chinese were more interested in their own remote past than were, for example, the Bedouins. But I was never able to convince him that the Chinese scholars who in the eighteenth and nineteenth centuries wrote about the geography and antiquities of Central Asia were anything more than what he called 'arm-chair archaeologists'; though they had in fact, as Generals and administrators, spent far more time in Central Asia and traveled far more widely than Stein himself. Pelliot did, of course, after his return from Tun-huang, get in touch with Chinese scholars; but he had inherited so much of the nineteenth-century attitude about the right of Europeans to carry off 'finds' made in non-European lands that, like Stein, he seems never from the first to last to have had any qualms about the sacking of the Tun-huang library.[13]

---

aeism in the Later Roman Empire and Medieval China, Mohr, 1985; 2nd ed., rev. and expanded, 1992.

[13] Arthur Waley, *Ballads and Stories from Tun-huang*, Allen and Unwin, 1960, 237–38. For a biography, see Jeanette Mirsky, *Sir Aurel Stein: Archaeologist, Explorer*, UChP, 1977; paperback, 1998. For the views of the keeper of Chinese books at the British Museum, see Lionel Giles, *Six Centuries of Tun-huang*, British Museum, 1944.

The French sinologist referred to by Waley, Paul Pelliot (1878–1945), arrived in 1908 and spent three feverish weeks selecting the cream of what was left in the temple library. He paid 500 taels (about 340 US$ of that time) for just over 6,000 hand-picked manuscripts. Others followed: assistants of Ôtani Kôzui (1876–1948) from Japan in 1911–12 and Sergei Oldenburg (1863–1934) and Captain Petr Kuz'mich Kozlov (1863–1935) from Russia.[14] Altogether, about 25,000 manuscripts were collected from Dunhuang and neighboring sites and exported; the remainder were taken to the Beijing Capital Library or found their way into the hands of other public or private collections. The total number of Dunhuang manuscripts (*Dunhuang yishu* 敦煌遺書 [or *xieben* 寫本 or *wenshu* 文書]) all over the world today comes to about 50,000 (including fragments). The majority of the manuscripts are on paper. They date from the early fifth to eleventh centuries. They form one of the largest collections of manuscripts on paper ever found in China. Their study has given rise to a new specialized field known as Dunhuang studies (*Dunhuangxue* 敦煌學). In addition to the written documents, there are a small number of printed works and rubbings. There are also many thousands of Buddhist paintings preserved on the walls of the Dunhuang and neighboring temples. Dunhuang has also been one of the main sites for the discovery of Han border documents (44.4.3).

Apart from the value of the Buddhist and Daoist texts, the Dunhuang manuscripts also include a considerable amount of popular literature. Because of the *baihua* 白話 movement in the decades after their discovery, it was the literary interest of the manuscripts that was emphasized. However, the sutras were often written on the back of all sorts of local documents, including fragments of ordinances, reports, purchase orders, contracts, and other materials, which have led to some of the most detailed researches into Chinese social and economic history of any period (*CHC*, vol. 4).

From 15,000 to 20,000 manuscripts on paper were also discovered at the end of the nineteenth and the beginning of the twentieth century near the modern city of Turpan (Tulufan 吐魯番) in Xin-

---

[14] Hopkirk, 1980 (42.2, *Early Twentieth Century*); "The German Expeditions, 1902–1914," in *Along the Ancient Silk Routes: Central Asian Art from the West Berlin State Museum*, John P. O'Neill, ed. in chief, Metropolitan Museum of Art, 1982, 25–55.

jiang, about 360 km (225 miles) to the northwest of Dunhuang. The documents date from the Jin to the Yuan. Between 1959 and 1975 another 2,000 documents were excavated, mainly from tombs nearby, including several copies of the *Lunyu*, the *Qianziwen* 千字文, calendars, and much else besides. They date from the fourth to eighth centuries.[15] About 2,000 Tangut manuscripts were found in 1907 by Kozlov in the ruins of Kharakhoto about 600 km (375 miles) to the northeast of Dunhuang. More were discovered in the 1980s (48.3).

For many years the Dunhuang (and Turpan) manuscripts were almost inaccessible since they were scattered all over the world and the publishing of scholarly catalogs and transcriptions for the most part proceeded slowly. It was in the late 1950s that Ikeda On 池田温, Kikuchi Hideo 菊池英夫, Dohi Yoshikazu 土肥義和, and other scholars at the Tôyô bunko in Tokyo, using microfilms, published a detailed catalog of non-Buddhist documents held in the British Museum. Volumes two, three, and four covered documents relating respectively to the institutional and economic aspects of Buddhism, to Daoism, and to literature. At the same time as the work in Tokyo, scholars in Kyoto also produced some of the first studies of social and economic history based on the Dunhuang documents.

Today, the entire corpus of the Dunhuang manuscripts from collections all over the world has been published (46.3.2), and many transcriptions and studies of selected manuscripts on Buddhist, Daoist, literary, and social and economic topics have appeared. Note that the documents on wooden tablets discovered in or around Dunhuang mainly date from an earlier period and are of an administrative rather than religious nature (44.4.3).

---

[15] Turpan also written Turfan, is one of the lowest, hottest, driest places on earth (its name is a transliteration of the original Uighur toponym meaning "low-lying ground"). For centuries Turpan was a key center on the silk road linking China to Persia. The more recently discovered manuscripts were found among several hundred tombs at Astana (Asitana 阿斯塔那), the graveyard of the old capital of the kingdom of Karakhoja (Qoco, Gaochang 高昌, 460–640) and its successors, 40 km (28 miles) to the east of Turpan.

46.3.1 Catalogs of Dunhuang Manuscripts

Bai Huawen 白化文, *Dunhuang wenwu mulu daolun* 敦煌文物目錄導論 (Guide to the Dunhuang catalogs), Taibei, 1991 (previously published by Hebei renmin in 1989). Good starting point.

Dunhuang yishu zuixin mulu 敦煌遺書最新目錄 (Latest catalog of manuscripts from Dunhuang), Huang Yongwu 黃永武, ed. in chief, Xinwenfeng, 1986. The most comprehensive catalog to date. Index of titles to the manuscripts in the old Beiping, Stein, Pelliot, Leningrad, and Ôtani collections, as well as 800 manuscripts in miscellaneous collections. It replaces the earlier *Dunhuang yishu zongmu suoyin* 敦煌遺書總目索引 (Index to general catalog of manuscripts from Dunhuang), Shangwu, 1962; Tokyo, 1963; corrected edition, Zhonghua, 1981, 1983.

The main catalogs of individual collections are:

National Library of China (former Peking Library): *Dunhuang jieyu lu* 敦煌劫餘錄 (An analytical list of the Dunhuang manuscripts in the National Library of Beijing), Chen Yuan 陳垣, comp. Beijing, 1931. Contains bibliographic notes on each manuscript included (condition of text, colophons, dates, seals, etc.).

British Library (formerly British Museum), London: *Descriptive Catalogue of the Chinese Manuscripts from Tunhuang in the British Museum*, Lionel Giles, comp., British Museum, 1957. Sections list 6,980 Buddhist, Daoist, and Manichaean texts, as well as secular texts and printed documents in the Stein collection at the Library. Cataloging now covers all the Stein Dunhuang manuscripts and printed texts. There are also important collections at the India Office Library.

Bibliothèque Nationale de France, Paris: Annotated catalog: *Catalogue des manuscrits chinois de Touen-Houang*, vol. 1 covering manuscripts nos. 2,001–2,500 (1970); vol. 3, 3,001–3,500 (1983); vol. 4, nos. 3,501–4,000 (1991); vol. 5, 4,001–6,040 (1995). The publication of vol. 2, which is to cover nos. 2,501–3,000, has been delayed for administrative reasons.

Institute of Oriental Studies of the Russian Academy of Sciences, St. Petersburg Branch (formerly the Institute of the Peoples of Asia under the Academy of Social Sciences, Leningrad branch): *Kitajskie rukopisi iz Dun'khuana* (Chinese Manuscripts from Dunhuang), L. N. Menshikov, 3 vols., 1963–83. Catalog of the documents collected by Oldenburg in the early twentieth century, many from Turpan. Chinese reprint by Shanghai guji, 2 vols., 1999.

Ômiya Library, Ryûkoku University 龍谷大學大宮圖書館: *Ôtani monjo shûsei* 大谷文書集成 (The Ôtani collection), Oda Yoshihisa 小田義久, comp., 2 vols., Hôzôkan, 1984, 1987. Includes documents from both Dunhuang and Turpan.

46.3.2 Turpan Documents

Tulufan chutu wenshu 吐魯番出土文書 (Documents excavated at Turpan), Zhongguo wenwu yanjiusuo 中國文物研究所, eds., vol. 1 (*yi* 壹), 1992; vol. 2 (*er* 貳), 1994; vol. 3 (*san* 叁), 1996; vol. 4 (*si* 肆), Wenwu, 1997. Facsimiles (upper half of the page) plus transcriptions (lower half of the page). Transcriptions of about 1,600 documents including not only edicts and memorials but also private contracts and letters (earlier published in *Tulufan chutu wenshu* 吐魯番出土文書 (Documents excavated at Turpan), Tan Changru 唐長孺, ed. in chief, 10 vols., Wenwu, 1981–91).

On the question of dating the documents, see Wang Su 王素, *Tulufan chutu Gaochang wenxian biannian* 吐魯番出土高昌文獻編年 (Chronology of the documents excavated at Karakhoja, Turpan), Xinwenfeng, 1997.

Tulufan chutu wenshu renming diming suoyin 吐魯番出土文書人名地名索引 (Personal and place-name index to *Tulufan chutu wenshu* [1981–91]), Li Fang 李昉 and Wang Su 王素 comps., Wenwu, 1997.

Xinchu Tulufan wenshu ji qi yanjiu 新出吐魯番文書及其研究 (Newly excavated Turpan documents and research), Liu Hongliang 劉洪亮, ed., Xinjiang renmin, 1998. 100 docs. discovered at Astana, 1975–90.

Berlin: many of the manuscripts collected by Albert Grünwedel (1856–1935) and Albert von Le Coq (1860–1930) were destroyed during WW II; about 6,000 Chinese documents survived and 8,000 in early Turkic languages. They have been published in the series *Berliner Turfantexte*, 17 vols., Akadamie Verlag, 1971–92; vols., 18–19, Turnhout: Brepols, 1996–97.

46.3.3 Photographs of Dunhuang and Turpan Manuscripts

For photographs of the original Dunhuang manuscripts, see:

Beijing daxue cang Dunhuang wenxian 北京大學藏敦煌文獻 (Dunhuang documents held at Peking University), 2 vols., Shanghai guji, 1995.

E cang Dunhuang wenxian 俄藏敦煌文獻 (Dunhuang documents held in Russia [at the Institute of Oriental Studies of the Russian Academy of Sciences, St. Petersburg Branch]), 9 vols., Shanghai guji, 1995–99;

vols. 10–15, forthcoming, 2000. Note also *E cang Dunhuang yishupin* 俄藏敦煌藝術品 (Dunhuang art objects held in Russia), 6 vols., Shanghai guji, 1997–99.

Facang Dunhuang Xiyu wenxian 法藏敦煌西域文獻 (Dunhuang and Western Region documents held in France), 8 vols., Shanghai guji, 1995–98.

Shanghai bowuguan cang Dunhuang Tulufan wenxian 上海博物館藏敦煌吐魯番文獻 (Dunhuang and Turpan documents held at the Shanghai Museum), 2 vols., Shanghai guji, 1995.

Shanghai tushuguan cang Dunhuang Tulufan wenxian 上海圖書館藏敦煌吐魯番文獻 (Dunhuang and Turpan documents held at the Shanghai Library), 2 vols., Shanghai guji, 1999.

Tianjinshi yishu bowuguan cang Dunhuang Tulufan wenxian 天津市藝術博物館藏敦煌吐魯番文獻 (Dunhuang and Turpan documents held at the Tianjin Art Museum), 7 vols., Shanghai guji, 1997–99.

Yingcang Dunhuang wenxian 英藏敦煌文獻 (Dunhuang manuscripts in British collections), 14 vols., Sichuan renmin and British Library, 1990–95. Non-Buddhist manuscripts rephotographed.

Dunhuang baozang 敦煌寶藏 (Treasures from Dunhuang), 140 vols., Xinwenfeng, 1981–86. Based on microfilm holdings from collections all over the world (except St. Petersburg). Not always legible, but is a major convenience until other series (e.g., that of Shanghai guji) are complete.

46.3.4 *Social, Economic, and Legal Dunhuang and Turpan Documents and Studies on Them*

Some of the most important collections of social, economic, and legal documents and studies on them are listed below:

Legal texts from Dunhuang and Turpan are typeset, punctuated, and collated in *ZZFDJ*, 1ˢᵗ series, vols. 3 and 4 (see 27.4).

Chûgoku kodai shahon shikigo shûroku 中國古代寫本識語集錄 (Collected colophons of ancient Chinese manuscripts); Ikeda On 池田温, ed., Tôbunken, 1990. Includes 2,623 entries, of which 1,703 date from the Tang and are mainly Buddhist texts. See *Chinese Civilization: A Sourcebook* (8.1), 102–4, for translations of five of them.

Dunhuang Tulufan wenshu chutan 敦煌吐魯番文書初探 (Preliminary investigations of Turpan documents), Tang Changru 唐長孺, ed. in chief, Wuhan daxue, 2 vols., 1983, 1990.

Dunhuang Tulufan wenxian yanjiu lunji 敦煌吐魯番文獻研究論集 (Collected research articles on Dunhuang and Turpan documents), Beijing daxue Zhongguo zhonggu yanjiu zhongxin, ed., Zhonghua, 1982; other research articles were published by the same center at Peking University under the same title in 1983, 1986, 1987 and 1990.

Dunhuang Tulufan chutu jingji wenshu yanjiu 敦煌吐魯番出土經濟文書研究 (Collected research articles on Dunhuang and Turpan economic documents), Han Guopan 韓國磐, ed., Xiamen daxue, 1986.

Liu Junwen 劉俊文, *Dunhuang Tulufan Tangdai fazhi wenshu kaoshi* 敦煌吐魯番唐代法制文書考釋 (Research on Tang dynasty Dunhuang and Turpan legal documents), Zhonghua, 1989.

Dunhuang shehui jingji wenxian zhenji shilu 敦煌社會經濟文獻真迹釋錄 (Photos and transcriptions of socioeconomic documents from Dunhuang), Shumu wenxian, 5 vols., 1986–90.

Dunhuang ziliao 敦煌資料 (Dunhuang materials), 1ˢᵗ collection, Zhonghua, 1961; rpnt., Daian, 1963. Reproduces documents such as household, name, and land registers and contracts. Transcriptions unreliable. Now largely superseded by the works listed above.

Zhongguo gudai jizhang yanjiu 中國古代籍帳研究, Gong Zexian 龔澤銑, tr. (from the Japanese original of Ikeda On 池田溫, 1977), Zhonghua, 1984.

46.3.5   *Guides to the Dunhuang and Turpan Documents*

The best overall introduction to the documents is contained in the comprehensive *Dunhuangxue da cidian* 敦煌學大辭典;[16] it describes all the main manuscripts in each category, the collections in which they are held, and the published catalogs, architecture, paintings, music, dance, geography, history, works of secondary scholarship, and the lives of the main scholars. Note the International Dunhuang Project whose aim is to promote the study and preservation of manuscripts and printed documents from Dunhuang and other Central Asian sites through international co-operation. IDP publishes a newsletter (*IDP News)*, which is available online.[17] See also the series *Tun-huang and Turpan Documents Concerning Social and*

---

[16] *Dunhuangxue da cidian* (Dictionary of Dunhuang studies), Ji Xianlin 季羡林, ed. in chief, Shanghai cishu, 1998;

[17] IDP was established in 1993. The secretariat is at the British Library in the Oriental and India Office Collections.

Economic History, edited by the Committee of Tunhuang Studies at the Tôyô bunko, 1978–87. Each consists of two volumes, (A) substantial introductions and notes (in English) on selected texts (transcriptions given) with bibliographies and (B) plates:

Legal Texts, Tatsuro Yamamoto, On Ikeda, and Makoto Okano, eds., 1978–80. Twenty-five legal texts.

Census Registers, Tatsuro Yamamoto and Yoshikazu Dohi, eds., 1984–85. One hundred and five examples of census registers.

Contracts, Tatsuro Yamamoto and On Ikeda, eds., 1986–87. Includes texts of 511 examples of all kinds of contracts including documents of sale and purchase, loans, leases, employment, adoption of sons, wills, divorce, and so on.

Social and Related Documents, Tatsuro Yamamoto, Yoshikazu Dohi, and Yusuku Ishida, eds. (forthcoming).

Other general introductions to the documents are also available; for example:

Wang Yongxing 王永興, *Dunhuang jingji wenshu daolun* 敦煌經濟文書導論 (Introduction to Dunhuang economic documents), Xinwenfeng, 1994. Leaves out private documents (notably those of Buddhist temples).

Jiang Boqin 姜伯勤, *Dunhuang shehui wenshu daolun* 敦煌社會文書導論 (Introduction to Dunhuang social documents), Xinwenfeng, 1992.

Gao Guofan 高國藩, *Dunhuang minsu ziliao daolun* 敦煌民俗資料導論 (Introduction to Dunhuang materials on popular customs), Xinwenfeng, 1993.

The nine-volume series *Kôza Tonkô* 講座敦煌 (Daitô, 1980–92) contains detailed introductions to every aspect of Dunhuang by leading Japanese and Chinese scholars, including the geographical setting (vol. 1), history (vol. 2), society (vol. 3), Daoism (vol. 4), Chinese-language documents (vol. 5), popular literature (vol. 6), Buddhism (vol. 7), Zen (vol. 8), and literature (vol. 9). Volume 5, under the editorial responsibility of Ikeda On, is particularly valuable as a starting point to all the many categories of Chinese-language documents found in the Dunhuang library.[18]

[18] Ikeda On, *Tonkô Kanbun bunken* 敦煌漢文文獻 (Dunhuang materials in Chinese), *Kôza Tonkô*, 5, Daitô, 1992.

Bibliography

Dunhuang Tulufanxue lunzhu mulu 敦煌吐魯番學論著目錄初篇日本部
分 (Bibliography of Dunhuang and Turpan studies, first part: Japanese part), Dunhuang Tulufan xue Beijing ziliao zhongxin, comp.,
Beijing tushuguan, 1999. Covers Japanese articles and studies, 1886–
1992.3.

Torufan, Tonkô shutsudo Kanbun monjo kenkyû bunken mokuroku 吐魯番
敦煌出土漢文文書研究文獻目錄 (Bibliography of studies on Tur-
pan and Tunhuang Chinese-language documents), Tôyô bunko, 1990.
This does not include scholarship on documents on bamboo strips or
tomb inscriptions.

Kuang Shiyuan 鄺士元, *Dunhuangxue yanjiu lunzhu mulu* 敦煌學研究論
著目錄 (Review of Tun-huang studies in the past century), Xinwenfeng, 1987. Contains citations to 6,084 works in Chinese, Japanese,
and Western languages arranged by topic. There is an author index
and date of publication index (through 1984).

Language

Dunhuang wenxian yuyan cidian 敦煌文獻語言詞典 (Dictionary of the
language of Dunhuang documents), Jiang Lihong 蔣禮鴻, comp.,
Hangzhou daxue, 1994. Dictionary of the language found in Dunhuang and Turpan manuscripts.

Jiang Lihong 蔣禮鴻, *Dunhuang bianwen ziyi tongshi* 敦煌變文字義通釋
(Comprehensive explanations of the meanings of characters in the
Dunhuang *bianwen*), 4th rev. edition, Shanghai guji, 1988.

Society and Journals

Dunhuang Tulufan xuehui 敦煌吐魯番學會 (Dunhuang Turpan society).
Publishes proceedings every two years or so (1983–).

Dunhuang Tulufan yanjiu 敦煌吐魯番研究 (1995– , annual), Beida

Dunhuangxue jikan 敦煌學輯刊 (1989– , irreg.), Lanzhou daxue lishixi
蘭州大學歷史系 (Lanzhou university, History department)

Dunhuang yanjiu 敦煌研究 (1981– , semiannual), Dunhuang yanjiuyuan
(Dunhuang academy), Dunhuang

46.4 Archaeology and Inscriptions

46.4.1 Archaeology

On the Sui canals linking north and south China, see 36.3.

Xi'an (the Tang capital Chang'an) has outstanding Tang monuments—for example, the Great Wild Goose Pagoda (Dayanta 大雁塔), originally built in 652 for the just-returned Xuanzang 玄奘 (41.5.1) to store the Buddhist scriptures that he had brought back from India.

The city also has rich collections of Tang artifacts. These are mainly at the Shaanxi History Museum (Shaanxi lishi bowuguan 陜西歷史博物館). Treasures include detailed murals from the tombs of relatives of the Tang emperors and more than 2,000 tomb figurines. In addition there is the Xi'anshi Tangdai yishu bowuguan 西安市唐代藝術博物館 (Xi'an municipal museum of the art of the Tang Dynasty) as well as the Xi'an beilin bowuguan 西安碑林博物館 (Museum of the forest of stelae) housed in the old Confucian Temple. It contains the largest collection of early stone inscriptions in China including the *Kaicheng shijing* 開成石經 of 837 (17.4). Elsewhere, you can even bathe near the pool where Yang Guifei 楊貴妃 (719–56) took the waters in a stone pool fed by hot springs in the Huaqing palace 華清宮 (excavation report: *Wenwu* 1990.5, 1991.9, and 1995.11; *CAAD* 2.1: 23–25 [1997]).

Parts of Tang Chang'an and Luoyang (secondary capital) have been excavated. So, too, has Yangzhou, an important Tang city (*Kaogu* 1990.1). The ruined city of Jiaohe 交河 (Yarkhoto) lies in the desert 10 km (6 miles) to the west of Turpan in Xinjiang. The city's history goes back to pre-Qin times, but most of the buildings that can be seen today date from the Tang. It was abandoned at the end of the Yuan. An eighth-century Lotus Sutra was found here in 1901.

The tomb of the founding emperor of the Sui, Wendi 文帝, may be seen in the southeastern part of Fufeng county 扶風縣. It is about 100 km (60 miles) from Xi'an. The tombs of 18 of the Tang emperors lie scattered around Xi'an.

Also at Fufeng is the Famensi 法門寺, a Buddhist temple which came under the direct personal patronage of many of the Tang emperors. It was famous for its Buddha relics (including Sakyamuni's finger bone). When the emperor Xianzong 憲宗 (778–820) gave instructions in 819 that this relic (*sheli* 舍利) be brought to the palace for temporary display and worship (as had been done every 30 years or so by his predecessors), Han Yu 韓愈 (768–824) condemned the practice in his diatribe "Lun fogu biao" 論佛骨表 (Memorial on the Buddha's bone), leading to his brief banishment to Chaozhou 潮

州.[19] In the tenth century the underground storage vault in the foundations of the pagoda was sealed up. Following the collapse of the pagoda in the Ming, the vault was completely built over. It was only discovered when the Ming pagoda fell over in 1981 and preparations were being made to rebuild the structure in 1987. The treasures found in the vault, which can be seen today in the temple museum, include not only the Buddha relic (in a solid gold casket encased in seven outer caskets), but 121 gold and silver dishes and a complete set of utensils for roasting, grinding, sorting, boiling, drinking, and storing tea. The utensils (of which 70 were presented by the emperors Yizong 懿宗, 833–73 and Xizong 僖宗, 862–88) are in perfect condition, as is the Buddha bone, which turns out to be a hollow piece of jade.

The Dunhuang murals and the finest carvings at the Longmen grottoes were mainly completed in the Sui and Tang (45.4). The largest stone statue of the Buddha in the world still stands where it was carved in the Tang out of the rock face of a hill outside Leshan 樂山 (modern Sichuan province). It took 90 years to complete (713–803). It is a few miles down the pilgrim route from Mt. Emei 峨眉, the westernmost of the four great Buddhist mountains (the other three are Wutaishan 五臺山 (Shanxi), Putuoshan 普陀山 (Zhejiang), and Jiuhuashan 九華山 (Anhui). Not long after the completion of the Leshan Buddha, fashions changed—huge Buddha statues were erected in urban temples, where special multi-storied towers were built to accommodate them.

Sui-Tang kaogu 隋唐考古 (Archaeology of the Sui and Tang), Qin Hao 秦浩, ed., Nanjing daxue, 1992; rpnt., 1996.

A Journey into China's Antiquity, vol. 3, *Sui-Tang-Song* (see 8.1 on this authoritative illustrated series).

Helga Stahl, *Gräber in Sichuan von der Tang bis zur Song-Zeit: Möglichkeiten einer Regionalgeschichte anhand von archäologischen Funden*, Forum, 1995.

---

[19] The excitement and religious fervor caused by the display of the relic in Chang'an led to extremes such as self-mutilation; see Kenneth K. S. Ch'en, *The Chinese Transformation of Buddhism*, PUP, 1973, 267–71.

46.4.2   Stone Inscriptions

The Tang is particularly rich in tomb inscriptions and more are being found all the time. They can be used to check or supplement the written record.[20]

For a comprehensive index of existing indexes, see *Tôdai boshi shozai sômokuroku* 唐代墓誌所在總目錄.[21] Arrangement is by date. There is no name index although the editor plans one. Altogether 5,826 tablets from 10 published collections are indexed, including *Beijing tushuguan cang Zhongguo lidai shike taben huibian* 北京圖書館藏中國歷代石刻拓本匯編 and *Shike tiba suoyin* 石刻題跋索引 (17.3, *Guides and Research Tools*). The other works indexed are:

Tangdai muzhi ming huibian fukao 唐代墓誌銘匯編附考, Mao Hanguang 毛漢光, ed., 18 vols., Shiyusuo, 1984–94 (3.7).

Qian-Tangzhi zhai 千唐誌齋, in Xin'an county 新安縣 near Luoyang, is the only museum dedicated to ancient tomb inscriptions, of which it has 1,413, the greater number of which (1,209) date from the Tang. The rubbings were published in *Qian-Tangzhi zhai cangzhi* 千唐誌齋藏誌, 2 vols., Wenwu, 1984; rpnt., 1991. There is also an index of the names of those recorded on the stelae, *Qian-Tangzhi zhai shizhizhu xingshi suoyin* 千唐誌齋石誌主姓氏索引 (An index to the names of those commemorated on the tomb tablets of the Tang thousand tomb inscriptions library).

Inscriptions tombales des dynasties T'ang et Song (d'après le fonds d'inscription possédées par l'École française d'Extrême-Orient), Jao Tsung-I (Rao Zongyi 饒宗頤), ed., EFEO and HKCUP, 1982. Annotated catalog of 388 tomb inscriptions, of which 370 are Tang, 5 Wudai, and 13 Song (up to 1125). Includes the texts of the inscriptions plus photographs of the rubbings. Arranged chronologically. Has name index and chronological index (arranged by reign name).

Sui Tang Wudai muzhi huibian 隋唐五代墓誌匯編, 9 parts in 30 vols., Tianjin guji, 1991–92. For a critical review, see Zhang Chenshi 張忱石, "*Sui Tang Wudai muzhi huibian* juzheng," 隋唐五代墓誌匯編舉

---

[20] Han Lizhou 韓理洲, "Xin chutu mubei muzhi zai Tangdai wenshi yanjiu fangmian de xueshu jiazhi" 新出土墓碑墓誌在唐代文史研究方面的學術價值 (The academic value of newly excavated Tang tomb inscriptions and tablets for the study of history and literature), *Xibei daxue xuebao* 3: 43–46 (1996).

[21] *Tôdai boshi shozai sômokuroku* (Comprehensive index to the whereabouts of Tang tomb tablets), Kigasawa Yasunari 氣賀澤保規, ed., Kyûko, 1997.

正 (Corrections to *Sui Tang Wudai muzhi huibian*), *Chutu wenxian yanjiu* 4: 274–98 (1998).

Luoyang chutu lidai muzhi jisheng 洛陽出土歷代墓誌輯繩 (3.7).

Tangdai muzhi huibian 唐代墓誌匯編, Zhou Shaoliang 周紹良, ed. in chief, 2 vols., Shanghai guji, 1992. Chronological arrangement, with a four-corner finding index at the end of vol. 2. Contains rubbings of 5,000 tomb tablets.

Xin Zhongguo chutu muzhi 新中國出土墓誌 (3.7).

46.5 Guides and Research Tools

46.5.1 Guides to Sources and Readers

The Tang, as one of the high points of the Chinese empire, has always attracted special attention, not only in China, but also in Japan and Korea, which modeled much of their higher culture, laws, and institutions on the Tang.

Denis Twitchett and Howard L. Goodman, *A Handbook for T'ang History*, 2 vols., Princeton Univ., Princeton Linguistic Studies, 1986. Contains a section on "Important T'ang Sources and T'ang Research Tools," 21–63. There are also annotated readings and notes on research topics, some general, but most linked to Tang history. Intended for beginning graduate students in Chinese studies.

Denis C. Twitchett, *The Writing of Official History Under the T'ang*, CUP, 1992. Concentrates on the compilation of the *Jiu Tangshu*, but also has important things to say on official history writing in general.

Wu Feng 吳楓, *Sui-Tang lishi wenxian jishi* 隋唐歷史文獻集釋 (Collected historical texts of the Sui and Tang with notes), Zhongzhou guji, 1987. Contains bibliographic annotations on 200 traditional written sources for the Sui and Tang arranged under 10 categories such as annalistic sources, miscellaneous notes, and so forth. An appendix lists the titles of more than 1,100 works written in the Tang arranged by *Sibu* classification. The list was drawn from the *Zhongguo congshu zonglu*.

Sui Tang Wudai jingji shiliao huibian jiaozhu 隋唐五代經濟史料匯編校注 (Collection of collated and annotated economic sources on the history of the Sui, Tang, and Wudai), part 1, 2 vols., Wang Yongxing 王永興, comp., Zhonghua, 1987. Excerpts from *wenji*, *shiji*, *biji*, inscriptions, Dunhuang and Turpan manuscripts. The excerpts are divided into seven subject categories, of which the first two (classes and class relations) are covered in these volumes.

Sui Tang Wudai shehui shenghuoshi 隋唐五代社會生活史 (A history of social life in the Sui, Tang, and Wudai), Li Bincheng 李斌城 et al., Shehui kexue, 1998. Contains much fascinating material (with references indicated) on population, food and drink, clothing, travel, women, marriage and burials, culture, customs, rituals, medicine, religion, *hangdi*, taboo names, and festivals in this period.

Suimo nongmin zhanzheng shiliao huibian 隋末農民戰爭史料匯編 (28.3).

Tang-Wudai nongmin zhanzheng shiliao huibian 唐五代農民戰爭史料匯編 (28.3).

Zhongguo lishi da cidian 中國歷史大辭典 contains a separate volume entitled *Sui Tang Wudai shi* 隋唐五代史, 1995. See 8.4.2, item 2, for comments on this encyclopaedia.

For guides to the Dunhuang and Turpan documents, 46.3.5.

46.5.2　Research Tools

Different types of special-purpose reference works for Sui, Tang, and Wudai-Shiguo history have already been introduced in the previous sections. Note also special-purpose reference works for all of Chinese history, which are also useful for these periods, for example, on weights and measures (7.3). Below are given a handful of indispensable references for the Sui, Tang, and Wudai-Shiguo on language, biography, official titles, geography, chronology, secondary sources, and societies and journals.

Language

Tang-Wudai yuyan cidian 唐五代語言詞典 (Dictionary of the Tang and Five Dynasties language), Shanghai jiaoyu, 1997, Jiang Lansheng 江藍生 and Cao Guangshun 曹廣順, eds. Contains about 5,000 entries drawn from the language of Dunhuang *bianwen* 變文, *Chanzong yulu* 禪宗語錄, and poetry as well as *biji* 筆記, historical biographies, documents, and so forth of the Tang and Five Dynasties. It is intended primarily for those interested in the development of the language between the seventh and tenth centuries and for readers of popular literature of the period. Arrangement is by *pinyin* and there is also a *pinyin* index. In the series *Jindai Hanyu duandai yuyan cidian xilie* (see 34.3, *Dictionaries*).

Biographies

Tang-Wudai renwu zhuanji ziliao zonghe suoyin 唐五代人物傳記資料綜合索引, Fu Xuancong 傅璇琮, Zhang Chenshi 張忱石, and Xu Yimin 許逸民, eds., Zhonghua and Tôhô, 1982; rpnt., 1987. Thorough index to biographical materials in 86 primary sources on some 30,000 figures. Names arranged by four-corner system.

Tôdai no denki sakuin 唐代の人傳記索引, Jinbun, 1951. An indexes to 17 works containing biographical information on Tang figures, in four categories: poets, Buddhists, Daoists, and painters. Entries are listed in four-corner sequence, with supplementary indexes for stroke count and Wade-Giles alphabetical order.

Zhongguo wenxuejia da cidian 中國文學家大辭典 (Dictionary of Chinese writers), *Tang-Wudai* 唐五代, Zhonghua, 1992.

Tangren hangdi lu 唐人行第錄 (Tang records of names by order of birth), Cen Zhongmian 岑仲勉, comp., 1962; Shanghai guji, 1978. Collects the names of many Tang literati with alternative names and has a finding table by stroke count.

Official Titles and Officeholders

In addition to *DOTIC*, see also the translations of Robert des Rotours, notably *Traité des fonctionnaires et traité de l'armée* (46.1).

Godai Sôsho hanchin nenpyô 五代宋初藩鎮年表 (Chronology of military commands in the Wudai and early Song), Kurihara Masuo 栗原益男, comp., Tôkyôdô, 1988.

Geography

Zhongguo lishi dituji 中國歷史地圖集, vol. 5, *Sui Tang Wudai shiqi* 隋唐五代時期 (Sui, Tang, and Five Kingdoms); see 4.3.2 on this essential series.

Tôdai no Chôan to Rakuyô 唐代の長安と洛陽 (Tang dynasty Luoyang and Chang'an), Hiraoka Takeo 平岡武夫, ed., *T'ang Civilization Reference Series*, 3 vols., Jinbun, 1956. Collects a very large amount of formal and informal writings on the two capitals during the Tang, plus maps and an index; Chinese translation, *Tangdai de Chang'an yu Luoyang* 唐代的長安與洛陽, Shanghai guji, 1989.

Yan Gengwang, 嚴耕望, *Tangdai jiaotong tukao* 唐代交通圖考 (Illustrated study of communications in the Tang), 5 vols., Shiyusuo, 1985–86.

Edward H. Schafer, *The Vermilion Bird: T'ang Images of the South*, UCP, 1967; rpnt., 1985.

Chronology

Tangdai de li 唐代的曆 (The Tang calendar), Hiraoka Takeo 平岡武夫, comp., Shanghai guji, 1990. (Chinese translation of Japanese original: *Tôdai no koyomi*, Jinbun, 1954.) Tabulates cyclical characters for every day from February 1, 618, to July 12, 907, fitting 10 months on each page. The right-hand column indicates the first and last days of the Western calendar month equivalents, as well as cyclical characters for the day of the solstices and equinoxes.

Edward H. Schafer, *Pacing the Void: T'ang Approaches to the Stars*, UCP, 1977.

Bibliographies of Secondary Scholarship

Sui Tang Wudai shi yanjiu gaiyao 隋唐五代史研究概要 (Guide to the history of the Sui, Tang, and Five Dynasties), Zhang Guogang 張國剛, ed. in chief, Tianjin jiaoyu, 1996. After a thorough discussion of the main themes in the history of these centuries with copious citation of modern Chinese scholarship (1–658), the authors introduce archaeology; Dunhuang studies, both in China and abroad (695–762); and historical sources and research tools (763–810). There follows a 374-page, unannotated bibliography of 8,000 books and articles of secondary scholarship in China (including Taiwan and Hong Kong), Japan, and the West.

Sui Tang Wudai shi lunzhu mulu 隋唐五代史論著目錄, Lishi yanjiusuo, eds., Jiangsu guji, 1985. Covers articles written between 1900 and 1981. A continuation goes up to the end of 1995: *Sui Tang Wudai shi lunzhu mulu* 隋唐五代史論著目錄 *1982–95*, Hang Gaoling 杭高霊 et al., Shanxi shifan daxue, 1997.

CHC, vol. 4, *Bibliographies* for vols. 3 and 4

"Viewpoints on T'ang China," *AA* 55 (1988). Special issue summarizing Japanese scholarship.

Godaishi kenkyû bunken mokuroku 五代史研究文獻目錄 (Catalog of studies on the history of the Five Dynasties), Yoshida Tora 古田寅 and Toriya Hiroaki 鳥谷弘昭, eds., Ritsumeikan daigaku, 1990. Covers 5,200 research articles and books in Japanese and Chinese up to 1988. There is an author index.

Bibliography on Parhae (Bohai-Bokkai): A Medieval State in the Far East, Norbert R. Adami, comp., Harrassowitz, 1994. Bohai (渤海), in northeast China, was an independent kingdom from 698 to 926.[22]

Societies and Journals

Zhongguo Tangshi xuehui 中國唐史學會 (Chinese society for Tang history). Founded in 1980.

Tôdaishi kenkyûkai 唐代史研究會 (Research society for Tang dynasty history, Tokyo). Has a publications series.

Tang yanjiu 唐研究 (1996–), Beida.

T'ang Studies (1982–). Journal of the T'ang Studies Society (Editorial, Boulder, Colorado).

Tangdai xuehui huikan 唐代學會會刊 (1990– , annual), Taibei.

[22] See also Johannes Reckel, *Bohai: Geschichte und Kultur eines mandschurisch-koreanischen Königsreiches der Tang-Zeit*, Harrassowitz, 1995.

47

Song

960–1279

| Northern Song 北宋 | 960–1127 |
| Southern Song 南宋 | 1127–1279 |

Most pre-Song and Song works survive today only in Song imprints and late copies and revisions of them. Indeed, it was the widespread use of printing that helped to ensure that more works (both official and private) survive from the Song than from any previous period.[1]

Throughout the Song there were alien dynastic regimes ruling over all or part of north China. The sources for these regimes (Liao, Xixia, Jin, and Yuan) are also important for the history of the Song, and vice-versa. For ease of presentation, the four are placed together with the Yuan in Chapter 48.

47.1   Main Historical Works

Song huiyao jigao 宋會要輯稿 (Draft recovered edition of the *Song huiyao*). The *Song huiyao* was recovered from the *Yongle dadian* in the early nineteenth century under the direction of Xu Song 徐松 (1781–1848), who also began the difficult task of trying to put it in order. Various other attempts were made to edit it until eventually his manuscript was published in a facsimile edition in 1936 under the title *Song huiyao jigao*.[2] The materials in the *Song huiyao* were taken from the Daily Records, no longer extant and

[1] On Song printing, see 18.4. On the archival system, see Wang Jinyu 王金玉, *Songdai dang'anguanli yanjiu* 宋代檔案管理研究 (Research on the administration of the Song archives), Zhongguo dang'an, 1997.

[2] *Song huiyao jigao*, photolithographic reproduction, 200 *ce*, Peiping tushuguan, 1936; reduced-size, facsimile reproduction, 8 vols., Zhonghua, 1957, 1987; Xinwenfeng, 1976.

the Veritable Records, also no longer extant, as well as the documents of the Six Ministries and of the Circuit Intendants.[3] It was compiled throughout the dynasty by the Important Documents Bureau (Huiyao suo 會要所). It contains the largest collection of documents from the Song with much information not available in the monographs of the *Songshi* 宋史, let alone in the *Wenxian tongkao* 文獻通考, especially on the economy. As such, it has been intensively studied and indexed.[4] It is arranged in chronological order within institutional categories and includes documents from 960 to 1220. There is an index to the table of contents which indicates subsections and the years covered in each, as well as the sources on which each subsection was based; it is usable with any of the editions of the *Song huiyao*:

Sô kaiyô kenkyû biyô-mokuroku 宋會要研究備要目錄 (Essentials for the study of the *Songhuiyao* table of contents), Tôyô bunko Sôdaishi kenkyû iinkai, Tôyô bunko, 1970.

Wenxian tongkao 文獻通考 is most detailed in the sections covering the Song. See also the *Tongzhi* 通志 (25.2).

Xu Zizhi tongjian changbian 續資治通鑑長編 (Long draft of the continuation of the *Zizhi tongjian*), Li Tao 李燾 (1114–83), 34 vols., Zhonghua punctuated and collated edition, 1979–95. Covers the years 960–1100 (i.e., the Northern Song) in great detail. The author spent 40 years working on it, using all available sources. In part it had to be recovered from the *Yongle dadian* during the course of editing the *Siku quanshu*. The first volume

[3] See Wang Yunhai 王雲海, *Song huiyao jigao kaojiao* 宋會要輯稿考校 (Study and collation of the *Song huiyao*), Shanghai guji, 1986; Chen Zhichao 陳智超, *Jiekai Song huiyao zhi mi* 解開宋會要之謎 (Solving the riddle of the *Song huiyao*), Shehui kexue wenxian, 1995.

[4] For lists of the dates of all the documents in the *Song huiyao* in chronological order, see *Sô kaiyô hennen sakuin* 宋會要編年索引 (Chronology of the *Song huiyao*), Umehara Kaoru 梅原郁, comp., Jinbun, 1995.

For a personal-name index to the *Song huiyao*, see *Song huiyao jigao renming suoyin* 宋會要輯稿人名索引, Wang Deyi 王德毅, comp., Xinwenfeng, 1978. There are also three Japanese indexes to the "Shihuozhi" in the *Song huiyao*: *Sô kaiyô shûkô shokka sakuin* 宋會要輯稿食貨索引 (1) personal names and book titles: *jinmei shomei-hen* 人名書名編; (2) dates and imperial edicts: *nengappi shôchoku-hen* 年月日詔勅編; (3) bureaucratic terms: *shokkan-hen* 職官編, Tôyô bunko Sôdaishi kenkyû iinkai, ed., Tôyô bunko, 1982, 1985, 1995.

of the Zhonghua edition contains an index and materials on Li
Tao's life.[5]

Jianyan yilai xinian yaolu 建炎以來繫年要錄 (Record of important
events in chronological order since the Jianyan reign period), Li
Xinchuan 李心傳 (1166–1243), comp., 4 vols., Shanghai guji,
1993. This edition contains also a personal-name index. Covers
the 36-year reign of Song Gaozong 宋高宗 (first emperor of
Southern Song, 1127–63). Recovered from the *Yongle dadian*
during the course of editing the *Siku quanshu*.[6]

Jianyan yilai chaoye zaji 建炎以來朝野雜記 (Miscellaneous records
of court and country since the Jianyan reign period), 1st collection, 1202; 2nd collection, 1216. Also by Li Xinchuan 李心傳.
Covers the last years of the Song.

Sanchao beimeng huibian 三朝北盟會編 (Collection of documents
on the treaties with the north during three reigns), Xu Mengxin
徐夢莘 (1126–1207), comp., 250 *juan*, 4 vols., Wenhai, 1966.[7]
This is an important source for the Song's relations with Jin
during the years 1101–60 (the three reigns of the title).

---

[5] There is a computerized concordance to the *Changbian*: *Changbian
quanwenben jiansuo xitong* 長編全文本檢索系統 (Complete computer concordance to the *Changbian*), Hebei daxue Lishi yanjiusuo 河北大學歷史研究所 and
Hanzi xinxi chuli yanjiusuo 漢字信息處理研究所, 1996. Also, Shiyusuo digital
library, forthcoming. See also *Zoku Shiji tsûgan chôhen jinmei sakuin* 續資治通
鑑長編人名索引 (Personal-name index to the *Changbian*), Umehara Kaoru 梅
原郁, comp., Dôhôsha, 1978, and idem, *Zoku Shiji tsugan chôhen goi sakuin* 續
資治通鑑長編語彙索引 (Glossary to the *Changbian*), Dôhôsha, 1989.

[6] John W. Chaffee discusses Li's work in his "The Historian as Critic: Li
Hsin-ch'uan and the Dilemmas of Statecraft in Southern Sung China," in *Or-
dering the World: Approaches to State and Society in Sung Dynasty China*, Robert
P. Hymes and Conrad Schirokauer, eds., UCP, 1993, 310–35. Vol. 4 of the
Shanghai guji edition (1992) of the *Siku* edition of *Jianyan yilai* contains an in-
dex of personal names (17–508) and authors and book titles (509–614). See also
Ken'en irai keinen yôroku jinmei sakuin 建炎以來繫年要錄人名索引, Umehara
Kaoru 梅原郁, comp., Dôhôsha, 1983.

[7] Name index to first 100 *juan*: "Sanchô hokumei kaihen jinmei sakuin" 三
朝北盟會編人名索引, Aso Mikio 安蘇幹夫, comp., *Hiroshima daigaku keizai
ronsô* 廣島大學經濟論叢 1.4: 55–83 (1979) for *juan* 1–40; 2.1, 2, 3: 55–88
(1979.12) for *juan* 41–100.

Songshi 宋史 (Standard History of the Song); editorship was credited to the chancellor Tuotuo (Toghto 脱脱, 1313-55), but the compiling was done by a group of officials from his office and from the Yuan Guoshi yuan 國史院 (Yuan Historiography Academy), 1343-45; 40 vols., Zhonghua, 1977; 3rd prnt., 1995. Covers the years 960-1279.[8] It is one of the largest of the 24 Standard Histories (thanks to the number of *guoshi* 國史 and documents which survived the fall of the Song), and it is particularly notable for the high standard of the monographs. Not surprisingly, the editors ensured that the coverage of the Yuan wars against the Song is seen more from a Yuan than a Song point of view. The *Songshi* contains references to about 100,000 people of whom 70,000 are relatives of the dynastic founder.[9]

Note the punctuated, indexed, and annotated editions of the monographs from all the Standard Histories (including the *Songshi*) given in 22.4. Below are listed a few of the translations and indexes for the monographs in the *Songshi* only:

Songshi shihuozhi buzheng 宋史食貨志補正 (Corrections and additions to the "Shihuozhi" of the *Songshi*), Liang Taiji 梁太濟 and Bao Weimin 包偉民, Hangzhou daxue, 1994. The authors have used many sources to supplement the *Songshi* "Shihuozhi," principally material from the *Song huiyao jigao* 宋會要輯稿.

Sôshi shokkashi yakuchû 宋史食貨志譯註 (Translation with notes of three of the fourteen chapters of the "Shihuozhi" of the *Songshi*: *Songshi, juan* 173-75), Wada Sei 和田清, ed., vol. 1, Tôyô bunko, 1960. This massive volume enlisted the aid of many experts on the Song economy; their work is in the tradition established by the leading Japanese economic historian of the Tokyo school of his generation, Katô Shigeru 加藤繁 (1880-1946)—to produce integral translations of all the *shihuozhi*. In the event only the revised translations of the monographs in the *Shiji* and in the *Qian Hanshu* and of those in the Standard Histories of the Tang and the Five Dynasties appeared in Katô's lifetime. The collective an-

[8] Hok-lam Chan (Chen Xuelin 陳學霖), "Chinese Official History at the Yuan Court: The Composition of the Liao, Chin and Sung Histories," in *China Under Mongol Rule*, John D. Langlois, ed., PUP, 1981, 56-106.

[9] *Songshi renming suoyin* 宋史人名索引 (Personal-name index to the *Songshi*), Yu Ruyun 俞如雲, comp., 4 vols., Shanghai guji, 1992.

notated translations edited by Wada of part of the "Shihuozhi" in the *Songshi* and the entire "Shihuozhi" in the *Mingshi* (49.2) are on a much grander scale. The detailed notes succeed in establishing the source for practically every statement in the *juan* translated. There are full indexes.[10]

Sôshi shokkanshi sakuin 宋史職官志索引 (47.4.2, *Official Titles and Officeholders*).

Sôshi senkyoshi sakuin 宋史選舉志索引 (Index to the monograph on the examination system in the *Songshi*), Saeki Tomi 佐伯富, comp., Dôhôsha, 1982.

Songshi xingfazhi suoyin 宋史刑法志索引 (Index to the monograph on law in the *Songshi*), Saeki Tomi 佐伯富, comp., Xuesheng, 1977.

Songshi bingzhi suoyin 宋史兵志索引 (Index to the monograph on the military system in the *Songshi*), Saeki Tomi 佐伯富, comp., Huashi, 1978.

Sôshi karyôshi sakuin 宋史河渠志索引 (Index to the monograph on rivers and canals in the *Songshi*), Saeki Tomi 佐伯富, comp., Seishin, 1979.

Songshi yiwenzhi, bu, fu pian, 宋史藝文志補附篇 (The *Songshi* "Yiwenzhi," its supplement, and related texts), Shangwu, 1957. Has author-title index.

Songshi yiwenzhi shibu yiji kao, 宋史藝文志史部佚籍考 (Study of lost works in the History branch of the *Songshi* "Yiwenzhi"), Liu Zhaoyou 劉兆祐, ed., 3 vols., Taibei: Guoli bianyiguan bianshen weiyuanhui 國立編譯館編審委員會, Zhonghua congshu 中華叢書, 1984. Also contains tables of lost and extant historical works in the "Yiwenzhi" and author-title indexes.

---

[10] Sudô Yoshiyuki 周藤吉之, "The Relationships Between the 'Shihuozhi' 食貨志 in the *Songchao guoshi* 宋朝國史 and the *Songshi* 宋史," *MTB* 19: 63–110 (1961); Deng Guangming 鄧廣銘, "*Songshi* 'Xingfazhi' kaozheng" 宋史刑法志考正 (Critical study of the monograph on law in the *Songshi*), *SYSJK* 20.II: 123–73 (1949) and the same author's "*Songshi* 'Zhiguanzhi' kaozheng" 宋史職官志考正 (Critical study of the monograph on official posts in the *Songshi*), *SYSJK* 10 (1948).

47.2   Other Textual Sources

The following list is in no sense intended to be exhaustive, but rather to give examples of the many additional Song sources available in different historical and literary genres.

History

Songshi quanwen xu Zizhi tongjian 宋史全文續資治通鑑, Yuan, anon. Annalistic history of the entire dynasty. Particularly valuable for its last 50 years or so. There is a photoreprint of a Ming edition; *Songshi ziliao cuibian* 宋史資料萃編, 2nd series, 5 vols., Wenhai, 1969.

Dongdu shilüe 東都事略, Wang Cheng 王稱. A twelfth-century *biannianti*-type history of the Northern Song. In some respects (e.g., biographies) it is more complete than the *Songshi*. There is a Wenhai photoreprint edition, 4 vols., 1967; also 14 *ce*, Yangzhou guji, 1990.

Geography

(Songben) Lidai dili zhizhang tu (宋本)歷代地理指掌圖 (Song edition of administrative maps, chronologically arranged), Shanghai guji, 1989. This is a photo-reproduction of an early Southern Song copy found in the Tôyô bunko; it is the earliest detailed work of Chinese administrative geography to have survived.

Taiping huanyu ji [*zhi*] 太平寰宇記[志] (Universal geography of the Taiping era, 976–83). This is the first extant Song comprehensive gazetteer. It is discussed in 4.4.3. On this and other Song geographical works, see *SB*, 128–68.

Yuanfeng jiuyu zhi 元豐九域志 (Gazetteer of the nine regions during the Yuanfeng period, 1078–86), Wang Cun 王存, presented 1080; published 1085; 2 vols., Zhonghua, 1984. This edition includes an index.

Yudi jisheng 輿地紀勝 (Records of famous places), Wang Xiangzhi 王象之, 1227; 32 *juan* missing; 8 vols., Zhonghua, 1992. This photoreprint of a Qing edition includes a four-corner index to personal names and toponyms and stone inscriptions. Describes the territories of the Southern Song with emphasis on culture. Arrangement is by *lu* 路, *zhou* 州, and *xian* 縣.

Fangyu shenglan 方輿勝覽 (Topography book for visiting places of scenic beauty), Zhu Mu 祝穆, 1239. There is a personal-name index attached to the Shanghai guji edition (1991).

Local Gazetteers

There are 30 Song local gazetteers extant. Twenty-four are described in *SB*, 131–49, which also lists the titles and contents of each.[11] Personal names in them are indexed in *Songren zhuanji ziliao suoyin zengdingben* (see 47.4.2, *Biographies*).

Travel and Diplomatic Missions

There are several famous Song accounts of trips inside China (4.8). Also, many of the Song embassies to neighboring regimes (Liao, Jin, or Mongol) recorded the mission in diary form or wrote it up on return to China (41.5.1). Others based their descriptions of foreign countries on the accounts of merchants.

Foreign missions to Song China are listed in Robert Hartwell, *Tribute Missions to China, 960–1126*, Philadelphia: copyright by the author, 1983. The Japan section is not complete.

Laws and Institutions

Song huiyao jigao xingfa 宋會要輯稿刑法 (27.4).

Song xingtong 宋刑統 (27.4).

Minggong shupan qingming ji 名公書判清明集 (27.4).

Tangyin bishi 棠陰比事 (27.4).

Qingyuan tiaofa shilei 慶元條法事類 (27.4).

Zhiyuan cuoyao 職源撮要 (27.6).

Sô-Gen kanshin sôgô sakuin 宋元官箴綜合索引 (Combined index to Song and Yuan *guanzhen*), Akagi Ryûji 赤城隆治, Satake Yasuhiko 佐竹靖彦, comps., Kyûko, 1987. Index to seven Song local administrative handbooks (27.6).

Xiyuanlu 洗冤錄 (27.6).

---

[11] See also James M. Hargett, "Song Dynasty Local Gazetteers," *HJAS* 56.2: 405–42 (1996). Contains in the appendix a listing of the 30 extant Song gazetteers. They are reprinted in *Song-Yuan fangzhi congkan* 宋元方志叢刊 (Collection of Song and Yuan gazetteers), 8 vols., Zhonghua, 1990. Facsimiles of 41 Song and Yuan gazetteers; see also Dahua, 1979, 1988; plus *xubian* 續編, 1990 (under title *Song-Yuan difangzhi congshu*).

Army

Wujing zongyao 武經總要 (Essentials of the military classics), Zeng Gongliang 曾公亮 (998–1078) and Ding Du 丁度 (990–1053), 1044; Jiefangjun, 1988. Important source on Song military institutions and strategic thinking (*SB*, 235–37).

Encyclopaedias

Taiping yulan 太平御覽 (31.1)

Cefu yuangui 册府元龜 (31.1)

Yuhai 玉海 (31.1)

Xiaoxue ganzhu 小學紺珠 (2.7)

For other Song encyclopaedias, of which there are several, as well as miscellaneous works, see *SB*, 319–49.

Edicts and Memorials

Song da zhaoling ji 宋大詔令集 (Collected edicts of the Song), compiled 1131–62, Zhonghua, punctuated ed., 1962, 1997. Out of the original 240 *juan*, 196 survive. They contain over 3,800 edicts of the Northern Song emperors, many of which are not to be found elsewhere.

Guochao zhuchen zouyi 國朝諸臣奏議 (or *Zhuchen zouyi* 諸臣奏議 or *Song mingchen zouyi* 宋名臣奏議), Zhao Ruyu 趙汝愚 (1140–96), comp; reprinted under the title *Songchao zhuchen zouyi* 宋朝諸臣奏議, Shanghai guji, 1990. The collection contains 1,630 memorials by 241 officials of the Northern Song; indexed in *Kokuchô shoshin sôgi mokuroku hoka* 國朝諸臣奏議目錄他 (Tables of contents for the *Guochao zhuchen zouyi etc.*), Yoshida Tora 吉田寅 and Tanada Naohiko 棚田直彦, comps., Tokyo kyôiku daigaku bungakubu Tôyôshi kenkyûshitsu Ajiashi kenkyûkai, 1957.

Lidai mingchen zouyi 歷代名臣奏議 (Memorials of leading officials of each period), 1416; 5 vols., Shanghai guji, 1964; rpnt., 1989. This work contains excerpts from memorials and quotes from other sources down to the Yuan arranged in a somewhat over-categorized 67 divisions. The Song and Yuan memorials account for 70 percent of the total. The 1989 reprint includes a summary giving the tentative name for each memorial and its author's name, as well as an author index.

Collections of Prose and Poetry

Quan Songwen 全宋文 (Complete Song prose works), Zeng Zaozhuang 曾棗莊 and Liu Lin 劉琳, eds. in chief, Ba-Shu, 1988–89. Designed to include all known literary works in prose written during the Song in a planned 150 volumes (including memorials, prefaces, postfaces, obituaries, letters, and so forth). Contains 100 million characters.

Quan Songshi 全宋詩 (Complete Song poetry), 72 vols., Beijing daxue, 1991–99. Designed to include all poems written during the Song dynasty, arranged chronologically by author. It contains more than 200,000 poems by over 8,900 poets.

Tang-Song ci baike da cidian 唐宋詞百科大辭典 (Encyclopaedia of Tang and Song *ci*), Wang Hong 王洪 et al., comps., Xueyuan, 1990. Includes table of contents under headings such as literary terms or first lines, but also relating to content such as customs (*minsu* 民俗).

Bieji 別集

The collected works of nearly 750 Song individuals have survived (unlike earlier dynasties from which most have been lost). This is reckoned to be about 10–20 percent of the total of those that were printed. The following are the main indexes for finding Song *bieji* and their contents. Famous individual authors such as Su Shi 蘇軾 or Zhu Xi 朱熹 have their own indexes; see *Research Tools for the Study of Sung History* (47.4.2).

Xiancun Songren bieji banben mulu 現存宋人別集版本目錄 (Catalog of extant collected works of Song individuals), Sichuan lianhe daxue guji zhengli yanjiusuo 四川聯合大學古籍整理研究所, ed., Ba-Shu, 1990. Arranged chronologically according to writer. Entries include title of extant work(s), edition(s) available (with details of *congshu* editions), and holding location. There are separate indexes for *congshu* collections based on the four-corner system; a list of holding libraries arranged by location (250 Chinese collections, 32 Japanese, and that of the Library of Congress); and authors' finding list by four-corner number.

Songren bieji xulu 宋人別集敘錄, Zhu Shangshu 祝尚書, Ba-Shu, 1997. More than 500 Song *bieji* in collections in China, Taiwan, Japan, Korea, and the United States.

An Index to Sung Dynasty Titles Extant in Ts'ung-shu, Brian E. McKnight, comp., CMC, 1977. Lists 4,500 titles, incl. variants, by 1,664 authors as found in *Zhongguo congshu zonglu* 中國叢書綜錄 (9.9).

Songdai Shuren zhuzuo cunyi lu 宋代蜀人著作存佚錄 (Catalog of extant and lost writings by Sichuanese authors of the Song period), Xu Zhaoding 許肇鼎, comp., Ba-Shu, 1986.

Nihon genson Sôjin bunshû mokuroku 日本現存宋人文集目錄 (Catalog of collected works of Song authors), Yoshida Tora 吉田寅 et al., eds., Tokyo, 1959; rev. edition, Kyûko, 1972. Lists the works of 528 individuals whose *bieji* are held in Japanese collections.

Sôdai bunshû sakuin 宋代文集索引 (Index to Song collected works), compiled under the direction of Saeki Tomi 佐伯富, Tôyôshi kenkyûkai, 1970; rpnt., Zongqing tushu, 1986. Contains 70,000 entries to personal names and toponyms, technical terms, and key words in 10 major and 23 supplementary collections of 10 Song literary figures: Fan Zhongyan 范仲淹 (989–1052), Hong Gua 洪适 (1117–84), Ouyang Xiu 歐陽修 (1007–72), Sima Guang 司馬光 (1019–86), Ye Shi 葉適 (1150–1223), Yin Zhu 尹洙 (1001/2–42), Zeng Gong 曾鞏 (1019–83), Zhang Fangping 張方平 (1007–91), Zhen Dexiu 真德秀 (1178–1235), and Zhu Xi 朱熹 (1130–1200).

A Guide to Sources of Chinese Economic History, AD 618–1368, Robert Hartwell, comp., UChP, 1964. Annotated index to materials of interest to the economic historian drawn from 112 collected works of Tang, Song, and Yuan authors included in the *Siku quanshu*.

Biji *Indexes*

In addition to the two Kyoto *biji* indexes (Chapter 31), there are two especially for the Song:

Tôkei mukaroku Muryôroku tô goi sakuin 東京夢華錄夢梁錄等語彙索引 (Index to *Dongjing menghua lu*, *Mengliang lu* and others), Umehara Kaoru 梅原郁, ed., Jinbun, 1979.

Liu Kuntai 劉坤太, *Diannaohua Songren biji jiansuo xitong* 電腦化宋人筆記檢索系統 (Computerized index to Song *biji*), The 50 titles in this database are listed in *Research Tools for the Study of Sung History*, 57 (47.4.2).

There is a repertory of the terminology in Tang and Song *biji*: *Tang-Song biji yuci huishi* 唐宋筆記語辭匯釋 (46.2, *Biji*). More useful, including for *biji*, is *Song yuyan cidian* 宋語言詞典 (47.4.2, *Language*).

Biji 筆記

Of the approximately 200 extant Song *biji* (see Chapter 31 on this genre), five titles have been selected as examples here:

Rongzhai suibi wuji 容齋隨筆五集 (Tolerant Study notebooks, five collections), Hong Mai 洪邁 (1123–1202), 2 vols., Shanghai guji, 1978. *H-Y Index 13: Rongzhai suibi wuji zonghe yinde* 容齋隨筆五集綜合引得 (Combined indices to the five collections of *Tolerant Study Notebooks*). Also indexed in *CZS*. Wide range of topics in 1,217 entries relating to civil service and intellectual life. There is a detailed description of the contents in *SB*, 292–308.

Dongjing menghua lu 東京夢華錄 (The eastern capital: A dream of splendors past), Meng Yuanlao 孟元老 (fl. 1090–1150), 1148; annotated and punctuated, Deng Zhicheng 鄧之誠, ed., Zhonghua, 1959; indexed in *CZS*. Lively and detailed descriptions of life in the Northern Song capital of Bianliang 汴梁 (Kaifeng) based on the author's reminiscences of his youthful years there. Umehara (1979) also indexes the *Dongjing menghua lu* as well as the *Mengliang lu*, the *Wulin jiushi*, and the other two key *biji* for the Southern Song capital of Lin'an 臨安 (Hangzhou), namely Nai Deweng 耐得翁, *Ducheng jisheng* 都城紀勝 (The famous sites of the capital) and Anon., *Xihu laoren fanshengji* 西湖老人繁勝記 (Description of the famous sites by the old man of the Western Lake); see *SB*, 150–52.

Mengliang lu 夢粱錄 (Record of the splendors of the capital city), Wu Zimu 吳自牧, Zhejiang renmin, 1983. Indexed in *CZS* and Umehara (1979). Reminiscences of the Southern Song capital of Lin'an 臨安 (Hangzhou) modeled after *Menghualu*. See, for example, *Daily Life in China on the Eve of the Mongol Invasion, 1250–1276*, Jacques Gernet, Allen and Unwin, 1962; SUP, 1970 (French original, 1959).

Wulin jiushi 武林舊事 (Former events in Wulin [Hangzhou]), Zhou Mi 周密 (1232–99 or 1308), 1280. Reminiscences of the Southern Song capital; see *SB*, 155–56. Indexed in *CZS* and in Umehara (1979).

Mengxi bitan 夢溪筆談 (Jottings from the Mengxi), Shen Kua 沈括 (1031–95), 1089–93. Mengxi was an area in Zhenjiang 鎮江, Jiangsu, to which Shen retired to write in 1088. Newly punctuated and corrected edition, *Xin jiaozheng 'Mengxi bitan'* 新校正夢溪筆談, Hu Daojing 胡道靜, ed., Zhonghua, 1957, 1975. One-third of the 507 notes record the author's observations of natural phenomena and the results of his experiments. A major work in the history of Chinese invention. Contains the first reference to the magnetic compass; see *SB*, 226–28.

Agriculture

Nongshu 農書, Chen Fu 陳敷, ed. (35.1)

47.3 Archaeology and Inscriptions

On the beginnings of the antiquarian study of inscriptions in the Song, see Chapter 17.

A Journey into China's Antiquity, vol. 3, *Sui-Tang-Song* (see 8.1 on this authoritative illustrated series).

Songling 宋陵 (Song tombs): the tombs of seven out of the nine emperors of the Northern Song may be visited at Gongyi city 鞏義市, Gong county 鞏縣, Henan, about 130 km (80 miles) to the north of Kaifeng. The two emperors not buried here were Huizong 徽宗 and his eldest son and successor, Qinzong 欽宗. Having been taken captive by the Jurchen in 1127, they died in captivity in what is now the province of Heilongjiang.

Valerie Hansen, "Inscriptions: Historical Sources for the Song," *Bulletin of Song-Yuan Studies* 19 (1987).

Dieter Kuhn, *A Place for the Dead: An Archaeological Documentary on Graves and Tombs of the Song Dynasty (960–1279)*, Forum, 1996.

Angela Schottenhammer, *Grabinschriften in der Song-Dynastie*, Forum, 1995.

Angela Schottenhammer, "Characteristics of Song Epitaphs," in *Burial in Sung China*, Dieter Kuhn, ed., Forum, 1994, 253–306.

One of the largest collections of rubbings of inscriptions contains eight volumes of Song inscriptions: *Beijing tushuguan cang Zhongguo lidai shike taben huibian* 北京圖書館藏中國歷代石刻拓本匯編 (17.3).

Annotated Bibliography to the Shike shiliao xinbian [New Edition of Historical Materials Carved on Stone], Dieter Kuhn and Helga Stahl, eds., Forum, 1991. Listing of stone inscriptions from the Song, Liao, and Jin. Arranged alphabetically by title; there is an author index.

Islamic Inscriptions in Quanzhou (Quanzhou Yisilanjiao shike 泉州伊斯蘭教石刻)*, Chen Dasheng 陳達生, ed., Chen Enming 陳恩明, tr., Yinchuan: Ningxia renmin and Fujian renmin, 1984. Contains transcriptions of more than 300 stelae with inscriptions in ancient Arabic and Persian from Quanzhou dating from the Song and Yuan with notes. In the 1990s, 20 more Islamic stelae were excavated in Quanzhou. They are mainly the tombstones of merchants.

47.4   Guides and Research Tools

47.4.1   Guides

For library catalogs (e.g., *Songshi* 宋史 "Yiwenzhi" 藝文志) and for collections compiled in the Song and Yuan, see 9.2 and 9.4.

SB. A Sung Bibliography, initiated by Etienne Balazs, Yves Hervouet, ed., HKCUP, 1978. *SB* is an annotated catalog of about 450 works written during the Song, with detailed descriptions of the contents and authors. The entries (80 percent of which are in English, the remainder in French) were written by 80 scholars from around the world. About 250 of the notices were written by Japanese contributors. Each entry outlines the nature of the work and gives bibliographic details. Yves Hervouet points out in his Introduction that the entries vary considerably in quality: "Some notices are outstanding, and are real miniature memoirs on the works described. Others are inadequate, and consist of a résumé of the notice in the *Ssu-k'u ch'üan-shu* or a re-writing of an article in a Japanese historical dictionary." Arrangement is by modified *Sibu* classification. There are separate indexes of books, personal names, and subjects. Since *SB* covers only works written in the Song, there are no entries for works such as the *Songshi* 宋史 (compiled in the Yuan).

Zhongguo lishi da cidian 中國歷史大辭典 (The great encyclopaedia of Chinese history), 14 vols., Shanghai cishu, 1983– , contains a separate volume on *Songshi* 宋史, Deng Guangming 鄧廣銘 (1907–98) and Cheng Yingliu 程應鏐, eds., 1984. See 8.4.2, item 2, for comments on this encyclopaedia.

Jan Yun-hua, "Buddhist Historiography in Sung China," *ZDMG* 114: 360–81 (1964).

Judith M. Boltz, *A Survey of Taoist Literature, Tenth to Seventeenth Centuries*, CCS, Univ. of California, Berkeley, 1987.[12]

47.4.2   Research Tools

Research Tools for the Study of Sung History, Peter Bol, ed., Sung-Yuan Research Aids (II), Binghamton, 1990, 2nd ed., Albany, 1996. A unique listing of indexes and other research tools for Song primary sources (1–82) plus bibliographies of secondary scholarship. There are Wade-

---

[12] See also Piet van der Loon, *Taoist Books in the Libraries of the Sung Period*, London: Ithaca Press, 1984.

Giles and Chinese indexes (83-99), followed by the chapter on the Song from *Ajia rekishi kenkyû nyûmon* アジア歴史研究入門 (8.2.3), which outlines both the primary sources and secondary scholarship (mainly Japanese) on the Song: Chikusa Masaaki 竺沙雅章, "Five Dynasties and the Song," Kenneth Chase, English tr. (103-41).

Language

Song yuyan cidian 宋語言詞典 (Dictionary of the spoken language during the Song dynasty), Yuan Bin 袁賓, ed. in chief, Shanghai jiaoyu, 1997. Contains over 4,000 entries covering mainly popular literature of the Song as well as *biji* 筆記, historical biographies, documents, and so forth. It is intended both for historical linguists and for readers of the popular literature of the period. Arrangement is by *pinyin* and there is also a *pinyin* index. In the series *Jindai Hanyu duandai yuyan cidian xilie* (see 34.3).

Robert Hartwell, "A Guide to Documentary Sources of Middle Chinese History: Documentary Forms Contained in the Collected Papers (*wenji*) of 21 T'ang and Sung Writers," *Bulletin of Song and Yuan Studies* 18: 133-82 (1986).

Note the appendix on Song official jargon in *Songdai guanzhi cidian* 宋代官制辭典 (Dictionary of Song dynasty official titles), Gong Yanming 龔延明, Zhonghua, 1997 (616-71).

Ô Anseki jiten 王安石事典 (Encyclopaedia of Wang Anshi), Higashi Ichio 東一夫, comp., Kokusho kankôkai, 1980.

Biographies

The *Songshi* contains references to about 100,000, people of whom 70,000 were related to the founding emperor, Zhao Kuangyin 趙匡胤 (for an index, see 47.1). If you cannot find a biography in *Sung Biographies* (item 1 below), then try items 2-4, which are indexes to biographical materials on well over 140,000 Song figures. Remember to search similar indexes for dynasties preceding, overlapping, and succeeding the Song (46.3 and Chapter 48). Biographical materials on newly unearthed stone inscriptions are indexed in item 3, but since inscriptions are continually being found, check the titles under *Collections of Inscriptions* (49.4.4).

Sung Biographies, Herbert Franke, ed., 4 vols., Steiner, 1976. Includes biographies of 441 people.

Songren zhuanji ziliao suoyin zengdingben 宋人傳記資料索引增訂本 (Index to biographical materials of Song figures), Chang Bide 昌彼德 et al., comps.; expanded by Wang Deyi 王德毅 and Cheng Yuanmin 程元敏, 6 vols., Taibei: Dingwen, 1976–80; Zhonghua, 1989, contains materials on 15,000 people, most with a short biographical notice. Should be used with the next item.[13]

Songren zhuanji ziliao suoyin bubian 宋人傳記資料索引補編, 3 vols., Sichuan daxue, 1994. Adds a further 14,000 names not found in *Songren zhuanji ziliao suoyin zengdingben* as well as supplementing 6,000 entries of the older work.

Songdai renwu ziliao suoyin 宋代人物資料索引 (Index to materials on Song figures), Shen Zhihong 沈治宏 and Wang Ronggui 王榮貴, eds., 4 vols., Sichuan cishu, 1997. Major index containing 140,000 entries drawn from four reprint collections of Song, Yuan and Ming gazetteers, namely, *Song-Yuan fangzhi congkan, Tianyige Mingdai cang fangzhi xuankan* and *Xubian*, and *Riben cang Zhongguo difangzhi congkan*. There is a *pinyin* index to the four-corner arrangement.

Songren nianpu jimu Songbian Songren nianpu xuankan 宋人年譜集目宋編宋人年譜選刊 (Bibliography of chronological biographies of Song personalities and selected Song *nianpu*), Wu Hongze 吳洪澤, ed., Ba-Shu, 1995.

Songren nianpu congkan 宋人年譜叢刊 (Collectanea of Song chronological biographies), Li Wenze 李文澤, Wu Hongze 吳洪澤, et al., eds., 12 vols., Ba-Shu, 2000. Reprints of 300 Song *nianpu* of 250 Song personalities.

Songren shengzu kao shili 宋人生卒考示例 (Verification of dates of birth and death of Song figures), Zheng Qian 鄭騫, Taibei: Huashi, 1977.

---

[13] It was based on two previous indexes: (1) *Song Biographical Index* compiled under the direction of Aoyama Sadao 青山定雄 by the Japanese Committee for the Song Project, *Sôjin denki sakuin* 宋人傳記索引, Tôyô bunko, 1968, which included dates (for some 8,000 Chinese who lived during the Song) as well as alternative names and the names of paternal ancestors for three generations if known (this last category is not reproduced in the Chang Bide index). The materials indexed include biographies and commemorative writings found in a wide variety of sources including local gazetteers, collected works, encyclopaedias, collections of epigraphy, etc.; (2) *Sishiqi zhong Songdai zhuanji zonghe yinde* 四十七種宋代傳記綜合引得 (Combined indices to 47 Song dynasty biographical collections), *H-Y Index* 34. Altogether, 9,024 figures are included. Arrangement is by ordinary names and by alternative names but does not give the other types of information included in Aoyama's index (1).

Tang-Song huajia renming cidian 唐宋畫家人名辭典 (Personal-name dictionary of Tang and Song painters), Zhu Zhuyu 朱鑄禹, Zhongguo gudian yishu, 1958.

Song Liao Jin huajia shiliao 宋遼金畫家史料 (Historical materials on Song, Liao, and Jin painters), Chen Gaohua 陳高華, Wenwu, 1984.

Official Titles and Officeholders

Songdai guanzhi cidian 宋代官制辭典 (Dictionary of Song dynasty official titles), Gong Yanming 龔延明, ed., Zhonghua, 1997. The definitive reference work for Song official titles. Particularly strong on alternative titles. Also contains an appendix on Song official jargon (616–71) as well as organization tables (672–731).

An Introduction to the Civil Service of Sung China: With Emphasis on Its Personnel Administration, Winston W. Lo, UHP, 1987. One of the important documents used by Lo is the *Libu tiaofa* 吏部條法 (Regulations of the Board of Personnel), of which nine chapters were reconstituted from the *Yongle dadian*. Edward Kracke, Jr., *Civil Service in Early Sung China*, HUP, 1953, includes the list of official titles and ranks of 1038.

Sôshi shokkanshi sakuin 宋史職官志索引 (Index to the monograph on official posts in the *Songshi*), Saeki Tomi 佐伯富, comp., Tôyôshi kenkyûkai, 1963. Arranged by Japanese reading; has stroke-order index. There is a useful introduction by Miyazaki Ichisada 宮崎市定, "Sôdai kansei josetsu: *Sôshi* shokkanshi o ikani yomubeki ka" 宋代官制序説宋史職官志を如何に讀むべきか (Introduction to the Song bureaucracy: How should the monograph on official posts in the *Songshi* be read?), 1–63. See also Umehara Kaoru, "Civil and Military Titles in Sung: The Chi-lu-kuan System," *AA* 50: 1–30 (1986). Useful for its chart showing ranking systems from different periods.

Les fonctionnaires des Song: Index des titres, Fu-jui Chang, Paris, 1962. Includes among the works indexed the *Songshi* "Zhiguanzhi" 宋史職官志 (Monograph on official posts in the *Songshi*).

Song zaifu biannian lu jiaobu 宋宰輔編年錄校補 (Chronology of Song chief and assisting counselors, revised), Wang Ruilai 王瑞來, ed., Zhonghua, 1986. Shows membership of the Council of State for the entire Song period, including documents of appointment and anecdotal information.

Bei Song jingfu nianbiao 北宋經撫年表 (Chronological tables of Northern Song civil and military intendants); *Nan Song zhifu nianbiao* 南宋制撫年表 (Chronological tables of Southern Song civil and military intendants), Wu Tingxie 吳廷燮, punctuated and corrected by Zhang

Chenshi 張忱石, Zhonghua, 1984. Includes all circuit-level intendants as well as prefects (*zhizhou* 知州) and gives dates of appointment. Arrangement by circuit and prefecture and by time. There is a personal-name index.

Geography

Zhongguo lishi dituji 中國歷史地圖集, vol. 6, *Song Liao Jin shiqi* 宋遼金時期 (Song, Liao, and Jin); see 4.3.2 on this essential series.

Aoyama Sadao 青山定雄, *Tô-Sô jidai no kôtsû to chishi chizu no kenkyû* 唐宋時代の交通と地志地圖の研究 (Collected studies on communications, gazetteers, and maps of the Tang and Song), Yoshikawa kôbunkan, 1963. There are also maps of Song communications (roads, grain transport, etc.), included.

Chronology

Zhongguo lishi dashi biannian: Wudai-Shiguo Song Liao Xia Jin 中國歷史大事編年五代十國宋遼夏金 (Chronology of major events in Chinese history: Five Dynasties, Ten Kingdoms, Song, Liao, Xia, and Jin), Beijing, 1987.

Sôdaishi nenpyô 宋代史年表 (Chronological table of events of the Song dynasty), Aoyama Sadao 青山定雄, ed. in chief, vol. 1, *Hoku-Sô* 北宋 (Northern Song), Tôyô bunko, 1967; vol. 2, *Nan-Sô* 南宋 (Southern Song), Tôyô bunko, 1974. Gives year-by-year tables of important events and cultural matters as well as corresponding dates for Korea, Liao, Xixia, Jin, and Yuan. Based on the basic annals of the *Songshi*.

Bibliographies of Secondary Scholarship

Yang Weisheng, "A Brief Survey of Song Studies in Chinese over the Last Ten Years," Lee-fang Ch'ien, tr., *Bulletin of Song-Yuan Studies* 20 (1988), 1–17.

Okazaki Hiroshi, "Japanese Studies in Chinese History (Song, Yuan, Ming and Qing), 1973–83," Joseph McDermott, tr., Tokyo Center for East Asian Cultural Studies, 1986.

Hasegawa Yoshio, "Trends in Postwar Japanese Studies in Sung History: A Bibliographical Introduction," *AA* 50: 95–120 (1986).

Peter J. Golas, "Rural China in the Song," *JAS* 39.2: 291–325 (1980).

Bibliographie et index des travaux en chinois sur les Song 1900–1975, Chen Qinghao 陳慶浩, comp., Paris, 1979. Arranged by subject. Has subject and author indexes.

Liao Song Xixia Jin shehui shenghuoshi 遼宋西夏金社會生活史 (A history of social life in the Liao, Song, Xixia, and Jin periods), Zhu Ruixi 朱瑞熙 et al., Shehui kexue, 1998. Contains much fascinating material (with references indicated) on food and drink, travel, birth and death, women and marriage, religion and ghosts, festivals, music and dance, education, medicine, and much else besides.

Societies and Journals

Journal of Sung-Yuan Studies (began as *Sung Studies Newsletter*, 1969–80, changed title to *Bulletin of Sung-Yuan Studies*, 1980–88 and adopted present title in 1989). Contains translations of the annual *Shigaku zasshi* state-of-the-field articles on Five Dynasties, Song, and Yuan studies and also has regular bibliographical updates of Chinese, Japanese, and Western scholarship on the Song period.

Songshi yanjiu tongxun 宋史研究通訊, 1985– , Shanghai shifan daxue.

Songshi yanjiuhui 宋史研究會 (Song history society), Nanjing; founded in 1980. *Songshi yanjiu lunwenji* 宋史研究論文集 (Collected research articles on Song history). Has been published about two years after the meetings (held every other year) since 1982.

Liao, Xixia, Jin, and Yuan

916–1368

Liao 遼 (*Qidan* 契丹, Khitan)	916–1125
Xixia 西夏 (*Dangxiang* 黨項, Tangut)	1038–1227
Jin 金 (*Nüzhen* 女真, Jurchen)	1115–1234
Yuan 元 (*Menggu* 蒙古, Mongol)	1260–1368

The difficulty of finding unbiased sources for the alien regimes of Liao, Xixia, Jin and Yuan is compounded by the fact that the *Liaoshi* 遼史 was written 200 years after the fall of the dynasty, long after its archives had been lost, and the Xixia was never counted as a legitimate dynasty and so had no Standard History. Until recently it has not attracted the attention of historians. The *Yuanshi* 元史 is generally reckoned to be one of the worse, if not the worst, of all the Standard Histories.

Given that the Liao, Xixia, and Jin fought against and coexisted with the Song and that the Yuan attacked the Song for over 50 years, it goes without saying that the basic sources for the Song are also important for these dynasties (see 47.1 and 47.2), as are those of the Ming for the Yuan (49.1). Only when there is explicit overlap in sources or research tools are the works introduced in the chapters on the Song and the Ming (47 and 49) repeated here.

There are a number of earlier references which cover the Liao, Jin, and Yuan—for example, biographical indexes. Not infrequently these have been superseded by research tools for a single dynasty.

48.1   Guides to Sources

Only those guides to two or more alien dynasties are listed in this section. *CHC*, vol. 6 is the best introduction to the history of the

Liao, Xixia, Jin, and Yuan between two covers. It also contains good bibliographies:

"Bibliographical Essays," in *CHC*, vol. 6. These are a good introduction to the traditional sources, Qing scholarship, and secondary sources (665–726).

Bu Liao Jin Yuan yiwenzhi 補遼金元藝文志 (9.4).

Zhongguo lishi da cidian 中國歷史大辭典 (The great encyclopaedia of Chinese history), 14 vols., Shanghai cishu, 1983– . Contains a separate volume on *Liao Xia Jin Yuanshi* 遼夏金元史, Cai Meibiao 蔡美彪, ed., 1986. See 8.4.2, item 2, for comments.

48.2 Liao

The Khitan kingdom was established in 916; Khitan was replaced with the dynastic name Liao in 948. In 983, Liao was changed back to Khitan, which in 1066 was called Liao again. Liao was the name of the river in the area in modern Liaoning which the Khitan counted as their home.

Liaoshi 遼史 (Standard History of the Liao), edited at the Yuan history office, 1343–44; 5 vols., Zhonghua, 1974; 6th prnt., 1996. It covers the years 916–1125.[1] The Liao dynasty (遼代, 916–1125) was only partially sinicized. It did not produce huge quantities of historical works in the first place, and its conquerors, the Jurchen Jin, did not compile a Standard History of the Liao. By the time the *Liaoshi* was written, the discussion of whether to include the dynasty in the legitimate succession had been going on for 200 years. The Liao archives were long since lost, and no *guoshi* 國史 or documents survived for the Yuan editors to work on. Despite the fact that it is one of the weakest of the Standard Histories, the *Liaoshi* is an essential source for a dynasty from which almost no documents survive. There is a full personal-name index[2] as well as a glossary.[3]

---

[1] "Bibliographical Essays, 1: The Liao," in *CHC*, vol. 6, 665–74.

[2] *Liaoshi renming suoyin* 遼史人名索引, Zhonghua, 1982.

[3] *Ryôshi sakuin* 遼史索引 (Index to the Standard History of the Liao), Jinbun, 1937. Cannot be relied upon for completeness.

The "Guoyujie" 國語解 chapter (at the end of the "Liezhuan" 列傳) contains important materials on the Khitan language.[4]

Karl A. Wittfogel and Feng Chia-sheng (Feng Jiasheng 馮家昇), *History of Chinese Society: Liao (907–1125)*, Philadelphia: American Philosophical Society, *Transactions*, n.s., 26 (1949). A massive study on the social, economic, and political institutions of the Liao period with many translated excerpts from the *Liaoshi* arranged by category. There is a thorough index.

"The 'Treatise on Punishments' in the Liao history," Herbert Franke, tr., *Central Asiatic Journal*, 27: 9–38 (1983). Translation of the monograph on law in the *Liaoshi*.

Other Textual Sources

Qidan guozhi 契丹國志 (Monograph on the Qidan kingdom), Ye Longli 葉隆禮, *jinshi* 1247, was written on the basis of Song sources. It is the only text used by the editors of the *Liaoshi* to have survived.[5] There is an integral translation into Russian with introduction and commentary.[6]

Koryŏ-sa 高麗史: for this and other Korean sources, see 42.5.

Liaoshi huibian 遼史彙編 (Collected documents on the history of the Liao), Yang Jialuo 楊家駱, ed., 10 vols., Dingwen, 1973.

Liaoshi huibianbu 遼史彙編補 (Supplement to *Liaoshi huibian*), Yang Jialuo 楊家駱, ed., Dingwen, 1974.

Quan Liaowen 全遼文 (Complete Liao writings), Chen Shu 陳述, ed., Zhonghua, 1982. Also includes inscriptions.

Qidan xiaozi yanjiu 契丹小字研究 (Studies on the Khitan script), Qingge'ertai 清格爾泰 et al., Shehui kexue, 1985.

Édouard Chavannes, "Voyageurs chinois chez les Khitans et les Joutchen." (41.5.1).

---

[4] *Qinding Liao Jin Yuan sanshi Guoyujie suoyin* 欽訂遼金元三史國語解索引 (Index to the national language glossaries in the Liao, Jin, and Yuan Histories), Taiwan: Shangwu, 1986.

[5] There is an index available: *Qidan guozhi tongjian* 契丹國志通檢, Wu Xiaoling 吳曉鈴 et al., comps., *CFS* 12, 1949; Chengwen, 1968.

[6] V. S. Taskin, *Istoriia gosudarstva Kidanei (Tsidan' go chzhi)*, Nauka, 1979.

Biographies

Liao Jin Yuan zhuanji sanshi zhong zonghe yinde 遼金元傳記三十種綜合引得 (Combined indices to 30 Liao, Jin, and Yuan biographical collections), *H-Y Index* 35. To be used with the Song biographical indexes, since the dynasties overlapped.

Ryô Kin Genjin denki sakuin 遼金元人傳記索引 (Index to biographies of Liao, Jin, and Yuan persons), Umehara Kaoru 梅原郁 and Kinugawa Tsuyoshi 衣川強 comp., Jinbun, 1972. There are 3,200 individuals listed; 130 *bieji* were consulted.

Archaeology

Liao art and artifacts, including excavated imperial capitals, imperial tombs, tomb frescoes, and architectural remains, have been intensively studied since the 1930s. The Liaoning Provincial Museum, one of the finest in China, includes a particularly rich collection.

Xiang Chunsong 項春松, *Liaodai lishi yu kaogu* 遼代歷史與考古 (Liao dynasty history and archaeology), Nei-Menggu renmin, 1996.

Liaodai shike wenbian 遼代石刻文編 (Liao dynasty inscriptions carved on stone), Xiang Nan 向南, comp., Hebei jiaoyu, 1995, contains transcriptions of more than 300 Liao inscriptions of all kinds, including many newly excavated.

Nancy Shatzman Steinhardt, *Liao Architecture*, UHP, 1997.

Societies and Journals

Liao Jin shi yanjiuhui 遼金史研究會 (Liao-Jin history society), Shenyang; founded in 1982.

48.3 Xixia

The Tangut Xia state ruled over a huge area extending from Mongolia to Xinjiang. It was situated between the Song, Liao, and Jin, and lasted for almost 200 years (ca. 982–1227). The Tanguts themselves used the Chinese name Da Xia 大夏.[7] In Tangut they used a name

---

[7] The ancestors of Li Yuanhao 李元昊, the founder of Da Xia 大夏, were enfeoffed by the Tang as Dukes of Xia (Xiaguo gong 夏國公) in 883 and at the same time appointed governors-general of the three northwestern prefectures of Xiazhou 夏州 (the capital of the short Xiongnu kingdom of Da Xia 大夏,

Footnote continued on next page

which translates into Chinese as Bai Gao Da Xia Guo 白高大夏國 (Great state of white and high). During the Song, the Chinese called it Xiaguo 夏國. From the Yuan it has been called Xixia 西夏 in Chinese sources (i.e., west of the Song). Some modern scholars prefer to call it Tangut Xia. The customary Chinese term Xixia is used throughout the manual. Xixia was never recognized as a legitimate dynasty and attracted little attention from historians.[8] Original sources are almost non-existent.[9] The main sources until modern times were the *liezhuan* chapters on the Xixia in the *Songshi*, *Liaoshi*, and *Yuanshi*. In the early twentieth century, considerable quantities of Tangut-language sources were discovered at the Xixia capital of Kharakhoto (Halahetuo 哈拉何托; Heishuicheng 黑水城; Heicheng 黑城 near modern Ejinaqi in Inner Mongolia) and Dunhuang, and later at other sites. Most of the early discoveries were made by Petr Kozlov in 1907, who took them back to Russia, where they are now housed in the Institute of Oriental Studies of the Russian Academy of Sciences, St. Petersburg. The Tangut documents were deciphered only in the 1970s and 1980s. The originals have been published by Shanghai guji:

E cang Heishuicheng wenxian 俄藏黑水城文獻 (Tangut documents from Heishuicheng held in Russia), 9 vols., Shanghai guji, 1997–99.

These documents offer the first chance of seeing the Xixia from the inside, a task made easier by the publication of a well-indexed dictionary containing definitions of 6,000 Tangut characters (including 107 variants) with explanations both in Chinese and in English.[10]

407–31), Suizhou 綏州, and Yinzhou 銀州. In 967, another ancestor was given the title King of Xia by the Song. Hence the choice of the dynastic name Da Xia on the establishment of the new empire in 1038; see *CHC*, vol. 6, 154–204. The main capital was Xingqing fucheng 興慶府城 near Yinzhou about 180 km (112 miles) to the west of Xiazhou.

[8] Ruth W. Dunnell, "The Recovery of Tangut History," *Orientations* 27.4: 28–31 (1996)

[9] "Bibliographical Essays, 2: The Hsi Hsia," in *CHC*, vol. 6, 674–78; Ruth Dunnell, "Who Are the Tanguts? Remarks on Tangut Ethnogenesis and the Ethnonym Tangut," *JAH* 18: 78–89 (1984).

[10] Li Fanwen 李范文, *Xia-Han zidian* 夏漢字典 (Tangut-Han dictionary), Ningxia renmin, 1997.

See Ruth W. Dunnell, "The Hsi Hsia," *CHC*, vol. 6, 154–204, as well as the following:

Ruth W. Dunnell, *The Great State of White and High: Buddhism and State Foundation in Eleventh-Century Xia*, UHP, 1996.

Ruth W. Dunnell, *Buddhism and the State in Eleventh Century Xia: Studies in the Sources of Early Tangut History*, UHP, 1995.

Xixiaxue gailun 西夏學概論 (Introduction to the study of the Xixia), Wang Tianshun 王天順, ed. in chief, Gansu wenhua, 1995, covers the language, culture, history, and archaeology of the Xixia.

Shi Jinbo 史金波 et al., *Xixia wenwu* 西夏文物 (Material culture of Xixia), Wenwu, 1988.

Wenhai yanjiu 文海研究, Shi Jinpo 史金波 et al., eds., Shehui kexue, 1983, contains a fragment of a rare Tangut-Chinese glossary, the *Wenhai* 文海 (anon, comp., 12th century) plus Chinese translation and index.

Li Fanwen 李范文, *Tongyin yanjiu* 通音研究 (Research on the *Tongyin* 通音), Ningxia renmin, 1986. Tangut dictionary of homophones.

E. I. Kychanov, *Izmenennyi i zanovo utverzhdennyi kodeks deviza tsarstvovaniia nebesnoe protsvetanie (1149–1169)*, vol.1, 1988; vol. 2, 1987; vol. 3, 1989; vol. 4, 1989. Translation and study of the almost complete Xia law code (*Tiansheng lüling* 天盛律令), of which a Chinese translation has been made: *Xixia Tiansheng lüling* 西夏天盛律令 in *ZZFDJ*. See also Shi Jinbo 史金波, "Xixia *Tiansheng lüling* lüelun" 西夏天盛律令略論, *Ningxia shehui kexue* 1 (1993).

Evgenii I. Kycanov (Kychanov) and Herbert Franke, *Tangutische und chinesische Quellen zur Militärgesetzgebung des 11. bis 13. Jahrhunderts*, Munich: Bayerischen Akademie der Wissenschaften, 1990.

Evgenii I. Kychanov, "Monuments of Tangut Legislation (Twelfth–Thirteenth Centuries)," in *Etudes tibétaines, Actes du XXIXe Congrès international des orientalistes*, July 1973, Paris: L'Asiathèque, 1976, 29–42.

Archaeology

The Xixia imperial mausolea are located in the desert about 35 km (22 miles) to the west of Yinquan 銀川 (the modern capital of the Ningxia Hui Autonomous Region). They extend over an area of 50 sq. km (20 sq. miles). There are nine imperial mausolea and 207 satellite tombs. Each of the imperial mausolea contains the ruins of eight different types of building, including "a corner tower, a magpie tower, a tablet pavilion, a moon city, a tomb park, towers on either side of the gate, a corner watch tower, a tomb top and a presentation hall." *Xixia ling* 西夏陵, Ningxia Wenkaosuo et al., eds., Dongfang, 1995, 164. Construction probably began in 1032 on the death of King Deming. The tomb site was destroyed in 1226 and 1227 during the Mongolian conquest of the Xixia.

48.4 Jin

"Anchuhu" 按出虎 in Jurchen means "gold" after the Anchuhu River (Ashihe 阿什河 in Heilongjiang province), which produces gold. This was the area from which the Jurchen came. Hence the dynastic name Jin 金.[11]

Jinshi 金史 (Standard History of the Jin), edited at the Yuan history office, 1343–44; punctuated and annotated edition, 8 vols., Zhonghua, 1975; 5th prnt., 1995. It covers the years 1115–1234.[12] One of the better edited of the Standard Histories, thanks to the efforts of Wang E 王鶚 (1190–1273), a senior Jin official who ensured that basic documents and historical works, including his own *Jinshi* 金史, were not lost at the fall of the Jin (see under Wang E, *Ru'nan yishi* below). One feature not found in other Standard Histories is the table of foreign embassies received at the Jin court. Another feature is the "Jinguo yujie" 金國語解 chapter at the end, which contains a list of non-Chinese names and terms with their Chinese equivalents. This is important for the study of the Jurchen language. There is a full personal-name

---

[11] See Hok-lam Chan (Chen Xuelin 陳學林), "Patterns of Legitimation in Imperial China," in *Legitimation in Imperial China: Discussions Under the Jurchen-Chin Dynasty*, Univ. of Washington Press, 1984, 19–48. Chan returns to the same question in "'Ta Chin' (Great Golden): The Origin and Changing Interpretations of the Jurchen State Name," *TP* 77.4–5: 253–99 (1991).

[12] Hok-lam Chan, "Bibliographical Essays, 3. The Chin Dynasty," in *CHC*, vol. 6, 678–89. Hok-lam Chan, "Chinese Official History at the Yuan Court: the Composition of the Liao, Chin and Sung Histories," in *China Under Mongol Rule*, John D. Langlois, ed., PUP, 1981, 56–106. Hok-lam Chan, "Patterns of Legitimation in Imperial China," Part I of Chan, *Legitimation*, 1984, 19–48. The author provides in Part III of this work a complete annotated translation of a Jin official collection of documents on the discussions on legitimate succession, 143–70.

index to the *Jinshi*[13] as well as a glossary of terms used in the entire work.[14]

Herbert Franke, "Chinese Texts on the Jurchen: Translation of the Jurchen Monograph in the *San ch'ao pei meng hui pien*," *Zentralasiatische Studien* 9: 119–86 (1975); "Chinese Texts on the Jurchen II: A Translation of Chapter One of the *Chin shih*," *Zentralasiatische Studien* 12: 413–52 (1978).

Da Jin guozhi 大金國志 supplements *Jinshi*. Indexed.[15]

Wang E 王鶚, *Ru'nan yishi* 汝南遺事 (Deeds of Ru'nan). For a fully annotated translation of the *Ru'nan yishi*, see Hok-lam Chan, *The Fall of the Jurchen Chin: Wang E's Memoir of Ts'ai-chou Under the Mongol Siege (1233–34)*, Steiner, 1996. Ru'nan was the ancient name of Caizhou 蔡州, to which the Jin court inadvisably fled after quitting Kaifeng. The last emperor committed suicide, and the Jin forces capitulated in February 1234.

Da Jin zhaoling shizhu 大金詔令釋注 (Edicts of the Jin, annotated and translated into Modern Chinese), Dong Kechang 董克昌, ed., Heilongjiang renmin, 1993.

Da Jin diaofa lu 大金弔伐錄 (Records of submission and attack under the great Jin), 1959. "A mine of information on the military and political situation during the collapse of the Northern Sung state," Chan (1994).

Comprehensive Literary Collection

Jinwen zui 金文最 (Complete collection of Jin literature), Zhang Jinwu 張金吾 (1787–1829), comp., 1895; rpnt., Chengwen, 1967.

Biji 筆記

Guiqian zhi 歸潛志 (Records written in retirement), Liu Qi 劉祁 (1203–50); Zhonghua, 1983. Life in Kaifeng during the last years of the Jin, including an eyewitness account of the Mongol siege. See Hok-lam

---

[13] *Jinshi renming suoyin* 金史人名索引, Cui Wenyin 崔文印, comp., Zhonghua, 1980.

[14] *Kinshi goi shûsei* 金史語彙集成 (Glossary to the *Jinshi*), Onogawa Hidemi 小野川秀美, 3 vols., Jinbun, 1960–62. Based on the *Bona* edition. Includes people, places, organizations, offices, etc.

[15] *Da Jin guozhi tongjian* 大金國志通檢, Wu Xiaoling 吳曉鈴 et al., comps., CFS 11, 1949; Chengwen, 1968.

Chan, "Liu Ch'i and His *Kuei-ch'ien chih*," in his *The Historiography of the Chin Dynasty: Three Studies*, Steiner, 1970, 121–88.

Biographies

Liao Jin Yuan zhuanji sanshi zhong zonghe yinde 遼金元傳記三十種綜合引得 (Combined indices to 30 Liao, Jin, and Yuan biographical collections), *H-Y Index* 35. To be used with the Song biographical indexes, since the dynasties overlapped.

Ryô Kin Genjin denki sakuin 遼金元人傳記索引 (Index to biographies of Liao, Jin, and Yuan persons), Umehara Kaoru 梅原郁 and Kinugawa Tsuyoshi 衣川強, comps., Jinbun, 1972. There are 3,200 individuals listed; 130 *wenji* were consulted.

Index to Biographical Material in Chin and Yuan Literary Works, Igor de Rachewiltz and Miyoko Nakano, comps., ANUP, 1st series, 1970; 2nd and 3rd series (with May Wang), 1972 and 1979.

Archaeology

Russian studies of pre-dynastic Jurchen archaeology are summarized in A. P. Okladnikov and V. E. Medvedev, "Chzhurchzheni Priamur'ia po dannym arkheologii," *Problemy Dal'nego Vostoka* 4: 118–28 (1974).

Nüzhenwen cidian 女真文詞典 (Dictionary of Jurchen), Jin Qicong 金啓孮, ed., Wenwu, 1984.

Secondary Studies

Herbert Franke, "The Chin Dynasty," *CHC*, vol. 6, 215–320.

Studies on the Jurchens and the Chin Dynasty, Herbert Franke and Hoklam Chan, Variorum, 1997. Collected articles.

Jing-shen Tao, *The Jurchen in Twelfth-Century China: A Study of Sinicization*, UWP, 1976.

Societies and Journals

Liao Jin shi yanjiuhui 遼金史研究會 (Liao-Jin history society), Shenyang; founded in 1982.

48.5 Yuan

The main sources for the rise of the Mongol empire and the history of the Yuan dynasty (1260–1368) are in Mongolian, Chinese, and Persian, supplemented by Korean works (in Literary Chinese) and accounts in Latin. The best introduction to the history of the rise of the Mongolian empire and to the Yuan dynasty is *CHC*, vol. 6, 321–664.

"Mongol" is derived from the Mengwu 蒙兀, a branch of the Shiwei 室韋 tribe, whose name first appears in Chinese sources in the ninth century. Thereafter, they are referred to as Menggu 萌古, Menggu 朦骨, Mengguli 蒙古里, Menggusi 蒙古斯, Mangguzi 盲骨子 (blind wretch, a favorite in Ming fiction), and so forth. The Mongols began using the name Menggu 蒙古 for all their tribes in the early thirteenth century. Chinggis khan named his kingdom Da Menggu guo 大蒙古國 and from this time onward it was abbreviated in Chinese as Menggu 蒙古.

Khubilai adopted the concept "Fundamental force" (*Yuan* 元) for the name of his dynasty from the opening lines of the *Yijing* 易經.[16]

48.5.1   Main Historical Works

Yuanshi 元史 (Standard History of the Yuan), Song Lian 宋濂 (1310–81) et al., comps., 1369–70; Zhonghua, 15 vols., 1976; 5th prnt., 1995. Covers the years 1206–1369. Edited in less than a year (faster than any other Standard History), it is incomplete and inaccurate (especially the *liezhuan*), yet nevertheless, in the words of Frederick Mote, it is "the modern historian's essential resource for the study of the Yuan period."[17] The fact that it is unpolished is a blessing in disguise in that many documents are preserved in their original or near-original state. This is especially true of the monographs. There is a glossary of terms used in the entire work and also a personal-name index.[18]

---

[16] Zhao Yi 趙翼 (1727–1814), "Yuan jian guohao shiyong wenyi" 元建國號始用文義 (In establishing their dynastic name, the Yuan began the practice of using literary meanings), *Nian'er shi zhaji* 廿二史劄記 (Critical notes on the twenty-two Standard Histories), 1799, *juan* 31. Zhao's brief essay is translated in full in Chan (1991), 254–56. See also *CHC*, vol. 6, 458; Herbert Franke, *From Tribal Chieftan to Universal God: The Legitimation of the Yuan Dynasty*, Bayerische Akademie der Wissenschaften, 1978.

[17] Frederick W. Mote "A Note on Traditional Sources for Yüan History," in *CHC*, vol. 6, 689.

[18] *Genshi goi shûsei* 元史語彙集成 (Glossary to the *Yuanshi*), Tamura Jitsuzô 田村實造, comp., 3 vols., Jinbun, 1961–63. Includes people, places, organi-

Footnote continued on next page

Economic Structure of the Yuan Dynasty: Translation of Chapters 93 and 94 of the Yüan shih, Franz Schurmann, HUP, 1956; rpnt., 1967. This is an annotated translation of the "Shihuozhi" of the *Yuanshi* plus introductions and index.

Un code des Yuan, Paul Ratchnevsky, vol., 1, Leroux, 1937; vol. 2 (PUF, 1972); vol. 3, (with Françoise Aubin), *Index* (PUF, 1977); vol. 4, Collège de France, Institut des Hautes Etudes Chinoises, 1985. This is an annotated translation with a long introduction (vol. 1) and index (vol. 3) of the monograph on law in the *Yuanshi* (*juan* 102–5).

The Military Establishment of the Yuan Dynasty, Ch'i-ch'ing Hsiao, HUP, 1978, contains a translation of *Yuanshi, juan* 98, "Bingzhi" 兵制 (military system) and *juan* 99, "Zhenshu" 陣屬 and "Suwei" 宿衛 (imperial guards).

Yuanchao bishi 元朝秘史 (The secret history of the Mongols). A Mongolian account of their own history, essential for the reigns of Chinggis khan and Ögödei. The Mongolian original having been lost, the text had to be reconstructed from a thirteenth-century phonetic transcription into Chinese characters.[19]

Shengwu qinzheng lu 聖武親征錄 (Record of the personal campaigns of the holy warrior) contains a more detailed chronological account of the reigns of Chinggis khan and Ögödei than found in the *Yuanshi*.[20] It was based on a Mongolian chronicle which was also used by Rashîd al-Din in the preparation of his chronicle,

---

zations, offices, etc. Cannot be relied upon for completeness. *Yuanshi renming suoyin* 元史人名索引, Yao Jing'an 姚景安, comp., Zhonghua, 1982.

[19] *The Secret History of the Mongols: For the First Time Done into English out of the Original Tongue, and Provided with an Exegetical Commentary*, Francis Woodman Cleaves (1911–95), tr., vol. 1, HUP, 1982 (set in type 1956). The author delayed publication for 26 years not wishing to disagree publicly with his teacher, William Hung, who had written some views on the Secret History in *HJAS* in 1951 with which he disagreed. Compare *The Secret History of the Mongols: The Life and Times of Chinggis Khan*, Urgunge Onon, tr. and ed., Curzon, 2000. Note *Index to the Secret History of the Mongols*, Igor de Rachewiltz, comp., IUP, 1972; see also *Menggu bishi* 蒙古秘史 (The secret history of the Mongols), originally called *Tuobu chiyan* 脫卜赤顏 (*Yuanchao bishi* 元朝秘史), Menggu renmin, 1980. *Yuanchao bishi tongjian* 元朝秘史通檢, Zhonghua, 1986.

[20] *Histoire des campagnes de Gengis Khan*, Paul Pelliot and Louis Hambis, trs., Brill, 1951.

Jâmi ʿal-Tavârîkh. Parts of Rashîd (on Ögödei, Güyüg, and Möngke) have been translated into English in John Boyle, *The Successors of Genghis Khan: Translated from the Persian of Rashîd al-Din*, Col. UP, 1971.

Yuan dianzhang 元典章 (Compendium of statutes and substatutes of the Yuan, or, more concisely, Institutions of the Yuan dynasty), 1322; the Shen Jiaben 沈家本 (1908) edition was superseded in 1972 with the publication of a facsimile of the original revised and expanded 1303 edition.[21] "The text consists of a huge collection of codes, ordinances, precedents, cases, and bureaucratic notes, thus reflecting the rich variety of the legal and social life of the Yuan dynasty."[22] Because so much of the text is "in the peculiar style of the Yüan period colloquial Chinese and further reflects, in many cases, the diction and grammar of Mongolian documents that underlie the Chinese texts, it has been difficult to read and also is offensive to cultivated Chinese because of the crudeness of its language."[23]

Gentenshô sakuin kô 元典章索引稿 (*Yuan dianzhang* draft index), 3 vols., Jinbun, 1957; Taibei rpnt., 1973.

Gentenshô nendai sakuin 元典章年代索引 (*Yuan dianzhang* chronological index), Uematsu Tadashi 植松正, ed., Dôhôsha, 1980.

48.5.2   Other Textual Sources

Da Yuan tongzhi tiaoge 大元通制條格 (Comprehensive regulations and statutes of the Yuan), 1321; 1930; rpnt., 2 vols., Taibei, 1968. There is a detailed but fragmentary index: *Tsûsei jôkaku. Kendai tsûki mokuji sakuin* 通制條格憲臺通記目次索引, mimeo., Kyoto, 1954. Annotat-

---

[21] *Da Yuan shengzheng guochao dianzhang* 大元聖政國朝典章, 16 *ce*, Taibei: Palace Museum, 1972. Uematsu Tadashi 植松正 reviews Japanese scholarship on the *Yuan dianzhang* in "*Institutions of the Yuan Dynasty* and Yuan Society," *Gest Library Journal* 5 (Spring 1992), 57–69.

[22] Paul Heng-chao Ch'en, *Chinese Legal Tradition Under the Mongols: The Code of 1291 as Reconstructed*, PUP, 1979. This is a reconstruction and translation of the *Zhiyuan xinge* 至元新格, a set of regulations rather than a formal code (*lü* 律).

[23] Frederick W. Mote, "A Note on Traditional Sources for Yüan History," in *CHC*, vol. 6, 697–98.

ed translation: *Tsûsei jôkaku no kenkyû yakuchû dai-issatsu* 通制條格の研究譯注第一册, Tokyo, 1964.

Jingshi dadian 經世大典 (Compendium for administering the empire), 1330–31. Only fragments survive.

Koryŏ-sa 高麗史: for this and other Korean sources, see 42.5.

Xin Yuanshi 新元史 (New Standard History of the Yuan), Ke Shaomin 柯劭忞 (1850–1933), 1922; Kaiming shudian, *Ershiwu shi*, Shanghai, 1935; Taibei, 1962–69. Covers the years 1206–1307.

Yuandai zouyi jilu 元代奏議輯錄 (Yuan memorials, compiled and edited), Chen Dezhi 陳得芝, Qiu Shusen 邱樹森, and He Zhaoji 何兆吉, eds., Zhejiang guji, 1998.

Note the sources used and the bibliographies in Paul Ratchnevsky, *Genghis Khan, His Life and Legacy*, Blackwell, 1991; and Morris Rossabi, *Khubilai Khan: His Life and Times*, UCP, 1988.

Bieji 別集

Yuanren wenji pianmu fenlei suoyin 元人文集篇目分類索引, Lu Junling 陸峻嶺, Zhonghua, 1979. Contains detailed indexes to the tables of contents of the *bieji* of 151 Yuan authors; three general collections; and 16 early Ming *bieji*. The contents of all these collections are indexed under three major categories: (1) biographical; (2) historical; (3) literary and miscellaneous. The first section is subdivided into men, women, Buddhists, Daoists, and those with a surname but no given name. The second contains items arranged under seven subdivisions, namely politics, taxes and labor service, education, army, law, manufacturing, and peasant uprisings. The third is arranged by *Sibu* categories. The miscellaneous section is subdivided into birds, beasts, insects, and fish; plants and trees; food and drink; utensils; and so forth.

Yuanren wenji banben mulu 元人文集版本目錄 (Catalog of editions of collected works of Yuan persons), Zhou Qingpeng 周清膨, Nanjing daxue, 1983.

Nihon genson Genjin bunshû mokuroku 日本現存人文集目錄 (Catalog of collected works by Yuan authors extant in Japanese libraries), Yamane Yukio 山根幸夫 and Ogawa Takashi 小川尚 compiled and published, Tokyo, 1970.

Genjin bunshû shiryô sakuin 元人文集史料索引 (Index to historical materials in Yuan collected works), Jinbun, mimeo., 1960. Indexes some 4,000 proper names and historical terms from 23 Yuan collected works.

Biji 筆記

Yuan *biji* are discussed by Herbert Franke in "Some Aspects of Chinese Private Historiography in the Thirteenth and Fourteenth Century," in *HCJ*, 115–34. For an example of one type of information which can be drawn from them, the social history of the Yuan, see Shi Weimin 史衛民, *Yuandai shehui shenghuoshi* 元代社會生活史.[24]

Shanju xinhua 山居新話 (New talk from a mountain dwelling), Yang Yu 楊瑀 (1285–1361), Herbert Franke, tr., *Beiträge zur Kulturgeschichte Chinas unter der Mongolenherrschaft*, Steiner, 1956.

Gengshen waishi 庚申外史 (Unofficial history of [the emperor born in] 1320), Quan Heng 權衡 (second half of fourteenth century), 1369. *Das Keng-shen wai-shih: Eine Quelle zur späten Mongolenzeit*, Helmut Schulte-Uffelage, tr. and ed., Akademie Verlag, 1963. Covers the years 1333–68 in annals style.

Chuogeng lu 輟耕錄 (Records compiled after returning from the farm), Tao Zongyi 陶宗儀 (?–1396), ca. 1366. *CFS Concordance* 13.[25]

Shuofu 說郛 (The domain of texts), Tao Zongyi 陶宗儀, comp.; preface dated 1370. Together with its early seventeenth-century continuation, *Shuofu xu* 說郛續, contains abstracts of mainly fictional *biji* from earliest times to the fourteenth and sixteenth centuries. See *Shuofukao* 說郛考, Chang Bide 昌彼德, Taibei: Wenshizhe, 1979.

Agriculture

Nongshu 農書, Wang Zhen 王禎 (35.1.2)

48.5.3 Archaeology

The Yuan capital of Shangdu 上都 (the Xanadu of Coleridge's poem "Kubla Khan," 1816) is situated near Dolon Nor (Zhenglan 正藍) in Inner Mongolia. In the 1950s military farms were built using the bricks from the city walls. Excavations of the palace were begun in 1992. It was the alternative or summer capital to Dadu 大都 (Khan-

---

[24] *Yuandai shehui shenghuoshi* (History of social life in the Yuan dynasty), Shehui kexue, 1996.

[25] See Frederick W. Mote, *T'ao Tsung-i and His "Cho Keng Lu"*, Ph.D, Univ. of Washington, 1954.

balik, modern Beijing) following a brief period (1260–63) when it was capital of the parts of China then controlled by Khubilai.

The excavations at Kharakhoto in 1983–84 brought to light a total of 3,000 documents, of which 2,200 are in Chinese; for a selection of 760 (dated 1295–1371), see *Heicheng chutu de wenshu* 黑城出土的文書 (Documents excavated at Kharakhoto), Li Yiyou 李逸友, ed., Kexue, 1991.

A Journey into China's Antiquity, vol. 4, *Yuan, Ming, Qing* (see 8.1 on this authoritative illustrated series).

48.5.4   Guides and Research Tools

The best introductions in English to the historiography of the Yuan are the "Bibliographical Essays" in *CHC*, vol. 6, 689–726. The first essay is "A Note on Traditional Sources for Yüan History," by Frederick W. Mote (689–99). See also Herbert Franke, "Chinese Historiography Under Mongol Rule," in *China Under Mongol Rule*, Variorum, 1994, 15–26.

Yuanshixue gaishuo 元史學概説 (Introduction to the study of Yuan history), Yang Zhijiu 楊志玖, Li Zhi'an 李治安 and Wang Xiaoxin 王曉欣, eds., Tianjin jiaoyu, 1989. Introduces primary sources and gives the state of the field in Chinese Yuan studies.

David M. Farquhar, *The Government of China Under Mongolian Rule: A Reference Guide*, Steiner, 1990. Contains brief but wide-ranging notes on all central and local government institutions.

Language

Yuan yuyan cidian 元語言詞典 (Dictionary of Yuan language), Li Chongxing 李崇興 et al., eds., Shanghai jiaoyu, 1998. Covers mainly popular literature of the Yuan as well as plays, poetry, *biji* 筆記, historical biographies, and so forth. It is intended both for historical linguists and for readers of the popular literature of the period. It replaces the not too reliable *Song-Yuan yuyan cidian* 宋元語言詞典 (Dictionary of Song and Yuan language), Long Qianan 龍潛庵, Shanghai cishu, 1985. Contains 11,000 entries drawn from nearly one thousand Song and Yuan sources including plays, novels, *biji*, poetry, and recorded sayings. In the series *Jindai Hanyu duandai yuyan cidian xilie* (34.3).

Biographies

In the Service of the Khan: Eminent Personalities of the Early Mongol Yuan Period (1200–1300), Igor de Rachewiltz, Hok-lam Chan, Hsiao Ch'i-ch'ing, and Peter W. Grier, Harrassowitz, 1993. Includes extensive biographies of 37 people.

Repertory of Proper Names in Yuan Literary Sources, Igor de Rachewiltz and May Wang, eds., 4 vols., SMC, 1988. Replaces two earlier indexes to biographical materials,[26] as well as complementing and supplementing other biographical indexes for the Yuan including:

Yuanren zhuanji ziliao suoyin 元人傳記資料索引 (Index to biographical materials of Yuan figures), Wang Deyi 王德毅, and Li Rongcun 李榮村, et al., comps., Xinwenfeng, 5 vols., 1979–82; Zhonghua, 1987. Contains materials on 16,000 people, from 800 sources. Vol. 5 contains a stroke-count index of alternative names.

Ryô Kin Genjin denki sakuin 遼金元人傳記索引 (Index to biographies of Liao, Jin, and Yuan persons), Umehara Kaoru 梅原郁 and Kinugawa Tsuyoshi 衣川強, comps., Jinbun, 1972. There are 3,200 individuals listed; 130 *bieji* were consulted.

Song-Yuan fangzhi zhuanji suoyin 宋元方志傳記索引 (Index to the biographies in Song and Yuan local gazetteers), Zhu Shijia 朱士嘉, Beijing, 1963. Includes 3,949 people in 33 gazetteers (47.4.2, *Biographies*).

Huizu renwu zhi, Yuandai 回族人物志·元代 (Biographies of Islamic people, Yuan dynasty), Bai Shouyi 白壽彝, Ningxia renmin, 1985. The first of four projected volumes of Islamic biographies.

Ch'en Yuan, *Westerners and Central Asians in China Under the Mongols: Their Transformation into Chinese*, tr. and annotated by Luther Carrington Goodrich, *MS* Monograph, Los Angeles: UCP, 1966; rpnt., Steyler, 1989.

Geography

Zhongguo lishi dituji 中國歷史地圖集, vol. 7, *Yuan-Ming shiqi* 元明時期 (Yuan and Ming); see 4.3.2 on this essential series.

Eleven gazetteers are known to have been compiled in the Yuan. For their titles, see Zhang Guogan 張國淦, *Zhongguo gu fangzhi kao* 中國古方志考 (Critical notes on old Chinese gazetteers), Zhonghua, 1962.

Societies and Journals

Journal of Sung-Yuan Studies (began as *Sung Studies Newsletter*, 1969–80, changed title to *Bulletin of Sung-Yuan Studies*, 1980–88; adopted the

---

[26] See *H-Y Index* 35 for Yuan collections as well as *Index to Biographical Material in Chin and Yuan Literary Works*, Igor de Rachewiltz et al., comps., ANUP, 3 vols., 1970–79.

present title in 1989). A good way of keeping up-to-date with new work in this field. Contains translations of the annual *Shigaku zasshi* state-of-the-field articles on Five Dynasties, Song, and Yuan.

Yuanshi yanjiuhui 元史研究會 (Yuan history society), founded in 1980, Lishisuo. Edits collected articles on Yuan history; see, for example, *Yuanshi luncong* 元史論叢 6, Shehui kexue, 1996.

49

Ming

1368–1644

Compared with its predecessors, the Ming is rather well documented. It is the first dynasty from which the Veritable Records of most of the reigns survive. More than 200 works of official history and many more private ones were written. The collected works of some 1,500 Ming authors are extant. There are also about 1,000 Ming local gazetteers.[1] Ming land deeds, merchant records, and other private documents have survived in small numbers. They are dealt with together with similar sources from the Qing (50.7).

49.1 Main Historical Works

Ming shilu 明實錄 (Veritable Records of the Ming). Official title: *Da Ming shilu* 大明實錄 or *Huang Ming shilu* 皇明實錄. Given the fact that almost none of the Ming central government archives have survived, the most important sources for Ming history are the Veritable Records of 13 of the 16 Ming reigns. They were compiled after the death of an emperor and were based on archival documents, especially edicts and memorials. The Ming was unusual in that the *Qijuzhu* 起居注 (Court Diaries), were not kept for 200 years, presumably out of a desire to maintain secrecy by excluding the note takers (see next main entry, *Wanli qijuzhu*). The *Ming shilu* are of an uneven quality because of the

---

[1] Zhu Yuanzhang 朱元璋, the first emperor of the Ming 明, took the dynastic name Ming from the title of his ward, the Red Turban leader Han Lin'er 韓林兒 (d. 1367), the Young Prince of Radiance (Xiao Mingwang 小明王). It was a word filled with the promise of the reappearance of the light of Manichaean (*Mingjiao* 明教) reversal and the coming of the Maitreya Buddha to rule the world; see *CHC*, vol. 7, 44.

biases of their compilers and the responsible grand secretary. Although they were not intended for publication, various drafts circulated and have survived (including some that made their way to Japan during the Edo period). The best modern edition is the reproduction of the manuscript in the former National Library of Beiping and now in the Shiyusuo: *Ming shilu* 明實錄, 3,045 *juan* in 133 vols., with appendixes (29 vols.) and corrections (21 vols.), Shiyusuo, 1961–66; Zhonghua, 1987. See *ISMH*, 30–33; *CHC*, vol. 7, 746–52.

There are a number of modern collections of excerpts from the Veritable Records—for example:

Mindai Man-Mô shiryô: Min jitsuroku shô Manshûhen Môkohen 明代滿蒙史料明實錄抄滿洲篇蒙古篇 (41.4.1).

Ming shilu Beijing shiliao 明實錄北京史料 (Historical materials from the Veritable Records of the Ming on Beijing), Zhao Qichang 趙其昌, ed., 4 vols., Beijing guji, 1995.

Ming shilu jingji ziliao xuanbian 明實錄經濟資料選編 (Selected economic materials from the Veritable Records of the Ming), Guo Hou'an 郭厚安, ed. in chief, Shehui kexue, 1989.

Ming shilu leizuan 明實錄類纂 (Veritable Records of the Ming by category), Li Guoxiang 李國祥 and Yang Chang 楊昶, eds., 20 vols., Wuhan, 1990–96. This large-scale series contains volumes of excerpts on numerous subjects such as the economy, officials, law, external relations, the examination system, science, natural disasters, biographies (more than 2,000 of them in the form in which they were entered in the *Shilu* under the date of their subject's death), Beijing, Anhui, Sichuan, Shandong, and women.

Ming shilu youguan Yunnan lishi ziliao zhaichao 明實錄有關雲南歷史資料摘抄 (for more titles, see 39.4 and 40.3.1).

Wanli qijuzhu 萬曆起居注 (Court Diaries of the Wanli era), 9 vols., Beijing daxue, 1988. These records, which were not kept for the first 200 years of the Ming, are an invaluable source for the years 1573–1615. They total 7,512 pages.

Mingshi 明史 (Standard History of the Ming), Zhang Tingyu 張廷玉 (1672–1755) et al., 1739, covers the years 1368–1644; 28 vols., Zhonghua, 1974; 5th prnt., 1995. The sections on Ming relations with the Jianzhou 建州 Jurchen should be treated with care. There are a number of studies of the process of compilation of

the *Mingshi*.[2] There is a personal-name index.[3] There are also a
number of translations of various parts of the *Mingshi*. Note especially:

Basic Annals of Ming T'ai-tsu, Romeyn Taylor, tr., CMC, 1975.

Minshi Shokkashi yakuchû 明史食貨志譯注 (Integral translation with
notes of the "Shihuozhi" in the *Mingshi*), Wada Sei 和田清
(1890–1963) and pupils, trs. and eds., 2 vols., Tôyô bunko, 1957;
new edition, Yamane Yukio 山根幸夫, ed., Kyûko, 1996. The
translation is in *Kanbun* 漢文 while the notes are in current
Japanese; the Chinese original is appended and there is an index.
In the new edition, errors have been corrected, the old bibliography removed, and updated references inserted into the text.

See also *Mingshi shihuozhi jiaozhu* 明史食貨志校注 (The *Mingshi*
"Shihuozhi," collated and annotated), Li Xun 李洵, ed., Zhonghua, 1982.

There are indexes and studies available to various other sections
of the *Mingshi*—for example, the monograph on law:

Minshi Keihôshi sakuin 明史刑法志索引, Noguchi Tetsurô 野口鐵郎,
Kokusho kankôkai, 1981.

Frank Münzel, *Strafrecht im alten China nach den Strafrechtskapiteln
in den Ming-Annalen*, Harrassowitz, 1968. Annotated translation
of the first section of *Mingshi* "Xingfazhi" 刑法志.

Guoque 國榷 (Evaluation of the work of our dynasty), Tan Qian 談
遷 (1594–1658), 1656; 6 vols., typeset edition, Guji, 1958. Useful
for basic chronology. Also in some cases it has a clearer account
than in the *Mingshi*, especially of Ming relations with the Jianzhou 建州 Jurchen.

[2] Thomas A. Wilson, "Confucian Sectarianism and the Compilation of the
Ming History," *LIC* 15.2: 53–84 (1994); Li Jinhua 李晉華, *Mingshi zuanxiu kao*
明史纂修考 (A history of the compilation of the Standard History of the
Ming), *Yenching Journal of Chinese Studies*, Monograph 3, 1933; rpnt., Shanghai
shudian, 1992.

[3] *Mingshi renming suoyin* 明史人名索引 (Index to personal names in the
Mingshi), Li Yumin 李裕民, comp., 2 vols., Zhonghua, 1985. Includes not only
all Ming names, but names from Song, Yuan, and Qing. References to *ce*, *juan*,
and page numbers of the Zhonghua punctuated edition of the *Mingshi* (1974).

Mingshi jishi benmo 明史紀事本末, Gu Yingtai 谷應泰 (1620–90), comp., 1658. Recounts 80 or so of the main events or *causes célèbres* of the dynasty.[4] Based in part on sources no longer extant.

Mingji 明紀 (Ming records), Chen He 陳鶴 (1757–1811) and Chen Kejia 陳克家 (d. 1860), 1871.

Ming tongjian 明通鑑(Comprehensive mirror of government under the Ming), Xia Xie 夏燮 (1799–1875), 1873. In part corrects errors and omissions in the *Mingshi*; includes copious references to the sources used.[5]

49.2   Other Textual Sources
Geography

Da Ming yitongzhi 大明一統志 (Gazetteer of the unified Great Ming), Li Xian 李賢 et al., comps., 1461; photographic reprint of original palace edition, 10 vols., Taibei, 1965; 2 vols., San-Qin, 1990.

Tianxia junguo libing shu 天下郡國利病書 (4.5.4).

Dushi fangyu jiyao 讀史方輿紀要 (4.5.4).

Local Gazetteers

About 1,000 gazetteers survive from the Ming. There is a listing of 900 of them in *ISMH*. Timothy Brook, *Geographical Sources of Ming-Qing History*, Michigan Monographs in Chinese Studies no. 58, Ann Arbor, 1988, covers also topographical and institutional gazetteers. Some gazetteers describe, or collect materials on, Nanjing and Beijing, for example, *Dijing jingwulüe* 帝京景物略 (Brief account of the sights of the imperial capital), Liu Tong 劉侗 (1594–1637), 1635. It covers gardens, temples, imperial tombs, famous sites, bridges, rivers, flora and fauna, insects and fish, anecdotes, and personalities of

---

[4] *Mingshi jishi benmo* (Major events of Ming history), 10 vols., Shangwu, 1935–37; Taibei Wanyou wenku rpnt., 1956; Zhonghua, 1985.

[5] There is a partial French translation of one of the continuations of the *Zizhi tongjian gangmu* 資治通鑑綱目 by L. C. Delamarre, *Histoire de la dynastie des Ming*, Paris, 1865. It is a translation of the first part of *Zizhi tongjian gangmu sanbian* 資治通鑑綱目三編 (1746), the third continuation of the *Gangmu*.

Beijing in the late Ming. There are also plenty of Ming *biji* recording city life (especially that of Nanjing; see below, *Biji*).

Tianyige cang Mingdai fangzhi xuankan 天一閣藏明代方志選刊 (Selected [107] Ming dynasty gazetteers from the Tianyige Library); 119 vols. Shanghai guji, 1963–65; 68 boxes, 1981–83; *Xubian* 續編, 144 vols., 1990. This famous, private Ningbo library originally held 435 Ming local gazetteers. Now the collection numbers 271. There are indexes to Song and Ming biographical materials and personal names in these gazetteers, see 47.4.2 and below under *Biographies*.

Nihon genson Mindai chihôshi mokuroku 日本現存明代地方志目錄, Yamane Yukio 山根幸夫, ed., Tôyô bunko, 1962; enlarged, 1971; new edition, Kyûko, 1995. Arranged by province; contains references to 710 Ming dynasty gazetteers held in Japanese collections.

Travel

The most famous traveler inside China of the Ming was Xu Xiake 徐霞客 (1586–1641), *Xu Xiake [Xu Hongzu] youji* 徐霞客[徐弘祖] 遊記 (4.8).

The most famous overseas Ming voyages were those of Zheng He 鄭和. The main sources on these and other Ming overseas travels are given in 41.5.1 (*Ming*).

Merchant Route Books (Luchengshu 路程書)

See 50.7.4.

Laws and Institutions

Start with John D. Langlois, Jr., "Ming Law," in *CHC*, vol. 8, 172–220.

Huang Ming zhishu 皇明制書, Zhang Lu 張鹵, ed., 1579; 2 vols., Koten kenkyûkai, 1966–67.

Ming Dagao yanjiu 明大誥研究 (Research on the great pronouncements of the Ming), Yang Yifan 楊一凡, Jiangsu renmin, 1988. Reprints, collates, and punctuates four different proclamations of the *Dagao*. See also the same author's *Hongwu falü dianji kaozheng* 洪武法律典籍考證 (Study of the legal codes of the Hongwu period), Falü, 1992.

Da Minglü 大明律 (The great Ming code), 27.3.

Da Mingling 大明令 (The great Ming statutes), 27.5.

Zhusi zhizhang 諸司職掌 (Handbook of government posts), 1393 and 1458.

Huang Ming tiaofa shilei zuan 皇明條法事類纂 (27.3).

Ming huiyao 明會要 (Table 32, 25.1).

Da Ming huidian 大明會典 (Collected statutes of the great Ming).
>   Four editions were compiled.[6] Two are extant: the first was completed in 1503 and revised in 1509 and printed in 1511 (the sixth year of *Zhengde* 正德). It is therefore referred to as the *Zhengde huidian*. It covers the years 1368 to 1479.[7] The second was ordered in 1576 and printed in 1587, and it is therefore referred to as the *Wanli* 萬曆 *huidian*. It covers the years 1479 to 1584.[8] The *huidian* were based on early statutes and regulations such as the *Da Mingling* (27.5). The *huidian* are not legal works, but collections of documents showing the workings of the main organs of government, their administrative procedures, precedents, and historical development. As such, they are very important sources for institutional and political history.

During the Ming dynasty, many individual branches of the administration printed their rules and regulations in handbooks, such as the *Nanjing hubu zhi* 南京戶部志[9] or the *Libu zhigao* 禮部志稿 (Draft monograph of the Ministry of Rites).[10] For a list of such works which have survived, see *ISMH*, 181–84.

Xu Wenxian tongkao 續文獻通考, Wang Qi 王圻, comp. (25.2).

---

[6] The first was ordered in 1474 and completed in 1479, but it was not printed and it has not survived; the third was ordered in 1529 and completed in 1550; it, too, has not survived.

[7] Rpnt., 3 vols., Kyûko, 1989.

[8] *Wanli huidian*, punctuated rpnt., 40 vols., Wanyou wenku, Shangwu, 1936; fac. rpnt., Taibei: Dongnan shubaoshe, 5 vols., 1963; Xinwenfeng, 1976; Zhonghua reduced-size edition, 1989. See Yamane Yukio 山根幸夫, "Min Shin no kaiten" 明清の會典 (The collected statutes of the Ming and Qing), ch. 17 of *CHKSK*.

[9] *Nanjing hubu zhi* (Monograph of the Nanjing Board of Finance), Xie Bin 謝彬, comp., 1550.

[10] *Libu zhigao* (Draft monograph of the Ministry of Rites), Yu Ruji 俞汝楫, ed. in chief, late Ming; see Jun Fang, "The Gazetteer of the Nanjing Ministry of Rites: The Record of an Auxiliary Capital Department in the Ming Dynasty," *The East Asian Library Journal* 7.1: 73–84 (1994).

Edicts and Memorials

Memorials, edicts, and many other documents may not have survived in the archives, but many thousands were collected and printed together during the Ming, either in general collections or in individual collections of an official (often in his collected works). *ISMH*, 119–75, lists approximately 300 collections of Ming memorials (arranged by author, by topic, or by period). To supplement *ISMH*, check the collected works of the officials whose memorials are being traced (see below under *Bieji*).[11]

Huang Ming jingshi wenbian 皇明經世文編 (Ming documents on statecraft), Chen Zilong 陳子龍 (1608–47) et al., comps., 1638.[12] The most important topically arranged collection of Ming memorials (and other writings). The 3,145 entries (which are quoted in full) were selected from hundreds of *bieji* and other sources written by 430 senior officials during the course of the Ming, both in the central government and in the provinces. Many of the sources quoted have since been lost, hence the value of this collection. The intention of the chief compilers (childhood friends from the Yangzi delta and Ming loyalists) was to concentrate their readers' minds at a time of impending disaster. The emphasis therefore is on practical matters of government and administration, especially national security. The arrangement is by author and by subject matter in a chronological frame. The book was banned during the Qing.

Huang Ming zhaoling 皇明詔令 (Edicts of the Ming), Fu Fengxiang 傅鳳翔, comp., 1539, 1548; 4 vols., Chengwen, 1967, contains edicts of Ming emperors between 1366 and 1547. For four other such collections, see *ISMH*, 199–200.

---

[11] Silas Wu, "The Transmission of Ming Memorials," *TP* 54: 275–87 (1968).

[12] *Ming jingshi wenbian* (based on four separate editions collated and photolithographically printed), 6 vols., Zhonghua, 1962 (includes a name-index); 3rd rpnt., 1997; Guofeng, photolithographic edition, 1964. Note *Mindai keiseibun bunrui mokuroku* 明代經世文分類目錄 (Classified index to Ming documents on statecraft), Tôyô bunko, 1986. Indexes 11 of the main Ming collections of essays on statecraft.

Bieji 別集

There are at least 1,500 extant collected works of individual Ming authors. Note that *ISMH* (126–70) lists 209 Ming *bieji* containing a minimum of three memorials.

Yuanren wenji pianmu fenlei suoyin 元人文集篇目分類索引, Lu Junling 陸峻嶺, Zhonghua, 1979. Contains detailed indexes to the tables of contents of the *bieji* not only of Yuan authors, but also of 16 early Ming *bieji*. For further details, see 48.5.

Zôtei Nihon genson Minjin bunshû mokuroku 增訂日本現存明人文集目錄 (Catalog of collected works by [1,400] Ming authors extant in Japanese collections), Yamane Yukio 山根幸夫, comp., enlarged and rev., Tôkyô joshi daigaku 東京女子大學, 1978.

Biji 筆記

ISMH (98–118) lists and comments on 75 Ming *biji* and *zashi* presenting direct information on the political and social history of the period. Xie Guozhen 謝國楨 in *Ming Qing biji tancong* 明清筆記談叢 discusses 19.[13] Below are listed 18 outstanding Ming *biji* (note also the examples of Ming *zashi* listed in Chapter 24 and the Kyoto *biji* indexes in Chapter 31):

Banqiao zaji 板橋雜記 (Miscellaneous records from Banqiao), Yu Huai 余懷 (1616–96), ca. 1695. Howard S. Levy, tr., *A Feast of Mist and Flowers*, Yokohama, 1966. Reminiscences of the Nanjing actors and singing girls encountered by the author in his youth before the Manchu conquest.

Chunming mengyu lu 春明夢余錄 (Record of dreams of the capital), Sun Chengze 孫承澤 (1592–1676), early Qing. Details on the buildings and institutions of Beijing in the Ming.

Diangu jiwen 典故紀聞 (Records of institutions and anecdotes), Yu Jideng 余繼登, Wanli; punctuated edition, Zhonghua, 1981. Exceptionally well informed. The author had access to the Wanli Court Diaries and also to the Veritable Records of the previous reigns; covers first 200 years of Ming history.

---

[13] *Ming Qing biji tancong* (Collection of notes on Ming-Qing *biji*), Shanghai: Zhonghua, 1960; enlarged edition, 1962; new edition, 1981. The author discusses 48 *biji*, of which 19 were written in the Ming.

Gengji bian 庚己編 (Written between 1510 and 1519), Lu Can 陸粲 (1494–1591); punctuated edition, Zhonghua, 1987. Printed together with *Kezuo zhuiyu* 客座贅語.

Jinling Fancha zhi 金陵梵刹志 (Monographs on the Buddhist temples of Nanjing), 1627.

Jinling suoshi 金陵瑣事 (Nanjing trifles), Zhou Hui 周暉, 1610. Indexed in *CZZS*. Notes on life in Nanjing to 1607.

Jinyan 今言 (Contemporary words), Zheng Xiao 鄭曉 (1499–1566), 1566; punctuated edition, Zhonghua, 1984. Mainly court and institutional matters of early Ming.

Kezuo zhuiyu 客座贅語 (Idle talk with guests), Gu Qiyuan 顧起元 (1565–1628), 1617; punctuated edition, Zhonghua, 1987. Notes on life in Nanjing. Printed together with *Gengji bian* 庚己編.

Qixiu leigao 七修類稿 (Draft arranged in seven categories), Lang Ying 郎瑛 (1487–1566); punctuated edition, Zhonghua, 1959. Historical and political notes. For index, see *CZS*.

Shaoshi shanfang bicong 少室山房筆叢 (Jottings from Shaoshi mountains study), Hu Yinglin 胡應麟 (1551–1602), punctuated edition, Zhonghua, 1958. The author's study was named after the Shaoshi mountains, Henan.

Shuidong riji 水東日記 (Diary written east of the river [Wusongjiang 吳淞江]), Ye Sheng 葉盛 (1420–74), punctuated edition, Zhonghua, 1980. Mainly historical and institutional subjects of early Ming plus snippets from Song, Yuan, and Ming writers.

Songchuang mengyu 松窗夢語 (Sleep talk from the window by a pine), Zhang Han 張瀚 (1511–93), Preface dated 1593; Shanghai guji, 1986. After retirement the author wrote 33 notes based on his experience as an official and also on conditions in his native Zhejiang. One of these notes, on merchants, has been translated (50.7.4).

[*Wanli*] *yehuo bian* [萬曆]野獲編 (Harvested in the wilds [during the Wanli period]), Shen Defu 沈德符 (1578–1642), punctuated edition, 3 vols., Zhonghua, 1959; 2nd ed., 1980; indexed in *CZZS*. One of the most famous of the Ming *biji*, it covers a wide variety of topics.

Wu zazu 五雜組 (Five-part miscellany), Xie Zhaozhe 謝肇淛 (1567–1624), 1616; punctuated edition, 2 vols., Zhonghua, 1959. The five categories referred to are the traditional heaven, earth, man, things, and events. Prime source on the late Ming; highly popular in Tokugawa Japan. For a translation of the chapters on painting, see

Sewall J. Oertling, *Painting and Calligraphy in the* Wu-tsa-tsu, CCS, Univ. of Michigan, 1997.

Yongchuang xiaopin 湧幢小品 (Trifles from the erectable study), Zhu Guozhen 朱國禎 (1558–1632), 1622; punctuated edition, Shanghai: Xinwenhua shushe 新文化書社, 1935; Zhonghua, 1959; *CZS*. Written between 1609 and 1621. On this title, see 9.9.

Yueshi bian 閱世編 (Seeing the world), Ye Mengzhu 葉夢珠 (1624–ca. 1693), punctuated edition, Shanghai guji, 1981. Songjiang 松江 conditions and institutions in the late Ming, early Qing. His comments on taxes and labor service have been translated by Clara Yu in *Chinese Civilization: A Sourcebook* (8.1), 282–86.

Yutang congyu 玉堂叢語 (Miscellaneous records from the Hanlin academy), Jiao Hong 焦竑 (1541–1620), 1618; punctuated edition, Zhonghua, 1981. The Yutang was one name for the academy.

Zaolin zazu 棗林雜俎 (Miscellaneous offerings from Zaolin), Tan Qian 談遷 (1594–1658), 1644; indexed in *CZZS*. Notes on a wide variety of subjects. The author's ancestors had taken refuge on several occasions at Zaolin in Hainingxian 海寧縣.

Agriculture
Nongzheng quanshu 農政全書 (35.1)

Merchants
On Ming merchants and route books, see 50.7.4.

Technology and Science
Bencao gangmu 本草綱目 (Chapter 36)
Tiangong kaiwu 天工開物 (Chapter 37, *Introduction*)
Lu Ban jing 魯班經 (37.4.1)

Foreign Works
The Korean Veritable Records (*Chosŏn wangjo sillok* 朝鮮皇朝實錄) were modeled after the Chinese and contain materials not found in Chinese sources. The Yi dynasty (1392–1910) covered almost the full span of the Ming and Qing. For excerpts from this and other sources, see 42.5.

49.3   Central Archives

The largest central archive during the Ming dynasty was the Hou-huku 後湖庫 in Nanjing. It was built in 1381 under the personal supervision of the Hongwu emperor on the islands of the Back Lake (the Houhu, present-day Xuanwu Lake 玄武湖) for security and as a precaution against fire. Here were stored growing mountains of *huangce* 黃冊 (yellow registers), and *yulin tuce* 魚鱗圖冊 (fish-scale registers) population counts, used for calculating labor services and maps for calculating land taxes. At the beginning of the dynasty, there were only six archive buildings. By the end of the sixteenth century, there were 667 buildings holding 1,790,000 records, but the system was beginning to break down. The windows were not regularly opened and broken shelving was left unrepaired. The entire archive eventually went up in flames at the collapse of the dynasty.[14]

The most prestigious archives built by the Ming were the imperial historical archives (Huangshicheng 皇史宬) just to the east of the palace in Beijing. They were built in 1534–36 and are still standing today, thanks to repairs carried out in 1568, 1807, and 1982. Only two windows light this massive brick and stone building, whose vault-like construction resembles a tomb, built to protect the contents from fire, floods, thieves, bandits, insects, and rats. The walls are two meters thick. The gables are open to the two high windows at either end of the vault to allow circulation of air. In the long interior, the only furnishings are 152 huge gilded, copper-clad storage chests made of camphor wood. Each weighs 155 kilo (70 lb). They rest on stone plinths like coffins. In them were stored imperial instructions (*xianxun* 賢訓), the *yudie* 玉牒 (Jade Registers, i.e., Imperial Genealogy), the Veritable Records of each reign; the one spare copy of the *Yongle dadian*; and various imperial portraits, congratulatory messages, seals, and gifts of foreign rulers (from which came the alternative name of the archives, Biaozhangku 表章庫). The Ming contents of the Huangshicheng were deposited in the Grand Secretariat archive by the Qing emperors, who stored exactly the same types of documents and objects in the archive as had the

---

[14] For a contemporary description of this archive at its height, see Zhao Weixian 趙惟賢, *Houhuzhi* 後湖志, preface dated 1513; punctuated ed., Jiangsu Guangling guji, 1987.

Ming. The Huangshicheng was partly destroyed by looting during the occupation of Beijing by the Eight Powers in 1900; in 1933, the remainder of the contents were sent to Nanjing; and in 1949, part of these went on to Taiwan, part eventually returned to Beijing. The Huangshicheng itself is today a museum open to the public. The original document chests stand empty. The remainder of the Qing contents are housed in the Yishiguan (50.1.2). Only about 3,600 Ming documents are extant, mainly from the Board of War dealing with the late Ming rebellion of Li Zicheng 李自成 and border defense against the Manchus. They were collected and stored in the early Qing in order to complete the Ming History. There are also some land and population records from the early Ming.[15]

In the Ming there were at least 300 provincial and prefectural archives. Most of their contents were destroyed in the fighting at the end of the dynasty. Nothing of them remains today. For lists of official Ming documents published in modern times, see 50.2.

49.4   Archaeology and Inscriptions

49.4.1   The Imperial Tombs

The founder of the dynasty, Zhu Yuanzhang, Ming Taizu 明太祖, is buried in the Ming Xiaoling mausoleum (明孝陵), Nanjing. In order to keep the entrance of the tomb vault secret, Zhu ordered that after his death coffins be carried out of 13 different city gates. He was buried together with his consort and 46 concubines in 1398. The above-ground buildings at Wanzhu 玩珠 peak on the southern slope of Zijinshan 紫金山 were burned down by soldiers in 1853; repairs were carried out in 1978. False claims of the discovery of the site of the tomb appear in the press from time to time. Thirteen of the remaining Ming emperors are buried at the Ming tombs (Ming shisan ling 明十三陵) at Changping county 昌平縣, north of Beijing; see Ann Paludan, *The Imperial Ming Tombs*, YUP, 1981. For references to the excavation of the tomb of the Wanli emperor, see 12.1. Just beyond the Ming tombs there are easily accessible sections of the Ming Wall, on whose strategic and cultural importance, see Arthur Waldron, 1992 (28.2).

---

[15] *Mingdai Liaodong dang'an huibian* 明代遼東檔案匯編, 2 vols., Liao-Shen shushe, 1985.

49.4.2   *The Forbidden City*

Beijing was formally named the capital (*jingshi* 京師) in 1420 (thereafter the previous *jingshi* was named Nanjing). Work had already begun on the new palace in Beijing for the Yongle emperor in 1406. It was completed in 1420. Although partly destroyed and reconstructed over five centuries, the palace retains today the essential Ming layout. It is four times the size of the palace of Versailles and is said to contain 9,000 rooms in 800 buildings. At the center is the Forbidden City (literally Pole Star forbidden city, *Zijincheng* 紫禁城) in which is situated the imperial palace (*huanggong* 皇宮). It stretches from Wumen 午門 in the north to Xuanwumen 玄午門 in the south and is surrounded by a moat.

The outer part of the palace or court (*qianchao* 前朝, *waichao* 外朝) was the seat of imperial government until February 1912. The inner quarters (*houqin* 后寢, *danei* 大內) remained the principal residence of the Ming and Qing emperors until the last emperor, Puyi was forcibly moved out in the winter of 1924 (51.14.2). In summer, the emperor and his suite were kept cool with blocks of ice placed in decorated containers (750 tons were stored every year). Heating in winter was from charcoal braziers; the *kang* 炕 (sleeping platforms) and day couches were heated with coal fires.

The Forbidden City stood at the center of the imperial city (*huangcheng* 皇城), around which stretched a wall six miles in circumference. The imperial city was surrounded to the north, east and west by the inner city (*neicheng* 內城), around which stood the city wall of Beijing. It was 25 km (15 miles) in circumference, 62 feet thick at the base, 34 feet at the top, and 40 feet high. After its removal in the 1970s, it became the path of the second ring road. In the nineteenth and early part of the twentieth century many western writers referred to the inner city as the "Tartar city." They called the outer city (*waicheng* 外城) the "Chinese city." It lay outside the southern section of the main city wall. Its heart was the area known today as Qianmenwai 前門外.

49.4.3   *Other Sites*

Two famous Ming sites that can still be visited today are the Imperial Archives (Huangshicheng 皇史宬) next to the palace in Beijing (50.1) and the Tianyige 天一閣 library in Ningbo (9.2).

49.4.4   Inscriptions

Construction and archaeology have turned up hundreds of tomb inscriptions, including many from the Ming (1,467 stelae are listed in one recent collection; see 3.7, Rong Lihua, 1993). Collections of inscriptions of all kinds for individual provinces and cities have also been published. Since the Ming inscriptions are often published with those of the Qing; for convenience they are listed in 50.7.6.

Illustrations

Wang Qi 王圻, *Sancai tuhui* 三才圖會 (38.1)

A Journey into China's Antiquity, vol. 4, *Yuan, Ming, and Qing* (see 8.1 on this authoritative illustrated series)

49.5   Guides and Research Tools

49.5.1   Guides to Sources

ISMH. An Introduction to the Sources of Ming History, Wolfgang Franke, Kuala Lumpur and Singapore: University of Malaya Press, 1968. *ISMH* is an indispensable annotated catalog of 800 primary sources written during the Ming. It also contains an unannotated list of 900 Ming local gazetteers. No other work in a Western language provides such an extensive listing of Ming primary sources. The introduction and the discussions of the nine different categories of historical writing in which the book is arranged have been reprinted with minor revisions as a long chapter in *CHC*, vol. 7, "Historical Writing During the Ming," 726–82.

The contributors to *CHC*, vols. 7 and 8, have written interesting "Bibliographic Notes" to their chapters in which they discuss not only the main primary sources they have used, but also some of their intellectual debts (783–815); there are eight short bibliographical notes in vol. 8, 987–1004.

DMB. Dictionary of Ming Biography, 1368–1644, L. Carrington Goodrich and Chaoying Fang, eds., 2 vols., Col. UP, 1976. Although the *DMB* is a biographical dictionary, it contains a great deal of information on a large number of the main works written or compiled during the Ming. There are detailed personal-name, book title, and subject indexes.

Ming History: An Introductory Guide to Research, Edward L. Farmer, Romeyn Taylor, and Ann Waltner, comps., University of Minnesota, Department of History, Ming Studies Research Series no. 3,

1994. Contains (1) explanations on such topics as the calendar, people and places (4–64); (2) main primary sources and reference works (65–125); (3) an annotated bibliography of secondary research (127–52); (4) 89 pages of selected Ming documents with 189 pages of vocabulary.

Mingshi yanjiu beilan 明史研究備覽 (Background to research on Ming history), Li Xiaolin 李小林 and Li Shengwen 李晟文, eds. in chief, Tianjin jiaoyu, 1988; rpnt., 1989. Contains an introduction to 330 primary sources, discussion of research themes, and a bibliography of secondary scholarship from the Ming period itself up to 1985 (including scholarship in Taiwan, Hong Kong, Japan, and the West).

Zhongguo lishi da cidian 中國歷史大辭典 (The great encyclopaedia of Chinese history), 14 vols., Shanghai cishu, 1983– , contains a separate volume on *Mingshi* 明史, Wang Yuquan 王毓銓 and Cao Guilin 曹貴林, eds., 1995. See 8.4.2, item 2, for comments.

49.5.2   Research Tools

Biographies

The *DMB* is the first reference to check for biographical information on any Ming figure. It contains some 659 biographies with bibliographic notes and includes foreigners active in China during the dynasty. See also:

Mingdai zhuanji congkan suoyin 明代傳記叢刊索引 (Index to biographical collections of the Ming dynasty), Zhou Junfu 周駿富, Mingwen, 1991, 3 vols. Now the most complete index to Ming biographical materials. Indexes the *Mingdai zhuanji congkan* 明代傳記叢刊 (a collection of 62 separate Ming biographical collections reprinted under Zhou's editorship in 1991 in 160 vols.). Ordinary names in vols. 2 and 3; alternative names in vol. 1; references to biographies of about 30,000 Ming figures. Supersedes *Bashijiu zhong Mingdai zhuanji zonghe yinde* 八十九種明代傳記綜合引得 (Combined indices to 89 Ming dynasty biographical collections); 3 vols., *H-Y Index* 24.

Mingren zhuanji ziliao suoyin 明人傳記資料索引 (Index to biographical materials of Ming figures), Chang Bide 昌彼德 et al., comps., 2 vols., Taibei: Zhongyang tushuguan 中央圖書館, 1965, 1978; Zhonghua, 1987. More than an index to biographical materials, these excellent volumes give short biographical sketches of some 10,000 individuals followed by detailed references to the sources (528 *bieji*; 65 historical biographies and *biji*, *nianpu*, accounts of conduct, and so forth).

ECCP includes several biographies and much important material on the late Ming (50.10.4).

Mingdai difangzhi zhuanji suoyin 明代地方志傳記索引, 2 vols., Dahua, 1986. Includes holdings of Taiwan and Japan and published material, thus expanding *Nihon genson Mindai chihôshi denki sakuin kô* 日本現存明代地方志傳記索引稿 (Draft index of people with biographies in Ming local gazetteers extant in Japanese collections), Yamane Yukio 山根幸夫, ed., Tôyô bunko, Mindai kenkyûshitsu, 1971 (includes references to biographies of some 30,000 people in 299 Ming gazetteers).

Tianyige cang Mingdai fangzhi xuankan: renwu ziliao renming suoyin 天一閣藏明代方志選刊人物資料人名索引 (Index to biographical materials and personal names in selected Ming dynasty gazetteers from the Tianyige Library), 2 vols., Huadong shifan daxue tushuguan Gujibu 華東師範大學圖書館古籍部, eds., Shanghai shudian, 1997.

Ming Qing jinshi timing beilu suoyin 明清進士題名碑錄索引 gives the names of the 51,624 *jinshi* of the Ming and the Qing and, most usefully, also indicates where biographical sources on them may be found (see 25.3).

Gujin tushu jicheng zhong Mingren zhuanji suoyin 古今圖書集成中明人傳記索引, HKCUP, 1963. Name index of biographical materials on 20,000 Ming figures in the *Tushu jicheng*.

Apart from checking the above items, remember to look in the index of *nianpu*, Xie, 1992 (3.8.4). On genealogies, including those of the Ming, see 3.5.

Official Titles and Officeholders

For official titles, use *DOTIC*, which incorporates the author's earlier work on Ming titles. Supplement with specialized tables, e.g.,

Ming dufu nianbiao 明督撫年表 (Table of Ming governors-general and governors), Wu Tingxie 吳廷燮, Zhonghua, 1982. Based on the table in *Ershiwushi bubian*, with corrections and the addition of an index.

Geography

Zhongguo lishi dituji 中國歷史地圖集, vol. 7, *Yuan Ming shiqi* 元明時期 (Yuan and Ming); see 4.3.2 on this essential series.

Mingdai zhengzhi dili yan'ge zongbiao 明代政治地理沿革總表 (Comprehensive tables of changing administrative areas in the Ming period), Niu Pinghan 牛平漢, Zhongguo ditu, 1997.

Chronology

A Synchronic Chinese-Western Daily Calendar, 1341–1661 AD, Keith H. Hazelton, Ming Studies Research Series no. 1, History Department, Univ. of Minnesota, 1984; corrected 1985. Computer-generated concordance for every day of the Ming dynasty using the Chinese calendar as the base. Each page contains one year.

Bibliographies and Catalogs of Primary Sources

Qianqingtang shumu 千頃堂書目 (Vast hall bibliography), Huang Yuji 黃虞稷 (1629–91). The most important contemporary catalog of Ming books. It was based on the author's own private library, which he built up from that of his father, and contains entries (many with brief annotations) for 14,907 works by Ming writers as well as 2,000 works by Song, Liao, Jin, and Yuan authors, many of which were lost as a result of the Qing literary purges. In the generally suspicious attitude toward the Ming, even this, the major catalog of books written during the Ming, had to circulate in manuscript form for 250 years and was printed only after the fall of the Qing in the *Shiyuan congshu* 適園叢書, 2nd series, 1912; rpnt., Shanghai guji, 1990; Wenwu, 1992; *Shumu congbian* 書目叢編, 1st series, Guangwen, 1967. Note *Senkeidô shomoku choshamei sakuin gojûonjun* 千頃堂書目著者名索引五十音順 (Qianqingtang bibliography author index ordered by the Japanese syllabary), Mindaishi kenkyû iinkai, Tôyô bunko, 1996. Includes a stroke-count index for surnames.

Mingshi 明史 "Yiwenzhi" 藝文志. Based on the *Qianqingtang shumu* (previous item) and the Zhonghua edition includes four other late Ming/early Qing catalogs. It is also indexed (9.4). Unlike the "Yiwenzhi" in previous Standard Histories, it includes only works written in the Ming and therefore does not include pre-Ming works even if they were still circulating in the Ming.

Mingdai shumu tiba congkan 明代書目題跋叢刊 (Collection of prefaces and colophons from Ming dynasty book catalogs), Feng Huimin 馮惠民 and Li Wanjian 李萬健, comps., 2 vols., Shumu wenxian, 1994.

Xinbian Tianyige shumu 新編天一閣書目 (Newly edited catalogs of the Tianyige library), Luo Zhaoping 駱兆平, Zhonghua, 1996. Includes the actual library holdings and what it was able to offer in the past, including for the *Siku quanshu*. On the Tianyige 天一閣, see 9.2.

Wan-Ming shiji kao 晚明史籍考, Xie Guozhen 謝國楨 (1901–82), Guoli Beiping tushuguan, 1933; rev. and enlarged edition, *Zengding Wan-Ming shiji kao* 增訂晚明史籍考, 3 vols., Shanghai guji, 1981. Annotated bibliography of 1,400 primary sources for the history of the late

Ming/early Qing (1621–62). Many of these sources do not appear in the standard Qing bibliographies. Xie also wrote various other works on Ming primary sources (see 49.2, *Biji*), as well as making collections of sources on *Mingdai shehui jingjishi ziliao xuanbian* 明代社會經濟史資料選編 (Selected social and economic materials from the Ming dynasty), 3 vols., Fujian renmin, 1980–81; *Mingdai nongmin qiyi shiliao xuanbian* 明代農民起義史料選編 (Selection of historical materials on peasant uprisings in the Ming), Fujian renmin, 1982.

Xuanlantang congshu 玄覽堂叢書, Zheng Zhenduo 鄭振鐸 (1897–1958), ed., 1ˢᵗ series, Shanghai, 1941; 2ⁿᵈ series, National Central Library, Nanjing; 3ʳᵈ series, National Central Library, 1948; rpnt., 1955. Zheng was the pioneer scholar in the field of popular literature. This collectanea reprints 57 works, mainly Ming. He also edited another collectanea of rare Ming works (using his alternative name of Renqiu zhuren 紉秋主人), *Mingji shiliao congshu* 明季史料叢書, 1944.

Bibliographies of Secondary Sources

Zhongguo jin bashi nian Mingshi lunzhu mulu 中國近 80 年明史論著目錄 (Catalog of research on the Ming during the last 80 years), Lishisuo, Mingshi yanjiushi 明史研究室, comp., Jiangsu renmin, 1981. Contains citations to some 9,400 Chinese articles and some 600 Chinese books on the Ming published 1900–1978. Includes Hong Kong and Taiwan publications. Arranged by subject (including historical geography and biography). Has author index.

Mindaishi kenkyû bunken mokuroku 明代史研究文獻目錄 (A classified bibliography of Ming studies in Japan with Korean Ming studies), Yamane Yukio 山根幸夫, comp., Tôyô bunko, 1960; rev., Kyûko, 1993. Includes references to 307 books in Japanese on the Ming and 5,000 articles mainly written between 1950 and 1993. In addition, 269 Korean articles and six books are cited. Has author index. Leaves out Chinese scholarship, because of the appearance of the preceding item. Supersedes Richard T. Wang, *Ming Studies in Japan, 1961–1981: A Classified Bibliography*, Minneapolis, 1985.

There are a number of state-of-the-field essays on Ming studies—for example:

Evelyn S. Rawski, "Research Themes in Ming-Qing Socioeconomic History—The State of the Field," *JAS* 50.1: 84–111 (1991).

Song Yuanqiang, "The Study of Regional Socio-Economic History in China: Retrospect and Prospects," *LIC* 12.1: 115–31 (1991). Surveys research in China.

Harriet T. Zurndorfer, "A Guide to the 'New' Chinese History: Recent Publications Concerning Chinese Social and Economic Development Before 1800," *International Review of Social History*; 33.2: 148–201 (1988). Covers from the Song to 1800. Includes a 16-page bibliography of Western books and articles published between 1970 and 1987.

William Rowe, "Approaches to Modern Chinese Social History," in Olivier Zunz, ed., *Reliving the Past: The Worlds of Social History*; Chapel Hill: Univ. North Carolina Press, 1985, 236–96. Also covers the first half of the twentieth century.

Noriko Kamachi, "Feudalism or Absolute Monarchism?: Japanese Discourse on the Nature of the State and Society in Late Imperial China," *Modern China* 16.3: 330–70 (July 1990). Summarizes and evaluates Japanese historiographical debates since World War II. Includes an eight-page bibliography.

Mori Masao, "A Survey of Ming Historical Studies in Japan: Past and Present," *Ming Studies*, 27: 67–83 (Spring 1989).

State and Society in China: Japanese Perspectives on Ming-Qing Social and Economic History; Linda Grove and Christian Daniels, eds., Univ. of Tokyo Press, 1984.

Societies and Journals

Late Imperial China (LIC: began in 1965 under the title *Ch'ing-shih wen-t'i*; adopted present title in 1985, semiannual), Society for Qing Studies, California Institute of Technology, Pasadena, California. Contains translations of *Shigaku zasshi* May issue review of Ming-Qing studies in Japan.

Mindaishi kenkyûkai 明代史研究會, Tokyo, 1967– . Journal: *Mindaishi kenkyû* 明代史研究 (1974–).

Ming Studies (1975– , semiannual), University of Minnesota, Minneapolis.

Zhongguo Mingshi xuehui 中國明史學會 (Chinese society for Ming history), 1980– .

Zhongguo Mingshi xuehui tongxun 中國明史學會通訊, 1990– .

Mingshi yanjiu 明史研究, Lishisuo, Mingshi yanjiushi (1991– , annual), Huangshan shushe. Previously *Mingshi yanjiu luncong* 明史研究論叢 (1981–90, irreg.).

Mingshi yanjiu zhuankan 明史研究專刊, 1978– , Taibei: Zhongyang wenhua yanjiuyuan. Annual, 1978–82; thereafter, semiannual.

50

Qing

1644–1912

Qing sources include many millions of documents (10 million from the central archives and some four million more from provincial and local archives). All forms of official publication as well as historical and literary genres have also survived in larger numbers than from all the previous centuries of Chinese history put together. There are also more non-Han language sources than available in previous dynasties—Manchu, Mongolian, Uighur, and Tibetan as well as Korean, Japanese, and Vietnamese sources written in Literary Chinese. In general, there are more sources from the later Qing (1840–1911) than from the early Qing (1644–1840), including new sources such as newspapers and magazines. European and American sources not only on relations with China, but also on internal developments also become important in the nineteenth century. That Qing sources are so plentiful is no doubt because of the relative proximity in time, the larger number of printed books in circulation, and the change in attitude toward archival documents that gradually took hold in the twentieth century.

Attention turns directly to the Qing archives, both central and local (50.1 and 50.3) and to publications of documents in them (50.2). Next come official historical works and compendia (50.4–5), the writings of individuals (50.6), and the private documents of merchants and landlords (50.7). The chapter ends with newspapers and periodicals, both Chinese and foreign (50.8), archaeology and inscriptions (50.9), and guides to sources and research tools not already mentioned (50.10).

Qing scholars were active in many fields, including history, philology, and phonology. Their studies are still important sources for earlier periods of Chinese history.

An index to Chapter 50 follows.

Index to Chapter 50

50.1 Central Archives

The imperial bureaucracy produced huge quantities of documents at the central government agencies, in the palace, and at the provincial and local yamens 衙門.[1] At least half a dozen copies were made of every routine memorial (*tiben* 題本) as it made its way from the originating official to the emperor. Upwards of two thousand copies were made of important edicts and other imperial pronouncements for distribution to the Six Boards and to every provincial, prefectural, and county yamen. Because of well-established traditions of compilation, a selection of these documents were excerpted or copied whole, particularly those considered to have a literary value. But few originals have survived from the Ming or earlier dynasties, either because of neglect or because of accidents such as fire or insects, or because they were deliberately destroyed to make storage space. Yet despite these hazards and despite all the fighting and destruction that preceded and followed the fall of the Qing, no fewer than 14 million original Qing documents have survived (mainly from archives in the capital, Beijing).[2] That they have done so is because of a number of different reasons, the most important being the new appreciation of the value of old government documents as antiquarian or historical items. This appreciation was nurtured by a small handful of collectors, bibliophiles, and scholars during the early Republican period, who eventually won the sup-

---

[1] The first recorded use of the word yamen in the English language according to the *OED* was in 1747: "Each magistrate great or small has his Tribunal or Yamen." The yamens of the later empire were the offices, both central and local, of all government departments dealing with all aspects of official business, not only legal affairs (in pre-Tang times, the phrase referred to military offices and was written *yamen* 牙門). In the provinces the yamen was also the residence of the presiding official. One of the best-preserved provincial yamens is that of the governor-general of Hebei (Zhili zongdu 直隸總督) at Baoding 保定, about 100 km (62 miles) south of Beijing. It was rebuilt in the early Qing and was the venue of major national and international events in the late Qing and Republic.

[2] Beatrice Bartlett (personal communication) points out that statistics on the numbers of documents held in archives need careful evaluation. Some documents were as short as two lines; others were extremely lengthy. A record book may contain details of hundreds of documents covering a year but be counted only as one item. For other examples of the care with which statistical statements about Chinese history should be treated, see 7.1.4.

port of the government. Since then the authorities both in Beijing and in Taibei have made efforts to collect, to preserve, to organize, and to publish the documents on a scale which would have been unthinkable under the old regime.

In 1900, when the allied forces entered Beijing, 50 to 60 percent of the archives of the Six Boards[3] were destroyed, as well as a considerable portion of the contents of the imperial archive, the Huangshicheng 皇史宬. The Russian troops appropriated the archives of the office of the Heilongjiang Military Governor and of three other subordinate military archives in the northeast.

At the fall of the dynasty in 1911, many millions of documents (mainly memorials, reports, rescripts, and memorial copies) still remained in the archives of the Junjichu 軍機處 (lit. Office of Military Plans, normally translated as Grand Council), the Neige 內閣 (Grand Secretariat), the Gongzhong dang'an 宮中檔案 (Palace Archives) and the Liubu 六部 (Six Boards). Most dated from the middle and late Qing, but there were several thousand from the end of the Ming, as well as quantities of materials on early Manchu history and the Shunzhi and Kangxi reigns. In the first years of the Republic, the Grand Council and Grand Secretariat archives remained in the palace. The documents of the Six Boards were inherited by their successor ministries.

As an example of the precarious state of the imperial archives, the story is often told of how a large part of the Grand Secretariat archives (Neige daku 內閣大庫) were sold and later saved.[4] In 1909, most of these documents had been moved to temporary storage in a courtyard of the palace. To make space, it was proposed, in line with past practice, to burn them. Zhang Zhidong 張之洞 (1837–1909), who was at that time the Grand Councilor in charge of the Board of Education, memorialized that the books in the archive be transferred to establish a new library in the Board and sent one of his officials, the bibliophile, scholar, and collector of ancient in-

---

[3] Libu 吏部, Hubu 戶部, Libu 禮部, Bingbu 兵部, Xingbu 刑部, and Gongbu 工部 (i.e., the Boards of Civil Office, Revenue, Rites, War, Punishments, and Public Works).

[4] This account is based on Ni Daoshan 倪道善, *Ming Qing dang'an gailun* 明清檔案概論 (An outline of the Ming-Qing archives), Sichuan daxue, 1990, 1992, 1–10; see also Lo Hui-min, "Some Notes on Archives on Modern China," in Leslie et al., eds., 1973 (20.3), 203–220.

scriptions, Luo Zhenyu 羅振玉 (1866–1940), to make the selection. While inspecting the books, Luo unscrolled some of the memorials and realized their worth as historical sources. So he persuaded Zhang to recommend storing the documents in order to prevent their being burned. As a result, not only the books found refuge in the Board's library (an early forerunner of the Guotu 國圖 housed at the Imperial Academy, Guozijian 國子監), but also the documents. In 1916, the library moved to the palace. The documents were placed in a little courtyard inside the Duanmen 端門 (between the present Tiananmen 天安門 and Wumen 午門). For five years they lay neglected. There were rumors that there were Song editions and even the bones of emperors among them. Much pilfering took place by self-appointed archaeologists of the Ministry of Education. Some perfunctory sorting was done by short-term laborers armed with pointed sticks. Eventually, in 1921 the museum decided to follow the example of most of the other ministries and to sell off a large part of the less than perfect of its Ming and Qing documents to paper merchants for pulp. The documents (weighing an estimated 75 tons), which had been placed by the sorters into 8,000 sacks, were sold for 4,000 *yuan* to a used paper shop in Xidan. One day, Luo Zhenyu was buying books and antiques in Liulichang when he came across the original of a congratulatory message to the emperor from the king of Korea, which he realized could only have come from the Grand Secretariat archives. After making inquiries he found out about the sale and bought back the documents from the paper shop for three times the price they had paid. The whole matter had reached the proportions of a public scandal, which later drew the celebrated remark from Lu Xun 魯迅, "Chinese public property really is difficult to keep; if the authorities are incompetent they ruin it, but if they are competent they steal it."[5]

---

[5] Lu Xun wrote his comment in 1927 and it was published in a weekly magazine in January 1928: "Tan suowei 'Danei dang'an'" 談所謂大內檔案 (On the so-called "imperial archives"); rpnt., *Ming Qing dang'an lunwen xuanbian* 明清檔案論文選編 (Selected articles on the Ming-Qing archives), Dang'an, 1985, 1–6. This wide-ranging selection of scholarly articles from the 1920s to 1980s on the archives was published on their sixtieth anniversary. A similar collection was published in 1995 containing articles written on the archives between 1985 and 1994: *Ming Qing dang'an yu lishi yanjiu lunwen xuan* 明清檔案與歷史研究論文選 (Selected articles on the Ming-Qing archives and historical research), 2 vols., Guoji wenhua, 1995.

Lu Xun was referring not only to the incompetence of the early Republican officials responsible for the neglect of the documents, but also to the appropriation of rare items by senior officials and their authorization for sale of the routine documents for pulp. In doing so, they demonstrated the common attitude that rare books were valuable and that archival documents, especially of a defunct and in this case, alien, dynasty, were junk. Indeed, Lu Xun himself was concerned more with the fate of the rare books than with the archives.

Partly as a result of the scandal and partly as a result of the reorganization of the cultural agencies of the government after 1925, the work of cataloging the documents began for the first time; it was undertaken in the 1920s and 1930s mainly by the Documents Repository (Wenxianguan 文獻館, 1928), of the Palace Museum, which gradually acquired most of what was left of the central government and court archives. The Shiyusuo acquired in 1928 half of Luo's collection (for slightly more than he had paid for the whole); Peking University and Qinghua had also bought documents and began editing and publishing them. Luo and his son Luo Fuyi 羅福頤 sponsored publication and cataloging of the part of their collection that they had taken to Tianjin.

No sooner had the work of cataloging (and to a certain extent, publishing) begun than the War of Resistance against Japan broke out and the work was halted. In 1949, the Republican government took several hundred thousand Qing documents to Taiwan (50.1.3). Ninety-five percent of the Qing archives stayed in China. Today, the Yishiguan holds something on the order of 10 million documents and an estimated additional four million are on deposit in various provincial archives, notably in Shenyang (50.1.5 and 50.3) and in Lhasa (50.3).

50.1.1 Catalogs and Guides to Ming-Qing Archives

A union catalog of Ming-Qing archival documents will no doubt be eventually completed. In the meantime the following catalogs and guides are recommended:

Zhonghua Ming Qing dang'an tonglan 中華明清檔案通覽 (Overview of the Ming-Qing archives of China), Quanguo Ming Qing dang'an mulu zhongxin 全國明清檔案目錄中心, ed., Dang'an, 2000. This is a large-scale (800-page) annotated guide to quanzong 全宗 (archive collections; record groups or *fonds*) in Beijing and in the provinces (including Taiwan) and the 14 million Ming-Qing documents they contain. Eventually, the conspectus will be completed by including the holdings of libraries and museums.

Zhonghua Ming Qing zhendang zhinan 中華明清珍檔指南 (Guide to the Ming-Qing archival treasures of China), Qin Guojing 秦國經, Renmin, 1994, 1996. Best available introduction to Ming-Qing archives (but see previous item).

Chinese Archives: An Introductory Guide, Ye Wa and Joseph W. Esherick, eds., China Research Monograph 45, Institute of Asian Studies, CCS, UCP, 1996. The principal aim of the authors is to describe many of the most important of the 3,500 archival collections in China today. The bulk of the contents of these archives is modern. Only a small number (181) hold Qing documents.

Zhongguo dang'anguan minglu 中國檔案館名錄 (Directory of Chinese archives), Dang'an, 1990, lists central and local archives with addresses.

50.1.2 Documents in the Yishiguan

The First Historical Archives (Zhongguo Diyi lishi dang'anguan 中國第一歷史檔案館, Yishiguan 一史館 for short) is the main repository of Ming-Qing original documents in China. They are housed in buildings just inside the Xihua gate (西華門) at the western entrance to the Forbidden City. The Yishiguan is the successor to the Wenxianguan 文獻館 (Documents Repository) of the Palace Museum (in the 1950s, they were called the Ming-Qing Archives or the Ming-Qing Department of the Central Archives).

The Yishiguan has prepared an on-line index of 600,000 documents (*jian* 件), which should be available to scholars shortly.[6]

About 70 percent of the 10 million documents in the Yishiguan come from five of the main Qing central archives, those of the Grand Secretariat, the Grand Council, the palace, the Imperial Household, and the Imperial Lineage. In addition, there are about 324,000 *juan* of documents from the Six Boards, mainly from the end of the dynasty and mostly from the Board of Punishments (320,000 *juan*), followed by the Army (2,500 *juan*) and the Board of

[6] The following description and list is drawn mainly from Ye and Esherick, 1996 and Qin, 1996 (50.1.1).

Revenue, Hubu 戶部 (1,000 *juan*). There are also extensive records from the Zongli Yamen 總理衙門 (1862–1901) and the Waiwubu 外務部 (Foreign Ministry), many of which have been published.[7]

The most interesting archives for the economic historian are those of the financial and monetary departments (item II.B in the breakdown starting on this page), of which the most plentiful are those of the Board of Revenue. These include records of government finances, coinage, population, taxes, granaries, and the salt industry.

For the social historian, as Ye and Esherick point out, the most interesting are probably the archives of the judiciary, supervisory, and civil administrative departments (item II.E).[8] Of these, those of the Board of Punishments (Xingbu 刑部) are the most extensive. They mainly date from 1870 to 1911. The materials are similar to the routine memorial copies in the censorial section of the Board of Punishments (Xingke 刑科 *tiben*) and have been similarly reorganized according to research and publication priorities of Chinese historians as set in the first thirty years of the People's Republic. Thus there are sections, for example, on prosecutions of leaders of peasant uprisings and secret societies, records of urban strikes and tax protests, anti-missionary cases, minority affairs cases, and so on. There are also records on property and credit disputes, robbery and theft, marital and family disputes, and corruption and smuggling.

The full extent of the scope of the coverage of the Yishiguan may be appreciated by glancing at the 75 *quanzong* 全宗 into which the documents are divided [*quanzong* numbers are given in square brackets]. Ming documents (which are discussed in 49.3) are in *quanzong* 1: *Mingchao dang'an* 明朝檔案. Note that each *quanzong* groups together the documents of a particular agency or person and therefore they vary in size between the largest (*quanzong* 2), the ar-

---

[7] Zongli Yamen 總理衙門 is the short form of the Zongli geguo tongshang shiwu yamen 總理各國通商事物衙門 (Office for the general management of affairs and trade with every country). It was also called Zongshu 總署 or Yishu 譯署 for short. Only a small part of the Ministry of Foreign Affairs archives covering the years 1901–11 are held at the Yishiguan. The larger part, as well as those of the Zongli Yamen, were taken to Taiwan in 1949 and are now housed there in the Jinshisuo (50.1.3).

[8] Nancy Park and Robert Anthony, "Archival Research in Qing Legal History," *LIC* 14.1: 93–137 (1993).

chives of the Neige with over 2.5 million documents, to that of *quanzong* 57, the mere handful of documents in the imperial stud archives.

The main breakdown is in the following broad categories:

I. Archives of the central organs of the imperial government (*Fubi huangdi de zhongshu jigou de dang'an* 輔弼皇帝的中樞機構的檔案)

II. Archives of the departments of the central government and of their dependent yamen (*Fenzhang guozheng ge buyuan yamen jiqi suoshu jigou de dang'an* 分掌國政各部院衙門及其所屬機構的檔案)

III. Archives of departments dealing with the imperial lineage and palace administration (*Zhangguan huangzu ji gongting shiwu jigou de dang'an* 掌管皇族及宮廷事務機構的檔案)

IV. Archives of local government organs, of individuals, and of princely establishments (*Difang jiguan ji geren he wangfu dang-an* 地方機關及個人和王府檔案)

V. Maps and plans (*Yutu huiji* 輿圖匯集)

These five categories are broken down into the following subcategories:

I. Archives of the central organs of the imperial government (*Fubi huangdi de zhongshu jigou de dang'an* 輔弼皇帝的中樞機構的檔案)

    1. *Neige dang'an* 內閣檔案 (Grand Secretariat archives) [*quanzong* 2]. Grand Secretariat archives (Neige dang'an 內閣檔案): a total of 2,714,851 edicts and memorials (Qin, 1996), of which the greater part are routine memorials (*tiben* 題本). About 1.5 million are in good condition (there are also a huge number of damaged ones). They cover all matters of civil and military government in great detail. They date from 1629 to 1911 and cover the years 1607–1911, with the majority falling towards the end of the period. Up to 1735, they are arranged by reign period and then divided topically. After 1735, they are grouped under each of the Six Boards, then arranged chronologically by reign, year, or even month, and subdivided by topic. The Neige archives also contain documents dealing with daily matters of in-

ternal administration and of the various official compiling offices (for example, of the statutes, the Court Diaries, and the
Veritable Records). They also contain separate catalogs of yellow registers (*huangce* 黃冊), the summaries of tax and head
counts and other statistical matters attached to the routine memorials. There are more than 230 volumes of catalogs of the
Neige documents. They are arranged by type of document, by
period, and by subject. Note that an additional 310,000 documents from the Neige archives are in the Shiyusuo in Taibei
(50.1.2).

2. *Junjichu dang'an* 軍機處檔案 (Grand Council archives) [*quanzong* 3]. Grand Council archives (Junjichu dang'an 軍機處檔
   案) covering the period 1730–1911: 793,000 documents, of
   which about 600,000 are memorial file copies (*lufu zouzhe* 錄副
   奏摺),[9] many in running script.[9] They were kept in the Grand
   Council reference collection as a means of keeping track of
   what had been sent to the emperor for comment or what he
   had commented or commanded (the original memorial with
   comments was returned to the sender). These copies supplement (and may sometimes duplicate) the 500,000 original palace
   memorials or edicts with imperial rescripts in vermilion (*zhupi
   zouzhe* 硃批奏摺 or *zhupi yuzhi* 硃批諭旨) kept in the palace
   collections described under item 3 below. In the 1950s they
   were organized according to eighteen subject categories: domestic administration, external relations, military affairs, finance,
   agriculture, water control, industry, commerce, communications, construction, culture and education, law, non-Han peoples' affairs, religion, astronomy and geography, suppression of
   revolutionary movements, imperialist aggression, and miscellaneous. Several of these subject categories have been cataloged in
   whole or in sub-categories. The routine memorials (*tiben*) normally entered the Grand Secretariat, where comments on the
   matters they contained were noted on slips. These along with
   the memorial were then sent to the emperor. His reaction was
   then recorded in red on the memorial by the secretaries for
   transmission back to the Board or originator for action. Such
   hongben 紅本 (as they were called) are quite different from the

---

[9] The basic study of the operations of the Council is Beatrice S. Bartlett,
Monarchs and Ministers: The Grand Council in Mid-Ch'ing China, 1723–1820,
UCP, 1991.

palace memorials with vermilion rescripts in the emperor's own hand (*zhupi zouzhe*).

3. *Gongzhong gechu dang'an* 宮中各處檔案 (Documents of the palace archives) [*quanzong* 4]. Palace archives (Gongzhongdang 宮中檔): mainly imperial edicts with vermilion rescripts (*zhupi yuzhi*) of which there are 500,000, and palace memorials with imperial rescripts (*zhupi zouzhe*). These are divided into the same categories as the memorial copies in the Junjichu archives. Total: about 715,000 documents.[10]

4. *Zeren Neige dang'an* 責任內閣檔案 (Archives of the Cabinet), 6,000 documents, 1911.4 to 1911.12 [*quanzong* 7]

5. *Bideyuan dang'an* 弼德院檔案 (Archives of the Privy Council), 107 documents, 1911.4 to 1911.12 [*quanzong* 8]

6. *Zizhengyuan dang'an* 資政院檔案 (Archives of the National Assembly), very few documents, 1910–11 [*quanzong* 50]

7. *Huiyi zhengwuchu dang'an* 會議政務處檔案 (Archives of the Bureau on Government Affairs), few documents, 1901–11 [*quanzong* 35]

8. *Xianzheng bianchaguan dang'an* 憲政編查館檔案 (Archives of the Committee for Drawing up Regulations for Constitutional Government), 100 *juan*, 1905–11 [*quanzong* 9]

II. Archives of the departments of the central government and of their dependent yamen (*Fenzhang guozheng ge buyuan yamen jiqi suoshu jigou de dang'an* 分掌國政各部院衙門及其所屬機構的檔案)

A. Archives of the Board of Civil Office concerning appointments and transfers of civilian officials (*Zhangguan wenguan renmian de Libu de dang'an* 掌管文官任免的吏部的檔案), over 1,000 *juan*, 1690–1911 [*quanzong* 12]

B. Archives of financial and monetary departments (*Zhangguan caizheng jinrong jigou de dang'an* 掌管財政金融機構的檔案)

1. *Hubu Duzhibu dang'an* 戶部度支部檔案 (Archives of the Board of Revenue and of the Ministry of Finance), over 1,000 *juan*, 1631–1911 [*quanzong* 13]

[10] Beatrice S. Bartlett, "Imperial Notations on Ch'ing Official Documents in the Ch'ien-lung (1736–1795) and Chia-ch'ing (1796–1820) Reigns," *National Palace Museum Bulletin* 7.2: 1–13 (1972) and 7.3: 1–13 (1972).

2. *Huikaofu dang'an* 會考府檔案 (Archives of the Department for Checking Money and Grain), very few documents, 1723–25 [*quanzong* 63]

3. *Qingli caizhengchu dang'an* 清理財政處檔案 (Archives of the Finance Clearing Section), very few documents, 1903–6 [*quanzong* 64]

4. *Shuiwuchu dang'an* 稅務處檔案 (Archives of the Section on Tax Affairs), 91 *juan*, 1906–11 [*quanzong* 44]

5. *Duban yanzhengchu dang'an* 督辦鹽政處檔案 (Archives of the Salt Supervisory Division), limited number of documents, 1909–11 [*quanzong* 25]

6. *Da Qing yinhang dang'an* 大清銀行檔案 (Archives of the Great Qing Bank), 49 *juan*, 1908–11 [*quanzong* 24]

C. Archives of the rites departments (*Zhangguan liyi jisi jigou de dang'an* 掌管禮儀祭祀機構的檔案)

1. *Libu dang'an* 禮部檔案 (Archives of the Board of Rites), very incomplete, 1631–1911 [*quanzong* 14]

2. *Lingqin Libu dang'an* 陵寢禮部檔案 (Archives of the Imperial Mausoleum Department), very few, 1742–1911 [*quanzong* 56]

3. *Yuebu dang'an* 樂部檔案 (Archives of the Board of Music), very incomplete, 1738–1911 [*quanzong* 55]

4. *Taichangsi dang'an* 太常寺檔案 (Archives of the Special Service for Sacrificial Rites to Altars and Temples), 32 *juan*, 1644–1906 [*quanzong* 58]

5. *Guanglusi dang'an* 光祿寺檔案 (Archives of the Special Food Supply Service), very few, 1644–1906 [*quanzong* 59]

6. *Honglusi dang'an* 鴻臚寺檔案 (Archives of the State Banquet Service), very few, 1644–1906 [*quanzong* 60]

D. Archives of the military and patrol departments (*Zhangguan junshi jigou de dang'an* 掌管軍事機構的檔案)

1. *Bingbu Lujunbu dang'an* 兵部陸軍部檔案 (Archives of the Army Board, Infantry Department), 2,500 *juan*, incomplete [*quanzong* 15]

2. *Taipusi dang'an* 太僕寺檔案 (Archives of the Imperial Stud), very few, Guangxu [*quanzong* 57]

3. *Baqi dutong yamen dang'an* 八旗都統衙門檔案 (Archives of the Eight Banners Yamen), over 900 *juan*, incomplete [*quanzong* 23]

4. *Bujun tongling yamen dang'an* 步軍統領衙門檔案 (Archives of the Capital Infantry Guards), 49 *juan*, 1853–1911 [*quanzong* 51]

5. *Guanli qianfeng hujun deng ying shiwu dachenchu dang'an* 管理前鋒護軍等營事務大臣處檔案 (Archives of the Office of the Minister in Charge of the Administration of the Vanguard and Other Divisions), very few, 1908–11 [*quanzong* 65]

6. *Jianruiying dang'an* 健銳營檔案 (Archives of the Light Division), very few and incomplete [*quanzong* 66]

7. *Huoqiying dang'an* 火器營檔案 (Archives of the Artillery and Musketry Division), very few, 1908 [*quanzong* 67]

8. *Shenjiying dang'an* 神機營檔案 (Archives of the Peking Field Force [Divine Mechanism Regiments]), very few, 1861–1911 [*quanzong* 40]

9. *Zongli lianbingchu dang'an* 總理練兵處檔案 (Archives of the Central Military Training Section), over 100 *juan*, 1908–11 [*quanzong* 39]

10. *Jingcheng xunfangchu dang'an* 京城巡防處檔案 (Archives of the Capital Patrol Division), very few, 1853–55 [*quanzong* 71]

11. *Jingfangyingwuchu dang'an* 京防營務處檔案 (Archives of the Capital Guards Division), very few, 1911 [*quanzong* 73]

12. *Jinji lujun ge zhendulian gongsuo dang'an* 近畿陸軍各鎮督練公所檔案 (Archives of the Training Boards of the Metropolitan Army Garrisons), very few, 1907–11 [*quanzong* 42]

13. *Jinwei jun xunlianchu dang'an* 禁衛軍訓練處檔案 (Archives of the Guards Training Division), very few, 1908–11 [*quanzong* 70]

14. *Junzifu dang'an* 軍諮府檔案 (Archives of the General Staff Office), very few, 1906–11 [*quanzong* 49]

E. Archives of the judiciary, supervision and civil administration (*Zhangguan sifa jiancha jigou de dang'an* 掌管司法監察機構的檔案)

1. *Xingbu Fabu dang'an* 刑部法部檔案 (Archives of the Board of Punishments and the Ministry of Justice), more than 32,000

juan, Kangxi to Xuantong, but mainly Guangxu and Xuantong [*quanzong* 16]

2. *Daliyuan dang'an* 大理院檔案 (Archives of the Supreme Court), very few, 1908–11 [*quanzong* 62]

3. *Xiuding Falüguan dang'an* 修訂法律館檔案 (Archives of the Legal Reform Office), 19 *juan*, 1905–11 [*quanzong* 10]

4. *Duchayuan dang'an* 都察院檔案 (Archives of the Censorate Office), very few, Shunzhi to Xuantong [*quanzong* 48]

F. Archives of the departments administering public works, agriculture and commerce (*Zhangguan gongjiao nongshang jigou de dang-an* 掌管工交農商機構的檔案)

1. *Gongbu dang'an* 工部檔案 (Archives of the Board of Works), more than 200 *juan*, very incomplete [*quanzong* 17]

2. *Nonggongshangbu dang'an* 農工商部檔案 (Archives of the Ministry of Commerce or the Ministry of Agriculture, Industry, and Commerce), more than 300 *juan*, 1903–11 [*quanzong* 20]

3. *Youchuanbu dang'an* 郵傳部檔案 (Archives of the Ministry of Posts and Communications), 65 *juan*, incomplete [*quanzong* 22]

G. Archives of the departments dealing with civil affairs and police (*Zhangguan minzheng jingwu jigou de dang'an* 掌管民政警務機構的檔案)

1. *Jingcheng shanhou xiexun zongju dang'an* 京城善後協巡總局檔案 (Archives of the Board for Restoring Security), very few, 1901–2 [*quanzong* 72]

2. *Xunjingbu dang'an* 巡警部檔案 (Archives of the Ministry of Public Security), more than 400 *juan*, 1905–6 [*quanzong* 37]

3. *Minzhengbu dang'an* 民政部檔案 (Archives of the Ministry of Civil Affairs), 1,000 *juan*, 1906–11 [*quanzong* 21]

4. *Jinyan zongju dang'an* 禁烟總局檔案 (Archives of the Opium Prohibition Bureau), very few, 1902–11 [*quanzong* 74]

H. Archives of departments dealing with culture and education (*Zhangguan wenhua ji jiaoyu jigou de dang'an* 掌管文化及教育機構的檔案)

1. *Guozijian dang'an* 國子監檔案 (Archives of the Imperial Academy), few, 1740–1906 [*quanzong* 54]

2. *Xuebu dang'an* 學部檔案 (Archives of the Ministry of Education), 400 *juan*, Guangxu and Xuantong periods [*quanzong* 19]

3. *Qintianjian dang'an* 欽天監檔案 (Archives of the meteorological division), very few, 1715–1908 [*quanzong* 53]

4. *Hanlinyuan dang'an* 翰林院檔案 (Archives of the Hanlin Academy), very few [*quanzong* 61]

5. *Guoshiguan dang'an* 國史館檔案 (Archives of the Historiography Institute), over 1,000 *juan*, mainly from after 1765; documents from 1703–1765 are in the Grand Secretariat archives [*quanzong* 11]

6. *Fanglüeguan dang'an* 方略館檔案 (Archives of the Military Campaigns Records Office) [*quanzong* 46]

I. Archives of nationalities and external affairs departments (*Zhangguan minzu waijiao jigou de dang'an* 掌管民族外交機構的檔案)

1. *Lifanbu dang'an* 理藩部檔案 (Archives of the Board of Dependencies), 700 *juan*, 1873–1911 [*quanzong* 45]

2. *Waiwubu dang'an baokuo Zongli geguo shiwu yamen* 外務部檔案包括總理各國事務衙門 (Archives of the Ministry of Foreign Affairs, including those of the Zongli Yamen), 5,000 *juan* [*quanzong* 18]

III. *Zhangguan huangzu ji gongting shiwu jigou de dang'an* 掌管皇族及宮廷事務機構的檔案 (Archives of departments dealing with the imperial lineage and palace administration)

1. *Zongrenfu dang'an* 宗人府檔案 (Archives of the Imperial Lineage), 430,000 documents dating from Yongzheng to Xuantong. They include birth, marriage, enfeofment, and genealogical records; they also cover Puyi's temporary residence in the palace after 1911 [*quanzong* 6]

2. *Neiwufu dang'an* 內務府檔案 (Archives of the Imperial Household), 189,500 documents, 1654–1924 [*quanzong* 5]. All kinds of documents dealing with the life and activities of the imperial household, including the imperial lineage genealogies, as well as a large collection of maps originally attached to incoming memorials. Total: about 1.9 million documents.

3. *Luanyiwei dang'an* 鑾儀衛檔案 (Archives of the Department of Protocol), over 500 *juan*, Qianlong to Xuantong [*quanzong* 36]

4. *Shiweichu dang'an* 侍衛處檔案 (Archives of the Imperial Bodyguards), very few, 1892–1909 [*quanzong* 68]

5. *Shangyu beiyongchu dang'an* 上虞備用處檔案 (Archives of the Imperial Parks), very few, incomplete [*quanzong* 69]

IV. Archives of local government organs, of individuals and of princely establishments (*Difang jiguan ji geren he wangfu dang-an* 地方機關及個人和王府檔案)

A. Archives of local government organs (*Difang jiguan dang'an* 地方機關檔案)

1. *Shuntianfu dang'an* 順天府檔案 (Archives of Shuntian Prefecture), 300 *juan*, post-Tongzhi [*quanzong* 28]

2. *Jingshi gaodeng shenpanting jianchating dang'an* 京師高等審判廳檢察廳檔案 (Archives of the Peking High Court and Prosecuting Attorneys' Office), over 150 *juan*, 1907–11 [*quanzong* 41]

3. *Beiyang dulianchu dang'an* 北洋督練處檔案 (Archives of the Beiyang military training department), very few, 1886–1911 [*quanzong* 52]

4. *Shandong xunfu yamen dang'an* 山東巡撫衙門檔案 (Archives of the Governor of Shandong), 200 *juan*, incomplete [*quanzong* 29]

5. *Heilongjiang jiangjun yamen dang'an* 黑龍江將軍衙門檔案 (Archives of the Office of the Heilongjiang Military Governor), 14,000 *juan*, 1684–1900 [*quanzong* 30]

6. *Ningguta fudutong yamen dang'an* 寧古塔副都統衙門檔案 (Archives of the Ningguta Manchu Brigade-General's Office), 1,000 *juan*, 1675–1900 [*quanzong* 31]

7. *Alechuke fudutong yamen dang'an* 阿勒楚喀副都統衙門檔案 (Archives of the Alachuke Manchu Brigade-General's Office), 400 *juan*, 1866–1899 [*quanzong* 32]

8. *Hunchun fudutong yamen dang'an* 琿春副都統衙門檔案 (Archives of the Hunchun Manchu Brigade-General's Office), 500 *juan*, 1737–1900 [*quanzong* 33]

9. *Changlu yanyun shisi dang'an* 長蘆鹽運使司檔案 (Archives of the Changlu Salt Distribution Commissioner), 3,000 *juan*, 1768–1914 [*quanzong* 34]

B. Archives of individuals and of imperial relatives (*Geren ji wangfu dang'an* 個人及王府檔案)

1. *Qing feidi Puyi dang'an* 清廢帝溥儀檔案 (Archives of the Deposed Emperor Puyi, 1906–67), 3,000 *juan*, 1911–31 [*quanzong* 26]

2. *Duanfang dang'an* 端方檔案 (Archives of Duanfang, 1862–1911), 140,000 *juan* [*quanzong* 27]

3. *Zhao Erxun dang'an* 趙爾巽檔案 (Archives of Zhao Erxun, 1844–1927), 622 *juan*, 1885–1912 [*quanzong* 75]

4. *Chun Qinwangfu dang'an* 醇親王府檔案 (Archives of the Princes Chun, including Yihuan 奕譞, 1840–91, and Zaifeng 載灃, 1883–1951), 200 *juan*, 1875–1926 [*quanzong* 38]

V. *Yutu huiji* 輿圖匯集 (Maps and plans), 7,000 of which do not fit into any of the other *quanzong* [*quanzong* 47]

50.1.3   Central Archives Held in Taibei

Of the many hundreds of thousands of documents shipped to Taibei in 1949, 346,776 are held at the Palace Museum.[11] The criteria for selection were that they be as old as possible and that they bear the emperor's personal comments. This is therefore a particularly valuable collection. There are two published catalogs; one lists all Chinese-language archival holdings from the Qing,[12] the other indexes biographies and biographical drafts.[13] There is also a computer database of the memorials enabling searches on the official memorializing, his office, the date, and the contents.

Much of the Shiyusuo collection of Neige documents are available on microfilm; about one-fifth (60,000) have been published (50.2.2) and the remainder are due out on CD-ROM.

---

[11] Many of the 153,215 palace memorials and 188,000 Grand Council reference copies (*lufu* 錄副) held at the Palace Museum have been published. Of the 39,824 record books, none has been published except late-Qing diaries; see Bartlett, "Ch'ing Documents in the National Palace Museum Archives. Part One, Document Registers: The *Sui-shou teng-chi*," *National Palace Museum Bulletin* 10.4: 1–17 (1975). Zhuang Jifa 莊吉發 describes the different types of document, their value for research, and their shelving in *Gugong dang'an shuyao* 故宮檔案述要 (Basic account of the Palace Museum Archives), Gugong bowuyuan 故宮博物院, 1983.

[12] *Guoli gugong bowuyuan Qingdai wenxian dang'an zongmu* 國立故宮博物院清代文獻檔案總目 (Catalog of Qing dynasty documentary archives in the National Palace Museum), Taibei: Gugong bowuyuan, 1982. Does not include Manchu holdings, for which see *Gugong wenxian* 2.3–3.3 (1971.6–1972.6).

[13] *Guoli gugong bowuyuan Qingdai wenxian zhuanbao zhuangao renming suoyin* 國立故宮博物院清代文獻傳包傳稿人名索引 (50.10.4, *Biographies*).

In addition to the documents from the Palace Museum and Shi-yusuo collections, the Guomindang (KMT) also shipped the archives of the Ministry of Foreign Affairs and many rare books from the National Central Library, the National Palace Museum, and the National Central Museum. The Jinshisuo has the Zongli Yamen 總理衙門 (1862–1901) and Waiwubu 外務部 (Foreign Ministry) documents (1901–11). About 10% have been published (see also 50.1.2, item I.2).

50.1.4　Central Archives Held in Japan

Nihon shozai Shindai dôan shiryô no shosô 日本所在清代檔案史料諸相 (On all aspects of Qing archive documents held in Japan), Kanda Nobuo 神田信夫, Tôyô bunko, 1993.

50.1.5　Shengjing Archives

Shengjing 盛京 (Shenyang) was the secondary capital of the Qing. Its Manchu name was Mukden. Documents relating to national as well as northeastern matters were stored in the archives there. Today, they are part of the Liaoning Provincial Archives, which have altogether about 200,000 Qing documents dating from 1789 to 1895. The Qing documents include 142 *juan* of imperial genealogy (*Yudie* 玉牒); 3,625 *juan* of Banner household and head counts (*Baqi bing-ding hukou ce* 八旗兵丁戶口冊), as well as other Banner documents; and 45,283 *juan* of northeastern documents. They also have a small holding of Ming documents (see 49.2).

50.2　Published Archival Documents

Sixty-five collections of documents from the Qing archives were published between the first collection put out by Luo Zhenyu in 1924 and 1948.[14] Since then, over 200 titles have appeared, ranging from single volumes to series in several hundred volumes. There is a considerable amount of overlap and repetition, but in recent years efforts have been made to integrate the published holdings in Taibei

[14] *Shiliao congkan chubian* 史料叢刊初編, Luo Zhenyu, ed., 10 *ce*, Shang-hai, 1924; Taibei, 1964. Wide variety of early Qing documents from the Grand Secretariat archives.

with those in Beijing. Large portions of the archives are already available on microfilm, and their publication on CD-ROM has also begun. Eventually no doubt, all the archives will be available on CD-ROM with complete indexes. For the time being, however, it is still necessary to look through a large number of catalogs and documents in order to track down those relevant to a particular research project.[15]

From the earliest days there has been a twofold trend in publications from the archives, either to group documents around a theme or to publish them chronologically in a series. Common themes have been Sino-foreign relations (50.2.7), popular uprisings (28.3), religious cases, the Opium and other wars (28.2), missionary cases, the anti-foreign movement, the Taipings (28.3), the Reform Movement, the 1911 revolution, natural disasters (36.4), documents of a particular province or of a particular archive. Important chronological publications have been many of the Qing Court Diaries, all the Veritable Records, and certain collected memorials of individual periods or individual officials (50.2.2).

A large number of indexes to the archives are available. For a start, the documents were indexed as they came in or went out or were copied or read. Some of these indexes have been used in the compilation of modern indexes.[16]

[15] The *Dang'an wenxian guangpan ku* 檔案文獻光盤庫, 120 discs, Chaoxing 超星, 1996. Part 1 (*Zhongguo Ming Qing dang'an ku* 中國明清檔案庫, 10 disks) contains works already published by the Yishiguan in book form (e.g., the imperially endorsed palace memorials of the Kangxi and Yongzheng reigns; the edicts of Qianlong reign (see 50.2.2); already published archives on selected themes, e.g., Opium and Sino-Japanese wars as well as the journal *Lishi dang'an* 歷史檔案 (1981–95). The remaining 110 disks contain materials on the Republic (37 disks) and People's Republic (73 disks).

[16] For example, *Qing Junjichu dang'an mulu* 清軍機處檔案目錄 (Catalog of record books in the Grand Council Archives), Beiping: Gugong wenxianguan, Gugong yinshuasuo, 1934. Lists year by year the record books (*dangce* 檔冊) and memorial bundles (*zhebao* 摺包) held by the Palace Museum; total of 7,969 of the former and 3,535 of the latter, containing some 800,000 documents in all. The memorials and other documents in this archive were copies of those passing to and from the emperor. A portion was removed to Taiwan.

50.2.1   Yishiguan *(Microfilms)*

Di'erci Yapian zhanzheng shiliao 第二次鴉片戰爭史料 (Historical materials on the Second Opium War), Yishiguan, comp., 14 reels, 1981. Records of Second Opium War (1856–60) covering 1853–60.

Gongzhong liangjiadan 宮中糧價單 (Crop price reports in the palace archives), Yishiguan, comp., 328 reels, 1990. Crop price reports covering each of the 28 provinces from Kangxi to 1911 (7.5).

Gongzhong lülipian 宮中履歷片 (Curricula vitae of officials in the palace archives), Yishiguan, comp., 6 reels, 1985. These abbreviated curricula vitae of officials taking up, or leaving, office were prepared for the emperor, and some contain his comments (from Kangxi to Xianfeng). They have been published in book form (50.2.4).

Gongzhong lüli yinjianzhe 宮中履歷引見摺 (Curricula vitae of officials in the palace archives), Yishiguan, comp., 27 reels, 1985. Curricula vitae of over 30,000 middle and lower-ranking officials, prepared for the occasion of their taking up or leaving office. Covering the years 1721–1911; they have been published in book form (50.2.4).

Gongzhong zhupi zouzhe caizhenglei 宮中硃批奏摺財政類 (Imperially rescripted memorials in the palace archives; financial category), Yishiguan, comp., 64 reels, 1986. These include 80,000 vermilion rescripted memorials on financial matters covering the years 1662 to 1911. The subjects covered are land and other taxes (*tianfu* 田賦), customs (*guanshui* 關稅), salt monopoly (*yanye* 鹽業), land and property rents (*dizu* 地租, *fangzu* 房租), miscellaneous taxes (*zashui* 雜稅), crop taxes (*liangshui* 糧稅), contributions (*sunshu* 損輸), grain stores (*zangchu* 藏儲), treasuries (*kuchu* 庫儲), expenses (*jingfei* 經費), and coinage and money (*huobi jinrong* 貨幣金融).

Heilongjiang jiang jun yamen dang'an 黑龍江將軍衙門檔案 (Archives of the Heilongjiang Brigade-General's Office), Yishiguan, comp., 193 reels, 1988. The archive has 12,800 records dating from 1684 to 1900. Most extensive are those of the Qianlong reign.

Hubu Duzhibu fengyin fengmice 戶部度植部俸銀俸米冊 (Board of Revenue, Revenue Section records of tribute silver and grain), Yishiguan, comp., 7 reels, 1985. Records of the silver and rice received by bannermen from 1760 to 1913; in 2,306 volumes.

Junjichu lufu zouzhe nongmin yundong lei 軍機處錄副奏摺農民運動類 (Grand Council memorial file copies in the peasant movement category), Yishiguan, comp., 7 reels, 1985.

Junjichu lufu zouzhe quanguo shuili yushui ziran zaihai ziliao 軍機處錄副奏摺全國水利雨水自然災害資料 (Memorial file copies in the Grand Council archives concerning materials on water control, rainfall, and natural calamities), Yishiguan, comp., 24 reels, 1992. Consists of 13,690 copies of weather reports covering the years 1736 to 1826. Includes also crop price reports.

Junjichu lufu zouzhe zhenya geming yundong lei 軍機處錄副奏摺鎮壓革命運動類 (Grand Council memorial file copies in the suppression of revolutionary movements category), Yishiguan, comp., 49 reels, 1991. Memorial copies collected by subject. This collection includes the Nian army (1814–1911); Taiping Heavenly Kingdom (1850–1864); the Boxers and the 1911 revolution.

Junjichu shangyudang 軍機處上諭檔 (Grand Council edicts), Yishiguan, comp., 394 reels, 1980. Covers the years 1723–1911.

Libu zaosong fengzeng xingshi ce 吏部造送封贈姓氏冊 (Record of those receiving titles prepared by the Board of Civil Office), Yishiguan, comp., 7 reels, 1985. This archive records the names of those people who received titles between 1862 and 1874 (family details—e.g., names of fathers and mothers and grandparents—are also given).

Manwen laodang 滿文老檔 (The old Manchu archives), Yishiguan, comp., 14 reels, 1983. The original is held in Taibei; these reels are taken from one of the six copies made in the Qianlong reign, four of which are in the Yishiguan and two in the Shenyang archives. See 50.2.6 for brief description of the *Manwen laodang*.

Manwen Nei guoshiyuan dang 滿文內國史院檔 (National History Office Manchu archives), Yishiguan, comp., 3 reels, 1989. These are the archives of the early Neige bureau responsible for the compilation of the National History (*Guoshi* 國史). The archive is arranged chronologically and covers the years 1633–43.

Neige Hanwen qijuzhu 內閣漢文起居注 (Court Diaries in Chinese from the Grand Secretariat), Yishiguan, comp., 223 reels, 1982. See 50.4.

Neige jingchace 內閣京察冊 (Grand Secretariat capital investigation records), Yishiguan, comp., 80 reels, 1985.

Neige Kangxichao qijuzhu 內閣康熙朝起居注 (Kangxi Court Diaries from the Grand Secretariat), Yishiguan, comp., 16 reels, 1985. See 50.4.

Neige Manwen qijuzhu 內閣滿文起居注 (Court Diaries in Manchu from the Grand Secretariat), Yishiguan, comp., 7 reels, 1985. See 50.4.

Neige Qiushen tiben 內閣秋審題本 (Grand Secretariat autumn assizes memorials), Yishiguan, comp., 212 reels, 1989. Covers the years 1736–95.

Qingdai Liuqiu dang'an shiliao 清代琉球檔案史料 (Historical materials from the Qing dynasty archives on the Ryukyus), Yishiguan, comp., 3 reels, 1992. Consists of 662 records taken from the memorial copies made in the Grand Council (1742–1898). For book publication, see 50.2.6, *Ryûkyû*.

Qingdai pudie dang'an 清代譜牒檔案 (Qing dynasty genealogies in the archives), Yishiguan, comp., 307 reels, 1983. Neiwufu personnel records covering 1754 to 1911 in 11,000 volumes. Details of the imperial house, bannermen, relatives, including not only family, but also economic conditions. Also palace personnel records, which cover everything from examination candidates to cases involving capital punishments in every province (1,200 volumes). Also Zongrenfu records, principally the imperial tree, which was revised every 10 years.

Xinhai geming dang'an shiliao 辛亥革命檔案史料 (Archive materials on the 1911 Revolution), Yishiguan, comp., 4 reels, 1983. A selection of 640 documents (indexed) relating to the 1911 Revolution, mainly from Qing official sources.

Zongrenfu hongqice 宗人府紅旗冊 (Red banner registers in the office of the Imperial Lineage archives), Yishiguan, comp., 87 reels, 1985. The red registers record the family conditions (births, deaths, marriages) of bannermen related on the distaff side of the imperial house. Covers the years 1857–98 in 1,500 volumes.

See also "Qing Archival Materials from the No. 1 Historical Archives on Microfilm at the Genealogical Society of Utah," *LIC* 9.2: 86–114 (1988).

50.2.2   General Publications

The dictionary of compilations containing documents and excerpts as well as modern publications from the archives (*Zhongguo dang'an wenxian cidian* 中國檔案文獻辭典, Box 6, Chapter 20) contains annotations on 1,700 such publications of Qing documents. This part of the book was edited by a team of historians and archivists led by Ni Daoshan 倪道善. To give an idea of the rich detail in the *Dang-an wenxian cidian*, it lists and annotates 75 published collections of documents from the 13 years of the Yongzheng reign alone, including contemporary eighteenth-century collections, later Qing collec-

tions, and modern publications from the Qing central and local archives.

Ming Qing shiliao 明清史料 (Ming-Qing historical materials), 100 vols., in
10 collections; first collection, Shiyusuo, 1930–31; collections 2–3,
Shanghai: Shangwu, 1935–36; vol 4, Zhongguo kexueyuan, 1951;
vols., 5–10, Shiyusuo, 1953–75; reprints by Shiyusuo: vol 1, 1997;
vols. 2–4 and 6–7, 1999; vol. 5, 1994. Consists of 8,200 typeset high-
quality documents from the Grand Secretariat dating from late Ming
and early Qing from the collection of the Shiyusuo. Included in the
next item.

Ming Qing dang'an 明清檔案 (Ming-Qing archives), 324 vols., Taibei:
Lianjing, 1986–95. The full title is *Zhongyang yanjiuyuan Lishiyuyan
yanjiusuo xiancun Qingdai Neige daku yuancang Ming Qing dang'an* 中
央研究院歷史語言研究所現存清代內閣大庫原藏明清檔案. This se-
ries was planned to number 1,500 folio volumes containing all of the
310,000 Neige documents in the Shiyusuo collection, arranged chronologically with annotations and an index. Having reached the 11th
year of Jiaqing (1806), the decision was taken to produce the remaining volumes on CD-ROM. Includes the previous item. For a brief description of the miscellaneous contents, see Wa and Esherick (1996),
330.

Ming Qing dang'an cunzhen xuanji 明清檔案存真選輯 (Selected materials
from the Ming-Qing archives: documents of the late Ming, early
Qing photolithographically printed), Li Guangtao 李光濤 et al., eds.,
3 vols., Shiyusuo, 1959–75; 1st vol., rpnt., 1992. Vol. 2 contains Manchu documents.

Ming Qing Neige daku shiliao 明清內閣大庫史料 (Historical materials
from the Grand Secretariat in the Ming and Qing), 1st collection,
Ming, 2 vols., Jin Yufu 金毓黻, ed., Dongbei tushuguan, 1949. Includes over 500 memorials dating from 1623 to 1644; the remainder
from early Qing.

Ming Qing shiliao huibian 明清史料匯編 (Collection of Ming-Qing historical materials), Shen Yunlong 沈雲龍, ed., 93 vols., in nine collections, Wenhai, 1967–84. Reprints all sorts of historical materials, especially on the late Ming, early Qing.

Kangxichao Hanwen zhupi zouzhe huibian 康熙朝漢文硃批奏摺彙編
(Collection of imperially rescripted palace memorials of the Kangxi
period in Chinese), Yishiguan, ed., 8 vols., Dang'an, 1984–85. Includes 3,119 memorials, of which 1,049 are in the Yishiguan and
2,070 are in the Palace Museum, Taibei, as published in the first
seven volumes of *Gongzhongdang Kangxichao zouzhe* 宮中檔康熙朝

奏摺 (Palace memorials of the Kangxi reign), Taibei: Gugong bowu-yuan, ed., 9 vols., 1976. The last two volumes of this collection are Yishiguan memorials in Manchu.

Yongzhengchao Hanwen zhupi zouzhe huibian 雍正朝漢文硃批奏摺彙編 (Collection of Chinese-language imperially rescripted palace memori-als of the Yongzheng period), Yishiguan, ed., 40 vols., Jiangsu guji, 1986. Contains more than 35,000 memorials of 1,200 senior officials. About 15,000 are from the Yishiguan; the remaining 20,000 are as re-produced in *Gongzhongdang Yongzhengchao zouzhe* 宮中檔雍正朝奏摺 (Palace memorials of the Yongzheng reign), Taibei: Gugong bo-wuyuan, ed., 32 vols., 1977–80. Note that already in the Yongzheng reign itself, an enormous collection of edicts was initiated: *Yongzheng chao zhupi yuzhi* 雍正朝硃批諭旨, 1738. It contains 7,000 imperial-rescripted edicts. Note also that the complete collection of vermilion-rescripted Yongzheng memorials in Manchu has been published in Chinese translation (50.2.6). See Beatrice S. Bartlett, "The Secret Me-morials of the Yung-cheng Period (1723–1735): Archival and Pub-lished Versions," *National Palace Museum Bulletin* 9.4: 1–12 (1974).

Yongzhengchao Hanwen yuzhi huibian 雍正朝漢文諭旨彙編 (Collection of Chinese-language vermilion-rescripted palace edicts of the Yong-zheng period), Yishiguan, ed., 10 vols., Guangxi shifan daxue, 1999.

Gongzhongdang Qianlongchao zouzhe 宮中檔乾隆朝奏摺 (Palace memo-rials of the Qianlong reign), Taibei: Gugong bowuyuan, ed., 68 vols., 1982–89. Contains 59,436 memorials arranged by date with undated ones placed at the end of the year.

Qianlongchao shangyu dang 乾隆朝上諭檔 (Qianlong reign imperial edicts), Yishiguan, ed., 18 vols., Zhongguo dang'an, 1991; rpnt., 1998.

Jiaqing Daoguang liangchao shangyu dang 嘉慶道光兩朝上諭檔 (Archive of imperial edicts from the reigns of Jiaqing and Daoguang), Yishi-guan, ed., 50 vols., Dang'an, 2000.

Guangxuchao zhupi zouzhe 光緒朝硃批奏摺 (Imperially rescripted palace memorials of the Guangxu reign), Yishiguan, ed., 120 vols., Zhong-hua, 1995–97. Arrangement of the more than 99,400 memorials (totaling 63 million characters) in this massive collection is by broad subject category. This includes the memorials in *Gongzhongdang Guangxuchao zouzhe* 宮中檔光緒朝奏摺 (Palace memorials of the Guangxu reign), Taibei: Gugong bowuyuan, ed., 26 vols., 1973–75.

Xianfeng Tongzhi liangchao shangyu dang 咸豐同治兩朝上諭檔 (Archive of Xianfeng and Tongzhi imperial edicts), Yishiguan, ed., 24 vols., Guangxi shifan daxue, 1998.

Guangxu Xuantong liangchao shangyu dang 光緒宣統兩朝上諭檔 (Archive of Guangxu and Xuantong imperial edicts), 37 vols., Guangxi shifan daxue, 1996. The edicts cover the years 1875 to 1911 and the arrangement is chronological.

Neige daku shudang jiumu 內閣大庫書檔舊目 (Catalog of book lists and lists of documents in the Grand Secretariat archives), Beiping, 1933. *Supplement*, Shanghai, 1936. Based on record books (*dangce* 檔冊) and book lists in the Shiyusuo holdings; supplement contains similar materials from Peking University and Palace Museum holdings.

Qingdai dang'an shiliao congbian 清代檔案史料叢編 (Historical materials from the Qing archives), Yishiguan, 14 vols., Zhonghua, 1978–90. Each volume concentrates on two or three themes, e.g., the financial circumstances of the Qing government at the time of the Taipings.

Zhanggu congbian 掌故叢編 (Collected historical documents), 10 *ce*, Gugong wenxianguan, Heji yinshuaju, 1928–29; rpnt., Guofeng, 1964. Mainly early Qing documents from Grand Council archives; after vol. 11, the name of the series was changed to *Wenxian congbian* 文獻叢編 (Collectanea from the Historical Records Office), 44 *ce*, Gugong wenxianguan, Gugong yinshuasuo, 1930–42; rpnt., Guofeng, 1963. Arrangement is by themes, e.g., materials on customs duties levied during the Yongzheng period in vols. 10–11 and 17–19. Vol. 37 contains an index to the first 36 *ce*; *Qing sanfan shiliao* 清三藩史料 (Materials on the revolt of the Three Feudatories), 6 vols., Gugong bowuyuan, 1932–33, was a side publication of the series. In addition, the Wenxianguan also published a periodical, *Shiliao xunkan* 史料旬刊 (Historical documents published every 10 days), 40 *ce*, Gugong wenxianguan, Jinghua yinshuju, 1930–31; rpnt., Guofeng, 1963.

Qingmo choubei lixian dang'an shiliao 清末籌備立憲檔案史料 (Historical materials from the archives on the preparations for the establishment of a constitution at the end of the Qing), Yishiguan, eds., 2 vols., Zhonghua, 1979.

50.2.3   Economic Documents

Catalogs

Qingdai zhupi zouzhe caizhenglei mulu 清代硃批奏摺財政類目錄 (Index of imperially rescripted palace memorials in the financial category), Qin Guojing, 秦國經 ed. in chief, 5 vols., Zhongguo caizheng, 1990–92. This was the first major catalog of the Yishiguan published since 1949. A total of 720,000 memorials are arranged chronologically. There is an index by memorialists.

Qing Neige jiucang Hanwen huangce lianhe mulu 清內閣舊藏漢文黃冊聯合目錄 (Union catalog of yellow registers in Chinese formerly stored in the archives of the Grand Secretariat), Wenxianguan, Beida wenke yanjiusuo and Shiyusuo, eds., 6 *ce*, Beijing daxue yinshuasuo, 1952. The yellow registers (*huangce* 黃冊) included not only population counts but also accounts relating to all types of labor service and payment. They were attached as numerical appendixes to memorials from officials working in any of the Six Boards or their subordinate departments. They often contain much fuller statistical materials than are found in the memorials themselves. This catalog includes a total of 17,033 *huangce*: 6,602 at Beida,[17] 7,000 at the Wenxianguan,[18] and 2,000 at the Shiyusuo. It is arranged by the Six Boards and then by subject matter. The introduction contains details of the subjects covered and numbers in each category. It has been reprinted in *Ming Qing dang'an lunwen xuanbian* 明清檔案論文選編, 173–92.

Jingji dang'an hanmu huibian 經濟檔案函目匯編 (51.1.3); archival holdings of Shiyusuo, mainly Republican period but some from 1903–11.

Collections

Diguozhuyi yu Zhongguo haiguan 帝國主義與中國海關 (Imperialism and the Chinese customs), parts 1–15, Zhongguo jindai jingjishi ziliao congbian weiyuanhui, eds., Kexue and Zhonghua, 1952–65.

Gongzhong liangjiadan 宮中糧價單 (Crop price reports in the palace archives), see 50.2.1 (Microfilm, no. 13).

Gongzhong zhupi zouzhe caizhenglei 宮中硃批奏摺財政類 (Imperially rescripted palace memorials on financial matters), see 50.2.1 (Microfilm, no. 12).

Guanyu Jiangning zhizao Caojia dang'an shiliao 關于江寧織造曹家檔案史料 (On the archives of the Cao family, Jiangning textile commissioner), Gugong Ming-Qing dang'anbu, eds., Zhonghua, 1975.

Haifang dang 海防檔 (Coastal defense archives), 9 vols., Jinshisuo, 1957. In the series *Zhongguo jindaishi ziliao huibian* 中國近代史資料匯編.

---

[17] *Qing jiuchao jingsheng baoxiaoce mulu* 清九朝京省報銷冊目錄 (Catalog of accounts forwarded to Beijing during nine reigns of the Qing dynasty), Qingdai Neige daku dang'an zhengli weiyuanhui, eds., 1935. Only the *huangce* of the first two reigns were published.

[18] *Neige daku xiancun Qingdai Hanwen huangce mulu* 內閣大庫現存清代漢文黃冊目錄 (Catalog of extant yellow registers in Chinese in the archive of the Grand Secretariat), Beijing, 1936.

Hanyeping gongsi 漢冶萍公司 (The Hanyeping Co.), vol. 1, Chen Xulu 陳旭麓 et al., Shanghai renmin, 1984.

Hubei kaicai meitie zongju Jingmen kuangwu zongju 湖北開采煤鐵總局, 荆門礦務總局 (The Hubei iron and coal mine dept. and the Jingmen coal department), Chen Xulu 陳旭麓 et al., Shanghai renmin, 1981.

Kuangwu dang 礦物檔 (Mining archives [1865–1911]), Jinshisuo, eds., 8 vols., 1960. In the series *Zhongguo jindaishi ziliao huibian* 中國近代史資料匯編.

Qingdai de kuangye 清代的礦業 (The mining industry in the Qing dynasty), 2 vols., Zhonghua, 1983.

Qingdai diqi dang'an shiliao (Jiaqing zhi Xuantong) 清代地契檔案史料嘉慶至宣統 (Historical materials on Qing land deeds, 1796–1911), Xiong Jingfeng 熊敬馮, ed., Sichuan Xindu dang'anju and Danganguan, 1988. Consists of 196 deeds from Xindu, Sichuan, dating from 1805 to 1911.

Qingdai diwang lingqin 清代帝王陵寢 (Imperial and princely tombs in the Qing dynasty), Yishiguan, ed., Dang'an, 1983.

Qingdai dizu boxue xingtai 清代地租剝削形態 (The exploitative land tax system in the Qing dynasty), Lishi yanjiusuo and Yishiguan, eds., 2 vols., Dang'an, 1981.

Qingdai Jilin dang'an shiliao xuanbian (gongye) 清代吉林檔案史料選編 (工業) (Selection of historical materials from the Qing dynasty Jilin archives [industry]), Jilin Dang'anguan, ed., 3 vols., Jilin Danganguan, 1985.

Qingdai Jilin dang'an shiliao xuanbian 清代吉林檔案史料選編 (Selection of historical materials from the Qing dynasty Jilin archives), Jilin Dang'anguan, eds., Jilin Dang'anguan, 1987.

Wu Xun dimuzhang 武訓地畝帳 (The land accounts of Wu Xun [1838–96]), Renmin, 1975.

Yuanming yuan 圓明園 (The summer palace), Yishiguan, ed., 2 vols., Shanghai guji, 1991.

Zhongguo jindai bingqi gongye dang'an shiliao 中國近代兵器工業檔案史料 (Historical materials on the history of the Chinese armaments industry in the modern period), Yishiguan, ed., 4 vols., Bingqi gongye, 1993.

Zhongguo jindai huobishi ziliao 中國近代貨幣史資料 (Materials on the history of Chinese coins and currency in the modern period), Zhongguo renmin yinhang canshi shi, ed., 2 vols., Zhonghua, 1964.

Zigong yanye qiyue dang'an xuanji 自貢鹽業契約檔案選輯 (Selected contracts from the archives of the Zigong salt industry), Zigongshi
Dang'anguan, ed., Shehui kexue, 1985. The materials cover the period 1732–1949.

50.2.4   Biographical Material

Zhongguo Diyi lishi dang'anguan cang 中國第一歷史檔案館藏, *Qingdai
guanyuan lüli dang'anguan bian*, 清代官員履歷檔案館編 (Holdings
of the Yishiguan of curricula vitae of Qing officials), Zhang Guisu
張桂素 et al., eds., 30 vols., Huadong shifan daxue, 1997. Contains
abbreviated curricula vitae of 55,883 individuals. The CVs were prepared for the emperor to read before receiving an official for an in-
terview. Vol. 30 is a name index (both by stroke count and by the
four-corner system). The Yishiguan holdings of these materials are
also available on microfilm (50.2.1).

50.2.5   Documents Relating to Taiwan

Taiwan's recorded history is remarkably short but the sources
available for tracing it from the seventeenth century onward are
unusually rich and varied (on the many different names for Taiwan
臺灣, see Table 6, 4.1). The first recorded Han visitor is in a late
fourteenth-century work, the *Daoyi zhilüe* 島夷志略 (41.5.1, *Yuan*).
At that time the island was inhabited by Malay-Polynesian peoples.
Starting from the seventeenth century, Han settlers from Fujian began arriving in small numbers. The northern part of the island was
briefly under Spanish control (1626–42). The Dutch period lasted
slightly longer (1624–62). They set up a trading post and camps in
the south and eventually drove the Spanish out. The Dutch were
succeeded by the Ming loyalist Zheng Chenggong 鄭成功 (1624–
62), whose family and forces controlled the island until their defeat
by a Qing admiral in 1683.[19] At that point the island was made a
prefecture. The population was roughly balanced between 100,000
people belonging to indigenous tribes and 100,000 Han settlers.
Shortly after being elevated to a province (1885), Taiwan was ceded
to Japan (1895; see 51.10). Each wave of settlers and conquerors left

---

[19] Zheng is commonly referred to as Koxinga (Guoxingye 國姓爺) the
name he acquired having been granted the use of the Ming imperial family
name, Zhu 朱, as a reward for his loyalty to the Ming. See Ralph C. Croizier,
Koxinga and Chinese Nationalism: History, Myth, and the Hero, HUP, 1977.

its mark, and from the seventeenth century, its own historical sources.[20] Japanese-language sources on Taiwan are dealt with in 51.11.2.

Qinggong yuezhe dang Taiwan shiliao 清宮月摺檔臺灣史料 (Taiwan historical sources in the monthly memorial registers in the Qing palace), Hong Anquan 洪安全, ed. in chief, 11 vols., Gugong, 1994–98.

Qinggong yuzhi dang Taiwan shiliao 清宮諭旨檔臺灣史料 (Taiwan historical sources in the imperial edicts in the archives of the Qing palace), Hong Anquan 洪安全, ed. in chief, 6 vols., Gugong, 1996–97.

Gugong Taiwan shiliao gaishu 故宮臺灣史料概述 (Introduction to Taiwan sources in the Palace Museum), Zhuang Jifa 莊吉發, comp., Taibei: Guoli Gugong bowuyuan, 1995.

Taiwan wenxian ziliao huibian 臺灣文獻資料匯編 (Taiwan documents and historical sources), 1ˢᵗ collection, 40 vols., Guoxue wenxian guan, Lianjing, 1993.

Ming Qing shiliao 明清史料 (50.2.2), collections 4–6 (*ding* 丁, *wu* 戊, *ji* 己), contain mainly documents related to Taiwan.

Taiwan wenxian congkan 臺灣文獻叢刊 (Collectanea of Taiwan documents and historical sources), 595 vols., Taiwan yinhang, 1957–72. Collection of excerpted and reprinted Chinese primary sources on Taiwan's history, including excerpts from imperial compilations, gazetteers, *biji*, and many others; mainly from the Qing.

50.2.6   Documents in Manchu

The terms "Manchu" and "Qing" are briefly discussed in Box 10. There are between 1.6 and 2 million Qing documents in Manchu (representing about one-sixth the total extant number of central Qing documents). They are mainly held at the Yishiguan and the Shenyang archives. There is also an important collection of over 200 boxes at the Palace Museum, Taibei (Chieh-hsien Chen, *Manchu Archival Materials*, Taibei: Linking Publishing Co., 1988). Published catalogs of the Manchu documents are becoming available, for example,

Qingdai bianjiang manwen dang'an mulu 清代邊疆滿文檔案目錄 (Catalog of Manchu documents relating to the borders in the Qing dynasty), Yishiguan et al, eds., 12 vols., Yishiguan, 1999. This detailed

[20] For Western-language sources on Taiwan, see 51.10.

catalog translates the titles of 156,500 Manchu documents and arranges them chronologically by region.

The oldest Qing documents in the Yishiguan are the private day-to-day records of the Qing imperial house over the years 1607–36, the *Manwen laodang* 滿文老檔 (Old Manchu archives). Six copies were made in the Qianlong reign. Today, four are in the Yishiguan and two in the Shenyang archives. The original is held in Taibei. A modern Chinese annotated translation has been published (see under *Manwen laodang* below). There is also a Japanese translation (*Manbun rôtô* 滿文老檔 (The old Manchu archives), Kanda Nobuo 神田信夫, ed., 7 vols., Tôyô bunko, 1955–63). The *Manwen laodang* are an essential source for Manchu history before the conquest of China. The Yishiguan also contains the Manchu version of the Court Diaries in 6,479 volumes. The remainder of the Manchu documents (some of which are in both Manchu and Chinese) date mainly from the earlier part of the dynasty and deal with military matters or with Mongolia, Tibet, or Xinjiang. Some have been translated into Chinese. Manchu materials in the archives are listed below in alphabetical order. Evaluations of the importance of Manchu documents as historical sources and references to other Manchu sources are given at the end of this subsection.

Hanyi Manwen jiudang 漢譯滿文舊檔 (Chinese translation of the old Manchu archives), Liaoning daxue lishixi, 3 vols., 1979. Translation in progress.

Manwen laodang 滿文老檔 (The old Manchu archives), 2 vols., Yishiguan and Shekeyuan, trs. and eds., Zhonghua, 1990. There are name- and place-indexes. This is a later version of the *Jiu Manzhou dang*. See Kanda Nobuo, "From *Man Wen Lao Tang* to *Chiu Man-chou Tang*," *MTB* 38 (1980).

Jiu Manzhou dang 舊滿洲檔 (The old Manchu archives), Gugong bowuyuan, 10 vols., Taibei, 1969. Photo-offset of the oldest version of this Manchu archive. Considerable portions have been translated into Chinese and published.

Manwen laodang 滿文老檔 (The old Manchu archives), see 50.2.1 (Microfilm, no. 16).

Manwen Nei guoshiyuan dang 滿文內國史院檔 (National History Office Manchu archives), see 50.2.1 (Microfilm, no. 15).

Box 10: The Origins of "Manchu" and "Qing"

As a means of consolidating his power on the eve of the conquest of China and in order to avoid any unfortunate associations with the past, the Jurchen ruler Hong Taiji 洪太極 (also referred to as Abahai 阿巴海 or Huang Taiji 皇臺吉, 1592–1643), promulgated in 1632 a revision of the new script (of 1599) and in 1636 adopted a new title; changed the name of the dynasty and started a new era (*gaiyuan* 改元). The alien name of his people was clearly no longer suitable for what was a fast-growing confederation including not only Jurchen, but also Mongols and Han, so the new name *Manju* (Manzhou 滿洲; Manchu in English) had been chosen the previous year. There are many theories as to the origin of this name (41.2.2). The characters represented the sounds of the original non-Han word (possibly the Manchu for "brave") with the added twist that both characters had the water signific.

There is no surviving evidence to explain why Qing 清 (also with the water signific) was chosen to replace the previous dynastic name (*guohao* 國號) of Jin 金 (Hou-Jin 後金). The similarity in pronunciation of the two probably influenced the choice. Qing in Manchu (Csing) is almost the same as Jin (Cin) or *xin* (*sin*) as in *Aixin* (*jueluo*) 愛新覺羅 (*Aisin gioro*), the name adopted by Nurhaci. The meaning of Cin is gold. But even if this is correct, it still does not explain the choice of the character Qing 清. It is tempting to speculate that Five-Phases theory (*wuxing* 五行, Box 7, 22.3.3) played a decisive role. It had last been much used in the debate over the legitimacy of the Jin dynasty. By the Ming, *wuxing* had lost its saliency as a political symbol, but it was still much used in society, for example, to rank siblings (3.2). According to the ancient "mutually overcoming cycle," fire overcomes metal, so Ming 明 (an era of fire as suggested by the sun signific) was set to prevail over Jin 金 (the metal signific). On the other hand, water overcomes fire, so Qing 清 (with the water signific) would have been a preferable choice for the Manchu to attract followers to their banner in the overthrow of the Ming rather than sticking with Jin. Also Qing 清 (clean or purify) may have seemed a good name for the new dynasty in contrast to the corrupt government which had characterized the last decades of the Ming.

We may never know for sure the reason for choosing Qing 清 because of the court's order to destroy the evidence in the sources, but the episode underlines the importance attached to choosing the right name and suggests some of the considerations that may have influenced the choice.

Qing Taizuchao lao Manwen yuandang 清太祖朝老滿文原檔 (Original Manchu documents from the archives of the reign of Qing Taizu), Guang Lu 廣祿 et al., eds., Shiyusuo, 2 vols., 1970–72.

Qingchu Nei guoshiyuan Manwen dang'an yibian 清初內國史院滿文檔案譯編 (Translated excerpts from the Manchu archives of the early Qing History Bureau), Yishiguan, ed., 3 vols., Guangming ribao, 1989.

Kangxichao Manwen zhupi zouzhe quanyi 康熙朝滿文硃批奏摺全譯 (Complete translation of Manchu Kangxi imperially rescripted palace memorials), Yishiguan, ed., Shehui kexue, 1996. Includes more than 5,000 memorials, including those held in Taibei.

Zheng Chenggong Manwen dang'an shiliao xuanji 鄭成功滿文檔案史料選輯 (Selected translations from the archives on Zheng Chenggong in Manchu), Yishiguan, ed., Fujian renmin, 1987.

Yongzhengchao Manwen zhupi zouzhe quanyi 雍正朝滿文硃批奏摺全譯 (Complete translation of Manchu Yongzheng imperially rescripted palace memorials), Yishiguan, eds., 2 vols., Huangshan, 1999. Includes more than 5,400 memorials, including those held in Taibei.

Shengjing Manwen dang'an zhong de lüling ji shaoshu minzu falü 盛京滿文檔案中的律令及少數民族法律 (Codes and statutes and laws relating to the national minorities from the Manchu-language archives at Shengjing [Shenyang]), Zhang Ruizhi 張銳智 and Xu Lizhi 徐立志, eds. in chief, 3rd series, vol. 2 of *ZZFDJ*. The Shengjing archive volume contains *Shengjing dang'an zhong de lüling* 盛京檔案中的律令 (Selections from laws in the Shenyang archives); *Menggu lüli* 蒙古律例 (Mongol laws and precedents); *Xining Qinghai fanyi chengli* 西寧青海藩夷成例 (Regulations for the commander of native affairs of Xining and Qinghai); *Qinding Hui-Jiang zeli* 欽定回疆則例 (Imperially approved regulations for the Moslems of Xinjiang).

Qingdai Xibozu Manwen dang'an shiliao 清代錫伯族滿文檔案史料 (Historical materials from the archives in Manchu on the Xibo people), Yishiguan, ed., 2 vols., Minzu, 1987.

The best general introduction to the Manchus is Pamela Kyle Crossley, *The Manchus*, Blackwell, 1997. Manchu documents and books can be used to check and supplement Chinese sources. On their importance for the historian of the Qing, see:

Pamela K. Crossley and Evelyn S. Rawski, "A Profile of the Manchu Language in Ch'ing History," *HJAS* 53.1: 63–102 (1993).

Joseph Fletcher, "Manchu Sources," in Leslie, Mackerras, and Wang (1973), 141–46.

Giovanni Stary, *Manchu Studies: An International Bibliography*, 3 vols., Harrassowitz, 1990 (vol. 3 is an author/subject index).

Hartmut Walravens, *Bibliographie der Bibliographien der mandjurischen Literatur*, Harrassowitz, 1996.

Beatrice Bartlett, "Books of Revelations: The Importance of the Manchu Language Archival Books for Research on Ch'ing History," *LIC*, 6.2: 25–36 (1985).

Quanguo Manwen tushu ziliao lianhe mulu 全國滿文圖書資料聯合目錄 (Union catalog of Manchu books and other materials), Huang Run-hua 黃潤華 and Qu Wensheng 屈文生, general eds., Shumu wenxian, 1991. Lists holdings in 49 collections in China of 1,015 Manchu books and 693 rubbings of Manchu inscriptions on stone.

50.2.7   Documents on Foreign Relations and Foreigners

Many of the important documents from the archives on late Qing external relations have been published. A small selection is listed below. After some general collections and reference tools, titles are arranged alphabetically under countries or regions. For a fuller listing covering the years 1840 to 1919, see *Zhongguo jindaishi wenxian bibei shumu* 中國近代史文獻必備書目 (50.10.1), 22–31. The selection begins with the *Chouban yiwu shimo* 籌辦夷務始末 collections, which were compiled during the dynasty. For Western and Japanese diplomatic archives and documentary collections on relations with the Qing, see 51.13.1. For other foreign sources, see 42.2 and 42.5. The extensive bibliographic essays on the border regions and external relations covering both primary and secondary sources in the *CHC* volumes on the Qing are listed at the end of 41.4.

Chouban yiwu shimo 籌辦夷務始末 (The management of barbarian affairs from A to Z), Gugong bowuyuan, eds., 260 *juan*, 1929–30. Facsimile of the three collections of foreign affairs documents compiled during the late Qing and covering the years 1836–74. A punctuated edition of two of them was put out by Zhonghua in 1964 (*Daoguangchao* 道光朝 *Chouban yiwu shimo*) and 1979 (*Xianfengchao* 咸豐朝 *Chouban yiwu shimo*); Beijing daxue, rpnt., 9 vols., 1981. Vol. 1 is an index. See also David Nelson Rowe, *Index to Ch'ing Tai Ch'ou Pan I Wu Shih Mo*, Shoestring Press, 1960.

Daoguang Xianfeng liangchao chouban yiwu shimo buyi 道光咸豐兩朝籌辦夷務始末補遺 (Supplement to the *Chouban yiwu shimo* of the Daoguang and Xianfeng reigns), 6 vols., Jinshisuo, ed., 1966. In the series *Zhongguo jindaishi ziliao huibian* 中國近代史資料匯編.

Qingji waijiao shiliao 清季外交史料 (Foreign affairs documents of the late Qing), 5 vols., Wang Yanwei 王彥威 (1843-1904) and Wang Liang 王亮, comps., 1932-35; Wenhai, 1963. Covers 1875-1911, thus carrying on from where the *Chouban yiwu shimo* left off. See *An Index to Diplomatic Documents of the Late Ch'ing Dynasty*, Robert L. Irick, Chinese Materials and Research Aids Center, Taibei, 1971.

Qingdai waijiao shiliao Jiaqing Daoguangchao 清代外交史料嘉慶道光朝 (Historical materials on Qing diplomacy: The reigns of Jiaqing and Daoguang), Beiping: Gugong bowuyuan, ed., 10 vols., 1933. In the series *Waijiao dang'an mulu huibian* 外交檔案目錄彙編 (Collection of catalogs of the diplomatic archives).

Waijiao dang'an hanmu huibian 外交檔案函目匯編 (Collection of the catalogues for documents on external relations), Jinshisuo, vol. 1, *1861-1901, 1901-11,* 1991 (for vol. 2, which covers 1912-26, see 51.1.3).

Zhongguo jindai duiwai guanxishi ziliao xuanji 中國近代對外關系史料選輯 (Selection of historical materials on China's modern external relations), Fudan daxue Lishixi, ed., 4 vols., Shanghai renmin, 1977.

Qingji geguo zhaohui mulu 清季各國照會目錄 (Catalog of the diplomatic notes of foreign states during the late Qing period), 4 vols., Gugong wenxianguan 故宮文獻館, ed., Gugong yinshuasuo, 1935-36. Contains 3,800 diplomatic notes.

Zhongguo duiwai tiaoyue cidian 中國對外條約辭典 (Dictionary of the foreign treaties of China), Zhu 朱寰 and Wang Hengwei 王恒偉, comps., Jilin jiaoyu, 1994. Includes brief notes on all of China's main treaties (and their negotiators) between 1689 and 1949. 3,571 entries.

Qingji Zhongwai shiling nianbiao 清季中外使領年表 (Tables of Chinese and foreign diplomats in the late Qing), Qin Guojing 秦國經 et al., eds., Zhonghua, 1986, 1997. Lists foreign consuls (from 1843) and Ministers (from 1860) as well as Chinese diplomats going abroad (ambassadors from 1875) and consuls (from 1877). There are personal-name indexes, including names in foreign languages.

The West

Siguo xindang 四國新檔 (New archives on the four [Great] Powers [1850–63]), Jinshisuo, ed., 11 vols., 1962. In the series *Zhongguo jindaishi ziliao huibian* 中國近代史資料匯編.

Jindai Zhongguo dui Xifang ji lieqiang renshi ziliao huibian 近代中國對西方及列強認識資料彙編 (Collection of materials on Chinese understanding of the West and the great powers in the modern period [1821–1911]), Jinshisuo, ed., 20 vols., 1972, 1984–90. In the series *Zhongguo jindaishi ziliao huibian* 中國近代史資料匯編.

Kangxi yu Luoma shijie guanxi wenshu 康熙與羅馬使節關係文書 (Documents on the relations of Kangxi and the ambassadors of Rome), Gugong bowuyuan, ed., 1932.

Siguo xindang [E Ying Fa Mei] 四國新檔[俄英法美] (New archival materials on four countries [Russia, England, France, America]), 4 vols., Jinshisuo, ed., 1966; 2 vols., 1992.

Britain

See 28.2 for a sampling of published historical and archival material on the Opium War.

Yingshi Mage'erni fang Hua dang'an shiliao xuanbian 英使馬戈爾尼訪華檔案史料選編 (Selected historical materials from the archives on the English Ambassador Macartney's visit to China), Yishiguan, ed., Guoji wenhua, 1996.

France

Qing Guangxuchao Zhong-Fa jiaoshe shiliao 清光緒朝中法交涉史料 (Historical materials on Sino-French relations during the Guangxu period), 11 vols., Gugong wenxianguan 故宮文獻館, ed., Gugong yinshuasuo, 1933.

Zhong Fa Yuenan jiaoshe dang 中法越南交涉檔 (Archive of Sino-French negotiations on Vietnam), 7 vols., Jinshisuo, ed., 1962. In the series *Zhongguo jindaishi ziliao huibian* 中國近代史資料匯編.

Zhong Fa zhanzheng 中法戰爭 (The Sino-French war [1883–85]), Gugong dang'anguan 故宮檔案館, ed., 7 vols., Xin zhishi, 1957. In the series *Zhongguo jindaishi ziliao congkan* 中國近代史資料叢刊. See Lloyd E. Eastman, *Throne and Mandarins: China's Search for a Policy During the Sino-French Controversy, 1880–1885*, HUP, 1967.

Zhong Fa zhanzheng 中法戰爭 (The Sino-French war), 2 vols., Zhonghua, 1995–96. In addition to Chinese, also French archival materials.

Germany

Deguo qinzhan Jiaozhouwan shiliao xuanbian 德國侵占胶州灣史料選編 (Selected historical materials on the German forced occupation of Jiaozhou Bay), Yishiguan, ed., Shandong renmin, 1987.

Jiao'Ao zhuandang 胶澳專檔 (Special archives on Jiaozhou Bay [1897–1912]), Jinshisuo, ed., 1991.

United States

Beatrice S. Bartlett, "Archive Materials in China on United States History," in *Guide to the Study of United States History Outside the U.S. 1945–80*, Lewis H. Hanke, ed., White Plains, New York: Kraus International, 1985, vol. 1, 504–66. Despite the title, this chapter provides a good general survey of the Qing and Republic up to 1937.

Zhong Mei guanxi shiliao 中美關係史料 (Historical materials on Sino-American relations), Jinshisuo, ed., 8 vols., 1968, 1988–90. In the series *Zhongguo jindaishi ziliao huibian* 中國近代史資料匯編.

Russia

On Sino-Russian relations, see Mark Mancall, *Russia and China: Their Diplmatic Relations to 1728*, HUP, 1971, and S. C. M. Paine, *Imperial Rivals: China, Russia, and Their Disputed Frontier*, Sharpe, 1996.

Gugong Ewen shiliao 故宮俄文史料 (Russian-language historical materials in the Palace Museum), Gugong wenxianguan, ed., Gugong yinshuasuo, 1936. Consists of 23 documents in Russian dating from the early seventeenth and eighteenth centuries.

Gugong Ewen shiliao 故宮俄文史料 (Russian-language historical materials in the Palace Museum), *Lishi yanjiu* editorial dept., *Lishi yanjiu*, 1964. Of the 202 documents dating from 1670 to 1849 here translated into Chinese, only the 23 Kangxi period documents had already been printed in the previous item.

Qingdai Zhong-E guanxi dang'an shiliao xuanbian 清代中俄關係檔案史料選編 (Selection of historical materials from the archives on Sino-Russian relations during the Qing period), 1st and 3rd collections, Yishiguan, ed., 5 vols., Zhonghua, 1979–81.

Deguo qinzhan Jiaozhouwan shiliao bianjie tiaoyue ji 中俄邊界條約集 (Collection of Sino-Russian border treaties), Shangwu, ed., Shangwu, 1973.

Zhong-E guanxi shiliao 中俄關係史料 (Historical materials on Sino-Russian relations [1917–21]), Jinshisuo, ed., 24 vols., 1959–75. In the series *Zhongguo jindaishi ziliao huibian* 中國近代史資料匯編.

Zhongyijun kang-E douzheng dang'an shiliao 忠義軍抗俄斗爭檔案史料 (Archival materials on the righteous army's struggle against the Russians), Liaoningsheng dang'anguan et al., ed., Liao-Shen, 1984.

Japan

There is a good guide to modern Sino-Japanese relations, which has very full citations for primary sources (both Chinese and Japanese): *Kindai Nit-Chû kankeishi kenkyû nyûmon* 近代日中關係史研究入門, Yamane Yukio 山根幸夫 et al., eds., Kenbun shuppan, 1992; enlarged edition, 1996. The first two chapters cover 1868–1911.

Jiawu Zhong-Ri zhanzheng 甲午中日戰爭 (The Sino-Japanese war of 1894–95), 2 vols., Shanghai renmin, 1982. From the papers of Sheng Xuanhuai 盛宣懷.

Qing Guangxuchao Zhong-Ri jiaoshe shiliao 清光緒朝中日交涉史料 (Materials on Sino-Japanese negotiations during the Guangxu reign), 44 vols., Gugong bowuyuan, ed., 1932.

Qingji Zhong Ri Han guanxi shiliao 清季中日韓關係史料 (Sino-Japanese-Korean relations during the late Qing period [1914–20]), Jinshisuo, ed., 11 vols., 1972. In the series *Zhongguo jindaishi ziliao huibian* 中國近代史資料匯編.

Zhong-Ri guanxi shiliao 中日關係史料 (Historical materials on Sino-Japanese relations), Jinshisuo, ed., multi-volume subseries arranged by subject and by period, 1972–97. In the series *Zhongguo jindaishi ziliao huibian* 中國近代史資料匯編.

Zhong-Ri zhanzheng 中日戰爭 (The Sino-Japanese war), Shixuehui, 7 vols., Xinzhishi, 1956. In the series *Zhongguo jindaishi ziliao congkan* 中國近代史資料叢刊.

Zhong-Ri zhanzheng 中日戰爭 (The Sino-Japanese war), Qi Qizhang 戚其章, ed. in chief, Zhonghua, 1989– . Continuation of the previous item. Collection of documents held in the Yishiguan. There are 11 vols. planned.

Korea

Qingdai Zhong-Chao guanxi dang'an 清代中朝關系檔案 (Archives on Sino-Korean relations in the Qing period), Yishiguan, ed., Guoji wenhua, 1996.

Ryûkyû (Liuqiu) 琉球

On Ryûkyû sources in general, see 42.5, and note:

Qingdai Zhong-Liu guanxi dang'an xuanbian 清代中琉關係檔案選編 (Selected historical materials from the archives on Sino-Ryûkyû relations during the Qing dynasty), Yishiguan, ed., Zhonghua, 1993; *xubian* 續編, 1994; *sanbian* 三編, 1996.

Qingdai Liuqiu guowang biaozou wenshu xuanlu 清代琉球國王表奏文書選錄 (Selected documents submitted by the Ryûkyû kings during the Qing dynasty), Yishiguan, ed., Huangshan, 1997.

Macao (Aomen 澳門*)*

The Yishiguan edited four collections of documents and one of maps to mark the return of Macao to China at the end of 1999. The most comprehensive was the six volume:

Ming Qing shiqi Aomen wenti dang'an wenxian huibian 明清時期澳門問題檔案文獻匯編 (Collection of archive documents on the Macao question during the Ming-Qing period).

Missionary Cases

Jiao'an shiliao bianmu 教案史料編目 (Bibliography of Chinese source materials dealing with local or international cases involving Christian missions), Wu Shengde 吳盛德 and Chen Zenghui 陳增輝, eds., Yanjing daxue, 1941.

Qingji jiaowu jiao'an dang 清季教務教案檔 (Archives on church affairs and disputes involving missionaries and converts), 21 vols., Jinshisuo, ed., 1974–81. Contains 10,090 documents dating from the years 1855–99.

Qingji jiao'an shiliao 清季教案史料 (Historical materials on missionary cases during the late Qing), Gugong wenxianguan et al., eds., part 1, 1937; part 2, 1948.

Qingmo jiao'an 清末教案 (Historical materials on missionary cases from the late Qing), Yishiguan and Fujian shifan daxue, Lishixi, eds., 3 vols., Zhonghua, 1998.

See 29.7.3 on the Protestants in China for further references.

Others

Huagong chuguo shiliao huibian 華工出國史料匯編 (Collection of historical materials on Chinese workers going abroad), Chen Hansheng 陳翰笙, ed. in chief, 10 collections in 11 vols., Zhonghua, 1980–85.

50.3   *Provincial and County Archives*

All provincial and county yamen kept extensive archives containing records of all aspects of official business and copies of official documents. Some idea of their extent can be gathered from the fragments of Qin and Han local archives that have survived (44.4). They show that extremely detailed records were kept even in small border outposts.[21] In the Qing there were about 2,000 local yamen whose officials were responsible for a huge range of routine reporting. The filing itself was done by the yamen clerks, each of whom kept the records of his own specialty along the lines of the sixfold division of the Boards (*Li* 吏, *Hu* 戶, *Li* 禮, *Bing* 兵, *Xing* 刑, *Gong* 工). In addition, various works of administrative law and regulations were also kept in the yamen.[22] Despite all this documentation, which is known to have been kept in original or in duplicate, no single county or provincial archive is known to have survived intact.[23] The volume of documents and the cost of constructing fire-, damp-, and insect-proof buildings were so great that local archives even at the best of times cannot have long survived, and in the twentieth century the collection and preservation of local archives never got under way because of the disturbed conditions. Indeed, many must have been destroyed in the upheavals of the last 100 years.

[21] Almost no trace of a local archive survives from the end of the Tang to the Qing. One exception is the letters and correspondence and office regulations from the Suzhou prefectural archive for the years 1162–64, which were found on the reverse side of the pages of one edition of Wang Anshi's papers, but this was a rare find: *Songren yijian* 宋人佚簡 (Lost records of a Song writer), Shanghai guji, 1994. Understandably, modern librarians are unwilling to unstitch valuable, old editions in order to retrieve what, if anything, may have been printed on the inside of the pages.

[22] T'ung-tsu Ch'ü, *Local Government in China Under the Ch'ing*, HUP, 1962.

[23] In 1729, as a security measure against fire losses, all yamen were ordered to make copies (*fuben* 副本) of all memorials, which were to be stored separately.

Furthermore, there was hardly a single historian at the end of the Qing or in the first half of the twentieth century who used local archives or who saw their value, unless the archive was an ancient one dating back to the Han or Tang. Small wonder that relatively few local documents from the Qing have survived.[24]

The paucity of surviving documents from provincial or local archives is somewhat mitigated by the fact that centuries before historians in the West emphasized the importance of archival as opposed to literary sources, Chinese historians were still drawing upon a long tradition of handling and quoting from original documents; thus not a few local documents were preserved in compilations higher up the administrative and historiographical hierarchy (Chapter 20, boxes 6 and 7). The same is also true of the local gazetteers (to a limited extent based on the local archives, although they were never intended to be a summary of them). They were compiled only on average two or three times a century and their primary purpose was to enshrine the people, places, and literary output of a locality (4.5).

As of the late 1990s, an estimated 4 million Qing documents were known to be held in provincial or regional archives, libraries and museums. By far the largest number, 2.4 million, are preserved in Lhasa at the Archives of the Tibet Autonomous Region, where the cold and possibly also the relative security of Tibet helped preserve them. The earliest documents date from the Yuan. Most are from the Qing and over 90 percent are in Tibetan. The remainder are in Chinese, Manchu, English, Russian, and Japanese. Over half a million documents have been sorted; it is reckoned that it will take 150 years to complete the sorting. Seventy percent of the holdings are available to researchers, but about 30 percent are in a serious state of deterioration. A selection of over 100 documents are reproduced in color and translated into English and Chinese in *A Collection of the Historical Archives of Tibet*, Wenwu, 1995 (see also 29.5.1 for Tibetan religious archives).

Other major local archives include:

---

[24] One exception is Sidney D. Gamble, who uses a series of exchange rates (cash/silver) extracted from yamen documents in Ding county 丁縣; see his *Ting Hsien: A North China Rural Community*, SUP, 1954, 1968.

Ba county archive (Baxian dang'an 巴縣檔案), Sichuan: 113,000 *juan* of documents. Their survival was by accident. During World War II they had been placed in a temple and were found again only in 1953. *Qingdai Qian dao Jia Baxian dang'an xuanbian* 清代乾到嘉巴縣檔案選編 (Selections from the Ba county archive, 1736–1850), 2 vols., Sichuan daxue, 1989 and 1996. They are now held in the Sichuan Provincial Archive at Chengdu. Other documents from the Ba county archives have also been published. See, for example,

> *Qingdai Baxian dang'an huibian* 清代巴縣檔案匯編乾隆卷 (Collection from the Ba county archive, Qianlong *juan*), Sichuansheng dang'anguan, 1991.

> Note Madeline Zelin, "The Rights of Tenants in Mid-Qing Sichuan: A Study of Land-Related Lawsuits in the Baxian Archives," *JAS* 45.3: 499–526 (1986). On other Sichuan archives, see *Lishi dang'an* (1983.2 and 1990.3).

Baodi county archive (Baodi xian dang'an 寶坻縣檔案), Shuntian 順天府 (capital) prefecture: kept at Yishiguan. Tax and case records cover nineteenth and early twentieth centuries; see

> Philip C. C. Huang, "County Archives and the Study of Local Social History: Report on a Year's Research in China," *Modern China* 8.1: 133–43 (1982).

> Philip C. C. Huang, *The Peasant Family and Social Change in North China*, SUP, 1985.

> Philip C. C. Huang, "Codified Law and Magisterial Adjudication in the Qing," in *Civil Law in Qing and Republican China*, Kathryn Bernhardt and Philip C. C. Huang, eds., SUP, 1994; SMC, 1997, 142–86.

Various Hebei counties, mainly Huolu 獲鹿 (pronounced Huailu). Landholding and tax assessment records *bianshence* 編審冊 (1,608 *juan* covering the years 1706–1911); see *Lishi dang'an* (1988.1); Wa and Esherick (1996), 120.

Guangdong provincial archives captured by British forces in 1858 (2,000 documents). They are cataloged in David Pong, *A Critical Guide to the Kwangtung Provincial Archives Deposited at the Public Record Office of London*, HUP, East Asia Research Center, 1975. See also *Lishi dang'an* (1983.1).

Shuangcheng 雙城縣, Heilongjiang, nearly 50,000 juan of nineteenth century local archives; Wa and Esherick (1996), 136.

Archives of Tamsui (Danshui) 淡水 subprefecture (northwest Taiwan) and Xinzhu 新竹 county (northwest Taiwan) containing 19,281 documents relating to 1,143 legal cases dating from 1789 to 1895 (Danshui subprefecture was divided in 1875 into Danshui and Xinzhu counties). Under the Japanese administration the archives were transferred to the central court and then to Taihoku Teikoku Daigaku 臺北帝國大學. In 1986, they were entrusted to the library of Taiwan University. Most of the cases were heard in the Tongzhi and Guangxu reigns. See *Dan-Xin dang'an* 淡新檔案, Zhang Xiurong 張秀榮, ed. in chief, 1st series, 4 vols., Taiwan daxue, 1995. The first series covers administrative cases; the second is planned to cover civil cases (4 vols.), and the third set, criminal cases (4 vols). Notes and indexes are planned for vols. 13 and 14. Note Mark A. Allee, "The Dan-Xin Archives," in his (ed.) *Law and Local Society in Late Imperial China*, SUP, 1994, 5–14, and the earlier David C. Buxbaum, "Some Aspects of Civil Procedure and Practice at the Trial Level in Tanshui and Hsinchu from 1789 to 1896," *JAS* 30.2: 255–79 (1971).

There are also more or less substantial holdings of Qing official documents, mainly from the end of the dynasty, in Henan (*Lishi dang'an* 1984.2), Yunnan, Gansu, Anhui (*Lishi dang'an*, 1984.3), Jilin, Shandong (*Lishi dang'an*, 1984.2) and Guizhou provincial archives. Some of these are available on microfilm or have been published (50.2.2). Parts of various provincial archives from Heilongjiang and Shandong are held at the Yishiguan (50.1.1, item IV.B).

The public papers of individuals were often published in their lifetimes, or posthumously. The Yishiguan holds extensive collections of the personal archives related to four individuals prominent at the end of the Qing. The documents consist mainly of memorials and official documents from 1875 to 1926 (50.1.1, item D.II).

50.4   Official Historical Works

Manwen laodang 滿文老檔 (The old Manchu archives), cover the years 1607–36; see 50.2.6 for further details of these and other Manchu-language sources.

Qijuzhu 起居注. Starting from 1629, various Court Diaries were kept. These contained a daily account of the emperor's activities and utterances. The record keeping was regularized early in the reign of Kangxi (1670) and continued both in Manchu and in Chinese until the end of the dynasty, one volume per month in the Kangxi period, rising to two per month from Yongzheng onward. Altogether, more than 12,000 *ce* of the Court Diaries are extant, some held in Taibei, some in Beijing. They form one of the most important basic sources for the history of the Qing dynasty. The diaries were secret documents, in theory not open even to the emperor. They were held in the archives of the Inner Court. Written at the most one year after the events they record, they contain reliable details not found in more public documents, including the Veritable Records, which were to a large extent based on them. Some are available in draft form; the Chinese versions of the following reigns have been printed (the Manchu versions are available on microfilm; see 50.2.1).

Kangxichao qijuzhuce 康熙朝起居注册 (Court Diaries of the Kangxi reign), typeset, punctuated edition, 3 folio vols., Zhonghua, 1983.

Yongzhengchao qijuzhuce 雍正朝起居注册 (Court Diaries of the Yongzheng reign), photolithographic edition, Yishiguan, 5 vols., Zhonghua, 1993.

Daoguangchao qijuzhuce 道光朝起居注册 (Court Diaries of the Daoguang reign), photolithographic edition, 100 vols., Lianhebao wenhua jijinhui Guoxue wenxianguan, Taibei: Lianjing chubanshiye gongsi, 1983.

Xianfengchao qijuzhuce 咸豐朝起居注册 (Court Diaries of the Xianfeng reign), photolithographic edition, 57 vols., Lianhebao wenhua jijinhui Guoxue wenxianguan, Taibei: Lianjing chubanshiye gongsi, 1983.

Tongzhichao qijuzhuce 同治朝起居注册 (Court Diaries of the Tongzhi reign), photolithographic edition, 43 vols., Lianhebao wenhua jijinhui Guoxue wenxianguan, Taibei: Lianjing chubanshiye gongsi, 1983.

Guangxuchao qijuzhuce 光緒朝起居注册 (Court Diaries of the Guangxu reign), photolithographic edition, 80 vols., Lianhebao wenhua jijinhui Guoxue wenxianguan, Taibei: Lianjing chubanshiye gongsi, 1987.

Qing shilu 清實錄 (Veritable Records of the Qing; the full title: *Da Qing lichao shilu* 大清歷朝實錄). Another very important basic historical source for the Qing. They are 30 percent longer than the *Ming shilu*, totaling altogether 60 million characters. Veritable Records were compiled for all 12 Qing emperors, with the exception of Puyi's reign (1909–11), for which the similar work is called *Xuantong zhengji* 宣統政紀 (Political records of the Xuantong reign). Each *shilu* was compiled under the instructions of the new emperor for the reign of his predecessor. There are two printed editions of the *shilu*:

Qing shilu 清實錄, 60 folio vols., Zhonghua, 1986–87. Based on the original copy preserved in the Huangshicheng 皇史宬, Beijing (now in the Yishiguan), collated with various parts and drafts of the *Qing shilu* held at Peking University, the Palace Museum, and the Liaoning (Shenyang) archives.

Tai Shin rekichô jitsuroku 大清歷朝實錄, 4,485 *juan* in 120 *han*, 1,220 *ce*. 300 copies printed and published for the Manchuria-Japan Cultural Association, Ministry of Finance, Tokyo, 1934–36. Photographic reproduction of the copy of the Veritable Records kept at the Shengjing 盛京 (Shenyang) palace. A complete facsimile reprint was made of all the *Shilu* with the exception of the *Xuantong zhengji* by Huawen, Taibei, 93 vols., 1963–64; Liaoning shekeyuan, 1980.

Other editions of the *shilu* were edited, including trilingual Manchu, Chinese, and Mongolian editions. Various portions were published separately, or especially for the government of Manchukuo (details may be found in the Introduction to the Zhonghua edition, which also discusses the process of drafting and publication of the *Qing shilu*). Some have been reprinted.[25]

There are a considerable number of published excerpts from the *Qing shilu*, which are potential time-savers—for example, *Qing shilu jingjishi ziliao* 清實錄經濟史資料.[26] The first three volumes contain excerpts on agriculture for the period 1644–1820 (vol. 1, population and land; vol. 2, agricultural production; vol. 3, part 1, agricultural taxes, and vol. 3, part 2 [in fact a fourth volume], living conditions and uprisings). Other selec-

---

[25] *Qing Taizu chao huangdi shilu gaoben sanzhong* 清太祖朝皇帝實錄稿本三種, Beijing, 1933–34.

[26] *Qing shilu jingjishi ziliao* (Historical materials on the economy from the Veritable Records of the Qing), Chen Zhenhan 陳振漢 et al., comps., 3 vols., Beijing daxue, 1989–93. Another selection of economic source materials is *Qing shilu jingji ziliao jiyao* 清實錄經濟資料輯要 (Excerpts from economic source materials from the *Qing shilu*), Nankai daxue Lishixi 南開大學歷史系, ed., Zhonghua, 1959. It is arranged under 75 topics.

tions of excerpts concentrate on individual provinces or regions—for example:

Da Qing lichao shilu Sichuan shiliao 大清歷朝實錄四川史料 (Historical materials on Sichuan from the *Qing shilu*), 2 vols., Dianzi keji daxue, 1988.

Qing shilu Dongbei shiliao quanji 清實錄東北史料全輯 (Collected
historical materials on the northeast from the *Qing shilu*), 10
vols., Jilin wenshi, 1988–90.

Qing shilu Ningxia ziliao jilu 清實錄寧夏資料輯錄 (Selected materials
on Ningxia from the *Qing shilu*), 3 vols., Ningxia renmin, 1986.

Qing shilu Xinjiang ziliao jilu 清實錄新疆資料輯錄 (Selected materials on Xinjiang from the *Qing shilu*), 12 vols., Xinjiang minzu
yanjiusuo, 1978.

Qing shilu Shaanxi ziliao huibian 清實錄陝西資料匯編 (Collection of
materials on Shaanxi from the *Qing shilu*), Shaanxi guji, 1996.

Qing shilu Jiang-Zhe-Hu dizhu ziliao xuan 清實錄江浙滬地主資料選
(Selection of materials from the *Qing shilu* on landlords of Jiangsu, Zhejiang, and Shanghai), Shanghai shekeyuan, 1989. Has an
index.

Qing shilu Shandongshi ziliao xuan 清實錄山東史資料選 (Selected
historical materials on Shandong from the *Qing shilu*), 3 vols.,
Qi-Lu, 1984.

Qing shilu Guangxi ziliao jilu 清實錄廣西資料輯錄 (Materials on
Guangxi collected from the *Qing shilu*), 5 vols., Guangxi renmin,
1988.

Qing shilu Yunnan shiliao jiyao 清實錄雲南史料輯要 (40.3.1).

For excerpts on non-Han peoples from the *Qing shilu*, see 40.3.1
and 41.4.1.

Donghualu 東華錄 (Records from within the Eastern Gate), Jiang
Liangqi 蔣良騏 (1723–89); punctuated edition, Zhonghua, 1980.
This important annalistic source (covering from 1644 to the
Yongzheng period) is so called from the fact that the first compiler, Jiang Liangqi, worked as an official in the Guoshi guan 國
史館 (Historiography Institute), which after 1765 was situated
inside the Donghua gate of the Forbidden City (the imperial archives, Huangshicheng [49.3 and 50.1], were just across the road
from it). The *Shiyichao Donghualu* 十一朝東華錄 covers the

years 1644–1874 and the much fuller *Guangxuchao Donghualu* 光緒朝東華錄, 5 vols., punctuated edition, Zhonghua, 1958, covers the years 1875–1908. Although less detailed than the Veritable Records (upon which they were mainly based), the various *Donghualu* are a quick way of finding sources in the Veritable Records; see Knight Biggerstaff, "A Note on the *Tunghua lu* and the *Shih-lu*," *HJAS* 4.2: 101–15 (1939).

Jingbao 京報 (Peking gazette). Nearly complete runs are extant for the second half of the nineteenth century (see 26.4). At least as important a source as the *Donghualu* of the same period.

Qingshigao 清史稿 (Draft Standard History of the Qing), Zhao Erxun 趙爾巽 (1844–1927) et al., comps., punctuated edition, 48 vols., Zhonghua, 1976–77; 5th prnt., 1996 (re-issued in reduced-size with biographical index, 4 vols., 1997). Covers the years 1644–1911. Work on the draft began at the instruction of Yuan Shikai 袁世凱 (1859–1916) in 1914.[27] The draft has never been fully accepted as one of the Standard Histories (it was proscribed by the Guomindang because it was compiled by Qing loyalists). The monograph on law has been published separately.[28] There is an annotated translation of part of the monograph on financial administration.[29] The Zhonghua edition of the *Qingshigao* is fully indexed in the Shiyusuo's *Nianwushi quanwen ziliaoku* 廿五史全文資料庫 (25 Histories full text database), 1988 (see 22.2). There is a name index to the basic annals, tables, and biographies sections: *Qingshigao ji biao zhuan renming suoyin* 清史稿紀表傳人名索引 (Personal-name index to the annals, tables, and biographies in the Draft History of the Qing), He Yingfang 何英芳, comp., 2 vols., Zhonghua, 1996.

---

[27] Thurston Griggs, "The Ch'ing Shih Kao: A Bibliographical Summary," *HJAS* 18: 105–23 (1955). Erich Haenisch, "*Das Ts'ing-shi-kao* und die sonstige chinesische Literatur zur Geschichte der letzten 300 Jahre," *AM* 6.4: 403–44 (1930). The biographies section was included among the materials indexed in *H-Y Index* 9.

[28] *Qingshigao xingfazhi zhujie* 清史稿刑法志註解 (Annotations to the *Qingshigao* monograph on law), Falü, 1957.

[29] Hoshi Ayao 星斌夫, *Shinshikô sôunshi yakuchû* 清史稿漕運志譯註 (Annotated translation of the section on tribute transportation of the monograph on financial administration in the *Qingshigao*), Kôbundô, 1962.

Qingshi 清史 (History of the Qing) was completed in 1962 by a committee in Taiwan.[30] It is largely based on the *Qingshigao*. It has a name index included in the last volume. Unfortunately, there are many errors. These were corrected in the *Renshou* edition of the Standard Histories.

Qing santong 清三通 (25.2):

> *Qingchao tongdian* 清朝通典; covers 1644–1785 (Table 33, 25.2).
>
> *Qingchao tongzhi* 清朝通志; covers 1644–1785 (Table 33, 25.2).
>
> *Qingchao wenxian tongkao* 清朝文獻通考; covers 1644–1785 (Table 33, 25.2).

Qingchao xu wenxian tongkao (1921), Liu Jinzao 劉錦藻. From 1786 to 1911. This is the best of the Qing continuations of the *Shitong* (Table 33, 25.2).

Fanglüe 方略 (28.2). Official publications of imperial campaigns against enemies at home and abroad. The titles of these works usually are in the form of *Pingding* 平定 ... *fanglüe* 方略 (Strategy for the pacification of ...), hence the generic title *fanglüe*. They were normally written immediately after a campaign and based on edicts, memorials, and battle reports. The form was *jishi benmo* (topically arranged).

50.5   Official Compendia

50.5.1   Geographical Works

Three *Da Qing yitongzhi* 大清一統志 (gazetteers of the unified Great Qing) were compiled. The proposal to begin the first was agreed by the Kangxi emperor in 1672, but it was completed only in 1743 because of the time taken to newly compile the provincial gazetteers upon which it was based:

Da Qing yitongzhi 大清一統志, Xu Qianxue 徐乾學 et al., comps., completed 1746.

Da Qing yitongzhi 大清一統志, Heshen 和珅 et al., comps., presented in 1784 and printed in 1790.

---

[30] *Qingshi*, 8 vols., Taibei: Guofang yanjiuyuan 國防研究院, 1961.

Da Qing yitongzhi 大清一統志, Muzhang'a 穆彰阿 et al., comps., completed in 1820 at the end of the Jiaqing period and thus referred to as the *Jiaqing chongxiu da Qing yitongzhi* 嘉慶重修大清一統志, printed in 1842; Shangwu reprint with this title with an index, Shanghai, 1934; Taibei, 1967; Shanghai shudian, 1981–84. The *Jiaqing yitongzhi* was the largest and most accurate of this type of Comprehensive Gazetteer. From it may be gained a detailed picture of the administrative geography of the entire empire at the beginning of the nineteenth century; more detailed information on individual places is of course available in the many thousands of extant Qing local gazetteers.[31]

In addition to the more than 5,600 local gazetteers that were compiled during the Qing (70 percent of all extant gazetteers, see 4.6), many guides and accounts of individual cities, especially the capital, have survived, for example the two works below (see *Biji* for other titles):

Rixia jiuwenkao 日下舊聞考 (Historical studies of Beijing), Yu Minzhong 于敏中 (1714–80), 1774; 4 vols., Beijing guji, 1985. Yu was the official in charge of the *Siku quanshu*. He expanded an earlier work, the *Rixia jiuwen* 日下舊聞 of Zhu Yizun 朱彝尊, 1629–1709, which quoted in 13 categories 1,449 sources on the history of Beijing from the earliest times to the end of the Ming.

Dumen zaji 都門雜記 (Miscellaneous notes on the capital), 1864. Issued under many different titles, it was intended as a guide to the capital for visiting scholars, officials, and merchants.

Works on Border Areas

Materials on the border regions have been excerpted from the *Qing shilu* (40.3.1 and 41.4.1). Many topographical or historical studies of border regions or border peoples were also compiled in the Qing—for example:

Songyun 松筠 (1752–1835) et al., *Xinjiang zhilüe* 新疆識略 (History of Xinjiang), 1821; Tongwenguan movable-type edition, 1882.

---

[31] G. M. H. Playfair, *The Cities and Towns of China: A Geographical Dictionary* (Hong Kong, 1879; 2nd ed., Kelly and Walsh, 1910; rpnt., Ch'eng-wen, 1965) is based on the *Jiaqing yitongzhi*; useful for locating better-known places, rivers, etc. (as of the late nineteenth century). It also gives coordinates.

Qi Yunshi 祁韻士 (1751–1815), *Huangchao fanbu yaolüe* 皇朝藩部要略 (Essentials on this august dynasty's barbarian territories [Mongolia, Xinjiang and Tibet]), 1846; Zhejiang shuju, 1884.

Menggu youmu ji 蒙古游牧記 (Record of nomad life in Mongolia), Zhang Mu 張穆 (1805–49); collated and added to by He Qiutao 何秋濤 (1824–62); completed, 1859; printed in 1867; included in *Guoxue jiben congshu* (9.6).

Shuofang beisheng 朔方備乘 (Historical sources on the northern Regions), He Qiutao 何秋濤, 1881. First major study of Sino-Russian relations.

Qingdai bianjiang shidi lunzhu suoyin 清代邊疆史地論著索引 (Index of books and articles on the historical geography of the border regions in the Qing dynasty), Zhongguo renmin daxue, Qingshi yanjiusuo, and Shekeyuan Zhongguo bianjiang shidi yanjiusuo, eds., Renmin daxue, 1988. Contains 8,000 articles and 1,200 books written 1900–1986, including those published in Taiwan and Hong Kong. Arrangement is by categories and by region.

50.5.2   Laws and Regulations

Huidian 會典 *and zeli* 則例. During the Qing, no commands (*ling* 令) were promulgated, but the Ming model for issuing very detailed *huidian* 會典 (collected statutes) was followed. There were five editions of such *huidian*, all of which were entitled *Da Qing huidian* 大清會典 (Collected statutes of the great Qing dynasty). Each carried the important administrative law put in force since the previous edition (in the form of *zeli* 則例 or *shili* 事例, precedents and regulations, substatutes) and each is referred to by the reign name in which it was compiled (in library catalogs they are entered under the actual title *Da Qing huidian* ... or *Qinding* 欽定 (Imperially authorized) *Da Qing huidian*.

Da Qing huidian 大清會典

Kangxi huidian 康熙會典, drafting began in 1684; completed in 1690, 162 *juan*, printed in 1696.

Yongzheng huidian 雍正會典, drafting began in 1624; completed in 1733, 250 *juan*, printed in 1734. Adds the institutions of 1687 to 1727 to the *Kangxi huidian*.

Qianlong huidian 乾隆會典, drafting began in 1747; completed in 1764; printed in 1768: *Qinding da Qing huidian* 欽定大清會典, 100 *juan* with *huidian zeli* 會典則例 (supplementary regulations and substatutes), 180 *juan*.

Jiaqing huidian 嘉慶會典, drafting began in 1801; completed in 1818; printed in 1822, 80 *juan*, plus *shili* 事例 (supplementary regulations and substatutes), 920 *juan*, plus *tu* 圖 (illustrations), 132 *juan*. Adds institutions since previous edition up to 1813.

Guangxu huidian 光緒會典, drafting began in 1886; completed in 1899, 100 *juan*; Shangwu, 1904, plus *shili*, 1,220 *juan*, plus *tu*, 270 *juan*; rpnt., Zhonghua, 14 vols., 1991, 1995. Adds institutions, supplementary regulations, and statutes between 1813 and 1896.

Zeli 則例

A very large number of works of early Qing administrative law as well as many editions of the regulations and substatutes of individual departments (*buli* 部例, *zeli* 則例) are extant. The titles of some of the most important (omitting the prefix *Qinding* 欽定 ... "Imperially authorized ...") are:

Baqi zeli 八旗則例 (Regulations and precedents for the Eight Banners), 1739; Xuesheng shuju, 1968; Dongbei shifan daxue punctuated edition, 1985.

Gongbu zeli 工部則例 (Regulations and precedents of the Board of Works), 1749, 1798; 2nd rev., 1891; Jiaqing edition (1798), 20 vols. photolithographic edition, Beijing tushuguan, 1997.

Guochao gongshi 國朝宮史 (History of the palace) completed in 1742; rewritten, 1769. One of the three MS copies was reprinted in a punctuated edition by Beijing guji in 1987. A continuation up to 1810 was published by the Palace Museum in 1932. Includes palace regulations, rituals, expenses, etc. See also the later *Gongzhong xianxing zeli* 宮中現行則例 (Presently applied regulations and precedents in the palace), 1856, 1888.

Hubu zeli 戶部則例 (Regulations and precedents of the Board of Revenue), 1776; thereafter 13 rev. eds. to 1851; 1864, Tongzhi rev. rpnt., Chengwen, 1966. More detailed regulations on different aspects of the work of the Board were also printed, for example, the *Hubu caoyun quanshu* 戶部漕運全書 (The Board of Revenue complete book of grain transport), 1735; 4th rev., 1876. Also the regulations for the separate provinces on customs, salt, famine relief, and canals.

Libu zeli 禮部則例 (Regulations and precedents of the Board of Rites), 1794; 2nd rev., 1841; rpnt., Chengwen, 1966.

Libu zeli 吏部則例 (Regulations and precedents of the Board of Civil Office), 1734; rev., 1742; rev., 1783; Daoguang, Tongzhi, and Guangxu revisions, Chengwen, 1966. More detailed regulations on different aspects of the work of the Board were also printed.

Lifanyuan zeli 理藩院則例 (Regulations and precedents of the Board of Colonial Affairs), 1789, 1817; 2nd rev., 1891, 1908.

Zongrenfu zeli 宗人府則例 (Regulations and precedents of the Office of the Imperial Lineage), 1739; 3rd rev., 1888.[32]

Shengli 省例

One of the unique features of Qing administrative law is that collections of provincial substatutes and cases (*shengli* 省例) relating to a single province were printed. In addition to the *shengli*, provincial yamen from the eighteenth century began printing the official regulations, which they received from the central government in works usually called *dingli* 定例 (established regulations) or *tiaoli* 條例 (itemized regulations or substatutes), some of which have survived.[33] The regulations for particular institutions at the provincial level, for example, the salt monopoly, have also survived, see under *Hubu zeli* above.

Fujian shengli 福建省例 (Substatutes of Fujian province), 1873; rpnt., Taiwan yinhang, 1964.

Hunan shengli cheng'an 湖南省例成案 (Substatutes and leading cases of Hunan province), Changsha, 1820. Largest and most interesting.

Jiangsu shengli 江蘇省例 (Substatutes of Jiangsu province), Nanjing, 1869; continuations published in 1875, 1883, and 1890.

Jinzheng jiyao 晋政輯要 (Extracts for governing Shanxi Province).

Xijiang zhengyao 西江政要 (Essentials of the governing Jiangxi province).

Yuedong shengli xinzuan 粵東省例新纂 (Newly edited substatutes of Guangdong province), Huang Enzheng 黃恩正, comp., 1846, 2 vols.,

---

[32] Most of these works went through many editions and many other regulations were also published. Ma Fengchen 馬奉琛 lists and briefly describes 500 such works in his *Qingdai xingzheng zhidu yanjiu cankao shumu* 清代行政制度研究參考書目 (Reference catalog for research on the Qing administrative system), Beijing daxue, 1935.

[33] See Fu-mei Chang Chen, "Provincial Documents of Laws and Regulations in the Ch'ing Period," *Ch'ing-shih wen-t'i* 3.6: 28–48 (1976).

Taibei, 1968. Not as interesting a work as the *Yuedong cheng'an chu-bian* 粵東成案初編 (First compilation of criminal and civil cases decided in Guangdong province), Guangzhou, 1832.

Zhi Zhe chenggui 治浙成規 (Regulations for governing Zhejiang province).[34]

See also:

Da Qing lüli 大清律例 (27.5)

Xing'an huilan 刑案匯覽 (27.5)

Fuhui quanshu 福惠全書 (27.6)

Qiangu beiyao 錢穀備要 (27.6)

50.5.3   Army and Uprisings

See Chapter 28 for Qing sources on the army, wars (28.2), and uprisings (28.3).

50.5.4   Edicts and Memorials

Da Qing shichao shengxun 大清十朝聖訓 (Sacred instructions and edicts of 10 Qing emperors, 1880). Most comprehensive collection for Qing; covers the years 1616 to 1874 in 922 *juan*. Arranged by topics.

(Yongzheng) zhupi yuzhi (雍正)硃批諭旨 (Vermilion-rescripted edicts of the Yongzheng period [1723–35], 1738, photolithographic rpnt., Beijing, 1930. Contains several thousand edicts directly dealt with by the emperor and carrying his personal comments and instructions in vermilion (hence the title).

Yongzheng shangyu neige 雍正上諭內閣 (Edicts of the Yongzheng reign issued through the Grand Secretariat), 1731 and 1741, Beijing. Arranged chronologically.

Shangyu baqi 上諭八旗 (Edicts of the Yongzheng reign to do with the Eight Banners, 1741). Arranged chronologically.

Many officials of the late Qing had their memorials printed. Many of these collections are listed in Ma Fengchen 馬奉琛, 1935 (50.5.2).

---

[34] Terada Hiroaki 寺田浩明, "Shindai no shôrei" 清代省例 (Provincial substatutes and cases in the Qing dynasty) in *CHKSK*, 657–714.

Huangchao jingshi wenbian 皇朝經世文編 (This august dynasty's documents on statecraft). Altogether 16 were published during the Qing. These collections contain the important memorials of well over 2,000 Qing officials and they have been conveniently indexed by the Kindai Chûgoku kenkyûkai iinkai (Seminar on Modern China at the Tôyô bunko), *Keisei bunpen sômokuroku sakuin* 經世文編總目錄索引, 3 vols., Tokyo, 1956. There is also an author index attached to volume three of the Zhonghua photolithographic edition: *Qing jingshi wenbian* 清經世文編, 3 vols., Zhonghua, 1992. The first volumes list the subject of each memorial (following the arrangement of the collections) while vol. 3 is an author index (with Wade-Giles finding list). Helen Dunstan, *Conflicting Counsels to Confuse the Age* (50.10.2) is an excellent introduction to these documents.

There is no list comparable to the *ISMH* for the Qing; but see Fairbank (1965), I: 39–105, for a list of some major collections of memorials and also the memorial collections published from the Qing archives in the 1930s and later (50.2.2). For a fuller listing of published collections and catalogs of memorials, reports, etc., from the Qing archives, see 50.2.

The following guides and indexes to the titles of the memorials of high late Qing officials are available:

Guide to the Memorials of Seven Leading Officials of Nineteenth-Century China, Chung-li Chang and Stanley Spector (1924–99), eds., UWP, 1955. Contains a useful subject index to the contents of the memorials of Zeng Guofan, Hu Linyi, Zuo Zongtang, Guo Songtao, Li Hongzhang, Zeng Guoquan, and Zhang Zhidong.

Sa Sôtô Chô Shidô Setsu Fusei Chô Ken sôgi mokuroku 左宗棠張之洞薛福成張謇奏議目錄 (Index of memorials by Zuo Zongtang, Zhang Zhidong, Xue Fucheng, and Zhang Qian), Seminar on Modern China, ed., Tôyô bunko, 1955.

Sei Senkai En Seigai sôgi mokuroku 盛宣懷袁世凱奏議目錄 (Index of memorials presented to the emperor by Sheng Xuanhuai and Yuan Shikai), Seminar on Modern China, ed., Tôyô bunko, 1955.

50.5.5 *Encyclopaedias and Collectanea*

Gujin tushu jicheng 古今圖書集成 (31.2)

Siku quanshu 四庫全書 (9.5)

50.6 Writings of Individuals

50.6.1 Agriculture

Bu Nongshu 補農書 (35.1)
Hengchan suoyan 恒產瑣言 (35.1)
Shoushi tongkao 授時通考 (35.1)
Gengzhi tu 耕織圖 (35.1)
Nongyan zhushi 農言著實 (35.1)

50.6.2 Bieji 別集

The final count of extant Qing collected works (including both collected works of individual authors, *bieji* 別集, and literary anthologies, *zongji* 總集) has not yet been made. The largest index (item 1 below) contains references to the works of 1,700 writers (it includes poetry collections as well as prose). The main indexes are:

Qingren shiwenji shulu 清人詩文集書錄 (Catalog of poetry and prose collections of Qing personalities), Ke Yuchun 柯愈春, comp., Zhonghua, 2000. Indexes 20,000–30,000 works of over 1,700 Qing writers. Includes collections in China, Taiwan, Japan, the USA, and Europe. The largest index to date.

Qingren wenji bielu 清人文集別錄 (Additional notes on the collected works of Qing authors), Zhang Shunhui 張舜徽, 2 vols., Zhonghua, 1963, 1980. The modest title suggests an annotated catalog, but it is more than that. Zhang has selected 599 of the cream of Qing *bieji* (perhaps between 5 and 10 percent of the total) and uses his notes to describe the life and works of each author. There is a personal-name index.

Qingdai wenji pianmu fenlei suoyin 清代文集篇目分類索引 (Subject index to tables of contents of Qing collected works), Wang Zhongmin 王重民 et al., comps., Guoli Beiping tushuguan 國立北平圖書館, 1935; Zhonghua, 1965; Guofeng, 1965. Indexes tables of contents in 428 collected works of individual Qing authors and 12 general collections; particularly useful because arranged by subject under the three broad categories of scholarly, biographical, and miscellaneous.

Nihon genson Shinjin bunshû mokuroku 日本現存清人文集目錄 (Catalog of collected works by Qing authors extant in Japanese libraries), Nishimura Genshô 西村元照, ed., Tôyôshi kenkyûkai, 1972.

50.6.3 Biji 筆記

In the Qing, the full variety of *biji* writing continued, ranging from failed scholars producing colorful guides to the big cities to famous scholars and historians, including Gu Yanwu, Zhao Yi, Qian Daxin, and Wang Mingsheng, recording some of their most interesting observations in their *biji*, often culled from a lifetime of reading (Chapter 31).[35] The selection of 17 Qing *biji* given below reflects this variety. Note also the two examples of *biji* guides to the capital under *Geography* above and also the selection of Qing *zashi* 雜史 in Chapter 24. The first seven listed below are the most famous Qing *kaozheng* 考證 (evidential research on historical and textual questions) *biji*.

Gaiyu congkao 陔餘叢考 (Mourning period miscellaneous notes), Zhao Yi 趙翼 (1727–1814), 1790; punctuated edition, Hebei renmin, 1990.

Guisi leigao 癸巳類稿 (Categorized draft of 1813), Yu Zhengxie 俞正燮 (1775–1840), 1813. Notes on many subjects touching on history, anthropology, folklore, geography, economics (there is a chapter on the different units for measuring land), and the classics (see *ECCP*, 936); reprinted in *Guoxue jiben congshu* (9.6).

Nian'er shi zhaji 廿二史劄記 (Classified notes on the twenty-two Standard Histories), Zhao Yi 趙翼, 1799; see 22.2.

Guisi cungao 癸巳存稿 (Leftovers from *Guisi leigao*), Yu Zhengxie. Contains mainly lighter subjects than those the author selected for his first collection of notes; also his study of the history of the *mu* 畝.

Rizhilu 日知錄 (Record of knowledge gained day by day), Gu Yanwu 顧炎武 (1613–82), Preface dated 1676, published 1695. Use *Rizhilu jishi* 日知錄集釋 (Collected notes on the *Rizhilu*), Huang Rucheng 黃汝成 (1799–1837), ed., 1795; rpnt. with punctuation, Yuelu, 1992, 1994. *Rizhi* 日知 in the title is taken from *Lunyu*, xix.5. In his Preface, Gu explained the basis for including some subjects and not others: "Since my childhood studies, I have always noted down what I perceived, and if it [turned out] to be incorrect, I revised it again and again, or if earlier men had said it before me, I omitted it entirely" (Liang Ch'i-

---

[35] Zhang Shunhui 張舜徽 has published notes taken from 100 Qing *biji* in *Qingren biji tiaobian* 清人筆記條辨 (Analysis by subject matter of the *biji* of Qing writers), Zhonghua, 1986. See also Xie Guozhen's notes on Ming-Qing *biji* (49.2, *Biji*).

ch'ao, 1959 [50.6.4], 31). *Rizhilu* contains 1,020 entries divided into philosophy, government, the examination system, popular customs, astronomy, and geography. Indexed in *CZS*.

Shijiazhai yangxin lu 十駕齋養新錄 (Record of self-renewal from the Ten Yokes Study), Qian Daxin 錢大昕 (1728–1804), 1804–6; Shangwu, 1937; rpnt., Shanghai shudian, 1982. Careful notes on the classics, phonology, philology, history, geography, and much else besides.

Shiqishi shangque 十七史商榷, Wang Mingsheng 王鳴盛 (1722–97); 22.2.

Chibei outan 池北偶談 (Chatting with visitors in the Chibei Book Depository), Wang Shizhen 王士禎 (1634–1711); 2 vols., Zhonghua, 1982 and 1984. Miscellaneous notes and comments by a famous scholar, poet, and bibliophile.

[*Dushutang*] *Xizheng suibi* [讀書堂]西征隨筆 (Notes of a western journey), Wang Jingqi 汪景祺 (1672–1726), 1723. Wang wrote these notes on his way to Shaanxi. His acerbic comments on the government and high officials, including the emperor, led to his execution in 1726.

Guangdong xinyu 廣東新語 (News from Guangdong), Qu Dajun 屈大均 (1630–96), 1680; punctuated edition, 2 vols., Zhonghua, 1985. Notes on conditions in Guangdong, mainly in the Ming.

Qingbai leichao 清稗類鈔 (Classified collection of Qing notes), Xu Ke 徐珂 (1869–1928), 13 vols., Zhonghua, 1984–86; rpnt., 1996. Gathers together excerpts from the author's observations as well as his reading notes in Qing *biji* and in late Qing and early Republican newspapers arranged by subject category. Indexed in *CZZS*.

Shiqu yuji 石渠餘記 (Left-over notes from the Stone Canal Pavilion), Wang Qingyun 王慶雲 (1798–1862), completed in the 1850s, Beijing guji, 1985. Unofficial history of finance and tax during the Qing. The Shiqu library was the name of the famous imperial library of the Western Han (see 9.2).

Xiaoting zalu 嘯亭雜錄 (Miscellaneous records of Xiaoting), Zhaolian 昭槤 (1776–1829), 1814 or 1815; *xulu* 續錄 (continuation), written 1817–26. Important supplement for Qing history, especially the years 1736–1821; punctuated edition, Zhonghua, 1980.

Yangzhou huafang lu 揚州畫舫錄 (The decorated boats of Yangzhou), Li Dou 李斗, 1795; Zhonghua, 1960. The author was from Yangzhou and provides a detailed guide to the sights and personalities of this great eighteenth-century commercial center at the height of its prosperity. Lucie Borota translates excerpts in *Renditions* 46 (1996), 58–68. See also Colin P. Mackerras, *The Rise of the Peking Opera, 1770–1870*, OUP, 1972, Chapter 3. Li's 17th chapter is a handbook on garden architecture and carpentry. It is discussed in Klaas Ruitenbeek, 1993 (37.4.2).

Yanpu zaji 簷曝雜記 (Miscellaneous records of Yanpu), Zhao Yi. A third collection of notes by the famous scholar-official.

Yuewei caotang biji 閱微草堂筆記 (Random jottings from the Cottage of Close Scrutiny), Ji Yun 紀昀 (1724–1805), 1800. Ji was chief editor of the *Siku quanshu* (9.5). Toward the end of his life, he wrote 1,200 fables and anecdotes many of them satirizing the pedantry and hypocrisy of his Neo-Confucian contemporaries. For a translation of more than 100 of the tales, see *Notes from the Hut for Examining the Subtle*, David L. Keenan, tr. and ed., Sharpe, 1998; and for a study, Leo Tak-hung Chan, *The Discourses on Foxes and Ghosts: Ji Yun and Eighteenth Century Literati Storytelling*, HKCUP, 1998.

Zi buyu 子不語 (What the master did not say), Yuan Mei 袁枚 (1716–97), 1788; Yuelu, 1985; Renmin wenxue, 1996. The title refers to the seventh book of the *Lunyu*: "The Master never talked of wonders, feats of strength, disorders of nature, or spirits" (*zi bu yu guaili luanshen* 子不語怪力亂神). Yuan Mei, on the other hand, was particularly fond of such matters. See *Censored by Confucius: Ghost Stories by Yuan Mei*, Kam Louie and Louise Edwards, trs., Sharpe, 1996. Yuan Mei arranged for his *suibi* to be published after his death.

50.6.4   Philology

The main scholarly endeavor of high Qing scholarship was to turn back to the Han texts of the classics and the early commentators. In this Chinese-style reformation, the *Hanxue* 漢學 scholars peeled away the later Neo-Confucian interpretations that they had inherited from the Song and the Ming. The Hanxuepai 漢學派 (as they later came to be called) used induction based on the careful accumulation of evidence. Typically, they applied *kaozheng* 考證 (evidential research) to the study of history and textual criticism, phonetics, and etymology. Examples of their work in the form of *biji* were cited in the previous section. The founder of the Hanxuepai was Gu Yanwu 顧炎武 (1613–82); see 4.5.4.[36] The main contribution of the

---

[36] For the academic background to *kaozheng*, see Benjamin Elman, *From Philosophy to Philology: Intellectual Aspects of Change in Late Imperial China*, Council on East Asian Studies, Harvard University, 1984, rpnt., 1990; Liang Ch'i-ch'ao, *Intellectual Trends in the Ch'ing Period*, tr. with introduction and notes by Immanuel C. Y. Hsü, HUP, 1959.

the Qing philologists was to lay the basis for the reconstruction of the phonology of Old Chinese; see Norman, 1988 (1.1), 42–48. Gu Yanwu was a pioneer. Thereafter, the biggest contribution was made by Duan Yucai 段玉裁, the most influential Qing scholar of the *Shuowen*. The Qing also saw the compilation of the largest dictionaries of characters and phrases compiled in imperial China (2.2), including of the common language (*Tongsu bian*; see below).

Duan Yucai 段玉裁 (1735–1815). After failing the metropolitan examination in 1761, he spent the remainder of his life as a teacher and scholar (his phonological studies are contained in his *Liushu yinyun biao* 六書音均表, 1775). His most influential work is *Shuowen jiezi zhu* 說文解字注, 1813–15; Shanghai guji, 1981.

Cui Hao 崔灝, *Tongsu bian* 通俗編 (Compilation of common usage), 1751; Shangwu, 1957. Contains more than 5,000 words, phrases, proverbs, and so forth arranged into 38 subject categories.

50.6.5   Fiction (see 34.3)

50.7   Documents of Merchants and Landlords

50.7.1   Introduction

Various local groups of merchants rose to prominence in the Ming and Qing. Their networks eventually extended all over the country.[37] The Huishang 徽商 (Huizhou merchants) were one of the most powerful groups in the south (50.7.2); the Jinshang 晋商 (Shanxi merchants) in the north (50.7.3). Ming-Qing route books and merchant manuals are the focus of 50.7.4. Ming-Qing land deeds and tenancy contracts from various other sources have been transcribed and published (50.7.5). Documents on stone inscriptions with a social or economic interest form a distinct category (50.7.6).

The largest private archive in China is the family archive of the direct descendants of Confucius of which 9,110 *juan* are extant; the documents date from 1522 to 1948. Many volumes of excerpts have been published. Most date from the Qing.[38]

---

[37] Their histories are told in the series *Zhongguo shida shangbang* 中國十大商幫 (The 10 great merchant groups of China), Shanxi renmin, 1993.

[38] *Qufu Kongfu dang'an shiliao xuanbian* 曲阜孔府檔案史料選編 (Edited selections from the archives of the Confucian estate, Qufu), Qufu xian wen-

Footnote continued on next page

A large archive of a Sichuan salt manufactory has survived.[39] A few account books of shops are known to have survived.[40] Some, notably traditional pharmacies, were sufficiently prosperous and long-lived to have left their mark. It is possible to trace back many of the leading Beijing pharmacies at least to the mid-nineteenth century, in some cases, even further. The Tongren tang 同仁堂, for example, was founded in the Ming, and it is still operating.

It is only very rarely that the personal financial accounts of individuals have survived.[41]

50.7.2   Huizhou Merchants

The Huizhou merchants of Anhui reached their high point in the early Qing. They have left behind the single largest extant body of historical documents, some going back to the Ming and even earlier. The first sighting of the documents was in the 1940s. Fang Hao 方豪, Fujii Hiroshi 藤井宏, Fu Yiling 傅衣凌 (1911–88), and Ho Ping-ti wrote about the region in the 1950s and 1960s.[42] The first report of the Huizhou documents was in 1957. The documents fall into three broad categories—contracts, rent books, and fish-scale registers. Their background is analyzed and discussed in Harriet T.

---

guanhui 曲阜縣文管會 et al., eds., 24 vols., Qi-Lu, 1980; *Kongfu dang'an xuanbian* 孔府檔案選編 (Selections from the Confucius family archive), 2 vols., Zhonghua, 1982.

[39] *Zigong yanye qiyue dang'an xuanji* 自貢鹽業契約檔案選輯 (Selected contracts from the Zigong salt industry), Shehui kexue, 1985. There are 30,000 documents from this industry held at the Zigong Municipal Archives, Sichuan.

[40] In 1934, the Beijing Library was presented with 468 volumes of account books dating from the late eighteenth and first half of the nineteenth century from Hebei province. These are the accounts of some 10 shops in Ningjin county 寧晉縣 and in Daliu market town 大留鎮 and their neighboring villages; see Yan Zhongping 嚴仲平, *Zhongguo jindai jingjishi tongji ziliao xuanji* 中國近代經濟史統計資料選輯 (Selected statistical materials on Chinese economic history in the modern period), Kexue, 1955.

[41] Zhang Dechang 張德昌, *Qingji yige jingguan de shenghuo* 清季一個京官的生活 (The life of a court official in the late Qing dynasty: a study of personal income and expenditure), HKCUP, 1970, which tabulates the expenditures of Li Ciming 李慈銘 for the years 1854–94.

[42] Michel Cartier, "Naissance de la Huizhoulogie," *RBS* VIII: 94–100 (1990); and Kang Zhao, "New Data on Landownership Patterns in Ming-Ch'ing China—A Research Note," *JAS* 40.4: 719–33 (1981).

Zurndorfer, *Change and Continuity in Chinese Local History: The Development of Hui-chou Prefecture*, Brill, 1989. Many of the Huizhou documents have been published, and there are also itemized and annotated catalogs:

Huizhou wenshu leimu 徽州文書類目 (Itemized catalog of the Huizhou documents), Wang Yuxin 王鈺欣 et al., Huangshan, 1999.

Huizhou lishi dang'an zongmu tiyao 徽州歷史檔案總目提要 (Annotated catalog of Huizhou historical archives), Yan Guifu 嚴桂夫 et al., 2 vols., Huangshan shushe, 1996. The first volume contains a description of the archives; the second, annotations on some 9,600 documents.

Huizhou qiannian qiyue wenshu 徽州千年契約文書 (A thousand years of contract documents from Huizhou), Zhou Shaoquan 周紹泉, ed. in chief, 40 vols., Huashan wenyi, 1991–93. Contains reproductions of the Huizhou documents held at the Lishisuo. The first 20 volumes reproduce 1,811 documents dating from 1242 to the end of the Ming; the second set of 20 volumes has over 1,400 from the Qing and Republic.

Ming Qing Huishang ziliao xuanbian 明清徽商資料選編 (Selected materials on the Ming-Qing Huizhou merchants), Zhang Haipeng 張海鵬 (1931–) and Wang Tingyuan 王廷元, eds., Huangshan shushe, 1985. This important collection contains 1,513 entries garnered from various sources, including Huizhou manuscripts and local genealogies.

Ming Qing Huishang ziliao xubian 明清徽商資料續編 (Second selection of materials on the Ming-Qing Huizhou merchants), Zhang Haipeng 張海鵬 and Wang Tingyuan 王廷元, eds., Huangshan shushe, 1997.

Ming Qing Huizhou shehui jingji ziliao congbian 明清徽州社會經濟資料叢編 (Ming-Qing socioeconomic materials from Huizhou), Anhuisheng bowuguan, ed., 1ˢᵗ selection, Shehui kexue, 1988; 2ⁿᵈ selection, Huizhou wenqi zhengli zu 徽州文契整理組, ed., Shehui kexue, 1990. The first selection contains transcriptions of 950 land and house purchase/sale/rental deeds of which 392 from the Ming; the second has 12 from the Song and Yuan and 685 from the Ming (originals held at the Lishisuo).

Zhongguo lidai qiyue huibian kaoshi 中國歷代契約匯編考釋 (50.7.4) contains many documents, including those from Huizhou held in the Peking University library.

There are now many analyses of the operations of the Huizhou merchants. A selection follows:

Zhang Haipeng 張海鵬 and Wang Tingyuan 王廷元, *Huishang fazhanshi* 徽商發展史 (History of the development of the Huizhou merchants), Huangshan, 1997.

Wang Zhenzhong 王振忠, *Ming Qing Huishang yu Huai Yang shehui bianqian* 明清徽商與淮揚社會變遷 (The Huizhou merchants and social change of the Huaiyang region in the Ming-Qing), Sanlian, 1996.

Zhang Haipeng 張海鵬 and Wang Tingyuan 王廷元, *Huishang yanjiu* 徽商研究 (Studies on the Huizhou merchants), Anhui renmin, 1995.

Huizhou shehui jingjishi yanjiu yiwenji 徽州社會經濟史研究譯文集 (Collection of translated articles on the socioeconomic history of Huizhou), Liu Miao 劉淼, ed., Huangshan, 1988.

Ming Qing Huizhou tudi guanxi yanjiu 明清徽州土地關係研究 (Land relations in Ming-Qing Huizhou), Zhang Youyi 章有義, ed., Shehui kexue, 1984.

Ye Xian'en 葉顯恩, *Ming Qing Huizhou nongcun shehui yu dianpuzhi* 明清徽州農村社會與佃僕制 (Ming-Qing Huizhou rural society and the tenant bondservant system), Anhui renmin, 1983. The first comprehensive study of the region.

On the Huizhou merchants as patrons of the arts, see 38.1.2.

50.7.3   Shanxi Merchants

The Jinshang 晋商 (Shanxi merchants), also called the Shanxi *piaohao* 山西票號 or *piaozhuang* 票莊 (Shanxi bankers), were one of the most powerful groups. At the height of their prosperity in the nineteenth century they ran 43 out of a known total of 51 *piaohao* in China. The wealthy and well-connected Nationalist politician and long-time finance minister, H. H. Kong (Kong Xiangxi 孔祥熙, 1881–1967) was from a Shanxi *piaohao* family. Twenty-two of the Shanxi *piaohao* had their headquarters in the county town of Pingyao 平遙. It is well-preserved. Several of the spacious courtyard houses have been restored and turned into museums.[43] The old city was made a UNESCO world heritage site in 1998. About a dozen film makers have used the location for films set in the Qing or Republic. The Zhang Yimou 張藝謀 film *Raise the Red Lantern* was filmed in the neighboring county of Qi 祁 in the residence of a

---

[43] *Jinshang zhaiyuan* 晋商宅院 (The Shanxi merchant courtyard houses): Qiao 喬, Wang 王, Cao 曹, and Qu 渠, 4 vols., Shanxi renmin, 1997.

Shanxi banker named Qiao 喬. At the height of their prosperity in the eighteenth century, 70 Qiao family members lived here with 170 servants. They operated 18 businesses trading in oil and vegetables, 200 shops, several coal mines, and a bank with 20 branches throughout China. The rise of Shanghai spelled the end of the Qiao and other Shanxi *piaohao* fortunes. See Zhang Zhengming 張正明, *Jin shang xingshuaishi* 晋商興衰史.[44]

50.7.4   Ming-Qing Route Books and Manuals

Numerous merchant route books (*luchengshu* 路程書) and manuals were published in the Ming and Qing. Some twenty to thirty are extant. They usually contain information on trade routes including time taken between stopping points, location of tax barriers and markets, and so on, as well as general knowledge for merchants, including information on differences between regional weights and measures, notes on different goods, and ethical maxims. The sections on routes were based on official administrative geographical works, and they are usually arranged according to the standard administrative hierarchy. Individual merchants or traveling officials using such works would, of course, have marked up their own copies with marginal notes. Use Timothy Brook, *Geographical Sources of Ming-Qing History*, Michigan Monographs in Chinese Studies no. 58, Ann Arbor, 1988, and for a thorough study containing a bibliography of more than 20 merchant manuals as well as of secondary scholarship in Chinese and Japanese on them, see Chen Xuewen 陳學文, *Ming Qing shiqi shangye shu ji shangren shu zhi yanjiu* 明清時期商業書及商人書之研究.[45]

Route Books

Huang Bian 黃汴, *Yitong lucheng tuji* 一統路程圖記 (Comprehensive illustrated route book of the empire), preface, 1570; reprinted in: Yang Zhengtai 楊正泰, *Mingdai yizhan kao* 明代驛站考 (Studies on the

---

[44] *Jinshang xingshuaishi* (The history of the rise and fall of the Shanxi merchants), Shanxi guji, 1995, 1996.

[45] *Ming Qing shiqi shangye shu ji shangren shu zhi yanjiu* (Research on business books and merchant books of the Ming and Qing periods), Hongye, 1997. See also Yamane Yukio 山根幸夫, "Mindai no roteisho ni tsuite" 明代の路程書について (On the route books of the Ming), *Mindaishi kenkyû* 4: 9-24 (1994).

Ming postal relay system), Shanghai guji, 1994. *Tianxia shuilu lucheng* 天下水陸路程 (Water and land routes of the empire) Yang Zhengtai 楊正泰, ed., Shanxi renmin, 1992, is almost the same book.

Shang Jun 商濬, *Shuilu lucheng* 水陸路程 (Water and land routes), preface dated 1617, rpnt. in Yang Zhengtai (1992). Appeared in numerous popular encyclopaedias and under various titles.

Tianxia lucheng Shiwo zhouxing 天下路程示我周行 (Guide to the land routes of the empire). Combines two typical merchant route books, with many dozens of copies extant. The earliest edition is dated 1694. Many reprints appeared, often with different compilers or titles.

Merchant Manuals

Shishang yaolan 士商要覽 (Essentials for scholar-merchants), early eighteenth century, Dan Yizi 儋漪子 ed. *Juan* 3 contains important materials on business ethics and methods of trading.

A Ming scholar's comments on merchants [from *Songchuang mengyu* 松窗夢語 (Sleep talk from the window by a pine), Zhang Han 張瀚 (1511–93)], has been translated by Lily Hwa in *Chinese Civilization: A Sourcebook* (8.1), 216–18. See also Timothy Brook, "The Merchant Network in 16th Century China—A Discussion and Translation of Zhang Han's 'On Merchants.'" *JESHO* 24.2: 165–214 (1981).

Maoyi xuzhi 貿易須知 (Essentials for merchants), Wang Bingyuan 王秉元, comp., mid-Qing, printed as appendix to Zhang Zhengming, 1995 (50.7.3), 335–50. Appears to be based on a late eighteenth-century manual for apprentices, *Shengyi shishi chujie* 生意世事初階 (First introduction to business), late eighteenth century, Wang Bingyuan 王秉元, comp., held at Nanjing daxue tushuguan 南京大學圖書館.

Dianye xuzhi 典業須知 (Essentials for the pawn industry), 1885, L. S. Yang, tr., *Xin shihuo*, 1.4: 231–43 (1971).

Ming-Qing Merchant Culture

In addition to the copious literature generated by the debates on the buds of capitalism (*ziben zhuyi mengya* 資本主義萌芽), note the following studies of merchants and the rise of urban consumption in late imperial China:

Timothy Brook, *The Confusions of Pleasure: Commerce and Culture in Ming China*, UCP, 1998, and the same scholar's chapter "Communications and Commerce," in *CHC*, vol. 8, 579–707, especially "Merchants in Ming society," 699–707.

Joanna Handlin Smith, "Gardens in Ch'i Piao-chia's Social World: Wealth and Values in Late-Ming Kiangnan," *JAS* 51.1: 5581 (1992).

Craig Clunas, *Superfluous Things: Material Culture and Social Status in Early Modern China*, Polity Press, 1991.

Ping-ti Ho, "The Salt Merchants of Yang-chou: A Study of Commercial Capitalism in Eighteenth-Century China," *HJAS* 17.1–2 (1954).[46]

Richard John Lufrano, *Honorable Merchants: Commerce and Self-cultivation in Late Imperial China*, UHP, 1997.

John Meskill, *Gentlemanly Interests and Wealth on the Yangtze Delta*, Association for Asian Studies, 1994.

50.7.5   Land Deeds and Tenancy Contracts

Selections of Ming and Qing private documents such as land deeds or tenancy agreements from areas other than Huizhou have been published. Some have been annotated and translated into Modern Chinese; most have not. General collections of sources sometimes include Ming and Qing private documents. Collections of land deeds and other types of contracts usually include Ming and Qing contracts. Note the works of historians such as Fu Yiling. He began his career with the discovery of a chest of Ming land deeds in a Fujian village (the earliest dating from the beginning of the sixteenth century) and quickly went on to pioneer the use of the documents of the Huizhou merchants (50.7.2). Occasional genealogies also contain private documents relating to land or goods. Japanese historians have analyzed land tenantry in the Ming and Qing using rent books and other such private sources. See, for example,

Muramatsu Yuji 村松祐次, *Kindai Kônan no sosen* 近代江南の租棧 (The bursaries of modern Jiangnan), Tokyo, 1970.

---

[46] Note *Zhongguo yanyeshi* 中國鹽業史 (History of the Chinese salt industry), Guo Zhengzhong 郭正忠, ed. in chief, 3 vols., Renmin, 1997. For a bibliography of Chinese and Japanese studies of the Chinese salt industry from the Han to the end of the Qing, see *Chûgoku engyôshi kenkyû bunken mokuroku* 中國鹽業史研究文獻目錄 (1926–88), Yoshida Tora 吉田寅, ed., Tokyo: Risshô daigaku Tôyôshigaku kenkyûshitsu, 1989. Also *Salt Production Techniques in Ancient China: The Aobo tu* [熬波圖], Yoshida Tora, ed., Hans Ulrich Vogel, tr., Brill, 1992.

Studies of Land Deeds and Tenancy Contracts

Valerie Hansen, *Negotiating Daily Life in Traditional China: How Ordinary People Used Contracts, 600–1400*, YUP, 1995. Analyzes all kinds of contracts in Chinese history from the Tang to the Ming. The first part deals with everyday life contracts, concentrating on the Dunhuang and Turpan materials; the second with afterlife contracts placed in tombs.

Zhongguo lidai qiyue huibian kaoshi 中國歷代契約會編考釋 (Collection of Chinese land deeds with notes and transcriptions), Zhang Chuanxi 張傳璽, ed., 2 vols., Beijing daxue, 1995. Includes 1,402 contracts from the Zhou dynasty to the Republic of China with transcriptions and translations into Modern Chinese. The introduction draws on a long article by the same author on the different types of contracts used at different periods of Chinese history and their value as historical sources: "Qiyue wenti" 契約問題 in *Qin Han wenti yanjiu* 秦漢問題研究 (Research on Qin and Han issues), rev. and enl. edition, Beijing daxue, 1995, 140–227.

Ming Qing tudi qiyue wenshu yanjiu 明清土地契約文書研究 (Studies on Ming-Qing land deeds), Yang Guozhen 楊國楨, ed., Renmin, 1988.

Transcriptions of Land Deeds

Chûgoku tochi keiyaku monjoshû. Kin–Shin 中國土地契約文書集・金-清 (Collection of texts of Chinese land deeds, Jin to Qing), Mindaishi kenkyûshitsu at the Tôyô bunko, ed., Tokyo, 1975. Gathers between two covers land deeds from 33 sources, including from Ming dynasty popular encyclopaedias.

Ming Qing Suzhou nongcun jingji ziliao 明清蘇州農村經濟資料 (Ming-Qing economic materials from Suzhou villages), Hong Huanchun 洪煥椿, ed., Jiangsu guji, 1988; 340 texts arranged under eight heads.

Ming Qing Fujian jingji qiyue wenshu xuanji 明清福建經濟契約文書選輯 (Selected Ming-Qing economic contracts from Fujian), Shanghai shifan daxue, 1996.

Minnan qiyue wenshu zonglu 閩南契約文書綜錄 (Comprehensive account of land deeds in southern Fujian), *Zhongguo shehui jingjishi yanjiu*, 1990, special issue.

Qingdai diqi dang'an shiliao (Jiaqing zhi Xuantong) 清代地契檔案史料嘉慶至宣統 (50.2.3).

Qing Hezhou qiwen huibian 清河州契文匯編 (Collection of contracts from Qinghe prefecture), Gansusheng Linxia Huizu zizhizhou danganguan, 甘肅省臨夏回族自治州檔案館, Gansu renmin, 1993. Contains 588 land deeds dating from 1819 to 1911.

Tôyô bunka kenkyûjo shozô Chûgoku tochi monjo mokuroku kaisetsu 東洋文化研究所所藏中國土地文書目錄解説, Hamashita Takeshi 濱下武志 et al., 2 vols., Tokyo, 1983–86. This contains (1) selections from 10 sets of Qing and Republican-period documents, with introductions and annotations and (2) a complete catalog of the 10 sets of documents (2,250 items in total).

Mizhixian Yangjiagou diaocha 米脂縣楊家溝調查 (Investigation of Yangjiagou, Mizhi county), Yan'an nongcun diaocha tuan 延安農村調查圖 (Yan'an investigation team), ed., Sanlian, 1957; rpnt., Renmin, 1980. Field study conducted in a north Shaanxi village in 1941.

Jing Su 景甦 and Luo Lun 羅崙, *Qingdai Shandong jingying dizhu de shehui xingzhi* 清代山東經營地主底社會性質, Shandong renmin, 1959; Endymion Wilkinson, tr.: *Landlord and Labor in Late Imperial China*, HUP, 1980. Land deeds and other records of landlord enterprises were used in this study, some dating from the eighteenth century.

Taiwan gongsi cang gu wenshu yingbian 臺灣公私藏古文書影編 (Copies of public and private documents from Taiwan), Wang Shiqing 王世慶, ed., series 1–10, 1983, Taibei.

Taiwan gu shuqi, 1717–1906 臺灣古書契 (Archaic land documents of Taiwan, 1717–1906), Lihong, 1997.

50.7.6 *Stone Inscriptions of Socioeconomic Interest*

Eduard B. Vermeer, *Chinese Local History: Stone Inscriptions from Fukien in the Sung to Ch'ing Periods*, Westview, 1991. Transcribes, translates and comments on 23 stone inscriptions.

Imahori Seiji 今堀誠二, *Chûgoku hôken shakai no kikô* 中國封建社會の機構 (Chinese feudal society: an intensive investigation of social groups in a county town from the early Qing on), Nihon gakujutsu shinkôkai, 1955. The stelae are included in an appendix, 701–837.

Jiangxi chutu muzhi xuanbian 江西出土墓志選編 (Selection of funerary texts excavated in Jiangxi), Chen Baiquan 陳柏泉, ed., Jiangxi jiaoyu, 1991; also includes 220 land deeds from the Tang to the Qing.

Ming Qing Foshan beike wenxian jingji ziliao 明清佛山碑刻文獻經濟資料 (Ming-Qing economic materials from Foshan stele and documents), Guangdong renmin, 1987.

Ming Qing yilai Suzhou shehuishi beikeji 明清以來蘇州社會史碑刻集 (Collected stelae on Suzhou social history since the Ming-Qing),

Wang Guoping 王國平 and Tang Lixing 唐力行, eds. in chief, Suzhou daxue, 1999. Contains 500 stone inscriptions; indexes list the inscriptions in the two previous Jiangsu/Suzhou collections: *Jiangsusheng Ming Qing yilai beike ziliao xuanji* 江蘇省明清以來碑刻資料選集 (Selection of Jiangsu stone inscriptions since Ming-Qing), Jiangsusheng bowuguan, ed., 3 vols., Sanlian shudian, 1959; rpnt., Daian, 1967, and *Ming Qing Suzhou gongshangye beikeji* 明清蘇州工商業碑刻集 (Collected Suzhou Ming-Qing stelae on industry and commerce), Suzhou bowuyuan et al., comps., Jiangsu renmin, 1981.

Ming Qing yilai Beijing gongshang huiguan beike xuanbian 明清以來北京工商會館碑刻選編 (Selected stele inscriptions from the Ming-Qing Beijing guild and Landsmannschaften), Li Hua 李華, ed., Wenwu, 1980, 1990.

Niida Noboru hakase shû Pekin kôshô girudo shiryôshû 仁井田陞博士輯北京工商ギルド資料集 (Materials on Beijing industrial and commercial guilds collected by Dr. Niida Noboru), 6 vols., Tôbunken, 1975–83.

Qingdai gongshang hangye beiwen jicui 清代工商行業碑文集粹 (Selection of the best Qing dynasty industrial and commercial guild stelae and documents), Peng Zeyi 彭澤益, comp., Zhongzhou guji, 1997.

Shanghai beike ziliao xuanji 上海碑刻資料選輯 (Selections from Shanghai stele inscriptions), Shanghai renmin, 1980. Contains 245 transcriptions of stele texts from the Song to the Qing.

Taiwan nanbu beiwen jicheng 臺灣南部碑文集成 (Collection of inscriptions from southern Taiwan), 6 vols., Taiwan yinhang, ed. and publisher, 1966, 1994. In the series *Taiwan wenxian yanjiu congkan* 臺灣文獻研究叢刊.

Taiwan zhongbu beiwen jicheng 臺灣中部碑文集成 (Collection of inscriptions from central Taiwan), Liu Zhiwan 劉枝萬, ed., Taiwan yinhang, 1962, 1994. In the series *Taiwan wenxian yanjiu congkan*.

50.8   *Newspapers*

The history of Chinese periodicals can be summed up in the handy terms *guanbao* 官報 (old-style official gazette) *waibao* 外報 (foreign periodical) and *minbao* 民報 (Chinese privately owned and managed paper). The nineteenth century was dominated by *waibao* and *guanbao*; from the 1890s, the *minbao* gained strength and then became dominant in the Republic (during which *guanbao* proliferated, *waibao* continued, and other categories appeared; see 51.3.1).

50.8.1   Guanbao 官報

The tradition of publishing official and unofficial gazettes of court and government news chiefly for the benefit of provincial officials, which dates from the Tang (26.4) was inherited by the Qing. Until 1638, the gazettes were normally hand-copied. After that date they were printed with movable type. By the Qing, the covers were normally yellow with the characters *Jingbao* 京報 (Peking gazette) in red on the front cover (hence the popular name *Huangpi jingbao* 黃皮京報). From the mid-Ming, the authors of miscellaneous notes and unofficial histories sometimes drew their material from the gazettes.[47] Translations of the late Qing gazettes appear intermittently in the *Chinese Repository* and the *North China Herald*. From 1872 to 1900, the *Herald* translated the gazettes *in toto*. Often these gazettes contain documents not found in the Veritable Records.[48] During the last years of the dynasty, the *Jingbao* was replaced with the daily *Zhengzhi guanbao* 政治官報 (Government gazette), 1907.10.26–1911.8.23. This was succeeded by the *Neige guanbao* 內閣官報 (Cabinet gazette), 1911.8.24–1912.2.12. Republican gazettes are listed in 51.3.8.

50.8.2   Waibao 外報

By the seventeenth century, irregular news sheets, privately published and often carrying a single item of news, were also becoming increasingly common in major cities. The first modern Chinese newspapers, however, were founded and edited by Protestant missionaries and businessmen. They began to appear in the early part of the century and carried missionary, commercial, and shipping news. Some were in Chinese, some in English, or Portuguese. The center of activities quickly moved from Southeast Asia (Malacca, Batavia) after the lifting of the ban prohibiting the propagation of Christianity in China in 1844. Presses were set up in Macao, Canton, Hong Kong, and Ningbo, and then Shanghai. Reflecting this relocation, the Chinese word for newspaper changed. At first the

[47] Yin Yungong, "Baozhi yu shixue 報紙與史學" (Newspapers and history), Yin, 1990 (see previous note), 165–73.

[48] Jonathan Ocko, "The British Museum's Peking Gazette," *Ch'ing-shih wen-t'i* 11.9: 35–49 (1973).

Cantonese coinage *xinwenzhi* 新聞紙 was used. Next, this was joined by the neologism *xinbao* 新報. By the end of the century both had been replaced by the Shanghai coinage *baozhi* 報紙 (but *xinwenzhi* is retained for "newsprint" and gave Japanese its word for newspaper, *shinbun* 新聞). Another indication of the preeminence of Shanghai as the center of modern Chinese printing, publishing, and journalism is that out of a total of 1,735 Chinese-language periodicals established between 1833 and 1911, 465 (24 percent) were published in Shanghai. Also, nearly all major innovations in printing technology from the 1840s to the first half of the twentieth century were first introduced into China by Shanghai publishers (18.5).

The Chinese word for periodicals *baokan* 報刊 (from *baozhi* 報紙 + *qikan* 期刊) refers to newspapers and periodicals. It is particularly suited to their history in the nineteenth and early twentieth century because no clear distinction was made between the two, hence in what follows (and in the section on the Republican press, 51.3.1), "periodicals" is used in this broad sense.

In addition to their Chinese names, most Chinese newspapers carried an official English name on their mastheads (occasionally also French). When this is the case, the foreign-language title is italicized in brackets in the following lists.

50.8.3   Chinese Periodicals, 1815–94

Malacca

Cha shisu meiyue tongji chuan 察世俗每月統記傳 (*A General Monthly Record, Containing an Investigation of the Opinions and Practices of Society*), founded by Robert Morrison. Issued 1815–26, first Chinese-language periodical ever issued. The reason that it appeared in Malacca was that the Qing authorities forbade the missionaries to print in China, so Morrison had invited a young printer, Liang Fa 梁發 (1789–1855) to set up shop with him in Malacca beyond the reach of the authorities. Several other Chinese-language periodicals were published in Southeast Asia and for the same reason (in Malacca and in Batavia [Jakarta]).

Macao

Yijing zashuo 依涇雜說, Macao, 1827. Published bilingually in English and in Chinese. Closed down by the government. First modern Chinese-language periodical published in China.

Canton

Dong Xi yang kao meiyue tongji chuan 東西洋考每月統記傳 (*Eastern Western Monthly Magazine*), founded by Karl Gützlaff (1803–51), 1833. More on Western science and culture and less Bible-related than the *Cha shisu meiyue tongji chuan*. In 1835, moved to Singapore.

Hong Kong

Xianggang Zhongwai xinbao 香港中外新報 (*Daily Press*), Hong Kong, 1858–1919, evening paper edited by Wang Tao 王韜 (1828–97). Earliest Chinese newspaper. From 1870s, the title was *Zhongwai xinbao* 中外新報. On Wang, see Paul A. Cohen, *Between Tradition and Modernity: Wang T'ao and Reform in Late Ch'ing China*, HUP, 1974. At its height the paper printed 10,000 copies.

Huazi ribao 香港華字日報, Hong Kong, 1872–1941. Began as Chinese version of the *China Mail*.

Xunhuan ribao 循環日報 (*Universal Circulating Herald*), Hong Kong, 1874–1941; 1945–47; 1959. First Chinese paper to contain political editorials (by Wang Tao). The press used was previously that of the London Missionary Society.

Shanghai

Shenbao 申報 (*Shanghai Journal* or "*The Shun Pao*"), founded by Ernest Major (ca. 1830–1908) and three friends, Shanghai, 1872–1949. The original name of the paper was *Shenjiang xinbao* 申江新報 (Shenjiang is the short form of the Chunshen jiang 春申江, the old name for the Huangpu jiang 黃浦江, Shanghai). The first print run was 600 copies on single 10 by 9-inch sheets printed on one side only. Major had come with his elder brother Frederick to Shanghai in 1862 to trade in tea and cotton. They also set up a pharmaceutical company. Using the profits from these ventures they established various pioneering and influential publishing ventures, including the first photolithographic publishing works in China, the Dianshizhai shiyinju 點石齋石印局 (see next item below); the Tushu jicheng qianyin shuju 圖書集成書鉛印局 (which published the *Tushu jicheng* using leaden type in 1884–88), and the Shenchang shuju 申昌書局. *Shenbao* became one of the most influential and longest lived newspapers in modern China. It innovated in printing technology (18.5), the use of the telegraph (50.8.4) the employment of a military correspondent (sent to cover the Sino-French War in Vietnam in 1884), and the use of the vernacular (*baihua* 白話) in the short-lived *Minbao* 民報, 1876. Before retiring to England in 1889, the two Major brothers formed a public company and they sold their shares for 100,000 taels. The company came under Chinese ownership in 1909 (on the later fortunes of the paper, see 51.3.1). The three publishing ventures of the Majors were combined with the Kaiming shudian 開明書店 in 1909 to form the Jicheng tushu gongsi 集成圖書公司, the largest and best equipped lithographic and leaden type printing establishment of its day in Shanghai.

Dianshizhai huabao 點石齋華報 (Illustrated paper from Lithograph Studio), published every 10 days, 1884–96 by *Shenbao* and printed at the Dianshizhai shiyinju 點石齋石印局 (Tien Shih Chai), established by the Major brothers in 1876. The first magazine published in China using lithography. Hugely successful and influential. Illustrates in detail the reception of Western science and technology and lifestyles in Beijing and Shanghai. Reprinted, HK: Guangjiaojing, 1983.

Shibao 時報 (*Eastern Times*), Shanghai, 1904.6.12–1939.9.1. See Joan Judge, *Print and Politics: 'Shibao' and the Culture of Reform in Late Qing China*, SUP, 1996.

Periodicals as a Source of New Learning

The Protestant missionaries pioneered periodicals on science, technology, medicine, and other subjects of the new learning (37.2). The three most influential of the missionary journals carrying the new knowledge were:

Liuhe congtan 六合叢談 (*Shanghai Serial*), founded and edited by Alexander Wylie (1815–87), Shanghai, monthly, Heihai shuguan 黑海書店 (Sea of ink bookstore, the London Missionary Society Press), 1857–63.

Wanguo gongbao 萬國公報 (*Chinese Globe Magazine*), founded by Young J. Allen (1836–1907) in 1868 (under the title *Jiaohui xinbao* 教會新報, [*Church Times*], 1868–74), Mei-Hua shuguan 美華書館 (American Presbyterian Missionary Press), Shanghai, weekly, 1868–1907 (ceased publication for lack of funds, 1883–89); 1889–1907, monthly, with same Chinese title but new English title, *A Review of the Times*. Began with a print-run of only 1,000; by 1894 this had increased to 4,000, and by 1899, 38,400, making it the most popular magazine of the day. Not to be confused with the short-lived reform periodical with the same name founded in Beijing in 1895 (50.8.4). See Adrian Arthur Bennett, *Research Guide to the* Wan-kuo kung-pao, CMC, 1976, and on Allen, idem, *Missionary Journalist in China: Young J. Allen and His Magazines, 1860–1883*, Athens: Ohio UP, 1983.

Gezhi huibian 格致匯編 (*The Chinese Scientific Magazine* and later, *The Chinese Scientific and Industrial Magazine*), monthly, 1876–79; ceased publication, 1880–82; monthly, 1882–86; quarterly, 1890–92; John Fryer (1839–1928), ed. in chief, Xu Shou 徐壽 (1818–84), editor, 1876–82. About 4,000 copies printed for national distribution. Previously *Zhong Xi wenjian lu* 中西聞見錄, W. A. P. Martin, ed., Beijing, 1872–76. On Fryer, see 37.2, and on Martin, see 42.2.

By the end of the century, Chinese newspapers and magazines were also introducing science and new ways of thinking, for example, between 1898 and 1915, more than 50 periodicals appeared devoted to women's issues and the number increased rapidly during the years of the New Culture movement (1915–25); see Jacqueline Nivard, "Women and the Women's Press," *Republican China* 10.1b: 37–55 (1984); see also Zheng Wang, 1999 (39.3.3).

50.8.4   Chinese Periodicals, 1895–1911

Chinese-language journalism flowered at the end of the nineteenth and beginning of the twentieth century for both political and technological reasons. Over 200 journals and papers advocating reform were founded. They are one of the main sources for research on this period, especially for intellectual and political history because they were used as vehicles for polemic and debate thus introducing the art of pamphleteering into China for the first time. They also began to disseminate news much faster than before thanks to the introduction of the telegraph. Until 1882, it took seven or eight days for a reporter to file copy from Beijing to Shanghai. On January 16 1882, a correspondent for *Shenbao* in Beijing sent news of an imperial decision by messenger to Tianjin and from there to Shanghai by the newly installed telegraph. It took one day.[49] Chinese communications and Chinese journalism were also transformed by the introduction of new printing techniques. For most of the second half of the nineteenth century, it took one hour to print 200–500 copies of a Chinese newspaper (using wooden movable type). The articles were still in *wenyan* 文言 and the papers were in book form on small folded sheets. In the last years of the Qing, letter-press print-

[49] Already on 1874.1.30, *Shenbao* had been the first newspaper in China ever to print a story from a foreign news cable. The details are given in *Zhongguo baokan cidian 1815–1949* 中國報刊詞典, 1991 (50.8.5), item 4, 507; for a technical history, see Erik Baark, *Lightening Wires: The Telegraph and China's Technological Development, 1860–1890*, Greenwood, 1997.

ing using leaden type enabled for the first time the printing of large-size newspaper sheets with daily print runs measured in the thousands (18.5). Not surprisingly, the introduction of the new technologies coincides with the first great boom in Chinese newspapers. Many of them were in the vernacular. Because of their reformist line, most were quickly closed by the government, so their life was short. Often the same title was used several times by different papers. To gain readers many published *fukan* 副刊 (literary supplements or *feuilleton*). These eventually developed into the influential literary journals and magazines of the May Fourth era (51.3.2). A comprehensive study of the modern printing press as an agent of change in China in the nineteenth and twentieth centuries remains to be written. In the meantime, see the suggestive pages in *CHC*, vols., 11–12.[50]

Selection of Periodicals Advocating Reform

Qiangxue bao 强學報 (*Self-Strengthening News*), founded by Kang Youwei 康有爲 (1858–1927), 1895–96. Official organ of the Qiangxuehui 强學會. Lasted three issues before being suppressed.

Wanguo gongbao 萬國公報, Kang Youwei 康有爲 and Liang Qichao 梁啓超, Beijing, 1895.8; in December changed name to *Zhongwai jiwen* 中外記聞; four months later suppressed by the Qing authorities.

Shiwu bao 事物報 (*Current Affairs* or *China's Progress*), founded by Kang Youwei 康有爲; edited by Liang Qichao 梁啓超, Shanghai, 1896.8–1898.8 (changed name to *Changyan bao* 昌言報 and moved to Shanghai). Began by printing 4,000 copies and at its height, 17,000 sold nationwide.

Xiangxue bao 湘學報, thrice-monthly, Changsha, 1897.4–1898.8 (the name was *Xiangxue xinbao* 湘學新報 from 1897.4–1897.11). National reputation. Complete original run held in the library of Beijing University. At its height sold 8,000 copies nationwide.

Zhixin bao 知新報, every five days; later, thrice-monthly, Macao, 1897–1901; photo-offset, 2 vols., Shanghai Shekeyuan, 1996.

Guowen bao, founded by Yan Fu 嚴復 (1854–1921) et al., Tianjin, 1897.10–1898.5.

[50] Hao Chang, "Intellectual Change and the Reform Movement, 1890–98," *CHC*, vol. 11, 274–338; Leo Ou-fan Lee, "Literary Trends I: The Quest for Modernity, 1895–1927," *CHC*, vol. 12, 452–501.

Xiangbao 湘報, daily (first in Hunan), Changsha, 1898.3–1898.10; rpnt., Zhonghua, 3 vols., 1965. At its height sold more than 6,000 copies nationwide.

Qingyi bao 情義報 (*The China discussion*), edited by Liang Qichao 梁啓超, Yokohama, every 10 days, 1898–1901.

Xinmin congbao 新民叢報 (*New People's Miscellany*), edited by Liang Qichao 梁啓超, fortnightly, 1902–7. Successor to previous item.

Selection of Periodicals Advocating Republican Revolution

Zhongguo ribao 中國日報 (Hong Kong, 1899–1913), daily. Organ of the Xingzhonghui 興中會 (Society for the Rebirth of China), 1894– .

Subao 蘇報 (*Jiangsu Tribune*), founded by Zhang Binglin 章炳麟 (Zhang Taiyan 章太炎, 1868–1936), daily, Shanghai, 1896–1903. Only became revolutionary after 1902.11.

Minbao 民報 (*The People*), Tokyo, 1905.11–1905.8; 1910.8. The organ of the Tongmenghui 同盟會 (United League), 1905– .

A number of major periodicals were inaugurated in the Qing and continued publication in the Republic. These included the following (for details see 51.3.1):

Huazi ribao 香港華字日報, Hong Kong, 1872–1941 (50.8.3)
Shenbao 申報, Shanghai, 1872–1949
Dagong bao 大公報, Tianjin, 1902–66
Dongfang zazhi 東方雜志, Shanghai, 1904–48
Shibao 時報, Shanghai, 1904–39
Shishi xinbao 時事新報, Shanghai, 1907–49
Shuntian shibao 順天時報, Beijing, 1901–30
Taiwan shibao, 臺灣時報, Taibei, 1909–45
Xinwen bao 新聞報, Shanghai, 1893–1949

50.8.5 References

For late-Qing Chinese-language newspapers and periodicals, start with Britton (1937), the first item in the following list of references. Because of the many hundreds of titles, the clearest presentation of the history of Chinese newspapers in the late Qing (and in the Republic) is not necessarily in conventional book form but itemized, as found, for example, in the volume in the great Chinese encyclopaedia on newspapers and publishing (item 2), or in dictionary form (items 3–4). For studies of late Qing periodicals, see items 5–6. For the contents of the leading late-Qing, early Republican periodicals, consult item 7. For union catalogs and other finding lists of Qing and Republican periodicals, see 51.3.5.

1. Roswell S. Britton, *The Chinese Periodical Press, 1800–1912*, Kelly and Walsh, 1937; rpnt., Ch'eng-wen, 1966.

2. *Zhongguo da baike quanshu* 中國大百科全書 (The great Chinese encyclopaedia), *Xinwen chuban juan* 新聞出版卷 (Newspaper and publishing volume); see 51.3.5 for details.

3. *Zhongguo jindai baokan minglu* (Annotated list of modern Chinese periodicals), Shi He 史和 et al., comps., Fujian renmin, 1991. Lists 1,753 Chinese-language periodicals and 136 foreign-language periodicals issued between 1815 and 1911. There are brief notes on the editors, dates and places of publication and contents. There are useful chronological and place-of-publication indexes. Unfortunately, dates are often miscalculated or misprinted.

4. *Zhongguo baokan cidian 1815–1949* 中國報刊詞典 *1815–1949* (Dictionary of the Chinese press, 1815–1949); see 51.3.5 for details.

5. *Xinhai geming shiqi qikan jieshao* 辛亥革命時期期刊介紹 (Introduction to periodicals of the period of the 1911 Revolution), Ding Shouhe 丁守和, Renmin, 1982–1987. Detailed introductions to 252 periodicals published between 1900 and 1918.

6. A Ying 阿英, *Wan Qing wenyi baokan shulüe* 晚清文藝報刊述略 (Brief account of late Qing literary journals and newspapers), Gudian wenxue, 1958.

7. *Zhongguo jindai qikan pianmu huilu* 中國近代期刊篇目匯錄 (Collected tables of contents of modern Chinese periodicals), Shangtu, ed., 6 vols., 1965–84. A useful reference; it gives the tables of contents of 495 Chinese periodicals and magazines published in Chinese between 1857 and 1918. Arranged chronologically. No index.

50.8.6 Foreign-Language China-Coast Periodicals

The first foreign-language China-coast newspaper was published in Portuguese, *A Abelha da Chine* (*Mifeng huabao* 蜜蜂華報), Antonio Frey, ed., Macao, 1822–23. In 1824, the name was changed to *Gazeta de Macao* (*Aomen bao* 澳門報), 1824–26. The first English-language periodical was the *Canton Register* (Canton, 1827–43). It was followed by the *Canton General Price Current*, Guangzhou, 1833; Macao, 1839. In 1843 it moved to Hong Kong (with the new name *Hong Kong Register*, enlarged to *The Overland Register and Price Current*, 1845–58). Some 16 similar English-language papers were published between 1840 and 1860 in Shanghai, Hong Kong, and Canton.

The first scholarly missionary journal was established in Canton: the *Chinese Repository* (1832–51). Its successor was the *Chinese Recorder* (1867–1941).[51] The most important and long lasting English-language newspaper was the *North China Herald*:

> *North China Herald* (*Beihua jiebao* 北華捷報), founded by Henry Shearman (d. 1856); weekly, Shanghai, 1850–1951; from 1864, daily with the title *North China Daily News* (*Zilin Xibao* 字林西報). The *North China Herald* was issued as a weekly supplement to the daily. Chinese version: *Shanghai xinbao* 上海新報 (1861–72), the first Chinese-language newspaper in Shanghai.

For a complete listing and evaluation of some 200 Western-language (mainly English) China-coast newspapers, see Frank H. H. King and Prescott Clark, *A Research Guide to China-Coast Newspapers, 1822–1911*, HUP, 1965. For a recent Chinese listing of the 136 main foreign-language newspapers issued between 1815 and 1911, including 67 English, 11 French, 3 German, 6 Portuguese, 20 Russian, and 28 Japanese ones, see Shi, 1991 (50.8.5), 372–88.

50.9   Archaeology

Plenty of monuments survive from the Qing. Many were first built in previous dynasties, but, like the Imperial Palace (Gugong 故宮) in Beijing, rebuilt or restored during the Qing. No attempt is made to list Qing monuments here. For Qing inscriptions, mainly of an economic or sociological nature, see 50.7.6. One of the best-preserved Qing provincial yamen is at Baoding, the capital of Zhili province (50.1); an unusually well-preserved and restored Qing county town in Shanxi, Pingyao 平遙 is introduced in 50.7.3.

Little remains of Qing Beijing with its walls within walls (the outer city enclosing the inner city, which in turn surrounded the imperial city with the palace at the center; see 49.4.2). To appreciate just how much has gone and how quickly, consult *In Search of Old*

---

[51] *The Chinese Recorder Index: A Guide to Christian Missions in Asia, 1867–1941*, Kathleen L. Lodwick, comp., 2 vols., Washington, Del.: Scholarly Resources Inc., 1986. For a list of Protestant journals in China, see Crouch, 1989 (29.7.3), 407–86.

Peking.[52] For photographs that capture some of the late Qing, early Republican atmosphere of the country and of the capital, including the imperial palace, see the works cited in 42.4.2. Other cities and monuments still carry some of the atmosphere of the Manchus—the palaces at Beijing and at Shengjing 盛京 (Shenyang) or at Rehe 熱河 (Chengde), for example.

The Qing emperors are buried in four places: the ancestors of Nurhaci at Yongling town 永陵鎮 in the Xinbin Manchu autonomous county 新賓滿族自治縣, Liaoning. This is 100 km (62 miles) due east of Shenyang in the heart of what was Jianzhou 建州 Jurchen territory. After the founding of the Qing, a 1,000 km (625 miles) road was built from the tombs to Beijing to enable the emperors to pay their respects to their ancestors. Five km (3 miles) west of Yongling are the vestiges of Hetu'ala 赫圖阿拉, the first capital established by Nurhaci; the tomb of Nurhaci himself is at the Fuling 福陵, east of Shenyang; Huang Taiji is buried at the Zhaoling 昭陵 in Shenyang. The Shunzhi, Kangxi, Qianlong, Xianfeng, and Tongzhi emperors are buried in the Eastern Qing tombs (Qing Dongling 清東陵) in Zunhua county 遵化縣, Hebei, about 125 km (78 miles) to the east of Beijing. The empress dowager, Cixi Taihou 慈禧太后, is also buried here. The Qing Dongling are the best preserved of all the Chinese imperial mausolea.

The Yongzheng, Jiaqing, Daoguang, and Guangxu emperors are buried at the Western Qing tombs (Qing Xiling 清西陵) about 120 km (75 miles) to the west of Beijing in Yi county 易縣, Hebei. The decision to be buried 250 km (156 miles) away from his father was made by the Yongzheng emperor. The Xiling are in a rustic setting and still preserve a certain splendor and are well worth the detour. They also contain the second largest echoing wall in China after that of the Temple of Heaven.

Illustrations

The fourth illustrated volume of the collections of the National Museum of Chinese History (*A Journey into China's Antiquity*) covers the Yuan, Ming, and Qing (see 8.1 on this authoritative illustrated series).

---

[52] L. C. Arlington and William Lewisohn, Vetch, Beiping, 1935; rpnt., HK: OUP, 1987 (with an introduction by Geremie Barmé).

50.10   Guides and Research Tools

50.10.1   Guides to Primary Sources

ECCP   Although a biographical dictionary (50.9.3), *ECCP* contains a great deal of information on a large number of the main works written or compiled during the Qing. There are detailed name, book title, and subject indexes.

Feng Erkang 馮爾康, *Qingshi shiliaoxue* 清史史料學 (The study of Qing historical sources), Taibei: Shangwu, 1993. Thorough introduction to most categories of Qing primary sources. Has an author-title index.

Lynne A. Struve, *The Ming-Qing Conflict, 1619–1683: A Historiography and Source Guide*, AAS Monograph 56, 1998. Full coverage of primary source materials in Chinese, Manchu, Japanese, Korean, and European languages.

Xie Guozhen 謝國楨, "Ming-Qing shiliao yanjiu" 明清史料研究 (Studies on Ming-Qing historical materials), in his *Ming Qing biji tancong* 明清筆記談叢 (Collection of notes on Ming-Qing miscellaneous notes), Zhonghua, 1962; Shanghai guji, 1981, 146–83. Provides a brief introduction to early Qing sources. In the rest of the work, he discusses 48 *biji*, of which 29 are from the Qing.

Du Weiyun 杜維運, *Qingdai shixue yu shijia* 清代史學與史家 (Qing historiography and historians), Dongda, 1984; Zhonghua, 1988.

Andrew J. Nathan, *Modern China, 1840–1972: An Introduction to Sources and Research Aids*, CCS, Univ. of Michigan, 1973.

Zhongguo jindaishi wenxian bibei shumu 中國近代史文獻必備書目 (Essential written sources for the history of modern China), Yao Zuoshou 姚佐綏 et al, comps., Zhonghua, 1996. Unannotated catalog of 5,600 published sources in Chinese for the period 1840 to 1919. Has both a title and a name index.

Zhongguo lishi da cidian 中國歷史大辭典 (The great encyclopaedia of Chinese history), 14 vols., Shanghai cishu, 1983– , has two volumes on the Qing: *Qingshi* 清史, vol. 1, Dai Yi 戴逸 and Luo Ming 羅明, eds.; vol. 2, Rong Mengyuan 榮孟源, ed., 1992. Vol. 1 contains just over 5,000 brief entries on the period 1644 to 1840; vol. 2 has the same number for the years 1840 to 1912. See 8.4.2 for comments.

Qing dynastic bibliographies are introduced in 9.4 and 9.5.

50.10.2 Documents

Introduction to Ch'ing Documents, Part One, Reading Documents: The Re-bellion of Zhong Rongjie, vol. 1, *Introduction, Vocabulary and Notes*; vol. 2, *Chinese Texts*, Philip Kuhn and John King Fairbank, eds., Fairbank Center, 1986; rev. edition, Harvard-Yenching, 1993. This republishes selected parts of the earlier now out-of-print *Ch'ing Documents: An Introductory Syllabus*, John King Fairbank, 1952; 3rd ed., rev. and enl., 2 vols., HUP, 1965; rpnt. with index, 1970.

Helen Dunstan, *Conflicting Counsels to Confuse the Age: A Documentary Study of Political Economy in Qing China, 1644–1840*, CCS, Univ. of Michigan, 1996. Carefully commented translation of 38 Qing docu-ments dealing with political economy, more especially the manage-ment of the grain supply in relation to the subsistence of the popula-tion. It is designed for undergraduate instruction, both on the se-lected topics and on the language of the documents translated (whose originals are not, however, included).

There are several important studies in English on the different types of documents in use in Qing government. See especially:

John K. Fairbank and Ssu-yü Teng, *Ch'ing Administration: Three Studies*, HUP, 1960.

Silas Wu, "The Memorial Systems of the Ch'ing Dynasty," *HJAS* (1967), 7–75.

Silas Wu, *Communication and Imperial Control in China: Evolution of the Palace Memorial System 1693–1735*, HUP, 1971.

Pei Huang, "The Confidential Memorial System of the Ch'ing Dynasty Reconsidered," *BSOAS* 57.2: 329–38 (1994).

50.10.3 Readers

The Search for Modern China: A Documentary Collection, Pei-kai Cheng and Michael Lestz with Jonathan D. Spence, comps., Norton, 1999. Translated passages from original sources many translated here for the first time. Organized under the same chapter headings as Jona-than D. Spence, *The Search for Modern China*, 2nd ed., Norton, 1999.

China's Response to the West: A Documentary Survey, 1839–1923, Ssu-yü Teng and John K. Fairbank, HUP, 1954; rev., 1963. See also the ac-companying *Research Guide for China's Response to the West: A Documentary Survey, 1839–1923*, HUP, 1954; 4th prnt., 1975.

50.10.4 Research Tools

Note that many reference works for modern Chinese history (*jindaishi* 近代史) cover both the late Qing (usually from 1840) and part of the Republic (usually to 1912-19, sometimes 1912-49). In such cases, depending on the emphasis, the reference is cited in full only in one Chapter (50 or 51) with a cross-reference in the other.

Dictionary

Shinmatsu Minshu monjo dokkai jiten, 清末民初文書讀解辞典 (Dictionary of documentary terminology used at the end of the Qing and beginning of the Republic), Yamakoshi Toshihiro 山腰敏寬, Kyûko, 1989. Contains definitions of some 4,900 terms and cites sources.

Ch'ing Administrative Terms: A Translation of The Terminology of the Six Boards with Explanatory Notes, E-tu Zen Sun (Ren Yidu 任以都, tr., HUP, 1961 (27.5).

Biographies

ECCP. Eminent Chinese of the Ch'ing Period, Arthur W. Hummel, ed., 2 vols., Washington, DC: Government Printing Office, 1943-44; SMC rpnt., 1991. *ECCP* includes authoritative biographies (many written by Fang Chaoying) of 800 leading officials, writers, and personalities active during the Qing. There are detailed name, book title, and subject indexes.

Biographical Dictionary of Chinese Women: The Qing Period, 1644-1911, Lily Xiao Hong Lee and Clara Lau, eds., Sharpe, 1998.

Qingdai zhuanji congkan suoyin 清代傳記叢刊索引 (Index to biographical collections of the Qing dynasty), Zhou Junfu 周駿富, 3 vols., Mingwen, 1986. Now the most complete index to Qing biographies. Indexes the *Qingdai zhuanji congkan* 清代傳記叢刊 (a collection of 150 separate Qing biographical collections reprinted under Zhou's editorship in 1985 in 202 vols.). The index gives citations to the names of 46,955 people compared to 27,000 in the *Sanshisan zhong Qingdai zhuanji zonghe yinde* 三十三種清代傳記綜合引得 (Combined indexes to 33 Qing dynasty biographical collections), *H-Y Index* 9, Beiping, 1932; 2nd ed., with corrections, Tôyô bunko, 1960.

Guoli gugong bowuyuan Qingdai wenxian zhuanbao zhuangao renming suoyin 國立故宮博物院清代文獻傳包傳稿人名索引 (Index of biographies and draft biographies in the Qing dynasty documentary archives in the National Palace Museum), Taibei: Gugong bowuyuan,

1982. Contains information on 15,000 people, of whom 5,000 are not covered in other Qing biographical collections.

Qingdai beizhuanwen tongjian 清代碑傳文通檢 (An index of Qing stele commemorative writings), Chen Naiqian 陳乃乾, comp., Shanghai: Zhonghua, 1959, 1999; pirated edition under the title *Qingren bieji qianzhong beizhuanwen yinde ji beizhuanzhu nianli pu* 清人別集千種碑傳文引得及碑傳主年里譜 (Index to 1,000 stele commemorative writings in Qing collected works with the dates of those with biographies), Taibei: Zhonghua wenhua shuyuan, 1965. This important index (mainly of *muzhiming*) supersedes the sections on commemorative writings in *Qingdai wenji pianmu fenlei suoyin* 清代文集篇目分類索引 (Subject index to tables of contents of Qing collected works), Wang Zhongmin 王重民 et al., comps., Guoli Beiping tushuguan, 1935; Zhonghua, 1965. Chen indexed more than twice as many collected works (altogether 1,025) and includes references to biographical materials on some 11,000 individuals, including those who died after 1644 or who were born before 1911. Dates are included.

Qingren shiming biecheng zihao suoyin 清人室名別稱字號索引 (Index to studio and alternative names of the Qing), Yang Tingfu 楊廷福 and Yang Tongfu 楊同甫, eds., 2 vols., Shanghai guji, 1988. Vol. 1 lists over 103,000 alternative names of 36,000 people. Vol. 2 is arranged by regular name and gives native place as well as alternative names. Arrangement in both parts is by stroke count.

Zhongguo jinxiandai renwu minghao da cidian 中國近現代人物名號大辭典, Chen Yutang 陳玉堂, ed., Zhejiang guji, 1993. Contains biographies of 10,112 people who lived between 1840 and 1949 with details of their literary names.

Hakki tsûshi retsuden sakuin 八旗通志列傳索引 (Index to the biographies in the gazetteer of the Eight Banners), Kanda Nobuo 神田信夫 et al., comps., Tôyô bunko, 1965.

Finally, note that at least 1,000 Qing *nianpu* are extant (about one quarter of the total from all periods). Use the standard *nianpu* index (Xie Wei, 1992, 3.8.4). There is no comprehensive index to the biographies in Qing gazetteers. Despite this lack, it is fairly easy to find the biography of a person since it is usually (but not invariably) included in the gazetteer of the county in which his family claimed its domicile. Note the curricula vitae of 55,883 officials (50.2.1–4).

Official Titles and Officeholders

The names of all holders of the *jinshi* degree in the Qing have been indexed in *Zengjiao Qingchao jinshi timingbei lu fu yinde* 增校清朝 進士題名碑錄附引得 (Index to the revised listing of stelae of Qing *jinshi* candidates), *H-Y Index*, Supplement 19. For well-indexed lists with the names of the 51,624 *jinshi* of the Ming and the Qing, see 25.3. On the examination system of the Qing, see Table 34, 25.3.

Qingdai zhiguan nianbiao 清代職官年表 (Chronological tables of office-holders in the Qing dynasty), Qian Shifu 錢實甫, ed., 4 vols., Zhong-hua, 1980, 1997. This massive work contains tables showing all of-ficeholders for 49 major posts. Useful both for biographical purposes and for understanding the functioning of the bureaucracy. There is a personal-name index starting from page 3,700.

Qingdai guanming biecheng 清代官名別稱 (Alternative forms of Qing official titles), Zhang Wode 張我德, ed., Renmin daxue, 1998.

Qingdai gedi jiangjun dutong dachen deng nianbiao 清代各地將軍都統大 臣等年表 (Chronological tables of generals, commanders-in-chief and senior officials in every province), Zhang Bofeng 章伯鋒 et al., comps., Zhonghua, 1965. Covers the years 1796–1911.

Qingdai daxueshi nianbiao 清代大學士年表 (The Grand Secretaries in Ch'ing China: A chronological list), Hung-ting Ku (Gu Hongting 古 鴻廷), CMC, 1980.

Qingji Zhongwai shiling nianbiao 清季中外使領年表 (50.2.6).

Present-Day Political Organization of China, H. S. Brunnert and V. V. Hagelstrom, comps.; revised by N. Th. Kolessoff; A. Beltchenko and E. E. Moran, trs., Kelly and Walsh, 1912; rpnt., Curzon, 2000. Based on *Da Qing huidian* 大清會典 (50.6.2). A useful supplement to *DOTIC* for the late Qing.

The Chinese Government: A Manual of Chinese Titles, Categorically Arrang-ed and Explained with an Index, W. F. Mayers, ed., Kelly and Walsh, 1897; rpnt., Ch'eng-wen, 1967. Based on the *Da Qing huidian*.

Zhongguo jindai guanzhi cidian 中國近代管制詞典 (Dictionary of mod-ern Chinese official titles), Qiu Yuanyou 邱遠猷, comp., Shumu wenxian, 1991. Covers late Qing, Taiping, Beiyang, etc. titles.

Geography

Zhongguo lishi dituji 中國歷史地圖集, vol. 8, *Qing shiqi* 清時期 (Qing); see 4.3.2 on this essential series.

Qingdai dili yan'ge biao 清代地理沿革表 (Tables of changing administrative units in the Qing period), Zhao Quancheng 趙泉澄, 1941; Shanghai: Zhonghua, 1955.

Chronology

Jindai Zhongguo shishi rizhi 近代中國史事日志 (Daily chronology of historical events in modern China), Guo Tingyi 郭廷以, comp., 3 vols., Zhengzhong, 1963; Zhonghua, 1987. Covers 1840–1911.

Modern China: A Chronology from 1842 to the Present, Colin Mackerras, with the assistance of Robert Chan, Thames and Hudson, 1982. For concordances, see 5.6.

Bibliographies of Secondary Scholarship

The bibliographical chapters and appendixes in the Qing volumes of the *CHC* are the best starting point, although some are already a shade out-of-date. See also the works listed at 42.3 and the biblliographies of Japanese scholarship in 51.11.

Qingshi lunwen suoyin 清史論文索引 (Index to articles on Qing history), Lishisuo and Zhongguo renmin daxue Lishixi, comps., Zhonghua, 1984. Covers articles written between 1900 and 1981 on the period 1644 to 1840. Taiwan and Hong Kong articles and books are included from 1949 onward. 24,000 articles are indexed.

Societies and Journals

Late Imperial China (*LIC*: began in 1965 under the title *Ch'ing-shih wen-t'i*; adopted present title in 1985, semiannual), Society for Qing Studies. Contains translations of *Shigaku zasshi* May issue review of Ming-Qing studies in Japan.

Qingshi luncong 清史論叢 (1979– , annual), Shekeyuan, Qingshi yanjiushi 清史研究室.

Qingshi yanjiu 清史研究 (1991– quarterly), Zhongguo renmin daxue Qingshi yanjiusuo 中國人民大學清史研究所; previous title, *Qingshi yanjiu tongxun* 清史研究通訊, 1981– .

51

The Republic

1912–1949

More historical sources survive from the 37 years of the Republic than from the preceding 3,000 years of Chinese recorded history. Proximity in time is the obvious reason. But the other main one is the development of a modern printing and publishing industry. It produced large enough print runs to ensure, for example, that copies of most of the 125,000 books that were published during the Republic have survived. The presses also made possible the production of much larger quantities of relatively new types of sources, notably print journalism. Newspapers (and periodicals) recorded events at both the national and the local levels in an abundance and quality which makes them one of the most important sources for the period. They were fed by a growing network of correspondents and agencies using the rapidly expanding telegraph system.

Proximity in time and modern techniques of recording have led to another new type of source—oral history. The recollections of many thousands of participants in national and local events are available. Even a few recordings of famous speakers have survived. Quantities of press and private photographs and cinema newsreels also from time to time provide an immediacy not found in the few carefully posed photographs that have survived from the late Qing.

Official documents burgeoned as never before. Not only because of a modern printing industry but also because throughout the Republic there were several governments and several political parties, each with its own printing press and archives. Many millions of documents, both central and local, have survived (for the first time they were no longer handwritten but printed).

Finally, foreign governments and foreign nationals became directly involved in Chinese affairs during the Republic on a much larger scale than ever before. They kept records of their work and analyses of events, which have survived in great quantities.

Much of the existing published material was produced in a highly politicized atmosphere to support various conflicting political positions all of which had in common the myth that the history of the Republic was an epic struggle between political parties or factions, each led by an omniscient leader. As the Republic fades further into the past and survivors record their memories of the reality they lived through rather than repeating the party line, official interpretations of the era in vogue up to the 1980s appear simplistic and dated. The fading of old sensitivities will no doubt lead to the further easing of access to archives still closed today. Coupled with the declining cost of publishing by using techniques such as CD-ROM, the volume of original sources to back new interpretations will no doubt greatly increase.

It is not the purpose of this chapter to attempt to list individual works falling into the different categories of extant primary sources. That would require a separate manual or annotated history. The aim is rather to provide a sampling of the different types of sources available and of the main reference tools for their use.[1] The sources could be presented in many different ways: by major events, for example, or by periods, political parties, political figures, intellectual leaders and creative writers, trends, or types—

> *events*: 1911 Revolution (October 10), May Fourth Movement (1919), Northern Expedition (1926–28), Long March (1934–35), Xi'an Incident (December 12, 1936), Marco Polo Bridge Incident (July 7, 1937). . . .

---

[1] Among the works that I found most useful in preparing this chapter was Andrew J. Nathan, *Modern China, 1840–1972: An Introduction to Sources and Research Aids*, CCS, Univ. of Michigan, 1973 (it and other guides are briefly listed in 51.14.1); *Zhongguo tongshi* 中國通史, Bai Shouyi 白壽彝, general editor, Shanghai renmin, 1986–99, vol. 21 (see 43.2 on this series); the *CHC* volumes on the Republic (12 and 13) and on the People's Republic (14 and 15) remain an important reference. They were, however, written in the late 1970s, early 1980s and therefore can be usefully updated by more recent surveys such as that contained in the special issue of *The China Quarterly* entitled *Reappraising Republican China*, CQ 150: 255–458 (1997).

political periods: early Republic (1912–16), Warlord era (1916–28), Nanking decade (1927–37), Jiangxi Soviet period of CCP (1931–34), Yan'an period of CCP (1936–47), Manchukuo (1932–45), Anti-Japanese war (1937–45), civil war (1945–49). . . .

armies and political movements: the military, the GMD (KMT), the CCP, and third parties. . . .

warlords: Wu Peifu 吳佩孚 (1874–1939), Yan Xishan 閻錫山 (1883–1960), Feng Yuxiang 馮玉祥 (1882–1948), Zhang Zuolin 張作霖 (1875–1928). . . .

political figures: Sun Yatsen 孫逸仙 (1866–1925), Yuan Shikai 袁世凱 (1859–1916), Jiang Jieshi 蔣介石 (1887–1975), Wang Jingwei 汪精衛 (1883–1944), Mao Zedong 毛澤東 (1893–1976). . . .

intellectual leaders and creative writers: Cai Yuanpei 蔡元培 (1868–1940), Chen Duxiu 陳獨秀 (1879–1942), Li Dazhao 李大釗 (1888–1927), Hu Shi 胡適 (1891–1962), Lu Xun 魯迅 (1881–1936), Guo Moruo 郭沫若 (1892–1978), Ba Jin 巴金 (1904–), Ding Ling 丁玲 (1904–86), Shen Yanbing 深雁冰 (Mao Dun 茅盾, 1896–1981). . . .

economic, social, and cultural trends: demography, economic development, the rise of an urban middle class, the rise of industrial manufacturing, the role of the military, the labor movement, the women's movement, changes in philosophical and political thinking, the introduction of modern science, technology, and medicine; experimentation with new styles of writing, painting, and music; the adoption of Western lifestyles. . . .

types: archival documents, books, newspapers and periodicals, oral histories, biographies, creative literature, foreign archives, and eyewitness accounts. . . .

This chapter is divided both by type of source and by subject. The 14 sections of the chapter are indexed on the following page.

Index to Chapter 51

Many other sections of the manual touch on other sources relating to the Republic, for example,

calendar (5.4.3)
foreign eyewitness accounts (42.3)
law (27.7)
local gazetteers (3.8.3 and 4.6)
population (7.2.4)
weights and measures (7.3)
women's studies (39.3.3)

A full listing of such references may be found in the subject index under "Republic."

Note the translation conventions used here and throughout the manual:

jindaishi 近代史 (modern history; from 1840 to 1919, or, according to others, 1911)

xiandaishi 現代史 (modern history; from 1919 to 1949, or from 1912 to post-1949)

dangdaishi 當代史 (contemporary history; from 1949 to present)

It is unlikely that these demarcations will hold much longer. For example, 1949 is beginning to look too remote to be regarded as ushering in the "contemporary."

On the transliteration conventions followed in the manual for names such as Sun Yatsen, see *Conventions* on page xix and individual entries in the name index.

51.1   Archives

51.1.1   Guides to Archives

Chinese Archives: An Introductory Guide, Ye Wa and Joseph W. Esherick, eds., China Research Monograph 45, Institute of Asian Studies, CCS, UCP, 1996. The authors describe the main archives in China and in Taiwan. They provide notes on the holdings of about 600 local archives in China (out of a total of 3,500). Invaluable.

State and Economy in Republican China: A Handbook for Scholars, 2000 (51.14.1). Part 2 contains an introduction to the main archives for economic and business history, namely, Ershiguan; the municipal archives of Beijing, Shanghai, Suzhou, Nantong, Chongqing, and Tianjin; the provincial archives of Jiangsu and Sichuan; the Shanghai Association of Industry and Commerce archives and other collections in Shanghai; other collections in Suzhou, Tianjin and Nantong; and in Taiwan, in addition to the collections listed in 51.1.3, the Taiwan Historical Materials Commission and the Taiwan Provincial Legislature Library. Invaluable.

Zhongguo dang'anguan minglu 中國檔案館名錄 (Directory of Chinese archives), Dang'an, 1990, lists central and local archives addresses.

Taiwan suocang Zhonghua minguo jingji dang'an 臺灣所藏中華民國經濟檔案 (Holdings of Republican period economic archives in Taiwan), Lin Manhong 林滿宏, ed., Jinshisuo, 1995.

51.1.2   Most Important National Archives

There is no single national archive in China. Nor is there even a single archive for modern history. Archives of different periods and different governments and organs are housed separately. These are in turn partly split between those in China and those in Taiwan. The main archives containing central government documents of the Republican period, only began to be open to researchers in the 1980s, and they are not yet all open. Prior to that, selections of documents from the archives on special subjects were published, and this practice continues. Given the often enormous quantities of documents, such collections of printed archival sources retain their usefulness (51.1.4). The main archives containing post-1912 central government documents are:

Zhongguo di'er lishi dang'anguan 中國第二歷史檔案館 (Second Historical Archives of China), Nanjing (the present name dates from 1964); Ershiguan 二史館 for short. Housed in the building of the GMD Party History Commission. Acquired the archives of the Guangzhou, Chongqing, and Beiyang governments and those parts of the GMD national history office and Party history committee archival holdings not taken to Taiwan by the GMD. Contains 1.8 million files in 900 *quanzong* (in 1985 the number of *quanzong* was 756 containing 1.4 million files). There is no published catalog of the files. The partially completed computer catalog is not open to researchers. See *Zhongguo di'er lishi dang'anguan zhinan* 中國第二歷史檔案館指南 (Guide to the Second Historical Archives of China), detailed edition (*xiangben* 詳本), Ershiguan, ed., Dang'an, 1994. This replaces the brief guide published by the archives in 1987 (whose contents are summarized in Wa and Esherick, 1996 [51.1.1], 45–51). The detailed guide has separate chapters on the main *quanzong*. It also has a name index and an institutional index. The Ershiguan edits and publishes documentary collections based on its holdings (51.1.4) and since 1985 has produced the quarterly journal *Minguo dang'an* 民國檔案. From time to time the Ershiguan publishes catalogs of publications, including photo-offset reprints and microfilms of its archival holdings.

Quanguo Minguo dang'an mulu zhongxin 全國民國檔案目錄中心 (National Catalog Center for Republican Archives). Based at the Ershiguan. Has begun to publish national indexes of Republican documents.

Zhongyang dang'anguan 中央檔案館 (Central Archives), Beijing. The present name dates from 1959. The official archives of the Chinese Communist Party (CCP). Situated about 30 km (20 miles) from Beijing at the foot of the Western Hills, the archives hold 660,000 files (containing eight million documents) of the Central Committee of the CCP and central government organs of the PRC, including 8,500 recordings. The time span covers from just before the May Fourth Movement to about 20 years before the present day (contemporary CCP documents are held in the archives of the CCP secretariat for 20 years before transferal to the Central Archives). Some 1.2 million documents have been put on computer index and the indexing continues. There are about 400,000 pre-1949 documents in the archives. Mao's library at the time of his death is still stacked on the shelves he used for them in Yan'an and in Zhongnanhai. The originals of all his known writings (30,000 documents) are also stored here. A considerable amount of the documents are written on poor-quality paper. Many of these have been microfilmed or put onto microfiches for long-term storage. The archives have published about 60 volumes of historical documents and three CDs of recordings of Mao, Zhou, and Deng (the earliest dates from 1949). The archives are not open to foreigners; approved Chinese research workers may have limited access to copies of original materials. The archives provide consultation services on those documents which are not restricted and catalog retrieval (access to the catalog is not granted). The fullest available description of the archives is in *Zhongyang dang'anguan jianjie* 中央檔案館簡介 (Concise introduction to the Central Archives), which was published for internal use in 1989. This has been translated in *CCP Research Newsletter* 8: 29–45 (1991) and is summarized in Wa and Esherick, 52–56.

Zhongyang dang'anguan guancang geming lishi ziliao zuozhe pianming suoyin 中央檔案館館藏革命歷史資料作者篇名索引 (Author index to materials on the history of the revolution in the Central Archives), 7 vols., Zhongyang dang'anguan, 1990–92.

Zhongguo renmin jiefangjun dang'an 中國人民解放軍檔案館 (Archives of the PLA), Beijing. Contains army archives from before 1949. See Wa and Esherick, 58.

Zhongguo zhaopian dang'anguan 中國照片檔案館 (Photography archives of China), Beijing. Includes a section containing photographs from 1832 to 1949. Computer cataloged. Open access.

Local Archives

There are extensive holdings of Republican era documents in city and county archives all over China. The best starting points are Kirby et al. (2000) and Wa and Esherick (1996). Since more and more local archives maintain web sites, it is worth checking the internet.

51.1.3   Archives in Taiwan

Guoshiguan 國史館 (Academia Historica). Main repository of Republican period documents in Taiwan. Established in 1947. Holds over five million items, including more than one million Ministry of Finance documents (1912–48); also more than 60,000 photographs. For holdings, see *Guoshiguan xiancang guojia dang'an gaishu* 國史館現藏 國家檔案概述 (Overview of national archives held at the Guoshiguan), Guoshiguan, 1996. Has a large document reprint series, including one of biographical materials and another covering events. For titles, see current edition of Guoshiguan, *Chuban mulu* 出版目錄 (Publications catalog). Apart from the Nationalist government archives (1925–48), the holdings include the archives of most of the central government ministries from the 1920s through the 1940s, Taiwan provincial, county and city archives.

Zhongguo Guomindang zhongyang weiyuanhui dangshi shiliao bianzuan weiyuanhui 中國國民黨中央委員會黨史史料編纂委員會 (Historical Commission of the GMD; Dangshihui 黨史會 for short). Contains 450,000 KMT documents, many of which are originals. Wa and Esherick (1996) suggest that the Dangshihui contains the world's largest collection of Republican era newspapers. There is an incomplete catalog of the Dangshihui and of the Jinshisuo's foreign affairs archives (which now have a full catalog; see under Jinshisuo). The title of the old catalog is

Zhongguo xiandaishi ziliao diaocha mulu 中國現代史資料調查目錄 (Check list of source materials on contemporary Chinese history), 11 vols., Jinshisuo, 1968–69.

Zhongguo xiandaishi ziliao diaocha mulu zongmu 中國現代史資料調查目錄總目 (Table of contents of *Checklist of Source Materials on Contemporary Chinese History*), CCRM, 1971.

Zhongyang yanjiuyuan Jindaishi yanjiusuo 中央研究員近代史研究所 (Institute of Modern History, Academia Sinica; Jinshisuo 近史所 for short). Holds part of the pre-1927 archives of the Ministry of Foreign Affairs of the Republic of China. These include a small number of Zongli yamen 總理衙門 (1861–1901) and Waiwubu 外務部 (1901–11) archives and also some of those of the Waijiaobu 外交部 (1912–26).

Waijiao dang'an hanmu huibian 外交檔案函目匯編 (Catalog of foreign affairs documents), Jinshisuo, vol. 2, *1912–1926*, 1991. For vol. 1 (covering 1861–1911), see 50.2.7. Since 1957, the Jinshisuo has been publishing selections from these two archives in the series *Zhongguo jindaishi ziliao huibian* 中國近代史資料匯編 (51.1.2).

The Jinshisuo also holds documents from various economics, agricultural and water control ministries and organs previously held by the Economics Ministry (*Jingjibu* 經濟部). Those documents (dated 1903–37) are mainly from the Nanjing decade. For catalogs, see

Jingji dang'an hanmu huibian 經濟檔案函目匯編 (Catalog of economic documents), Jinshisuo, vol., 1, 1987; vol. 2, *Ministry of Economic Affairs, 1938–48*; *National Resource Committee, 1936–52*, 1993; vol. 3, *Water Conservancy, 1934–48*; *Agriculture and Forestry, 1940–49*; *Salt, 1670s–1950s*, 1994.

Sifabu diaochaju 司法部調查局 (Bureau of Investigation of the Ministry of Justice), Taibei. Includes an important collection on CCP history; see *Chinese Communist Materials at the Bureau of Investigation Archives, Taiwan*, Peter Donovan et al., comps., CCS, Michigan, 1976.

Daxi dang'an 大溪檔案. Jiang Jieshi's personal archives. Contains a huge number of documents covering the years 1923 to 1952. Now open as the Presidential Archives.

See 51.10 for the archival holdings of Taiwan collections on Taiwan history in the twentieth century and 51.11.1 for Japanese sources on the period 1905–45.

51.1.4   Published Archival and Other Source Materials

Source materials are published in many different forms in China. Most basic (and often the most useful) are the meticulously edited collections of archival documents, which are published in complete runs for a particular archive class, period, or topic, often in the form of a multivolume series or collectanea (*huibian* 匯編, *congkan* 叢刊, *congshu* 叢書). Sometimes the editing consists of annotations and various indexes, although the latter is still comparatively rare. The documents may be photo-offset or typeset and punctuated. For a "dictionary" of publications from the archives, see:

Zhongguo dang'an wenxian cidian 中國檔案文獻辭典, 1994 (Box 6, Chapter 20). It includes annotations on over 1,600 documentary collections (published either during the Republic or in China and Taiwan between 1949 and the end of 1990).

Some examples of the huge variety of published sources from Republican era archives of all kinds at both national, provincial, municipal, and local levels are given below and also in many of the other sections of the chapter, notably, 51.4, 51.7–9, and 51.12.

Another type of collection or series consists of general historical source materials (. . . *shi ziliao* 史資料, *shiliao* 史料). These may be archival materials (*dang'an ziliao* 檔案資料) or published contemporary sources. Such collections vary enormously in quality depending on their compiler's intentions (usually expressed either in the preface or in the afterword). Sometimes the net is cast wide, sometimes, less so: and the intent is to make a special point or support an already drawn conclusion. Often the collections published in China in the 1950s and 1960s are national in coverage and arranged by themes intended to teach a particular lesson. The sound of axes grinding is rarely less than overwhelming. From the 1970s collections became more sophisticated, regional, local, precise, and useful.

Selected source materials are usually indicated as such in the title with a phrase like *xuanbian* 選編, *xuanji* 選集, or *xuanji* 選輯.

Source materials are often published in collectanea or series (*huibian* 匯編, *congkan* 叢刊, *congshu* 叢書), some of which contain several thousand volumes. These may simply be reprints of books, for example, of the Republican period, or they may be selected from hundreds of different sources. In either case they can be very useful. A tiny sample of collectanea containing Republican sources is listed below:

Zhongguo jindaishi ziliao congkan 中國近代史資料叢刊 (Collectanea of materials on modern Chinese history), Zhongguo shixuehui, ed.,

Shenzhou guogang; Xin zhishi; Shanghai renmin, eleven titles in 64 vols., 1951–79. This series helped kick-start the study of nineteenth and early twentieth-century history by making widely available archival and other sources on eleven key events, uprisings, wars, or movements (reference is made to seven of the eleven titles in sections 28.2–3 and 50.2.7). There is an index to the series: *Zhongguo jindaishi ziliao congkan suoyin* 中國近代史資料叢刊索引 (Index to collectanea of materials on modern Chinese history), Renmin daxue tushuguan, ed., 2 vols., 1983. Some titles in the series have been superseded by better selected, more detailed, or more comprehensive documentary collections. Many of these are referred to in the appropriate section of the manual.

Zhongguo jindaishi ziliao huibian 中國近代史資料匯編 (Collection of materials on modern Chinese history), Jinshisuo, 1957– . Unlike the previous item, all the volumes in this long-lasting series contain archival documents (from the Jinshisuo holdings; see 51.1.3). More than 30 titles in over 130 volumes were published between 1957 and 1998. Reference is made to many of the titles in this series in the appropriate section.

Jindaishi ziliao 近代史資料 (1954–61, semiannual; 1961– , quarterly), Jindaisuo, ed., Kexue, 1954–61; Zhonghua, 1962–81; Shehui kexue, 1981– . Reprint series of primary sources on modern history.

Jindai Zhongguo shiliao congkan 近代中國史料叢刊 (Collectanea of materials on modern Chinese history), Shen Yunlong 深雲龍, ed. in chief, 1,278 vols., Wenhai, 1966–73. Reprints of mainly late Qing, early Republican source materials.

Jindai Zhongguo shiliao congkan xubian 近代中國史料叢刊續編 (Collectanea of materials on modern Chinese history: continuation), Shen Yunlong 深雲龍, ed. in chief, 1,000 vols., Wenhai, 1974–82.

Jindai Zhongguo shiliao congkan sanbian 近代中國史料叢刊三編 (Third collectanea of materials on modern Chinese history), Shen Yunlong 深雲龍, ed. in chief, 1,006 vols., Wenhai, 1979–86.

Zhonghua minguo ziliao conggao 中華民國資料叢稿 (Draft series of historical materials on the Republic of China), Lishisuo, ed., Zhonghua, 1974– . Zhonghua has published a large number of titles in this reprint and translation series.

Minguo congshu 民國叢書 (Republican collectanea), Zhou Gucheng 周古城, ed. in chief, 500 vols. in five collections, Shanghai shudian, 1989–99. Contains reprints of 1,500 titles written and published during the Republic. Three further collections of 100 vols. each are planned.

51.2 *Books*

Proximity in time and the introduction of modern techniques of printing have ensured that many more books are extant from the 37 years of the Republican period than from the previous 3,000 years of Chinese recorded history:

Number of Extant Books

All of Chinese history to 1890s:	50,000 (approx)
1912–49 (the 37 years of the Republic):	125,000
1950–87 (first 37 years of the People's Republic):	1,236,000

The two most important publishers of the Republican period were the Shangwu yinshuguan 商務印書館 (The Commercial Press, 1897–) and the Zhonghua shuju 中華書局 (The Chung Hwa Book Company, 1912–). Both began in Shanghai and quickly became rivals. Between them they published over 16 percent of the 125,000 books published during the Republican period. The Commercial Press began as a printshop for commercial stationery (hence the name). In 1902, the company established editing, printing, and distribution functions, which it combined under one roof (the model was the American Presbyterian Mission Press; see 18.5). It thus became the first modern Chinese publishing house. Many others quickly followed the same "three-in-one" model.[2]

Minguo shiqi zong shumu 民國時期總書目 (Comprehensive catalog of Republican period books), Beijing tushuguan, ed., 21 vols., Shumu wenxian, 1991–97. Lists over 124,000 books published between 1911 and October 1949. This represents about 90 percent of all books published in the Republican period. Archaeology, history, geography, and biography are covered in two volumes. They contain a total of 11,029 titles on these subjects. There is a *pinyin* index.

---

[2] The Commercial Press published 15,116 titles in 28,058 volumes (not counting titles in its collectanea) between 1902 and 1950; see *Shangwu yinshuguan tushu mulu (1897–1949)* 商務印書館圖書目錄 (Catalog of Commercial Press books, 1897–1949), Shangwu, 1981. Note also the study by Jean-Pierre Drège, *Le Commercial Press de Shanghai*, Collège de France, 1978. The Zhonghua shuju published over 5,700 titles (not counting titles in its collectanea) between 1912 and 1949; see *Zhonghua shuju tushu zongmu (1912–1949)* 中華書局 圖書總目 (Comprehensive catalog of Zhonghua shuju books, 1912–49), Zhonghua, 1987.

Kang Ri zhanzheng shiqi chuban tushu lianhe mulu 抗日戰爭時期出版圖書聯合目錄 (Union catalog of books published during the period of the war against Japan), Chi Chunyang 赤春陽, ed. in chief, Sichuan daxue, 1992. Lists 28,000 *"kangzhanben"* 抗戰本 titles published between 1937.7 and 1949.9. Does not include string-bound books, children's comics, periodicals, or individual titles in collectanea.

Jiefangqu genjudi tushu mulu 解放區根據地圖書目錄 (Catalog of books in the liberated base areas), Zhongguo renmin daxue tushuguan 中國人民大學圖書館, ed., Renmin daxue, 1989. Publications in the base areas between 1937 and 1949.

Zhongguo jindai xiandai congshu mulu 中國近代現代叢書目錄 (9.6).

51.3 *Newspapers and Periodicals*

Newspapers are one of the prime sources for the history of the Republic because they record on a daily basis the political and social views having the most impact at the time. New telegraph and telephone networks now linked Chinese cities together and with the outside world, giving greater immediacy and efficiency in news reporting than had previously been possible. New printing presses were introduced, enabling single editions of up to 150,000 to be run off in a single day. Editorial bias needs to be taken into account; as Andrew Nathan well puts it, Republican newspapers "enjoyed a free and rather gossipy atmosphere . . .; they provide rich resources on political and military history, social (especially urban) change, finance, banking, and the history of journalism itself. They need, of course, to be read with due attention to problems of accuracy caused by a rumor-laden atmosphere and most newspapers' adherence to one or other political group. Nor do newspapers provide the inside view of political events that can sometimes be gained from private and government archives when these are available" (Nathan, 1973, 33).

There were about 125 newspapers in 1901; the 1911 Revolution stimulated the founding of many new ones—by 1913, there were 495; following closures by the government of Yuan Shikai, the number dropped to 130. By the next year, the numbers had risen again to 500. After the May Fourth Movement, many hundreds more started up. By 1921, there was an estimated national total of 1,137 (of which just under half were daily newspapers). For a general introduction, see Lee-hsia Hsu Ting, *Government Control of the Press in Modern China, 1900–1949*, HUP, 1974. For the early history of newspapers in China, see 26.4 (Tang to Qing), 50.8 (late Qing), 18.5 (introduction of new printing techniques), and 51.3.5 for reference works to help find Republican period newspapers.

51.3.1   Main Periodicals Published During the Republic

Periodicals flourished in the Republic. *Minbao* 民報 (Chinese privately owned and managed papers) took the lead. New types of *guanbao* 官報 (official gazettes) reflecting new organizations came into being, such as *jiguan bao* 機關報 (institutional periodicals), for example, those of political parties (*dangbao* 黨報), and *zhuanye bao* 專業報 (professional journals). *Waibao* 外報 (foreign periodicals) continued to thrive. Learned journals (*xuebao* 學報) appeared for the first time. The following is a select list of 50 out of the several thousand periodicals published during the Republic (academic and professional journals are treated separately in 51.3.7).[3] Titles are listed under each of four periods depending on their date of first publication. Within each period the order is alphabetic. The four periods are: pre-1912 (only those periodicals which continued during most of the Republican period); 1912–26, 1927–37, and 1938–49. When a periodical carried a foreign name on its masthead this is shown in brackets in italics after the Chinese name. Note that Shanghai continued to be the center of the modern printing, publishing, and newspaper industry in China:

Shanghai xinwenshi (1850–1949) 上海新聞史, *1850–1949* (The history of Shanghai newspapers, 1850–1949), Ma Guangren 馬光仁, ed. in chief, Fudan daxue, 1996. There is a chronology (pp. 1097–141) but this hardly makes up for the lack of an index to this important work.

Founded Pre-1912

Dagong bao 大公報 (*L'Impartial*), Tianjin, 1902–66. Edited at various times in Shanghai, Hankou, Hong Kong, Guilin, and Chongqing; after 1949, in Shanghai up to 1966. The Hong Kong *Daogong bao* is still in business. Important source on the 1920s and 1930s.

Dongfang zazhi 東方雜志 (*Eastern Miscellany*), Shangwu, Shanghai, 1904–48. Longest-running large-scale, general periodical. Monthly for the first 16 years, thereafter, bimonthly. Reprinted by Taiwan Shangwu,

---

[3] The selection of the Communist titles in the list is based on the one in Tony Saich, 1996 (51.9.2).

1976, with a combined index to the original 44 volumes and the six volumes which appeared in Taiwan, 1948–54. For tables of contents (1904–48), see *Dongfang zazhi zongmu* 東方雜志總目, Sanlian, 1957, 1980.

Huazi ribao 華字日報, Hong Kong, 1872–1941 (50.8.3).

Manshû nichinichi shimbun 滿洲日日新聞 (*Manchuria Daily News*), Dairen and Shenyang, 1907–45. The most influential Japanese newspaper in Manchuria. Important source for the history of Manchuria; see Suleski, 51.11.3 (1994), 52.

Shenbao 申報 (*Shanghai Journal* or "*The Shun Pao*"), founded by the British entrepreneur Ernest Major (1830?–1908) in Shanghai. Issued 1872–1949. It became the most influential Shanghai paper and is often quoted as an "encyclopaedia" of modern Chinese history. By the early 1920s its circulation was 50,000; by the end of the decade, 100,000, and by the mid 1930s, 150,000. For an index, see *Shenbao suoyin* 申報索引 (1872.4–1949.5), Shanghai shudian, 1988. On the beginnings of the paper, see 50.8.3.

Shibao 時報 (*Eastern Times*), Shanghai, 1904–39 (50.8.3).

Shishi xinbao 時事新報 (*The China Times*), Shanghai, 1907.12–1949.5. Major rival of *Shenbao*. Famous *fukan*, *Xuedeng* 學燈 (51.3.2). Moved to Chongqing in 1937.

Shuntian shibao 順天時報, Beijing, 1901–30. In 1905, the paper's founder, Nakajima Masao 中島真雄, entrusted it to the office of the Japanese Minister in Beijing. Thereafter, the *Shuntian shibao* was taken to reflect Gaimushô views on China policy and events (it was therefore sometimes nicknamed the *Nitian shibao* 逆天時報, "Disobeying heaven times"). At its height 12,000 copies were printed. Nakajima went to Manchuria and there founded the *Manzhou ribao* 滿洲日報 and the *Shengjing shibao* 盛京時報 (1906–45); see Suleski, 1994 (51.11.3), 2.4.1. Nakajima later wrote his memoirs: *Tai-Shi kaikoroku* 對支回顧錄 (Memoirs about China), 2 vols., Tôa dôbunkai, 1936; rpnt., 1968 (Suleski, 1994 [51.11.3], 5.2.15).

Taiwan shibao 臺灣時報, Taibei, 1909–45; 11 CD-ROM, 1998; for index, see *Taiwan shibao zong mulu* 臺灣時報總目錄, 1997.

Xinwen bao 新聞報 (*The News*), Shanghai, 1893.2–1949.5. Largest circulation Shanghai paper.

Founded 1912–26

Buersheweike 布爾什維克 (*The Bolshevik*). Shanghai, 1927.10–1932.7. Weekly organ of the CCPCC; changed to a bi-monthly and finally a monthly. An underground journal. 52 issues appeared.

Chenbao 晨報 (*Morning Post*), founded by the Jinbu dang 進步黨 (Progress Party) led by Liang Qichao 梁啓超, Beijing, 1916.8–1936 (up to 1918 called *Chenzhong bao* 晨鐘報). Influential in north China. Famous *fukan* (51.3.2).

Dangbao 黨報 (*The Party Paper*). The CCP's first internal party paper. It began publication in 1923.11 with an unspecified periodicity. It is unclear when it ceased publication, but one issue appeared in 1924.6.

Gongchandang 共產黨 (*The Communist*). The monthly publication of the first party group in Shanghai, 1920.11–1921.7.

Guowen zhoubao 國文周報 (*Kuo-wen Weekly, Illustrated*), Shanghai, 1924–37. For tables of contents, see *Guowen zhoubao zongmu* 國文周報總目, Sanlian, 1957, 1980.

Jiefang 解放 (*Liberation*), Yan'an, 1937.4–1941.5. Began as a weekly of the CCPCC; later changed to a bi-monthly. 134 issues were published.

Jingbao 京報 (*Peking Press*), founded by Shao Piaoping 邵飄萍 (1886–1926), Beijing, 1918.10 (ceased publication 1937.7). Famous *fukan* (51.3.2).

Laodongzhe 勞動者 (*Laborer*), Guangzhou, weekly, 1920.10–1921.1.

Litou 犁頭 (*The Plow*). Began publication in Canton on 1926.1.25 as the organ of the Guangdong Peasant Association. Initially, it was published every ten days but subsequently was changed to a weekly. The last issue (no. 23) was published on 1927.1.27. Generally pro-CCP.

Meizhou pinglun 每周評論 (*Weekly Review*), Beijing, 1918.12–1919.8.

Minguo ribao 民國日報 (*Min Kuo Yir Pao*), Shanghai, 1916.1–1931.12. In 1924, it was made the official GMD organ; then superseded by *Zhongyang ribao*. Famous *fukan* (51.3.2).

Qianfeng 前鋒 (*Vanguard*). Official organ of CCPCC. Secretly printed in Shanghai, 1923.7–1924.2. Only three issues were published.

Rexue ribao 熱血日報 founded by the CCP, Shanghai, 1925.6.4–6.27. First CCP daily newspaper.

Shenghuo (*Life*), Shanghai, 1925–33. Edited by Zou Taozhen 鄒韜奮. Circulation rose from 2,000 to 155,000, the record at the time (see under *Shenghuo ribao* in next subsection for some details on Zou).

Xiangdao 向導 (*The Guide*), CCP Central Committee weekly, Shanghai, 1922.9–1927.7. In all, 201 issues were published. At its height, more than 100,000 copies were printed.

Xianqu 先驅 (*The Pioneer*). 1922.1–1923.8. The fortnightly journal of the Youth League. There were many other periodicals for youth, e.g., *Zhongguo qingnian* 中國青年, 1923.10–1927.10.

Xin qingnian 新青年 (*La Jeunesse*). Launched in September 1915 in Shanghai, it had a major impact on progressive thinkers during the May Fourth Movement. Originally called *Qingnian zazhi* 青年雜志 (*Youth Magazine*), its name was changed in September 1916. From September 1920 it was operated as a publication of the Shanghai communist small group and became an organ of the CCP after its foundation. In July 1922 it temporarily stopped publication, reappearing in June 1923 as the party's theoretical organ. It ceased publication in July 1926 after five irregular issues, 1925–26.

Yishibao 益世報 (*Social Welfare*), founded by Frederick Lebbe (1877–1940), a Belgian Vincentian and naturalized Chinese citizen (he took the name Lei Mingyuan 雷鳴遠), Tianjin, 1915.10–1949.1; the paper moved to Kunming, Chongqing, Xi'an, Beiping, and Shanghai.

Zhongguo nongmin 中國農民 (*The Chinese Peasant*). 1926.1–1927.7. Published by the Central Peasant Department of the GMD. The general editor was Mao Zedong. In December 1926, it temporarily ceased publication but was revived briefly in Hankou in July 1927.

Zhongyang ribao 中央日報 (*The Central Daily News*), Hankou, 1927.3; Shanghai, 1927–29; Nanjing, 1931.2–1948; rpnt., Jiangsu guji, 60 vols., 1997. Official organ of the Guomindang 國民黨 (GMD) Central Committee. Continued publication in Taibei after 1949.

1928–37

Datong ribao 大同日報, founded in Manchukuo, Changchun, 1932.

Douzheng 斗爭 (*Struggle*). Organ of the Central Bureau of the CCP, weekly, 1933.2–1934.9. It was widely disseminated in the base areas.

Hongqi 紅旗, Shanghai, 1928.11–1930.8; amalgamated with the *Shanghai bao* 上海報 and called *Hongqi ribao* 紅旗日報 (see next item).

Hongqi ribao 紅旗日報 (*Red Flag Daily*). An organ of the CCPCC Shanghai, 1930.8. Starting on 1931.3.9, its name was changed to *Hongqi zhoubao* (see next item).

Hongqi zhoubao 紅旗周報 (*Red Flag Weekly*). The successor to the previous item, 1931.3–1934.3 (in August 1933, it became a bi-monthly). Because it was an underground publication, it often had a fake cover.

Hongse Zhonghua 紅色中華 (*Red China*). Ruijin 瑞金, Jiangxi, 1931.12–1934.10. Organ of the Central Soviet government. Rose to 40,000 copies per issue. After the evacuation of the base area, its publication effectively stopped; revived in the Shaan-Gan-Ning base area. From 1937.1.27, its name was changed to *Xin Zhonghua bao* 新中華報 (*New China*).

Jiuwang ribao 救亡日報 (*Jiuwang Daily*), Shanghai, 1937.8–1941.2.

Qunzhong 群眾 (*The Masses*). An open weekly CCP publication for the GMD-ruled areas and Hong Kong, Hankou (later Chongqing), 1937.12–1946. In June 1946, it began publication in Shanghai but was forced to stop by the GMD in 1947.3. In Hong Kong it was published as a weekly from 1947.1 until it voluntarily ceased publication in 1949.10.

Saodang bao 掃蕩報, Guomindang military, Nanchang, 1932.6; Hankou, 1934; Chongqing, 1938.10; Kunming, 1943. Changed name to *Heping ribao* 和平日報 in 1945.11. Moved to Taibei in 1949.9. Ceased publication in 1950.

Shenghuo ribao 生活日報 (*Life Daily News*), founded by Zou Taofen 鄒韜奮 (1895–1944), Hong Kong, 1936. Zou was founder of the Shenghuo shudian 生活書店 in Shanghai (1932), which later became one of the partners in the Sanlian shudian (Sanlian: Shenghuo. Dushu. Xinzhi sanlian chubanshe 生活.讀書.新知三聯出版社, 1945–).

Shibao 實報 (*Truth Post*), Beiping, 1928.10–1944.4. Printruns of up to 100,000 copies.

Shihua 實話 (*True Words*). The organ of the CC, it was set up in Shanghai in 1930.9. It was superseded by *Hongqi ribao* 紅旗日報 (*Red Flag Daily*).

Xin Zhonghuabao 新中華報 (*New China News*). A publication of the Central Soviet government published in Yan'an as a successor to *Hongse Zhonghua* 紅色中華 (*Red China*), it began publication on 1937.1.29 In 1939.1, it became a publication of the CCPCC, while continuing as a publication of the Shaan-Gan-Ning Border Region Government. It published a total of 230 issues, ending publication on 1941.5.15.

Xinyue 新月 (*New Crescent*), Shanghai, 1928–33.

Zhonghua ribao 中華日報, Shanghai, 1932.4–1937.11; restarted 1939.7–1945.8. Printruns of 50,000 copies. Newspaper of the Wang Jingwei 汪精衛 government.

1938–49

Balujun junzheng zazhi 八路軍軍政雜志 (Military and political journal of the Eighth Route Army), 1939.1–1942.3. Organ of the General Political Office of the Eighth Route Army.

Gongchandangren 共產黨人 (*The Communist*). Yan'an, 1939.10–1941.8. Internal CCP paper published nineteen times.

Jiefang ribao 解放日報 (*Liberation Daily*). Set up as a publication of the CCPCC, Yan'an, 1941.5. It was the major paper for the base areas, and many other publications were halted to allow concentration on it. Publication ended in 1947.3. There were altogether 2,130 issues. See Patricia Stranahan, *Molding the Medium: The Chinese Communist Party and the* Liberation Daily, Sharpe, 1991. For indexes, see *Jiefang ribao suoyin* 解放日報索引, Renmin ribao, 1956, and *Jiefang ribao renming suoyin* 解放日報人名索引, Shumu wenxian, 1983. The second index contains references to 9,000 Chinese and foreigners mentioned in the paper. Note there were several other papers with the same name.

Kangzhan ribao 抗戰日報, Changsha, 1938.

Renmin ribao 人民日報 (*People's Daily*). Started as the organ of the North China Bureau of the CCP, 1946.6, with the fusion of the *Jin-Cha-Ji ribao* 晋察冀日報 (*Jin-Cha-Ji Daily*) and the *People's Daily*, both published in the Jin-Ji-Lu-Yu base area. In 1949.3 publication was moved to Beijing, and in August it became the official organ of the CCPCC.

Xinhua ribao 新華日報 (*New China Daily*), CCPCC, Wuhan, 1938.1. Continued printing in various places until finally ceased in Chongqing in 1954.8; use *Xinhua ribao suoyin* 新華日報索引, Beijing tushu guan, 1963–64.

Xinmin bao 新民報, founded by the Xinminhui 新民會, Beijing, 1938.1–1944.4. Pro-Japanese.

51.3.2   Supplements

Many newspapers sought to attract readers with literary supplements. The four most famous of the May Fourth era were:

Chenbao fukan 晨報副刊 (1918–28; in 1921 the name was changed to *Chenbao fujuan* 晨報副鎸); photo-offset rpnt., Renmin, 1991.

Jingbao fukan 京報副刊 (1918–26, 1928–37)

Xuedeng 學燈 (*fukan* of *Shishi xinbao* 時事新報), 1918–47

Juewu 覺悟 (*fukan* of *Minguo ribao*), 1919–29

51.3.3   News Agencies

Zhongyang tongxunshe (gufen youxian gongci) 中央通訊社股份有限公司. Normally referred to as Zhongyangshe 中央社 (Central China News or CNA), 1924.4, Guangzhou; 1927.5 moved to Nanjing. The GMD news agency, 1927–49.

Xinhua tongxunshe 新華通訊社, CCP, 1931– .

Guoji xinwenshe 國際新聞社, 1937/38–49.

51.3.4   Journalist Associations

There were 10 main journalist associations active between 1912 and 1949. The three most important were

Beida xinwenxue yanjiuhui 北大新聞學研究會, 1918–20

Zhongguo zuoyi xinwenjizhe lianmeng 中國左翼新聞記者聯盟 (Jilian 記聯 for short), 1932–36

Zhongguo qingnian xinwenjizhe xuehui 中國青年新聞記者學會, 1937–49

51.3.5   References

Because of the many hundreds of titles, the clearest presentation of the history of Chinese newspapers is not in conventional book form but itemized, as found, for example, in the excellent volume in the great Chinese encyclopaedia on newspapers and publishing (item 1 below), or in dictionary form (item 2).

For the contents of the leading late-Qing, early Republican periodicals, consult item 3.

Items 4 and 5 are examples of introductions to the periodicals of specific periods, in this case those of the May Fourth era.

For union catalogs, see items 6 and 7. For finding lists of the important holdings of late Qing and Republican periodicals in Guotu and Shangtu, use items 8–10. Item 11 is a catalog of newspaper supplement holdings in the Shanghai Library.

Items 12–14 are indexes to selected groups of periodicals.

Item 15 is one example of the many reprint series available.

1. *Zhongguo da baike quanshu* 中國大百科全書 (The great Chinese encyclopaedia), *Xinwen chuban juan* 新聞出版卷 (Newspaper and publishing volume), Da baike quanshu, 1992; 3rd prnt., 1998. Excellent brief articles on the main periodicals, newspapers, magazines, editors, journalists, printers, and publishers, plus reproductions of the front

pages of all leading periodicals. A good starting point. There is a *pinyin* index, a Chinese-English glossary of standard printing terminology, and a chronology of main events in the development of Chinese newspapers and publishing. Coverage is worldwide.

2. *Zhongguo baokan cidian* 中國報刊詞典, 1815–1949 (Dictionary of the Chinese press), Wang Huilin 王檜林, Zhu Hanguo 朱漢國, eds. in chief, Shuhai, 1991. Gives brief annotations on all 3,707 *baokan* (newspapers and serials) founded between 1815 and 1949. The arrangement is chronological with a stroke-count index. In addition, there are short profiles of 357 prominent newspaper and periodical editors, owners, editorialists, and writers. A useful appendix gives pen names (Lu Xun [his best-known pseudonym] wins the prize with over 120).

3. *Zhongguo jindai qikan pianmu huilu* 中國近代期刊篇目匯錄 (Collected tables of contents of modern Chinese periodicals), Shangtu, ed., 3 parts in 6 vols., 1965–84. A most useful reference; it gives the tables of contents of 495 Chinese periodicals and magazines published in Chinese 1857–1918. Arranged chronologically. There is no index.

4. *Wusi shiqi qikan jieshao* 五四時期期刊介紹 (Introduction to periodicals of the May Fourth era), Zhonggong zhongyang Ma Lie Si zhuzuo pianyiju yanjiushi 中共中央馬恩列斯著作編譯局研究室 (Research room for the redaction and translation of the works of Marx, Lenin, and Stalin Bureau of the Central Committee), ed., 3 vols., Renmin, 1958–59, rpnt., Sanlian, 1979. Details of 240 May Fourth periodicals.

5. Tse-tung Chow, *Research Guide to the May Fourth Movement: Intellectual Revolution in Modern China*, HUP, 1963. Details of about 600 periodicals of the years 1915–23 in Part 1. Indexed.

6. *Quanguo Zhongwen qikan lianhe mulu 1833–1949 zengdingben* 全國中文期刊聯合目錄 *1833–1949* 增訂本 (Revised union catalog of Chinese periodicals, 1833–1949), 1961; rev. edition, Shumu wenxian, 1981. Catalogs 19,115 periodicals in 50 Chinese libraries (incl. in Taiwan). There is a *pinyin* index. A supplement was published in 1994 (see next item).

7. *Quanguo Zhongwen qikan lianhe mulu bubianben* 1833–1949 全國中文期刊聯合目錄補編本 (Supplement to the union catalog of Chinese periodicals, 1833–1949), Beijing tushuguan and Shanghai tushuguan, eds., Shumu wenxian, 1994. Contains an additional 16,400 titles.

8. *Beijing tushuguan guancang baozhi mulu* 北京圖書館館藏報紙目錄, (Catalog of newspaper holdings in the Peking Library), Shumu wen-

xian 1981. Provides holding information for some 1,800 Chinese and 1,000 foreign-language newspapers. Chinese-language titles are put into pre-1949 and post-1949 sections and then arranged by province. A separate section lists Hong Kong, Macao, and overseas Chinese titles, arranged by country. Foreign-language titles are arranged by country. Has stroke-count title indexes.

9. *Shanghai baokan tushuguan Zhongwen qikan mulu* 上海報刊圖書館中文期刊目錄 (Periodical and newspaper holdings of Shanghai newspaper and periodical library), 2 vols. Shanghai, 1956–57. Vol. 1, 1888–1949, 8,037 titles; vol. 2, 1949–56, 1,300 titles.

10. *Shanghai tushuguan guancang Zhongwen baozhi mulu (1862–1949)* 上海圖書館館藏中文報紙目錄 (Catalog of Chinese newspaper holdings in the Shanghai Library), Shanghai tushuguan, 1982. Catalogs 3,543 Chinese newspaper titles. There is a *pinyin* index to the first character of each title and an index of titles arranged by place of publication.

11. *Shanghai tushuguan guancang Zhongwen baozhi fukan mulu (1898–1949)* 上海圖書館館藏中文報紙復刊目錄 (Catalog of holdings of Chinese newspaper supplements in the Shanghai Library), Shanghai tushuguan, 1985. Companion volume to previous item. It catalogs 7,098 titles of supplements (special issues, magazine sections, photogravure sections, etc.) to over 1,400 newspapers. There is a *pinyin* index to the first character of the title as well as an index of titles arranged by subject and an index of titles arranged by the title of the newspaper in which the supplements appeared.

12. *Shijiu zhong yingyin geming qikan suoyin* 十九種影印革命期刊索引 (Index to 19 revolutionary periodicals), Renmin ribao Library, ed., Renmin ribao, 1959. Includes *Xin Qingnian*, *Meizhou pinglun*, etc.

13. *Ershiliu Zhong yingyin geming qikan suoyin* 二十六種影印革命期刊索引 (Index to 26 revolutionary periodicals), Zhongguo geming bowuguan 中國革命博物館, ed., Renmin ribao, 1988.

14. *Xinminzhu zhuyi geming shiqi yingyin geming qikan suoyin (Kang Ri zhanzheng shiqi)* 新民主主義革命時期影印革命期刊索引 (抗日戰爭時期), Dangxiao, 1987.

15. *Zhonghua minguo shiliao congshu* 中華民國史料叢編 (Collectanea of Republican period materials), Luo Jialun 羅家倫, Huang Jilu 黃季陸, and Qin Xiaoyi 秦孝儀, eds., Dangshi hui, 1968– . Reprint series of late Qing, early Republican periodicals.

51.3.6   Foreign-Language Newspapers

Numerous English and other foreign-language newspapers were published during the Republic, mainly in Shanghai, but also in other Chinese cities. Three of the most influential were:

North China Daily News, Shanghai, 1864–1951 (50.8.6)

North China Herald (*Beihua jiebao* 北華捷報), Shanghai, 1850–1951 (a weekly supplement to the above; see 50.8.6)

South China Morning Post (*Nanhua zaobao* 南華早報), Hong Kong. 1903.11– .

Manshû nichinichi shimbun 滿洲日日新聞 (51.3.1)

For a listing of 20 more English titles, see *CHC*, vol. 12, p. 834.

51.3.7   Learned Journals

There was a huge flowering of scholarship during the short period of the Republic between the removal of the imperial censor and before the imposition of new orthodoxies in 1949. This flowering was stimulated by the desire to reappraise the Chinese tradition in the light of modern ways of thinking and scientific approaches imported from the West. Much of the new thinking appeared in scholarly journals. These can be classified either as secondary sources (if they are used for their scholarship on earlier periods) or as primary sources (if they are used as an indication of the intellectual history of the Republican period or as sources on contemporary events). The leading scholarly journal was the *Shehui kexue zazhi* 社會科學雜志 (*Quarterly Review of Social Sciences*), Academia Sinica, 1930–37; rpnt., CCRM, 1969. For bibliographies of Republican learned journals, see Skinner and Hsieh, 1973; Howard, 1962; Sun and de Francis, 1952 (10.2.3). For some of the main professional journals, see 51.4.

51.3.8   Government Gazettes (gongbao 公報)

"Gazette" (*gongbao* 公報) was used in the British sense of an official publication containing announcements or bulletins. It could also contain "communications received and answers sent, reports made, decisions, regulations, proceedings of sessions, agenda, appointments and promotions" (Nathan, 1973, 49). For the translated table of contents of some early ones, see item 1 below. The *guanbao* 官報

of earlier centuries were similar, although they were intended for a much smaller readership (see 26.4 and 50.8.1). The main Republican national level *gongbao* were:

Government Gazettes of the Republic of China, 1912–1914: A Grand Table of Contents, CCRM, 1971.

Linshi gongbao 臨時公報 (Provisional gazette), Nanjing, 1912.2.13–1912.4.5; photo-offset, 8 vols., Jiangsu renmin.

Linshi zhengfu gongbao 臨時政府公報 (Gazette of the provisional government), Nanjing, 1912.1.29–1912.4.5; photo-offset, 12 vols., Jiangsu renmin.

Zhengfu gongbao 政府公報 (Gazette of the [Beiyang] government), Beijing, 1912.5.1–1928.6; photo-offset, 240 vols., Shanghai shudian.

Junzhengfu gongbao 軍政府公報 (Gazette of the revolutionary military government), Guangzhou, 1917.9.17–1918.5.14.

Lu haijun da yuanshuai da benying gongbao 陸海軍大元帥大本營公報 (Gazette of the headquarters of the marshal of the army and navy), Guilin, 1922.1–1926.6. Succeeded by next item.

Guomin zhengfu gongbao 國民政府公報 (Gazette of the National government), Guangzhou, 1925.7–1926.12; Nanjing, 1927.5–1937.11; Chongqing, 1937.11–1948.5; rpnt., 222 vols., Guoshiguan.

Many of the provinces, cities, and individual departments also issued *gongbao*, for example, the *Anhui gongbao* 安徽公報, 1912–48, *Shanghaishi zhengfu gongbao* 上海市政府公報 (irregular), or the *Caizheng gongbao* 財政公報, 1927.8–1937.6, Nanjing; *Caizhengbu gongbao* 財政部公報, Chongqing, 1940.1–1945.6.

For notes on 61 *gongbao*, see *Zhongguo dang'an wenxian cidian* 中國檔案文獻辭典, 1994 (Box 6, Chapter 20), 451–60.

51.4   Economic Sources and Statistics

The archives of the national government economic ministries and departments contain the most detailed statistics on the period. They have begun to be cataloged, and some have been published. They have not yet been fully exploited. Given the political unrest, it is hardly surprising that there are no reliable published statistical series for the Republic. Possibly the only exception are foreign trade statistics, at least up to the end of the 1930s. For Republican population statistics, such as they are, see 7.2.4.

51.4.1   Yearbooks, Annuals, Handbooks, and Directories

The first annual in China was published by the maritime customs. It appeared continuously for the better part of a century: *Haiguan Zhongwai maoyi niankan* 海關中外貿易年刊 (51.4.2).

Next to appear were state-of-the-country yearbooks compiled for treaty port readers. The most useful to the modern researcher is *The China Year Book*, H. G. W. Woodhead (1883–1959), ed., annual, 1912–39.[4] In addition to statistics and governmental profiles, each volume has a biographical section.

The leading Shanghai newspaper, *Shenbao* 申報, published a retrospective on its 50th anniversary in 1923 and thereafter, on an annual basis.

A leading Shanghai banking journal also began publishing a statistical annual in 1923:

Zhonghua minguo 12 nianfen jingji tongji 中華民國12年份經濟統記 (Economic statistics of the 12th year of the Republic), Shanghai yinhang zhoubaoshe, 1923. This annual was subsequently published in 1924, 1925, 1930, and 1931.

The Nationalist government itself began to publish a considerable number of yearbooks (*nianjian* 年鑑) and handbooks (*shouce* 手冊) during the Nanjing decade in the 1930s. As Nathan (1973) points out, they constitute a useful supplement to the government gazettes because they are more selective and compact. They were published by central government ministries, by provinces, and by cities.

China Handbook 1937–44, Chinese Ministry of Information, Chongqing, 1944; rpnt., Chengwen, 1971.

Shanghaishi nianjian 上海市年鑑 (*Greater Shanghai Annual*), Shanghaishi tongzhiguan, 1935, 1936, 1937.

Statistics of Shanghai (*Shanghaishi nianjian* 上海市年鑑), The Shanghai Civic Association, 1933.

Diyici Zhongguo jiaoyu nianjian 第一次中國教育年鑑 (First yearbook of Chinese education), 1934; rpnt., Zhuanji, 1971.

---

[4] Tianjin: Routledge, 1912–21; Tianjin: Tsientsin Press, 1921–30; Shanghai: The North China Daily News and Herald, 1931–39. Note no volumes of the *Year Book* were published for 1915, 1917–18, 1920, 1927, and 1937.

Di'erci Zhongguo jiaoyu nianjian 第二次中國教育年鑑 (Second yearbook of Chinese education), Shangwu, 1948.

Higher Education in China, n.d. (probably Nanjing, 1936).

Zhongguo shiyezhi 中國實業志 (Industrial gazetteers of China), Shiyebu 實業部, comp. and published, Shanghai, 1933–34. Separate volumes for each province. Only the volumes for Hunan (1935), Shandong (1934), Shanxi (1937), Jiangsu (1933), and Zhejiang (1933) were published.

Several yearbooks were published in Japanese in Tokyo, in Taiwan and in Manshûkoku:

Shina nenkan 支那年鑑 (China yearbook), Tôa dôbunkai, ed. and published, Tokyo, 1912, 1917, 1918, 1920, 1927, and 1942.

Man-Mô bunka nenkan 滿蒙文化年鑑 (Yearbook of Manchu-Mongolian culture), Man-Mô bunka kyôkai 滿蒙文化協會, ed., Dairen, 1923. Further volumes were published during 1932–45 (Suleski, 1994, 2.1.5).

The Manchuria Yearbook, Tôa keizai chôsa kyoku, ed. and published, 1931, 1932 (Suleski, 1994, 31–38).

51.4.2   Published Archival Material and Other Sources

The Imperial Maritime Customs published annual and decennial reports and also special series on subjects such as the cotton or silk trade. There were five decennial reports covering the years 1882–91, 1892–1901, 1902–11, 1912–1921, and 1922–31. The annual reports form a continuous series covering 90 years:

Haiguan Zhongwai maoyi niankan 海關中外貿易年刊 (*Reports and Returns on Trade*), Imperial Maritime Customs, annual, 1859–1948; photo-offset, 220 vols., Nanjing chubanshe, 1991. See Liang-lin Hsiao, *China's Foreign Trade Statistics, 1864–1949*, HUP, 1954.

Zhonghua minguo gongshang shuishou shiliao xuanbian 中華民國工商稅收史料選編 (Selection of historical material on trade tax receipts of the National government), Jiangsusheng Zhonghua minguo gongshang shuishoushi bianxiezu 江蘇省中華民國工商稅收史編寫組 and Ershiguan, eds., Nanjing daxue, 8 vols., 1994–96.

Guomin zhengfu caizheng jinrong shuishou dang'an shiliao (1927-1937 nian) 國民政府財政金融稅收檔案史料 (Archival sources on the finances, currency, and tax receipts of the National government), Caizhengbu Caizheng kexue yanjiusuo 財政部財政科學研究所, Ershiguan, ed.,

Zhongguo caizheng jingji, 1997. In the series *Zhonghua minguoshi dang'an ziliao congshu*.

Zhongguo jindai jingjishi yanjiu zongshu 中國近代經濟史研究綜述 (General outline of research in modern Chinese economic history), Mi Rucheng 宓汝成, ed., Tianjin jiaoyu, 1987. A useful introduction.

Zhongguo jindai jingjishi cankao ziliao congkan 中國近代經濟史參考資料叢刊 (Collection of reference materials for modern economic history), Zhongguo kexueyuan Jingji yanjiusuo, ed., various publishers. Seven collections in all, of which three follow.

Zhongguo jindai jingjishi tongji ziliao xuanji 中國近代經濟史統計資料選輯 (Selected statistical materials on modern Chinese economic history), Yan Zhongping 嚴中平 (1909–91) et al., comps., 2 vols., Kexue, 1955. Covers the years 1796–1898. A planned supplementary volume never appeared.

Zhongguo jindai nongyeshi ziliao 中國近代農業史資料 (Historical materials on modern Chinese agriculture), Zhang Youyi 章有義 and Li Wenzhi 李文治, comps., 3 vols., Sanlian, 1957. Covers 1840–1938.

Zhongguo jindai shougongyeshi ziliao 中國近代手工業史資料 (Materials on Chinese handicraft industries in the modern period), Peng Zeyi 彭澤益, ed., 4 vols., Sanlian, 1957; Shanghai: Zhonghua, 1962.

Zhongguo jindai waizhaishi tongji ziliao 中國近代外債史統記資料 (Statistical materials on the history of foreign loans to China in the modern period), Xu Yisheng 徐義生, comp., Zhonghua, 1962; rpnt., Hong Kong, 1978. Covers 1853–1927.

Jiu Zhongguo gongzhaishi ziliao 舊中國公債史資料 (Historical materials on public debt in old China), Qian Jiaju 千家駒, comp., Caizheng jingji, 1955; Zhonghua, 1984.

Zhongguo gongshang hanghuishi ziliao 中國工商會史資料 (Materials on the history of China's chambers of commerce and industry), Peng Zeyi 彭澤益, ed., 1995.

Zhongguo jindai gongyeshi ziliao 中國近代工業史資料 (Source materials on the history of modern industry in China), Chen Zhi 陳真 and Yao Luogong 姚洛共, comps., 6 vols., Sanlian, 1957–61.

Zhongguo xiandaishi tongji ziliao xuanbian 中國現代史統計資料選編 (Selected statistical materials on contemporary Chinese history), Beijing daxue Guoji zhengzhixi 北京大學國際政治系, comp., Henan renmin, 1985.

Note the following works of Sydney D. Gamble (1890–1968):

Peking: A Social Survey, New York: George H. Doran, 1921.

Prices, Wages and the Standard of Living in Peking, 1900–1924, co-authored with T'ien-p'ei Meng, Beijing Express Press, 1926.

Household Accounts of Two Chinese Families, New York: China Institute in America, 1931.

"Daily Wages of Unskilled Chinese Laborers, 1807–1902," *FEQ* 3 (1943).

Specialized government and professional journals are an important source on statistics and the economy:

Tongji yuekan 統記月刊 (*Statistical Monthly*), Beijing, Cabinet Bureau of Statistics.

Tongji yuebao 統記月報 (*The Statistical Monthly*), Bureau of Statistics, Legislative Yuan, 1929–49.

Zhongyang yuekan 中央月刊 (*Bank of China Monthly Review*), 1930–38.

Yinhang zhoubao 銀行周報 (*Bankers' Weekly*), Shanghai, 1917–50. Founded by Zhang Jia'ao (51.4.5).

Shanghai zong shanghui yuebao 上海綜商會月報 (*Journal of the General Chamber of the Shanghai Chamber of Commerce*), monthly, 1921–27; after 1928, changed name to *Shangye yuebao* 商業月報.

51.4.3   Business History

National and municipal libraries contain the archives of private and public businesses and business-related organizations such as chambers of commerce. Consult *State and Economy in Republican China: A Handbook for Scholars*, 2000 (51.14.1).

The Labor Movement

Ming K. Chan, *Historiography of the Chinese Labor Movement, 1895–1949: A Critical Survey and Bibliography of Selected Chinese Source Materials at the Hoover Institution*, Hoover Institution Press, 1981.

Dictionnaire biographique du mouvement ouvrier international, la Chine, Lucien Bianco, ed., Editions ouvrières et Presses de la Fondation nationales des sciences politiques, 1985.

51.4.4   The Rural Economy

Among the most thorough surveys of the rural economy were those made by Japanese research institutes (51.11.1) and at Nanking University:

John Lossing Buck (1890–1962), *Land Utilization in China: A Study of 16,786 Farms in 168 Localities, and 38,256 Farm Families in Twenty-Two Provinces in China, 1929–1933*, 3 vols., Nanjing: University of Nanking; UChP, 1937; rpnt., Paragon, 1964.

Randall E. Stross, *The Stubborn Earth: American Agriculturalists on Chinese Soil, 1898–1937*, UCP, 1986.

See also the two main works of Sydney Gamble on village life:

Ting Hsien: A North China Rural Community, New York: Institute of Pacific Relations, 1954.

North China Villages: Social, Political, and Economic Activities Before 1933, UCP, 1963.

General collections of historical land deeds contain samples from the Republic (50.7.5). Several collections of Republican land deeds have been published; see, for example,

Minguo diqi shiliao 民國地契史料 (Republican land deeds sources), Xiong Jingdu 熊敬篤, ed., Xinduxian dang'anju 新都縣檔案局, 1985.

Tôyô bunka kenkyûjo shozô Chûgoku tochi monjo mokuroku kaisetsu 東洋文化研究所所藏中國土地文書目錄解説 (Annotated catalog of Chinese land documents in the library of the Tôbunken), Hamashita Takeshi 濱下武志 et al., eds., 2 vols., Tokyo, 1983–86. Contains (1) selections from 10 sets of Qing and Republican period documents, with introductions and annotations and (2) a complete catalog of the 10 sets of documents (totalling 2,250 items).

There are large reprint series of Republican rural surveys, for example,

Minguo ershiniandai Zhongguo dalu tudi wenti ziliao 民國二十年代中國大陸土地問題資料 (Sources on the land question in mainland China in the 1920s), Xiao Zheng 蕭錚, ed., Chengwen, 200 vols., 1977.

51.4.5 Prices and Inflation

Chang Kai-ngau (Zhang Jia'ao 張嘉璈, 1889–1979), *The Inflationary Spiral: The Experience of China, 1939–1950*, MIT Press and Wiley, 1958. Zhang was the younger brother of Carsun Chang (Zhang Junmai 張君勱 [Zhang Jiasen 張嘉森] 1886–1969, a leading proponent of the third way during the New Culture era). Zhang Jia'ao was a central figure in the development of a modern Chinese banking system and general manager of the Bank of China, 1929–35. He was also deeply involved in Chinese railroad financing and development (*Biographical Dictionary of Republican China*, vol. 1, 26–30). In 1917 he founded the *Bankers Weekly* in Shanghai (51.4.2). From May 1947 to March 1948 he was governor of the Bank of China and therefore particularly well placed to write about the climax of China's inflation. He migrated to the United States in 1953. See also the next item.

Last Chance in China: The Diary of Chang Kia-ngau, Donald Gillin and Ramon H. Myers, eds., Hoover Institution Press, 1989.

Hsun-hsin Chou, *The Chinese Inflation, 1937–1949*, Col.UP, 1963.

Zhonghua minguo huobishi ziliao 中華民國貨幣史資料 (Materials on the monetary history of the Republic), Zhongguo renmin yinhang canshi shi 中國人民銀行參事室 (Office of the advisor to the People's Bank), ed., 2 vols., Shanghai renmin, 1991.

51.5   Biographical Materials and Oral History

A huge amount of new biographical sources on those who lived during the Republic became available in the last quarter of the twentieth century. Despite the fact that both the leading English-language biographical dictionaries for the Republic were published before this, they are still the best starting point when looking up anybody falling into the top 1,300 or so personalities:

Biographical Dictionary of Republican China, Howard L. Boorman, ed., Richard C. Howard, associate ed., 5 vols., Col. UP, 1967–71. The 5th vol. is a personal-name index compiled by Janet Krompart, Col. UP, 1979. Includes biographies of 600 leading personalities active in the years 1911–49. There is some overlap with *ECCP* because almost all the subjects of this dictionary were born at the end of the Qing, and some had already made their mark before the establishment of the Republic. The editors have included cross-references to *ECCP*.

Biographical Dictionary of Chinese Communism, 1921–1965, Donald W. Klein and Anne B. Clark, eds., 2 vols., HUP, 1971. Contains 433 main biographies. Data on some 700 additional persons are provided in the text and 450 more in the appendixes. The appendixes also give breakdowns of the biographees into different categories (date of birth, women, military education abroad, etc.) and what they participated in, for example, early CCP activities and organizations (including lists of members of the Politburo, 1920s–1955 and Central Committee to 1945), important events, communist armies, Soviets (1927–37), and border regions and liberated areas (1937–49).

Since the Republic, ever larger biographical dictionaries and collections of biographical materials have been compiled on personalities active in the period. Often these commemorate followers of the GMD or the CCP (items 1–9). Much of the detail in these works is based on information in the considerable number of biographical dictionaries which were published during the Republic in Chinese (and also in Japanese or English and other Western languages). A small selection is given below (items 7–9). To a limited extent oral history material is also incorporated (51.5.9). There are also numerous newly compiled specialized biographical dictionaries, of women soldiers or of industrialists, for example, or of distinguished personalities from a particular region, province, city, college, or school. These can be easily located by searching on the identifying key words in online library catalogs.

One problem in using Chinese biographical data is that individuals used many different types of alternative name. Traditional alternative names are examined in 3.2.4 and modern ones in 51.5.2 and 51.6.

Xinhai yilai renwu zhuanji ziliao suoyin 辛亥以來人物傳記資料索引 (Index to biographical materials on persons active after the 1911 revolution), Fudan daxue Lishixi ziliaoshi, comp., Wang Genming 王根明, ed., Shanghai cishu, 1990. 80,000 entries containing biographical materials (mainly from Chinese, Taiwanese, and Hong Kong newspapers, 1900–85) on 18,000 people who lived 1911–49.

Zhongguo jin xiandai renwu zhuanji ziliao suoyin 中國近現代人物傳記資料索引 (Index to biographical materials on persons active in the modern and contemporary periods), Wang Jixiang 王繼祥, ed. in chief, Dongbei shifan daxue tushuguan, 1988. 24,000 entries containing biographical materials on 10,000 people active 1840–1949.

Minguo renwu da cidian 民國人物大辭典 (Dictionary of Republican personalities), Xu Youchun 徐友春 et al., eds., Hebei renmin, 1991. Contains short biographies of 12,000 people.

Geming renwuzhi 革命人物志 (Records of revolutionary personalities), Dangshihui, ed., 23 vols., 1969–83. Biographies based on the main GMD archives.

Guoshiguan xiancang Minguo renwu zhuanji shiliao huibian 國史館現藏民國人物傳記史料匯編 (Collection of biographical materials on Republican personalities from the Guoshiguan), 17 vols., 1988–1998.

Minguo gaoji jiangling liezhuan 民高級將領列傳 (Biographies of high-ranking military officers of the Republic), Wang Chengpin 王成品 et al., eds., Jiefangjun, 1988– . Multivolume series in progress.

Zhongguo gongchandang mingren lu 中國共產黨名人錄 (Record of famous CCP personalities), Sichuan renmin, 1997. Contains short biographies of about 11,400 party members.

Zhonggong dangshi renwu zhuan 中共黨史人物傳 (Biographies of personalities in the history of the Chinese Communist Party), Zhonggong dangshi renwu yanjiuhui, ed., 60 vols., Shaanxi renmin, 1980–96.

Gendai Shina jimmeikan 現代支那人名鑒 (Biographical dictionary of contemporary Chinese), Gaimushô jôhôbu 外務省情報部 (Public Information Bureau, Ministry of Foreign Affairs), ed., Tôa dobunkai, 1916, 1924, 1928. The 1924 edition is the best. There is an index in Wade-Giles. See next entry.

Dong sansheng guanshenlu 東三省官紳錄 (Prominent officials and gentry of the three eastern provinces), Tanabe Tanejirô 田邊種治郎, ed., Dong sansheng guanshenlu kanxingju, 1924. Over 943 biographical sketches (on this and other biographical dictionaries for Manchukuo, see Suleski, 1994, 39–41).

Gendai Chûkaminkoku Manshûkoku jimmeikan 現代中華民國滿洲國人名鑒 (Prominent persons in the Republic of China and Manchukuo), Gaimushô jôhôbu 外務省情報部 (Public Information Bureau, Ministry of Foreign Affairs), ed., Tôa dôbunkai, 1932, 1937, 1942. Each volume contains short biographies of between 2,500 and 7,000 people, with a considerable number of new names appearing in each collection. Entries in the volumes starting with that of 1932 are divided between Chinese people active in the Republic (part 1) and in Manchukuo (part 2). See also 51.11.

Who's Who in China: Biographies of China's Leaders, Shanghai: The China Weekly Review, 1st ed., 1918–19; 2nd ed., 1920; 3rd ed., 1925 (enl., 1928); 4th ed., 1931 (enl., 1933); 5th ed., 1936, (enl., 1940); 6th ed., 1950. Contains biographies and photographs of a total of about 2,900 personalities. For an index, see *Who's Who in China, 1918–50*, comp., Tony Cavanagh, 3 vols., CMC, 1982.

51.5.2   Aliases, Pen Names, and Alternative Names

In the modern period most of the old types of alternative names were used and some new terms were coined, for example, pen name (*biming* 筆名) and alias (*huaming* 化名). A selection of the many reference works to identify these and other types are listed below. Section 50.6 contains reference works for identifying the pen names of writers:

Zhongguo jinxiandai renwu bieming cidian 中國近現代人物別名辭典 (Alternative names of Chinese personalities in the modern period), Xu Weimin 徐爲民, ed. in chief, Shenyang, 1993. Brief details of 14,000 people (1840–1949) using 40,000 *bieming*.

Minguo renwu bieming lu 民國人物別名錄 (Alternative names of personalities in the Republic), Zhongguo youyi, 1989. Alternative names of over 10,000 people.

Qingmo Minchu zhongyao baokan zuozhe biming zihao tongjian 清末民初 重要報刊作者筆名字號通檢 (Index of pen names and literary names used by authors at the end of the Qing and the beginning of the Republic in important newspapers and periodicals), Zhang Jinglu 張靜 廬 et al., comps., Zhongshan tushu, 1965. Originally appeared in *Wenshi* 1 and 4 (1962 and 1965).

Wusi yilai lishi renwu biming bieming lu 五四以來歷史人物筆名別名錄 (Record of pen names and alternative names of historical personalities since the May Fourth movement), Zhang Jingru 張靜如, comp., Shaanxi renmin, 1986.

Zhonggong dangshi renwu bieming lu 中共黨史人物別名錄 (Record of alternative names of personalities in the history of the Party), Chen Yutang 陳玉堂, ed., Hongqi, 1985. Listing of the pseudonyms and pen names of 185 CCP members and eight foreigners.

Minguo renwu beizhuan ji 民國人物碑傳記 (Stele biographies of personalities of the Republic), Shekeyuan Jindaishi ziliao bianjibu 社科院 近代史資料編輯部, Sichuan renmin, 1997.

For the pen names of writers only, see 51.6.

51.5.3 Collected Works of Individuals

Many politicians and intellectuals continued the old practice (30.3) of publishing their selected (or collected) works during their lifetimes (*xuanji* 選集, *wenji* 文集, *quanji* 全集, *yanlunji* 言論集). These could include all types of writing, for example, speeches, essays, letters, telegrams, or longer works. Often more complete collected works were published after an individual's death. Also many different editions were published, some more complete than others. *Wenji* are one of the basic biographical sources for thousands of people who lived during the Republic.

Ma Fengchen 馬奉琛, 1935 (50.5.2), 186–272 and 467–584, lists the collected papers of noted Qing statesmen published up to 1934.

Zhongguo jindaishi wenxian bibei shumu 中國近代史文獻必備書目 lists the collected works and collected poems (*shiji* 詩集) of 1,000 individuals who lived between 1840 and 1919 (50.10.1).

51.5.4   Diaries

Diaries in the Republic begin to break out of the traditional mode of recording the hour of rising, the weather, guests, and excursions (3.6.1). For the first time they can be a used as a source for the emotional and intellectual development of an individual. The diaries of the famous were often intended as a public statement. There are a number of collections, for example,

Minguo mingren riji congshu 民國名人日記叢書 (Collectanea of diaries of personalities of the Republic), Jiangsu guji and Ershiguan, 1992– . Includes the diaries of Feng Yuxiang 馮玉祥 (1882–1948), Jiang Zuobin 蔣作賓 (1884–1942) et al.

51.5.5   Letters

The advent of a modern postal system in the nineteenth century and the spread of education, coupled with the relative proximity in time of the Republican period, means that much larger numbers of letters survive from the Republic than from previous periods. They can be a useful biographical source.

51.5.6   Autobiographies and Memoirs

Autobiographies and memoirs begin to become much more self-revealing in the Republic. See, for example, the first two items below:

Two Self-Portraits: Liang Ch'i-ch'ao and Hu Shih, Li Yu-ning and William Wycoff, Outer Sky Press, 1993. Based on Liang and Hu's own partial autobiographies.

The Autobiography of a Chinese Historian, Arthur W. Hummel, tr., Brill, 1931. The autobiography of Gu Jiegang 顧頡剛 (29.1).

Susan Chan Egan, *A Latterday Confucian: Reminiscences of William Hung (1893–1980)*, Harvard East Asian Monograph, 131, 1980.

An Oppositionist for Life: Memoirs of the Chinese Revolutionary Zheng Chaolin, Gregor Benton, ed. and tr., Atlantic Highlands, N.J.: Humanities Press, 1997. Zheng was born in 1901.

51.5.7   Chronological Biographies

The old form of *nianpu* 年譜 (chronological biography) continues to be written for Republic personalities.

51.5.8   Political Figures: Collected Works and Other Sources

The selected works of many of the main political figures were published in their lifetimes. Much more comprehensive collections (or in some cases complete works) were published after their deaths. There is also an enormous quantity of writing about leading political figures. These include not only traditional forms such as *nianpu* 年譜, but also reminiscences and political memoirs, sometimes even revelations. One does not have to be a believer in the two competing heroic versions of modern Chinese history to treat these sources with the attention they deserve. A sampling of the writings by, in the name of, or about Yuan Shikai, Sun Zhongshan (Sun Yatsen), Jiang Jieshi (Chiang K'ai-shek), Wang Jingwei, and Mao Zedong are listed below.

Yuan Shikai 袁世凱 *(1859–1916)*

Yuan Shikai weikan shuxin shougao 袁世凱未刊書信手稿 (Unpublished handwritten drafts of Yuan Shikai's calligraphy and letters), Beijing: Zhonghua quanguo tushuguan wenxian suowei fuzhi zhongxin, 3 vols., 1998.

Yuan Shikai zouyi 袁世凱奏議 (Memorials of Yuan Shikai), Tianjin tushuguan and Tianjin shekeyuan Lishi yanjiusuo, ed., Liao Yizhong 廖一中, Luo Zhenrong 羅真容 checked, 3 vols., Tianjin guji, 1987. Note the index to Yuan's memorials to the emperor in 50.5.4.

Yuan Shikai zouzhe 袁世凱奏折 (Memorials of Yuan Shikai), 8 vols., 1970. In the series *Guoli gugong bowuyuan Gugong wenxian* 國立故宮博物院故宮文獻, special publication 1.

Yuan Shikai Tianjin dang'an shiliao xuanbian 袁世凱天津檔案館史料選編 (Selections on Yuan Shikai from the Tianjin archives), Tianjin jinshi dang'anguan, ed., vol. 1, Tianjin guji, 1990.

Sun Yatsen 孫逸仙 (1866–1925)

Sun Yatsen is the name by which Sun is best known in the West. It is the old transcription of the Cantonese pronunciation of one of his later literary names. In China he is usually referred to as Sun Yixian (the standard pronunciation of Sun Yatsen), Sun Wen 孫文 (his given name), or Sun Zhongshan 孫中山 (another literary name, derived from his Japanese alias Nakayama Shô 中山樵).

Bibliography of Sun Yat-sen in China's Republican Revolution, 1885–1925, Sidney H. Chang and Leonard H. D. Gordon, comps. and eds., with the assistance of Elaine P. Chang and Marjorie J. Gordon, University Press of America, 1991; 2nd ed., 1998. Contains 2,581 entries on or by Sun Yatsen in 19 languages arranged in the following categories: bibliography and reference, writings of Sun Yatsen, books, articles, papers and symposia, translated works of Sun, documentary collections, doctoral dissertations and masters theses, selected newspapers, magazines and special reports, and audio-visual reports. There are author and subject indexes.

Prescriptions for Saving China: Selected Writings of Sun Yatsen, Julie Lee Wei, Ramon H. Myers, and Donald G. Gillin, eds., Hoover Institution Press, 1994.

Guofu quanji 國父全集 (Complete works of the father of the nation), Dangshihui, ed., 3 vols., Taibei; rev. ed., 6 vols., 1965.

Sun Zhongshan quanji 孫中山全集 (Complete works of Sun Yatsen), Zhongshan daxue Lishixi and Guangdongsheng Sheke Jindai yanjiusuo, eds., 11 vols., 1981–86.

Jiang Jieshi 蔣介石 (1887–1975)

Jiang Jieshi 蔣介石, *Jiang zongtong sixiang yanlun ji* 蔣總統思想言論集 (Collection of President Jiang's thoughts and speeches), 30 vols., Zhongyang wenwu, 1966.

Jiang Jieshi 蔣介石, *Jiang zongtong milu* 蔣總統秘錄 (Secret records of President Jiang), 15 vols., Zhongyang ribao, 1974–78.

Wang Jingwei 汪精衛 (1883–1944)

From 1940 to his death in 1944, Wang was head of the Japanese-sponsored government in Wuhan opposed to the Nationalist government led by Jiang Jieshi in Chongqing. Note that the official newspaper of the Wang Jingwei government was *Zhonghua ribao* 中華日報 (51.3.1, 1928–37) and the government gazette was called the

Zhengfu gongbao 政府公報 and later the *Guomin zhengfu gongbao* 國民政府公報, photo-offset, Jiangsu guji, 15 vols., 1991.

Ô Chômei zenshû 汪精衛全集 (Complete works of Wang Jingwei), Kawakami Jun'ichi, tr., Tôa kôronsha, 1939– .

Poems of Wang Ching-wei, Seyuan Shu, tr., into English with a preface and notes, Allen & Unwin, 1938.

Wang Jingwei xiansheng zhengzhi lunshu 汪精衛先生政治論述 (Mr. Wang Jingwei's talks on politics), 15 vols., Taibei, 1990.

Mao Zedong 毛澤東 *(1893–1976)*

The originals of all known writings of Mao are kept at the Zhongyang dang'anguan (51.1.2). The most complete collection of Mao Zedong's writings covering the period 1912 to 1949 is *Mao's Road to Power: Revolutionary Writings, 1912–1949*, Stuart R. Schram, ed., Sharpe, 1992– . By its comprehensiveness, the accuracy of the translations, and the thoroughness of the annotations, it replaces previous published collections in Chinese, Japanese, and English. Subsequent changes in Mao's works in successive editions of his *Selected Works* are noted. The volumes are:

1　*The Pre-Marxist Period, 1912–1920*, 1992
2　*National Revolution and Social Revolution, December 1920–June 1927*, 1995
3　*From the Jinggangshan to the Jiangxi Soviets, July 1937–December 1930*, 1995
4　*The Rise and Fall of the Chinese Soviet Republic, 1931–1934*, 1997
5　*Toward the Second United Front, January 1935–July 1937*, 1999
6　*The New Stage, August 1937–December 1938*, 2000
7　*New Democracy, 1939–1941*, 2000
8　*Rectification, 1942–July 1945*, 2001
9　*From Victory to Civil War, August 1945–June 1947*, 2001
10　*Toward the Conquest of Power, July 1947–October 1, 1949*, 2001

Mao Zedong ji 毛澤東集 (Collected writings of Mao Zedong), Takeuchi Minoru 竹內實, ed., 10 vols., Hokubôsha, 1970–72. Reviewed by Stuart Schram in *CQ* 46: 366–69 (1971).

Mao Zedong ji pujuan 毛澤東集補卷 (Supplements to the collected writings of Mao Zedong), Takeuchi Minoru 竹內實, ed., 10 vols., Hokubôsha, 1980–86.

Mao Zedong nianpu 毛澤東年譜 (Chronological biography of Mao Zedong), 3 vols., Renmin, 1993. A daily account of Mao's activities.

For a bibliography of English-language works on Mao Zedong, see *Mao Zedong: A Bibliography*, Alan Lawrence, comp., Greenwood, 1991.

51.5.9 Oral History

Wenshi ziliao 文史資料

In 1959, the prime minister, Zhou Enlai, launched the idea that those over 60 years of age in the People's Consultative Conferences all over China record their reminiscences of historic events from 1898 to 1948. Wenshiguan 文史館 (Institutes of culture and history) were formed all over the country. Enrollment was enlarged after 1978. By 2000, over one billion words of reminiscences were recorded and published. There is a catalog of the open publications of *Wenshi ziliao* for the years 1960–90 (item 1 below). Numerous selections have been made (items 2 and 3, for example). Many of the collections are on special topics, for example, the 1911 Revolution (item 4 below). Quality is uneven, but they deserve more attention from historians than they have received:

Quanguo geji zhengxie wenshi ziliao pianmu suoyin 全國各級政協文史資料篇目索引 (Index to tables of contents of literary and historical materials at each level CPPCC), 5 vols., Wenshi, 1992.

Wenshi ziliao xuanji 文史資料選輯 (Selections of literary and historical materials), 72 vols., Zhongguo renmin zhengzhi xieshang huiyi quanguo weiyuanhui Wenshi ziliao yanjiu weiyuanhui 中國人民政治協商會議全國委員會文史資料研究委員會 (Literary and History Materials Committee of the Chinese People's Political Consultative Conference), ed., Zhonghua, 1960–80.

Zhonghua wenshi ziliao wenku 中華文史資料文庫 (Chinese literary and historical materials trove), 20 vols., Zhongguo wenshi, 1996. Contains 30 million words. Volumes are organized by broad subject category.

Xinhai geming huiyilu 辛亥革命回憶錄 (Reminiscences of the 1911 Revolution), Zhongguo renmin zhengzhi xieshang huiyi quanguo weiyuanhui Wenshi ziliao yanjiu weiyuanhui, ed., 6 collections, Zhonghua, 1961–63.

Other Collections of Reminiscences

Besides *Wenshi ziliao* 文史資料, various other oral history projects were launched:

Hongqi piaopiao 紅旗飄飄 (The red flag waves), Zongguo qingnian, 32 collections, 1957–93. Revolutionary reminiscences.

Geming huiyi lu 革命回憶錄 (Revolutionary reminiscences), Renmin, 21 collections, 1980–87.

Xinghuo liaoyuan 星火燎原 (A single spark can light a prairie fire), 10 vols., Beijing renmin wenxue, 1958–63; 2nd ed., rev., Jiefangjun, 1997. Military reminiscences.

Taiwan

Koushu lishi congshu shumu 口述歷史叢書書目 (Catalog of oral history series), Shiyusuo, 1999. The series to date contains over 70 volumes, each containing the recorded reminiscences of a participant in modern Chinese history. The Shiyusuo also publishes a journal on oral history:

Koushu lishi qikan 口述歷史期刊 (1989– , annual), Jinshisuo.

The Guoshiguan 國史館 (51.1.3) also publishes an oral history series. As of 1999, 12 titles had been published.

USA

Many Chinese nationalists and some early communist leaders left China and settled in America. Quite a number recorded their reminiscences or wrote their memoirs.

Chinese Oral History Project, Columbia University. The project was initiated by C. Martin Wilbur and Franklin L. Ho in 1958. Over the next 20 years, 17 interviews were conducted with outstanding figures of the Republican period. They are now held in the university's rare books and manuscripts library (published catalog: *The Oral History Collection of Columbia University*, Elizabeth L. Mason and Louis M. Starr, eds., Oral History Research Office, Columbia University, 1979). In the 1980s the transcripts of the interviews were published in microfiche form. Some have been also published in book form.

For an excellent example of the immediacy to be gained from oral history, see the interviews conducted with four members of the Shanghai Wenshiguan in Zheng Wang, 1999 (39.3.3).

51.6 Creative Literature, 1900–49

Start with the handy Wilt Idema and Lloyd Haft, *A Guide to Chinese Literature*, CCS, Univ. of Michigan, 1998. For more detail, use:

A Selective Guide to Chinese Literature, 1900–1949: The Novel, Milena Do-
lezelova-Velingerova, ed., Brill, 1988.

A Selective Guide to Chinese Literature, 1900–1949: The Short Story, Zbig-
niew Slupski, ed., Brill, 1988.

A Selective Guide to Chinese Literature, 1900–1949: The Poem, Lloyd Haft,
ed., Brill, 1989.

A Selective Guide to Chinese Literature, 1900–1949: The Drama, Bernd
Eberstein, ed., Brill, 1990.

Chih-Tsing Hsia, *A History of Modern Chinese Fiction: Third Edition*, Indiana UP, 1999 (originally published YUP, 1961; 2nd ed., 1971). Covers from May Fourth to the Cultural Revolution.

Modern Chinese Literary Thought: Writings on Literature, 1893–1945, Kirk
A. Denton, ed., SUP, 1996.

Biographies of Writers

The four volumes of the *Selective Guides* series listed above contain
biographic details on a great many writers, as does the *Zhongguo
wenxue da cidian* 中國文學大詞典 (30.4).

A Biographical Dictionary of Modern Chinese Writers, Yang Li,
ed. in chief, New World Press, 1994, contains brief biographies and
lists of major works of over 700 writers active between the May
Fourth Movement and the mid-1980s.

Biming 筆名 (Pen Names)

Modern writers usually used not one but several pen names, depending on the occasion (Lu Xun used well over 120, an extreme
case). The reasons that they did so were varied:

1. Lack of confidence when publishing for the first time
2. Different names for different styles
3. Delight in strange names or to express a personal view (cf.
   shiming 室名; 3.2.4)
4. If more than one article or essay was published in one issue
   of a journal, editors often assigned a second name
5. To stimulate a dialog or to create the effect of public support
   for views expressed in a previous work
6. To avoid political repression

This list is drawn from the first item below:

Twentieth Century Chinese Writers and Their Pen Names, Chu Pao-liang
(Zhu Baoliang 朱寶梁), comp., Hanxue yanjiu zhongxin, G. K. Hall,

1977; enlarged ed., 1989. Contains the 17,940 assumed names of 6,784 persons. Real names arranged by Wade-Giles in majuscule followed by pen names in minuscule (with characters shown).

Zhongguo xiandai wenxue zuozhe biming lu 中國現代文學作者筆名錄 (Pen names of contemporary Chinese writers), Xu Naixiang 徐乃翔, Qin Hong 欽鴻, comps., Hunan wenyi, 1988. Includes pen names of 7,000 writers active 1917–49.

For more references for looking up alternative names, see 51.4.2.

Anthologies

Columbia Anthology of Modern Chinese Literature, Joseph S. M. Lau, ed., Col.UP, 1995.

Straw Sandals: Chinese Short Stories, 1918–1933, Harold Isaacs, ed., Foreword by Lu Xun, MIT, 1974.

Writing Women in Modern China: An Anthology of Women's Literature from the Early Twentieth Century, Amy D. Dooling and Kristina M. Torgeson, eds., Col. UP, 1998.

On women and literature, see Barlow 1994 and Lu 1993 (39.3.3).

Bibliographies, Translations

1500 Modern Chinese Novels and Plays: Present Day Fiction and Drama in China, Jos. Schijns et al., eds., Beiping: Catholic University Press, 1948.

A *Bibliography of Studies and Translations of Modern Chinese Literature, 1918–1942*, Donald Gibbs and Yun-chen Li, comps., HUP, 1975.

51.7   Warlords and the Military, 1912–49

The military filled the vacuum between the breakdown of the empire and the restoration of a strong civilian government. Records were not always kept, and many were destroyed. Not all archives have been fully opened, although much more is being published from them. A great deal of biographical material has survived, and an increasing amount of autobiographies, memoirs, reminiscences, and veteran interviews has been published.

Writing on the warlords, the civil wars, and the eight-year anti-Japanese war tends to fall into one of two types. The first is campaign history, the second attempts to evaluate the military as a political and social phenomenon and its effects on society and the economy. Most work tends to fall into the first type and adopts a partisan framework, depending on whether the author is writing in a GMD or CCP context.

Given the passage of time and the wealth of new sources, it should now be possible to give warfare its rightful place at the fore-front of modern Chinese history without feeling obliged immediately to take sides. As Diana Lary puts it in a slightly different way, "The Guomindang lost control of China because its armies lost, first to the Japanese and then to the Communists. The Communists came to power not because their ideology appealed to the people, but because their conventional (not guerrilla) armies triumphed in large, set-piece battles. These are important correctives for a field in which the study of political systems and of ideology has loomed much larger than the study of military history and the history of warfare" (*JAS* 57.1 [1998], 185).

In studying the causes, the course, and the effects of warfare in these years it is as well to remember that not all parts of the country were affected in the same ways.[5] The fighting was concentrated in particular places. In the 224 years between 1616 and 1840, there were 735 major battles scattered rather evenly all over China (the average is three battles per year). The intensity of warfare rose in the 70 years between 1840 and 1911, which saw 1,968 battles (an average of 28 per year). Just over 50 percent of them were located in the six provinces of Anhui, Jiangsu, Zhejiang, Hubei, Guizhou, and Jiangxi. The upsurge continued in the early part of the Republic (1912–1931), broadly speaking, the warlord years, which saw 679 battles (35 per year). During the period 1931–1945, there were 2,035 battles (135 per year). Finally, the peak was reached during the five years 1945–50, which saw 1,246 battles (249 per year). Different provinces suffered during these years, but 54 percent of the fighting from 1912 to 1949 was in just six provinces (Hebei, Shandong, Shanxi, Henan, Jiangsu, and Hubei).

The 1911 Revolution

Delin Liu (劉德麟) and Shuangsheng He (何雙生) discuss the sources on the 1911 Revolution under the following headings: col-

---

[5] Jin Lin 金麟, "Zhongguo jin xiandai zhanzheng de dili fenbu" 中國近現代戰爭的地理分布 (The distribution of battles in China in the modern period), *Lishi dili* 15: 177–88 (1999).

lections of general source materials, source material collections on specialized topics, collections of archival source materials (both Chinese and foreign), reminiscences, collected writings of individuals, chronological biographies, and miscellaneous works, including periodicals and reference works.[6]

The first two studies below were among the first to stress the interpretation of the 1911 Revolution as a military event rather than emphasizing its ideological or political content. In following a movement as complex and geographically dispersed as the 1911 Revolution, a good historical atlas is essential (item 3):

Edmund Fung, *The Military Dimension of the Chinese Revolution*, UBCP, 1980.

Edward A. McCord, *The Power of the Gun: The Emergence of Modern Chinese Warlordism*, UCP, 1993.

Xinhai gemingshi dituji 辛亥革命史地圖集 (Collection of maps on the history of the 1911 Revolution), Xinhai geming Wuchang qiyi jinian guan, comp., Zhongguo ditu, 1991. The commentary to the maps is illustrated with photographs and diagrams.

Beiyang Warlords

During the 12 years 1916 to 1928, there were nine changes of government, 24 changes of cabinet, and 26 prime ministers. Real power lay with the regional armies led by warlords. The Beiyang warlords (*Beiyang junfa* 北洋軍閥) were originally officers loyal to Yuan Shikai. In 1917, they split into the Anhui and Zhili cliques. Lai Xinxia 來新夏 divides the sources on them into eight categories: archives, biographical materials, special collections, local gazetteers, miscellaneous notes, treatises, published collections of historical sources, and newspapers and periodicals.[7] The archives of Yuan Shikai (51.5.8) and many other historical sources on the Beiyang warlords are held in Tianjin. An increasing amount are being published:

---

[6] "A Brief Account of the Publications of Historical Source Materials on the 1911 Revolution Since 1949," in *The Chinese Revolution of 1911: New Perspectives*, Chün-tu Hsüeh (Xue Jundu 薛君度), ed., HK: Joint Publishing, 1986, 175–204.

[7] "Guanyu Beiyang junfashi de wenxian" 關于北洋軍閥史的文獻 (On the materials on the northern warlords), *Zhongxue lishi* 中學歷史 2 (1982).

Beiyang junfa shiliao 北洋軍閥史料 (Historical materials on the Beiyang warlords), Tianjin guji, 6 collections in 36 vols., 1991– .

Beiyang junfa 北洋軍閥 (The Beiyang warlords), Lai Xinxia 來新夏, 5 vols., Shanghai renmin, 1988.

Beiyang junfa 北洋軍閥 (The Beiyang warlords), Zhang Bofeng 章伯鋒 and Li Zongyi 李宗一, Wuhan, 6 vols., 1990.

Beiyang junfashi yanjiu ziliao suoyin (1900–1983.6) 北洋軍閥史研究資料索引 (Index to research materials on the history of the Beiyang warlords), Fujian shifan daxue tushuguan qingbao ziliaoke 福建師範大學圖書館情報資料科 and Lishixi ziliaoshi, 歷史系資料室, eds. and printed, 1983.

For a study of how war affected the course of modern Chinese history, see Arthur Waldron, *From War to Nationalism: China's Turning Point, 1924–1925*, NY: CUP, 1995. The outcome of the second Zhili-Fengtian War (the subject of this study) was to remove some of the GMD's strongest opponents and thus pave the way for its rise to power.

Archives and sources on the warlords are often held locally. Even when they are not, publications on them are often local. There is now a specialized literature on most of the leading warlords and on many of the minor ones. Often helpful guides to the sources have been published as, for example:

Zhang Xueliang ziliao suoyin 張學良資料索引 (Index of materials on Zhang Xueliang), Liaoning wenshi ziliao weiyuanhui, ed., Liaoning renmin, 1986. More than 700 entries.

The Rise and Influence of the Military

Ralph L. Powell, *The Rise of the Chinese Military*, PUP, 1955.

F. F. Li, *A Military History of Modern China*, PUP, 1956.

Hans van de Ven, "The Military in the Republic," *CQ* 150: 352–74 (1997).

Introductions to the Warlords and Their Politics

David Bonavia, *China's Warlords*, HK: OUP, 1995.

Diana Lary, *Warlord Soldiers: Chinese Common Soldiers, 1911–1937*, CUP, 1985.

Jerome Ch'en, *The Military-Gentry Coalition: China Under the Warlords*, University of Toronto, York University, Joint Center on Modern East Asia, 1979.

Hsi-sheng Ch'i, *Warlord Politics in China, 1916–1928*, SUP, 1976.

Lucien W. Pye, *Warlord Politics: Conflict and Coalition in the Modernization of Republican China*, Praeger, 1971.

James E. Sheridan, "China's Warlords: Tigers or Pussycats?" *Republican China* 10.2 (1985).

James E. Sheridan, "The Warlord Era: Politics and Militarism Under the Peking Government, 1916–1928," in *CHC*, vol. 12, 284–321.

Hans J. Van de Ven, "Public Finance and the Rise of Warlordism," *Modern Asian Studies* 30.4 (1996).

Anthony B. Chan, *Arming the Chinese: The Western Armaments Trade in Warlord China,1920-1928*, UBCP, 1982.

William Kirby, *Germany and Republican China*, SUP, 1984.

Warlord Dictionaries

Zhongguo jindai junfashi cidian 中國近代軍閥史辭典 (Dictionary of warlords in modern China), Tian Ziyu 田子渝 and Liu Dejun 劉德軍, eds. in chief, Dang'an, 1989.

Zhongguo jindai junfashi cidian 中國近代軍閥史辭典 (Dictionary of warlords in modern China), Li Kaiyun 李開沅, ed. in chief, Wuhan, 1991. Contains 2,139 entries covering the years 1895 to 1937.

Guide to Secondary Sources

Zhongguo jindai junshishi yanjiu gailun 中國近代軍事史研究概論, Zhang Yiwen 張一文, ed., Tianjin jiaoyu, 1991.

Bibliography of Secondary Sources

Zhongguo jindai junshishi lunwen suoyin 1910–1986 中國近代軍事史論文索引 (Index of articles on Chinese military history in the modern period, 1910–86), Fudan daxue, Lishixi, Junshi kexue, 1986.

51.8 Selection of Published GMD Documents

The Zhongguo geming tongmenghui 中國革命同盟會 (Tongmenghui 同盟會 for short) was founded in Tokyo in 1905 with Sun Wen (better known in English by his Cantonese name, Sun Yatsen) as president. In English the Tongmenghui is sometimes referred to as

the United League or the Revolutionary Alliance. In 1912 it united
with four other parties to form the Nationalist Party (Guomindang
國民黨 or GMD [KMT] for short). In January 1924, the GMD was
reorganized on the Soviet model. After the death of Sun in March
1925, Jiang Jieshi (usually referred to in English by the Cantonese
form of his name, Chiang K'ai-shek) became the dominant leader.
One of the essential tools in following the work of the GMD is the
calendar of the party plenums:

Zhongguo Guomindang lici daibiao dahui ji zhongyang quanhui 中國國民
黨歷次代表大會及中央全會 (Successive meetings of the GMD congresses and central plenums, 1924–49), 2 vols., Rong Mengyuan 榮孟
源, comp., Guangming, 1986.

Note the official GMD gazette, newspapers, and news agency:

Zhonghua minguo guomin zhengfu gongbao 中華民國國民政府公報 (51.3.9)
Minguo ribao 民國日報 (51.3.1, 1912–26)
Zhongyang ribao 中央日報 (51.3.1, 1912–26)
Saodang bao 掃蕩報 (51.3.1, 1928–37)
Zhongyangshe 中央社 (51.3.3)

Zhongguo guomindang lishi shijian renwu ziliao jilu 中國國民黨歷史事件
人物資料輯錄 (Collection of historical events, personalities, and materials connected to the KMT), Ma Qibin 馬齊彬 et al., Jiefangjun,
1988.

Geming wenxian 革命文獻 (Documents on the revolution), Dangshihui,
151 vols., 1953–89. Continues the pre-1949 GMD series *Geming wenxian congkan* 革命文獻叢刊.

Zhonghua minguoshi dang'an ziliao huibian 中華民國史檔案資料匯編
(Collection of Republican historical materials from the archives), Ershiguan, ed., 54 vols., Jiangsu renmin, 1979–86; Jiangsu guji, 1986– .

Zhonghua minguoshi dang'an shiliao changbian 中華民國史檔案資料長編
(Collection of Republican historical materials from the archives), Ershiguan, ed., 70 vols., Nanjing daxue, 1993.

Zhonghua minguoshi dang'an ziliao changbian 中華民國史檔案資料長編
(Collection of Republican historical materials from the archives), Ershiguan, ed., 100 vols., Guangxi shifan daxue, 1997.

Zhonghua minguoshi dang'an ziliao congkan 中華民國史料檔案叢刊 (Collection of Republican historical materials from the archives), Ershiguan, ed., Dang'an, 1980– . Archives on different topics published by
various publishers.

Zhonghua minguoshi dang'an ziliao congshu 中華民國史料檔案叢書 (Collectanea of Republican historical materials from the archives), Ershiguan, ed., Dang'an, 1993- .

Kang Ri zhanzheng shiqi Guomindang jun jimi zuozhan riji 抗日戰爭時期國民黨軍機密作戰日記 (The top secret war diary of the GMD during the anti-Japanese War), Ershiguan, ed., Wan Renyuan 萬仁元 and Fang Qingqiu 方慶秋, eds. in chief, 3 vols., Zhongguo dang'an, 1995.

Riben diguo zhuyi qin Hua dang'an ziliao xuanbian 日本帝國主義侵華檔案資料選編 (Selection of historical materials from the archives on Japanese imperialism's invasion of China), Ershiguan, Jilin Shekeyuan, and Zhonghua, 1988- . Documents from the Nationalist archives in the Ershiguan.

Zhonghua minguo zhongyao shiliao chubian-dui Ri kangzhan shiqi 中華民國重要史料初編-對日抗戰時期 (First selection of historical materials on the Republic of China—the period of the war against Japan), Qin Xiaoyi 秦孝儀, ed., Dangshihui, 1981-88. Documents from the Nationalist archives in the Dangshihui.

51.9 Selection of Published CCP Documents

51.9.1 Histories of the CCP

James P. Harrison, *The Long March to Power: A History of the Chinese Communist Party, 1921–1972*, Praeger, 1972.

Lucien Bianco, *The Origins of the Chinese Revolution, 1915–1949*, Muriel Bell, tr., SUP, 1971.

New Perspectives on the Chinese Communist Revolution, Tony Saich and Hans van de Ven, eds., Sharpe, 1995.

History of the Chinese Communist Party-A Chronology of Events, FLP, 1991. This is a translation of *Zhonggong dangshi dashi nianbiao* 中共黨史大事年表, Zhonggong zhongyang dangshi yanjiushi 中共中央黨史研究室 (Party History Research Center of the CCP CC), ed., Renmin, 1987. The Party's own view of its history (as of the early 1990s) set out in annalistic form.

Zhongguo gongchangdang lishi 中國共產黨歷史 (History of the CCP), Zhonggong zhongyang dangshi yanjiushi, ed., Jiefangjun, 1987.

Zhonggong dangshi zhishi shouce 中共黨史知識手冊 (Handbook of knowledge about party history), Zheng Fulin 鄭福林, ed. in chief, Beijing chubanshe, 1987. Historical events, terminology, personalities, party plenums, army battle order, and historical materials.

51.9.2 Documentary Sources for the History of the CCP

Until recently the difficulty in researching the history of the Communist Party of China (CCP) was that many of the main documents were not available. In the first 30 years of the PRC, only those archival documents which supported the orthodox view of party history were printed, usually in selected or excerpted form. Since the 1980s, more materials from CCP archives, both central and local, have been released, often printed in full. But the archives are not yet entirely open. For a guide to the sources, see Zhang Zhuhong 張注洪, *Zhongguo xiandai gemingshi shiliaoxue* 中國現代革命史史料學 (The study of the primary source materials for modern Chinese revolutionary history), Zhonggong dangshi ziliao, 1987. It has been translated into English in *Chinese Studies in History* 23.4 (1990) and 24.3 (1991) and *Chinese Sociology and Anthropology* 22.3-4 (1990). The main selection of CCP documents in English and the single best starting point is:

The Rise to Power of the Chinese Communist Party: Documents and Analyses, Tony Saich, ed., with a contribution by Benjamin Yang, Sharpe, 1996. This huge collection of 212 translated documents replaces earlier collections such as *A Documentary History of Chinese Communism*, Conrad Brandt, Benjamin Schwartz and John K. Fairbank, trs., HUP, 1952. It contains an important introduction on CCP history by Saich, a chronology, and analytic comments on each of the eight periods (1920–49) into which the documents are arranged. There is a selective bibliography, which has been useful in compiling the following list of essential published collections of party documents.

Zhonggong zhongyang wenjian xuanji neibuben 中共中央文件選集內部本 (Selected documents of the CCP CC, internal volumes), Zhongyang dang'anguan 中央檔案館 (Central Party Archives), ed., Dangxiao, 1982-87. Vols. 1–14 cover the period 1921–49. The next item is an open (*gongkai* 公開) version of the same collection.

Zhonggong zhongyang wenjian xuanji 中共中央文件選集 (Selected documents of the CCP CC), Zhongyang dang'anguan, ed., 18 vols., Dangxiao, 1989-92. Vols. 1–14 cover the period 1921–49.

It has become established practice that each party plenum publishes the major documents issued during the lifetime of the preceding plenum. These have been published for those plenums falling within the years 1921–49 (and later):

Zhongguo gongchandang di yici Quanguo daibiao dahui wenjian huibian 中國共產黨第一次全國代表大會文件匯編 (Collection of documents on the First Congress of the CCP), Zhongyang dang'anguan, ed., Renmin, 1980–81.

Zhongguo gongchandang di erci zhi di liuci Quanguo daibiao dahui wenjian huibian 中國共產黨第二次至第六次全國代表大會文件 (Collection of documents on the Second to Sixth congresses of the CCP), Zhongyang dang'anguan, ed., Renmin, 1980–81.

Liuda yiqian dang de lishi cailiao 六大以前黨的歷史材料 (Before the Sixth Party Congress, Party historical materials), Zhonggong zhongyang shujichu 中共中央書記處 (Secretariat of the CCP CC), ed., Yan'an, 1940; republished, Renmin, 1952, 1981.

Liuda yilai dangnei mimi wenjian 六大以來黨內秘密文件 (Since the Sixth Party Congress: secret inner party documents), Zhonggong zhongyang shujichu, Yanan, 1941; republished, Renmin, 1952, 1981.

Zunyi huiyi wenxian 遵義會議文獻 (Documents on the Zunyi Conference), Renmin, 1985.

The Kiangsi Soviet Republic, 1931–1934: A Selected and Annotated Bibliography of the Ch'en Ch'eng Collection, Tien-wei Wu, comp., Harvard-Yenching Library, 1981.

51.9.3 Documentary Collections on Particular Events or Areas

Apart from documentary collections of national-level events, there are also several ongoing collections for individual events or particular areas of the country. Important series for events include:

Zhonggong dangshi ziliao congkan 中共黨史資料叢刊 (Collection of materials on the history of the CCP), Zhongyang dangxiao.

Zhongguo xiandai gemingshi ziliao congkan 中國現代革命史資料叢刊 (Collection of source materials for modern Chinese revolutionary history), Renmin.

Zhongguo gongchandang lishi ziliao congkan 中國共產黨歷史資料叢刊 (Collection of source materials on the history of the CCP), Zhongyang dangshi.

Huge quantities of sources from regional and local CCP archives began to be published from the early 1980s. For the first time they allow a closer look at the diversity of the CCP experience in different parts of China. Two examples out of many follow:

Shaan-Gan-Ning geming genjudi shiliao xuanbian 陝甘寧革命根據地史料
選輯 (Selected materials on the history of the Shaan-Gan-Ning revolutionary base area), Gansu shekeyuan, ed., Gansu renmin, 1981– .

Shaan-Gan-Ning zhengfu wenjian xuanbian 陝甘寧政府文件選輯 (Selected Shaan-Gan-Ning government documents), 13 vols., Dang'an,
1986–90.

51.9.4   Communist Armies and Battles

Zhongguo renmin jiefangjun dashiji 中國人民解放軍大事記, 1927–1982
(Chronology of the Chinese People's Liberation Army, 1927–82),
Junshi kexue, 1983.

Zhongguo jiefangjun zhanshi 中國解放軍戰史 (The battle history of the
PLA), Junshi kexueyuan junshi lishi yanjiubu, ed., 3 vols., Junshi
kexue, 1987.

Zhongguo renmin jiefangjun zhanyi zhanlie xuanbian 中國人民解放軍戰
役戰烈選編 (Selection of campaigns and battles of the Chinese People's Liberation Army), 5 vols., Jiefangjun zhengzhi xueyuan, 1984.

Zhongguo renmin jiefangjun lishi ziliao congshu 中國人民解放軍歷史資
料叢書 (Collectanea of historical materials on the Chinese People's
Liberation Army), Jiefangjun, 225 vols., 1988– .

Zhongguo renmin jiefangjun lishi ziliao congkan 中國人民解放軍歷史資
料叢刊 (Collectanea of historical materials on the Chinese People's
Liberation Army), Jiefangjun. Precise details of major battles.

51.10   Taiwan

Shortly after Taiwan was ceded to Japan (by the Treaty of Shimonoseki, 1895), the Han population of the island stood at about 3
million while the indigenous tribal peoples numbered something
less than 100,000. Taiwan remained part of the Japanese colonial
empire until 1945. In 1949, the second great influx of Han settlers
arrived in the form of the defeated GMD government and an army
of 800,000. For sources on the indigenous peoples, see 40.3.2; for
the Han settlement of Taiwan, see 7.2.3; and for Taiwan under the
Qing, see 50.2.5. Japanese-language sources on Taiwan are dealt
with in 51.11.2.

Taiwan wenxian ziliao lianhe mulu chugao 臺灣文獻資料聯合目錄初稿
(Draft union catalog of Taiwan documents and historical sources), 3
vols., Taiwan fenguan, 1991.

Zhongwen Taiwan ziliao zongmu 中文臺灣資料總目 (General catalog of Chinese-language materials on Taiwan), Taiwan fenguan, 1993.

Guancang Taiwan wenxian qikan lunwen suoyin 館藏臺灣文獻期刊論文索引 (Index to articles in Taiwan periodicals held in the library), 7 vols., Taiwan fenguan, 1995–97.

Taiwanshi yanjiu yibai nian: huigu yu yanjiu 臺灣史研究一百年回顧與研究 (One hundred years of research on Taiwan history: retrospect and research), Huang Fusan 黄福三 et al., eds., Zhongyang yanjiuyuan Taiwanshi yanjiusuo choubeiju, 1997. A good introduction to the sources for many different aspects of Taiwan history.

See also the two volumes based on a series of 26 lectures delivered in 1991–94 by various scholars under the sponsorship of the Wu Sanlian foundation for Taiwan historical sources (Wu Sanlian Taiwan shiliao jijinhui 吳三連臺灣史料基金會):

Taiwanshi yu Taiwan shiliao 臺灣史與臺灣史料 (Taiwan history and Taiwan historical sources), Zhang Yanxian 張炎憲 et al., eds., vol. 1, Zili wenhuabao she, 1993; 2nd prnt., 1994; vol. 2, 1995.

Taiwan wenxian ziliao hezuo fazhan yantao huiyi baogao 臺灣文獻資料合作發展研討會議報告 (Reports of the study meeting on the development of cooperation on Taiwan documents and materials), 1991, Central Library, Taiwan fenguan. Contains brief descriptions of the main resources in libraries and collections in Taiwan for Taiwan studies.

Catalogs of Taiwan Historical Sources

Xianzhuang shu mulu 綫裝書目錄 (Catalog of thread-bound books), Guo-li zhongyang tushuguan, Taiwan fenguan 國立中央圖書館臺灣分館, compiled and published, 1991.

Taiwan wenxian lianhe mulu chugao 臺灣文獻聯合目錄初稿 (Draft union catalog of materials on Taiwan), Taiwan fenguan, ed. and published, 3 vols., 1990. Volume 3 is a name index.

Wang Shih-ch'ing (Wang Shiqing 王世慶) and William M. Speidel, "An Introduction to Resources for the Study of Taiwan History," *Ch'ing-shih wen-t'i* 3 (1976), 90–116.

Wang Shiqing 王世慶, *Taiwan yanjiu Zhongwen shumu* 臺灣研究中文書目 (Chinese bibliography for Taiwan studies), Huanqiu, 1976.

Taiwan wenxian ziliao mulu 臺灣文獻資料書目 (Catalog of Taiwan documents and historical sources), Guojia tushuguan, 1997.

Taiwan wenxian shumu jieti 臺灣文獻書目解題 (Annotated historical materials and books on Taiwan), Wang Shiqing 王世慶, ed. in chief, Taiwan fenguan, 1987–97. This multi-volume series of annotated catalogs covers local histories, maps, official gazettes, genealogies, language, and biography.

Japanese-Language Sources

See 51.11.2.

Western-Language Sources (17ᵗʰ–20ᵗʰ Centuries)

The following entries are either primary sources or catalogs.

Cao Yonghe曹永和, "Helan shiqi Taiwan shiliao jieshao" 荷蘭時期臺灣史料介紹 (Introduction to historical sources for the Dutch period), in *Taiwanshi yu Taiwan shiliao* 臺灣史與臺灣史料, vol. 1, 1–21.

De Dagregisters Van Het Kasteel Zeelandia, Taiwan. Deel 1, 1629–1641, J. Leonard Blussé et al., eds., The Hague: M. Nijhoff, 1986; *Deel 2, 1641–1648*, 1995; *Deel 3, 1648–1655*, 1996; *Deel 4, 1655–1662*, 1999.

Xiwen Taiwan ziliao shumu 西文臺灣資料書目 (Catalog of Western sources on Taiwan), Taiwan fenguan, 1993.

A Bibliography of English-language sources for Taiwan History, Chen Ruoshui, comp., Taibei: Lin Muyuan Zhonghua wenhua jiaoyu jijinhui, 1995. Covers from the seventeenth century to 1991.

Geography

Taiwan diming cishu 臺灣地名辭書 (Dictionary of Taiwan place names), Taiwansheng wenxian weiyuanhui, ed. and published, multivolume series, 1984– (vol. 21, 1999).

China's Island Frontier: Studies in the Historical Geography of Taiwan, Ronald G. Knapp, ed., UHP, 1980; SMC, 1995.

Institutes and Commissions

Taiwanshi yanjiusuo 臺灣史研究所, Zhongyang yanjiuyuan

Taiwansheng wenxian weiyuanhui 臺灣省文獻委員會 (Taiwan Historical Materials Commission)

Journals

The main scholarly journals on Chinese history edited in Taiwan are listed in 10.2.5. For journals specializing in the history of Taiwan, see

Taiwanshi yanjiu 臺灣史研究 (1994– , semiannual), Institute of Taiwan History, Zhongyang yanjiuyuan.

Taiwan shiliao yanjiu 臺灣史料研究 (1993– , semiannual). A learned journal devoted to exploring a Taiwanese interpretation of Taiwan history sponsored by the Wu Sanlian foundation (see above).

Taiwanshi tianye yanjiu tongxun 臺灣史田野研究通訊 (1994– , semiannual), Zhongyang yanjiusuo, Taibei.

Taiwan kin-gendaishi kenkyû 臺灣近現代史研究, Taiwan Kin-gendaishi kenkyûkai, ed., Ryûkei, 1978– .

51.11   Japanese Sources

Apart from documents produced by government departments in Tokyo, including the military and the foreign ministry (51.12.1), Japanese academic institutions produced all kinds of publication which are now important primary sources, not only for Japanese activities in China but also for conditions in China during the Republic. The main ones (in order of establishment) are listed in 51.11.1. In addition to the work of the academic institutions, the Japanese colonial governments in Taiwan, Manshûkoku, the Kwantung Leased Territories, and Korea established special commissions, investigation departments (*chôsaka* 調查科) or research institutes (*kenkyûjo* 研究所) to conduct practical investigations of landholding conditions, legal and commercial practices, religious beliefs, and local customs. Much of their work was published in multi-volume reports or journals. They form one of the most important supplementary categories of historical sources on Chinese history between 1890 and 1945 (51.11.2–3). For the historical background, see the three conference volumes:

The Japanese Colonial Empire, 1895–1945, Ramon H. Myers and Mark R. Peattie, eds., PUP, 1984.

The Japanese Informal Empire in China, Peter Duus, Ramon H. Myers, and Mark R. Peattie, eds., PUP, 1989.

The Japanese Wartime Empire, 1931–1945, Peter Duus, Ramon H. Myers, and Mark R. Peattie, eds., PUP, 1996.

For an annotated listing of many of the sources produced by Japanese academic institutions and Japanese colonial governments between 1898 and 1945, see

Modern Chinese Society, 1644–1970: An Analytical Bibliography, vol. 3, *Publications in Japanese,* G. W. Skinner and Shigeaki Tomita, comps., SUP, 1973. Volumes 1 and 2 of this bibliography also contain useful material on the Qing (10.4.1 and 10.2.3).

Japanese Studies of Modern China: A Bibliographical Guide to Historical and Social Science Research on the 19ᵗʰ and 20ᵗʰ Centuries, John K. Fairbank, Masataka Banno, and Sumiko Yamamoto et al., comps., Tuttle, 1955; 2ⁿᵈ prnt., HUP, 1971. This is updated in the next item.

Japanese Studies of Modern China Since 1953: A Bibliographical Guide to Historical and Social Science Research on the Nineteenth and Twentieth Centuries: Supplementary Volume for 1953–1969, Noriko Kamachi, John K. Fairbank, and Ichiko Chûzô et al., eds., HUP, 1975.

51.11.1 Japanese Research Institutions in China

Nisshin bôeki kekyûjo 日清貿易研究所 (Institute for research in Sino-Japanese trade, Shanghai, 1890).

Tôa dôbunkai 東亞同文會 (East Asia common culture society), Tokyo, 1898. The impetus for the society's establishment was to seek common ground on the basis of the shared written characters; see Douglas R. Reynolds, "Training Young Chinese Hands: Tôa dôbun shoin and Its Precursors, 1886–1945," in Duus et al., 1989 (51.11) 210–71.

Tôa dôbun shoin 東亞同文書院 (Common culture college), Shanghai, 1901–45. In all just under 5,000 Japanese students were graduated.

Beiping Renwen kexue yanjiusuo 北平人文科學研究所 (Pekin Jimbun kagaku kenkyûjo), Beijing, 1927–45. Set up using the Japanese Boxer indemnity funds (9.7).

Tôhô bunka gakuin kenkyûjo 東方文化學院研究所 (Institute for Oriental Culture), Tokyo, 1929. Financed with the Japanese Boxer indemnity funds. Formerly opened in 1933. Forerunner of Tokyo University's Tôyô bunka kenkyûjo (which name dates from 1949).

Tôhô bunka gakuin kenkyûjo 東方文化學院研究所 (Institute for Oriental Culture), Kyoto, 1929. Financed with the Japanese Boxer indemnity funds. Opened in 1930. One of the forerunners of Kyoto University's Jinbun kagaku kenkyûjo (which name dates from 1949).

Examples of Publications

Shina shôbetsu zensho 支那省別全誌 (Comprehensive gazetteer of the individual provinces of China), Tôa dôbunkai, 1918–1920; *Shinshû* 新集

(new series), 1941–44. Based on data gathered on field trips by students from the Tôa dôbun shoin 東亞同文書院, Shanghai.

Chûgoku nôson kankô chôsa 中國農村慣行調查, Chûgoku nôson kankô chôsa kankôkai 中國農村慣行調查刊行會, ed., 6 vols., Niida Noboru, ed., Iwanami, 1952–58; rpnt., 1981. The research was conducted by the Mantetsu Hokushi keizai chôsajo 滿鐵北支經濟調查所 (SMRC institute for investigation of north China villages) in villages of Hebei, Shandong, and Shanxi between the years 1940 and 1944. For studies that uses these materials, see Perkins, 1969 (7.2.1); Ramon H. Myers, *The Chinese Peasant Economy: Agricultural Development in Hopei and Shantung, 1890–1949*, HUP, 1970; Philip Huang, *The Peasant Economy and Social Change in North China*, SUP, 1985.

Shina keizai zensho 支那經濟全書 (A compendium on the Chinese economy), Tôa dôbunkai hensan kyoku, ed., 12 vols., Tokyo: Tôa dôbunkai, 1908–11.

Apart from the institutes listed at the beginning of this section, the Japanese colonial authorities established two imperial universities (in Taibei and Seoul) and several higher commercial schools (Kôtô shôgyô gakko 高等商業學校). These published investigations and studies and academic journals.

51.11.2 *Taiwan*

The main archive of the Japanese government general in Taiwan is handwritten in grass script in a formal official style. It is now kept in the Taiwan wenxian shiliaoguan 臺灣文獻史料館:

Taiwan sôtokufu kôbun ruisan 臺灣總督督公文類纂 (Public documents of the government general of Taiwan), 13,855 volumes.

Taiwan shiryô no kôbun 臺灣史料稿文 (Draft Taiwan historical sources), Taiwan sôtokufu shiryô henzankai 臺灣總督督史料編纂會 (Committee for the editing of historical sources of the Taiwan government general), ed., 1929–33. The materials were drawn from government gazettes and digests; covers the years 1899–1919. A convenient condensation of this huge collection is provided by the next item.

Taiwan shiryô kôbun 臺灣史料綱文 (Outlines of *Taiwan shiryô*), Nagoya: Chûkyô daigaku shakai kagaku kenkyûjo 中京大學社會科學研究所, ed., Seibundô, 1986–89.

Taiwan zongdufu wenshu mulu 臺灣總督撫文書目錄 (Catalog of the documents of the Taiwan government general), 4 vols., 1993–98.

Taiwan zongdufu dang'an zhongyiben 臺灣總督撫檔案中譯本 (Chinese translations from the Taiwan government general archives), 11 vols., 1994–98.

Other archives have survived including some of the county administration archives and part of the archives of the Taiwan development company.

Several research and investigation organs were established in Taiwan by the colonial government under the direction of Gôto Shimpei 後藤新平 (1857–1929), the founder of Japanese research-based colonial development policy; see Yukiko Hayase, *The Career of Gôto Shimpei: Japan's Statesman of Research, 1857–1929*, Ph.D, Florida State University, 1974. Similar ones were also set up elsewhere in the empire. The main Taiwan research organs were

Rinji Taiwan tochi chôsa kyoku 臨時臺灣土地調查局 (Special bureau for the investigation of land holding in Taiwan), Taibei, 1898.

Rinji Taiwan kyûkan chôsakai 臨時臺灣舊慣調查會 (Special commission for the investigation of old customs in Taiwan), 1901. See Okamatsu Santarô 岡松參太郎 (1871–1921), *Provisional Report of Investigation of Laws and Customs in the Island of Formosa Compiled by Order of the Governor-General of Formosa*, Kobe: Kobe Herald Office, 1902; Chengwen, 1971; Ramon H. Myers, "The Research of the Commission for the Investigation of Traditional Customs in Taiwan," *Ch'ing-shih wen-t'i* 2.6: 24–54 (1971).

Rinji Taiwan kokô chôsabu 臨時臺灣户口調查部 (Special department for the investigation of the population of Taiwan).

Taiwan sôtokufu Chûô kenkyûjo 臺灣總督撫中央研究所 (Central research institute of the Taiwan Government-general).

Taiwan sôtokufu kanbô chôsaka 臺灣總督撫官房調查科 (Investigation section of the Secretariat of the Taiwan Government-general).

Some of the most important reports include:

Shinkoku gyôseihô 清國行政法 (Administrative laws of the Qing dynasty), Report of the Rinji Taiwan kyûkan chôsakai, 6 parts in 8 vols., Taibei: 1903–11; 7 vols., Tokyo and Kobe: 1910–14; rpnt., Daian, 1965–66; index, 1967; Kyûko, 1972; 7 vols., SMC, 1989. This contains plenty of original documents. It was based on documentary research and field work carried out not only in Taiwan, but all over China.

Taiwan shihô 臺灣私法 (Private law of Taiwan), Rinji Taiwan kyûkan chôsakai, ed., 6 vols.; *Taiwan shihôfuroku sankôsho* 臺灣私法附錄參

考書 (Reference materials attached to *Taiwan shihô*), 7 vols., 1910–11; 13 vols., SMC, 1995.

Rinji Taiwan tochi chôsa kyoku 臨時臺灣土地調查局. Set up to conduct a cadastral survey in preparation for land registration, 1898–1901. Collected many landholding documents and contracts. Various reports based on the survey were published. The registers themselves (*Tochi shinkôsho* 土地申告書) are filed under the administrative divisions of the time and held in the Taiwan wenxian shiliaoguan 臺灣文獻史料館; for a study that uses these materials, see Chih-ming Ka, *Japanese Colonialism in Taiwan: Land Tenure, Development, and Dependency, 1895–1945*, Westview, 1995.

Bibliographies and Catalogs

Riwen Taiwan ziliao shumu 日文臺灣資料書目 (Catalog of Japanese sources on Taiwan), Taiwan fenguan, 1993.

Nihon teikoku ryôyûki Taiwan kankei tôkei shiryô mokuroku 日本帝國領有期臺灣關係統計史料目錄 (Catalog of historical statistics of Taiwan under Japanese rule), Hitotsubashi daigaku Keizai kenkyûjo Nihon keizai tokei bunken sentâ, 1985. The documents are mainly available in Japanese collections.

Riju shidai Taiwan jingji tongji wenxian mulu 日據時代臺灣經濟統計文獻目錄 (Annotated bibliography of Taiwanese economic statistical documents from the Japanese era), Wu Congmin 吳聰敏 et al., eds., Guoli Taiwan daxue jingjixi, 1995. The documents are mainly available in Taiwan collections.

51.11.3   Manshûkoku

The English name Manchuria (northeast China) is derived from the Chinese Manzhou 滿洲 (itself probably based on a Manchu word; see Box 10, 50.2.6). In everyday Chinese, from the late Qing, the three provinces of Fengtian 奉天, Jilin 吉林, and Heilongjiang 黑龍江 in northeast China were referred to as Dongbei sansheng 東北三省, Dongsansheng 東三省, or simply Dongbei 東北. The name of the Japanese puppet state Manshûkoku 滿洲國, 1932–45 (Manchukuo in English) is also derived from Manzhou 滿洲.

The editor of an excellent bibliography of Manchuria in the early Republic, Ronald Suleski, identifies the main sources for the history of Manchuria in the early twentieth century as being government archives, scholarly monographs and articles, statistical yearbooks, and biographical dictionaries; see idem, *The Moderniza-*

tion of Manchukuo: An Annotated Bibliography, HKCUP, 1994, xvii. In this work Suleski annotates 421 items (about 40 percent Japanese language, 30 percent in Chinese, and 30 percent in English).

The main Japanese research organ in Manchuria was the Minami Manshû tetsudô kabushiki kaisha chôsabu 南滿洲鐵道株式會社調查部 (Research Department of the South Manchurian Railway Company; Mantetsu or SMRC for short), 1907–45, see John Young, *The Research Activities of the South Manchurian Railway Company, 1907–1945: A History and Bibliography*, East Asian Institute, Columbia University, 1966. The Research Department of the SMRC carried out studies and conducted surveys on all aspects of the economy of northeast China. This bibliography lists 6,000 items produced by the SMRC. For this and other bibliographies of Manchuria, see Suleski, 1994, 48–50. One of the first reports conducted by the SMRC was similar to those produced elsewhere in the empire:

Manshû kyûkan chôsa hôkoku 滿洲舊慣調查報告 (Report of the investigation of Manchu old customs) Minami Manshû tetsudô kabushiki kaisha chôsabu, ed., 9 vols., 1912–15.

A few of the main reference books produced during the Manshûkoku years are mentioned elsewhere in this chapter, namely:

Man-Mô bunka nenkan 滿蒙文化年鑑 (51.4.1)

The Manchuria Yearbook (51.4.1)

Dong sansheng guanshenlu 東三省官紳錄 (51.5.1)

Gendai Chûkaminkoku Manshûkoku jimmeikan 現代中華民國滿洲國人名鑒 (51.5.1)

The government gazette has been republished:

Wei Manzhouguo zhengfu gongbao 偽滿洲國政府公報, 120 vols., Liao-Shen, 1990.

51.12 External Relations

A considerable part of the surviving Chinese diplomatic source material for the years 1840–1949 has been published, often grouped around the relations with a particular partner (for late Qing diplomatic documents, see 50.2.7):

Jindai Zhongwai guanxishi yanjiu gailan 近代中外關系史研究概覽 (General outline of research in the history of modern Chinese external relations), Xia Liangcai 夏良才, ed., Tianjin jiaoyu, 1991. A useful introduction.

Zhonghua minguo waijiao cidian 中華民國外交辭典 (Dictionary of Republican diplomacy), Shi Yuanhua 石源華, ed., Shanghai guji, 1996.

Zhongguo duiwai tiaoyue cidian 中國對外條約辭典 (Dictionary of the foreign treaties of China), Zhu Huan 朱寰 and Wang Hengwei 王恒偉, comps., Jilin jiaoyu, 1994. Includes brief notes on all of China's main treaties (and their negotiators) between 1689 and 1949. 3,571 entries.

Zhonghua minguo waijiaoshi ziliao xuanbian 中華民國外交史資料選編 (Selection of historical materials on Republican diplomacy), Cheng Daode 程道德, ed., Beijing daxue, 2 vols., 1985.

Zhongwai tiaoyue jibian 中外條約集編 (Collection of treaties between the Republic of China and foreign states), Waijiaobu, ed., 3 vols., Taibei: Zhonghua, 1957; rev., 1965. Gives texts of treaties entered into by the Nationalist government between 1927 and 1964. Includes both Chinese and foreign-language texts of the treaties.

Since the 1980s, sources on the external relations of the CCP have increased enormously. They include memoirs, documentary collections, and a burgeoning secondary scholarship in Chinese. The opening of the Soviet archives provides new materials. See:

Towards a History of Chinese Communist Foreign Relations, 1920s–1960s: Personalities and Interpretive Approaches, ed., Michael H. Hunt and Niu Jun, Washington: Woodrow Wilson Asia Program, n.d.

Michael H. Hunt, *The Genesis of Chinese Communist Foreign Policy*, Col. UP, 1996.

51.13   Foreign Archival Sources on China, 1840–1949

Most Western countries maintain national archives which are open to researchers and in which are deposited the records of central government departments. On their establishment, the archives usually inherited the official papers of individual departments of the central government until then held separately. In some cases these date back many centuries. Archives are usually open for researchers but most countries have a rule preventing access to documents less than 30 years old (the US is more liberal). Some of the national archives were established as early as the late eighteenth or early nineteenth centuries. The first were the Archives nationales de France, 1794;

next came the Public Record Office in Britain, 1838. The US National Archives were established in 1934. The Republic of China established the Guoshiguan in 1947 and the People's Republic set up the Zhongyang dang'anguan in 1959.

China keeps extant governmental documents dating from all periods prior to 1949 in a number of different archives (50.1 and 51.1). In addition, a significant number of pre-1949 documents are held in Taiwan (50.1.3). The first attempts to publish the archival record in its entirety began in Germany in 1826 and it has continued in most other modern countries with some success for the earlier periods of their histories, from which fewer documents survive. In China, too, the practice of publishing archival sources has developed, sometimes *in toto* (especially for the earlier periods), but often in edited form to document a particular event, period, or point of view (51.1.4).

Finding out about the holdings of national archives in the West has been greatly eased by the publication of calendars (document inventories) and catalogs, put online in the late 1990s. One category of Western archives which are essential for the study of China's international relations (and often, too, for domestic conditions) are diplomatic archives.

51.13.1   Diplomatic and Other Government Archives

Almost all Western diplomatic documents and official correspondence relating to the late Qing and Republican period are publicly available and cataloged. The greater part are not in print, but they are usually available on microfilm. The foreign ministries of most countries publish comprehensive annual series of diplomatic documents, a practice that began in the nineteenth century. Such series run into dozens of volumes and are ongoing. Many other governmental agencies with a say in foreign affairs, for example, the military and the intelligence services, also publish selections from their historical archives. In the following entries, the first item is usually the published diplomatic series.

Britain

British archives, including those of the Foreign Office, are stored at the Public Record Office (PRO), London. There is a comprehensive guide to the holdings, which includes an alphabetical index: *Guide to the Public Record Office*, PRO: microfiches, 1999. All FO papers on China from 1815 through to the end of the Republic are open. Most are on microfilm. The important classes are:

FO 17 (*China general political correspondence, 1815–1905*)
FO 371 (*China general political correspondence, 1906–32*)
FO 228 (*China general consular correspondence, 1834–1930*)

Various selections have been published from these classes, for example,

Taiwan Political and Economic Reports, 1861–1960, Robert L. Jarman, ed., 10 vol., Archive Editions, 1997. Includes all regular and occasional reports from British consular officials stationed in Taiwan, including annual trade reports. The originals are kept in the PRO in classes FO 371 and FO 228. The first eight volumes cover the years up to 1949.

There are many other classes covering correspondence relating to specific activities or types of record, for example, the records of the criminal court at Shanghai and from missions in different parts of China. The FO publishes an index to the main classes of correspondence addressed to London, and this has been partly reproduced:

Index to the Correspondence of the Foreign Office for the Year . . . , 1920–1940, 86 vols., Kraus-Thomson, 1969–71.

The index is also available on microfilm.

The FO itself continuously printed selected papers and memoranda for the information of British missions overseas. These are called confidential prints. There is a published index of them covering the years 1840–1937 (item 2 below). It includes a subject index for the years 1840–1914:

FO 405 (*Confidential Prints on China, 1848–1954*).

Foreign Office Confidential Papers Relating to China and to Neighbouring Countries, 1840–1914, with an Additional List, 1915–1937, Lo Hui-min, ed., Mouton, 1969.

Confidential prints were also used for diplomatic "blue books" (documents presented by command either to the House of Commons, to the House of Lords, or to both houses and called parliamentary papers). The nineteenth century blue books on China have been reprinted: *British Parliamentary Papers: China*, Irish University Press Area Studies Series, 42 vols., Shannon: Irish University Press, 1971.

The years covered are 1833–99. The contents of the volumes are as follows:

1	Civil disorder	27-28	Military affairs
2	Consular establishments	29	Missionaries
3-4	Coolie emigration	30-31	Opium War
5	Diplomatic affairs	32	Taiping Rebellion
6-21	Commercial reports	33-35	Treaty of Tientsin
22	Explorations	36-40	Trade
23	Foreign concessions	41	Western China
24-26	Hong Kong	42	Miscellaneous

The PRO also includes part of the Guangdong provincial archives, see Pong, 1975 (50.3), and considerable correspondence in Chinese from various sources, including the office of the Chinese secretary in the Beijing Embassy:

Hsin-pao Chang and Eric Grinstead, "Chinese Documents of the British Embassy in Peking, 1793-1911," *JAS* 22:354–56 (1963).

Dilip K. Basu, "Ch'ing Documents Abroad: From the Public Record Office in London," *Ch'ing-shih wen-t'i* 2.8: 3-30 (1972).

Anglo-Chinese Relations, 1839–1860: A Calendar of Chinese Documents in the British Foreign Office Records, J. Y. Wong, ed., OUP, 1983.

Europe

For the diplomatic archives of Western Europe, see

The New Guide to the Diplomatic Archives of Western Europe, Daniel H. Thomas and Lynn M. Case, eds., University of Pennsylvannia Press, 1975 (the previous edition was published in 1959).

Faguo waijiaobu yikaifang de youguan Zhongguo dang'an mulu 法國外交部已開放的有關中國檔案目錄 (Catalog of French archives on China already opened to the public), Liu Zhenkun 劉振鶤 in *Jindaishi yanjiu* 1981.1.

Bibliographie zu den deutsch-chinesischen Beziehungen, 1860–1945, Alfons Faser, ed., München: Minerva, 1984.

Soviet Union and East Europe

Since the breakup of the Soviet Union, access to party, diplomatic, and other government archives has made available a whole new category of primary sources on CCP foreign policy, including the years prior to 1949.

Japan

Diplomatic and other Japanese government documents are made public after the lapse of 30 years. Diplomatic documents not yet published in the series *Nihon gaikô monjo* (see below) may be inspected in microfilm at the Gaimushô Shiryôkan 外務省史料館.

Nihon gaikô monjo 日本外交文書 (Documents on Japanese foreign policy), Gaimushô 外務省, 1936– , in progress. Covers from 1868 on (by 1999, the coverage had reached the year 1934). A huge, selective collection of documents from the Gaimushô archives. Volumes are indexed and from time to time more detailed indexes are published.

As with other foreign ministries, the Gaimushô frequently publishes not only the annual volumes but also all the documents relating to a particular incident or event, for example,

Nihon gaikô bunsho, Manshû jihen 日本外交文書満洲事變 (Japanese foreign policy documents, the Manchurian incident), Gaimushô, 1977.

There is a smaller collection (various editions) containing only the most important documents:

Nihon gaikô nianpyô oyobi shuyô monjo, 日本外交年表并重要文書 (Diplomatic chronology with important documents), Gaimushô, ed., 3 vols., Hara, 1983–85.

Note the following early checklists and research guide:

Checklist of Archives in the Japanese Ministry of Foreign Affairs, Tokyo, Japan, 1868–1945, Cecil H. Uyehara, comp., Library of Congress, 1954.

Checklist of Microfilm Reproductions of Selected Archives of the Japanese Army, Navy, and Other Government Agencies, 1868–1945, Georgetown University Press, 1959.

Japan's Foreign Policy, 1868–1941: A Research Guide, James W. Morley, ed., Col.UP, 1978.

United States

The following is a sampling of what is available in the US National Archives, which get richer as the time draws closer to the present.

Papers Relating to the Foreign Relations of the United States, 1861– , United States Department of State, ed., Government Printing Office, 1862– . Usually referred to as *Foreign Relations of the United States* (*FRUS*), the series has constituted the official record of the foreign policy and diplomacy of the United States since 1861. It is compiled by State Department historians who collect, arrange, and annotate the principal documents constituting the record. As with other foreign ministries, documents relating to particular events or countries, for example, China, are frequently published separately, either independently or by the department:

1945, The Far East, China, vol. 7, pub. 8442, GPO, 1969.

American Diplomatic and Public Papers, The United States and China, 3 series, Jules Davids, ed., Scholarly Resources, 1973–81:

1 *The Treaty System and the Taiping Rebellion, 1842–1860*, 21 vols.
2 *The United States, China, and Imperial Rivalries, 1861–1893*, 18 vols.
3 *The Sino-Japanese War to the Sino-Russian War, 1894–1905*, 14 vols.

United States Relations with China, with Special Reference to the Period 1944–1949, United States Department of State, ed., GPO, 1949; reissued as *China White Paper*, with introduction and index by Lyman Van Slyke, 2 vols., SUP, 1967.

United States National Archives and Records Service, *Dispatches from United States Ministers to China, 1843–1906*, Records of the Department of State, General Services Administration, Microfilm series 92, Washington, DC.

Records of the United States Department of State Relating to the Internal Affairs of China, 1910–1949, GPO, Washington, DC. Four indexes and guides cover the years 1910–49:

Records of the Department of State Relating to the Internal Affairs of China, 1910–1929: A Descriptive Guide and Subject Index to Microcopy No. 329, Mordechai Rozanski, ed., Scholarly Resources, 1979. Scholarly Resources also makes available indexes for 1930–39 (published, 1985), 1940–44 (1986), 1945–49 (1986).

OSS/State Department Intelligence and Research Reports, 1941– .

Catalogue of National Archives Microfilm Publications, US National Archives, Records Service, 1974– .

US Army in World War II, multiple volumes, various dates, US Department of the Army, Historical Division.

US Military Intelligence Reports, China, 1911–1941, 15 microfilm reels, Paul Kesavis, ed., University Publications of America, 1983.

Note the many records and reports of the hearings of the executive sessions of the Senate Foreign Relations Committee and of congressional hearings on China.

51.13.2   Nonofficial Archives

Nonofficial archives include missionary society archives and the archives of individual missionaries, business archives, and the archives of private individuals.

Missionary Societies

See 29.7.

Companies and other Private Institutions

If a company or organization (for example, chamber of commerce) still exists, the quickest way is to ask directly the location of their archives. If not, then check bibliographies and guides such as:

Kwang-ching Liu, *Americans and Chinese: A Historical Essay and a Bibliography*, HUP, 1963. The bibliography is based on the holdings of some 75 US libraries. It lists English-language archival materials on US-China relations, including the private papers of individuals.

A Guide to Manuscripts and Documents in the British Isles Relating to the Far East, N. Mathew and M. D. Wainwright, SOAS, 1977.

51.14   Guides and Research Tools

51.14.1   Guides

The Republic is covered in the selected list of guides to the modern period below. There are also chapters on the Republic in general guides to Chinese history such as Yamane (8.3.2). See, too, the bibliographical notes and bibliographies in the *CHC*, vols. 11–13 (43.1).

State and Economy in Republican China: A Handbook for Scholars, William C. Kirby, Man-houng Lin, Jame Chin Shih, and David A. Pietz, eds., HUP, 2000. Part 1 lists useful research aids for the general history of the period; part 2 contains an introduction to the main archives for economic and business history (and for other types of history); see 51.1.1 for details of the archives covered; part 3 is a reader of selected Republican business and economic history documents with copious annotations. An invaluable guide for anyone researching the economic or political history of Republican China.

Andrew J. Nathan, *Modern China, 1840–1972: An Introduction to Sources and Research Aids*, CCS, Univ. of Michigan, 1973.

Zhongguo jindaishi wenxian bibei shumu 中國近代史文獻必備書目 (Essential written sources for the history of modern China), Yao Zuoshou 姚佐綏 et al., comps., Zhonghua, 1996. Unannotated catalog of 5,600 published sources in Chinese for the period 1840 to 1919, many from the first eight years of the Republic. Has both a title and a name index.

Zhonghua minguoshi cidian 中華民國史辭典 (Dictionary of Republican China), Chen Xulu 陳旭麓 and Li Huaxing 李華興, eds., Shanghai renmin, 1991.

Contemporary China: A Research Guide, Peter Berton and Eugene Wu; Howard Koch, Jr., ed., Hoover, 1967. Covers reference works and sources in all languages. Indispensable for China, 1949–65, and Taiwan, 1945–65.

Research Materials on Twentieth-Century China: An Annotated List of CCRM Publications, Ping-kuen Yü (Yu Bingquan) 余秉權, et al. eds., Washington, DC: Center for Chinese Research Materials, Association of Research Libraries, 1975. The CCRM was established in 1968 and funded by the Ford and Mellon Foundations. A total of 979 titles are in the catalog (of which 926 were reproduced and published by the CCRM, including many newspapers and periodicals).

Modern China: A Bibliographical Guide to Chinese Works, 1898–1937, John K. Fairbank and Kwang-ching Liu, HUP, 1950; corrected rpnt., 1961. Intended to be suggestive rather than comprehensive.

Zhongguo xiandaishi shuji lunwen ziliao juyao 中國現代史書籍論文資料舉要 (Notes on books and articles on modern Chinese history), Hu Pingsheng 胡平生, 2 vols., Xuesheng, 1999. Extremely detailed, annotated lists of secondary scholarship in Chinese, English, and some Japanese arranged by chronological themes from 1911 to 1995. The years 1917–28 are covered in 1,500 pages. Unfortunately, the layout looks as if all paragraph markers had been removed. The result is that titles and authors run together in a continuous, barely readable stream of print.

Chûgoku kindaishi kenkyû nyûmon 中國近代史研究入門 (Guide to research on modern Chinese history), Shingai kakumei kenkyûkai 辛亥革命研究會, Kyûko, 1992.

51.14.2   Research Tools

Chronology

Zhonghua minguo shishi jiyao 中華民國史事紀要 (Abstract of main historical events of the Republic of China), Zhonghua minguo shiliao zhongxin, ed., Guoshiguan, 1974. This hugely detailed, day-by-day chronology (with documentary excerpts) from 1894 to the present covers the years 1894–1949 in 77 large volumes. The 1949 volume was published in 1996.

Zhonghua minguo da shiji 中華民國大事記 (Chronology of main events in the Republic of China), Han Xinfu 韓信夫 and Jiang Kefu 姜克夫, eds. in chief, 5 vols., Zhongguo wenshi, 1997. A day-by-day chronology of events, 1905–49. Less bulky than the preceding item but still enormous.

Zhonghua minguo shishi rizhi 中華民國史事日志 (Daily chronology of historical events in the Republic of China), Guo Tingyi 郭廷以, comp., 3 vols., Jinshisuo, 1979–84. Covers 1912–49. The same historian published a chronology of 1840–1911 (50.10.4, *Chronology*).

Atlases and Historical Maps

China Postal Atlas Showing the Postal Establishments and Postal Routes in Each Province (*Zhonghua youzheng yütu* 中華郵政輿圖), China: Directorate General of Posts, 1903, 1908, 1919, 1936.

Zhonghua minguo xin ditu 中華民國新地圖 (New atlas of the Republic of China), Ding Wenjiang 丁文江 et al., comps., 1934. Index contains 34,000 toponyms.

Zhongguo xiandaishi dituji 中國現代史地圖集 (Collection of maps on the history of modern China), Wu Yuexing 武月星, ed. in chief, Zhongguo ditu, 1999. Major collection of more than 200 maps of the years 1919–49; includes military campaigns and also has commentary illustrated with photographs, tables, and diagrams.

Official Posts

The first three reference works below cover slightly different sets of officeholders. The fourth covers Chinese diplomats stationed overseas during the Republic. The first item covers all main central and provincial government officials of all the main administrations active in China, 1912–48. It is also conveniently indexed. The second covers the same plus GMD party officials, 1925–49. The third includes civil and military officials, 1912–49. The information in all three is drawn from government gazettes (*gongbao* 公報; 51.3.8) and directories of officials (*zhiyuanlu* 職員錄, for which see Suleski, 5.11 [1994], 39–43).

Minguo zhiguan nianbiao 民國職官年表 (Chronological tables of Republican period officials), Liu Shoulin 劉壽林 et al., comps., Zhonghua, 1995. An essential reference work for all serious students of the Republic. The compilers provide detailed tables of officeholders in both central and provincial governments, 1912–49, with dates of taking up and leaving office when known. The administrations covered are the various provisional governments and local assemblies of the early Republic, the Canton revolutionary government, the Peking government, the Nationalist government, Manchukuo, the Wang Jingwei regime, and the three military governments that ruled Mongolia and Xinjiang in the years 1936–45. There is a stroke-count index of the 12,000 officials in the tables showing their place of origin. There is also a convenient finding index of their literary names.

Guomin zhengfu zhiguan nianbiao 國民政府職官年表 (Tables of office holders in the National government [1925-49]), Zhang Pengyuan 張朋園 et al., eds., 4 vols., Jinshisuo, 1987– . Includes party officials.

Zhonghua minguo guomin zhengfu junzheng zhiguan renwuzhi 中華民國國民政府軍政職官人物志 (Military and civilian officials during the Nationalist government), Liu Guoming 劉國銘, ed. in chief, Chunqiu, 1989. Lists 29,500 people active, 1925–48. Includes military officers and members of national and provincial assemblies.

Zhongguo zhuwai shiling nianbiao (1912–1949) 中國駐外使領年表 (Table of Chinese ambassadors and consuls stationed abroad, 1912–49), Jindaisuo Nanjing zhengli chu, ed. and published, 1963.

Organization of the Governments of the Republican Period

Minguo shiqi zhongyang guojia jigou zuzhi gaishu 民國時期中央國家機構組織概述 (Introduction to the organization of the offices of central national departments in the Republican period), Ershiguan, ed., Dang'an, 1994. Essential reference for understanding the structure and functioning and dates of establishment of all major offices of all the many national governments during the Republic.

Societies

There are national research societies on most of the main events and personalities of the Republican period. One association for the whole period is the Nanjing Zhonghua minguoshi yanjiuhui 南京中華民國史研究會 (Nanjing Republican period research society). Note also the Zhonggong dangshi xuehui 中共黨史學會 (CCP History Association), which puts out a biweekly Newsletter entitled *Dangshi xinxibao* 黨史信息報 (Shanghai).

Journals

There are a large number of specialized journals and newsletters for particular types of twentieth-century Chinese history. What follows

below is only a small sampling of some of the leading journals on
modern history, on CCP history and on historical archives. For a
much fuller listing of historical journals and bibliographic tools for
finding research results, see Chapter 10.

China Quarterly, The (1960–), London

Dang'an yu lishi 檔案與歷史, Shanghai Municipal Archives

Dangde wenxian 黨的文獻 (1988– , bimonthly)

Guoshiguan guankan 國史館館刊 (1947– , biannual; 1987– , trimesterly),
    Guoshiguan

Jiangsu lishi dang'an 江蘇歷史檔案, Nanjing

Jindai Zhongguo 近代中國 (1977– , bimonthly), Dangshihui

Jindai Zhongguoshi yanjiu tongxun 近代中國史研究通訊 (1986– , semi-
    annual), Jinshisuo

Jindaishi yanjiu 近代史研究 (1979– , bimonthly), Jindaishisuo

Kang Ri zhanzheng yanjiu 抗日戰爭研究 (1991)

Minguo dang'an 民國檔案 (1985– , quarterly), Ershiguan, Nanjing

Republican China (1984– , semi-annual; from 1975 to 1983 was called
    Chinese Republican Studies Newsletter)

Sichuan dang'an shiliao 四川檔案史料 (Chongqing)

Xianggang Zhongguo Jindaishi xuehui huikan 香港中國近代史學會會刊
    (1985– , annual), Hong Kong

Zhonggong dangshi yanjiu 中共黨史研究 (1987– ; from 1980 to 1987 ap-
    peared under the title *Dangshi yanjiu* 黨史研究, bimonthly), Central
    Party School, Beijing

Zhonggong dangshi ziliao 中共黨史資料, Party History Research Center

Zhongyang yanjiuyuan Jindaishi yanjiusuo jikan 中央研究員近代史研究所
    季刊 (1969– , annual)

APPENDIX

Appendix

Publishers

Academy Editions, London
Akademie Verlag, Berlin
Aldine, Chicago
Allen and Unwin, London
American Philosophical Society, Philadelphia
Anhui renmin chubanshe 安徽人民出版社, Hefei
ANU Press, Australian National University Press, Canberra
Aolinpike 奧林匹克, Beijing
Athlone Press, University of London
Atheneum, New York
Aubier: Françoise Aubier, Paris
Baihuazhou wenyi chubanshe 白洲文藝出版社, Nanchang
Ballantine Books, New York
Ba-Shu shushe 巴蜀書社, Chengdu
Bayi chubanshe 八一出版社, Beijing
Beifang funü ertong chubanshe 北方婦女兒童出版社, Changchun
Beijing chubanshe 北京出版社, Beijing
Beijing daxue chubanshe 北京大學出版社, Beijing
Beijing haowang shudian 北京好望書店, Beijing
Beijing shumu wenxian chubanshe 北京書目文獻出版社, Beijing
Beijing tushuguan chubanshe 北京圖書館出版社, Beijing
Beijing yuyan xueyuan chubanshe 北京語言學院出版社, Beijing
Bikashoin 美華書院, Tokyo
Blackwell: Basil Blackwell, Oxford
Brill: E. J. Brill, Leiden
British Museum Press, London
Carl Hauser Verlag, München/Wien
Cehui chubanshe 測會出版社, Beijing
Century Books, New York
Ch'eng-wen, *see* Chengwen
Changchun chubanshe 長春出版社, Changchun
Chengdu chubanshe 成都出版社, Chengdu
Chengwen 成文 publishing co., Taibei
Chongqing chubanshe 重慶出版社, Chongqing
China Building Industry Press, see Zhongguo jiancai gongye chubanshe
Chinese Language Research Association, Presidio, Monterey, California
Chûbun shuppansha 中文出版社, Kyoto
Clarendon Press: Oxford University Press, Oxford
Clio Press, Santa Barbara and Oxford
CMC: Chinese Materials Center, Taibei and San Francisco
Col. UP: Columbia University Press, New York City, New York

Commercial Press, see under Shangwu
Corn. UP: Cornell University Press, Ithaca, New York
CUP: Cambridge University Press, Cambridge, England
Curzon Press, Richmond, Surrey, England
Da baike quanshu; see Zhongguo da baike quanshu chubanshe
Dahua shuju 大化書局, Taibei
Daian 大安, Tokyo
Daitô shuppansha 大東出版社, Tokyo
Dali chubanshe 大立出版社, Taibei
Daxiang chubanshe 大象出版社, Zhengzhou
Dangxiao: see under Zhonggong zhongyang dangxiao
Dang'an chubanshe 檔案出版社, Beijing
Dianzi keji daxue chubanshe 電子科技大學出版社, Chengdu
Dingwen shuju 鼎文書局, Taibei
Ditu chubanshe 地圖出版社, Beijing
Dizhen chubanshe 地震出版社, Beijing
Dôhôsha 同朋舍, Kyoto
Dôyûsha 同友舍, Kyoto
Dongbei shifan daxue chubanshe 東北師範大學出版社, Changchun
Dongbei shifan daxue tushuguan 東北師大圖書館, Changchun
Dongda: Dongda tushu youxian gongsi 東大圖書有限公司, Taibei
Doubleday Inc., New York
Dover: Dover Publications, Inc., Mineola, New York
DUP: Duke University Press, Durham, North Carolina
Dunhuang wenyi chubanshe 敦煌文藝出版社, Lanzhou
Edinburgh UP, Edinburgh University Press
Editions Derouaux Ordina, Liège
Elanders Boktryckeri Artiebolag, Göteborg
Facts on File Inc., New York
Falü chubanshe 法律出版社, Beijing
Fangzhou chubanshe 房舟出版社, Taibei
FLP: Foreign Languages Press (Waiwen chubanshe 外文出版社), Beijing
Forum, Edition Forum, Heidelberg
Free Press, Glencoe, New York
Fujian kexue jishu chubanshe 福建科學技術出版社, Fuzhou
Fujian renmin chubanshe 福建人民出版社, Fuzhou
Fukutake Shoten 福武書店, Tokyo
G. K. Hall, Boston, Mass
Gansu wenhua chubanshe 甘肅文化出版社, Lanzhou
Gansu yinxiang chubanshe 甘肅音像出版社, Lanzhou
Garland Publishing, Inc., New York
Gongyi meishu chubanshe 工藝美術出版社, Beijing
Greenwood Press, Westport, Conn
Guangdong jiaoyu chubanshe 廣東教育出版社, Guangzhou
Guangdong renmin chubanshe 廣東人民出版社, Guangzhou
Guangdongsheng ditu chubanshe 廣東省地圖出版社, Guangzhou
Guangjiaojing chubanshe 廣角鏡出版社, Hong Kong
Guangming ribao chubanshe 光明日報出版社, Beijing
Guangwen shuju 廣文書局, Taibei
Guangxi jiaoyu chubanshe 廣西教育出版社, Nanning
Guangxi renmin chubanshe 廣西人民出版社, Nanning, Guangxi

Guangxi shifan daxue chubanshe 廣西師範大學出版社, Nanning
Gudian wenxue chubanshe 古典文學出版社, Beijing
Gugong bowuyuan 故宮博物院, Taibei
Guji chubanshe 古籍出版社, Shanghai
Guofang daxue chubanshe 國防大學出版社, Beijing
Guofeng chubanshe 國風出版社, Taibei
Guoji wenhua chuban gongsi 國際文化出版公司, Beijing
Hacker Art Books Inc., New York
Hainan guoji xinwen chuban zhongxin 海南國際新聞出版中心, Haikou
Haiyang chubanshe 海洋出版社, Beijing
Hakluyt Society, Cambridge and London
Hanxue yanjiu ziliao ji fuwu zhongxin 漢學研究資料及服務中心, Taibei
Hanyu da cidian chubanshe 漢語大詞典出版社, Shanghai
Hara shobô 原書房, Tokyo
Harrassowitz: Otto Harrassowitz Verlag, Wiesbaden
Hauser: see Carl Hauser Verlag
Haworth Press, New York
Hebei daxue chubanshe 河北大學出版社, Shijiazhuang
Heibonsha 平凡社, Tokyo
Heilongjiang kexue jishu chubanshe 黑龍江科學技術出版社, Harbin
Heilongjiang renmin chubanshe 黑龍江人民出版社, Harbin
Henan daxue chubanshe 河南大學出版社, Kaifeng
Henan renmin chubanshe 河南人民出版社, Zhengzhou
Heirakuji shoten 平樂寺書店, Tokyo
HKCUP: Chinese University Press, Shatin, N. T., Hong Kong
HKUP: Hong Kong University Press, Hong Kong
Holos Verlag, Heidelburg
Hongqi chubanshe 紅旗出版社, Beijing
Hongqiao chubanshe 紅橋出版社, Taibei
Hongye wenhua shiye youxian gongsi 紅葉文化事業有限公司, Taibei
Hoover Institution Press, Stanford
Hôzôkan 法藏館, Kyoto
HRAF: Human Resource Area Files Press, New Haven
Huadong shifan daxue chubanshe 華東師範大學出版社, Shanghai
Huangshan shushe 黃山書社, Hefei
Huanqiu shushe 環球書社, Beijing
Huashan wenyi cubanshe 華山文藝出版社, Hefei
Huashi chubanshe 華事出版社, Taibei
Huawen shuju 華文書局, Taibei
Huayu jiaoxue chubanshe 華語教學出版社, Beijing
Huaxia chubanshe 華夏出版社, Beijing
Hubei cishu chubanshe 湖北辭書出版社, Wuhan
Hubei jiaoyu chubanshe 湖北教育出版社, Wuhan
Hunan chubanshe 湖南出版社, Changsha
Hunan renmin chubanshe 湖南人民出版社, Changsha
Hunan shifan daxue chubanshe 湖南師範大學出版社, Changsha
HUP: Harvard University Press, Cambridge, Mass
H-Y Institute: Harvard-Yenching Institute, Beiping and Cambridge, Mass
IUP: Indiana Unversity Press, Bloomingdale, Indiana
Iwanami shoten 岩波書店, Tokyo
Jiangong chubanshe 建軍出版社, Beijing

Jiangsu guangling guji keyinshe 江蘇廣陵古籍刻印社, Yangzhou
Jiangsu jiaoyu chubanshe 江蘇教育出版社, Nanjing
Jiangsu kexue jishu chubanshe 江蘇科學技術出版社, Nanjing
Jiangxi jiaoyu chubanshe 江西教育出版社, Nanchang
Jiaotong daxue chubanshe 交通大學出版社, Shanghai
Jiefangjun chubanshe 解放軍出版社, Beijing
Jilin daxue chubanshe 吉林大學出版社, Changchun
Jilin jiaoyu chubanshe 吉林教育出版社, Changchun
Jilin kexue jishu chubanshe 吉林科學技術出版社, Changchun
Jilin wenshi chubanshe 吉林文史出版社, Changchun
Jinbun kagaku kenkyûjo 人文科學研究所, Kyoto
Jingguan jiaoyu chubanshe 警官教育出版社, Beijing
Jingji ribao chubanshe 經濟日報出版社, Beijing
Kagaku shoin 科學書院, Tokyo
Kaiming shudian 開明書店, Shanghai (unless otherwise indicated)
Kansai daigaku shuppansha 關西大學出版社, Suita
Kelley, Augustus M., Publishers, New York
Kelly and Walsh, Shanghai
Kenbun shuppan 研文出版, Tokyo
Kexue chubanshe 科學出版社, Beijing
Kluwer Academic Publishers, Dortrecht
Knopf, New York
Kôbundô shoten 光文堂書店, Yamagata
Kôdansha 講談社 Intl., Tokyo
Kokudosha 國土社, Tokyo
Kokusho kankôkai, 國書刊行會, Tokyo
Koten kenkyûkai 古典研究會, Tokyo
Kraus Reprint Ltd., Nendeln, Leichtenstein
Kyûko shoin 汲古書院, Tokyo
Kyôtô daigaku bungakubu 京都大學文學部, Tôyôshi kenkyûkai 東洋史研究會,
    Kyoto
Lanzhou daxue chubanshe 蘭州大學出版社, Lanzhou
Leroux: Ernest Leroux, Paris
Lianjing: Lianjing chuban shiye gongsi 聯經出版事業公司, Taibei
Liaoning jiaoyu chubanshe 遼寧教育出版社, Shenyang
Liaoning minzu chubanshe 遼寧民族出版社, Shenyang
Liaoning renmin chubanshe 遼寧人民出版社, Shenyang
Liao-Shen shushe, 遼沈書社, Shenyang
Lihong chubanshe 利宏出版社, Taibei
Lingnan daxue tushuguan 嶺南大學圖書館, Guangzhou
Linye chubanshe 林業出版社, Beijing
Liren shuju 里仁書局, Taibei
Longwood Academic, Nashua, New Hampshire
Lund Humphries, London
Lüyou chubanshe 旅遊出版社, Beijing
Macmillan, London
Maisonneuve: Adrien-Maisonneuve, Paris
McGaw-Hill, Inc., New York
Meitan gongye chubanshe 煤炭工業出版社, Beijing
Meitoku shobô 明德書房, Tokyo
Mellen: Edwin Mellen Press, Lampeter

Minglun chubanshe 明論出版社, Taibei
Mingwen shuju 明文書局, Taibei
MIT Press, Cambridge, Mass
Morning Glory Publishers (Zhaohua chubanshe 朝華出版社), Beijing
Mouton de Gruyter, Berlin and New York
Mouton et Cie, Paris and the Hague
John Murray, London
Museum of Far Eastern Antiquities (Östasiatiska Samlingarna), Stockholm
Nanjing daxue chubanshe 南京大學出版社, Nanjing
Nei Menggu renmin chubanshe 內蒙古人民出版社, Huhehaote
New World Press, Beijing
Nigensha 二玄社, Tokyo
Nihon gakujutsu shinkôkai 日本學術新興會, Tokyo
Ningxia renmin chubanshe 寧夏人民出版社, Yinchuan
Nongye chubanshe 農業出版社, Beijing
Norton: W. W. Norton and Co., New York
Ochanomizu shobô 御茶の水書房, Tokyo
Octagon Books, London
Ohio University Press, Athens, Ohio
Open Court, Chicago and La Salle, Illinois
OUP: Oxford University Press, Oxford
Outer Sky Press, Bronxville, New York
Paradigm Publications, Brookline, Mass
Paragon Book Reprint Corp., New York
Penguin Books, Harmondsworth, Middlesex
Pennsylvania State University Press, University Park, Pennsylvania
People's China: see Renmin Zhongguo chubanshe
Praeger, New York
Prentice Hall, Englewood Cliffs, N.J.
Probsthain: Arthur Probsthain, London
PUF: Presses Universitaires de France, Paris
PUP: Princeton University Press, Princeton, N.J.
Qi-Lu shushe 齊魯書社, Ji'nan
Qingdao chubanshe 青島出版社, Qingdao
Qingnian: see Zhongguo qingnian chubanshe
Qunyan chubanshe 群言出版社, Beijing
Qunlian chubanshe 群聯出版社, Shanghai
Random House, New York
Reaktion, London
Renmin chubanshe 人民出版社, Beijing
Renmin daxue: see Zhongguo renmin daxue
Renmin meishu 人民美術, Beijing
Renmin Weisheng chubanshe 人民衛生出版社, Beijing
Renmin Zhongguo chubanshe 人民中國出版社, Beijing
Rider and Co., London
Robalde: Ward Robalde Press, Los Angeles
Ronald Press, New York
Routledge & Kegan Paul, London
Routledge Intl., London
Ryôgen shoten 燎原書店, Tokyo
Ryûkei shosha 龍溪書舍, Tokyo

Saika Shorin 菜華樹林, Nagoya
Sanlian: Shenghuo. Dushu. Xinzhi sanlian chubanshe 三連.讀書.新知三聯 出版社, Beijing
San-Qin chubanshe 三秦出版社, Xi'an
Scholarly Resources, Wilmington, Delaware
Science Press, see Kexue chubanshe
Seibundô 精文堂, Tokyo
Seuil: Editions du Seuil, Paris
Scarecrow Press, Lanham, Maryland (formerly Metuchen, New Jersey)
Shaanxi guji chubanshe 陝西古籍出版社, Xi'an
Shaanxi lüyou chubanshe 陝西旅遊出版社, Xian
Shaanxi renmin jiaoyu chubanshe 陝西人民教育出版社, Xi'an
Shambhala Publishers Inc., Boulder, Colorado; Boston, Mass
Shandong daxue chubanshe 山東大學出版社, Ji'nan
Shandong jiaoyu chubanshe 山東教育出版社, Ji'nan
Shandong renmin chubanshe 山東人民出版社, Ji'nan
Shandong wenyi chubanshe 山東文藝出版社, Ji'nan
Shandong youyi shushe 山東友誼書社, Ji'nan
Shanghai cishu chubanshe 上海辭書出版社, Shanghai
Shanghai guji chubanshe 上海古籍出版社, Shanghai
Shanghai jiaoyu chubanshe 上海教育出版社, Shanghai
Shanghai renmin chubanshe 上海人民出版社, Shanghai
Shanghai shudian chubanshe 上海書店出版社, Shanghai
Shanghai wenhua chubanshe 上海文化出版社, Shanghai
Shanghai yuandong chubanshe 上海遠東出版社, Shanghai
Shangwu: Shangwu yinshuguan 商務印書館, Beijing and Shanghai
Shangwu Intl.: Shangwu guoji youxian gongsi 商務國際有限公司, Beijing, Hong Kong, Taiwan, Singapore and Kuala Lumpur
Shanxi shifan daxue chubanshe 山西師範大學出版社, Taiyuan
Sharpe: M. E. Sharpe, Armonk, New York
Shehui kexue chubanshe: see Zhongguo shehui kexue chubanshe
Shehui kexue wenxian chubanshe 社會科學文獻出版社, Beijing
Seishin shobô 省心書房, Tokyo
Shenzhou guoguangshe 神州國光社, Shanghai
Shijie shuju 世界書局, Shanghai; also Taibei
Shoestring Press, Hamden, Conn
Shoseki Jôhôsha 書籍情報社, Tokyo
Shogakukan Shuppansha 小學館出版社, Tokyo
Shoudu Shifan daxue chubanshe 師範大學出版社,
Shuhai chubanshe 書海出版社, Taiyuan
Shumu Wenxian chubanshe 書目文獻出版社, Beijing
Sichuan Cishu chubanshe 四川辭書出版社, Chengdu
Sichuan daxue chubanshe 四川大學出版社, Chengdu
Sichuan renmin chubanshe 四川人民出版社, Chengdu
Sichuan Shehui kexue chubanshe 四川社會科學出版社, Chengdu
Sinolingua, see Huayu Jiaoxue chubanshe
SMC: Nantian shuju youxian gongsi 南天書局有限公司, Taibei
Sôbunsha 創文社, Tokyo
Sôgensha 創元社, Kyoto
Springer Verlag, Berlin and Hamburg
St Martin's Press, London; New York

Steiner: Franz Steiner Verlag, Stuttgart
Steyler: Franz Steyler Verlag, Nettetal
Student Book Company: *see* Xuesheng shuju
Studio Editions, London
SUNY: State University of New York Press, Albany, New York
SUP: Stanford University Press, Stanford, California
Suzhou renmin chubanshe 蘇州人民出版社, Suzhou
Taishûkan shoten 大修館書店, Tokyo
Thames and Hudson, London
Tianjin jiaoyu chubanshe 天津教育出版社, Tianjin
Tianjin renmin meishu chubanshe 天津人民美術出版社, Tianjin
Tianhua chubanshe 天花出版社, Taibei
Tôhô shoten 東方書店, Tokyo
Tôkyô daigaku shuppankai 東京大學出版會, Tokyo
Tôkyôdô shuppan 東京堂出版, Tokyo
Tôsui shobô 刀水書房, Tokyo
Tôyô bunko 東洋文庫, Tokyo
Tuanjie chubanshe 團結出版社, Beijing
Tuttle: Charles E. Tuttle, Vermont and Tokyo
Twayne, New York
UAP: University of Arizona Press, Tucson
UBCP: University of British Columbia Press, Vancouver
UChP: University of Chicago Press, Chicago
UCP: University of California Press, Berkeley
UHP: University of Hawaii Press, Honolulu
UMP: University of Michigan Press, Ann Arbor, Michigan
UWP: University of Washington Press, Seattle
University of Kansas Press, Lawrence
University Publications of America, Frederick, Md
Unwin Hyman, London
Variorum, Aldershot, England
Vetch: Henri Vetch, the French Bookstore, Peking and Hong Kong
Waiyu jiaoxue yu yanjiu chubanshe 外語教學與研究出版社, Beijing
Wanjuanlou tushu gongsi 萬卷樓圖書公司, Taibei
Weatherhill, Tokyo and New York
Wenhai chubanshe 文海出版社, Taibei
Wenjin chubanshe 文津出版社, Taibei
Wenwu chubanshe 文物出版社, Beijing
Wenxing shudian 文星書店, Beijing
Westview Press, Boulder, Colorado, USA
White Lotus Co. Ltd., Bangkok
Wild Peony, Broadway, New South Wales, Australia
Wiley: John Wiley, New York
William Sloane Associates, New York
Wuhan daxue chubanshe 武漢大學出版社, Wuhan
Wunan tushu chuban gongsi 吳南圖書出版公司, Taibei
Xi'an ditu chubanshe 西安地圖出版社, Xi'an
Xibei daxue chubanshe 西北大學出版社, Xian
Xinhua shudian 新華書店, Beijing
Xinwenfeng chuban gongsi 新文豐出版公司, Taibei
Xinxing chubanshe 新星出版社, Beijing

Xizang renmin chubanshe 西藏人民出版社, Lhasa
Xuelin chubanshe 學林出版社, Shanghai
Xuesheng shuju 學生書局, Taibei
Xueyuan chuban gongsi 學苑出版公司, Beijing
Yamakawa shuppansha 山川出版社, Tokyo
Yamamoto shoten 山本書店, Tokyo
Yiwen yinshuguan 藝文印書館, Taibei
Yoshikawa kôbunkan 吉川弘文館, Tokyo
Yuelu shushe 岳麓書社, Changsha
Yunnan jiaoyu chubanshe 雲南教育出版社, Kunming
Yunnan renmin chubanshe 雲南人民出版社, Kunming
YUP: Yale University Press, New Haven
Yurindô 有鄰堂, Tokyo
Yuwen chubanshe 語文出版社, Beijing
Yuzankaku 雄山閣, Tokyo
Zhejiang guji chubanshe 浙江古籍出版社, Hangzhou
Zhejiang renmin chubanshe 浙江人民出版社, Hangzhou
Zhejiang sheying chubanshe 浙江攝影出版社, Hangzhou
Zhengzhong shuju 正中書局, Taibei
Zhishi chubanshe 知識出版社, Shanghai
Zhonggong zhongyang dangxiao chubanshe 中共中央黨校出版社, Beijing
Zhonggong zhongyang dangxiao tushuguan 中共中央黨校圖書館, Beijing
Zhongguo caizheng jingji chubanshe 中國財政經濟出版社, Beijing
Zhongguo chengshi chubanshe 中國城市出版社, Beijing
Zhongguo da baike quanshu chubanshe 中國大百科全書出版社, Beijing
Zhongguo ditu chubanshe 中國地圖出版社, Beijing
Zhongguo duiwai fanyi chubanshe 中國對外翻譯出版社, Beijing
Zhongguo gongren chubanshe 中國工人出版社, Beijing
Zhongguo guangbo dianshi chubanshe 中國廣播電視出版社, Beijing
Zhongguo guoji guangbo chubanshe 中國國際廣播出版社, Beijing
Zhongguo huanjing kexue chubanshe 中國環境科學出版社, Beijing
Zhongguo huaqiao chubanshe 中國華僑出版社, Beijing
Zhongguo jiancai gongye chubanshe 中國建材工業出版社, Beijing
Zhongguo jianzhu gongye chubanshe 中國建築工業出版社, Beijing
Zhongguo kexueyuan, Beijing Tianwentai 中國科學院北京天文臺, Beijing
Zhongguo kuangye daxue chubanshe 中國礦業大學出版社, Hangzhou
Zhongguo qingnian chubanshe 中國青年出版社, Beijing
Zhongguo renmin daxue chubanshe 中國人民大學出版社, Beijing
Zhongguo renmin gong'an daxue chubanshe 中國人民公安大學出版社, Beijing
Zhongguo renshi chubanshe 中國人事出版社, Beijing
Zhongguo shangye chubanshe 中國商業出版社, Beijing
Zhongguo shehui kexue chubanshu 中國社會科學出版社, Beijing
Zhongguo shudian 中國書店, Beijing
Zhongguo wenhua yanjiusuo 中國文化研究所, Taibei
Zhongguo wenlian chuban gongsi 中國文聯出版公司, Tianjin
Zhongguo wenshi chubanshe 中國文史出版社, Beijing
Zhongguo wenxue chubanshe 中國文學出版社, Beijing
Zhongguo xueshu chubanshe 中國學術出版社, Beijing
Zhongguo youyi chuban gongsi, Hong Kong
Zhongguo yuyan wenhua daxue chubanshe 中國語言文化大學出版社, Beijing
Zhongguo Zangxue chubanshe 中國藏學出版社, Beijing

Zhonghua ditu xueshe 中華地圖學社, Shanghai
Zhonghua: Zhonghua shuju 中華書局, Beijing
Zhongshan daxue chubanshe 中山大學出版社, Guangzhou
Zhongshan tushu gongsi 中山圖書公司, Hong Kong
Zhongyi guji chubanshe 中醫古籍出版社, Shanghai
Zhongyi xueyuan chubanshe 中醫學院出版社, Shanghai
Zhongzhou guji chubanshe 中州古籍出版社, Zhengzhou
Zhuanji wenxueshe 傳記文學舍, Taibei
Zijincheng chubanshe 紫禁城出版社, Beijing

INDEXES

Index of Terms Explained

Index of Names

Index of Book

and Periodical Titles

Subject Index

Harvard-Yenching Institute Monograph Series
(titles now in print)